DATE			

THE
COLUMBIA ANTHOLOGY
OF TRADITIONAL CHINESE
LITERATURE

TRANSLATIONS FROM THE ASIAN CLASSICS

THE
Columbia Anthology of Traditional Chinese Literature

VICTOR H. MAIR, EDITOR

COLUMBIA UNIVERSITY PRESS / NEW YORK

Columbia University Press wishes to express its appreciation of assistance given
by the Pacific Cultural Foundation toward the publication of this book.

Columbia University Press
New York   Chichester, West Sussex
Copyright © 1994 Columbia University Press
All rights reserved

Library of Congress Cataloging-in-Publication Data

The Columbia anthology of traditional Chinese literature / Victor H.
  Mair, editor.
        p.   cm. — (Translations from the Asian classics)
     ISBN 0–231–07428–X
     1. Chinese literature—Translations from Chinese.   I. Mair,
  Victor H.   II. Series.
  PL2658.E1C65   1994
  895.1′08—dc20   93–48174
                                                                CIP

For list of permissions see pages 1326–1330.

TRANSLATIONS FROM THE ASIAN CLASSICS

For Jing

CONTENTS

Criticism and Theory

PART 2. VERSE

Classical Poetry

PART 3. PROSE

Documents

History

Moral Lessons

Parallel Prose

Letters

Biographies, Autobiographies, and Memoirs

Fictional and Fictionalized Biographies and Autobiographies

PART 4. FICTION

Rhetorical Persuasions, Parables, and Allegories

Anecdotal Fiction

Tales of the Strange

PART 5. ORAL AND PERFORMING ARTS

PREFACE

The primary purpose of this anthology is to provide a broad selection of expertly translated texts from the widest possible variety of sources while staying within the limits of a portable one volume text. My aim throughout has been to give a sense of the full range of Chinese literature. The editorial principles I have employed do not restrict literature to belles-lettres in the narrowest sense. For the purposes of this anthology, literature is construed very broadly as vivid or imaginative writing. Literature may be driven by a lyrical impulse or generated by a narrative intent; it may even be chiefly descriptive or expository. A text may be concerned with any subject matter or be written in virtually any genre or form; so long as it has esthetic merit or genuine emotional appeal (apart from its original purpose), it is capable of being considered literature. This anthology demonstrates that many different types of written texts might be regarded as literature.

The conception of "Chinese literature" has up until now been rather narrow and prescriptive; the canon needs to be enlarged. To a certain extent, then, this is meant to be an iconoclastic anthology. As we free ourselves from the customary constraints imposed by the concept of "classical," we discover an enormous number of interesting texts available for consideration. Throughout history, the tradition was constantly being reshaped in response to a host of literary and nonliterary factors, and, in retrospective fashion, will go on being remade in response to similar factors. Chinese literature, like Chinese culture as a whole, is not a seamless, monotonous fabric. Anthologists and literary historians who emphasize only standard genres and elite writers are responsible for perpetuating a false image of what Chinese literature might be for our own age.

It is sometimes thought, for instance, that Chinese literature is almost exclusively puritanical, but China has a long tradition of pornographic literature as explicit as any in the world. I have decided not to include the most egregious types of pornography but have chosen a few examples that display unusual irony or wit. With the pornography as with all other types of literature included here, I have not bowdlerized or prettified.

I have attempted to choose texts that reveal what people from all levels and sectors of society in China thought, felt, believed, and did. The China of this anthology is not an idealized picture formed by thinkers and scholars isolated from the lives of the masses. The full literary record in China offers a rich fund of information, images, and impressions to complement that of the official historiographers and Confucian bureaucrats. A conscious effort has been made to include material by and about women, minorities, farmers, soldiers, merchants, physicians, and many other types of people.

On the other hand, I have by no means avoided the most sophisticated, mannered, and abstruse texts that are so important a part of Chinese culture as a whole. China's literati-officials were the greatest bureaucrats the world has ever seen. They created a stable institutional system that, despite the vicissitudes of periodic war and recurrent dynastic change, persisted for more than two thousand years until 1911. They were also accomplished poets and essayists with roots in the social and political thinkers of the Warring States period, among whom the most distinguished were Confucius, Mencius, Hsün Tzu, and Han Fei Tzu. An abiding characteristic of premodern China was that the bureaucracy and the intelligentsia were very nearly identical. To be a respected statesman, one was almost always required to be a passable poet. It was only with the arrival of massive Western influence that the old institutions of literati dominance and control disintegrated beyond all hope of repair.

Before China was confronted by Western ideas and things in the late nineteenth and twentieth centuries—with a nearly complete capitulation to such notions as science, democracy, and communism and the resultant collapse of literati authority—the West had already begun to influence Chinese thought, learning, literature, and technology since the sixteenth century. Indeed, my second goal in compiling this volume has been to show that China was never separated from the rest of the world. China-watchers (and many Chinese themselves) have long accepted a Middle Kingdom ideology according to which this great East Asian empire was allegedly sealed off from the rest of the world. Nothing could be further from the truth, as is amply shown by the cosmopolitan character of many of the texts collected here.

A third guideline I have followed in putting together this anthology is to avoid a preponderance of works overanthologized in the past. I have assiduously sought out previously untranslated works, although a few old favorites (such as T'ao Ch'ien's famous essay on "The Peach Blossom Spring" and Su Shih's two inimitable Red Cliff rhapsodies) could not be excluded. This collection contains many exciting pieces never published in English and others scarcely known even in China but richly deserving of fuller recognition.

Fourth, I have introduced new translators. Aside from instances where earlier translators are chosen for special effect, all the translators in this volume are attuned to the spirit and needs of students at the turn of the twenty-first century. This choice is not meant to denigrate the splendid achievements of our predecessors, but I see little reason to anthologize yet again translations from a century or half century ago.

Fifth, whole texts are used as much as possible in order not to mystify the reader with omissions and paraphrases. Several novella-length works are printed in their entirety to give an idea of how an extended Chinese narrative progresses. For long novels, usually an entire chapter or two is offered. The same is true for drama where, with only a couple of exceptions, whole scenes or plays are presented rather than bits and pieces. Chinese verse being what it is, most of the poems gathered here are short, although I have made a special effort to include a number of the longest poems in Chinese literature. I have tried to strike a balance between long and short pieces to give a truthful impression of the character of Chinese literature and to prevent monotony.

As seen from the table of contents, the works are divided into several broad categories and many subcategories, which should be considered only as one possible scheme among many for the classification of Chinese literature. Even a distinction between prose and poetry is inadequate when attempting to deal with Chinese literary texts. There are, for instance, genres such as the rhapsody (*fu*) and parallel prose (*p'ien-t'i-wen*) that seem to straddle the boundary between prose and poetry. And what do we do with the ubiquitous prosimetric or chantefable form of popular literary texts in which verse sections regularly alternate with prose? Such problems are the despair of theorists and historians aspiring to a neat classification scheme that will embrace all Chinese literature. Nonetheless, by arranging this anthology according to type and genre instead of stubbornly following a chronological scheme, students will be able to grasp more readily that Chinese literature is not just one indistinguishable mass of unfamiliar names and titles. Within the various sections of the anthology, a chronological and authorial scheme is adopted. Particularly for the earlier texts, however, dating is uncertain.

The reader will observe that biography and autobiography are particularly well represented in this anthology. The reasons for this are many. Chief among them is that much of the finest literature in China was written in the form of biographies; in terms of sheer literary merit, biography deserves a prominent position in any anthology of Chinese literature. Furthermore, a goodly proportion of Chinese history, both official and unofficial, was written in the form of biography. Consequently, several biographical pieces selected can also be placed under that category.

Two other types of literature proportionately better represented here than in other general anthologies of Chinese literature are the rhapsody and various popular genres derived from prosimetric oral storytelling. The former is stressed because it constitutes the first flowering of descriptive and imaginative literature, albeit one that often appears under a thin veil of didacticism. The latter is emphasized because it was from the oral and performing arts that fiction and drama in China took their lifeblood. In addition to a generous selection of works that derive from the oral and performing arts, I have also included texts in other genres that describe performers and their profession. In spite of the fact that next to nothing survives of genuine, unadulterated folk literature from the premodern period, I have selected a number of texts that adumbrate its qualities and concerns. I have also given due consideration to folk and popular literature in this anthology because it is through them that the tradition was continuously rejuvenated and rescued from stultification.

Chinese literature was overwhelmingly dominated by men until this century. Nonetheless, I have made a particular attempt to include works by and about women. Except where noted, however, all authors in this volume are male.[1]

This is an integrated compilation in the sense that the various works collected are viewed not as separate entities but as part of an organic whole. Each text or group of texts is numbered for ease of reference. Extensive cross-referencing is provided, for most of the texts refer or allude to one or more of the other texts. By structure and design, the entire anthology is an exercise in intertextual analysis. In the notes the translators and I have pointed out themes and images that recur in different genres dating from different periods. It is surprising, for example, how often tidal bores and cockfighting reappear in texts widely separated from one another in time. But that such motifs and allusions (as well as hundreds of others) keep coming back again and again in a self-referential way is an interesting feature of Chinese literature that should not be overlooked.

Another facet of Chinese literature to which we pay especial attention is its interrelationship with the other arts. For example, I offer several poems about specific paintings and several others actually inscribed on paintings, together with a couple that discuss the subject of painting as a whole. Reactions to different kinds of music and dance and appreciations of the skill of craftsmen also appear. Moreover, I have included an extensive section on literary criticism and theory. This is somewhat unusual for an anthology of Chinese literature but nonetheless vital for understanding what the Chinese themselves thought of their own literary tradition.

Many of the texts are chosen for their potential in stimulating classroom discussion. College and university students might become excited by reading a Chinese text for many reasons. One of these is its similarity to or contrast with something from their own tradition. For example, the transformation text on Maudgalyāyana's journey to hell in search of his mother bears fruitful comparison with Dante's *Inferno* and parts of Milton's *Paradise Lost*. The narrative poem about the girl warrior Mulan immediately calls to mind Joan

---

1. The principles concerning the matters discussed in the above paragraphs are more fully developed in my "Anthologizing and Anthropologizing: The Place of Non-Elite and Non-Standard Culture in the Chinese Literary Tradition," *Working Papers in Asian / Pacific Studies* (Durham: Duke University Asian / Pacific Studies Institute, 1992).

of Arc. Li Ju-chen's "The Women's Kingdom" is strongly reminiscent of chapters from Jonathan Swift's *Gulliver's Travels*.

The reader needs no prior knowledge of Chinese languages, script, or history to use this anthology. It is designed not just for students at large research universities with many sinologists on the faculty and with extensive library resources. It is also created to satisfy the needs of students at small colleges that may have only one faculty member on their staff who handles all aspects of Chinese civilization (and often of other Asian civilizations as well). I would certainly be gratified if readers who have no academic affiliation become acquainted with and learn to appreciate Chinese literature through this book.

Two decades of teaching Chinese literature to undergraduates at Tunghai, Harvard, and the University of Pennsylvania have taught me that it does not pay to overwhelm students with too much material. A deluge of texts by a host of authors is not nearly so effective as a few carefully chosen items by a smaller number of the most interesting writers. Students absorb much better a limited amount of material from an unfamiliar culture than a massive quantity thrown at them all at once. It makes no sense to strive for utter comprehensiveness in a book of this sort. This is, after all, an anthology, and it is the business of the anthologist to pick and choose. At the same time, I recognize both my obligation to provide the reader with a representative sample of the entire breadth of Chinese literature in all its abundance and my desire to satisfy the different interests of as many instructors and students as possible. Beyond striving judiciously to fulfill both responsibilities, I wish to offer a few pleasant surprises for those who may already have become somewhat jaded by reading too much in one small corner of the universe of Chinese literature or who have prematurely succumbed to stereotypes about its supposed exoticism and overrefinement. My hope is that this anthology will be one that everyone will be enticed to dip into, if not necessarily devour from cover to cover (although that, too, would be nice).

In the end, the responsible anthologist can do no more than select from the vast abundance that confronts him those items he is prepared to justify on the grounds of literary excellence or lasting significance. While trying to cover as many genres and types of subject matter as feasible within the liberal confines of 1,300–odd pages, I have also kept a sharp lookout for quality. I have searched for pieces that are animated and esthetically pleasing, since these are often the most attractive and memorable for undergraduates. Unless a text has demonstrable literary virtues or provides valuable insights and remarkable impressions (whether these be social or intellectual), I have not considered it for inclusion. The same holds for the most sophisticated examples of belles-lettres and for the most vibrant, earthy texts from the folk and popular realms. Above all, I did not want this anthology to be a stale collection of the same old chestnuts presented over and over as the quintessence of Chinese literature. I hope the reader will for the first time be exposed to the true richness of the Chinese literary tradition, not just a preconceived notion of what is "elevated."

I view this anthology as a companion volume for *Sources of Chinese Tradition*, also published by Columbia University Press. As such, it scrupulously avoids duplicating the types of material available in *Sources*. Texts dealing with religion, thought, philosophy, institutions, and so forth have not been included in the present volume unless they demonstrate literary merit or significance. This anthology can very well be used as the primary textbook for a one-semester general course on traditional Chinese literature or as an ancillary text for introductory courses on Chinese history, civilization, society, and culture. Nevertheless, because of the high literary quality and unavailability elsewhere of the new translations it offers, many instructors may also wish to assign it, perhaps together with other materials, for more specialized courses on Chinese literature.

Apart from five or six texts specified in the annotations, all the selections in this anthology were originally written in one of the four following languages:

1. Classical Chinese (also called Literary Chinese or Literary Sinitic) in a wide variety of styles
2. Medieval Vernacular Sinitic, also in a number of variants
3. Early Mandarin, with extremely rare admixtures from the nonstandard Sinitic topolects and from non-Sinitic languages
4. Buddhist Hybrid Sinitic

The task of preparing another anthology of Chinese folk, popular, and "minority" literature to include texts written in the many other Sinitic and non-Sinitic languages of China remains to be fulfilled, although Mark Bender and I have taken the initial steps in preparing such a compilation.

With a handful of exceptions (for example, a professor at Oxford University, a retired schoolteacher from Shanghai, two distinguished American poets, a deceased British missionary-sinologist, a deceased British military officer who was also a student of Chinese religion, a Chinese author of international stature), the vast majority of translators represented are professional sinologists teaching in American universities. All highly skilled, they have their own distinctive styles of translation, some striving more for utmost accuracy and others being more concerned with felicity of expression. No matter what their preferences, however, all are subject to a universal rule for translators of Chinese texts: the highly elliptical nature of written Sinitic languages, especially Classical Chinese, makes it necessary for any translator of a work of Chinese literature to add numerous components in order for the final product to make sense in English. Where a Chinese sentence will often omit the subject or other parts of speech in a sentence and may not specify gender, number, tense, mood, and the like, the requirements of English grammar generally demand that such things be supplied. In strictly sinological translation, there are precise conventions (mainly the use of parentheses and brackets) for designating which elements have been added and which were already present in the original text. So as not to interfere with the smooth reading of these texts by nonspecialists, all such technical apparatus has been removed, except in rare circumstances where its retention is deemed appropriate to convey significant information for the general reader. Occasionally, other minor changes are made in the translations so that readers will not be confused by varying conventions.

Similarly, sinological translations are often studded with Chinese characters (i.e., sinographs). Since they would clearly be useless and out of place in an anthology of this nature, all sinographs have been removed except in one text that deals with the nature of the writing system itself. Likewise, there is no point in providing long strings of transcribed Chinese syllables for readers to whom they would only be so many meaningless sounds. Hence, titles of poems, essays, and so forth are normally given only in translation, although the titles of important books are also provided in romanized form for ease of reference.

Save when a consecutive group of translations is done by one person (in which case the translator's name appears at the end of the series), the names of the translators of all the selections in this anthology are given at the bottom of each piece.

Aside from half a dozen special cases (to be discussed below), annotations are held to a minimum. This is partly to keep an already large book within managcable limits but also because overly detailed notes and commentaries would only distract from the pleasure of reading the works themselves and not be assimilable by the typical reader. Indeed, my intention has been to devise translations that can stand on their own as literary texts in English without elaborate notes. In two cases fuller annotations are called for. First, we demonstrate how traditional Chinese commentators read and explicated literary texts. Second, we provide more explanatory notes when the original work is too densely allusive or highly symbolic to understand without extensive commentary. In general, the notes avoid technicalities and do not deal with such narrow matters as textual emendations and various identifications of place names.

In the following, I shall discuss several additional technical and mechanical aspects of this anthology. First and foremost is how to represent the sounds of sinographs. The pronunciation of Chinese characters varies greatly through history and across the geographic expanse of this great empire. It is only a convention that we use Modern Standard Mandarin (hereafter MSM) to represent the sinographs in our writings about China. In many ways, MSM is the least satisfactory of all Sinitic languages for reading out traditional Chinese texts. Certainly it would be better to recite early poetry in Cantonese or Fukienese, which preserve significant features of the old phonology. This is ironic since languages such as Cantonese and Fukienese are farther removed from the center of Sinitic civilization and were incorporated relatively late into the cultural sphere of China. The main explanation for this phenomenon lies in the fact that peripheral extensions of a cultural entity frequently tend to be the most conservative. Furthermore, the north of China was often dominated to one extent or another by non-Sinitic peoples. For example, Särbi, Tibetan, Tabgatch, Tangut, Khitan, Jürchen, Mongol, and Manchu rulers (not an exhaustive list) established dynasties or kingdoms that controlled all or part of north China. The latter two groups, in fact, succeeded in gaining control over the whole of China for considerable periods of time and expanded the military and political might of the empire beyond the limits of what it had been under ethnic Han rulers. A heavy Altaic impact—lexical, grammatical, phonological, and otherwise—on northern Sinitic languages such as Mandarin was unavoidable in these circumstances. Consequently, Mandarin as spoken today is furthest removed from the older stages of Sinitic and thus least suitable for representing the language of most of the works of literature collected here. Yet a nearly universal practice among scholars who write about Chinese history in alphabetic languages is to use the sounds of MSM as the sole phonetic realization of the sinographs. I believe that sinology in the twenty-first century will almost certainly progress to a stage where references to proper nouns relating to earlier periods and regional cultures will routinely be provided in reconstructions or transcriptions that appropriately and accurately reflect their actual pronunciation instead of in MSM.

Granting that we are presently obliged, because of inadequate historical reconstructions and a paucity of topolectical handbooks, to use MSM as the sole phoneticization of the sinographs, we are faced with the necessity of making a choice among numerous competing transcriptions of MSM. That adopted for the present anthology is a slightly modified form of Wade-Giles, the old sinological standard.[2] Wade-Giles romanization of MSM is still used

---

2. A few special spellings have been adopted. *Chow* is used to transcribe the name of the depraved and tyrannical last emperor of the Shang dynasty to distinguish him from the succeeding Chou dynasty. *Wey* is used to differentiate the Chou dynasty state from the Warring States kingdom Wei. *Yi* is used throughout instead of *I* so as not to be confused with the first-person English pronoun (except for *Yee*, which signifies the name of a freehold during the Shang period, and *Yih*, which stands for the name of a high official under the legendary ruler Yü, as distinguished from the famous archer Yi). *Yüh* is used as the alternative name for the legendary ruler Shun to differentiate him from Yü who controlled the flood. The old reconstructions *Viet* and *Ngwa* are used to signify the ancient southern states of Yüeh and Wu to distinguish them from other homophonous names in MSM or to emphasize that the original inhabitants of these regions spoke non-Sinitic languages. (No specific claims are made for their relatedness to any other ancient or modern peoples.) *Tuo* is sometimes used for To to avoid confusion with the English preposition. Finally, following the preference of several of the translators, hyphens are occasionally omitted between syllables.

by the overwhelming majority of sinologists and virtually all major academic research libraries in English-speaking countries. Furthermore, the vast bulk of scholarly writing in English about Chinese literature employs Wade-Giles romanization. It would be terribly confusing and difficult for students without any background in the study of Mandarin (the typical student who will use this book) to try to follow up the readings with any sort of research if another romanization system were chosen. Pinyin (the official romanized script of the People's Republic of China), however, has lately become widely current in the mass media and many introductory Mandarin courses use it exclusively, so I have included a conversion chart from Wade-Giles to Pinyin for those already familiar with the latter. It should be noted that a few of the translations selected here originally employed Pinyin or other transcription systems; these have been uniformly converted to Wade-Giles for consistency. As more than a hundred translators are involved in the making of this anthology, it is virtually impossible to attain absolute uniformity with regard to capitalization, hyphenation, and diacritics. Each translator brings to the task of translation his or her own expertise and style. This is a distinct advantage for a work in which a wide variety of literary texts must be interpreted, but the difficulty of dissimilarities in usage cannot always be overcome with complete satisfaction for all parties concerned.

For ease of reference, line numbers are usually provided for poems eight or more lines in length, except when they are clearly divided into easily identifiable stanzas or when they possess a strong narrative content. The lines of lyrics and arias have not been numbered; nor have those of rhapsodies unless the translator has specifically requested that they be so treated.

Chinese authors may have many different names, such as soubriquets, styles, studio names, pen names, nicknames, fancy names, cognomens, and milk (i.e., baby) names. Even in this century, a well-known author like Lu Hsün (not his real name!) employed more than a hundred aliases. To avoid hopeless confusion, I have usually referred to authors and other individuals only by the name by which they are best known.

I have found it convenient to introduce one new English word in the translations, namely, *tricent*. This means "three hundred paces" (approximately one third of a mile) and is modeled on the word *mile* (from Latin *mille*, i.e., "[a] thousand [paces]"). Sinologists have long felt the need for such a word to render accurately the Chinese unit of length, *li*, because the same syllable is also used to transcribe the following frequently cited terms: *principle, rites / ritual / etiquette / ceremony / civility, benefit / profit / gain, ward*, as well as another smaller unit of length (⅓ millimeter), a unit of weight (.05 grams), a unit of area (.666 square meters), a monetary unit (one thousandth of a Chinese dollar), a unit of monthly interest (.1 percent), and so forth. Simply to transcribe *li* would, at best, be meaningless for an American reader and, at worst, ambiguous or misleading. *Tricent* is an exact equivalent of *li* in the sense of a third of a mile and represents a happy solution to a difficult problem in sinological translation that the majority of contributors whom I have consulted welcome warmly. (To convert tricents to miles, divide by three.)

BIBLIOGRAPHICAL NOTE

The most important source of information for the brief introductory notes is *The Indiana Companion to Traditional Chinese Literature* (Bloomington: Indiana University Press, 1986; rev. rpt. Taipei: Southern Materials Center, 1988), William H. Nienhauser, Jr. (editor and compiler), Charles Hartman (associate editor for poetry), Y. W. Ma (associate editor for fiction), and Stephen H. West (associate editor for drama). While not without the blemishes that one might expect from such a massive and complicated work, this is a magnificent reference tool and the first one to which readers should turn in pursuit of questions raised by the texts in this anthology. (Perhaps the next best place for readers to turn to would be the guides to Chinese prose, poetry, drama, and fiction published by G. K. Hall.) The entries in Nienhauser et al. are succinct and authoritative; in many cases it has been impossible to simplify them further. The ample bibliographies provide citations to the best available scholarship in English, French, German, Russian, Chinese, Japanese, and other languages. My debt to *The Indiana Companion* is great, and I wish to acknowledge it explicitly.

Other works frequently consulted in drawing up the annotations include Helwig Schmidt-Glintzer's *Geschichte der chinesischen Literatur: Die 3000-jährige Entwicklung der poetischen, erzählenden und philosophisch-religiösen Literatur China von den Anfängen bis zur Gegenwart* (Bern, München, Wien: Scherz, 1990). The most comprehensive single-volume history of Chinese literature, it is current, full of valuable insights, and extensively documented. Also useful has been Eugen Feifel, *Geschichte der chinesischen Literatur: Mit Berücksichtigung ihres geistesgeschichtlichen Hintergrundes* (Hildesheim, Zürich, New York: Georg Olms, 1982). This compact volume, which is packed with detailed information, is based upon Nagasawa Kikuya's *Shina gakujutsu bungeishi* but has expanded upon it considerably. Relying heavily on the excellent Czech school of sinology is the *Dictionary of Oriental Literatures*, Vol. 1, East Asia (New York: Basic Books, 1974), Jaroslav Průšek (general editor) and Zbigniew Słupski (volume editor). While the coverage of this volume is limited and bibliographies are minimal, the entries, high in quality, merit careful reading. Finally, there is the old standby, *Topics in Chinese Literature: Outlines and Bibliographies*, Harvard-Yenching Institute Studies, Vol. 3 (Cambridge: Harvard University Press, 1953 rev. ed.) by James Robert Hightower. Although the bibliographies are completely out of date, the series of seventeen essays on various genres reveals the hand of a master. This remains the best brief survey of Chinese literature for someone who desires a perceptive overview of the field.

Certain annotations are based on more specialized works. Among these are John Timothy Wixted's translation of Yoshikawa Kōjirō's *Five Hundred Years of Chinese Poetry, 1150–1650: The Chin, Yuan, and Ming Dynasties* (Princeton: Princeton University Press, 1989) and Lois Fusek's *Among the Flowers* (New York: Columbia University Press, 1982). I am especially indebted to the rich fund of folklore and historical data in Anne Birrell's two volumes, *Popular Songs and Ballads of Han China* (London, Sydney, Wellington: Unwin Hyman, 1988; rev. ed., Honolulu: University of Hawaii Press, 1993) and *New Songs from Jade Terrace: An Anthology of Early Chinese Love Poetry* (London: George Allen and Unwin, 1982; rev. ed., Harmondsworth: Penguin, 1986); they have served as the basis for a number of annotations in this anthology. The commentaries and notes in Harold Shadick's *A First Course in Literary Chinese*, 3 vols. (Ithaca, London: Cornell University Press, 1968) have also been helpful. For the brief biographical notices of poets, I have relied heavily on Burton Watson, *The Columbia Book of Chinese Poetry: From Early Times to the Thirteenth Century* (New York: Columbia University Press, 1984) and Jonathan Chaves, *The Columbia Book of Later Chinese Poetry* (New York: Columbia University Press, 1986). The introductions to the commentaries in Professor Watson's other numerous translations of Chinese literary texts have also been extensively relied upon.

ACKNOWLEDGMENTS

I am deeply grateful to everyone, including the translators, who has contributed annotations for the various selections in the anthology or made suggestions about how to improve the annotations. In many instances when a translation was previously published, I have adapted the introductory note and annotations from their original source. Often, however, the translators have provided new notes, or I have written them myself because the old ones were not suitable for this anthology.

I am indebted to all of the translators, editors of journals, and publishers who have made their works available to me. If, by chance, I have inadvertently overlooked someone/thing or failed to give sufficient credit where it is due, I can only plead that it was unintentional and beg the indulgence of those concerned. Where such omissions may have unfortunately occurred, they will be promptly corrected in future printings if called to my attention.

The following people have been particularly kind in making suggestions for improvements to the notes or for making occasional corrections to the translations: Derk Bodde, Stephen R. Bokenkamp, Daniel Bryant, James Crump, Robert Joe Cutter, Kenneth DeWoskin, Milena Doleželová-Velingerová, Glen Dudbridge, Elling Eide, Patrick Hanan, Valerie Hansen, James Hargett, Charles Hartman, Robert Hegel, James Robert Hightower, Dale R. Johnson, Paul W. Kroll, Richard Kunst, Richard Mather, Tsu-Lin Mei, William H. Nienhauser, Jr., Charles Orzech, Stephen Owen, Stuart Sargent, Phyllis Brooks Schafer, Jerry Schmidt, Chung-wen Shih, Richard Strassberg, and John Wang.

I wish especially to thank the following for offering valuable advice concerning possible selections: Alan Berkowitz, Gloria Bien, Derk Bodde, Peter Bol, E. Bruce Brooks, Daniel Bryant, Susan Bush, K. C. Chang, Jonathan Chaves, Yu-shih Chen, Min-chih Chou, Alvin Cohen, James Crump, Kenneth DeWoskin, Albert Dien, Milena Doleželová-Velingerová, Elling Eide, Jeannette Faurot, Michael Fuller, Patrick Hanan, Valerie Hansen, Donald Harper, Charles Hartman, Robert Hegel, James Robert Hightower, Wilt Idema, Dale R. Johnson, David Keightley, David Knechtges, Andrew Kopecki, Peter Li, Richard Lynn, Y. W. Ma, Richard Mather, David McCraw,

Lev Nikolaevich Men'shikov, Lucien Miller, William H. Nienhauser, Jr., Stephen Owen, Andrew Plaks, Stuart Sargent, Wayne Schlepp, Jerry Schmidt, Jerome Seaton, Harold Shadick, Edward Shaughnessy, Jonathan Spence, Richard Strassberg, Lynn Struve, Frederic Wakeman, C. K. Wang, John Wang, Ellen Widmer, Charles Wivell, Timothy Wixted, Timothy C. Wong, Philip Yampolsky, and Pauline Yu. While I consider the advice from these and other scholars to be of great value, it has been impossible for me to accommodate all the excellent suggestions put to me. Thus, the final responsibility for choices made and the manner of their treatment rests solely with the editor. I sincerely wish that I had been able to include all their suggestions, but the result would have been an unwieldy and unaffordable behemoth of little practical use to anyone, least of all the teachers and students to whom this book is directed.

Some selections have been chosen because of their immense popularity (e.g., Lin Yutang's translation of Shen Fu's *Six Chapters of a Floating Life*, which has been suggested by my colleagues more than any other text). Many of the selections, however, reflect my own preferences and strong desire to represent all segments of society and all parts of the Chinese empire.

Thomas Lawton, Senior Research Scholar at the Freer Gallery of Art (Smithsonian Institution), has provided me with important information concerning the peach-stone boat described in selection 209. I deeply appreciate his willingness to take time from a busy schedule to do research for me and I am indebted to my colleague Nancy Steinhardt for introducing me to him.

Thanks are due to Zhu Hong for having read over my translation of the "Ballad of the Maiden of Lan-ling" and for making a good suggestion about how to improve it. I am also indebted to Achilles Fang, William Hung, and Lien-sheng Yang for having offered helpful comments on an early draft translation of the tenth story in the "Chi Yün Sampler."

I want to acknowledge the kindness of Irene Bloom in permitting me to use Richard Lynn's translation from *Ts'ang-lang's Discussions of Poetry*, which was originally prepared for her forthcoming edited volume entitled *Sources of Neo-Confucian Tradition*.

Naturally, an anthology of this scope would not have been possible without the cooperation of the numerous contributors. My thanks to each of them for kindly consenting to let their work become a part of this anthology. I am especially indebted to those contributors who have prepared new translations expressly for this anthology or who have permitted me to use translations they hope to publish themselves later on. Many of the works appearing here for the first time are available nowhere else.

Some of the translations have already appeared in various books and journals. I wish to register here my particular gratitude to their publishers and editors for granting permission to reprint in this anthology.

Most of the editorial work on this volume was carried out while I was a fellow at the National Humanities Center (1991–92). The entire staff of the center was extremely helpful in all phases of the project, and I consider myself extraordinarily fortunate to have been chosen to spend a year in that wonderfully stimulating environment. In particular, I wish to register my thanks to the librarians, Alan Tuttle, Rebecca Vargha, and Jean Houston, who kept me supplied with a steady flow of books, and to the manuscript typists, Karen Carroll and Linda Morgan, who performed wonders of decipherment for me on an almost daily basis. My residency at the National Humanities Center was funded by the National Endowment for the Humanities and the Mellon Foundation; without their generous support this anthology could never have become a reality.

In a work of this magnitude, which has involved correspondence with hundreds of people, it is likely that I have overlooked others who have given me assistance in its compilation. If such be the case, I beg their forgiveness and will make amends for the oversight on some future occasion if it is brought to my attention.

I wish to take this opportunity to express my gratitude to Jennifer Crewe, senior executive editor at Columbia University Press, for the expert guidance and sympathetic understanding she has given me at all stages of this project, from the very inception of the anthology to its appearance in print. Thanks are also due to Jessica Rosenthal Benson, Eve Bayrock, and Adam Tibbs, editorial assistants, for many kind favors. Anne McCoy, managing editor of the press, took a great interest in the manuscript, and Amy Lui-Ma edited it meticulously. I deeply appreciate the contributions both of them have made to this book.

For reading through portions of the manuscript and for providing intellectual stimulation, I am profoundly grateful to Jing Wang. My brothers, Joseph, Thomas, and Denis, gave me much love and encouragement when I despaired of completing this large project. The latter two also helped with the proofreading, as did my son, Thomas. Finally, to my wife, Li-ching, I am forever indebted for many years of support and understanding.

Victor H. Mair

HEILUNGKIANG

KIRIN

MONGOLIA

LIAONING

INNER

Yellow River

NINGHSIA

KOREA

• Peking
Tientsin

HOPEI

Taiyuan

SHANSI

Tsinan Tsingtao
▲ Mt. T'ai
SHANTUNG

Yellow Kaifeng
Loyang Chengchow

Sian
(Ch'ang–an)

SHENSI

HONAN

Huai R.

KIANGSU

JAPAN

Yangchow

Nanking

Soochow
Shanghai

HUPEI

ANHWEI

Ch'ien-
t'ang
R.

Hangchow

Yangtze River

Chungking

Tung–t'ing
Lake

Mt.
Lu

P'o–
yang
Lake

CHEKIANG

Changsha

KIANGSI

KWEI–
CHOW

HUNAN

FUKIEN

Chuanchow

KWANGSI

KWANGTUNG

TAIWAN

Canton

HAINAN

CHINA

ᵒᵒᵒ Long
Walls

ⱇⱇⱇ Grand
Canal

PART I

Foundations and Interpretations

Divinations
and Inscriptions

I
A Late Shang Divination Record

Oracle Bone (early 12th century B.C.E.).

(**Preface:**) Crack-making on *chia-shen* (day twenty-one), Ch'üeh divined: (**Charge:**) "Lady Hao will give birth and it will be good." (**Prognostication:**) The king read the cracks and said: "If it be on a *ting* day that she give birth, it will be good. If it be on a *keng* day that she give birth, there will be prolonged luck." (**Verification:**) After thirty-one days, on *chia-yin* (day fifty-one), she gave birth. It was not good. It was a girl.

The kings of the late Shang period (c. 1200–1050 B.C.E.) attempted to communicate with the spiritual forces that ruled their world by reading the stress cracks in cattle scapulas and turtle plastrons. They and their diviners produced these cracks by applying a heated brand or poker to the bones or shells, intoning, as they did so, a charge that conveyed their intentions, wishes, or need to know. After the divination ritual was over, a record of the topic and, sometimes, of the prognostication and the result, was engraved into the bone. Those inscriptions, recovered only within the last hundred years by archeologists and painstakingly deciphered by paleographers, provide a direct contact with many of the Shang kings' daily activities and concerns. This inscription, like many, shows that the Shang king himself, in this case Wu Ting (ca. 1200–1180 B.C.E.), read the oracle. The ritual and spiritual ability to foretell the future was generally a royal monopoly; the diviners, such as Ch'üeh, rarely prognosticated in this way.

The inscriptions on the oracle bones represent the earliest written Sinitic texts. Since the script is in essence fully formed when it first appears and there are few if any indigenous precursors in the rich archeological record for the preceding millennia that reveal its gradual development, the origins of writing in China remain deeply puzzling. New discoveries and directions in research, however, are expected to throw light on this question.

For more information on the Chinese writing system, see selection 199.

(Preface:) Crack-making on *chia-shen* (day twenty-one), Ch'üeh divined: (Charge:) "Lady Hao will give birth and it may not be good." (Verification:) After thirty-one days, on *chia-yin* (day fifty-one), she gave birth. It really was not good. It was a girl."

Translated by David N. Keightley

2
Two Bronze Inscriptions of the Western Chou

To Yu ting [Tripod]

To Yu (Late Western Chou)

It was the tenth month; because the Hsien-yün arose and broadly attacked the Ching Garrison it was reported back to the king, who commanded Duke Wu: "Dispatch your premier troops and pursue at Ching Garrison." Duke Wu commanded To Yu to lead the duke's chariotry in pursuit at Ching Garrison. On *kuei-wei* (day twenty), the belligerents attacked Hsün, taking captives. To Yu westwardly pursued. On the morning of *chia-shen* (day twenty-one), striking at Mai, To Yu cut off heads and manacled prisoners to be interrogated; in all, using the duke's chariotry to cut off the heads of two hundred and . . . five men, manacling twenty-three prisoners to be interrogated, capturing one hundred and seventeen of the belligerents' chariots, and taking back the captives from among the people of Hsün. And then striking at Kung, he cut off the heads of thirty-six men, manacled two prisoners to be interrogated, and captured ten chariots. Following in pursuit and striking at Shih, To Yu again cut off heads and manacled prisoners to be interrogated. Then he raced in chase as far as Yang-chung, where the duke's chariotry cut off the heads of one hundred and fifteen men and manacled three prisoners to be interrogated. The captured chariots could not be taken and were burned, with only the horses driving the wounded and the recovered prisoners from the Ching

The first of these two recently discovered inscriptions on bronze artifacts, the "To Yu *ting* [Tripod]," dates toward the beginning of the reign of King Hsüan (r. 827–782 B.C.E.; the exact date may be 816 B.C.E.) of the Chou dynasty and commemorates quite graphically a series of battles between a Chou army and a Hsien-yün army. The second inscription, on the "Shih Ch'iang *p'an* [Basin]," dates somewhat earlier, to the reign of King Kung (r. 917–900 B.C.E.) and may well represent the first conscious historical writing in the Chinese tradition. It should be noted, however, that these two inscriptions are not really representative in terms of their rather unusual length, narrative quality, and historiographical significance.

Garrison. To Yu then presented the captives, heads, and prisoners to be interrogated to the duke. Duke Wu then presented them to the king, who addressed Duke Wu, saying: "You have pacified the Ching Garrison; I enrich you, awarding you lands and fields." On *ting-yu* (day thirty-four), Duke Wu was at the Presentation Hall and commanded Hsiang-fu to summon To Yu, who then entered the Presentation Hall. The duke personally addressed To Yu, saying: "I began by giving you sanctuary; you have not transgressed but have succeeded in affairs and made a great catch. You have pacified the Ching Garrison; I award you one tessera, one set of golden bells, and one hundred catties of *hao-yu*-bronze." To Yu dares to respond to the duke's beneficence and herewith makes this precious cauldron with which to befriend him; may [my] sons and grandsons eternally treasure and use it.

Translated by Edward L. Shaughnessy

Shih Ch'iang p'an [Basin]

Wei Ch'iang (Middle Western Chou)

Accordant with antiquity was King Wen! He first brought harmony to government. The Lord on High sent down fine virtue and great security. Extending to the high and low, he joined the ten thousand states.

Capturing and controlling was King Wu! He proceeded and campaigned through the four quarters, piercing Yin and governing its people. Eternally unfearful of the Ti (Distant Ones), oh, he attacked the Yi minions.

Model and sagely was King Ch'eng! To the left and right he cast and gathered his net and line, therewith opening and integrating the Chou state.

Deep and wise was King K'ang! He divided command and pacified the borders.

Vast and substantial was King Chao! He broadly tamed Ch'u and Ching; it was to connect the southern route.

Reverent and illustrious was King Mu! He patterned himself on and followed the great counsels.

Continuing and tranquil is the Son of Heaven! The Son of Heaven strives to carry on the long valor of kings Wen and Wu. The Son of Heaven is diligent and without flaw, faithfully making offerings to the spirits above and below, and reverently glorifying the great plans. Heavenly radiant and incorruptible, the Lord on High, Hou Chi, and the witch protectors give to the Son of Heaven an extensive mandate, thick blessings, and abundant harvests. Among the borderland peoples and the *man*-savages, there are none who do not hasten to appear at court.

Pure and retiring was the High Ancestor! He was at the numinous place of Wei. When King Wu had already defeated Yin, the Wei scribes and valorous ancestors came to present themselves in audience to King Wu. King Wu then commanded the Duke of Chou to dispense to them domicile at a low place of Chou.

Happy and helpful was Ancestor Yi! He assisted and served his ruler, distantly planning with belly and heart his son's acceptance.

Clear-eyed and bright was Grandfather Hsin of the branch lineage! Transferring the lineage and nurturing sons and grandsons, he had abundant good fortune and many blessings. Even-horned and redly gleaming, appropriate were his sacrifices.

Extending and even was my cultured deceased father, Duke Yi! Strong and bright, he obtained purity. Without owing agricultural harvests, surpassing shoots were the openings of the new fields.

Filial and convivial is Scribe Ch'iang! Morning and night not dropping, may he daily have his merits acknowledged. Ch'iang does not dare to stop, and in response extols the Son of Heaven's illustriously beneficent command, herewith making this treasured, sacrificial vessel. Would that his valorous ancestors and cultured deceased father grant favor and give Ch'iang vibrant freshness, fortunate peace, blessed wealth, a yellowing old age, and a prolonged life so that he may be worthy to serve his lord! May he for ten thousand years eternally treasure and use it.

Translated by Edward L. Shaughnessy

3

The Book of Changes of the Chou People

1. Ch'ien (Heaven)[1]

Anonymous (Western Chou?)

1.0 Grand treat.[2]
     A favorable determination.[3]

The *Changes*, known in modern Chinese as *Yi-ching (I-ching), The Classic of Changes*, or *Chou-yi (The Changes of Chou)*, is one of China's oldest books. Originally a diviner's manual, it was used in conjunction with a type of divination in which stalks of the yarrow plant were manipulated in groups of four to arrive at a series of numbers that were keys to lines in the text. The text itself was probably orally transmitted and elaborated by many generations of diviners in the Shang and Chou dynasties in the first two millennia B.C.E., and came to be written down in

1.1 A submerged dragon.[4]
Do not use it.[5]

substantially its present form in the early centuries of the Chou dynasty, which nominally ruled from about 1100 B.C.E. until about 200 B.C.E. The oldest known version of the text, which is the basis of this translation, consists of sixty-four brief "chapters" associated with sixty-four hexagrams as identifying labels, each hexagram being one of the sixty-four possible combinations of six solid or broken lines. Each hexagram-chapter is composed of a hexagram text and six (or, in two cases, seven) line texts. The texts are filled with a variety of omens and images which, often in rhyme and probably involving word-magic, are based upon puns on like-sounding words, obscure allusions to historical episodes such as "curiosity killed the cat," and folk wisdom such as "step on a crack and break your mother's back." Perhaps as the diviners manipulated the yarrow stalks and kept obtaining the same hexagrams and lines in connection with certain omens or situations of their clients, they might have begun to keep track of these *synchronicities*, along with their actual outcomes—auspicious, threatening, unfortunate, and so on—so as to improve their predictive power. These diviners' notes formed the core of the *Changes*.

Centuries later, in the Warring States period of the late Chou dynasty and Han dynasty, commentaries were added by urbane scholars of the day to the original text to explain the meaning of what had become a very archaic and obscure work in terms comprehensible to the more sophisticated Chinese society of their day. These commentaries gradually found their way into the canon itself, adding a new and more philosophical layer of meaning to the once simple classic. Two of the most important of these commentaries are offered in selection 4. This sort of reinterpretation continued through the centuries; important commentaries were written that recast the *Changes* in a Taoist, Buddhist, or Neo-Confucian light, with the *Changes* reaching a pinnacle of importance in the Neo-Confucian thought of the Sung dynasty. Art, literature, natural philosophy, and even the martial arts have all drawn heavily from the tradition of the *Changes* for their theoretical framework and terminology.

1. Almost all the names of the sixty-four hexagram-chapters in the *Changes* originated as tags designating a hexagram by selecting a prominent word in the hexagram or line texts, and writing it at the beginning of the hexagram text if it did not already occur at that position. Thus Ch'ien occurs in the line text 1.3 reduplicated as an echoic adverb of manner, describing the vigorous appearance of a nobleman. In later eras each hexagram name took on a rich symbolic significance. The most famous pair of these symbols were Ch'ien and K'un. Ch'ien became the symbol of Heaven, the yang principle, the active and creative, while K'un became its counterpart, the symbol of Earth, the yin principle, the passive and receptive.

2. The "grand treat" was a sacrificial offering accepted by the gods. The notation "grand treat" or just "treat" appears frequently throughout the *Changes*, particularly in the hexagram texts which begin each hexagram-chapter. It is a mildly imperative "treat!", which is a mandate to the diviner consulting the stalks to offer a sacrificial treat.

3. The word translated here as "determination" occurs often in the text of the *Changes*. It started out as a technical term inherited from the oracular tradition of the Shang dynasty, in which it always preceded a divinatory charge to the oracle bone or turtle plastron involving a proposition to be tested, an issue to be settled. From this original sense of "resolution of doubt," referring to a divinatory determination, it later evolved into a personal moral quality of "firm resolution" or "perseverance." Note that the English words "determination" and "resolution" themselves wear these two semantic hats. "Favorable determination" came to mean that when this line was encountered in manipulating the stalks, it would be favorable to be firm and determined.

4. The Chinese dragon was overall an auspicious beast, which usually dwelt in water. We are free to understand the dragons here as powerful mythic symbols, as do the Chinese.

5. This probably means that one should not use the outcome of the divinatory determination in action.

1.2 See a dragon in a field: it will be favorable to see a big man.[6]

1.3 Nobles throughout the day are *g'ian-g'ian* vigorous, but at night they are wary.[7]

Threatening, but there will be no misfortune.

1.4 Or it leaps in the deep: no misfortune.

1.5 A dragon flying in the sky: it will be favorable to see a big man.

1.6 A dragon in a gully: there will be trouble.

1.7 See a group of dragons without heads: auspicious.[8]

2. *K'un (Earth)*

2.0 Grand treat.

A determination favorable for a mare.

A noble who is going somewhere will first lose his way and later find a host.

Favorable to the west and south—one will find a friend. To the east and north he will lose a friend.

Auspicious in a determination about security.

2.1 When one steps on the frost, the solid ice is coming.[9]

2.2 Straight and square, big and not doubled up:[10] there is nothing for which this is unfavorable.

2.3 Hold a jade talisman in the mouth.

---

6. The society of the early Chou dynasty was divided into an aristocratic class, referred to in the *Changes* as "nobles" or "big men," and the common people, referred to as "small men." The class society of early Chou was later reinterpreted by Confucius and his contemporaries in ethical terms, just like the word "noble" in English. "Noble" came to mean noble in behavior, not in birth, while a small man was mean-spirited and lacking in the Confucian virtues.

7. *G'ian-g'ian* is the reduplicated Old Chinese pronunciation of the hexagram name Ch'ien.

8. The first two hexagram-chapters in the traditional order, Ch'ien and K'un, both have an extra—seventh—line text, the original purpose of which is not clear. These lines are labeled "use nine" and "use six" in the text. One explanation of this usage is that the seventh line is consulted when all the lines one obtains in manipulating the yarrow stalks are "nines" (in the first hexagram Ch'ien) or "sixes" (in the second hexagram K'un).

9. Many of the line texts of the *Changes* are in rhyme, either internally or with a rhyming word in each of successive line texts. In the hexagram-chapter K'un, the words "frost" in 2.1, "square" in 2.2, "jade talisman" in 2.3, "pouch" in 2.4, "skirt" in 2.5, and "yellow-bright" in 2.6 all rhyme—even in modern Mandarin. The rhyme is also echoed by the notation "grand treat" and the word "going" in the hexagram text 2.0. Sound symbolism could have led to each of the rhyming emblems being collected in this hexagram-chapter, all linked by their sound with one another and with the "grand treat" sacrifice.

10. This might have been a description of the shape of a crack made by a diviner in an oracle bone. One scholarly view holds that the tradition of the *Changes* originated as a supplement to the oracle bone divination of the Shang and early Chou dynasties. Thus the *Changes* was a quick and literally "easy" (*yi*) way to prognosticate a crack.

Can be determined.[11]

If someone pursues the service of the king, there will be no completion; there will be an end.

2.4 Bind up a pouch: there will be no misfortune and no honor.

2.5 A yellow skirt: very auspicious.

2.6 Dragons battle in the open country. Their blood is dark and yellow-bright.[12]

2.7 Favorable in a long-range determination.[13]

63. *Chi-chi (Already across the stream)*

63.0 Treat.

A somewhat favorable determination.

Auspicious for the beginning, but a tangle at the end.[14]

63.1 He trails along the spun thread.[15]

It wets its tail.[16]

There will be no misfortune.

63.2 A matron loses her wig. Do not search for it. She will get it in seven days.

63.3 The High Ancestor[17] attacked the Kuei[18] border tribe and conquered it in three years.

11. This is the strict grammatical sense, but the line may simply mean "an acceptable determination," i.e., the action divined about can be taken.

12. The hexagram-chapters of the *Changes* are divided into odd-and-even pairs, which are linked through their hexagram signs. The signs are related either by being reverse images of each other, with the yin-yang polarity of unbroken and broken lines reversed, as is the case with Ch'ien and K'un, or by being inverse, top-to-bottom mirror images of each other, as is the case with the last two hexagram chapters, no. 63 Chi-chi and no. 64 Wei-chi below. The pairs are sometimes semantically linked through common images in the line texts. Here the dragon image continues the imagery of the Ch'ien hexagram-chapter.

13. See note 8.

14. The word translated as "tangle" originally meant a tangle of thread, from which a general sense of "disorder" or "chaos" was derived. The Chinese character used to write this word shows two hands separating tangled silk threads on a frame. The omen of the tangled ends of silk strands, symbolic of disorder at the end of one's affairs, fits in with the images taken from spinning in the following line texts.

15. This must have been an omen associated with spinning technology. Spun or twisted thread could be a fishing line, as in song 226 the *Classic of Odes*, in which there is the line "This gentleman went fishing, I twisted the line for him." "He trails the line" would be a parallel image with the fox wetting his tail. Spinning images appear as a leitmotif throughout the line texts of the pair of hexagram-chapters composed of this and the following one, mingled with the images of the fox crossing the stream and various other historical anecdotes.

16. This probably refers to the "small fox" which is explicitly named in the hexagram text 64.0 of the paired hexagram below.

17. Probably a reference to the greatest king of the preceding Shang dynasty, King Wu-ting, who reigned c. 1200 B.C.E. See selection 1.

18. Although the character *kuei* later was used to write a word meaning "devil" or "ghost," it

A small man should not use this.

63.4 For a jacket there are those who wear worn-out silk floss.
Be cautious throughout the day.

63.5 The neighbors to the east slaughter an ox. It does not compare with the
summer sacrifice of the neighbors to the west in really receiving
their blessings.

63.6 It gets its head wet. Threatening.

64. *Wei-chi (Not yet across the stream)*

64.0 Treat.
The small fox is on the point of crossing the stream and wetting its tail:
there is nothing for which this is favorable.

64.1 It wets its tail: distress.

64.2 He trails along the spun thread.
The determination is auspicious.

64.3 It has not yet crossed the stream.
Ominous for an attack.
Favorable for wading across a big river.

64.4 The determination is auspicious. Troubles will go away.
Chen[19] used this to attack the Kuei border tribe and in three years was
rewarded in the great state.[20]

64.5 The determination is auspicious. There will be no trouble.
It will be glory for the nobles. There will be a capture.[21]
Auspicious.

---

probably refers here to the historically documented Hsien-pei (Šärbi) Altaic tribe, the Kuei, or
Kuei-jung.

19. *Chen* means "to thunder," "to shake." Here it appears to be the name of a historical
figure ("The Shaker"?), perhaps a general who took part in the attack referred to in lines 63.3
and 64.4. In the annals of the Shang dynasty, recorded more than a thousand years later in the
Han period history *Records of the Grand Historian (Shin Chi,* see selection 190), a certain Chen
is cited as an ancestral king of the Shang, while in a later history, the *Bamboo Annals,* quoted in
the *History of the Later Han (Hou Han Shu),* it is recorded that "in the thirty-fifth year of the
reign of Wu-yi, the Chou duke Chi-li attacked the western tribe, the Kuei-jung, and captured
twenty Ti tribe chieftains." The Shang king Wu-yi was great-grandson to King Wu-ting. So
Chen the Shaker might also have been the Chou chieftain Chi-li, who, generations before the
Chou people conquered the Shang and founded their own dynasty, helped the Shang attack the
Kuei, and was subsequently rewarded by the Shang, referred to here as "the great state." Most
likely, this line is a conflation of several historical traditions.

20. Perhaps a reference to the state of Shang, the dominant state in north China in the late
second millennium B.C.E.

21. The word *fu,* rendered here as "capture," is used frequently in bronze inscriptions and
other early Chou period texts to refer to the capture in battle of enemy prisoners or booty.
Captives in the Shang and early Chou often became either sacrificial victims or forced labor.
Later in the tradition of the *Changes,* the same word, still written with its archaic form now

64.6 There will be a capture while drinking wine.
     There will be no misfortune.
     It gets its head wet.
     There will be a capture.
     He will lose the ladle.[22]

Translated by Richard A. Kunst

---

unique to the *Changes*, is invariably interpreted as meaning "trustworthiness" or "sincerity." The link between the older and later usage is vague, but seems to turn on the concept of "reliability." Perhaps "capture" became "be captured," which became "be captivated by," which became "regard as reliable, trustworthy," which became "trustworthy, sincere." The transitional stage could be reflected in this line from the *Classic of Documents* (Chün-shih, 9): "Therefore, when the One Man (the king) had sacrificial services to the four quarters, if he performed the divinations with oracle bones and yarrow stalks, there were none which did not captivate him," i.e., there were none which were not reliable. It has also been proposed that this semantic shift might have been based on the ancient Chinese practice of taking hostages to ensure the reliability of one's enemies.

22. Reading the character *shih* of the received text as the original form of the word *ch'ih* ("ladle") would make this line similar to the earlier line "Do not lose ladle and aromatic spirits" (51.0). Retaining the common sense of *shih*, the phrase would instead mean "He will lose his decorum."

4
Two Early Commentaries on the *Classic of Changes*

Explaining the Trigrams

Anonymous (Han?)

1. In the distant past the way that the Sage[1] made the *Changes* is as follows: He was mysteriously assisted by the gods and so initiated the use of yarrow stalks. He made Heaven three and Earth two and so provided the numbers with a basis. He observed the flux between yin and yang and so established the trigrams. As the trigrams are begun and are dispersed due to the movement of the hard and soft lines, he initiated the use of the moving lines. He was in complete accord with the Way and its Virtue, and the principles involved conform to rightness. He exhausted principles to the ut-

1. Here the *sheng* (sage/sages) is identified by traditional commentators as the mythical culture-hero Fu-hsi.

most and dealt thoroughly with human nature, and in doing so arrived at the workings of fate.

2. In the distant past, the way the sages[2] made the *Changes* was as follows: It was to be used as a means to stay in accord with the principles of nature and of fate. It was for this reason that they determined what the Way of Heaven was, which they defined in terms of yin and yang, what the Way of Earth was, which they defined in terms of hard and soft, and what the Way of Man was, which they defined in terms of benevolence and righteousness. They brought these three powers together and doubled them; this is why the *Changes* forms its hexagrams out of six lines. They provided yin allotments and yang allotments, so their functions alternate between soft and hard; this is why the *Changes* forms its patterns out of six positions.

3. As Heaven (*Ch'ien*,[3] Pure Yang), and Earth (*K'un*, Pure Yin) establish positions, as Mountain (*Ken*, Restraint) and Lake (*Tui*, Joy) have material force flow between them, as Thunder (*Chen*, Quake) and Wind (*Sun*, Compliance) give rise to each other, and as Water (*K'an*, Water Hole) and Fire (*Li*, Cohesion) do not fail to complement each other, the Eight Trigrams combine with one another in such a way that to reckon the past one follows the order of their progress, and to know the future one works backward through them. Therefore, the *Changes* allows us to work backward from the future and reckon forward from the past.

4. It is by Thunder (*Chen*, Quake) that things are caused to move, by Wind (*Sun*, Compliance) that they are dispersed, by Rain (*K'an*, Water Hole) that they are moistened, by the Sun (*Li*, Fire, Cohesion) that they are dried, by Restraint (*Ken*) that they are made to stop, by Joy (*Tui*) that they are made happy, by Pure Yang (*Ch'ien*, Heaven) that they are provided with a Sovereign, and by Pure Yin (*K'un*, Earth) that they are harbored.

5. The Divine Ruler comes forth in Quake (*Chen*) and sets all things in order in Compliance (*Sun*), makes them visible to one another in Cohesion (*Li*, also Fire, Brightness), gives them maximum support in Pure Yin (*K'un*, also Earth), makes them happy then in Joy (*Tui*), has them do battle in Pure Yang (*Ch'ien*), finds them thoroughly worn out in Water Hole (*K'an*), and has them reach final maturity in Restraint (*Ken*).

The myriad things come forth in Quake (*Chen*); Quake corresponds to the East. They are set in order in Compliance (*Sun*); Compliance corresponds to the Southeast. "Set in order" means that they are fresh and neat. *Li* (Cohesion) here means Brightness. That the myriad things are made visible to one another signifies the trigram of the South. The fact that the Sage faces the South to listen to the whole world and turns toward the Brightness there to rule is

2. It is likely that *sheng* now refers to the ancient sages collectively: Fu-hsi, King Wen (founder of the Chou dynasty), and the Duke of Chou.

3. The italicized transcriptions here and in the following paragraphs are the names of the eight trigrams in the *Changes* used to form the sixty-four hexagrams.

probably derived from this. *K'un* (Pure Yin) here means the Earth. The myriad things are all nourished to the utmost by It. This is why it says "gives them maximum support in *K'un*." *Tui* (Joy) here means "Autumn at its height," something in which the myriad things all find cause to rejoice. This is why it says "makes them happy then in Joy (*Tui*)." In "has them do battle in Pure Yang (*Ch'ien*)," *Ch'ien* is the trigram of the Northwest. This signifies where yin and yang exert pressure on each other. *K'an* (Water Hole) means Water. It is the trigram of due North, the trigram of wearisome toil. It is here that the myriad things all find refuge. This is why it says "finds them thoroughly worn out in Water Hole (*K'an*)." *Ken* (Restraint) is the trigram of the Northeast. It is here that the myriad things reach the end of their development, but it is also the beginning of that development. This is why it says "has them reach final maturity in Restraint (*Ken*)."

6. As for the numinous, it is the term used for that which invests the myriad things with the marvel of what they are and do. Of forces that make the myriad things move, none is swifter than Thunder. Of forces that make the myriad things bend, none is swifter than Wind. Of forces that make the myriad things dry, none is a better drying agent than Fire. Of forces that make the myriad things rejoice, none is more joy-giving than Lake. Of forces that moisten the myriad things, none is more effective than Water. Of forces that provide the myriad things with ends and beginnings, none is more resourceful than Restraint. This is why Water and Fire drive each other on, why Thunder and Wind do not work against each other, and why Mountain and Lake have material force flow between them. Only in consequence of all this can flux and transformation take place, thus allowing the myriad things to become all that they can be.

7. *Ch'ien* (Pure Yang) means strength and dynamism; *K'un* (Pure Yin) means submissiveness and pliancy; *Chen* (Thunder) means energizing; *Sun* (Compliance) means accommodation; *K'an* (Water Hole) means pitfall; *Li* (Cohesion) means attachment; *Ken* (Restraint) means cessation; and *Tui* (Joy) means to delight.

8. *Ch'ien* (Pure Yang) has the nature of the horse, *K'un* (Pure Yin) that of the ox, *Chen* (Thunder) that of the dragon, *Sun* (Compliance) that of the cock, *K'an* (Water Hole) that of the pig, *Li* (Cohesion) that of the pheasant, *Ken* (Restraint) that of the dog, and *Tui* (Joy) that of the sheep.

9. *Ch'ien* (Pure Yang) works like the head, *K'un* (Pure Yin) like the stomach, *Chen* (Thunder) like the foot, *Sun* (Compliance) like the thigh, *K'an* (Water Hole) like the ear, *Li* (Cohesion) like the eye, *Ken* (Restraint) like the hand, and *Tui* (Joy) like the mouth.

10. *Ch'ien* (Pure Yang) is Heaven, thus it corresponds to the father; and *K'un* (Pure Yin) is Earth, thus it corresponds to the mother. As for *Chen* (Quake), [*K'un*] here seeks [from *Ch'ien*] for the first time and gets a son, thus we call it the Eldest Son; and as for *Sun* (Compliance), [*Ch'ien*] here seeks

[from *K'un*] for the first time and gets a daughter, thus we call it the Eldest Daughter. As for *K'an* (Water Hole), [*K'un*] here seeks [from *Ch'ien*] for the second time and gets a son, thus we call it the Middle Son; and as for *Li* (Cohesion), [*Ch'ien*] here seeks [from *K'un*] for the second time and gets a daughter, thus we call it the Middle Daughter. As for *Ken* (Restraint), [*K'un*] here seeks [from *Ch'ien*] for the third time and gets a son, thus we call it the Youngest Son; and as for *Tui* (Joy), [*Chien*] here seeks [from *K'un*] for the third time and gets a daughter, thus we call it the Youngest Daughter.

11. *Ch'ien* (Pure Yang) is Heaven, is round, is the sovereign, is father, is jade, is metal, is coldness, is ice, is pure red, is a fine horse, is an old horse, is an emaciated horse, is a piebald horse, and is fruit of the tree.

K'un (Pure Yin) is Earth, is mother, is cloth, is a cooking pot, is frugality, is impartiality, is a cow with a calf, is a great cart, is the markings on things, is the multitude of things themselves, and is the handle of things. In respect to soils, it is the kind that is black.

Chen (Quake) is thunder, is the dragon, is black and yellow, is overspreading, is the great highway, is the Eldest Son, is decisiveness and impetuosity, is a green, lush bamboo, and is the reed plants. In respect to horses, it is those which excel at neighing, those which have white rear legs, those which work the legs (i.e., run fast), and those which have white foreheads. In respect to cultivated plants, it is the kind that grows back (i.e., pod sprouting plants, legumes, etc.). At the end point of its development it is soundness and sturdiness (i.e., it turns into *Ch'ien*, Pure Yang), and is luxuriant and fresh growth.

Sun (Compliance) is wood, is the wind, is the Eldest Daughter, is the straightness of a marking cord, is the carpenter (or carpenter's square), is the spotless and pure, is the lengthy, is the high, is the advancing and receding, is the unresolved, and is odor. In respect to men, it is the balding, the broad in forehead, the ones with much white in their eyes, and the ones who keep close to what is profitable and who market things for threefold gain. At the end point of its development it is the trigram of impetuosity (i.e., it turns into *Chen*, Quake).

K'an (Water Hole) is water, is the drains and ditches, is that which lies low, is the straightening and bending, and is the bow and the wheel. In respect to men, it is the increasingly anxious, the sick at heart, and the ones with earaches. It is the trigram of blood and of the color red. In respect to horses, it is those with beautiful backs, those which put their whole hearts into it, those that keep their heads low, those with thin hooves, and those that shamble along. In respect to carriages, it is those that often have calamities (breakdowns, accidents). It is penetration, is the moon, and is the stealthy thief. In respect to trees, it is those that are strong with dense centers.

Li (Cohesion) is fire, is the sun, is lightning, is the Middle Daughter, is mail and the helmet, and is the halberd and the sword. In respect to men, it is those with big bellies. It is the trigram of dryness. It is the turtle, is the crab, is the snail, is the clam, and is the tortoise. In respect to trees, it is the hollow ones with tops withered.

Ken (Restraint) is the mountain, is the footpath, is the small stone, is the gate tower, is the tree fruit and vine fruit, is the gatekeeper and the palace-guard, is the fingers, is the dog, is the rat, and is the black maws of species [of birds and beasts of prey]. In respect to trees, it is the kind that is sturdy and much gnarled.

Tui (Joy) is the lake, is the Youngest Daughter, is the shamaness, is the mouth and tongue, is the deterioration [of plant life], and is the breaking off of what had been attached. In respect to soils, it is the kind that is hard and alkaline. It is the concubine and is the sheep.

Translated by Richard John Lynn

The Great Treatise (Appended Phrases)

Anonymous (Warring States or Early Western Han)

Part I, Chapter 12 (Summary)

The *Changes* says: "Heaven will assist him as a matter of course; this is good fortune, and nothing will be to his disadvantage." The Master said: "*Yu* (divine assistance) means help." One whom Heaven helps is someone who is in accord with It. One whom people help is someone who is trustworthy. Such a person treads the way of trustworthiness, keeps his thoughts in accord with Heaven, and also thereby holds the worthy in esteem. This is why "Heaven will assist him as a matter of course; this is good fortune, and nothing will be to his disadvantage."

The Master said: "Writing does not exhaust words, and words do not exhaust ideas. If this is so, does this mean that the ideas of the sages cannot be discerned?" The Master said: "The sages established images in order to express their ideas exhaustively. They established the hexagrams in order to treat exhaustively the true innate tendency of things and their counter tendencies to spuriousness. They attached phrases to the hexagrams in order to exhaust what they had to say. They let flux occur and achieve free flow in order to exhaust the potential of the benefit involved. They made a drum of it, made a dance of it, and so exhausted the potential of its numinous power."

Ch'ien and *K'un*, do they not comprise the arcane source for change? When *Ch'ien* and *K'un* form ranks, change stands in their midst, but if *Ch'ien* and *K'un* were to disintegrate, there would be no way that change could manifest itself. If change could not manifest itself, this would mean that *Ch'ien* and *K'un* might almost be on the verge of extinction!

Therefore, what is prior to physical form pertains to the Way, and what is subsequent to physical form pertains to concrete objects. That which transforms things and regulates them is called flux. By extending this to practical action one may be said to achieve complete success. To take this up and integrate it into the lives of the common folk of the world is called the great task of life.

Therefore, as for the images, the sages had the means to perceive the mysteries of the world and, drawing comparisons for them with analogous things, made images out of those things which seemed appropriate. In consequence of this, they called these "images." The sages had the means to perceive the activities taking place in the world and, observing how things come together and go smoothly, enacted statutes and rituals accordingly. They appended phrases to the hexagram lines in order to judge the good and bad fortune involved. This is why these are called line phrases. These line phrases speak to the most mysterious things in the world, and yet one may not feel aversion toward them; they speak to the things in the world which are most fraught with activity, and yet one may not feel confused about them.

To plumb the mysteries of the world to the utmost is dependent on the hexagrams; to drum up people to action all over the world is dependent on the phrases; to transform things and regulate them is dependent on flux; to start things going and carry them out is dependent on the free flow of flux; to be aware of the numinous and bring it to light is dependent on the men involved; to accomplish things while remaining silent and to be trusted without speaking is something intrinsic to virtuous conduct.

Translated by Richard John Lynn

Philosophy, Thought, and Religion

5
Kuan Tzu

Inner Workings

Attributed to Kuan Chung (?–645 B.C.E.)

I.1

It is ever so that the vital essence of things is what gives them life.
Below, it gives life to the five grains; above, it creates the ranked stars.
When floating between heaven and earth, we call it ghost or spirit,
When stored in the breast, we call it sageliness.

"Inner Workings" is a lengthy hortatory text, for the most part in rhyme, which might have been chanted orally and probably existed in different versions long before it came to be written down, which must have occurred no later than about 300 B.C.E. It is chapter 49, one of the four so-called *Hsin shu* ("Arts of the Mind") chapters in the *Kuan Tzu*. All four chapters deal with aspects of Taoist quietism and, except for the *Lao Tzu* (selection 10) and the *Chuang Tzu* (selection 9), represent the richest source for the study of early quietist thought. Among these chapters, "Inner Workings" is arguably the most important from a purely philosophical point of view, since it includes some of China's earliest discussions on the workings of the mind and the practice of breath and dietary controls. Students of Indian philosophy will recognize many resonances with the Yogic tradition.

The *Kuan Tzu* is an enormous, heterogeneous work attributed to Kuan Chung, an illustrious prime minister who served under Duke Huan of the state of Ch'i. The text as we have it now, however, was largely put together by the busy Han period editor, Liu Hsiang (see selections 238 and 242). Although the *Kuan Tzu* is difficult to characterize and date, it is a treasury of Warring

I.2

Thus, man's vital force—
How bright! As if mounting the heavens.
How dark! As if entering an abyss.
How vast! As if filling the ocean.
How compact! As if contained within the self.

I.3

Thus, this vital force—
Never to be restrained by physical strength, it may be brought to rest by
    spiritual Power;[1]
Never to be summoned by one's call, it may be made welcome by one's
    powers of awareness.
Respectfully preserve and never lose it, such is called perfecting one's
    Power.
Power being perfected, wisdom develops, and all things may be fully
    comprehended.

II.1

It is ever so that the mind's gestalt
Is naturally full and naturally replete,
Naturally born and naturally perfected.
Should its function be impaired,
It is certain to be due to sorrow and happiness, joy and anger, desire and
    profit-seeking.
If we can rid ourselves of sorrow and happiness, joy and anger, desire and
    profit-seeking,
The mind will revert to its flawless state.

II.2

The mind's inner reality is benefited by rest and quiet.
Avoid being harassed or confused, and its harmony will naturally be
    complete.
How clear! As if right at our side.
How nebulous! As if beyond comprehension.
How expansive! As if exhausting the limitless.
This mind, if we search for it, is not far, and we may daily use its Power.

States thought, including the earliest economic theory from China and discernible strands of
proto-Confucian political ideals.

    1. The word translated as "Power" here is *te*. It is usually rendered as "virtue" and has
also been interpreted as "integrity." Etymologically speaking, perhaps the closest equivalent
is "doughtiness."

III

Now the Way is what fills the mind's gestalt, but men cannot hold it in
    place.
Going, it may not return; coming, it may not stay.
How still! No one hears its sound.
How immediate! Residing within our minds.
How obscure! No one sees its form.
How bounteous! Together with us born.
We cannot see its form,
We cannot hear its sound,
Yet it is orderly in its completeness.
Such we call the Way.

IV.1

It is ever so that the Way has no fixed place,
Yet in a good mind it will peacefully settle.
The mind quiescent, and the vital force well managed,
The Way can then be made to stay.

IV.2

The Way is never far removed;
By obtaining it, people live.
The Way is never detached;
By relying on it, people become harmonious.
Thus, how immediate! As if one were bound together with it.
How distant! As if it were exhausting infinity.

IV.3

That Way's inner reality
Rejects sound and speech.
Only after cultivating one's mind and quieting one's powers of awareness
May the Way be comprehended.

V

That which is the Way,
The mouth cannot express, the eye cannot see, and the ear cannot hear.
It is the means to cultivate the mind and rectify its gestalt.
Losing it, men die; having it, they live.
Losing it, undertakings fail; having it, they succeed.

VI.1

It is ever so that the Way
Has neither roots nor stalks,

Neither leaves nor blossoms.
Yet what to all things gives life
And brings them to fruition
Is termed the Way.

VI.2

The supreme quality of Heaven is regularity;
Of Earth, it is equity;
Of man, it is quiescence.
Spring and autumn, summer and winter are Heaven's seasons.
Mountains and hills, rivers and valleys provide Earth's resources;
Joy and anger, taking and giving underlie man's schemes.
For this reason, the sage—
In accordance with the times, is ever changing, but never transformed;
In accordance with things, he is ever moving, but never inconsistent.

VI.3

Able to be correct and quiescent,
He is thus able to remain stable.
There being a stable mind within,
His ears and eyes are sharp and clear.
His four limbs strong and firm,
He can serve the vital essence as a dwelling place.
The vital essence is the essence of the vital force.
When the vital force permeates, there is life, and with life comes thought;
With thought comes knowledge, and with knowledge comes a stopping point.

VII.1

It is ever so that the mind's gestalt,
On being inundated with too much knowledge, loses its vitality.
What is at one with things and able to bring about their transformation is
    called the Spirit;
What is at one with affairs and is able to bring about changes in them is
    called wisdom.
To transform without altering one's vital force,
To change without altering one's wisdom—
Only the man of quality who grasps the One is able to do this!
Grasping the One and never losing it,
He is able to become prince over all things.
The man of quality manipulates things, but is never manipulated by them.
This is because he comprehends the One's inherent order.
A well-regulated mind lies within, well-regulated words issue from his
    mouth, and well-regulated policies are applied to men;

Hence the world is well regulated.
"With one word comprehended,
The world submits;
With one word firmly established,
The world obeys."
This saying clearly expresses the meaning.

VII.2

When the mind's gestalt is not correct, the Power will not come;
When the self within is not quiescent, the mind will not be well regulated.
Rectify the mind's gestalt and hold on to the Power,
Then the beneficence of Heaven and righteousness of Earth in bounteous
    fashion will naturally arrive.
The supremacy of the Spirit—how brilliant!—
    it knows all things.
Preserve it within, and do not go to excess.
Do not let things confuse the senses;
    do not let the senses confuse the mind.
This is called internalization of the Spirit.

VII.3

The Spirit independently exists.
Its going and coming,
No one is able to contemplate.
Lose it, and the mind is certain to be confused; obtain it, and the mind is
    certain to be well regulated.
Respectfully keep clean its abode, and its vital essence will naturally come.
Quiet your thoughts in order to contemplate it;
Rest your mind in order to keep control of it.
Maintain a dignified appearance and respectful attitude,
Then its vital essence will of itself become stable.
Obtain it and never let it go,
Your ears and eyes will never go astray, nor will your mind become occupied
    with irrelevant concerns.
When a correct mind lies within, all things attain their proper measure.

VIII.1

The Way fills the whole world,
Existing wherever people dwell.
Yet people are incapable of knowing it.
With the one word understood,
Above, one may explore Heaven,

Below, reach the extremities of Earth,
Circulating about, cover the whole of the nine regions.
What do we mean by understanding it?
This lies in the mind's regulation.

VIII.2

When our minds are well regulated,
Our sense organs are also well regulated;
When our minds are at ease,
Our sense organs are also at ease.
What regulates them is the mind;
What sets them at ease is the mind.
The mind therefore contains an inner mind;
That is to say, within the mind there is another mind.

VIII.3

In that mind's mind.
Awareness comes before sound;
After awareness come forms;
After forms come names;
After names comes putting the mind to use;
After putting the mind to use comes its regulation.
Without proper regulation, there is certain to be confusion;
If there is confusion, there is certain to be death.

VIII.4

When the vital essence is present, it naturally produces life.
Outwardly it produces a restful glow;
Stored within, it becomes a fountainhead.
Floodlike, harmonious, and smooth, it becomes the vital force's wellspring.
So long as the wellspring does not run dry,
The four parts of the body will remain firm;
So long as the wellspring is not exhausted,
The passages of the nine apertures will remain clear.
Thus it is possible to explore the limits of Heaven and Earth and cover the
    four seas.
Within, there will be no delusions; without, there will be no calamities.
His mind complete within, his form complete without,
Encountering neither Heaven-sent calamities nor man-made harm—
Such a person, we call a sage.

IX.1

When man is capable of being correct and quiescent,
His flesh is plump and full, his ears and eyes are sharp and clear;
His muscles become taut, and his bones sturdy.
Thus he is able to wear on his head the great circle and plant his feet on the
    great square.[2]
He finds his reflection in the Great Purity and is comparable to the great
    luminaries.

IX.2

Respectful and cautious, and avoiding excesses, he daily renews his Power.
He comes to understand everything in the world, and explores its four
    extremities.
The respectful development of his inner well-being is what we call
    internalization of the Spirit.
Being like this and never retrogressing, his is a life without excesses.

X.1

It is ever so that the Way is certain to be dense and close,
Certain to be broad and expansive,
Certain to be strong and firm.
Preserve the good and never let it go;
Rid yourself of licentiousness and discard frivolity.
Having come to understand its supremacy,
You may return to the Way and its Power.

X.2

When a complete mind lies within, it cannot be concealed;
It may be ascertained from one's bearing and observed from one's
    complexion.
If you greet men with good intent, they will become dearer than brothers;
If you greet them with evil intent, they will become more harmful than
    weapons.
The unspoken is more startling than a thunderclap.
The manifestations of the mind and the vital force are more illuminating
    than the sun and moon, more discerning than a father or mother.
Rewards are not enough to encourage goodness; punishments are not enough
    to discipline evil.
But when awareness of the vital force is attained, the whole world will
    submit;
When awareness of the mind is firmly rooted, the whole world will obey.

2. The "great circle" refers to Heaven and the "great square" to Earth.

XI.1

If you concentrate your vital force until you become like the Spirit,
Your grasp of all things will be complete.
Can you concentrate your mind?
Can you focus your powers of awareness?
Without resorting to tortoise shells and divining stalks, can you foretell bad
    fortune from good?
Can you tell where to stop?
Can you tell when to desist?
Rather than seeking it in others, can you find it within yourself?
Think about it! Think about it!
Again, think about it!
If you still cannot fathom it, ghosts and spirits will help you fathom it.
This is not because of their powers;
It is because the vital essence and its vital force are supreme.

XI.2

The four parts of the body will be in correct order:
Your pulse and breath will become quiet;
You will focus your powers of awareness and concentrate your mind;
Your ears and eyes will not be distracted;
And even though things be distant, they will appear as if near at hand.

XI.3

Thought and inquiry produce knowledge;
Slackness and carelessness produce sorrow;
Violence and arrogance produce resentment;
Sorrow and melancholy produce illness;
Sickness and trouble bring death.
If you continue to think with no relaxation,
Inwardly you will be troubled, and outwardly you will grow thin;
If you do not make early plans to prevent this,
Your life will relinquish its abode.

XI.4

When eating, it is best not to overindulge;
When thinking, it is best not to overdo.
When there is a suitable equilibrium,
Long life will naturally be achieved.

XII

It is ever so that in man's life,
Heaven produces his vital essence.

Earth produces his form.
These combine in order to produce man.
When they are in harmony, there is life;
Without harmony, there is no life.
If one searches for the way to it,
Its inner reality cannot be seen, its outward manifestation cannot be
    classified.
However, when equanimity and correctness dominate the breast and engulf
    the mind, this brings long life.
If joy and anger are excessive,
Deal with them in a planned manner.
Moderate the five desires [3] and get rid of the two violent emotions. [4]
Be neither joyous nor angry, then equanimity and correctness will dominate
    your breast.

XIII

It is ever so that man's life
Is certain to depend on equanimity and correctness.
Its loss is certain to be because of joy and anger, sorrow and suffering.
Thus, for arresting anger, nothing is better than poetry;
For getting rid of sorrow, nothing is better than music.
For moderating music, nothing is better than rules of propriety;
For preserving rules of propriety, nothing is better than respect;
For preserving respect, nothing is better than quiescence.
Inwardly quiescent and outwardly respectful,
You may revert to your true nature,
And it will become completely stable.

XIV.1

It is ever so that concerning eating habits,
With too much gorging, the breath will be harmed
And the form will be unable to hold it all;
If there is too much abstention, the bones will dry up
And the blood will congeal.
Between gorging and abstention, there is a happy medium called moderation.
It provides a place for the vital essence to dwell and for knowledge to develop.
If hunger or overindulgence is excessive,
Deal with it in a planned manner.
When too full, quickly move about; when hungry, relax your thoughts; when
    old, forget your worries.

3. The five desires stem from the action of the five organs: ears, eyes, nose, mouth, and
heart/mind, involving hearing, seeing, smelling, tasting, and love and hate.
4. The two violent emotions are joy and anger.

If, having eaten too much, you do not quickly move about,
The breath will not circulate to your four extremities.
If, being hungry, you do not relax your thoughts,
Your hunger will not be alleviated.
If, being old, you do not forget your worries, when troubled, you will be
    quickly exhausted.

XIV.2

Expand your mind, and you will feel release;
Deepen your breathing, and you will feel relaxed.
Your form will be at ease and never restless;
You will be able to focus your powers of awareness, and dispose of the
    myriads of minor irritations.
On seeing profit, you will not be enticed;
On seeing harm, you will not be frightened.
Being relaxed and humane, you will find happiness within yourself.
This is called setting in motion the vital force;
The movement of your powers of awareness will be like Heaven.

XV.1

It is ever so that man's life is certain to depend on his being content.
Through sorrow he loses his guiding thread; through anger he loses his
    beginnings.
In sorrow and melancholy, joy and anger,
The Way can find no resting place.
Love and desires—quiet them!
Stupidity and confusion—rectify them!
Do not pull! Do not push!
Happiness will naturally be restored.

XV.2

That the Way will naturally come
Is something you can count on and plan for.
If you are quiescent, you will obtain it;
If you move hastily, you will lose it.
The spiritual force within the mind sometimes arrives and sometimes
    departs.
So fine that nothing can exist within it; so large that nothing can exist beyond
    it.
The reason we lose it is because haste is harmful.
When the mind is able to retain a state of quiescence,
The Way will naturally become stable.
For the man who comprehends the Way,

The lines of his face effuse a sense of harmony, and his hair exudes it.
Within his breast there is nothing corrupt.
Since he practices this method of moderating desires, nothing ever causes
    him harm.

Translated by W. Allyn Rickett

Duties of the Student

Attributed to Kuan Chung (?–645 B.C.E.)

The teacher presents his teachings; students take them as their
    standards.
By being docile and reverential, and keeping their minds completely
    open, their learning is maximized.
On seeing goodness, they follow it; on hearing of righteousness, they
    submit to it.
Docile and compliant, filial and respectful toward their elders, they
    never display arrogance or resort to physical force.
5   Never false or depraved in purpose, their conduct is certain to be correct
    and straightforward.
Observing constant standards whether abroad or at home, they are
    certain to seek out those who are virtuous.
Their features being well composed, their inner thoughts are certain to
    be exemplary in their correctness.
Though they awaken early and go to bed late, their dress is certain to be
    tidy.
Mornings being devoted to enhancing their learning and evenings to
    practicing what they have learned, they are ever cautious of doing
    anything wrong.
10   Being ever diligent in concentrating on these things, such are the
    standards for study.

Young students in rendering service are late to bed and early to rise.
When sweeping the floor in front of the teaching mat, washing their
    hands, and rinsing their mouths, they conduct themselves in a
    respectful manner.

This essay constitutes chapter 59 of the *Kuan Tzu*, but it also circulated independently.
"Duties of the Student" has received considerable attention from Chinese scholars ever since
Han times. It is one of the earliest discussions on education in China. The nature of the ritual
described is rudimentary compared with the detailed works of Han Confucianists, such as the
Record of Ritual (Li chi). Several phrases incorporated from the *Classic of Odes (Shih ching)*
indicate that the text probably dates from the third or fourth century B.C.E. and represents a
common tradition that was operative in the thousands of local schools and larger academies
functioning during that period, rather than being a specifically Confucian statement.

Once they have finished dressing and prepared the wash-basin for the
    teacher, he also rises.
When he has completed his toilet, the students remove the basin,
    sprinkle and sweep the floor, and adjust the teacher's mat.
15   The teacher then seats himself, and the students in going out or coming
    in are as respectful as if they were greeting guests.
They sit in a dignified manner facing the master, their features
    composed and never changing.

For receiving instruction, there are guidelines:
The eldest student must come first.
The first time around, it is like this, but thereafter it is not.
20   The first time students recite their lessons, they must stand, but
    thereafter they do not.
If a student arrives late, his fellow students on either side will stand.
Should there appear a guest,
A student will immediately arise.
Since a guest cannot be denied,
25   The student will welcome him and hurry to carry out his wishes,
Rushing to the teacher for instruction.
Even though the person the guest seeks is not there, the student will still
    report back to him.
He then returns to his seat and resumes his studies.
If a student has a question,
30   He will raise his hand to ask it.
When the master leaves, everyone stands.
In his every word and action, the student takes moderation as his guide.
Those who were to flourish in the past were certain to begin like this.

At mealtimes, when the teacher is about to eat, a student prepares food
    for him.
35   Having pulled up his sleeves, washed his hands, and rinsed his mouth,
    the server then kneels down to present the food.
When the sauces, grain, and various dishes are set forth, it must be
    done in an orderly fashion.
Vegetable stews are served before dishes of fowl, meat, fish, or turtle.
Both the stews and sliced meat dishes are placed in the middle but kept
    separate.
Meat dishes having been placed in front of the sauces, the entire setting
    forms a square.
40   The grain is served last; on the left is the wine, on the right is the soy.[1]

1. This may, however, refer to another word that is homophonous and is written with a
similar graph. This alternative reading signifies water in which a little rice or millet has been
boiled for some time and which is used for rinsing the mouth after a meal.

Having reported that everything is ready, the student withdraws and,
cupping his hands before him in obeisance, stands to one side.
The normal meal consists of three servings of grain and two dippers of
wine,
The student holds in his left hand a pottery serving dish, in his right
chopsticks or a ladle.
He refills the various dishes in order as soon as he sees they are
becoming empty.

45 If two dishes become empty at the same time, he refills them in the
order they were originally served.
Having refilled all the dishes, he begins the cycle again.
Since his serving implement has a foot-long handle, he does not need
to kneel. Such are the guidelines for making refills.

When the teacher has finished eating, the student clears everything
away,
And hastens to bring in a basin for the teacher to rinse his mouth,
sweeps the floor in front of the mat, and gathers together the
sacrificial utensils.

50 Once the teacher gives the order, the students then begin their meal.
They arrange themselves properly according to age, and are certain to
sit at the very front of the mat.
Grain must be picked up and eaten with the fingers, but stews are not
eaten with the hands.
It is permissible for them to rest their hands on their knees, but not to
lean on their elbows.
Having eaten to the full, they should cup their hands and touch the
edges of their mouths to see if any food particles remain there,

55 Shake their skirts to get rid of any food crumbs, brush them off the mat,
and having completed their meal, rise from their places.
Gathering up their clothing, they step down from the mat and turn to
face it.
Each person then clears away the remains of his food as though he were
a guest.
Having cleared the food, they put away the utensils,
And then return to their positions before the mat.

60 Whenever sweeping the floor in front of the teaching mat, students
should use the following method:
They should fill a basin with water and roll up their sleeves to the
elbow.
In a large hall, they may sprinkle the water by tossing it widely about; in
a small room, they should sprinkle by taking only a little in their
hands.

When holding the dustpan, the tongue should be pointed toward the
sweeper; in the middle is placed the broom.
The sweeper, on entering the door, stands for a while to make sure his
demeanor is without fault.
65   He holds the broom in his hand, and lowers the dustpan, leaning it
against the doorjamb.
For sweeping in front of the teaching mat, there are guidelines:
The sweeper must begin with the southwest corner;
Moving back and forth with his back bent in the shape of a bent chime,
He makes certain that he does not knock into anything;
70   From the front of the room, he works backward,
Collecting the dirt just inside the door.
Then squatting down, he gathers up the dirt by pushing it into the
dustpan with his hand.
He points the tongue of the dustpan toward himself and places the
broom across it.
Should the teacher rise from his place on the mat, the sweeper will
straighten up and excuse himself.
75   Then, after squatting down to grasp the dustpan and broom, he
reassumes a standing position and proceeds to remove them.
Having finished with his sweeping, the sweeper then returns to his
position—this all being in accord with the object of his studies.

During the evening meal, the students repeat the morning's ritual.
At dusk they light the torches, in each corner sitting and holding them.
The method for placing the faggots is to lay them crosswise to the torch
holder's sitting position.
80   When the torch has burned down to an appropriate length, he lights a
new one by pacing it at right angles to the old one like a carpenter's
square.
He leaves a faggot's width between them, the one that is already
burning being just below the one being lit.
At the same time he holds up a basin to catch falling embers.
Then with his right hand grasping the old torch,
He trims the burning end with his left, but should any embers be about
to drop, another student will replace him in holding the torch.
85   When exchanging seats, students must not turn their backs on those
who hold positions of honor.
Subsequently, the burned ends are taken out and discarded.

When the teacher is about to retire, the students all stand.
They respectfully present him with his pillow and mat, and ask him
where he would like to place his feet.

The first time they arrange his sleeping mat, they request this
    information, but once the pattern has been established, they do not.
90 After the teacher has retired, each student seeks out his friends;
Dissecting and polishing,
Each one strengthens his arguments.
The day's routine having been completed, the next day it begins anew.
Such are the guidelines for students.

Translated by W. Allyn Rickett

6
Mo Tzu

Chapter 31: On Ghosts, 3

Mo Ti (480?–400? B.C.E.)

Mo Tzu said: With the passing of the sage-kings of the Three Dynasties, the world lost its righteousness and the feudal lords took might as right. The superior and the subordinates are no longer gracious and loyal; father and son,

Mo Ti, i.e., Master Mo or Mo Tzu (Mecius), neglected throughout much of Chinese history, was an original and very important thinker nonetheless. Mo Tzu was opposed to aggressive wars and stressed the development of defensive weaponry. He and his followers wrote extensively on optics and other technical fields. But he is known primarily for his doctrine of universal love, which bears a striking resemblance to Christian thought, and which has led Western theologians and religious historians to be particularly fascinated by him. He also displays numerous affinities with Spartan philosophers and, indeed, more than any other early Chinese thinker, comes closest to qualifying as a genuine philosopher. It was he, for example, who developed logic more fully than anyone else in China before the advent of Buddhism. Thus, there have been a series of vigorous debates on the identity and background of this intriguing individual whose name, it has been argued, may indicate that he was a carpenter or even that he was a foreigner.

Mo Tzu was diametrically opposed to Confucius (see the next selection) on virtually every issue the two men discussed. Where Confucius advocated an extended mourning period, for example, Mo Tzu emphasized the need for simplicity in funerals. Where Confucius held music in highest esteem, Mo Tzu condemned it as luxurious and corrupting. Where Confucius was skeptical about the existence of ghosts and spirits (in any event, he certainly preferred not to discuss such subjects; see selections 106 [unnumbered note] and 248), Mo Tzu came out strongly in favor of their existence. Since ghosts and spirits have played such an important role in the development of imaginative literature in China, we have selected from the works of Mo Tzu this chapter on ghosts. It is one of three chapters on the subject attributed to the thinker, the other two having been lost, and is probably the first systematic analysis of the world of spirits written in

elder and younger brother are no longer affectionate and filial, brotherly and respectful, virtuous and kind. The rulers do not attend diligently to government and the artisans do not attend earnestly to their work. The people practice immorality and wickedness, and become rebellious. Thieves and bandits with weapons, poison, water, and fire hold up innocent travelers on the highways and the bypaths, robbing them of their carts and horses, coats and fur coats, to enrich themselves. All these start therewith (with the passing of the sage-kings). And so the world falls into chaos.

Now what is the reason for this confusion? It is all because of the doubt of the existence of ghosts and spirits, and the ignorance of their being able to reward virtue and punish vice. If all the people in the world believed that the spirits were able to reward virtue and punish vice, how could the world be in chaos? Those who deny the existence of spirits proclaim: "Of course, there are no spirits." And from morning till evening they teach this doctrine to the people of the empire. They bewilder the people, causing them all to doubt the existence of ghosts and spirits. In this way the empire becomes disorderly. Therefore Mo Tzu said: If the rulers and the gentlemen of the world really desire to procure benefits for the empire and remove its calamities, they must understand whether ghosts and spirits exist or not.

Since we must understand whether ghosts and spirits exist or not, how can we find out? Mo Tzu said: The way to find out whether anything exists is to depend on the testimony of the ears and eyes of the multitude. If some have heard it or some have seen it, then we have to say it exists. If no one has heard it and no one has seen it, then we have to say it does not exist. So, why not go to some village or some district and inquire? If from antiquity to the present, and since the beginning of man, there are men who have seen the bodies of ghosts and spirits and heard their voices, how can we say that they do not exist? If none have heard them and none have seen them, then how can we say they do? But those who deny the existence of the spirits say: "Many in the world have heard and seen something of ghosts and spirits. (Since they vary in their testimony,) who are to be accepted as really having heard and seen them?" Mo Tzu said: As we are to rely on what many have jointly seen and what many have jointly heard, the case of Tu Po is (to be accepted).[1]

King Hsüan of Chou (827–783 B.C.E.) put his minister Tu Po to death though he was innocent. Tu Po remarked: "The king puts me to death while I am innocent. If man loses his consciousness after his death, then all is over.

Chinese. We may contrast it with what Wang Ch'ung, a rationalist and skeptic of the Han period, has to say on the same subject (see selection 11).

1. In the following paragraphs Mo Tzu cites a number of cases to support the existence of spirits. Most of the people and occasions mentioned are historical, but the details seem to have come from the fairy tales current at his time.

If I shall still retain my consciousness after death, I shall let the king know of this within three years." In three years, King Hsüan assembled the feudal lords at P'u T'ien. There were several hundred carts. Attendants numbered by the thousand, and the multitude covered the fields. At noon Tu Po in red garments and headgear appeared riding in a plain chariot drawn by a white horse, holding a red bow and carrying red arrows. He pursued King Hsüan and shot him on his chariot. The arrow pierced his heart and broke his back. He fell and died prostrate. At the time all the people of Chou who were there saw it and those far away heard of it. It was recorded in the *Spring and Autumn*[2] of Chou. Rulers instructed their ministers with it and fathers warned their sons with it, saying: "Be careful, be respectful. All who kill the innocent are speedily and severely visited by misfortune and punished by the ghosts and spirits like this." Judging from what is recorded here, how can we doubt that ghosts and spirits exist?

Not only does the record in this book prove it to be so. Formerly, Lord Mu of Ch'in[3] (c. 640 B.C.E.) was once in the temple at noon. A spirit entered and alighted. He had the face of a man but the body of a bird. His attire was plain and dark. His appearance was dignified. Seeing him, Lord Mu became afraid and was rushing away. The spirit said: "Do not be afraid. God cherishes your intelligent virtue, authorizing me to prolong your age by nineteen years, and ordaining your state to be prosperous and your descendants to be many and not to lose Ch'in." Lord Mu saluted him repeatedly and bowed, saying: "May I ask the name of my god?" He answered: "I am Kou Mang." If we are to accept what Lord Mu of Ch'in had seen personally as reliable, then how can we doubt that ghosts and spirits exist?

Not only does the record in this book[4] prove it to be so. Formerly Lord Chien of Yen (c. 500 B.C.E.) put his minister Chuang Tzu Yi to death while he was innocent. Chuang Tzu Yi remarked: "The lord puts me to death though I am innocent. If man loses his consciousness after death, then all is done. If I shall still retain my consciousness after death, I shall let the Lord know of this within three years." In a year, Yen[5] was going to repair to Tsu. Such ceremonies were the occasions of large assemblages of men and women. At noon Lord Chien was riding on the road to Tsu. Chuang Tzu Yi carried a red staff and struck and prostrated him. At the time all the people of Yen who were there saw it and all those who were far away heard of it. It was recorded in the *Spring and Autumn* of Yen. The feudal lords circulated the news around, and remarked: "So speedy and severe are the misfortunes and punish-

---

2. *Spring and Autumn* (see introductory note to selection 191) was then not a proper name, title of the annals of Lu, but a common name for any annals.

3. The text says Lord Mu of Cheng, but the incident historically belongs to Lord Mu of Ch'in.

4. That is, the historical record of Ch'in.

5. Yen is the name of the state, but here means the lord of Yen, who is its representative.

ment from the ghosts and spirits upon him who kills the innocent." Judging from the record in this book, how can we doubt that ghosts and spirits exist?

Not only does the record in this book prove it to be so. Anciently, in the reign of Lord Wen of Sung, whose name was Pao (610–589 B.C.E.), there was a master of ceremonies by the name of Kuan Ku. While he was working in the temple, a wizard[6] carrying a cane appeared and said to him: "Kuan Ku, why don't the jades and stones measure up to the standard, and why are the cakes and wine unclean, the victims imperfect and not fat, and the sacrifices not in season? Did you do this or did Pao do this?" Kuan Ku answered: "Pao is still small and in his swaddle-clothes. What does he have to do with this? It is all done by the official in charge, Kuan Ku." Thereupon the wizard lifted his cane and struck him, prostrating him on the altar. At the time those people who were present all saw it, and those far away heard of it. It was recorded in the *Spring and Autumn* of Sung. The feudal lords circulated the news and remarked: "So speedy and severe is the punishment from the ghosts and spirits to him who is not reverent in performing sacrifices!" Judging from the record of this book, how can we doubt that ghosts and spirits exist?

Not only does the record in this book prove it to be so. Formerly, Lord Chuang of Ch'i (794–731 B.C.E.) had two ministers, Wang Li Kuo and Chung Li Chiao, who were engaged in a lawsuit. For three years no judgment could be reached. The Lord of Ch'i thought of putting both of them to death, but was afraid to slay the innocent; he thought of acquitting both of them but was afraid to let loose the guilty. So he let them provide a lamb and take oath on the altar of Ch'i. The two men agreed to take the oath of blood. The throat of the lamb was cut and its blood sprinkled on the altar. The case of Wang Li Kuo was read all through. But before half of the case of Chung Li Chiao was read, the lamb arose and butted at him, broke his leg, and prostrated him on the altar. At the time all the people of Ch'i who were present saw it, and those far away heard of it. It was recorded in the *Spring and Autumn* of Ch'i. The feudal lords circulated the news around and remarked: "So speedy and severe is the punishment from the ghosts and spirits to him who takes an oath in insincerity!" Judging from the record in this book, how can we doubt that ghosts and spirits exist?

Therefore Mo Tzu said: One may not act disrespectfully even in woods, valleys, or solitary caves where there is no man. The ghosts and spirits are watching everywhere.

Those who deny the existence of spirits ask: "Are the senses of hearing and sight of the multitude sufficient to decide a doubt? How can people strive to be learned gentlemen while they continue to trust the senses of hearing and sight of the multitude?"

---

6. The wizard is represented here as a medium of the spirits.

Mo Tzu said: If the senses of hearing and sight of the multitude are thought to be not trustworthy, we may ask if such men as the sage-kings of the Three Dynasties, Yao, Shun, Yü, T'ang, Wen, and Wu, are trustworthy? Of course, about this all people above the mediocre will say such men as the ancient sage-kings of the Three Dynasties, Yao, Shun, Tü, T'ang, Wen, and Wu, are trustworthy. If the ancient sage-kings of the Three Dynasties are trustworthy, we may review some of their deeds.

In ancient times, having captured Yin and punished Chow, King Wu let the feudal lords share in the worship (of the ancestors of Yin). Those more closely related were to partake in the temple sacrifices and those less closely related in the outdoor sacrifices. So King Wu must have believed there were ghosts and spirits. Therefore, after capturing Yin and punishing Chow, he let the feudal lords share in the worship. If there were no ghosts and spirits, why did King Wu assign the duties of worship?

Not only does the deed of King Wu prove it to be so. When the ancient sage-kings distributed rewards, it had to be before their ancestors. When they meted out punishments, it had to be before the altar. Why were rewards distributed before the ancestors? To submit to their fairness. Why were punishments meted out before the altar? To submit to their justice.

Not only does the record in this book prove it to be so. On the day the ancient sage-kings of the Three Dynasties of Yü, Hsia, Shang, and Chou[7] first established their empire and built their capitals, they invariably chose the central altar on which to build the ancestral temple. They would pick out the luxuriant and elegant among the trees to plant in the temple of agriculture. They would select the affectionate and filial, virtuous and kind among the elders of the country to be masters of ceremonies. They would pick out the victims among the six animals by their fatness, perfection, and color of their wool. The jades and stones were to be appropriate in material and satisfactory in measurement. The cakes and wine were to be prepared with the most fragrant and yellow grain, so the quality of cakes and wine would vary with the abundance of the year. That is to say, in the government of the ancient sage-kings, ghosts and spirits had priority over people. Before the offices and courts were completely established, the sacrificial vessels and sacrificial robes must have all been stored in the storehouse, the masters and attendants of ceremonies must have all been installed in court, and the victims must have been kept apart from the original flock. Since the government of the ancient sage-kings was like this, the ancient sage-kings must have believed in the existence of ghosts and spirits.

Deep was their own interest in the welfare of ghosts and spirits. Yet they were afraid their descendants might not understand it. Thus they recorded it on bamboos and silk to bequeath to them. Fearing that these might rot and

7. The Three Dynasties denotes only the last three.

disappear so the descendants might not learn it, they engraved it on plates and cups, and cut it in metals and stones. They feared also that the descendants might not be reverent and obtain blessing, and so among the books of the ancient kings and the records of sages, testimonies to the existence of ghosts and spirits occur time and again, even on a single foot of silk or a single sheet in the books. Why was this? Because the sage-kings were interested in it. Those who deny the existence of spirits are opposing the interest of the sage-kings, and such is not the way of the superior man.

Those who deny the existence of spirits might say: "Among the books of the ancient kings not a foot of silk or a sheet is found that testifies to the existence of ghosts and spirits once and again. Then where are these testimonies?"

Mo Tzu replied: They are found (for instance) in the "Ta Ya" of the books of Chou. "Ta Ya" tells: "The rule of King Wen over the people pleased Heaven. Although Chou is an old country, it is newly commissioned by Heaven. Chou does not appear showy. The commission from God does not appear to be seasonable. King Wen reached high and low; he was on the left and the right of God. How active was King Wen! He dispensed his intelligent virtue without ceasing."[8] If ghosts and spirits did not exist, then how could King Wen be "on the left and right of God" since he was already dead? Here we have a testimony of ghosts in the book of Chou.

If there are testimonies only in the books of Chou and none in those of Shang, still it could not be reliable. But we find among the books of Shang the following: "Oh! Anciently, before Hsia was visited by misfortune, of the various animals and insects and even birds none deviated from their proper course. As to those who have faces of men, who dare be divergent in heart? Even the ghosts and spirits of hills and rivers dared not be insurgent."[9] If one were respectful and sincere one could maintain harmony in the world and stability to the lower earth. Now it was to assist Yü that ghosts and spirits of hills and rivers dared not be insurgent. Here we have a testimony of ghosts in the book of Shang.

If there are testimonies of ghosts only in the books of Shang and none in those of Hsia, it is still not reliable. But we have the "Speech at Kan"[10] among the books of Hsia running thus: "In the midst of the war at Kan, the Emperor called the six associates to receive instructions in the headquarters. He said: 'The Prince of Hu violated the five elements and disused the three calendars. Heaven decreed to exterminate his life!' And he continued: 'At noon I shall

8. This quotation is from the ode "King Wen" in the collection "Greater Elegantiae" from the *Classic of Odes* (see selection 22).

9. The quotation is from the "Instructions of Ĕ" in the *Classic of Documents* (see selection 188).

10. The text says "Speech of Yü." Some ancient writers seem to use both titles for the same work. In the present text of the *Classic of Documents*, the essay is called "Speech at Kan."

grapple with the Prince of Hu for the fate of the day. But (mind you), you ministers and people, it is not because I covet their land and treasures. I am only carrying out the punishment in obedience to Heaven. If you on the left do not do your part on the left, you will be disobeying my orders; if you on the right do not do your part on the right, you will be disobeying my orders; if you charioteers do not manage your horses according to orders, you will be disobeying my orders. Rewards will be distributed before my ancestors and punishments will be meted out before the altar.' "[11] Why were rewards distributed before the ancestors? To submit their fairness. Why were punishments meted out before the altar? To submit their justice. Because the ancient sage-kings must reward virtue and punish vice with ghosts and spirits, they distributed rewards before the ancestors and meted out punishments before the altar. Here we have a testimony of ghosts in the books of Hsia.

Now, first in the books of Hsia and next in the books of Shang and Chou, testimonies to the existence of ghosts and spirits occur again and again. What is the reason for this? Because the sage-kings were interested in it. Judging from the records of these books, how can we doubt that there are ghosts and spirits?

Anciently, on the propitious day of *ting-mao*,[12] Chou offered thanksgiving to Earth and the Four Quarters, and their ancestors. They did this to prolong their age. If there were no ghosts and spirits, how could their age be prolonged?

Mo Tzu said: As to the fact that ghosts and spirits can reward virtue as well as punish vice, if it could be proclaimed to the whole country and to all the people, it would really be a source of orderliness in the country and blessing to the people. The corruption of the officials in their public charges and the immorality among men and women will all be seen by ghosts and spirits. The vice of those who, with weapons, poisons, and water and fire, waylay innocent travelers and rob them of their carts and horses, coats and fur coats to enrich themselves will be seen by ghosts and spirits. Thereupon the officials will not dare be corrupt in office, withholding reward when they find the virtuous or withholding punishment when they find the wicked. Those among the people who commit vice and cruelties and, with weapons, poisons, and water and fire, waylay innocent travelers, robbing them of their carts and horses, coats and fur coats to enrich themselves—all these will be no more and the world will have order. Really, the intelligence of ghosts and spirits cannot be combated. Even in solitary caves, big ponds, woods, and valleys, ghosts and spirits are watching. The punishments from ghosts and spirits cannot be evaded.

11. This is almost the whole of the "Speech at Kan." But in many places the text differs greatly from that in the extant *Classic of Documents*. The same is true of the "Instructions of Ě" mentioned in note 9.

12. *Ting-mao* is the name of the day according to the Chinese calendar then in use.

Even wealth and great numbers, daring and strength, strong armor and sharp weapons will be frustrated by the punishment of ghosts and spirits.

If this is doubted, look at the story of the ancient King Chieh of Hsia. He was an emperor in honor and possessed the whole empire in wealth. He cursed Heaven, blasphemed against the spirits above, and destroyed the multitudes below.[13] Thereupon Heaven commissioned T'ang to carry out the judicious punishment. With nine chariots,[14] T'ang arranged the Bird Formation and the Wild Goose March. He climbed Ta Tsan,[15] scattered the forces of Hsia, and entered its land. And he captured T'ui Yi Ta Hsi. Now, King Chieh of Hsia was an emperor in honor and possessed the whole empire in wealth. In his service was the man of great daring and strength, T'ui Yi Ta Hsi, who had torn apart a buffalo alive. He could kill a man at the move of a finger. The number of those killed amounted to a million, and they were thrown into lakes and mountains. Yet, for all this, Chieh could not evade the punishment from ghosts and spirits. This is why I say even wealth and numbers, daring and strength, strong armor and sharp weapons cannot combat the punishment from ghosts and spirits.

Not only is this so. Anciently, King Chow of Yin was also an emperor in honor and possessed the whole empire in wealth. He cursed Heaven, blasphemed against the spirits above, and destroyed the multitudes below. He exposed the aged, murdered the children, tortured the innocent, and opened a pregnant woman. The common people and the widows and widowers cried aloud but were not heard. Thereupon Heaven commissioned King Wu to carry out the judicious punishment. With a hundred selected chariots and four hundred warriors, King Wu appointed his officials and reviewed his forces. He battled the armies of Yin in the Wilderness of Mu. He captured Fei Chung and Ě Lai, and the multitude deserted and ran away. King Wu rushed into the palace.[16] He executed Chow and hanged him on a red ring with his crimes published on a white flag to punish him for the feudal lords in the empire. Now King Chow of Yin was an emperor in honor and possessed the whole empire in wealth. He had men of such daring and strength as Fei Chung, Ě Lai, and Duke Hu of Ch'ung,[17] who could kill a man at the move of a finger. The number of those killed amounted to a million, and they were thrown into the lakes and mountains. Yet, for all this, Chow could not evade the punishment from ghosts and spirits. This is why I say even wealth and

13. There is a sentence in the text following this which does not seem to make any sense as it stands, and is therefore not translatable.

14. Each chariot unit consists of twenty-five men. It seems there should be "ninety" chariots instead of "nine."

15. Ta Tsan is most likely the name of a pass.

16. The four graphs following this do not seem to have anything to do with this narration.

17. All these men are the vicious associates of Chow.

numbers, daring and strength, strong armor and sharp weapons cannot frustrate the punishment from ghosts and spirits.

Moreover, Ch'in Ai has said: "No virtue is too small; no extermination of a lineage is too big." This is to say, in distribution of rewards by ghosts and spirits, no man is too insignificant to be rewarded for his virtue; in the meting out of punishments by ghosts and spirits, no man is too great to be punished.

Those who deny the existence of spirits say, "If one did not work for the blessing of one's parents but worked for their destruction, would one still be a filial son?"

Mo Tzu explained: The ghosts and spirits of all times may be divided into spirits of Heaven, spirits of hills and rivers, and ghosts of men after their death. It is true that there are sons who die before their fathers, and younger brothers before their elder brothers. But, as the saying in the world goes: "He who is born first dies first." So those who die first would be the mother if not the father, and the elder sister if not the elder brother.

At any rate, we should prepare clean cakes and wine reverently to do sacrifice. If ghosts and spirits do exist, then it is to serve father and mother, elder sisters and elder brothers with food and drink. Is this not a great blessing? If ghosts and spirits did not exist, it would seem to be a waste of material for the cakes and wine. But such use is not just to throw it into the ditch or gully. For the relatives from the clan and friends from the village and district can yet eat and drink them. So, even if there were really no ghosts and spirits, a sacrifice would still gather together a party, and the participants could enjoy themselves and befriend the neighbors. Those who hold there are no ghosts say: "Of course there are no ghosts and spirits, and therefore I should not expend my wealth on the cakes and wine and victims. This is not because I am miserly about my wealth on the cakes and wine and victims, but because I do not see what I can accomplish with it." This is opposed to the records of the sage-kings above and opposed to the practice of the filial sons among the people. Yet they claim to be superior men in the empire. This is no way to be superior men. But Mo Tzu said: For me to offer sacrifice is not to throw it into the ditch or the gully. It is to bless the ghosts above, gather a party, enjoy ourselves, and befriend the neighbors below. If spirits did exist, I would be serving my father and mother and brother with food. Is this not a great blessing in the world?

Therefore Mo Tzu said: If the rulers and the gentlemen of the world really desire to procure benefits for the world and eliminate its calamities, they must believe in and teach the existence of ghosts and spirits. This is the way of the sage-kings.

Translated by Yi-pao Mei

7

Confucian *Analects*

Book 2

Anonymous (5th–4th centuries, B.C.E.)

I

1. Governing by the light of one's conscience is like the pole star which dwells in its place, and the other stars fulfill their functions respectfully.

II

1. He[1] said: The anthology of three hundred poems can be gathered into the one sentence: Have no twisty thoughts.

III

1. He said: If in governing you try to keep things leveled off in order by punishments, the people will, shamelessly, dodge.

2. Governing them by looking straight into one's heart and then acting on it (on conscience) and keeping order by the rites, their sense of shame will bring them not only to an external conformity but to an organic order.

IV

1. He said: At fifteen I wanted to learn.
2. At thirty I had a foundation.
3. At forty, a certitude.
4. At fifty, knew the orders of heaven.
5. At sixty, was ready to listen to them.
6. At seventy, could follow my own heart's desire without overstepping the T-square.

V

1. Meng Yi-tzu asked about filiality. He said: Don't disobey.
2. Fan Ch'ih was driving him, and he said: Meng-sun asked me about filiality, I said: It consists in not disobeying (not opposing, not avoiding).
3. Fan Ch'ih said: How do you mean that? He said: While they are alive,

The *Analects* is a body of sayings, brief discourses, and conversations attributed primarily to Confucius and secondarily to his disciples. Although the words of Confucius and his disciples reported are sometimes accompanied by short anecdotes, the collection otherwise provides very little context for the occasions upon which they were spoken. Critical scholarship has shown that the *Analects* is as multifarious in its origins and dating as the *Bible*.

1. Confucius.

be useful to them according to the proprieties; when dead, bury them according to the rites, make the offerings according to the rites.

VI

1. Meng Wu the elder asked about filiality. He said: A father or mother is only worried as to whether a child is sick.

VII

1. Tzu-yu asked about filiality. He said: Present-day filial piety consists in feeding the parents, as one would a dog or a horse; unless there is reverence, what difference is there?

VIII

1. Tzu-hsia asked about filiality. He said: The trouble is with the facial expression. Something to be done; the junior takes trouble, offers food first to his elders; is that all there is to filiality?

IX

1. He said: I have talked a whole day with Hui and he sits quiet as if he understood nothing, then I have watched what he does. Hui is by no means stupid.

X

1. He said: Watch a man's means, what and how.
2. See what starts him.
3. See what he is at ease in.
4. How can a man conceal his real bent?

XI

1. If a man keep alive what is old and recognize novelty, he can, eventually, teach.

XII

1. The proper man is not a dish.

XIII

1. Tzu-kung said: What is a proper man? He said: He acts first and then his talk fits what he has done.

XIV

1. He said: A proper man is inclusive, not sectary; the small man is sectarian and not inclusive.

XV

1. He said: Research without thought is a mere net and entanglement; thought without gathering data, a peril.

XVI

1. He said: Attacking false systems merely harms you.

XVII

1. He said: Yu, want a definition of knowledge? To know is to act knowledge, and when you do not know, not to try to appear as if you did, that's knowing.

XVIII

1. Tzu-chang was studying to get a paid job.
2. He said: Listen a lot and hide your suspicions; see that you really mean what you say about the rest, and you won't get into many scrapes. Look a lot, avoid the dangerous and be careful what you do with the rest, you will have few remorses. Salary is found in a middle space where there are few words blamed, and few acts that lead to remorse.

XIX

1. Duke Ai asked how to keep the people in order. He said: Promote the straight and throw out the twisty, and the people will keep order; promote the twisty and throw out the straight and they won't.

XX

1. Chi K'ang asked how to instill that sincere reverence which would make people work. He said: Approach them seriously [verso il popolo]; be respectful and deferent to everyone; promote the just and teach those who just cannot, and they will try.

XXI

1. Someone asked Confucius why he was not in the government.
2. He said: The Historic Documents say: filiality, simply filiality and the exchange between elder and younger brother that spreads into government; why should one go into the government?

XXII

1. He said: Men don't keep their word. I don't know what can be done for them: a great cart without a wagon-pole, a small cart and no place to hitch the traces.

XXIII

1. Tzu-chang asked if there were any knowledge good for ten generations.

2. He said: Yin, because there was wisdom in the rites of Hsia, took over some and added, and one can know this; Chou, because it was in the rites of Yin, took over some and added, and one can know what; someone will thread along after Chou, be it to an hundred generations one can know.

XXIV

1. He said: To sacrifice to a spirit not one's own is flattery.

2. To see justice and not act upon it is cowardice.

Translated by Ezra Pound

8

Mencius

Bull Mountain

Meng K'o (372–289 B.C.E.)

Mencius said, "Bull Mountain was once beautifully wooded. But, because it was close to a large city, its trees all fell to the axe. What of its beauty then? However, as the days passed things grew, and with the rains and the dews it was not without greenery. Then came the cattle and goats to graze. That is why, today, it has that scoured-like appearance. On seeing it now, people imagine that nothing ever grew there. But this is surely not the true nature of a mountain? And so, too, with human beings. Can it be that any man's mind naturally lacks Humanity and Justice? If he loses his sense of the good, then he loses it as the mountain lost its trees. It has been hacked away at—day after day—what of its beauty then?

"However, as the days pass he grows, and, as with all men, in the still air of the early hours his sense of right and wrong is at work. If it is barely perceptible, it is because his actions during the day have disturbed or destroyed

The *Mencius* consists of the rather full discussions of the "Second Sage" (Mencius) of Confucianism with rulers and rival thinkers. The present edition was established by Chao Ch'i in 201 B.C.E. This text has greater literary value but less authority than the *Analects* (see preceding selection), which is supposed to represent the words and thoughts of the "First Sage" (Confucius) himself.

The two section titles are supplied by the editor.

it. Being disturbed and turned upside down the 'night airs' can barely sustain it. If this happens he is not far removed from the animals. Seeing a man so close to an animal, people cannot imagine that once his nature was different—but this is surely not the true nature of the man? Indeed, if nurtured aright, anything will grow, but if not nurtured aright, anything will wither away. Confucius said, 'Hold fast to it, and you preserve it; let it go and you destroy it; it may come and go at any time—no one knows its whereabouts.' Confucius was speaking of nothing less than the mind."

Translated by W. A. C. H. Dobson

Fish and Bear's Paws

Mencius said, "I am fond of fish, but, too, I am fond of bear's paws. If I cannot have both, then I prefer bear's paws. I care about life, but, too, I care about Justice. If I cannot have both, then I choose Justice. I care about life, but then there are things I care about more than life. For that reason I will not seek life improperly. I do not like death, but then there are things I dislike more than death. For that reason there are some contingencies from which I will not escape.

"If men are taught to desire life above all else, then they will seize it by all means in their power. If they are taught to hate death above all else, then they will avoid all contingencies by which they might meet it. There are times when one might save one's life, but only by means that are wrong. There are times when death can be avoided, but only by means that are improper. Having desires above life itself and having dislikes greater than death itself is a type of mind that all men possess—it is not only confined to the worthy. What distinguishes the worthy is that he ensures that he does not lose it.

"Even though it be a matter of life or death to him, a traveler will refuse a basket of rice or a dish of soup if offered in an insulting manner. But food that has been trampled upon, not even a beggar will think fit to eat. And yet a man will accept emoluments of ten thousand *chung* regardless of the claims of Propriety and Justice. And what does he gain by that? Elegant palaces and houses, wives and concubines to wait on him, and the allegiance of the poor among his acquaintance! I was previously speaking of matters affecting life and death, where even there under certain conditions one will not accept relief, but this is a matter of palaces and houses, of wives and concubines, and of time-serving friends. Should we not stop such things? This is what I mean by 'losing the mind with which we originally were endowed.' "

Translated by W. A. C. H. Dobson

9

Chuang Tzu

Chuang Chou (355?–275 B.C.E.)

Once upon a time, Chuang Chou[1] dreamed that he was a butterfly, a butterfly flitting about happily enjoying himself. He didn't know that he was Chou. Suddenly he awoke and was palpably Chou. He didn't know whether he were Chou who had dreamed of being a butterfly, or a butterfly who was dreaming that he was Chou. Now, there must be a difference between Chou and the butterfly. This is called the transformation of things.

Of all early Chinese thinkers, Master Chuang possessed the most fertile imagination, and his highly creative literary style had a greater impact on later writers throughout history than any other figure from the pre-Ch'in period. While the *Chuang Tzu* is invariably characterized as a Taoist text both by Taoists and by others, the positions espoused in the book are so diverse and protean they defy easy classification. Certainly the book is not by one author. The seven "Inner Chapters" are generally considered most clearly associated with the shadowy individual named Chuang Chou. While some of the fifteen "Outer Chapters" and eleven "Miscellaneous Chapters" also include passages of great interest, much of the material in them consists of thinly disguised Confucianism and Legalism, as well as other more conventional ideologies that are at odds with the unconstrained playfulness of the more genuine chapters.

1. Master Chuang (Chuang Tzu). The surname Chuang means "sedate" and Chou, his personal name, signifies "[all] round" or "whole."

The emperor of the Southern Sea was Lickety, the emperor of the Northern Sea was Split, and the emperor of the Center was Wonton.[1] Lickety and Split often met each other in the land of Wonton, and Wonton treated them very well. Wanting to repay Wonton's kindness, Lickety and Split said, "All people have seven holes for seeing, hearing, eating, and breathing. Wonton alone lacks them. Let's try boring some holes for him." So every day they bored one hole, and on the seventh day Wonton died.

1. The undifferentiated soup of primordial chaos. As it begins to differentiate, dumpling-blobs of matter coalesce. Wonton soup probably came first as a type of simple early fare. With the evolution of human consciousness and reflectiveness, the soup would have been adopted as a suitable metaphor for chaos.

Chapter 17: Autumn Floods

When the time of the autumn floods arrived, the hundred tributaries poured into the Yellow River. Its onrushing current was so huge that one could not discern an ox or a horse on the opposite side or on the banks of its islets. Thereupon the Earl of the River[1] delightedly congratulated himself at having

1. The god of the Yellow River.

complete and sole possession of all excellences under heaven. Following along with the current, he went east until he reached the North Sea. There he looked eastward but could not see the water's end, whereupon he crestfallenly gazed across the surface of the sea and said with a sigh toward its Overlord,[2] "There is a proverb which says, 'He who has heard the Way a hundred times believes no one may be compared with himself!' This applies to me. Furthermore, when I first heard those who belittle the learning of Confucius and disparage the righteousness of Po-yi, I did not believe them. But now that I behold your boundlessness, I realize that, had I not come to your gate,[3] I would have been in danger[4] and ridiculed forever by the practitioners of the great method."[5]

The Overlord of the North Sea said, "You can't tell a frog at the bottom of a well about the sea because he's stuck in his little space. You can't tell a summer insect about ice because it is confined by its season. You can't tell a scholar of distorted views about the Way because he is bound by his doctrine. Now you have ventured forth from your banks to observe the great sea and have recognized your own insignificance, so that you can be told of the great principle.

"Of all the waters under heaven, none is greater than the sea. The myriad rivers return to it ceaselessly, but it never fills up; the drain[6] at its bottom endlessly discharges, but it never empties. Spring and autumn it never varies, and it knows nothing of flood and drought. Its superiority to such streams as the Yangtze and the Yellow River cannot be measured in numbers. Yet the reason I have never made much of myself on this account is because I compare my own form to that of heaven and earth and recall that I received my vital breath from yin and yang. Midst heaven and earth, I am as a little pebble or tiny tree on a big mountain. Since I perceive of myself as being small, how then can I make much of myself? May we not reckon that the four seas in the midst of heaven and earth resemble the cavity in a pile of stones lying in a huge marsh? May we not reckon that the Middle Kingdom[7] in the midst of the sea is like a mustard seed[8] in a huge granary? When we designate the number of things there are in existence, we refer to them in terms of myriads, but man occupies only one place among them. The masses of men occupy the nine regions,[9] but wherever grain grows and wherever boats and

2. Whose name was Jo.
3. To learn from you instead of from the Confucians.
4. Of continuing in my delusion.
5. The Way (Tao).
6. More literally, "tail-confluence (Wei-lü)," a hole with a gigantic stone plug at the bottom of the sea whence its waters are removed.
7. To this day, this is still China's name for itself.
8. The Chinese text has a bisyllabic term meaning "tares" or "panic grass."
9. The ancient Chinese conceived of their realm as being divided into nine sections, somewhat like a tic-tac-toe diagram.

carriages reach, the individual occupies only one place among them. In comparison with the myriad things, would he not resemble the tip of a downy hair on a horse's body? The succession of the five emperors, the contention of the three kings, the worries of humane men, the labors of the committed scholars all amount to no more than this. Po-yi declined it for the sake of fame. Confucius lectured on it for the sake of his erudition. This is because they made much of themselves. Is this not like you just now making much of yourself because of your flooding waters?"

"This being so," asked the Earl of the River, "may I take heaven and earth as the standard for what is large, and the tip of a downy hair as the standard for what is small?"

"No," said the Overlord of the North Sea. "Things are limitless in their capacities, incessant in their occurrences, inconstant in their portions, uncertain in their beginning and ending. For this reason, great knowledge observes things at a relative distance; hence it does not belittle what is small or make much of what is big, knowing that their capacities are limitless. It witnesses clearly the past and the present; hence it is not frustrated by what is far off or attracted by what is close at hand, knowing that their occurrences are incessant. It examines fullness and emptiness; hence it is not pleased when it obtains or worried when it loses, knowing that their portions are inconstant. It understands the level path; hence it is not enraptured by life or perturbed by death, knowing that beginnings and endings are uncertain. We may reckon that what man knows is less than what he doesn't know; the time when he is alive is less than the time when he is not alive. When he seeks to delimit the boundaries of the extremely large with what is extremely small, he becomes disoriented and can't get hold of himself. Viewed from this vantage, how do we know that the tip of a downy hair is adequate to determine the parameters of the extremely small? And how do we know that heaven and earth are adequate to delimit the boundaries of the extremely large?"

"The deliberators of the world," said the Earl of the Yellow River, "all say, 'That which is extremely minute has no form; that which is extremely large cannot be encompassed.' Is this true?"

"If we look at what is large from the viewpoint of what is minuscule," said the Overlord of the North Sea, "we won't see the whole. If we look at what is minuscule from the viewpoint of what is large, we won't see the details. Now, that which is minute is the smallest of the small; that which is enormous is the largest of the large. Hence their differences are suitable and in accord with their circumstances. Yet, the minute and the coarse are both dependent upon their having a form. That which has no form is numerically indivisible; that which cannot be encompassed is numerically undelimitable. That which can be discussed in words is the coarseness of things; that which can be conceived of in thought is the minuteness of things. That which can neither be discussed in words nor conceived of in thought is independent of minuteness and coarseness." [10]

"How, then," asked the Earl of the Yellow River, "are we to demarcate the value and magnitude of a thing, whether it be intrinsic or extrinsic?"

The Overlord of the North Sea said, "Observed in the light of the Way, things are neither prized nor despised; observed in the light of things, they prize themselves and despise others; observed in the light of the common lot, one's value is not determined by oneself. Observed in the light of gradations, if we consider to be large that which is larger than something else, then the myriad things are without exception large; if we consider to be small that which is smaller than something else, then all the myriad things are without exception small. If we regard heaven and earth as a mustard seed and the tip of a downy hair as a mountain, we can perceive the numerousness of their relative gradations. Observed in the light of merit, if we grant whatever merit they have, then the myriad things without exception have merit; if we point to whatever merit they lack, then the myriad things lack merit. If we recognize that east and west, though opposites, cannot be without each other, their shared merit will be fixed. Observed in the light of inclination, if we approve whatever they approve, then the myriad things without exception may be approved; if we condemn whatever they condemn, then the myriad things without exception may be condemned. If we recognize that Yao and Chieh approved of themselves but condemned each other, we can perceive their controlling inclinations.

"Long ago, Yao yielded his throne to Shun and the latter became emperor, but when K'uai yielded his throne to Tzu Chih [11] they were both cut down. T'ang and Wu became kings through contention, but the duke of Po con-

---

10. The following lengthy paragraph has been inappropriately inserted at this point:

> Therefore the conduct of the great man is not aimed at hurting others, yet he does not make much of his humaneness and kindness. When he moves, it is not for profit, but he does not despise the porter [a] at the gate. He does not wrangle over goods and property, yet he does not make much of his declining and yielding. In his affairs, he does not rely upon others and does not make much of utilizing his own strength, but he does not despise those who are avaricious and corrupt. His conduct may differ from that of the common lot, but he does not make much of his eccentricity. His behavior may follow that of the crowd, but he does not despise the glib flatterer. All the titles and emoluments in the world are not enough to encourage him, nor are penalties and shame enough to disgrace him. He knows that right and wrong are indivisible, that minuscule and large are undemarcatable. I have heard it said, "The Man of the Way is not celebrated; the man of ultimate virtue is not successful; the great man has no self." This is the pinnacle of restraint.

> a. Who is always looking out for a tip or a bribe.

11. In the year 316 B.C.E., King K'uai of Yen yielded his throne to his minister, Tzu Chih, in conscious imitation of Yao handing over his throne to Shun. This led to three years of internal strife and the invasion of Yen by the state of Ch'i.

tended and was destroyed.[12] Viewed in this light, the etiquette of contending and yielding, the conduct of Yao and Chieh, may be either prized or despised in accord with the times, but may not be taken as constants. A beam or a ridgepole may be used to breach a city wall, but it cannot be used to plug a hole, which is to say that implements have specific purposes. A Ch'i-chi or a Hua-liu[13] may gallop a thousand tricents in a day, but for catching rats they're not as good as a wild cat or a weasel, which is to say that creatures have different skills. An owl can catch fleas at night and discern the tip of a downy hair, but when it comes out during the day it stares blankly and can't even see a hill or a mountain, which is to say that beings have different natures. Therefore, when it is said 'Make right your teacher, not wrong; make good government your teacher, not disorder,' this is to misunderstand the principle of heaven and earth and the attributes of the myriad things. It would be like making heaven your teacher and ignoring earth, like making yin your teacher and ignoring yang. The unworkability of this is clear. Still, if one goes on talking like this and does not give it up, one is either being stupid or deceptive. The emperors and kings of old had different modes of abdication, and the rulers of the three dynasties had different modes of succession. He who acts contrary to the times and contravenes custom is called a usurper; he who accords with the times and conforms to custom is called a disciple of righteousness. Keep silent, oh Earl of the Yellow River! How could you know about the gate of honor and baseness and about the practitioners of small and large?"[14]

"Then what am I to do?" asked the Earl of the Yellow River, "and what am I not to do? With regard to rejecting and accepting, taking and giving, how should I behave?"

"Viewed in the light of the Way," said the Overlord of the North Sea,

> "What is prized and what is despised
> May be referred to as alternating developments of each other.
> Do not persist in following the dictates of your will,
> For it will bring you into great conflict with the Way.
>
> 5   What is few and what is many
> May be referred to as reciprocal extensions of each other.

12. T'ang and Wu were the founding kings of the Shang and Chou dynasties respectively. The duke of Po was the grandson of King P'ing of Ch'u. His father, the crown prince, was demoted when the king became infatuated with a woman from the state of Ch'in. He fled to Cheng and married a woman who gave birth to the duke of Po. When the latter grew up, he returned to Ch'u and raised an armed insurrection in 479 B.C.E. to take revenge for his father, but was defeated and eventually committed suicide.

13. The Chinese counterparts of Bucephalus and Pegasus.

14. The words "gate" and "practitioners" here are resonant with their occurrence in the Earl of the Yellow River's first speech at the beginning of the chapter.

Do not be inflexibly monotonous in your behavior,
For it will put you at odds with the Way.

Be solemn as the lord of a state
10   Whose integrity is impartial;
Be self-composed as the officiant of a sacrificial altar
     Whose blessings are impartial;
Be broad-minded as the immensity of the four directions
     Which have no borders.

15   Embosom all the myriad things,
Taking each one under your protective wings.
This may be referred to as universality.[15]
The myriad things will be equally regarded,
There being no long or short among them.

20   The Way has neither beginning nor end,
But things have life and death.
Not being able to presume upon their completion,
They are now empty, now full,
Without stability in form.

25   The years cannot be advanced,
Nor can time be stayed.
Dissolution and generation, fullness and emptiness—
Whatever ends has a beginning.

Thus may we
Speak of the secret of the great purport,[16]
30   Discuss the principle of the myriad things.

The life of things
Is like the cantering and galloping of a horse—
They are transformed with each movement,
They change with each moment.
35   What are you to do?
What are you not to do?
Just let things evolve by themselves."

"Then what is to be prized about the Way?" asked the Earl of the Yellow River.

The Overlord of the North Sea said, "She who knows the Way must

15. More literally, the text has "nonlocality."

16. It would be totally out of keeping with this magnificent dialogue between the Overlord of the North Sea and the Earl of Yellow River to translate *yi* here in its restricted Confucian sense of "righteousness."

apprehend principle; she who apprehends principle must be clear about contingency; she who is clear about contingency will not harm herself with things. She who has ultimate integrity will neither be burned by fire nor drowned in water, will neither be harmed by cold and heat nor injured by bird and beast. This does not mean that she belittles these things, but rather that she examines where she will be safe or in danger. She is tranquil in misfortune or in fortune; she is careful about her comings and goings, so that nothing can harm her. Therefore it is said, 'The heavenly is within, the human is without; integrity lies in heaven.' When you know the operation of the heavenly and the human, you will root yourself in heaven and position yourself in contentment. Then you will be hesitant and flexible, reverting to what is important and bespeaking perfection."

"What do you mean by heavenly, and what do you mean by human?"

The Overlord of the North Sea said, "Oxen and horses having four feet is what is meant by 'heavenly.' Putting a halter over a horse's head or piercing through an ox's nose is what is meant by 'human.' Therefore it is said,

'Do not destroy the heavenly with the human;
Do not destroy destiny with intentionality;
Do not sacrifice your good name for attainments.' [17]
If you guard this carefully and do not lose it,
You may be said to have returned to the truth."

The unipede envies the millipede; the millipede envies the snake; the snake envies the wind; the wind envies the eye; the eye envies the mind.

The unipede said to the millipede, "I go hippity-hopping along on my one foot but barely manage. How is it, sir, that you can control myriad feet?"

"It's not so," said the millipede. "Haven't you seen a person spit? When they spew forth, the big globs are like pearls, the droplets are like a mist. All mixed up together, the number that falls is immeasurable. Now, I just move by my natural inner workings but don't know why it is so."

The millipede said to the snake, "I go along on my multitudinous feet, but I'm not as fast as you who have no feet. How come?"

"How could we change the movements of our natural inner workings?" asked the snake. "What use do I have for feet?"

The snake said to the wind, "I go along by moving my spine and ribs, thus I have a shape. But you, sir, who arise with a whoosh from the North Sea and alight with a whoosh in the South Sea, have no shape at all. How can this be?"

"It's true that I arise with a whoosh from the North Sea and alight in the

---

17. Most commentators interpret the last clause as meaning "do not sacrifice yourself for the sake of fame," but this totally ignores both the syntax and diction of the sentence. The problem with the present interpretation is that we would not expect the Overlord of the North Sea to care the slightest about name or fame. One suspects, therefore, a lapse on the part of the author.

South Sea," said the wind, "but whoever points at me vanquishes me, and whoever treads upon me vanquishes me. Nonetheless, only I can snap big trees and blow down big houses. Therefore, the great vanquishing depends upon a host of minor defeats. It is only the sage who can be a great vanquisher."

When Confucius was traveling in K'uang, the local militia[18] surrounded him several layers deep,[19] but he kept right on singing and playing his lute. Tzu-lu went over to see him and said, "How can you be so cheerful, master?"

"Come!" said Confucius, "I shall tell you. Long have I shunned adversity, but have not been able to avoid it: that's my destiny. Long have I sought success, but have not been able to achieve it; that's the times. In the age of Yao and Shun, there was no one under heaven who met with adversity, but their achievements were not due to their knowledge. In the age of Chieh and Chow, there was no one under heaven who met with success, but their failures were not due to their lack of knowledge. It was because of the times and the circumstances they encountered.

"To travel on water yet not flee from crocodiles and dragons is the courage of the fisherman; to travel on land yet not flee from rhinoceroses and tigers is the courage of the hunter; to have naked blades cross before him yet view death as calmly as life is the courage of the ardent warrior; to know that adversity is due to destiny and that success is due to the times yet face great difficulty without fear is the courage of the sage. Just sit tight, Tzu-lu. I am under the control of my destiny."

Shortly afterwards, the leader of the armed men came over and apologized, saying, "We thought you were Tiger Yang,[20] and so we surrounded you. Now that we know you're not, please accept our apologies, and we shall retreat."

Kung-sun Lung[21] inquired of Prince Mou of Wei, saying, "When I was young I studied the Way of the former kings, and when I grew up I understood the conduct of humaneness and righteousness. I joined sameness and difference, separated hardness from whiteness, asserted the unassertable, and affirmed the unaffirmable.[22] I perplexed the thinkers of the hundred schools and refuted the disputers of the manifold persuasions. I considered myself to be ultimately accomplished. But now I have heard the words of Master Chuang and am

18. The Chinese text has "people of Sung" instead of "local militia," but this incident actually occurred in the state of Wey, just across the border from Sung. K'uang was the name of a place in the state of Wey.

19. This remarkable incident is recounted at greater length elsewhere in the *Chuang Tzu*.

20. A notorious marauder whose forces had raided the area not long before.

21. An ancient Chinese sophist whose forte was paradoxes.

22. These are all references to Kung-sun Lung's celebrated sophistries.

bewildered by their oddity. I don't know whether it's because my powers of discussion are not up to his or because my knowledge is less than his. Now I feel that I can't even make a peep. I venture to ask what strategy I should adopt."

Prince Mou leaned against his table and heaved a great sigh. Then he looked up to heaven and, smiling, said, "Haven't you heard about the frog in the broken-down well? 'I really enjoy myself here!' it said to a turtle of the Eastern Sea. 'If I want to go out, I jump along the railing around the well, then I come back and rest where the brick lining is missing from the wall. I enter the water till it comes up to my armpits and supports my chin. When I slop through the mud, it covers my feet and buries my toes. Turning around, I see crayfish and tadpoles, but none of them are a match for me. Furthermore, I have sole possession of all the water in this hole and bestraddle all the joy in this broken-down well. This is the ultimate! Why don't you drop in some time, sir, and see for yourself?'

"But before the turtle of the Eastern Sea could get his left foot in, his right knee had already gotten stuck. After extricating himself, he withdrew a little and told the frog about the sea, saying, 'A distance of a thousand tricents is insufficient to span its breadth; a height of a thousand fathoms is insufficient to plumb its depth. During Yü's time, there were floods nine years out of ten, but the water in it did not appreciably increase; during T'ang's time, there were droughts seven years out of eight, but the extent of its shores did not appreciably decrease. Hence, not to shift or change with time, not to advance or recede regardless of amount—this is the great joy of the Eastern Sea.' Upon hearing this, the frog in the broken-down well was so utterly startled that it lost itself in bewilderment.

"Furthermore, when you, whose knowledge is inadequate to understand the limits of 'right' and 'wrong', still wish to see through the words of Master Chuang, it's like making a mosquito carry a mountain on its back or an inchworm race against the Yellow River—they won't be up to the task. Still further, aren't you, whose knowledge is inadequate to understand the words for discussing the uttermost mysteries and who satisfy yourself with a moment's profit, like the frog in the broken-down well?

"Master Chuang, however, marches through the Yellow Springs[23] one moment and ascends to the empyrean the next.

With him, there is neither north nor south,
But only untrammeled release in all four directions
And absorption in the unfathomable;
There is neither east nor west,
Beginning as he does in darkest obscurity
And returning to grand perceptivity.

23. The Chinese equivalent of Hades.

But you, sir, bewilderedly seek something with which to quiz him and grope for a means to dispute him. This is simply like peering at heaven through a tube or pointing at the earth with an awl—too small for the purpose. Be gone, sir! Haven't you heard of the young lad from Shou-ling[24] who tried to learn to walk the way people do in Han-tan.[25] Before he had acquired this new skill, he had forgotten how he used to walk, so all he could do was come crawling home on all fours. If you don't go away now, sir, you'll forget what you used to know and lose your profession."

Mouth agape and tongue-tied, Kung-sun Lung fled in consternation.

Master Chuang was fishing in the P'u River.[26] The king of Ch'u dispatched two high-ranking officials to go before him with this message: "I wish to encumber you with the administration of my realm."

Without turning around, Master Chuang just kept holding on to his fishing rod and said, "I have heard that in Ch'u there is a sacred tortoise that has already been dead for three thousand years. The king stores it inside a hamper wrapped with cloth in his ancestral temple. Do you think this tortoise would rather be dead and have its bones preserved as objects of veneration, or be alive and dragging its tail through the mud?"

"It would rather be alive and dragging its tail through the mud," said the two officials.

"Begone!" said Master Chuang. "I'd rather be dragging my tail in the mud."

When Master Hui was serving as the prime minister of Liang, Master Chuang set off to visit him. Somebody said to Master Hui, "Master Chuang is coming and he wants to replace you as prime minister." Whereupon Master Hui became afraid and had the kingdom searched for three days and three nights.

After Master Chuang arrived, he went to see Master Hui and said, "In the south there is a bird. Its name is Yellow Phoenix.[27] Have you ever heard of it? It takes off from the South Sea and flies to the North Sea. It won't stop on any other tree but the kolanut; won't eat anything else but bamboo seeds;[28] won't drink anything but sweet spring water. There was once an owl which, having

24. A place in the state of Yen.
25. The capital of the state of Chao. The people there were said to have a stylishly distinctive strut.
26. In Shantung.
27. The precise meaning of the name *yüan-ch'u* is uncertain, although the second graph seems to indicate that the bird in question was young.
28. Since bamboo flowers (and hence produces seeds) only rarely—some species as seldom as once a century—the implication is that the Yellow Phoenix (which itself only appears at great intervals) is very particular about its food. Another interpretation of the sinographs in question yields "fruits of the *Melia azedarach*," said to be favored by the phoenix and the unicorn but

got hold of a putrid rat, looked up at the Yellow Phoenix as it was passing by and shouted 'shoo!' Now, sir, do you wish to shoo me away from your kingdom of Liang?"

Master Chuang and Master Hui were strolling across the bridge over the Hao.[29] "The hemiculters[30] have come out and are swimming[31] so leisurely," said Master Chuang. "This is the joy of fishes."

"You're not a fish," said Master Hui. "How do you know what the joy of fishes is?"

"You're not me," said Master Chuang, "so how do you know that I don't know what the joy of fishes is?"

"I'm not you," said Master Hui, "so I certainly do not know what you do. But you're certainly not a fish, so it is irrefutable that you do not know what the joy of fishes is."

"Let's go back to where we started,"[32] said Master Chuang. "When you said, 'How do you know what the joy of fishes is?', you asked me because you already knew that I knew. I know it by strolling over the Hao."[33]

shunned by the dragon. Common names for this plant are pride of India, pride of China, and chinaberry.

29. In Anhwei.

30. Small fish found in rivers and lakes. They are only a few inches long with thin, flat bodies that, according to old Chinese texts, are "shaped like a willow leaf."

31. Note that this is a rendering of the same graph translated in the previous sentence as "strolling" and elsewhere in the *Chuang Tzu* as "wandering" or occasionally as "traveling".

32. More literally, "to the root [of the problem/argument]."

33. Although not so protracted and elaborate, the entire style of argumentation in this famous passage bears an uncanny resemblance to many philosophical arguments found in the works of Plato. Chapter 17 ends here.

In seeds there are germs. When they are found in water they become filaments. When they are found at the border of water and land they become algae.[1] When they germinate in elevated places they become plantain. When the plantain is found in fertile soil it becomes crow's foot.[2] The crow's foot's roots become scarab grubs and its leaves become butterflies. The butterflies soon evolve into insects that are born beneath the stove. They have the appearance of exuviae and are called "house crickets." After a thousand days the house crickets became birds called "dried surplus bones."[3] The spittle of the dried surplus bones becomes a misty spray and the misty spray becomes

1. The Chinese expression may be rendered more literally as "clothing of frogs and oysters."

2. This is a literal translation of the two sinographs forming the name. The plant in question is commonly called blackberry lily in English.

3. The precise identification of this and several of the following terms is impossible because they are colloquial names lost to the tradition of classical explication.

mother of vinegar. Midges are born from mother of vinegar; yellow whirligigs are born from fetid wine; blindgnats are born from putrid slimebugs. When goat's queue couples with bamboo that has not shooted for a long time, they produce greenies. The greenies produce panthers; panthers produce horses; horses produce men; and men return to enter the wellsprings[4] of nature. The myriad things all come out of the wellsprings and all reenter the wellsprings.

4. The sinograph for "wellsprings [of nature]" includes within it the graph for "germs," which occurs at the beginning of this bizarre romp through evolution. There is little doubt that the two words are etymologically related in Sinitic. This has prompted many scholars to equate the two as they occur in the passage.

Duke Huan[1] was hunting in the marshes with Kuan Chung[2] as his charioteer when he saw a ghost. Grabbing hold of Kuan Chung's hand, he asked, "Did you see something, Father[3] Chung?"

"Your servant saw nothing," was the reply.

After the duke returned he babbled incoherently and became ill, so that he did not go out for several days. There was a scholar of Ch'i named Master Leisurely Ramble who said to him, "Your Highness is harming yourself. How could a ghost harm you? If an embolism of vital breath caused by agitation disperses and does not return, what remains will be insufficient; if it rises and does not come back down, it will cause a person to be easily angered; if it descends and does not come back up, it will cause a person to forget easily; if it neither rises nor descends, it will stay in the center of a person's body, clogging his heart, and he will become ill."

"Yes," said Duke Huan, "but are there ghosts?"

"There are. In pits there are pacers; around stoves there are tufties. Fulgurlings frequent dust piles inside the door; croakers and twoads hop about in low-lying places to the northeast; spillsuns frequent low-lying places to the northwest. In water there are nonimagoes; on hills there are scrabblers; on mountains there are unipedes; in the wilds there are will-o'-the-wisps; and in marshes there are bendcrooks."

"May I ask what a bendcrook looks like?" said the duke.

"The bendcrook," said Master Ramble, "is as big around as the hub of a chariot wheel and as long as the shafts. It wears purple clothes and a vermilion cap. This is a creature that hates to hear the sound of rumbling chariots. When it does, it stands up holding its head in its hands. He who sees it is likely to become hegemon."

Duke Huan erupted in laughter and said, "That was what I saw." Where-

1. Of the state of Ch'i, the first of the five hegemons who imposed their will on the other feudal states.

2. Prime minister of Duke Huan and the ostensible author of the book entitled *Master Kuan* (*Kuan Tzu*, see selection 5).

3. A term of address used to show respect.

upon he adjusted his clothing and cap, and had Master Ramble sit down with him. Before the day was over, his illness left him without his even being aware of it.

Translated by Victor H. Mair

10

The Classic Book of Integrity and the Way: *Tao Te Ching*

Attributed to Lao Tzu (c. 250 B.C.E.?)

1
(38)

The person of superior integrity
      does not insist upon his integrity;
For this reason, he has integrity.
The person of inferior integrity
      never loses sight of his integrity;
For this reason, he lacks integrity.

The person of superior integrity takes no action,
    nor has he a purpose for acting.
The person of superior humaneness takes action,
    but has no purpose for acting.
The person of superior righteousness takes action,
    and has a purpose for acting.

The *Tao Te Ching* is probably the best-known Chinese book in the world, having been translated hundreds of times into dozens of languages. This slender tome of approximately five thousand sinographs divided—sometimes rather arbitrarily—into eighty-one brief "chapters," has had an important influence on religion and thought that is hugely out of proportion to its size. Although the text is held by Taoist believers to have been composed by Lao Tzu in the sixth century B.C.E., the available evidence indicates that it was actually not committed to writing until sometime in the third century. Furthermore, there is no reliable biographical information concerning Lao Tzu. The name, which means "Old Master," is most likely a general designation for a number of venerable sages who actively promoted one brand or another of quietist thought. The authorship of the *Tao Te Ching* may thus be said to be composite in nature.

For the word translated here as "integrity," see note 1 in selection 5.

The present translation is based on silk manuscripts discovered in 1973 at Ma-wang-tui in Hunan province. These, approximately half a millennium older than the earliest editions previously available, permit the solution of many difficult textual problems. The chapter numbers are those of the Ma-wang-tui manuscripts; the traditional chapter numbers are given in parentheses.

The person of superior etiquette takes action,
    but others do not respond to him;
Whereupon he rolls up his sleeves
    and coerces them.

Therefore,
    When the Way is lost,
        afterward comes integrity.
    When integrity is lost,
        afterward comes humaneness.
    When humaneness is lost,
        afterward comes righteousness.
    When righteousness is lost,
        afterward comes etiquette.

10
(47)

Without going out-of-doors,
    one may know all under heaven;
Without peering through windows,
    one may know the Way of heaven.

The farther one goes,
The less one knows.

For this reason,
    The sage knows without journeying,
            understands without looking,
            accomplishes without acting.

24
(61)

A large state is like a low-lying estuary,
    the female of all under heaven.
In the congress of all under heaven,
    the female always conquers the male through her stillness.
Because she is still,
    it is fitting for her to lie low.
By lying beneath a small state,
    a large state can take over a small state.
By lying beneath a large state,
    a small state can be taken over by a large state.

Therefore,
    One may either take over or be taken over by lying low.

Therefore,

> The large state wishes only to annex and nurture others;
> The small state wants only to join with and serve others.

Now,

> Since both get what they want,
> It is fitting for the large state to lie low.

30
(80)

Let there be a small state with few people,
> where military devices find no use;
Let the people look solemnly upon death,
> and banish the thought of moving elsewhere.

They may have carts and boats,
> but there is no reason to ride them;
They may have armor and weapons,
> but there is no reason to display them.

Let the people go back to tying knots
> to keep records.
Let their food be savory,
> their clothes beautiful,
> their customs pleasurable,
> their dwellings secure.

Though they may gaze across at a neighboring state,
> and hear the sounds of its dogs and chickens,
The people will never travel back and forth,
> till they die of old age.

41
(76)

> Human beings are
> > soft and supple when alive,
> > stiff and straight when dead.

> The myriad creatures, the grasses and trees are
> > soft and fragile when alive,
> > dry and withered when dead.

Therefore, it is said:
> The rigid person is a disciple of death;
> The soft, supple, and delicate are lovers of life.

> An army that is inflexible will not conquer;
> A tree that is inflexible will snap.

The unyielding and mighty shall be brought low;
The soft, supple, and delicate will be set above.

45
(1)

The ways that can be walked are not the eternal Way;
The names that can be named are not the eternal name.
The nameless is the origin of the myriad creatures;
The named is the mother of the myriad creatures.

Therefore,
    Always be without desire
        in order to observe its wondrous subtleties;
    Always have desire
        so that you may observe its manifestations.

    Both of these derive from the same source;
    They have different names but the same designation.

    Mystery of mysteries,
    The gate of all wonders!

50
(6)

The valley spirit never dies—
        it is called "the mysterious female";
The gate of the mysterious female
        is called "the root of heaven and earth."
Gossamer it is,
        seemingly insubstantial,
        yet never consumed through use.

54
(10)

While you
    Cultivate the soul and embrace unity,
        can you keep them from separating?
    Focus your vital breath until it is supremely soft,
        can you be like a baby?
    Cleanse the mirror of mysteries,
        can you make it free of blemish?
    Love the people and enliven the state,
        can you do so without cunning?
    Open and close the gate of heaven,
        can you play the part of the female?

Reach out with clarity in all directions,
     can you refrain from action?

It gives birth to them and nurtures them,
It gives birth to them but does not possess them,
It rears them but does not control them.
     This is called "mysterious integrity."

55
(11)

Thirty spokes converge on a single hub,
     but it is in the space where there is nothing
          that the usefulness of the cart lies.
Clay is molded to make a pot,
     but it is in the space where there is nothing
          that the usefulness of the clay pot lies.
Cut out doors and windows to make a room,
     but it is in the spaces where there is nothing
          that the usefulness of the room lies.
Therefore,
     Benefit may be derived from something,
          but it is in nothing that we find usefulness.

72
(28)

Know masculinity,
Maintain femininity,
     and be a ravine for all under heaven.
By being a ravine for all under heaven,
Eternal integrity will never desert you.
If eternal integrity never deserts you,
You will return to the state of infancy.

Know you are innocent,
Remain steadfast when insulted,
     and be a valley for all under heaven.
By being a valley for all under heaven,
Eternal integrity will suffice.
If eternal integrity suffices,
You will return to the simplicity of the unhewn log.

Know whiteness,
Maintain blackness,
     and be a model for all under heaven.
By being a model for all under heaven,

Eternal integrity will not err.
If eternal integrity does not err,
You will return to infinity.

When the unhewn log is sawn apart,
    it is made into tools;
When the sage is put to use,
    he becomes the chief of officials.

For

Great carving does no cutting.

Translated by Victor H. Mair

11
Balanced Discussions

Chapter 28: Taoist Untruths

Wang Ch'ung (27–90?)

In the books of the Literati it is stated that[1] Huang Ti[2] exploited the copper mines of Mount Shou,[3] and out of the ore cast tripods at the foot of the Ching Mountain.[4] When the tripods were completed, a dragon with a long beard

Balanced Discussions (Lun heng) represents a position of extreme skepticism and rationalism that was rare for its day. The author, Wang Ch'ung, is critical of virtually all established systems of thought. It is not surprising that his work soon fell into an oblivion from which it was rescued only in the nineteenth century. Wang Ch'ung wrote in and advocated the use of a simple, unadorned style. His other major works were lost, including *Satires against Customs and Usages* (*Chi su chieh yi*), in which it is reported that he advocated the use of the vernacular as opposed to the classical / literary language in writing. Had such a proposal been adopted, it would have had salutary, liberating consequences for Chinese thought and literature, but the entrenched power of the literati and their vested interest in the maintenance of the difficult, artificial book language obviously precluded such an eventuality until the revolutions of the present century.

The *Balanced Discussions* includes several sections that may be characterized as the first attempts to analyze the nature of literature in China. Wang Ch'ung reserves a special place for the rhapsody and the ode as having expressive properties that distinguish them from other more utilitarian types of writing.

1. The following story is taken from the *Records of the Grand Historian* (see selection 225), chapter 28, where an official relates it to Emperor Wu of the Han.
2. The Yellow Emperor.
3. In Shansi province, near P'u-chou.
4. The mountain lies in Shensi, near Sian.

came down, and went to meet Huang Ti. Huang Ti mounted the dragon. His whole suite including the harem, over seventy persons in all, mounted together with him, whereupon the dragon ascended. The remaining smaller officials, who could not find a seat on the dragon, all got hold of the dragon's beard, which they pulled out. Huang Ti's bow fell down. The people gazed after him until he disappeared in the sky. Then they hugged his bow and the dragon's beard and moaned. Therefore later ages named the place Tripod Beard/Lake[5] and the bow of the emperor Raven's Cry.[6]

The Grand Annalist in his eulogy on the Five Emperors[7] also says that, having performed the hill-sacrifice, Huang Ti disappeared as a genius, and that his followers paid their respect to his garments and cap, and afterward buried them.[8] I say that this is not true.

What does Huang Ti really mean? Is it an appellative or a posthumous title? Being a posthumous title it must be some praise bestowed upon him by his subjects, for this kind of title is a glorification of what the deceased had done during his lifetime. Huang Ti was a votary of Tao[9] and subsequently, as they say, rose to Heaven. If his subjects wanted to honor him, they ought not to have styled him Huang, but ought to have given him a title implying his ascension as an immortal.

According to the rules for honorary titles, the pacification of the people would be called Huang, which means that he who is styled so kept the people at peace,[10] but the word does not denote the acquisition of Tao. Among the many emperors, those given to arts and literature were called *wen*, i.e., scholarly, and those fond of war, *wu*, i.e., warriors. Both designations had their real basis. They served to exhort others to do the like.

If at the time of Huang Ti posthumous titles were not yet given according to qualities, of what generation were those who first called him Huang Ti? Huang Ti's own subjects must have known their prince, and later generations could trace his doings. Although our doubts about the existence of appellatives and posthumous titles at Huang Ti's time may not be set at rest, in any event it is evident that Huang cannot mean an Immortal who rose to Heaven.

A dragon does not rise to Heaven. If Huang Ti rode on a dragon, it is clear that he could not have ascended to Heaven either. When a dragon rises, clouds and rain appear simultaneously and carry it along. As soon as the

5. Ting-hu. A place by this name actually exists in Honan.

6. Wu-hao.

7. Huang Ti, Chuan Hsü, K'u, Yao, and Shun. Other enumerations are also given.

8. *Records of the Grand Historian*, chapter 28.

9. The Way, the fundamental principle of Taoism. Whether mistakenly or not, the Taoists have always claimed Huang Ti as one of theirs; hence the legend of his ascension to heaven.

10. This seems to be a fanciful etymology. *Huang* is "yellow," but never means "to pacify." The Yellow Emperor was called yellow from the color of the earth, over which he ruled. Thus the name is generally explained, whether correctly is doubtful. Recent scholars have argued, on the basis of archeology and historical linguistics, that he may have had "yellow" (blond) hair.

clouds disperse and the rain stops, the dragon comes down again and reenters its pond. Should Huang Ti really have ridden on a dragon, he would have been drowned with the dragon in the pond afterwards.

Huang Ti was interred in the Chiao Mountain,[11] and still they say that his officials buried his garments and cap. If he actually went up to Heaven on a dragon, his garments and cap could not have separated from his body; and if he became a genius after the hill-sacrifice and vanished, he could not have left his garments and cap behind either. Had Huang Ti really become a genius who could not die but rose to Heaven, his officers and people must have seen it with their own eyes. Having thus witnessed his ascension to Heaven, they decidedly knew that he did not die. Now, to bury the garments and cap of somebody who did not die would have been as if he had died. Such a thing would not have been in accordance with the feelings of the officials, who were aware of the real state of affairs and could distinguish between life and death.

It is on record that the seventy-two sovereigns who ascended Mount T'ai[12] had troubled and toiled, worrying themselves over the state of the empire. Subsequently, their efforts were crowned with success and things settled, so that universal peace reigned throughout the land. When there was universal peace, the whole empire enjoyed harmony and tranquility. Then they ascended Mount T'ai and performed the hill-sacrifices. Now, the pursuit of Tao and the struggle for immortality are different from the vexations of official life and business. He whose thoughts all center in Tao forgets worldly affairs, because to trouble about them would injure his nature.[13] They say that Yao looked dried up and Shun withered. Their hearts were sorrowful, and their bodies feeble and careworn. If Huang Ti brought about universal peace, his appearance must have been similar to that of Yao and Shun. Since Yao and Shun did not attain to Tao, it cannot be true that Huang Ti rose to Heaven.[14] If Huang Ti in his pursuit of Tao neglected all worldly affairs, his mind would have been equanimous, and his body fat and strong. Then he would have been quite different from Yao and Shun, and consequently his achievements could not have been the same. In that case the universe would not have enjoyed universal peace. Without universal peace, his sacrifice on the mountain would not have taken place.[15]

11. Some say that this mountain is situated in the province of Kansu, and others, more eastward in the province of Shensi.

12. China's most sacred mountain in Shantung.

13. Taoism inculcates contemplation and quietism, and abhors an active life.

14. Only he who possesses Tao becomes immortal and can ascend to heaven. If the model emperors Yao and Shun did not attain to Tao, why would Huang Ti, provided that he worked as hard as Yao and Shun?

15. The hill-sacrifice (*feng-shan*) was not performed unless the empire enjoyed peace, and peace could not be secured without hard work. Hard work precluded a Taoist life, and without Tao, Huang Ti (the Yellow Emperor) could not ascend on high.

The Five Emperors and Three Rulers were all remarkable for their wisdom and virtue, Huang Ti not more so than the others. If all the sages became genii, Huang Ti would not be one alone; and if the sages did not become genii, why should Huang Ti alone be a genius? People seeing that Huang Ti was very partial to magical arts, which are practised by genii, surmised that he was a genius.

Moreover, on finding the name Tripod Beard/Lake, they said that Huang Ti exploited the copper of Mount Shou and cast it into tripods, and that a dragon with a floating beard came to meet him. This explanation would be on the same line with that of the Kuei-chi Mountain.[16] The purport of the name of this mountain is said to be that the emperor Yü of the Hsia dynasty, on a tour of inspection, held a meeting and a review on this mountain, whence its name Kuei-chi.[17] Yü went to Kuei-chi for the purpose of regulating the water courses, but not on a tour of inspection, just as Huang Ti was addicted to magic, but did not ascend to heaven. There was no such thing like a meeting or a review, as there was no casting of tripods, nor a dragon with a long beard. There is a village called "Vanquish Mother." Does that mean there was really a son who vanquished his mother? A city is called "Morning Song." Are we to infer that its inhabitants used to sing when they rose in the morning?

The books of the Literati relate that the Prince of Huai-nan[18] in his study of Taoism assembled all the Taoists of the empire, and humbled the grandeur of a princedom before the expositors of Taoist lore. Consequently, Taoist scholars flocked to Huai-nan and vied with one another in exhibiting strange tricks and all kinds of miracles. Then the prince attained to Tao and rose to heaven with his whole household. His domestic animals became genii, too. His dogs barked up in the sky, and the cocks crowed in the clouds. That means the drug of immortality was so plentiful that dogs and cocks could eat of it and follow the prince to Heaven. All who have a fad for Taoism and who would learn the art of immortality believe in this story, but it is not true.

Man is a creature. His rank may be ever so high, even princely or royal,

16. In the province of Chekiang.

17. This fanciful "etymology," like those of so many place names and proper nouns in traditional China, is the result of the erroneous—but almost universal—practice of interpreting terms on the basis of the surface signification of the sinographs used to write them. Kuei-chi was undoubtedly the transcription of some non-Sinitic word, the meaning of which was lost when the local languages died out under the massive impact of Han (Sinitic) civilization as it expanded outward from its Yellow River valley base.

18. Liu An, prince of Huai-nan, commonly known as Huai-nan Tzu, a Taoist philosopher and alchemist of the second century B.C.E. He was a prince of the imperial family of the Han emperors.

but his nature cannot be different from that of other creatures. There is no creature who does not die. How could man become an immortal? Birds, having feathers and plumes, can fly but they cannot rise to Heaven. How should man, without feathers and plumes, be able to fly and rise? Were he feathered and winged he would only be equal to birds, but he is not; how then should he ascend to Heaven?

Creatures capable of flying and rising are provided with feathers and wings; others fast at running have hoofs and strong feet. Swift runners cannot fly, and flyers not run. Their bodies are organized differently according to the fluid they are endowed with. Now, man is a swift runner by nature, and therefore does not grow feathers or plumes. From the time he is full grown until his old age, he never gets them by any miracle. If among believers in Taoism and the students of the art of immortality some became feathered and winged, they might eventually fly and rise after all.

If the nature of creatures could be changed, it ought to be possible that metal, wood, water, and fire could also be altered.[19] Frogs could be changed into quails, and sparrows could dive into the water and become clams.[20] It is the upshot of their spontaneous, original nature, and cannot be attained by the study of Tao. Lest the Taoists should be put on a level with the aforesaid animals, I say that, if men could have all the necessary feathers and plumage, they might ascend to Heaven.

Now, the growth and development of creatures are not abrupt, and their changes are not violent but brought about gradually. If the Taoists and students of immortality could first grow feathers and plumes several inches long so that they could skim over the earth and rise to the terraces of high buildings, one might believe that they could ascend to Heaven. But they do not show that they are able to fly even a small distance. How can they suddenly acquire the faculty of flying such a long way through the study of their miraculous arts without any gradual progress? That such a great result might really be effected by means of feathers and wings cannot be ascertained.

The human hair and beard and the different color of things when young and old afford another cue. When a plant comes out, it has a green color; when it ripens, it looks yellow. So long as a man is young, his hair is black; when he grows old, it turns white. Yellow is the sign of maturity, white of old age. After a plant has become yellow, it may be watered and tended ever so much, but it does not become green again. When the hair has turned white no eating of drugs nor any care bestowed upon one's nature can make it black again. Black and green do not come back; how could age and decrepitude be laid aside?

---

19. The elements of which the bodies of all creatures are composed cannot be transformed, therefore those creatures cannot change their nature.

20. These and similar metamorphoses are mentioned in ancient works.

Yellow and white are like the frying of raw meat and the cooking of fresh fish. What has been fried cannot be caused to become raw again; and what has been cooked, to become fresh. Fresh and raw correspond to young and strong; fried and cooked, to weak and old. Heaven, in developing things, can keep them vigorous until autumn but not further on till next spring. By swallowing drugs and nourishing one's nature, one may get rid of sickness, but one cannot prolong one's life and become an immortal. Immortals have a light body and strong vital energy, and yet they cannot rise to heaven. Light and strong though they be, they are not provided with feathers and wings and therefore not able to ascend to Heaven.

Heaven and earth are both bodies. As one cannot descend into the earth, one cannot ascend into Heaven. Such being the case, where would the road be leading up to Heaven? Man is not strong enough to enter and pass through Heaven's body. If the gate of Heaven is in the northwest, all people rising to Heaven must pass by the K'un-lun Mountain. The state of Huai-nan Tzu being situated in the southeast of the earth, he must, if he really ascended to Heaven, first have gone to K'un-lun with all his household, where he would have found an ascent. Provided that the Prince of Huai-nan flew straight across the land to the northwestern corner, flapping his wings, then he must have had feathers and wings. But since no mention is made of his passing by K'un-lun, nor of feathers and wings growing out of his body, the mere assertion of his ascension cannot be but wrong and untrue.

Liu An, prince of Huai-nan, lived contemporaneously with the emperor, Hsiao Wu Ti.[21] His father, Liu Chang, was banished to Yen-tao[22] in Shu[23] for some offense, but died on the road to Yung-chou.[24] Liu An, who succeeded him in his princedom, bore a grudge against the emperor for having caused his father's death in exile and thought of making rebellion. He attracted all sorts of schemers and intended great things. Men like Wu Pei filled his palaces, busy in writing books on the Taoist arts and publishing essays on the most miraculous subjects. They were bustling about and putting their heads together.

In the *Memoir of the Eight Companions*,[25] they wished to prove supernatural forces as if they had attained to Tao. But they never reached it and had no success. Then Huai-nan Tzu plotted a rebellion with Wu Pei. The scheme was discovered, and he committed suicide or, as some say, was put to death. Whether this be the case or he committed suicide is about the same. But

21. 140–86 B.C.E.
22. The modern Ya-chou-fu.
23. An old kingdom in Szechwan.
24. One of the nine provinces into which the legendary emperor Yü divided the empire, comprising Shensi and Kansu.
25. The eight principal Taoist associates of Huai-nan Tzu, one of whom was Wu Pei.

people finding his writings very deep, abstruse, and mysterious, and believing that the predictions of the *Memoir of the Eight Companions* had been fulfilled, divulged the story that he had become a genius and went up to heaven, which is not in accordance with the truth.

It is chronicled in the books of the Literati[26] that Lu Ao,[27] when wandering near the Northern Sea,[28] passed the Great North, and through the Dark Gate[29] entered upon the Mongolian[30] plateau. There he beheld an individual with deep eyes, a black nose, and the neck of a wild goose. Lifting his shoulders, he soared up, and rapidly came down again, gamboling and disporting all the time against the wind. When he caught sight of Lu Ao, he suddenly lowered his arms and sought refuge under a rock. Lu Ao saw him there, resting on the back of a tortoise and eating an oyster.

Lu Ao accosted him, saying, "Sir, I believe that, because I have given up what the world desires, separating from my kindred and leaving my home in order to explore what is outside of the six cardinal points,[31] you will condemn me. I began traveling in my youth. When I had grown up, I did not care for the ordinary duties of man but managed to travel about. Of the four poles, the Great North is the only one that I have not yet seen. Now unexpectedly I find you here, sir. Shall we not become friends?"

The stranger burst out laughing and said, "Why, you are a man from China. You ought not to come as far as this. Yet sun and moon are still shining here. There are all the stars, the four seasons alternate, and yin and yang are still at work. Compared to the Nameless Region, this is only like a small hill. I travel south over the Weary Waste, and halt north in the Hidden Village. I proceed west to the Obscure Hamlet, and pass east through the Place of Dimness. There is no earth beneath, and no heaven above. Listening, one does not hear, and to the onlooker, objects flit away from sight. Beyond that region, there is still shape. Where that ends, one advances ten million tricents by making one step. I could not yet get there. You, sir, reached only this place in your travels but speak of exploring. Is that not an exaggeration? But, please, remain. I have to meet Han Man[32] on the ninth heaven[33] and

26. The following story is taken from *Huai-nan Tzu*.
27. A traveler of the third century B.C.E.
28. This expression can mean the Gobi.
29. The Great North and the Dark Gate are Taoist fanciful names.
30. It is interesting to note the name Mongol here. The Mongols were already known to the Chinese under their actual name in the second century B.C.E. when they were living in the north of China.
31. To wit, the four quarters, above, and below.
32. This is probably the name of a genius ("transcendent being").
33. According to the belief of the Taoists there are nine superposed stages or spheres of the heavens.

cannot stay longer." The stranger then raised his arms, gave his body a jerk, and off he went into the clouds.

Lu Ao stared after him until he became invisible. His heart was full of endless joy, and at the same time he was grieved, as though he had lost somebody. "Compared with you, my master," said he, "I am nothing more than an earthworm is to a wild goose. Crawling the whole day, I do not advance more than some feet, but myself consider it far. It is pitiable indeed."

Such as Lu Ao held that dragons alone have no wings, but when they rise, ride on the clouds. Had Lu Ao said that the stranger had wings, his words might be credible. But he did not speak of wings. How could the other, then, ascend to the clouds?

Those creatures who, with agility, rise into the clouds do not take human food or human drink. The dragon's food is different from that of snakes, hence its movements are not the same as those of snakes. One hears that the Taoists drink an elixir made of gold and gems, and eat the flowers of the purple boletus. These extremely fine stuffs make their bodies light, so that they become spirits and genii. The stranger ate the flesh of an oyster. Such is the food of ordinary people, by no means fine, or rendering the body light. How could he, then, have given himself a jerk and ascended to heaven?

I have heard that those who feed on air do not take solid food, and that the latter do not eat air. The above-mentioned stranger ate something substantial. Since he did not live on air, he could not be so light that he might have risen on high.

It may be that Lu Ao, studying Tao and trying hard to become an immortal, traveled to the Northern Sea. Having left human society and gone far away, he felt that he did not succeed in acquiring Tao. He was ashamed and afraid, lest his fellow countrymen should criticize him. Knowing that things would certainly turn out so, that everybody would reproach him, he invented these extravagant stories. He said that he met with a stranger. The meaning of the whole story is that his efforts to become immortal were not successful, and that time had not yet come.

In the case of Liu An, Prince of Huai-nan, who suffered death as a punishment of rebellion, all people heard of it and at that time saw it; yet the books of the Literati say that he obtained Tao and disappeared as a genius, and that his cocks and dogs went up to heaven also. We cannot be surprised, then, that Lu Ao, who alone went to a far-off country, leaving no trace, should speak obscure and mysterious words. His case is similar to that of Hsiang Man-tu of P'u-fan [34] in Ho-tung. [35]

Hsiang Man-tu was a follower of Tao and a student of spiritism. He abandoned his family and went away. When after three years' absence he came back, his people asked him what had happened to him. Hsiang Man-tu

34. The modern P'u-chou in Shansi.
35. A circuit comprising the southern part of Shansi.

replied "I have no clear recollection of my departure, but I suddenly found myself as if lying down. Several genii appeared, who took me up to Heaven, until we were at a few tricents' distance from the moon. I saw that all was dark above and beneath the moon, so that I could not distinguish east and west. Where we stopped near the moon, it was bitter cold. I felt hungry and wished to eat, when a genius gave me a cupful of morning-red to drink. After having taken one cup, one does not feel hunger for several months. I do not know how many years or months I stayed there nor what fault I committed, for suddenly I found myself asleep again and brought down to this place."

The Ho-tung people gave him the surname of Fallen Angel. But dealing thoroughly with the subject, we find that this story is impossible. If Hsiang Man-tu could rise to Heaven, he must have become a genius. How could he return after three years' time? If a man could leave his kindred and ascend to heaven, his vital fluid and his body must have undergone a change. Now, all creatures that have been metamorphosed do not return to their previous state. When a chrysalis has changed into a cricket and received its wings, it cannot be transmuted into a chrysalis again. All creatures that fly up have wings. When they fly up and come down again, their wings are still there as before. Had Hsiang Man-tu's body had wings, his tale might be reliable; but since it had not, his talk is futile and not more trustworthy than Lu Ao's.

Perhaps it was known at this time that Hsiang Man-tu was a fervent believer in Tao who stealthily left his home and wandered about in distant lands. At last, when he achieved nothing, and felt his strength exhausted and his hope gone, he stealthily returned home. But being ashamed if he had nothing to say, he told the story of his ascension to Heaven, intimating thereby that Tao⁻ could be learned and there really were genii, and that he himself was degraded for some fault after having reached the goal, first rising to Heaven and then coming down again.

The books of the Literati contain the statement that the king of Ch'i being dangerously ill, a messenger was sent to Sung to fetch Wen Chih.[36] When he arrived and saw the king's sickness, he said to the heir apparent: "The king's illness can certainly be cured, but when it has been, the king is sure to kill me."

The heir apparent inquired what for, and Wen Chih replied, "Without anger the king's illness cannot be cured, but when the king gets angry, my death is certain."

The heir apparent bowed his head, and entreated him, saying, "Should you cure the king's sickness, myself and my mother are going to restrain the king

36. A famous doctor who ostensibly could have lived later than the third century B.C.E. for he is mentioned in *Lieh Tzu*, but see selection 12 for the complicated problems of dating this heterogeneous text.

forcibly at the cost of our lives. The king will certainly please my mother. We are wishing that you, master, shall have no trouble."

Wen Chih gave his consent and said that he was prepared to die. The king with his eldest son fixed a time. Thrice the physician was expected but did not come so that the king of Ch'i was already very angry. When he came at last, he did not take off his shoes, but walked upon the bed and tread upon the sheets. He asked the king about his sickness, but the king was so furious that he did not speak with him. Then he said something which but aggravated the king's wrath. The king abused him, and rose up, and his disease was gone. He was so enraged and so little pleased that he wished to boil Wen Chih alive. The heir apparent and the queen forthwith interfered but could obtain nothing. Wen Chih was actually boiled alive in a cauldron. After three days' and three nights' cooking, his appearance had not yet changed. Wen Chih said, "If one really is anxious to kill me, why does one not put on the lid to intercept the yin and yang fluids."

The king had the lid put on, whereupon Wen Chih died. Wen Chih was a Taoist, in water he was not drowned, and in fire he did not burn. Hence he could remain three days and three nights in the kettle without changing color.

This is idle talk. Wen Chih was boiled three days and three nights without changing color. If, then, only in consequence of the lid being put on was he choked and died, this proves that he was not in possession of Tao. All living and breathing creatures die when deprived of air. When they are dead and boiled, they become soft. If living and breathing creatures are placed in vessels with a lid on, having all their fissures carefully filled so that the air cannot circulate and their breath cannot pass, they die instantaneously. Thrown into a kettle with boiling water, they are also cooked soft. Why? Because they all have the same kind of body, the same breath, are endowed by heaven with a similar nature, and all belong to one class. If Wen Chih did not breathe, he would have been like a piece of metal or stone, and even in boiling water not be cooked soft. Now he was breathing, therefore, when cooked, he could not but die.

If Wen Chih could speak, he must have made sounds that require breathing. Breathing is closely connected with the vital force that resides in bones and flesh. Beings of bones and flesh, when cooked, die. To deny that is the first untruth.

Provided that Wen Chih could be cooked without dying, he was a perfect Taoist, similar to metal or stone. To metal or stone it makes no difference, whether a lid be put on or not. Therefore, to say that Wen Chih died when the lid was put on is the second untruth.

Put a man into cold water that is not hot like boiling water and he will die for want of breath after a short interval, his nose and mouth being shut out from the outer air. Submerged in cold water, a man cannot remain alive; how much less in bubbling, boiling water, in the midst of a violent fire? To say that Wen Chih survived in the boiling water is the third untruth.

When a man is submerged in water, so that his mouth is not visible outside, the sound of what he says is inaudible. When Wen Chih was cooked, his body was certainly submerged in the kettle and his mouth invisible. Under those circumstances, one could not hear what he said. That Wen Chih should have spoken is the fourth untruth.

Had a man who after three days' and three nights' cooking not died and not changed color, even ignorant people would have been amazed. If the king of Ch'i was not surprised, the heir apparent and his ministers should have noticed this wonderful fact. In their astonishment at Wen Chih, they would have prayed that he be taken out, granted high honors, and be venerated as a master from whom one might learn more about Tao. Now three days and three nights are mentioned, but nothing is said about the officials asking for his release. That is the fifth untruth.

At that time it was perhaps known that Wen Chih was actually cooked and that his death was caused by it. People noticing that he was a Taoist invented the story that he lived a subtle life and did not die, just as Huang Ti really died, whereas the reports say that he rose to heaven and, as the prince of Huai-nan, suffered the punishment of rebellion, while the books say that he entered a new life. There are those who like to spread false reports. Hence the story of Wen Chih has been propagated until now.

There are no instances of anyone having obtained Tao, but there have been very long-lived persons. People remarking that those persons, while studying Tao and the art of immortality, become over a hundred years old without dying call them immortals, as the following example will show.

At the time of Han Wu Ti,[37] there lived a certain Li Shao-chün, who pretended that by sacrificing to the Hearth and abstaining from eating grain he could ward off old age. He saw the emperor, who conferred high honors upon him. Li Shao-chün kept his age and the place where he was born and had grown up secret, always saying that he was seventy years old and could effect that things did not grow old. On his journeys, he visited all the princes around and was not married. On hearing that he could manage that things did not age, people presented him with much richer gifts than they would otherwise have done. He always had money, gold, dresses, and food in abundance. As people believed that he did not do any business and yet was richly provided with everything, and as nobody knew what sort of man he really was, there was a general competition in offering him services.

Li Shao-chün knew some clever maneuvers and some fine tricks, which did not fail to produce a wonderful effect. He used to feast with the Marquis

37. 140–85 B.C.E.

of Wu-an.[38] In the hall there was a man of over ninety years. Li Shao-chün indicated to him the places which his grandfather frequented when shooting. The old man knew them, having visited them as a child with his father. The whole audience was bewildered.

When Li Shao-chün saw the emperor, the emperor had an old bronze vase, about which he asked him. Li Shao-chün replied that, in the fifteenth year of the reign of Duke Huan of Ch'i,[39] it was placed in the Po-ch'in hall. The inscription was examined, and it was found out that it was indeed a vessel of Duke Huan of Chi'i. The whole Court was startled, and thought that Li Shao-chün was several hundred years old. After a long time, he died of sickness.

Those who nowadays are credited with the possession of Tao are men like Li Shao-chün. He died amongst men. His body was seen, and one knew, therefore, that his nature had been longevous. Had he dwelled in mountain forests or gone into deserts, leaving no trace behind him, he would have died a solitary death of sickness amidst high rocks. His corpse would have been food for tigers, wolves, and foxes, but the world would again have believed him to have disappeared as a real immortal.

The ordinary students of Tao do not have Li Shao-chün's age. Before reaching a hundred years, they die like all the others. Yet uncultured and ignorant people still hold that they are separated from their bodies and vanish, and that, as a matter of fact, they do not die.

What is understood by separation from the body? Does it mean that the body dies and the spirit disappears, or that the body does not die but drops its coil? If one says that the body dies and the spirit is lost, there is no difference from death, and everyone is a genius. If one believes that the body does not die but throws off its coil, one must admit that the bones and flesh of all the deceased Taoists are intact and nowise different from the corpses of ordinary mortals.

When the cricket leaves its chrysalis, the tortoise drops its shell, the snake its skin, and the stag its horns, in short, when the horned and skinned animals lose their outward cover, retaining only their flesh and bones, one might speak of the separation from the body. But even if the body of a dead Taoist were similar to a chrysalis, one could not use this expression, because, when the cricket leaves the chrysalis, it cannot be considered as a spirit with regard to the chrysalis. Now, to call it a separation from the body, when there is not even a similarity with the chrysalis, would again be an unfounded assertion missing the truth.

The Grand Annalist was a contemporary of Li Shao-chün. Although he was not among those who came near Li Shao-chün's body when he had

38. A district in Honan. The name of the marquis was T'ien Fen.
39. Duke Huan of Ch'i reigned from 683–641 B.C.E. The fifteenth year of his reign was 669.

expired, he was in a position to learn the truth. If Li Shao-chün really did not die but only parted with his body, the Grand Annalist ought to have put it on record and would not have given the place of his death.

The reference to the youth of the nonagenarian in the court would prove Li Shao-chün's age. Perhaps he was fourteen or fifteen years old when the old man accompanied his grandfather as a boy. Why should Li Shao-chün not know this if he had lived two hundred years? [40]

Wu Ti's time is very far from Duke Huan's, when the bronze vase was cast, [41] and Li Shao-chün could not have seen it. Perhaps he heard once that in the palace there was an old vessel, or he examined the inscription beforehand to speak upon it, so that he was well informed when he saw it again. When our amateurs [42] of today see an old sword or an antique crooked blade, they generally know where to place it. Does that imply they saw how it was wrought?

Tung-fang Shuo is said to have also been possessed of Tao. His name was Chin and his style Man-ch'ien, but he changed his names and for a time took office with the Han dynasty. Outwardly he was considered an official, but inwardly he passed to another existence.

This is wrong, too. Tung-fang Shuo lived, together with Li Shao-chün, under the reign of Wu Ti, and must have been known to the Grand Annalist. Li Shao-chün taught Tao and a method to keep off old age by means of sacrificing to the "Hearth." He determined the period of a tripod cast under Duke Huan of Ch'i, and knew the places frequented by the grandfather of a nonagenarian when hunting, yet he did not really attain to Tao. He was only a long-lived man who died late. Moreover, Tung-fang Shuo was not as successful as Li Shao-chün in magical arts, wherefore, then, was he credited with the possession of Tao? Under Wu Ti there were the Taoists Wen Ch'eng and Wu Li and others of the same type, who went to sea in search of the genii and to find the physic of immortality. Because they evidently knew the Taoist arts, they were trusted by the emperor. Tung-fang Shuo undertook no mission at sea, nor did he do anything miraculous. If he had done so, he would only have been a man like Li Shao-chün or on a level with Wen Ch'eng and Wu Li. Nevertheless, he had the chance to be credited with the possession of Tao. He again resembled Li Shao-chün, insomuch as he made a secret of his birthplace and the courtiers did not know his origin. He exaggerated his age. People finding that he looked rather strong and young and was of phlegmatic temper, that he did not care much for his office, but was well versed in divination, guessing, and other interesting plays, called him, therefore, a man possessed of Tao.

40. Why two hundred years? Li Shao-chün would have known the nonagenarian's grandfather if he was about ninety years old himself.

41. The interval is upwards of five hundred years.

42. Connoisseurs.

There is a belief that by the doctrine of Lao Tzu one can transcend into another existence. Through quietism and dispassionateness, one nourishes the vital force and cherishes the spirit. The length of life is based on the animal spirits. As long as they are unimpaired, life goes on, and there is no death. Lao Tzu acted upon this principle. Having done so for over a hundred years, he passed into another existence and became a true Taoist sage.

Who can be more quiet and have fewer desires than birds and animals? But birds and animals likewise age and die. However, we will not speak of birds and animals, the passions of which are similar to the human. But what are the passions of plants and shrubs, that they are born in spring and die in autumn? They are dispassionate and their lives do not extend further than one year. Men are full of passions and desires, and yet they can become a hundred years old. Thus the dispassionate die prematurely, and the passionate live long. Hence Lao Tzu's theory to prolong life and enter a new existence by means of quietism and absence of desires is wrong.

Lao Tzu was like Li Shao-chün. He practiced his theory of quietism, and his life happened to be long of itself. But people seeing this, and hearing of his quietism, thought that by his art he passed into another existence.

The idea prevails that those who abstain from eating grain are men well versed in the art of Tao. They say, for example, that Wang Tzu-ch'iao[43] and the like, because they did not touch grain and lived on different food than ordinary people, had not the same length of life as ordinary people; insofar as having passed a hundred years, they transcended into another state of being and became immortals.

That is another mistake. Eating and drinking are natural impulses with which we are endowed at birth. Hence the upper part of the body has a mouth and teeth, the inferior part orifices. With the mouth and teeth one chews and eats; the orifices are for the discharge. Keeping in accord with one's nature, one follows the law of heaven; going against it, one violates one's natural propensities and neglects one's natural spirit before heaven. How can one obtain long life in this way?

If Wang Tzu-ch'iao had no mouth, teeth, or orifices at birth, his nature would have been different from that of others. Even then one could hardly speak of long life. Now, the body is the same, only the deeds being different. To say that in this way one can transcend into another existence is not warranted by human nature.

For a man not to eat is like not clothing the body. Clothes keep the skin warm and food fills the stomach. With a warm epidermis and a well-filled belly, the animal spirits are bright and exalted. If one is hungry and has nothing to eat, or feels cold and has nothing to warm one's self, one may

43. A magician of the sixth century B.C.E., son of King Ling of the Chou dynasty. He is reported to have been seen as an immortal riding through the air on a white crane.

freeze or starve to death. How can frozen and starved people live longer than others?

Moreover, during his life man draws his vital force from food, just as plants and trees do from earth. Pull out the roots of a plant or a tree and separate them from the soil, and the plant will wither and soon die. Shut a man's mouth so that he cannot eat, and he will starve but not be long-lived.

The Taoists exalting each other's power assert that the "pure man" eats the fluid; that the fluid is his food. Wherefore the books say that the fluid-eaters live long and do not die; that, although they do not feed on cereals, they become fat and strong by the fluid.

This too is erroneous. What kind of fluid is understood by fluid? If the fluid of the yin and yang be meant, this fluid cannot satiate people. They may inhale this fluid so that it fills their belly and bowels, yet they cannot feel satiated. If the fluid inherent in medicine be meant, man may use and eat a case full of dry drugs or swallow some ten pills. But the effects of medicine are very strong. They cause great pain in the chest but cannot feed a man. The meaning must certainly be that the fluid-eaters breathe, inhaling and exhaling, emitting the old air and taking in the new. Of old, P'eng Tsu[44] used to practice this. Nevertheless he could not live indefinitely, but died of sickness.

Many Taoists hold that by regulating one's breath one can nourish one's nature, pass into another state of being, and become immortal. Their idea is that, if the blood vessels in the body be not always in motion, expanding and contracting, an obstruction ensues. There being no free passage, constipation is the consequence, which causes sickness and death.

This is likewise without any foundation. Man's body is like that of plants and trees. Plants and trees growing on the summits of high mountains, where they are exposed to the squalls of wind, are moved day and night, but do they surpass those that are hidden in mountain valleys and sheltered from wind?

When plants and trees, while growing, are violently shaken, they are injured and pine away. Why then should man by drawing his breath and moving his body gain a long life and not die? The blood arteries traverse the body, as streams and rivers flow through the land. While thus flowing, the

44. The Chinese Methusaleh, believed to have lived over eight hundred years around the middle of the third millennium B.C.E. and to have been a great-grandson of the legendary Emperor Chuan Hsü.

latter lose their limpidity and become turbid. When the blood is moved, it becomes agitated also, which causes uneasiness. Uneasiness is like the hardships man has to endure without remedy. How can that be conducive to a long life?

The Taoists sometimes use medicines with a view to rendering their bodies more supple and their vital force stronger, hoping thus to prolong their years and to enter a new existence.

This is a deception likewise. There are many examples that by the use of medicines the body grew more supple and the vital force stronger, but the world affords no instance of the prolongation of life and a new existence following.

The different physics cure all sorts of diseases. When they have been cured, the vital force is restored, and then the body becomes supple again. According to man's original nature, his body is supple of itself, and his vital force lasts long of its own accord. But by exposure to wind and wetness, he falls a victim to hundreds of diseases, whence his body becomes heavy and stiff, and his force is weakened. By taking an efficacious remedy, he restores his body and the vital force. This force is not small at the outset or the body heavy, and it is not by medicine that the force lasts long or the body grows supple and light. When first received,[45] they already possess those qualities spontaneously. Therefore, when by medicines the various diseases are dispelled, the body made supple, and the vital force prolonged, they merely return to their original state. But it is impossible to add to the number of years, let alone the transition into another existence.

Of all the beings with blood in their veins there are none but are born, and of those endowed with life there are none but die. From the fact that they were born, one knows that they must die. Heaven and Earth were not born, therefore they do not die. The yin and the yang were not born, therefore they do not die. Death is the correlate of birth, and birth the counterpart of death. That which has a beginning must have an end, and that which has an end must necessarily have had a beginning. Only what is without beginning or end lives forever and never dies.

Human life is like water. Water frozen gives ice, and the vital force concentrated forms the human being. Ice lasts one winter, then it melts; man lives a hundred years, then he dies. Bid a man not to die, can you bid ice not to melt? All those who study the art of immortality and trust that there are means by which one does not die must fail as sure as one cannot cause ice never to melt.

Translated by Alfred Forke

---

45. Received by man at birth, when heaven endows him with a body and the vital fluid.

12

Lieh Tzu

The Stupid Old Man Who Moved a Mountain

Attributed to Lieh Yü-k'ou (third century B.C.E.?)

The mountains T'ai-hsing and Wang-wu are seven hundred miles square and seven hundred thousand feet high. They stood originally between Chi-chou on the north and Ho-yang on the south. When Mister Simple of North Mountain was nearly ninety, he was living opposite them. It vexed him that, with the north flank of the mountains blocking the road, it was such a long way round to come and go. He called together the family and made a proposal: "Do you agree that we should make every effort to level the high ground, so that there is a clear road straight through to South of Yü and down to the south bank of the Han river?"

They all agreed. But his wife raised difficulties: "You are too weak to reduce even the smallest hillock; what can you do with T'ai-hsing and Wang-wu? Besides, where will you put the earth and stones?"

They all answered: "Throw them in the tail of the gulf of Chih-li, north of Yin-t'u."

Then, taking his son and grandson as porters, he broke stones and dug up earth, which they transported in hods and baskets to the tail of the gulf of Chih-li. The son of their neighbor Mr. Ching-ch'eng, born to his widow after his death and now just cutting his second teeth, ran away to help them.

Mister Simple did not come home until the hot season had given way to the cold. Old Wiseacre of River Bend smiled and tried to stop him, saying: "How can you be so unwise? With the last strength of your declining years, you cannot even damage one blade of grass on the mountains; what can you do to stones and earth?"

Master Lieh and his text, traditionally dated to the fourth century B.C.E., are both doubtful, although we do find references to a Lieh Yü-k'ou as early as the third century B.C.E. The book that carries his name is a collection of stories, sayings, and brief essays grouped in eight chapters, each loosely organized around a single theme. Among these, the "Yang Chu" chapter preaches a hedonism out of keeping with the rest of the book, but the remaining seven chapters constitute the most important Taoist document after the *Tao Te Ching* (see selection 10) and *Chuang Tzu* (see selection 9). While the book does contain material dating to around the third century B.C.E., the scholarly consensus is that it assumed its present form as late as 300 C.E. or even later. One of the reasons for this consensus is that the book contains Indian tales that can be traced to specific Buddhist works introduced to China only after that date.

The *Lieh Tzu* is the most easily intelligible of the Taoist classics for its straightforward prose style. When the same story appears in both the *Lieh Tzu* and the *Chuang Tzu* (as is often the case), the version in the *Lieh Tzu* is inevitably easier to understand.

The section title is supplied by the editor.

Mister Simple of North Mountain breathed a long sigh, and said: "Certainly your mind is set too firm for me ever to penetrate it. You are not even as clever as the widow's little child. Even when I die, I shall have sons surviving me. My sons will beget me more grandsons, my grandsons in their turn will have sons, and these will have more sons and grandsons. My descendants will go on forever, but the mountains will get no bigger. Why should there be any difficulty about leveling it?"

Old Wiseacre of River Bend was at a loss for an answer.

The mountain spirits, which carried snakes in their hands, heard about it, and were afraid he would not give up. They reported it to God who, moved by his sincerity, commanded the two sons of K'ua-erh to carry the mountains on their backs. They put one in Shuo-tung and the other in Yung-nan. Since then there has been no high ground from Chi-chou in the north to the south bank of the Han river.

Translated by A. C. Graham

13

Lotus Sūtra

Chapter 3: Parable

Translated by Kumārajīva (fl. 385–409)

At that time Śāriputra[1] danced for joy, then straightway rose and, joining his palms and looking reverently at the August Countenance,[2] addressed the

The *Lotus Sūtra* or *Saddharmapuṇḍarīkā-sūtra (Scripture of the Lotus Blossom of the Fine Dharma)* is by any standard among the most influential scriptures of Mahāyāna (Great Vehicle) Buddhism, and one of the few for which a Buddhist Sanskrit text survives. Hence it is possible to reconstruct much of the Sanskrit technical terminology (explained in the following notes) upon which the Chinese text is based. Chinese translations of the *Lotus* are known to have been made in the years 255, 286, 290, 335, 406, and 601. Of these, only the third, fifth, and sixth translations have survived, but the sixth is scarcely more than a revision of the fifth. The third was done by Dharmarakṣa (c. 223–300), a descendant of Iranians. The fifth, on which the present translation is based, is that of Kumārajīva, who ranks among the most outstanding of translators of Buddhist texts into Chinese. Kumārajīva's father was a Kashmiri, and his mother was a princess of the Central Asian city-state of Kucha. He did not go to China voluntarily, but was carried off by the Chinese general Lü Kuang as a booty of war in 385. Dharmarakṣa presumably did his translation without help, being perfectly at home in both Buddhist Sanskrit and Chinese. Kumārajīva, on the other hand, was the head of the most elaborate state-sponsored translation bureau yet to exist in China. Judging from the clarity of style, the method of

Buddha, saying: "Now that I have heard this Dharma[3]-sound from the World-Honored One, I have in my heart the thought of dancing for joy. I have gained something I never had before. What is the reason? Formerly, when I heard such a Dharma as this from the Buddha, I saw the bodhisattvas[4] receive the prophecy that they should become Buddhas; but we had no part in this. I was sore grieved that I was to miss the incalculable knowledge and insight of the Thus Come One.[5] World-Honored One, in the past I have dwelled alone in mountain forests and at the foot of trees; and, whether sitting or walking, I always had this thought: 'We have all entered identically into Dharmahood. How is it that the Thus Come One shows us salvation by resort to the Dharma of the Lesser Vehicle?[6] This is our fault, not that of the World-Honored One. What is the reason? Had we waited for him to preach that on which the achievement of anuttarasamyaksaṃbodhi[7] is based, then without fail we should have attained salvation through the Greater Vehicle.[8] However, since we did not understand that the preaching had been based on expedient devices and accorded with what was appropriate to the particular circumstances, when we first heard the Buddha's Dharma, directly we had encountered it, we believed it, accepted it, had thoughts about it, and based conclusions on it.' World-Honored One, from of old, day long and into the night I have been reproaching myself. But now that I have heard from the Buddha what I had never heard before, a Dharma that has never been before, I have cut off my doubts and second thoughts; my body and mind are at ease, and happily I have gained peace. This day, at long last, I know that I am truly the Buddha's son, born of the Buddha's mouth, born of Dharma-transformation. I have gained a portion of the Buddha's Dharma."

---

translation the bureau employed must have been quite efficient. Kumārajīva's version provides easier reading than Dharmarakṣa's, which helps explain why and how it eclipsed the latter totally.

The present chapter on simile and parable in the expedient teaching of Buddhist doctrine is a good example of the fine literary quality of the *Lotus Sūtra*.

1. An important disciple of the Buddha.

2. This, and "World-Honored One" below, are two of the many epithets used to refer to the Buddha.

3. Doctrine or Truth of the Buddha. When not capitalized, it may refer to a constituent of existence (a phenomenon), or even to a mere thing.

4. A being who, himself well on the way to Buddhahood, puts off final attainment of that goal in order to save others.

5. Tathāgata, a frequent epithet of the Buddha, who has trodden the same path to supreme enlightenment as all the other Buddhas.

6. Hīnayāna; Buddhism of the saints and sages (arhats), which emphasizes self-cultivation and austerity.

7. Supreme perfect enlightenment, that of a Buddha.

8. Mahāyāna, Buddhism of the bodhisattvas (see note 4), which emphasizes salvation and faith. The third vehicle, the middle one, is Madhyamayāna, Buddhism of the pratyekabuddhas, which emphasizes ascetically attained Buddhahood for the self.

At that time Śāriputra, wishing to restate this meaning, proclaimed gā-thās,[9] saying:

Having heard this Dharma-sound, I
    Have gained that which I never had before.
My heart harbors a great joy,
    And the network of my doubt is completely cleared away.
From of old, having received the Buddha's doctrine,
    I have never lost the Greater Vehicle.
The Buddha's voice is very rare,
    Able to clear away the agonies of the beings.
Having already gained the extinction of the outflows,[10]
    Upon hearing this, I also cleared away my cares and agonies.
Dwelling in mountains and valleys,
    Or being at the foot of trees in forests,
Whether seated or walking about,
    I constantly thought of these things.
"Ah!" said I in profound self-reproach,
    "How can I have so deceived myself?
Though all sons of the Buddha,
    Entered alike into dharmas without outflows,
We shall not all be able in the future
    To expound the Unexcelled Path.
The thirty-two marks—the gold color,
    The ten strengths, and the various deliverances —[11]
Are all together within one Dharma;
    Yet I have not gained these things.
The eighty kinds of the wondrously good,
    The eighteen unshared dharmas,
And such excellences as these though there be,
    Yet have I missed them all.
When I go about alone,
    I see the Buddha present in the great multitude,
His name being bruited about in all ten directions,
    Broadly benefiting the beings.
I think to myself that I have lost this advantage,
    For I imagine I have been deceiving myself.
I constantly, day and night,
    Think repeatedly about these things.

9. Verses.

10. Impurities of the body.

11. Aspects and characteristics of a Buddha. See Edward Conze, ed., *The Large Sutra on Perfect Wisdom* (London: Luzac, 1961), chapter 16, for further references to technical expressions occurring in this section.

I wish to question the World-Honored One about them,
    Whether I have missed them or not.
I constantly see the World-Honored One
    Praising the bodhisattvas:
Thus day and night
    Do I constantly weigh and measure matters such as these.
Now I hear the Buddha's voice
    Preaching the Dharma in accord with what is appropriate for
    the moment.
With what is free of outflows, hard to conceive or to discuss,
    He causes the beings to reach the Platform of the Path.[12]
Formerly I, attached to wrong views,
    Was a teacher of brahmans.[13]
The World-Honored One, knowing my thoughts,
    Uprooted the wrongs and preached nirvāṇa.[14]
I, completely clearing away my wrong views,
    Directly witnessed the empty dharmas.
At that time, in my heart I said to myself
    That I had contrived to reach the passage into extinction.
But now, at last, I am aware
    That this is no real passage into extinction.
When I contrive to become a Buddha,
    When I am fully endowed with the thirty-two marks,
When a multitude of gods, men, and yakṣas,[15]
    As well as dragons, spirits, and the like, do me honor,
At that time—and not before—shall I be able to say
    That I am forever and completely extinguished
    without residue.
The Buddha, in the midst of the great multitude,
    Says that I shall become a Buddha.
When I hear a Dharma-sound such as this,
    My doubts and second thoughts are completely cleared away.
When first I heard the Buddha's preaching,
    In my heart I was greatly alarmed:
'Surely Māra[16] is playing Buddha,
    Confusing my thoughts!'

12. The *bodhimaṇḍa*, seat of enlightenment; the name given to the spot under the bodhi tree on which the Buddha sat when he became enlightened.
13. High-caste Hindus.
14. Extinction, the end of reincarnation and the goal of all Buddhists.
15. A supernormal being; demon.
16. The Destroyer, the Evil One, who tempts men to indulge their passions and is thus the great enemy of the Buddha and his teaching.

The Buddha, by resort to various means,
    Parables, and cunning phrases, preaches,
But his thought is as calm as the sea;
    When I hear him, my network of doubt is severed.
The Buddha says that in ages gone by,
    Incalculable Buddhas, now passed into extinction,
Dwelling securely in the midst of expedient devices,
    Also preached this Dharma, every one of them;
That the Buddhas of the present and the future,
    Their numbers past all reckoning,
Also, by resort to expedient devices,
    Set forth a Dharma such as this one,
Just as, in the present, the World-Honored One—
    Beginning with his birth and going through his departure
        from the household life,
His attainment of the Path, and his turning of the Dharma-wheel[17]—
    Has also preached by resort to expedient devices.
The World-Honored One preaches the Real Path,
    While Pāpīyaṃs[18] has none of this.
By this token, I know for a certainty
    That this is no Māra playing Buddha,
But that I, through having fallen into a net of doubt,
    Thought this was the work of Māra.
When I hear the Buddha's gentle voice,
    Profound, far removed from the ordinary understanding,
        and extremely subtle,
Setting forth the pure Dharma,
    My heart is overjoyed,
My doubts and second thoughts are cleared away forever,
    And I dwell securely in the midst of real knowledge, saying:
'Of a certainty I shall become a Buddha,
    Revered by gods and men;
I shall turn the unexcelled Dharma-wheel,
    Teaching and converting bodhisattvas.' "

At that time, the Buddha declared to Śāriputra: "I now speak in the midst of the great multitude of gods, men, śramaṇas,[19] Brahmans, and the like. Formerly, I, in the presence of two myriads of millions of Buddhas, for the sake of the Unexcelled Path was constantly teaching and converting you. And you, throughout the long night of time, following me, received my instruc-

17. Symbol of the preaching of the doctrine by the Buddha.
18. The "More Evil One," i.e., Mara.
19. "Ascetic," specifically a Buddhist monk.

tion. It is because I led you hither by resort to expedient devices that you have been born into my Dharma. Śāriputra, long ago I taught you to aspire to the Buddha Path. You have completely forgotten. Accordingly, you say to yourself that you have already gained passage into extinction. Now once again, wishing to cause you to recall the path you trod in keeping with your former vow, for the voice-hearers'[20] sakes I preach this scripture of the Greater Vehicle, named the Lotus Blossom of the Fine Dharma, a Dharma preached to bodhisattvas, one which the Buddha keeps in mind.

"Śāriputra, you, in an age to come, beyond incalculable, limitless, inconceivable kalpas,[21] having made offerings to several thousands of myriads of millions of Buddhas, having upheld the True Dharma and having acquired to perfection the Path trodden by bodhisattvas, shall be able to become a Buddha named Padmaprabha (Flower Glow), a Thus Come One, worthy of offerings, of right and universal knowledge, your clarity and conduct perfect, well gone, understanding the world, an unexcelled Worthy, a Regulator of men of stature, a Teacher of gods and men, a Buddha, a World-Honored One.

"That Buddha's realm shall be named Viraja (Free of Defilements). Its land shall be flat and even, clean, well adorned, tranquil, rich, and abounding in gods and men. It shall have vaiḍūrya[22] for soil in an eightfold network of highways, each bordered with cords of pure gold. At their sides shall be columns of seven-jeweled trees, constantly bearing blossoms and fruit.

"Flower Glow, the Thus Come One, shall furthermore by resort to the Three Vehicles teach and convert the beings. Śāriputra, though the time of that Buddha's emergence shall not be an evil age, by reason of his former vow he shall preach the Dharma of the Three Vehicles. His kalpa shall be named Mahāratnapratimaṇḍita (Adorned with Great Jewels). Why shall it be named Adorned With Great Jewels? Because in that realm bodhisattvas shall be taken for great jewels. Those bodhisattvas shall be incalculable, limitless, past reckoning and discussion, beyond the reach of number or parable, such that—except with the power of Buddha-knowledge—none shall be able to know them.

"When they are about to walk, jeweled blossoms shall spring up to receive their feet. These bodhisattvas shall not have just launched their thoughts, but all shall have long since planted the roots of excellence, and shall cultivate brahman-conduct purely, in the presence of incalculable hundreds of thousands of myriads of millions of Buddhas, being constantly the objects of the Buddhas' praise, ever cultivating Buddha-knowledge, acquiring thoroughly

20. *Śrāvaka* ("auditor"), a person already on the way to Buddhist salvation, a salvation to be gained for himself alone by hearing the preachings of a Buddha.
21. Cosmic ages or eras.
22. A cat's-eye gem. The word "beryl" is cognate with this.

great spiritual penetration, knowing well the gateways of all the dharmas, straightforward and honest, without deception, firm in intent and mindfulness. Such bodhisattvas as these shall fill that realm.

"Śāriputra, the life-span of the Buddha Flower Glow shall be twelve minor kalpas, excluding the time during which he shall be a prince, having not yet become a Buddha. The life-span of the people of his realm shall be eight minor kalpas. Flower Glow, the Thus Come One, when twelve minor kalpas have passed, shall present a prophecy of anuttarasamyaksaṃbodhi to the bodhisattva Dhṛtiparipūrṇa (Hard-Full). I tell you bhikṣus[23] that this bodhisattva Hard-Full shall in turn become a Buddha, who shall be called Padmavṛṣabhavikrāmin (He Whose Feet Tread Securely on Blossoms). His Buddha-realm shall also be of the same sort.

"Śāriputra, after the passage into extinction of this Buddha Flower Glow, his True Dharma shall abide in the world for thirty-two minor kalpas, and his Counterfeit Dharma shall abide in the world also for thirty-two minor kalpas."

At that time, the World-Honored One, wishing to restate this meaning, proclaimed gāthās, saying:

Śāriputra, in an age to come,
    You shall be venerated for your achievement of
        the universal wisdom of a Buddha.
Your name shall be called Flower Glow,
    And you shall save incalculable multitudes,
Having made offerings to numberless Buddhas,
    Having perfected bodhisattva conduct,
The ten strengths, and other such meritorious qualities,
    And having borne direct witness to the Unexcelled Path.
When incalculable kalpas have passed,
    The kalpa shall be named Adorned with Great Jewels.
The world shall be named Free of Defilement,
    Being pure and without blemish,
Having vaiḍūrya for its soil,
    Setting off its highways with golden cords,
Its particolored trees of seven jewels
    Constantly blooming and bearing fruit.
The bodhisattvas of that realm
    Shall be ever firm of intent and mindfulness,
Their supernatural penetrations and pāramitās[24]
    All having been thoroughly perfected,

23. "Mendicant [monk]" is, together with śramaṇa ("ascetic," see note 19), the most common Buddhist Sanskrit designation for a Buddhist monk.
24. Perfections.

And they themselves, in the presence of numberless Buddhas, having
    Learned well the bodhisattva-path.
Great worthies such as these
    Shall have been converted by the Buddha Flower Glow.
When a prince, the Buddha,
    Forsaking his realm and setting aside his honors,
In his final body
    Shall leave the household life and achieve the Buddha Path.
The Buddha Flower Glow shall abide in the world
    For a life-span of twelve minor kalpas.
The people of his realm
    Shall have a life-span of eight minor kalpas.
After the Buddha shall have passed into extinction,
    His True Dharma shall abide in the world
For thirty-two minor kalpas,
    Broadly saving the living beings.
When his True Dharma is completely extinct,
    There shall be a Counterfeit Dharma for thirty-two
        minor kalpas
His śarīra[25] shall be spread far and wide,
    And gods and men everywhere shall make offerings to it.
What the Buddha Flower Glow shall do
    Shall all be as I have said.
That One Sainted and Venerable among Two-Legged Beings[26]
    Shall be most distinguished, without his like.
He shall be none other than you yourself:
    You should and ought to be delighted.

At that time the fourfold multitude—bhikṣus, bhikṣunīs, upāsakas, and upāsikās,[27] as well as a great multitude of gods, dragons, yakṣas, gandharvas,[28] asuras,[29] garuḍas,[30] kinnaras,[31] mahoragas,[32] and the like—seeing Śāriputra receive in the Buddha's presence a prophecy of anuttarasamyaksaṃbodhi, danced endlessly for joy of heart and, each removing the uppermost garment he was wearing, presented it to the Buddha as an offering. Śakro Devānām

25. "Body," specifically the relics of a Buddha when he has attained *nirvāṇa*.
26. Human beings.
27. Mendicant monks and nuns, lay brothers and sisters.
28. Musician-demigods.
29. Demons of the first order, in perpetual hostility with the gods, more or less equivalent to the Greek Titans.
30. Mythical birds.
31. Mythical creatures reckoned as being part horse and part human, sometimes associated with the heavenly musicians (see note 28).
32. Great serpents.

Indraḥ[33] and Brahmā,[34] the king of the gods, together with numberless sons of gods, also made offerings to the Buddha of their fine divine garments and of divine māndārava and mahāmāndārava[35] flowers. The divine garments they had scattered remained stationary in the open air, then turned about by themselves. Divine musicians, all together, at once made music of a hundred thousand myriads of kinds in the open air and, raining down many divine flowers, spoke these words: "The Buddha, in former times in Vārāṇasī,[36] first turned the Dharma-wheel. Now, at long last, he is again turning the unexcelled and supremely great Dharma-wheel." At that time the sons of gods, wishing to restate this meaning, proclaimed gāthās, saying:

Formerly, in Vārāṇasī,
    You turned the Dharma-wheel of the Four Truths,[37]
With discrimination preaching the dharmas,
    The origination and extinction of their Five Collections.[38]
Now again you are turning the most subtle,
    Unexcelled great Dharma-wheel.
This Dharma is profound and recondite,
    For few there are who can believe in it.
From of old, we
    Have often heard the World-Honored One preach,
But have never before heard such
    A profound and subtle superior Dharma.
When the World-Honored One preaches this Dharma,
    We are all delighted accordingly.
The greatly wise Śāriputra
    Has now been able to receive an august prediction.
We also, in this way,
    Shall certainly be able to become Buddhas,
In all the worlds
    Most venerable and having none superior.
The Buddha Path, beyond reckoning and discussion,
    We shall preach by resort to expedient devices and in accord
        with what is peculiarly appropriate.

33. "The Able One, Lord of the Gods," i.e., Indra.
34. The creator god and ultimate ground of all being in Hinduism.
35. The blossom of the coral tree, but in all likelihood referring in this text to some mythical flower. *Mahā* means "great."
36. Benares, the great holy city lying midway on the Ganges.
37. The four noble truths are: 1. suffering is a necessary attribute of sentient existence, 2. the accumulation of suffering is caused by the passions or desires, 3. the passions can be extinguished, 4. the Buddhist Way leads to the extinction of the passions.
38. These are 1. *rūpa*, visible matter or form, 2. *vedanā*, sensation, 3. *saṃjñā*, notion or perception, 4. *saṃskāra*, constituent impulses, and 5. *vijñāna*, cognition.

What meritorious deeds are ours,
    Whether in the present age or in ages gone by,
As well as the merit of having seen Buddhas,
    We divert completely to the Buddha Path.

At that time, Śāriputra addressed the Buddha, saying: "World-Honored One! I now have no more doubts or second thoughts, since I have been personally enabled to receive in the Buddha's presence a prophecy of anuttara-samyaksaṃbodhi. These twelve hundred who freely control their own thoughts formerly dwelled on the level of learners. The Buddha constantly taught them, saying, 'My Dharma can separate one from birth, old age, sickness, and death,[39] making possible the complete achievement of nirvāṇa.' These people, the learners, and those who had nothing more to learn also thought, on the grounds that they had separated themselves from the view of 'I' and from the view of 'there is' and 'there is not,' that they had attained nirvāṇa. Yet now, in the presence of the World-Honored One having heard what they had never heard before, they have fallen into doubt and uncertainty. Very well, O World-Honored One! I beg you, for the sake of the fourfold multitude, to explain the causes and conditions, thus separating them from their doubts and second thoughts."

At that time the Buddha declared to Śāriputra: "Did I not say formerly that the Buddhas, the World-Honored Ones, by resort to a variety of explanations of causes and conditions, parables, words and phrases, and expedient devices, preach the Dharma; that all is for the purpose of anuttarasamyaksaṃbodhi? This is because these preachings are all effected in order to convert bodhisattvas. However, Śāriputra, I shall now, once again, by resort to a parable clarify this meaning. For they who have intelligence gain understanding through parables.

"Śāriputra, imagine that a country, or a city-state, or a municipality has a man of great power, advanced in years, of incalculable wealth, and owning many fields and houses as well as servants. His house is broad and great; it has only one doorway, but great multitudes of people—a hundred, or two hundred, or even five hundred—are dwelling in it. The halls are rotting, the walls crumbling, the pillars decayed at their base, and the beams and ridgepoles precariously tipped. Quite suddenly, throughout the house and all at the same time, a fire breaks out, burning down all the apartments. The great man's sons—ten, or twenty, or thirty of them—are still in the house.

"The great man, directly seeing this great fire break out from four directions, is alarmed and terrified. He then has this thought: 'Though I was able to get out safely through this burning doorway, yet my sons within the burning house, attached as they are to their games, are unaware, ignorant,

---

39. According to Buddhist doctrine, these are the four types of suffering characteristic of human life.

unperturbed, and unafraid. The fire is coming to press in upon them; the pain will cut them to the quick. Yet at heart they are not horrified, nor have they any wish to leave.'

"Śāriputra, this great man has the following thought: 'I am a man of great physical strength. I might, in the folds of my robe or on top of a table, take them out of the house.' He thinks: 'This house has only one doorway, which, furthermore, is narrow and small. The children are young and, as yet having no understanding, are in love with their playthings. They may fall victim to the fire and be burned. I must explain the terror of it to them. This house is already on fire. They must make haste and get out in time. I must not let this fire burn them to death.' When he has had these thoughts, then in accord with his decision he says explicitly to the children, 'Get out quickly, all of you!' Though the father, in his compassion, urges them with explicit words, yet the children, attached as they are to their games, will not deign to believe him or to accept what he says. Unalarmed and unafraid, they have not the least intention of leaving. For they do not even know what a 'fire' is, or what a 'house' is, or what it means to 'lose' anything. All they do is run back and forth, looking at their father.

"At that time, the great man has this thought: 'This house is already aflame with a great fire. If we do not get out in time, the children and I shall certainly be burned. I will now devise an expedient, whereby I shall enable the children to escape this disaster.' The father knows the children's preconceptions, whereby each child has his preferences, his feelings being specifically attached to his several precious toys and unusual playthings.

"Accordingly, the father proclaims to them, 'The things you so love to play with are rare and hard to get. If you do not get them, you are certain to regret it later. Things like these—a variety of goat-drawn carriages, deer-drawn carriages, and ox-drawn carriages—are now outside the door for you to play with. Come out of this burning house quickly, all of you! I will give all of you what you desire.' The children hear what their father says. Since rare playthings are exactly what they desire, the heart of each is emboldened. Shoving one another aside in a mad race, all together in a rush they leave the burning house.

"At this time, the great man, seeing that his children have contrived to get out safely and that all are seated in an open space at a crossroads, is no longer troubled. Secure at heart, he dances for joy. Then the children all address their father, saying: 'Father, the things you promised us a while ago—the lovely playthings, the goat-drawn carriages, deer-drawn carriages, and ox-drawn carriages—give us now, if you please.'

"Śāriputra, at that time the great man gives to each child one great carriage. The carriage is high and wide, adorned with a multitude of jewels, surrounded by posts and handrails, little bells suspended on all four sides. Also, on its top are spread out parasols and canopies. Further, it is adorned with an assortment of rare and precious jewels. Intertwined with jeweled cords and hung with flowered tassels, having heaps of carpets decorated with strips of cloth as well as vermilion-colored cushions, it is yoked to a white ox, whose skin is pure white, whose bodily form is lovely, whose muscular strength is great, and whose tread is even and fleet like the wind. This ox also has many attendants serving and guarding it. What is the reason? Because this great man, of wealth incalculable, his various storehouses all full to overflowing, has this thought: 'My wealth being limitless, I may not give small, inferior carriages to my children. Now these little boys are all my sons. I love them without distinction. I have carriages such as these, made of the seven jewels, in incalculable numbers. I must give one to each of them with undiscriminating thought. I may not make distinctions. What is the reason? I take these things and distribute them to the whole realm, not stinting even then. How much more should I do so to my own children!' At this time, the children, each mounting his great carriage, gain something they have never had before, something they have never hoped for. Śāriputra, what do you think? When this great man gives equally to all his children great carriages adorned with precious jewels, is he guilty of falsehood or not?"

Śāriputra said: "No, World-Honored One! This great man has but enabled his children to escape the calamity of fire, thus preserving their bodily lives. He is guilty of no falsehood. Why? Because the preservation whole of their bodily lives means that they have already received a lovely plaything. For what reason is that? All the other playthings, O Blessed One, were taken in exchange for their very lives. How much more so when, by resort to an expedient device, he has rescued them from that burning house! World-Honored One! Had this great man given them not one tiny carriage, he would still be no liar. Why? Because this great man first thought: 'By resort to an expedient device I will enable the children to get out.' For this reason he is guilty of no falsehood. How much more is this true when the great man, knowing that his wealth is incalculable and wishing to confer advantage on his children, gives to all equally a great carriage!"

The Buddha proclaimed to Śāriputra: "Good! Good! It is as you say! Śāriputra, the Thus Come One is also like this. That is, he is the Father of all the worlds. To fear, terror, debilitation, anguish, care, worry, ignorance, and obscurity he puts an absolute end. Also, completely achieving the might of incalculable knowledge and insight, as well as fearlessness; having great spiritual power and the power of wisdom; perfecting the pāramitās of practical expedients and of wisdom, as well as of great good will and great compassion; constantly unflagging; and constantly seeking the good, he benefits all. Thus he creates the old and rotten burning house of the three worlds[40] and, in order to save the beings from the fires of birth, old age, sickness, death, worry, grief,

---

40. *Trailokya* or *triloka*, the three realms of sensuous desire, form, and formlessness.

woe, agony, folly, delusion, blindness, obscurity, and the three poisons,[41] he teaches and converts them, enabling them to attain anuttarasaṃyaksambodhi. He sees that the beings are scorched by birth, old age, sickness, death, care, grief, woe, and anguish. They also, thanks to a fivefold desire[42] for wealth, suffer a variety of woes. Also, since they adhere greedily to their views and seek persistently what they desire, they currently suffer many woes, and shall hereafter suffer the woes of hell, beasts, and hungry ghosts or, if they are born above the heavens or in the midst of men, suffer woe in the straits of destitution, or the woe of separation from what they love, or the woe of union with what they hate. It is in the midst of such various woes as these that the beings are plunged, yet they cavort in joy, unaware, unknowing, unalarmed, unafraid, neither experiencing disgust nor seeking release. In this burning house of the three worlds, they run about hither and yon, and though they encounter great woes they are not concerned.

"Śāriputra, having seen this, the Buddha then thinks: 'I am the Father of the beings; I must rescue them from their woes and troubles, and give them the joy of incalculable and limitless Buddha-wisdom, thus causing them to frolic.'

"Śāriputra, the Thus Come One also has this thought: 'If merely by resort to my spiritual power and the power of my knowledge, and casting aside expedient devices, for the beings' sake I praise the Thus Come One's power of knowledge and insight and his fearlessness, the beings cannot thereby attain salvation. What is the reason? These beings, who have not yet escaped from birth, old age, sickness, death, care, grief, woe, and anguish, are being burned in the flaming house of the three worlds. How can they understand the Buddha's wisdom?'

"Śāriputra, just as that great man, though physically strong, did not use his strength, but, by resort to a gentle practical expedient, rescued his children from the troubles of the burning house, then gave each of them a great carriage adorned with precious jewels, just so does the Thus Come One in the same way, though he has various sorts of strength and fearlessness, refrain from using them, but merely, by resort to wisdom and practical expedients, rescue the beings from the burning house of the three worlds, preaching to them Three Vehicles—those of voice-hearer, of pratyekabuddha, and of Buddha—and saying to them: 'You all are to have no desire to dwell in the burning house of the three worlds. Have no lust for coarse and broken-down visible matter, sounds, smells, tastes, and tangibles! If, clinging to them greedily, you display lust for them, then you shall be burned. Quick, get out of the three worlds! You shall get three vehicles—those of voice-hearer,

41. The three defilements of *rāga* (lust for the unwholesome), *dveṣa* (hatred for the wholesome), and *moha* (delusion).

42. Desires or passions that arise from the five sense organs (eyes, ears, nose, tongue, and body).

pratyekabuddha, and Buddha. I now guarantee it, and I am never false. All you need do is strive earnestly with effort.' By such devices as this, the Thus Come One attracts and urges the beings. He also says: 'You all are to know that the dharmas of these three vehicles are praised by the saints, and they who mount them are their own masters, unbound, depending on nothing, and seeking nothing. Mounted on these three vehicles, one gains for oneself the pleasure of faculties, strengths, intuitive perceptions, paths, dhyāna[43]-concentrations, deliverances, samādhis,[44] and the like, all without outflows, then gets incalculable tranquil joys.'

"Śāriputra, if there are beings who within are wise by nature; who, having heard the Dharma from the World-Honored One, believe and accept it; who, earnestly striving and wishing to leave the three worlds, seek nirvāṇa for themselves—these are named Those Who Mount the Vehicle of the Voice-Hearers. They are like those children who left the burning house in quest of goat-drawn carriages. If there are beings who, having heard the Dharma from the World-Honored One, believe and accept it; who, earnestly striving and seeking the knowledge that is so of itself, desire the quietude that is content with its own goodness, and are deeply aware of the causes and conditions of the dharmas—these are called Those Who Mount the Vehicle of the Pratyekabuddhas. They are like those children who left the burning house in quest of deer-drawn carriages. If there are beings who, having heard the Dharma from the World-Honored One, believe and accept it; who, vigorously practicing and striving, seek All-Knowledge, Buddha-knowledge, the knowledge which is so of itself, the knowledge without a teacher, the knowledge and insight of the Thus Come One, his strengths, and his fearlessness; who, mercifully recalling and comforting incalculable living beings and benefiting gods and men, convey all to deliverance—these are named Those Who Mount the Great Vehicle. It is because the bodhisattvas seek this Vehicle that they are named Mahāsattvas.[45] They are like those children who leave the burning house in quest of ox-drawn carriages. Śāriputra, just as that great man, seeing his children safely out of the burning house and in a place of safety, and thinking that he himself has wealth incalculable, presents his children equally with great carriages, just so does the Thus Come One in the same way, being the Father of all living beings, when he sees incalculable thousands of millions of beings going through the gateway of the Buddha's doctrine off the painful, fearful, and precipitous pathway of the three worlds, there to gain the joy of nirvāṇa—just so, I say, does the Thus Come One at that time have this thought: 'I have a treasure house of incalculable, limitless

43. Meditation or contemplation. This Sanskrit word is transcribed as Zen in Japanese (from which it has been borrowed into English) and as Ch'an in Modern Standard Mandarin.
44. Concentration preparatory to meditation.
45. "Great beings."

knowledge, strengths, various sorts of fearlessness, other such Buddhadharmas. These living beings are all my children.' Then he gives the Great Vehicle equally to all, not allowing any of them to gain passage into extinction for himself alone, but conveying them all to the extinction of the Thus Come One. To all these living beings who have escaped the three worlds he gives the Buddhas' dhyāna-concentration, their deliverances, and other devices of enjoyment, all of one appearance, of one kind, all praised by the saints, all able to bring about the prime, pure, and subtle joy. Śāriputra, just as that great man, first having enticed his children with three carriages and then having given them only one great carriage, adorned with jewels and supremely comfortable, is yet not guilty of falsehood, just so is the Thus Come One free of falsehood in the same way, though he first preached the three vehicles in order to entice the beings, then conveyed them to deliverance by resort to only the One Great Vehicle. Why? Because the Thus Come One, having a treasure house of incalculable wisdom, strengths, various sorts of fearlessness, and other dharmas, is able to give the Dharma of the Great Vehicle to all living beings; but they are not all able to accept it. Śāriputra, for these reasons, be it known that the Buddhas, by resort to the power of expedient devices, divide the One Buddha Vehicle and speak of three."

The Buddha, wishing to restate this meaning, proclaimed gāthās, saying:

Suppose that, for example, a great man
    Had a great house.
The house, since it was old,
    Was in a state of collapse:
The halls were lofty and precarious,
    The bases of the pillars crumbling and rotten,
The beams and ridgepoles aslant,
    The stairways and landings disintegrating,
The walls and partitions cracked,
    The clay and paint peeling off,
The thatch worn thin and in disarray,
    The rafters and eavepoles coming loose,
Totally misshapen
    And full of assorted filth.
There were five hundred persons
    Dwelling within.
Kites, owls, and eagles,
    Crows, magpies, pigeons, and doves,
Newts, snakes, vipers, and gribbles,
    Centipedes and millipedes,
Lizards and myriopods,
    Weasels, badgers, and mice,

And other malignant beings
  Milled back and forth in a crisscross.
Places stinking of feces and urine
  Overflowed with their filth,
With May-bugs and other insects
  Clustered on them.
Foxes, wolves, and jackals[46]
  Gnawed at, trampled on,
And chewed up corpses,
  Leaving the bones and flesh a mess.
Thereupon bands of dogs,
  Racing to the spot, seized them,
Hungry, weak, and terrified,
  Seeking food here and there,
In their struggle, snatching and pulling one another,
  Snarling, gnashing their teeth, and howling.
That house's terrors
  And strange sights were of this kind.
Here and there and all about
  Were ghosts and demons,
Yakṣas and evil spirits,
  Eating human flesh;
Varieties of poisonous insects
  And other malignant birds and beasts
Hatched from eggs,
  All defending themselves against one another.
The yakṣas would race to the spot,
  Vying with one another to seize and eat them.
When they had eaten their fill,
  Their wicked thoughts would be all the more intense;
The sound of their quarrels
  Was terrifying.
The *kumbhāṇḍa*-demons[47]
  Would squat on high ground,
Or, at times, would rise above the earth
  A foot or two,
Then would wander back and forth,
  Amusing themselves according to their own fancy,

---

46. The word translated as "jackals" is *yeh-kan,* said to be a type of blind, emaciated tree-dweller somewhat resembling a fox.
  47. A kind of demon having testicles the shape of water jars.

Seizing two legs of a dog,
    Or beating it so that it lost its bark,
Or trampling on its neck,
    Terrifying the dog for their own amusement.
Again, there were demons
    Tall of body,
Naked, dark, and emaciated,
    Constantly dwelling there,
Emitting loud and baneful sounds,
    Howling in their quest for food.
Again, there were demons
    Whose throats were the shape of needles,
Again, there were demons
    Whose heads were the shape of ox-heads,
Who would now eat human flesh,
    And would then devour dogs,
The hair of their heads in a tousle,
    Harmful, malignant, and dangerous,
Hard pressed by hunger and thirst,
    Howling as they ran back and forth.
The yakṣas and hungry demons,
    The malignant birds and beasts,
Facing all four ways in their acute hunger,
    Would peer through windows.
The likes of these were the troubles
    And terrors incalculable.
This old and decayed house
    Belonged to one man.
The man had gone a short distance from the house
    When, before he had been gone very long,
In the rear apartments
    Suddenly a fire broke out,
From all four sides at once
    Raging in flame.
The ridgepoles and beams, the rafters and pillars,
    Shaking and cracking with the sound of explosion,
Broke asunder and fell,
    While the walls and partitions collapsed.
The ghosts and demons
    Raised their voices in a scream;
The eagles and other birds,
    As well as the kumbhāṇḍas,

Milled about in a panic,
    Unable to get out.
The malignant beasts and poisonous insects
    Hid in crevices;
While the *piśāca*-demons,[48]
    Who also dwelled therein,
Being of slight merit,
    When they were hard pressed by the fire,
Wrought harm on one another,
    Drinking blood and devouring flesh.
Since the bands of jackals
    Were already dead,
The great malignant beasts,
    Racing to the spot, devoured them.
Stinking smoke, with its foul odor,
    Filled the place on all four sides.
Centipedes and millipedes,
    As well as varieties of poisonous snakes,
Being burned by the fire,
    Vied with one another to get out of their holes,
And the kumbhāṇḍaka-demons,
    Seizing them at will, devoured them.
Also, the hungry demons,
    The tops of their heads aflame,
And tormented by hunger, thirst, and heat,
    Ran about in agonized panic.
In this way, that house was
    Extremely frightening,
With calamities, conflagrations,
    And many other troubles, hardly just the one.
At that time, the householder,
    Standing outside the door,
Heard someone say,
    "Your children
A while ago, in play,
    Entered this house.
Being little and knowing nothing,
    They are enjoying themselves and clinging
        to their amusements."
Having heard this, the great man
    Entered the burning house in alarm,

48. Ogres, goblins, or sprites.

To save them
    From the catastrophe of burning.
He uttered a warning to his children,
    Explaining the many calamities:
"Malignant demons, poisonous insects,
    And conflagrations are rampant.
A multitude of woes, in succession,
    Shall follow one another unceasingly.
The poisonous snakes, the newts and vipers,
    As well as the yakṣas
And kumbhāṇḍa-demons,
    The jackals, the foxes, and the dogs,
The eagles, the kites, and the owls,
    And the varieties of centipedes,
Beside themselves with hunger and thirst,
    Are most frightening.
This is a woeful and troublesome place;
    How much the more so with a great fire!"
The children, knowing nothing,
    Though they heard their father's admonitions,
Still, addicted as before to their pleasures,
    Amused themselves ceaselessly.
At that time, the great man
    Had this thought:
"The children, being this way,
    Make my cares even more acute.
Now this house
    Has not one pleasant feature,
Yet the children,
    Steeped in their games
And not heeding my instructions,
    Will surely be injured by the fire."
Then straightway, intentionally
    Devising some expedients,
He announced to the children:
    "I have various
Precious playthings—
    Lovely carriages adorned with fine jewels,
Goat-drawn carriages, deer-drawn carriages,
    And carriages drawn by great oxen—
Now outside the door.
    Come out, all of you!

For your sakes, I
    Have made these carriages,
Following the desire of your own thoughts.
    You may amuse yourselves with them"
When the children heard him tell
    Of carriages such as these,
Straightway, racing one another,
    They ran out at a gallop,
Reaching an empty spot
    And getting away from woes and troubles.
The great man, seeing his children
    Able to get out of the burning house
And abiding at a crossroads,
    Sat on his lion throne
And joyfully said to himself,
    "Now I am happy!
These children
    Were very hard to bring into the world and raise.
Foolish, little, and knowing nothing,
    They entered a dangerous house,
Where there were many poisonous insects,
    Frightful spirits,
And raging flames of great fires
    Rising together from all four sides,
Yet these children
    Were addicted to their games.
I have already saved them,
    Enabling them to escape trouble.
It is for this reason, O men,
    That I am now happy,"
At that time, the children,
    Knowing that their father was serenely seated,
All went before their father
    And addressed him, saying:
"We beg you to give us
    The three kinds of jeweled chariots
That you promised us a while ago, saying,
    'Children, come out!
I will use three kinds of carriages
    To accord with your wishes.'
Now is the right time.
    Please give them to us!"

The great man, being very rich,
   And having treasure houses filled with
Gold, silver, and vaiḍūrya,
   Giant clamshells and agate,
From many precious objects
   Had several carriages made—
Decked with ornaments,
   Surrounded with handrails and shielding,
With little bells hanging from all four sides
   And golden cords intertwined;
With pearl-studded netting
   Stretched out over the top,
And gold-flowered tassels
   Dropping down here and there;
With assorted ornaments in many colors
   Encircling them all around;
With soft and fine silk and cotton
   Made into cushions;
With superbly fine mats,
   Their value in the thousands of millions,
Pure white and spotlessly clean,
   Covering them;
With great white oxen,
   Fat and in the prime of life, and endowed with great strength,
Their physical form lovely,
   Yoked to the jeweled carriages;
With many footmen, fore and aft,
   Attending them.
These lovely carriages
   He gave equally to all the children.
The children, at this time,
   Dancing for joy
And mounting these jeweled carriages,
   Cavorted in all four directions,
Playing and enjoying themselves,
   Completely at ease and feeling no encumbrances.
I tell you, Śāriputra:
   I, too, am like this,
Being the Most Venerable among many saints,
   The Father of the World.
All the living beings,
   All my children,

Are profoundly addicted to worldly pleasure
   And have no wise thoughts.
The three worlds, completely insecure,
   Are just like a house afire,
Being full of many woes
   Most frightful,
Constantly marked by birth, old age,
   Sickness, death, and care—
Fires such as these,
   Raging without cease.
The Thus Come One, having already left
   The burning house of the three worlds,
Is quiet and unperturbed,
   Dwelling securely in forest and field.
Now these three worlds
   Are all my possession;
The living beings within them
   Are all my children.
Yet, now these places
   Have many cares and troubles,
From which I alone
   Can save them.
Even though I teach and command,
   Yet they neither believe nor accept;
But to their tainting desires
   Are so profoundly addicted that I,
By resort to an expedient device,
   Preach the three vehicles to them,
Causing the beings
   To know the woes of the three worlds,
And demonstrating and setting forth
   The Supramundane Way.
If these children,
   With fixed thought,
Acquire fully the three wisdoms[49]
   And the Six Supernatural Penetrations,[50]
They shall include among them those who can be
      cause-perceivers
   And nonbacksliding bodhisattvas.

49. The second, fifth, and sixth of the supernatural penetrations (see note 50).
50. The powers to be anywhere at will, to see anything anywhere, to hear any sound anywhere, to know the thoughts of any mind, to know past lives, and to eradicate illusions.

O, Śāriputra!
  For the beings' sake, I,
By resort to this parable,
  Preach the One Buddha Vehicle;
All of you, if you can
  Believe and accept these words,
Shall without exception
  Completely attain the Buddha Path.
This Vehicle is fine,
  Supremely pure,
In all the worlds
  Having not its master.
It is a thing which they whom the Buddha gladdens,
  All living beings,
Should praise,
  To which they should make offerings and do obeisance.
It is incalculable thousands of millions
  Of strengths and deliverances,
Dhyāna-concentrations and modes of knowledge,
  And other dharmas of the Buddhas.
If they can gain this kind of Vehicle,
  I enable those children,
Night and day, for a number of kalpas,
  Ever to amuse themselves,
With bodhisattvas
  And the multitude of voice-hearers
To mount this jeweled Vehicle,
  And to arrive directly at the Platform of the Way.
For these reasons,
  Seek as you will in all ten directions: [51]
There is no other vehicle,
  Apart from the expedient devices of the Buddhas.
I tell you, Śāriputra,
  You men
Are all my children,
  And I am your Father.
For kalpa upon kalpa, you
  Have been scorched by multitudinous woes,
And I have saved you all,
  Causing you to leave the three worlds.
Although earlier I said
  That you would pass into extinction,

51. The eight compass points, plus up and down.

This was to be a mere end to birth and death,
     And no true extinction.
What you should now achieve
     Is nothing other than Buddha-wisdom.
If there are bodhisattvas
     In the midst of this multitude,
They can listen single-mindedly
     To the Buddhas' real Dharma.
Even though the Buddhas, the World-Honored Ones,
     Resort to expedient devices,
The living beings whom they convert
     Are all bodhisattvas.
If there are persons of slight understanding
     Profoundly addicted to lust and desire,
For their sakes,
     I preach the Truth of Suffering,
And the beings rejoice at heart
     That they have gained something they never had before.
The Buddha's preaching of the Truth of Suffering
     Is reality without falsehood.
If there are beings
     Who, not knowing the origin of woe,
Are profoundly addicted to the causes of woe,
     Unable to cast them off even for a moment,
For their sakes,
     By resort to an expedient device, I preach the Path:
That the origin of all woes
     Is desire, which is their basis.
If one extinguishes desire,
     They have nothing on which to rest.
The extinction of woes
     Is called the Third Truth.
For the sake of the Truth of Extinction,
     One cultivates the Path.
Separation from the bonds of woe
     Is called the attainment of deliverance.
As for these ignorant men, whereby
     Do they attain deliverance?
It is the mere separation of self from falsehood
     That is called "deliverance."
In fact, however, they have not yet attained
     Total deliverance.

The Buddha says that these men
    Are not yet truly extinguished,
For these men have not yet attained
    The Unexcelled Path.
At heart, I have no wish
    To cause them to attain passage into extinction.
I am the Dharma King,
    With respect to the Dharma acting completely at will.
To bring the gift of tranquillity to the beings
    Is why I have appeared in the world.
You, Śāriputra!
    As for this Dharma-seal of mine,
I wish to benefit the world,
    And therefore I preach it.
Wherever you go,
    Do not propagate it recklessly.
If there is a listener
    Who, with due rejoicing, receives it upon the crown of his head,
You are to know that that man
    Is an *avivartika*. [52]
If there is one who believes and accepts
    This Scripture-Dharma,
That man has already, in times gone by,
    Seen Buddhas of the past,
Deferentially made offerings to them,
    And also heard this Dharma.
If among men there is one who can
    Believe what you preach,
Then it means that he sees me
    And also sees you
And the *bhikṣusaṃgha*, [53]
    As well as the bodhisattvas.
This Scripture of the Dharma Blossom
    Is preached for those of profound knowledge;
Those of shallow perception, if they hear it,
    Shall go astray and not understand.
For all voice-hearers
    And pratyekabuddhas,
The content of this scripture
    Is beyond the reach of their faculties.

52. "One not to be turned back."
53. Company of monks.

You, Śāriputra,
    Even you, where this scripture is concerned,
Gained entry through faith.
    How much the more so the other voice-hearers!
Those other voice-hearers,
    By virtue of their belief in the Buddha's Word,
Accept this scripture;
    It does not fall within the range of their own knowledge.
Also, Śāriputra,
    To the proud, arrogant, lazy, and indolent,
To those who reckon on terms of "I,"
    Do not preach this scripture.
To the ordinary fellow of shallow perception,
    Profoundly addicted to the five desires,
Hearing yet unable to understand,
    Also do not preach.
If a man, not believing,
    Maligns this scripture,
Then he cuts off all
    Worldly Buddha-seeds.
Or, again, he may, with contorted face,
    Harbor doubts and uncertainties.
You are now to hear me tell
    Of that man's retribution for his sins.
Whether the Buddha be in the world,
    Or whether after his passage into extinction,
There shall be those who malign
    Such scriptures as this one,
And who, seeing that there are readers and reciters,
    And copiers and keepers of this scripture,
Shall, in disparagement, deprecation, hatred, and envy of them,
    Harbor grudges against them.
The retribution for these men's sins
    You are now to hear:
These men, at life's end,
    Shall enter the Avīci hell,[54]
Where they shall fulfill one kalpa.
    When the kalpa is ended, they shall be reborn there;
In this way, spinning around
    Throughout kalpas unnumbered, and then
From hell emerging,
    They shall fall into the rank of beasts.

54. The lowest and most terrible of all the hells.

If they are dogs or jackals,
    Their forms shall be hairless and emaciated,
Spotted and scabbed,
    Things from which men shrink.
They shall also by men be
    Detested and despised,
Ever suffering from hunger and thirst,
    Their flesh and bones dried out and decayed.
While living, they are pricked by poisonous thistles;
    When dead, they are covered with tiles and stones.
It is because they have cut off the Buddha-seed
    That they suffer these retributions for their sins.
If they become camels,
    Or if they are born among asses,
On their bodies they shall ever carry heavy loads
    And suffer the blows of rods and whips,
Thinking only of water and grass
    And knowing nothing else.
For maligning this scripture
    They shall suffer punishments such as these.
If they are those who become jackals,
    They shall enter human settlements,
Their bodies spotted and scabbed,
    Also missing one eye,
By the children
    Beaten,
Suffering all manner of woe and pain,
    At times to the point of death.
Having died in this form,
    They shall then be endowed with the bodies of
        monster serpents,
Their forms long and huge,
    To the extent of five hundred yojanas,[55]
Deaf, stupid, and legless,
    Writhing about on their bellies,
By little insects
    Pecked at and eaten,
Day and night, suffering woe
    And enjoying no respite.
For maligning this scripture
    They shall suffer punishments such as these.

---

55. A unit of distance, supposed to measure several miles.

If they contrive to become humans,
>   They shall be obscure and dull of faculties,
Short, mean, bent over, and crippled,
>   Blind, deaf, and hunched.
If they have anything to say,
>   Men shall neither believe nor accept it.
The breath of their mouths ever stinking,
>   They shall be possessed by ghosts,
Poor and lowly,
>   Doing men's bidding,
Much plagued by headache and emaciation,
>   Having nothing on which to rely.
Though they may personally attach themselves to men,
>   Men do not have them in their thoughts.
If they gain something,
>   Shortly afterward they shall leave it behind.
If they practice the way of medicine,
>   Tending disease in accord with prescription,
They shall but aggravate the illnesses of others,
>   At times bringing them even to the point of death.
If they themselves have diseases,
>   No man shall be able to save them;
Even if they take good medicine,
>   The sickness shall be all the more acute.
Or others may attack them,
>   Snatching, pillaging, stealing, or robbing.
Such are the sins
>   Into whose misfortune they shall fall by their own willful acts.
Sinners such as these
>   Shall never see the Buddha,
The King of the many saints,
>   Preaching the Dharma, teaching, and converting.
Sinners such as these
>   Shall ever be born in places of trouble.
Mad, deaf, and confused of thought,
>   They shall never hear the Dharma.
For kalpas as numberless
>   As Ganges' sands,
Whenever born, they shall be deaf and dumb,
>   Of defective faculties,
Ever dwelling in hell
>   As if amusing themselves in a pleasure garden
Or being in other evil paths
>   As if in their own homes.

Camels, asses, pigs, and dogs—
    These shall be their companions.
For maligning this scripture
    They shall suffer punishments such as these.
If they contrive to become human beings,
    They shall be deaf, blind, and dumb,
Poor, destitute, and in general decrepit,
    Yet adorning themselves withal.
Swollen with water or dried out and wizened,
    Scabs, boils,
And ills like these
    They shall have for their dress.
Their bodies a constant stench,
    Filthy and unclean,
Profoundly addicted to the view of "I,"
    They shall magnify their anger.
Their lust being acute,
    There shall be nothing to choose between them and birds
        or beasts.
For maligning this scripture
    They shall suffer punishments such as these.
I say to you, Śāriputra,
    Of those who malign this scripture
That, if I were to tell their punishments,
    Even if I should exhaust a kalpa, I should not finish them.
For this reason,
    I expressly tell you,
When you are in the midst of ignorant men,
    Do not preach this scripture.
If there are those of keen faculties,
    Of knowledge clear and bright,
Of much learning and strong memory,
    Who seek the Buddha Path,
For men like these—
    And only for them—may you preach.
If a man, having formerly seen
    Hundreds of thousands of millions of Buddhas,
Has planted seeds of goodness,
    His profound thought being firm,
For a man like this—
    And only for him—may you preach.
If a man strives,
    Constantly cultivating thoughts of good will
And not begrudging his own body or his own life,

Then for him alone may you preach.
If a man is deferential
    And has no other thoughts,
Separating himself from common fools
    And dwelling alone in mountains and marshes,
For men like him—
    And only for them—may you preach.
Also, Śāriputra,
    If you see that there is a man
Who rejects evil acquaintances
    And clings to good friends,
For men like him—
    And only for them—may you preach.
If you see a son of the Buddha
    Keeping a discipline as pure
As a bright jewel
    And seeking the scriptures of the Great Vehicle,
For men like him—
    And only for them—may you preach.
If a man, having no anger,
    Is honest and gentle,
Ever pitying all
    And venerating the Buddhas,
For men like him—
    And only for them—may you preach.
Again, there may be a son of the Buddha
    In the midst of the great multitude
Who, with pure thought
    And by resort to various means,
Parables, and phrases,
    Preaches the Dharma, unobstructed,
For men like him—
    And only for them—may you preach.
If there is a bhikṣu
    Who, for the sake of All-Knowledge,
Seeks the Dharma in all four directions,
    With joined palms receiving it on the crown of his head,
Desiring merely to receive and keep
    The scriptures of the Great Vehicle,
Not accepting so much
    As a single gāthā from the other scriptures,
For men like him—
    And only for them—may you preach.

As a man wholeheartedly
   Seeks the Buddhaśarīra,
So may one seek the scriptures
   And, having found them, receive them on the crown of one's
      head.
Such a person shall never again
   Wish to seek other scriptures,
Nor has he ever before thought
   Of the books of the unbelievers,
For men like him—
   And only for them—may you preach.
I say to you, Śāriputra,
   That I, in telling of this sort
Of seekers of the Buddha Path,
   Could spend a whole kalpa and still not finish.
If they are men of this sort,
   Then they can believe and understand,
And for their sakes you may
   Preach the Scripture of the Fine Dharma Flower.

Translated by Leon Hurvitz

14

Abhidharma-mahāvibhāṣā-śāstra

Chapter 99: The Sins of Mahādeva

Translated by Hsüan-tsang (600–664)

Once upon a time, there was a merchant in the kingdom of Mathurā. He married while still a youth and soon his wife gave birth to a baby boy. The child, who had a pleasing appearance, was given the name Mahādeva.

Before long, the merchant went on a long journey to another country, taking with him rich treasures. Engaging in commercial ventures as he wended his way, a long time passed without his return. The son, meanwhile, had grown up and committed incest with his mother. Later on, he heard that

This text, the title of which has been supplied by the editor, is taken from chapter 99 of the *Abhidharma-mahāvibhāṣā-śāstra*, which is said to have been compiled 400 years after the Buddha entered Nirvana. It was translated from Sanskrit into Chinese by the famous pilgrim

his father was returning and he became fearful at heart. Together with his mother, he contrived a plan whereby he murdered his father. Thus did he commit his first cardinal sin.[1]

This deed of his gradually came to light, whereupon, taking his mother, he fled to the city of Pāṭaliputra where they secluded themselves. Later, he encountered a monk-arhat from his native land who had received the support of his family. Again, fearing that his crime would be exposed, he devised a plan whereby he murdered the monk. Thus did he commit his second cardinal sin.

Mahādeva became despondent. Later, when he saw that his mother was having illicit relations, he said to her in a raging anger: "Because of this affair, I have committed two serious crimes. Drifting about in an alien land, I am forlorn and ill at ease. Now you have abandoned me and fallen in love with another man. How could anyone endure such harlotry as this?" Thereupon he found an opportune time to murder his mother. He had committed his third cardinal sin.

Inasmuch as he had not entirely cut off the strength of his roots of goodness, Mahādeva grew deeply and morosely regretful. Whenever he tried to sleep, he became ill at ease. He considered by what means his serious crimes might be eradicated. Later, he heard that Buddhist monks were in possession of a method for eradicating crimes. So he went to the monastery known as Kukku-ṭārāma.[2] Outside its gate, he saw a monk walking slowly and meditating. The monk recited a hymn which went:

> If someone has committed a serious crime,
> He can eradicate it by cultivating goodness;
> He could then illuminate the world,
> Like the moon emerging from behind a screen of clouds.

When Mahādeva heard this, he jumped for joy. He knew that, by converting to Buddhism, his crimes could certainly be eradicated. Therefore he went to visit a monk in his quarters. Earnestly and persistently, Mahādeva entreated the monk to ordain him as a novice. When the monk saw how persistent Mahādeva's entreaties were, he ordained him as a novice without making an investigation or asking any questions. He allowed him to retain the name

---

Hsüan-tsang (see selections 250, 270, and 259) during the years 656–659. The Chinese title of the scripture is *A-p'i-ta-mo ta-p'i-p'o-sha lun.*

The oedipal dimensions of the Mahādeva story are fascinating, but its main import is as a vivid narrative statement of sectarian differences.

1. There are five such sins altogether: parricide, matricide, killing an arhat (advanced Buddhist disciple or saint), injuring the body of Buddha, and causing disunity in the *saṃgha* (community of monks).

2. "Chicken Garden Monastery," built by Aśoka, the great king and patron of Buddhism.

Mahādeva, and offered him instruction in the Buddhist precepts and prohibitions.

Now Mahādeva was quite brilliant and so, not long after he had entered the priesthood, he was able to recite and adhere to the text and the significance of the Buddhist canon. His words were clear and precise and he was adept at edifying others in the faith. In the city of Pāṭaliputra, there were none who did not turn to Mahādeva in reverence. The king heard of this and repeatedly invited him into the inner precincts of the palace. There he would respectfully provide for Mahādeva's needs and invite him to lecture on the Law of the Buddha.

Mahādeva subsequently went to live in the monastery. There, because of improper thoughts, he sometimes had nocturnal emissions. But he had previously declared himself an arhat and so he commanded a disciple to wash his soiled clothing. The disciple addressed Mahādeva: "The arhat is one in whom all outflows have been exhausted.[3] How, then, master, can you endure such a thing as this to persist?"

Mahādeva informed him, saying, "It was the Wicked One[4] who tempted me. You should not think this something unseemly. Outflows, however, may broadly be classified in two categories; the first results from delusions and the second from impurity. The arhat is without outflows due to delusion. But he is yet unable to avoid those due to impurity. And why is this? Although the arhat may put an end to delusion, how can he be without urine, bowels, tears, spittle, and the like? Furthermore, the Wicked Ones are ever hatefully jealous of the Buddha's Law. Whenever they see someone who is cultivating goodness, they invariably attempt to ruin him. Even the arhat is tempted by them. This was the cause of my emission. It was all their doing—you should not be skeptical in this regard." This is termed "the origin of the first false view."[5]

Again, Mahādeva wished to make his disciples like him and be intimately attached to him. He cleverly created opportunities whereby he was able to note and differentiate the degree of achievement each monk had attained along the four stages of religious perfection. Whereupon one of his disciples

3. Sanskrit *āsrava-kṣaya*. This term generally implies "outflow from the mind," hence "passion." But because of the context, we may understand it in the bare, literal meaning of the Chinese *lou* ("leak, drip, effluvia, discharge, emission").

4. Sanskrit *Deva māra*. He delights in obstructing the Buddhist saints as they strive to achieve the truth by sending his daughters to seduce them.

5. Altogether there are five views, *pañca dṛṣṭayaḥ*: 1. The arhat may ejaculate while asleep. 2. The arhat may remain subject to certain forms of ignorance. 3. The arhat may still have doubts. 4. The arhat may be made aware of his level of enlightenment by someone other than himself. 5. The arhat shouts at the moment of enlightenment. The upshot of all this is a loss of dignity for the arhat and, conversely, a move toward equality for the laymen vis-à-vis the *religieux*. It is, in sum, the beginning of the division between so-called Hīnayāna and Mahāyāna, the "Greater" and "Lesser" vehicles of the Buddhist faith.

kowtowed to him and said: "The arhat ought to have experiential knowledge. How is it that none of us have this sort of self-awareness?"

Mahādeva informed him, saying, "But arhats also have ignorance. You should not, then, lack faith in yourselves. I tell you that, of the various forms of ignorance, there are broadly two types. The first is that which is defiling; the saint is without this type. The second is that which does not defile; the saint still has this type of ignorance. On account of this, you are unable to have full awareness of yourselves." This is termed "the origin of the second false view."

At another time, his disciples said to him: "We have heard that the sages have transcended all doubts. How is it that we still harbor doubts in regard to the truth?"

Again, Mahādeva informed them, saying, "The arhat also has his doubts and suspicions. Of doubts, there are two types. The first is that of muddleheadedness; the arhat has excised this type. The second derives from mistakes in judgment; the arhat has not yet excised this type. The self-englightened have made great accomplishments in spite of this. How, then, can you who are mere listeners be without doubt regarding the manifold truths and thereby allow yourselves to feel humbled?" This is termed "the origin of the third false view."

Later, when the disciples opened the sūtras to read, they learned that the arhat is possessed of the eye of sage wisdom. Through self-emancipation he is able to attain experiential knowledge of self. And so they spoke to their master, saying, "If we are arhats, we ought to have experiential knowledge of self. How is it, then, that we must be initiated by our master into that fact and are without the direct insights that would enable us to have experiential knowledge of the self?"

To this, Mahādeva replied: "Though one is an arhat, he must still be initiated by others. He cannot rely on self-awareness. Even for the likes of Śāriputra who was foremost in wisdom and Maudgalyāyana who was foremost in supernatural power, if the Buddha had not remarked upon their abilities, they would not have gained self-awareness. How, then, can those who are initiated by others into that fact have self-understanding of it? Therefore you should not be endlessly inquiring in regard to this." This is termed "the origin of the fourth false view."

Mahādeva had, indeed, committed a host of crimes. However, since he had not destroyed his roots of goodness, during the middle of the night he would reflect upon the seriousness of his crimes and upon where he would eventually undergo bitter sufferings. Beset by worry and fright, he would often cry out, "Oh, how painful it is!" His disciples who were dwelling nearby were startled when they heard this and, in the early morning, came to ask him whether he were out of sorts.

Mahādeva replied, "I am feeling very much at ease."

"But why," asked his disciples, "did you cry out last night, 'Oh, how painful it is!'?"

He proceeded to inform them: "I was proclaiming the holy way of the Buddha. You should not think this strange. In speaking of the holy way, if one is not utterly sincere in the anguish with which he heralds it, it will never become manifest at that moment when one's life reaches its end. Therefore, last night I cried out several times, 'Oh, how painful it is!' " This is termed "the origin of the fifth false view."

Mahādeva subsequently brought together the aforementioned five false views and made a hymn:

Enticement by others, ignorance,
Hesitation, initiation by another,
The Way is manifested because one shouts:
This is called the genuine Buddhist teaching.

With the passage of time, the Theravāda[6] monks in the Kukkuṭārāma gradually died off. Once, on the night of the fifteenth of the month when the monks were holding their regular spiritual retreat, it was Mahādeva's turn to ascend the pulpit and give the reading of the prohibitions. He then recited the hymn which he had composed. Of those in the company of monks at that time, be they learners or learned, be they of much wisdom, attentive to the precepts, or cultivators of wisdom, when they heard what Mahādeva said, there was no one who refrained from reproving him: "For shame! Stupid man! How could you say such a thing? This is unheard of in the canon." Thereupon they countered his hymn, saying:

Enticement by others, ignorance,
Hesitation, initiation by another,
The Way is manifested because one shouts:
What you say is not the Buddhist teaching.

Upon this, an unruly controversy erupted that lasted the whole night long. By the next morning, the factions had become even larger. The folk of all classes, up to and including important ministers, came from the city one after another to mediate but none of them could bring a halt to the argument.

The king heard of it, and himself went to visit the monastery. At this point, the two factions each stated their obstinate position. When the king had finished listening, he too, became filled with doubt. He inquired of Mahādeva, "Who is wrong and who is right? With which faction should we align ourselves?"

6. A purist doctrine to which elders adhere.

"In the *Sūtra on Regulations*," replied Mahādeva, "it is said that, if one wishes to terminate controversy, one should go along with the voice of the majority."

The king proceeded to order the two factions of monks to separate themselves. In the faction of the saints and sages, although there were many who were elders, the total number of monks was small. In Mahādeva's faction, although there were few who were elders, the total number of common monks was large. So the king followed the majority and allied himself with Mahādeva's crowd. The remainder of the common monks were reproved and made to submit. The matter concluded, the king returned to his palace.

The controversy in the Kukkuṭārāma, however, did not cease. Afterward, the monastery split into two groups in accordance with the two different views. The first was called Sarvāstivāda and the second was called Mahāsaṃghika. When the saints and sages realized that the mass of monks were going counter to their principles, they departed from the Kukkuṭārāma with the intention of going to another place.

As soon as the ministers heard of this, they rushed to the king and reported. Hearing this, the king was outraged and issued an edict to his ministers which stated: "Let them all be taken to the edge of the Ganges River. Put them in a broken boat so that they will capsize in midstream. By this means, we shall test whether this lot is made up of saints or commoners."

The ministers carried out the test as directed by the king's words. The saints and sages each brought into play his spiritual powers. They were like the Goose King[7] vaulting through space. Furthermore, using their miraculous strength, they rescued from the boat those who had left the Kukkuṭārāma with them but who had not yet attained supernatural power. They manifested many miraculous transformations and assumed various shapes and forms. Next they mounted the heavens and went off to the northwest. When the king heard this, he was deeply abashed. Stifled with regret, he fell on the ground in a swoon and revived only when water was splashed on his face. He swiftly dispatched a man to find out where they had gone. Upon the return of the envoy, the king learned that they were in Kashmir. He persistently entreated them to return but the monks all refused to obey his command. The king then donated to them the whole of the land of Kashmir and constructed monasteries to accommodate the large group of saints and sages. The monasteries were given names in accordance with the various shapes the monks had assumed during their flight—for example, "Pigeon Garden." Altogether there were five hundred such monasteries. Again he dispatched envoys to contribute precious jewels and make arrangements for the articles of daily living so that the monks would be provided for. Ever after this, the land of Kashmir has had large

---

7. An epithet of the Buddha.

numbers of saints and sages who have upheld the Law of the Buddha. Its transmission and reformulation there are still very much in evidence to this day.

Having lost this large group of monks, the king of Pāṭaliputra took the initiative in providing for the monks of Kukkuṭārāma. After some time, as Mahādeva was making an excursion into the city, a physiognomist chanced to see him and secretly told his fortune: "Seven days from today, the life of this disciple of Buddha will certainly come to an end."

When Mahādeva's disciples heard this, they were frightfully worried and informed him of it. He then declared to them, "I have known this for a long time already."

After they had returned to the Kukkuṭārāma, he sent his disciples to spread out over the whole of the city of Pāṭaliputra. When the king, his ministers, and the ascetics heard the words, "In seven days I shall enter Nirvāṇa," there was none but who sighed with grief.

With the arrival of the seventh day, Mahādeva died as he had predicted. The king, his ministers, and the folk of all classes from the city were saddened and filled with affectionate longing. They all undertook to provide fragrant firewood as well as ghee, floral incense, and similar materials. These were assembled in a given place where the cremation was to take place. Each time the man who held the fire to light the wood approached it, his fire would go out. All sorts of plans were devised but it simply would not light. A soothsayer who was present spoke to the crowd: "The deceased cannot consume such splendid crematory materials as those you have provided. It is fitting that the excrement of dogs be smeared on him."

They acted in accordance with his words and the fire erupted in flames. In seconds, the blaze had burned itself out. Suddenly, there was nothing but ashes. In the end, a howling wind blew by and scattered them everywhere till nothing was left. This is due to his having been formerly the originator of the false views. All who have wisdom ought to pay heed to this example.

Translated by Victor H. Mair

15

Pu-k'ung pa-so t'o-lo-ni tzu-tsai wang ch'ou ching[1]

from *The Scripture of Amoghapāśa Dhāraṇī, the Sovereign Lord of Spells*

Translated by Ratnacinta (d. 721)

The *Dhāraṇī*[2]
Namo ratnatrāya namo āryāmitābhāya tathāgatāya namo āryāvalokiteśvarāya bodhisattvāya mahāsattvāya mahākāruṇikāya tad yatha. Oṃ amogha pratihata hūṃ hūṃ phaṭ svāhā.

Section 9: Siddhi[3] *to Make a Corpse Fetch Concealed Treasure*

At that time the sage Bodhisattva Avalokiteśvara discussed the method of fetching concealed treasure. If one wishes to fetch something that has been

These two sections of this late seventh-century translation are representative of a kind of text and interest crucial to the development and spread of Buddhist culture in China. One of the great attractions of Buddhism at all levels of Chinese society was its dual goal of enlightenment and worldly benefit. This dual goal and the promise of ready success were especially prominent in Esoteric Buddhist texts and teachings (also known as Tantric Buddhism or Vajrayāna) which began to appear in China from the third century onward. During the seventh and eighth centuries, Esoteric Buddhism had a significant impact on Chinese literature and art in general.

The Scripture of the Amoghapāśa Dhāraṇī, the Sovereign Lord of Spells is such a tantric text. It amounts to a small toolbox of religious rituals designed to serve a variety of religious needs ranging from curing illness, to prolonging life, to worshiping Amoghapāśa in a quest for enlightenment. Amoghapāśa, "the Unfailing Lasso," is a manifestation of Avalokiteśvara (the Bodhisattva of Compassion), whose devices—including the lasso or lifeline—save those in danger. Texts such as this, which may be expanded and contracted or modified as need and local concern dictate, were common as Esoteric Buddhism spread across India, Central Asia, and into China. This text was among the last to be translated before the propagation of a complete system of esoteric teachings *(Chen-yen)* by Śubhākarasiṃha, who arrived in Ch'ang-an in 717, and Vajrabodhi and his disciple Amoghavajra, who arrived in the T'ang capital during the year of Ratnacinta's death, 721.

Ratnacinta was reputedly descended from a line of Kashmiri kings and entered the Buddhist order as a boy. He excelled at chanting and meditation and developed a reputation as a strict follower of the Vinaya (rules of the discipline). He came to Loyang in 693, where he was lodged in a succession of monasteries, translating scriptures until he moved to the T'ien-chu ("India") monastery at Lung-men in 707. From that time until his death at the age of over one hundred years in 721, he lived a simple life in quarters constructed entirely in the Indian fashion. During this period, he did not work on translation, though other Indians living with him made grammatical improvements on his earlier translations, particularly on the *Amoghapāśa Dhāraṇī*.

buried, the spellman[4] should first chant the spell to protect his own body. Then proceed into a tumulus and select an adult male corpse—a body without the marks of boils or lesions on it.[5] It should next be given a thorough washing. Then daub incense and flowers on its feet as offerings and simply chant the spell commanding the corpse to arise.[6] Having done so, he asks, "Reverend master, what is your business with me?" The corpse then demands paper, brush, and ink, and the spellman provides the corpse with paper and so forth. Then, according to plan, the corpse will transcribe the rite for obtaining hidden jewels and present it to the spellman. If the spellman is illiterate,[7] then he should tell the corpse, "You should fetch them for me." The corpse will get them and bring them as commanded. The precious jewels obtained in this way should be accepted and, according to the Teaching, be used as an offering to the Three Jewels[8] to be shared with all beings. The corpse will obey the spellman and if the precious jewels which were obtained are used up, then the corpse can be sent for more. However, if you do not distribute them to the Three Jewels, the śramaṇas (monks), brahmans, and poor people, then he should not be sent for more.[9]

If the spellman does not wish to go into the tomb himself and, what is more, does not wish to make a corpse arise, but knows the place where the treasure is buried, then he should go there to collect it at night. He should take along a companion who loves virtue, who is of like mind and behavior,

---

Ratnacinta's translation of the *Amoghapāśa Dhāraṇī* is especially noteworthy in that its classical Chinese is anything but elegant and has to be described as "broken." Comparing it with a later, polished version of the same text, the reader is struck by its tortured and obviously Indian syntax, a quality which, though it may have repelled many, would nonetheless have been fascinating for its exotic quality.

1. Two versions of the text exist. The first, on which this translation is based, is by Ratnacinta. The second is a nearly identical but grammatically more polished version of this text attributed to the Brahman Li Wu, who worked with Ratnacinta in the early eighth century.

2. A *dhāraṇī* is a brief spell used to focus the mind of the meditator and, properly employed, is said to yield great benefits. The term is sometimes used indiscriminately to refer as well to *mantra*, which some commentators regard as being shorter than *dhāraṇī*. The Sanskrit *dhāraṇī* that follows is typical in its respectful invocation of the Buddha and the bodhisattva as well as in its utterance of various sacred syllables. This particular *dhāraṇī* is dedicated to Amoghapāśa ("He of the Unfailing Lasso").

3. *Siddhi*, "accomplishment" or "success," indicates a supernormal achievement or "magi-cal" power. A "corpse" can refer to a wicked or corrupt monk, a meaning that seems unlikely here.

4. Literally "one who holds the spell," rendered here with the archaic word "spellman."

5. The polished version of the text specifies that the body should not be decayed.

6. Following the reading in Li Wu's polished version.

7. Literally, if the spellman has no use for the transcription, or does not use transcription.

8. The "Three Jewels" are the Buddha, the Teaching (Dharma), and the Community (saṃgha).

9. The polished version simply says that if it is not used for the benefit of the community and so forth, you will be unable to achieve this *siddhi* again.

who is terrified of sinful karma, who well comprehends the sūtras (Buddhist scriptures) and śāstras (authoritative commentaries), and who is understanding and wise. First, it is imperative that you perform the auspicious rites and protect your body with spells. Then smear a cloth with tallow to make a candle.[10] Chant the Lord of Spirit-Spells, the *Amoghapāśahṛdaya*, one hundred and eight times, and, using aspen brush,[11] light a big fire. On behalf of all beings, give rise to the comprehensive vow to cut off forevermore poverty, suffering, afflictions, and so on. Then take the tallow candle and pitch it into the air. Though the place of concealment be vast, the candle will drop down and remain in the air at a height equivalent to the depth at which the precious thing is buried. It will wait for the spellman to come to the place of concealment so to recognize clearly and delimit the spot. The candle will go out and you will know where the treasure is buried.

Later, when you want to fetch it, you should take chyle, linseed, and congee[12] as a sacrifice to heaven and the spirits. After the sacrifice, go with your companion and fetch it. Having obtained the jewels, divide them into three parts: one portion for yourself, one to be given to your companion, and one to be offered with your companion to the Three Jewels, as is fitting. Then take your own portion and together with your companion dedicate it for the use of all beings. Thus you will be able to have your portion, and so long as the spellman's lifetime is not yet up, you may use it indefinitely.

Translated by Charles D. Orzech

Section 10: Siddhi *for Entering the Princess*[13] *Grotto*

At that time, the sage Bodhisattva Avalokiteśvara explained the method of the *siddhi* for entering the princess grotto. If the spellman wishes to enter such a place, he should take along an intimate companion. First, you should com-

10. The polished version specifies a kind of votary candle burned before a Buddha image.

11. The polished version gives *kou-chi*, which some sources identify as *Lycium chinense* ("matrimony vine").

12. According to the *American Heritage Dictionary*, chyle is "a thick white or pale yellow fluid, consisting of lymph and emulsified fat, that is taken up by the lacteals from the intestine in digestion." Congee is a watery gruel made of rice.

13. The character used here for "princess" *(ts'ai)* is rare and poorly attested. Indeed, given the nature of the events described in the text, "princess" seems a somewhat inaccurate and misleading translation. A variant orthography pronounced *yin* commonly refers to lewd women, i.e., prostitutes. Followed by the character for palace *(kung)* it refers to Maithuna (a goddess found in the Garbhadhatumaṇḍala) and to the ritual practice of sexual intercourse. The polished version of the text substitutes the character for "grotto" *(k'u)* for "chambers" *(shih)* in the title and glosses this as a dwelling of the "titans" *(asura)*. In Indian mythology, the titans wage constant warfare against the gods and some of the weaker of their number live in a cave in the western mountains. Thus, the princesses of this text are "titan" princesses and one of the aims of the rite is to attain the status of ruler of the titans.

plete the auspicious rites using the spell on your own body. Then go to the
grotto. The grotto is lovely and usually has flowing springs, bathing pools, all
sorts of flowers and fruits, and musical instruments. People of this world
regard these grottoes as the dwelling place of powerful immortals. Now, when
you wish to enter it, the spellman should, on the fifteenth day of the waxing
moon, keep the eight prohibitions, bathe, eat vegetarian food, and don clean
white clothes. Afterward, go to where the spring issues forth. You should take
rice and millet, barley and wheat, soybeans, lentils and sesame, i.e., all the
seven types of grains as well as curds and cheese. Chant the Lord of Spirit-
Spells, the *Amoghapāśahṛdaya*. On each and every iteration take the grain
and scatter it in a fire. This will cause the door of the grotto to open by itself.
When the spellman sees the grotto door open he must not be frightened and
should not hastily get up, but rather should continue chanting. One by one,
princesses bearing all sorts of flowers and incense will emerge from the grotto
and address you, saying. "Well come, Worthy One! Do you wish to accept
these flowers and incense from me?" The spellman should not be hasty to
accept them. Only on the third request should the spellman say, "Well come,
sister! Just as you have come to receive me, will you grant the incense
and flowers to my companion?" The companion contemplates the princess,
immediately loves her, and grasps her hand to take her as a wife. Because the
princess knows the man's heart is very loving, she accepts the matter like a
maidservant. The companion forthwith wants an opportunity to indulge the
passions as he pleases. His shape and appearance become as youthful as a
lad's.[14] Then they amuse themselves in the world of the senses.

If you wish to abandon the human body immediately to attain the celestial
body of an Accomplished Spell Immortal,[15] the spellman should chant the
spell and obtain five hundred additional wonderful princess-wives. Emerging
from the grotto, holding every sort of clothing, adornments, incense, and
flowers, they will pay obeisance to the spellman and say, "Excellent Sage, take
pity on us." It will go on like this for a while, with them saying that they only
want you to accept his clothing, and so on. After the third request, the
spellman, wishing to subdue the passions of all the spell immortals, should
thence accede to their requests. Then there will not be anything which the
spellman and princesses cannot manifest, and one will have achieved the state
of *cakravartin* of the spell immortals.[16]

If you abandon the human body to attain a body in heaven, all the spell
immortals will gather and bow their heads at your feet. They will proclaim

14. The polished version notes that even if he is heavyset his appearance becomes youthful,
and so on.

15. The polished version indicates that one thus gains the body of a "Spell Immortal," likely
that of a titan, while below, attaining a heavenly body indicates that of a god *(deva)*.

16. *Cakravartin* or "world-ruler" here means the adept will be the ruler of the spell immortals.

and praise your good fortune, and wish that you constantly dwell there. They will play all sorts of music and perform all the songs and dances. They will erect a hundred thousand bejeweled streamers and canopies for your delight and satisfaction. The spellman will freely receive the recompense of a king of heaven with a peaceful and joyful mind, and will continually contemplate the Buddha to the end and not forget him. Performing the acts of a Bodhisattva, you will attain knowledge of your previous lives and transcend all evil rebirths. Moreover, you will not be addicted to the world of the five passions and will constantly attain vision of all the Buddhas and Bodhisattvas. You will be able to teach and transform limitless beings in the unsurpassed Bodhi Way, and will enter the unfailing knowledge of the *samādhi*[17] gate of all *dhāraṇī*.

Translated by Charles D. Orzech

17. Concentrated contemplation or meditation.

Criticism and Theory

16
Classic of Odes

The Great Preface

Anonymous (Late Western Han)

1. As for the "Kuan-chü"[1]—[it is to be understood in terms of] the virtue of the Consort.

2. It is the first of the Airs,[2] and it is that whereby the world is transformed, and husband and wife put right. So it was performed at the village meetings and at the gatherings of the feudal lords.

3. "Air" means "suasion"; it means "teaching." Suasion is exerted in order to move [one's prince?], and teaching aims to transform [the people].

This brief but difficult and confusing text serves as the preface to the so-called Mao recension of the *Classic of Odes* (see selection 22). It is attached to the first ode and begins by commenting on it, but has general implications for the whole collection. The compilation and authorship of the preface are both highly vexed (guesses as to its date range from the fifth century B.C.E. to the third century C.E.). Furthermore, it is so recondite that several later scholars were prompted to rewrite it, the most noted reorganization being that of the famous neo-Confucian thinker, Chu Hsi (1130–1200). In spite of its obscurity, "The Great Preface" is important because it is the first instance of what may be considered literary criticism in China. It stresses the moralistic purpose and value of the *Classic of Odes*. We may say that this preface summarizes the traditional Confucian concept of the role of poetry in society.

1. "Call of the Osprey," the first poem in the *Classic of Odes*. See selection 276 for a humorous spoof on the exegesis of this poem.

2. Or "It is the beginning of the suasion."

4. The Ode is where the aim goes. While in the heart, it is the aim; manifested in words, it is an Ode.

5. Emotion moves within and takes shape in words. Words are not enough, and so one sighs it. Sighing it is not enough, and so one draws it out in song. Drawing it out in song is not enough, and so all unawares one's hands dance it and one's feet tap it out.

6. Emotion is manifested in the voice. When voice is patterned, we call it tone.

7. The tones of a well-governed age are peaceful and happy; its government is harmonious. The tones of a chaotic age are resentful and angry; its government is perverse. The tones of a lost state are sorrowful and longing; its people are suffering.

8. So for putting right the relations of gain and loss, moving heaven and earth, and affecting the manes and spirits, nothing comes close to the Odes.

9. The early kings therefore used them to regulate the relations between husbands and wives, to perfect filiality and respect, to enrich human relations, to beautify the tutelary transformation [of the people], and to change mores and customs.

10. So the Odes have Six Arts. The first is called "Air" [feng]. The second is called "recitation" [fu]. The third is called "analogy" [pi]. The fourth is called "stimulus" [hsing]. The fifth is called "Elegantia" [ya]. The sixth is called "Laud" [sung].

11. Superiors use the Airs to transform those below. Those below use the Airs to spur their superiors on. They strive for delicacy and thus remonstrate obliquely: the speaker does not offend, and still the hearer takes warning. Thus they are called "Airs." [3]

12. When the kingly way decayed and rites and righteousness were discarded, when the teaching of government was lost so that states had different governments and families different customs, then the Changed Airs and Changed Elegantiae were made.

13. The state historians were knowledgeable about the records of success and failure. They were pained at the desuetude of correct human relations and appalled by the cruelty of government by punishments. They sang of what they felt in order to sway their superiors.

14. They know how things had changed and longed for the old customs. So the Changed Airs derive from feelings and yet stop within [the bounds of] ritual and righteousness. That they derive from feelings is because that is how people are. That they stop within ritual and righteousness is all due to the beneficence of the early kings.

15. Thus it is that when the affairs of an entire state are tied to the person of a single individual, we deem it an "Air." When [an Ode] articulates the

---

3. That is, they are called "Airs" (feng) because they sway (feng) their hearers.

affairs of the empire, giving form to the mores of the four quarters, we deem it an "Elegantia."

16. "Elegantia" means "correctness." They tell of the reasons for the rise and fall of kingly government. In government there are [matters] greater and lesser; and so there are the Greater Elegantiae and the Lesser Elegantiae.

17. The Lauds raise the forms and visage of flourishing virtue. They tell the ancestral manes of its successes.

18. These are the four beginnings. They represent the perfection of the Odes.

19. Thus the transformation of the "Kuan-chü" and "Lin-chih"[4] derive from the suasion of the kings; they are associated with the Duke of Chou. That they are called "south" is because the transformation proceeded from north to south. The virtues of the "Ch'üeh ch'ao"[5] and the "Chou-yü"[6] derive from the suasion of the feudal lords. They derive from what the early kings taught; they are associated with the Duke of Shao.

20. The Chou-nan (Chou South) and the Shaonan (Shao South) represent the way of right beginning; they are the foundation of the kingly transformation.

21. Thus in the "Kuan-chü" there is joy in getting a good girl to marry to the lord and concern in advancing the worthy, [but] no abandonment in her beauty. There is sorrow in her seclusion—that is, concern for talent—but no harm to the [essential] goodness of the heart. This is the significance of the "Kuan-chü."

Translated by Steven Van Zoeren

4. "The Feet of the Unicorn," no. 11 in the *Odes*, the final Air of the Chou-nan section. The *lin* ("unicorn") was the portent of an age of sagacious rule.

5. "The Magpie's Nest," no. 12 in the *Odes*, the first Air of the Shao-nan section. Chou and Shao were the fiefs from which the transformative virtue of King Wen spread, assisted by the famous Duke of Chou in the former case and the Duke of Shao in the latter.

6. "Grooms and Gamesters," no. 25 in the *Odes*, the final Air in the Shao-nan section.

17

Rhymeprose on Literature

Lu Chi (261–303)

Preface
(*in Unrhymed Prose*)

Each time I study the works of great writers, I flatter myself I know how their minds worked.

Certainly expression in language and the charging of words with meaning can be done in various ways.

Nevertheless, we may speak of beauty and ugliness, of good and bad in each literary work.

Whenever I write myself, I obtain greater and greater insight.

5 Our constant worry is that our ideas may not equal their objects and our style may fall short of our ideas.[1]

The difficulty, then, lies not so much in knowing as in doing.[2]

I have written this rhymeprose on literature to expatiate on the consummate artistry of writers of the past and to set forth the whence and why of good and bad writings as well.

May it be considered, someday, an exhaustive treatment.

Now, it is true, I am hewing an ax handle with an ax handle in my hand: the pattern is not far to seek.[3]

Known to his contemporaries as a statesman and a general, Lu Chi was among the more prolific authors of his time, but his literary fame rests solely on the single work selected here. The "Rhymeprose on Literature" is the first systematic and reasonably comprehensive treatise on literary criticism written in China. It is somewhat unusual in that it is itself written in one of the most distinctive Chinese literary genres, the rhymeprose or rhapsody (see unnumbered note in selection 149). While Ts'ao P'i (187–226; see selection 170 [unnumbered note]), in his short "Discussion of Literature" (*Lun wen*), should be credited with establishing the independence of belles-lettres from pedestrian types of writing, he was more concerned with ranking the merits of contemporary authors than with describing the nature of literature and literary creativity.

1. Essentially a restatement of the Confucian saying in the "Great Treatise" of the *Classic of Changes*: "Writing cannot express words completely; words cannot express thoughts completely." See selection 4.

2. The incommensurability supposed to exist between knowledge and action had already found expression twice in the *Chronicle of Tso* (see selection 190) and in several other early Chinese works. The Socratic identification of knowledge with action, which became the keynote of post-Renaissance writers and an item in the credo of many Marxists, was seldom affected by Chinese thinkers until the time of Wang Shou-jen, commonly known as Wang Yang-ming (1472–1528), nor does it seem to have left any lasting impression on the Chinese intellectual world. At any rate, when Sun Yat-sen, the founder of the modern Chinese nation, reversed the ancient tag and propounded his thesis of knowledge being difficult and action easy, he was leaving the identity thesis severely alone.

3. Allusion to a line from the *Classic of Odes*, no. 158, which is also quoted in the *Doctrine of the Mean*.

10   However, the conjuring hand of the artist being what it is, I cannot
        possibly make my words do the trick.
      Nevertheless, what I am able to say I have put down here.

Text

I: Preparation

Taking his position at the hub of things, [the writer] contemplates the
mystery of the universe; he feeds his emotions and his mind on the
great works of the past.

Moving along with the four seasons, he sighs at the passing of time;
gazing at the myriad objects, he thinks of the complexity of the
world.

He sorrows over the falling leaves in virile autumn; he takes joy in the
delicate bud of fragrant spring.

With awe at heart, he experiences chill; his spirit solemn, he turns his
gaze to the clouds.

5   He declaims the superb works of his predecessors; he croons the clean
fragrance of past worthies.

He roams in the Forest of Literature, and praises the symmetry of great
art.

Moved, he pushes his books away and takes the writing brush, that he
may express himself in letters.

II: Process

At first he withholds his sight and turns his hearing inward; he is lost in
thought, questioning everywhere.

His spirit gallops to the eight ends of the universe;[4] his mind wanders
along vast distances.

10   In the end, as his mood dawns clearer and clearer, objects, now clean-
cut in outline, shove one another forward.

He sips the essence of letters; he rinses his mouth with the extract of the
Six Arts.[5]

Floating on the heavenly lake, he swims along; plunging into the nether
spring, he immerses himself.

Thereupon, submerged words wriggle up, as when a darting fish, with
the hook in its gills, leaps from a deep lake; floating beauties flutter

4. Extremities of the eight directions (north, south, east, west, and northeast, northwest,
southeast, and southwest).

5. Either the six arts of the *Rituals of Chou* (*Chou li*, these being ceremonies, music,
archery, horsemanship, calligraphy, and mathematics) or the six Confucian arts (the *Classics* of
Odes, *History/Documents*, and *Changes*, *Ceremonies*, *Music*, and the *Spring and Autumn*).

down, as when a high-flying bird, with the harpoon-string around its
wings, drops from a crest of cloud.

He gathers words never used in a hundred generations; he picks rhythms
never sung in a thousand years.

15   He spurns the morning blossom, now full blown; he plucks the evening
bud, which has yet to open.

He sees past and present in a moment; he touches the four seas in the
twinkling of an eye.

III: Words, Words, Words

Now he selects ideas and fixes them in their order; he examines words
and puts them in their places.

He taps at the door of all that is colorful; he chooses from among
everything that rings.

Now he shakes the foliage by tugging the twig; now he follows the waves
to the fountainhead of the stream.

20   Sometimes he brings out what was hidden; sometimes, looking for an
easy prey, he bags a hard one.

Now the tiger puts on new stripes, to the consternation of other beasts;
now the dragon emerges, and terrifies all the birds.

Sometimes things fit together, and are easy to manage; sometimes they
jar each other, and are awkward to manipulate.

He empties his mind completely to concentrate his thoughts; he collects
his wits before he puts words together.

He traps heaven and earth in the cage of form; he crushes the myriad
objects against the tip of his brush.

25   At first they hesitate upon his parched lips; finally they flow through the
well-moistened brush.

Reason, supporting the matter [of the poem], stiffens the trunk; style,
depending from it, spreads luxuriance around.

Emotion and expression never disagree: all changes [in his mood] are
betrayed on his face.

If the thought touches on joy, a smile is inevitable; no sooner is sorrow
spoken of than a sigh escapes.

Sometimes words flow easily as soon as he grasps the brush; sometimes
he sits vacantly, nibbling at it.

IV: Virtue

30   There is joy in this vocation; all sages esteem it.

We [poets] struggle with Non-Being to force it to yield Being; we knock
upon Silence for an answering Music.

We enclose boundless space in a square foot of paper; we pour out a
deluge from the inch-space of the heart.
Language spreads wider and wider; thought probes deeper and deeper.
The fragrance of delicious flowers is diffused; exuberant profusion of
green twigs is budding.

35   A laughing wind will fly and whirl upward; dense clouds will arise from
the Forest of Writing Brushes.

V: *Diversity*

1: The Poet's Aim

Forms vary in a thousand ways; objects are not of one measure.
Topsy-turvy and fleeting, shapes are hard to delineate.
Words vie with words for display, but it is mind that controls them.
Confronted with bringing something into being or leaving it unsaid, he
groans; between the shallow and the deep, he makes his choice
resolutely.

40   He may depart from the square and deviate from the compasses; for he
is bent on exploring the shape and exhausting the reality.
Hence, he who would dazzle the eyes makes much of the gorgeous; he
who intends to convince the mind values cogency.
If persuasion is your aim, do not be a stickler for details; when your
discourse is lofty, you may be free and easy in your language.

2: Genres

Shih (lyric poetry) traces emotions daintily; *fu* (rhymeprose) embodies
objects brightly.[6]
Pei (epitaph) balances substance with style; *lei* (dirge) is tense and
mournful.

45   *Ming* (inscription) is comprehensive and concise, gentle and generous;
chen (admonition), which praises and blames, is clear-cut and
vigorous.
Sung (culogy) is free and easy, rich and lush; *lun* (disquisition) is
rarefied and subtle, bright and smooth.
Tsou (memorial to the throne) is quiet and penetrating, genteel and
decorous; *shuo* (discourse) is dazzling bright and extravagantly
bizarre.
Different as these forms are, they all forbid deviation from the straight,[7]
and interdict unbridled license.

6. The ten literary genres discussed in this and the four following couplets do not, of course,
exhaust the literature of Lu Chi's day, and yet they seem to be the most important ones.

7. An allusion to the Confucian dictum on the design of the three hundred Odes: "Having
no twisty (i.e., depraved) thoughts." See selection 7.

Essentially, words must communicate,[8] and reason must dominate;
   prolixity and long-windedness are not commendable.

VI: *Multiple Aspects*

50   As an object, literature puts on numerous shapes; as a form, it
       undergoes diverse changes.
     Ideas should be cleverly brought together; language should be
       beautifully commissioned.
     And the mutation of sounds and tones should be like the five colors of
       embroidery sustaining each other.
     It is true that your moods, which come and go without notice,
       embarrass you by their fickleness,
     But if you can rise to all emergencies and know the correct order, it will
       be like opening a channel from a spring of water.
55   If, however, you have missed the chance and reach the sense belatedly,
       you will be putting the tail at the head.
     The sequence of dark and yellow being deranged, the whole broidery
       will look smudged and blurred.

VII: *Revision*

     Now you glance back and are constrained by an earlier passage; now
       you look forward and are coerced by some anticipated line.
     Sometimes your words jar though your reasoning is sound; sometimes
       your language is smooth while your ideas make trouble.
     Such collisions avoided, neither suffers; forced together, both suffer.
60   Weigh merit or demerit by the milligram; decide rejection or retention
       by a hairbreadth.
     If your idea or word has not the correct weight, it has to go, however
       comely it may look.

VIII: *Key Passages*

     Maybe your language is already ample and your reasoning rich, yet
       your ideas do not round out.
     If what must go on cannot be ended, what has been said in full cannot
       be added to.
     Put down terse phrases here and there at key positions; they will
       invigorate the entire piece.
65   Your words will acquire their proper values in the light of these phrases.
     This clever trick will spare you the pain of deleting and excising.

   8. Another Confucian dictum from the *Analects*.

IX: *Plagiarism*

It may be that language and thought blend into damascened gauze—
    fresh, gay, and exuberantly lush;
Glowing like many-colored broidery, mournful[9] as multiple chords;
But assuredly there is nothing novel in my writing, if it coincides with
    earlier masterpieces.
70 True, the arrow struck my heart; what a pity, then, that others were
    struck before me.
As plagiarism will impair my integrity and damage my probity, I must
    renounce the piece, however fond I am of it.

X: *Purple Patches*

It may be that one ear of the stalk buds, its tip standing prominent,
    solitary and exquisite.
But shadows cannot be caught; echoes are hard to bind.
Standing forlorn, your purple passage juts out conspicuously; it cannot
    be woven into ordinary music.
75 Your mind, out of step, finds no mate for it; your ideas, wandering
    hither and thither, refuse to throw away that solitary passage.
When the rock embeds jade, the mountain glows; when the stream is
    impregnated with pearls, the river becomes alluring.
When the hazel and arrow-thorn bush is spared from the sickle, it will
    glory in its foliage.
We will weave the market ditty into the classical melody; perhaps we
    may thus rescue what is beautiful.

XI: *Five Imperfections*

1: In Vacuo

Maybe you have entrusted your diction to an anemic rhythm; living in
    a desert, you have only yourself to talk to.
80 When you look down into silence, you see no friend; when you lift your
    gaze to space, you hear no echo.
It is like striking a single chord—it rings out, but there is no music.

---

9. With regard to "mournful[ness]," it may be remarked here that a tragic note seems to have prevailed in Chinese poetics since the last days of the Han dynasty; in fact, it seems to have become a frame of reference with which to judge poetry (see "sad[ness]" in line 87 below). As gaiety was a quality not excluded in Confucian poetics (compare the *Analects*, 3.20), it would be worth investigating how and exactly since when sadness has become the key mood of Chinese poetry.

2: Discord

Maybe you fit your words to a frazzled music; merely gaudy, your
   language lacks charm.
As beauty and ugliness are commingled, your good stuff suffers.
It is like the harsh note of a wind instrument in the courtyard below;
   there is music, but no harmony.

3: Novelty for Novelty's Sake

85   Maybe you forsake reason and strive for the bizarre; you are merely
   searching for inanity and pursuing the trivial.
Your language lacks sincerity and is poor in love; your words wash back
   and forth and never come to the point.
They are like a thin chord violently twanging—there is harmony, but it
   is not sad

4: License

Maybe by galloping unbridled, you make your writing sound good; by
   using luscious tunes, you make it alluring.
Merely pleasing to the eye, it mates with vulgarity—a fine voice, but a
   nondescript song.
90   It reminds one of Fang-lu and Sang-chien,[10]—it is sad, but not
   decorous.

5: Insipidity

Or perhaps your writing is simple and terse, all superfluities removed—
So much so that it lacks even the lingering flavor of a sacrificial broth;[11]
   it rather resembles the limpid tune of the "vermilion chord."[12]
"One man sings, and three men do the refrain";[13] it is decorous, but it
   lacks beauty.

Is this tearfulness merely geographical? The elegies of Ch'u are by no means joyous jingles;
could it be, then, that the South has been responsible for the whining note in Chinese poetry?

10. The names of these apparently "licentious" songs from a defunct state would seem
to mean "Guarding against Dew" and "Amidst the Mulberries." Otherwise, the reference
is unclear.

11. Sacrificial broth was neither salted nor spiced; that is to say, it was bland.

12. "Vermilion chord" refers to the zithers played in ancestral temples.

13. An allusion to ceremonial zithers described according to the *Record of Ritual (Li chi)* as
in the previous note.

XII: Variability

As to whether your work should be loose or constricted, whether you
should mold it by gazing down or looking up,
95 You will accommodate necessary variation, if you would bring out all
the overtones.
Maybe your language is simple, whereas your conceits are clever;
maybe your reasoning is plain, but your words fall too lightly.
Maybe you follow the beaten track to attain greater novelty; maybe you
immerse yourself in the muddy water—to reach true limpidity.
Well, perspicacity may come after closer inspection; subtlety may ensue
from more polishing.
It is like dancers flinging their sleeves in harmony with the beat or
singers throwing their voices in tune with the chord.
100 All this is what the wheelwright Pien[14] despaired of ever explaining; it
certainly is not what mere language can describe.

XIII: Masterpieces

I have been paying tribute to laws of words and rules of style.
I know well what the world blames, and I am familiar with what the
worthies of the past praised.
Originality is a thing often looked at askance by the fixed eye.
The *fu*-gems and jade beads, they say, are as numerous as the "pulse in
the middle of the field,"[15]
105 As inexhaustible[16] as the space between heaven and earth, and growing
co-eternally with heaven and earth themselves.
The world abounds with masterpieces; and yet they do not fill my two
hands.[17]

XIV: The Poet's Despair

How I grieve that the bottle is often empty; how I sorrow that Elevating
Discourse is hard to continue.
No wonder I limp along with trivial rhythms and make indifferent
music to complete the song.

14. The story of wheelwright Pien, a master craftsman who could not transmit to others the
secret of his art, occurs at the end of the thirteenth chapter in the *Chuang Tzu* (see selection 9).
15. *Classic of Odes*, no. 196: "In the midst of the plain there is pulse,/ And the common
people gather it." (Translated by James Legge)
16. Like the bellows in chapter 5 of the *Tao Te Ching* (see selection 10).
17. This refers to a line from the *Classic of Odes*, no. 226: "All morning I gather the king-
grass,/ And do not collect enough to fill my hands."

I always conclude a piece with a lingering regret; can I be smug and
self-satisfied?

110   I fear to be a drummer on an earthen jug; the jinglers of jade pendants
will laugh at me.

XV: *Inspiration*

1

As for the interaction of stimulus and response, and the principle of the
flowing and ebbing of inspiration,
You cannot hinder its coming or stop its going,
It vanishes like a shadow, and it comes like echoes.
When the Heavenly Arrow is at its fleetest and sharpest, what confusion
is there that cannot be brought to order?

115   The wind of thought bursts from the heart; the stream of words rushes
through the lips and teeth.
Luxuriance and magnificence wait the command of the brush and the
paper.
Shining and glittering, language fills your eyes; abundant and
overflowing, music drowns your ears.

2

When, on the other hand, the Six Emotions[18] become sluggish and
foul, the mood gone but the psyche remaining,
You will be as forlorn as a dead stump, as empty as the bed of a dry
river.

120   You probe into the hidden depth of your soul; you rouse your spirit to
search for yourself.
But your reason, darkened, is crouching lower and lower; your thought
must be dragged out by force, wriggling and struggling.
So it is that when your emotions are exhausted you produce many
faults; when your ideas run freely you commit fewer mistakes.
True, the thing lies in me, but it is not in my power to force it out.
And so, time and again, I beat my empty breast and groan; I really do
not know the causes of the flowing and the not flowing.

XVI: *Coda—Encomium*

125   The function of style is, to be sure, to serve as a prop for your ideas.
(Yet allow me to expatiate on the art of letters:)

18. The six emotions are perhaps like and dislike, pleasure and anger, sorrow and joy.

It travels over endless miles, removing all obstructions on the way; it
  spans innumerable years, taking the place, really, of a bridge.
Looking down, it bequeaths patterns to the future; gazing up, it
  contemplates the examples of the ancients.[19]
It preserves the way of Wen and Wu, about to fall to the ground;[20] and
  it propagates good ethos, never to perish.
No path is too far for it to tread; no thought is too subtle for it to
  comprehend.
130 It is a match for clouds and rain in yielding sweet moisture; it is like
  spirits and ghosts in bringing about metamorphoses.[21]
It inscribes bronze and marble to make virtue known; it breathes
  through flutes and strings, and is new always.

Translated by Achilles Fang

19. This line is derived from the *Classic of Documents:* "I wish to see the emblematic figures
of the ancients—the sun, the moon, the stars, the mountains, the dragon, and the flowery fowl,
which are depicted on the upper garment. . . ." (Translated by James Legge)

20. This line alludes to the *Analects,* 19.22: "The doctrines of Wen and Wu have not yet
fallen to the ground." (Translated by James Legge)

21. The couplet refers to the *Classic of Changes:* the first half compares style with the
omnipotent Ch'ien (heavenly) principle, by virtue of which "the clouds move and the rain is
distributed"; the second half may allude to a Confucian saying, "He who knows the method of
change and transformation may be said to know what is done by that spiritual power." (Translated by James Legge)

18
Literary Selections

Preface

Hsiao T'ung (501–531)

When we look to the first beginnings and scrutinize from afar those primordial
conditions—in times of winter caves and summer nests when men devoured

Literary Selections (Wen hsüan) is by far the most important and influential anthology of
Chinese literature. Indeed, as a bisyllabic word in modern Sinitic languages, its title has come
to mean simply "anthology." The preface to *Literary Selections* is included here as a relatively
concise statement of the large number of genres and subgenres of elite Chinese literature that
existed in the early sixth century. Hsiao T'ung (Prince Chao-ming of the Liang dynasty) and his
collaborators most probably drew extensively upon the formulations established by Liu Hsieh (c.
465–c. 520) in his *The Literary Mind and the Carving of Dragons* [i.e., Ornate Rhetoric] *(Wen-
hsin tiao-lung),* the first book-length treatment in Chinese of the major issues involved in the

undressed game and drank blood[1]—times then were rude and people plain; writing had not yet appeared. Then we come to the rule of Fu-hsi, who first traced the Eight Trigrams and invented writing to take the place of government by knotted cords; from this time written records came into being.[2]

The *Classic of Changes* says, "Observe the patterns in the sky to discover the seasons' changes; observe the patterns among men to transform All-Under-Heaven"—so far-reaching are the times and meanings[3] of pattern (*wen*)![4] Now the Imperial Chariot had its origin in the oxcart, but the Imperial Chariot has none of the crudeness of the oxcart. Thick ice is composed of accumulated water, but accumulated water has not the coldness of thick ice. Why so? The original form is preserved but elaborated on, or the essential nature changed through intensification. This is true of things, and it is also true of literature (*wen*). It changes with passing time, and to describe it is no easy task. But to make the attempt:

The Preface to the *Classic of Songs* says,[5] "There are six modes of the Songs. The first is instruction (*feng*); the second is description (*fu*); the third is simile (*pi*); the fourth is metaphor (*hsing*); the fifth is ode (*ya*); the sixth is hymn (*sung*)." Later poets deviated from the ancient [practice], and of the [six

---

study of literature. Whereas the latter was partially inspired by certain Buddhist ontological and epistemological concepts, Ts'ao P'i, Lu Chi (for these two literary critics, see selection 17), and Hsiao T'ung seem to have remained more or less immune—at least consciously so in their critical formulations—to the theoretical positions of this foreign religion.

It should be noted that this preface is not simply a straightforward piece of expository prose. It is written, rather, in the mannered parallel style (see selections 195 and 196), and logical exposition frequently gives way before the demands of symmetry.

1. "Formerly the ancient kings had no houses. In winter they lived in caves, which they had excavated, and in summer in nests, which they had framed. They knew not yet the transforming power of fire, but ate the fruits of plants and trees, and the flesh of birds and beasts, drinking their blood, and swallowing also the hair and feathers." (From the *Record of Rites [Li chi]*, translated by James Legge)

2. This is quoted verbatim form the opening lines of the "Preface" to the *Classic of Documents* attributed to K'ung An-kuo (fl. c. 156–c. 74 B.C.E.; a descendant of Confucius in the eleventh generation). There are conflicting legends and myths concerning the invention of writing in China (compare selection 199).

3. The same encomium occurs repeatedly in the *Classic of Changes*.

4. The word for literature and writing (*wen*) originally meant "pattern."

5. It is impossible to translate the terms satisfactorily, for they have meant many things to different commentators, but at least the nature of the difficulty can be defined. Three of the six items—*feng*, *ya*, and *sung*—are the names of the chief divisions of the present *Classic of Odes*, and while there is no general agreement about their significance there, they are certainly not the names of tropes. *Fu*, *pi*, and *hsing* are variously interpreted and inconsistently applied by the commentators on the *Classic of Odes*. For our present purposes, the important question is how Hsiao T'ung understood the items, and it is apparent from the rest of this paragraph that he was concerned solely with the occurrence of the word *fu* as something associated with the *Classic of Odes*. It provides his point of departure in sketching the development of the *fu* genre, though he must have been aware that the genre was not identical with the trope, as indeed his statement in the next sentence ("the moderns took over only the term *fu*") implies.

modes of the] ancient poetry, the moderns took over only the term *fu*. It appeared first of all in the works of Hsün Tzu[6] and Sung Yü,[7] and was continued subsequently by Chia Yi[8] and Ssu-ma Hsiang-ju;[9] from this time on the ramifications were many. Descriptive of cities and sites there are [the *fu* of Chang Heng and Ssu-ma Hsiang-ju with their imaginary interlocutors His Honor] Insubstantial[10] and [Master] No-Such[-Person].[11] Directed against hunting are the "Ch'ang-yang"[12] and "Hunting with Plumes" [*fu* of Yang Hsiung]. When it comes to *fu* describing one event or celebrating a single object (such as those on Wind, Clouds, Plants, and Trees, or the ones about Fish, Insects, Birds, and Beasts), considering their range, it is quite impossible to list them all.

There was also the Ch'u poet Ch'ü Yüan, who clung to loyalty and walked unsullied; the prince would not accept it when the subject offered advice unwelcome to his ears. Though his understanding was profound and his plans far-reaching, in the end he was banished south of the Hsiang River. Injured for his unbending integrity and with no one in whom to confide his sorrow, he stood on the verge of the abyss, determined to embrace the stone; he sighed by the pool, haggard in appearance.[13] It is from him that the writings of the *sao* poets derive.

Poetry is the product of the emotions: the feelings are moved within and take form in words.[14] In "The Osprey" and "The Unicorn" appears the Way of the Correct Beginning;[15] "The Mulberry Grove" and "On the Banks of the Pu" represent the music of a defunct state.[16] Truly the way of the *feng* and the *ya* may be seen in them at its most brilliant. From the middle period of Fiery Han[17] the paths of poetry gradually diverged. The Retired Tutor (Wei Meng) wrote his "Poem in Tsou,"[18] and the surrendered general (Li Ling) wrote the

6. In spite of their shared name, the riddles in rhyme of the "Fu" chapter of the *Hsün Tzu* have nothing in common with the *fu* ("rhapsody" or "rhymeprose") of Han times.

7. Four *fu* attributed to Sung Yü (see selection 149) are included in the *Literary Selections*.

8. Chia Yi's "Owl *fu*" (see selection 150) is the earliest *fu* of which the text is given in a contemporary Former Han period source (*Records of the Grand Historian*; see selection 225).

9. See selection 151.

10. A character in the "Rhapsody on the Western Capital" by Chang Heng (78–139).

11. Occurs in selection 151 by Ssu-ma Hsiang-ju.

12. Titled after the palace of that name at Ch'ang-an where the game was brought in cages and released.

13. Paraphrased from Ch'ü Yüan's biography in the *Records of the Grand Historian*, ch. 84.

14. See selection 16.

15. *Classic of Odes* (see selection 22), nos. 1 and 11.

16. As stated in the *Record of Ritual (Li chi)*.

17. The Han dynasty ruled by virtue of the Fire element.

18. Wei Meng (second century B.C.E.) was tutor to three generations of princes of Ch'u, the last of whom he found intractable and against whom he "wrote a satirical poem as a remonstrance." He retired to his native Tsou, where he wrote another poem, presumably the one referred to by Hsiao T'ung.

poem on the bridge;[19] with them the four-word and five-word [meters] became [recognized as] distinct classes. In addition, there were [meters] with as few as three words and as many as nine words, the several forms developing at the same time, [like horses] galloping together though on separate traces.

Eulogy (*sung*) serves to broadcast virtuous deeds; it praises accomplishment. Chi-fu made his pronouncement "How stately!";[20] Chi-tzu exclaimed "Oh, perfect!"[21] Elaborated as poetry it was expressed like that; composed as eulogy it is also this way.

Next are Admonition (*chen*), which arises from ameliorating defects, and Warning (*chieh*), which derives from setting to rights. Disquisition (*lun*) is subtle in making logical distinctions, and Inscription (*ming*) is generous in narrating events. When a good man dies, a Dirge (*lei*) is made; when a portrait is painted, an Appreciation (*tsan*) is supplied.

Further, there are these branches: Proclamation (*chao*), Announcement (*kao*), Instruction (*chiao*), and Command (*ling*); these types: Memorial (*piao*), Proposal (*tsou*), Report (*chien*), and Memorandum (*chi*); these categories: Letter (*shu*), Address (*shih*), Commission *(fu)*,[22] and Charge (*chi*); these compositions: Condolence (*tiao*), Requiem (*chi*), Threnody (*pei*), and Lament (*ai*); these forms: Replies to Opponents (*ta k'o*) and Evinced Examples (*chih shih*); these texts: Three Word (*san yen*) and Eight Character (*pa tzu*); Song (*p'ien*), Elegy (*tz'u*), Ditty (*yin*), and Preface (*hsü*); Epitaph (*pei*) and Columnar Inscription (*chieh*); Necrology (*chih*) and Obituary (*chuang*). A multitude of forms have shot up like spear-points; diverse tributaries have joined the main stream. Yet they might be compared to musical instruments made of different materials—some of clay, some from gourds, yet all are to give pleasure to the ear; or to embroideries of different colors and designs—all are to delight the eye. This accounts for just about all that writers have written.

When not busy with my duties as Heir Apparent, I have spent many idle days looking through the garden of letters or widely surveying the forest of literature, and always I have found my mind so diverted, my eye so stimulated,

---

19. Referring to his farewell poem to Su Wu (c. 143–60 B.C.E.), which begins: "We clasp hands on the river bridge / By nightfall where will the traveler have gone?" It is now generally accepted that all the Li Ling (d. 74 B.C.E.) poems in the *Literary Selections* are forgeries.

20. *Classic of Odes*, no. 260: "Chi-fu has made this eulogy, / Stately its clear melody." This poem is a eulogy of Chung Shan-fu, but it is not in the "Lauds" section of the *Odes*; nor is the preceding eulogy of the prince of Shen (*Odes* no. 259) with its similar concluding lines.

21. Chi-tzu is the "Duke's-son Chao of Wu," who came on a state visit to Lu. The *Chronicle of Tso* (see selection 190) gives a long account of his reception, particularly of the musical performance which he requested and which included selections from the major sections of the *Odes*. After each piece he made appropriate remarks. His exclamation "Oh, perfect!" came after he had heard the "Lauds" section of the *Odes* and is followed by an enthusiastic catalog of its perfections.

22. This is written with a different sinograph than that for "rhapsody" or "rhymeprose" discussed extensively above.

that hours have passed without fatigue. Since the Chou and the Han, far off in the distant past, dynasties have changed seven times and some thousands of years have elapsed. The names of famous writers and men of genius overflow the green bag;[23] the scrolls of winged words and flowing brushes fill the yellow covers. If one does not leave aside the weeds and select the flowers, it is impossible, even with the best intentions, to get through the half.

Now the writings of the Duke of Chou and the works of Confucius are on a level with sun and moon, as mysterious as ghosts and spirits. They are the models of filial and respectful conduct, guides to the basic human relationships; how can they be subjected to pruning or cutting?

The works of Chuang Tzu and Lao Tzu, of Kuan Tzu and Mencius are devoted primarily to establishing a doctrine; they are not immediately concerned with literary values. In the present anthology they, too, have been omitted.

When it comes to the excellent speeches of the sages and the straightforward remonstrances of loyal ministers, the fine talk of the politicians and the acuity of the sophists,[24] these are "ice melting[25] and the fountain leaping,[26] gold aspect and jade echo."[27] They are what are referred to as "sitting on Mount Chü and debating beneath the Chi Gate."[28] Chung-lien's making Ch'in's army withdraw,[29] Yi-ch'i's getting Ch'i to submit,[30] the Marquis of Liu's raising eight difficulties,[31] the Marquis of Ch'ü-ni's proposing the six strate-

23. A reference to Hsün Hsü (d. 289) who devised the four bibliographic categories to include all books, which he stored in green bags and tied with yellow cords.

24. A reference to *Han Ying's Illustrations of the Didactic Application of the Classic of Odes* (*Han shih wai chuan*): "The superior man avoids the three points: he avoids the brush-point of the literary man; he avoids the spear-point of the military man; he avoids the tongue-point of the sophist."

25. Probably refers to *Tao Te Ching* (see selection 10), ch. 15: "Yielding as ice as it starts to melt," where it is used to characterize the excellent officers of antiquity.

26. This may refer to a line from the Grave Inscription for Ts'ao Ch'üan ("Plans like a spring gushing") by Tseng Chao.

27. This probably alludes directly to Wang Yi's preface to "Encountering Sorrows" (see selection 148): "The writings of Ch'ü Yüan are truly far-reaching in their influence. . . . Of them it can be said that their aspect is of gold, their substance of jade, peerless in a hundred generations."

28. A lost work, *Lu Lien Tzu*, is quoted by the distinguished annotator of the *Literary Selections*, Li Shan (630?–689): "T'ien Pa, a sophist of Ch'i, argued on Mount Chü and debated beneath the Chi-cheng Gate. He defamed the Five Emperors and incriminated the Three Kings, in one day putting down a thousand opponents."

29. In the *Intrigues of the Warring States* (see selection 238), it is told how Lu Chung-lien dissuaded Chao from recognizing the ruler of Ch'in as emperor (as advocated by the general Hsin Yüan-yen of Wei), and the report of his indictment of Ch'in led the latter state to withdraw its armies which were besieging Han-tan.

30. In the *Records of the Grand Historian*, it is told how Li Yi-chi persuaded Ch'i to join with Liu Pang in the wars that led to the founding of the Han dynasty.

31. Further in the *Records of the Grand Historian*, it is told how Chang Liang, marquis of

gies:[32] their accomplishments were famous in their own time and their speeches have been handed down from a thousand years. But most of them are found in the records or appear incidentally in the works of the philosophers and historians. Writings of this sort are also extremely numerous, and though they have been handed down in books, they differ from belles-lettres, so that I have not chosen them for this anthology.

As for histories and annals, they praise and blame right and wrong and discriminate between like and unlike. Clearly they are not the same as belles-lettres. But their eulogies and essays concentrate verbal splendor, their prefaces and accounts are a succession of flowers of rhetoric; their matter derives from deep thought, and their purport places them among belles-lettres. Hence I have included these with the other pieces.

From the Chou House of long ago down to this Holy Dynasty, in all it makes thirty chapters. I have named it simply the *Anthology*. The following texts are arranged by genres. Since poetry and *fu* are not homogeneous, these are further divided into categories. Within each category the sequence is chronological.

Translated by James Hightower

Liu, dissuaded the Han emperor Kao Tsu from reestablishing the Six Feudal States (as Li Yi-chi had advocated) by citing eight precedents and pointing out the differences in circumstances.

32. Ch'en P'ing (see selection 257, note 1), marquis of Ch'ü-ni, became chief minister under the Han emperor Kao Tsu. According to Ssu-ma Ch'ien in his *Records of the Grand Historian*, the Six Strategies had been kept secret and he had no way of knowing what they were.

19
Record of the Classification of Old Painters

Preface

Hsieh Ho (fl. c. 500–535?)

Now by classification of painters is meant the relative superiority and inferiority of all painters. As for painters, there is not one who does not illustrate some

The *Record of the Classification of Old Painters (Ku-hua p'in-lu)* is a short work, but it has had a seminal impact on all later theories of art in China. In it, Hsieh Ho laid down the six fundamental principles for Chinese painting theory. Although they are extremely difficult to interpret (it would appear that Hsieh Ho himself had not fully assimilated them), it is highly probable that there is some connection with the *ṣaḍaṅga* ("six limbs") of Indian painting theory since the two sets correspond virtually one for one. A close correspondence should also be noted

exhortation or warning, or show the rise and fall in man's affairs. The solitudes and silences of a thousand years may be seen as in a mirror by merely opening a scroll.

Even though painting has its Six Elements,[1] few are able to combine them thoroughly; and from ancient times until now each painter has excelled in one particular branch. What are these Six Elements? First, Spirit Resonance, which means vitality; second, Bone Method, which is a way of using the brush; third, Correspondence to the Object, which means the depicting of forms; fourth, Suitability to Type, which has to do with the laying on of colors; fifth, Division and Planning, that is, placing and arrangement; and sixth, Transmission by Copying, that is, the copying of models.

Only Lu T'an-wei[2] and Wei Hsieh[3] were thoroughly proficient in all of these.

But, while works of art may be skillful or clumsy, esthetics knows no ancient and modern. Respectfully relying upon remote and recent sources and following their classifications, I have edited and completed the preface and citations. Hence what is presented is not too far-ranging. As for the origins of painting, it is merely reported that it proceeded from gods and immortals, but none was witness to such.

Translated by Susan Bush and Hsio-yen Shih,
based on the translation of William Acker

---

between ideas expressed in this preface and in concepts common to early Chinese literary theory such as *The Literary Mind and the Carving of Dragons* (see unnumbered note to selection 20).

Hsieh Ho may have been related to the famous progressive poets of the Southern Dynasties, Hsieh Ling-yün (see selection 30) and Hsieh T'iao (464–499).

1. More literally, "laws."
2. Fifth century.
3. Active late third to early fourth century.

20
Ts'ang-lang's Discussions of Poetry

An Analysis of Poetry

Yen Yü (c. 1180–c. 1235)

1. For the student of poetry, judgment is the most important thing. His introduction must be correct and his ambition must be set high. He should

The *Ts'ang-lang shih-hua* is a manifold and complex text. Nonetheless, it seems to engage in essentially four different arguments:

take the Han, Wei, Chin, and High T'ang as his teachers and not wish to be someone who has lived after the K'ai-yüan (713–741) and T'ien-pao (742–755) eras. If he yields, he will have the devil of inferior poetry enter his bosom because he did not set his ambition high enough. If one has not yet reached the end of a journey, he can increase his efforts, but, as soon as he goes off the road, the more he hurries the more he will go astray because his introduction was not correct. For, as it is said: "If one studies the very best of something, he will only manage to achieve half of it, but, if one studies second-rate achievements, it will result in something truly inferior." It is also said: "If one's judgment surpasses that of his teacher, only then will it be worthy of being handed down to posterity, but, if it merely equals that of his teacher, when handed down it will consist of the teacher's virtues diluted by half!" One's efforts must proceed from the top and work down and cannot proceed from the bottom and work up. First, one must thoroughly recite the Elegies of Ch'u[1] and sing them morning and night so as to make them his basis. When he goes on to recite *The Nineteen Ancient Poems*,[2] the *Music Bureau Ballads in Four Sections*,[3] and the pentasyllabic verse of Li Ling (d. 74 B.C.E.) and Su Wu (c. 143–60 B.C.E.) and that of the Han and the Wei, he must do them all thoroughly. After that, he will take up the collected poetry of Li Po and Tu Fu[4] and read them until, lying on top of one another, they become his pillows, just as people today study the Classics. Next, he will

1. The Poetry of the High T'ang masters (Li Po, Tu Fu, and their contemporaries) is the perfect realization of the true law or Dharma of poetry.
2. Perfect poetry depends upon spontaneity, which Yen Yü, the author, characterizes in terms of enlightenment, a term borrowed from Ch'an/Zen Buddhism.
3. Not all T'ang poetry is worthy of emulation, however, since after the High T'ang period poetry underwent deviation, and some Middle T'ang (766–834) poetry and Late T'ang (835–907) poetry is a product of what Yen calls "false enlightenment." As the High T'ang period corresponds analogously to the "orthodoxy" of the Lin-chi School of Ch'an, so does much of the poetry of the Middle and Late T'ang eras correspond to the heterodoxy of the Ts'ao-tung School, and the "lesser" (and therefore "false") attainments of the Hīnayāna tradition as a whole to the Śrāvaka and Pratyeka, and so on (see notes 7 and 8 below).
4. To a considerable extent, Yen's work of criticism is a diatribe against the poetry of his own era, against Sung period poetry in general, and in particular against the poetry of the Chiang-hsi School. He condemns Sung poetry essentially on two grounds: it is not "enlightened" (i.e., spontaneous), and it does not embody the true Dharma (law) of poetry.

Little is known about the author except that he was a native of Shao-wu (in modern Fukien), that he was in touch with several prominent poets of his day, and that he left behind a small collection of poetry. His fame, however, rests securely on the insightful critical work from which the beginning is excerpted here.

1. *Ch'u tz'u* (see selection 148).
2. See selection 165.
3. An unknown collection of ballad poetry (for *yüeh-fu*, see selection 164).
4. See selections 45 and 48.

comprehensively take up the famous masters of the High T'ang. Once he allows all this to ferment in his bosom for a long time, he will be enlightened spontaneously. Although he might not attain the ultimate end of study, still he will not go off the correct road. This is nothing less than to work from the basis of the very highest attainments, and I say that it is the "one road that leads upward," that it "cuts straight to the foundation," that it is "the gateway to immediate enlightenment," and that it is "the single sword-thrust to the heart."

2. There are five aspects to the Dharma[5] of poetry: formal structure, power of formal style, personal style, inspired feeling, and intonation and rhythm.

3. There are nine modes in poetry: the lofty, the antique, the profound, the remote, the ever-flowing, the heroic-and-powerful, the elated-and-transcendent, the sad-yet-resolute, and the forlorn-yet-gracious. There are three dimensions of poetry to which one must pay special heed: to the openings and closures of poems, to syntax, and to crucial elements of diction. There are two absolutely essential characteristics of poetry: it must flow freely and not be restricted, or it must be thoroughly imbued with deeply moving expression. There is one ultimate attainment in poetry: enter the spirit. When poetry enters spirit, it is perfect and complete, and nothing more can be added to it. Only Li Po and Tu Fu managed to do this, and if others ever do they will be very few indeed!

4. In the tradition of the Ch'anists, there are the Greater and the Lesser Vehicles, the Southern and the Northern Schools, and the heterodox and orthodox Ways. There, the student must follow the Very Highest Vehicle, embody the Correct Dharma Eye, and experience enlightenment of the first order. However, if it is Lesser Vehicle Ch'an, the fruit of the Śrāvaka[6] or the Pratyeka,[7] it will never be orthodox. Discussing poetry is just like discussing Ch'an/Zen. The poetry of Han, Wei, Chin, and the High T'ang represents enlightenment of the first order. Poetry from the Ta-li era on (after 766) corresponds to the Lesser Vehicle and has fallen into enlightenment of the second order. The Poetry of the Late T'ang is Śrāvaka or Pratyeka. He who studies the poetry from the time after the Ta-li era is as if he were an adherent of the Ts'ao-tung School.[8] For the most part, the Way of Ch'an is concerned with marvelous enlightenment and the Way of Poetry is also concerned with marvelous enlightenment. Thus, Meng Hao-jan[9] was far inferior to Han Yü[10] in knowledge, that is, in everything but poetry where he was the superior, and

5. This might be rendered as Law or, less literally, Way.

6. "A hearer." This generally refers to a practitioner of so-called Hīnayāna ("Lesser Vehicle") Buddhism.

7. One who attains enlightenment solely for himself.

8. The "orthodox" Lin-chi School regarded the Ts'ao-tung School as teaching "false" enlightenment.

9. See selection 42.

10. See selection 53.

this was all due to its sense of marvelous enlightenment. Only when one is enlightened can he be a real expert and show his natural color. However, there are different depths and different scopes of enlightenment. There is thoroughly penetrating enlightenment, and there is enlightenment which only achieves partial understanding. The Han and the Wei are indeed supreme! They did not have to depend upon enlightenment at all! Poets beginning with Hsieh Ling-yün[11] and including the masters of the High T'ang possessed thoroughly penetrating enlightenment; although there were others who might have achieved enlightenment, it was never that of the first order. The way I have evaluated the tradition of poetry is not presumptuous and the way I have discriminated among poets and eras is not reckless. The world has always had people it could do without, but there has never been anything written it could afford to ignore. The Way of Poetry is just like this, and, if anyone believes this not to be so, then his view of poetry is not sufficiently broad and his examination of poetry is not sufficiently deep. If one tries to take up the poetry of the Chin and the Sung and thoroughly examines it, then tries to take up the poetry of the Southern and Northern dynasties and thoroughly examines it, then tries to take up the poetry of Shen Ch'üan-ch'i (d. c. 713), Sung Chih-wen (d. c. 713), Wang Po,[12] Yang Chiung (d. 692), Lu Chao-lin (c. 641–c. 680), and Lo Pin-wang[13] and thoroughly examines it, then especially tries to take up the poetry of Li Po and Tu Fu and thoroughly examines it, then tries to take up the poetry of the Ta-li era and thoroughly examines it, then tries to take up the poetry of the Yüan-ho era (806–820) and thoroughly examines it, and then finally takes up the poetry of Su Shih and Huang T'ing-chien[14] of the present dynasty and that of their respective followers and thoroughly examines it, then what is right and what is wrong will be unable to remain hidden. If there is still any poetry not listed here, it must consist of wild-fox heterodoxy and will obscure true knowledge of poetry, so that one will be unable to save himself and thus never reach enlightenment.

5. Poetry is concerned with a different kind of talent which has nothing to do with books and involves a different kind of interest which has nothing to do with Principle, but if one does not read books widely and thoroughly investigate Principle, he will never be able to attain the ultimate meaning of poetry. That which has been called "don't travel on the road of Principle and don't fall into the fish trap of words"[15] is the superior way. Poetry is the expression

11. See selection 30.
12. See selection 196.
13. See selection 37.
14. See selections 72 and 73.
15. This alludes to the *Chuang Tzu*, ch. 26:

A fish-trap is for catching fish; once you've caught the fish, you can forget about the trap. A rabbit-snare is for catching rabbits; once you've caught the rabbit, you can forget about the snare. Words are for catching ideas; once you've caught the idea, you can forget about the

of one's original nature and the poets of the High T'ang were solely concerned with inspired feeling. They were like antelopes who hung by their horns, leaving no tracks by which they might be found.[16] Their poetry is utterly marvelous because it is transparent as crystal, and thus, like echoes in the air, the play of color in phenomenal appearance, like the moon reflected in water or an image seen in a mirror, their words come to an end, but their meaning is limitless. Modern writers make bizarre interpretations and so consider poetry to consist of language or of talent and learning, or think that it is a kind of reasoned discourse. They certainly are not unskillful, but their poetry will never manage to reach the attainments of that of the ancients because it always lacks the tone made by "one singing and three joining in."[17] Moreover, in composing poems, they too often spend all their attention on allusions while remaining unconcerned with inspiration. Their every word must have a precedent in the sources, and every rhyme they employ must have been used before. Even if one reads them over and over again from beginning to end, it is still impossible to grasp what they are trying to do; the worst of them actually scream and growl, a practice completely against the principle of magnanimity, and almost go so far as to make up poetry out of abusive language! When poetry has reached such a state, it can certainly be called a disaster! However, is there no poetry of modern times that can meet with our approval? Yes, there is, but I grant approval only to that which is in accord with the poetry of the ancients. Thus poetry at the beginning of our dynasty still carried on the tradition of the T'ang poets, and Wang Yü-ch'eng (954–1001) emulated Po Chü-yi,[18] Yang Yi (974–1020) and Liu Yün (fl. c. 1016) emulated Li Shang-yin,[19] Sheng Tu (d.1041) emulated Wei Ying-wu (736–c. 790), Ou-yang Hsiu[20] emulated the ancient style verse of Han Yü, and Mei Yao-ch'en[21]

---

words. Where can I find a person who knows how to forget about words so that I can have a few words with him?

Translated by Victor H. Mair

16. The image of the antelope that hangs by its horns from a tree branch and leaves no tracks was often employed by certain Ch'an masters of the T'ang period. For instance, Master Tao-ying (d. 902) addressed his disciples: "You are like good hunting dogs who only know how to find animals that leave tracks and who now have come across an antelope that hangs by its horns; not only are there no tracks, you don't even recognize its scent!" From the *Record of the Transmission of the Lamp (Ch'uan-teng lu)*.

17. What these Ch'an masters are saying is: "If you want to learn, you cannot get caught up in the precise, literal meaning of what we have been saying. Sense and reason are useless since we leave no tracks for you to follow." Yen Yü here implies that this is true in great poetry as well, the real significance of which lies beyond sense and reason and the literal meaning of language.

18. See selection 180.

19. See selection 65.

20. See selection 206.

21. See selections 53 and 70.

emulated the even-and-bland quality of certain of the T'ang poets, but when Su Shih and Huang T'ing-chien began to bring forth their own ideas in order to make up poetry, this style based on that of the T'ang poets was changed.[22] The efforts made by Huang T'ing-chien were especially intense, and later on his teaching was extremely influential and its adherents became known throughout the world as the Chiang-hsi Sect. In more recent times, poets such as Chao Shih-hsiu (fl. c. 1195–1224) and Weng Chüan (fl. c. 1195–1224) took their sole delight in the poetry of Chia Tao[23] and Yao Ho (fl. c. 831) and to some extent drew near to a pure-and-perservering style. The Poets of Rivers and Lakes[24] mostly emulated their style and called themselves for a time the T'ang School. However, not realizing that they had become the offspring of the Śrāvaka and the Pratyeka, how could they ever think that they had come to possess the True Dharma Eye of the Great Vehicle of the Masters of the High T'ang! Alas! It has been a long time since the transmission of the True Dharma Eye has been interrupted! Although no one has yet begun to chant the doctrine of T'ang poetry, the Way of T'ang poetry may yet one day become manifest, whereas they are now chanting their style, calling it "T'ang poetry," and students will consequently say that T'ang poetry is truly limited to this alone! Can it be possible that the Way of poetry must suffer this double misfortune![25] Therefore, without any particular thought to my own limitations, I always try to determine the main tenets of poetry; borrowing Ch'an as an analogy, and making a careful analysis from the Han and the Wei on, I say with complete determination that we must take that of the High T'ang as representing the Dharma of poetry, and even if I offend all good gentlemen in the world in doing so, I will not recant!

Translated by Richard John Lynn

22. Became deviant, heterodox.
23. See selection 59.
24. This appellation refers to "commoner poets."
25. The first misfortune was to have poetry develop a non-T'ang "heterodox" style at the hands of Su Shih and Huang T'ing-chien and their followers, and the second misfortune was this present trend to emulate the poetry of the Late T'ang.

21
Poems on Poetry, No. 30

Yüan Hao-wen (1190–1257)

I know my foolishness, a mere ant trying to shake a tree;
Such is the tyro's urge, ever to criticize.
With old age, leaving behind a thousand poems—
By whom will their strengths and weaknesses be judged?

Translated by John Timothy Wixted

Yüan Hao-wen was the most notable literary personage of the Chin (Jürchen) dynasty, under which he was also a high-ranking official. He is best known for his poems mourning the fall of the Chin dynasty to the Mongols and for his three series of poems on poetry, which constitute a rather unusual body of literary criticism. In the latter he praised the northern (more heroic, technically oriented) tradition of which he was a part and disparaged the southern (more intuitional, Zen-like) tradition, for which see selection 20.

With Chang Hung-lüeh,[1] Court Attendant, Discussing Literature

Yüan Hao-wen

Writing issues from pained reflection;
But who writes with pained reflection?
Even if there were one of pained reflection,
4   In all the world, how many would recognize him?
Skillful prose and skillful poetry
Are very like the chess of a champion master;
Though a grand master may respond casually,
8   There is a knack to his every move.
Unless one looks on, move by move,
It will be the same as peeking at the sky through a tube.
A text has to be written character by character;
12   It should also be read character by character.
Mulling over places where there is an aftertaste,
A hundred readings will not suffice.
If, by effort, one achieves full comprehension,
16   Its language will become like next-of-kin.

1. Brother of the poet Chang Hung-fan (1238–1280).

It was only allowed Kuang and K'uei,[2]
Hearing plucked strings, to discern proper music.
Men of today, going through texts,
20   Sweep over ten lines at a glance.
A stuffy nose cannot distinguish fragrant from foul;
Bad eyesight confuses red and green.
If the tiniest part is overlooked,
24   The perceived object could be Ch'u or Shu.[3]
No wonder that at the foot of Ching Mountain,
One often hears the weeping of the maimed one.[4]

Translated by John Timothy Wixted

2. Two famous musicians of ancient times.
3. Two widely separated states, here signifying disparateness.
4. Pien Ho (eighth century B.C.E.) was from the state of Ch'u. Having discovered a fabulous piece of jade, he presented it to the king. The jade, however, was judged to be of inferior quality, so he was subjected to being maimed by having his left foot cut off. When a new king came to the throne, he presented the jade again, but again the jade was considered to be of inferior quality and he suffered the penalty of having his right foot cut off. When still another king came to the throne, Pien Ho, weeping tears of blood, once more presented it to the monarch. On this occasion, the true worth of the jade was recognized. The king accepted it and Pien Ho was duly rewarded.

PART II

Verse

Classical Poetry

<hr>

22
Classic of Odes

Anonymous (c. 840–620 B.C.E.)

1
Kuan-kuan call the ospreys
  perched there on a river isle.
A pure maid, so alluring,
  a mate worthy of a nobleman.

The *Shih ching* (the *Classic of Odes, Book of Songs,* or *Poetry Classic*) is the most ancient anthology of Chinese poetry. The 305 poems—more properly, songs, since they were lyrics accompanied by tunes now lost—date approximately from the late Western Chou to the middle of the Spring and Autumn period (c. 840–620 B.C.E.), although they appear to have undergone substantial editing and regularization in the following centuries. They are divided into four parts: 160 *Kuo feng* ("Airs of the States"), 74 *Hsiao ya* ("Lesser Ya"), 31 *Ta ya* ("Greater Ya"), and 40 *Sung* ("Temple Hymns"). Of these, the oldest are the Greater and Lesser Ya, and the youngest are the Airs of the States.

The "Airs of the States" preserve an array of folk images and themes. Included in this selection are: 1, an account of the frustrated pursuit of a desirable and mysterious woman; 6, a celebration of the virtues of a new bride; 8, a brief lesson on gathering a fertility herb, punningly named "babes-in-a-pot"; 9, a warning about dealing with those possessed of exceedingly superior qualities, exemplified by a metaphorical allusion to the river goddesses called "the Floating Maids of the Han"; 23, a glimpse at a seduction; 28, an emotional leave-taking; 39, an almost comical account of the consequences of listening to advice from the inexperienced; 42, an evocation of a woman, or perhaps a goddess, of great beauty; 43, a warning of the ugliness that results when one is obsessed with the pursuit of beauty; 57, another celebration of feminine beauty; 58, a wife's bitter complaints about her husband's mistreatment of her; 63, an expression

5   Long and short the water fringe;
       to left and right I hunt it.
    A pure maid, so alluring,
       awake and asleep I seek her.

    Seeking but not finding,
10   awake and asleep with her I long to lie.
    I long, oh, how I long,
       tossing and turning from side to side.

    Long and short the water fringe;
       to left and right I pick it.
15 A pure maid, so alluring,
       as lute with zither, I befriend her.

    Long and short the water fringe;
       to left and right I cull it.
    A pure maid so alluring,
20   as bell with drum, I delight her.

---

of pity for someone alone and impoverished; 64, a sketch of a courtship ritual in which fruit is exchanged for girdle pendants; 76, a girl's plea that her ardent lover restrain himself; 113, a complaint about greedy landowners; 154, a poetical almanac outlining court rituals and agrarian activities; and 158, a miniature lesson on how a marriage should be conducted.

The "Lesser Ya" and "Greater Ya"—which perhaps take their name from the *ya* or "elegant pronunciation" used in chanting them—seem more concerned with life at the royal court. Selected from the "Lesser Ya" are: 191, an entreaty begging that a high court official fulfill his responsibilities to protect the realm; and 210, a paean to an unnamed king praising him and the harvest. From the "Greater Ya" are: 245, an account of the miraculous birth and accomplishments of "Lord Millet," mythical founder of the Chou house; 253, a plea that the king and officials be more mindful of their suffering population; and 256, a lengthy remonstrance whose philosophical content makes it a precursor to such verse texts as the *Lao Tzu* (see selection 10) and the "Nei Yeh" chapter of the *Kuan Tzu* (see selection 5).

The "Temple Hymns" are represented by one poem: 280, a description of a Chou musical performance presented both to celebrate and please the royal ancestors.

Traditionally, the *Shih ching* has been regarded as a canonical collection of important moral truths and lessons. Confucius saw in its content and language a guide for moderation in speech and action. Later followers of Confucius's teachings read the poems as if they were a detailed chronicle of praise of the heroes and heroines or blame of the villains of early Chinese history. Such interpretations are codified in the official prefaces, glosses, and commentaries written during the late Chou and the Han dynasties (see selection 16 for the first and most famous of these). Much later, during the Sung dynasty, there was a reaction against such historical and political explications, especially of the "Airs of the States." There thus emerged the view that most of the pieces are folk songs devoid of political intent and historical judgment—a view of the text that remains prominent today.

The *Shih ching* established the basis for the long and glorious tradition of Chinese classical poetry (*shih*), which was practiced continuously as the preferred form of literati verse until this century. Other genres of verse (*tz'u, ch'ü, yüeh-fu,* and so on, for which see the following sections) competed with it in succeeding centuries, but *shih* always reigned supreme.

6

That peachtree so frail,
   radiant are its blossoms.
That girl come to marry,
   she is right for this house-and-home.

5   That peachtree so frail,
   swollen is its fruit.
That girl come to marry,
   she is right for this home-and-house.

That peachtree so frail,
10   its leaves are dense.
That girl come to marry,
   she is right for this whole family.

8

So plentiful, the babes-in-a-pot,
   I pick them!
So plentiful, the babes-in-a-pot,
   I hold them!

5   So plentiful, the babes-in-a-pot,
   I squeeze them!
So plentiful, the babes-in-a-pot,
   I caress them!

So plentiful, the babes-in-a-pot,
10   I press them to my blouse!
So plentiful, the babes-in-a-pot,
   I press them to my bodice!

9

The lofty trees of the south
   may not be rested beneath.
The Floating Maids of the Han
   may not be enticed.
5   The Han so broad,
   cannot be waded.
The Chiang so long,
   cannot be traveled by raft.

When a bundle of kindling is too prickly
10   you trim its thorns.
When a betrothed girl is to be married

one feeds her horse.
The Han so broad,
cannot be waded.
15   The Chiang so long,
cannot be traveled by raft.

When a bundle of kindling is too prickly
you trim its points.
When a betrothed girl is to be married
20   one feeds her colt.
The Han so broad,
cannot be waded.
The Chiang so long,
cannot be traveled by raft.

23

On the offering mound, a dead roe,
white floss grass wraps it up.
There is a girl who longs for spring,
an auspicious knight leads her forward.

5   In the grove, a trembling oak,
on the offering mound, a dead deer.
White floss grass binds and ties them.
The girl is like jade.

"Whoa, gently, gently.
10   Do not move my apron,
and make the shaggy dog bark."

28

The swallow flies away,
irregularly flapping its wings.
That child goes to be wed,
I escort her far, here to this wild mound.
5   My stares reach her not,
my tears are like rain.

The swallow flies away,
its neck lowered then raised.
That child goes to be wed,
10   far I accompany her.
My stares reach her not,
I linger long and cry.

The swallow flies away,
its cry low then high.

15 That child goes to be wed,
    I escort her far, here to the south.
My stares reach her not,
    this exhausts my heart.

"Lady Second-born of the House of Jen,
20   Her heart staunch and sincere.
Always mild and kind,
    pure and true her person.
Her thinking of our former lord
    exhorts me, the orphan."

39

Cautiously bubbles that spring water;
    still, it flows into the Ch'i.
My love is in Wei,
    no day but I desire him.
5 Clever are those old maids named Chi,
    with them I consult:

"Upon departing, lodge at Tzu,
    and offer libations at Ni.
When a young lady goes to be married,
10   she leaves parents and brothers far behind."
I ask the maiden aunts,
    and next my elder sisters:

"Upon departing, lodge at Kan,
    and offer libations at Yen.
15 Grease the wheels and insert the linchpins
    before the bridal carriages set out.
If you speed to Wei,
    you will no doubt be hurt."

I think of the forked spring,
20   my sighs and laments multiply.
I think of the towns of Hsü and Ts'ao,
    my heart does so yearn.
Yoking the horses I wander aimlessly,
    to put aside my sorrows.

42

The Chaste Maiden, shining scarlet,
    awaits us at Wall-Nook.

Obscure, invisible,
   scratching her head, immobile.

5 The Chaste Maiden, so clever,
    has given us the Vermilion Stalk.
The Vermilion Stalk glows bright red
    in celebration of a maiden's beauty.

From our shepherd we offer young floss grass,
10   sworn to be beautiful and rare.
Made not in payment for the maiden's beauty,
    but to praise the kind one's gift.

43

The Restored Terrace is new and fresh,
    the River's water is full and swelling.
When it is the pleasing and genial one seeks,
    hideous swaybacks abound.

5 The Restored Terrace towers high,
    the River's water stretches flat.
When it is the pleasing and genial one seeks,
    hideous swaybacks come.

When a fishnet is set out,
10   a wild goose gets tangled in it.
When it is the pleasing and genial one seeks,
    one finds but ugly hunchbacks.

57

The large-headed beauty, head so alluring,
    wears embroidery neath a grasscloth shroud.
Child of the Marquis of Ch'i,
    wife of the Marquis of Wei,
5 Sister of the Eastern Palace Heir;
The Lord of Hsing calls her sister-in-law,
    she calls the Sire of T'an brother-in-law.

Hands like frail reeds,
    skin like congealed fat.
10 Neck like a tree-grub,
    teeth like melons seeds.
A cicada head, moth eyebrows.
Her cunning smile a pale green,
    the lovely eyes so black and white.

15   The large-headed beauty towers proud,
         offering prayers at the farmer's altar;
     The four stallions are tall,
         their vermilion tassels bushy;
     She rides to court screened by pheasant feathers.
20   Grand officers retire early,
         lest they tire their lord.

     The water of the River swells,
         its northerly flow rushes.
     Stretched nets still the water, *gwat-gwat!*
25   sturgeons beat their tails, *pwat-pwat!*
     Rushes and sedges reach high.
     Attendant ladies, hair coiffed high,
         attendant knights, so forceful.

     58

     It takes a very stupid dolt
         to bring cloth to trade for silk.
     He didn't come to trade for silk,
         he came to bargain for me!
5   I'll escort you sir across the Ch'i,
         till we come to Heap Hill.
     Its not that I want to prolong the date,
         but sir you have no go-between.
     I beg you sir be not angry,
10   let's make it autumn that we wed.

     I climb that broken-down wall
         to look for your return to the barrier;
     When I do not see your approach
         my tears flow unccasingly.
15   When I've seen your return to the barrier,
         then I smile, then I chatter;
     You divine with shells, divine with stalks,
         the signs contain no evil words.
     You come with your cart
20   to remove me and my dowry.

     Before the mulberry has shed,
         its leaves are so glossy!
     Beware, oh dove!
         eat not the fruits of the mulberry!
25   Beware, oh girl!
         dally not with a knight!

A knight's dalliances are overlooked,
    but a girl's are never forgiven.

When the mulberry sheds,
30   its leaves turn yellow and fall.
Since I went with you,
    for three years I have swallowed poverty.
When the Ch'i floods,
    it wets the curtains of a carriage.
35   The girl didn't change,
    though the knight was deceiving.
The knight was inconstant,
    his favors cast this way and that.

For three years I was your wife,
40   without tiring of household chores.
Early to rise and late to bed,
    without a morning's leisure.
I have stayed on here
    only to meet with this cruelty.
45   My brothers ignore me,
    if they knew they'd jeer at me.
When I calmly ponder it,
    I see I have hurt myself.

We were to grow old together as one
50   but growing old has made me an object of scorn.
The Ch'i has its banks,
    the marsh has its sides.
During the gay times of hair tied in girlish horns,
    the chatter and laughter were so pleasant.
55   The promises and oaths were so earnest,
    I never thought it'd change.
That it would change was unthinkable to me
    and now all is ended.

63

Foxes move in pairs
    on the dam in the Ch'i.
Oh, how worried is my heart,
    that child has no skirt.

5   Foxes move in pairs
    on the stones in the Ch'i.
Oh, how worried is my heart,
    that child has no belt.

Foxes move in pairs
10   by the side of the Ch'i.
Oh, how worried is my heart,
    that child has no coat.

64

Throw me a quince
    and I'll repay you with carnelian.
Though not a worthy repayment,
    long may you find pleasure in it.

5   Throw me a peach,
    and I'll repay you with turquoise.
Though not a worthy repayment,
    long may you find pleasure in it.

Throw me a plum
10   and I'll repay you with obsidian.
Though not a worthy repayment,
    long may you find pleasure in it.

76

Please, Sir Second-born,
    don't jump our village wall,
    don't break our planted willows.
Would I dare begrudge them?
5   I simply fear my parents.
Though you, Sir, I cherish,
    I also fear my parents' words.

Please, Sir Second-born,
    don't jump our outer wall,
10   don't break our planted mulberries.
Would I dare begrudge them?
    I simply fear my elder brothers.
Though you, Sir, I cherish
    I also fear my brothers' words.

15   Please, Sir Second-born,
    don't jump our garden wall,
    don't break our planted spindletrees.
Would I dare begrudge them?
    I simply fear the gossip of other people.
20   Though you, Sir, I cherish,
    I also fear the gossip of other people.

113

Big rats! Big rats!
    Don't eat our millet!
For three years we've spoiled you,
    but none of you has requited us.
5   It's got to the point where we'll leave you
    and go to that happy land.
Happy land! Happy land!
    There we'll find a place.

Big rats! Big rats!
10   Don't eat our wheat!
For three years we've spoiled you,
    but none of you has rewarded us.
It's got to the point where we'll leave you
    and go to that happy state.
15 Happy state! Happy state!
There we'll find a proper place.

Big rats! Big rats!
    Don't eat our sprouting grain!
For three years we've spoiled you,
10   but none of you has thanked us.
It's got to the point where we'll leave you
    and go to that happy frontier.
Happy frontier! Happy frontier!
    Who moans and groans there?

154

In the seventh month, declining is the Fire Star;
    in the ninth month, you must distribute clothes.
If not, in the days of the first month, when the cold wind blows,
    in the days of the second month, when the chill air stirs,
5   noblemen will lack their robes, the poor will lack their flannels.
    How then will they end the year?
In the days of the third month, attend to the plow;
    in the days of the fourth month, raise high your heel.
Our assembled wives and children
10   bring food offerings to those southern fields;
The Chief of the Fields comes and enjoys the banquet.

In the seventh month, declining is the Fire Star;
    in the ninth month, you must distribute clothes.
When the spring days become warm
15   and singing is the oriole,

the women grasp their deep baskets
  and follow along tiny paths,
there to seek tender mulberry leaves.
"As the spring days lengthen
20   we gather in crowds to pick the multiflora."
The girl's heart is deeply pained,
  but she'll meet a young nobleman and join him in marriage.

In the seventh month, declining is the Fire Star;
  in the eighth month, the rushes and sedges are prepared.
25 In the silkworm month, separate the branches of the mulberry;
  Take those axes and hatchets,
use them to cut the branches that extend far and reach high,
  and bundle those mulberry shoots.
In the seventh month, singing is the shrike;
30   when it is the eighth month, then spin,
  spin both black and yellow.
My vermilion dye is very bright,
  I make a skirt for a young nobleman.

In the fourth month, seeding is the *yao* grass;
35   in the fifth month, singing is the cicada.
In the eighth month you should harvest;
  in the tenth month, the trees shed and leaves fall.
In the days of the first month, go and hunt badgers;
  Catch those foxes and raccoon-dogs
40   and make fur garments for a young nobleman.
In the days of the second month, you should go on the joint hunt
  and thus augment your military prowess;
Keep for yourselves the year-old boars
  but present to your sire the three-year-old boars.
45 In the fifth month, the locusts shake their legs;
  in the sixth month, the grasshoppers flutter their wings.
In the seventh month, it is in the barrens;
  and in the eighth month, under the eaves.
In the ninth month, it is at the doorway;
50   and in the tenth month, the cricket enters and stays beneath the bed.
Stop up the holes and smoke out the rats;
  block the northern window and plaster the door.
Oh, wife and children!
  Because we are passing into a new year,
55   enter this shelter and stay here.

In the sixth month, eat wild plums and cherries;
  in the seventh month, boil the mallows and pulse.

In the eighth month, harvest the dates;
   in the tenth month, reap the rice.
60 Make this spring wine
   with which to increase vigorous old age.
In the seventh month, eat melons;
   in the eighth month, cut gourds.
In the ninth month, gather hemp seeds,
65   pick bitter herbs, chop ailanto into firewood,
   thus help nourish our chief husbandman.

In the ninth month, ram the earth of the threshing floor;
   and in the tenth month, bring in the harvest:
the glutinous millet and the panicled millet,
70   the late-ripening grains and those that ripen early,
   the hemp, the pulse, and the wheat.
Oh, chief husbandman!
   Our harvest is gathered together;
   Enter and manage the tasks of the palace.
75 If at dawn you attend to the floss grass,
   at dusk you weave the ropes.
Quickly mend the thatch on the roof
   and start to scatter the myriad grains.

In the days of the second month,
80   cut chunks of ice, *dong-dong!*
In the days of the third month,
   store them in the ice house.
In the days of the fourth month,
   rise early to present lamb and offer onions.
85 In the ninth month, things shrivel with the frost;
   in the tenth month, clean the threshing floor.
Twin wine vessels are offered as a feast
   and then slaughter lambs and sheep.
Enter that Noble Hall
90   and lift in a toast the rhino cup:
   May you live forever and without end!

158

How do you cut an ax-handle?
   Only an ax can do it!
How do you take a bride?
   Only a go-between can succeed!
5 In cutting an ax-handle, in cutting an ax-handle,
   the model is near at hand.

I have joined with that girl;
  basket and platter are aligned.

191

Towering is that southern mountain,
  its rocks are piled high;
So eminent is Master Yin,
  the people all gaze at you.
5 Their grieved hearts are burning
  and they dare not even joke or chat.
The state is on the verge of ruin,
  Why do you not attend to your duties?

Towering is that southern mountain,
10   its vegetation grows luxuriantly.
So eminent is Master Yin,
  how come your inequities?
Heaven sends repeated plagues,
  death and chaos increase and multiply.
15 The people have no praise for you
  and nobody prohibits their curses.

Sir Yin, Grand Master:
Be the foundation of the Chou
  and maintain the state's stability.
20 The Four Quarters—these hold together;
  the Son of Heaven—him assist.
Keep the people from being disloyal.
Oh, Bright Heaven, you are merciless!
  It is not right that you deplete our armies.

25 The ruler is neither personal nor close;
  so the mass of people are not reliable.
He does not inquire and does not consult;
  may the people not cheat their superiors.
Be just, be moderate,
30   and you will avoid the danger of petty men.
The paltry relatives by marriage,
  these should not be generously employed.

Oh, Bright Heaven, because he is not fair,
  sends down this excess of quarrels;
35 Oh, Bright Heaven, because he is not harmonious,
  brings about great discord.
If the ruler is moderate
  he brings rest to the people's hearts;

If the ruler is easy,
40   animosity and hatred—these are averted.

Oh, Bright Heaven, you are merciless!
    There is no end to the turmoil,
Oh, it grows by the month
    and causes the people to know no peace.
45 Their grieving hearts are as if drunk;
    who maintains the integrity of the state?
If you do not personally govern,
    in the end you will make the Hundred Names toil.

I yoke those four stallions;
50   but the four stallions swell their necks in resistance;
I gaze at the four quarters;
    but there is no place at all to go.

Now you let your evil flourish;
    I see your lances.
55 When we have peace, when we have ease,
    then you will witness our requital.

Oh, Bright Heaven, there is no peace.
    Our king is not tranquil;
He does not examine his own heart,
60   but contrarily resents his chief officers.

An elder has made his lament,
    to set forth entirely our quarrels with the king.
Oh, change your heart
    and thereby nurture the myriad states.

210

Extensive the lands flanking that southern mountain—
    it was Yü who laid out the ground for tillage;
Arable the plains and wetlands—
    the distant descendant made them into fields.
5 We draw boundaries and establish divisions,
    making acreage to the south and to the east.

The sky above has been filled with clouds:
    a very heavy winter snowfall
was followed by spring showers.
10   The soil is damp, it is moist!
It is soaking, it is wet!
    It gives birth to our myriad grains!

The borders-and-bounds are well regulated,
   the millet crop abundant.
15 The harvest tax collected by the distant descendant
      he makes into liquor and food
which he gives the impersonator and guests.
   May he enjoy a long life of ten thousand years!

In the inner fields are huts,
20   gourds grow along the borders-and-bounds;
These he slices and these he pickles
   and presents them to the august ancestors.
Long life to the distant descendant;
   may he receive good fortune!

25 He offers first the pure liquor
      and follows it with a red bull;
These are for the enjoyment of the ancestral elders.
   He grasps the knife with jingling bells
to lay open the furry hide of the victim
30   and he takes its blood and fat.

These he presents and these he offers—
   they are fragrant and sweet-smelling.
The offering rites are very bright;
   grandly come the ancestors.
35 They reward him with great blessings—
      a long life without end!

245

The one who first gave birth to our people,
   this was Chiang Yüan.
How did she give birth to our people?
   She knew to make the Yin and Ssu offerings,
5 thereby to eliminate her barrenness.
   She trod on the toe-print made by God.
She was the one enriched, the one on whom the blessing rested.
   She became pregnant, she refrained from sex;
She gave birth to him, she nurtured him—
10   He was Lord Millet.

Truly she went her full term;
   her first-born came forth easily like a lamb.
He did not tear, he did not rend;
   there was no injury, no harm.

15   Thus, He made evident his magic power.
          Did not God-on-High give her comfort?
      Did He not enjoy her Yin and Ssu offerings?
          For tranquilly she gave birth to the child.

      Truly she placed him in a narrow lane
20   where oxen and sheep protected and cherished him;
      Truly she placed him in a forested plain
          where he was met with by woodcutters;
      Truly she placed him on cold ice
          where birds covered him with their wings—
25   When the birds left,
          Lord Millet bawled!

      He sat up, he cried out,
          and his voice was already strong;
      Truly he crawled about,
30   able to raise himself up expectantly and stand resolutely erect.
      And when he sought to feed himself
          he planted giant beans.
      The giant beans grew tall,
          the ears of grain grew luxuriantly;
35   The hemp and wheat grew thick,
          the gourds were abundant.

      Truly Lord Millet's husbandry
          was a divinely aided method.
      He cleared the thick grasses,
40   and planted the fields with the yellow crop.
      It grew evenly, it became luxuriant,
          it grew singly, it grew tall;
      It flowered, it eared,
          it was firm, it was fine;
45   Its ears ripened, its kernels hardened.
          Accordingly he took T'ai for his house-and-home.

      Truly God sent down the blessed grains:
          the black millet, the double-kerneled;
      the millet vermilion-sprouted and white.
50   He spread the black millet and the double-kerneled,
      these he reaped and gathered by the acre;
          He spread the vermilion and white millet,
      these he carried on his shoulder and on his back.
          He brought them home and made an offering.

55 Truly, how do we make our offerings?
    Some pound the grain, others bale it out;
Some sift, some tread;
    We wash it—sop sop,
and boil it till it's steamy.
60   We plan and we ponder;
We pick southern wood and offer fat,
    take a ram to offer to the spirit of the road;
Then we roast and we broil,
    to initiate the new year.

65 High we load the footed vessels;
    we place it on the footed vessels and stands.
Its aroma starts to ascend
    and God-on-High, well pleased, savors it:
"What smell is this, so pure and good?"
    Lord Millet inaugurated the offerings,
and without our suffering any blame or regret,
    they have continued till now.

253

The common people are very weary
    and now might be allowed a little repose;
Be kind to this Central Kingdom
    and thereby comfort the four quarters.
5 Indulge not the wily and obsequious
    and so instill care in the wicked;
Crush the robbers and tyrants
    for they have not respected your brightness.
Be gentle to those far off, be good to those nearby,
    and so make our king secure.

The common people are very weary
    and now might be allowed a little rest;
Be kind to this Central Kingdom
    so that the people will gather here.
15 Indulge not the wily and obsequious
    and so instill care in the catcallers;
Crush the robbers and tyrants
    so the people will not be made to suffer.
Neglect not your labors
20   so our king will enjoy rest.

The common people are very weary
    and now might be allowed a little respite;

Be kind to this Capital City
  and thereby comfort the four states
25 Indulge not the wily and obsequious
  and so instill care in the excessive;
Crush the robbers and tyrants,
  prevent them from doing evil.
Be mindful of your awesome bearing
30 and so bring near the virtuous.

The common people are very weary
  and now might be allowed a little relief;
Be kind to this Central Kingdom
  so that the people's cares will drain away.
35 Indulge not the wily and obsequious
  and so instill care in the evil;
Crush the robbers and tyrants,
  let them not ruin the upright.
Although you are but as small children
40 your effect is vast and great.

The common people are very weary
  and now might be allowed a little peace;
Be kind to this Central Kingdom
  so that it will suffer no injury.
45 Indulge not the wily and obsequious
  and so instill care in the parasites;
Crush the robbers and tyrants,
  let them not overturn the upright.
Oh, king, I wish to make you like jade,
50 and so have resorted to this great remonstrance.

256

Make quiet, so quiet, your awesome bearing,
  verily it is the counterpart to virtue.
Others, too, have a saying,
  "All the wise are stupid."
5 The stupidity of the commoners
  is merely a natural flaw from which they suffer;
The stupidity of the wise
  is because they fear committing an offense.

The man who is not contentious—
10 the four quarters receive instruction from him;
The virtuous acts that are restrained—
  the four states obey them.

Boldly scheming and giving orders
　　his plans are far-seeing and his announcements timely;
15　Be careful and watchful of your awesome bearing,
　　verily be the model of the people.

He who presides over us now
　　promotes confusion and chaos in government;
He upsets and overturns his virtue
20　　and is wildly steeped in liquor.
Although you are steeped in pleasure and looseness,
　　ought you not think of your descendants?
Should you not broadly seek your royal predecessor
　　so that you can embrace his holy pattern?

25　That is why Heaven does not now support you.
　　Be like yon spring that flows;
　　be not channeled into oblivion.
Rise at dawn and sleep at night.
　　Wash and sweep within the courtyard;
30　　Verily be the standard for the people.
Tend well your carriages and horses,
　　your bows, arrows, spears, and swords.
These prepare you should war arise
　　and control you the lands of the barbarian Man.

35　Come to terms with your men and people,
　　be heedful of the measures by which you rule;
　　these prepare you for the unexpected.
Be watchful of the orders you give,
　　be careful of your awesome bearing,
40　　in all ways be mild and good.
A flaw in white jade
　　may still be polished away;
But a flaw in your words
　　cannot be repaired.

45　Be not careless in issuing orders;
　　do not say, "It does not matter.
None can restrain my tongue."
　　Orders cannot be made to disappear.
There is no order that is not answered,
50　　no act of kindness not repaid.
Be generous with friends and acquaintances,
　　the common people, the very young.

May sons and grandsons form an unbroken line,
    and the myriad people all obey.

55 When seen befriending a gentleman,
    you make your countenance harmonious and mild,
    not far off are there transgressions.
  Be observant and attentive of your house—
    Are you still not fearful in your curtained enclosure?
60 Do not say, "It is not public.
    No one meets me here."
  The arrival of the spirits, oh,
    can never be predicted, oh,
    how much less may they be ignored, oh.

65 Regulate your acts of leniency,
    make them admirable, make them praiseworthy;
  Be sincerely attentive to your demeanor,
    make no errors in your bearing;
  Be not untrustworthy, be not injurious,
70   and few will fail to follow you.
  "If someone throws me a peach,
    I repay him with a plum."
  But that youngster who butts with his horns,
    he is a troublesome knave.

75 Because the pliant wood is soft and tender,
    one strings it with silk;
  Because the reverent man is warm and genial,
    he is the fundament of virtue.
  A wise man, when I instruct him with my words,
80   adheres to the course of virtue;
  But he who is stupid
    contrarily calls me untrustworthy.
  Each kind of person has his own mind.

  Oh, you young one!
85   You do not recognize the good from the bad.
  If I am not leading you by the hand,
    I am having to show you;
  If I am not ordering you face-to-face,
    I am pulling you by the ear.
90 Some people excuse you saying you still lack understanding,
    But you have already held your own son!

When the people are dissatisfied,
    who can learn of it in the morning,
    but wait till evening to settle it?

95   Shining Heaven is bright,
    but my life lacks joy;
When I see you so benighted,
    my heart is so dejected.
I teach you earnestly
100   but you listen to me heedlessly;
You do not take my words as a means to govern
    but take them as a means to oppress.
Some people excuse you saying you still lack understanding.
    But you have already reached senility!

105 Oh, you little one!
    I instruct you in the old manners.
Heed and use my advice
    and have no cause for great regret!
Heaven is now causing difficulties
110   and hence will cause him to lose his state.
I have picked analogies that are not exotic.
    Shining Heaven does not err.
But he twists and perverts his own virtue
    and causes the people great anxiety.

280

The blind musicians, the blind musicians,
    are here in the courtyard of Chou.
In place are the cross-board and post of the bell-frame,
    protruding teeth and erect feathers decorate them,
5   There are the drums small and large, the hanging drums,
    the tambourines and lithophones, the sounding-box and scraper.
When all is readied, then they play:
    the panpipes and flutes all begin.
Ringing are their sounds,
10   solemn and harmonious the blend of notes;
    our forebears and ancestors listen to it.
Our guests have come,
    long they look upon their accomplishments.

Translated by Jeffrey Riegel

23

The Needle and Thread

Pan Chao (45–120?)

Strong spirit of pure steel, from autumn's metal cast;[1]
Incarnate body of power, slight and subtle, straight and sharp!
To pierce, then to enter gradually in, that is your nature;
Things far apart all strung into one,[2] that is your task.

Only your ordered footprints, you wonderful needle and thread,
Attest the quantity, the variety, the universality of your work.
You retrace, you sway, you twist in your path to mend flaws,
Until the results resemble the pure wool of the lamb.[3]

What measure or basket suffices to count the pieces of your work?
All, all together these are your memorials.
They are found in the village home;
They ascend into the stately hall.

Translated by Nancy Lee Swann

This poem (actually labeled as a "rhapsody" [*fu*]) should be read in conjunction with the same author's *Lessons for Women* (selection 194), with which it shares many points of agreement concerning the character and morals deemed appropriate for women of the upper classes during the first century.
   1. Of the five elements or phases (wood, fire, water, metal, and earth), autumn is associated with metal.
   2. Echoes two passages in the *Analects* (selection 7), where Confucius claims that his way is to string things together into one.
   3. In China the lamb, which always kneels when suckled by the dam, was associated with filial piety.

24

Seven Sorrows

Wang Ts'an (177–217)

The Western Capital[1] is disordered and lawless;
Wolves and tigers have brought on disaster.

The Six Dynasties author and critic Shen Yüeh (see selection 31) praised this poem (the first of two by the poet with the same title) as one of the best in the tradition in his land-

I'll leave behind the Middle Kingdom
4 And stay far away among the tribes of Ching.[2]
Relatives face me sadly;
Friends hang on and cling.
Out of the city gate I see nothing
8 But white bones covering the plain.
By the road a starving woman
Embraces her child, then leaves it in the weeds.
She looks back, hears it bawl and cry,
12 Wipes her tears without going back.
"I don't know where I shall die myself;
How could I save the two of us?"
Spurring my horse, I leave her behind,
16 Not bearing to hear such words.
To the south, I climb the Pa-ling mound,[3]
Turn my head, and gaze[4] upon Ch'ang-an.
Understanding now the poet of "The Lower Springs,"[5]
20 I heave a painful sigh.

Translated by Richard W. Bodman

---

mark "Afterword to the Biography of Hsieh Ling-yün" in *History of the Sung*, ch. 67. Wang Ts'an is considered the most brilliant of the Seven Masters of the Chien-an Reign (196–220) who enjoyed the patronage of the powerful Ts'ao family (see selection 170).

"Seven Sorrows" is a formal verse category beginning with either Wang Ts'an or Ts'ao Chih (see selection 26). This is the first of a set of three in this formal category (or subgenre) of verse. The content of Wang Ts'an's poem is historical; it refers to the fall of Ch'ang-an and the poet's self-exile in 193 C.E.

1. The Western Capital was Ch'ang-an, which means "Long[-lasting] Peace."

2. Ching, an old name for Ch'u, lay to the south and the southwest.

3. Pa-ling was the funeral mound of Emperor Wen of the Han dynasty, whose reign (179–156 B.C.E.) was noted for its political and economic stability.

4. The word *wang* ("to look, gaze") can also mean "to hope." Hence this line can also be read: "Turning my head, I hope for long-lasting peace."

5. This phrase alludes to poem no. 153 of the same title in the *Classic of Odes* (selection 22), the first stanza of which reads: "Cool is that down-flowing spring, / It overflows the bushy *lang* plants; / Moaning I awake and sigh, / I think of that capital of Chou." Scholars in the Han period interpreted this poem as a longing for political stability. "Lower Springs" could also be interpreted as "Nether Springs" or "Netherworld." The last two lines incorporate several ambiguities and permit several different translations: 1. "I understand the author of the 'Lower Springs,' who sighs and breaks his heart"; 2. "I understand the man beneath the nether springs (i.e., Han emperor Wen) who sighs and breaks his heart (at the state of the world today)"; 3. "I understand the men beneath the nether springs (i.e., all the dead); we/they sigh and break our/their hearts." Hence the last couplet incorporates a moment of understanding and even epiphany, in which the poet realizes his identity with the poets of the past and his sympathy with all the dead, present and past.

25
Poem Without a Category

Liu Chen (d. 217)

Office work: a wearisome jumble;
ink drafts: a crosshatch of deletions and smears.
Racing the writing brush, no time to eat,
4   sun slanting down but never a break;
swamped and muddled in records and reports,
head spinning till it's senseless and numb—
I leave off and go west of the wall,
8   climb the height and let my eyes roam:
square embankments hold back the clear water,
wild ducks and geese at rest in the middle—
Where can I get a pair of whirring wings
12   so I can join you to bob on the waves?

Translated by Burton Watson

The title may also be rendered as "Miscellaneous Poem." A great deal of the poetry written during the latter part of the Eastern Han dynasty, as well as later, was occasional in nature, that is to say, it was composed at banquets, outings, or farewell parties, or was addressed to a particular individual and sent with, or in lieu of, a letter. The title "Miscellaneous Poem" was applied to pieces which did not fit into any of the various categories of occasional poetry but which represent the private musings of the poet. They tend to be introspective, charged with feeling, and at times couched in highly metaphorical language. Liu Chen was an official in the service of the Ts'ao family who, at the time this poem was written, shortly before 217, were feudal rulers with their capital in the city of Yeh in Honan. Like Wang Ts'an (see selection 24), Liu Chen was a distinguished member of the Seven Masters of the Chien-an Reign who were patronized by Ts'ao Ts'ao (see selection 170) and his two literarily minded sons, Ts'ao Chih (see selection 26) and Ts'ao P'i (see note to selection 17).

Cockfight

Liu Chen

The cinnabar cockerels sport resplendent hues,
Their paired spurs like tips of blades.
Ready to parade their blazing might,
4   They join in battle on this courtyard path.

Sharp claws test the jade steps,
Glaring eyes are infused with fiery light;
Long tail-feathers lift in a startling wind,
8   Hackle quills spread in display.
They spring and wield bent beaks,
Strike like lightning and again fly back.

Translated by Robert Joe Cutter

26
Ballad of the Orioles in the Fields

Ts'ao Chih (192–232)

The tall trees are full of sad wind;
The sea water rises in billows.
Without a keen sword in hand,
4   What's the use of plentiful ties of friendship?
Don't you see the oriole in the hedge?
Seeing a hawk, he tumbles into the net.
The fowler is glad to get the oriole.
8   A young man is sad to see the bird caught;
He grasps his sword and cuts the net away.
The oriole gets free, he flies and flies;
He flies and flies, upward, touching the blue sky
12   And down again, to thank the young man.

Translated by Hans H. Frankel

Despite the complex family relationships, Ts'ao Chih is usually said to be the third son of Ts'ao Ts'ao (see selection 170), the famous general and later king of the late Eastern Han and Three Kingdoms period. Ts'ao Chih was kept in political isolation by his older brother, Ts'ao P'i, designated heir to their father's throne. This accounts for the sadness that informs much of his writings, but it did not prevent him from being active in literary circles.

27
Songs of My Soul

Juan Chi (210–263)

1

It is the middle of the night—I cannot sleep,
I sit up to pluck my dulcet lute;
Through thin curtains, I view the bright moon,
A soothing breeze blows at my lapels.

A lone goose cries in the wild beyond,
A soaring bird sings in the woods to the north;
Pacing to and fro, I wonder what my future will bring—
Anxious and alone, my poor heart is broken.

49

My steps lead me to a junction of three roads,
I ruefully recall the object of my thoughts;
Could it be that I shall see him this morning?
Verily, he would seem to appear nebulously.

In the marsh a towering pine tree grows,
I cannot hope for its span of ten thousand generations;
The high-flying birds brush against the sky,
Happily they roam together above the clouds.

But here I am, a lonely man walking along the road;
Tears falling, I bemoan the days gone by.

50

The lucent dew congeals into frost,
Flowering grasses give way to mugwort and goosefoot;
Who says that the ruler's sagacity
And perspicuity can long endure?

Juan Chi was a member of the Seven Sages of the Bamboo Grove, a group of poet-intellectuals noted for their eccentric behavior and aloofness from official life. His most famous poems, a series of eighty-two pieces called "Songs of My Soul," evince a mood of deep pessimism and sorrow in keeping with the atmosphere of the times. He made extensive use of symbolic language, probably to avoid the suspicions of those in power. Juan Chi lamented the shortness of life as well as the stupidity and ill will of his contemporaries. He longed for liberation or, at least, a true friend to console him in his melancholy.

So I'll mount a cloud and summon immortal Sung and Wang,
Who will teach me how to respire[1] and live forever!

56

Whether one is eminent or humble depends on Fate,
Success and failure each has its own season.

Genial, glib-tongued good-for-nothings
Cheat each other in pursuit of profit;
Ingrates degrade grace bestowed,
And expose it to the scorn of slanderers.

The wagtail chirrups among the clouds,
Flying continuously with nothing to hope for,
How could one expect that the man who kept aloof
One day would be unable to preserve himself?

59

An elder lives by the side of the river,
He weaves baskets of reeds and throws away pearls;[2]
He finds pigweed and pulse sweet to his taste,
And enjoys his hut of wattle and thatch.

How could he ape those fine, young dandies,
Who go riding in light chariots drawn by fine horses?
In the morning, they are born beside the best highways,
In the evening, they are buried at the edges of byways.

Before our joy and laughter have come to an end,
We find ourselves sighing and sobbing in the twinkling of an eye;
As I observe these flighty fellows,
I express my indignation with these words.

60

The Confucianist is versed in the Six Arts,[3]
Once his mind is made up, nothing can sway him;
He will do nothing which contravenes the Rites,
And will say nothing which is contrary to the Law.

If he is thirsty, he drinks from a pure stream,
And, even when hungry, eats but a bamboo bowl of rice in two days.

---

1. A reference to the Yogic breathing techniques of the Taoist practitioners. Sung is Ch'ih
Sung Tzu, Master Red Pine; Wang is Wang-tzu Ch'iao. Both were Taoist transcendents.
2. An allusion to the penultimate parable in the *Chuang Tzu*, ch. 32 (see selection 9).
3. Ritual or ceremony, music, archery, charioteering, writing, numbers.

He has nothing to sacrifice at the seasons of the year;
Through his clothing he often feels the bitter cold.

Shuffling along in his sandals, he chants "South Wind,"
In his coarse gown, he laughs at the fancy chariots;
He has faith in the Way and holds fast to *Poetry* and *History*,
Righteously he will not accept a single free meal.

But his criticism is so caustic
That Lao Tzu could only heave a long sigh of despair.

71

The hibiscus grows lushly on the grave mounds,
It shines with scintillating brilliance;
But when the bright sun plummets into the forest,
Its petals flutter forlornly by the roadside.

The cricket chirrups by my windowsill,
The cicada buzzes amidst the brambles;
Ephemerids' play lasts only three mornings,
Then they die in a teeming heap of pretty wings.

For whom do they put on all their finery?
It is just self-preening as they drift with the time;
Ah! How very short is life's alloted span!
Still, impassioned, each being pours forth all of its energy.

Translated by Victor H. Mair

28

Poem on the Wandering Immortal[1]

Kuo P'u (276–324)

Kingfishers frolic among the orchid blossoms,
each form and hue lending freshness to the others.
Green creepers twine over the tall grove,
4   their leafy darkness shadowing the whole hill.

The poet was a Taoist mystic, geomancer, collector of strange tales, editor of old texts, and erudite commentator.

1. The word for "immortal" *(hsien)* is elsewhere in this anthology sometimes translated as "transcendent." Neither translation is entirely satisfactory for rendering this technical term which signifies someone highly accomplished in various Taoist arts for prolonging life. Translations such as "fairy" or "god" are even less suitable.

And in the midst, a man of quiet retirement
softly whistles, strokes the clear lute strings,
frees his thoughts to soar beyond the blue,
8   munches flower stamens, dips from a waterfall.
When Red Pine[2] appears, roaming on high,
this man rides a stork, mounting the purple mists,
his left hand holding Floating Hill's sleeve,
12   his right hand patting Vast Cliff on the shoulder.
Let me ask those short-lived mayflies,
what could they know of the years of the tortoise and the crane?

Translated by Burton Watson

2. Red Pine, Floating Hill, and Vast Cliff are all legendary immortals of ancient times.

29
Substance, Shadow, and Spirit

T'ao Ch'ien (365–427)

Noble or base, wise or stupid, none but cling tenaciously to life. This is a great delusion. I have put in the strongest terms the complaints of Substance and Shadow and then, to resolve the matter, have made Spirit the spokesman for naturalness. Those who share my tastes will all get what I am driving at.

I *Substance to Shadow*

Earth and heaven endure forever,
Streams and mountains never change.
Plants observe a constant rhythm,
4   Withered by frost, by dew restored.
But man, most sentient being of all,
In this is not their equal.
He is present here in the world today,
8   Then leaves abruptly, to return no more.
No one marks there's one man less—
Not even friends and family think of him;

T'ao Ch'ien, also called T'ao Yüan-ming, lived in the Six Dynasties, a period of disunity when northern China had fallen into the hands of non-Chinese leaders. The south, where T'ao lived, was ruled by a succession of weak and short-lived dynasties that had their capitals in modern Nanking.

The things that he once used are all that's left
12   To catch their eye and move them to grief.
I have no way to transcend change,
That it must be, I no longer doubt.
I hope you will take my advice:
16   When wine is offered, don't refuse.

II *Shadow to Substance*

No use discussing immortality
When just to keep alive is hard enough.
Of course I want to roam in paradise,

Of Hsi ancestry (that is, of non-Han origins), the poet was born into a family of a minor official. He was proud of his distinguished great-grandfather T'ao K'an, who had been enfeoffed as Duke of Ch'ang-sha for his services to the Chin dynasty. His maternal grandfather, Meng Chia, was a close associate of Huan Wen, a powerful figure in China at the time. Feeling an obligation to continue the family tradition of government service, T'ao Ch'ien had served as secretary or adviser to various generals, but none of the positions was very satisfying to him; he continually yearned to return to the pastoral life. In the year 415, through the assistance of an uncle, he was appointed magistrate of P'eng-tse, a post he held only for eighty days before retiring from public service for good. For twenty-two years after that, T'ao Ch'ien led a farmer's life and experienced all the hardships that it entailed. He was much admired, both by his contemporaries and by succeeding generations, for never compromising his ideals. But now he is recognized even more for the greatness of his poetry and essays.

The immediate source of the poem entitled "Substance, Shadow, and Spirit" has been sought in the Buddho-Taoist polemics of the poet's own times, and it is quite possible that T'ao Ch'ien may have found there his inspiration for the labels he gave his three components of a man. Substance focuses on the inescapable fact of human mortality, acceptable only by recourse to the wine bottle. He speaks of techniques for "transcending change" (from later chapters of the *Classic of Documents*, see selection 188, or, more likely, from *Lieh Tzu*, see selection 12), which would seem to make him a believer in that sort of Taoism which went in for alchemy, dietary regimens, and breath control in search of longevity. Shadow is clearly Confucian in desiring a reputation for good deeds that will live after him. Spirit, having claimed for himself a special position among the three, brushes aside the proposals of the others and comes out for a stoical acceptance of life and death. Substance, Shadow, and Spirit can thus each be regarded as a spokesman for a philosophy of life, though the omission of a representative of a Buddhist point of view seems odd unless we accept that the poet ultimately rejects it in favor of a more indigenous outlook. There are, however, more distant—but still unmistakable—parallels to a poem entitled "Warning, to Be Pure," attributed to Kao Yi-fang of the Later Han period, who is otherwise unknown:

Heaven is eternal and earth endures
But human life is different from these. . . .
Drinking wine harms my nature
Pensive thought injures my spirit. . . .
Body and breath leave one another.
Once gone there's no returning again. . . .

4   But it's a long way there and the road is lost.
    In all the time since I met up with you
    We never differed in our grief and joy.
    In shade we may have parted for a time,
8   But sunshine always brings us close again.
    Still this union cannot last forever—
    Together we will vanish into darkness.
    The body goes; that fame should also end
12 Is a thought that makes me burn inside.
    Do good, and your love will outlive you;
    Surely this is worth your every effort.
    While it is true, wine may dissolve care
16 That is not so good a way as this.

III *Spirit's Solution*

    The Great Potter[1] cannot intervene—
    All creation thrives of itself.
    That Man ranks with Earth and Heaven
4   Is it not because of me?
    Though we belong to different orders,
    Being alive, I am joined to you.
    Bound together for good or ill
8   I cannot refuse to tell you what I know:
    The Three August Ones[2] were great saints
    But where are they living today?
    Though P'eng-tsu[3] lasted a long time
12 He still had to go before he was ready.
    Die old or die young, the death is the same;
    Wise or stupid, there is no difference.[4]
    Drunk every day you may forget,
16 But won't it shorten your life span?
    Doing good is always a joyous thing
    But no one has to praise you for it.
    Too much thinking harms my life;

    1. A Taoist metaphor for the creator of the universe and all within it.
    2. The first three emperors according to Chinese myth (Fu-hsi, the Divine Farmer, and the Yellow Emperor).
    3. The Chinese equivalent of Methuselah.
    4. These two lines reflect a passage from *Lieh Tzu* (see selection 12): "Among the living there are wise and foolish, noble and mean: this is how they differ. Dead there is corruption and extinction: it is in this that they are the same. . . . Ten-year-olds die and centenarians die, the good and the saintly die, and the wicked and the stupid die."

20   Just surrender to the cycle of things,
     Give yourself to the waves of the Great Change,
     Neither happy nor yet afraid.
     And when it is time to go, then simply go
24   Without any unnecessary fuss.

Translated by James Robert Hightower

Poems After Drinking Wine (No. 5)

T'ao Ch'ien

     I built my hut beside a traveled road
     Yet hear no noise of passing carts and horses.
     You would like to know how it is done?
4   With the mind detached, one's place becomes remote.
     Picking chrysanthemums by the eastern hedge
     I catch sight of the distant southern hills:
     The mountain air is lovely as the sun sets

It is easy to understand why this is one of T'ao Ch'ien's most famous poems and one of the most celebrated and oft-quoted poems in the whole of the Chinese literary tradition. It conveys admirably the detachment and repose of the Great Recluse who makes his home among men yet remains uncontaminated by the world, whose communion with nature occurs as readily through the chrysanthemums by the eastern hedge as through the distant mountain scenery. A fundamental truth seems to have been communicated, even as the post suggests, without having been formulated in words.

Some such reading of the poem seems to have inspired the seven pages of effusions by traditional commentators in the *Collected Criticisms*. That it is an inadequate understanding of a poem considerably more complex than that is best demonstrated by a detailed examination; essentially the clue is in the allusion that underlies lines 5–6.

The first line begins with an expression *chieh lu*, which suggests "thatched hut," though the verb *chieh* is common enough in combination with words meaning "building" or "house." Actually the line says nothing about a "traveled road"; a closer translation would be, "I built my hut in an inhabited area" (i.e., not off by itself in the wilds).

T'ao Ch'ien attributes his ability to ignore the world while living in it to a "mind that is far away," and the next couplet tells what his absent mind is concerned with. He is picking chrysanthemums, not to put in a vase for decoration, but to use as medicine, probably in a wine infusion. The purpose of such a concoction is to prolong life ("Chrysanthemum is tonic against growing old," as he wrote in another poem, "Living in Retirement on the Double Ninth Festival."), and the Southern Mountain which catches his eye as he is picking the petals is not an irrelevant piece of scenery but a prime symbol of the thing he has in mind. "Longevity like the Southern Mountain" is the irresistible associative link from the *Classic of Odes*, one of T'ao Ch'ien's favorite texts. It provides a touch of irony as much as of reassurance, however, for even a confirmed believer in potions and exercises (which T'ao Ch'ien was not) could hardly hope for

8   And flocks of flying birds return together.
    In these things is a fundamental truth
    I would like to tell, but lack the words.

Translated by James Robert Hightower

---

long life of such dimensions. At the same time, this particular Southern Mountain had for T'ao Ch'ien another not unrelated meaning, which made the Mountain of Long Life the prospective site for his grave.

In Praise of Ching K'o

T'ao Ch'ien

Prince Tan of Yen knew how to treat a man—
His aim was vengeance on mighty Ying.
He long had looked for the man worth a hundred
4   And then as the years ran out he got Ching K'o.
"A gentleman will die for one who knows his worth;
With sword in hand I will leave Yen's capital,
My pallid charger whinnying through the streets
8   As they escort me, filled with high resolve."
The hero's hair thrusts through his high hat,
His valor saturates the long capstring.
A farewell cup beside the River Yi,
12 Around him sit the heroes of the realm.
Kao Chien-li strikes the sad guitar,
Sung Yi sings the high-pitched mournful song.
A plaintive wind begins its lonely wail,
16 The cold waves surge in the swelling flood.
With the Shang mode tune the tears flow fast
When the note *yü* is struck the hero is startled:
He knows he will leave and never return
20 But after him his name will live forever.
He mounted his carriage and never once looked back.
Canopy flying, he headed for the court of Ch'in.

This poem celebrates one of the most famous events of ancient times, Ching K'o's attempted assassination of the First Emperor of Ch'in, the unifier of the Chinese empire. Ssu-ma Ch'ien told the story in a very dramatic form in his *Records of the Grand Historian* (see selection 225), which provides the historical background for a full understanding and appreciation of this poem.

Straight for his goal he dashed, ten thousand miles
24   Around and through a thousand towns he drove.
When the chart unrolled, the thing was there—
Even the intrepid ruler drew back in fear.
Alas, that his swordsmanship was faulty
28   And left the unimaginable deed undone!
Although the man is long since dead and gone,
After a thousand years he inspires us still.

Translated by James Robert Hightower

On Reading the *Seas and Mountains Classic*

T'ao Ch'ien

I

In early summer when the grasses grow
And trees surround my house with greenery,
The birds rejoice to have a refuge there
4   And I, too, love my home.
The fields are plowed and the new seed planted
And now is time again to read my books.
This out-of-the-way lane has no deep-worn ruts[1]
8   And tends to turn my friends' carts away.
With happy face I pour the spring-brewed wine
And in the garden pick some greens to cook.
A gentle shower approaches from the east
12   Accompanied by a temperate breeze.
I skim through the *Story of King Mu*
And view the pictures in the *Seas and Mountains Classic.*

This limpid lyric introduces the series by recreating the ideal occasion for a farmer's reading, the time of leisure after the spring planting. The poet does not expect visitors and finds an excuse for his friends' neglect; philosophically he pours himself a drink and turns to his favorite books. Nothing better dramatizes the dearth of works of the imagination in early Chinese literature than the two which he seizes upon. Both the *Story of King Mu* and the *Seas and Mountains Classic* are the products of fantasy; they freely introduce magic and marvels, but in a form closer to Baedeker than Malory. The first pretends to be history, the second geography; only a mind starved for fiction could rejoice in either. T'ao Ch'ien's enthusiasm is contagious; and if only the books had been safely lost, we could easily share his pleasure. We still can, if we are content to do it vicariously.

1. Deep ruts are a sign of traffic, particularly of the kind of carriage driven by officials.

A glance encompasses the ends of the universe—
16 Where is there any joy, if not in these?

Translated by James Robert Hightower

Blaming Sons

T'ao Ch'ien

White hair shrouds both my temples,
my skin and flesh have lost their fullness.
Though I have five male children,
4   not one of them loves brush and paper.
A-shu's already twice times eight—
in laziness he's never been rivaled.
A-hsüan's going on fifteen
8   but cares nothing for letters or learning.
Yung and Tuan are thirteen
and can't tell a 6 from a 7!
T'ung-tzu's approaching age nine—
12 all he does is hunt for chestnuts and pears.
If this is the luck Heaven sends me,
then pour me the "thing in the cup"!

Translated by Burton Watson

30

On My Way from South Mountain to North Mountain, I Glance at the Scenery from the Lake

Hsieh Ling-yün (385–433)

At dawn I set out from the sunlit cliffs,
At sunset I take my rest by the shaded peaks.

The poet was a descendant of an illustrious and affluent northern émigré family of the Southern Dynasties. He was especially well known for his landscape poetry but was also noted as a devout Buddhist, and many of his works combine his interest in Buddhism with his attachment to the beauties of nature, especially mountains (see introductory note to selection 214). Hsieh

Leaving my boat, I turn my eyes upon the distant sandbars,
4   Resting my staff, I lean against the lush pines.
The small mountain paths are far and deep,
The ring-like islets are beautiful and pleasing.
I view the twigs of tall trees above,
8   I listen to the torrents in the deep valley below.
The rocks lie flat, and the river divides its flow;
The forest is dense, tracks are buried and lost.
What is the effect of Nature's "deliverance" and "becoming"?
12   All things growing are lush and thriving.
Young bamboos are wrapped in green sheaths,
Fresh rushes embrace their purple flowers;
Seagulls play by the springtime banks,
16   Wild pheasants sport in the gentle breeze.

Translated by Kang-i Sun Chang

was censured by literary critics of his own day and succeeding generations for being difficult because he made frequent use of allusion, ambiguity, and parallelism. His work is highly imaginative yet full of natural imagery. He wrote several philosophical prose pieces and was also involved in the translation of key Buddhist scriptures. A headstrong individual, Hsieh was repeatedly banished to the far south and finally executed.

On Climbing the Highest Peak of Stone Gate Mountain

Hsieh Ling-yün

In the morning with my staff I sought the topmost crag;
In the evening I rested in my mountain nest.
Distant peaks oppose my lofty lodge;
4   The facing range looks over twisting streams.
A long grove screens the courtyard door;
Tumbled rocks crowd the entry steps.
Interlinking cliffs make one feel the road is blocked;
8   Dense bamboo makes the paths lose their way.
Arriving guests forget the new-made track;
And departing are misled by an older trail.

Compare this poem with selection 214.

Huo-huo the evening torrents rush;
12　*Chiao-chiao* the nocturnal gibbons howl.
Deep and darkly sunk in meditation, for what better reason
Than never swerving from holding on to the Way?
My heart interlocks with the hardy trunks of autumn;
16　My eyes delight in the tender buds of spring.
Living in man's ordinary lot, I await my end;
In the midst of flux at peace with the world.
How I regret there is no like-hearted traveler
20　With whom to climb the ladder of blue clouds!

Translated by Richard W. Bodman

31
Harmonizing with a Poem by Left Assistant Yü Kao-chih Requesting Sick Leave

Shen Yüeh (441–513)

At year's end is there anything one can depend on?
Helter-skelter, grief and sickness come by turns.
Were it not for bath-leave, who could ever find relief?
4　How to preserve oneself has surely never been transmitted.
If you clutch an orchid, it will vainly fill your grasp;
If you await the water-clock, it never flows completely out.
Tumult and uproar both are rife before our eyes,
8　While records and directives multiply upon our laps.
What use is there for eloquence that talks of heaven?
A futile exercise to dream of being given a brush to write great things.

Shen Yüeh was renowned as the deviser of the basic rules for regulated verse, which became the prestige form of poetry in the T'ang and later periods. He achieved this by adapting metrical Sanskrit prosody to the tonal features of Sinitic languages. Shen successfully experimented with these revolutionary ideas in his own verse. In addition, he was the editor of the *History of the [Liu] Sung* which, as might be expected from someone of Shen Yüeh's inclinations, includes an unusually large number of literary biographies for an official dynastic history. Imbued with a transcendent Taoist sentiment, he was also deeply attracted to Buddhism for its compassion and spirituality. At the same time, he responded to the Confucian call to public service.

Hang up your cap, as Feng Meng did beside the Eastern City Gate;
12   Why ever come again out of the hills and forests?

Translated by Richard Mather

Seeing the Beloved in a Dream

Shen Yüeh

Last night I heard your long-drawn sighs,
And knew that in your heart were memories.
Then, actually and of its own accord, the Gate of Heaven opened;
4   Our two souls were joined—I saw you face to face.
Not only did you proffer me the pillow of Shamanka Mountain,
But you also brought a meal held level with your brow.
I stood to look, and then lay down again,
8   When suddenly I woke to find you were not by my side.
How could you know that for this spirit-wounded one
A flood of tears has soaked my breast?

Translated by Richard Mather

Returning to My Garden Home:
In Respectful Response to the Master of
Hua-yang[1]

Shen Yüeh

Early on I wished to seek out famous mountains,
But the date awaited the completion of my son's and
     daughter's weddings.
Then, although these two events were over,
4   Quite aside from these, I still was of two minds.
But suddenly I heard the Dragon Chart of a new dynasty had come,
And even now I see its glorious radiance spread.
Assisting at the court, I head the Eight High Officers;

1. The Taoist Scholar T'ao Hung-ching (see selection 32).

8   I've opened land, am paid with taxes from a thousand households.
    My official capstrings never have been bathed in dew,
    Nor have the wind and rain yet combed my hair;
    But tinkling jades resound within the recessed palace gates,
12 And gold cicada pendants gleam in sunlight at dawn audiences.
    I'm ashamed I have not even made a petty man's requital,
    Yet, unworthy, I enjoy the highest rank.
    It's not that I've forgotten all those lifetime dreams;
16 Just that there is no respite—no time even for regret!

Translated by Richard Mather

Listening to Gibbons at Rock-Pool Creek

Shen Yüeh

Yow! Yow! Night gibbons cry.
Soft, soft, dawn mists mesh.
Are their voices far? nearby?
Just see mountains piled up high.
Having liked the East Hill's song,
I now await West Cliff's reply.

Translated by Richard W. Bodman

32

Poem Written in Answer to His Majesty's Question: "What Is There in the Mountains?"

T'ao Hung-ching (452–536)

"What is there in the mountains?" you ask—
Many a white cloud on mountain peaks.

But these are pleasures for me alone,
I can't take and send them to my Prince.

Translated by Stephen Owen

The poet was an eminent Taoist patriarch and scholar.

33
Describing a Dream for Someone

Wang Seng-ju (465–522)

I've known fancies turn into dreaming,
but never believed a dream could be like this:
she was fair, fair, immaculate,
4 she was pure, pure perfection,
as she sat, intimate, by hibiscus cushions,
as she turned back the joy-of-love quilt,
and her elegant footsteps were so lovely,
8 her whispered words most enchanting.
What I describe didn't seem to happen fast,
but then, strangely, became a momentary thing,
and I woke to nothingness,
12 aware that all is empty illusion.

Translated by Anne Birrell

Wang Seng-ju was from a poor family but he rose to the rank of censor under the Liang rulers. The name Seng may denote a formal connection with Buddhist religious life. The wit of his poem stems from his intelligent and lively use of well-known Buddhist concepts such as nothingness, dreams, and empty illusion.

34
Spring Day

Yü Chien-wu (487–550)

Peach blossoms are red, willow catkins white,
Shimmering in the sun and swaying in the wind;
Their shape emerges beyond the vermilion walls,
4 Their fragrance goes back to the blue hall.
Mirrored in the water, parasitic bamboos,

One of the foremost exponents of the so-called "palace-style poetry" which focused on courtly themes in the broadest sense, including the lives, emotions, and manners of the inhabitants of the women's apartments. He was the father of the poet Yü Hsin, the author of the famous "Rhapsody of Lament for the South," a history in rhymeprose of the Liang dynasty and its fall.

Lying across the hill, a half-dead paulownia tree;
The list of awardees announced, I realize the great bounty;
8   Grasping my writing tablet, I am chagrined by my paltry talent.
          Translated by Victor H. Mair and Tsu-Lin Mei

35
A Pheasant on His Morning Flight

Hsiao Kang (503–551)

The dawning sun shines upon the royal wheat fields,
A spring fowl crosses the deserted plain;
At times raising his plumicorns to elude the falcon,
He suddenly wheels aslant to spite the mounds.

Young men serve on distant campaigns,
Resentful, their thoughts brim with rebellion;
Better follow after a profligate courtier,
Whose silken sleeves brush the robes of ministers.
          Translated by Victor H. Mair and Tsu-Lin Mei

    The author was both crown prince and center of a flourishing literary salon in the Eastern Palace of the Liang royal establishment. The efforts of the circle of poets around him resulted in the development of a palace-style poetry (see selection 34). Hsiao Kang was quite likely the sponsor of the epochal collection of love poetry entitled *New Songs from Jade Terrace* (compiled c. 545 by the court poet Hsü Ling) that enshrined this style of verse. His own brother, Hsiao T'ung, was the editor of the famous *Wen-hsüan* (*Literary Selections*, see selection 18), the seminal anthology of traditional Chinese prose and verse that was intended to stand in opposition to the current literary fashion as exemplified by *New Songs from Jade Terrace*. Curiously, however, the *Jade Terrace* collection is also noted for its preservation of a number of earlier popular songs and ballads (see, for example, selections 162–165).

36

Untitled

Brahmacārin Wang (c. 7th–8th centuries)

I have a couple acres of land
Planted on the slopes of South Mountain;
There are four or five blue pines
And two vines of green beans.

When it's hot, I bathe in the pond,
When it's cool, I sing by its banks;
Rambling about, I take my satisfaction,
Completely unaffected by others.

Translated by Victor H. Mair

The vast majority of the poems attributed to Wang Fan-chih (= Sanskrit Brahmacārin ["Lay Buddhist devotee or ascetic with his mind set on purity"]) were recovered only in the early part of this century among the Tun-huang manuscripts (see selection 266). They are important for the large amount of vernacularisms they employ. Like the Cold Mountain poems (see selection 58) with which they share so many similarities, the oeuvre of Wang Fan-chih was almost certainly not written by a single individual, but rather represents a certain type of popular poetry with proto-Zen tendencies.

37

On the Cicada: In Prison

Lo Pin-wang (Before 640–684?)

The Western Course: a cicada's voice singing;
A southern cap: longing for home intrudes.

The poet's youth was spent in poverty. He enlisted in the army and was stationed in the Western Regions and in Szechwan. Lo is considered to be one of the four most important poets in the early part of the T'ang period.
Paraphrase by the translator:

When the sun moves through the Western Course of the heavens, a sign of autumn, the cicada sings. Its singing causes homesickness in me, like that once felt by Chung Yi of Ch'u, wearing his southern cap as a memento of his homeland when a prisoner in the state of Ch'in. Like him, I am a southerner imprisoned in the North. How can I bear that those wings of the cicada, so often used to describe the curls of beautiful ladies, come to listen to my "Song of White Hair," like that which Cho Wen-chün (see selection 158) sang when

How can I bear those shadows of black locks
4   That come here to face my "Song of White Hair"?
Dew heavy on it, can fly no farther toward me;
The wind strong, its echoes easily lost.
No one believes in nobility and purity—
8   On my behalf who will explain what's in my heart?

Translated by Stephen Owen

Ssu-ma Hsiang-ju abandoned her? Those black cicada wings like curls remind me of youth and attractive beauty, unbearable to one who is growing old and feels rejected by his ruler. Futhermore, since the singing of the cicada is a reminder of autumn, the season associated with the coming of old age, how can I bear that it come any closer to me, reminding me of my own aging? But perhaps I have misunderstood the cicada: associated with purity and old age, it may be a kindred spirit. If my ruler hears it, it may remind him of *my* purity and old age, and thus obtain my release. In this respect, its singing is like pleading my case to the throne. But it, like me, is caught up in the autumn situation that it represents: the dew is so heavy upon it that it can fly no farther and thus will not be able to get into the palace and reach the ruler's ears. Furthermore, though I might hope that its singing will be heard from outside, the autumn wind is so strong that its voice will be drowned out. Even if his singing, or my own in this poem, were to reach near the throne, it would do no good, because no one believes any more in nobility or purity—neither mine, my innocence of crime, nor that of the cicada. Thus there is no one to state my case for me.

38
Written Impromptu upon Returning to My Hometown

Ho Chih-chang (659–744)

I left home as a youth and am returning an old man—
The sounds of my hometown have not changed,
    yet the hair on my temples is receding;
The children look at me but do not recognize me—
Laughing, they ask, "Guest, where have you come from?"

Translated by Victor H. Mair

From the lower Yangtze valley, Ho Chih-chang was a high official in the capital, Ch'ang-an, who befriended the young Li Po (see selection 45) and became a boon drinking companion of the latter.

39

Poems of Reflection on the Vicissitudes of Life

Ch'en Tzu-ang (661–702)

5

The men in the market pride themselves on their knowledge and craft,
But they are as ignorant as babes in regard to the Way;
Amidst the press and grab, they make boastful display of luxury—
They know not where their bodies will one day end up.

How could they ever see the Master of Dark Purity,
Who observed the world in a jade pot?
Frustrated, he left behind him heaven and earth,
And entered Infinity mounted on Transformation.

10

I dwell in seclusion and observe the creative process,
Inarticulate, my jaws quiver in an effort to speak;
Speakers of slander devour each other,
Profit and loss are fraught with deception.

Disputatious are the sycophants,
They contend with each other for glory;
Wu Kuang turned down the rule of the empire,
But a merchant will compete for a penny.

Have done with it all! Go pick the magic mushroom,
Ten thousand generations will be as a moment.

13

I dwell in the forest nursing a long illness,
The water and trees accentuate the solitude and stillness;
I lie here idly observing the changes in nature,
And meditate absentmindedly on ending rebirth.

In spring, buds are just beginning to show,
Then summer's red sun arrives in all its fullness;
But death and decline begin from that moment—
Oh, when will my sorrowful sighs come to rest?

Translated by Victor H. Mair

Though he successfully passed the highest civil service examination in 684, Ch'en Tzu-ang was more than once unjustly imprisoned on various charges, and he eventually died while incarcerated. He was the forerunner of early T'ang literary reforms which rejected the decadent style of the Six Dynasties period, advocating in its place the masculine style of the Han and Wei periods. There are a total of thirty-eight poems in this series.

40

Poems of Reflection on the Vicissitudes of Life

Chang Chiu-ling (673–740)

I close my door and trace the transformations of nature,
Living in the forest, I focus on the object of my thoughts;
I sigh for the tree in the winter cold,
For in days gone by it was lushly fragrant.

In the morning sun, where is the phoenix?
At sunset, the cicada is sad and alone;
My thoughts overwhelm me in the middle of the night,
Deeply I sigh, asking myself whom I await.

What I had cherished has surely gone forever,
And since it is gone, it cannot be retrieved;
Eating from bronze tripods is no affair of mine,
Life on a clouded mountain has been my hope.

The north is so very distant from the south—
And how my chariot horses do tarry!
Heaven and earth are totally alien to each other—
Silently I lie within my curtains.

Translated by Victor H. Mair

The poet became a Presented Scholar (comparable to the academic doctorate in the West) in 702 after passing the highest civil service examination. He served as an able prime minister for emperor Hsüan Tsung. Chang Chiu-ling's poems greatly influenced the development of a type of poetry that reflects upon the landscape while revealing the inner mind. This is the last in a series of twelve poems.

41

Climbing the Stork Pavilion

Wang Chih-huan (688–742)

The white sun leaning on the mountain disappears,
The Yellow River flows on into the sea;

The author was born into a family of officials. He himself served as a county magistrate and held other minor posts. Most of his poetic works have been lost, only six quatrains surviving.

To stretch your gaze a thousand leagues,
Climb up still another story.

Translated by Richard W. Bodman

These, however, have been sufficient to establish him as a significant figure in discussions of T'ang period literature.

42

Seeking out Master Chan on Incense Mountain

Meng Hao-jan (689?–740)

On a morning ramble I visit a great mountain,
The mountain far away in the empty azure.
Billowing mist spreads over a hundred leagues;
4   As the sun goes down I reach my goal at last.
At the valley's mouth I hear a bell sound;
By the wood's edge scent a breath of incense.
Leaning on my staff, I seek an old friend;
8   Having loosened the saddle, give my mount a rest.
The stone gate is hard by a chasm's brink;
A bamboo-lined path winds through the forest depths.
I enjoy meeting with a "Companion in the Law";[1]
12   In "Pure Talk"[2] we stay up until dawn.
All my life I have respected true reclusion,
For days on end sought spiritual mysteries.
An old rustic goes to his fields at dawn;
16   A mountain monk returns to his temple in the evening.
There are many pure notes in pines and streams;
These moss-grown walls are wrapped in a feeling of antiquity.
How I would like to retire to this very mountain,
20   "Casting off both self and world alike."

Translated by Daniel Bryant

Meng Hao-jan was the oldest of the leading poets of the High T'ang period. Unlike many others, he had never passed the official examinations or obtained a position in the civil service. Despite his lack of success in official employment, he became acquainted with many highly placed men in the government. He also gained the respect of a number of outstanding younger poets. Wang Wei, Li Po, and Tu Fu all wrote moving tributes to him (see, for example, the first poem in selection 45), although Tu Fu does not seem to have met him personally.

1. Someone who pursues a religious, usually Buddhist, life.
2. Abstruse, witty discourse that is often associated with Taoists.

Spring Dawn

Meng Hao-jan

Asleep in spring unaware of dawn,
And everywhere hear the birds in song.
At night the sound of wind and rain,
You'll know how much from the flowers gone.

Translated by Elling Eide

Passing Seven-League Rapids

Meng Hao-jan

I heed the warning not to "sit beneath the eaves,"[1]
A thousand coins are not to be taken lightly.
Finding great pleasure in hills and streams,
4   I have made many journeys, drifting in boats.
On the Five Sacred Mountains I have sought Shang Tzu-p'ing.[2]
By the Three Rivers Hsiang, mourned for Ch'ü Yüan.[3]
Lakes—I have crossed the breadth of Tung-t'ing;[4]
8   Rivers—I enter the clear Hsin-an.[5]

And now I hear the rapids of Yen Kuang,
For they lie on the course of this very stream.
Through layered ridges for hundreds of leagues,
12   Back and forth with no constant direction.
Verdure and raven-black swirl and billow together,
In parted streams pouring and tumbling at random.
The fishing reef is level enough for a seat,
16   But the mossy steps are slippery and hard to walk.

1. The sort of scion who should not "sit beneath the eaves" lest something fall from the roof and injure him was one from a family that held a thousand coins (or ingots).
2. A semi-legendary recluse.
3. See selection 148.
4. A large lake in central China.
5. A tributary of the Che. Shortly below where it joins the main stream is a stretch of rough water called the Seven-league Rapids. It was here that Yen Kuang, once a youthful companion to the man who later became emperor Kuang-wu, restorer of the Han dynasty, retired to fish from a broad boulder above the river, refusing to join the government of his erstwhile companion.

Monkeys drink from pools below the rocks,
And birds return to the sun-rimmed trees.
I gaze on this wonder and regret that I came so late,
20   Rest on my oar and lament that darkness comes.
Swirling my hands, I dally with the swift-moving waters,
Washed clean henceforth of all dusty cares.

Translated by Daniel Bryant

43
Silent at Her Window

Wang Ch'ang-ling (698–756)

Too young to have known the meaning of sorrow,
in her spring dress she climbs the tower chamber.

New leaves on all the willows wound her;
She sent him off to war for nothing but a title.

Translated by Sam Hamill

Though from humble circumstances, Wang Ch'ang-ling became a Presented Scholar in 727.
He is recognized as a poet as well as an astute esthetician and prosodist.

44
Climbing Pien-chüeh Temple

Wang Wei (701–761)

A bamboo path leads through the First Stage
Where the City of Illusion appears from Lotus Peak.

Wang Wei was a painter, musician, and calligrapher as well as a writer. The scion of a
distinguished family, he passed the highest civil service examination in 721 at an early age and
entered upon a long and distinguished career in government interspersed with periods of
banishment and voluntary withdrawal to the countryside. He is best remembered for his descriptions of life at his country retreat. Wang Wei was a devout Buddhist who called himself
Vimalakīrti (Wei represents the first syllable of that Sanskrit name), after the saintly Indian
Buddhist layman.

"Climbing Pien-chüeh Temple" illustrates the progress of the soul from the illusion of the
physical world to the extinction of self in Nirvāṇa. The beauty of the temple landscape serves

Up in its windows all Ch'u[1] is encompassed,
4   Above its forests Nine Rivers[2] lies level.
Pliant grasses accepted for sitting in meditation,
Tall pines echo with sūtra chanting.
Then, dwelling in void, beyond the Clouds of Law,
8   Observe the World, attain Non-Life.

Translated by Stephen Owen

---

only to draw the deluded soul along the right path: it is the "City of Illusion" of the Buddhist parable (from the *Lotus Sūtra*; see selection 13).

1. Included parts of the modern provinces of Kiangsi, Anhwei, Kiangsu, and Hupeh.
2. The nine affluents of the Yangtze River or a port on the Yangtze below the city of Hankow.

Second Song for the Worship of the Goddess at Yü Mountain: "Bidding the Goddess Farewell"

Wang Wei

In a swirl they come forward and bow
     there before the hall,
Eyes filled with love-longing
     toward the sacred mats like jade.
She came but did not speak,
     Her will was not made known;
4   And she is the evening rain,
     makes the empty mountains somber.
The pipes grieve in shrillness,
Flurried strings throb with longing;
The carriage of the goddess
     is about to turn majestically.
8   In a flash clouds draw back,
     the rain ceases;

In this poem we encounter the theme of exile within the description of a shamanistic performance near Chi-chou. The model was the "Nine Songs" from the *Elegies of Ch'u* (see selection 148): the accepted interpretation of these poems in the T'ang period was that Ch'ü Yüan had composed them as revisions of the popular shamanistic performances that he had seen in his exile. In Wang Wei's poem, there is a silent literary-historical context, a tacit assumption of enacting the role of Ch'ü Yüan in his own unjust exile.

And green stand the mountains
amid water's splashing flow.

Translated by Stephen Owen

Deer Enclosure

Wang Wei

On the empty mountain, seeing no one,
Only hearing the echoes of someone's voice;
Returning light enters the deep forest,
Again shining upon the green moss.

Translated by Richard W. Bodman and Victor H. Mair

45

To Meng Hao-jan

Li Po (701–762)

I love the Master, Meng Hao-jan,
A free spirit known the whole world through.
In the flush of youth he spurned the cap and carriage,
4   And rests now, white-haired with age, among clouds and pines.
Drunk in moonlight, often "smitten by the sage,"

Li Po seems to have been born in Central Asia and might have had Turkic or other non-Han ancestors. When he was five, the family returned to China proper, settling in Mien-chou in modern Szechwan. At age twenty-five, he began to travel extensively in central and eastern China, and became popular both for his abundant talent and for his eccentricity. He was recommended to the imperial court and summoned to the capital, Ch'ang-an, by Emperor Hsüan Tsung. There he became a favorite until his unconstrained behavior eventually proved offensive and he was let go. His later life was one of constant drifting and difficulty.

More than nine hundred of Li Po's poems are still extant today, and many possess an unusual combination of boldness and grace. His works are full of the romantic and the fantastic: he had a unique ability to conceive and execute grand visions. Aptly eulogized as "a transcendant banished from heaven," Li Po is universally recognized as one of the greatest Chinese poets of all times.

Li Po's poem of praise echoes Meng Hao-jan's own poetry throughout, as if to prove that the figure in the poem is indeed Meng Hao-jan (see selection 42). In line 5, "sage" is strong wine.

Or led astray by flowers, he does not serve his lord.
The highest mountain—how can I look to climb it?
8   I can do no more than kneel to his pure fragrance.

Translated by Stephen Owen

Up into the Clouds Music

Li Po

West of the golden sky,
Where the white sun sinks away,
Old K'ang,[1] the Barbarian Birdie,[2]
[Stanza continues.]

This poem describes a Wen-k'ang performance, a kind of mummery with music, dance, and song that served as the grand finale for certain rather elaborate musical entertainments. (At the Sui court a Wen-k'ang used twenty-two performers.) In origin, the name Wen-k'ang ("Cultured and Stalwart") was the posthumous title of Yü Liang (289–340), a Chin dynasty statesman whose sister was married to an emperor. At his death, his household entertainers made themselves up in his likeness and performed a memorial dance with banners. Performances of this sort came to be called "Wen-k'ang musicales," and the performer in one could be called a "Wen-k'ang," meaning, essentially, "a mummer." The Wen-k'ang musicale that Li Po describes was probably sponsored by a local official or a nobleman living in the provinces to celebrate either the recovery of Ch'ang-an from An Lu-shan's rebels in 757 or a subsequent birthday of the new emperor, Su Tsung, who had replaced his fleeing father, Hsüan Tsung, on August 12, 756. The poem was probably commissioned by the sponsor of the celebration and may have been recited during the performance. The religious symbolism is a mixture of Buddhism, Taoism, a little Confucianism, and several independent traditions of mythology; in short, it is Chinese popular religion.

1. People surnamed K'ang were often foreigners from the K'ang-chü kingdom located in the vicinity of modern Tashkent and Samarkand. Scholars today think the name may have been derived from *kānkuk*, the Tocharian word for "stone," but if Li Po, who knew Turkish, assigned any meaning to "K'ang," he more likely thought of it as one of the Turkish words for "father."

2. There are several T'ang references to performers—usually flute players and presumably foreign—who were called "Barbarian Birdie" (*Hu-ch'u*, literally "foreign fledgling"). This name (or nickname) may have been partly a suggestion of their musical talents and partly an approximation of some Turkish name such as *quščuk*, "little bird," or *quti*, "his blessedness or good fortune." "Little bird" seems likely to have been in the background here, but an original *Qang Quti*, meaning "a father's good fortune," is also a possibility. In the Later T'ang there was a Turkish general named K'ang Fu, *Fu* being the Chinese word for "blessing or good fortune."

3. Literally "moon cave," but this means the cave of "the moon people," who may have been the Uti mentioned by Pliny. They were possibly Indo-European Tocharians, but it is conventional to call them "Scythians" since we do not really know who the Scythians were either. Chinese tradition puts the cave in P'o-li ("rock crystal") Mountain, located in what is now northern Afghanistan, and holds that it is the source of the famous "heavenly horses." Li Po, himself born in Central Asia, named his younger son P'o-li. Elsewhere he associates his own

Was born in that Scythian cave[3] of the moon.
Awesome and craggy the features of his face;
Measured and precise his manner of bearing.
Green jade glowing, glowing, the pupils of his eyes;
Yellow gold curling, curling, the hair upon his temples.

Flowery canopies[4] hang down to his lower lashes,
A lofty mountain[5] looms over his upper lip.
Not seeing his strange, uncanny form,
How could you know the Lord of Creation?
The Great Way was this mummer's stern father,
Primal Ether this mummer's elderly kin.
He played with P'an-ku,[6] patting his head,
And pushing the carriage turned Heaven's wheels.
He says he saw when the sun and the moon were born,
Cast from water-silver[7] and the essence of fire.
While the solar crows had not yet come out of the valley
And the lunar rabbit was still a half-hidden form,[8]
Nü-wa[9] toyed with the yellow earth
And lumped it into ignorant humans,
Scattering them to the Six Directions,
Thick, thick, like dust and sand.
When birth and death go on endlessly,
Who could guess that this barbarian is a realized immortal?

Since the Jo Tree was planted by the Western Ocean
And the Fu Mulberry was set in the Eastern Sea,[10]
To the present day, how great the time?
The twigs and leaves are ten-thousand miles long.
The Middle Kingdom had Seven Sages,[11]
[Stanza continues.]

---

origin with the cave, but the "Scythian cave" really represents the far west in general rather than any specific place.

4. His bushy eyebrows.

5. His foreign nose.

6. The demiurge who brought order out of chaos to create the world. Old K'ang patted him on the head, so Old K'ang must be "older than creation."

7. The element mercury.

8. In Chinese mythology, a rabbit lives on the moon, and there were once ten suns, each inhabited by a crow.

9. The sister and wife of the legendary ruler Fu-hsi. The two are usually depicted with snake-like bodies. In some accounts they were the parents or creators of the human race.

10. Two of the three or four "world trees" in Chinese mythology. In some accounts the sun rises from the Fu Mulberry and sets in the Jo Tree (see selection 148, section II, line 46).

11. The T'ang emperors prior to Su Tsung. In reality, there were eight of them. From a line in his "Rhymeprose on the Great Hunt," we can tell that Li Po *is counting* the almost forgotten

Then along the way collapsed into chaos.[12]
His Majesty answered the upturn of fortune,
And a dragon flew into the city of Hsien-yang.[13]
As when the Red Eyebrows[14] set up their Tub,[15]
And White Water restored the Glory of Han,[16]
So, angrily seething, the Four Seas moved,
And for Him great spreading waves arose.
When He stepped to tread the Purple Tenuity,[17]
Heaven's Gates[18] opened of their own accord,
And the old barbarian responding to Utmost Virtue[19]
Came east to present his immortal actors:
Lions in the five colors,
Phoenixes with the nine perfections.[20]
These are the old barbarian's poultry and hounds;
[Stanza continues.]

Li Ch'ung-mao, who reigned for only about two weeks, but he is *not counting* Empress Wu, who reigned memorably as China's unique female *emperor*. Empress Wu was, after all, a woman, she usurped the throne, she briefly changed the name of the dynasty, and she was not family.

12. A reference to the An Lu-shan rebellion that almost toppled the T'ang dynasty.

13. The Ch'in dynasty capital. Here it represents the T'ang capital, Ch'ang-an. The dragon flying in represents the recovery of the capital by imperial troops in 757.

14. Peasant rebels who distinguished themselves by painting their eyebrows red. They rose in Shantung in 18 C.E. during the reign of Wang Mang, who had ended the Former Han dynasty by usurping the throne in 9 C.E. In 23 C.E., they sacked the capital and killed Wang Mang.

15. Liu P'en-tzu (Little Tub Liu), a distant relative of the Han emperors, was set up as emperor by the Red Eyebrows in 25 C.E. There is some humor here, not only because the funny name seems to anticipate "White Water" in the next line, but also because "setting up the ritual tripod vessels" means "establishing a new dynasty," and therefore "setting up a tub" seems perfect for an unsuccessful attempt to found or restore a dynasty.

16. In 25 C.E., Liu Hsiu, who had lived near White Water in what is now Hupei province, restored the Han by founding the dynasty we know as the Later Han. Liu, a descendant of the first Han emperor, was given the posthumous title "Gloriously Martial." His connection with the place called White Water became memorable because of a neglected omen. Wang Mang disliked the "metal knife" coins of the Former Han because the characters for "metal" and "knife" are the main elements in the character for "Liu," the surname of the Han royal family. To avoid this bad omen, he minted new coins bearing the words "currency of commerce," not realizing that those characters could be broken apart into characters reading "Immortal Man of White Water."

17. When Su Tsung became the "eighth" T'ang emperor and returned to Ch'ang-an. The "Purple Tenuity," a circumpolar constellation containing stars that are part of Draco, is the realm of God, the Emperor of Heaven. Here it represents Ch'ang-an.

18. A star in the Northern Dipper. The sense of the line is, "The country is at peace, the borders are safe, travel is possible."

19. The first reign title or year period proclaimed by Emperor Su Tsung: August 12, 756 to March 17, 758.

20. Probably mummers so dressed.

Singing and dancing they have flown to God's Town;[21]
Proudly prancy, swirly whirly,
Advancing, retreating, and dressing on line.

He is good at barbarian songs. He offers up Chinese wine,
He kneels upon two knees. He presses both elbows together.
Scattering flowers,[22] pointing to Heaven,
raising his pallid arms.
He worships the Dragon Countenance,
He offers long life to The Sage.[23]

Northern Dipper may wobble. South Mountain may fall.
But, O Son of Heaven, as nine nines[24] are eighty-one
and so many times ten thousand years,
long may You drain the ten thousand years cup.

Translated by Elling Eide

21. The Purple Tenuity, but also Ch'ang-an.

22. This must have been a special moment in the performance. The processional music for a Wen-k'ang musicale was called "Road with a Single Crossing"; the dance music was called "Scattering Flowers." The scattering of flowers was especially associated with the Western Paradise of Amitābha, the Buddha of Eternal Life.

23. "Dragon Countenance" and "The Sage" both refer to the emperor.

24. Nine is an especially auspicious number because it is a homonym of the word meaning "eternal."

Late Bloomer at the Front of My Garden

Li Po

A Queen Mother of the West[1] peach tree is planted in my yard;
After three thousand warming springs,
it finally had a flower.
This strain and delay producing a fruit
was laughed at all around,
But when I climbed up to pick it, aah, aah, I sighed aloud.

Translated by Elling Eide

1. The Queen Mother of the West (see selection 187, note 5) was famous for her peaches of immortality. The trees she grew only fruited once every three thousand years.

To Send to Tu Fu[1] as a Joke

Li Po

I ran into Tu Fu by a Rice Grain Mountain,
In a bamboo hat with the sun at high noon.
Hasn't he got awfully thin since our parting?
It must be the struggle of writing his poems.

Translated by Elling Eide

1. For Li Po's great contemporary, Tu Fu, see selection 48.

Drinking Alone in the Moonlight[1]

Li Po

Beneath the blossoms with a pot of wine,
No friends at hand, so I poured alone;
I raised my cup to invite the moon,
Turned to my shadow, and we became three.
Now the moon had never learned about my drinking,
And my shadow had merely followed my form,
But I quickly made friends with the moon and my shadow;
To find pleasure in life, make the most of the spring.

Whenever I sang, the moon swayed with me;
Whenever I danced, my shadow went wild.
Drinking, we shared our enjoyment together;
Drunk, then each went off on his own.
But forever agreed on dispassionate revels,
We promised to meet in the far Milky Way.

Translated by Elling Eide

1. This is the first in a series of four poems under this title.

Autumn Cove

Li Po

At Autumn Cove, so many white monkeys,
bounding, leaping up like snowflakes in flight!
They coax and pull their young ones down from the branches
to drink and frolic with the water-borne moon.

Translated by Burton Watson

A pentasyllabic quatrain.

Viewing the Waterfall at Mount Lu

Li Po

Sunlight streaming on Incense Stone kindles violet smoke;
far off I watch the waterfall plunge to the long river,
flying waters descending straight three thousand feet,
till I think the Milky Way has tumbled from the ninth height of Heaven.

Translated by Burton Watson

The second of two poems under this title. Mount Lu is in Kiangsi. Incense Stone (more literally, "Incense Burner") is one of its peaks.

Still Night Thoughts

Li Po

Moonlight in front of my bed—
I took it for frost on the ground!
I lift my head, gaze at the bright moon,
lower it and dream of home.

Translated by Burton Watson

This pentasyllabic quatrain used to be known by virtually all Chinese schoolchildren.

Poems in an Old Style

Li Po

1

Ages have passed since the stately Odes flourished,
I am growing old and there is no one else to present them;
The folk songs became tangled with creeping grasses,
In the Warring Kingdoms, thorny bushes grew thickly.

Dragons and tigers devoured each other,
Armed hostilities lasted until rabid Ch'in;
How feeble had the orthodox tradition grown!
In its place arose the sad and complaining bard.

Yang and Ssu-ma revived Ch'ü Yüan's declining ripples,[1]
And opened a new current which reached a boundless swell;
Although there has been a myriad of changes in its fortune,
Ars *poetica* finally sank into oblivion.

Ever since the Chien-an period at the end of the Han,
Prettiness itself has not been considered fine enough;
In our own hallowed age, we have returned to antiquity,
Our majestic monarch values purity and truth.

The assembled talents are handsome and smart,
"They have mounted fate's carriage and joined the leaping dragons";
Style and substance glitter together—
A host of stars spread over the Autumn Sea.

My determination is but "to edit and transmit,"[2]
So that this brilliance may shine through a thousand springs;
If my task is accomplished, I would hope, like the sage,
To lay down my brush with the capture of the unicorn.

21

There was a sojourner in Ying who intoned "White Snows,"
The reverberations flew to the cerulean sky;
His effort was wasted in singing this tune,
In the whole world, there was no one who could follow his song.

But when he tried "Scamp from Szechwan,"
Those who joined him numbered in the thousands;

---

1. Referring to the rhapsodic tradition (see selection 149 and following items) that is held to have begun with the southern *Elegies of Ch'u* (see selection 148).
2. What Confucius is alleged to have said of his own role in the compilation of the *Classic of Odes* (see selection 22).

He swallowed his grief but what could he say?
In vain was his sorrowful sighing.

54

My sword at my waist, I climb a high tower,
Pensive, I view the springtime scenery;
Dense thickets cover the layered mounds,
Rare grasses have gone into hiding in deep valleys.

The phoenix sings by the Western Sea,
It wishes to roost but has found no suitable tree;
The jackdaw, however, has a place to dwell,
Beneath the mugwort it gathers in teeming flocks.

As when the fortunes of Chin daily diminished,
I am like Juan Chi[1] weeping bitterly at the road's end.

Translated by Victor H. Mair

1. See selection 27.

46

The Streets of Ch'ang-an

Ch'u Kuang-hsi (707–760?)

Cracking whips, off to the wine shop,
in flashy clothes heading for the whorehouse door;
a million cash spent in an hour—
expressionless, they never speak a word.

Translated by Burton Watson

From Kiangsu, the poet became a Presented Scholar in the year 726. He wrote conventional court poetry, but sometimes gave it a surprisingly ironic or reflective twist. He also wrote bucolic poems, a foil for his absorption in the courtly life of the capital.

47

Rejoicing that the Zen Master Pao Has Arrived from Dragon Mountain

Liu Chang-ch'ing (709?–785?)

What day did you come down from that former place,
spring grasses ready to turn green and fair?
Still it faces the mountain moon,
but who listens now to its rock-bound stream?
Monkey cries tell you night is fading;
blossoms that open show you the flowing years.
With metal staff you quietly come and go,
mindless—for everywhere is Zen.

Translated by Burton Watson

Liu Chang-ch'ing achieved the rank of Presented Scholar in 733 and served as censor. He wrote primarily pentasyllabic regulated verse. Many of his poems deal with personal suffering in a time of tremendous social upheaval, but he also wrote simple pastoral poetry and quiet Buddhist verse. Note that a disposition toward Buddhism by no means precluded association with Taoists, as is evidenced by the following poem.

Sent to the Taoist of Dragon Mountain, Hsü Fa-leng

Liu Chang-ch'ing

On and on in the white clouds
he lives alone, guest of the verdant mountains;
Midday in the grove he lights the incense,
and with the cassia blossoms shares the stillness.

Translated by William H. Nienhauser, Jr.

48
Spring View

Tu Fu (712–770)

The nation is ruined,   but mountains and rivers remain.
This spring the city   is deep in weeds and brush.
Touched by the times   even flowers weep tears.
Fearing leaving   the birds tangled hearts.
Watch-tower fires   have been burning for three months
To get a note from home   would cost ten thousand gold.
Scratching my   white hair thinner
Seething hopes   all in a trembling hairpin.

Translated by Gary Snyder

Tu Fu sat for the highest civil service examinations but failed to attain the coveted rank of Presented Scholar. Only in 755 was he given a minor post as a district police commissioner (which he actually rejected), and he never succeeded in gaining the higher echelons of government to which he aspired. Eventually he moved his family to Ch'eng-tu, Szechwan, where he built a thatched cottage that has become a famous symbol of his poetic sensibility.

In his verse, the poet reflects poignantly on the pressing issues of his own times while grounding himself solidly in the poetic tradition that he inherited. Where Li Po (see selection 45), the other most celebrated poet of the T'ang period (the Golden Age of Chinese poetry), revealed a Taoistic predisposition, Tu Fu was more conventionally Confucian in his outlook.

A Guest Arrives

Tu Fu

North and south of my cottage, spring waters everywhere—
All I can see are a flock of terns that come day after day;
The flowery path has not been swept for any guests,
Only today do I finally open my gate for you.

The market is far, so our supper platter lacks variety,
Our family is poor, so the wine flask holds but old home-brew;
If you're willing to sing with the gaffer next door,
I'll call across the fence for him to finish the last cup.

Translated by Victor H. Mair

Journey North

Tu Fu

I

The second year of the emperor's reign, in autumn
during the Extra Eighth Month, on Beginning Luck[1]
I, Master Tu   about to journey north
vast, vague   wonder about my home

These times have brought us hardship, sorrow
in or out of court, there are few free days
yet (I feel shame for favors specially granted)
a decree permits a return to my vines and brambles

I bow farewell,   pay respects in the palace
10 fearful, alarmed   a long time before I come out
Although I lack the temperament to admonish
I fear the Ruler may still have some errors left:
the Ruler truly is lord of our rising again
about state affairs certainly diligent
but the Eastern Hu[2] rebellion is not yet over
so his servant Fu is anxious about what is pressing

I wipe my tears   long for the Travel Locale[3]
on roads and trails   still muddled
the universe   endures its gaping wounds
20 sadness, sorrow   when will it ever end?

II

Slow, slow   we cross paddy paths
men, smoke   sparse in the desolation
those we meet   most of them wounded
groaning, sobbing   and even bleeding

1. The extra or intercalary eighth month in the second year of the T'ang emperor Su Tsung's reign begins on the day corresponding to September 18, 757, of the Western calendar. "Beginning Luck" is a term used in ancient times for the first week of a month, but here Tu Fu might be using it for the first day.

2. Throughout the poem, Tu Fu refers to the rebels as Hu, a derogatory term for non-Chinese to the west and sometimes to the north, because An Lu-shan was of Sogdian and Turkish descent. The Sogdians were one of the major Iranian groups in Central Asia during medieval times. For the An Lu-shan rebellion, see selections 180 and 181.

3. The emperor's provisional court during exile is euphemistically called the "Travel Locale."

I turn my head back toward Feng-hsiang[4] town:
its pennons and banners at dusk grow bright, go out
On and up   into folds of wintry hills
often we come across   grottoes where horses are watered

The land around Pin[5]   goes deep into the earth
30   waters of the Ching   crash in its midst
a fierce tiger   stands in front of us
gray cliffs   at his roar, split

Chrysanthemums hang   blossoms of this autumn
rocks carry   ruts of ancient chariots
blue clouds   move me to elation
secluded things   are, after all, a joy

Mountain berries   most of them tiny, delicate
spread and grow   mixed with acorns and chestnuts
some red   like dust of cinnabar
40   some black   like dots of lacquer
wherever rain or dew moisten
whether sweet or bitter, all bear fruit
My longing thoughts   are by Peach Spring[6]
more sighing   for the clumsiness of my life's course

Hilly land   and I gaze at Fu Altar[7]
cliffs and valleys   emerge and disappear
my own path   has reached to the bank of the stream
my servant   is still in the tips of the trees

An owl   calls from a brown mulberry
50   field mice   fold their paws in a mess of nests

The night is deep   and we pass through a battlefield
the wintry moon   shines on white bones
at T'ung Pass[8]   a million warriors
at that time   why did they scatter so fast?
thus it happened   and half the people of Ch'in
were broken, wounded   or turned into other beings

4. Feng-hsiang, site of the emperor's court in exile, is about a hundred miles to the west of Ch'ang-an, the Western Capital.
5. At about a third of the total distance from Feng-hsiang to his wife's place in Fu-chou in the north, Tu Fu comes to the town of Pin, through which flows the Ching.
6. Referring to T'ao Ch'ien's essay on the Peach Blossom Spring (see selection 204).
7. A landmark near where Tu Fu's family had moved.
8. The poet-historian cannot help thinking of the disastrous battle fought earlier during An Lu-shan's rebellion at T'ung Pass, in an area also known by its ancient name, Ch'in, where nearly 200,000 loyal troops were killed—euphemistically, "turned into other beings."

But what about me?   I fall into Hu dust
and now go home   my hair all flecked with white

III

It's been over a year   I arrive at my thatched house
60 wife and children   clothes with a hundred patches
our bawling   returns with sounds of pines
a sad brook   shares our stifled sobs
Our son, spoiled all his life
face whiter than snow
sees his dad   turns his back and weeps
dirty, grimy   feet unsocked

In front of the bed   our two little girls
patched tatters   barely passing their knees
a seascape   broken ripples and waves
70 from an old embroidery   out-of-line crooks and snaps
Sky Wu   and Purple Phoenix[9]
upside down   on the coarse cloth of their jackets

An old man   sick in mind and chest
vomiting, diarrhetic   I lie down several days

"How could I not have   in my satchel, silks
to save you   from the cold, the shivering?"
powder and eye-black   also unwrapped from their parcels
quilts and curtains   gradually displayed
and my thin wife   has her face aglow again
80 our silly daughters   their hair they comb themselves
they copy their mother   there's nothing they don't do
morning makeup   free-handedly smeared
at another time   I give them rouge and powder
and they messily paint   their eyebrows wide

Come back alive   I face the children
it's as though I'm about   to forget the hunger and thirst
they ask questions   and fight to pull my beard
who could bring himself   to shout at them?

I turn back my thoughts   to the sadness of being among rebels
90 and sweetly submit   to a disorderly din

9. One of the things that catches Tu Fu's attention upon returning home is the condition of his children's clothes of coarse fabric, torn and patched with fine embroidery cut and resewn in such manner that the lines of waves and background patterns are disturbed and some of the images such as those of the mythological animals Purple Phoenix and Sky Wu, the water spirit, are inverted.

newly come home   ready to be comforted
—how can I bring up our making a living?

IV

The Most Revered is still covered with dust [10]
how many days before he stops training the troops?

I look up and see   the sky's colors have changed
I sit and sense   weird vapors dispersed
A dark wind comes out of the northwest
sad, dull, following the Uighurs.
Their king wants to help, as an ally
100   their folk are good at the "galloping ambush" [11]
He sends soldiers, five thousand men
and fast horses, ten thousand mounts

Of such people,   just a few would be best
everyone agreed to this brave decision
Using them, always as "eagle steeds"
will smash the enemy faster than an arrow
The Holy Heart waits with great composure
but at current discussions, spirits begin to flag

At the Yi and the Lo   a finger-palm recovery
110   the Western Capital   not needing to be stormed [12]
The government armies ask to penetrate deeply:
their latent valor can be released all at once!
Then will you rise and open up Ch'ing and Hsü
whirl your gaze, capture the Heng and the Chieh [13]

A vast sky   piles up frost and dew
a corrective spirit   includes stern destruction

10. The emperor—the "Most Revered"—is still covered with the dust of exile.

11. The year before (756), the king of the Uighur allies in the northwest sent troops to help the loyal forces in a campaign that was so successful that the T'ang emperor, who was then Su Tsung, made the Uighur prince ceremonial brother to Su Tsung's son, an honor not lost on the foreign noble. The Uighurs were expert horsemen, one of whose most successful maneuvers was the "galloping ambush." The descendants of the Uighurs, an important federation of Turkic peoples during the medieval period, are still active in Central Asia today.

12. Loyang, the Eastern Capital, located between the Yi and the Lo rivers, will be recaptured by loyal forces in an operation that is as easy as pointing a finger toward a palm: Ch'ang-an, the Western Capital, will be recovered in an operation taking less effort than it takes a hand to pluck a weed.

13. Ch'ing-chou occupies what is now Shantung; Hsü-chou was the adjacent state to the south. Heng Mountain and Chieh-shih Mountain recall another ancient state, northwest of Ch'ing-chou, near the homeland of the Hu, the heart of the rebel nation.

misfortune reversed   it's the year to destroy the Hu
the force is gathered   it's the month to take the Hu
Hu destiny   can it last for long?
120 The imperial stand   was never meant to be broken!

V

Recall how before, when   things got out of control
matters were different from those of ancient times
the vicious minister has been chopped to bits
his companions in evil have since then been dispersed
We do not hear that the Hsia and the Yin declined
because they themselves put Pao and Ta to death [14]
Chou and Han achieved their reconstruction
Hsüan and Kuang were indeed clear-sighted and wise [15]
Martial, martial is General Ch'en [16]
130 grasping his battle-ax, roused in his loyal zeal:
had it not been for you, all men would have ceased to be
today, the nation still lives!

Desolate   is great Unity Hall
quiet, quiet   White Beast Gate
men of the capital   look for kingfisher splendor
as the auspicious spirit   moves toward the Golden Tower [17]
the parks and tombs   truly have their gods
are swept, sprinkled   often and without fail
bright, bright   the Great Founder's deed
140 his establishing   most broad and pervasive!
Translated by Hugh M. Stimson

14. The Hsia and Yin (or Shang) dynasties fell because of the moral failings of their last rulers, reflected in their preoccupation with their beautiful consorts. Ta Chi, a concubine of the last ruler of Yin, was an accomplice in his unkingly revels and helped bring about the downfall of that dynasty. Pao Ssu was a favored concubine and later queen of King Yu of the Chou dynasty, who was assassinated because of an instance when he catered to her whims.

15. The T'ang dynasty, like the dynasties of Chou and Han benefiting respectively from the efforts of reconstruction of King Hsüan and Emperor Kuang-wu, is destined to continue in civil peace.

16. During Emperor Hsüan Tsung's journey into exile at the time of An Lu-shan's rebellion, it was General Ch'en Hsüan-li who engineered the death of the minister Yang Kuo-chung and who persuaded the emperor to have Yang Kuei-fei executed.

17. The emperor, Su Tsung, on his return to the capital (Great Unity Hall and White Beast Gate) and his residence in the Golden Tower will, so Tu Fu hopes, bring good luck to the nation so that the imperial tombs can then renew their ritual lustrations, and the great work of the founder of the T'ang dynasty can be continued.

Recruiting Officer of Shih-hao

Tu Fu

At dusk I sought lodging at Shih-hao village,
When a recruiting officer came to seize men at night.
An old man scaled the wall and fled,
His old wife came out to answer the door.

How furious was the officer's shout!
How pitiable was the woman's cry!
I listened as she stepped forward to speak:
"All my three sons have left for garrison duty at Yeh;
From one of them a letter just arrived,
10   Saying my two sons had newly died in battle.
Survivors can manage to live on,
But the dead are gone forever.
Now there's no other man in the house,
Only a grandchild at his mother's breast.
The child's mother has not gone away;
She has only a tattered skirt for wear.
An old woman, I am feeble and weak,
But I will gladly leave with you tonight
To answer the urgent call at Ho-yang—
20   I can still cook morning gruel for your men."

The night drew on, but talking stopped;
It seemed I heard only half-concealed sobs.
As I got back on the road at daybreak,
Only the old man was there to see me off.

Translated by Irving Y. Lo

Seven Songs Written While Living at T'ung-ku in 759

Tu Fu

1

There's a wanderer, there's a wanderer, his name is Tzu-mei.[1]
His head is white, his tangled hair tumbles past his ears.

1. The courtesy name of the poet.

He lives all year on acorns he gathers like Master Tsu the monkey trainer,[2]
Under the cold sky at dusk in mountain valleys.
There is no news from the Central Plain; he cannot return.
His hands and feet are frostbitten, his skin and flesh numb.

Alas! This is my first song, oh! a song already sad;
A pitying wind comes to me from the sky.

2

Long hoe, long hoe, with your raw wooden handle,
I entrust my life to you, you are my only provider.
The yams have no shoots, the mountain snow is deep.
I pull down my short coat many times; it won't cover my shins.
Today we return empty-handed, you and I;
My son groans, my daughter moans, the four walls are quiet.

Alas! This is my second song, oh! I begin to sing it loud.
My neighbors' faces are distressed on my behalf.

3

I have younger brothers, I have younger brothers, all far away.
All three were sickly: have any gotten stronger?
We live apart, drifting farther; we never see each other.
Tartar dust obscures the sky, the road back is long.
Wild geese fly east, then the cranes follow;
Can they carry me to your side?

Alas! This is my third song, oh! I sing it three times.
Will you know where to come to find your elder brother's bones?

4

I have a younger sister, I have a younger sister, she lives in Chung-li.[3]
Her husband died young, her children are all giddy.
The waves are high on the long Huai,[4] and the dragon rages.
Ten years without a meeting: when will it ever come?
I long to go in my little boat, but arrows are all I see;
The South is dark and far away, filled with soldiers' flags.

Alas! this is my fourth song, oh! I sing it four times,
And the apes in the forest cry for me in broad daylight.

2. Alluding to the story from the *Chuang Tzu* (see selection 9) about Master Tsu, the keeper of monkeys, who outwits his herd into obedience by promising them four chestnuts in the morning and three in the afternoon, when they had been displeased with his original offer of three in the morning and four in the afternoon.
3. In modern Anhwei province.
4. A large river that drains part of Honan and northern Anhwei.

5

The wind blows in the mountains around, the creeks run fast.
Cold rain falls in sheets, withered trees are sodden.
Yellow weeds grow on the old city wall below unbroken clouds.
White foxes jump around, yellow foxes stand.
Why must I pass my life in this lonely valley?
At midnight I rise, beset by countless cares.

Alas! This is my fifth song, oh! I draw the notes out long,
But I cannot call back my soul that it might return home.

6

There is a dragon in the South, oh! in a mountain pool.
The old trees round about, their branches intertwined.
Their leaves turn yellow and fall; then the dragon sleeps.[5]
A poisonous snake comes from the east, roaming the waters.
I walk in fear: how dare I go out?
I draw my sword to strike, but it may be better to wait.

Alas! This is my sixth song, oh! a singer's thought lingers.
May the creeks and valleys show their spring colors again for my sake.

7

I am a man who's made no name, already I've grown old,
Wandering hungry three years on barren mountain roads.
In Ch'ang-an the ministers are all young men;
Wealth and fame must be earned before a man grows old.
In the mountains here are scholars who knew me long ago;
We only think of the good old days, our hearts full of pain.

Alas! This is my seventh song, oh! with sorrow I end the refrain,
Looking up to the wide sky where the white sun rushes on.

Translated by Geoffrey Waters

5. So the dragon will come out of hibernation and eat the snake. Some critics believe that the dragon refers to the emperor, and the snake, the rebel Shih Ssu-ming.

Thinking of My Little Boy

Tu Fu

Pony Boy   though it's spring we're still apart
oriole songs   in the warmth are at their fullest

separation   seasonal change upsets me
4   quick and clever   who chatters with you now
a canyon stream   a road in the empty mountains
a rough gate   a village among old trees
I think of you   I grieve and almost sleep
8   toasting my back   I lean on the sunny rail

Translated by David Lattimore

Jade Flower Palace

Tu Fu

Where the stream winds   pine winds linger
scutter of gray rats   over ancient tiles
who knows   what king had his palace here
4   ruined buildings   under the sheer cliff
dim rooms   where ghost-fires flicker green
a broken road   washed out by grieving torrents
ten thousand crannies   make your true pipe organs
8   autumn colors   your genuine high fashion
when lovely girls   have turned to yellow earth
what use now   their art of kohl and powder
of all attending   the golden chariot
12   not a remnant   but for these stone horses
sorrow's got me   I sit upon the grass
flood over with singing   tears drench my hands
step by step   we trudge the journey
16   who if any   lives till old

Translated by David Lattimore

At the Sky's End, Thinking of Li Po

Tu Fu

Cold winds   rise from the edge of heaven
True Gentleman   how fares your thought

Tu Fu was forty-seven years old when he wrote this poem in the year 759. He had just quit his disappointing career in the state bureaucracy and had begun the wanderings that would

```
       wild geese      what hour is your arrival
  4    river and lake      swell with autumn waters
       literature      is adverse to good fortune
       marsh trolls      relish the passerby
       you ought to share      a word with the slandered spirit
  8    hurl a poem      to him in the Mi-lo River
```

Translated by David Lattimore

occupy the rest of his life. His first stop was Ch'in-chou on the northwestern frontier of China, at the "edge of heaven."

Writing from Ch'in-chou, Tu Fu thinks of his elderly friend and mentor, the poet Li Po (see selection 45), who has been exiled (unjustly, Tu Fu believes) to the far south, and who now lives near Lake Tung-t'ing on the middle Yangtze, that is, in the region of "river and lake" (line 4). Tu Fu would like to know what thoughts Li Po has for him. But the autumn winds and waters rise—it is not a time of easy communication. In folklore, migrating geese can carry a letter from a loved one far away; but as it is now fall, the geese are going in the wrong direction. Not until spring can they deliver a letter to Tu Fu from his friend in the south.

Tu Fu's poem contains two folkloric references: to goose-messengers and to "trolls" of marshes (such as those around Lake Tung-t'ing) and mountain pools. These references make a gesture of courteous sympathy toward Li Po's characteristic themes, which especially include folklore, fantasy, and sublime scenery peopled with legendary beings. Goose-messengers also suggest intense affection for Li Po, since geese carry news between lovers or spouses.

Two other references in the poem express an extreme respect for Li Po.

First, in line 2 Tu Fu addresses Li Po not as *chün* ("milord") but, even more deferentially, as *chün-tzu*, a term which in Confucius and Mencius signifies the True Gentlemen. We are reminded that Li Po's poetry, besides its aspect of Taoist fantasy and self-abandon, displays as well a complementary aspect of Confucian earnestness and social concern, shown especially in his series of fifty-nine poems written to ancient airs or evoking an ancient atmosphere (see selection 45, last group).

Second, Tu Fu implies a likeness between Li Po and Ch'ü Yüan (see selection 148), earliest of Chinese poets to have come down to us with a distinct persona. Ch'ü Yüan is mentioned here as the "slandered spirit" (line 7). As writers, a certain similarity exists between the often extravagant Li Po and the rhapsodic, visionary, mythopoetic Ch'ü Yüan. From the more austere viewpoint of the Central Plain, both were poets of romantic outer regions: Li Po of Shu in the west (Szechwan), Ch'ü Yüan of Ch'u in the south (Hunan). Between the two there was also a relationship of contiguity, since Li Po now lived, as had Ch'ü Yüan, in the region of Ch'u.

There is a further similarity between Ch'ü Yüan and Li Po—as slandered spirits. Ch'ü Yüan, a minister to the king of Ch'u, had been slandered to his ruler and dismissed. He eventually drowned himself in the Mi-lo River (line 8), south of Lake Tung-t'ing. More than a thousand years later, Li Po had served, perhaps under duress, in the entourage of an illegitimate claimant to the throne, for which he had been jailed and later exiled. The charge that his friend had voluntarily joined a rebellion was regarded by Tu Fu as slanderous. Unstated is the fact that Tu Fu, an unappreciated loyal critic of the ruler—in which respect he, too, resembled Ch'ü Yüan—had reason to regard himself likewise as a slandered spirit. As such, he sends a poem to his fellow-spirit Li Po, suggesting that Li in turn offer a poem to their antique fellow sufferer in his watery resting place.

Li Po was pardoned in 759 but continued to live in the Yangtze area. Tu Fu now warns his reckless old friend that what happened before can happen again. Poets are their own worst enemies; their compulsive candor makes the literary life "adverse to good fortune" (line 5). But poets have external enemies too, envious slanderers or "trolls" (line 6) always happy to pounce upon and devour the straying traveler.

For Tu Fu's posthumous readers his lines have a poignancy that Li Po, because he predeceased Tu Fu, could not have felt—if in fact he ever received the poem. Twelve years after he wrote this poem and eight years after Li Po had died, Tu Fu's late wanderings, richly chronicled in his verses, carried him at last to the region of Ch'u. There he, too, died while traveling the rivers south of Lake Tung-t'ing. Ch'ü Yüan, Li Po, and Tu Fu, who with T'ao Ch'ien (see selection 29) and Su Shih (see selection 72) rank as China's most famous poets, all concluded their lives of adversity in the land of rivers and lakes.

49
Maple Bridge Night Mooring

Chang Chi (fl. 756)

Moon set, a crow caws
      frost fills the sky
River, maple, fishing-fires
      cross my troubled sleep.
Beyond the walls of Soochow
      from Cold Mountain temple
The midnight bell sounds
      reach my boat.

Translated by Gary Snyder

The poet was native of Hsiang-chou (present-day Hsiang-yang in Hupei). He became a Presented Scholar in 753 and assumed a series of lower and middle-level posts in government. About forty poems attributed to him are still extant. Of these, his considerable fame rests exclusively on the one selected here.

50

A Song of the Running Horse River: Presented on Saying Farewell to the Army Going on Campaign to the West

Ts'en Shen (715–770)

Don't you see how the Running Horse River flows along the edge of the Sea
    of Snow,[1]
Where vast and wild the brown of level sands reaches to the sky?

The wind howls at night in the ninth month over Lun-t'ai,
And a river full of broken boulders big as bushel baskets
Covers the earth with careening stones blown before the wind.

The Hsiung-nu[2] grass turns yellow now, their horses fit and plump;
West of the Altai[3] Range we see the dust of rebellion fly;
A general of the House of Han campaigns in the distant west.

Ts'en Shen, whose father died when he was still a child, came from an impoverished family.
Nonetheless, he became a Presented Scholar in the year 744 and served for many years as an
official on the western frontiers of the empire. Thus he had a personal understanding of army
life in remote places and under difficult conditions. He also became familiar with the customs
of non-Han peoples. This experience, unusual for a reputable Chinese author, is reflected in
his poems.

    The district of An-hsi, where Ts'en served for some years, was located in the far west, in what
is now Sinkiang or Chinese Turkestan. It has even been suggested that Ts'en may have
been present at the fateful battle of Talas (751), when Arab armies defeated the Chinese still
farther to the west. Ts'en's return to court and appointment as Omissioner was the result of a
petition signed by a number of officials including the poet Tu Fu. This took place at a crucial
juncture in T'ang history, for Ts'en joined the court in Ling-wu, where the new Emperor
Su Tsung was rallying forces for the battle against An Lu-shan, whose army had occupied the
capital.

    1. The geography of this poem is, if not fanciful, at least difficult of precise definition. The
Running Horse River and the Sea of Snow are entirely unidentifiable. One source places them
both in Russian Turkestan. More likely, they are either long forgotten local names or fictitious
ones used for effect.

    2. The Hsiung-nu (Huns) were the most important nomad enemies of the Chinese during
the Han dynasty. Although they were ancient history by Ts'en's day, he uses the name to refer to the frontier barbarians of his own time. This practice of referring to contemporary persons
and events in the guise of their Han dynasty counterparts was extremely common among
T'ang poets.

    3. "Altai" here translates the term "Metal Mountains." Of the various explanations offered
for this name, the Altai mountain range is the closest to the general area, but it is uncertain if
Ts'en is referring to this range or to any particular place at all. Context suggests that it may be
equivalent to T'ien-shan ("Heavenly Mountains").

The general[4] leaves his iron armor on throughout the night;
Troops move out at midnight to the sound of rattling halberds—
The wind cuts like a knifeblade, faces feel the slash.

Snow clings to the horses' coats, their sweat ascends in steam,
Only to turn to ice again on dappled and piebald backs;
Urgent dispatches are drafted in tents, the ink congeals on the stone.

When the Hunnish horsemen hear, their hearts will tremble within;
We know they will not dare to cross their swords and spears with ours:
At the west gate of Chü-shih[5] camp we await the display of your spoils.

Translated by Daniel Bryant

4. General Feng Chang-ch'ing, who appears in the titles of several of Ts'en's poems, was at the time military governor of the western frontier with the title Protector General of Pei-t'ing. His predecessor, the Korean Kao Hsien-chih, lost the battle of Talas to the Arabs in 751. While their victory at Talas was as much the extreme point of Arab expansion into central Asia as their defeat at Tours had been of their advance into western Europe a few years before, the Arabs failed to follow up their advantage. The Chinese were put on the defensive by the defeat and began losing ground to the local nomads from this time on. Ts'en Shen joined Feng's staff in 754 at the age of forty. He hoped, by doing so, to rise to a high place in the government, an ambition that had remained frustrated while he was in metropolitan China, despite his literary talents and distinguished family background. All this may help explain the respectful and laudatory tone with which Ts'en describes his commander's exploits. General Feng's career came to an unhappy end within a few years. He was defeated by the rebel An Lu-shan and subsequently put to death.

5. Chü-shih was the Han name for the area around the eastern part of the T'ien-shan in modern Dzungaria and Turfan.

51
In Illness, Dismissing My Singing Girl

Ssu-k'ung Shu (fl. 788)

Ten thousand things wound my heart when you're before my eyes,
I, lean and withered, to sleep facing such a flower!
I've used up all my yellow gold teaching you songs and dances—
go stay with someone else now, make a young man happy.

Translated by Burton Watson

Ssu-k'ung Shu attained the rank of Presented Scholar after success in the highest level of the civil service examinations. During and after the An Lu-shan rebellion (see selection 180), he was forced to move around quite a lot, including a period of banishment to Ch'ang-lin in Hupei. He was one of the "Ten Talents of the Ta-li Era" (766–779).

52

On Failing the Examination

Meng Chiao (751–814)

The dawn moon struggles to shine its light,
the man of sorrows struggles with his feelings.
Who says in spring things are bound to flourish?
4   All I see is frost on the leaves.
The eagle sickens, his power vanishes,
while little wrens soar on borrowed wings.
But leave them be, leave them be!—
8   these thoughts like wounds from a knife!

Translated by Burton Watson

The poet lost his wife fairly early in their marriage and his three sons all died young. He became a Presented Scholar only in 796 and, because of his unsuitability for officialdom, never had a successful career in government. Consequently, his was a life of poverty and ill fate. This is reflected in the themes of his poetry: the inconsistency of human relations, the suffering of the people, and personal misfortunes. Meng Chiao was a bitter and unhappy man.

53

The Girl of Mount Hua

Han Yü (768–824)

In streets east, streets west, they expound the Buddhist canon,
clanging bells, sounding conches, till the din invades the palace;
"sin," "blessing," wildly inflated, give force to threats and deceptions;
4   throngs of listeners elbow and shove as though through duckweed seas.
Yellow-robed Taoist priests preach their sermons, too,

Orphaned at an early age, Han Yü was brought up by his elder brother and sister-in-law. He became a Presented Scholar in the year 792 and subsequently held a number of official posts, including that of teacher at the Imperial College (see selection 205). Han Yü was twice exiled, the second time for a famous memorial submitted to the emperor reprimanding him for his devotion to Buddhism.

Han Yü was a major figure in the development of traditional Chinese literature. He proclaimed and put into practice a literary theory called *ku-wen* (the writing of antiquity or ancient-style writing) that resulted in a revitalized style of writing based on ancient ideals of clarity, conciseness, and utility. To this end, Han Yü incorporated elements of colloquial rhythm, diction, and syntax into both his prose and poetry, at the same time reaffirming the Confucian

but beneath their lecturns, ranks grow thinner than stars in the flush
    of dawn.
The girl of Mount Hua, child of a Taoist home,
8   longed to expel the foreign faith, win men back to the Immortals;
she washed off her powder, wiped her face, put on cap and shawl.
With white throat, crimson cheeks, long eyebrows of gray,
she came at last to ascend the chair, unfolding the secrets of Truth.
12 For anyone else the Taoist halls would hardly have opened their doors;
I do not know who first whispered the word abroad,
but all at once the very earth rocked with the roar of thunder.
Buddhist temples were swept clean, no trace of a believer,
16 while elegant teams jammed the lanes and ladies' coaches piled up.
Taoist halls were packed with people, many sat outside;
for latecomers there was no room, no way to get within hearing.
Hairpins, bracelets, girdle stones were doffed, undone, snatched off,
20 till the heaped-up gold, the mounds of jade glinted and glowed in
    the sunlight.
Eminent eunuchs from the heavenly court came with a summons
    to audience;
ladies of the six palaces longed to see the Master's face.
The Jade Countenance[1] nodded approval, granting her return;
24 dragon-drawn, mounting a crane, she came through blue-dark skies.
These youths of the great families—what do they know of the Tao,
milling about her a hundred deep, shifting from foot to foot?
Beyond cloud-barred windows, in misty towers, who knows what
    happens there

---

classics as the basis of education and good writing. His transformation of the contemporary
literary style still based on early medieval (third to seventh century) models, together with his
animosity toward popular Buddhism and Taoism, mark Han Yü as an important forerunner of
the Neo-Confucian movement of the Sung dynasty.

This trenchant poem, written in heptasyllabic "old poetry" form, gives a good idea of Han
Yü's narrative style, while displaying his well-known contempt for Buddhism and Taoism. The
poem begins with a description of the immense popularity of the Buddhist preachers of Ch'ang-
an, who had drawn the crowds away from their Taoist rivals, and of a sudden reversal of the
situation when the "girl of Mount Hua," a beautiful young Taoist priestess, appeared in the
capital to attract the attention even of the emperor himself. In the closing section, the poet
chides the rich young men of the capital who flock about the priestess for other than spiritual
reasons, and hints that her favors are reserved for more exalted personages. The bluebird in the
last line, bearer of love notes, is the messenger of the immortal spirit Hsi Wang-mu, the Queen
Mother of the West (see selection 187, note 5), to whom the priestess is compared. We have no
way of knowing whether Han Yü's insinuations were justified, though it might be recalled that
Yang Kuei-fei, the renowned favorite of Emperor Hsüan Tsung, originally entered the palace as
a Taoist priestess.

   1. The emperor.

28   where kingfisher curtains hang tier on tier and golden screens are deep?
The immortal's ladder is hard to climb, your bonds with this
   world weighty;
vainly you call on the bluebird to deliver your passionate pleas!

Translated by Burton Watson

54

Three Poems by the Most Eminent Woman Poet of the T'ang Period

Hsüeh T'ao (770?–832?)

Wind

Seeking marsh
orchids, a light
zephyr ranges.

It wafts over strings;
they cry out,
one chord.

Twigs in the woods
sing in whistles and rustles.

Along paths through the pine trees:
night-bracing
fresh.

Translated by Jeanne Larsen

The poet was born into a respectable family from the T'ang capital, Ch'ang-an. Her father, a minor official, died in Szechwan, leaving his family stranded with no secure source of support. The adolescent Hsüeh T'ao joined the entertainers' guild and became well known for her poetry and wit. She was summoned to serve as a courtesan-hostess for the military governor of Szechwan. Her reputation continued to spread, and she exchanged poems with some of the most famous poets of the day. Hsüeh T'ao retired to an independent life as an artisan. Her name is still associated with sheets of beautiful paper on which poems may be written. Of about five hundred poems by Hsüeh T'ao once in circulation, no more than ninety survive.

Listening to a Monk Play the Reed Pipes

Dawn cicadas choke back sobs,
Evening orioles grieve.

Lively language,
quick,
precise,
from ten fingers' tips.

He's done with reading holy texts;
He wants to play a bit.

His tune floats after
temple chimes
to gild clear autumn's air.

Translated by Jeanne Larsen

This beautifully musical poem takes on the special problem of music played by a Buddhist monk. Strictly speaking, from the Buddhist standpoint such an attractive, emotionally stirring art form ought to be shunned: it fosters attachment to the world of illusion. Yet a plaintive or ethereal melody can mingle an austere awareness with its appeal to the senses.

The opening images remind the reader of the melancholy associations of reed pipes, which came to China from the north. Though the poem moves to a less lugubrious metaphor, comparing the melody to the rise and fall of human speech, the final image points out the tension between attachment and nonattachment in this Buddhist music. The metal chimes struck to mark the sections of the day have autumnal and transcendent associations of long standing. Their notes, and those of the pipes, are depicted as scattering through the sky like precious gold leaf applied to a maṇḍala, (Buddhist painting usually having a circular form) or a copy of a sūtra (Buddhist scripture). But "to gild" (ni) also implies "to muddy" (ni).

Lotus-Gathering Boat

Lotus-laden,
pushing through,
a single windblown leaf

tells the news: it's fall again,
time to fish
and sport.

The moon-hare runs, the sun-crow flies,
human chatter stills.

Hsüeh T'ao describes this scene in terms that mingle the human world with the green realm of plants. The pink or red sleeves suggest both women in appealing clothing and the rosy petals of the blossoms on the stream. The single leaf blown before the wind is, of course, the lotus gatherers' skiff. The original describes the boat with an ambiguous phrase; it is simultaneously

Pink tinted sleeves fill up the brook
and poling songs
begin

Translated by Jeanne Larsen

_____

presented as "weighed down by" gathered lotuses and as pushing its way through others yet un-
plucked.

The amatory air of many poems on the topic invites us to read Hsüeh's with the old
association of fishing and sexuality in mind. The movements of the mythic rabbit in the moon
and the three-legged sun-crow (see selection 148, section II, line 68) remind us of time's passing.

55
River Snow

Liu Tsung-yüan (773–819)

These thousand peaks cut off the flight of birds
On all the trails, human tracks are gone.
A single boat—coat—hat—an old man!
Alone fishing chill river snow.

Translated by Gary Snyder

Liu Tsung-yüan became a Presented Scholar in the year 793. His official career was
meteoric. Joining a group of political reformers some years later, Liu gained power for a short
while prior to the death of the emperor who had supported change. The new emperor distrusted
the reform coterie, and Liu was demoted to a position subordinate to the prefect of Yung-chou.
Still later, he was made prefect of Liu-chou, another appointment far removed from the centers
of power. Liu often satirized the meanness and corruption of officialdom. One of the finest prose
stylists of the T'ang period, he was a master of the ancient-style essay (see introductory note to
selection 53). A sensitive poet as well, many of his most memorable pieces describe the scenes of
his exile and the complicated feelings of a northerner banished to the distant south.

56
Presented to the Taoist Paragon Mao

Cheng Huan (776–839)

The ultimate Tao is nameless;
The ultimate man lives long.

By surveying the range of depicted things
4   We may seem to deduce his true form.
Square mouth richly glossed with vermilion;
Thick eyebrows brushed with blue.
The bearing of a pine—from stock full blown;
8   The substance of a crane—by nature weightless.
In the Tao and its force—divinely transcendent;
In his inward store—numinous of heart.
Pink flesh and silky hair;
12   External blazons floriate and vital.
Complexion as if embodying fragrance;
Aspect like a harmony of lights.
Embryonic—hermetic—fashioning mutations;
16   Ingesting yin, emitting yang.
I have heard that An Ch'i[1]
Is hidden or visible—unpredictably.
He may be down in our world;
20   He may be roving up in the expanse of blue.
Vivat! This perfect being!
Could he not be An Chi's later incarnation,
Repeated here those sylphine bones?—
24   Long to endure without wasting away.
Like moonlight his shining pupils,
Clear-seeing as if just new;
Soft and plump his youthful features,
28   Fresh and glittering like the spring:
The equal of metal or stone,
Or indelible vermilion and azure.[2]
Were he upon a Heaven-piercing Platform,
32   To be seen there by ordinary folk,
Even common gentry would regard him with reverence,
Aware that they themselves are shrouded in dust;
While noble men would take his full measure—
Ah, with what reverence! As if a god!

Translated by Edward H. Schafer

Cheng Huan became a Presented Scholar in 794.
   1. A legendary transcendent of antiquity.
   2. As here, the poem is full of images and terms relating to painting. It would seem that Mao is an artist who has painted an Ultimate Man (the Taoist ideal person) and is himself being praised as one by the poet.

57
Apotheosis

Wu Yün (?–778)

Nine dragons—how fluent their undulations!—
Bear me aloft by nebulous sky-stays.
I look down with slanted glance, missing my old country,
4   But wind and dust blend it in featureless verdure.
Gently, easily, I separate from the human domain;
Away, away, drawing near to the town of God.
Surmounting the strands of starry chronograms above,
8   Observing the lights of sun and moon below.
Swiftly now, past the Grand Tenuity:[1]
The blaze of a sky dwelling—gleaming, glittering.

Translated by Edward H. Schafer

Wu Yün, one of the best-known Taoist adepts of Hsüan Tsung's reign (712–756), was called to court for his expertise in spiritual matters as well as his poetic brilliance. His most interesting poems celebrate, as this one, the adept's ecstatic travels through the celestial regions. Wu Yün's sponsorship was influential in earning the imperial summons that brought the famous bard Li Po (see selection 45) to court. He is also known as the author of several essays on the cultivation of the Tao (Way).

1. The southern palace of the Lord of Heaven at the autumnal equinox (formerly in Leo and Virgo).

58
Untitled Poems

Cold Mountain (Ninth century)

2

whoever reads my poems
must guard his purity of heart

We may think of Cold Mountain as a state of mind rather than as an individual poet. The Cold Mountain collection consists of 307 poems written during the seventh through the ninth centuries. A notable feature of these poems is the relatively large proportion of vernacular elements they include, although they are by no means written in a purely vernacular style. Their Zen Buddhist orientation has made them very popular in the present century, which has experienced a worldwide resurgence of this sect of intuitive Buddhism. As such, they have

his greed at once be modesty
flattery suddenly honesty
banish and be rid of evil karma[1]
trust and accept his true nature
get his buddha body today
hurry as if these were orders

16

people ask the way to Cold Mountain
roads don't reach Cold Mountain
summer the ice never melts
sunup the fog is thick
how did someone like me arrive
our minds aren't the same
if they were
you could get there then

29

pole your three winged galleons[2]
ride your thousand-mile stallions
you still won't reach my home
it's called the darkest wild
cliff cave deep in the mountains
clouds and thunder come down all day
I'm not Master Confucius
I have nothing to offer others

128

a graceful handsome youth
well versed in classics and histories
everyone calls him sir
they all address him scholar
but he hasn't been able to get a position
and he doesn't know how to handle a plow
this is how books fool us

---

attracted some of the very best translators of Chinese poetry. Red Pine's versions are unique in capturing the spirit of the originals, perhaps because he comes close to living the life espoused in these crazy, but wise, poems.

1. The word "karma" includes the act (to be banished) as well as its result (to be rid of) and is said to be evil when its result is suffering.

2. The Chinese had three sizes of a large yet fast, and hence winged, warship that used oars and poles.

173

raise girls but not too many
once born you have to train them
smack their heads and yell watch out
beat their behinds and shout shut up
and before they learn how to work a loom
they won't touch a basket or broom
Old Lady Chang advised her young jenny
you're big but no match for your Mother

183

they laugh at me hey farm boy
your cheeks are a little rough
your hat's not very high
and your belt sure is tight
it's not that I don't catch the trends
no money I can't catch up
but one day I'll be rich
and stick a stupa[3] on my head

200

the unfortunate human disorder
a palate that's never weary
of steamed piglet with garlic sauce
roast duck with pepper and salt
deboned raw fish mince
unskinned cooked pork cheek
unaware of the bitterness of others' lives
as long as their own are sweet

201

reading won't save us from death
and reading won't free us from want
then why do we like to be literate
the literate lord it over others
if a grown man can't read
where can he live in peace
squeeze garlic juice in your crowfoot[4]
and you'll forget it's bitter

---

3. A stupa is a conical structure erected over the relics of a Buddha.
4. *Coptis chinensis*, a very bitter medicinal herb.

228

his mind is as high as a mountain
his ego doesn't yield to others
he can preach the Vedic Canon[5]
or discuss the Three Religions[6]
in his heart no shame
he breaks precepts and flouts the Vinaya[7]
boasts a law for superior men
and claims to be the first
fools all praise and sigh
wise men clap and laugh
a mirage of flower in the sky
how can he avoid growing old
better to know nothing at all
to sit quiet and have no cares

246

yesterday I went to a cloud observatory[8]
and met some Taoist priests
star caps and moon capes askew
they said we inhabit hill and stream
I asked them the art of immortality
they said how could we presume
for what's called the spirit sublime
the elixir must be the secret of the gods
till death we wait for a crane
and they said we'll ride off on a fish[9]
later I thought this through
and concluded they were crazy
just look at an arrow shot into space
in a moment it falls back down
even if they do become immortals
they'll just be corpse-haunting ghosts
the moon of the mind is so perfectly clear
how can phenomena compare
if you want to know the art of immortals
within yourself is the first of spirits

5. The *Vedas* include the sacred literature of Hinduism.
6. Confucianism, Taoism, and Buddhism.
7. That portion of the Buddhist canon dealing with regulation of moral behavior by precept.
8. Taoists indicated their hermitages by the word "observatory."
9. The immortal, Wang Tzu-ch'iao (see selection 203, note 7), rode off on a crane to the land of immortals, while Ch'in Kao rode off on a carp.

don't follow Masters of the Yellow Turban[10]
holding onto idiocy maintaining doubt

267

ever since I left home
I've developed an interest in yoga
contracting and stretching the four-limbed Whole
attending intently the six-sensed All
wearing rough clothes all year
eating coarse food morning and night
hard on the trail even now
I'm hoping to meet the Buddha

283

one Budding-Talent Wang[11]
laughs at my prosody[12]
he says I don't know a wasp's waist
much less a stork's knee[13]
I can't control my flats and leans[14]
all my words come helter-skelter
I laugh at the poems he writes
a blind man's songs of the sun

307

whoever has Cold Mountain's poems
is better off than reading sūtras[15]
paste them up on your screen[16]
and read them from time to time

Translated by Red Pine

10. The Yellow Turbans were a Taoist sect of the Han dynasty whose name later became associated with those Taoists whose practice emphasized alchemy and magic.

11. A Budding Talent was roughly equivalent to our Bachelor of Arts. Although the designation as an official degree ceased to be employed as of 651, it continued to be used with reference to men-of-letters throughout the T'ang.

12. In his *Poetics*, Shen Yüeh (see selection 31) set forth a number of prosodic tonal errors.

13. When the second and fifth syllables in a pentasyllabic line have the same tone, it is called a "wasp's waist." When the fifth and fifteenth syllables of the poem have the same tone, it is called a "stork's knee."

14. Referring to tones that are level/even and slanted/contoured.

15. Buddhist scriptures.

16. The Chinese used to place inside their rooms folding frames inset with paper or silk backed with wood to protect them from drafts.

59
Looking for a Recluse but Failing to Find Him

Chia Tao (779–843)

Under the pines I questioned the boy.
"My master's off gathering herbs.
All I know is he's here on the mountain—
   clouds are so deep, I don't know where. . . ."

Translated by Burton Watson

The poet came from a humble family. He stayed for a while in a Buddhist temple and became a monk. Later, he gave up monkhood to make several attempts at the civil service examinations. Having failed them all, he continued to live a life of constant frustration and misfortune. Chia's poetry, mostly in the form of presentations and responses to Buddhist and Taoist monks or recluses, is full of understated oddities and mysteries.

60
Pitying the Farmer

Li Shen (780–846)

He hoes the grain under a midday sun,
sweat dripping down on the soil beneath the grain.
Who realizes that the food in the food bowl,
every last morsel of it, is bought with such toil?

Translated by Burton Watson

Li Shen was one of the initiators of the new ballad movement.

61

To Patriarch Sun at Hua-yang[1] Grotto

Li Te-yü (787–849)

I

In what place is one most free of bonds?
At Hua-yang, eighth of the Heavens.
The wind in the pines carries dew in all its clarity;
The moon, through the bearded lichen, is cleansed of mist.
Suddenly startled—a crane at the gemmy altar;
Humming in season—cicadas on the jeweled tree.
I long to post my thoughts from a thousand tricents:
"My only love is the spring at Phoenix Gate."

II

The torrent-iris on the stone puts out purple floss;
The dark blue hills clumped in seclusion—the waters swollen full.
Sweetflag flowers are fixed there, where no men are;
On such a day in spring one must meet only a "feathered visitor."[2]

III

Searching alone on the sand-bar with its orchids, diverted by dilatory beams
    of light;
Leaning at ease on the window with its pines, gazing off at blue-misted hills;
Imagining afar the spring mountains in the pale glow of the luminous moon,
And the clear lithophones at a jadestone altar—where you return from
    "Pacing the Void."[3]

Translated by Edward H. Schafer

A noted parallel prose stylist, Li Te-yü became a leader of an important court faction to which many excellent writers were attached. These included authors of some of the most memorable classical language short stories, for instance, Li Kung-tso (see selection 253). Like many politicians of his day, Li Te-yü had Taoist predilections.

1. "Golden-altared" Hua-Yang is a grotto-heaven hidden at the roots of Mao Shan, a mountain sacred to Taoists. See selections 31 and 32.

2. A Taoist divinity, or, by courtesy, a priest or mature initiate.

3. A traditional chant about the transit of space by a Taoist adept.

62
At Ch'ang-ku,[1] Reading: To Show to My Man Pa

Li Ho (790–816)

Echo of insects where the lamplight thins;
the cold night heavy with medicine fumes:
because you pity a broken-winged wanderer,
through bitterest toil you follow me still.

Translated by Burton Watson

Li Ho came from a good family and enjoyed the patronage of Han Yü (see selection 53), but was disappointed in his aspirations to forge a career in government service. As his dates indicate, he died at a young age. The works of the youthful genius, written in an old style, seek to recapture some of the mysteries and myths of the shamanic songs in *The Elegies of Ch'u* (see selection 148). A general aura of eeriness and allusiveness informs much of his imagery, which he uses to criticize the ills of his own times.

1. Ch'ang-ku, the poet's country home, was west of Loyang. This poem was probably written shortly before his death.

My Man Pa Replies

Li Ho

Big-nose looks best in mountain-coarse clothes;
bushy-brows should stick to his poetry toils!
Were it not for the songs you sing,
who would know the depths of autumn sorrow?

Translated by Burton Watson

In this poem, Li Ho imagines how his servant might answer the previous quatrain. It picks up the heavy melancholic tone of the first poem and gently mocks it.

Ravine on a Cold Evening

Li Ho

White foxes[1] howl at mountain wind beneath the moon;
Its autumn cold sweeps up clouds and leaves a sapphire void.

1. White animals, especially foxes, often appear as manifestations of the supernatural in Chinese lore.

Jade mists shimmering wet are white as curtains;
The Silver Channel's[2] arcing swell flows to the eastern sky.
By the stream a sleeping egret dreams of migrating geese;
Faint ripples, without a murmur, drift slowly by.
Twisting cliffs of layered hills, dragons coil on coil;
Bitter bamboo[3] sound for a stranger their sighing flutes.

Translated by Maureen Robertson

2. The River of Heaven or Milky Way.
3. A variety of bamboo used in the manufacture of song-flutes.

63
The Robe of Golden Thread

Autumn Maid Tu (T'ang)

I urge you, milord, not to cherish your robe of golden thread;[1]
Rather, milord, I urge you to cherish the time of your youth.
When the flower is open and pluckable, you simply must pluck it;
Don't wait till there are no flowers, vainly to break branches.

Translated by Victor H. Mair

The poet was a celebrated beauty of Chin-ling (present-day Nanking) who became the concubine of Li Ch'i, the military commissioner of Chen-hai (present-day Chekiang province). Li was executed for treason about the year 807, whereupon Tu Ch'iu-niang (Autumn Maid) became a favorite in the imperial palace. The poet Tu Mu (see selection 64), in a biography of her, relates how she became intoxicated after drinking wine from a jade cup and wrote this poem to encourage Li Ch'i to relax and enjoy himself. Li was reported to have been quite fond of the song and sang it often.

1. Your official career and dignity.

64
Red Embankment[1]

Tu Mu (803–852)

Stalagmites in spring caves rise to more stalactites;
Ponds avoid the turning cliffs' dog-toothed edges.

Tu Mu came from an established background of nobility. His grandfather was Tu Yu, compiler of an important encyclopedia. When he was in his adolescence, however, his father

I smile at myself curling into the womb, horns on my head pulled in,
Returning coiled up on the misty steps, just like a snail!

Translated by John M. Ortinau

---

died and the family fortunes declined. He became a Presented Scholar in 828. Later, frustrated in his political career by factionalism at court, he turned his attention to beautiful women. Tu Mu had a strong sense of Confucian idealism and a deep love of the past. He is counted among the finest of the late T'ang poets.

1. Chu-p'o, located at Fan-ch'uan, the poet's childhood home.

65
Boasting of My Son

Li Shang-yin (c. 813–c. 858)

Kun-shih, my pride, my son,
Is handsome and bright without a match.
In swaddling clothes, less than a year old,
4   He already could tell six from seven.
In his fourth year he knew his name,
And never cast his eyes on pears and chestnuts.[1]
My friends and acquaintances often look at him
8   And say, "This child is a young phoenix![2]
Even in a previous age when looks were esteemed,
He would have been placed in the first class!"

The poet lost his father at age nine and had an unsettled early life. He became a Presented Scholar in 837, but he never attained high rank and died out of office. Li Shang-yin's poems are full of bizarre fantasy and evoke a mood of subtle sentimentality that is highly symbolic yet romantic. This strange and obscure quality is enhanced by a language that is both archaic and colloquial. Also a master of parallel prose, Li is said to be the author of an extremely earthy and witty *Miscellany* (see selection 219).

1. Lines 4–6 allude to the following excerpt from T'ao Ch'ien's (365–427) humorous poem "Reproaching My Sons":

Yung and Tuan are both thirteen,
But cannot tell six from seven;
T'ung-tzu is nearly nine,
But only looks for pears and chestnuts.

By relating the opposite, Li Shang-yin shows his own son's superiority. For T'ao Ch'ien's poem, see selection 29.

2. For young phoenix, the original has "vermilion cave," alluding to the legend that phoenixes live on the Vermilion Cave Mountain. The phoenix is, of course, one of the noblest and most auspicious creatures in Chinese mythology and symbolism.

Or else, "He has the air of an immortal!"
12   Or, "He has the bone structure of a swallow or a crane!"[3]
How could they have said such things?
Just to comfort me in my declining years!
In a beautiful and mild month of spring,
16   He joins my nephews and nieces at play,
Rushing round the hall and through the woods,
Bubbling with noise like a golden cauldron boiling!
When a worthy guest comes to the door,
20   He will rashly ask to go out first;
When the guest asks what he wants,
He will hedge and not tell the truth.
Then he'll come back to mimic the guest,
24   Breaking through the door and holding Father's tablet;[4]
He'll ridicule the guest for being dark like Chang Fei,[5]
Or laugh at him for stuttering like Teng Ai.[6]
One moment he is a heroic eagle with bristling feathers,
28   Next moment he is a brave horse in high spirits;
Having cut a thick bamboo pole,
He rides on it and runs with wild abandon.
Suddenly he starts to play the stage bully,[7]
32   Calling the servant in a measured voice.
Then, at night, by the gauze lantern,
He bows his head and worships the Buddha's image.
He raises his whip to catch a spider's web,
36   Or bends his head to suck the honey from a flower;
He vies with the butterflies in agility,
And does not yield to the floating catkins for speed.
Before the steps he meets his elder sister,
40   And loses heavily in a game of draughts.[8]
So he runs away to play with her dressing case,
And pulls off all its golden knobs!
Held by her, he struggles and stumbles,
44   But his angry pride cannot be subdued.

3. According to Chinese physiognomy, a "swallow's chin" and a "crane's bone structure" betokened a noble destiny.

4. *Hu*, a long and narrow tablet held by officials, was originally for writing on but later became a purely ceremonial ornament.

5. A famous general (d.221), a household name even now among Chinese children.

6. Teng Ai (197–264) was a witty and able official and general who suffered from stuttering.

7. Literally, "military counselor," the protagonist in a type of comic skit known as the "military counselor play," in which the protagonist, dressed like an official, would bully the deuteragonist, dressed as a servant (see line 32).

8. A board game played with six black and six white pieces.

He bends down and pulls open the carved window;
Then spits on the zither to wipe its lacquered surface!
Sometimes he watches me practicing calligraphy,
48   Standing upright, without moving his knees.
The ancient brocade he wants for a coat;
The jade roller,[9] too, he begs to have.
He asks Father to write on a "spring banner";[10]
52   The "spring banner" is suitable for a spring day.
The slanting banana leaves roll up the paper;
The magnolia[11] flowers hang lower than the brush.
My son, your father was formerly fond of studying;
56   He worked earnestly and hard at his writings.
Now, haggard and wan, and nearly forty,[12]
He has no flesh left and fears fleas and lice.
My son, don't follow your father's example
60   In studying hard and seeking A's and B's![13]
Look at Jang-chü[14] with his *Art of War*,
Or Chang Liang with what he learned from the Yellow Stone:[15]
They became teachers of kings overnight,
64   And no longer had to bother about trifling things!
Moreover, now in the west and in the north,
The Ch'iang and Jung[16] tribes rampage unchecked;
The Court can neither kill nor pardon them,
68   But allows them to grow like an incurable disease.
You, my son, should quickly grow up,
And go to the tiger's den to look for cubs![17]
You should become a marquis of ten thousand households;
72   Don't stick to a bag of classical books!

Translated by James J. Y. Liu

9. For a scroll of painting or calligraphy.

10. A banner with auspicious expressions written on it and hung up to welcome spring.

11. Also called "tree-brush," since its budding flowers are pointed like Chinese writing brushes. The poet here contrasts the brushlike flowers with the real brush.

12. It was not uncommon for Chinese poets to moan about getting old at such an early age, and one should remember that the general expectancy of life then was low.

13. Referring to the classification of successful candidates at the civil service examinations.

14. A general of the fourth century B.C.E. after whom a book on the art of war was named.

15. Chang Liang (d. 189 B.C.E.), a military strategist, was reported to have received a book on the art of war from an old man who said he was the spirit of a yellow stone. Chang was one of the main supporters of the first emperor of the Han dynasty and was enfeoffed Marquis of Liu.

16. Ancient names for certain Central Asian tribes, used here to refer to disturbances caused by the Tang-hsiang (a Ch'iang tribe) and the Uighurs in 849 and 850.

17. The line alludes to a famous remark by Pan Ch'ao (33–103), conqueror of Central Asia: "If you do not enter the tiger's den, how can you get the tiger's cubs?"—a saying that has remained proverbial to the present day. The allusion is particularly appropriate since the poet is exhorting his son to grow up and fight the Central Asian tribes.

Master Chia [1]

Li Shang-yin

To the audience hall [2] the worthy banished minister was recalled;
Master Chia's talents were matchless in the world.
Alas, in vain did the Emperor move his seat forward at midnight—
Instead of asking about the people, he asked about the gods!

Translated by James J. Y. Liu

The poem is a satire on the superstitions of the T'ang emperors, many of whom tried to obtain the elixir of life. The poet shows his disapproval by deploring the fact that when Emperor Wen of Han recalled the banished Chia Yi to court, all he wanted to learn from Chia was the nature of spirits and gods instead of the life of the people.

1. Chia Yi (201–169 B.C.E.) was a famous scholar and statesman who was banished from the court of Emperor Wen of Han but later recalled. When the emperor asked him about the gods, Chia embarked on a discourse on the subject. It so interested the emperor that he moved his sitting mat forward and listened until midnight (see selection 150).

2. The main hall of the Wei-yang Palace in Han times, where the emperor summoned Chia Yi.

Alone by the Autumn River

Li Shang-yin

All spring, my sorrows grew like lotus leaves,
now they wither and my autumn sadness grows.

Grief is as long and as wide as life.
I watch the autumn river. I listen to it flow.

Translated by Sam Hamill

66
Impromptu on a Hangover

P'i Jih-hsiu (c. 833–883)

I block out the midday brightness with a screen depicting dark woods,
burn a stick of heavy incense, nursing my hangover.

P'i Jih-hsiu became a Presented Scholar in 867 but was a recluse before embarking upon an official career. Much of his early prose and poetry is concerned with social injustice (see, for

What's this? As evening comes I'm ready for a drink again!
Beyond the wall I hear the cry of someone selling clams.

Translated by Burton Watson

example, selection 231) and advocates the moral philosophy of Mencius (see selection 8) and Han Yü (see selection 53). But during a sojourn in Soochow as a virtual guest of Lu Kuei-meng (?–c.881, see selection 236), a fellow bard, he indulged himself in pleasure and the study of Taoism. He made a return to his early social commitment by joining a rebel group, but was executed by its leader for his forthright criticism.

67
Oxhead Temple

Ssu-k'ung T'u (837–908)

From my favorite place in the Chung-nan Mountains,
The chanting of the monks emerges into the dark sky.
Groves of trees stand out clearly in the somber solitude,
Thin mist floats in the desolate void.

Translated by Hellmut Wilhelm

Ssu-k'ung T'u is famous as the author of the long poetic work entitled "Twenty-four Categories of Poetry" (*Erh-shih-ssu shih p'in*), considered one of the most important works of T'ang period literary criticism. As the T'ang dynasty collapsed, he retreated to an isolated valley in Shansi. There he wrote exquisite poems of his own about the landscape and about the monks and temples of the area.

68
On a Visit to Ch'ung-chen Taoist Temple I See in the South Hall the List of Successful Candidates in the Imperial Examinations

Yü Hsüan-chi (c. 844–c. 868)

Cloud-capped peaks fill the eyes
In the spring sunshine.

Yü Hsüan-chi is the most celebrated woman poet of the T'ang period after Hsüeh T'ao (see selection 54). She had been a courtesan and the concubine of a government official, but later

Their names are written in beautiful characters
And posted in order of merit.
How I hate this silk dress
That conceals a poet.
I lift my head and read their names
In powerless envy.

Translated by Kenneth Rexroth and Ling Chung

---

took up residence in a Taoist convent. She is said to have been executed for murdering a maid of hers who had become intimate with one of her gentlemen callers.

Exceedingly few women gained literacy in traditional China and, of those who did, virtually none of them took part in the vaunted civil service examinations. The ability to write passable poetry was considered to be a requisite for becoming a successful bureaucrat in old China. Yü Hsüan-chi was a poet, but her gender disqualified her from becoming an official.

69

A Locust Wood Mallet for Papermaking

—*Given to Chou T'ai-ch'u*

Lin Pu (967–1028)

Light and dry,
Fit to the hand,
It's from an ancient locust.
A few blows:
Pure echoes
Penetrate pool and terrace.

Besides the mallet
The "fish-netting" of the mold
Is slick and sleek.
When you write a new poem
Perhaps you will send me a copy.

Translated by Paul Hansen

A reclusive poet of Hangchow, Lin Pu remained unmarried throughout his life. He was a lover of nature and devoted admirer of the beautiful scenery of the West Lake region, where he lived on the island of Orphan Mountain.

70

Sharing Lodging with Hsieh Shih-hou[1] in the Library of the Hsü Family and Being Much Bothered by the Noise of Rats

Mei Yao-ch'en (1002–1060)

The lamp burns blue, everyone asleep;
from their holes the hungry rats steal out:
flip-flop—a rattle of plates and saucers;
clatter-crash!—the end of my dream.
I fret—will they knock off the inkslab on the desk?
worry—are they gnawing those shelves of books?
My little son mimics a cat's miaowing,
and that's a silly solution for sure!

Translated by Burton Watson

The author, one of the best-known early Sung poets, held a series of minor government posts. He wrote in a simple, unpretentious style about the details of daily life and about various social ills. An admirer of Han Yü (see selection 53), he participated with Ou-yang Hsiu (see selection 206) and others in the revival of Confucianism. The poet and critic Liu K'e-chuang (1187–1269) characterized him with a technical term for the founder of a Buddhist sect as "the Mountain-opening Patriarch of the poetry of this dynasty." The tragic deaths of his first wife and two young children led Mei to write poems of great pathos. He stressed the "flat and bland" (*p'ing-tan*) and wrote about reality as opposed to Buddhist and Taoist mysticism and enlightenment.

1. Hsieh was a nephew of the poet's wife, who had died earlier in the year this poem was written (1044) in K'aifeng. He was married to a daughter of the Hsü family. The poet and his two little children were spending the night at the Hsü home.

Shih-hou Pointed out to Me that from Ancient Times There Had Never Been a Poem on the Subject of Lice, and Urged Me to Try Writing One

Mei Yao-ch'en

A poor man's clothes—ragged and easy to get dirty,
easy to get dirty and hard to keep free of lice.
Between the belt and the lower robe is where they swarm,

ascending in files to the fur collar's margin.
They hide so cleverly—How can I ferret them out?—
dining on blood, making themselves at home.
My world, too, has its sallies and withdrawals;
why should I bother to pry into yours?

Translated by Burton Watson

Sad Remembrance

Mei Yao-ch'en

From the time you came into my house
you never seemed to mind being poor,
every evening sewing till midnight,
lunch ready a little past noon.
Ten days and nine we ate pickles;
one day—a wonder—we dined on dried meat.
East and west for eighteen years,
the two of us sharing bitter and sweet,
counting all along on a hundred years' love—
who'd have thought you'd be gone in one night!
I still remember when the end came,
how you held my hand, not able to speak—
this body, though it lives on,
at the last will join you in dust.

Translated by Burton Watson

Memories of the poet's first wife, a daughter of a well-to-do family, who had died the year before this poem was written (1045).

The Dappled Horse

Mei Yao-ch'en

The boat moored, lunch in a lonely village;
on the far bank I see a dappled horse,
in lean pasture, gaunt with hunger;

scruffy birds flocking down to peck his feed.
Pity is powerless—I have no bow;
again and again I try to pelt them with clods
but I haven't the strength to manage a hit,
face sweaty and hot with chagrin.

Translated by Burton Watson

Written on a journey by river boat.

Marrying Again

Mei Yao-ch'en

Some days ago I remarried,
delighting in now, sorrowful for the past;
someone to entrust the household to,
no more my lone shadow under the moon.
Force of habit—I call the wrong name;
as of old, something weighing on my heart.
How lucky I am—gentle and mild:
to have found two women with natures like this!

Translated by Burton Watson

An Offering for the Cat

Mei Yao-ch'en

Since I got my cat Five White
the rats never bother my books.
This morning Five White died.
4   I make offerings of rice and fish,
bury you in mid-river
with incantations—I wouldn't slight you.
Once you caught a rat,
8   ran round the garden with it squeaking in your mouth;
you hoped to put a scare into the other rats,
to clean up my house.

Written on a river journey.

When we'd come aboard the boat
12   you shared our cabin,
      and though we'd nothing but meager dried rations,
      we ate them without fear of rat piss and gnawing—
      because you were diligent,
16   a good deal more so than the pigs and chickens.
      People make much of their prancing steeds;
      they tell me nothing can compare to a horse or donkey—
      enough!—I'll argue the point no longer,
20   only cry for you a little.

Translated by Burton Watson

71

Bald Mountain

Wang An-shih (1021–1086)

My duties took me to a spot by the sea—
there to gaze upon a mountain isle I stopped my boat
as I wondered who had denuded it so;
4   a villager explained it to me and I quote:

"One monkey on the mountain did chatter,
another followed in playful pursuit;
they mated and gave birth to a son—
8   a host of sons—and still more grandsons to boot.

Lush vegetation covered the mountain,
roots and berries, at first, they easily took;
they clambered up to the highest places
12   and, crouching, ferreted out every nook.

Wang An-shih was famous for the enormously controversial reforms in all spheres of government that he instituted during his period in power at the Sung court. He was intent on rectifying social mores, the deterioration of which he believed had led to the imminent disintegration of the state. The measures that he advocated, however, were too harsh and their implementation was too rapid, causing a strong reaction even from those, such as Su Shih (see selection 72), who were sympathetic with his aims.

In his earlier poetry, Wang focused on social and political problems and stressed Confucian ideals. After retirement, his works became more intimate and reflective. He is also considered to be one of the eight prose masters of the T'ang-Sung period.

Each in this host of monkeys made himself sleek and fat,
while the mountain was utterly ravished;
wrangling with each other to fill their stomachs,
16   on talk of conservation no leisure was lavished.

The big monkeys found the going tough,
the small monkeys were, of course, all the more constrained;
little by little, they nipped and they nibbled,
20   till not a single blade of grass remained."

Though the monkey possesses superhuman craft,
he isn't adept at wielding hoe and plow himself;
the craving he has for fruit and grain
24   is invariably satisfied through pelf.

Alas for this mountain encircled by sea!
On all four sides they spy, but there's nowhere to flee;
while the progression of life goes on without cease
28   and the year draws to a close, what plan will there be?

Translated by Victor H. Mair

Confiscating Salt

Wang An-shih

From the local office, orders flying thicker than comb's teeth:
along the seacoast, salt confiscation stricter than ever.
Poverty moans and sobs under a broken roof
while boatloads of inspectors patrol back and forth.
Islands of the ocean, from times past lean and barren;
island folk struggling just to keep alive:
boil sea water or starve to death;
who can sit unmoving, not try to escape?
And now they say there are pirates hereabouts
who murder traveling merchants, scuttle their boats—
The life of one subject weighs heavier than the realm!
What true man would vie with others for a hairbreadth's gain?

Translated by Burton Watson

Salt was a government monopoly and the officials made every effort to prevent people living
on the seacoast from boiling water and extracting salt for private profit. The poem attacks the
government for depriving the people of a possible livelihood and competing with them for profit.

72

White Crane Hill

Su Shih (1037–1101)

At my new place on White Crane Hill we dug a well forty feet deep. We struck a layer of rock partway down, but finally broke through and got to water.

Seacoast wears you out with damp and heat;
my new place is better—high and cool.
In return for the sweat of hiking up and down
4   I've a dry spot to sleep and sit.
But paths to the river are a rocky hell;
I wince at the water-bearer's aching back.
I hired four men, put them to work
8   hacking through layers of obdurate rock.
Ten days and they'd gone only eight or ten feet;
below was a stratum of solid blue stone.
Drills all day struck futile sparks—
12   when would we ever see springs bubble up?
I'll keep you filled with rice and wine,
you keep your drills and hammers flying!
Mountain rock must end some time—
16   stubborn as I am, I won't give up.
This morning the houseboy told me with joy
they're into dirt soft enough to knead!
At dawn the pitcher brought up milky water;
20   by evening, it was clearer than an icy stream.
All my life has been like this—
what way to turn and not run into blocks?
But Heaven has sent me a dipper of water;
24   arm for a pillow,[1] my happiness overflows.

Translated by Burton Watson

For a note on Su Shih, see selection 156.

In 1097, the year before he wrote this poem, the poet had bought some unused land at White Crane Hill overlooking the Tung River in Hui-chou. There he built a house, which he completed in the second month of this year.

1. An allusion to *Analects* (see selection 7), 7.15: "The Master said, 'With coarse grain to eat, water to drink, and my bended arm for a pillow—I still have joy in the midst of these things. Riches and honor unrighteously acquired are to me as a floating cloud.' "

Who Says a Painting Must Look Like Life?

Su Shih

Written on paintings of flowering branches by Secretary Wang of Yen-ling:
two poems.

Who says a painting must look like life?
He sees only with children's eyes.
Who says a poem must stick to the theme?
Poetry is certainly lost on him.
Poetry and painting share a single goal—
clean freshness and effortless skill.
Pien Luan's[1] sparrows live on paper;
Chao Ch'ang's flowers breathe with soul.
But what are they beside these scrolls,
bold sketches, with spirit in every stroke?
Who'd think one dot of red
could call up a whole unbounded spring!

Translated by Burton Watson

The full name and identity of Secretary Wang are unknown. This is the first of two
pentasyllabic poems dated 1087, probably written to accompany a picture of a branch of
flowering plum, the symbol of early spring.
    1. Pien Luan lived in the late eighth century; Chao Ch'ang's dates are 998–1022.

When Yü-k'o Painted Bamboo

Su Shih

Written on paintings of bamboo by Wen Yü-k'o in Ch'ao Pu-chih's collection:
three poems.

When Yü-k'o painted bamboo,
He saw bamboo only, never people.
Did I say he saw no people?
So rapt he forgot even himself—
He himself became bamboo,

Written in 1087 when the poet was in the capital serving as a member of the imperial Han-
lin Academy, which drafted government documents, and acting as tutor to the young ruler,
Emperor Che Tsung. Wen Yü-k'o or Wen T'ung (1018–1079) was a cousin of the poet's from

Putting out fresh growth endlessly.
Chuang Tzu[1] no longer with us,
Who can fathom this uncanny power?

Translated by Burton Watson

Szechwan and a painter noted for his works of bamboos. Ch'ao Pu-chih (1053–1110) was one of the poet's leading disciples. This is the first poem of the series.

  1. See selection 9.

Reading the Poetry of Meng Chiao

Su Shih

Night: reading Meng Chiao's poems,
Characters fine as cow's hair.
By the cold lamp, my eyes blur and swim.
4   Good passages I rarely find—
Lone flowers poking up from the mud—
But more hard words than the *Odes*[1] or "Li sao".[2]
Jumbled rocks clogging the clear stream,   ∘
8   Making rapids too swift for poling.
My first impression is of eating little fishes—
What you get's not worth the trouble;
Or of boiling tiny mud crabs
12   And ending up with some empty claws.
For refinement he might compete with monks
But he'd never match his master Han Yü.
Man's life is like morning dew,
16   A flame eating up the oil night by night.
Why should I strain my ears
Listening to the squeaks of this cold cicada?
Better lay aside the book
20   And drink my cup of jade-white wine.

Translated by Burton Watson

Written in 1078 when Su Shih was governor of Hsü-chou in the northwest corner of Kiangsu. Meng Chiao (see selection 52), a well-known T'ang poet, was a disciple of the even better known poet and statesman, Han Yü (see selection 53). Su was probably reading a printed edition of the so-called small character variety. This is the first of two pentasyllabic poems with the same title.

  1. See selection no. 22.
  2. See selection 148.

Black Clouds—Spilled Ink

Su Shih

6th month, 27th day. Drunk at Lake Watch Tower, wrote five poems.

Black clouds—spilled ink half blotting out the hills;
pale rain—bouncing beads that splatter in the boat.
Land-rolling wind comes, blasts and scatters them:
below Lake Watch Tower, water like sky.

Translated by Burton Watson

Written at Hangchow in 1072, this is the first of a series of five poems.

Lament of the Farm Wife of Wu [1]

Su Shih

Rice this year ripens so late!
We watch, but when will frost winds come?
They come—with rain in bucketfuls;
4   the harrow sprouts mold, the sickle rusts.
My tears are all cried out, but rain never ends;
it hurts to see yellow stalks flattened in the mud.
We camped in a grass shelter for a month by the fields;
8   then it cleared and we reaped the grain, followed the wagon home,
sweaty, shoulders sore, carting it to town—
the price it fetched, you'd think we came with chaff.
We sold the ox to pay taxes, broke up the roof for kindling;
12   we'll get by for the time, but what of next year's hunger?
Officials demand cash now—they won't take grain;
the long northwest border tempts invaders.
Wise men [2] fill the court—why do things get worse?
16   I'd be better off bride to the River Lord! [3]

Translated by Burton Watson

1. Wu is the region around the mouth of the Yangtze River.
2. "Wise men" is literally Kung (Sui) and Huang (Pa), two officials of Han times who worked for the welfare of the peasants.
3. This line refers to the ancient custom of sacrificing a young girl each year as a "bride" to the River Lord, the god of the Yellow River. See note 15 to selection 156.

Eastern Slope

Su Shih

A little stream used to cross my land,
came from the mountain pass back there,
under city walls, through villages—
4   the current sluggish and choked with grass—
feeding finally into K'o Clan Pond,
ten sixth-acres stocked with fish and shrimp.
Drought this year dried it up,
8   its cracked bed plastered with brown duckweed.
Last night clouds came from hills to the south;
rain soaked the ground a plowshare deep.
Rivulets found the channel again,
12   knowing I'd chopped back the weeds.
In the mud a few old roots of cress
still alive from a year ago.
If white buds will open again,
16   when spring doves come I'll make a stew!

I planted rice before Spring Festival
and already I'm counting joys!
Rainy skies darken the spring pond;
20   by green-bladed paddies I chat with friends.
Transplanting takes till the first of summer,
delight growing with wind-blown stalks.
The moon looks down on dew-wet leaves
24   strung one by one with hanging pearls.
Fall comes and frosty ears grow heavy,
topple, and lean propped on each other.
From banks and dikes I hear only
28   the sound of locusts like wind and rain.
Rice, newly hulled, goes to the steamer,
grains of jade that light up the basket.
A long time I've eaten only government fare,
32   old rusty rice no better than mud.
Now to taste something new—
I've already promised my mouth and belly.

Translated by Burton Watson

Two of a series of eight poems describing a small farm at Eastern Slope (whence the poet's
style) in Huang-chou, Hupei, where Su Shih lived in exile after his release from prison. He had
been incarcerated for "slandering the emperor," that is, writing poetry considered too critical of
the government.

73

To Go with Shih K'o's[1] Painting of an Old Man Tasting Vinegar

Huang T'ing-chien (1045–1105)

Old lady Shih, braving acerbity, pokes in her three-foot beak;
old man Shih, vinegar-tasting, face in a hundred wrinkles:
who knows how it feels to scrunch up your shoulders, shivering clear to the
    bone?
A painting not to be surpassed even by the brush of Master Wu![2]

Translated by Burton Watson

Huang T'ing-chien, who became a Presented Scholar in 1067, was a disciple of Su Shih (see selection 72) and shared his interest in Zen Buddhism. Huang, fastidious in his use of language, was accomplished both as a poet and lyricist (see selection 121). He was also one of the most eminent Sung period calligraphers.

1. A tenth-century painter noted for his treatment of humorous and supernatural subjects. The painting, as we know from other sources, actually depicted an elderly couple.
2. The famous T'ang painter Wu Tao-tzu.

74

Written on a Cold Evening

Yang Wan-li (1127–1206)

The poet must work with brush and paper,
but this is not what makes the poem.
A man doesn't go in search of a poem—
the poem comes in search of him.

Translated by Jonathan Chaves

The poet was born shortly after the Jürchens established the Chin dynasty in the north of China. He became a Presented Scholar in 1154. Yang's emphasis on the development of a personal style was undoubtedly influenced by Zen Buddhism, which advocates enlightenment attained through individual insight and effort. Often called "the colloquial poet" for the rough quality of his diction, he paid great attention to the small details of everyday life.

Don't Read Books!

Yang Wan-li

Don't read books!
Don't chant poems!
When you read books your eyeballs wither away,
    leaving the bare sockets.
When you chant poems your heart leaks out slowly
    with each word.
People say reading books is enjoyable.
People say chanting poems is fun.
But if your lips constantly make a sound
    like an insect chirping in autumn,
you will only turn into a haggard old man.
And even if you don't turn into a haggard old man,
it's annoying for others to have to hear you.

It's so much better
    to close your eyes, sit in your study,
    lower the curtains, sweep the floor,
    burn incense.
It's beautiful to listen to the wind,
    listen to the rain,
    take a walk when you feel energetic,
    and when you're tired go to sleep.

Translated by Jonathan Chaves

Watching a Village Festival

Yang Wan-li

The village festival is really worth seeing—
mountain farmers praying for a good harvest.

Flute players, drummers burst forth from nowhere;
laughing children race after them.
Tiger masks, leopard heads swing from side to side.
Country singers, village dancers perform for the crowd.

I'd rather have one minute of this wild show
than all the nobility of kings and generals.

Translated by Jonathan Chaves

Songs of Depression

Yang Wan-li

1

I don't feel like reading another book,
and I'm tired of poetry—that's not what I want to do.
But my mind is restless, unsettled—
I'll try counting raindrop stains on the oilcloth window.

2

I finish chanting my new poems and fall asleep—
I am a butterfly journeying to the eight corners of the universe.
Outside the boat, waves crash like thunder,
but it is silent in the world of sleep.

Translated by Jonathan Chaves

75

Blue Rapids

Lu Yu (1125–1210)

A hundred men shouting at once, helping to rattle the oars;
in the boat, face to face, we can't even hear ourselves talk.
All at once the men have scattered—silence, no more scuffle;
the only sound, two winches reeling out hundred-yard tow-lines:
whoo-whoo, whaa-whaa—how fast the winches unwind,
boatmen already standing there on the sandy shore!
Fog lifts from reedy villages, red in the setting sun;
rain ended, from fishermen's huts the damp smoke of cooking fires.
I turn my head, look toward home, now a thousand mountains away;
a trip up the gorges—we've just passed rapids number one.

As Su Shih (see selection 72) was the most important poet of the Northern Sung period, so was Lu Yu the most important poet of the Southern Sung period. Lu, noted for his passionate patriotism, made repeated calls for mounting military strikes against the Tungusic Jürchen who had occupied the northern Chinese heartland in the middle of the 1120s. Many of his poems were written explicitly in this very public vein, but a wholly different mood prevails in his other poems, which describe the quiet joys and experiences of quotidian existence.

Lu Yu was extraordinarily prolific, having left behind close to ten thousand poems in his collection. There is also good evidence that he had destroyed thousands of others. This stupen-

When I was young I used to dream of the joys of official travel;
older now, I know just how hard the going can be.

Translated by Burton Watson

---

dous figure was partly due to his longevity but mostly because of a huge reservoir of determination and energy. Arranged chronologically, Lu Yu's poems constitute a virtual poetic biography.

"Blue Rapids" was written in 1170 while the poet was ascending the Three Gorges of the
Yangtze. The drumming noise of the oars signaled the departure of the boat.

At Ta-an I got sick from wine and had to lay over for half a day. Governor Wang invited me to his place again but I didn't go, so he sent me some wine to help me get over my hangover. Accordingly, I drank a little at River Moon Inn.

Lu Yu

River inn spring hangover—half a day's delay,
plus troubling the governor to send over wine so I could clear my head.
Masses and masses of willow flowers on the banks of the Chia-ling;
something special—at sky's end, today's case of the dumps!

Translated by Burton Watson

Written in 1172 while on the way to Hsing-yüan in Shensi.

The Merchant's Joy

Lu Yu

The wide wide Yangtze, dragons in deep pools;
wave blossoms, purest white, leap to the sky.
The great ship, tall-towered, far off no bigger than a bean;
4   my wondering eyes have not come to rest when it's here before me.
Matted sails: clouds that hang beyond the embankment;

Written in 1187. Compare with selection 82.

lines and hawsers: their thunder echoes from high town walls.
Rumble rumble of oxcarts to haul the priceless cargo;
8   heaps, hordes to dazzle the market—men race with the news.
In singing-girl towers to play at dice, a million on one throw;
by flag-flown pavilions calling for wine, ten thousand a cask;
the Mayor? the Governor? we don't even know their names;
12   what's it to us who wields power in the palace?
Confucian scholar, hard up, dreaming of one square meal;
a limp, a stumble, prayers for pity at His Excellency's gate;
teeth rot, hair falls out—no one looks your way;
16   belly crammed with classical texts, body lean with care—
See what Heaven gives me—luck thin as paper!
Now I know that merchants are the happiest of men.

Translated by Burton Watson

Written in a Carefree Mood

Lu Yu

Old man pushing seventy,
in truth he acts like a little boy,
whooping with delight when he spies some mountain fruits,
laughing with joy, tagging after village mummers;[1]
with the others having fun stacking tiles to make a pagoda,
standing alone staring at his image in the jardiniere pool.
Tucked under his arm, a battered book to read,
just like the time he first set off for school.

Translated by Burton Watson

Written in 1192 in Shao-hsing (Chekiang), this is the first of two poems with the same title.
1. Villagers dressed up in costume who go from house to house at the beginning of spring to drive out evil spirits.

The Stone on the Hilltop

Lu Yu

Autumn wind: ten thousand trees wither;
spring rain: a hundred grasses grow.
Is this really some plan of the Creator,
this flowering and fading, each season that comes?
Only the stone there on the hilltop,
its months and years too many to count,
knows nothing of the four-season round,
wearing its constant colors unchanged.
The old man has lived all his life in these hills;
though his legs fail him, he still clambers up,
now and then strokes the rock and sighs three sighs:
how can I make myself stony like you?

Translated by Burton Watson

Written in 1193.

To Show to My Sons

Lu Yu

In death I know well enough all things end in emptiness;
still I grieve that I never saw the Nine Provinces[1] made one.
On the day the king's armies march north to take the heartland,
at the family sacrifice don't forget to let your father know.

Translated by Burton Watson

This is Lu Yu's deathbed poem, written in 1209 when he was eighty-four years old.
1. The divisions of China in ancient times.

76
Chin-ling Post Station

Wen T'ien-hsiang (1236–1282)

Grasses enclose the old palaces as waning sunlight shifts.[1]
A lone wind-tossed cloud stops briefly: on what can it depend?
The view here, mountains and rivers, has never changed,
Yet the people within the city walls already are half gone.[2]
The reed flowers that fill the land have grown old with me,
But into whose eaves have the swallows of my former home flown?[3]
Now I depart on the road out of Chiang-nan;[4]
Transformed into a weeping cuckoo, reeking of blood, I shall return.[5]

Translated by Michael A. Fuller

Wen T'ien-hsiang was a great statesman and general who fought a losing war to defend the Southern Sung emperor from the invading Mongol (Yüan) armies. This poem was probably written when the poet was captured and being taken north to the Yüan capital.

1. Chin-ling (modern Nanking) was a secondary capital during the Southern Sung.
2. This relates to a story about a Taoist adept, Ting Ling-wei, who turned himself into a crane and returned to his home town after being away for ten years. While he perched on a roost, a youth of the town shot an arrow at him. As he flew away, he sighed, "The town is as of old, but the people are not."
3. This bird imagery—part of a series in the poem—alludes to a famous couplet by the T'ang poet Liu Yü-hsi (see selection 110): "The swallows that in former day flew before the courtyards of the great Wang and Hsieh clans/Have flown into the houses of common folk."
4. That is, he is about to head north, across the Yangtze.
5. There is much lore on the cuckoo. In one story, Tu Yü, a king of Shu (part of the modern province of Szechwan), ceded his throne to his very able minister and then left the country. Later he regretted this noble deed, and after his death his soul transformed into a cuckoo that returned to Shu. Its plaintive cry was said to sound like spitting blood as well as the words, "It's best to return."

77
Miscellaneous Poem on Rural Life

Liu Yin (1249–1293)

Sunset was thick with the feel of rain
And a happy glow filled the southern acres.

Liu Yin was rare among the northern Chinese living under the Mongols in expressing opposition to the Yüan dynasty. Indeed, he went even further to assert that the three non-Han

Who expected an all-night wind
Would bring forth the willows beyond the gate?

Translated by John Timothy Wixted

---

dynasties from the Liao and Chin onward were all illegitimate, not just the Yüan. A veritable curmudgeon, he criticized Wang Wei (see selection 44) for his fondness toward Buddhism. In addition to being an accomplished poet, Liu was also a proponent and practitioner of old-style prose.

78

To a Pyrotechnist

Chao Meng-fu (1254–1322)

This wondrous art in the human realm
          rivals nature's skill:
concocting formulas, igniting lanterns,
          turning night to day!
Willow catkins flutter downwards,
          carpeting earth in white;
peach blossom petals drop and scatter,
          covering courtyards with red.
Bursting, spreading, scintillating—
          just like stars that fall;
bubbling, boiling, roaring, blasting—
          like warfare by fire!
Some other night, again you will unfurl brocade of flowers:
no need to grieve that they have scattered in the eastern wind.

Translated by Jonathan Chaves

A master poet, painter, and calligrapher, Chao Meng-fu set new standards in all these fields. He was a descendant of the Sung imperial family. His willingness to serve the Yüan government and subsequent rise to eminence led to an uncertainty about his reputation in later Chinese historiography.

79
Shipboard Song

Yüan Chüeh (1266–1327)

White reeds grow on chilly sands;
Their remnant flowers wave old brooms.
A million houses of Yen-ching
Depend on you for their kindling.
Though unobtrusive and born of the lowest,
Your usefulness is well worth praise.
You outshine the peach and plum blossoms,
Each striving to appear prettiest of all.

Translated by John Timothy Wixted

The poet was from Ssu-ming (modern Ningpo) in Chekiang. Like Chao Meng-fu (see selection 78) before him, he became a high official in the imperial Han-lin Academy under the Mongols. The emperor spent summers at the Upper Capital of K'ai-p'ing (Doloonuur), and Yüan would sometimes accompany him and compose poems about desert scenes. He adopted the literary name Ch'ing-jung chü-shih (Pure Countenance Lay Believer). Yüan Chüeh's poems are scholarly in nature and rich in descriptive power.

This poem is one of a series of pentasyllabic old-style poems, "Shipboard Songs," written as a journal of his trip to the capital. The poems tell variously of scenes and products of the north that he was seeing for the first time. In this selection, the water surface on both sides of the boat, as it approaches Yen-ching (the Peking area), is covered with white reeds, the capital's fuel source.

80
Mating

Yang Wei-chen (1296–1370)

Eyebrow mounds dark, facing the spluttering lamp,
Her billowy half bun spills over pillow's edge.
Arms and legs joined with another's, fetchingly about to sob,
She grasps the fine silk, nearly kneading it to pieces.

Translated by John Timothy Wixted

The poet became a Presented Scholar in 1327, after which he held several minor positions under the Yüan dynasty. As the foremost figure in classical poetry of his time, Yang Wei-chen represents a break from the stiffness and rationality of much Northern Sung poetry. This poem is about the pleasures of the night.

81

Inscribed on a Painting by Myself

Ni Tsan (1301–1374)

On the eastern seacoast lives a sick man
who calls himself mad and deluded.
He writes on walls and paints silk and paper:
surely he is more than insane.

Translated by Jonathan Chaves

One of the most innovative painters in the history of Chinese art, Ni Tsan was also an excellent poet. The understated, spare diction of his verse may be linked with the same qualities in his painting.

82

The Merchant's Joy

Chang Yü (1333–1385)

All year long, he never visits his home town:
by nature, he loves to be a traveler!
So he has entrusted his livelihood to the rivers and lakes,
4   never refusing a distant journey for the sake of profit.
Burning magic money, pouring libations of wine,
            he prays for good winds at dawn;
he makes friends everywhere he goes, east or west.
In this floating home of his, there's nothing to tie him down,
8   and his name has never been entered
            in the tax-collector's books!
On board his huge ship, with its two enormous sweeps,
his major concubine can sing for him,
            and his minor concubine can dance!
He buys fine wines every day at the wineshops along the river,
12   and knows nothing of the pain of parting in the ordinary world.
There are many houses of pleasure on both banks of the Yangtze:

Chang Yü was one of the freshest voices in Ming period poetry. The serene tone of much of his poetry belies the turmoil of his political life during the stormy transition from the Yüan to the Ming.

a thousand doors, ten thousand gates—
            he has passed through them all!
    What other human is as happy as the merchant:
16   aside from stormy weather, what problems does he have?

Translated by Jonathan Chaves

83
To a Hermit in the Mountains

Hsü Pen (1335–1380)

You've lived there long, away from the trappings of office,
your mind at peace, cut off from the world.
In jars: herbs, handed down by your teacher.
In bags: elixir, refined by your own hand.
You whistle out loud beyond the thousand peaks,
walk quietly along a hundred streams.
You resent even the intrusions of woodcutters and shepherds,
so now you want to move still deeper into the clouds.

Translated by Jonathan Chaves

Like Chang Yü (see selection 82), Hsü Pen was among a number of great poets who hailed from Soochow. Hsü led a checkered political life but conjured up a world of serene detachment in his simple, profound poems.

Saying Goodbye to a Monk from Japan

Hsü Pen

Thousands of miles away—the Fu-sang Tree,[1]
            among the faint colors of dawn!
Vast ocean sky, seen by few travelers.
No need to follow the tides with your wooden bowl:
you can fly toward the sun on your golden staff!
You'll go on eating Chinese food as you travel back east,
but you'll put on native clothes again after you reach home.

    1. In Chinese mythology, a tree at the easternmost point of the sky, from which the sun rises.

Your countrymen are sure to ask: "How's the Dharma[2] doing there?"
Just show them the palm-leaf manuscripts[3] you're bringing back
         with you.

Translated by Jonathan Chaves

2. The Buddhist law or doctrine.
3. Buddhism originally came to China from India. The presence in China of Sanskrit palm-leaf manuscripts of the original Buddhist scriptures would seem to indicate that China was still in touch with the motherland of Buddhism. The Japanese monk may, however, have been given some manuscripts that had already been in China for centuries.

84

Written on Seeing the Flowers, and Remembering My Daughter

Kao Ch'i (1336–1374)

I grieve for my second daughter.
Six years I carried her about,
Held her against my breast and helped her eat,
4   Taught her rhymes as she sat on my knee.
She would arise early and copy her elder sister's dress,
Struggling to see herself in the dressing-table mirror.
She had begun to delight in pretty silks and lace,
8   But in a poor family she could have none of these.
I would sigh over my own recurring frustrations,
Treading the byways through the rain and snow.
But evenings when I returned to receive her greeting
12   My sad cares would be transformed into contentment.
What were we to do, that day when illness struck?
The worse because it was during the crisis;
Frightened by the alarming sounds, she sank quickly into death.
16   There was no time even to fix medicines for her.

Kao Ch'i is still another of the fine poets produced by the Yangtze Valley city of Soochow. Executed on the dubious grounds that he was peripherally involved in a rebellion, Kao was one of the many victims of the repressive atmosphere fostered by the uncouth founder of the Ming dynasty, Chu Yüan-chang, who distrusted even his closest associates.

The poet spent several months during the spring and early summer of 1367 in a city under siege. His five-year-old little girl died during that difficult period. The following spring, seeing the flowers bloom again reminded him of an incident that called her to mind. This prompted him to write the above poem.

Distraught, I prepared her poor little coffin;
Weeping, accompanied it to that distant hillside.[1]
It is already lost in the vast void.
20   Inconsolate, I still grieve deeply for her.
I think how last year, in the spring,
When the flowers bloomed by the pond in our old garden
She led me by the hand along under the trees
24   And asked me to break off a pretty branch for her.
This year again the flowers bloom.
Now I live far from home, here by this river's edge.
All the household are here, only she is gone.
28   I look at the flowers, and my tears fall in vain.
A cup of wine brings me no comfort.
The wind makes desolate sounds in the night curtains.

Translated by F. W. Mote

1. This probably took place some months after both her death and the end of the siege.

The Song of the Man of Green Hill

Kao Ch'i

On the river lies Green Hill. I moved to the south of it, and so gave myself the name "The Man of Green Hill." Here I have lived an uneventful life, spending the entire day painstakingly chanting poems. In spare moments, I have written this Song of the Man of Green Hill to express my feelings and to rebut those who mock me for being a "poetry fanatic."

Man of Green Hill,
gaunt and pure,
originally an official of the immortals
        beneath the Pavilion of Five-Color Clouds:
what year was he sent down in exile
        to this world below?
5   He won't tell people his family or name.
Hiking in sandals? He's tired of distant trips.
Shouldering a hoe? Too lazy to farm!
He owns a sword, but lets it rust,
and books which lie scattered in confusion.
10   Unwilling to bend his waist
        for five pecks of rice,

unwilling to wag his tongue
            to persuade cities to surrender.
He only enjoys searching for verses,
chanting to himself, with himself exchanging poems.
Through the fields, he drags his cane
            and wears a rope belt:
15   onlookers don't know who he is,
                they just laugh and mock!
They take him for the crazy scholar of Lu,
            the wild man of Ch'u.
But when the Man of Green Hill hears,
            he pays them no heed:
the sounds of chanting leave his lips
                endlessly, humming a steady stream.
20   Chanting in the morning, he forgets his hunger;
chanting in the evening, to calm his unease.
And as he painstakingly chants,
he goes into a trance as if drunk.
His hair he has no time to comb;
25   family matters he can't bother to attend.
If baby cries, he feels no compassion.
If guests come, he doesn't even greet them.
He has no fear of running out of food, like Hui,[1]
nor does he admire the full coffers of Mr. Yi.[2]
30   He feels no shame in wearing coarse garments,
    nor does he envy flowery hatstrings.
He pays no heed to dragons and tigers
            bitterly fighting,
or the Crow and Frog[3] as they hastily run their course.
Along the water's edge alone he sits
35   or in the woods alone he walks.
He hews out Primal Vapor
and explores the Primal Essence.
So hard for the Creator and ten thousand creatures
            to conceal themselves from him!
Throughout the eight corners of the universe
            sweeps the blade of his mind,
40   causing that which has no image
            to produce a sound.

1. Yen Hui, Confucius' favorite disciple who nevertheless suffered poverty.
2. Yi Tun, a legendary millionaire.
3. These creatures were believed to inhabit the sun and moon respectively.

Minute! Like shooting a louse, hanging
                  from a hair;
Gigantic! As if butchering a whale.
So pure, like sipping immortal nectar;
dangerous, as though steep cliffs were piled high.
45   Burgeoning, clouds gathering in the sky;
issuing, shoots of plants through frost.
Climbing high to the root of Heaven,
                  exploring the moon's caves;
rhinoceros horn illuminating Ox Island Abyss
                  where ten thousand monsters appear!
Subtle meanings suddenly comprehended,
                  as if by a spirit;
50   lovely landscapes always competing
                  with the mountains and streams.
Stars and rainbows contribute to the luster;
mists and fogs moisten flowery bloom.
Listen to the music—harmonies of Shao,[4]
savor the taste—he's mastered the Great Broth.[5]
55   There's nothing else here in this world
                  that pleases me,
only sounds of metal and stone
                  chiming and ringing together.
In my thatched hut beside the river,
                  clearing after wind and rain,
I close my door, wake fresh from sleep,
                  and finish a new poem.
Beating on a jar, I sing out loud,
60   not caring if vulgar ears are shocked.
I want to call the old father from Mount Chün[6]
                  to bring with him the long flute played by the immortals,
and harmonize with this song of mine,
                  playing in the moonlight.
I only fear that suddenly waves will arise,
birds and beasts will howl in fear
                  and mountains crumble away.
65   If God hears this, He'll be angry
and send down a white crane to bring me back,
not leaving me to do my mischief in this world,

4. The name of an archaic, classical music long since lost in Kao's day.
5. See selection 9, the second passage, footnote 1.
6. According to an old story, he taught a traveling merchant how to play three magic flutes.

> but again to tie on my pendant of jade
> and fly to the Jasper Capital!

Translated by Jonathan Chaves

Silkworm Song of Torchlit Fields

Kao Ch'i

In eastern village and western village
               they celebrate New Year's Eve:
towering torches, a thousand of them,
               light the fields all red!
The old people pray with smiles,
               the young folk sing songs:
"We wish for a year good for silkworms
               and also good for wheat."
In bright starlight strange shadows are cast,
               startling the perched crows;
flames from torches burn off the cold,
               giving birth to spring.
Late at night, torches all burned out,
               the people return to their homes;
they all say prognostications
               show a prosperous year ahead.

Translated by Jonathan Chaves

85

On the Hall of Precious Virtue

Yang Shih-ch'i (1365–1444)

The cock crows—cock-a-doodle-doo!—the east grows bright;
from every house, people rush out to slave for profit!

    The holder of the exalted position of Grand Secretary under four emperors, Yang Shih-ch'i
was a brilliant political tactician. Few officials in Chinese history who rose to such prominence
also achieved such a high degree of authority as poets.

They dash to the east, hustle to the west,
                    tumbling over each other:
thousands of dollars? tens of thousands? No amount is enough!
In your noble hall you sit calmly, not doing a thing;
clumps of green trees overhang limpid wavelets.
Wearing colorful clothes,[1] you pour wine
                    for your compassionate father:
elder brothers and younger brothers, all truly happy.
In human life, poverty doesn't matter if the Way is present:
a mountain of yellow gold is no treasure at all.

Translated by Jonathan Chaves

1. A reference to the well-known tale of Lao Lai Tzu, who, at the age of seventy, put on colorful children's clothes and played like a child before his parents so that they would feel young again.

Night Rain: A Wall Collapses

—Sent to My Neighbors

Yang Shih-ch'i

A heavy rain crumbles a wall of my house;
I rise at night, grab my clothes, and run!
The wind enters the room, flapping the curtains;
water pours in a stream down the stairs.
The pots beneath the stove still not inundated;
quickly, I run to save the books on my desk.
If only I could be like my eastern and western neighbors:
calmly sleeping, not a thing to worry about.

Translated by Jonathan Chaves

86

Song of Cursive Calligraphy

Hsieh Chin (1369–1425)

Ten years of my life, spent at the window or beneath the lamp,
practicing calligraphy day and night without a break!
Beside the "ink pond"[1] I've used up an oceanful of water;
my worn-out brushes, piled high, would make a Mount Omei!
5   When the spirit moves me, I pour out
                 eight hundred gallons of wine,
get drunk, go wild, and let my brush do whatever it will.
Rabbit-hairs[2] in hand, I let the tip loose,
and sweep my way through a million sheets of tinted phoenix paper.
One stroke across,
10 one stroke down:
a gold spear thrust into the ground, an awl stuck through the wall.
A brilliant rainbow arching across a blue autumn sky,
a waterfall rushing down the stones of a cinnabar cliff.
One dot large,
15 one dot small:
at midnight, a falling star, dazzling as it follows the moon;
flying through the air, a crossbow pellet, reaching toward the clouds!
A black pearl from the sea, glittering in a vast sky!
As lovely as: a beautiful woman, gathering flowers,
               displaying her new makeup;
20 as bold as: a courageous soldier, grasping a spear,
               on the battlefield!
As vibrant as: multicolored rocs and purple phoenixes
               trying to outfly each other;
as swift as: autumn serpents and spring snakes
               darting away. . . .
Forms like those of thick clouds in a million transformations,
postures like those of lightning bolts, flashing
               across a clear sky!
25 Wild geese flying in formation against the autumn clouds;
dragons doing battle in the surging waters of a spring river!

Like Yang Shih-ch'i (see selection 85), Hsieh Chin was also a Grand Secretary, the most powerful office in early Ming government, but he was arrested by political enemies and later died in prison. He is one of the chief compilers of the enormous collection of documents known as the *Yung-lo ta tien*.

1. Chang Chih of the Later Han dynasty, the father of cursive calligraphy as an art form, practiced so much that the pond he used to sit beside turned black from his discarded ink.

2. See selection 235.

Don't you recall why Wang Hsi-chih³
            was a man who loved to raise geese?
 A true artist should have the same ambition:
beneath his brush, gods and spirits must appear!

Translated by Jonathan Chaves

3. Wang Hsi-chih (see selection 200) was the greatest of Chinese calligraphers. From watching the elegant lines of the geese's necks as they swam, he derived inspiration for his calligraphy.

87
[Written on a Landscape Painting in an Album]

Shen Chou (1427–1509)

White clouds encircle the waist of the hills like a belt;
A stony ledge soars into the void, a narrow path into space.
Alone, I lean on my thornwood staff and gaze calmly into the distance,
About to play my flute in reply to the song of this mountain stream.

Translated by Daniel Bryant

Another Ming notable who hailed from Soochow (compare selections 83 and 84), Shen Chou was one of the greatest painters in the history of Chinese art. He was also a poet of significance who lived an uneventful life devoted to painting and literature. This untitled poem is found on one of his paintings, a landscape album leaf in the Nelson Gallery in Kansas City.

The Taoist Huang Has Died of Alcoholism

Shen Chou

Your master died from drinking too much;
now you have followed in his steps.
A mound of dregs will be your grave,
your tombstone inscribed with the "Ode in Praise of Wine."

Unsteady on your feet, you tripped and stumbled, °
your face flushed, your liver wasted.
Now you are gone, not even your shadow remains;
there is only your portrait, drawn in my poem.

Translated by Jonathan Chaves

88

On a Painting of Fish Being Caught, a Song

Li Tung-yang (1447–1516)

Poor people fish mostly with snare nets;
Rich people fish mostly with seine nets.
The poor don't manage as well as the rich;
4   One seine net can bring in tens of feet of fish.
When river flowers line the banks and the river is low,
That is when a foot-long fish is worth an inch of gold.
With banks high and snare nets small, not enough gets heaved in,
8   And the stifled sobs of fishermen's songs sadden the heart.
Along the riverbank, family after family sells its catch;
Large boats, small boats, too numerous to count.
Large boats bearing good fish bring in lots of cash;
12   Small boats linger on, through the day and night.
A Ch'ang-sha wanderer,[1] I think of my native land—
How I'd like to be there, sitting and watching along the stream:
I'd buy some fish, purchase wine, and, facing the bright moon,
16   Bring myself to raise a cup, though hardly a drinker myself.
Living here west of Lake Bridge,
Court messengers bring fish long as large chopsticks.
But can I, by myself, eat food most residents have never tasted?
20   From my railing, I have them tossed back in.
There are things in life that interest me, but not fish;
Enough now of unrolling this scroll to look at the scene.
With neither home nor land to call my own, one need hardly ask—
24   My only wish: with the common people of the Four Seas to share fat,
        fresh fish.

Translated by John Timothy Wixted

Although his ancestral home was Ch'a-ling in Hunan, Li Tung-yang's more immediate forebears resided in Peking and were attached to the imperial household. Recognized as a child prodigy, Li was presented to the emperor at the age of three, and when only seven was placed in the service of the palace. After becoming a Presented Scholar at the unusually young age of sixteen, he served as a leading official in the emperor's entourage. Because he frequently served as chief examiner for the metropolitan examinations, many junior officials became his disciples. Thus exercising great power in both the literary and political world, he was a man of considerable influence. A characteristic of Li Tung-yang's poetry is its large scale, which was commensurate with his high position.

1. In the southern province of Hunan.

89

Inscribed on the Doors of My Bookshelves

Yang Hsün-chi (1456–1544)

Mine was a trading family
Living in Nan-hao district for a hundred years.
I was the first to become a scholar,
4   Our house being without a single book.
Applying myself for a full decade,
I set my heart on building a collection.
Though not fully stocked with minor writings,
8   Of major works, I have nearly everything:
Classics, history, philosophy, belles-lettres—
Nothing lacking from the heritage of the past.
Binding up the volumes one by one in red covers,
12   I painstakingly sew them by hand.
When angry, I read and become happy;
When sick, I read and am cured.
Piled helter-skelter in front of me,
16   Books have become my life.
The people of the past who wrote these tomes,
If not sages, were certainly men of great wisdom.
Even without opening their pages,
20   Joy comes to me just fondling them.
As for my foolish family, they can't be helped;
Their hearts are set on money alone.
If a book falls on the floor, they don't pick it up;
24   What do they care if they get dirty or tattered?
I'll do my best by these books all my days,
And die not leaving a single one behind.
There are some readers among my friends—
28   To them I'll give them all away.
Better that than have my unworthy sons
Haul them off to turn into cash.

Translated by John Timothy Wixted

In Soochow and its environs there were probably several thousand people writing poetry in the second half of the fifteenth century, and their activities were centered around Shen Chou (see selection 87) and his disciples. Among them Yang Hsün-chi was one. Born into a trading family without a single volume in the house, he turned into a true bibliophile. He became a Presented Scholar in 1484. A few years later, rather than continuing to serve as an official, he feigned illness and returned to Soochow to devote himself to his books. In this pentasyllabic old-style poem, he relates his progress from bookless son to literary scholar.

90

A Fan from Korea

Chu Yün-ming (1460–1526)

This oriental country, year after year,
      sends its long-journeying ships;
presenting a tribute of wind and moonlight,
      they come to China.
I trust you will not view this as some trifling affair:
the world now is a single family.

Translated by Jonathan Chaves

    Chu Yün-ming is recognized as the most important calligrapher of the Ming period. His verse owes much to the expressive diction of T'ang poetry, but possibly even more to the unostentatious depiction of everyday life characteristic of Sung poetry.

91

Ballad of Selling a Child

Wang Chiu-ssu (1468–1551)

    The village woman brings her five-year-old son
    to sell to our household for four and a half measures of grain.
    I ask her, "Why do you wish to sell your son?"
4   And she answers me, with repeated sighs:
    "My husband is old, sick in bed, and blind in both eyes;
    from morning to evening, there's no telling if he'll live or die.
    Our five acres near the village are only poor land.
8   and our two rooms, circled by a wall, are falling apart.
    My eldest son is thirteen, and he can push a plow,
    but our fields are few, our profit meager, so we don't have enough
      to eat.
    Last winter we were late with our tax payments:
12 the officials came knocking at our door, pressuring us to pay.
    Only when a rich family made us a loan did we manage to get through,
    but thinking back, that only made our life more difficult than before.

    Wang Chiu-ssu was a master of long narrative poems with a moralizing tendency. At the same time, he was interested in the eccentric T'ang Buddhist poet Han Shan (see selection 58). This indicates how difficult it is to establish a simple dichotomy of stuffy orthodoxy versus eccentric individualism in Ming poetry.

My second son, eight years old, knows oxen and sheep,
16   so the eastern neighbor bought him to care for his herds.
Meanwhile, the rich people demand payment of our debt, as if they
    expected us to pay with our lives,
and my sick husband coughs and wheezes, his stomach completely
    empty.
Come to such a pass, we realized we had no choice at all,
20   and so I've brought my youngest son here to exchange for grain.
Half this grain will be used to repay the rich folks' loan,
half will be used to make some gruel to feed my poor husband."
When the village woman stopped speaking, she prepared to leave,
24   but her son tugged at her clothes, crying his mother's name.
The woman, miserable, lingered for a while,
and borrowed the use of a spare bed, so she could pass the night with
    her son.
When the morning drums beat solemnly, and the roosters cried their
    wild cry,
28   the woman rose, and hesitated as she watched her son in his
    sound sleep.
Then, stifling her sobs, holding back the tears, she left the city walls
with the grain that would at least alleviate her terrible suffering.
When the boy woke up, he called for his mother, but she was nowhere
    to be seen,
32   so he walked around the house, crying out loud, unsteady on his feet.
Everyone who saw him wept tears at the sight,
everyone who heard him knit his brow.
Alas! The wild tiger does not eat its cub,
36   and the old ox will lick the calf.
How can we throw away this pearl we hold in the palm of our hand,
cutting away this flesh from our heart!

Please realize:
    The rich grow crueler as their fields increase,
40   and they buy servants and slaves with their wealth.
Then, one day, they curse them in anger,
whipping them unfeelingly until their blood flows!
Don't they know that all flesh and bone comes from the same womb,
44   that another's son and my son are of one form?
Alas! Will the four seas and the nine continents ever share the same
    springtime,
so there will be no more people who must sell their daughters and sons?
Translated by Jonathan Chaves

92

Ballad of the Government Granary Clerk

Ho Ching-ming (1483–1521)

Spiked thorns all over, and a thirty-foot wall;
towering entrance with iron bolts
　　　　double doors sealed shut.
The minor clerk of the granary
　　　　with gray whiskers and green shirt
writes out ten columns of vermilion characters
　　　　on the wood-plank board.
Standing in front of an official banner,
　　　　all day he reads out loud;
with clipped tallies, people form lines,
　　　　and listen to the numbers being called.
The rich families get plenty of grain,
　　　　piles of it like hills;
their big carriages go creaking off,
　　　　taking two oxen to pull;
A hungry man from the countryside
　　　　stands beneath the wall:
he too wants to come forward for grain,
　　　　but the clerk just curses at him.

Translated by Jonathan Chaves

A leader of the archaist movement of the mid-Ming period, Ho Ching-ming particularly
excelled in long, expansive poems about paintings. At his best, Ho could infuse his poems,
founded though they were on High T'ang models, with dynamic energy and life.

93

[Title Lost]

Huang Ě (1498–1569)

Pearl-teardrops roll and gather,
　　　water in the inkstone;

This poem is by Huang Ě, the second wife of Yang Shen (see selection 142). From a
respectable family, she was well educated.

broken-hearted, how can I write
    broken-hearted poems?
Ever since that distant day
    when we last held hands
right to this time I've been too lazy
    to paint in my eyebrows.

There is no medicine that can cure
    my grief through the long nights;
I do have money, but can't buy back
    the time when we were young!
Earnestly I entrust my message to the mountain birds:
soon, fly down, south of the river,
    urge him to return!

Translated by Jonathan Chaves

94
A Trip to a Mountain Village

Li K'ai-hsien (1501–1568)

I break off a branch, and prod my lazy donkey;
the bags are torn—my books fall out on the road.
Hungry, haggard—two village servants
4   with shirts so short they don't reach their pants!
Dry and hot, exactly noon,
as we struggle along the dusty road.
One servant is still quite strong,
8   but the other has no strength left.
The strong man sings mountain songs;
the tired man just sighs out loud.
Suddenly, the road ends, and a wood appears;
12   they say we have reached the mountain village.
Earthen walls supporting thatched roofs:
lanes and alleys, here, against the cliffs!

From a family of officials in Shantung, Li K'ai-hsien became a Presented Scholar in 1529. Like Yang Shen (see selection 142), he was an individualist writer difficult to categorize. Li was friendly with a number of orthodox poets but was far more innovative and idiosyncratic. He was instrumental in the revival of Yüan drama in the later Ming period. A playwright of romances (*ch'uan-ch'i*, see selection 274), Li also wrote suites of arias and a variety of prose works.

When it is learned that distant travelers have arrived,
16   the farmers happily welcome us.
To go with the millet, a chicken must be killed—
but the chicken has flown into the neighbor's courtyard!
A jug is opened, and thick wine poured out;
20   wild vegetables are cut, and brought in a basket.
Drunk and sated, I lie on a rope-bed,
and dream at once that I have traveled to paradise.
When I wake, the mountain moon is high;
24   I rise and walk where my steps take me.
The night air seems fresher than ever;
suddenly, I realize my cares have disappeared.
If I didn't fear burdening my host,
28   I'd stay here for a month, and not go home!

Translated by Jonathan Chaves

A Parable

Li K'ai-hsien

There was a man who studied the art of disappearing.
Before he had mastered the technique, he boasted to his wife:
"Tell me, can you see my body now?"
4   The wife laughed: "My eyes have not been taken by a ghost!
Your face is right in front of mine, just inches away;
it's not as though you're at the neighbor's or behind a fence!
Since you have a body, why shouldn't I be able to see it,
8   unless you were clever enough to pull off some trick!"
The man was outraged at his wife's frank words;
he kicked her, slapped her, and cursed her out.
Then he asked the same thing of his concubine, and she pretended to
    be amazed:
12   she looked all around behind her, then stared straight ahead.
Lying, she said, "Master, what art is this!
Your body is hidden away—I only hear your voice!"
The man, delighted, went to town, and stole something from a shop.
16   At first the shopkeeper was too startled to move—then he
    became furious,

In his ability to turn defeat into apparent victory, Li's "master of invisibility" foreshadows the main character of Lu Hsun's "The True Story of Ah Q," written in 1921.

and gave the man a worse beating than the man had given his wife,
screaming and cursing with a voice like a thunderclap.
As for the "master of invisibility," he yelled too: "Go ahead, beat me up,
20 but if you want to *see* my body, you'll have a hard time!"
Now I once lived in the capital, where I became stuck-in-the-mud.
I was afraid to visit the ministers and high officials.
I was rejected, sent away—but still I didn't change . . . ,
24 Until I escaped, and held my old fishing rod again.

Translated by Jonathan Chaves

Earthquake

Li K'ai-hsien

The earthquake covered Shansi and Shensi;
millions of people died or were hurt.
Homes were flattened to the ground,
and skeletons could be seen lying everywhere.
The prognostication? "Too much Yin."[1]
Perhaps this is an omen of some fault in government.[2]
Three lifelong friends of mine
in one night fell to the dust.[3]

Translated by Jonathan Chaves

One poem from a group of ten, all to the same rhymes.
Poet's notes:

1. "The prognostication says, 'An earthquake occurs when there is an excess of yin.' "

2. "Local officials submitted a memorial, saying, 'The land here is usually quiet, but now it has moved: this is because we officials have not been doing our duty.' "

3. "Yang Shou-li, the Secretary, Han Pang-ch'i, the Investigator, and Ma Li, the Lord of the Imperial Banquets: taken by surprise, they were all crushed to death."

Yang Shou-li (1484–1555), Han Pang-ch'i (1479–1555), and Ma Li (1474–1555) all died in the quake. Han Pang-ch'i had earlier memorialized to the effect that another earthquake was a sign of inadequacy in government, which is in accordance with the Confucian idea that the moral state of human society exerts an influence upon nature.

On the Cold Food Festival,[1] Entertaining at the Southern Estate—the Guests Were Li Chiu-ho, Ma Nan-yeh, Wei Tung-kao, Li Hu-ch'uan, Huang K'ung-ts'un, Li Lung-t'ang, and Hu Hu-shan

Li K'ai-hsien

Singing, dancing—handsome actors entertain;
guests have been invited to the courtyard.
The singers' mats hold the setting sun;
the dancers' sleeves flap in the east wind.
Lakeside willows—this smoky mist is hard to prohibit!
Flowering peach—a fire burning red by itself!
Village women come to ride the swing;
when they're done kicking, their hair is a mess![2]

Translated by Jonathan Chaves

1. The Cold Food Festival was reckoned as occurring one hundred and some-odd days after the winter solstice. It was, in essence, a spring festival. The wit of lines 5 and 6 in the present poem is based upon the practice of prohibiting any kind of fire for cooking during the festival. The swinging of the penultimate line was a game performed by women and associated with this festival. In other cultures, too—for example, in India—swinging by women has connotations of fertility and even eroticism. As such, it is a frequent theme in Indian painting, forming a striking parallel to the use of swinging to symbolize the second or the third month of the lunar year in two series of twelve paintings each by the late-Ming painter, Wu Pin.

2. The last line of the poem contains the verb *ts'u* ("to kick"), which is interpreted here as referring to the swinging, but which may actually refer to another game connected with the Cold Food Festival and often mentioned by Li K'ai-hsien together with swinging, *ts'u-chü*, or "kick-ball." This game is played to this day in Japan, where it is called *kemari*, as a ritual to usher in the spring.

Watching the Swinging

Li K'ai-hsien

To the east touching Hui-chün, to the north, the Yellow River, there is a village called Ta-kou-yai. On the day of the Ch'ing-ming Festival,[1] they set

One poem from a set of two.

1. Starting two days after the Cold Food Festival, this is the spring festival *par excellence*, and is also characterized, among other things, by the playing of such ritual games as swinging. (See notes to the previous poem.)

up several high frames for swings, and the women and girls from the neighboring villages happily gather there. I happened to be passing by on some other business, and I was moved to write these poems.

The colorful frames are erected beside the Yellow River;
the women laugh and sing.
Their bodies are as light as a passing bird,
their hands are as nimble as a shuttle on the loom.
In the villages, few fires burn;[2]
on the swings, many techniques!
A passerby suddenly feels a chill of fear:
could his career be as precarious as this?

Translated by Jonathan Chaves

2. Poet's note: "This refers to the fact that many of the people have fled as refugees—it is not only because of the prohibition against cooking fires for the Cold Food Festival."

Sent to the Master Physician, "Almond Orchard" Shih

Li K'ai-hsien

"Almond Orchard" Shih has been famous as a doctor for a long time in the Ts'ao and P'u regions. Recently, I learned about him from a poem sent to me by Ch'en Yüeh-shan. Not a day goes by without sick people requesting his services, but he has been declining on the grounds of his own illness with increasing frequency each year so he can devote himself to planting almond trees. Ch'en has already written a poem for him, and I don't want to be the only one to ignore him, so I've written one of my own.

Master Shih's medical fame, because of Master Ch'en,
has now reached here, to me.
In the mountains he walks, collecting herbs,
then sits in the market, with gourds of them to sell.
He has loved almond trees for over ten years,
and has planted a grove of several hundred.
As for me, my one illness is my craze for chess:
tell me, can your arts cure this?

Translated by Jonathan Chaves

Thanking Doctor Jen

Li K'ai-hsien

My daughter was extremely beautiful—but she suffered from *lei-li*.[1] When I heard that the specialist in external medicine, Jen Mien-shan, could cure this ailment, I sent a letter to him by messenger, which reached him at Ch'ing-ch'üan prefecture. Upon arrival, he treated the *lei-li*, and it disappeared at his touch! But because of a complicating fever, my daughter died. It was Fate! When the doctor left, I thanked him with this poem, which was only the proper thing to do. I have always tried to cultivate tranquility, and forget worldly cares, but in this affair I could hardly avoid extreme suffering. If I were to have a son now, perhaps that would alleviate my grief. I may be old, but I must strive to this end.

Master Jen has long been famous
        for treating external ailments.
I send him a letter by messenger,
        and immediately he responds.
The *lei-li* completely vanishes—
        a beautiful daughter again!
But her bones are steamed with fever,
        and she loses her life.
People say you can doctor an illness,
        but you cannot doctor Fate!
I thought I had transcended emotion,
        but oh! the emotion now!
I loved this daughter as if she were a son—
        now she is lost;
only a son would be consolation
        for my sorrowful life.

Translated by Jonathan Chaves

1. Defined as "scrofula" in the dictionaries; some form of glandular swelling in the neck is involved.

95

A Buddhist Monk Cut and Burned His Own Flesh to Make the Rains Stop—a Man from His Native Place Asked Me to Write a Poem to Send to Him

Hsü Wei (1521–1593)

The sky extends upward for ninety thousand miles.
When it wants to be clear it is clear,
        when it wants to rain it rains.
For the rain god and the sun god
        it's as easy as herding sheep:
they receive their orders and carry them out;
        who would presume to complain?
So what kind of man is this Buddhist monk,
daring to set up an altar with banners and drums?
With his cracking whip he stands up to Heaven
and cries out to Hsi-ho[1] to bring back the chariot of the sun!
The immortal Chang in broad daylight flew up into the sky—
now this monk has a chance to do even better than that!
All he does is to burn a bit of incense on an inch of his flesh
and the ocean calls the clouds back to the kingdom of water.
The local alchemists are all impressed by what the monk has done,
and the magistrate gives him a piece of red silk.
But still, this man, virtuous as King Aśoka,[2]
        must bear the pain with his own body
while the farmers all bow down to the Inspector of Fields.

Translated by Jonathan Chaves

    Hsü Wei was one of the most original painters and calligraphers of the Ming period. His poetry provided inspiration for the burgeoning of poetic creativity in the late Ming period, and he was also noted for his plays. Hsü was a most unstable individual; having attempted suicide by smashing his testicles (pretending insanity at the time), he murdered his third wife, was put into prison, and was sentenced to death. After seven years, however, he was released.

    This poem provides a rare example of a member of the scholar-official class taking interest in the practices of folk religion.

    1. The mythical charioteer of the sun.

    2. See selection 208.

A Kite

Hsü Wei

A man who lives by the sea tells of a young boy who, preparing to eat some candy, tied the string of his kite around his waist. Suddenly, a great wind started to blow, sweeping the kite off toward the sea. The boy fell to his death. When his body was recovered, the candy was found still clutched in his hand.

(The kite speaks:)

When the wind is gentle
    and I want to rise
        I cannot rise.

When the wind is strong
    and I want to land
        I cannot land.

Can I cross the ocean?—Depend on me
    to make it by myself;

What a shame that I have carried a boy—
    as he ate some candy—
        to his death.

Translated by Jonathan Chaves

One poem from a group of twenty-five.

96
Song of Selling Flowers

Tsung Ch'en (1525–1560)

People who buy flowers in Ch'ang-an[1]
pay millions for just a few stems.
Beside the road there is a hungry man:
they don't give him a single cent.

Translated by Jonathan Chaves

Tsung Ch'en's poetry is consistent with the orthodox program of writing in emulation of High T'ang models, although he brings in effective references to contemporary events and has a refreshingly direct touch in his shorter poems (see also selection 198).

1. Present-day Sian, Ch'ang-an served as the capital for many dynasties.

97

Saying Good-bye to a Singing Girl Who Has Decided to Become a Nun

Mo Shih-lung (c. 1539–1587)

You have called at the gate of the True Vehicle,
                your worldly self is no more.
You have said farewell forever
                to the golden chambers,
                                the wind and the dust.
Lightly you wield the yak-tail whisk;
                your singing fan lies on the floor.
You learn to adjust your meditation cushion,
                and laugh at the dancer's mat.
No more resentment when rouge fades
                like red flowers;
no longer will the feathered hairdo appear in your mirror.
Mist, light, water—quiet Zen mind:
I know a new springtime
                will bloom
                        in the Realm of Emptiness.

Translated by Jonathan Chaves

To the Monk Wu-hsia on the Occasion of His Editing the *Lotus Sūtra* [1]

Mo Shih-lung

You have edited a thousand pages of palm-leaf manuscripts;[2]
for years now, your mind has been devoted
                to the Buddhist canon.

Famous as a painter and a theoretician of art, as a poet Mo Shih-lung demonstrates a delicate lyricism of considerable evocative power.
    1. See selection 13.
    2. See note 3 to the second poem in selection 83. Both here and there, "palm-leaf manuscripts" may simply function as a pious trope for Buddhist scriptures, even those written in Chinese.

I ask you the true meaning
                of Bodhidharma's[3] trip to China:
no written word has ever explained this mystery.

Translated by Jonathan Chaves

3. The founding patriarch of the Zen sect who came to China from India.

98
Twenty-Two Quatrains on Receiving the Obituary Notice for My Son Shih-ch'ü[1]

T'ang Hsien-tsu (1550–1617)

My son, you loved telling the story of Prince Naṭa[2]
who stripped off his own flesh, returned it to his mother,
                and gave his father his bones!
Now your flesh has gone to the Ninefold Springs[3]
                —does your mother understand?
and your father must gather your bones
                and bring them home.

Translated by Jonathan Chaves

Possibly the greatest dramatist of the Ming dynasty, T'ang Hsien-tsu is especially well known for his masterpiece, *The Peony Pavilion (Mu-tan t'ing)* (see selection 276). He was a friend of Yüan Hung-tao (see selection 99) and other figures in the late Ming individualist movement and shared with them an appreciation for romantic love. Somewhat surprisingly, however, the arias in *The Peony Pavilion* are, if anything, more erudite and even bookish than the writings of the orthodox masters themselves—virtually every line has embedded in it a literary allusion, and the play is therefore a kind of scholarly *tour de force*. T'ang's poetry, far less familiar, is beautifully crafted and shares with his arias an interesting fusion of lyrical tone and density of diction.

One poem from the group of twenty-two.

1. The poet's son died in 1600 in Nanking, where he had gone to take the official examinations.

2. According to a Buddhist text of the Sung dynasty, *Wu-teng hui-yüan* (ch. 2), "Prince Naṭa (the son of the guardian king of the north, Vaiśravaṇa) stripped off his own flesh and returned it to his mother, and took out his bones and returned them to his father. Only then did he manifest his True Body, wield his great spiritual power, and expound the dharma (law/doctrine) to his parents."

3. The underworld.

On the day of Washing the Buddha[1] in the year
ting-wei (1607), I dreamed that my late son Shih-
ch'ü was holding a book and appeared to be quite
happy.[2] He said that he had earned his *chin-shih*
degree in the underworld. After we sighed and
laughed together for a long time, I woke up and
wrote this poem.

T'ang Hsien-tsu

I have burned ten thousand volumes
           as paper money[3] for you!
I have grieved at the death of such a talented son.
But do they really have an examination system
           down in the Yellow Springs?
How many of your fellow students
           have ascended to the Sixth Heaven[4] of Desire?

Translated by Jonathan Chaves

1. On the eighth day of the fourth month in the lunar calendar, which was believed in China to be Buddha's birthday, images of Buddha would be washed in celebration.
2. Shih-ch'ü had died seven years earlier in Nanking. He had gone there to take examinations leading eventually to the bestowal of the Presented Scholar's degree, which would allow the candidate to enter the official bureaucracy. T'ang had been sending his son books to study from by burning them instead of the usual paper money, hoping that the books will reach him in the underworld (Yellow Springs).
3. Chinese traditionally burn paper money, printed specially for the purpose, as gifts for the souls of their ancestors.
4. In Buddhist mythology, the Sixth Heaven is the highest heaven in the Realm of Desire. T'ang uses it as an image for obtaining the Presented Scholar's degree.

99

The "Slowly, Slowly" Poem

—*Playfully inscribed on the wall*

Yüan Hung-tao (1568–1610)

The bright moon slowly, slowly rises,
the green mountains slowly, slowly descend.
The flowering branches slowly, slowly redden,
4   the spring colors slowly, slowly fade.
My salary slowly, slowly increases,
my teeth slowly, slowly fall out,
my lover's waist slowly, slowly expands,
8   my complexion slowly, slowly ages.

We are low in society
              in the days of our greatest health,
our pleasure comes when we are no longer young.
The Goddess of Good Luck
              and the Dark Lady of Bad Luck
12   are with us every step we take.
Even heaven and earth are imperfect
and human society is full of ups and downs.
Where do we look for real happiness?
16   —Bow humbly, and ask
              the Masters of Taoist Arts.

Translated by Jonathan Chaves

   Yüan Hung-tao was the leader of the late Ming Kung-an School of literature, so named for
the subprefecture in Hupei province where he was born. Tsung-tao (1560–1600) and Chung-tao
(1570–1624), his elder and younger brothers, were also important members of this influential
literary circle. Known as an individualist, Yüan is a highly eccentric figure within the context of
Ming literature. But his eccentricity falls well within the parameters of Chinese tradition and
can even be seen as weighing the balance back toward moderation after decades of domination
of the cultural scene by the extreme archaism of the orthodox masters.

On Receiving My Letter of Termination

Yüan Hung-tao

The time has come to devote myself to my hiker's stick:
I must have been a Buddhist monk in a former life!

Sick, I see returning home as a kind of pardon.
A stranger here—being fired is like being promoted.
In my cup, thick wine; I get crazy-drunk,
eat my fill, then stagger up the green mountain.
The southern sect, the northern sect, I've tried them all:
this hermit has his own school of Zen philosophy.

Translated by Jonathan Chaves

100
The Broken Lampstand

Wu Wei-yeh (1609–1671)

I remember when you shared my insomnia:
how can I bear to cast you off today?
In joy, you were with me, beside the chilly window;
in sorrow, you added to the depth of my old room.
Now I must read in neighbors' reflected light;
I will sink into dream beneath Buddha's altar lamps.
I've no regrets that the orchid-oil is gone—
those clever rats no longer will invade.

Translated by Jonathan Chaves

Wu Wei-yeh is one of the later writers most worthy of being considered a major figure in the history of Chinese poetry. He especially excelled at lengthy narrative poems unparalleled in the Chinese literary tradition for their unique use of oblique narrative technique and lyrical evocativeness to convey historical events as experienced by concubines and other peripheral participants in one of the most tumultuous periods of Chinese history—the transition from late Ming to early Ch'ing.

101
The Grain-Barge Wife

Wu Chia-chi (1618–1684)

Autumn winds blow along the river,
blow upon a man in hunger;

Disillusioned with the moral failure of the Ming leadership, Wu Chia-chi turned to the common people around him for exemplars of loyalty and filial piety, key Confucian virtues, and

he has a wife lovely as a flower,
4   but no means to put food on her plate!
Toward sunset with great clamor
a grain barge moors in the harbor.
The officer in charge sits at the prow;
8   gazing about, he sees the lovely face.
He sends a man with an urgent message:
"I have plenty of clothes and food.
You are going to starve to death—
12   why not join me, and we'll work together.
Work with me for one year,
and I'll send you home for a fee.
Work with me for three years,
16   and I'll send you home for free!"
The husband pleads with his wife:
"I urge you to do what he asks.
If you don't, we will starve to death,
20   and then we'll be parted forever."
He lifts his wife—lifelong companion—to her feet;
her tears fall like drops of rain.
One day a wife in her bedchamber,
24   the next, a boatman's mistress!
When the man's cronies hear he may have a son,
they prepare a feast, the fatted calf and wine.
They come in boats from south of the river;
28   they come in boats from north of the river.
The boatman is delighted in his heart;
with his own hand he pours out goblets of wine.
He tells himself that lovely piece of goods
32   is like a bird, caught within his nets.
But the netted sparrow has a mate,
the woman has a husband.
How could they know this woman's will
36   could never be bent or broken?
Her husband, weeping, clings to her:
"Follow what he says, lower your eyes!
Work for him for three years' time,
40   and he'll let you return for free."

---

recorded acts of such people which he believed bore testimony to the ongoing vitality of these virtues. His medium-length narrative poems are distinguished by a stark, uncompromising power.

The woman remains silent, not a word;
   as people sleep, the moon sinks at the window.
   Quickly she leaves the boatman's place,
44   determined to seek ghostly companions.
   Clutching a rock, she jumps into the Grand Canal:
   the waves stop flowing for her.
   Passersby wipe their tears and stare
48   at her body floating in the water.

Translated by Jonathan Chaves

102

Singing of the Source of Holy Church

Wu Li (1632–1718)

Before the firmament was ever formed,
      or any foundation laid,
high there hovered the Judge of the World,
      prepared for the last days!
This single Man from His five wounds
      poured every drop of blood;
a myriad nations gave their hearts
      to the wonder of the Cross!
The heavenly gates now have a ladder
      leading to their peace;
demonic spirits lack any art
      to insinuate deception.
Take up the burden, joyfully
      fall in behind Jesus,
look up with reverence towards the top of that mountain,
      follow His every step.

Translated by Jonathan Chaves

This is among the earliest known Chinese poems that deal explicitly with Christian themes. The poet, Wu Li, is famous as one of the Six Orthodox Masters of painting in the early Ch'ing period. His works hang in such major American museums as the Freer Gallery, Metropolitan Museum of Art, Cleveland Museum of Art, and William Rockhill Nelson Gallery of Art. His poems, though little known, are worthy of attention for his bold experiment in creating virtually from scratch a Chinese Christian poetry. Having converted to Catholicism and entered the Society of Jesus in 1682, Wu Li was one of the first Chinese to be ordained a priest, in 1688.

103

Composed at the West Wall of Tsou-p'ing[1] Three Days After the Festival of Pure Brightness[2]

Wang Shih-chen (1634–1711)

Rain now stopped on the plain to the west,
It is all orioles and blossoms, charming in every way.
Green hills surround the city walls,
White birds burst through the stream's mist.
A little village there beyond its clear flow,
Gardens here at the front of the bright, rain-washed scene.
Thinking way back to those guests at Orchid Islet,[3]
Wistfully I stroll through the sunset of this spring day.

Translated by Richard John Lynn

Wang Shih-chen was a native of Hsin-ch'eng, Shantung. He had a long, successful career in the state bureaucracy, in which he rose to become president both of the Censorate and the Board of Punishments. His literary career was equally illustrious. As one of the most prominent writers of the entire Ch'ing era, his poetry, essays, works of literary criticism and theory, and literary anthologies made an enormous impact then and continue to be widely studied and admired today.

1. A district seat in the northeastern part of Tsinan prefecture in Shantung.

2. The Festival of Pure Brightness (Ch'ing-ming) was celebrated on March 24, 1656, the year in which this pentasyllabic poem was composed. This festival occurs after the spring equinox and heralds the advent of warmer, more pleasant weather. As such, it is a favorite day for outings.

3. The "guests at Orchid Islet" refers to Wang Hsi-chih (303–379) and his famous gathering of poets for "Rites of Purification" on the third day of the third lunar month of 353 at the Orchid Pavilion (Lan-t'ing) on Orchid Islet, Shao-hsing district, Chekiang (see selection 200).

After Snow, Longing for Elder Brother Hsi-ch'iao[1]

Wang Shih-chen

Atop the bamboo grove slants sunset's glow,
The narrow lane free of carriage tracks.[2]

1. Wang Shih-lu (1626–1673), the poet's eldest brother. At the time of this poem (1659), Shih-lu was Prefect Director of Schools in Lai-chou, Shantung, and the poet himself was in Peking. Although Shih-Chen had obtained the Presented Scholar *(chin-shih)* degree the previous

Across a thousand miles of evening I think of him
And face the empty garden's snow all alone.[3]

Translated by Richard John Lynn

year, he did not receive his first official appointment until 1659. In the meantime, he was observing the workings of the Board of War and living at the Temple of Compassionate Benevolence.

2. This line is reminiscent of a line in T'ao Ch'ien's (365–427) "Returning to Live in the Country": "In my humble lane cart wheels and horses' halters are scarce." Compare with selection 154.

3. The last line is reminiscent of a line in Liu Tsung-yüan's (773–819) "River Snow": "He fishes in the cold river's snow all alone." See selection 55.

Ch'ai-kuan[1] Mountain Pass

Wang Shih-chen

It's early when we set out on the Ch'en-ts'ang Road,[2]
Our horses' hooves churning up the clouds and mist.
On and on, we finally reach the Ch'ai-kuan where
4   Clouds hang low and rain pours down,
The center of the crazy road potholed and jagged,
And all around a cloak of bamboo forest, thick and dark.
A great rock stands right in the middle of the pass,
8   Shaped like a fierce tiger crouching.
There is no Flying General[3] now in the world,
So why do you gnash your teeth in anger?
Dragons[4] scaled and unscaled frolic right next to us,
12   Startling us out of our wits, making us gasp for breath.
From time to time, strange birds give a cry—
We hear them but don't know where they are.
The Black River[5] in the distance sweeps down,
16   A myriad torrents rushing along all at once.

1. Ch'ai-kuan Pass in the northwestern part of Liu-pa district in Shensi, through which goes the route that connects with the high road into Szechwan. The poet at this time (1672) was on his way to Szechwan to direct the provincial examination there.

2. Goes through Pao-chi district in Shensi and leads to the Ch'ai-kuan.

3. An allusion to Li Kuang of the Han dynasty, who is said to have once shot at a rock during a night march, thinking it was a tiger. His arrow was later found buried up to its feathers in the rock.

4. The dragons are fanciful references to lightning.

5. South of the Ch'ai-kuan, it flows toward the southwest.

I've often heard that Purple Cypress Mountain[6]
Is a place where immortals wander and dwell.
If we once chanced upon some Essence of Stone,[7]
20   In broad daylight we could sprout feathers.[8]
Who caused me, when I had the form of a wild crane,
Scattering my feathers, to fall into the trap?
As the True Creator cannot be asked questions,
24   Let me start out again toward the vast, vague distances.

Translated by Richard John Lynn

6. North of Feng district in Shensi. The seventy-two caves at its summit are supposedly inhabited by immortals.
7. An elixir of immortality.
8. Transformation into an immortal, usually in the form of a wild crane. Compare with the second rhapsody in selection 156.

Medicine

Wang Shih-chen

What do we know about the efficacy of medicine?
Full of worries, one's easy prey to sickness and old age.
Now, my eyes are cried dry weeping for my children[1]
And heart broken by chanting poignant ballads.
Who knows when letters from home might arrive,
As autumn waves run deep both day and night.
While here, the apes of Pa[2] are most inconsiderate,
For crying so sadly in the maple forest.

Translated by Richard John Lynn

1. By this time (1672) the poet had lost two children to illness.
2. Pa is an old name for Szechwan.

Pure Sound Pavilion [1]

Wang Shih-chen

With clothes shaken out at Pure Sound Pavilion,
Pines and cassias singing softly in the breeze,
I sit and face the great peak of Mount Omei, [2]
As clouds disperse, revealing the remaining snow.

Translated by Richard John Lynn

1. On South Mountain, it is within the precincts of the Temple that Soars Atop the Clouds, Chia-chou district, Szechwan. Tradition has it that Su Shih (see selection 156) gave it its name.
2. One of the most famous mountains in China, both because of its scenic beauty and as a place sacred to Buddhism and Taoism (see selection 216).

104
Lines in Praise of a Self-Chiming Clock

K'ang-hsi (1654–1722)

The skill originated in the West,
But, by learning, we can achieve the artifice:
Wheels move and time turns round,
Hands show the minutes as they change.

Red-capped watchmen, there's no need to announce dawn's coming.
My golden clock has warned me of the time.
By first light I am hard at work,
And keep on asking, "Why are the memorials late?"

Translated by Jonathan Spence

This poem was written by the Manchu emperor K'ang-hsi about 1710. He was an ardent supporter of scholarship, literature, and the arts in general throughout his six-decade reign (1661–1722).

105
Song of Surfing on the Bore[1]

Cheng Hsieh (1693–1765)

The boys of Ch'ien-t'ang practice riding the bore:
with firm poles and long oars they stroke and plunge!
One boy, alone, stands on each deck as if cast in iron,
face the color of ashes, his eyes unblinking, fixed.
The bore rolls in like a mountain—they shoot their boats ahead;
masts and sculls flip over sideways
        as the boats stand up on end!
Then—suddenly, they all disappear, without a trace . . .
then reappear on the slow after-waves, a fleet of boats again.
Now the bore has gone down, the waves flow softly,
        the boats follow the gulls.
The boys sing and laugh, the mountains are green,
        the blue water laps the shore.
This is the way we all should go through the troubles of life:
put up with them while they last—calm waters lie ahead.

Translated by Jonathan Chaves

One of the Eight Eccentrics of Yang-chou, Cheng Hsieh had a highly distinctive style both as a painter and a calligrapher. His poetry is full of humor and has a bold search for unusual subject matter, though not without a noticeable moralizing tendency.

1. "An abrupt rise of the tide which breaks in an estuary, rushing violently up the channel" (*The American College Dictionary*). In China, the mouth of the Che River at Hangchow (also known as the Ch'ien-t'ang River at this location) is famous for this phenomenon (see selection 217).

106
On the Way to Pa-ling

Yüan Mei (1716–1797)

From Lake Tung-t'ing we travel west
        to the Shrine of the Goddess;
here to comfort weary travelers
        are women with painted brows.

Yüan Mei became a Presented Scholar in 1739 when he was only twenty-three years old. He was appointed to the imperial academy and instructed to learn the Manchu language, but failed

The mountain town is desolate,
> shops close at early hours;
the fortress tower's light still far,
> we're late to moor our boat.
The dialect here I do not speak—
> I'll hire interpreters;
such strange birds—I don't know their names,
> ashamed as a scholar of the *Odes*.[1]
How rare to find a boatman
> who understands my heart:
each time I open the cabin window
> there's a branch of blossom on shore.

Translated by Jonathan Chaves

----

the Manchu examinations miserably. After other minor appointments, he resigned from public life and devoted himself to writing and teaching.

One of the most attractive of the later poets and essayists, Yüan Mei combines humor with affection for mundane detail. His *Poetry Talks from the Sui Garden (Sui yüan shih-hua)* is one of the best compilations of poetic criticism from the later period and a veritable treasure-trove of insightful discussions of poems and poets.

Yüan Mei had an extremely broad range of interests. For example, he wrote several fine essays on the culinary arts. He also advocated education for young women and even served as the director of a school for female poets whose works he published, for which he was sternly rebuked by many of his more orthodox contemporaries.

Although critical of Li Yü (see selection 211) as being effete and ill-considered, Yüan Mei himself sponsored a traveling troupe of actors and had extraordinarily close relationships with the more handsome among them

Last, but not least, Yüan Mei was an ardent fan of strange tales in the tradition of P'u Sung-ling (see selection 247) and Chi Yün (see selection 248). He collected and published several volumes of these, the most famous being *What the Master* [i.e., Confucius] *Would Not Discuss (Tzu pu yü)*.

1. One of the benefits to be derived from studying the classic *Shih ching* (*Odes*, see selection 22), according to instructions by Confucius to his disciples, is that the reader learns the names of animals and birds.

Miscellaneous Feelings in the Sui Garden[1]

Yüan Mei

I

Joy and anger are not caused by outside things:
they simply happen to arise in the heart.

1. The ostensible meaning of the name of Sui Garden is "Follow Garden," although it actually derives from the first syllable of the sinographic transcription of a former owner, Suihete.

Rising and falling are not matters of fate:
one simply happens to encounter them.
Reading a book and finding nothing there,
I drop the volume, get up, and take a walk.
I think I'll go to the bamboo grove
where I can listen to the springtime water flow.

2

Let them knock at the bramble gate—
the host is in a dream!
Startled awake, I search for my socks;
I must have lost them east of the thatched hut.
At night, with nothing on my mind,
in dream I watched the bamboo growing tall.
Should guests arrive now at my garden,
barefoot I will see them off.

3

Classics, Histories, Philosophers, Belles-Lettres:
these the four branches of literature.
Pavilions I have built, libraries—
one for each kind in four different spots.
In each one I have placed an inkstone
as well as several brushes to write.
Mornings I rise, wash my face,
then let my feet lead me where they will.
Circulating among all four,
happily I pass the day's twelve hours.

4

When they hear me stop reading out loud,
the farmers come from all around.
The healthy ones shoulder hoe and plow,
the fragile ones wear their hempen shoes.
The happy ones bring piles of bamboo mats,
the tired ones have bundled firewood.
They invite me to sit with them under the trees:
we all open our hearts to each other!

Yüan Mei asserted that the garden was the model for Grand Prospect Garden (Ta-kuan Yüan) that figures so centrally in the novel, *Dream of Red Towers* (see selection 263). In any event, the garden, under Yüan Mei's leadership, was certainly a focus of flourishing literary activity during the second half of the eighteenth century. It also figures in the title of his perceptive book of criticism, *Poetry Talks from the Sui Garden* (see unnumbered note above).

"This year we've suffered from wind and rain,
and still can't plant good sprouts.
We hear you chanting out loud from books:
could it be you prepare for exams?"
I love these people, their true, sincere nature,
and the way they speak, like little children!
Each one drinks a cup of wine
and we lie in a heap on the moss.

5

Do not mock me for building this tower tall:
of course a tower should be tall!
If you approach from three miles away,
already I'll see you from here.
When you visit, come not in a carriage:
the carriage's racket will terrify my birds.
And when you visit, don't come on a horse:
the horse's teeth will decimate my grass.
Also, when you visit, please, don't come at dawn:
we mountain folk hate to rise too early.
And when you visit, don't wait until dusk:
by then the flowers will all have withered away.

6

The Master of Sui Garden in the past
first built buildings here beside these hills.
Terraces, pavilions summoned clouds and mist;
wine cups glittered in the candlelight.
The old men here all say to me
that this Master was no vulgar man.
He took this garden and passed it on—to whom?
How could he know it would be me!
Long, long the thirty years;
and now I come, to help the flowers and bamboo.
"Follow Garden": the meaning timely now;
no need to change the garden's name at all.
Consider my present-day happiness
continuation of the Master's joy.
Does it really just all "pass away"?
Past and present, still the same chess game!
And who will follow after I have left?
I ask the mountain, but it does not say.

Translated by Jonathan Chaves

Lyrics and Arias

A Suite in the *Ch'ing-p'ing* Mode[1]

Attributed to Li Po (701–762)

Part One

As clouds think of her clothing, as blossoms think of her face,
Spring wind caresses the railings
and dew is thick on the flowers.
[Stanza continues.]

This is one of the earliest sets of lyrics, "lyric" (also called "lyric meter" or "song lyric" in English) here being used as a technical term equivalent to the Chinese literary genre *tz'u*. All the poetry in the previous section of the anthology belongs to the genre known as *shih* and is of quite a different nature from that of *tz'u*. *Shih* normally consist of lines of equal length, usually pentasyllabic or heptasyllabic, and may be thought of as prosodically "square" in shape. One of the most common words for "character" in Mandarin is *fang-k'uai-tzu* ("square graph" or "tetragraph"). The square shape of a regular number of graphs in the lines of a poem results in a square or rectangular shape for the poem as a whole. It also invites abundant use of such literary devices as parallelism and antithesis in matching lines and couplets. Traditionally, however, Chinese texts—whether poetry or prose—were written out in continuous strings of sinographs without any indication of line length or punctuation, these being determined during the act of reading.

Tz'u, or lyrics, usually consist of lines of unequal length. Originally, the length of each line was determined by the music to which these lyrics were sung. Such tunes frequently entered the repertoire from Central Asia and other surrounding regions or from the popular culture, especially the entertainment world, of various localities within China. A suite of matching or grouped tunes was said to belong to a given "mode" *(tiao)*, which may be regarded as analogous to a musical "key" (i.e., several related *tz'u*-tunes were "in the mode/key of . . ."). The whole system of Chinese lyrical tunes and modes bears certain resemblances to Indian ragas and, indirectly through Indianized Central Asian and South Asian musical sources, may have been

If you do not find her by the Mountain of Numerous Jewels,[2]
You may head for the Jasper Terrace[3]
to meet her beneath the moon.

Part Two

A branch of red voluptuousness, the dew congealed perfume,
For clouds and rain on Sorceress Mountain,[4]
why go breaking your heart?

_____

[Stanza continues.]

influenced by them and by other Indian musical and prosodic conventions. With the passage of time, the musical quality of the tunes and modes in China was forgotten, but the syllabic lengths and prosodic quality of the lines became fixed, arbitrary patterns to which new lyrics could be fitted. Thus lyrics may be said to be "to the tune of . . . ," even though the actual tunes were lost while only the line lengths and certain tonic, syntactic, grammatical, and other characteristics were retained.

The subject matter of the earliest lyrics was often related to the titles of the tunes to which they were written. Before very long in the evolution of the genre, however, there developed a complete divorce between the meaning of tune title and the content of a given lyric. Indeed, a separate title apart from the tune title was often provided for each new lyric. Many translators simply transcribe the tune titles because of their irrelevance to content and because they are often extremely difficult to understand. This is particularly the case for the later stages in the development of the tradition where the relationship between the tune title and the content of a lyric or aria is usually meaningless.

It is not just the structure of the *tz'u*-lyric that is so different from that of the *shih*-poem. The themes and diction are also distinctive. The lyric, for example, is typically far less allusive than a classical poem. In contrast, the language of the lyric may often be more effusive. Where the classical poem is largely governed by the quasi-monosyllabic nature of the literary (written) language, the lyric is full of polysyllabic words from the vernacular (oral) language. It is commonplace for the lyric, furthermore, to be spoken in the persona of a woman, even though most lyrics, like the vast majority of all Chinese verse, were written by men. A constant theme of the lyric is love, normally considered an unworthy or trivial subject in the tradition of classical poetry.

The lyric had its precursors in the T'ang period and its heyday in the Five Dynasties and Sung periods but was replaced by the aria (see selections 130 ff.) during the Yüan period. The genre continued to be practiced by scattered authors during the Ming and Ch'ing periods. Mao Tse-tung, the founder of the People's Republic of China, was an avid practitioner of *tz'u*-lyrics.

The question of the authorship of "A Suite in the *Ch'ing-p'ing* Mode" is a thorny one. One problem with the set is that each of the three parts is actually written as though it were a regular heptasyllabic poem. Yet this is in keeping with the early involvement of literati poets with the lyric. Often their regular verse would be adapted to the irregular line lengths of lyric meters by the addition of filler words and syllables.

For a note on the poet, see selection 45.

1. These lyrics are believed to have been written at imperial command on an occasion in 743 or 744 when Emperor Hsüan Tsung and Precious Consort Yang (Yang Kuei-fei) were enjoying the tree peonies in the imperial gardens.

2. In the wonderful realm of the mythical Queen Mother of the West, who is attended by beautiful immortals.

3. The palace of the Queen Mother of the West.

4. "Clouds and rain" are the usual figure for delicately suggesting sexual intimacy. The original dalliance that resulted in sex being associated with clouds and rain took place on Sorceress Mountain (Wu Shan) in southwest China.

I wonder who could be compared in the palaces of the Han?
Would it be dear Flying Swallow[5]
trying new powder and rouge?

Part Three

Beauty to topple a nation in the company of famous flowers,
They always succeed with His Majesty
making him turn with a smile.
Knowing that the spring wind may bring regrets unending,
North of the Aloeswood Pavilion
they lean on the balustrade.

Translated by Elling Eide

5. Chao Fei-yen. A beautiful Han dynasty dancer who caught the eye of Emperor Ch'eng and ultimately became his empress in 16 B.C.E. It is said that Li Po was banished from court when the eunuch Kao Li-shih called it slanderous to compare Precious Consort Yang with Flying Swallow.

108
Four Lyrics from Tun-huang

Anonymous (8th–9th century)

Tune: "Eternal Longing"

I

He was a traveler west of the river,
with wealth and eminence rare in this world.
All day long in vermilion towers[1]
. . . . . dancing and singing songs.[2]

The cup filled again and again, till he's drunk as mud;
lightly, lightly trading golden goblets,
wearing out the day tasting joys, pursuing pleasures—
Some people are rich and never go home.

Approximately five hundred lyrics, mostly dating to the tenth century or somewhat earlier, were discovered at Tun-huang (see selection 266). Except for three or four known T'ang poets, all are anonymous, but in some cases the names of the singers were given. The Tun-huang lyrics include a total of sixty-nine different tune titles. They are extremely important for understanding the early history of lyric meters.
    1. Multistoried houses of entertainment.
    2. Two characters are missing on the manuscript at the beginning of this line.

2

He was a traveler west of the river;
only he knew how lonely he was,
dust and dirt covering his face,
all day long being cheated by others.

Morning after morning standing by the west gate of the market,
the wind blowing the tears that came down in two streams,
gazing toward his native land so many roads away—
Some people are poor and never go home.

3

He was a traveler west of the river,
then he took sick, lay an inch away from death.
Still he stayed on, looking for news,
though as time went by it seemed he'd have to depart.

The villagers dragged him to the west side of the road—
his father and mother knew nothing about it—
tied a tag on his body with his name written on it—
Some people die and never go home.

Tune: "Magpie on the Branch"

4

I can't stand the wily magpie and all his extravagant stories!
He brings me good news, but what proof does he ever have?
One of these times when he flies by, I'll grab him, capture him live,
shut him up in a golden cage to put a stop to his chatter!

With the best of intentions I went to her, delivered my good news—
who'd have thought she'd shut me up in a golden cage?
I only hope her soldiering husband comes home soon
so she'll lift me up, turn me loose to head for the blue clouds!

Translated by Burton Watson

109

Tune: "Memories of the South"
A Reminiscence

Po Chü-yi (772–846)

I

The beauty of the South!
Once I was familiar with all its sights and sounds.
At sunrise, river flowers redder than flame,
In spring, river waters the blue of indigo.
Can I help remembering the South?

II

Memories of the South!
Most fondly I remember Hangchow.
Visiting temples in the hills in quest of cassia seeds dropped from the moon;
Watching the Tidal Bore[1] from my pillow in the pavilion of my office.
When shall I ever revisit Hangchow?

III

Memories of the South!
Next I recall the stately mansions of Wu.
A cup of fine Wu vintage—
The color of spring bamboo leaf;
Wu damsels dancing in pairs—
Lotus blossoms flushed with wine.
When shall I meet them again?

Translated by Jiaosheng Wang

For a note on Po Chü-yi, see selection 180.
1. See selections 105 and 217.

110
Tune: "Memories of the South"
A Spring Lyric After Po Chü-yi

Liu Yü-hsi (772–842)

Spring is going, gone!
Having thankfully bid adieu
To the people of Loyang.
Willow tendrils quivering in the breeze
Wave good-bye;
Clustered orchids drip dew
To wet their handkerchiefs.
And she sits alone,
Knitting her moth-eyebrows.

Translated by Jiaosheng Wang

Imbued with Confucianism through his family tradition and upbringing, Liu Yü-hsi became a Presented Scholar in 793 at the age of twenty. However, a setback in his official career occurred when he wrote a number of poems thought to be politically offensive. Liu was one of the earliest literati poets to experiment with the prosodic arrangements of popular songs. He was also influenced by non-Sinitic folk songs with which he came to be familiar during two periods of banishment.

111
Tune: "Deva-Like Barbarian"

Wen T'ing-yün (?–866)

The mountains on the screen shimmer in the golden dawn;
A cloud of hair brushes the fragrant snow of her cheek.
Lazily, she rises and paints mothlike brows;
Slowly, tardily, she gets ready for the day.

A native of T'ai-yüan in Shansi, Wen T'ing-yün failed the highest civil service examination many times. An accomplished musician on the flute and zither, he was able to create new tunes of his own. Most lyrics attributed to earlier literati poets are barely distinguishable from "square" or "rectangular" classical poetry in form. Performers relied heavily on so-called "padding words" to flesh them out so that they would fit the irregular contours of popular tunes. Wen's lyrics, in contrast, are full-fledged with a sprightly rhythm unlike that of classical poetry. The first major poet to produce unabashedly a substantial number of genuine lyrics, it was Wen who did the most to legitimize the lyric as an appropriate genre for literati. Sixty-six of his seventy extant

Mirrors, front and behind, reflect a flower,
Face and flower shining each upon the other.
Stitched in the silk of her bright new coat,
Golden-threaded partridges fly pair by pair.

Translated by Lois Fusek

lyrics are preserved in the *Among the Flowers Collection (Hua chien chi)*, the famous anthology of lyrics about love and separation compiled by Chao Ch'ung-tso (fl. 934–965). This is by far the largest number of poems by which any author is represented in this highly significant collection. Ou-yang Chiung, who (like most of the poets included in the collection) was from Shu (present-day Szechwan), wrote a preface dated 940 that attempted to justify this new effete and ornate style of verse as an appropriate vehicle for the expression of literati sentiment.

The lyric selected here is from a group of fourteen by Wen to the same tune title. Although the sinographs usually used to write the tune title *P'u-sa man* seem to mean "Bodhisattva Southwesterners," there is much controversy over their correct interpretation. One modern literary historian, Elling Eide, gives evidence that they should be rendered as "Strings of Jewels for Bodhisattvas," and that the lyrics to this tune were originally all strings of couplets about beautiful women. A Bodhisattva is a savior figure in Mahāyāna ("Great Vehicle") Buddhism and "deva" (the translation given for the same word by the translator of Wen T'ing-yün's lyric) is simply a Sanskrit word for "deity." The same tune title (*P'u-sa man*) is rendered as "The Bodhisattva Foreigner" for the second lyric by Wei Chuang in selection 112.

112

Tune: "Thinking of the Imperial Capital"

Wei Chuang (836–910)

Out strolling on a spring day,
Almond blossoms flutter and fill her hair.
"On the field path, who is that young man
  So dashing?
I'd like to be his wife
  My whole life long!
Even if he heartlessly abandoned me,
  I'd feel no shame."

Translated by John Timothy Wixted

Wei Chuang hailed from Tu-ling in Shensi. He was the great-great-grandson of the poet Wei Ying-wu. His parents, however, passed away when he was but a child, and he grew up in reduced circumstances. By 894 when he became a Presented Scholar, the T'ang dynasty was already in serious decline, so there was little hope of a meaningful career in officialdom. For this and for other personal reasons, his verses are filled with melancholy. Forty-eight of his lyrics are included in the *Among the Flowers Collection*, which shows that he was one of the more

Tune: "The Bodhisattva Foreigner"

Wei Chuang

Recalling now the pleasures of the South,
When I was young in light spring tunic—
Astride my horse by the sloping bridge,
Red-sleeved ones beckoned from every storied house.

By gilt-hinged kingfisher screens,
Drunk, I'd enter the flower groves to spend the night.
Seeing such flower twigs now,
Though gray-haired, I swear I'd not go home.

Translated by John Timothy Wixted

active literati practitioners of the new genre. He was also the author of the celebrated poem, "Lament of the Lady of Ch'in," an account of the sack of Ch'ang-an by the rebel Huang Ch'ao. This long, dramatic piece, which was phenomenally popular shortly after its composition, was lost for over a thousand years and recovered only in this century among the Tun-huang manuscripts (see selections 108 and 266). While living in Szechwan, Wei purchased and lived in the former house of the great poet Tu Fu (see selection 48).

113
Tune: "Drunk Among the Flowers"

Mao Wen-hsi (fl. 930)

Don't ask any questions!
I'm afraid of questions!

Questions add all the more to my suffering.
The waters of spring are flooding the pond.
Mandarin ducks still seek each other there.

Last night, the rains fell in an icy sleet.
At a time near dawn, it was extremely cold.
I think of him in the frontier guard tower.
No news has come for such a very long time.

Translated by Lois Fusek

The lyricist was a native of Kao-yang in Shantung. He obtained the title of Presented Scholar and entered government service under the Earlier Shu dynasty (907–925) in Szechwan. The lyric selected here is the first of two by the author composed to the same tune title.

114

Tune: "Offering Congratulations to the Enlightened Reign"

Ou-yang Chiung (896–971)

I remember the day when we first met among the flowers.
I lifted my red sleeve to hide my face,
And so frivolously turned my head away.
I played with the sash on my red skirt,
And quite deliberately with my slender,
Jadelike fingers, I began to pick away,
A pair of phoenixes stitched with gold.

The green *wu-t'ung*[1] trees are locked deep in the garden.
Who could know how much we would love one another?
Will there be a time when we can be forever close?
I envy the mated swallows that come in the spring.
Flying, they descend to the jade tower,
Where day and night, they are together!

Translated by Lois Fusek

A native of the culturally and historically important town of Hua-yang in Szechwan, Ou-yang Chiung served as a high-ranking official under both the Earlier Shu (907–925) and Later Shu (934–965) dynasties, as well as under the Sung government which reunified China after the Five Dynasties. He was the author of a noteworthy preface to the *Among the Flowers Collection* (see selection 111), from which this lyric is taken. It is the first of two by him to the same tune title.

1. The scientific name for the *wu-t'ung* is *Sterculia platanifolia* or *Firmiana platanifolia*. In English, it is called the kolanut or Chinese parasol tree. An ornamental tree frequently found growing in the courtyards of Chinese temples and houses, its large leaves afford excellent shade. As a literary trope, it occurs constantly in poems and plays to evoke feelings of sadness experienced by someone who hears raindrops lugubriously falling upon its broad leaves. Here, we may also interpret its name as a homophone for "we-together."

115
Tune: "The Crow's Nocturnal Cry"

Li Yü (937–978)

Last night there was rain with a soughing wind.
In the air was the sound of autumn,
And the screens and curtains rustled.
Again and again I turned on my pillow,
As the candlelight waned, and the clepsydra stopped dripping.
Nor could I compose myself when I sat up.

Worldly affairs simply drift away
In the wake of the running stream:
Methinks my life is but a floating dream.
Fittest to frequent—
The calm Land of Drunkenness.
Other than it, there's no path
I can bear to travel.

Translated by Jiaosheng Wang

Li Yü was the last emperor of the Southern T'ang dynasty. Apparently ineffective as a ruler, he was a true esthete. A painter, calligrapher, and lyricist, he favored Buddhism and tried his best to avoid war. But his dynasty was quickly conquered and replaced by the Sung, with the result that much of his later verse dwells upon lost glory. Li Yü enlarged the scope of writing in lyric meters beyond the previously normal confines of the teahouse and women's apartments. With him, it became possible to use the lyric as a vehicle for writing about such subjects as the downfall of his own dynasty, the shortness of life, and the futility of human endeavor.

Tune: "Beating Silk Floss"
Autumn Boudoir

Li Yü

In the sequestered court quiet reigns,
Within the small yard not a soul stirs.
An intermittent breeze wafts the intermittent thudding of a cold mallet.[1]
There's no helping these drifting notes
That invade my chamber curtains the livelong night
And will not let me go to sleep—
A bright moon looking on.

Translated by Jiaosheng Wang

1. The sound of beating silk floss.

Tune: "New Bounty of Royalty"[1]

Li Yü

There's no helping
Autumn colors slipping imperceptibly by.
Dusk descends on courtyard steps
Strewn with fallen petals and leaves.
Once more the Double Ninth Festival[2] returns,
And I ascend the terrace pavilion
Letting fade the fragrance of dogwood.

Aroma of chrysanthemum wine
Wafting by the hall entrance;
Drizzling rain robed in evening mist.
Wild geese just come back
Honking drearily in the chill air.
Regrets untold—from year to year unchanging.

Translated by Jiaosheng Wang

1. After the loss of his empire to the Sung dynasty, Li Yü was imprisoned in the Sung capital. Later, the Sung emperor T'ai Tsung granted him a pardon, and he was allowed to live in a separate residence. This lyric was presumably written during that period of comparative ease. In some later poems, however, he expressed the strong nostalgic feelings of a deposed monarch. This enraged the Sung emperor, who not long afterward ordered him to be poisoned.

2. The ninth of the ninth lunar month, a festival celebrated by climbing a hill and drinking wine. It is also associated with longevity and thus becomes an appropriate occasion for drinking an infusion of chrysanthemum petals in wine, a concoction thought to confer long life.

Tune: "Joy of Encounter"
Autumn Boudoir

Li Yü

Wordless, alone I ascend the West Tower.
The moon, a beautiful crescent,
Shines on a clump of lonely parasol-trees
That lock up serene autumn
In a secluded courtyard.

Sorrows of parting—a jumble of raveled thread:
Try to cut it—it defies severing;
Sort it out—and it tangles again.

A taste with a queerness
There's no savoring
Save in the depth of one's heart.

Translated by Jiaosheng Wang

Tune: "Pure Serene Music"

Li Yü

Spring is half gone since we parted.
My heart breaks when I see
Snowy plum petals at the foot of the stairs in disarray
That all but cover my body
For all my brushing.

Wild geese come back—can I trust the message they bring?
The way so long—no use to dream of returning.
The pain of separation is just like the spring grass:
The more it grows, the farther away you are.

Translated by Jiaosheng Wang

Tune: "Sand Washed by Waves"

Li Yü

Outside the curtain rain trickles on.
Spring already on the decline,
And my satin quilt is scarcely proof
Against the chill of dawn.
In my dreams I was still avid for moments of pleasure,
Feeling captive no longer.

Gaze not alone from the balustrade!
My beautiful homeland—
A boundless expanse of hills and streams
All too lightly parted with,
Now so hard to catch a glimpse of.
The river glides on—
Flowers fade—

Spring is gone!
A gulf between heaven and earth.

Translated by Jiaosheng Wang

Tune: "Joy of Encounter"

Li Yü

Woodland flowers lose their vernal color
Too soon, all too soon!
How can they stand
Heartless evening blasts and chill rain at dawn?

Rouged tears, how they make one linger and drink one's fill;
Rosy blossoms, when will they reappear?
Regret, long-lasting, this life of ours—
A river of melancholy waters
That ever eastward flows.

Translated by Jiaosheng Wang

Tune: "Sand Washed by Waves"

Li Yü

Things bygone engender nothing but unbearable sorrow,
With present scenes before my very eyes.
Autumn wind blows on courtyard steps
O'ergrown with moss,
Pearl blinds hang idly unfurled under the eaves.
Who will come to visit
This livelong day?

Sunk and buried is the iron-girded chain[1] in the Yangtze;
Gone to waste long since my imperial sway.
Evening cool, a cloudless sky, luminous moonrise—
Reminders of jade towers and jeweled palaces of old

1. A strong iron chain fixed along the Yangtze under orders of Li Yü in a futile attempt to stop the advancing Sung army from crossing the river.

That now cast their shadows over the Ch'in-huai[2]
All in vain.

Translated by Jiaosheng Wang

2. A river, famed as a luxurious pleasure resort, which flowed through the lost territory of the Southern T'ang.

Tune: "The Beauty of Yü"
A Reminiscence

Li Yü

The vernal breeze returns to refresh
The rank grass in the small courtyard with green.
Young leaves dreamy-eyed
Keep sprouting from the willows.
And I lean wordless by myself against the railing.
For hours on end,
Brooding over bamboos
That whisper under a new moon
As in days of old.

Piping and song not yet done;
The wonted cups and jars still there.
Ice on the pond beginning to thaw,
Candles in the deep painted hall
Glowing in scented darkness—
Hard to bear for one with
Temples turned the color of hoarfrost and snow.

Translated by Jiaosheng Wang

Tune: "Memories of the South"
A Reminiscence

Li Yü

Regrets untold!
In a dream last night
I was again out touring High Park

As in days of old:
Luxurious coaches in streams,
Fine steeds soaring like dragons—
A blaze of moonlight and flowers
In the balmy breezes of spring.

Translated by Jiaosheng Wang

116
Tune: "Bells Ringing in the Rain"
Sadness of Parting

Liu Yung (987?–1053)

It was at the roadside pavilion that we were to bid adieu.
A sudden evening rain had just come to a lull,
Lugubrious the chirp of cicadas in the chill air.
At the farewell dinner outside the city gate,
We drank in low spirits,
Unable to tear ourselves away at the boatman's summons.
Hand in hand we gazed at each other's tear-stained eyes,
Words choked on the verge of utterance,
As we brooded over the misty waves
That swept a thousand tricents away,
And a dusky haze silhouetted against
A wide southern sky.

Parting with a loved one has ever been painful since days of old,
Let alone in the season of bleak autumn.
Where shall I be this evening when I sober up?
On a bank o'ergrown with willows—
The moon waning, the wind of dawn blowing.[1]

Liu Yung came from the southeastern coastal region of Fukien. He achieved the rank of Presented Scholar in 1034 at the relatively late age of forty-seven but never energetically embarked upon an official career. Liu spent a lot of his early years frequenting the demimonde of Pien-ching (modern K'aifeng), the Northern Sung capital, where he became well known among the courtesans for whom he wrote new lyrics. He is noted for creating the subgenre of long lyrics (*man-tz'u*). Liu's works depict urban life and make free use of colloquial language. He was considered by other lyricists to be unconventional and even vulgar, but was also capable of employing highly refined literary language when he felt it appropriate.

1. In the original Chinese, this line is traditionally considered to be famous for its poignant picturesqueness.

Once parted, year after year must elapse
When to relive pleasant hours and gay scenes
Will be but an illusion,
And even though I have a thousand delicate sentiments,
To whom can I bare my aching heart?

Translated by Jiaosheng Wang

Tune: "Eight Beats of a Kan-chou Song"

Liu Yung

Facing me, the blustering evening rain besprinkles the sky over
the river,
    Washing the cool autumn air once more.
    Gradually, the frosty wind rises chilly and hard,
        The landscape looks more forlorn,
        The fading sun falls on the balcony.
    Everywhere, the red withers and the green fades away:
        One by one, the glories of nature cease.
        Only the water of the Long River[1]
        Flows in silence to the east.

I cannot bear to climb high and look far,
    For to gaze at my native land in the dim distance
        Would release endless homeward thoughts.
I sigh over the past year's wanderings;
Why should I desperately linger on?
        I imagine the fair one
Is now gazing, head raised, from her chamber.
        How often has she
Mistaken a returning boat on the horizon for mine?
        How would she know that I,
    Leaning here on the railings,
    Should be congealed with sorrow like this?

Translated by James J. Y. Liu

1. The Yangtze.

117
Tune: "Sumuche[1] Dancers"

Fan Chung-yen (989–1052)

Blue cloud sky
Yellow leaf ground
Autumnal waves
Under cold blue mist.
Hills catch the setting sun, sky and water merge.
Unfeeling, fragrant grasses grow
On and on past the setting sun.

Unhappy homesick soul
Obsessed with travel cares—
Night brings no relief
Except when pleasant dreams prolong the sleep.
Don't look out the high window when the moon shines—
The wine in your melancholy heart
Will turn to tears of longing.

Translated by James Robert Hightower

Fan Chung-yen's father died when he was still very young and he took the surname Chu
when his mother remarried. He studied in a rural Buddhist temple and received the assistance of
a number of generous patrons, with the result that he was able to pass the examinations for
Presented Scholar in 1015. He became the leader of an initial reform of Northern Sung
institutions and thus prepared the way for the major reforms of Ou-yang Hsiu (see selection 206)
and Wang An-shih (see selection 71). Not a prolific author, his poems, prose pieces, and lyrics
(especially his short lyrics) are nonetheless highly appreciated.

1. The name is probably the transcription of some Central Asian word, whence the tune
originally came.

Tune: "Trimming the Silver Lamp"

Fan Chung-yen

Last night I was reading the *Chronicle of the Three Kingdoms*[1]
And laughed at Ts'ao Ts'ao, Sun Ch'üan, Liu Pei.[2]
They tried every stratagem,
Used up their hearts' strength,

1. Compare with selection 258, which is a fictionalized version of this history.
2. Key figures in the history of the Three Kingdoms.

And all any one got was a third of the country.
Tot it up on your fingers, reflect—
Was it worth one drink with Liu Ling?[3]

Human life never lasts a hundred years.
Young, you are too foolish; old, you get decrepit.
There's only the few good years
In between.
How can you stand to tie them to an empty name?
The highest rank, a thousand of gold—
Ask your white hairs,
Can it make them retreat?

Translated by James Robert Hightower

3. Liu Ling (c.221–300) was one of the seven bohemian sages of the Bamboo Grove. A famous toper and author of "Hymn to the Virtue of Wine," Liu declared that he would not mind being buried so long as he died drunk. His abstinence-advocating wife once compelled him to renounce wine before the gods, but he tricked her by persuading her to prepare an offering of meat and wine for the celestial spirits and then guzzling down the alcoholic beverage by himself.

118
Tune: "Spring in the Jade House"

Yen Shu (991–1055)

Green willows and fragrant grass by the posthouse road
Where the young man left me without a pang.
An unfinished dream at the fifth watch bell
The sorrow of parting under the blossoms in a third month rain.

Insensitive misses susceptible's bitterness,
Whose every inch turns into a thousand myriad strands.
The sky's edge, earth's corner—sometime they come to an end;
It's just this longing that is never done.

Translated by James Robert Hightower

The lyricist, who was from Lin-ch'uan in Kiangsi, passed the Presented Scholar examination at the incredibly young age of fourteen and soon thereafter received an official appointment. By the age of forty-four, he had become Grand Councilor and was one of the few southerners to achieve such a high rank at the Northern Sung court. A true statesman-poet, Yen sponsored a literary salon in his own home. He was particularly skilled in composing short lyrics and followed the tradition of the Southern T'ang lyricists.

Tune: "Treading on Fragrant Grass"

Yen Shu

A path strewn with a sprinkling of red;
A broad plain carpeted all over with verdure.
Hue of trees, lush and dark, hazy around the high tower.
The spring breeze knows not how to stop
Willow catkins blowing in a fine drizzle
On the wayfarer's face.

Leaves emerald-green—the orioles are hidden from view;
Pearled blinds drawn—the swallows are denied entrance.
Incense smoke calmly ascends
To whirl round with the floating gossamer.
Fumes of wine gone, I wake from a troubled dream
To find the slanting sun
Shining on a courtyard profoundly secluded.

Translated by Jiaosheng Wang

Tune: "Sand of Silk-Washing Brook"
A Reminiscence

Yen Shu

A goblet of wine.
A verse newly composed:
The same old terrace and pavilion,
The same weather,
As last year's.
The westering sun—
When will it be here again?

Swallows coming back seem to be old acquaintances;
Flowers fade away, do what one may.
Inside the small garden,
Up and down the scented footpath,
Alone I pace.

Translated by Jiaosheng Wang

119
Tune: "Gathering Mulberry Leaves"

Ou-yang Hsiu (1007–1072)

A gaudy boat with wine on board: West Lake is at its best.
Pipes and strings to play a tune,
Cups of jade to pass around.
Riding steady, it permits a tipsy nap.

The moving clouds are below the moving boat.
Air and water so completely clear—
I look up there and look down here,
Wondering if that's another sky in the lake.

Translated by James Robert Hightower

For a note on Ou-yang Hsiu, see selection 206.

Tune: "Magnolia Flower" (short version)

Ou-yang Hsiu

There's no keeping back spring—
The swallow has aged, the warbler is tired and nowhere to be found.
Tell departing spring,
Once old, no one ever turned young again.

The breeze is mild, the moon is fine,
If you've got the money, buy a smile.
Make the best of the fragrant hour—
Don't wait until the flowers are gone before you break the branch.

Translated by James Robert Hightower

Tune: "Drunk in Fairyland"

Ou-yang Hsiu

Shyly she knits her brows
And shows a face delicately rouged:

Supple waist in white silk
Beside the peony balustrade.
Vexed, she won't let him approach—
Half hiding her coy face,
Her voice low and shaking,
She asks, "Does anyone know?"
Smoothing her silk skirt,
She steals an upward glance
And takes a step or two away.

Then she asks,
"If I do it and then
My hair comes all undone
And mother guesses what's up?
No, I am going home—
You leave me alone for now.
Besides, I've needlework to do for mother;
She'll scold me if I don't get it done.
Wait until late tonight,
And come again
Under the shadows of the courtyard trees, okay?"

Translated by James Robert Hightower

120
Tune: "Calming Windswept Waves"

Su Shih (1037–1101)

Prefatory note: On the seventh day of the third month, I was caught in a downpour en route to Sandy Lake. Those carrying the rain gear had gone ahead. My companions all felt downhearted, but I didn't. Presently it became fine, and I wrote these lines.

Listen not to the rain piercing the woods, pelting the leaves!
I might as well stroll leisurely along
Making verses impromptu and whistling at ease.
More relaxing than a saddle are straw sandals and bamboo staff.
  Why be afraid

For a note on Su Shih, see selection 156.

To spend my whole life with abandon,
In straw raincape, in mist and rain?

A keen spring wind sobers me up from wine, leaves me with
       A bit of chill,
Now I see the slanting sun beckoning to me
From the top of the hill.
I turn my eyes to the scene of the late storm, and
       Go back!
I say, to where you will be troubled
By neither rain nor shine.

Translated by Jiaosheng Wang

Tune: "A Riverside Town"
Hunting at Mi-chou

Su Shih

Left hand leading a yellow hound,
In the right a gray falcon,
I feel rejuvenated with the vigor of youth.
Cavalrymen in sable coats and helmets of brocade
Cross the thousand-tricent level ridge in one powerful sweep.
Let the whole town turn out at the prefect's[1] clarion call,
To watch him shoot the tiger at bay,
Emulate the prowess of King Sun of Wu![2]

Now I have drunk my fill,
My spirits rise to their highest:
What though my temples are streaked with gray?
When will be dispatched here
An envoy with the imperial tally?[3]

    This romantic lyric was written in a forceful style, presumably to refute the flowery style of the contemporary poet Liu Yung that was then much in vogue. In a letter to a friend, Su Shih expressed satisfaction at having composed a lyric in his own romantic style which produced an effect that rivaled, if not surpassed, that of Liu's effusions.

    1. At the time of writing, Su was prefect of Mi-chou, a minor post far removed from the capital, to which he had been demoted for a trivial offense.

    2. When King Sun Ch'üan of the state of Wu in the period of the Three Kingdoms (220–265) was out riding, his horse was injured by a tiger. He bravely attacked the tiger with his halberd.

    3. A wooden label issued by the ruler either as a credential or as a decree for the pardon of an offender.

I am all impatience to bend my bow like a full moon,
And, aiming northwest, shoot down the Wolf[4]
Running riot in the sky!

Translated by Jiaosheng Wang

4. The Wolf here refers to the star Sirius, taken to represent the Liao invaders to whom the Northern Sung had lost much of its territory.

Tune: "Partridge Sky"
Written While Banished to Huang-chou

Su Shih

Where the forest breaks,
Hills emerge into view;
Where the walled courtyard is hidden in bamboo,
Obstreperous cicadas riot over a small pond o'ergrown with withered grass.
Frequent is the appearance of white birds looping in the air,
Delicate the fragrance of pink lotus blooms mirrored in water.

Beyond the village houses,
Beside the ancient town,
Cane in hand, a leisurely stroll I take
In the wake of the slanting sun.
Thanks to last midnight's bounteous rain,
My floating life[1] now enjoys one more day of delicious cool.

Translated by Jiaosheng Wang

1. An expression meaning "precarious life" which originates from Chuang Tzu (see selection 9).

Tune: "Butterflies Lingering over Flowers"

Su Shih

Faded the last red blossoms,
Small the new-born green apricots.
Where emerald waters wind about the house

Swallows are on the wing.
Let willow catkins dwindle after one more blast!
There's nowhere on earth but sweet grass will grow.

Within the wall there's a swing, without the highway.
A passerby without is struck by
A girl's sweet laughter within.
Silence prevails as the laughter fades away,
And the enchanted for the unfeeling enchantress
Can only heave a sigh.

Translated by Jiaosheng Wang

Tune: "Water Mode Song"

Su Shih

How many times has the moon shone full?
Lifting my cup I ask the blue sky.
In the palaces and towers of Heaven
What season is it tonight, I wonder.
I should like to ride there on the wind,
But I fear I could not stand the cold
Of those crystal domes and jade halls on high.
I rise and dance and make my shadow move:
How much nicer it is here!

Over vermilion chambers,
Through curtained windows
Shining on the sleepless—
The moon should not be blamed.
But why always full when friends are separated?
Men are happy or sad, apart or together,
The moon is obscured or clear, waxing or waning:
In this world perfection seldom comes.
I only hope that we can live long
And both enjoy the moon's beauty, though a thousand miles apart.

(Mid-autumn, 1076, written after an all-night party, very drunk,
    remembering my brother, Tzu-yu)

Translated by James Robert Hightower

Tune: "River Town"

Su Shih

Lost to one another, the living and the dead, these ten years.
I have not tried to remember
What is impossible to forget.
Your solitary grave is a thousand miles away,
No way to tell you my loneliness.
If we were to meet, you would not recognize me—
Face covered with dust,
Hair like frost.

Last night in a dark dream I was all at once back home.
You were combing your hair
At the little window.
We looked at one another without speaking
And could only weep streaming tears.
Year after year I expect it will go on breaking my heart—
The night of the full moon
The hill of low pines.

(The twentieth of the first month, 1075, to record a dream)

Translated by James Robert Hightower

Tune: "Fragrance Fills the Courtyard"

Su Shih

Vainglory in Snailhorn,
Petty profit on Flyshead:
It all adds up to effort wasted.
If everything is determined in advance,
Then who is weak, who is strong?
With what time I have left before I am old,
Let me be irresponsible for a little bit.
In my hundred years,
I'd still like to be drunk
Thirty-six thousand times.

Reckon it up—
How much can you have,

With worry and grief, wind and rain
Taking away a good half?
But why
Go on till you die, talking about the short end and the big deal?
Here we have a fresh breeze and a bright moon,
The moss-mat spread,
The cloud-curtain drawn—
It's good here in the south:
A thousand measures of fine wine
And "Fragrance Fills the Courtyard"[1] for a song.

Translated by James Robert Hightower

1. The tune title of this lyric. Compare selection 121, the first lyric.

Tune: "Immortal by the River"

Su Shih

I drank at night on East Slope, sobered up, got drunk again.
When I came home it was sometime past midnight,
The houseboy was already snoring like thunder.
I pounded on the gate and got no response,
Then leaned on my staff and listened to the river noises.

I have long deplored that this body is not one's own.
When can I forget the restless striving?
The night is late, the wind still, the ripples smooth.
In a little boat I shall put out from here,
Entrusting my remaining days to river and sea.

Translated by James Robert Hightower

Tune: "Always Having Fun"

Su Shih

The bright moon like frost,
A fair breeze like water,
The scene in all directions perfectly sharp:

Leaping fish in the winding stream
Round lotus leaves washed with dew—
All is silent and deserted.
Like the roll of the third watch drum,
A single leaf rustles
And the dark dream-cloud is rudely broken.
In all the vastness of night,
No place to seek her out again.
Awake, I pace around the little garden.

The weary traveler at the world's end,
Whose road back lies through mountains,
Has stared his heart's eyes out toward the garden at home.
Swallow Tower is empty—
Where is the beautiful Pan-pan?
Only swallows now in the locked hall.
Past and present are like a dream,
A dream from which we never awake.
The old joy, the new grief are still there.
In another age,
They will visit Yellow Tower by night
And heave their sighs for me.

(Written after passing the night in Swallow Tower and dreaming of Pan-pan)

Translated by James Robert Hightower

121
Tune: "The Courtyard Full of Fragrance"
Tea

Huang T'ing-chien (1045–1105)

Spring wind in North Park—
Square tablet, round disk of jade,
Fame that stirs capital and frontier a myriad miles away;

For information on Huang T'ing-chien, see selection 73.

A panegyric on tea. North Park in Fukien produces a famous tea, pressed into round or square cakes for transport, as was the Sung custom. To prepare an infusion, the cake had to be broken and ground to powder: this is the sacrifice that makes the tea deserve at least a commemorative tablet. It wins at the banquet for being the last comestible consumed. It banishes fatigue and the necessity of a springtime nap, and for the Chinese, too, it was the cup that cheers. It

Shattered body, powdered bones—
Achievements worthy of the Ling-yen Hall of Heroes.
At the banquet it wins the palm of refinement,
Downs spring sleep,
Pushes back the boundary of grief.
Offered by slender hands,
Rubbed to paste and whipped to milky froth.
Golden thread, partridge-striped.

Ssu-ma Hsiang-ju, though sick of thirst,
Produced a song for every flask—
We have poets here,
And it will support them by the lamp—
Drunken jade, toppling mountain.
Rummage through your memory of a thousand volumes,
And pour forth your inexhaustible spring of poetry;
When I go home at last,
Wen-chün is waiting up
By the little window, to sit with me.

Translated by James Robert Hightower

---

should be served by the pretty maid who prepared the brew by whipping up the powder into a frothy, creamy beverage familiar today only in the Japanese ceremonial tea.

    Ssu-ma Hsiang-ju was said to suffer from an ailment—possibly diabetes—that made him thirsty. In spite of his disability, he could still drink enough wine to be inspired to write poems. The same is expected of the talented guests at the banquet, who, supported by a drink of the sobering tea, are exhorted to write poetry though so drunk they are ready to collapse, like Hsi K'ang (223–362; see selection 203), a crumbling mountain of jade. Back home the poet will find his faithful wife, like Hsiang-ju's Cho Wen-chün (see selection 158), waiting for him, so that they can have a cup of tea together before retiring.

Tune: "Joy of Returning to the Fields"

Huang T'ing-chien

Evening rain drips on the steps,
The clock moves slowly
Building up the dreary solitude—
Every drop seems to shatter my heart.
I hate you and love you,
Resent you and like you—
Whatever is the right thing to do?

I had thought our happiness would last,
And here is this present misery I can't cope with.
Smart as he is,
He's worth pining away for.
And really in my sleep,
In my dream, in my heart,
For a long time I shed speechless tears.

Translated by James Robert Hightower

Tune: "Joy of Returning to the Fields"

Huang T'ing-chien

The spring scene finds me thinner still:
She was the one who flirted with me,
But there was also love in my heart.
She thinks of me and calls me up,
Then when we meet she scolds me—
How in Heaven's name can a person stand it?

She will treat me specially nice,
And then at the party she knits her brows.
People are surprised
And blame me for being too soft.
All right, I've decided I'll give you up!
Definitely it's the end this time—
But then when we meet again it will be as it always was.

Translated by James Robert Hightower

Tune: "A Thousand Autumns"

Huang T'ing-chien

The best thing in the world
Is precisely being together like this;
The nights getting longer,

The weather cool,
The rain dripping a bit outside the curtain,
The molded incense in the burner—
I've long dreamed about it
And now it's really happening.

Our joy reached its peak and she turned lovely limp;
The jade was soft, the flower drooped and fell,
Her hairpin dangling on my sleeve,
Her hair piled on my arm.
The lamp lights her ravishing eyes,
Wet with perspiration, intoxicated—
Sleep, sweetheart, sleep;
Sweetheart, sleep.

Translated by James Robert Hightower

122
Tune: "Sand of Silk-Washing Brook"
A Spring Morning[1]

Ch'in Kuan (1049–1100)

A suggestion of chill pervades the little bower,
The haze of dawn sulky as though it were deep autumn.
On the painted screen, thin mist hovering over a running brook—
A scene tranquil and serene.

Fallen petals flying at ease—ethereal like dreams;
Mizzling rain in an endless stream—fine as sorrow.
The jeweled curtain hung up idly on a little hook of silver.

Translated by Jiaosheng Wang

Ch'in Kuan became a Presented Scholar in 1085. He served as an editor in the imperial library and an officer of the bureau of compilation. He was demoted when his sponsor Su Shih (see selection 156) fell from power in 1095. Ch'in is especially noted for perfecting the poetic language of the lyric without disregarding its musical requirements.

1. In the opinion of the critic Wang Kuo-wei (see selection 147), this is one of the most noteworthy of Ch'in Kuan's short lyrics.

Tune: "Perfumed Garden"
Bidding Adieu

Ch'in Kuan

Mountains wreathed in wisps of light cloud;
Withered grass stretches to meet the far horizon.[1]
Muted the sound of bugles on the gate tower;
Ready to depart, a boat moored at the river's edge.
How many things bygone at the Fairy Pavilion
Return to mind in a misty haze,
As listlessly we drain our cups to bid adieu!
Beyond the setting sun, a scattering of crows in the cold air
Are winging above a stream
That winds round a solitary village.[2]

Heart-rending this moment of separation
When the scented bag is tenderly given away as a memento,
And the silk girdle untied in token of farewell.[3]
All this, however, has but earned me the name of a fickle lover,
A drifter in the Green Mansions.[4]
Once parted, who can say when we'll meet again?
On my coat and sleeves are stains of tears shed in vain.
It grieves me to see the lofty city-walls
Receding from view in the lurid lights of evening.

Translated by Jiaosheng Wang

1,2. These lines in the original Chinese are widely recited.
3. The scented bag was worn at his waist by a man as a mark of affection for the girl he loved, and the silk girdle worn by the girl had a knot which she would cut should the romantic relation come to an end.
4. A euphemism for brothels.

Tune: "Happiness Approaches"

Ch'in Kuan

Rain sets more flowers blooming
On the spring pathway.
And the flowers stir up the hill
Into a blaze of vernal color.

Where the rivulet deepens
You come on orioles
In their hundreds and thousands.

Clouds scudding overhead—
A host of sturdy dragons and snakes
Dancing and whirling in an azure sky.
Dead drunk, I lie asleep
In the shade of an ancient wisteria—
Utterly unconscious of
Facing north or south.

Translated by Jiaosheng Wang

Tune: "Rouged Lips"
Peach Blossom Springs [1]

Ch'in Kuan

Drunk, I let my skiff
Float aimlessly down the stream
To where peach flowers are blossoming in deep seclusion.
Ensnared by worldly cares,
To me it is not given
To be a dweller among the flowers.

The sun sets on
Misty waters stretching, boundless,
A thousand tricents away.
Hills innumerable,
Pink and red scattered like rain.
Lost to memory—
The way I came.

Translated by Jiaosheng Wang

1. Echoes the celebrated utopian essay and poem of T'ao Yüan-ming (see selection 204).

Tune: "Spring in the Painted Hall"

Ch'in Kuan

Fallen petals carpet the garden walk,
The pond full to the brim.
Fine rain drizzles, mocking the sun;
The apricot orchard languishing where cuckoos cry.
Spring will soon be fled,
Do what one may.

Alone I ascend the painted pavilion beyond the willows,
And twist a spray of bloom leaning against the balustrade.
Wordless, I let drop the flower, facing the declining sun:
The pain in my heart—who will know?

Translated by Jiaosheng Wang

123
Tune: "The Diviner"

Li Chih-yi (fl. 1071)

I live at the head of the Long River,[1]
You live along its lower reaches;
Day after day I think of you but cannot see you,
Yet we both drink the waters of the Long River.

When will these waters ever cease?
When will this yearning ever end?
I wish only that your heart will be like my heart,
And that you will never repudiate our mutual affection.

Translated by Victor H. Mair

The poet, a successful scholar-official, was a follower of Su Shih (see selection 72).
1. The Yangtze.

124

Tune: "Nien-nu Is Charming"

Chu Tun-ju (1080?–1175?)

Old age has come and I am glad;
I've experienced what the world holds
And know too well the way things are,
Have seen through the shams.
The sea of sorrow, the mount of pain,
All shattered in a trice.
No longer misled by flowers
Or led into trouble by wine,
I know all the scores now.
When full I look to take a nap;
Awake again, I play the role called for.

Don't talk of time a-passing!
In this old man's heart
Is no wish to meddle much in affairs.
I don't try to become a Taoist immortal
Or flatter the Buddha
Or imitate the busy Confucius.
I have no wish to compete with worthy men;
Let them laugh—
This is just the way I am.
When the play is over,
I will leave my costume for the dumb actors.

Translated by James Robert Hightower

A reclusive poet and painter of the Southern Sung period, Chu Tun-ju was born into a family of bureaucrats from Loyang. He attained the rank of Presented Scholar in 1135 but declined several appointments offered to him. He settled in Canton after the Jürchen took control of the north of China and established the Chin dynasty, displacing the Sung to the south. Chu Tun-ju's works are filled with nature imagery and nostalgia for the north.

125
Tune: "Rouged Lips"
Naivete

Li Ch'ing-chao (1084–c. 1151)

Stepping down from the swing,
Languidly she smooths her soft, slender hands,
Her flimsy dress wet with light perspiration—
A slim flower trembling with heavy dew.

Spying a stranger, she walks hastily away in shyness:
Her feet in bare socks,
Her gold hairpin fallen.
Then she stops to lean against a gate,
And looking back,
Makes as if sniffing a green plum.

Translated by Jiaosheng Wang

Li Ch'ing-chao is universally recognized as China's greatest woman poet and one of the foremost lyricists in her own right. She was born in Li-ch'eng (modern Tsinan in Shantung province; see selection 265, chapter 2, note 3) of an outstanding literary family. Her father was a noted writer of prose and a literary associate of Su Shih (see selection 156). Her mother, also a poet, was descended from a distinguished family. Li Ch'ing-chao was already recognized as a talented voice in her adolescence. In 1101 she married Chao Ming-ch'eng, a student in the imperial academy. The couple shared compatible tastes in literature, painting, and calligraphy, and she wrote warmly of their mutual joys. Later, however, she experienced the traumatic events surrounding the fall of the Northern Sung to the Jürchen and the transfer of the dynasty to the Southern Sung. This dislocation was attended by much personal loss (see selection 203), and she wrote sensitively of her suffering and sadness during this period.

Tune: "Magnolia Flowers" (short version)

Li Ch'ing-chao

From the flower vendor I bought
A sprig of spring just bursting into bloom—
Sprinkled all over with teardrops
Still tinged with traces of
Roseate clouds and morning dew.

Lest my beloved should think
I'm not so fair as the flower,

I pin it slanting in my cloud hair,
And ask him to see
Which of us is the lovelier:
The flower or I.

Translated by Jiaosheng Wang

Tune: "Fisherman's Pride"[1]
A Dream

Li Ch'ing-chao

Billowing clouds surging across the heavens
Merge into dawn's hazy mist.
Sails in their thousands toss and dance
As the Milky Way recedes.
In a vision I find myself before the Heavenly Ruler,
Who asks solicitously
Where I wish to be off to.

"My journey is a long one," I reply.
"The sun is setting all too soon.
And my brilliant poetic attempts, alas!
Have come to no purpose."
Presently a whirlwind rises, and lo!
The Mighty Roc[2] is winging to the Empyrean
On a flight of ninety thousand tricents.
Blow, O Whirlwind! Blow on without cease.
Blow my tiny craft to the three far-off isles[3]
Where the Immortals dwell.

Translated by Jiaosheng Wang

1. Among Li Ch'ing-chao's lyric poems, this one is unique in style and content. Written probably after the fall of the Northern Sung dynasty, when she found herself an exile in South China with all her hopes and aspirations frustrated, it is a work of pure romance, conceived in a trance, and worthy of the greatest masters of romantic lyric poetry. It shows the versatility of her genius in producing a masterpiece in a style other than that of the elegantly restrained lyric of which she was generally recognized as the foremost exponent. Among its most enthusiastic admirers was Liang Ch'i-ch'ao, a great essayist and critic in the last years of the Ch'ing dynasty.

2. A fabulous bird first described in the works of Chuang Tzu (see selection 9). When migrating to the South Seas it is said to strike the waters for three thousand tricents before soaring to a height of ninety thousand tricents on a whirlwind. Hence the popular saying "Roc's Journey" used by Chinese to this day to congratulate someone embarking on a career of lofty aspirations.

3. The three legendary isles, P'eng-lai, Fang-chang, and Ying-chou in the Po-hai Sea.

Tune: "Airing Inmost Feelings"
I Smell the Fragrance of Faded Plum Blossoms by My Pillow

Li Ch'ing-chao

Last night, dead drunk, I dawdled
While undoing my coiffure,
And fell asleep with a sprig of
Faded plum blossom in my hair.
The fumes of wine gone,
I was woken out of my spring sleep
By the pungent smell of the petals,
And my sweet dream of far-off love
Was broken beyond recall.

Now all voices are hushed.
The moon lingers and softly spreads her beams
Over the unfurled kingfisher-green curtain.
Still, I twist the fallen petals,
I crumple them for their lingering fragrance,
I try to recapture a delicious moment.

Translated by Jiaosheng Wang

Tune: "The Charm of a Maiden Singer"
Spring Thoughts

Li Ch'ing-chao

Slanting wind, misty rain
Once more assail a courtyard bleak and desolate.
The double gate needs must be shut.
Favorite flowers, darling willows:
Cold Food Day approaches,
With unsettling weather in all its changing moods.
I finish a poem with difficult rhymes,
Sober up from the fumes of strong wine
With a queer sense of listlessness.
My multitude of thoughts—who will convey them
Now the wild geese have all winged out of sight?

Spring chill fills the upper rooms,
For days on end the curtains are drawn on all sides:
I am too languid to lean over the balustrade.
The incense burnt out, my quilts feel cold
As I wake from a new dream.
No dawdling in bed for one who comes to grief
When Spring is calling with all its diversions:
Young parasol-trees sprout new leaves;
Clear dew trickles in the first flush of dawn.
Now the sun is riding high, the fog withdraws.
Still I'd rather wait,
To see whether the day will really be fine.

Translated by Jiaosheng Wang

Tune: "Partridge Sky"
To the Cassia Flower

Li Ch'ing-chao

Fair Flower!
Dark, pale, light yellow in color,
Soft and gentle by nature.
Aloof and remote,
A subtle fragrance trails behind you.
What need for light green or deep crimson,
You choicest of flowers!

Let plum blossoms be envious,
Chyrsanthemums be ashamed!
You are crowned Queen of Mid-autumn
At the Grand Exhibition of Flowers.
How unfeeling of the poet Ch'ü Yüan
To be so cold toward you
As to deny you a place
In his masterpiece.[1]

Translated by Jiaosheng Wang

1. An allusion to "Encountering Sorrow" (*Li sao*), a long poem in Ch'ü Yüan's *Elegies of Ch'u*, in which he listed many precious flowers and plants as symbolic of men of high virtue but omitted the cassia flower, presumably out of bias (see selection 148).

Tune: "On the Trail of Sweet Incense"

Li Ch'ing-chao

Golden chrysanthemums just in bloom
Tell of the approach of the Double Ninth Festival.
A bounteous gift from Heaven these autumnal tints,
Which however bring sadness in their train
As circumstances change.
I try on my thin dress, taste new-brewed wine,
Aware that I am in for
A spell of wind,
A spell of rain,
A spell of cold.

Yellowing twilight fills my rooms
With gloom and anxiety.
Memories of heartrending sorrow
Overwhelm me as I sober up from wine.
An unending night,
A full moon flooding an empty bed.
In my ears the dull thud
Of mallets on the washing blocks,
The feeble chirp of crickets,
The monotonous dripping of the clepsydra.

Translated by Jiaosheng Wang

Tune: "Joy of Eternal Union" [1]
Lantern Festival

Li Ch'ing-chao

The setting sun—a pool of molten gold;
Evening clouds—disks of emerald jade.
Where is he—the one in my thoughts?
Spring willows robed in hazy mist;
"Falling Plum Blossoms" wafted by a plaintive flute:
Lovely springtime—how far is it advanced?

1. The advent of the Lantern Festival revived memories of the poet's happy days in the Northern Sung capital, the loss of which to the Tartars was always in her thoughts.

Warm sunshiny weather at the Lantern Festival—
Who knows but it may be
A prelude to wind and rain?
My old wine and poetry companions send
Perfumed coaches, fine horses to take me for a ride,
But I decline all their invitations.

Sweet are memories of our old capital in its heyday!
Young ladies with time to spare
Made the Lantern Festival a special occasion for joy.
In kingfisher-feather caps and
Gold-thread jeweled hair ornaments,
They vied with one another for loveliness.
Now worn with care,
My hair windblown and temples frosty,
I dread going out on festive evenings.
I'd much prefer to stay behind the screen
And listen to youthful talk and laughter
As people pass by.

Translated by Jiaosheng Wang

A Long Melancholy Tune (Autumn Sorrow)[1] Despair

Li Ch'ing-chao

Searching, seeking,[2]
    Seeking, searching:
What comes of it but
    Coldness and desolation,
A world of dreariness and misery
And stabbing pain!
As soon as one feels a bit of warmth

1. In this poem, Li Ch'ing-chao expresses her sentiments with rapidity and abandon but none of the characteristics of the elegant, restrained style in which most of her lyrics are written. The poem is in fact rather like a rhapsody that recalls to mind Ou-yang Hsiu's famous prose-poem "Autumn Sounds" (see selection 206).

2. This masterpiece of Li Ch'ing-chao's is admired, among other things, for the three groups of reiterated characters at the beginning of the poem. The three groups are ingeniously interrelated, with the second group being the result of the first, and the third the result of the second. This arrangement heightens the pathos.

A sense of chill returns:
A time so hard to have a quiet rest.
What avail two or three cups of tasteless wine
Against a violent evening wind?
Wild geese wing past at this of all hours,
And it suddenly dawns on me
That I've met them before.

Golden chrysanthemums in drifts—
How I'd have loved to pick them,
But now, for whom? On the ground they lie strewn,
Faded, neglected.[3]
There's nothing for it but to stay at the window,
Motionless, alone.
How the day drags before dusk descends!
Fine rain falling on the leaves of parasol-trees—
Drip, drip, drop, drop, in the deepening twilight.
To convey all the melancholy feelings
Born of these scenes
Can the one word "sorrow" suffice?[4]

Translated by Jiaosheng Wang

3. Some commentators interpret the above lines as follows:

"Golden chrysanthemums in full bloom,
Their fallen petals in drifts —
Who would pick them
Now I'm withered and worn?
On the ground they lie strewn, neglected."

4. Instead of using hyperboles in the conventional way, Li Ch'ing-chao shows great creativity in saying that the word "sorrow" is inadequate to convey a multitude of melancholy feelings.

Tune: "Spring at Wu Ling"[1]
Spring Ends

Li Ch'ing-chao

The wind has subsided,
Faded all the flowers:
In the muddy earth

1. Written in 1135, six years after her husband's death, when the poet was living at Chin-hua in today's Chekiang province as a temporary refuge from the Chin invasion.

A lingering fragrance of petals.
Dusk falls. I'm in no mood to comb my hair.
Things remain, but all is lost
Now he's no more.
Tears choke my words.

I hear Twin Brooks[2] is still sweet
With the breath of spring.
How I'd, too, love to go for a row,
On a light skiff.
I only fear at Twin Brooks my grasshopper of a boat
Wouldn't be able to bear
Such a load of grief.[3]

Translated by Jiaosheng Wang

2. A stream in the southeast of Chin-hua often visited by poets in T'ang and Sung times as a scenic resort.
3. A line (three lines in the format presented here) famed for the beauty and freshness of its imagery.

126
Tune: "Immortal at the Riverbank"
A Reminiscence

Ch'en Yü-yi (1090–1138)

It was at the Noon Bridge we were drinking—
Most of us men of high talent and ambition.
The stream below with a shimmering moon in its lap
Was gliding silently away into the distance;
In the sparse shadows of blossoming apricot
Wafted the notes of a flute till daybreak.

Twenty-odd summers gone by fleet as a dream,
    unsettling—to find myself here still.
Idly I ascend the small tower
For a view of the scene after rain,

Ch'en Yü-yi became a Presented Scholar in 1113. Shortly afterward the northern part of China was occupied by the Jürchens, whereupon he moved south to become a high official under the first Southern Sung emperor. He was proficient both as a writer of classical poems and as an author of lyrics.

Regaled with snatches of the fishermen's midnight song
Telling of the vicissitudes of past and present.

Translated by Jiaosheng Wang

127
Tune: "Spring in the Ch'in Garden" (About to swear off drinking, he warns the wine cup to go away)

Hsin Ch'i-chi (1140–1207)

Cup, you come here!
Your old man has been
Looking himself over today.
For years on end he's had a thirst
With a throat like a scorched pot.
But now he's ready to go to sleep and snore like thunder.
You say, "Liu Ling[1]
Was the great philosopher of all time.
Once drunk, what did it matter if he died and was buried on the spot."
A shame you're so ruthless
With your very best friend.

Worse, you're in league with song and dance.
I reckon you are man's worst poison.
What's more, the thing we hate, a lot or a little,
Is what we once loved.

Like Li Ch'ing-chao (see selection 125), Hsin Ch'i-chi was born in Li-ch'eng (modern Tsinan, Shantung). He was passionate and insistent in his patriotic advocacy of a more determined effort to recapture the north of China from the Jürchens who had established the Chin dynasty there. Hsin was a friend of the renowned neo-Confucian scholar Chu Hsi (1130–1200) and entertained at his villa near the Fukien-Kiangsi border many of the greatest thinkers and statesmen of his day. His youthful espousal of Confucian virtues gave way to a more Taoist view in later life, and he held great store by the writings of Chuang Tzu (see selection 9). Hsin was primarily responsible for developing the lyric as a more erudite, expansive, and allusive genre than it had been. The most prolific Sung period author of lyrics, of which 626 by him survive, he also played a large role in the ultimate divorce of the metrical patterns of the genre from their once musical background. After Hsin, the lyric became a vehicle for the display of technical virtuosity, where it had once been the voice of popular songs.

1. See selection 117, second lyric, note 3.

Nothing itself is good or bad,
It's excess makes the trouble.
Here's my ultimatum:
Don't stay, go away fast.
I have the strength to dispose of you.
The cup bowed and said,
"If you say so, I'll leave;
I'll come again when you call me."

Translated by James Robert Hightower

Tune: "Pure Serene Music"
Rural Life

Hsin Ch'i-chi

Low hang the eaves of the thatched hut,
Green, green grows the grass beside the brook.
To whose family belongs that tipsy white-haired couple,
Chatting and merry-making in the dulcet accents of the south?

Their eldest son is hoeing the bean-field east of the brook,
The second is busy weaving a hen-coop;
But the one they think most lovable is the youngest, that scamp of a boy:
Lo! he is sprawled on the bank peeling lotus pods!

Translated by Jiaosheng Wang

Tune: "Pure Serene Music"
En Route to Po-shan

Hsin Ch'i-chi

Swiftly riding past the willows,
My traveling cloak heavy and wet with dew.
Lone shadow of a roosting egret astir
As it drowsily eyes the sandbank—
Fish and shrimp haunting its dreams.

Bright moon, a sprinkling of stars
Bathe the stream in a blaze of light.
Graceful the shadow of a young washer of silks:
A bashful smile to passersby,
And she is off to
Where her baby is crying at the door.

Translated by Jiaosheng Wang

Tune: "Picking Mulberry Seeds"
Written on a Wall en Route to Po-shan

Hsin Ch'i-chi

As a lad I never had any idea of the taste of sorrow,
But loved to go up the tallest towers.
Loved to go up the tallest towers,
To compose new verses simulating sorrow.

Now that of sorrow I have tasted my fill,
I hesitate on the verge of utterance.
I hesitate on the verge of utterance,
And would rather say,
What a nice cool autumn, with tints lovely and mellow!

Translated by Jiaosheng Wang

Tune: "Partridge Sky"
At Po-shan Monastery

Hsin Ch'i-chi

Not for the Imperial City am I bound.
I'd rather put the monks to the trouble of entertaining me.
I take delight in seeking flavor out of the flavorless;
And passing my days simulating talent
With no pretensions to talent.

Rather remain my usual self than be a high official.
Having seen my fill of this mundane world,
I'd much prefer returning to be a tiller of the fields—
With pines and bamboos for my true friends,
And mountain birds and flowers as kindred spirits.

Translated by Jiaosheng Wang

Tune: "Partridge Sky"
For a Friend [1]

Hsin Ch'i-chi

Mulberries at the roadside break into bud,
The eggs of the east neighbor's silkworms are just hatching.
A brown calf on the smooth, grassy slope gives a contented low,
A sprinkling of dusky crows dot the chill wood in the slanting sun.

Hills far and near,
Footpaths crisscrossed between the fields,
And a wineshop with its blue pennon fluttering.
Spring is here with the shepherd's purse at the brookside,
While peach and plum in town are still assailed by wind and rain.

Translated by Jiaosheng Wang

1. Written presumably to air his feelings to friends worrying about the poet's life in the countryside after his demotion.

Tune: "The Dark Clouds of Ch'u"
Visiting the Rainy Crag Alone

Hsin Ch'i-chi

At the brookside I stroll
Accompanied by my shadow mirrored in the limpid stream.
At the bottom of the stream lies the blue sky,
Where clouds are drifting by,
I in their midst.

Who will join me in vibrant song?
In the empty valley a clear note rises.
Methinks 'tis neither from a fairy nor from a ghost,
But the echo of
The "Song of Peach Blossom Stream"
When the waters all around are in spate.[1]

Translated by Jiaosheng Wang

1. According to the *Book of Rites*, when peach flowers bloom in spring, mountain torrents from ravines pour down and flood all nearby rivers and streams.

Tune: "The Bodhisattva's Golden Headdress"

Hsin Ch'i-chi

Past Yü-ku Tower glides the river Ch'ing[1]—
Laden with tears shed by how many suffering wayfarers?
And I gaze northwest toward the lost capital,
To my dismay barred by countless intervening hills.

Futile for green hills to bar the way!
To the east the river ever freely flows.
But my heart is heavy as evening descends on the stream,
To hear partridges calling deep in the hills.

Translated by Jiaosheng Wang

1. A famous scenic spot of Sung Times overlooking the Ch'ing river, where the fleeing Northern Sung empress dowager escaped capture by the invaders, who wrought great havoc among the people.

128
Tune: "Rouged Lips"
Rain Just Over on the
Night of the Lantern Preview

Wu Wen-ying (c. 1200–c. 1260)

Dark clouds have rolled clean away.
Goddess of the Moon looks down after her evening toilet,
Laying the dust and moistening the ground
That Fairy Maidens tread.

Back again in the bustling thoroughfare,
I feel myself reliving
Scenes of jolly lantern shows of other days.
With nostalgic feelings tender as water,
What can I do but retrace my steps to the small chamber,
Where under heated quilts
I'm soon lost in spring dreams,
Still haunted by the din of music and song.

Translated by Jiaosheng Wang

Only scanty biographical information is available about the poet. Wu Wen-ying lived during the period when the Southern Sung was about to collapse before the Mongols. Oddly, most of his works seem to deal with his own concerns, especially his affection for two favorite concubines. A different reading of his subtly stated works, however, reveals a concern for his country and his people. After Hsin Ch'i-chi (see selection 127), Wu was the second most prolific Sung period author of lyrics with approximately 350 known pieces to his credit.

Tune: "Sand of Silk-Washing Brook"
A Reminiscence

Wu Wen-ying

Gateway buried deep in flowers—
Happy times bygone a mere dream.
The setting sun wordless, swallows return with a mournful air;
Curtain-hooks quivering where a slender hand's touch has left its perfume.

Fallen catkins mutely shed tears for the departing spring;
Moving clouds cast shadows to cover up the moon's bashfulness.
The east wind toward evening chills more than the bleakness of autumn.

Translated by Jiaosheng Wang

129
Tune: "Pure Serene Music"

Chang Yen (1248–c. 1320)

All of a sudden my delight in sightseeing wanes,
Now the maidens gathering flowers
Are nowhere to be found.
Away from home one cares little
For spring outings,
Distracted by composing mournful verses.

Under whose roof are the swallows
That last year were roaming the ends of the earth?
I'd rather not listen to the patter of evening rain:
Late spring is no time to speed
The blossoming of flowers.

Translated by Jiaosheng Wang

Chang Yen was a native of Hangchow. Though descended from a Southern Sung nobleman, he experienced so many misfortunes in life that at one time he had to support himself as a fortune-teller in the market place of the city of Ningpo. Chang spent forty years studying music and wrote an important work on the theory and history of lyric meters entitled *Sources of the Lyric (Tz'u yüan)*. His summation of the genre in this work also represents its culmination. After him, the waning lyric gave way to the newly exuberant aria and was only revived sporadically much later during the Ming and Ch'ing periods.

130

In the Southern Mode, to the Tune "A Sprig of Flowers" The Refusal to Get Old

Kuan Han-ch'ing (c. 1220–c. 1307)

I've plucked every flower that grows over the wall,
And gathered every willow overhanging the road;[1]
The tenderest buds were the flowers I picked,
And the willows I gathered, of the supplest green fronds;
A wastrel, gay and dashing,
Trusting to my willow gathering, flower plucking hand,
I kept at it till the flowers fell and the willows withered;
Half my life I've been willow gathering and flower plucking
And for a whole generation slept with flowers and lain among the willows.

Yellow Bell Coda

But I am an
Un-steam-soft-able, un-boil-through-able,
Un-pound-flat-able, un-bake-dry-able
Rattling plunkety-plunk coppery old bean.[2]
Who said you young gentlemen could intrude upon her
Un-hoe-up-able, un-cut-down-able,
Un-disentwine-able, un-cast-off-able,
Intricate, thousand-fold brocade snare?[3]
As for me, I can take pleasure in the Liang-yüan[4] moon,

Like the majority of the better-known Yüan dramatists, Kuan Han-ch'ing hailed from Ta-tu (modern Peking). A professional actor himself, Kuan is regarded as the greatest playwright of the Yüan period and the virtual creator of the genre generally referred to as Yüan drama (*tsa-chü*, literally "variety show"; see selections 272 and 273). Kuan was not only the best but also the most productive Yüan playwright, there being sixty titles associated with his name, eighteen of which are extant. His main characters are mostly female, which is atypical of Yüan drama. Kuan's arias employ highly colloquial language and deal primarily with romantic themes, often in a humorous vein, as is the case here.

For a note on the new general verse called the aria *(ch'ü)*, which became popular during the Yüan period, see selection 132.

1. Throughout the poem flowers and willows refer to courtesans.

2. Literally, "copper garden pea"—Yüan slang for a libertine who is somewhat past his prime.

3. A courtesan's methods of getting a man into her clutches.

4. Liang-yüan was a vast park built in Han times by Prince Hsiao of Liang, here suggesting sophisticated tastes.

Drink no less than East Capital[5] wine,
Enjoy the flowers of Loyang,
And pluck the willow of Chang-t'ai.[6]
Besides, I can compose poems, write ancient script,
Play the lute and play the flute;
I know how to sing the Che-ku, dance the Ch'ui-shou,[7]
Drive game for the hunt, kick the football,
Play chess and roll dice;
Even if you knock out my teeth, stretch my mouth out of shape,
Lame my legs, break my arms,
Even if heaven afflicted me with these several ills and disabilities,
I'd still not give up;
Not unless Yama[8] himself gives the order
And the evil spirits themselves come to hook out
My three souls and return them to hell,
My seven shades and consign them to oblivion,[9]
Only then
Will I retire from the path of mist and flowers.[10]

Translated by Wayne Schlepp

5. The Eastern Capital, i.e., Loyang, was noted for its luxuriance and beauty. See also note 1 on flowers and willows.
6. A district of Ch'ang-an, the Western Capital, where a famous T'ang courtesan named Liu (i.e., "willow") lived. *Chang-t'ai liu* is often used in reference to courtesans generally.
7. *Che-ku* ("Partridge") or *Che-ku t'ien* ("Partridge Sky") is the name of a lyric verse form. *Ch'ui-shou* is the name of a song to which one danced, hands hanging down the while.
8. King of the underworld.
9. The belief that one dies only after the evil spirits have hooked out of one's body all ten of its souls.
10. The gay life among courtesans.

131
Tune: "Shua Hai-erh"
Country Cousin at the Theater

Tu Shan-fu (fl. 1230)

When the rains are in season and the wind sets fair
Nothing is better than the farmer's share.
Our silkworms had mulberries to spare.

Our grains had been reaped to the final stook
And the tax men had left us more than they took.
Since my village had a vow at the temple to pay,
They sent me to redeem it on market day.
As I reached the high road by the top of the town
I saw a paper banner they had just hung down.
On it was writing with designs in between
And below it the biggest gaggle I had ever seen.

(Liu-sha)

Among 'em was the one who was working a door,
Yelling, "This way, this way, pay your fee before
The whole place is full and you can't find a bench!
Our first act's a *yüan-pen*[1] called *Seductive Wench*,
This is followed by a short *yao-mo*,[2]
It's easy on the stage to make time go
But hard to get applause for doing so."

(Wu-sha)

Then, without a pause in his hullabaloo,
He snapped up my coppers and shoved me through.
Now inside the door was a cliff made of wood
Where layers of people sat around or stood.
Like inside a bell-tower I would have said
When I stood at the bottom and lifted up my head.
But looking the other way it seemed as though
I was watching a whirlpool down below
Of people sitting everywhere.
And a bunch of women sitting there
Watching a platform—it was not a god's day,
But the drums and the cymbals were a-crashing away!

(Ssu-sha)

On the floor came a girl who capered, and then
Went off and led on a bunch of her men.
One of that gang you could tell right away

Little is known of the author of this folksy set of arias.
1. A type of variety play or skit; forerunner of the full-fledged Yüan drama.
2. Reprise.

Spelled trouble if you met him whatever the day.
His head was wrapped in a jet-black cloth
With some kind of brush-pen stuck in the swath.
(One look at him and you couldn't go wrong,
You knew right away how *he* got along)
His whole face was limed an ashy white
With some black streaks on top of that—
Now there was a sight!
He wore on his body one of those kinds
Of tunics covered with big designs.

(San-sha)

Well, he
Recited some verses and one or two rhymes,
Then he spoke a kind of *fu*[3] and sang a few times.
His mouth kept on goin' right through every verse!
He wasn't *real* good, but I've heard a lot worse.
And the memory he'd got I wish I had—
To tell all those jokes and japes wouldn't be bad.
Then he came to the end:
"That's all," he said.
Then he slapped his feet around a bit and bowed his head.
And that was all for one part, so the music played.

(Erh-sha)

Now in comes "Little Brother" and "Squire Chang,"
The last tellin' the first one just where he's wrong.
They cross the stage and go round and roun'
All the time sayin' they're walking into town.
Then they say they're in town (though they went nowhere!)
And they spy a young girl under the awning there.
Old Chang's got to have her if it costs him his life.
And he sets right out tryin' to get her to wife.
He's sure in a hurry and just that keen
That he teaches Little Brother how to be go-between.
But she wants silk and satin, millet and rice,
And ol' Squire Chang?—she won't look at him twice.

3. Rhapsody or rhyme-prose (see selections 149 ff.).

(Yi-sha)

Squire Chang backs up 'cause forward won't do
And with his right foot in the air he hoists his left one too!
Poor Chang is whipsawed fro and to
Till he's so hotted up he don't know what to do,
So he
Bangs his meat-club on the ground and snaps it right in half
And I nearly bust my side while I double up and laugh.

(Wei)[4]

Now the lawsuits would start just as sure as there's rain,
But I got such a bladderful I'm dyin' in pain,
I keep hangin' on and hangin' around to see the thing through.
Just to listen to them talk and to see what they would do,
But my bladder is achin' so I can't catch my breath—
Those crazy pizzles made me leave—
Else I'd have laughed myself to death!

Translated by James I. Crump

4. The section titles signify "six" through "one" and "coda," the last.

132
Tune: "Heaven-Cleansed Sands"
Autumn Thoughts

Ma Chih-yüan (1250?–1323?)

Withered wisteria, old tree, darkling crows—
Little bridge over flowing water by someone's house—
Emaciated horse on an ancient road in the western wind—
Evening sun setting in the west—
Broken-hearted man on the horizon.

Translated by Victor H. Mair

With this epochally memorable piece (note that it lacks a single verb), we may mark the shift from the lyric (*tz'u*) to the aria (*ch'ü*). Although other poets were writing arias before him (see selections 130 and 131), it was from Ma Chih-yüan that dominance of the new genre began.

The aria in many respects is similar to the lyric but employs a separate corpus of tunes and is used to express different sentiments. As with the lyric, aria verses are written to song music. Distinctively a product of the period of Mongol rule in China, the aria undoubtedly owes much to the specific political and cultural configuration of that era. The aria, for example, typically employs more colloquial expressions than even the most earthy of the lyrics, yet the form remains hospitable to both literary and vernacular phrase and structure. The subject matter of the aria is diverse, but lovesongs probably preponderate, as with the lyric. The full range of the arias contain nearly every literary device found in the historical arsenal of Chinese verse.

Several arias are sometimes grouped together in sets or suites, with all the tunes in a given suite belonging to the same mode or key. Altogether, there are some five hundred known tune titles which were part of the public domain and to which arias were composed. Arias may range in length from pithy twenty-character gems to long narrative confections of ten or twelve songs in a suite. They were the favored form of entertainment for the age, whether sung by themselves or incorporated in the flourishing musical dramas (see selections 272 and 273). Perhaps because of their show-business history, however, they were much underrated by Chinese literary scholars until the beginning of the twentieth century.

Ma Chih-yüan, a native of Ta-tu (modern Peking), is generally recognized as the most distinguished author of arias and aria sequences and an outstanding playwright. His most famous dramatic work, *Autumn in the Han Palace (Han kung ch'iu)*, tells of the forced marriage of a Han dynasty court beauty to a Tartar chieftain as part of a diplomatic maneuver. His other plays are mostly about Taoism and reclusion.

133
[Untitled]

Chang Yang-hao (1269–1329)

Ch'ü Yüan's "sorrow"[1]
none can explain
yet its meaning is
clear as the sun and the moon.
the sorrow remains
the man is gone
to feed
     the shrimp and crabs of the river Hsiang.
that gentleman was silly
I'll stay in this green mountain shade
singing wild
     and drinking till it hurts
here's *joy*
     that's boundless.

Translated by Jerome P. Seaton

A native of Tsinan, Shantung, Chang Yang-hao was an official who held several important positions. He wrote most of his arias after retirement.

1. See selection 148.

134

Tune: "Rapt with Wine, Loudly Singing— Joy in Spring's Coming"

My Love

Kuan Yün-shih (1286–1324)

Natural demeanor warm and soft,
Winsome face demure.
When we chance to meet, her sidelong glances encourage me,
Kindling the pangs of my lovesickness.

Matchmaker bees and go-between butterflies fail to coax her:
Swallows or orioles can't do as they please.
Just like a sprig of red almond blossoms peeping over a wall
She lies beyond the reach of plucking hand.
How I feel, in vain, that for those blossoms' sake the wind
    and rain bear shame!

Translated by Richard John Lynn

Kuan Yün-shih was a Sinicized Uighur (a Central Asian Turkic people) whose original name was Sävınč Qaya. He was an excellent horseman, hunter, and warrior. After serving briefly in the Mongol military establishment, he became a student of the leading Confucian scholar of his time, Yao Sui (1239–1314). Significantly, he wrote a *Vernacular Exegesis on the Classic of Filial Piety* and served as tutor to the heir apparent. Toward the end of his life he developed an interest in Zen and alchemy.

135

Tune: "Tsui-chung T'ien"

To the Giant Butterfly

Wang Ho-ch'ing (Yüan)

This butterfly escaped, it seems,
From the chrysalis of Chuang Tzu's dreams,[1]

The wag of his times, Wang Ho-ch'ing composed occasional—and probably impromptu—pieces. This song is said to have been written in response to the sudden appearance of a species of large butterfly in the environs of the capital.

1. See selection 9.

Spread two great wings upon the spring air,
Then sucked three hundred gardens bare!
Might not elegant creatures such as these
Shame to death our simple honeybees?
Or, giving their wings a tiny shake,
Blow our flower vendors in the lake?!

Translated by James I. Crump

Tune: "Po Pu-tuan"
Long-Haired Little Dog

Wang Ho-ch'ing

Ugly as a jackass
But the size of a pig.
This curious thing
Is nowhere to be found
In the *Shan-hai Ching.*[1]
Head to toe and everywhere—
Body completely covered with hair.
I believe you're a wicked household sprite—
The Malevolent Dustmop with a bite!

Translated by James I. Crump

1. *The Classic of Mountains and Seas,* an ancient work that includes descriptions of fantastic and faraway people, places, and creatures (see selection 29, fourth poem).

Tune: "Po Pu-tuan"
Fat Couple

Wang Ho-ch'ing

A rather obese Master Shuang[1]
Bore off an overweight Su Niang.[2]

1. His name means "double" or "pair."
2. Miss Su.

(Each one of that pair
Was the size of a bear.)

On the wings of romance, off they sped,
But paused a while at Yü-chang³ to pant—
These lovebirds the size of an elephant—
And bang their bellyskins in bed!

Translated by James I. Crump

3. A name for Kiangsi.

136
Tune: "San-fan Yü-lou Jen"

Anonymous (Yüan)

Wind disturbing the eave-chimes again.
Cloth at the window rustles with rain.
That empty pillow,
Cold counterpane
All tangled up with me,
I curse with fine particularity.
My emotions are confused and dim
But the darker thoughts are reserved for him!
Oh, wait until he comes back here,
Then won't I pick a fight!
And scratch his face!
And twist his ear!
"And where did *you* sleep all last night!"

Translated by James I. Crump

137

Tune: "Hung Hsiu-hsieh"
To a Flea

Yang Na (Yüan)

Small as he is he can nimbly dance
From fold of collar to waist of pants.
The prick of a lance
Is this creature's bite,
And he can elude the keenest sight.
How can one capture a creature who
With a somersault can vanish from view?!

Translated by James I. Crump

138

Tune: "Wu Yeh-erh"
Twitting the Teller of Tall Tales

Anonymous (Yüan)

In Easton a certain citizen
Had a Phoenix born to his hen!
In Southville there was a paradox,
Someone's horse turned into an ox!
August is the month for fur coats,
On a pile of tile you can plant a tree,
A dry-gulch[1] is good for sailing boats.
Our dumplings are bigger than soup-tureens;
We grow barrel-sized aubergines.

Translated by James I. Crump

1. *Yang-kou* ("open ditch") was also the name of a famous fighting cock.

139

In the Chung Mode, to the Tune of "P'u T'ien Lo"

Anonymous (early 14th century?)

I thought when he hadn't been there for two or three days—
When he walks in the door I'll really bawl him out!
He'll come over to me, full of excuses,
Spluttering, making no sense, stuttering;
The slippery devil will try to worm out of it, how can anyone trap him!
I can't describe how I long for him to ask for my favors;
But I'll put him out of mind, and when I've got over it, I'll tell him we're
    through.
If we're through, we're through, but even if he's sorry I won't be able to tell
    whether he really means it.
But then he boldly came up and asked me how I'd been,
And all I could do was smile back, keep in my temper for fear he'd get angry,
So when he leaves and doesn't come back again for a couple of days, I'll be
    looking for someone to go and hunt him up.

Translated by Wayne Schlepp

140

[Untitled]

Yün-k'an Tzu (late Yüan)

out of chaos,
            Chang Kuo-lao[1] popped
riding his white ass backwards
through illusion
born in purple clouds
coiled in ruby mist
every night he folded that old ass up
swallowed it
            to sleep in bliss.

Translated by Jerome P. Seaton

The poet's name is obviously a pseudonym, but nothing else is known about him.
    1. One of the eight immortals of Taoism. This is part of a series of poems by the same poet about these legendary individuals.

141
Lazy Cloud's Nest 1

Ali Hsiying (late Yüan)

write poems when I'm sober, and sing when I'm drunk
I leave my fancy lute untuned,
throw down my book, and sleep.
I don't dream dreams of empire
to have a little idle time is good enough
the sun and moon race like the weaver's shuttle
wealth and rank are blossoms, bloom and fall
spring goes
why not enjoy it?

Translated by Jerome P. Seaton

Ali Hsiying was a Moslem, the son of Ali Haiyai.

Lazy Cloud's Nest 2

Ali Hsiying

If someone came what would I do
dozing here with my clothes on
completely at ease, feeling frisky
human life? What can you say
rank is above me a bit
wealth, I don't need it
haha, you laugh
I laugh, haha.

Translated by Jerome P. Seaton

142
Tune: "Moon over West River"

Yang Shen (1488–1559)

I've brewed myself a whole bunch of trouble,
and all because of feelings of love!
The spring dream in this house of passion
                    never really formed:
I wasted days and evenings
                    of "rain-and-cloud." [1]

The swallow—what does he know
                    of my feelings?
It's the oriole who seems to call her name!
To get rid of this passion
                    I can talk about the Void—
or turn within to look at my own heart.

Translated by Jonathan Chaves

Yang Shen wrote poetry in all the major genres, but his lyrics, including the one chosen here, are among the most expressive examples after the Sung period.
1. A traditional euphemism for sexual intercourse.

143
Tune: "Dreaming of Southland"
Thinking of Someone

Liu Shih (1618–1664)

1

He is gone,
Gone somewhere west of Feng-ch'eng. [1]

Liu Shih's beginnings are obscure. What we know for sure is that she became an accomplished courtesan and poet-painter while still in her teens, and many literati in the Chiang-nan area (south of the Yangtze) came to admire her literary achievements. That several portraits of her were made by Ming-Ch'ing literati painters is proof of her standing among her male contemporaries. She published her first collection of poems at the age of twenty and enjoyed the reputation of being a courtesan of superb talent and beauty. Her intense love relationship with

A thin rain dampens my red sleeves,
New weeds lie as deep as my jade brows are low,
The butterfly is most bewildered.[2]

2

He is gone,
Gone from the Isle of Egrets.
Lotus blossoms turn to emerald remorse,
Willow catkins rise to join the zither's grief,
Behind the brocade curtain—the early autumn startles.

3

He is gone,
Gone from the painted chamber tower.
No longer lustrous and beautiful, I sit idle,
Why bother about rouge powder and jade hairpin?
Only the wind coming at night.[3]

4

He is gone,
Gone from the small water pavilion.
Would you say we "have not loved enough"?
Or that we "have little to regret"?
All I see is trodden moss.

---

the young poet Ch'en Tzu-lung (1608–1647) and her later marriage to the literary giant Ch'ien Ch'ien-yi (1582–1664) made her a legendary figure in the field of literature. Most important, her numerous love poems to Ch'en Tzu-lung—and for that matter, Ch'en's to her—engendered a whole new interest in the lyric, a genre characterized by the intensity of emotion. Since traditionally a proficiency in song lyrics was closely associated with the courtesan culture, Liu Shih, as might be expected, greatly influenced the late-Ming revival of the lyric genre.

Liu Shih and Ch'en Tzu-lung's lyric poetics was clearly patterned on the late-Ming notion of reciprocal love. Her numerous poetic exchanges with Ch'en—in some cases her poems are more elaborate in scope and length than Ch'en's—are framed as personal letters, telling the secrets of a passion felt by two equally talented poets. She was no longer a mere singer like the earlier courtesans, whose prime duty was to perform song lyrics for men. As a poet herself, she has acquired a personal voice. In her perhaps most brilliant song-series, "Dreaming of Southland" (subtitled "Thinking of Someone," twenty poems), she tells a moving story of her relationship with Ch'en, narrating her struggles with love's agonized passion.

1. Most likely refers to the hometown of the late Ming scholar-official and loyalist, Ch'en Tzu-lung, with whom the poet was closely associated over a long period of time.

2. A reference to Chuang Tzu's famous dream experience (see selection 9).

3. This song alludes to one of Li Shang-yin's (see selection 65) love poems: "Last night's stars, last night's winds/By the wall of the painted chamber tower, east of the hall of cassia."

5

He is gone,
Gone from the green window gauze.
All I gain is frail sickness. Lighter than a swallow,
Pitiful is my lone self, now that we are far apart.
Secretly we hide sweet memories in our hearts.

6

He is gone,
Gone, leaving the jade pipe cold.[4]
Phoenix pecked at the scattered tiny red beans,
Pheasants, joyfully embracing the censer, gazed at us,[5]
Apricot was the color of my spring dress.

7

He is gone,
Gone from the shadow of the green *wu-t'ung*[6] tree.
I can't believe this has earned us a heartbreaking tune,
Still I wonder why our love has failed.
Whence this brooding grief? No need to look.

8

He is gone,
Gone from the small Crab-apple Hall.
I force myself to rise; the fallen petals are quivering,
A few red parting tears still remain,
Outside the door, willows leaning against one another.

9

He is gone,
Gone, yet dreams of him come even more often.
Recalling the past: our shared moments were mostly wordless,
But now I secretly regret the growing distance.
Only in dreams can I find self-indulgence.

10

He is gone,
Gone, and the nights are longer.

4. This line alludes to Li Ching's (916–961) line: "In the small chamber the song of the jade flute has become cold." By this allusion, Liu Shih's line is a subtle reference to the chamber in the Southern Villa where she lived with Ch'en Tzu-lung during the spring and summer of 1635.
5. The pheasant designs of the incense-burner.
6. For a note on the *wu-t'ung* ("we-together") tree, see selection 114.

How can this jeweled belt warm my thoughts about the black steed?[7]
Gently putting on the silk robe in chill jade moonlight,
Behind the rosy curtain, a single wisp of incense.

11

Where was he?
On the Isle of Smartweed.
The duck-censer burning low, the fragrant smoke warm,
Spring mountains winding deeply in the painted screen,
The golden sparrow ceased to weep.

12

Where was he?
At the middle pavilion.
Recall once after washing his face,
His carefree laughter seemed so unconcerned—
Who knows for whom he smiled?

13

Where was he?
In the moonlight.
In the middle of the night, I clutched his priceless arm,
Lethargic, I looked at the lotus flowers again and again,
My inner sentiments, how hazy!

14

Where was he?
In the magnolia boat.
Often talking to herself when receiving guests,
Feeling more lost while combing her hair,
This beauty still broods over his charms.

15

Where was he?
At the magnificent banquet.
My perfumed arms fluttered up and down,
Words issued in song, like profound thoughts,
Chiefly from my faintly glossed lips.

---

7. The "jeweled belt" might be a gift from Ch'en Tzu-lung. The "black steed," a symbol of the male lover, is metaphorically connected with Ch'en here.

16

Where was he?
At the Autumn Crab-apple Hall.
Fun was playing hide-and-seek,
Round after round, no need to linger for long.
Again, how many sunsets have gone by!

17

Where was he?
On the Lake of Misty Rain.
Water rippled by the bamboo oar, the moon shining bright in the lustrous
    and gentle spring,
Our storied boat filled with wind and daphne fragrance,
Willows caressing the delicate waves.

18

Where was he?
At the jade steps.
No fool for love, yet I wanted to stay,
Overly sensitive to any sign of indifference,
It must be that I feared love would run too deep.

19

Where was he?
Behind the curtain patterned with thrushes.
A parrot dream ends in a black otter's tail,
Incense smoke lingers on the tip of the green spiral censer,
Delicate were the pink jade fingers.

20

Where was he?
By my pillow side.
Nothing but endless tears at the quilt edge—
Wiping off secretly, but only inducing more,
How I yearn for his pity and love.

Translated by Kang-i Sun Chang

144

Tune: "Happily Flitting Oriole"

From Music of Harmonious Heaven in Reverent Thanks to
the Lord of Heaven

Wu Li (1632–1718)

Late in Han
God's Son came down from Heaven
to save us people
and turn us toward the good.
His grace goes wide!
Taking flesh through the virginity
        of the Holy Mother,
                in a stable He was born.
Joseph too came to present Him in the temple:
there to offer praise was
Simeon.
They say He can
save our souls from their destructiveness
and sweep away the devil's wantonness.

Translated by Jonathan Chaves

For information on the poet and his creation of a Chinese Christian poetry, see selection
102. This particular poem is in the aria *(ch'ü)* form.

145

Tune: "Partridge Sky"
I Rejoice to Meet a Friend
Visiting at My Rustic Study

Ch'iao Lai (1640–1694)

There's no occasion for knocking at an out-of-the-way door;
What good fortune brings an old friend to tap at my thatch gate?

From Pao-ying in Kiangsu, Ch'iao Lai achieved the status of Presented Scholar in 1667. He
became one of the highest-ranking scholars of the early Ch'ing period as a compiler and editor

Set amidst hills, the house is half hidden in a mantle of moss;
Felled to serve as a bridge, the gnarled tree still puts forth new leaves.
Young bamboo shoots sprout in the gentle noonday breeze;
Drifting petals fall into my tea-stove by mistake.
Our feelings calm as water, the two of us sit relaxed
Facing each other in the woods,
Regaled with the birdsong of Spring.

Translated by Jiaosheng Wang

at the imperial court. As a youth, he had been a follower of Wang Shih-chen (see selection 103), who both influenced and promoted him.

146
Tune: "Sand of Silk-Washing Brook"
In Memoriam

Nara Singde (1655–1685)

Who else will care for me
Alone in the chill west wind,
Now that my idle window is shut
Amid the dreariness of yellow leaves?
Under the declining sun's gaze
I stand deep in thought
Of happy times gone by.

Worry not when your sweet wine-intoxicated self
Is overwhelmed with heavy spring slumber!
Book-guessing games with splashing of fragrant tea [1]
Will suffice to beguile the waking hours—
Things I then thought to be nothing out of the ordinary.

Translated by Jiaosheng Wang

Nara Singde was a thoroughly Sinicized Manchu of aristocratic birth. He accompanied the K'ang-hsi emperor (see selection 104) in his travels to distant parts of the empire, including his ancestral homeland in Inner Asia. Nara's finely crafted verse is filled with inexplicit Buddhist sentiments and melancholy thoughts. He lived a tragically short but highly productive and active life. Nara may well be regarded as the most significant writer of lyrics after the Sung period and was certainly a major figure in the revival of the genre.

1. An allusion to the pastimes which the Sung poet Li Ch'ing-chao, of whom the author was a great admirer, used to enjoy with her husband in their days of happiness (see selections 125 and 202).

Tune: "As If in a Dream"

Nara Singde

In a myriad arched yurts, the men are drunk.
Stars' reflections quiver, about to drop.
 My homing dream, sundered by Wolf River,[1]
Is then shaken to bits by the river's roar.
     Back to sleep!
     Back to sleep!
Well I know that in waking there's no savor.

Translated by David McCraw

"As If in a Dream" is famous for its opening strophe.
 1. The White Wolf River flows east from White Wolf Mountain (near Ling-yüan, Liaoning) into the Pohai Sea.

Tune: "Butterflies Lingering over Flowers"

Nara Singde

Then and now rivers and mountains have no certain lot.
     In the painted bugle's cry,
  Herd upon herd of horses come and gone.
This view abrim with barren chill, who could express?
The west wind has blown all the scarlet maples old.

Hidden griefs from long ago, where could I find the words?
     Ironclad steeds, gold-tipped spears,[1]
  A green tomb by the road at yellow dusk.[2]
My feelings grow ever deeper,[3] who knows how deep?
Setting sun deep in mountains, rain deep in autumn.

Translated by David McCraw

 1. Nara alludes first to Hsin Ch'i-chi's (see selection 127) lyric to the tune "Joy of Eternal Union":

Gold-tipped spears and ironclad steeds,
Tigerish esprit bolting a thousand leagues.

 2. An allusion to Wang Chao-chün, a Chinese court lady forced by politics to marry the khan of a northern nomadic tribe, from the third of Tu Fu's "Expressing My Thoughts on Ancient Sites" (see selection 48): "Alone she left behind a green tomb to face the yellow dusk."
 3. Whenever Huan Yi (d.392?) heard an a cappella song, he would wail: "What's to be done?" Hsieh An remarked: "Tzu-yeh (i.e., Huan Yi) certainly is a man whose 'feelings grow ever deeper!' "

147
Tune: "Sand of Silk-Washing Brook"

Wang Kuo-wei (1877–1927)

Faded hibiscus and its leaves
Wilt side by side
Artemisia that stood high above the wall
Now half-decayed
Under the slanting sun's gaze
Someone in a lonely lodge
Is prone to heart-rending sorrow.

Sit and you sense the broad sweep
Of clear returning autumn;
Watch and you are dazzled by
The brilliance of the departing sun
How can the human world ever
Live out these lengthening nocturnal hours?

Translated by Jiaosheng Wang

Wang Kuo-wei was a wondrously learned philosopher and literary critic-historian of the late Ch'ing and early Republican period. Possessing a magnificent blend of traditional Chinese scholarship and modern Western theories (Nietzsche and Kant were two of his favorite thinkers from youth), Wang made startlingly fresh and fundamental contributions to research on such difficult and varied subjects as the origins of Chinese drama, the decipherment of oracle shell and bone inscriptions, and the essence and development of lyric meters, and carried out a profoundly creative analysis of the novel *Dream of Red Towers* (see selection 263) in which he applied the concept of the will put forward by Schopenhauer. Wang, however, was deeply exasperated by Chinese reformers who attempted to use Western ideas merely as expedient tools without attempting to comprehend their universal value. A political conservative, Wang was loyal to the Ch'ing royal family long after the dynasty had collapsed in the 1911 revolution. Whether his suicide by drowning on June 2, 1927 is related to his disappointment with political events or personal crises (of which there were indeed many) remains a mystery. As a lyricist, he is considered the finest exponent of the genre after Nara Singde (see selection 146).

Tune: "Sand of Silk-Washing Brook"

Wang Kuo-wei

A hazy mountain temple hides away behind the setting sun.
Dusk falls before birds on the wing get halfway up to the top.

From above, a single chime of the temple bell
Brings the passing clouds to a halt.

I try to climb the lofty peak to steal a look at the bright Moon.
Maybe she is in the mood to open the Eye of Heaven for a peep at the
   mundane world.
Pity is that I am but a mortal in her heavenly eyes.

Translated by Jiaosheng Wang

Tune: "Rouged Lips"

Wang Kuo-wei

Of late it has dawned on me that it's futile
To do away with longing altogether.
For, try to stop it as you may,
It will steal upon you, all unawares,
In Dreamland.

Terraces and towers appear
And then vanish with your dreams.
And you wake only to find
A garden of snowy lilacs outside the western window,
Bathed in pools of cool moonlight.

Translated by Jiaosheng Wang

Elegies and Rhapsodies

148
Heavenly Questions

Attributed to Ch'ü Yüan (340?–278 B.C.E.)

I

'Tis said:

>   At the beginning of remote antiquity,
>   Who was there to transmit the tale?
>   When above and below had not yet taken shape,
> 5 By what means could they be examined?

Ch'ü Yüan is the first Chinese poet known by name and about whom a modicum of biographical information is available. A member of the royal family of the southern kingdom of Ch'u, he was a loyal official to two of its rulers. But the intrigues and slanders of other courtiers who were jealous of him led to his banishment to the even more distant south. There he eventually committed suicide by drowning himself in the Mi-lo river out of despair over the capture of the capital of Ch'u by armies of the state of Ch'in.

The "Heavenly Questions" (*T'ien wen*—this title might also be rendered as "Celestial Riddles" or "Divine Conundrums"), like "Encountering Sorrows" (*Li sao*—the title may also be interpreted as "Departing Sorrows"), Ch'ü Yüan's anguished poem of longing for his idealized ruler, forms a part of the collection of early southern verse known as the *Elegies of Ch'u (Ch'u tz'u)*. Edited by Wang Yi (d. 158 C.E.), who was also its first and most influential commentator, *Elegies* includes works written by and attributed to Ch'ü Yüan as well as works from the Han period composed in imitation of his style.

Upon first encounter, "Heavenly Questions" is one of the most unusual and baffling texts in all of Chinese literature. It consists entirely of a long series of mysterious and essentially unanswered queries concerning the origin and nature of the universe, the founding of civilization by various semidivine beings, and the complicated affairs of the rulers of the legendary and

> When darkness and light were obscured,
> Who could fathom them?
> When primal matter was the only form,
> How could it be recognized?

historical kingdoms right up to the time of the poet himself. Most of the questions are of such maddening obscurity that they are extremely difficult to interpret, let alone answer.

Aside from merely being puzzled or flabbergasted by the "Heavenly Questions," there are a number of productive approaches that the reader may take to this intriguing text. One may view it as offering guideposts to a fragmentary mythology, as evidence for a lost religiosity, as a matrix for comprehending archeological discoveries, and so forth. There have also been several traditional explanations of the text, such as that it represents an expression of personal frustration or that it constitutes a key to early narrative wall paintings. This type of explanation is hard to sustain however, for it is usually based on sheer conjecture or misinterpretation of the text.

The seeming impenetrability of the "Heavenly Questions" has by no means prevented commentators and annotators from attempting to provide a complete set of answers to them. Unfortunately, these answers are almost invariably based on Han period and later legends, so they lack validity and the power to convince. Indeed, many of the explications in Han and later works were created at least partly with the intention of making sense of the "Heavenly Questions," so naturally they cannot serve as reliable explanatory devices for the very text upon which they are premised.

In recent decades, a completely new strategy for comprehending the "Heavenly Questions" has been applied with increasing success. Both the context and the content of the text can be partially reconstructed through the use of comparative mythology. For this interpretive scheme to function successfully, however, it is necessary to abandon the notion that early Chinese civilization developed entirely in isolation from the rest of the world. There are, for example, such obvious indications of linkages with other civilizations as the rabbit in the moon or the tortoise bearing blissful isles on its back, both of which betray Indian influence. Even more striking is the very form of the genre itself. The "Heavenly Questions" shares a whole set of resemblances to the Indo-European wisdom texts commonly known as "riddles."

The authors of the ancient Vedic hymns, the earliest of which date to roughly the beginning of the first millennium B.C.E., were often deliberately cryptic (e.g., Ṛg Veda, I.164). The subject matter of their riddles is, furthermore, virtually the same as that of the "Heavenly Questions" (e.g., Atharva Veda, X.7–8). The Upaniṣads, which followed the Vedas, are even more similar to the "Heavenly Questions." The Śvetāśvatara Upaniṣad begins with a series of comparable questions and the Praśna Upaniṣad (literally, the "Upaniṣad [Secret Session] of Questions") consists entirely of all sorts of difficult and profound questions that are put to a ṛṣi ("seer"). Elsewhere in the Upaniṣads and in the Brāhmanas as well, there are series of questions concerning cosmology and mythology that are quite like the "Heavenly Questions."

In the ancient Iranian Zend-Avesta, doctrine is presented in a series of questions and answers between Zarathustra and Ahura Mazda. In "Yasna" 44, for example, the questions posed by Zarathustra are astonishingly reminiscent of those in the opening portion of the "Heavenly Questions": "Who is it that supported the earth below and the sky above so that they do not fall?" "Who is it that joined speed with wind and welkin?" "Who is it that created blessed light and the darkness?" Even at the far northwestern end of the Indo-European range, the same types of riddles persist in some of the earliest of the poetic Edda. In "Vafthrudnismāl," questions between Gangrath (Wodan) and Wabedrut focus on the origins of heaven and earth. Similar questions abound in "Fiölvinnsmāl," "Alvissmāl," and other songs in the Edda.

J. Huizinga, in chapter VI ("Playing and Knowing"), pp. 105–118, of his classic *Homo Ludens: A Study of the Play-Element in Culture* (Boston: Beacon, 1955; tr. from the German

10   Brightness became bright and darkness dark;
     What has caused them to be like this?
     Yin and yang commingle;
     What was basic, what transformed?

---

ed. of 1944), has analyzed such question series as related to cult indoctrination and sacrifices. In this sense, they function as a sort of catechism. The tradition of imparting and testing knowledge through a series of riddles is prominent throughout the ancient Indo-European tradition, especially its Indo-Iranian and Germanic branches. The texts consisting of questions cited above (and many others like them) may thus be viewed as vestiges of ancient riddle-solving contests, the contestants in which were rewarded or punished (sometimes with their lives), depending upon their performance in responding to the questions. The emphasis on cattle in the "Heavenly Questions" also indicates an Indo-European connection.

But the pan-Eurasian quality of the "Heavenly Questions" would appear not to be limited solely to their increasingly obvious Indo-European affinities. Within the past couple of decades, Chinese scholars have written enormous studies detailing numerous other apparently foreign elements in the *Elegies of Ch'u* in general and in the "Heavenly Questions" in particular. Especially to be noted are Su Hsüeh-lin, *T'ien wen cheng chien (The Authentic Text of "T'ien Wen")* (Taipei: Kuang-tung, 1974), who occasionally overstates her case, and Hsiao Ping, *Ch'u tz'u hsin t'an [New Investigations on the Elegies of Ch'u]* (Tientsin: T'ien-chin ku-chi, 1988), pp. 43–49, 56–74, and 503–805, who is an extremely careful and thorough scholar. Su, Hsiao, and others have pointed out many close parallels between the "Heavenly Questions" on the one hand and West Asian, North African, and European mythologies and symbol systems on the other. Another outstanding study of this type is Joseph Fontenrose's masterful *Python: A Study of Delphic Myth and Its Origins* (Berkeley and Los Angeles: University of California Press, 1959), especially appendix 3. Although *Python* is by no means specifically devoted to the "Heavenly Questions" or even to the Chinese tradition at all, it provides an extraordinarily well documented and extremely revealing comparison of the combat and flood myths in China and elsewhere in the Eurasian ecumene.

The only old literary text in Chinese that is remotely comparable to the "Heavenly Questions" may be found at the beginning of the thirteenth chapter of the *Chuang Tzu*, "Heavenly Revolutions." Not only is the title manifestly similar to that of the "Heavenly Questions," but the reader is actually met with a barrage of questions that is remarkably like those of the "Heavenly Questions" in asking about the origins and nature of the universe. It is significant that, after the presentation of the riddles at the opening of "Heavenly Revolutions," a magus proceeds to answer them. There is solid evidence that Iranian magi were at the Chou court by 800 B.C.E. and quite possibly were also active in Shang ruling circles by around 1200 B.C.E. See Victor H. Mair, "Old Sinitic *mʸag*, Old Persian *maguš*, and English 'Magician,' " *Early China* 15 (1990): 27–47. We should also note that, like the "Heavenly Questions," the *Chuang Tzu* had close associations with Ch'u culture.

The reader will observe that few notes have been provided for the first parts of the "Heavenly Questions" but that more of them are given for the later parts of the text. The reason for this is simple, namely, there are more accurate historical sources available for the Chou dynasty and Warring States periods than for the beginning of the world and the invention of civilization. "Heavenly Questions" is the *locus classicus* for much of the lore that it mentions. Rather than speculate on unanswered questions concerning cosmology and mythology, it is better to let the text speak for itself unless there are other trustworthy materials available. As we get closer to the time when the piece was written down, it becomes progressively easier to fill in the answers.

"Heavenly Questions" is divided into eleven main sections according to their subject matter. Within each section, stanzas are determined by rhyme breaks.

Round heaven with its nine layers,
15 Who managed and measured it?
What sort of achievement was this?
Who was the first to make it?

How was the Cord tied to the Hub?
How was the Heavenly Pole added to them?
20 What did the Eight Pillars hold up?
Why was there a gap in the southeast?

The borders of the ninefold heavens—
Where do they stretch: where do they join?
Many are their corners and angles—
25 Who knows their number?

Upon what are the heavens folded?
Where are the twelve stages divided?
How are the sun and moon attached?
How are the constellations arrayed?

30 The sun emerges from the morning vale,
It comes to rest on the crepuscular horizon.
From dawn until dusk,
How many miles does it travel?

What virtue hath the moon,
35 That it dies and then is reborn again?
What benefit is there
To harbor a bunny in its belly?

The goddess of fertility had no mate;
How did she get nine sons?
40 Where does the god of pestilence dwell?
Where does the benign wind breathe?

What closes and brings darkness?
What opens and brings light?
Before the Horn rises in the east,
45 Where does the numinous sunlight hide?

II

Kun was incapable of controlling the flood;
Why did the masses esteem him?
Everyone said, "There's no need to worry.
Why not let him try to carry it out?"

5   The linked hawk-turtles dragged along;
     What did Kun learn from them?
     He completed the work in accord with the will of the people;
     Why did Deus punish him?

     Eternally imprisoned at Feather Mountain,
10   Why did Kun's corpse not disintegrate after three years?
     Lord Yü was born from the belly of Kun;
     How did this transformation occur?

     Taking up the thread of his predecessor,
     Yü thereupon completed the dead father's work;
15   How did he continue the original enterprise,
     Even though his plan was different?

     The floody abyss was extremely deep—
     How did he fill it in?
     Nine were the regions of square earth—
20   How did he pile them up?

     What did the respondent dragon draw on the ground?
     Where were the lakes and rivers channeled off?

     What was it that Kun had managed?
     What was it that Yü completed?
25   When the tumultuous thunder rumbled,
     Why did the earth tilt toward the southeast?

     How were the nine continents laid out?
     Where were the stream beds sunk?
     They flow to the east but never fill the sea—
30   Who knows the reason why?

     From east to west or from north to south,
     Which length is greater?
     The earth is elliptical from north to south—
     What is its breadth?

35   The hanging gardens of K'un-lun,
     Where does their base lie?
     With nine layers of tiered walls,
     How many tricents is its heights?

     The gates of the four directions—
40   Who is it that passes through them?
     When the northeast gate opens,
     What air breezes through it?

Where does the sun not reach?
Where does the incandescent dragon not shine?

45   Before Hsi-ho, the solar charioteer, has risen,
Whence cometh the light of the Jo flower?

In what place is the winter warm?
In what place is the summer cold?
Where is the forest of stones?
50   What beast can speak?

Where is there a hornless dragonet,
That roams about carrying a bear on its back?

The horrible hydra with nine heads—
Where does it flit about so swiftly?
55   Where is the place of immortality?
What do the giants guard?

The spreading nine-stemmed nuphar,
And the cannabis flowers, where do they grow?
The snake that can swallow elephants—
60   How big must it be?

Black Waters, Dark Toes,
And Three Dangers—where are they?
The years extend without death;
What is the limit of longevity?

65   Where does the merman live?
Where does the monster bird dwell?
Why did Yi shoot down the suns?
Why did crow feathers fall from them? [1]

III

Yü's energy was devoted to his work, [2]
Having descended to inspect the land below.
How did he get that T'u mountain maid,
And unite with her midst the terraced mulberries?

5   Yearning for a consort, he mated with her,
From whose body was born a successor.

---

1. A mythological explanation of maculae (sunspots). The great archer-prince Yi, hero of
the Chuang people (Moz Yiz Daihvuengz), shot down nine extra suns that once appeared in the
sky and scorched the earth.
2. Draining the land (see above, line II.14).

Why did he crave different tastes,
And feel satisfied with a morning's delight?

Ch'i[3] replaced Yih[4] as the lord,
10   But suddenly encountered troubles.
How did Ch'i suffer from sorrow,
And yet avert his predicament?

All returned to hunting and husbandry,
So that no harm came to his[5] person.
15   Even though Yih made these reforms,
Why was it Yü's line that was passed down?

Ch'i paid court to Deus with lance dance and damsels,
Receiving from him the "Nine Disputations" and the "Nine Songs."
Why did the diligent son slay his mother,
20   So that her stone corpse split upon the ground?

Deus sent down Yi of the East
To remove the troubles of the Hsia people;
Why did Yi shoot the god of the Yellow River
And take for wife the goddess of the Lo River?

25   With full-drawn pearl-inlaid bow and nimble thimble,
Yi shot the great wild boar;
When he presented the fat of the sacrificial meat,
Why was Lord Deus not pleased?

Cho[6] married Sable Fox;
30   Deluded by his wife, he plotted against Yi.
How is it that Yi could shoot through leather,
Yet he was swallowed up by conspiracy?

Traveling westward on a perilous journey,
How did he[7] cross the mountain cliffs?
35   When he[8] was transformed into a yellow bear,
How did the magus bring him back to life?

Everyone sowed black millet,
And exploited the rushes and reeds;

3. Son of Yü.
4. A high official of Yü, who had been chosen to succeed him as ruler of the Hsia dynasty.
5. Yih's, that is.
6. Minister of Yi.
7. This may refer to Yi.
8. Kun.

For what reason did they scatter in all directions,
40   And why was the enmity against Kun so long-lasting?

With white rainbow skirts and cloudlike adornments,
What is she doing in this hall?
Where did he get the excellent medicine
That he could not hide securely?

45   Heaven's framework spans the vertical and the horizontal;
When the vital yang breath dissipates, death will ensue.
Why did the great bird call?
How did it lose its body?

The pluvial sprite causes rain to fall;
50   How does he bring it about?
The god of wind has a deer's head and a bird's body;
How did he receive it?

When giant turtles bearing islands on their backs stir,
How do they keep them steady?
55   If one launches a boat to cross the land,
By what means does it move?

When Ao[9] stood before his sister-in-law's door,
What was he seeking from her?
Why did Shao-k'ang[10] go in pursuit of him with hounds,
60   But end up decapitating her?

The woman Ch'i sewed his lower garment,
And he rested with her in the same house;
How did the wrong head fall by mistake,
When she herself met disaster?

65   Ao planned to reorganize his troops;
How did he strengthen them?
After he capsized the boats of Chen-hsün,[11]
By what method was he taken?

IV

There were portents at the beginning;
By whom were they predicted?
A jade terrace ten stories tall;
By whom was it erected?

9. Son of Cho.
10. A ruler of the mid-Hsia dynasty.
11. A feudal state of the Hsia royal family.

5   Fu-hsi [12] was established as Deus;
    By what principle was he raised up?
    Woman Wa [13] was embodied with a serpent's tail;
    Who was it that created her?

    Shun was tormented at home;
10   Why did his father let him remain a bachelor?
    If Yao did not inform Shun's father,
    How could he marry his two daughters to him?

    Shun deferred to his younger stepbrother,
    Who harmed him nonetheless.
15   How could the stepbrother unleash his brutish instincts,
    But never be endangered himself?

    Ngwa's heritage reaches into the past,
    Having been founded among the southern peaks;
    Who would have expected that, fleeing to this place,
20   Two princes [14] Ngwa would gain?

        V

    When Chieh attacked Meng-shan,
    What did he get thereby? [15]
    How was Mo-hsi dissipated?
    Why did T'ang kill her?

5   From a tripod trimmed with swans and ornamented with jade,
    Lord Deus was feted;
    How did he receive the plans against Chieh of Hsia,
    Who was finally destroyed?

    When Deus descended to survey the world,
10   There below he encountered Yi Yin;

12. The first ancient sage-king, he is almost certainly related to the flood-hero, Phu-Hay, of the Hmong (i.e., Miao) people.

13. She shares a number of similarities with Eve, the first woman of the Judaeo-Christian tradition.

14. Chung-yung and T'ai-po of the Chou royal house. They had ceded their rights to the throne in favor of a younger half-brother. The name of the southern kingdom transcribed here as Ngwa would be transcribed as Wu in Modern Standard Mandarin.

15. The answer is two beautiful women presented to him by the conquered state of Meng-shan as a form of appeasement. Chieh was the last king of the Hsia dynasty. After he returned with the two concubines, his deserted queen, Mo-hsi, had a conspiratorial affair with his servant, Yi Yin, and assisted T'ang, the first ruler of the Shang dynasty, to overthrow the Hsia.

When Chieh was banished to Ming-t'iao for his crimes,
Why did the black-hairs[16] rejoice so greatly?

VI

Chien Ti[17] was on a tall terrace;
Why did K'u think that she was suitable?
A dark bird made a gift to her;
Why was the woman happy?

5   Hai[18] inherited Chi's virtues,
For his father was a good man;
Why was he finally murdered in the freehold of Yee,
Where he pastured his cattle and sheep?[19]

When he danced for her with his shield,
10   Why did she cherish him?
With his smooth loins and sleek skin,
How did he seduce her?

In the freehold of Yee there were herdsmen;
How did they encounter him?
15   They struck the bed, but he went out first;
Whose command were they following?

Heng inherited Chi's virtues;
How could he have retrieved their docile cattle?
Why was he concerned only with position and pay,
20   And did not even come back for them?

Meritorious Wei traced his father's footsteps,
And the freehold at Yee had no peace;
How numerous were his soldiers, like birds flocking to brambles,
When the responsible son gave vent to his emotions?

16. From West Asia to East Asia, this was a standard way of referring to the commoners during antiquity. Some modern languages, such as Russian, still retain this expression.

17. Deus K'u, divine ancestor of the Yin (Shang) rulers, presented her with an egg brought to her nine-storied terrace by a dark bird. She swallowed the egg and became pregnant. The son she gave birth to was Hsieh, Minister of Education for Shun, who helped Yü control the floods and who was the founder of the house that later established the Yin dynasty.

18. Said to be the first herdsman, he was the brother of Heng and the father of Wei, through whom the Yin line was passed on.

19. The answer is that he apparently developed a licentious relationship with the wife of the ruler of this freehold. One version of the story says that his own brother, Heng, was also having an affair with the same woman and so killed Hai out of jealousy. In any event, with the death of Hai, the family lost their cattle in the freehold of Yee until Hai's son, Wei, recovered them. In the following stanzas, there is an undercurrent of censure against Heng for not taking action to retain the cattle himself.

25 The deluded younger brothers were all profligate,
    And threatened the older brother;
    How did he transform them through deception,
    So that their descendants met with lasting success?

    T'ang[20] the Achiever toured the east,
30 And reached the freehold at Hsin;
    How is it that he requested a servant,
    But instead got an auspicious wife?[21]

    From a tree by the water's edge,
    They got the little boy,[22]
35 Why, then, did they hate him,
    And send him away as an escort for the lady from Shen?

    T'ang was released from the Double Springs prison;
    Now what was his crime?
    He overcame his inhibitions and attacked the monarch;[23]
40 Now who was it that incited him?

    At first, Yi Yin was T'ang's servant,
    But afterwards was accepted as councilor;
    How was he T'ang's minister to the very end,
    Later receiving offerings along with the ancestors of the Shang?

    VII
    To Yin was given all under heaven;
    How was the throne bestowed upon Chou?
    Yin had prospered but then was lost;
    What was Chow's crime?[24]

5   Though Chow was of kingly stature,
    Who caused him to be foolish and deluded?
    Why did he hate his close councilors,
    While trusting in slanderers and flatterers?

20. Seven generations after Wei, he was the founder of the Yin (Shang) dynasty.
21. T'ang requested from the freeholder of Hsin the talented Yi Yin who was later instrumental in helping him overthrow the Hsia dynasty. Although his request was not granted, he married the freeholder's daughter and Yi Yin came along as part of her entourage.
22. Legend holds that Yi Yin's mother turned into a mulberry tree when she was fleeing from a flood that engulfed her village. The night before, she had been warned in her dream by a god not to look back, but she could not keep herself from doing so.
23. Here referring to Chieh, who had imprisoned him.
24. This section deals with the toppling of the last ruler of the Shang, Chow.

How did Pi Kan [25] offend,
10   So that he was suppressed?
How did Lei K'ai truckle,
So that he was enfeoffed?

How can sages who are of equal virtue
End up behaving so differently?
15   Chow made mincemeat of Mei Po for his directness,
Master Chi feigned madness to preserve his life.

They convened at dawn and swore fealty;
How was this face-to-face appointment actualized? [26]
Like flocks of gray hawks they came flying;
20   Who was it that caused them to assemble?

They vied to mobilize their offensive weaponry;
How was this carried out?
They rushed forward together with their wings of attack,
How were the troops led?

25   When Chow's body was mutilated,
Why was Uncle Tan unhappy? [27]
When Wu personally directed the operations,
Why were there sighs of admiration?

VIII

Lord Millet [28] was the firstborn son;
Why did Deus [29] detest him?
Thrown out upon the ice,
How did the birds keep him warm?

25. Pi Kan was the loyal uncle of King Chow. The latter was much annoyed by the frequent admonitions of his uncle. When someone told him that a sage's heart has seven openings, he had Pi Kan's heart cut out so that he could see for himself.

26. King Wu, who became the first king of the Chou dynasty, was joined by eight hundred feudal lords whom he convened at a great meeting. The character *wu*, which many commentators interpret as a first-person pronoun indicating King Wu, actually stands for a homonymous cognate meaning "meet face to face." The only first-person reference in the "Heavenly Questions," quite properly, comes in the section dealing with Ch'u (see line XI.12), the home state of the presumed author. The "Wu" of the king's title is a separate sinograph meaning "martial."

27. "Uncle Tan" is an appellation of the Duke of Chou who was so important in helping to establish the Chou dynasty. His name was Tan and he was the younger brother of King Wu. From the viewpoint of the succeeding generation, then, he was "Uncle Tan." The Duke of Chou was upset at King Wu's treatment of Chow's corpse because the Shang dynasty had been sanctioned by Heaven. Even though Chow was a tyrant, as an incarnation of Deus, he should have been treated with due respect.

28. Hou Chi, the first ancestor of the clan that later established the Chou dynasty.

29. See line VI.1 and the note there.

5   How was it that he, drawing his bow full and grasping his arrows,
     Had the unique ability to be a general?
     Since he had startled Deus and made him agitated,
     Why did he encounter lasting success?

     The Earl of the West[30] gave orders while Yin declined;
10   He grasped a whip and acted as herdsman.
     Who ordered the transfer of the altar to the earth to Ch'i,[31]
     To take over the mandate of the Yin state?

     When the tribal elders moved to Ch'i,
     What made the people willing to follow them?
15   In Yin there was a bewitching woman;
     How did she cause him to be censured?[32]

     When Chow bestowed upon him the mincemeat of a vassal,[33]
     The Earl of the West reported it to Heaven above.
     How did he personally deliver the punishment of Exalted Deus,
20   So that the mandate of Yin could not be saved?

     When Preceptor Wang was in the butchery,
     How did the Earl of the West recognize him?
     He drummed with his knife and raised his voice in song;
     Why was his lord so happy?

25   When King Wu set forth to kill Chow of the Yin,
     What was it that made him so grieved?
     Carrying a corpse,[34] he assembled his warriors;
     What was it that made him so hasty?

     Kuan Shu[35] hung himself in the arbor vitae grove;
30   What was the reason for that?
     How was Heaven moved and the earth agitated?
     Who was frightened by this?

30. Po Ch'ang, the future King Wen, who laid the groundwork for the Chou state.

31. The cradle of Chou culture, whence Hou Chi's descendants moved to escape annihilation by the Dik tribesmen. This move was suggested by the "Old Duke, Father T'an," also known as King T'ai, who was the grandfather of King Wen.

32. The beguiling woman of Yin was Ta-chi, King Chow's concubine. Chow was so infatuated by her that his ears were deaf to all protests.

33. See line VII.15.

34. That of the Earl of the West, his father, who was posthumously canonized as King Wen after the founding of the Chou.

35. After the overthrow of Chow, Kuan Shu was one of the representatives of the Chou dynasty established in the eastern part of the kingdom to oversee the remnants of the Shang aristocracy. Implicated in a plot to cause dissension among the new rulers by casting aspersions against the loyalty of the Duke of Chou, he was forced to commit suicide.

When August Heaven bestowed the mandate,
What warning was given?

35   One may receive control of all under heaven,
Until another is caused to replace one.

Lord Chao [36] embarked on a royal tour,
Journeying all the way to the southern land.
What benefit did he receive

40   By meeting that white pheasant?

King Mu [37] was cunningly covetous;
What was his purpose in traveling all around?
When he made a circuit of all under heaven,
For what was he seeking?

45   A strange couple dragged along their wares;
What were they hawking in the market? [38]
Who executed King Yu? [39]
How did he obtain Pao Ssu?

IX

The mandate of Heaven shifts from side to side;
Whom does it punish, whom protect?
Duke Huan of Ch'i [40] nine times convened his vassals,
Yet even he was murdered in the end.

5   Ho the Valiant [41] was the grandson of Meng; [42]
As a youth, he met with rejection. [43]

36. Fourth of the Chou kings. He traveled to Ch'u in pursuit of southern rareties, but drowned while crossing a river.

37. Fifth king of the Chou, he was celebrated in legend for his love of horses and for his many long journeys, especially to the distant west.

38. During the reign of King Hsüan, the eleventh of the Chou rulers, a prophecy was heard in a children's song that the dynasty would fall because of a wild mulberry bow and a wicker quiver. A peasant couple were caught selling these items in the market, but they made good their escape. As they were fleeing, they rescued a baby who had been abandoned by an unmarried palace maid. The little girl grew up to be Pao Ssu, the demanding queen of King Yu, who was the twelfth and last ruler of the Western Chou.

39. The answer is the so-called "Dog Barbarians" who were able to penetrate the neglected defenses of the capital because of King Yu's preoccupation with Pao Ssu.

40. During the Eastern Chou period, when the dynasty was in decline, numerous city-states contested for power. The strongest of these during the seventh century B.C.E. was Ch'i, whose duke was nine times chosen to be leader of the feudal lords.

41. Ho Lü, king of Ngwa (r. 514–496 B.C.E.).

42. King of the powerful southern state of Ngwa.

43. Ho Lü was the legitimate heir to the Ngwa throne, but was passed over in a complicated, irregular succession. After a period of exile when he was young, Ho Lü had his cousin, who occupied the throne, assassinated and finally became king himself.

How did he gain military might in his prime,[44]
So that he could spread his prowess across the land?[45]

Progenitor P'eng[46] cooked a pheasant;
10 How did Deus partake of it?
He received lasting longevity;
How could he exist so long?

X

They pastured their livestock together in the center;[47]
Why was the lord[48] angry?
Their lives were slight as those of bees and ants;
How could their power persist?

5 The goddess was startled to see them picking ferns;[49]
How did a deer[50] protect them?
North they traveled to the bend in the river;
Why were they happy to congregate there?

The elder brother[51] possessed Dog Mound;
10 Why did the younger brother[52] desire it?
In exchange, he was offered a hundred chariots,[53]
And ended up losing his entitlements.

44. Through the assistance of the talented minister, Wu Tzu-hsü.
45. Like Duke Huan of Ch'i, King Ho Lü of Ngwa acted as one of the five hegemons during the Spring and Autumn period.
46. P'eng Keng or P'eng Tsu, the Chinese counterpart of Methuselah, was a practitioner of Yogic breath control and an excellent chef.
47. At the beginning of the Chou dynasty, the Ch'in tribe, which would ultimately supplant it roughly a thousand years later, was still a small group who shared the pastures of the Chou heartland.
48. King Wu of the Chou dynasty.
49. King Wu pushed the Ch'in northward out of the center of the Chou kingdom into less hospitable territory. There they were for a time forced to subsist by foraging off the sparsely vegetated land.
50. Fei-lien, the antlered god of the wind (see line III.51), who was also thought of as the first ancestor of the Ch'in people. Fei-lien (*piwər-gliam) may merely be the binomial spelling of the Sinitic word for "wind" (MSM *feng*, ancient reconstruction *pium).
51. Master Fei, an important ancestral figure of the Ch'in house. He was responsible for reestablishing the Ch'in at Dog Mound after they had wandered in the inhospitable wilds of the north.
52. Master Fei's stepbrother, Ch'eng, whose mother was the daughter of the powerful Marquis of Shen.
53. King Hsiao, the eighth ruler of the Chou dynasty, refused to enfeoff Ch'eng as lord of Dog Mound. Instead, he presented him with a hundred chariots and appointed him as ambassador to the distant Western Jung tribe. This move was designed to defuse the conflict between the two brothers and resulted in Ch'eng's losing his regular feudal entitlements.

XI

Midst evening thunder and lightning,
Why was he [54] afraid to return?
His majesty could not be maintained;
What was Deus seeking?

5   He [55] hid away in caves;
How can his predicament be described?
Illustrious Ch'u raised armies;
How did it take the lead? [56]

Recognizing the errors of his predecessor, [57] he [58] corrected them;
10   What more can be said?
Ho Lü vied to conquer our state;
Long was he victorious over us.

She circled round the village gates and passed through the altars to the
      earth,
Till she reached the burial mounds.
15   She was licentious, she was wanton,
And consequently gave birth to Tzu-wen. [59]

It was reported that Hsiung [60] would not reign long;
How did Tzu-wen chasten his superior [61] and renounce himself,
Thereby making his loyal name all the more illustrious?

Translated by Victor H. Mair

54. This refers to King Ling of the southern state of Ch'u, the home of the author of "Encountering Sorrow" and "Heavenly Questions." Once when the king went on an excursion, his younger brother took advantage of the situation to usurp the throne and install himself as King P'ing. The latter was an evil despot who, among other dastardly deeds, killed his loyal adviser Wu She, father of Wu Tzu-hsü (see note 44), and relied upon the unscrupulous Fei Wu-chi instead.

55. King P'ing's son and successor, King Chao, was forced to flee when the armies of the state of Ngwa entered the Ch'u capital.

56. King Chuang, grandson of King Ch'eng (see notes 60 and 61) brought his state to eminence and served as hegemon.

57. King P'ing.

58. King Chao.

59. The result of an illicit union, Tzu-wen was abandoned in the wilds. There a tigress suckled him and he grew up to be the able minister of King Ch'eng of Ch'u.

60. The text has *tu-ao*, a transcription of the Ch'u word for a monarch who rules but a short time. Hsiung ("Bear") was both the surname and the totem of the Ch'u royal family. Hsiung Chien was the son of King Wen of Ch'u and the older brother of King Ch'eng.

61. Hsiung Yün (later King Ch'eng) who was in conflict with his brother, Hsiung Chien, over the succession. Since Hsiung Yün was privy to the excellent advice of Tzu-wen, he emerged the victor and led Ch'u to glory.

149
The Wind

Attributed to Sung Yü (290?–222 B.C.E.)

King Hsiang of Ch'u was taking his ease in the Palace of the Orchid Terrace, with his courtiers Sung Yü and Ching Ch'a attending him, when a sudden gust of wind came sweeping in. The king, opening wide the collar of his robe and facing into it, said, "How delightful this wind is! And I and the common people may share it together, may we not?"

But Sung Yü replied, "This wind is for Your Majesty alone. How could the common people have a share in it?"

"The wind," said the king, "is the breath of heaven and earth. Into every corner it unfolds and reaches; without choosing between high or low, exalted or humble, it touches everywhere. What do you mean when you say that this wind is for me alone?"

Sung Yü replied, "I have heard my teacher say that the twisted branches of the lemon tree invite the birds to nest, and hollows and cracks summon the wind. But the breath of the wind differs with the place which it seeks out."

"Tell me," said the king. "Where does the wind come from?"

Sung Yü answered:

> "The wind is born from the land
> And springs up in the tips of the green duckweed.
> It insinuates itself into the valleys
> And rages in the canyon mouth,
> Skirts the corners of Mount T'ai

The *fu* ("rhapsody," "rhymeprose," or "prose-poem") stands at the very beginning of the most important anthology of traditional Chinese literature, *Literary Selections* (see selection 18) and fully one quarter of the entire large volume is devoted to this genre. The prominence awarded to *fu* by the editor of *Literary Selections* is not accidental, for this is the first genre to have afforded Chinese authors broad scope in which to display their narrative, descriptive, and lyrical talents. It is highly significant that both the elegy (see selection 148) and the rhapsody, which constitute the earliest forms of imaginative and expressive belles-lettres in China, were invented and matured in the peripheral southern state of Ch'u which was fundamentally of non-Sinitic origins and, in any event, culturally quite dissimilar from the northern homeland of the Chinese people.

The "Rhapsody on the Wind" is attributed to Sung Yü, a writer of the third century B.C.E. who served at the court of Ch'u and was a disciple of the famous elegiac poet and statesman, Ch'ü Yüan (see selection 148). Whether or not it is actually by Sung Yü, it nonetheless represents an important type in rhapsodic literature, the poetic description of a particular object or phenomenon—in this case, the wind. The poem may be intended simply to delight the reader with its gusty portrait of the winds of the land of Ch'u. But, if traditional commentators are to be believed, a more serious purpose underlies it, namely, the expression of veiled reproaches against a king whose way of life is so far removed from that of his impoverished subjects that the very winds that blow upon them are of a different nature.

And dances beneath the pines and cedars.
Swiftly it flies, whistling and wailing;
Fiercely it splutters its anger.
It crashes with a voice like thunder,
Whirls and tumbles in confusion,
Shaking rocks, striking trees,
Blasting the tangled forest.
Then, when its force is almost spent,
It wavers and disperses,
Thrusting into crevices and rattling door latches.
Clean and clear,
It scatters and rolls away.
Thus it is that this cool, fresh hero wind,
Leaping and bounding up and down,
Climbs over the high wall
And enters deep into palace halls.
With a puff of breath it shakes the leaves and flowers,
Wanders among the cassia and pepper trees,
Or soars over the swift waters.
It buffets the mallow flower,
Sweeps the angelica, touches the spikenard,
Glides over the sweet lichens and lights on willow shoots,
Rambling over the hills
And their scattered host of fragrant flowers.
After this, it wanders into the courtyard,
Ascends the jade hall in the north,
Clambers over gauze curtains,
Passes through the inner apartments,
And so becomes Your Majesty's wind.
When this wind blows on a man,
At once he feels a chill run through him,
And he sighs at its cool freshness.
Clear and gentle,
It cures sickness, dispels drunkenness,
Sharpens the eyes and ears,
Relaxes the body and brings benefit to men.
This is what is called the hero wind of Your Majesty."

"How well you have described it!" exclaimed the king. "But now may I hear about the wind of the common people?" And Sung Yü replied:

The wind of the common people
Comes whirling from the lanes and alleys,

Poking in the rubbish, stirring up the dust,
Fretting and worrying its way along.
It creeps into holes and knocks on doors,
Scatters sand, blows ashes about,
Muddles in dirt and tosses up bits of filth.
It sidles through hovel windows
And slips into cottage rooms.
When this wind blows on a man,
At once he feels confused and downcast.
Pounded by heat, smothered in dampness,
His heart grows sick and heavy,
And he falls ill and breaks out in a fever.
Where it brushes his lips, sores appear;
It strikes his eyes with blindness.
He stammers and cries out,
Not knowing if he is dead or alive.
This is what is called the lowly wind of the common people."

Translated by Burton Watson

150
The Owl

Chia Yi (201–169 B.C.E.)

Chia Yi had been Tutor to the Prince of Ch'ang-sha[1] for three years when one day an owl flew into his house and perched in a corner of his room. (In

"The Owl" by Chia Yi is the earliest work in the rhapsody form whose authorship and date of composition are reasonably certain. The text is recorded in the biography of the poet in chapter 84 of the *Records of the Grand Historian* by Ssu-ma Ch'ien, compiled around 100 B.C.E. (see selection 225). The prefatory note accompanying "The Owl" is based upon Ssu-ma Ch'ien's description of the circumstances under which the work was composed. The position of tutor to the King of Ch'ang-sha, in a remote region (modern Hunan) of the Yangtze Valley, was actually a form of banishment. This fact, along with the poet's failing health, accounts for the air of gloom that pervades the work. Using the owl as his mouthpiece, Chia Yi preaches himself a fervently Taoist sermon on the equality of life and death. His poem, far more personal and overtly philosophical than most of the other early rhapsodies, stands apart from the mainstream of literary development, its tone too somber for the social uses to which the rhapsody form was customarily put, its intense conviction inimitable by anyone not afflicted as its author was. One of the most intriguing aspects of this rhapsody on "The Owl" is its uncanny resemblance to Edgar Allan Poe's "The Raven," a work which it predates by more than two millennia.

1. In Hunan.

Ch'u the word for owl is *fu;* it is a bird of ill omen.)[2] This was after he had been banished to Ch'ang-sha (Ch'ang-sha is a low, damp place), and he was greatly depressed at what he took to be a sign that he had not much longer to live. On this occasion he wrote a rhapsody to console himself. It reads as follows:

> The year was *tan-wo,*[3] it was the fourth month, summer's first,
> The thirty-seventh day of the cycle,[4] at sunset, when an owl alighted in
>   my house.
> On the corner of my seat it perched, completely at ease.
> I marveled at the reason for this uncanny visitation
> 5   And opened a book to discover the omen. The oracle yielded the
>   maxim:
> "When a wild bird enters a house, the master is about to leave."
> I should have liked to ask the owl: Where am I to go?
> If lucky, let me know; if bad, tell me the worst.
> Be it swift or slow, tell me when it is to be.
> 10 The owl sighed; it raised its head and flapped its wings
> But could not speak.—Let me say what it might reply:
> All things are a flux, with never any rest
> Whirling, rising, advancing, retreating;
> Body and breath do a turn together—change form and slough off,
> 15 Infinitely subtle, beyond words to express.
> From disaster fortune comes, in fortune lurks disaster[5]
> Grief and joy gather at the same gate, good luck and bad share the same
>   abode.
> Though Wu was great and strong, Fu-ch'ai met with defeat;
> Yüeh was driven to refuge on K'uai-chi, but Kou-chien became
>   hegemon.[6]

2. This is quite obviously an aside which introduces both a linguistic fact and a relevant custom from the far southern setting of the work. The following parenthetical sentence is of a similar nature.

3. There are varying opinions—175, 174, and 173 B.C.E.—as to which year this is meant to indicate.

4. This corresponds to the twenty-eighth day of the fourth lunar month, 173 B.C.E., and to the twenty-third day of the fourth lunar month, 174 B.C.E. The fourth lunar month of 175 B.C.E. had no such cyclical date.

5. Shortened from *Tao Te Ching* (selection 10), chapter 58.

6. The rivalry between Wu (Ngwa) and Yüeh (Viet) provides one of the most dramatic examples of the reversals of fortune that Chia Yi is illustrating. Fu-ch'ai, the last ruler of Wu, failed to take advantage of his opportunity to destroy Yüeh when Kou-chien's army was surrounded on top of Mount K'uai-chi (or Kuei-chi). Years later the situation was reversed and Yüeh destroyed Wu. Under King Kou-chien, Yüeh became the leading state among those contending for supremacy during the breakup of the Eastern Chou dynasty.

20   Li Ssu emigrated to become minister, but in the end he suffered the
      Five Punishments.[7]
      Fu Yüeh was once in bonds, before he was minister to Wu-ting.[8]
  So
      Disaster is to fortune as strands of a single rope,
      Fate is past understanding—who comprehends its bounds?[9]
      Force water and it spurts, force an arrow and it goes far.[10]
25   All things are propelled in circles, undulating and revolving—
      Clouds rise and rain falls, tangled in contingent alternation.
      On the Great Potter's wheel creatures are shaped in all their infinite
         variety.
      Heaven cannot be predicted, the Way cannot be foretold,
      Late or early, it is predetermined; who knows when his time will be?
  Consider then:
30   Heaven and Earth are a crucible, the Creator is the smith;[11]
      Yin and yang are the charcoal, living creatures are the bronze:
      Combining, scattering, waning, waxing—where is any pattern?
      A thousand changes, a myriad transformations with never any end.
      If by chance one becomes a man, it is not a state to cling to.
35   If one be instead another creature, what cause is that for regret?
      A merely clever man is partial to self, despising other, vaunting ego;
      The man of understanding adopts the larger view: nothing exists to take
         exception to.
      The miser will do anything for his hoard, the hero for his repute;
      The vainglorious is ready to die for power, the common man clings to
         life.
40   Driven by aversions and lured by desires, men dash madly west or east;
      The Great Man is not biased, the million changes are all one to him.
      The stupid man is bound by custom, confined as though in fetters;

7. Li Ssu was instrumental in preparing the way for the establishment of the Ch'in dynasty which succeeded in establishing a unified state.

8. Fu Yüeh spent time as a convict, but he became a star in the sky after being adviser to the Shang ruler Wu-ting.

9. In the *Tao Te Ching*, this question follows immediately after the line about fortune and calamity (compare with note 5).

10. This proverbial expression occurs in the *Huai-nan Tzu* and in *The Springs and Autumns of Mr. Lü*. In the former it is used to emphasize the need for effort at the right time: the best arrow needs a bow to send it far, etc. In the latter it is a warning against attempting to cope with that which is "stirred up," in particular a ruler. In the present context the arrow and water are examples of things at the mercy of an outside force: even so all of creation, man included, is driven by the impersonal workings of the Way.

11. This line and lines 33, 34, 36, 37, 38, 39, 50, and 51 are all based on sentences from the *Chuang Tzu*. It is clear that Chia Yi was inspired by the ideas and images of Master Chuang in creating this rhapsody.

The Perfect Man is above circumstance, Tao is his only friend.
The mass man vacillates, his mind replete with likes and dislikes;
45   The True Man is tranquil, he takes his stand with Tao.
Divest yourself of knowledge and ignore your body, until, transported,
     you lose self;
Be detached, remote, and soar with Tao.
Float with the flowing stream, or rest against the isle,
Surrender to the workings of fate, unconcerned for self,
50   Let your life be like a floating, your death like a rest.
Placid as the peaceful waters of a deep pool, buoyant as an unfastened
     boat,
Find no cause for complacency in life, but cultivate emptiness and
     drift.
The Man of Virtue is unattached; recognizing fate, he does not worry.
Be not dismayed by petty pricks and checks!

                                   Translated by James Robert Hightower

151

Sir Fantasy

Ssu-ma Hsiang-ju (c. 179–118 B.C.E.)

When Ch'u dispatched Sir Fantasy as its envoy to the state of Ch'i, the king
of Ch'i called out all the knights within his domain and, providing the party

Ssu-ma Hsiang-ju (see also selection 158) in his youth served at the court of King Hsiao of
the state of Liang, a prince of the Han imperial house. King Hsiao had gathered around him an
illustrious group of poets and rhetoricians, which included Mei Ch'eng (see selection 152). Ssu-
ma wrote the first part of this rhapsody while attached to the court of King Hsiao, and it
subsequently came into the hands of Emperor Wu, who exclaimed, "What a pity that I could
not have lived at the same time as the author of this!" When informed that the author was still
alive, the emperor summoned Ssu-ma to the capital and provided him with writing materials so
that he could continue his literary labors. The poet thereupon revised and expanded his earlier
rhapsody to produce the present work—sometimes treated as a single piece entitled "Sir Fantasy"
and sometimes as two items, the second entitled "Rhapsody on the Shang-lin (Hunting Park)."
   Like many early rhapsodies, this one is cast in the form of a debate, the participants being
three officials with names that emphasize their fictitious nature, each speaking in praise of his
master. In the first part of the rhapsody, presumably composed at an earlier date, Sir Fantasy of
the fief of Ch'u and Master No-such of Ch'i describe the hunts and outings of their respective
lords. In the second part, Lord Not-real, spokesman for the supreme ruler, the Son of Heaven
(i.e., the emperor), overwhelms his companions with a magnificent description of the Shang-lin
Park on the outskirts of Ch'ang-an and the imperial hunts and entertainments that take place

with carriages and horsemen, went out with the envoy on a hunt. After the hunt was over, Sir Fantasy was describing the wonders of the event to Master No-such, while Lord Not-real stood by. When the three of them had taken their seats, Master No-such asked, "Did you enjoy the hunt today?" "Very much!" replied Sir Fantasy. "Did you have a large catch?" Master No-such asked, to which Sir Fantasy answered, "No, the catch was rather meager." "If the catch was small, then what did you find so enjoyable?" he pressed. "What I enjoyed was the way the king of Ch'i was endeavoring to impress me with the great number of carriages and horsemen, while for my part I described to him the hunts that we have at Yün-meng in Ch'u." "Would you perhaps tell us about these hunts of Ch'i and Ch'u?" asked Master No-such, to which Sir Fantasy replied:

"Surely!
The king of Ch'i rode forth with a thousand carriages,
Selecting to accompany him ten thousand horsemen,
To hunt on the borders of the sea.
The ranks of men filled the lowlands;
Their nets and snares covered the hills.
They seized the hares and ran down the deer,
Shot the tailed deer with arrows and snared the feet of the unicorns.
They raced along the briny coves,
The new-felled game staining their carriage wheels.
Their arrows found their mark and the catch was plentiful;
The king grew proud and began to boast of his achievements.
He turned in his carriage and said to me,

" 'Does the state of Ch'u also have its hunting lands, its wide plains and stretching lowlands, as rich and joyous as these? Can the hunts of the king of Ch'u rival these of mine?'

"I dismounted from my carriage and replied, 'I am only a humble inhabit-ant of the land of Ch'u. I have served the king ten years or more, and at times have accompanied him on his travels; I have attended him in the hunting parks of the capital of Ch'u and seen in person what they are like; yet I have not seen all by any means, and I can hardly speak of his hunts in the distant lowlands.'

" 'Be that as it may,' said the king of Ch'i, 'tell me in general what you have seen and heard!' and I replied, 'Of course, of course.

" 'In Ch'u, they say, there are seven lowlands. Of these I have visited only one; the other six I have never seen. The one I have visited is the smallest of

there. Surprisingly, the work ends with a passage in which the emperor is shown renouncing such pleasures, opening his parks and ponds to the use of the common people, and adopting a policy of frugality in government.

them all, called Yün-meng. It is nine hundred tricents square, and in the center there is a mountain.

" 'A mountain which winds and twists upward,
Rearing its lofty crags on high,
Covered with jagged jutting peaks
That blot out the sun and moon
And entangle them in their folds;
Its crest pierces the blue clouds,
Its slopes roll and billow downward,
Reaching to the Yangtze and the rivers around.
Its soil is colored cinnabar and blue, copper and clayey white,
With yellow ochre and white quartz,
Tin and jade, gold and silver,
A mass of hues, glowing and shining,
Sparkling like the scales of a dragon.
Here too are precious stones: carnelians and garnets,
Amethysts, turquoises, and matrices of ore,
Chalcedony, beryl, and basalt for whetstones,
Onyx and figured agate.
To the east stretch fields of gentians and fragrant orchids,
Iris, turmeric, and crow-fans,
Spikenard and sweet flag,
Selinea and angelica,
Sugar cane and ginger.
On the south lie broad plains and wide lowlands,
Rising and falling in gentle slopes,
Secluded hollows and rolling leas,
Hemmed in by the great Yangtze
And bounded by Witch's Mountain.
On the high, dry crests grow
Indigo, broom, and sage,
Basil, sweet fern, and blue artemisia;
In the low, damp places,
Mallows, henbane, cattails, and bulrushes,
Marsh roses and bog rhubarb,
Water lilies, cress, and mare's-tail,
Wormwood and swamp cabbage.
All manner of plants are here,
Too numerous to be counted.
To the west, bubbling springs and clear pools
Spread their restless waters,
Lotus and water chestnut blooming on their borders,

Huge rocks and white sand hidden in their depths,
Where live sacred turtles, dragons, and water lizards,
Terrapins and tortoises.
Northward rise dense forests and giant trees—
Medlar, cedar, and camphor,
Cinnamon, prickly ash, and anise tree,
Chinese cork, wild pear, red willow,
Hawthorn, chinaberry, jujube, and chestnut,
Mandarins and citrons, breathing forth their fragrance.
In their branches live apes, gibbons, and langurs,
Phoenixes, peacocks, and pheasants,
Flying lizards and lemurs.
Beneath their shade prowl white tigers and black panthers,
Leopards, lynxes, and jackals.[1]
The king of Ch'u orders his brave warriors
To seize these beasts with their bare hands,
While he mounts behind four piebald horses,
Riding in a carriage of carved jade.
From pliant staffs of whalebone
Stream banners studded with moon-bright pearls.
He grasps his stout lance forged by Kan Chiang.
At his left side hangs the painted bow of the Yellow Emperor;
On his right are strong arrows in a quiver of the Hsia kings.
A companion as wise as Yang-tzu of old stands by his side;
A driver as skilled as Hsien-a holds the reins.
Though the steeds are reined in to any easy pace,
They gain on the wily beasts;
The carriage wheels run down asses,
The steeds kick at onagers,
Spears pierce wild horses, axle points cut down wild mares,
As the hunters behind their powerful steeds shoot at fleeing jackasses.
Swiftly, relentlessly,
Like thunder they move, like the whirlwind they advance,
Streaming like comets, striking like lightning.
No shot leaves their bows in vain
But each must pierce the eye of the game,
Burrow in the breast, strike through the side,
And sever the cords of the heart,
Till the catch becomes a rain of beasts,
Covering the grass and filling the ground.
With this the king of Ch'u slackens his pace and gazes about,

1. Two lines, mentioning rhinoceroses and elephants and repeating the name of one of the
beasts above, have been omitted, as they appear to be a later addition.

Raising his head with lofty composure;
He looks toward the dark forest,
Observes the fierceness of his brave huntsmen
And the terror of the wild beasts,
Then spurs after the exhausted game, striking those that are spent,
Watching the aspect of every creature.
Next come the lovely maidens and fair princesses,
Robed in fine silk cloth
And trailing rich silks and crepes,
Girdled in sheer netting
And draped with scarves like mist,
Beneath which their skirts, gathered in close pleats,
Gently swirl and sway,
Falling in deep and pliant folds,
So long and full
That they must gather up the hems demurely.
With flying beads and dangling pendants,
They bend and sway in their carriages,
Their robes and scarves rustling softly,
Brushing the heads of the orchids below
Or fluttering against the feathered carriage tops,
Tangling in their kingfisher hairpins
Or twining about the jeweled carriage cords.
Lightly and nimbly they come
Like a vision of goddesses.
Together the groups set out to hunt in the fields of marsh orchids;
Scrambling through the thick grasses
And ascending the stout embankments of the river,
They surprise kingfishers
And shoot crow pheasants,
Fix fine cords
To their short arrows
To shoot the white geese
And the wild swans,
Bring down a pair of egrets
Or a black crane.
Tiring of these sports, they embark
To sail upon the clear lake,
And drift over the surface in their pelican-prowed boats.
They lift their cassia oars,
Spread kingfisher curtains,
And raise feathered canopies;
With nets they snare terrapins

And angle for purple mollusks;
They strike golden drums
And sound the wailing flutes,
As the songs of the boatmen
Echo across the water.
The lake insects are startled
By the waves of their wake,
As the bubbling springs gush forth,
A turmoil of water,
And the boulders in the depths grate together
With a dull, reverberating roar
Like the voice of thunder
Resounding a hundred miles.
To signal the huntsmen to rest from their labors,
The sacred drums are sounded
And beacon fires raised;
The carriages draw up in ranks,
The horsemen form in battalions,
And all take their places in proper order,
Range themselves once more in position.
Then the king of Ch'u ascends the Terrace of the Bright Clouds,
Where he rests in perfect repose,
Takes his leisure in perfect ease
And, flavoring his dishes with herbs and spices,
Sits down to feast.
The king of Ch'u is not like Your Highness,
Who counts it a pleasure to race all day,
Never descending from your carriage to rest,
Slashing at game and staining your carriage wheels with blood.
If I may speak from what I have seen,
The hunts of Ch'i cannot match those of Ch'u!' "

"With this the king of Ch'i fell silent and did not answer me."

"How can you speak in such error?" exclaimed Master No-such. "You have not considered a thousand miles too long a journey, but have been gracious enough to visit our state of Ch'i. On this occasion the king of Ch'i, calling out all the knights within his domain and providing them with a multitude of carriages and horsemen, has set forth to the hunt, hoping that by these efforts he might secure a plentiful catch and bring enjoyment to the guests at his court. How can you call it a mere boastful show? When he inquired whether you have such hunting lands in Ch'u, it was his wish to hear of the stalwart customs of your great kingdom and to listen to your discourses. Now, instead of praising the virtues of the king of Ch'u, you lavish your words on the glories of Yün-meng and describe to us in rich phrases the wanton pleasures and reckless extravagances that take place there. For your sake, I cannot help wishing you had not done this. Even if these entertainments are as you describe them, they hardly reflect to the credit of Ch'u. If they exist, for you to speak of them is only to spread abroad the fame of your ruler's faults; and if your reports are false, then you do but injure the trust we bear you. To expose the evils of one's ruler or to place trustworthiness in jeopardy—neither action can be approved. By speaking as you have, you must certainly invite contempt from the king of Ch'i and cause embarrassment to the state of Ch'u.

"As for Ch'i, it is bounded on the east by the vast ocean,
And on the south by the mountains of Lang-ya.
We may take our pleasure upon Mount Ch'eng
And shoot game on the slopes of Chih-fu;
Sail upon the Gulf of Po-hai
And roam the marsh of Meng-chu.
Northeast of us lies the land of the Su-shen,
And east of this we border the Valley of Boiling Water.
In autumn we hunt in the region of the Green Hills,
Sailing far away over the seas;
Our state could swallow eight or nine of your Yün-mengs
And they would never even tickle its throat.
As for the wonders and marvels you speak of,
The strange creatures of other regions,
The rare beasts and odd birds—
All manner of beings are gathered here in Ch'i
In such abundance within our borders
That I could not finish describing them,
Nor could the ancient sage Emperor Yü give them names
Or his minister Hsieh write them all down.
Yet, since the king of Ch'i is but a vassal of the emperor,
He does not consider it right to speak of the joys of travel
Or describe the magnificence of his parks and gardens.
Moreover, you are here as his guest,
And this is why he declined to reply to your words.
How could you think it was because he had no answer?"

Thereupon Lord Not-real broke into a smile and said, "The spokesman for Ch'u has spoken in error, while the case for Ch'i leaves much to be desired. When the emperor demands that the feudal lords bear their tribute to his court, it is not that he desires the goods and articles they bring, but that his vassals may thereby 'report on the administration of their offices';[2] and when

2. Reference to Mencius (see selection 8), chapter 1, part 2, section 4.

he causes mounds to be raised on the borders of states and their boundaries to be marked off, these are not for the purpose of defense, but so that the feudal lords may not trespass upon each other's lands. Now, although the king of Ch'i has been enfeoffed in the east to serve as a bastion to the imperial house, he is carrying on secret contacts with the Su-shen and jeopardizing his own state by crossing his borders and sailing over the sea to hunt in the Green Hills, actions which are a violation of his duties. Both of you gentlemen, instead of attempting in your discussions to make clear the duties of lord and subject and striving to rectify the behavior of the feudal lords, vainly dispute with each other over the joys of hunting and the size of parks, each attempting to outdo the other in descriptions of lavish expenditures, each striving for supremacy in wanton delights. This is no way to win fame and gain praise, but will only blacken the names of your rulers and bring ruin to yourselves. Moreover, what do the states of Ch'i and Ch'u possess, that they are worth speaking about? You gentlemen perhaps have never laid eyes upon true splendor. Have you not heard of the Shang-lin Park of the Son of Heaven?

"To the east of it lies Ts'ang-wu,
To the west the land of Hsi-chi;
On its south runs the Cinnabar River,
On its north, the Purple Deeps.
Within the park spring the Pa and Ch'an rivers,
And through it flow the Ching and Wei,
The Feng, the Hao, the Lao, and the Chüeh,
Twisting and turning their way
Through the reaches of the park;
Eight rivers, coursing onward,
Spreading in different directions, each with its own form.
North, south, east, and west
They race and tumble,
Pouring through the chasms of Pepper Hill,
Skirting the banks of the river islets,
Winding through the cinnamon forests
And across the broad meadows.
In wild confusion they swirl
Along the bases of the tall hills
And through the mouths of the narrow gorges;
Dashed upon boulders, maddened by winding escarpments,
They writhe in anger,
Leaping and curling upward,
Jostling and eddying in great swells
That surge and batter against each other;
Darting and twisting,

Foaming and tossing,
In a thundering chaos;
Arching into hills, billowing like clouds,
They dash to left and right,
Plunging and breaking in waves
That chatter over the shallows;
Crashing against the cliffs, pounding the embankments.
The waters pile up and reel back again,
Skipping across the rises, swooping into the hollows,
Rumbling and murmuring onward;
Deep and powerful,
Fierce and clamorous,
They froth and churn
Like the boiling waters of a caldron,
Casting spray from their crests, until,
After their wild race through the gorges,
Their distant journey from afar,
They subside into silence,
Rolling on in peace to their long destination,
Boundless and without end,
Gliding in soundless and solemn procession,
Shimmering and shining in the sun,
To flow through giant lakes of the east
Or spill into the ponds along their banks.
Here horned dragons and red hornless dragons,
Sturgeon and salamanders,
Carp, bream, gudgeon, and dace,
Cowfish, flounder, and sheatfish
Arch their backs and twitch their tails,
Spread their scales and flap their fins,
Diving among the deep crevices;
The waters are loud with fish and turtles,
A multitude of living things.
Here moon-bright pearls
Gleam on the river slopes,
While quartz, chrysoberyl,
And clear crystal in jumbled heaps
Glitter and sparkle,
Catching and throwing back a hundred colors
Where they lie tumbled on the river bottom.
Wild geese and swans, graylags, bustards,
Cranes and mallards,
Loons and spoonbills,

Teals and gadwalls,
Grebes, night herons, and cormorants
Flock and settle upon the waters,
Drifting lightly over the surface,
Buffeted by the wind,
Bobbing and dipping with the waves,
Sporting among the weedy banks,
Gobbling the reeds and duckweed,
Pecking at water chestnuts and lotuses.
Behind them rise the tall mountains,
Lofty crests lifted to the sky;
Clothed in dense forests of giant trees,
Jagged with peaks and crags;
The steep summits of the Nine Pikes,
The towering heights of the Southern Mountains,
Soar dizzily like a stack of cooking pots,
Precipitous and sheer.
Their sides are furrowed with ravines and valleys,
Narrow-mouthed clefts and open glens,
Through which rivulets dart and wind.
About their base, hills and islands
Raise their tall heads;
Ragged knolls and hillocks
Rise and fall,
Twisting and twining
Like the coiled bodies of reptiles;
While from their folds the mountain streams leap and tumble,
Spilling out upon the level plains.
There they flow a thousand miles along smooth beds,
Their banks lined with dikes
Blanketed with green orchids
And hidden beneath selinea,
Mingled with snakemouth
And magnolias;
Planted with yucca,
Sedge of purple dye,
Bittersweet, gentians, and orchis,
Blue flag and crow-fans,
Ginger and turmeric,
Monkshood, wolfsbane,
Nightshade, basil,
Mint, ramie, and blue artemisia,
Spreading across the wide swamps,

Rambling over the broad plains,
A vast and unbroken mass of flowers,
Nodding before the wind;
Breathing forth their fragrance,
Pungent and sweet,
A hundred perfumes
Wafted abroad
Upon the scented air.
Gazing about the expanse of the park
At the abundance and variety of its creatures,
One's eyes are dizzied and enraptured
By the boundless horizons,
The borderless vistas.
The sun rises from the eastern ponds
And sets among the slopes of the west;
In the southern part of the park,
Where grasses grow in the dead of winter
And the waters leap, unbound by ice,
Live zebras, yaks, tapirs, and black oxen,
Water buffalo, elk, and antelope,
'Red-crowns' and 'round-heads,'
Aurochs, elephants, and rhinoceroses.
In the north, where in the midst of summer
The ground is cracked and blotched with ice
And one may walk the frozen streams or wade the rivulets,
Roam unicorns and boars,
Wild asses and camels,
Onagers and mares,
Swift stallions, donkeys, and mules.
Here the country palaces and imperial retreats
Cover the hills and span the valleys,
Verandahs surrounding their four sides;
With storied chambers and winding porticos,
Painted rafters and jade-studded corbels,
Interlacing paths for the royal palanquin,
And arcaded walks stretching such distances
That their length cannot be traversed in a single day.
Here the peaks have been leveled for mountain halls,
Terraces raised, story upon story,
And chambers built in the deep grottoes.
Peering down into the caves, one cannot spy their end;
Gazing up at the rafters, one seems to see them brush the heavens;
So lofty are the palaces that comets stream through their portals

And rainbows twine about their balustrades.
Green dragons slither from the eastern pavilion;
Elephant-carved carriages prance from the pure hall of the west,
Bringing immortals to dine in the peaceful towers
And bands of fairies to sun themselves beneath the southern eaves.[3]
Here sweet fountains bubble from clear chambers,
Racing in rivulets through the gardens,
Great stones lining their courses;
Plunging through caves and grottoes,
Past steep and ragged pinnacles,
Horned and pitted as though carved by hand,
Where garnets, green jade,
And coral abound;
Agate and marble,
Dappled and lined;
Rose quartz of variegated hue,
Spotted among the cliffs;
Rock crystal, opals,
And finest jade.
Here grow citrons with their ripe fruit in summer,
Tangerines, bitter oranges and limes,
Loquats, persimmons,
Wild pears, tamarinds,
Jujubes, arbutus,
Cherries and grapes,
Almonds, damsons,
Mountain plums and litchis,
Shading the quarters of the palace ladies,
Ranged in the northern gardens,
Stretching over the slopes and hillocks
And down into the flat plains;
Lifting leaves of kingfisher hue,
Their purple stems swaying;
Opening their crimson flowers,
Clusters of vermilion blossoms,
A wilderness of trembling flames
Lighting up the broad meadow.
Here crab-apple, chestnut and willow,
Birch, maple, sycamore and boxwood,
Pomegranate, date palm,

3. In much the same way as the European aristocrats delighted in picturing themselves as
rustic shepherds and shepherdesses, their Chinese counterparts loved to imagine that they were
carefree immortals riding about on dragons and sipping dew in airy mountain retreats.

Betel nut and palmetto,
Sandalwood, magnolia,
Cedar and cypress
Rise a thousand feet,
Their trunks several arm-lengths around,
Stretching forth flowers and branches,
Rich fruit and luxuriant leaves,
Clustered in dense copses,
Their limbs entwined,
Their foliage a thick curtain
Over stiff and bending trunks,
Their branches sweeping to the ground
Amidst a shower of falling petals.
They tremble and sigh
As they sway with the wind,
Creaking and moaning in the breeze
Like the tinkle of chimes
Or the wail of flageolets.
High and low they grow,
Screening the quarters of the palace ladies;
A mass of sylvan darkness,
Blanketing the mountains and edging the valleys,
Ascending the slopes and dipping into the hollows,
Overspreading the horizon,
Outdistancing the eye.
Here black apes and white she-apes,
Drills, baboons, and flying squirrels,
Lemurs and langurs,
Macaques and gibbons
Dwell among the trees,
Uttering long wails and doleful cries
As they leap nimbly to and fro,
Sporting among the limbs
And clambering haughtily to the tree-tops.
Off they chase across bridgeless streams
And spring into the depths of a new grove,
Clutching the low-swinging branches,
Hurtling across the open spaces,
Racing and tumbling pell-mell,
Until they scatter from sight in the distance.
Such are the scenes of the imperial park,
A hundred, a thousand settings

To visit in the pursuit of pleasure;
Palaces, inns, villas, and lodges,
Each with its kitchens and pantries,
Its chambers of beautiful women
And staffs of officials.
Here, in late fall and early winter,
The Son of Heaven stakes his palisades and holds his hunts,
Mounted in a carriage of carved ivory
Drawn by six jade-spangled horses, sleek as dragons.
Rainbow pennants stream before him;
Cloud banners trail in the wind.
In the vanguard ride the hide-covered carriages;
Behind, the carriages of his attendants.
A coachman as clever as Sun Shu grasps the reins;
A warrior as brave as Lord Wei stands beside him.
His attendants fan out on all sides
As they move into the palisade.
They sound the somber drums
And send the hunters to their posts;
They corner the quarry among the rivers
And spy them from the high hills.
Then the carriages and horsemen thunder forth
Startling the heavens, shaking the earth;
Vanguard and rear dash in different directions,
Scattering after the prey.
On they race in droves,
Rounding the hills, streaming across the lowlands,
Like enveloping clouds or drenching rain.
Leopards and panthers they take alive;
They strike down jackals and wolves.
With their hands they seize the black and tawny bears,
And with their feet they down the wild sheep.
Wearing pheasant-tailed caps
And breeches of white tiger skin
Under patterned tunics,
They sit astride their wild horses;
They clamber up the steep slopes of the Three Pikes
And descend again to the river shoals,
Galloping over the hillsides and the narrow passes,
Through the valleys and across the rivers.
They fell the 'dragon sparrows'
And sport with the *chieh-ch'ih,*

Strike the *hsia-ko*[4]
And with short spears stab the little bears,
Snare the fabulous *yao-niao* horses
And shoot down the great boars.
No arrow strikes the prey
Without piercing a neck or shattering a skull;
No bow is discharged in vain,
But to the sound of each twang some beast must fall.
Then the imperial carriage signals to slacken pace
While the emperor wheels this way and that,
Gazing afar at the progress of the hunting bands,
Noting the disposition of their leaders.
At a sign, the Son of Heaven and his men resume their pace,
Swooping off again across the distant plains.
They bear down upon the soaring birds;
Their carriage wheels crush the wily beasts.
Their axles strike the white deer;
Deftly they snatch the fleeting hares;
Swifter than a flash
Of scarlet lightning,
They pursue strange creatures
Beyond the borders of heaven.
To bows like the famous Fan-jo
They fit their white-feathered arrows,
To shoot the fleeing goblin-birds
And strike down the griffins.
For their mark they choose the fattest game
And name their prey before they shoot.
No sooner has an arrow left the string
Than the quarry topples to the ground.
Again the signal is raised and they soar aloft,
Sweeping upward upon the gale,
Rising with the whirlwind,
Borne upon the void,
The companions of gods,
To trample upon the black crane
And scatter the flocks of giant pheasants,
Swoop down upon the peacocks
And the golden roc,
Drive aside the five-colored *yi* bird
And down the phoenixes,

4. These appear to be mythical beasts. From this point on, Ssu-ma Hsiang-ju's description
of the hunt becomes more and more fanciful.

Snatch the storks of heaven
And the birds of darkness,
Until, exhausting the paths of the sky,
They wheel their carriages and return.
Roaming as the spirit moves them,
Descending to earth in a far corner of the north,
Swift and straight is their course
As they hasten home again.
Then the emperor ascends the Stone Gate
And visits the Great Peak Tower,
Stops at the Magpie Turret
And gazes afar from the Dew Cold Observatory,
Descends to the Wild Plum Palace
And takes his ease in the Palace of Righteous Spring;
To the west he hastens to the Hsüan-ch'ü Palace
And poles in a pelican boat over Ox Head Lake.
He climbs the Dragon Terrace
And rests in the Tower of the Lithe Willows,
Weighing the effort and skill of his attendants
And calculating the catch made by his huntsmen.
He examines the beasts struck down by the carriages,
Those trampled beneath the feet of the horsemen
And trod upon by the beaters;
Those which, from sheer exhaustion
Or the pangs of overwhelming terror,
Fell dead without a single wound,
Where they lie, heaped in confusion,
Tumbled in the gullies and filling the hollows,
Covering the plains and strewn about the swamps.
Then, wearied of the chase,
He orders wine brought forth on the Terrace of Azure Heaven
And music for the still and spacious halls.
His courtiers, sounding the massive bells
That swing from the giant bell rack,
Raising the pennants of kingfisher feathers,
And setting up the drum of sacred lizard skin,
Present for his pleasure the dances of Yao [5]
And the songs of the ancient Emperor Ko;
A thousand voices intone,
Ten thousand join in harmony,
As the mountains and hills rock with echoes

---

5. A mythical emperor.

And the valley waters quiver to the sound.
The dances of Pa-yü, of Sung and Ts'ai,
The Yü-che song of Huai-nan,[6]
The airs of Tien and Wen-ch'eng,
One after another in groups they perform,
Sounding in succession the gongs and drums
Whose shrill clash and dull booming
Pierce the heart and startle the ear.
The tunes Ching, Wu, Cheng, and Wei,
The Shao, Huo, Wu, and Hsiang music,
And amorous and carefree ditties
Mingle with the songs of Yen and Ying,
'Onward Ch'u!' and 'The Gripping Wind.'
Then come actors, musicians, and trained dwarfs,
And singing girls from the land of Ti-ti,
To delight the ear and eye
And bring mirth to the mind;
On all sides a torrent of gorgeous sounds,
A pageant of enchanting colors.
Here are maidens to match
The goddesses Blue Lute and Fu-fei:
Creatures of matchless beauty,
Seductive and fair,
With painted faces and carved hairpins,
Fragile and full of grace,
Lithe and supple,
Of delicate feature and form,
Trailing cloaks of sheerest silk
And long robes that seem as though carved and painted,
Swirling and fluttering about them
Like magic garments;
With them wafts a cloud of scent,
A delicious perfume;
White teeth sparkle
In engaging smiles,
Eyebrows arch delicately,
Eyes cast darting glances,
Until their beauty has seized the soul of the beholder
And his heart in joy hastens to their side.

"But then, when the wine has flowed freely and the merriment is at its height, the Son of Heaven becomes lost in contemplation, like one whose

6. These are all various countries or regions of the Chinese empire.

spirit has wandered, and he cries, 'Alas! What is this but a wasteful extravagance? Now that I have found a moment of leisure from the affairs of state, I thought it a shame to cast away the days in idleness and so, in this autumn season, when heaven itself slays life, I have joined in its slaughter and come to this hunting park to take my ease. And yet I fear that those who follow me in ages to come may grow infatuated with these sports, until they lose themselves in the pursuit of pleasure and forget to return again to their duties. Surely this is no way for one who has inherited the throne to carry on the great task of his forebears and insure the rule of our imperial house!'

"Then he dismisses the revelers, sends away the huntsmen, and instructs his ministers, saying, 'If there are lands here in these suburbs that can be opened for cultivation, let them all be turned into farms in order that my people may receive aid and benefit thereby. Tear down the walls and fill up the moats, that the common folk may come and profit from these hills and lowlands! Stock the lakes with fish and do not prohibit men from taking them! Empty the palaces and towers, and let them no longer be staffed! Open the storehouses and granaries to succor the poor and starving and help those who are in want; pity the widower and widow, protect the orphans and those without families! I would broadcast the name of virtue and lessen punishments and fines; alter the measurements and statutes, change the color of the vestments, reform the calendar and, with all men under heaven, make a new beginning!'

"Then, selecting an auspicious day and fasting in preparation,
He dons his court robes
And mounts the carriage of state,
With its flowery pennants flying
And its jade bells ringing.
He sports now in the Park of the Six Arts,
Races upon the Road of Benevolence and Righteousness,
And scans the Forest of the *Spring and Autumn Annals*.[7]
His archery now is to the stately measures of 'The Fox Head'
And 'The Beast of Virtue';[8]
His prey is the Dance of the Black Cranes,
Performed with ceremonial shield and battle axe.
Casting the heavenly Cloud Net,[9]
He snares the songs of the *Classic of Odes*,

7. These three lines list skills (etiquette, music, archery, charioteering, writing, and mathematics), virtues, and an important text that should be mastered by the Confucian gentleman.

8. Musical compositions supposed to have been played at the archery contests of the king and the feudal lords respectively in ancient times.

9. The name of a constellation.

Sighs over 'The Felling of the Sandalwood' [10]
And delights in the ruler who 'shares his joy with all.' [11]
He mends his deportment in the garden of *Rites*
And wanders in the orchard of the *Classic of Documents*.
He spreads the teachings of the *Classic of Changes*,
Sets free the strange beasts penned in his park,
Ascends the Bright Hall,
And seats himself in the Temple of the Ancestors. [12]

"Then may his ministers freely present before him their proposals for the betterment of the empire, and within the four seas there is no one who does not share in the 'spoils' of this new hunt. [13] Then is the empire filled with great joy; all men turn their faces toward the wind of imperial virtue and harken to its sound. As though borne upon a stream, they are transformed to goodness; with shouts of gladness they set forth upon the Way and journey to righteousness, so that harsh punishments are set aside and no longer used. Finer is this ruler's virtue than that of the Three Sages [14] of antiquity, more plenteous his merits than those of the Five Emperors. [15] When a ruler has achieved such virtue, then may he enjoy himself at the hunt without incurring blame. But to gallop from morn to night in sunshine or rain, exhausting the spirit and tiring the body, wearing out the carriages and horses, draining the energies of the huntsmen and squandering the resources of the treasury; to think only of one's own pleasure before sufficient benefits have been bestowed upon others; to ignore the common people and neglect the government of the nation, merely because one is greedy for a catch of pheasants and hares—this no truly benevolent ruler would do! Thus, from what I can see, the kings of Ch'i and Ch'u merit only pity. Though their domains are no more than a thousand tricents square, their hunting parks occupy nine tenths of the area, so that the land cannot be cleared and the people have no space to grow food. When one who is no more than a feudal prince attempts to indulge in extravagances fit only for the supreme ruler, then I fear it is the common people who will suffer in the end!"

10. A song from "Airs from the State of Wei," in the *Classic of Odes* (see selection 22), said to express censure of a greedy ruler who fails to make use of wise men.

11. From the song "Sang-hu," "Lesser Odes," in the *Classic of Odes*.

12. Two of the most important imperial structures; the former was used for sacrifices to the highest deity and the latter for sacrifices to the royal ancestors.

13. In the passage above the poet uses the hunting metaphor to describe the ideal ruler: a student of the Classics and the arts, amusing himself with the stately dances and songs of antiquity and thinking always of the welfare of his people instead of indulging in extravagant pleasures. Thus, after having dazzled the emperor with his rhetoric, the poet delivers his "message."

14. The mythical heroes Yao, Shun, and Yü.

15. The mythical rulers T'ai Hao, Yen Ti, Huang Ti, Shao Hao, and Chuan Hsü.

At these words Sir Fantasy and Master No-such abruptly changed countenance and looked uneasily about, quite at a loss for words. Then, backing off and rising from their places, they replied, "We are uncouth and ignorant men who do not know when to hold our tongues. Fortunately today we have received your instruction, and we shall do our best to abide by it."

Translated by Burton Watson

152
Seven Stimuli

Mei Ch'eng (d. 140 B.C.E.)

The Crown Prince of Ch'u having fallen ill, a guest from Wu[1] went to ask after his health.

"I have heard," said the guest, "of Your Highness' discomfort, and was wondering whether you might have improved somewhat?"

"I am exhausted," said the Prince. "Thank you ever so much for your concern." The guest, accordingly, seized this opportunity to offer his advice:

> "Presently,
>> The kingdom is at peace;
>> everywhere, there is harmony.
> And you are,
>> at this moment, in the prime of your life.
> Yet, I should imagine that
>> you have long been besotted with pleasures,
>> day and night indulging yourself without limit.
>> An irruption of noxious humors
>> has balled up inside of you.
>> Distracted you are and listless;
>> distraught and crapulous,
>> fearful and timorous,

This prose-poem occupies an important place in the early development of the *fu* ("rhapsody" or "rhymeprose"), which established itself as a genre of lush verbiage and elaborate description. The rhapsody enabled Chinese writers to expand the scope of their literary creativity far beyond the limits of the traditional short, lyrical verse and usually utilitarian prose. As such, it is a key genre in the history of imaginative belles-lettres in China. Still, like virtually all of the other major *fu*, "Seven Stimuli" makes a perfunctory nod toward didacticism at the end to justify its existence in the highly moralistic Confucianism of its day.

1. The author himself was from the Wu (Ngwa) area (Huai-yin).

> you lie in bed but cannot sleep.
> Debilitated and dull of ear,
> you detest hearing the sound of another's voice.
> Your vitality dissipated,
> a hundred illnesses befall you at the same time;
> your senses confused,
> joy and anger become imbalanced.
> If you persist much longer this way,
> your life itself may be imperiled.

Could it be, Crown Prince, that this is your plight?"

"Thank you ever so much for your concern," said the Prince. "Relying on my father's royal grace, I do, from time to time, enjoy such pleasures, but not to the degree which you have described."

> "Nowadays,"
>   said the guest,
>   "The sons of good families
>   are sure
>   to hide away
>   in the inner recesses of palaces.
>   Within, they have governesses to look after them,
>   without, they have preceptors to instruct them;
>   though they wish to make friends, they have not the
>   wherewithal.
> Their food and drink
>   is smooth, savory, sweet, and crisp;
>   their meat is fat, their wine is thick.
> Their clothing
>   is endlessly varied, light but warm;
>   they swelter and suffocate in it as in the heat of summer.
>   Even something
>   as durable as metal or stone,
>   would soon
>   fuse and dissolve
>   in the face of such
>   heat:
> need
>   I say
>   what becomes of flesh
>   and bone?
> Therefore, it is said:
>   he who

gives free rein
> to his sensual desires
and dissipates
> himself in physical pleasures
will damage
> the equilibrium of his circulatory system.

What's more,
> riding a chariot or carriage no matter where one goes
is called
> a 'paralytic portent.'
> Cave-like winter rooms and airy summer palaces
are called,
> likewise, 'aguish agents.'
> Pearly teeth and moth-eyebrows
are called
> 'hatchets to trim the tree of life.'
> Things sweet, crisp, oily, and syrupy
are called,
> likewise, 'rot-gut reagents.'

Now
> you, Crown Prince,
>> have a pallid, pasty complexion.
>> Your arms and legs move sluggishly,
>> your muscles and bones have lost tone and fiber,
>> your blood pressure is much too high,
>> your hands and feet are infirm.
>> Yüeh lasses wait upon you in front,
>> Ch'i maidens attend you behind;
>> you are forever engaged in dalliance or banqueting.
You dissipate yourself
> in
>> hidden rooms and private
>>> parlors,
All this
> is willingly to dine on poison;
playing
> with the claws and teeth
>> of savage
>>> beasts.
But the effects
> of your past activities
>> are very deep-seated,

and you have postponed,
>> for such a long time,
>>> the abandonment of these ways.
Thus, though one should command
>> Pien-ch'üeh[2] to treat you internally
>> and Shaman[3] Hsien to treat you externally,
>> what good would it do?

Now,
>> an illness such as Your
>>>> Excellency's
surely calls for
>> the superior men of our age—
>> men of broad learning and strong memory.
>> They should, when occasion allows, offer their opinions,
>> thus changing your habits and altering your ideas.
>> They should never leave your side,
>> and should serve as your assistants.
>> These pleasures in which you wallow,
>> the intemperance which holds your mind,
>> the apathy which stifles your will—
>> how could they then
>>>> arise?"

"Very well," said the Crown Prince. "When I am over my illness, I shall carry out these instructions of yours."

"But your illness," said the guest, "has now reached the point that neither plant nor mineral medicines, acupuncture nor cauterization can cure you. Only through the exposition of essential apothegms and marvelous maxims may you be rid of it. Wouldn't you like to hear them?"

"Yes," said the Crown Prince, "I am desirous of hearing your exposition."

The guest spake:

>> "The paulownia of Dragon Gate Mountain
> reaches
>>> a height of one hundred feet
>>>> before it branches.
>> Its center
>>> has a tightly packed mass
>>>> of concentric rings;

2. A famous physician of old.
3. Recent research has shown that it would be more accurate to identify him as a magus.

                    its roots
                            spread out
                                    in all directions.
            Above it,
                            there are thousand-meter peaks;
            below,
                            it looks over hundred-fathom canyons.
                            The backwash from the rising current
                            swashes and swirls against it.
            Its roots
                            are half-dead, half-alive.

In winter,
sleet and snow driven by fierce winds
                            assail
                                            it;
in summer,
    resounding peals of thunder and lightning
                            shake
                                            it.
Mornings,
                    the yellow oriole and the bulbul sing
                                            there;
evenings,
                    the mateless hen and birds which have gone astray roost
                                            there.

                    The solitary snow-goose calls out at daybreak
                                            above it;
                    the heath-cock
                            sadly chirps as it flutters about
                                    beneath it.

            Then,
                    with autumn behind and winter coming on,
send
    the Lutemaster Chih to chop it down and make it into a lute.
    Filaments from the cocoons of wild silkworms are used for its strings,
    the buckle of an orphan child is used as an ornamental inlay,
    the pearl eardrops of the widowed mother of nine are used for its frets.
            Command
                    Master T'ang to play on it 'All Things Pleaseth,'
                    Po-ya[4]
                            to accompany him with a song.

4. A distinguished lutanist of ancient times.

The words of the song are:
  'The bearded spikes of the wheat do ripen, the pheasant flies up in the
    morn—
  heading for a desolate valley, it sets its back to the withered locust tree;
  it skirts along deserted lands, peers down upon twisting mountain
    streams.'

Hearing this song, flying birds
  fold their wings—they cannot go on;
    hearing this song, wild beasts
  droop their ears—they can proceed no farther;
    hearing this song, daddy longlegs, caterpillars, crickets
      and ants
  prop their proboscises—they cannot advance.

This, indeed, is the most lugubrious music in the world! Could you force
yourself to rise and listen to it?"

"I am still ill," replied the Crown Prince, "and am, as yet, unable to
get up."

The guest spake:

"A fatty stomach-cut of veal
with bamboo shoots and rush stems to go with it;
a blended mixture of plump dog
and edible lichens for a potage.
Whether rice from Miao Mountain in Ch'u
or wild rice of the zizania grass,
it is so sticky it can be patted into balls,
so slippery it dissolves upon touching your tongue.
Then,
  call upon
    Yi Yin to sauté and simmer,
    Yi-ya to season and spice.[5]
    There will be well-stewed bear's paw
    prepared with a finely flavored sauce.
    You shall have thinly sliced sections of roast loin
    and fresh strips of minced carp,
    perilla plucked in autumn when it is yellow,
    vegetables succulent from the white dews of late summer.
    This will be followed by wine made fragrant with orchid
      petals
    which you may pour for a mouthwash.

5. These lines mention two famous cooks from the past.

> At last, you will dine on hen pheasant
> and fetus of domesticated panther.
> Whether you eat but little or sup a lot,
> it will digest as quickly as hot water poured upon snow.

These, indeed, are the most delectable dishes in the world! Could you force yourself to rise and partake of them?"

"I am still ill," replied the Crown Prince, "and am, as yet, unable to get up."

The guest spake:

> "You shall have stallions from Chung and Tai,[6]
> chosen at the prime age, they will pull your chariot.
> From the front, they seem like Flying Duck coursers,
> behind, they appear to be mythical mules.
> Panic-grass and wheat their provender,
> they are restless within and chafe without.
> They are harnessed with strong reins
> and stick to the good roads.

Thereupon,
> Po-le[7] examines the steeds front to back,
> Wang Liang and Tsao-fu[8]
> serve as the charioteers,
> Ch'in Ch'üeh[9] and Lou Chi[10]
> ride on the right as guards.

These two
> can stop runaway
> horses,
> can raise overturned
> chariots.

Therefore,
> you could make
> a bet
> of one thousand pounds
> on a race
> of a thousand miles.

These, indeed, are the finest steeds in the world! Can you force yourself to rise and ride in the chariot they pull?"

6. Two small states noted for producing excellent horses.
7. A celebrated horse-trainer of antiquity.
8. Two famous charioteers.
9. A fleet warrior in ancient times.
10. A great jumper.

"I am still ill," replied the Crown Prince, "and am, as yet, unable to get up."

The guest spake:

"Or you could mount
          the Ching-yi observation tower,
          gaze south to Thorn Mountain,
          gaze north across the Ju River.
          On the left, the Yangtze, on the right, Tung-t'ing Lake—
          the pleasures such a view affords are unexcelled.

Thereupon,
      you should call
          elocutionists with broad learning
          to expound on the origins of the rivers and mountains
          and to name all of the grasses and trees,
          finding analogies and making allusions,
          categorizing and classifying.
          Let your eye roam and your gaze drift,

then come down from the tower and have wine prepared
          in
              Heart's Pleasure Palace,
              with its corridors leading in all four directions,
              its terraced walls and storied structures,
              all decorated with variegated colors;
              with its crisscross carriageways,
              its winding lakes and pools.
              There are dabchicks and egrets,
              precious peacocks and sylvan swans,
              birds of paradise and flamingoes—
              a riot of bluish-green crowns and purple necks.
              Hens and cocks, stipple-crested and speckle-breasted,
              warble harmoniously in flocks.
              Sunfish jump and leap,
              fins flapping and scales skittering.
              Beside still waters grow scizanthus and smartweed,
              creeping grasses and aromatic licorice,
              supple mulberries and riverside tamarisks—
              a profusion of silken-white leaves and purple stems.
              The ginkgo and the camphor
              have branches which reach to the very heavens;
              firmiana and coir palm
              make forests which stretch as far as the eye can see.
              An almost palpable assembly of fragrant aromas

mingles with the breezes which come from all directions.
The trees sway lazily with the wind,
their leaves showing, by turns, light bottoms and dark
    tops.
As we take our places on the banquet mats, let wine flow
    freely
and lilting strains bring joy to our hearts!
Let Ching Ch'un[11] assist with the wine,
Tu Lien[12] be in charge of the music,
Let all sorts of gustful flavors be spread before us,
an assortment of cooked meats, fish, and cereals be
    prepared.
Refined hues will delight our eyes,
lilting strains give pleasure to our ears.

Thereafter,
    the orchestra strikes up
        the dance tune
            for the Whirling Ch'u,[13]
    wafts aloft
        the dazzling songs
            of Cheng and Wei.[14]
Send for
    Hsi-shih
        Cheng Shu,
          Yang Wen,
          Tuan-kan,
    Wu-wa
        Lü-chü
        Fu Yü,[15]
        such handsome lads and lovely ladies as these.
In their kaleidoscopic skirts and trailing swallow-tails,
they cast flirtatious glances which show their hearts have
    already given in.
    The luster of their eyes flows in ripples,
        they are imbued with the scent of turmeric;
        they are as though covered with stardust,
        and have anointed themselves with orchid pomade.

11. Mentioned in the *Mencius* (see selection 8).
12. A famous lutanist.
13. A regional style of dance.
14. Two kingdoms noted for their talented female singers.
15. All seven names refer to legendary beauties or attractive men.

Having changed into something comfortable,
they come to wait on you.
These, indeed, are the world's most
luxurious, extravagant,
and sumptuous delights!

Can you force yourself to rise and enjoy them?"
"I am still ill," said the Crown Prince, "and am, as yet, unable to get up."

The guest spake:

"For you, Crown Prince,
I should like
to train
prancing piebald horses,
harness them
to a chariot with streamers flying from the hubs,
or have you ride
in a fine carriage and four.
In your right hand
are sharp-pointed arrows from
Emperor Hou's [16] quiver,
in your left hand,
the decorated bow known as
'Crow Call.'
You wend your way through
the Dream-cloud Forest,
make a quick circuit around
moors where orchids grow,
slow your pace when you come to
the Yangtze's banks.

Bending the sedge as you pass,
you head into the soothing breezes;
drunk on the sunny air,
you revel in the ardor of spring.
You chase down crafty beasts,
gather in fleet-winged fowl.
Then,
you give full play
to the ability of your dogs and horses.
Weary
are the legs of the wild animals,

16. Great Yü, queller of the flood.

as full scope is given
    to the knowledge and skill
        of the guides and charioteers.
        They strike terror in the tiger and leopard,
        cause birds of prey to cower in fright.
    The bells on the bits of the pursuing horses tinkle,
    causing fish to leap in nooks along the river's edge.
    They trod upon roe and rabbit,
    trample over elk and deer.
    Sweat dripping, froth dropping,
    the quarry succumbs to the relentless pressure.
    Those which die without even being
        wounded
are quite
    enough to fill the carts in the
        rear.

This is the grandest sort of martial hunt. Could you force yourself to rise and join the chase?"

"I am ill," said the Crown Prince, "and am, as yet, unable to get up."

But this time a sunny sparkle appeared in the space between his brows and gradually spread till it almost covered his entire face. The guest saw that the Crown Prince had a happy look and so pressed forward:

"The fire in the dark of night lights the skies,
the army-carts trundle thunderously;
banners and pennants flutter aloft,
an imposing array of feathers and fur.
Galloping, racing, they contend for the lead;
caught in their zest for the hunt, each strives to be first.
Vast stretches are scorched to intercept the game;
as one gazes across it,
    the land stands out in relief.
Immaculate, intact sacrificial animals
are presented at the gates of the feudal princes."

"Excellent!" exclaimed the Crown Prince. "I'd like to hear more."

"I'm not finished yet," said the guest.
    "Then,

in dense forests and deep marshes,
'neath a murky layer of mists and clouds—
aurochs and tigers sally forth together.
But the gladiators are ferocious—
bodies bared to the waist, they grapple with the beasts.

Naked swords gleam and glitter,
spears and lances cross in a tangle.
The game is collected and achievements noted,
rewards of gold and silk are presented.
Sedge is pressed down and turmeric spread over it
as a mat to be used by the Breeder for State Sacrifices.
There are excellent wines and delectable dishes,
savory meats barbecued and roasted,
to entertain the honored guests.
Brimming beakers are raised together,
pledges rouse the heart and excite the ear.
Sincere and honorable, they have no regrets;
whether in consent or refusal, they are decisive.
The cast of genuine trust on their faces
is embodied in the music of metal bells and stone
          chimes.
Loudly they sing, clearly they shout:
'Long live the Crown Prince!' and never weary of it.

This, Crown Prince, is what you really delight in! Can you force yourself
to rise and join us?"

"I should very much like to take part," said the Crown Prince. "It is just
that I am afraid I would be a great burden to the high officials." But it looked
as though he were about to get up.

The guest spake:

"On the fifteenth of the eighth month, together with the nobles and your
aquaintances and brothers who come from afar, we shall go to view the tidal
bore[17] at Winding River in Kuang-ling. When we first get there, we won't be
able to see the shape of the tidal flood itself. But simply viewing the force of
the water which precedes it is startling enough to terrify the beholder.

Viewing
          the way it
                    o'erleaps
                              itself,
          the way it
                    plucks itself
                              up,
          the way it
                    flaunts its
                              turbulence,

17. A rare phenomenon that occurs in certain rivers where a wall of water moves inland at
times of high tide (see selection 217).

the way it
　　whirls and
　　　　swirls,
　　the way it
　　　　washes and
　　　　　　swishes,
though one have
　　　a clear impression in his mind of what it is and be gifted
　　with words,
he still could not describe in detail its intrinsic quality.
　　　　Blurred—vague—
　　　　frightful—terrifying—
　　　　a confused rumble;
　　　　hazy—fuzzy—
　　　　swelling—cresting—
　　　　vast and extensive—
　　　　o'erstepping into the boundless.

　　The beholder fixes his mind
　　　　　on South Mountain,
　　from there, gazes all the way
　　　　　to the Eastern Sea;
　　The waters conjoin
　　　　　with the azure sky,
　　imagination is exhausted in trying to distinguish
　　　　　where the horizon ends.

　　After scanning this limitlessness,
　　turn your attention to Aurora's bed.

　　Rushing waves
　　　　borne by the counter-current
　　　　　come bearing down—
one hardly knows
　　　where they will halt.
　　Or perhaps,
　　　　in a tumultuous tangle,
　　　　　the waves break.
　　Suddenly,
　　　　resolved, they go off,
　　　　　never to return.
　　As the water approaches
　　　　Crimson Creek on the southern bank
　　　　　and then flows into the distance,

inside,
one feels empty, troubled,
and rather enervated.
From evening,
when the tide recedes
until it rises again in the
morning,
in his mind's eye,
he retains an impression of it
without even trying.
And then,
having experienced this catharsis of the spirit
and purgation of his internal organs,
his hands are laved, his feet are bathed,
his hair shampooed, his teeth brushed.
He renounces indolence, relinquishes sloth,
discards impurity, divests filth,
sunders suspicion, dispatches doubt,
opens ear, illumines eye.

At the time of the bore,
even though
one's illness be chronic, his infirmity protracted,
be he
hunchbacked, he would straighten himself, crippled, he
would rise and walk,
blind, his eyes would open, deaf, his ears would hear,
so as to behold this
spectacle.
This is all the more true of these who merely
have traces of melancholy and trivial ennui,
suffer from crapulence or oenomania
and the like!
Therefore, I say that
relief from stupor and deliverance from torpor
are not even worthy of
mention."

"Splendid," exclaimed the Crown Prince. "But just what is the essence of this bore?"

"There are no records in the ancient books," the guest replied, "but I have heard from my teacher that there are three aspects wherein it seems almost as though it were divine:

Its urgent

thunder can be heard hundreds of furlongs away;
the river's waters flow in reverse,
the ocean's waters go upstream with the tide;
the mountains exhale and inhale vapors
all day and all night without cease.

Welling and swelling, the tidal race picks up speed,
its waves surge

and its billows rise.

At the very beginning,

it is a cascading

torrent,

like

the downward swoop

of white egrets.

After it has progressed

a short while,

it becomes a vast expanse of dazzling whiteness,

like

a silk-white chariot drawn by white horses,

curtains and canopy unfurled.

The bore's

waves surge

in nebulous confusion,

tumultu-

ous

as though

the three regiments were

plunging into preparedness.

It

spreads out to the sides
and suddenly rears

up,

airily and graceful-

ly

as

the light chariot

of a commander marshalling his troops.

The bore is harnessed to six flood-dragons,
and follows close upon Great White, the god of the river.

It is high and mighty, whether resting or racing,
continuous and unbroken from front to back.
The waves are enormous, towering,
consecutive and recurring—
jos-jostling, ca-capering.
Row after row of stout bulwarks and ramparts,
multitudinous
     as the ranks of an army.
with the stentorian and cacophonous roar,
they surge uncurbed across the breadths;
the fount of this flood is not to be stayed!

Observing both banks of the river,
we see there a
     convulsive, boiling, brooding, seething,
     troublous, roiling, jolting, heaving;
     it smashes upward, flings boulders below.
There is, about it, something which resembles
     a valiant, mighty warrior
     bursting with rage
          and completely undaunted.
It tramples revetments, bursts through ferry-crossings,
inundates inlets and courses coves,
then leaps its banks, spills over its dikes.

     He who encounters it perishes;
     that which blocks it is destroyed.

The bore has its beginning
     along the shore of
          Surrounding Site.
     Diverted by foothills, dividing in valleys,
     it swirls past Green Splint,
     is muzzled at Sandalwood Signpost.
It slackens its pace
     at sacred-to-the-son Wu Tzu-hsü [18] Mountain,
marches on past
     mother of Tzu-hsü Arena.
        It shoots beyond Red Bank,
        Sweeps by Mulberry Brushwood.

It runs amok
     like stalking thunder.

18. The bore was considered to be a manifestation of Wu Tzu-hsü's spirit, which was outraged at his dead body having been disrespectfully thrown into the river in a leather sack (see selection 182).

Truly aroused is its warlike energy,
as though it were moved with anger!
Rumble, rumble, grumble, grumble,
it has the appearance of galloping horses;
grumble, grumble, rumble, rumble,
its sound is like thundering drums.
Enraged when checked, it boils over,
clear waves arch up and leap across;
river-spirit Yang-hou's billows stir and shake.
They all join battle at
the gorge known as Clashcrash.
Birds are unable to fly away in time,
fish are unable to turn back in time,
animals are unable to flee in time.
There is a flurry of fins, feathers, and fur
amidst the surging waves and chaotic clouds.

The bore takes the southern hills by storm,
then attacks the northern bank at its back;
it overturns hillocks and mounds,
levels flat the western riverside.

Perilous!   Precipitous!
Storage basins collapse, reservoirs break—
only with decisive victory does it leave off.

Yet it gurgles, bubbles, murmurs, ruffles;
displaying its spray, flaunting its splash,
it is the extreme of perversity.
Fish and turtles lose their bearings in it—
they are tossed and turned topsy-turvy;
disoriented and bewildered,
they stumble, tumble, fumble, bumble.
Since even sprites are left spellbound,
there is no way adequately to describe it.

It is quite simply enough to bowl a person
over,
reeling in the gloom of
consternation,

This is the world's most
extraordinary and wondrous
spectacle!
Can you force yourself to rise and enjoy it?"

"I am ill," said the Crown Prince, "and am, as yet, unable to get up."

The guest spake:

"I should like to introduce to you men who are practitioners of the occult, who are capable and learned,
                    such as

Chuang Chou [19]
Wei Mou [20]
Yang Chu [21]

Mo Ti [22]

P'ien Chüan [23]
Chan He

and the like.

I would have them
        expound upon
            the mystic profundity of
                the world,
        argue about
            the morality of
                all creation.

            Confucius and Lao Tzu will be moderators and observers;
    Mencius
        will verify by manipulating
                tallies;
        not once in ten thousand times will a mistake be made.

Theirs, indeed, are the most essential apothegms and most marvelous maxims in the world. Wouldn't you like to hear them?"

Thereupon, the Crown Prince, supporting himself on a small table, rose and declared: "I feel enlightened as though I had already heard the words of the sages and dialecticians." Then he broke out in great beads of sweat and, all of a sudden, his illness was ended.

Translated by Victor H. Mair

19. See selection 9.
20. A Warring States thinker.
21. An egoist thinker, foil for the pragmatist Mo Tzu (see note 22).
22. Mo Tzu, for whom see selection 6.
23. This and the following figure, Chan He, were apparently comparable to Izaak Walton.

153
Rhapsody on Whistling

Ch'eng-kung Sui (231–273)

I

The secluded gentleman,

1   In sympathy with the extraordinary,
    And in love with the strange,
2   Scorns the world and is unmindful of prestige.
    He breaks away from human endeavor and leaves it behind.
3   He gazes up at the lofty, longing for the days of old;
    He ponders lengthily, his thoughts wandering afar.

He would

4   Climb Mount Chi in order to maintain his moral integrity;
    Or float on the blue sea to amble with his ambition.

II

5   So he invites his trusted friends,
    Gathering about himself a group of like-minded.
6   He gets at the essence of the ultimate secret of life;
    He researches the subtle mysteries of Tao and Te.
7   He regrets that the common people are not yet enlightened;
    He alone, transcending all, has prior awakening.
8   He finds constraining the narrow road of the world —
    He gazes up at the concourse of heaven, and treads the high vastness.
9   Distancing himself from the exquisite and the common, he abandons
        his personal concerns;
    Then, filled with noble emotion, he gives a long-drawn whistle.

III

Thereupon,

10   The dazzling spirit inclines its luminous form,
     Pouring its brilliance into Vesper's Vale.

The technique of transcendental whistling in old China (also in Turkey, where it was still extant in the 1960s, and some other countries) was a kind of nonverbal language with affinities to the spiritual aspects of meditation. There were many famous whistlers in Chinese history before the composition of this definitive rhapsody on the subject. Among them were Liu Ken (first or second century) and Sun Teng and Juan Chi (both third century C.E.).

The notes for this selection are keyed to the numbered verses.

4. A mountain in Honan where Ch'ao-fu and Hsü Yu retired when Yao offered them the empire. Po Yi also went there to avoid Yü's son.

6. This verse touches on the very essence of the theory of whistling as a process of self-cultivation. The two key texts alluded to are the *Tao Te Ching*, especially chapter 1, and several critical passages in the appendices to the *The Classic of Changes* (see selections 3, 4, and 10).

11   And his friends rambling hand in hand,
      Stumble to a halt, stepping on their toes.
12   He sends forth marvelous tones from his red lips,
      And stimulates mournful sounds from his gleaming teeth.
13   The sound rises and falls, rolling in his throat;
      The breath rushes out and is repressed, then flies up like sparks.
14   He harmonizes 'golden *kung*' with 'sharp *chiao*,'
      Blending *shang* and *yü* into 'flowing *chih*.'
15   The whistle floats like a wandering cloud in the grand empyrean,
      And gathers a great wind for a myriad miles.
16   When the song is finished, and the echoes die out,
      It leaves behind a pleasure that lingers on in the mind.
17   Indeed, whistling is the most perfect natural music,
      Which cannot be imitated by strings or woodwinds.

      IV

Thus, the Whistler
18   Uses no instrument to play his music,
      Nor any material borrowed from things.
19   He chooses it from the near-at-hand—his own Self,
      And with his mind he controls his breath.

      V

20   By moving his lips, there is a melody;
      By pursing his mouth, he makes the sounds.
21   For every category he has a song;
      To each thing he perceives, he tunes a melody.

14. The notes of the Chinese pentatonic scale (*fa, sol, la, do, re*).

15. The grand empyrean is another word for the transcendental void. The wandering is a metaphor for the illusory individual self.

19. The text comes from *The Classic of Changes*, appendix 2.2. The word *shen* ("Self") here is more than just "body" or "person." The whistler finds the music and the means of producing it within himself; this refers to meditation. The sages of *The Classic of Changes* and the Taoist adepts could cognize anything and achieve anything from within themselves without leaving their seat or going out of their "room." Everything is available within the Self. The breath and the mind are closely linked. By cultivating the flow of his attention, he simultaneously gains control over the flow of his breath.

21. The key principle here is found in the continuation of *The Classic of Changes*, appendix 2.2: "The sages make the eight trigrams to comprehend the power of pure consciousness and to categorize the conditions of all things." From any given point of view, each object or situation fits into a category for which there is a corresponding hexagram. Each hexagram consists of yin and yang lines, which may be interpreted as patterns of sound. These are the "songs." So, whenever the whistler perceives something, he immediately transposes it into a "melody." With his control of the vital breath (*ch'i*), he can manipulate these sounds and thereby control any phenomena.

The Music is

22 Loud, but not raucous,
   Tenuous, but not terminated.

23 Pure, surpassing both reed and mouth-organ,
   Richly harmonious with lute and harp.

24 Its mystery is subtle enough to unfold fully pure consciousness and
   enlighten creative intelligence;
   Its essence is refined enough to explore completely the hidden and
   plumb the depths.

25 It holds back the distressing abandon of a Whirling Ch'u melody;
   It regulates the extravagant dissipation of a Northern Ward song.

26 It turns floods into drought,
   And turns Pure Creativity into Solid Intelligence.

   VI

27 Since the cantos induce all possible transformations,
   The applications of the tunes are unbounded.

28 The harmonious and happy are made joyful and satisfied;
   The grieved and wounded are torn within.

29 At times it is deep and dispersed—about to break off;
   At other times it is strong and harsh—filled with high spirits.

30 It wanders slowly to and fro, persuasive and clear;
   It rises swiftly in a crescendo, complex and intricate.

31 Though you be lost in thoughts, it can bring you back to your Mind;
   Though you be distressed, it will never break your Heart.

32 Whistling combines the eight sounds into perfect harmony;
   Indeed, it stabilizes extreme pleasure without going to excess.

   VII

Now, if

33 You climb your lofty terrace to look out at the view;
   You open your study door and let your gaze roam the distances;

24. "Mystery" and "subtle" recall the first chapter of the *Tao Te Ching*. In the remainder of this verse, the author weaves in the vocabulary of *The Classic of Changes*, appendix 2.5.

25. Two celebrated dance tunes from antiquity.

26. "Solid" may more literally be rendered as "redoubled." It refers to the second hexagram (*K'un*) of *The Classic of Changes*, which is made of the *K'un* trigram redoubled. The phrase "Pure Creativity" (more literally, "indomitable or excessive yang") refers to the sixth line of the first hexagram (*Ch'ien*). The sense here is that yang has reached its maximum when we have six solid yang lines forming *Ch'ien*. The power of the whistle can turn the pure yang hexagram, *Ch'ien*, inside out to form the pure yin hexagram, *K'un*. This shows the capacity of whistling to take us from one pole of creation to the opposite pole.

32. Eight kinds of musical sounds—produced from the calabash (gourd), earthenware, stretched hides, wood, stone, metal, silk strings, and bamboo.

34   With a gasp you raise your head to look up and tap the rhythms;
      With a din your long-drawn canto resonates with reverberations.
35   Sometimes the melody rolls out easily and turns back by itself;
      Sometimes it hesitates, and then lets loose again.
36   Sometimes it is soft and yielding, tender and pliant;
      Sometimes it is rushing and vigorous, like the sound of waves and
          gushing water.
37   Unexpectedly, the echo is suppressed and the torrent dries up;
      Then a pure note floats out, limpid and bright.

      VIII

38   Now excessive vitality stirs up an effusion,
      A confusing mixture, interchanging and intertwining,
39   Like a rising whirlwind, *lieh-lieh*,
      Tracing echoes, *chiu-chiu*;
40   Or like the long-drawn neighing of a tatar horse,
      Facing into the cold wind of the northern steppes.
Or also like
41   The wild goose leading her little ones;
      The flock cries out as it flies over the desert wastes.

      IX

Thus, the Whistler can
42   Create tones based on the forms,
      Compose melodies in accordance with affairs;
43   Respond without limit to the things of Nature,
      Trigger his inspiration, sending echoes rushing off,
44   Like a turbulent torrent bursting forth,
      Or clouds piling up endlessly,
45   Now breaking up, now running together,
      About to die out—and then continuing.

      X

46   Fei Lien, the Wind God, swells out of his deep cavern,
      And a fierce tiger replies with a howl in the central valley.

38. The expression rendered as "interchanging and intertwining" also happens to be a technical term for the way the hexagrams of *The Classic of Changes* interrelate.

39. The italicized bisyllabic words in this line, here somewhat anachronistically given in their MSM pronunciation, are onomatopoeic descriptions of how the whirlwind rose and the echoes were traced. A fairly common device in ancient Chinese poetry, it probably derives from the vernacular realm. Especially in highly colloquial or topolectical speech, many Chinese are still fond of employing such expressions.

46. For the Wind God, compare selection 148, line III.51 and note 50.

47   The Southern Sieve moves in the vaulted sky,
      And a bright whirlwind quivers in the lofty trees.
48   It shatters our crammed-up cares and scatters them,
      Purging the turbid constipations of life's dusty cloud.
49   It works the changes of yin and yang in perfect harmony,
      And transforms the base vulgarity of lewd customs.

        XI

Now if the Whistler
50   Wanders over lofty ridges and crags,
        crossing a huge mountain,
51   And, at the edge of a gorge,
        overlooking a purling stream,
52   Sits down on a massive rock,
      And rinses his mouth with the sparkling spring;
53   Or leans into a luxuriant profusion of marsh-orchids,
      In the shade of the elegant charm of tall bamboos—
54   Then his warble pours forth,
      An endless succession of echoing reverberations.
55   He unfolds the melancholic thoughts harbored mutely in his mind;
      And arouses his most intimate feelings, which have long been knotted
        up.
56   His heart, cleansed and purified, is carefree;
      His mind, detached from the mundane, is sylphlike.

        XII

Should he then
57   Imitate gong and drum,
      Or mime clay vessels and gourds;
58   There is a mass of sound like many instruments playing—
      Like reed pipe and flute of bamboo—
59   Bumping boulders trembling,
      An horrendous crashing, smashing, rumbling.
Or should he
60   Sound the tone *chih*, then severe winter becomes steaming hot;
      Give free play to *yü*, then a sharp frost makes summer fade;
61   Move into *shang*, then an autumn drizzle falls in springtime;
      Strike up the tone *chiao*, then a vernal breeze soughs in the bare
        branches.

        47. The Southern Sieve is a constellation.
        60–61. See note to verse 14 for the identification of these four musical tones.

XIII

62   The eight sounds and five harmonies constantly fluctuate;
     The melody follows no strict beat.
63   It runs, but does not run off;
     It stops, but does not stop up.
64   Following his mouth and lips, it expands forth;
     Floating on his fragrant breath, it travels afar.
65   The music is terse and exquisite, with flowing echoes;
     The sound stimulates brilliance, with its clear staccatos.
66   Indeed, with its supreme natural beauty,
     It is quite distinguished and incomparable!
67   It transcends the music of Shao Hsia and Hsien Ch'ih;
     Why vainly find the exotic in Cheng and Wei?

XIV

For when the Whistler performs,
68   Mien Chü holds his tongue and is distraught;
     Wang Pao silences his mouth and turns pale.
69   Duke Yü stops singing in the middle of a song;
     Master Ning restrains his hands from tapping and sighs deeply.
70   Chung Ch'i abandons his lute and listens instead;
     Confucius forgets the taste of meat and stops eating.
71   The various animals all dance and stomp their feet;
     The paired phoenixes come with stately mien and flap their wings.
72   They understand the magnificent beauty of the long-drawn Whistle;
     Indeed, this is the most perfect of sounds!

Translated by Douglass A. White

62. Compare note 6 to selection 161.

67. Whistling is more sublime than the music of Shao Hsia and Hsien Ch'ih, two musicians of the mythical Yellow Emperor. It is more wild and exotic than the music of Cheng and Wei, two states known for the dissipation of their music.

68. Mien Chü was famous for singing in a prolonged manner whereas Wang Pao was noted for singing in an abrupt manner.

69. Duke Yü was a great singer of the Han period whose voice shook the rafters and raised the dust. Master Ning was remembered for singing a deeply moving, sad song.

70. Chung Ch'i was a celebrated lutanist. It is said that Confucius forgot the taste of meat for three months after hearing the music of Shao.

154
The Return

T'ao Ch'ien (365–427)

I was poor, and what I got from farming was not enough to support my family. The house was full of children, the rice-jar was empty, and I could not see any way to supply the necessities of life. Friends and relatives kept urging me to become a magistrate, and I had at last come to think I should do it, but there was no way for me to get such a position. At the time I happened to have business abroad and made a good impression on the grandees as a conciliatory and humane sort of person. Because of my poverty an uncle offered me a job in a small town, but the region was still unquiet and I trembled at the thought of going away from home. However, P'eng-tse[1] was only thirty miles from my native place, and the yield of the fields assigned the magistrate was sufficient to keep me in wine, so I applied for the office. Before many days had passed, I longed to give it up and go back home. Why, you may ask. Because my instinct is all for freedom, and will not brook discipline or restraint. Hunger and cold may be sharp, but this going against myself really sickens me. Whenever I have been involved in official life I was mortgaging myself to my mouth and belly, and the realization of this greatly upset me. I was deeply ashamed that I had so compromised my principles, but I was still going to wait out the year, after which I might pack up my clothes and slip away at night. Then my sister who had married into the Ch'eng family died in Wu-ch'ang,[2] and my only desire was to go there as quickly as possible. I gave up my office and left of my own accord. From mid-autumn to winter I was altogether some eighty days in office, when events made it possible for me to do what I wished. I have entitled my piece "The Return"; my preface is dated the eleventh moon of the year *Yi-ssu* (405).

> To get out of this and go back home!
> My fields and garden will be overgrown with weeds —
>   I must go back.
> It was my own doing that made my mind my body's slave
> Why should I go on in melancholy and lonely grief?
> 5 I realize that there's no remedying the past
> But I know that there's hope in the future.
> After all I have not gone far on the wrong road
> And I am aware that what I do today is right, yesterday wrong.
> My boat rocks in the gentle breeze

For information on the author, see selection 29.

1. Just southeast of the present-day town of the same name and ten miles east of the present-day town of Hu-k'ou in Kiangsi.

2. In modern Hopei.

10   Flap, flap, the wind blows my gown;
      I ask a passerby about the road ahead,
      Grudging the dimness of the light at dawn.
      Then I catch sight of my cottage —
          Filled with joy I run.
15   The servant boy comes to welcome me
          My little son waits at the door.
      The three paths[3] are almost obliterated
          But pines and chrysanthemums are still here.
      Leading the children by the hand, I enter my house
20   Where there is a bottle filled with wine.
      I draw the bottle to me and pour myself a cup;
      Seeing the trees in the courtyard brings joy to my face.
      I lean on the south window and let my pride expand,
      I consider how easy it is to be content with a little space.
25   Every day I stroll in the garden for pleasure,
      Although there is a gate, it is always shut.
      Cane in hand I walk and rest,
      Occasionally raising my head to gaze into the distance.
      The clouds aimlessly rise from the peaks,
30   The birds, weary of flying, know it is time to come home.
      As the sun's rays grow dim and disappear from view
      I walk around a lonely pine tree, stroking it.

      Back home again!
      May my friendships be broken off and my wanderings come to an end.
35   The world and I shall have nothing more to do with one another.
      If I were again to go abroad, what should I seek?
      Here I enjoy honest conversation with my family
      And take pleasure in books and cither to dispel my worries.
      The farmers tell me that now spring is here
40   There will be work to do in the west fields.
      Sometimes I call for a covered cart,
      Sometimes I row a lonely boat,
      Following a deep gully through the still water
      Or crossing the hill on a rugged path.
45   The trees put forth luxuriant foliage,
      The spring begins to flow in a trickle.
      I admire the seasonableness of nature

3. An allusion to Chiang Yü, an official who became a recluse rather than serve Wang Mang (usurper of the Han dynasty). Chiang had a hut in a bamboo grove, to which he cleared three paths. He sought only the company of two bosom friends; both were men of principle who renounced fame and refused to come out of retirement.

And am moved to think that my life will come to its close.
    It is all over —
50 So little time are we granted human form in the world!
Let us then follow the inclinations of the heart:
Where would we go that we are so agitated?
I have no desire for riches
And no expectation of Heaven.
55 Rather on some fine morning to walk alone
Now planting my staff to take up a hoe,
Or climbing the east hill and whistling long[4]
Or composing verses beside the clear stream:
So I manage to accept my lot until the ultimate homecoming.
60 Rejoicing in Heaven's command, what is there to doubt?

Translated by James R. Hightower

4. For the type of "long whistling" that the author probably engaged in, see selection 153.

155
Rhymeprose on the Sword Gallery[1]

To Send My Friend Wang Yen on His Way to Shu[2]

Li Po (701–762)

South of Hsien-yang,[3]
gazing in a straight line for five thousand miles,
I see the soaring crags and spires of clouded ranges.
There before me the Sword Gallery cuts across,
Suspended from the sky
to provide a passage through the center.

For information on the rhapsodist, see selection 45. It is obvious from their form that this and the following selection are not typical of the *fu* ("rhapsody," "rhymeprose") genre. Indeed, the term came to be used for a wide variety of literati and folk genres that were not classifiable as prose or verse.

1. A difficult mountain pass north of Ch'eng-tu in Szechwan, on the road between Ch'eng-tu and the T'ang capital at Ch'ang-an.
2. An old name for Szechwan in southwest China.
3. The Ch'in dynasty capital, near Ch'ang-an. Often, as here, the name is used to represent Ch'ang-an itself.

Up above are
pine winds that rustle, whistle, sough, and sigh;
And there the gibbons of Pa,[4] sadly crying to one another.
On every side
flying chutes rush through the chasms,
Spattering stones, splashing the Gallery,
surging and gushing with frightening thunder.
Sending off my beautiful friend. Now the parting!
I wonder when that day. His coming home!

While gazing after him—what end to feelings?
With sad notes deep inside—I sigh and moan.
I watch as the azure waves go coursing eastward,
And grieve as the white sun is hidden in the west.
A wild goose takes leave of Yen[5]—those autumn noises.
The clouds bring sorrow to Ch'in[6]—this evening light.
But, oh, when the bright moon appears above
the Sword Gallery,
Let us have some wine together in our two villages,
thinking of one another.

Translated by Elling Eide

4. An old name for a part of what is now Szechwan.
5. An ancient state in northeast China. Autumn comes early there, and the migrating geese are among the reminders that time and life are passing.
6. The ancient state that unified China to create the Ch'in dynasty in 221 B.C.E. Here it represents north-central China and the area around Ch'ang-an.

156
Red Cliff Rhapsodies, 1 and 2

Su Shih (1037–1101)

1

In the fall of the year *jen-hsü* in the seventh month on the day after the full moon,[1] I traveled in a boat with some guests to the foot of Red Cliff.[2] A light wind wafted by, and not a ripple was stirred. I poured wine for my guests as

Su Shih or Su Tung-p'o ("Eastern Slope" Su) was one of the dominant figures in Chinese literati culture, influencing not only prose and poetry but also esthetic theory, painting, and calligraphy as well. He was born into a gentry family of limited means and educated primarily by his father, Su Hsün (1009–1066), later famous as a political essayist, and also by his mother,

we chanted the poem about the bright moon and sang the song about the graceful maiden.[3] Before long, the moon appeared over East Mountain and lingered by the constellations Dipper and Ox.[4] White dew extended over the Long River; the water's gleam mingled with the sky. We let our reed of a boat follow its course as it traversed myriad acres[5] of expanse. I felt boundless, as if gliding through the void, not knowing where I might land; I felt as if I were soaring about, having left the world behind to stand alone as I sprouted wings to become a transcendent.

---

née Ch'eng. He and his younger brother, Su Ch'e (1039–1112), were regarded as newly discovered talents after passing the Presented Scholar examination in 1057 under Ou-yang Hsiu (see selection 206). In 1061, Su Shih passed the special examination held to recruit new officials and began his career as a Case Reviewer at the Court of Judicial Review. During these early years, he wrote numerous memorials identifying critical national problems in areas of finance and military defense. Although supportive of reform, he opposed the overly rapid implementation and Legalist approach of the statesman Wang An-shih's (see selection 71) New Policies. Between 1079 and 1100, depending upon which ruler was on the throne and which faction was in power, Su Shih experienced a series of exiles and pardons.

Though an activist Confucian official, Su Shih was eclectic in his intellectual interests. He was deeply influenced by Zen Buddhist ideals of enlightenment, yet searched for transcendence through engagement with social reality and the natural environment. Such themes as the equivalence of objective and subjective viewpoints, the Tao as a ceaseless alternation between change and constancy, the affirmation of happiness in this life, equanimity toward fate, and ceaseless curiosity about the natural world pervade his prolific writings. His classical poems (*shih*) alone number almost 2,800, of which those containing perceptions of nature and his philosophical views are the most widely read. His lyrics (*tz'u*), numbering about 350, expanded the range of content in this genre and are considered innovative examples of an attitude of "heroic abandon." One of the "Eight Masters of T'ang and Sung Prose," Su was further canonized by the literary tradition as the personification of the Northern Sung *Zeitgeist*—an expansive, optimistic personality who later was celebrated in drama, painting, and the decorative arts. His two pieces on Red Cliff were written during his exile in Huang prefecture. They soon became monuments of Chinese literature and calligraphy, and established the place as a literary shrine.

1. The date is equivalent to August 12, 1082 in the Western calendar.

2. Located in modern Huang-kang, Hupei. Su Shih noted elsewhere that Red Cliff was located several hundred paces from his residence in Huang prefecture, but he was unsure whether it was the same Red Cliff where the famous naval battle in 208 occurred between the forces of Wei under Ts'ao Ts'ao (155–220) and those of Wu under the general Chou Yü (175–210, see selection 258). In fact, the battle site was located elsewhere along the Long River, in modern P'u-ch'i, Hupei. According to some sources, Su Shih's Red Cliff was originally named "Red Nose" because of its color and shape; the names were thought to have been confused because of their similar pronunciation.

3. The poem about the bright moon is traditionally identified as "The Moon Appears" from the *Classic of Odes*, in which the moon is a beautiful woman whose unattainability provokes longing and anxiety. The poem about the graceful maiden is " 'Kuan-kuan' Cry the Ospreys," also from the *Classic of Odes*, in which a nobleman courts a virtuous lady for his palace. See selections 22 (poem 1) and 16.

4. These constellations lie above the northern horizon, indicating that Su was looking toward the northeast.

5. The Chinese word used is actually a unit of measure equal to approximately sixteen acres.

Then we drank more wine and reached the height of joy. I beat out a rhythm against the side of the boat and sang:

Cassia-wood oars,
Magnolia-wood rudder,
Stroke the moon's pure reflection
As we glide upstream on its shimmering light.
Ever distant, the object of my longings.
I gaze at the beautiful one
In a faraway corner of heaven. [6]

One of the guests could play the flute and accompanied my song.[7] Yet his sounds—*wu-wu*—were plaintive, yearning, weeping, accusing. The lingering notes meandered through the air, drawn out like silken threads. They would have aroused a submerged dragon to whirl around in the cavernous depths, and caused a widow to weep in her lonely boat.

I was saddened. Straightening my clothes, I sat up and asked my guest, "Why are you playing this way?" He replied,

"The moon is bright, stars are few,
Crows and magpies are flying south.[8]

"Isn't this from the poem by Ts'ao Meng-te? Look westward and there is Hsia-k'ou. Look east and there lies Wu-ch'ang.[9] The mountains and the river encircle one another; how dense the viridian growth! Yet is this not the place where Meng-te was trapped by Chou Yü?[10] He had just conquered Ching-chou and sailed down to Chiang-ling[11] as he followed the course of the river eastward. His fleet stretched bow to stern for a thousand tricents; his banners and flags blotted out the sky. As he drank wine by the bank of the river, he lay down his lance crosswise and composed this poem. Indeed, he dominated his

6. In the traditional Confucian interpretation of poetry, such imagery of the distant beauty personified as the moon can be read as the exile's longing for the imperial court. Naturally, other more erotic and metaphysical interpretations are also possible.

7. Later commentators have identified this guest as Yang Shih-ch'ang, a Taoist known for his expert playing of the *hsiao* (vertical bamboo flute).

8. A quote from a poem by Ts'ao Ts'ao, courtesy name Meng-te. Ts'ao wrote two ballads entitled "Short Song" ("Tuan-ko hsing") sometime after the Battle of Red Cliff in 208. The first, from which these lines are taken, begins with melancholy observations about the futility of human ambition and the shortness of life but ends with a renewed determination to unify the country.

9. The city of Hsia-k'ou, built by the Wu emperor Sun Ch'üan (reigned 222–252) in 223, was located in modern Wu-ch'ang, Hupei; ancient Wu-ch'ang was located in modern Ŏ-ch'eng district, Hupei and was not the modern city of the same name.

10. A reference to the Battle of Red Cliff in 208.

11. Ching-chou refers to a city, now Hsiang-yang, Hupei, which administered a region in the Later Han covering much of modern Hupei and Hunan provinces. Ts'ao Ts'ao was able to obtain this strategic place by the surrender of the commander without a fight. Chiang-ling was located in modern Chiang-ling, Hupei.

age, yet where is he now? And what about you and me conversing here by the riverbank like a fisherman and a woodcutter, joined by fish and shrimp with the deer as our companions? We ride on a boat no bigger than a leaf as we drink to each other out of simple gourds. We exist no longer than mayflies between heaven and earth, and are of no more consequence than a kernel in the vast ocean. I grieve that my life is but a moment and envy the Long River's endless flow. If only I could grasp hold of a flying transcendent and wander with him through the heavens to embrace the bright moon and live forever. But, I realize this cannot be attained so I confide these lingering sounds to the sad autumn wind."

I said, "Do you really understand the water and the moon? Here, it flows by yet never leaves us; over there, it waxes and wanes without growing or shrinking. If you look at things as changing, then heaven and earth do not last for even the blink of an eye. If you look at them as unchanging, then I along with everything am eternal. So why be envious? Moreover, each thing within heaven and earth has its master. If I did not possess it, then I would not take even a hair of it. However, the pure wind over the river becomes sound when our ears capture it, and the bright moon between the mountains takes on form when our eyes encounter it. There is no prohibition against our acquiring them, and we can use them without ever consuming them. They are from the inexhaustible treasury of the Creator of Things, which you and I can enjoy together."

My guest became happy and laughed. We washed out the cups and drank again. Soon the food was gone, and the cups and plates were strewn about. We lay down in the boat, leaning against each other for pillows, unaware that it was becoming light in the east.

2

In the tenth month of the same year on the day of the full moon,[12] I walked from Snow Lodge back toward Lin-kao.[13] Two guests accompanied me as we crossed over Yellow Clay Slope. Frost and dew had already fallen; the leaves had all dropped off from the trees. Our shadows lay on the ground as we gazed up at the bright moon. We looked around us, delighted by the scene, and sang songs for each other as we walked along.

After a while, I sighed, "I have guests but no wine, and even if I had wine, there is no food to go along with it. The moon is white, the wind, gentle. But how can we enjoy such a fine evening?" One of the guests replied, "Today at twilight, I cast a net and caught a fish with a large mouth and fine scales. It

12. The date is equivalent to November 7, 1082.
13. The Snow Lodge, located in the east of modern Huang-kang, Hupei, was a small villa built by Su Shih. Snow fell during its construction and the interior was then decorated with murals of snow scenes. Lin-kao was the location of Su Shih's main residence beside the Long River in the southern part of Huang-kang, Hupei.

resembles a Pine River perch.[14] But where can we obtain some wine?" I went back and discussed this with my wife, who said, "I have some wine which I have stored for quite a while in case you should ever need it."

So we took along the wine and the fish, and traveled once again to the foot of Red Cliff. The river flowed audibly, the cleaved banks rose a thousand feet. The mountain was high, the moon, small. The water level had fallen, rocks protruded. How long had it been since my last visit? The scene was no longer recognizable! I lifted up my robe and alighted. I made my way among sharp crags, parting the overgrowth to crouch on rocks shaped like tigers and leopards, and to climb up trees twisted like horned dragons. I pulled myself up to the precarious nests of falcons, and peered down at the hidden palace of the River God P'ing Yi.[15] My two guests were unable to follow me this far. I suddenly let out out a sharp cry. The plants and trees were startled and shook; mountains resounded, valleys echoed. Winds arose, and the water became agitated. For my part, I became hushed and melancholy, awed and fearful. Then I began to tremble so that I could no longer remain there. I returned, got back on board, and had the boat steered into the mainstream. We let it drift until it stopped and rested there.

By then, it was toward midnight. All around us it was serenely silent. Just then, a solitary crane came toward us across the river from the east. Its wings traced cartwheels in the air. It seemed as if dressed in a white jacket over a black gown, and let out a long, piercing cry as it swept past our boat and headed west.

A short while later, the guests left and I fell asleep. I dreamed of two[16] Taoists fluttering about in feathered gowns. As they passed below Lin-kao, they greeted me and asked, "Did you enjoy your journey to Red Cliff?" When I asked their names, they looked down without answering. "Oh! Now I understand! Last night, was it not you who called out as you flew by?" The Taoists turned back at me and laughed. And then I suddenly awakened. I opened the door and looked outside but saw no trace of them.

Translated by Richard Strassberg

14. The Pine River (Sung-chiang; modern Wu-sung-chiang) flows from the Great Lake into the Huang-p'u River in modern Shanghai. It was noted for its tasty perch.

15. According to legend, P'ing Yi, originally a human, drowned and became the River God Ho-po.

16. There has been considerable textual controversy over the centuries as to whether Su Shih had written that he had dreamed of one or two Taoists. Both alternatives have appeared in printed versions, calligraphic copies, and paintings. However, the earliest printed edition, used here, mentions two Taoists and the change to one may well have been a mistaken editorial emendation.

Folk and Folklike Songs, Ballads, and Narrative Verse

157
Song of the Great Wind

Liu Pang (256–195 B.C.E.)

A great wind arises—billowing clouds fly;
His majesty dominating all within the seas, he returns to his old hometown.
Where can he find brave warriors to guard the four directions?

Translated by Victor H. Mair

The poet was founder of the Han dynasty.

158
Cock-Phoenix, Hen-Phoenix

Ssu-ma Hsiang-ju (c. 179–118 B.C.E.)

Preface

While Ssu-ma Hsiang-ju was traveling through Lin-ch'iung, a rich man there named Cho Wang-sun had a daughter, Wen-chün, who had recently

Two songs set to the accompaniment of the lute.
The author hailed from Ch'eng-tu, the old capital of Shu in modern Szechwan. Very poor until his literary talent was finally recognized by the Han emperor Wu, he was the author of

been widowed. She hid behind a screen and peeped through. Hsiang-ju won
her heart with these songs:

Cock-Phoenix

Cock-phoenix, cock-phoenix goes back to his hometown
From roaming the four seas in search of his hen.
Unlucky days—he found no way to meet her.
What a surprise! Tonight up in this hall,
In this very place is a girl sweet and pretty.
My bedroom so near, she so far—it pains my heart.
How can we be mandarin ducks caressing neck to neck?

Hen-Phoenix

Hen-phoenix, oh hen-phoenix, come nest with me!
Tail to tail we'll breed, be my bride forever!
Passionately entwined, bodies ones, hearts united,
At midnight come with me! Who will ever know?
Let's rise together wing to wing and fly on high.
Unmoved by my love she makes me pine.

Translated by Anne Birrell

---

several famous rhapsodies, a genre popular in the Han era, the best known of these being "Sir
Fantasy" and "Shang-lin Park" (see selection 151).

159
Ground-Thumping Song

Anonymous (Western Han?)

When the sun comes up we work,
when the sun goes down we rest.
We dig a well to drink,
plow the fields to eat—
the Emperor and his might—what are they to us!

Translated by Burton Watson

Reputed to be a song of very early times sung by peasant elders as they beat on the ground to
keep time. In irregular meter.

160
A Song

Li Yen-nien (c. 140–87 B.C.E.)

In the north there is a lovely woman,
Beyond compare, unique.
One glance destroys a man's city,
A second glance destroys a man's kingdom.
Would you rather not know a city and kingdom destroyer?
Such beauty you won't find twice!

Translated by Anne Birrell

Li Yen-nien was a court musician and entertainer in the reign of the Han emperor Wu. He had a beautiful sister whose praises he sang before the emperor in this poem. The emperor was introduced to her and she became his favorite concubine. She received the title of *Fu-jen*, translated as "Lady," and Li Yen-nien was promoted to the rank of Harmonizer of the Tones. His poem, considered to be the earliest example of the pentasyllabic meter, belongs to the *ko-shih* ("song-poem") category. It alludes in lines 3–4 to poem no. 264 of the *Classic of Odes*, and itself became a much quoted verse.

161
We Have Chosen a Timely Day

Anonymous (Western Han)

We have chosen a timely day,
We wait with hope,
Burning fat and artemisia
To welcome the Four Directions.[1]
Ninefold[2] doors open
For the Gods' journey forth,

This poem is part of a cycle entitled "Songs for Suburban Sacrifice, in Nineteen Parts." The entire cycle describes worshippers at a seasonal vigil awaiting the consecrated moment when the gods will come down to the altar and bless the people. This type of hymn is similar to the liturgy of welcoming a god in the "Nine Songs" of the southern kingdom of Ch'u (see selection 148) dating from about the fourth century B.C.E. The two closest parallels are "Lord of the East, The Great One" and "Thou Amid the Clouds."

1. The four points of the compass.
2. Nine is a mystic number, here referring perhaps to nine symbolic doors of the altar that would admit the gods into the presence of humans.

They send down sweet grace,
Bounteous good fortune.
The chariot of the Gods
Is hitched to dark clouds,
Yoked to flying dragons,
Feather pennants amassed.

The coming down of the Gods
Is like wind-driven horses;
On the left turquoise dragon,[3]
On the right white tiger.[4]

The coming of the Gods
Is divine! What a drenching!
First bringing rain
Which spreads in sheets.

The arrival of the Gods
Is lucky shade within shade.[5]
All seems confused,
Making hearts tremble.

The Gods are now enthroned,
The Five Tones[6] harmonize.
Happy till the dawn
We offer the Gods pleasure.

Ritual calves with budding horn bumps,
Vessels of millet sweet,
Goblets of cassia wine,
We host the Eight Quarters.[7]

The Gods serenely linger,
We chant "Green" and "Yellow."[8]
All round meditate on this,
Gaze at the green jade hall.
A crowd of beauties gathers,
Refined, perfect loveliness:
Faces like flowering rush,

3. Presides over the eastern sky as a guardian spirit.
4. Presides over the western sky as a guardian spirit.
5. *Yin-yin*, suggesting mysterious darkness and the female cosmic principle.
6. The five notes of the ancient Chinese musical scale.
7. Of the universe.
8. These hymns probably refer to the green color symbolic of spring and the yellow of the earth.

Rivals in dazzling glamor,
Wearing flowery patterns,
Interwoven misty silks,
With trains of white voile,
Girdles of pearl and jade.
They bear Blissful-night and Flag-orchid,
Iris and orchid perfumed.
Calm and peaceful
We offer up the blessed chalice.

Translated by Anne Birrell

162
Lost Horizon

Attributed to Hsi-chün (fl. 110 B.C.E.)

Preface

In the reign of Emperor Wu of the Han dynasty during the years 110–104 B.C.E., the emperor made Hsi-chün, daughter of the king of Chiangtu,[1] a princess and married her off to Kunmi, the ruler of the Wusun tribe.[2] When she reached their land, she settled in Kunmi's palace. Through all those years she only met him once or twice, but did not speak to him. The princess became melancholy and composed a song[3] that went like this:

My family married me to a lost horizon,
Sent me far away to the Wusun king's strange land.
A canvas hut is my mansion, of felt its walls,
Flesh for food, mare's milk to drink.
Longing ever for my homeland, my heart's inner wound.
I wish I were the brown goose going to its old home.

Translated by Anne Birrell

1. Liu Chien. Being the daughter of the prince of Chiangtu, this made her a relative of Emperor Wu.
2. The apparently Indo-European Wusun people were located in the region of modern Lake Balkash and northwestern Sinkiang province.
3. This poem features the caesural sound-carrier particle *hsi* (ancient pronunciation *gig) in each line, reminiscent of the *sao*-song style of *The Elegies of Ch'u* (see selection 148).

163

Song of the Viet Boatman

Anonymous (1st century B.C.E.)

Preface

The ruler of Ngo kingdom in the state of Ch'u, Tzu-hsi, was traveling in a blue-plumed boat with a kingfisher awning. The Viet oarsman fell in love with Tzu-hsi, and sang a Viet song as he plied the oars. The ruler of Ngo was touched. Full of desire, he raised his embroidered quilt and covered the boatman. His song went like this:

Tonight, what sort of night?
I tug my boat midstream.
Today, what sort of day?
I share my boat with my lord.
Though ashamed, I am loved.
Don't think of slander or disgrace!
My heart will never fail,
For I have known my lord.
On a hill is a tree, on the tree is a bough.
My heart delights in my lord, though he will never know.

Translated by Anne Birrell

Initially recorded in the first century B.C.E. by Liu Hsiang, this poem apparently derives from an earlier oral tradition of the southern state of Viet (pronounced Yüeh in Modern Standard Mandarin), and was then rendered in the Ch'u language (another southern tongue), whence it seems to have been translated into Sinitic, i.e., Chinese. It has in its present form elements of the *sao*-song style, similar to some poems in *The Elegies of Ch'u* (see selection 148). This poem is thought by many critics to offer evidence of homosexuality in ancient China.

164

Mulberry up the Lane

Anonymous (c. 100 C.E.)

Sunrise at the southeast corner
Shines on our Ch'in [1] clan house.

The first of six old folk-songs preserved in the *Jade Terrace* anthology (see selection 35), this is the famous narrative poem concerning Ch'in Lofu, about whom refrains occur in many later love poems. It goes by several other titles, including "The Sun Rises from the Southeast Corner

The Ch'in clan has a fair daughter,
She is called Lofu.

Lofu is good at silkworm mulberry,
She picks mulberry at the wall's south corner.
Green silk is her basket strap,
Cassia her basket and pole.

On her head a twisting-fall hairdo,
At her ears bright moon pearls.
Green silk is her lower skirt,
Purple silk is her upper shirt.

Passersby see Lofu,
Drop their load, stroke their beard.
Young men see Lofu,
Take off caps, put on headbands.
The plowman forgets his plow,
The hoer forgets his hoe.
They come home cross and happy—
All from seeing Lofu.

A prefect from the south is here,
His five horses stand pawing the ground.
The prefect sends his servant forward
To ask, "Whose is the pretty girl?"
"The Ch'in clan has a fair daughter,
Her name is Lofu."
"Lofu, how old is she?"

Suite" and "The Lofu Love-Song Suite." A "suite" is a series of related stanzas linked to make one long poem. Ch'in Lofu is also mentioned as a model of feminine decorum in the still longer and more famous narrative poem entitled "A Peacock Southeast Flew" (see selection 173).

"Folk-song" is used as a general reference for the poetic form called *yüeh-fu*. Often translated simply as "ballad," this term originally signified the Bureau of Music re-established by the Han emperor Wu about 120 B.C.E. on the model of an earlier office set up by the Ch'in dynasty. It then came to mean those anonymous folk-songs collected by officials attached to this bureau. Still later, the term indicated folk-songs in general, whether they were genuine folk pieces or polished imitations by named poets. They are characterized by narrative, formulaic, and musical elements, as well as by simple diction, bold imagery, and punning devices. The earlier type of *yüeh-fu* was metrically irregular, while the later version was metrically inseparable from the old poem *(ku-shih)*.

1. Ch'in Lofu, the daughter of the Ch'in clan from Hantan, capital of the Chao state. She married a man called Wang Jen. One day the king of Chao caught sight of her from the pillars and parapet of his palace terrace when she was picking mulberry up the lanes. He was so attracted to her that he asked her to drink with him. She eluded his advances by composing a song for the lute, "Mulberry up the Lane," in which she praised her husband and rejected the casual love of a passing official. The king then desisted from his efforts to seduce her.

"Not yet quite twenty,
A bit more than fifteen."

The prefect invites Lofu,
"Wouldn't you like a ride with me?"
Lofu steps forward and refuses:
"You are so silly, Prefect!
You have your own wife, Prefect,
Lofu has her own husband!
In the east more than a thousand horsemen,
My husband is in the lead.
How would you recognize my husband?
His white horse follows black colts,
Green silk plaits his horse's tail,
Yellow gold braids his horse's head.
At his waist a Lulu dagger [2]—
Worth maybe more than ten million cash.

"At fifteen he was a county clerk,
At twenty a court official,
At thirty a chancellor,
At forty lord of his own city.

"As a man he has a pure white complexion,
Bushy whiskers on both cheeks.
Majestic he steps into his office,
Dignified he strides to the courtroom,
Where several thousand in audience
All say my husband has no rival!"

Translated by Anne Birrell

2. A dagger with a hilt shaped like the pulley of a well. The word for the ring of the pulley, a pun for return or reunion, naturally evoked romantic associations for lovers who were separated.

165

From the "Nineteen Old Poems"
Green, Green Riverside Grass

Anonymous (Han)

Green, green riverside grass,
Lush, lush willow in the garden,
Sleek, sleek a girl upstairs,
White, white faces her window.
Fair, fair her rouge and powder face,
Slim, slim she shows her white hand.

Once I was a singing-house girl,
Now I am a playboy's wife.
A playboy roves, never comes home,
My empty bed is hard to keep alone.

Translated by Anne Birrell

This is the second of the celebrated "Nineteen Old Poems," an anonymous set of fine poems in the new pentasyllabic form evidently dating from the Eastern Han period, although eight of them have been attributed to Mei Ch'eng of the Western Han period (see selection 152). It was imitated numerous times by later poets in succeeding centuries.

Frail, Frail Lone-Growing Bamboo

Anonymous (Han)

Frail, frail, lone-growing bamboo,
  roots clasping the high hill's edge;
  to join with my lord now in marriage,
4 a creeper clinging to the moss.
  Creepers have their time to grow,
  husband and wife their proper union.
  A thousand miles apart, we made our vow,
8 far far—mountain slopes between us.
  Thinking of you makes one old;

This is the seventh of the "Nineteen Old Poems."

your canopied carriage, how slow its coming!
These flowers sadden me—orchis and angelica,
12 petals unfurled, shedding glory all around;
if no one plucks them in blossom time
they'll wilt and die with the autumn grass.
But if in truth you will keep your promise,
16 how could *I* ever be untrue?

Translated by Burton Watson

166
They Fought South of the Wall

Anonymous (Han?)

They fought south of the wall,
died north of the outworks,
lie dead in the fields unburied,
4 fine food for the crows.
Tell the crows for me,
weep for these strangers!
Dead in the field, if no one buries them,
8 how can their rotting flesh hope to escape you?
Waters are deep, swift and strong,
rushes and reed banks cluster darkly;
the brave horsemen have fought and died,
12 their weary mounts wander here and there, neighing.
On the bridge they built sentry huts—
how could we go south? how could we go north?
And if we do not gather in the grain and millet,
16 what will our lord have to eat?
We want to be loyal subjects, but what can we do?
I think of you, good subjects,
good subjects, how I remember—
20 at dawn you set off to battle;
night fell, but you never came back.

Translated by Burton Watson

A music bureau ballad in irregular meter.

167

Crows on City Walls
A Children's Ditty from the Early Years
of the Reign of the Later Han Emperor Huan.

Crows on city walls,
Tails down in retreat.
Father became an officer,
Son became a conscript.
One soldier dies,
One hundred chariots.
Chariots clatter, clatter
As they enter Ho-chien.[1]
At Ho-chien a pretty girl is skilled at counting cash,
With her cash she makes a mansion, with gold she makes a hall.

Ssu-ma Piao (240–306) included this song in his "Treatise on the Five Elements." He dated the origin of the ditty at around 150 C.E. and the events it "foretold" at around c. 167 C.E. He attached this interpretation to it:

> This is a children's ditty circulating in the capital in the early part of Emperor Huan's reign. It refers to government greed. "Crows on city walls,/ Tails down in retreat" means to occupy a position of great advantage and eat on one's own, refusing to share with those beneath one, which refers to those in authority who amass a great fortune. "Father became an officer,/ Son became a conscript" says that when the Man and Yi tribes rebelled, a father had to become an officer in the army, while his son became a conscript and went out to attack them. "One soldier dies,/ One hundred chariots" says that when one man dies in the punitive expedition against the Huns, behind him are another hundred war chariots. "Chariots clatter, clatter/ As they enter Ho-chien" says that when Emperor Huan was about to die, chariots clattered into Ho-chien to welcome Emperor Ling. "At Ho-chien a pretty girl is skilled at counting cash,/ With her cash she makes a mansion, with gold she makes a hall" means that when Emperor Ling ascended the throne his mother, the Yung-lo Dowager Empress, loved to amass gold to make a hall. "On the stone-mill, greedy, greedy, she pounds yellow millet" says that although the Yung-lo Dowager Empress piled up gold and cash, she was so greedy she never had enough and she made the people pound yellow millet for her own use. "Under the rafter there is a hanging drum./ I want to strike it, but the minister will be angry" says that the Yung-lo Dowager Empress ordered Emperor Ling to sell offices as a source of cash, and that those who received official emoluments were not the right people. It says that we are loyal and sincere; we are men of honor who look on all this with resentment and want to strike the hanging drum in order to seek an audience. But the chief minister is the one who controls the drum, and he for his part is a flatterer and toady. He is angry and stops me from striking the drum in protest.

1. The place name Ho-chien is the only detail that permits a link beteen the song and historical events. Ssu-ma Piao's interpretation focuses on two targets in the late Later Han: social upheaval caused by war and the greed of the emperor's mother. Ho-chien was an ancient province in the state of Chao, modern Hopei. It became a kingdom in the Han and was ruled by members of the royal family.

On the stone-mill, greedy, greedy, she pounds yellow millet.
Under the rafter there is a hanging drum.
I want to strike it, but the minister will be angry.

Translated by Anne Birrell

168
Watering Horses at a Long Wall[1] Hole

Anonymous or Attributed to Ts'ai Yung (133–192)

Green, green riverside grass.[2]
Skeins, skeins of longing for the far road,
The far road I cannot bear to long for.
In bed at night I see him in dreams,
Dream I see him by my side.
Suddenly I wake in another town,
Another town, each in different parts.
I toss and turn, see him no more.

Withered mulberry knows wind from the skies,
Ocean waters know chill from the skies.
I go indoors, everyone self-absorbed,
Who wants to speak for me?

A traveler came from far away,
He brought me a double-carp.[3]

Ts'ai Yung, from Honan, was a well-known poet, musician, and calligrapher. He was well versed in astronomy and musical theory, and redacted the authorized version of the six Confucian classics. Later he incurred the displeasure of the authorities and was condemned to death, the sentence being commuted to having his hair pulled out. Eventually Ts'ai became a recluse. When the warlord Tung Cho challenged the Han dynasty he summoned Ts'ai to court, inviting him to take office and ennobling him as a marquis. At Tung's defeat, Ts'ai was again imprisoned for an indiscreet remark, and he died in jail. He was known by the colorful nickname "Drunken Dragon" for his drinking bouts. Ts'ai was the subject of a play by the fourteenth-century playwright Kao Ming, who portrayed him in less than flattering terms. The title of the play is "The Lute" (see selection 274).

1. The "long wall" was part of a system of defensive fortifications that was built starting from the Chou period and was linked up more closely during the Ch'in period. It ultimately came to be part of the group of fortified barriers now known collectively as the Great Wall.

2. Compare the first line of selection 165.

3. In the old poems a letter was sometimes carried in a container shaped like a fish, which was said to be "cooked" when opened. The carp is a prolific fish, and the double carp was probably an emblem of fertility or wedded bliss.

I call my children and cook the carp.
Inside there is a white silk letter.
I kneel down and read the white silk letter.
What does it say in the letter, then?
Above it has, "Try and eat!"
Below it has, "I'll always love you."

Translated by Anne Birrell

169

Song: I Watered My Horse at the Long Wall Caves

Ch'en Lin (d. 217)

I watered my horse at the Long Wall caves,
water so cold it hurt his bones;
I went and spoke to the Long Wall boss:
  "We're soldiers from T'ai-yüan[1]—will you keep us here forever?"
  "Public works go according to schedule—
  swing your hammer, pitch your voice in with the rest!"
A man'd be better off to die in battle
than eat his heart out building the Long Wall!
The Long Wall—how it winds and winds,
winds and winds three thousand tricents;

here on the border, so many strong boys;
in the houses back home, so many widows and wives.
I sent a letter to my wife:
  "Better remarry than wait any longer—
  serve your new mother-in-law with care
  and sometimes remember the husband you once had."

Ch'en Lin, from Kiangsu, was one of the Seven Masters of the Chien-an Reign (196–220; see selections 24 and 25). He lived in an age of almost incessant warfare and, as a courtier in the service of the Ts'ao family (see selections 26 and 170), he may have hoped with this "song" to draw the attention of his patrons to the terrible hardship that military and *corvée* labor service inflicted on the common people. This poem, which follows the same theme as the preceding ballad, shows how literati poets could take material and ideas from the popular tradition and reshape them according to their own perspectives. It uses a mixture of pentasyllabic and heptasyllabic lines that skillfully suggests, without actually copying, the metrical irregularity of the old ballads.

  1. An important city in Shansi.

In answer her letter came to the border:
    "What nonsense do you write me now?
    Now when you're in the thick of danger,
    how could I rest by another man's side!"
[He] If you bear a son, don't bring him up!
    But a daughter—feed her good dried meat.
    Only *you* can't see, here by the Long Wall,
    the bones of the dead men heaped about!
[She] I bound up my hair and went to serve you;
    constant constant was the care of my heart;
    too well I know your borderland troubles;
    and I—can I go on like this much longer?

Translated by Burton Watson

170

Song on Enduring the Cold

Ts'ao Ts'ao (155–220)

North we climb the T'ai-hang Mountains;[1]
the going's hard on these steep heights!
Sheep Gut Slope dips and doubles,
enough to make the cartwheels crack.

Stark and stiff the forest trees,
the voice of the north wind sad;
crouching bears, black and brown, watch us pass;
tigers and leopards howl beside the trail.

Few men live in these valleys and ravines
where snow falls thick and blinding.
With a long sigh I stretch my neck;
a distant campaign gives you much to think of.

    This poem was probably written early in 206, when Ts'ao Ts'ao was crossing the T'ai-hang Mountains between Shansi and Hopei to attack a rival. The author was the founder of the Wei dynasty and father of the noted poets Ts'ao Chih (see selection 26) and Ts'ao P'i (187–226). Ts'ao P'i was also the first critic in China to treat literature as a medium of esthetic expression rather than as a mere vehicle for political propaganda and didactic instruction. Ts'ao Ts'ao is the antihero of the novel entitled *Romance of the Three Kingdoms* (see selection 258).
    1. A large mountain system stretching through several of China's northern provinces.

Why is my heart so downcast and sad?
All I want is to go back east,
but waters are deep and bridges broken;
halfway up, I stumble to a halt.

Dazed and uncertain, I've lost the old road,
night bearing down but nowhere to shelter;
on and on, each day farther,
men and horses starving as one.

Shouldering packs, we snatch firewood as we go,
chop ice to use in boiling our gruel—
That song of the Eastern Hills[2] is sad,
a troubled tale that fills me with grief.

Translated by Burton Watson

2. *Odes* 156, a song describing the hardships of a military campaign.

171
Pity Me!

Fu Hsüan (217–278)

Pity me! my body is female,
My lowly state is hard to describe.
A boy faces door and gate,
Comes down on earth with a natural birthright,
His manly heart burns for the four seas,
Ten thousand leagues he yearns for windy dust.

A girl is born, there is no celebration,
She is not her family's prized jewel.
Grown up she is hidden in private rooms,
Veils her head, too shy to look on others.

Shedding tears she marries in another village,
Sudden like a cloudburst of rain.
With bowed head she calms her features,
White teeth clenched beneath red lips.
She kneels down countless times

Born in Shensi, the poet rose from poverty and obscurity to wealth and fame through his literary talent. He served as censor and lord chamberlain under the Chin emperor Wu.

To maids and concubines like grim guests.
Happy love is like Cloudy Han,[1]
Like mallow or bean that leans toward spring sun.
Loving hearts in conflict are worse than water on fire,
One hundred wrongs are heaped upon the girl.

Her jade face with the years alters,
Her husband takes many new loves.
Once they were form and shadow,
Now they are Hun and Chinese.
Hun and Chinese sometimes see each other.
Love once severed is remote as Antares and Orion.[2]

Translated by Anne Birrell

1. The celestial river, counterpart of the Milky Way in the West. It is also called Starry River, Long River, Long Han, Sky River, or River of Heaven. It was believed that the Yellow River on earth flowed from the Han River in the sky. This reference usually conjures up ideas of the amorous legend of the Weaver Girl and Herdboy stars. The Han River is seen as an obstacle between the stellar lovers as it is in full flood every night of the year except the seventh night of the seventh month. On that night the waters ebb, allowing the lovers to meet. Weaver Girl is sometimes called the Girl of the Han River.

2. In Chinese lore, these two astronomical bodies are believed to be quareling brothers who never meet. In equinoctial opposition, they symbolize estranged lovers or friends.

172
Midnight Songs

Anonymous (late 4th century)

1

The sun sinks low. I
go to my front gate,
and look long, and see
you passing by.

Tradition has it that these untitled poems were written by a woman known as Tzu-yeh or Midnight. She lived sometime before the end of the fourth century and evidently made her living as a professional singer. Her dialect was of southeast China, a region known for its women poets.

The originals of these translations appear in a group of forty-two poems attributed to Midnight. The number for each poem here simply reflects its position in the collection. These lyrics might actually be the work of more than one person; and probably many female entertainers

Seductive face,
so many charms,
such hair!
—and sweet perfume
that spills
in from the road.

    2

My perfume?
No more
than incense leaves.
Seductive face?
You really think I'd dare?

But heaven doesn't rob us
of desires:
that's why it's sent me
here, why I've
seen you.

---

composed such popular poems using the sad melody—now lost—to which the words were originally sung.

    Other sequences, such as the seventy-five "Midnight Songs on the Four Seasons," testify to the continuing popularity of poetry in this voice. Later poets—including men of the educated class—found the poems moving, artistically satisfying, and well worth imitating. As witty, fluent examples of the five-syllable quatrain form, they had a significant influence on the poetry of ensuing centuries.

    The poems display a range of attitudes toward love and desire. Sometimes the speaker expresses heartbreak, and other times, intense physical longing. At times she is playful, cynical, or wry. Often the original texts can as easily be read in the third person as in the first. However, they do use personal pronouns—such as a colloquial word for "I" or for "you, my love"—more than the poetry of elite writers generally does.

    The Midnight songs employ a folk-songlike—usually female—voice: they are rich in puns on words related to love and passion. The best example in this selection is poem number 7, which uses "silk" as a traditional pun on "thoughts [of love]," along with a word that can be understood as either "a mate" or "a length of cloth." The translation here is necessarily much freer than in the other poems: the last line of the original simultaneously says, "How could I have known [those threads] wouldn't become a length of cloth?" and ". . . [we] wouldn't become mates?"

    Certain phrases recur in the poems. See, for example, the opening words of numbers 28 and 33. This may be evidence that the lyrics were created, and circulated, orally. At any rate, in the first two poems, repeated phrases make it possible to read poem number 2 as an answer to number 1.

    After the Midnight songs, the next significant source for poems by women is the mid-sixth-century anthology entitled New Songs from a Jade Terrace (Yü-t'ai hsin-yung; see selection 35) edited by the court poet Hsü Ling. Out of the one hundred and five poets represented in this celebrated anthology, thirteen are women. See selection 175 for an erotic poem by one of them.

3

Night after night, I do not
comb my hair. Silky
tangles hang
across my shoulders.

I stretch my limbs
around that young man's
hips. Is there any
place on him
I could not
love?

7

When I started wanting
to know that man,
I hoped our coupled hearts
would be like one.

Silk thoughts threaded
on a broken loom—
who'd have known
the tangled snarls to come?

9

So soon. Today, love, we
part. And our re-
union—when
will that time come?

A bright lamp
shines on an empty place,
in sorrow and longing:
not yet, not yet, not
yet.

12

Through the front gate,
my morning thoughts
take off; from river-
isles out back,
at twilight, they return.

Talk and
laughter—who

shall I share them with?
Deep in my belly, dark and
damp, I think of you.

16

Seize the moment!—
while you're still young.
Miss your chance—
one day, and you've grown old.

If you don't
believe my words, just look
out at those grasses
underneath the frost.

28

Night so
long. Can't get
to sleep. Turn
on my side, and hear
the nightwatch drum.

No reason for it, love,
and yet we met:
it leaves a bitter taste
down in my guts.

33

Night so
long. Can't get
to sleep. Bright
moon blazes into bloom.

In thought, I hear
a call from a windblown
voice. And to the empty
sky, make hollow answer,
yes.

42

Morning's sun
shines through windows draped
in brocade sewn
with coins. Light

breezes move those pure
white silks.

An artful smile: a pair
of lush, curved, crimson
horns.
Lovely eyes: soft
moth-brows fall
and rise.

Translated by Jeanne Larsen

173

A Peacock Southeast Flew

Anonymous (5th century)

Preface

At the close of the Han Dynasty, during the years of 196–220 C.E., the wife of Chiao Chung-ch'ing, the magistrate of Luchiang prefecture, whose maiden name was Liu, was dismissed from home by her husband's mother. She swore to herself that she would never remarry, but her own parents and family brought a great deal of pressure to bear on her. So she committed suicide by drowning herself. When her husband, Chung-ch'ing, learned of

This is a long narrative poem—rare in Chinese literature (it is unique for this early period). Usually assigned to the third or fourth century, linguistic evidence points to a somewhat later period. The extreme length and narrative properties of the poem, as opposed to the brief lyrical and descriptive quality of typical Chinese verse, have prompted some historians to posit Indian influence. Kan Pao (fl. 317 C.E.), however, records in scroll 11 of *Search for the Supernatural* (see selection 243) a story of marital fidelity that contains numerous parallels: a devoted couple, the wife torn from her husband, vows of eternal love despite separation, separate suicides, graves joined by overarching trees, sad chorus of mandarin ducks, and the sympathy of the public for the dead couple. The content of the narrative would therefore appear to be Chinese, unless Kan Pao's tale (like many others in his collection) was also influenced by a foreign source. Indeed, many of the themes and features in this extraordinary poem, including the regal bird mentioned in the title and first line, would seem to indicate some sort of connection with India.

The poem also goes by another, more Chinese-sounding, title: "An Old Poem Written for Chiao Chung-ch'ing's Wife." The formulaic opening of the narrative contains an image popularly used in the folk-song tradition—a bird which becomes separated from its mate or its flock. The theme of separation is echoed toward the end of the story when Chiao Chung-ch'ing commits suicide on a "southeast" bough of a garden tree.

The preface, of unknown date, appears to have been composed separately. The Luchiang prefecture mentioned in the preface was located in what is now Anhwei province.

this, he also committed suicide by hanging himself from a tree in the garden. A contemporary poet felt deep sympathy for these two and composed a poem about them. It goes as follows:

A peacock southeast flew,
After five leagues it faltered.

"At thirteen I could weave white silk,
At fourteen I learned to make clothes.
At fifteen I played the many-stringed lute,
At sixteen recited *Odes* and *History*.[1]
At seventeen I became your wife
And my heart was full of constant pain and sorrow.

"You became a government clerk,
I kept chaste, my love never straying.
At cockcrow I went in to weave at the loom,
Night after night found no rest.
In three days I cut five lengths of cloth,
Mother-in-law still nagged at my sloth.
It wasn't my weaving that was too slow,
But it's hard to be a wife in your home.
I don't want to be driven out,
But there's no way I can stay on here.
So please speak with your mother
To let me be sent home in good time."

The clerk heard these words
And up in the hall spoke with his mother.
"As a boy my physiognomy chart was unlucky,
I was fortunate to get such a wife as she.
We bound our hair,[2] shared pillow and mat,
Vowed to be lovers till Yellow Springs.[3]
We both have served you two years or three,
From the start not so long a time,
Yet the girl's conduct is not remiss,
Why do you treat her so unkindly?"

His mother said to the clerk,
"How can you be so soft!
This wife has no sense of decorum,

1. Two of the Confucian classics.
2. At the age of puberty, boys and girls bound their hair. The phrase comes to mean marriage. It is sometimes used with another ritual, the first wine of marriage.
3. The land of the deceased that lies beneath the earth.

Whatever she does she goes her own way.
I've borne my anger for a long time now,
You must not just suit yourself!
Our east neighbors have a good daughter,
Her name is Ch'in Lofu.[4]
So pretty her body, beyond compare,

Your mother will seek her for your wife.
It's best to dismiss this one as soon as we can,
Dismiss her, we won't let her stay!"

The government clerk knelt down in reply,
"Now I only have this to say, Mother.
If you dismiss this wife today,
For the rest of my life I will not remarry!"
His mother heard these words,
Thumped her bed, then in a fierce rage:
"My son, have you no respect?
How dare you speak in your wife's defense!
I have lost all feeling for you,
On no account will I let you disobey me!"

The government clerk silent, without a word,
Bowed twice and went back within their doors.
He started to speak to his new wife,
Stammered, unable to talk.
"I myself would not drive you away,
But there's my mother, scolding and nagging.
You just go home for a little while,
Today I must report to the office.
It won't be for long, I'll soon be coming home,
And when I come back I'll be sure to fetch you.
So let this put your mind at rest.
Please don't contradict me!"

His new wife said to the clerk:
"No more of this nonsense!
Long ago in early springtime
I left home to come to your gates.
Whatever I did I obeyed your mother,
In my behavior never dared do as I pleased.
Day and night I tried hard at my work.
Brought low I am caught in a vice of misery.
My words have been blameless,

4. See selection 164.

I fulfilled my duties diligently.
Why then, as I'm being summarily dismissed,
Do you still talk of my coming back here?
I have embroidered tunics,
Gorgeous they shine with a light of their own;
Red silk funnel bedcurtains,
At the four corners hang scent sachets;
Dressing cases sixty or seventy,
Green jasper, green silk cord;
Many, many things, each of them different,
All sorts of things in these boxes.
I am despised, and my things also worthless,
Not worth offering your next wife,
But I'll leave them here as gifts.
From now on we'll never meet again,
But it will be a constant comfort for me,
If you never, never forget me!"

The cock crew, outside it was getting light.
The new wife got up and carefully dressed.
She puts on her broidered lined gown
And four or five different things.
On her feet she slips silk shoes;
On her head tortoise-shell combs gleam;
Round her waist she wears flowing silk white,
On her ears wears bright moon pendants.
Her hands are like pared onion stems,
Her mouth seems rich scarlet cinnabar.
Svelte, svelte she walks with tiny steps,
Perfect, matchless in all the world.

She went up the high hall, bowed to Mother.
The mother heard she was leaving, didn't stop her.
"Long ago when I was a child,
I grew up in the countryside.
I had no schooling from the start,
On both counts would shame the man of a great house.
I received from you, Mother, much money and silk,
I do not want to be summarily dismissed;
Today, though, I am going back home.
I am afraid I have brought trouble to your house."

She withdrew and took leave of her sister-in-law.
Tears fell, beads of pearl.
"When I first came as a bride

You were beginning to lean on the bed.
Now as I am being dismissed,
You are as tall as I, sister.
Care for Mother with all your heart,
Be nice and help all you can.
On the first, seventh, and last ninth [5] of the month,
When you're enjoying yourself, don't forget me!"

She left the gates, climbed the coach, departed,
Tears fell in more than a hundred streams.
The clerk's horse was in front,
The new wife's coach behind.
Clatter-clatter, how it rumbled, rumbled!
They met at the mouth of the main road,
He dismounted, got into her coach.
With bowed head he whispered these words in her ear:
"I swear I won't be parted from you,
Just go home for a little while.
Today I am going to the office,
But I'll return before long.
I swear by Heaven I'll not betray you!"

His new wife said to the clerk:
"I feel you love me fondly,
And you seem to hold me in high esteem.
Before long I hope you will come for me.
You must be rock firm,
I must be a pliant reed.
The pliant reed is supple as silk,
The firm rock will not be rolled away.
I have my father and brothers,
Their temper is wild as thunder;
I fear they will not abide by my wishes,
But oppose me, destroy my hopes."
They raised their hands in a long, long farewell,
For both loves the same wistful longing.

She entered the gates, went up the family hall,
Approaching, withdrawing with expressionless face.
Her mother beat her fist loud:
"We didn't plan for you to return on your own!
At thirteen I taught you to weave,

5. On the seventh and twenty-ninth days of each lunar month, women were permitted to rest from their work.

At fourteen you could make clothes,
At fifteen you played the many-stringed lute,
At sixteen you knew ceremonial rites,
At seventeen I sent you off in marriage,
Telling you to swear not to give offense.
What have you done wrong now that
Uninvited you come home yourself!"
"I, Lanchih, have brought shame on my mother,
But your child has truly done no wrong."
Her mother's heart was broken with deep sorrow.

She had been home more than ten days
When the district magistrate sent a matchmaker.
He said, "We have a third young master,
Charming beyond compare in all the world!
He is barely eighteen or nineteen,
Eloquent, very talented he is!"

Mother said to daughter:
"Go, you may answer 'yes.' "
Her daughter choked back the tears:
"When I, Lanchih, first came home,
The clerk showed me great kindness,
Swore on oath he'd never desert me.
If I were now to betray our love,
I fear this act would be wrong.
Let's break off the betrothal talks.
In good time we'll discuss the matter again."

Her mother explained to the matchmaker:
"In all humility, I do have such a daughter,
She went away in marriage, but is returned to our gates.
She was reluctant to be an official's wife,
How would she please a fine gentleman's son?
I hope you will be successful with other inquiries.
We cannot at present give permission."

The matchmaker was gone many days,
Then a deputy was sent for, asked to reconsider.
"They say they have a daughter, Lanchih,
Whose forefathers for generations have held office.
Say, 'My master says he has a fifth son,
Elegant, refined, not yet married.
My deputy I've sent as matchmaker,
And a secretary to bring his message.' "

Immediately they put their case: "The prefect's family
Has such a fine son,
He wishes to take solemn vows of marriage
And so we are sent to your house."

The mother refused the matchmaker:
"My daughter has already sworn an oath.
What dare a mother say?"
When her brother learned of this
He was disappointed and furious in his heart.
He broached the matter, telling his sister:
"In these arrangements, why are you so unreasonable?
First you married a government clerk,
Later you might marry a squire.
Fortune is like Heaven and Earth,
It can bring glory to your person.
Not to wed this lord now,
What will happen in the future?"

Lanchih looked up and replied:
"In fact what my brother says is right.
I left home to serve my bridegroom.
Midway I returned to my brother's gates.
It's my place to follow my brother's wishes,
Why would I do as I please?
Though I made a vow with the government clerk,
I may never chance to meet him again.
Tell them straight away I agree to marry,
They may arrange a betrothal."

The matchmaker got down from the ritual couch:
"Yes, yes!" and "Quite, quite!"
He went back to the office and explained to the prefect:
"Your servant has carried out your command.
Our discussion has met with great success!"
When the prefect heard this
He rejoiced in his heart.
He scanned the calendar, opened the almanac:
"It will be auspicious this month,
The Six Cardinal Points are in conjunction.
The luckiest day is the thirtieth,
Today it's now the twenty-seventh,
You may go and conclude the nuptials."

Discussions on both sides hastened the wedding gifts,
In succession like floating clouds.
A green sparrow and white swan boat,
At the four corners were dragon banners
Softly curling in the wind.
A gold coach of jade its wheels,
Prancing piebald horses,
Colored silk threads and gold stitched saddles.
A wedding gift of three million cash,
All strung on green cord.
Assorted silks, three hundred bolts,
From Chiaokuang[6] a purchase of fine fish.
A retinue of four or five hundred men
Densely massed set out to the palace.

Mother said to daughter:
"I have just received a letter from the prefect,
Tomorrow he will come to invite you in marriage.
Why aren't you making your clothes?
Don't fail to start now!"
Her daughter, silent, without a word,
Sobbed with her kerchief stifling her mouth.
Tears fell as if poured.
She moved her seat of lapis lazuli,
Set it near the window.
Her left hand held shears and rule,
Her right hand took the sheer silk.
By morning she finished an embroidered robe,
Later she finished an unlined dress of silk.
Dim, dim, the sun was about to darken,
With sad thoughts she left the gates and wept.

When the government clerk heard of this affair
He asked for furlough to go home a while.
Before he had come two or three leagues
His wearisome horse sadly whinnied.
His new wife recognized his horse's whinny,
Slipped on her shoes and met him.
Sadly from a distance they gazed at each other,
She knew it was her long lost one coming.
She raised her hand, patted his horse's saddle,
Her loud sighs tore his heart.

6. Chiao-chou and Kuang-chou on the far southern seacoast.

"Since you parted from me
Unimaginable things have happened!
Things have turned out not as we once wished,
Nor could I make you understand.
I have had my parents—father and mother,
Bringing pressure to bear joined by my brother,
To make me consent to marry another man.
You have come back, what do you hope for?"

The government clerk said to his new wife:
"Congratulations for winning such high promotion!
The firm rock square and strong
Could have endured a thousand years.
The pliant reed, once so supple,
Is reduced to this in the space of dawn to dusk!
You may reign supreme like the sun,
I will face Yellow Springs alone."

His new wife said to the government clerk:
"What do you mean by such words?
Together we have suffered this great crisis,
First you, and then your wife.
Down in Yellow Springs we will meet,
Don't betray our vow made this day!"
They held hands, then went their separate ways,
Each returning to their different gates.
For the living to make a parting unto death
Is more hateful than words can tell.
They think of their farewell from this world,
Never in a million years to be brought back to life.

The government clerk went back home,
Up in the hall he bowed to his mother:
"Today the great wind is cold,
Cold winds have crushed a tree,
Harsh frosts grip the garden orchid.
Your son today goes to darkness,
Leaving Mother to survive alone.
For I must carry out a most unhappy plan;
Torment our souls no more!
May your life be like South Mountain's[7] rock,
Your four limbs healthy and strong!"

7. Occurs early on in the *Classic of Odes*, poem 172, where the blessings of long life and happiness are invoked. A symbol of longevity, the mountain stood south of Ch'ang-an.

When his mother heard these words
Teardrops fell with each word:
"You are the son of a great family,
With official position at galleried courts.
Don't die for the sake of that wife!
About noble and base are you so naive?
Our east neighbor has a good daughter,
Meek and mild, the loveliest in town.
Your mother will seek her for your wife,
All will be arranged between dawn and dusk."

The government clerk bowed twice and went back
Sighing long sighs in his empty rooms.
The plan he made was fixed as ever.
He turned his head toward the door,
Slowly he watched, grief's oppressive rage.

That day horses and cattle lowed,
His new wife goes into her green hut.
After dusk had fallen
A quiet hush, people start to settle down.
"My life will end today,
My soul will vanish, my corpse will linger a while."
She lifts her skirt, removes her silk shoes,
Stands up and goes toward the clear lake.

When the government clerk hears of this act,
His heart knows it is the long separation.
He hesitates under a garden tree,
Hangs himself from a southeast branch.

The two families asked for a joint burial,
A joint burial on the side of Mount Hua.[8]
East and west were planted pine and cypress,
Left and right catalpa were set.
Branch with branch joins to form a canopy,
Leaf with leaf meets in wedlock.
Among them is a pair of flying birds,
Called mandarin ducks, drake and hen,
Lifting their heads they call to each other,
Night after night until the fifth watch.[9]
Passersby stay their steps to listen,
Widows get out of bed and pace to and fro.

8. A sacred mountain in Shensi (see selection 53).
9. Just before dawn (3–5 a.m.).

Be warned, men of the future,
Learn this lesson and never forget!

Translated by Anne Birrell

174
Magic Cinnabar[1]

Pao Chao (415–466)

The king of Huainan[2]
Craving immortality
Drank potions, ate health foods, read arcane tomes.
Of lapis lazuli his drug bowls, of ivory his plates;
Gold cauldron, jade ladle, he mixed magic cinnabar,
Mixed magic cinnabar,
Pleasured in purple rooms,
In purple rooms where exotic girls fondle bright earrings.
Paradise birdsong, phoenix dance broke his heart.

Translated by Anne Birrell

From Kiangsu, Pao Chao served in several posts under the Liu-Sung emperor Hsiao-wu, the poet Liu Chün. His ambitions were frustrated by the rigid class distinctions of his day, which barred him from the high places that his genius might otherwise have earned him. Compelled to spend his life as a staff writer and administrator for various aristocrats, he was eventually assassinated by rioting soldiers when one of his patrons was forced to commit suicide for rebellion. He is generally regarded as a major poet of the Southern Dynasties, especially for his ballads and his innovative developments in the folk-song genre.

1. A red mineral used in preparing elixirs of immortality.

2. "South of the Huai [River]"; an area that lies mostly within the modern province of Anhwei. A brilliant group of scholars assembled there by the king of Huainan, Liu An (d. 122 B.C.E.), a member of the royal family of the Han dynasty who upheld Taoism, wrote some of the earliest Chinese texts on cosmology.

Going out Through the North Gate of Chi,[1] A Ballad

Pao Chao

Winged bulletins arise from frontier outposts;
Beacon fires extend to the city of Hsien-yang.[2]
Cavalry are sent to garrison Kuang-wu;
4   Infantry dispatched to the aid of Shuo-fang.[3]
Rigorous autumn stiffens bows and shafts;
Hunnish squadrons are spirited and strong.
The Son of Heaven lays a hand on his sword in anger;
8   Couriers catch sight of one another in the distance.
Climbing stony roads in echelon formation,
Crossing over flying bridges in single file.
Flutes and drums flow with memories of Han;
12   Banners and armor are covered with nomad frost.
A howling wind rises to assail the frontier;
Sand and grit soar aloft and float.
Horses' coats are stiff as hedgehogs';
16   Horn-trimmed bows cannot be drawn.
In perilous times appear steadfast officials;
In disordered ages, we know the loyal and the good.
Giving up their lives in the service of a noble ruler,
20   Their own deaths are offered as a sacrifice to the nation.

Translated by Daniel Bryant

1. An old name for the region around Peking.
2. The capital of the Western Han dynasty, located near modern Sian in Shensi.
3. Frontier districts located in northern Shansi and inside the bend of the Yellow River.

175
Added to a Letter Sent to a Traveler

Pao Ling-hui (fl. c. 464)

Since you went away, oh,
I lean on the porch-rail, my face tense.

The female poet Pao Ling-hui was the younger sister of the poet Pao Chao, and like her brother wrote in the style of refined imitation of Han dynasty folk-songs and ballads (see selection 174).

Nights, no block and pounder sound;
Noontimes, my high gate stays closed.
Within the curtains of my bed, a stream of fireflies;
Out front in the courtyard, a bloom of purple orchids.
Nature's things dry up: they sense the season's changed—
Wild geese arrive: they know a traveler's chill.
Your journey may end at winter's close—
Though spring wears on, I'll wait for your return.

Translated by Jeanne Larsen and Anne Birrell

As its opening line, this poem borrows from "Bedroom Longing" by Hsü Kan (171–218 C.E.), a poem of sixty lines by a member of the literary circle under the patronage of the Ts'ao royal family in the Wei dynasty. Pao Ling-hui's poem develops in a very different way from her predecessor's—where he is meditative, she is observant; where he is verbose, she is succinct. The images of the silent block and pounder in line 3 function as surprisingly coarse puns, given the generally decorous eroticism of *New Songs from a Jade Terrace* (*Yü-t'ai hsin-yung*), the mid-sixth-century anthology in which this poem is preserved (see selection 35). The block (*chen*) was a heavy stone on which wet clothes were beaten by a wooden pounder (*ch'u*) to clean and thicken the cloth. Another name for the block was *kao-chen*, also called a *fu*, which is a pun for a man, lover, or husband (*fu*). The tactile, auditory, and visual imagery of the two objects combines to simulate lovemaking.

176
The Ballad of Mulan

Anonymous (5th–6th century)

Click, click, forever click, click;
Mulan sits at the door and weaves.
Listen, and you will not hear the shuttle's sound,
4 But only hear a girl's sobs and sighs.
"Oh tell me, lady, are you thinking of your love,
Oh tell me, lady, are you longing for your dear?"
"Oh no, oh no, I am not thinking of my love,
8 Oh no, oh no, I am not longing for my dear.

Mulan (old pronunciation Muklan) was a member of the Särbi (Hsien-pei) people. This celebrated ballad tells of her resolve to take her father's place in fending off the encroaching Jou-jan nomads. She is often compared with Joan of Arc, although the two do not share much more in common than the fact that they were both women warriors. The people and places in the ballad are all from the far northern borderlands of China, and it is likely that this remarkable work was first conceived in one of the languages of that land of nomads.

But last night I read the battle-roll;
The Khan has ordered a great levy of men.
The battle-roll was written in twelve books,
12   And in each book stood my father's name.
My father's sons are not grown men,
And of all my brothers, none is older than me.
Oh let me to the market to buy saddle and horse,
16   And ride with the soldiers to take my father's place."
In the eastern market she's bought a gallant horse,
In the western market she's bought saddle and cloth.
In the southern market she's bought snaffle and reins,
20   In the northern market she's bought a tall whip.
In the morning she stole from her father's and mother's house;
At night she was camping by the Yellow River's side.
She could not hear her father and mother calling to her by her name,
24   But only the song of the Yellow River as its hurrying waters hissed and
        swirled through the night.
At dawn they left the River and went on their way;
At dusk they came to the Black Water's side.
She could not hear her father and mother calling to her by her name,
28   She could only hear the muffled voices of Scythian horsemen riding on
        the hills of Yen.
A thousand leagues she tramped on the errands of war,
Frontiers and hills she crossed like a bird in flight.
Through the northern air echoed the watchman's tap;
32   The wintry light gleamed on coats of mail.
The captain had fought a hundred fights, and died;
The warriors in ten years had won their rest.
They went home; they saw the Emperor's face;
36   The Son of Heaven was seated in the Hall of Light.
To the strong in battle lordships and lands he gave;
And of prize money a hundred thousand strings.
Then spoke the Khan and asked her what she would take.
40   "Oh, Mulan asks not to be made
        A Counsellor at the Khan's court;
She only begs for a camel that can march
        A thousand leagues a day,
44   To take her back to her home."

When her father and mother heard that she had come,
They went out to the wall and led her back to the house.
When her little sister heard that she had come,
48   She went to the door and rouged her face afresh.

When her little brother heard that his sister had come,
He sharpened his knife and darted like a flash
51 Toward the pigs and sheep.

She opened the gate that leads to the eastern tower,
She sat on her bed that stood in the western tower.
She cast aside her heavy soldier's cloak,
55 And wore again her old-time dress.
She stood at the window and bound her cloudy hair;
She went to the mirror and fastened her yellow combs.
She left the house and met her messmates in the road;
59 Her messmates were startled out of their wits.
They had marched with her for twelve years of war
And never known that Mulan was a girl.
For the male hare has a lilting, lolloping gait,
63 And the female hare has a wild and roving eye;
But set them both scampering side by side,
And who so wise could tell you "This is he"?

Translated by Arthur Waley

177
Song of the Tölös

Hulü Chin (fl. mid-6th century)

Along the Tölös River,
Beneath the Shady Mountain,
The sky seems like a vaulted yurt,
Covering the wilderness all around.

The sky is azure,
The wilderness is vast,
And when the wind blows, the grasses bend to reveal cattle and goats.

Translated by Victor H. Mair

Hulü Chin, the chieftain of a northern Turkic tribe known as the Tchirek, was attached to the courts of Eastern Wei (534–550) and Northern Ch'i (550–557). His song was said to have originally been sung in the Särbi (Hsien-pei) language current in those courts and subsequently translated into Chinese. Compare the introductory notes to selections 163, 176, and 178.

178
Song of the Breaking of the Willow

Anonymous (6th century?)

Far off I see the River[1] at Meng Ford,
willows thick and leafy there.
I am the son of a captive family
and cannot understand the Han man's[2] song.

Translated by Burton Watson

Written from the point of view of a non-Han prisoner in the north, it is obvious from the last line that this song must have originally been sung in a non-Sinitic language.
1. The Yellow River.
2. "Han" is a term for the largest ethnic group among the Chinese.

179
Army Ballad

Wang Wei (701–761)

The bugle blows, setting the marchers moving,
A grumbling hubbub as the soldiers rise.
Fifes screech, a tumult of neighing horses
As they struggle to ford the Golden River.[1]
Sunset at the edge of a great desert,
Sounds of battle within the dust and mist.
Having bound up the necks of all the famous chieftains,
They return to report to the emperor.

Translated by Stephen Owen

For a note on Wang Wei, see selection 44.
1. This geographical feature fixes the setting of the ballad along the northern borderlands. Unlike the previous three selections, however, it is clearly written from a Chinese point of view.

180

The Song of Lasting Regret

Po Chü-yi (772–846)

Monarch of Han,[1] he doted on beauty, yearned for a bewitching temptress;[2]

"The Song of Lasting Regret" is the romanticized retelling of the love affair between the great emperor Li Lung-chi (reigned 712–756, posthumously known as Hsüan Tsung) and Yang Yü-huan, the lady raised by him in 742 to the high rank of "Precious Consort" (*kuei-fei*).

The emperor's infatuation with Lady Yang and his virtual abandonment of governmental affairs (first to the dictatorial Li Lin-fu, who held sway as Minister of State until 752, and then to the equally grasping Yang Kuo-chung, a distant cousin of Lady Yang) have long been regarded in both official and popular history as the main factors leading to the ruin of Hsüan Tsung's long reign and the near-destruction of the dynasty itself. The effective instrument of overthrow was a Sogdian-Turkic general with the sinicized name An Lu-shan who, as a personal favorite of both the emperor and his consort, gradually accumulated supreme military power in the northeast border region (near modern Peking) and, in December 755, turned his troops against the government. By July of 756 the rebel forces were in position to overrun the capital city, Ch'ang-an. In the face of this imminent threat, the emperor and his immediate entourage and military guard fled the capital in the early morning of July 14, intending to take refuge in Shu (present-day Szechwan) in the southwest, where Yang Kuo-chung had built up a private stronghold and sphere of influence. The next day, at the Ma-wei post-station (located some thirty miles west of the capital), the imperial troops killed Yang Kuo-chung and refused to move on unless the emperor put Lady Yang to death as well. Hsüan Tsung was compelled to appease the soldiers, and Lady Yang submitted to being strangled to death with a cord wielded by Kao Li-shih, chief eunuch and the emperor's oldest confidant. After this event the emperor moved on to sanctuary in Shu, while the heir-apparent Li Heng (posthumously known as Su Tsung, reigned 756–62) broke off from the main party with a contingent of soldiers to progress northwest and organize a base of loyalist resistance to the rebels. Shortly thereafter, Li Heng proclaimed himself emperor; Hsüan Tsung had no choice but to acknowledge his now emeritus status. About a year and a half later, Ch'ang-an was retaken by T'ang forces, and Su Tsung invited the old emperor to return to the capital, where he would live out his remaining years in sad remembrance of earlier glories. But it was not until 763 that the rebellion begun by An Lu-shan would be fully quelled. When the state was finally reunified, and the forty-four-year reign of Hsüan Tsung—unprecedented in its splendor—was but a memory, it seemed to most that a great turning point in history had been passed. Notwithstanding more serious political and military causes for the disaster, that a reign of such magnificence could end with such a crash confirmed most members of the traditionally misogynist mandarinate in the view that the root cause of the debacle was lodged in the emperor's allegedly shameful relationship with Precious Consort Yang.

This is the view adopted by Po Chü-yi in his poem. But Po is as interested in the sentimental aspects of the tale as he is in its political implications. Indeed, it is primarily, in his telling, a love story—one which he allows himself license to embroider at times with incidents contrary to fact (such as the trampling of Lady Yang under the army's horses and the emperor's reduced entourage passing by Mount Omei) as well as the insertion of scenes of pure fantasy (such as the Taoist adept's visit to Lady Yang's ethereal essence in the isles of the immortals and his conversation with her there).

The poem was written early in 807 C.E. and was originally supplemented with a more historically accurate prose recitation of events, "Tale of the Song of Lasting Regret" by Po's

Through the dominions of his sway, for many years he sought but did
not find her.
There was in the family of Yang a maiden just then reaching fullness,
4   Raised in the women's quarters protected, unacquainted yet with others.
Heaven had given her a ravishing form, impossible for her to hide,
And one morning she was chosen for placement at the side of the
sovereign king.
When she glanced behind with a single smile, a hundred seductions
were quickened;
8   All the powdered and painted ones in the Six Palaces[3] now seemed
without beauty of face.

In the coolness of springtime, she was permitted to bathe in the Hua-
ch'ing[4] pools,
Where the slickening waters of the hot springs washed over her firm
flesh.
Supported as she rose by a waiting-maid, she was so delicate, listless:
12   This was the moment when first she acceded to His favor and
beneficence.

Cloud-swept tresses, flowery features, quivering hair-pendants of gold,
And behind the warmth of lotus-bloom drapings, they passed the
springtime nights—

---

friend, Ch'en Hung. Composed in 120 heptasyllabic lines, the poem is organized in a series of
vignettes set forth in rhyming couplets and in quatrains. These short, lilting units are framed by
octets at the beginning and the end of the poem. Rhyme changes in the original are indicated as
stanza-breaks in the translation.

Po Chü-yi became a Presented Scholar in 799 but, because of his uncompromising honesty
and forthrightness, his official career was not smooth. He settled in Loyang in his later years,
where he formed a society with some Buddhist monks of Fragrant Hill temple and styled himself
"Lay Buddhist of Fragrant Hill." Po left behind more than three thousand poetic works, making
him the most prolific of all T'ang poets. His language was plain and relatively easy to understand,
a cause for scorn by literary critics inclined to more mannered and pretentious styles. A story
about Po tells of how he would not consider a poem finished if it could not be understood when
read aloud to a washerwoman. Perhaps it is his comprehensibility and naturalness that contribute
to making him by far the best-known Chinese poet in Japan.

1. Po Chü-yi here adopts the convention—often used by T'ang poets when writing of
contemporary political matters—that he is speaking of the first great Chinese imperium, the
Han.

2. "Bewitching temptress" is literally "state-toppler," i.e., a beauty for whom one would
lose everything.

3. The dwellings of the imperial concubines.

4. The Hua-ch'ing ("Floriate Clear") Palace on Mount Li, some fifteen miles east of Ch'ang-
an, included several hot springs. Hsüan Tsung was particularly fond of this imperial retreat. He
had the buildings, grounds, and pools refurbished, and removed there with Lady Yang and
necessary court officials at increasingly frequent intervals during the later years of his reign (see
also lines 28–29).

Springtime nights so grievously brief, as the sun rose again high!
16   From this time onward the sovereign king no longer held early court.

Taken with pleasure, she attended on the feasts, continuing without let;
Springtime followed springtime outing, evening after evening she
   controlled.

Of the comely beauties of the rear palace,[5] there were three thousand
   persons,
20   And preferments and affection for all three thousand were placed on her
   alone.
In her golden room, with makeup perfect, the Delicate One[6] serves for
   the night;
In a tower of jade, with the feast concluded, drunkenness befits love in
   spring.

Her sisters and brothers, older or younger, all were enfeoffed with land;[7]
24   The most enviable brilliance and glory quickened their doorways and
   gates.
Then it came to pass, throughout the empire, that the hearts of fathers
   and mothers
No longer valued the birth of a son but valued the birth of daughters.

The high sites of Mount Li's palace reached into clouds in the blue,
28   And transcendent music, wafted on the wind, was heard there
   everywhere.

Measured songs, languorous dancing merged with sound of strings and
   bamboo,
As the sovereign king looked on all day long, never getting enough . . .
Until, out of Yü-yang,[8] horse-borne war-drums came, shaking the
   earth,
32   To dismay and smash the melody of "Rainbow Skirts and Feathered
   Vestments."[9]

*   *   *

5. The women's quarters, whose numerous maidens are now wholly neglected by the emperor, for whom Lady Yang is the only woman that exists.

6. The "Delicate One" (*chiao*) figures Lady Yang in the person of Ah-chiao, beloved of Emperor Wu of Han (Han Wu Ti) in his youth and about whom he once said, "If I could have Ah-chiao, I should have a room of gold made in which to treasure her."

7. Besides Yang Kuo-chung, other relatives of Lady Yang, including most conspicuously three of her sisters, received lavish conferments and marks of favor from the emperor.

8. An Lu-shan's headquarters, about seventy miles east of present-day Peking.

9. The new name given by Hsüan Tsung to an exotic Indo-Iranian melody that he rescored and to which Lady Yang danced in a costume made to resemble the fairy garments of moon maidens. According to one tradition, the emperor brought the melody back with him from a mystical voyage to the moon.

By the nine-layered walls and watchtowers, dust and smoke arose,
And a thousand chariots, ten thousand riders moved off to the southwest.[10]

The halcyon-plumed banners jounced and joggled along, moving and stopping again,
36   As they went forth westward from the metropolis' gates, something more than a hundred tricents.
And then the Six Armies would go no farther—there was no other recourse,
But the fluently curved moth-eyebrows[11] must die before the horses.

Floriform filigrees were strewn on the ground, to be retrieved by no one,
40   Halcyon tailfeathers, an aigrette of gold, and hairpins made of jade.
The sovereign king covered his face—he could not save her;
When he looked back, it was with tears of blood that mingled in their flow.

*   *   *

Yellowish grit spreads and scatters, as the wind blows drear and doleful;
44   Cloudy walkways turn and twist, climbing Saber Gallery's[12] heights.
Below Mount Omei[13] there are very few men who pass by;
Lightless now are the pennons and flags in the sun's dimmer aura.

Waters of Shu's streams deepest blue, the mountains of Shu are green—
48   For the Paragon, the Ruler, dawn to dawn, night upon night, his feelings:
Seeing the moon from his transient palace—a sight that tears at his heart;
Hearing small bells in the evening rain—a sound that stabs his insides.[14]

*   *   *

Heaven revolves, the days roll on, and the dragon carriage was turned around;

10. The emperor and his personal retinue are fleeing the capital.
11. Those of Lady Yang.
12. The lofty pass that connects the territory of Ch'in (in which Ch'ang-an is located) with that of Shu (see selection 155).
13. About one hundred miles southwest of Chengtu, this is the most important mountain in Szechwan. It was officially ennobled in T'ang times for its supernatural potency (see selection 216).
14. The sight of the moon pains him because he remembers other nights when he and Lady Yang enjoyed it together, just as he recalls the music she used to play as he hears the plaintive sound of little bells tinkling in the rain under the eaves of a roof.

52   Having reached the spot, faltering he haltered, unable to leave it again.
      But amidst that muddy earth, below Ma-wei Slope,
      Her jade countenance was not to be seen—just a place of empty death.

      Sovereign and servants beheld each other, cloaks wet from weeping;
56   And, looking east, to the metropolis' gates, let their horses take them
         homeward.

*   *   *

      Returned home now, and the ponds, the pools, all were as before—
      The lotuses of Grand Ichor Pool, the willows by the Night-is-Young
         Palace.[15]

      The lotus blossoms resemble her face, the willow branches her eyebrows;
60   Confronted with this, would it be possible that his tears should not fall?
      From the day that peach and plum flowers open, in the springtime
         breezes,
      Until the leaves of the "we-together"[16] tree are shed in the autumn
         rain. . . .

      The West Palace and the Southern Interior[17] were rife with autumn
         grasses,
64   And fallen leaves covered the steps, their red not swept away.
      The artistes, once young, of the Pear Garden[18] have hair gone newly
         white;
      The Pepper Room[19] attendants and their budding nymphs are become
         aged now.

      Fireflies flit through the hall-room at dusk, as he yearns in desolation;
68   When all the wick of his lone lamp is used, sleep still fails to come.
      Ever later, more dilatory, sound the watch-drum and bell in the
         lengthening nights;
      Fitfully sparkling, the River of Stars[20] streams onward to the dawn-
         flushed sky.

15. Both were famous Han-time sites. The House of T'ang had its own pool of this name within the grounds of the emperor's Palace of Great Light.

16. The *Wu-t'ung* (*Sterculia platanifolia*). Its name is homophonous with the phrase "we together" (*wu t'ung*), and the falling of its leaves in the autumn rain suggests to Hsüan Tsung the extinction of the love he once shared with Lady Yang.

17. Referring respectively to the Sweet Springs Hall in the "palace city" and the Palace of Ascendant Felicity near Ch'ang-an's east market-ward. Both were the residences assigned by Su Tsung to the retired emperor who was not permitted to live in the grander compound of the Palace of Great Light again.

18. This garden had housed Hsüan Tsung's group of private musicians in the years of his glory and pleasure.

19. The dwelling of the chief consort.

20. The Milky Way.

The roof-tiles, paired as love-ducks, grow chilled, and flowers of frost
  grow thick;
72 The halcyon-plumed coverlet is cold—whom would he share it with?
Dim-distanced, far-faded, are the living from the dead, parted more
  than a year ago;
Neither her soul nor her spirit have ever yet come into his dreams.

*   *   *

A Taoist adept from Lin-ch'iung,[21] a visitor to the Hung-tu Gate,[22]
76 Could use the perfection of his essential being to contact souls and
  spirits.
Because of his broodings the sovereign king, tossing and turning, still
  yearned;
So he set to task this adept of formulas, to search for her sedulously.

Cleaving the clouds, driving the ethers, fleeting as a lightning-flash,
80 Ascending the heavens, entering into the earth, he sought her out
  everywhere.
On high he traversed the sky's cyan drop-off,[23] and below to the Yellow
  Springs;[24]
In both places, to the limits of vision, she was nowhere to be seen.

Of a sudden he heard rumor then of a transcendent mountain in the
  sea,
84 A mountain resting in void and nullity, amidst the vaporous seemings.

High buildings and galleries shimmer there brightly, and five-colored
  clouds mount up;
In the midst of this, relaxed and unhurried, were hosts of tender sylphs.
And in *their* midst was one, known as Greatest Perfection,[25]
88 Whose snow-white skin and flower-like features appeared to resemble
  hers.

In the western wing of the gatehouse of gold, he knocked at the jade
  bolting,

21. In modern Szechwan.
22. A Han dynasty designation for one of the capital portals.
23. The distant deep-blue reaches of the sky, and more specifically—to Taoist initiates—the region bearing that name in the Heaven of Nascent Azure.
24. The traditional Chinese underworld destination of one's *p'o* or carnal (earth-bound) souls.
25. "Greatest Perfection" (T'ai-chen) was the religious name adopted by Lady Yang when she briefly took orders as a Taoist priestess, prior to being recognized with a formal title as sharer of Hsüan Tsung's bed. Yang Yü-huan had originally been the wife of Hsüan Tsung's eighteenth son, Li Mao (Prince Shou). Her short period as a Taoist priestess, while not entirely a sham (Hsüan Tsung was intimately interested in Taoist teachings), served to "purify" her for attachment to the emperor.

In turn setting in motion Little Jade who made report to Doubly
    Completed.[26]
When word was told of the Son of Heaven's envoy, from the House of
    Han,
92   Then, within the nine-flowered drapings, her dreaming spirit startled.

She searched for her cloak, pushed pillow aside, arose, walked forth
    distractedly;
Door-screens of pearl, partitions of silver, she opened out one after
    another.
With her cloud-chignon half-mussed to one side, newly awakened from
    sleep,
96   With flowered cap[27] set awry, down she came to the ceremonial hall.

Her sylphine sleeves, puffed by a breeze, were lifted, flared and
    fluttering,
Just the same as in the dance of "Rainbow Skirts and Feathered
    Vestments."
But her jade countenance looked bleak, forlorn, crisscrossed with
    tears—
100   A single branch of pear blossom, in springtime laden with rain.

Restraining her feelings, focusing her gaze, she asked her sovereign
    king's indulgence:
"Once we were parted, both voice and face were lost to limitless
    vagueness.
There, within Chao-yang Basilica,[28] affection and favor were cut short,
104   While here in P'eng-lai's[29] palaces, the days and months have
    lengthened.

"Turning my head and looking down to the sites of the mortal sphere,
I can no longer see Ch'ang-an, what I see is dust and fog.
Let me take up these familiar old objects to attest to my deep love:
108   The filigree case, the two-pronged hairpin of gold, I entrust to you to
    take back.

"Of the hairpin but one leg remains, and one leaf-fold of the case;
The hairpin is broken in its yellow gold, and the case's filigree halved.

26. "Little Jade" (Hsiao-yü) and "Doubly Completed" (Shuang-ch'eng) are T'ai-chen's
maids. The latter was known in Taoist tradition as an attendant of the goddess Hsi Wang-mu
("Queen Mother of the West," see selection 187, note 5); the former was the beautiful daughter
of King Fu-ch'ai (reigned 495–473 B.C.E.) of the ancient state of Wu.
    27. That worn by Taoist priests and priestesses.
    28. The Chao-yang ("Splendid Sunshine") Basilica was one of the halls occupied by imperial
consorts during the Han.
    29. Named after the Taoist isles of immortality in the eastern ocean.

But if only his heart is as enduring as the filigree and the gold,
112 Above in heaven, or amidst men, we shall surely see each other."

As the envoy was to depart, she entrusted poignantly to him words as
    well,
Words in which there was a vow that only two hearts would know:
"On the seventh day of the seventh month, in the Hall of Protracted
    Life,[30]
116 At the night's mid-point, when we spoke alone, with no one else
    around—
'In heaven, would that we might become birds of coupled wings!
On earth, would that we might be trees of intertwining limbs! . . .' "
Heaven is lasting, earth long-standing, but there is a season for their
    end;
120 *This* regret stretches on and farther, with no ending time.

Translated by Paul W. Kroll

30. The Hall of Protracted Life (Ch'ang-sheng tien) was part of the Hua-ch'ing complex on Mount Li. Its name was used as the title of a famous early Ch'ing drama about the ill-fated love affair between Hsüan Tsung and "Precious Consort" Yang, ten years and three drafts in the writing by Hung Sheng (1650?–1704).

181
Iranian Whirling Girls

Po Chü-yi

1

Presented by the kingdom of Sogdiana at the end of the Heavenly Jewel reign period.[1]

    The poets Po Chü-yi (see selection 180) and Yüan Chen (see selection 252) did not simply fabricate these happenings. Records exist in the official *T'ang History* (*T'ang shu*) of the presentation of whirling dancers at court as tribute in 718, 719, 727, and 729. They came from Keš (hear Tashkent), Samarkand, Maimargh, and Khumdeh, all of which lay within Sogdiana, hence we are justified in referring to them as Sogdian or northeast Iranian whirlers. Such vigorous, rapidly twirling dances were common among the Iranian peoples. Compare, for example, the sacred whirling dance of the Sufi dervishes, most of whom were Iranians or who modeled themselves after Iranian styles. As for the pseudo-Iranian whirlers at the T'ang court, the history of the intrigues surrounding them is described in the introductory note to selection 180.

    1. 742–755.

An admonition against contemporary morals.

Iranian whirling girl, Iranian whirling girl—
Her heart answers to the strings,
Her hands answer to the drums.
At the sound of the strings and drums, she raises her arms,
5   Like swirling snowflakes tossed about, she turns in her twirling dance.
Whirling to the left, turning to the right, she never feels exhausted,
A thousand rounds, ten thousand circuits—it never seems to end.
Among men and living creatures, she is peerless;
Compared to her, the wheels of a racing chariot revolve slowly and a
    whirlwind is sluggish.

10   When the tune is over she bows twice in gratitude to the Son of
        Heaven,
And the Son of Heaven smiles a bit of a toothsome smile for her.

Iranian whirling girl,
You came from Sogdiana.
In vain did you labor to come east more than ten thousand tricents.
15   For in the central plains there were already some who could do the
        Iranian whirl,
And in a contest of wonderful abilities, you would not be their equal.

In the closing years of the Heavenly Jewel reign period, the times were
    about to change,
Officials and concubines all learned how to circle and turn:
Within the palace was the favorite Precious Consort Yang, without was
    Roxshan,
20   The two were most highly acclaimed for being able to do the Iranian
        Whirl.
She was registered as a consort in the Pear Garden for entertainment,
He was treated as a son in the intimacy of the Golden Pheasant Screen.
Roxshan entranced the ruler with his Iranian Whirl,
His soldiers had crossed the Yellow River before the emperor suspected
    him of rebellion.
25   The Precious Consort stole the ruler's heart with her Iranian Whirl,
And when she was murdered by mutinous troops at Ma-wei, he thought
    of her all the more.
From then on, heaven and earth have been out of kilter,
And for fifty years it has been impossible to suppress the dissolution.

Iranian Whirling girl,
30   Don't dance to no purpose;
Sing this song several times to enlighten our illustrious sovereign.

Translated by Victor H. Mair

II

Yüan Chen (779–831)

When the Heavenly Jewel reign period was about to end and the
    Iranian[2] wished to rebel,
Iranians presented to the emperor a girl who could do the Iranian
    Whirl.
She whirled so well that, before he knew what was happening, the
    illustrious monarch was captivated by her,
And, before long, the bewitching Iranian had moved in with him in the
    Palace of Long Life.

5 The world does not know the meaning of the Iranian Whirl,
But I can tell you what the appearance of the Iranian Whirl is like:

A tumbleweed nipped from its root by the frost and blown wildly by a
    twister,
A red platter balanced at the top of a pole and dazzling as a wheel of
    fire.
Black-dragon pearl earrings fly out like shooting stars,
10 Rainbow halo of a light scarf fast as a flash of lightning.

A submerged whale inhales in the dark, causing the ocean waves to dip
    inward,
A wildly dancing whirlwind, sleet in space.

After ten thousand passes, who can distinguish beginning from end?
Among those seated around her in the audience, who can discern back
    from front?

15 The lower-ranked concubines who look on say to one another:
"The way to win our lord's favor is through circular transformations."
Right and wrong, good and bad—they all depend on what the lord says,
North, south, east, west follow upon the lord's glance.

Supplely do her sashes cling to her body,
20 Flying to and fro, they wrap around her like so many bracelets.

Hearing of this, deceitful officials turn over schemes in their hearts,
They confuse the mind of the lord with smooth talk while the lord's
    eyes are bedazzled.

If the lord's words seem to bend, then she crouches like a hook,
If the lord's words favor the straight, she releases as an arrow.

---

2. Referring to the rebellious general, An Lu-shan (Chinese transcription for Roxshan the
Arsacid [i.e., Persian/Iranian]), who was of mixed Sogdian and Turkic ancestry.

25   Nimbly she pursues the shadows of the moonlight everywhere they
           wend,
       Skillfully she mimics the manifold warblings of the oriole in springtime.

       Using the lord's power, they overthrow heaven and subvert earth,
       Fearful the lord might discover them, they are busily concerned with
           covering up.

       The imperial banners travel south to Ten Thousand Mile Bridge,[3]
30   Finally Emperor Hsüan Tsung realizes that things have gone awry.
       This holds a message for those who whirl the eye and whirl the heart:
       Everyone in the nation ought to join in rebuking them!

                                                  Translated by Victor H. Mair

   3. On his flight to Szechwan.

182
Poem of Medicine Puns

Anonymous (9th century?)

His wife then composed a poem with the names of medicines its theme and,
by means of it, asked him a series of questions:

   "I, Belladonna, am the wife of a man named Wahoo,
   Who early became a mandrake in Liang.

   This *tour de force* of punning is taken from the Tun-huang (see selection 266) story of Wu
Tzu-hsü. The hero was a fugitive from his home state of Ch'u to the state of Wu (Ngwa) during
the latter part of the sixth century B.C.E. The king of Ch'u executed his father and brother
because they had remonstrated with him over his disreputable conduct. On his flight, Wu Tzu-
hsü happens to stop where his wife was living at the time. We should note that Wu Tzu-hsü has
been separated from her for a long time because of his official duties. Although he is in need of
food and shelter, as soon as Wu realizes that it is his wife's house that he has come to, he wishes
to hurry on without being recognized by her, for fear that any knowledge of his identity might
lead to apprehension by the authorities. Wu, however, has prominent front teeth, and his wife
is more than suspicious about who this visitor really is.

   Each line of the poem bears at least one pun on the name of a medicine, most of which are
herbs. During the Sung period, there was a category of storytelling which consisted entirely of
such puns. The present text is the earliest and most elaborate example known of this genre. All
of the medicines mentioned in these lines are identified in Victor H. Mair, *Tun-huang Popular
Narratives* (Cambridge: Cambridge University Press, 1983), pp. 275–279.

   The Tun-huang story of Wu Tzu-hsü was probably originally composed around the first
quarter of the eighth century, but the actual copy that has been miraculously preserved for us
must date from the late ninth or early tenth century.

Before our matrimonyvine could be consomméted, he had to go back,
Leaving me, his wife, to dwell here ruefully alone.
5   The mustard has not been cut, the flaxseed bed remains unvisited—
Hemlocked in here without any neighbors, I raised my head and sighed
        for my Traveler's Joy:
'Parsley, sage, rosemary, and thyme—
I pray that he'll forget me not!'
Gingerly, I hoped, but I recently heard that the King of Ch'u,
10   Acting without principle and unleashing a bitterroot heart,
Slaughtered my pawpaw and brother-in-law with a jalap! jalap!
Clovered with shame, weak as a wisp of straw,
And arrowhead-swift, my husband fled with fear as a dog would.
Quick as a periwinkle, he became a fungative,
15   And hid amongst the stinkbushes;
But hiding became a hell-of-a-bore.
He seemed like a jackal pursued by horehounds;
Laudanum almighty, how he hopsed and hyssopped like a
        jack-in-the-pulpit!
When I think of it, bittersweet tears stain my bleedingheart;
20   I am arti-choked with antimony.
At nightshade when I sleep, it's hard to endure till the morning's glory;
I recite his name all day until my tongue curls up like a sliver of
        cypress.
His voice, begging balm, so ingenuous entered my ears;
Drawn by aniseedent causes, I dillied up to the visitor,
25   And, seeing it was my long orrised honeysuckle whom I mint at the
        gate,
Sloed down my steps to a hibiscus pace.
And then I saw your toothwort smile;
It reminded me of my husband's dog's tooth violets.
Borax you don't remember me but, no madder what caper you're up to,
30   I'm willing to lay out my scurvy Butter and Eggs."

Tzu-hsü answered in the same cryptic vein:

"Potash! Nitre am I this fellow Wahoo whom you speak of,
Nor am I a fungative from injustice.
Listen while I tell you the currant of my travels.
I was born in Castoria and grew up in Betony Wood;
5   My father was a Scorpio, my mother a true Lily-of-the-valley.
Gathering up all of my goldenrod and silverweed,
This son of theirs became a Robin-Run-Around.
Rose Hips was my low-class companion,
Nelson Rockyfeldspar my uppercrust chum.

10   Together with them, I waded Wild Ginger Creek,
      And caught cold in its squilling, wintergreen waters;
      Saffronly, of the three of us, I found myself alone.
      Day after day, my lotus-thread hopes dangled tenuously;
      My thoughts were willows waving in the wind.
15   All alone, I climbed Witch Hazel Mountain;
      How hard it was to cross the slippery elms and stone roots!
      Cliffs towering above me, I clambered over stoneworts and rockweeds;
      Often did I encounter wolfsbanes and tiger thistles.
      Sometimes I would be thinking of soft spring beauties,
20   But suddenly would meet up with a bunch of pigsheads;
      My thoughts would linger over midsummer vetches,
      Yet I could never see an end to my tormentils.
      So I reversed my steps, feeling compelled to spurry back;
      Fennelly, I arrived here.
25   I grow goatsbeard,
      Not dog's tooth violets.
      Methinks you've scratched a fenugreek but found no tartar,
      So furze tell me what you mean and don't make such a rhubarb."

                                    Translated by Victor H. Mair

183

Ballad on the Investigation of a Disaster

Yao Chen (1448–1478)

Having heard that an official was coming to investigate the disaster,
The starving people stood near the head of his horse.
"Are you starving?" asked the official.
"This is a rich village," replied his clerk.
"Our food is already exhausted," said the people.
"There is some extra grain," said the lictor.

Hearing the words of his assistants,
He turned away, unwilling to enter the village.
Starvation and repletion depend upon clerks and lictors;
The official merely holds on to the register in his hand.

Before the investigation, in some cases the people had enough to eat,
Having stored up extra rice during the twelfth month of the previous year;
After the investigation, all the people were starving.

When an official passes by, tax money must be handed over completely;
When he leaves, he will report on his diligent labors—
While the starving people will be weeping together in the night.

Translated by Victor H. Mair

184

The Half-and-Half Song

Li Mi-an (16th century?)

By far the greater half have I seen through
This floating life—ah, there's the magic word—
This "half"—so rich in implications.
It bids us taste the joy of more than we
Can ever own. Halfway in life is man's
Best state, when slackened pace allows him ease.

A wide world lies halfway 'twixt heaven and earth;
To live halfway between the town and land,
Have farms halfway between the streams and hills;
Be half-a-scholar, and half-a-squire, and half
In business; half as gentry live,
And half related to the common folk;
And have a house that's half genteel, half plain,
Half elegantly furnished and half bare;
Dresses and gowns that are half old, half new,
And food half epicure's, half simple fare;
Have servants not too clever, nor too dull;
A wife who is not too ugly, nor too fair.

—So then, at heart, I feel I'm half a Buddha,
And almost half a Taoist fairy blest.
One half myself to Father Heaven I
Return; the other half to children leave—
Half thinking how for my posterity
To plan and provide, and yet minding how
To answer God when the body's laid at rest.

"This is the soundest and most mature philosophy of living comprised in a single poem that I know, although I know, too, that it is one of the most exasperating to the hundred-percenters" (Lin Yutang).

He is most wisely drunk who is half drunk;
And flowers in half-bloom look their prettiest;
As boats at half-sail sail the steadiest,
And horses held at half-slack reins trot best.

Who half too much has, adds anxiety,
But half too little, adds possession's zest.
Since life's of sweet and bitter compounded,
Who tastes but half is wise and cleverest.

Translated by Lin Yutang

185

Mountain Songs

Feng Meng-lung (1574–1645)

My Old Man's Small

1

My old man's small, shriveled and shrunk;
When a crummy horse has no bridle, who enjoys the ride?
The river swells, the boat rides high,
Too bad his pole is short.
How will he ever touch bottom?

2

My old man's small and unromantic;

The modern literary historian, Y.W. Ma, has called Feng Meng-lung "the personification of popular Chinese literature" who did more to champion and preserve this sorely neglected field than any other individual in premodern times. A native of the Soochow area in the lower Yangtze basin, he was devoted to the collection and publication of the literature of the people, something otherwise almost unheard of for a Chinese scholar until the twenties and thirties of this century. It is indicative of the culturally subversive nature of his enterprise that Feng Meng-lung felt compelled to do his writing, compiling, and editing under dozens of different pseudonyms.

Feng is best known for the three highly acclaimed volumes of vernacular fiction, each including forty short stories, that he collected (see selections 255 and 256). He was also involved in the authorship of several historical novels and in the composition of a still larger number of plays. Feng's eclectic interests extended to the compilation of joke books (see selection 224) and the writing of rule books for cards and other games. The folk-songs presented here were originally sung in the Wu topolect and are of great linguistic importance even in Feng's imprecise sinographic transcriptions (compare the unnumbered first note to selection 193).

We share the same bedcurtains but not the same pillow.
I joined to your household a fine patch of land;
Too bad you don't know how to plant it.
Every year the harvest of its flowers will be reaped by others.

No Old Lady

People laugh at me for having no old lady.
But they don't know that "when you scrub rice in a busted sieve, you get a lot
    outside."
Just like a wild mountain cock that spends the night along the road,
The old bird without a nook always manages to squeeze in somewhere.

Fooling Mom

Last night I spent beside my lover
While Mom slept by my feet.
I said, "Lover, when boating on the Yangtze, to get rice from the pot,
Lightly, lightly slip the scoop in.
The iron shovel's rough and bulky,
So slowly, slowly, draw it out."

Smart

Mom is smart,
But her daughter's smart too.
Mom sifted ashes all across the floor,
But I rashly carried my lover into bed and out again,
The two of us sharing a single pair of shoes.

Feeling the Itch

I itched inside and caught my lover's eye,
But once he came to me he wouldn't leave me alone.
From the prow down to the cabin, the deck began to burn;
Luckily my lover put out the fire in my stern.

Translated by Richard W. Bodman

186

A Lament for Fortune's Frailty

from *Cantonese Love-Songs*

Chiu Tsz-yung (fl. 1820–1830)

Man is lonely: the moon shines all the brighter.
Those sinful debts of the sea of lust and of the heaven of love are still
    unpaid.
Since parting and meeting, sorrow and gladness, have their season:
Why is there at all times a blight on famous flowers?
5   Look you! Yöng Fê's[1] jade bones were buried beside the mountain
    track.

The Cantonese love-song was in essence created single-handedly by the poet-official Chiu
Tsz-yung (Chao Tzu-yung in Modern Standard Mandarin [MSM] pronunciation). The genre
was written in a mixture of three languages: vernacular Cantonese (the poet's native language),
classical Chinese (an archaic book language), and Mandarin (the artificial language of the
officials [i.e., the Mandarins] based on the speech of the capital [Peking at the time when Chiu's
book was written, probably around 1828]).

The proper names in the extensive notes are rendered in Cantonese pronunciation to show
that the various regions of China had their own greatly different ways of reading the sinographs.
Mandarin equivalents are provided in parentheses for those who are not familiar with Cantonese.

1. Yöng Kwai-fê (MSM Yang Kuei-fei), celebrated as the all-powerful favorite of the Emperor
Thong Yün Tsung (T'ang Hsüan-tsung, reigned 713–756 C.E.). She was the daughter of Yöng
Yün-yím (Yang Hsüan-yen), a petty functionary of Shukchau (Shu-chou) in western China, and
bore the childhood name Yuk Wán (Yü-huan, Jade Bracelet/Ring), to which there is no doubt
an allusion in the "jade bones" of the text. Having attracted notice by her surpassing beauty, she
became in 735 one of the concubines of Prince Shau (Shou Wang), the emperor's eighteenth
son. Three years later, on the death of the then imperial favorite, the ministers of Yün Tsung
cast their eyes upon the lovely Princess Yöng. No sooner had the emperor obtained a sight of his
daughter-in-law than he became violently enamored of her, and caused her to be enrolled
among the ladies of his seraglio, bestowing in exchange another consort on his son. In 745, she
was raised to the rank of Kwai-fê (Kuei-fei), a title second in dignity to that of the empress only.
Year after year the emperor abandoned himself more completely to amorous dalliance with his
concubine, ransacking tributary kingdoms for gems to enhance her beauty and sparing no
extravagance to gratify her caprices. These days of licentious enjoyment terminated in the
rebellion of Oan Luk-shán (An Lu-shan), the emperor's unworthy minion. During the hurried
flight of the court before the advancing insurgents in 756, the imperial cortège halted at the
entrenched position of Má Ngai (Ma-wei). The beaten and famished soldiery rose in revolt, and
satiated their vengeance in the blood of the imperial consort. With unutterable anguish, the still
fondly enamored monarch was constrained to order his faithful attendant, the eunuch Kô Lek-
sz (Kao Li-shih) to strangle Yöng Fê (some say she was hanged on a pear tree) and bury her by
the roadside (compare with selections 180 and 181).

2. Wong Chhiû-kwan (Wang Chao-chün), a famous heroine of romance. She was said to
have been taken into the harem of Hoan Yün Tai (Han Yüan-ti) in 48 B.C.E., where, however,
she was hidden from the notice of her imperial lord through the malice of his treacherous
minister Mô Yín-shau (Mao Yen-shou). On a report of her beauty reaching the court, Mô was

The grass remained green above Chhiû-kwan's[2] tomb.
In fallen fortune Siû Tsheng[3] sadly mourns o'er her likeness.
Shap Nöng[4] drank of misery abundant as water.
In fine, from birth to womanhood more than the half among rosy girls
    are ill-fated:
10   How much the more are we, flowers and paint of love's arbor, injured
    by lustful passions.

---

commissioned to bring her to the palace, and she was found by him to be of surpassing loveliness, the daughter of poor but worthy parents. Her father refused to pay a bribe demanded by Mô Yín-shau, who in revenge presented to Hoan Yün Tai a portrait so little like the original that the emperor conceived no wish to see the new addition to his seraglio. She thereby languished in oblivion for years, until chance threw the emperor across her path, when he at once became enamored of her beauty. The faithless minister, his wiles discovered, fled from the court and took refuge with the Khan of the Hung Nô (Hsiung-nu; Huns), to whom he showed the real portrait of Chhiû-kwan. The Khan, fired by the hope of obtaining possession of so peerless a beauty, invaded China in irresistible force, and only consented to retire beyond the Great Wall when the lady was surrendered to him. She accompanied her savage captor, bathed in tears, until the banks of the Amur were reached, when, rather than go beyond the fatal boundary, she plunged into the waters of the stream and was drowned. Her corpse was interred on the banks of the river, and it is related that the tumulus raised above her grave remained covered with undying verdure, whence the tomb is called "Green Mound." Another version, perhaps nearer to the truth, has her bearing the Khan children and staying with him until old age. This pair of versions constitutes but one of countless examples in Chinese literature of the constant interplay between self/center/Han and other/periphery/"barbarian."

3. The tragedy of this brilliant heroine has been recorded in a book of popular love stories as follows: "Siû Tsheng was the concubine of a certain graduate of Fúlam: her home was in Kwongleng. Because her surname was the same as that of her lover, it has been suppressed. The girl is only known as Siû Tsheng (Hsiao Ch'ing, 'Little Green'), and her second names were Wan Nöng (Yün-niang, 'Cloud Lass'). Unusually intelligent, when ten years of age she met an old woman who taught her the *Prajñâpâramitâ-hṛdaya-sûtra* (*Heart Sūtra*). After reading it once, she was word-perfect. The old woman said: 'This girl is precocious in learning, but her fortune will be fragile.' " This prophecy came true, for Siû Tsheng and her lover's wife became bitter enemies. One day, after a passionate quarrel, in which the wife carried the day, the story proceeded as follows: "Siû Tsheng said to her maids: 'Bid the artists' studios send me a good portrait painter.' The painter came, and she bade him paint her portrait. When he had finished it, she took a mirror, and, gazing long into it, she said: 'The likeness is there, but not the expression.' So she set it aside. When a second portrait had been painted, she said: 'The expression is there, yet it lacks vivacity. Perhaps it is because the melancholy of my face deceives you.' So she again set it aside, and bade him take his brush and stand beside her, while she spoke to her maids, looked at them, talked and laughed, or fanned the tea-stove, or chose a book, or plucked at her clothes, or ground paints for the artist. Soon the portrait was painted, surpassing in grace and loveliness. She smiled and said: 'That will do.' When the painter left, she took the picture and made obeisance to it at her bedside, burning joss-sticks and pouring a libation of pear-wine before it. Then with a cry—'Siû Tsheng! Siû Tsheng! Was this your fate?'—she fell back upon a chair, weeping like rain, and with the cry she died."

4. Tô Mê (Tu Mei) was the tenth among her brothers and sisters and so was called Tô Shap Nöng (Tu Shih-niang, "Daughter [Who Is] Tenth [Among the] Tô [Children]"). She lived during the years 1573–1620. At the age of thirteen she became a courtesan and at the age of

Since we are willow blossoms, more than the half of us are weak as
water:
How can we learn to start stainless from the mire, ever displaying
ourselves strong and pure?
I fear, I do but fear, that sad autumn will whirl the elm leaves into the
golden well:[5]
Therefore I must ever be as the winter plum tree which steadfastly
endures the spite of snow and frost.
15   Methinks in all four seasons flowers and trees are as a happy land.
Only sad men, in face of one another, gulp down their grief and stifle
their words.
Ah! needs must I myself be wakeful.
Who can bear witness to fortune's frailty?
I were best recount my way of life o'er the Tomb of a Hundred
Flowers.[6]

Translated by Cecil Clementi

nineteen, when already rich with her earnings, she met in Peking a certain Leï Yü-sin (Li Yü-hsin) whose father, the lieutenant-governor of Chekiang, had sent him there to advance his studies for the civil service examinations. Leï and Shap Nöng fell deeply in love. After a year in Peking, the student had spent all his money, and his father, hearing of his son's doings, ordered him to return home. Shap Nöng went with her lover, and on their way they met a wealthy acquaintance of Leï Yü-sín, named Sün Fû (Sun Fu), who, availing himself of the poverty of Leï and his fear of his father's anger, induced the lover to sell his mistress for the sum of a thousand dollars. Shap Nöng, learning of the bargain, brought with her a casket when she was passed from the ship of her lover to that of Sün Fû the next morning. Before the eyes of both Leï and Sün, she opened the casket, showing them its contents of priceless jewels. Then, reproaching her lover for his cruelty and avarice, she held the casket in her arms, sprang into the river, and was drowned.

5. Compare the line of Wang Ch'ang-ling (see selection 43): "Yellow in autumn are the elm leaves over the golden well." The story is told of a certain Portuguese astronomer at the imperial Chinese court, who, when asked by a rival astronomer about the day on which summer changed to autumn, replied: "In Hok-kung (Hsüeh-kung, the Palace of Learning) is a well: beside this well is an elm, which, if autumn has not yet come, does not lose its leaves. Take a golden bowl and place it at the edge of the well: then, when the exact day comes, an elm-leaf will fall into the bowl. That is the day!"

6. In a book of Cantonese legends, we read the following: "In the time of Shung Chen (Ch'ung-chen, 1628 C.E.), there was a famous courtesan named Chöng Khîû (Chang Ch'iao). Upon her death, each of her lovers planted a flower on her tomb. In all there were some hundred flowers. The colors of the flowers were variegated and beautiful. It was within sight of the Jasmine Hill and was called the Tomb of Flowers."

187
Ballad of the Maiden of Lan-ling[1]

Chin Ho (1818–1885)

After the general had broken the blockade at Hsüan-chou,[2]
'Midst triumphal songs he sped along the road;
Marching eastward until he reached the Lai river,[3]
He constructed an opulent encampment.
Portable screens ten layers deep were arrayed with fine silks,
Feathery tassels by the hundreds were hung with strings of pearls;
Carpets with mythical creatures were spread on the ground,
Trees of coral and jade reflected brilliantly in the lamplight.
There were bowls made of tortoise shell and cups fashioned from mollusks,
Pepper flower wine was brewed and lambkins were fatted;
Seated in their furs and embroidery were the toast of the time,
The assembled grandeur of those present was rare for that age.
'Twas said that the general would conclude a wedding ceremony,
The damsel whose betrothal was arranged long ago would join him today;
A matchmaker sent to distant Lan-ling to fetch her
Directed the Soochow boatmen along the rivers swollen with spring rain.

This ballad is unusual for its expansive narrative quality and great length (compare the introductory notes to selections 173 and 176). The combination of folkish diction and high literary flavor in this rhymed work of uneven line lengths is also uncommon, if not altogether unprecedented, in the Chinese literary tradition. Chin Ho was, indeed, one of the most original and forward-looking poets of the nineteenth century. He foreshadowed many of the developments that took place around the end of the Ch'ing dynasty and the beginning of the Republican period when innovative writers strove to break free from the constraints of traditional norms for versification.

This long verse tale describes the chaotic conditions in the Yangtze valley during its occupation by the revolutionary armies of the T'ai-ping T'ien-kuo ("Heavenly Kingdom of Great Peace"), a massive convulsion which shook central China to its foundations during the middle of the nineteenth century and in the course of which millions of people died. The efforts of the Ch'ing government to retake the area were not without their own ill effects. Like the opium wars which followed it, the T'aiping rebellion was a major contributing factor in the final collapse of the imperial system. The author of this ballad himself lost over half his family in the depradations of the long struggle between the Manchu government and the T'ai-ping rulers. Many of his works severely criticize both the rebels and the imperial forces sent to quash them. Aside from its scathing denunciation of the military leaders, this particular poem is also distinguished by the vivid depiction of the heroine who may in one sense be said to foreshadow the phenomenally popular characters in Chinese novels of knight errantry still being turned out in large quantities today.

1. In Kiangsu province, about thirty miles northwest of Wu district.
2. Modern Hsüan-cheng district in Anhwei province.
3. The modern Li River in Kiangsu province.

On a beautiful morning with a bright sun and a gentle breeze,
The snow had melted on the warm sandbanks and the waves shone
    aquamarine;
The children at Twin Bridges[4] vied in their cries of joy,
The new year's plum and willow were suffused with spring.
At the stroke of noon, from afar were heard the sounds of bugle and drum,
The vanguard announced that the lady would soon arrive;
Smiling, the general came down the terrace steps to meet her,
Silent, the guests waited in a walled circle around him.
No sooner had her gaily decorated boats docked at the general's gate,
Than a maiden debarked with simian swiftness and hawkish determination.
She was dressed plainly yet elegantly, eschewing ornamentation,
Her expression was as ingenuous as that of a divine being;
If she were not a princess in the retinue of the Queen Mother of the West,[5]
She surely was the Weaving Maid[6] come down from her heavenly palace.
Her tall, slender body standing erect,
A look of troubled apprehension on her face,
She smoothed her dress politely and spoke to the assembled guests:
"You who have come to this hall are all from high-ranking families,
And I am not without my own upbringing;
Allow me to explain clearly from the very beginning.
I am the daughter of an official from Lan-ling,
Whose family encountered many difficulties in these troubled times;
Now I have just my mother and two brothers,
Trying to make do in an out-of-the-way place.
A while back, as I was watering the vegetables on our meager plot,
The general fixed his gaze upon me as he was passing by;
Carrying my buckets, I returned home quickly and closed the door,
Not having exchanged a single word with him.
Yesterday, two officers came to our house,
Bearing coffers overflowing with gold and other presents;
They said that we were already engaged,
And that my mother had previously given her consent.
Today they came a-rowing to bring me here,
Saying that the wedding would be soon and that I should take care not to
    resist.
When my brother merely asked what was going on,
They rebuffed him with loud voices that shook the foundations;
Several dozen soldiers brandished their swords,

---

4. A place approximately three miles south of Ch'un district in Kiangsu.
5. A mythical matriarch who was said to live in splendor by a jadelike pool in the far-off K'un-lun Mountains.
6. Vega in the constellation of Lyra, around whom many touching legends grew up.

Then milled about menacingly like wolves and tigers.
A command was barked and they swiftly regrouped,
Frightening the travelers on the road outside our door;
The situation was so intimidating that,
Even if I had wings, I would not have been able to get very far.
Had I not agreed to come with them,
The startled souls of our whole family would not have died in peace;
Now that I have come with them,
I wish to ask the general what this is all about."

Seething with anger as she unleashed this torrent of words,
The maiden suddenly reached out with one hand and grabbed the general;
With her other hand resting on a sword that she was about to draw, she
    continued:[7]
"Have I spoken the truth or not?
Have your ears heard me or not?
I want to take you to Soochow,[8]
To accuse you point by point before the governor's tribunal,
Entreating him to inform our sage ruler on behalf of a commoner.
From old, how many famous generals have had their glorious deeds inscribed
    in bronze?
Aside from all of the feudal titles, estates, and rewards of money and silk
    presented by the nation to show its gratitude,
Have they ever been permitted to ravish innocent, defenseless women in
    recognition of their achievements?
When an imperial proclamation comes from the capital, which seems far but
    is actually quite near,
Supposing that it instructs me to marry you,
Wouldn't you be content?
Without the mandate of the Son of Heaven,
There's absolutely no way to solve this dispute.
In your rage you may kill me,
Like a wee, tiny flea or mosquito that has landed on a pile of manure;
Or perhaps I shall take your life with my sword,
And before I have gone five steps, the blood gushing from your neck will
    instantly splatter my homespun skirt.
On the long embankment outside the gate, there are countless wild crab-
    apple trees,
Beneath them there's lots of empty land for us to build you a lecherous
    general's grave;

7. The maiden's impassioned speech is delivered in a plainer style than that of the rather
florid language which precedes it.
8. The capital of Kiangsu province.

Make up your mind fast whether you want to live or die,
What's the point of hanging your head in abject silence as though you were
    shy?"

The general, who usually shouted thundrously,
And who could casually toss a stone weighing hundreds of pounds,
At this moment wore a deathly, ashen pallor,
Then flushed red like a man in a drunken stupor.
His subordinates and bodyguards boiled with fury,
Clenched their fists, bared their claws, and gnashed their teeth;
But the general was in the maiden's hands,
And they could not be separated rashly.
"When throwing something at a mouse, watch out for the plates and
    saucers"—
It was impossible for them to unleash their spears and lances.
Flailing his arms left and right, the general directed his men to back off,
And looked beseechingly at the assembled guests as though pleading with
    them to intervene.

After their initial shock, the guests regained composure
And went forward to bow before the maiden, saying,
"Listening to your ladyship's words,
We were so outraged that our hair stood on end;
In the end, we can only hope
That this was originally not the general's intention.
To seek your hand in marriage is one thing,
But would he dare be so unprincipled as to take you by force?
Because of their ineptness and lack of understanding,
The fault lies with the people he employed;
Those two officers, for example,
Will certainly be severely bastinadoed for feigning orders.
Now there's nothing else to say,
But that you should be sent back to your village.
The general will himself go to your gate,
Where, baring his shoulders, he will beg a thousand pardons;
He will present some humble gifts,
Delicacies to offer your mother.
The matter will pass over like the misty clouds
That leave no stain upon the sky;
Please return to the boat at once,
And then it will be plain as day if he goes back on his word."

The maiden frowned at the assembled guests and said with a laugh,
"Sirs, do you take me for a child?

I've lost all confidence in him now;
How could anyone with such a wild nature become gentle?
Even mountain spooks always search for their enemies,
So it's unlikely that someone who harbors evil thoughts will turn humane.
How painful to think that, since the armed uprisings,
Troops have been killing the people everywhere;
They consider that killing the people is like killing thieves,
And this poisonous attitude has spread across the land.
On the highway to Lan-ling,
They come and go in droves;
If it's not on a frosty evening,
Then it's on a rainy morning.
Our house is but a few rooms,
A pile of kindling buffeted by the barren winds;
Our family is but a few kin,
Pitiful fish confined to a cauldron.
At a snap of the fingers, turmoil arises,
In the blink of an eye, all becomes dust and ashes.
Would one rather that the seeds of disaster be sown,
To end up a grieving will-o'-the-wisp?
Who knows whether Yama[9] exists,
And who can you complain to in the tomb of endless night?
Better to cry out before the ninefold empyrean,[10]
Heaven will certainly not make a partial judgement;
Perhaps if I take decisive action,
Public opinion will naturally prove true.
I knew clearly when I came here,
That I was like a mantis trying to block a huge chariot with its forelegs;[11]
Do you think that I would seek to preserve my life at the expense of my
    honor,
Or that I cherish this insignificant, little body?
Your efforts to mediate, sirs,
Are but so much verbiage that I cannot go along with."

The assembled guests again went forward and bowed, saying,
"Please do not be so angry.
The general has a worthy name
And has all along treasured his plumage;
His every thought is to emulate the Confucian literati,

9. The Buddhist king of the underworld, who is supposed to judge the souls sent there.
10. In the *Elegies of Ch'u* (see selection 148), it was thought that heaven was nine layers deep. Here heaven stands for the emperor.
11. From a parable in the twelfth chapter of the *Chuang Tzu* (see selection 9).

His broadminded character is particularly sincere.
This affair was most improper;
Once news of it gets out,
Ten thousand mouths will proclaim the injustice,
And will surely rebuke him endlessly.
A bad reputation will come of its own accord—
He may wish to defend himself, but he'll scarcely be able to open his mouth;
A piece of white jade that has sullied itself
Is not worth a string of cash.
Realizing that there may be no time to regret his error,
He laments the fact that he has nothing to cover his face with.
The elders of the lower Yangtze
Will be too ashamed to recognize him when they meet,
How much less would he be willing to confront the anger of the masses,
And raise troops because of a marriage!
His crime would be so great that it obliterates the teaching of the sages—
He would no longer be counted a human being.
This man is by no means ordinary,
He fights the bandits tirelessly in all directions;
Though his great talent may not be equal to that of Kuan Chung and Yüeh
    Yi,[12]
His heroism is a match for Chao She and Lien P'o.[13]
Since your ladyship comes from an old family of officials,
Be so kind as to pardon a brave servant of the court.
As to the affairs of another day, we can assure you with one voice,
That so-and-so will be appointed to government office and so-and-so will be
    made a member of the gentry.
Together we kneel before you and beg for the general's life,
May your ladyship be forgiving as a transcendent, a Buddha, or a heavenly
    spirit."

The maiden realized that it would be difficult to ignore the sentiments of the
    guests, so she said,
"For you, sirs, I will yield.
For the moment, let us set aside all that you have just said,
I ask only to borrow one thing from you, sirs.
I have heard that the general owns an excellent steed named 'White Fish,'
Who can travel a thousand tricents per day with ease.
From the time I left Lan-ling

12. Two famous generals of the Spring and Autumn and the Warring States periods respectively to whom the celebrated strategist of the Three Kingdoms, Chu-ke Liang, often compared
himself.
    13. Two outstanding generals of the Warring States period.

And said goodbye to my family, it has already been more than four days;
My old mother must be leaning against the village gate crying bitterly,
My two brothers must be clasping their arms in our courtyard sighing vainly.
If I ride this horse back to my home,
I can reach there by early nightfall.
Henceforth, we will abandon our humble hut,
And take up residence in a Peach Blossom Spring not of this world;[14]
There I shall wait upon my mother attentively,
And read Yellow Stone's[15] book on strategy with my brothers—
No foolish fisherman from Wu-ling[16] will be able to find us.
Three or four days later,
After we have moved,
From the shrine of Chiang Tzu-wen,[17]
I'll send you back the horse, all right?"

The general seldom rode this horse,
But now his only fear was that she would not leave on it;
Hurriedly, he called out to his attendants to bring the horse forward,
Its four legs white as snow and flossy hair dangling from its ears.
Verily, not in vain was it a Soochow stepper,[18]
'Twas descended from the wind that Master Lieh[19] used to ride.
As soon as the maiden took one look at this horse,
Her brows unfurled with a touch of joy;
Finally releasing the general's clothes from her grasp,
She was already in the saddle before anyone saw her leap.
With a long, drawn-out "Thanks!" she burst through space and was gone,
Like a flash of lightning or a shooting star, she left not a trace.

For several days after the girl had gone, the army did not stir,
Because the general displayed courage and prowess in restoring them to
    order.
His encampment encircled the sides of Mount Chung;
There guests and advisers came to pay their respects to the general,
Encouraging him to quaff the new vintage,

14. A utopian refuge (see selection 204).
15. A hermit who lived during the Ch'in and Han dynasties, he bequeathed his book to Chang Liang, who in turn used the teachings in it to help Liu Pang found the Han dynasty.
16. Another reference to T'ao Ch'ien's utopian essay about the Peach Blossom Spring (see note 14).
17. Located in modern Nanking, the shrine commemorates a high-ranking officer of the ancient kingdom of Wu (Ngwa).
18. An allusion to a fleet steed of antiquity.
19. The Taoist Master Lieh was thought to be able to ride on the wind (see selection 12). This allusion and the one mentioned in note 18 are missing in some editions of the text, an indication that their scholarly quality makes them suspect in such a popular ballad.

While gongs and pipes continuously blared forth a medley.
Out of the cloudy distance appeared a lone horse in a dusty clatter,
Glistening and without blemish it came onrushing;
Her word was as good as gold, the contract was redeemed,
The general went forward to take the reins and led the horse back to its stable.
Covered with bloodlike sweat, it gave a long whinny;
On its back was bound crosswise a bulging, twisted object three feet high,
'Twas the bundle of betrothal presents brought that day by the two officers,
Returned with its seal unbroken and not the slightest thing missing.
When the bundle of betrothal presents was unloaded, beneath it there lay
In addition, like the single slip of a shallot, a knife,
Light flashing from its razor-sharp blade.
Transfixed by the sight, for many nights the general did not sleep soundly.

Translated by Victor H. Mair

PART III

Prose

Documents

188
The Great Announcement

from the *Classic of Documents*

Anonymous (early Chou period)

I

The king speaks to the following effect:—"Ho! I make a great announcement to you, the princes of the many States, and to you, the managers of my affairs.—Unpitied am I, and Heaven sends down calamities on my House, without exercising the least delay. It greatly occupies my thoughts, that I, so very young, have inherited this illimitable patrimony, with its destinies and domains. I have not displayed wisdom, and led the people to tranquility, and how much less should I be able to reach the knowledge of the decree of Heaven!

This selection is taken from the *Classic of Documents* or *Book of History* (*Shu ching*), one of the main Confucian classics. It is a collection of documents, mainly speeches, attributed to various rulers and ministers of high antiquity. The documents, however, contain almost no information concerning the circumstances under which they were composed, nor is there any historical narrative relating one document to another. The work is thus more an archive of source materials—some of dubious derivation—than a connected history. "The Great Announcement" is considered by scholars to be one of the more authentic items in this collection of materials from diverse origins and periods.

The prefatory note states, "When King Wu died, the three overseers and the wild tribes of the Huai rebelled. The Duke of Chou acted as prime minister to King Ch'eng and, having proposed to make an end of the house of Yin [i.e., the Shang dynasty], composed 'The Great Announcement.'"

"Yes, I who am but a little child am in the position of one who has to cross a deep water;—it must be mine to go and seek how to cross over. I must diffuse the elegant institutions of my predecessor, and augment the appointment which he received from Heaven;—so shall I be not forgetful of his great work. Nor shall I dare to restrain the majesty of Heaven seen in the inflictions it sends down.

II

"The Tranquilizing king[1] left to me the great precious tortoise,[2] to bring into connection with me the intelligence of Heaven. I consulted it, and it told me that there would be great trouble in the region of the west, and that the western people would not be still. Accordingly we have the present senseless movements.

"Little as the present prosperity of Yin is, its prince greatly dares to take in hand its broken line. Though Heaven sent down its terrors on his House, yet knowing of the evils in our kingdom, and that the people are not tranquil, he says—'I will recover my patrimony'; and so he wishes to make our State of Chou a border territory again.

"One day there was a senseless movement, and the day after, ten men of worth among the people appeared to help me to go forward to restore tranquility and to perpetuate the plans of my father. The great business I am engaging in will have a successful issue, for I have divined and always got a favorable intimation. Therefore I tell you, the princes of my friendly States, and you, the directors of departments, my officers, and the managers of my affairs,—I have obtained a favorable reply to my divinations. I will now go forward with you from all the States, and punish those vagabond and transported ministers of Yin.

III

"And now, you the princes of the various States, and you the various officers and managers of my affairs, all retort on me, saying, 'The hardships will be great, and that the people are not still has its source really in the king's palace, and in the mansions of those princes of the troubled State. We, little ones, and the old reverent men as well, think the expedition ill-advised. Why does your majesty not go contrary to the divination?'

"I, in my youth, think also continually of the hardships, and say, Alas! these senseless movements will deplorably afflict widowers and widows! But I am the servant of Heaven, which has assigned me this great task, and laid this hard duty on my person. I therefore, the young one, do not pity myself, and it would be right in you, the princes of the States, and in you, the many

---

1. This presumably refers to King Wu, father of King Ch'eng, who is ostensibly the speaker of the announcement.
2. Signifying the rights and ability to consult the oracle (see selection 1).

officers, the directors of departments, and the managers of my affairs, to soothe me, saying, 'Do not be distressed with sorrow. We shall surely complete the plans of your Tranquilizing father.'

"Yes, I, the little one, dare not disregard the charge of God. Heaven, favorable to the Tranquilizing king, gave such prosperity to our small State of Chou. The Tranquilizing king divined and acted accordingly, and so he calmly received his great appointment. Now Heaven is helping the people;— how much more must I follow the divinations! Oh! the clearly intimated will of Heaven is to be feared:—it is to help my great inheritance."

IV

The king says, "You, who are the old ministers, are fully able to examine the long-distant affairs;—you know how great was the toil of the Tranquilizing king. Now where Heaven shuts up and distresses us is the place where I must accomplish my work;—I dare not but do my utmost to complete the plans of the Tranquilizing king. It is on this account that I use such efforts to remove the doubts and carry forward the inclinations of the princes of my friendly States. Heaven also assists me with sincere expressions of attachment, which I have ascertained among the people;—how dare I but aim at the completion of the work formerly begun by the Tranquilizer? Heaven moreover is thus toiling and distressing my people, so that it is as if they were suffering from disease;— how dare I allow the appointment which the Tranquilizer, my predecessor, received, to be without its happy fulfillment?"

The king says, "Formerly, at the initiation of this expedition, I spoke of its difficulties, and revolved them in my mind daily. But when a deceased father, wishing to build a house, had laid out the plan, if his son be unwilling to raise up the hall, how much less will he be willing to complete the roof! Or if the father had broken up the ground, and his son is unwilling to sow the seed, how much less will he be willing to reap the grain! In such a case will the father, who had himself been so reverently attentive to his objects, be willing to say, 'I have an heir who will not abandon the patrimony'?—How dare I, therefore, but use all my powers to give a happy settlement to the great charge entrusted to the Tranquilizing king?

"If a father have those among his friends who attack his child, will the elders of his people encourage the attack, and not come to the rescue?"

V

The king says, "Oh! Take heart, ye princes of the various States, and ye managers of my affairs. The enlightening of the country was from the wise, even from the ten men who obeyed and knew the decree of God, and the sincere assistance given by Heaven. At that time none of you presumed to change the royal appointments. And now, when Heaven is sending down calamity on the State of Chou, and the authors of these great distresses appear as if the inmates of a house were mutually to attack one another, you are without any knowledge that the decree of Heaven is not to be changed!

"I ever think and say, Heaven in destroying Yin is doing husbandman's work;—how dare I but complete the business of my fields! Heaven will thereby show its favor to the former Tranquilizer.

"How should I be all for the oracle of divination, and presume not to follow your advice? I am following the Tranquilizer, whose purpose embraced all the limits of the land. How much more must I proceed, when the divinations are all favorable! It is on these accounts that I make this expedition in force to the east. There is no mistake about the decree of Heaven. The indications of the divinations are all to the same effect."

Translated by James Legge

189

The Contract for a Youth

Wang Pao (fl. 61–54 B.C.E.)

Wang Tzu-yüan of Shu Commandery[1] went to the Chien River on business, and went up to the home of the widow Yang Hui, who had a male slave named Pien-liao. Wang Tzu-yüan requested him to go and buy some wine. Picking up a big stick, Pien-liao climbed to the top of the grave mound and said: "When my master bought me, Pien-liao, he only contracted for me to care for the grave and did not contract for me to buy wine for some other gentleman."

Wang Tzu-yüan was furious and said to the widow: "Wouldn't you prefer to sell this slave?"

Yang Hui said: "The slave's father offered him to people, but no one wanted him."

Dating to in 59 B.C.E., this powerfully written and at times funny text must have been meant as a parody. The author was a literatus who served in the imperial court. A native of Yi-chou in the present-day province of Szechwan, Wang Pao (styled Tzu-Yüan) became prominent for three panegyrics celebrating the virtues and accomplishments of the emperor and his ministers, which he wrote at the request of the governor of the region. He also wrote a fourth panegyric as an exegesis of the first three. These compositions much ingratiated him with the emperor. The simple, slightly vernacular style of "The Contract for a Youth," however, stands in striking contrast to his other more florid compositions.

1. Szechwan. All of the place names in the text are located in this province, except for Yi-chou which is in Yunnan.

Wang Tzu-yüan immediately settled on the sale contract, etc.

The slave again said: "Enter in the contract everything you wish to order me to do. I, Pien-liao, will not do anything not in the contract."

Wang Tzu-yüan said: "Agreed!"

The text of the contract said:

Third year of Shen-chiao, the first month, the fifteenth day,[2] the gentleman Wang Tzu-yüan, of Tzu-chung, purchases from the lady Yang Hui of An-chih village in Chengtu, the bearded[3] male slave, Pien-liao, of her husband's household. The fixed sale price is 15,000 cash. The slave shall obey orders about all kinds of work and may not argue.

He shall rise at dawn and do an early sweeping. After eating he shall wash up. Ordinarily he should pound the grain mortar, tie up broom straws, carve bowls and bore wells, scoop out ditches, tie up fallen fences, hoe the garden, trim up paths and dike up plats of land, cut big flails, bend bamboos to make rakes, and scrape and fix the well pulley. In going and coming he may not ride horseback or in the cart, nor may he sit crosslegged or make a hubbub. When he gets out of bed he shall shake his head to wake up, fish, cut forage, plait reeds and card hemp, draw water for gruel, and help in making *tsu-mo* drink.[4] He shall weave shoes and make other coarse things, catch birds on a gummed pole, knot nets and catch fish, shoot wild geese with arrows on a string, and shoot wild ducks with a pellet bow. He shall ascend the mountains to shoot deer, and go into the waters to catch turtles. He shall dig a pond in the garden to raise fish and a hundred or so geese and ducks; and shall drive away owls and hawks. Holding a stick, he shall herd the pigs. He shall plant ginger and rear sheep; rear the shotes and colts; remove manure and always keep things clean; and feed the horses and cattle. When the drum sounds four he shall arise and give them a midnight addition of fodder.

In the second month at the vernal equinox he shall bank the dikes and repair the boundary walls of the fields; prune the mulberry trees, skin the palm trees, plant melons to make gourd utensils, select eggplant seeds for planting, and transplant onion sets; burn plant remains to generate the fields, pile up refuse and break up lumps in the soil. At midday he shall dry out things in the sun. At cockcrow he shall rise and pound grain in the mortar, exercise and curry the horses, the donkeys, and likewise the mules—three classes.

When there are guests in the house he shall carry a kettle and go after wine; draw water and prepare the evening meal; wash bowls and arrange

2. February 18, 59 B.C.E.

3. The word used here would seem to indicate that the slave was of non-Han extraction.

4. Apparently a fine brew made from the skimmings of boiled butter.

food trays; pluck garlic from the garden; chop vegetables and slice meat; pound meat and make soup of tubers; stew fish and roast turtle; boil tea[5] and fill the utensils. When the dinner is over he shall cover and put away leftovers; shut the gates and close up the passageways for dogs; feed the pigs and air the dogs.

He shall not argue or fight with the neighbors. The slave should only drink bean-water and may not be greedy for wine. If he wishes to drink good wine he may only wet the lips and rinse the mouth; he may not empty the dipper or drain the cup. He may not go out at dawn and return at night, or have dealings with close chums.

Behind the house there are trees. He should hew them and make a boat, going downriver as far as Chiang-chou and up to Chien-chu. On behalf of the storehouse assistants he shall seek spending money, rejecting the strings of cash which are defective. He shall buy mats at Mien-t'ing, and when traveling between Tu and Lo he should trade in the small markets to get powder for the ladies. When he returns to Tu he shall carry hemp about on his pole, transporting it out to the side markets. He shall lead dogs for sale and peddle geese. At Wu-yang he shall buy tea, and he shall carry lotus on his pole from the Yang family pool. When he travels to market assemblies he shall carefully guard against the practice of theft. When he enters the market he may not squat like a barbarian, loll about, or indulge in evil talk and cursing. He shall make many knives and bows, and take them into Yi-chou to barter for oxen and sheep. The slave shall teach himself to be smart and clever, and may not be silly and stupid.

He shall take an axe and go into the mountains; cut memorandum tablets and hew cart shafts; if there are leftovers he should make sacrificial stands, benches, and wooden shoes, as well as food pans for pigs. He shall burn wood to make charcoal; collect stones and heap them into retaining walls, make huts and roof houses; and whittle books to take the place of commercially prepared writing tablets. On his return at dusk he should bring two or three bundles of dry wood.

In the fourth month he should transplant; in the ninth month he should reap; and in the tenth month gather in the beans. He shall gather quantities of hemp and rushes and stretch them into rope.

When it rains and there is nothing to do, he should plait grass and weave reeds. He shall plant and cultivate peach, plum, pear, and persimmon trees. He shall set out mulberry trees, one every thirty feet in rows eight feet apart, and fruit trees in corresponding sequence with the rows and intervals

---

5. There is some doubt whether the Chinese knew tea this early. The graph used to write the word is ambiguous and may simply mean "bitter [sauce]." Tea did not become a popular drink in China—certainly not in the heartland—until the T'ang period (see selections 121 and especially 229).

matching. When the fruit is ripe and is being picked or stored he may not suck or taste it.

At night if the dogs bark he should arise and warn the neighbors, block the gate and bar the doors, mount the tower and beat the drum, don his shield and grasp his spear. Returning down he shall make three circuits of inspection.

He shall be industrious and quick-working, and he may not idle and loaf. When the slave is old and his strength spent, he shall plant marsh grass and weave mats. When his work is over and he wishes to rest he should pound a picul of grain. Late at night when there is no work he shall wash clothes really white. If he has private savings they shall be the master's gift or from guests. The slave may not have evil secrets; affairs should be open and reported. If the slave does not heed instructions, he shall be bastinadoed a hundred strokes.

The reading of the text of the contract came to an end. The slave was speechless and his lips were tied. Wildly he beat his head on the ground, and beat himself with his hands; from his eyes the tears streamed down, and the drivel from his nose hung a foot long.

He said: "If it is to be exactly as master Wang says, I would rather return soon along the yellow-soil road,[6] with the grave worms boring through my head. Had I known before I would have bought the wine for master Wang. I would not have dared to do that wrong."

Translated by C. Martin Wilbur

6. In the underworld.

History

190

Two Brothers of Cheng and the Mother Who Doted on the Younger

from *The Commentary of Mr. Tso*

Attributed to Tso Ch'iu-ming (3rd century B.C.E.?)

Duke Yin First Year (722 B.C.E.)

In the past, Duke Wu of Cheng had taken a bride from the state of Shen, known as Lady Chiang of Duke Wu.[1] Lady Chiang gave birth to the fu-

The putative author of the *Tso chuan* or *Tso shih chuan* (*The Chronicle* or, more accurately, *Tradition* or *Commentary of Mr. Tso*) is Tso Ch'iu-ming. No biographical information exists concerning him, however, and his relationship to the work that bears his name remains unknown. The word *chuan* in the title implies that the work was considered a commentary on the *Spring and Autumn Annals* (*Ch'un-ch'iu*), but it is uncertain whether the *Tso chuan* was originally compiled for that purpose. Nonetheless, because the period of time that it covers (722–468 B.C.E.) is almost the same as that of the *Annals* (722–481 B.C.E.) and it contains detailed accounts of events referred to in the latter, the *Tso chuan* can conveniently serve as a commentary on the *Annals*—even though the entries do not always match.

The *Annals*, one of the five main classics of the Confucian tradition, provides a bare record of the events in the various feudal states. The entries are extremely brief, consisting mostly of notices of accessions to rule, marriages, deaths, diplomatic meetings, wars, and other events in the lives of the ruling dukes of the state of Lu and the other feudal states with whom they interacted, along with notations on unusual occurrences in the natural world such as earthquakes, comets, droughts, insect plagues, and so forth, all of which were thought to reflect the political condition of the realm. The *Tso chuan*, on the other hand, consists of thirty densely

ture Duke Chuang and to his brother, Tuan of Kung. Duke Chuang was born wide awake and consequently greatly startled Lady Chiang.[2] Therefore she named him Born Awake and came to hate him. But she loved his younger brother Tuan and wished to have him declared heir to the throne of Cheng. Repeatedly she begged Duke Wu to do so, but he would not agree.

Later, when Duke Chuang became ruler of Cheng (743 B.C.E.), Lady Chiang asked him to assign the city of Chih to his younger brother Tuan. But the duke replied, "Chih is a strategic city, the place where Kuo Shu[3] met his death. Any other city you have only to ask for."

She then requested that Tuan be given the city of Ching, and he was accordingly sent to reside there. He came to be called the T'ai-shu or Grand Younger Brother of Ching City.

Chai Chung, a high official of Cheng, said to the duke, "If any of the major cities have walls exceeding a hundred *chih* in length, they pose a danger to the capital.[4] According to the regulations of the former kings, even the largest cities should not exceed one third the size of the capital, while middle-sized cities should be one fifth and small cities one ninth. Now the city of Ching does not fit these dimensions and violates the regulations. You may find yourself unable to endure the consequences!"

---

written chapters and is China's oldest work of narrative history. Its entries provide a year-by-year—often month-by-month—account of happenings only mentioned in the *Annals*. The narratives focus primarily on political, diplomatic, and military affairs, but also contain considerable information on economic and cultural developments.

The original form of the *Tso chuan* is unknown. The narratives may initially have been grouped under the various states but later broken up and appended to the year-by-year entries of the *Annals* that focused on the reigns of the dukes of Lu. This rearrangement may have been made in the latter part of the third century C.E. Linguistic and philological evidence, however, indicates that the text was originally composed sometime during the third century B.C.E., considerably later than the date of 463 B.C.E. when it was supposed to have been completed. In spite of the mysteries surrounding its composition, the *Tso chuan* is a masterpiece of the early prose tradition and has had an immense influence on later Chinese literature and historiography. From the first century on, it was numbered among the texts of the enlarged Confucian canon.

The present selection is the first extended narrative from the *Tso chuan* and deals with the aftermath of a difficult breech delivery.

1. Shen was ruled by a branch of the Chiang family, hence the bride was referred to as Lady Chiang.

2. The phrase *wu-sheng*, translated here as "born wide awake," is also interpreted to mean born just as his mother was waking up, or born feet first. To help explain the mother's loathing for the child, Ssu-ma Ch'ien in *Records of the Grand Historian* (see selection 223), ch. 42, the account of the state of Cheng, adds that the birth was a difficult one.

3. An evil ruler of the nearby state of Kuo who made his capital at Chih and behaved evilly until overthrown by Cheng. Duke Chuang fears his younger brother will do likewise.

4. According to commentators, one *chih* represents a section of city wall one *chang* in height and three *chang* (or, according to another theory, five *chang*) in length. One *chang* is said to equal ten feet.

The duke said, "Lady Chiang would have it that way—how can I avoid the danger?"

"There is no end to what Lady Chiang would have!" replied Chai Chung. "Better tend to the matter at once and not let it grow and put out runners, for runners can be hard to control. If even plants that have put out runners cannot be rooted out, how much more so the favored younger brother of a ruler!"

The duke said, "If he does too many things that are not right, he is bound to bring ruin on himself. I suggest you wait a while."

After some time the T'ai-shu ordered that the western and northern border regions acknowledge fealty to him as well as to the duke. The ducal son Lü,[5] an official of Cheng, said to the duke, "The state cannot tolerate a system of double fealty! What do you intend to do? If you sanction what the T'ai-shu has done, then I beg leave to serve him rather than you. If you do not intend to sanction it, then I urge you to do away with him before he stirs up the hearts of the people!"

"No need," said the duke. "He will bring on his own downfall."

The T'ai-shu proceeded to take over the cities that had previously acknowledged double fealty and make them his own, extending his control as far as Lin-yen. The ducal son Lü said, "Now is the time to act! If he expands his territory, the people will go over to his side."

The duke replied, "If he acts wrongly, no one will side with him.[6] Though he expands his territory, he will face ruin."

The T'ai-shu completed the building of his walls, called together his men, mended his armor and weapons, equipped his foot soldiers and chariots, and prepared for a surprise attack on the capital of Cheng. Lady Chiang was to open the city to him. When the duke learned the date planned for the attack, he said,"Now is the time!" He ordered the ducal son Lü to lead a force of two thousand chariots and attack Ching. Ching turned against the T'ai-shu Tuan, who took refuge in Yen. The duke attacked him at Yen, and on the day *hsin-ch'ou* of the fifth month, the T'ai-shu fled the state and went to Kung.[7]

In the end the duke confined his mother, Lady Chiang, in Ch'eng-ying and took a vow, saying, "Not until we reach the Yellow Springs[8] shall we meet again!"

Later he regretted the vow. Ying K'ao-shu, a border guard of Ying Valley,

5. *Kung-tzu*, "ducal son," is a designation used for sons of feudal rulers; *kung-sun*, "ducal grandson," is used for grandsons; descendents in the next generation were given a surname of their own. Both Kung-tzu and Kung-sun later became surnames.

6. Or, following Tu Yü's (222–284) interpretation, "He is acting wrongly and in an unbrotherly manner."

7. At this point there appears a passage explaining the wording of the *Spring and Autumn Annals* entry pertaining to these events. In the present translation passages of this type have been omitted.

8. The springs within the yellow earth, a term for the land of the dead.

hearing of this, presented gifts to the duke, and the duke in turn had a meal served to him. He ate the meal but set aside the meat broth. When the duke asked him why, he replied, "Your servant has a mother who shares whatever food he eats, but she has never tasted your lordship's broth. I beg permission to take her some."

"You have a mother to take things to. Alas, I alone have none!" said the duke.

"May I venture to ask the meaning of that?" said Ying K'ao-shu.

The duke explained why he had made the remark and confessed that he regretted his vow.

"Why should your lordship worry?" said the other. "If you dig into the earth until you reach the springs, and fashion a tunnel where the two of you can meet, then who is to say you have not kept your vow?"

The duke did as he suggested. As the duke entered the tunnel he intoned this verse:

> Within the great tunnel,
> genial, genial is my joy!

When Lady Chiang emerged from the tunnel she intoned this verse:

> Outside the great tunnel,
> far-flung, far-flung is my joy!

So in the end mother and son became as they had been before.

The gentleman remarks:[9] Ying K'ao-shu was a man of utmost filial piety. He loved his mother, and succeeded in inspiring a similar feeling in Duke Chuang. Is this not what the *Book of Odes* means when it says:

> While filial sons are unslacking,
> forever shall be given you good things.[10]

Translated by Burton Watson

---

9. The *Tso chuan* frequently introduces didactic comments on the events of its narrative in this fashion. Though it has been asserted that "the gentleman" refers to Confucius, this is clearly impossible in many cases. These remarks are presumably judgments made by the author or authors of the *Tso chuan*, though some may have been added by later hands. There are eighty-four such passages in the *Tso chuan*.

10. This is from ode 247 of the *Classic of Odes* (see selection 22).

191

The Passing of Kung Sheng

from *History of the Han*

Pan Ku (32–92)

When Wang Mang took control of the government, Kung Sheng and Ping Han together petitioned to resign from office on account of their age and health. Earlier, during the time of Emperor Chao,[1] when Han Fu of Cho commandery came to the capital having been summoned for audience on account of his virtuous conduct, he was presented with an imperial document of entitlement and rolls of bundled silk, and was dispatched to return home. The emperor issued an edict saying: "We feel compunction about burdening him with the affairs of official duties. Let him endeavor to cultivate filial devotion and brotherly respectfulness, and so edify his district and town. On his journey home, he shall stay at the government relay lodges, and the local hostels will provide him with wine and meat, and feed his entourage and horses. The Senior Subaltern shall seasonally pay him visits, and shall present him one head of sheep and two *hu*[2] of wine yearly in the eighth month. In the case of something untoward,[3] he shall be presented with one set of burial shroud and coverlet, and sacrificed to with the medium offering."[4]

Wang Mang then, in accordance with the precedent, announced he would dismiss Sheng and Han. The imperial document read: "Today, the fourth day of the sixth month of the second year of the Yüan-shih reign,[5] the two elders,

Wang Mang's founding of a new dynasty has been condemned throughout Chinese history as an unrightful act of usurpation. The portrayal of Kung Sheng's conduct evinces the general commendation of acts against "usurpers" and the specific disparagement of Wang Mang that was common throughout all periods of imperial China, especially during the Later Han. The account of Kung Sheng was composed during the second half of the first century C.E., and thus merely some fifty years after Wang Mang's "usurpation" and his subsequent overthrow resulting in the reinstitution of "legitimate" rule. The construction of Kung Sheng's life and career, and the approbatory portrayal of Kung's righteous self-sacrifice, reflect the sentiments of a historiography wherein praise and blame are accorded retrospectively in compliance with the dominant values of the historian and his time. Thus, Kung Sheng is portrayed as a humble savant who, especially later in his career, accepted appointments with great reluctance and, even then, only until such time as he was able to retire on the excuse—or pretext—of age and health. At the advent of "illegitimate" rule, Kung Sheng withdrew in moral protest.

For the compilation of the *History of the Han* (also called the *History of the Former Han*), see selection 226.

1. In 80 B.C.E.
2. Approximately 40 liters.
3. I.e., death.
4. Of a sheep and a pig.
5. Equivalent to the first of July, 2 C.E.

Imperial Household Grandee[6] and Grand Palace Grandee,[7] shall cease their duties due to age and illness." The Grand Empress Dowager sent the Supervisor of the Receptionists to issue an imperial edict to them, which said: "It is heard that of old, when those holding office came to advanced age, they retired from office; in this way their resignation was respected and their energies not exhausted. At the present, the Grandees' years have advanced, and We would feel compunction at troubling them with the affairs of official duties. Let them present their sons, as well as one each of grandchildren, brothers, and sons of brothers. Let the Grandees cultivate their persons and cleave to the Way, and thus finish their long years. They shall be granted bundled silk and the privilege of lodging in the official guesthouses while on their journey, and at the new year be granted a sheep, wine, a tunic, and a cloak, all in accordance with the Han Fu precedent. The male progeny they present all shall be selected for the office of Gentleman." Thereupon, Sheng and Han returned to grow old in their native districts. . . .[8]

When Wang Mang usurped the rule of the country,[9] he dispatched the Commanding General of the Five Awesome Armies to conduct the conventional observances throughout the empire. The Commanding General personally paid respects to Sheng, offering him a sheep and wine. On the New Year,[10] Mang sent an emissary to go to Sheng and confer upon him the appointment of Chancellor of Academicians. On the pretext of illness, Sheng did not comply to the summons to audience.

Two years later, Mang again dispatched emissaries to present a document bearing the imperial seal, and the seal and seal-cord of the office of Academic Chancellor for the Preceptors and Companions of the Heir Designate, and he sent a comfortable quadriga[11] to receive Sheng. They went forward to accord respect and to confer the rank of Superior Chancellor, presenting in advance the amount of six months' emolument to facilitate his transfer to the capital. The emissaries along with the Grand Administrator of the commandery, the Senior Subaltern of the prefecture, the district elders, the sundry officials and those known for their conduct and fealty, as well as their students, in all amounting to a thousand men and more, entered Sheng's hamlet to present the edict.

The emissaries wished to induce Sheng to come forward and greet them, and so stood long outside the gate. Sheng claimed aggravated illness and prepared a bed in his quarters, below the southern window in the room west of the entry. He lay his head to the east, neatly spread his court attire and

6. Kung Sheng.
7. Ping Han.
8. The text here breaks to discuss an unrelated matter.
9. On January 10, 9 C.E.
10. Five days later.
11. Outfitted with rush-padded wheels so as to ride smoothly.

drew up his sash.[12] The emissaries passed through the entry, filed west and stood facing south. They presented the edict to which was attached the document with the imperial seal, removed to the courtyard, twice did obeisance and offered up the seal and seal-cord of office. They brought in the comfortable quadriga and went forward to address Sheng, saying, "The sage court has never been neglectful of you, lord; when the codes and regulations were not yet established at the advent of the new dynasty, we waited for you to formulate the government, hoping to hear that what we had wished for could come to be realized, and thus bring peace to all between the seas."

Sheng responded, "I have always been unclever, and adding to that being advanced in years and afflicted with illness, liable to expire at any moment. Were I to follow your lordships the emissaries and take to the road, I would be certain to die during the journey. This would be without benefit, to the greatest degree." The emissaries sought to persuade him of the importance of this appointment, going so far as advancing to place the seal and seal-cord upon Sheng's body. But Sheng pushed the articles aside and would not accept them.

The emissaries then memorialized: "We are just in full summer's torrid heat, and Sheng ails from asthenia; possibly he could be allowed to wait for autumn's coolness before setting out." This was approved by imperial edict. Once each five days, one of the emissaries went together with the Grand Administrator to inquire as to his daily welfare. They said to Sheng's two sons and his disciple Kao Hui and others, "The court humbly wishes to accord your lordship ceremonial entitlement. Though he be afflicted with illness, it would be better to set out and move to the official relay lodge, to demonstrate his intention to go. This would assure for his sons and grandsons a legacy of great endeavors." Hui and the others related the words of the emissaries.

Sheng realized that he would never be listened to, and addressed Hui and the others: "I was the recipient of great favor from the House of Han, but there was nothing with which I could repay it. Now I am old in years, and imminently will be put into the earth. In my opinion, how could I with my single life serve two ruling houses, and face my former rulers below?" Sheng then gave instructions on the matter of mourning, and on restraint in terms of the coffin: "The shroud surrounds the body; the coffin surrounds the shroud. You are not to follow vulgar custom and stir up my grave, nor plant cypresses, nor erect a memorial hall." When he had finished speaking, he did not again open his mouth to drink or eat. When fourteen days had passed he died; he was seventy-eight years[13] old at death.

The emissaries and the Grand Administrator oversaw the restraint in funeral matters, and presented the double burial coverlet and sacrificial memorial services according to the law. Disciples, hemp-clad mourners, and funeral

12. This description alludes to the way in which an ill Confucius insisted on correct posture and dress; it is taken from *Analects* 10.13.

13. The text has "seventy-nine *sui*."

participants were counted by the hundreds. An elderly fellow came to mourn, whose wailing was extremely grave. Presently he said, "Alas, incense burns itself up on account of its fragrance; oil depletes itself on account of its brightness. Master Kung in the end cut off prematurely his appointed years— he was no cohort of mine." He then left in a hurry; nobody knew his identity.

Sheng's residence was at Lien hamlet[14] in P'eng-ch'eng.[15] Those of later ages engraved stone tablets to mark the gates of his hamlet.

Translated by Alan J. Berkowitz

14. Hamlet of the Incorrupt.
15. Modern Hsü-chou in Kiangsu province.

192

Činggis Qahan Subdues the Naiman

from *The Secret History of the Mongols*

Anonymous (c. 1228)

Again, when Činggis Qahan[1] made a decree, he made a decree, saying, "Let the quiverbearers, the guards which are dayguards, the cooks, the keepers of

The predominant ethnic group in China today is that of the Han, yet the multiethnic, multiracial composition of the Chinese populace has been a significant factor throughout the history of the nation. Indeed, it is probable that non-Han rulers have occupied the throne of imperial China more often than not, and many of the most distinguished generals, statesmen, scholars, and artisans have had non-Han or partially non-Han backgrounds. Given the ethnic variety of the Chinese people, it is not surprising that works originally composed in non-Han (i.e., non-Sinitic) languages would have had a considerable impact on the development of Chinese literature. Studies on this aspect of Chinese literary history are still in their infancy but promise significant revelations for future researchers.

The Secret History of the Mongols was composed in Mongolian around 1228. It was originally written in the Mongolian script, which was derived from the Old Uighur script (which, in turn, was derived from the Syriac script). The Mongolian text, however, was preserved only in a sinographic transcription, from which this English translation has been made. A vernacular Sinitic translation, prepared between about 1368 and 1404, was important for the compilation of later Chinese historical works dealing with the rise of the Yüan dynasty. *The Secret History* provides a vivid account of the forging of the Mongol nation and is an excellent example of the absorption of non-Han materials into the mainstream of Chinese civilization that has been going on for millennia.

Five special pronunciation symbols are used in this translation: č is pronounced as *ch*; š is pronounced as *sh*; γ and q are pronounced *g* and *k* far back in the throat; and ǰ is pronounced like the *j* in "jump."

1. Also commonly romanized as Genghis Khan ("Universal Ruler"), this is the title of Temujin.

doors, and the keepers of geldings take their turn in the daytime and, before that the sun setteth, retire for the nightguards and, going out to their geldings, pass the night. Let the nightguards, at night, make to lie those of their men that shall lie round about the tent and make to stand in turn those of their men that shall stand at the door. Let the quiverbearers and the dayguards, the next day, when We take broth, tell unto the nightguards that they are come and then let the quiverbearers, the dayguards, the cooks, and the keepers of doors go each unto his daily task. Let them sit upon their seats. Let them,[2] completing their days of turn of three nights and three days and passing the three nights in the very same manner, changing places with those who relieve them, be nightguards the night which followeth their being relieved. Let them pass the night lying round about." And so, making an end of dividing the army into thousands so as to form thousands, appointing stewards, enrolling eighty nightguards and seventy guards which are dayguards, choosing *ba'atud*[3] for Qasar,[4] when, from Keltegei Qada of Mount Or Nu'u of the Qalqa River, he set forth against the Naiman people, the sixteenth day of the first moon of summer, on the "red circle" day,[5] the year of the rat [1204], when Činggis Qahan, having sprinkled the standard,[6] set forth, being gone up along the Kelüren River, making Ĵebe[7] and Qubilai[8] to be spies, when he reached the Sa'ari Steppe, at the head of Mount Qangqarqan, the watchmen of the Naiman were there. The Naiman watchmen pursuing unto our watchmen, one from our watchmen—one which had a white horse and a rather bad saddle—was taken by the watchmen of the Naiman. When the watchmen of the Naiman, taking that horse, spake unto one another, they said unto one another, "The geldings of the Mongγol are lean." When ours, reaching the Sa'ari Steppe and halting there, said unto one another, "What shall we do?" then, when Dodai Čerbi gave advice unto Činggis Qahan, he gave advice, saying, "We are, indeed, few in number. Over and above the fact that we are few in number we are come, being exhausted. Thus, indeed, halting, until our geldings be satiated, pitching, spreading ourselves in this Sa'ari Steppe, every person be he but alive lighting fires at the rate of five places a man, we shall terrify them by the fire. The Naiman people are said to be many. Their *qan*[9] is called a weakling which is not yet come out from in his tent. While we confuse them by fire, our geldings also will become satiated. Making our geldings to become satiated, having pursued the watchmen of the Naiman, if,

2. I.e., "my guards (*kešigten*)."
3. Valiant men.
4. Arqai Qasar of the Ĵalayir, a son of Seče Domoγ.
5. The sixteenth of the fourth lunation, an auspicious day.
6. With mare's milk. A ceremony performed on the eve of battle.
7. The name means "weapon." It was given by Činggis Qahan to the warrior Jirγo'adai of the Tayiči'ud tribe.
8. Of the Barula tribe; captain of a thousand and one of the "four dogs" (see note 37).
9. Ruler or Sovereign.

following hard upon them, making them to unite themselves at their middle, we join battle in that confusion, will it not do?" when, approving this word, Činggis Qahan made a decree, he proclaimed an ordinance unto the soldiers, saying, "So, then, make ye one to light fires." And so, pitching, spreading themselves in the Sa'ari Steppe, one made every man were he but alive to light fires at five places. At night the watchmen of the Naiman, from the head of Mount Qangqarqan, at night seeing the many fires, having sent unto Tayang Qan,[10] said, "Was one not saying that the Mongγol are very few in number? They have fires which are more than the stars." Giving unto him the little white horse which had the rather bad saddle, they sent, saying, "The soldiers of the Mongγol have pitched until the Sa'ari Steppe is covered. Are they not increasing on each day? They have fires which are more than the stars."

Receiving this message of the watchmen, Tayang Qan was at the Qačir Usun[11] of the Qangγai. Having suffered one to bring this message, when he sent, telling it unto his son Güčülüg Qan,[12] he sent, saying, "The geldings of the Mongγol are lean. One saith, 'They have fires which are more than the stars.' Hence the Mongγol are many. Now,

> If we join battle in earnest,
> Will it not be difficult to separate ourselves from them?
> If we join battle in earnest,
> They will not wink with their black eyes—those.

> If we join battle
> With the hard Mongγol
> Which draw not back,
> Even if they are pierced
> In the cheek;
> Even if the black blood
> Issue,
> Will it do?

The geldings of the Mongγol are said to be lean. We, making our people to pass over the Altai[13] and rolling them back, removing, reforming our army, marching, enticing them,[14] marching, fighting dogfights,[15] until we arrive at the foot of the Altai—our geldings are fat—making the bellies to be pulled

10. Emperor of the Naiman.
11. Qačir Water (River).
12. Qan of the Naiman.
13. An important mountain range in Central Asia, whence the Altaic language family (including Turkic and Mongolian languages) takes its name.
14. I.e., the Mongγol.
15. Skirmishes.

up[16] and waiting until the geldings of the Mongγol be exhausted, we shall pour out our army at their faces."[17] At that word, when Güčülüg Qan spake, saying, "The woman Tayang of always! When his heart hath failed him, he hath spoken these words. The many of the Mongγol of whom ye speak would be come from whence? The more part of the Mongγol are with Jamuγa[18] here in the hands of us. When the heart of the woman Tayang

> Which is not yet gone out to the place where a woman heavy with
>   child pisseth;[19]
> Which is not yet arrived at the pasture of the calf of the wheel[20]

failed him, came he not, speaking these words?" he sent, speaking by a messenger till his father was pained, till he was injured. At this word, Tayang Qan being mentioned by his son in such a manner that he himself was compared unto a woman, when Tayang Qan spake, he said, "Let the mighty, courageous Güčülüg, the day when the enemy and we shall encounter one another and when the enemy and we shall kill one another, not put away, perhaps, this his courage. When, in earnest, the enemy and we shall have encountered one another and shall have joined battle, to separate ourselves from them will, perhaps, be difficult." At that word, when Qori Sübeči,[21] the great chief who governed under Tayang Qan, spake, having said, "Thy father Inanča Bilge Qan[22] shewed not the back of man or the rump of gelding unto a companion[23] which was equal.[24] Now, thou, it having yet been the morning early,[25] how faileth thee thy heart, thou? If we had known that thy heart would thus fail thee, even though she be but a woman, would we, bringing Gürbesü,[26] thy mother, not have made her to set the army in order? Čima![27] Alas! Why by Kögse'ü Sabraγ[28] must we be made to suffer the effect of his

16. "This expression means 'to do so that the belly diminishes in volume.' The horses fattened in pasture cannot furnish violent and prolonged efforts without being spoiled. It is why the Mongols, during a certain number of days, let them graze only a very short time, until, rid of superfluous fat, they are in good form." (Antoine Mostaert)

17. I.e., "we shall deploy before them."

18. Son of Qara Qada'an of the Jajirad.

19. I.e., "who has not yet gone so far from the tent as a pregnant woman who, because of her pregnancy, does not go any farther from the tent to urinate than is absolutely necessary."

20. I.e., "who has not gone so far from the tent as the calf which, during the day, is tied to the wheel of a cart in the vicinity of the tent in order to prevent it from following its mother and sucking her milk, because a cow which has a calf is milked every day."

21. A watchman of the Naiman.

22. Of the Naiman.

23. I.e., enemy.

24. I.e., "He never took flight." In other words, he was not a coward before his peers.

25. I.e., "Whereas it is still long before the battle will be joined."

26. Mother of Tayang Qan of the Naiman.

27. Like *ayi* several sentences below, this is a sighing sound.

28. Of the Naiman.

waxing old? The ordinances of our army are become lax. It is the time and the destiny of the Mongɣol. It is not become favorable for us. *Ayi! Turluɣ*[29] Tayang, thou art but as if thou art not able." Having struck his quiver,[30] he trotted elsewhere.

At that, Tayang Qan, being wroth, spake, saying, "A life which dieth and a body which suffereth[31] are one and the same for all. If it be so, let us fight." Removing from the Qačir Usun, being gone down along the Tamir River, passing over the Orqon, passing by the eastern skirt of Naqu Qun,[32] at the moment when, arriving, he was drawing nigh unto Čakirma'ud, the watchmen of Činggis Qahan seeing him, as they brought a message, said, "The Naiman, arriving, draw nigh." Having suffered them to bring this message, Činggis Qahan made a decree, saying, "The issue will be adversities either which are more than many or which are fewer than few."[33] Setting forth against them, having driven away their watchmen, when he set the army in order, he said, "Marching the 'qaraɣana' march, arraying ourselves in the 'lake' array, let us fight the 'chisel' fight."[34] Having so said, Činggis Qahan, going himself as a spy, made Qasar to set the middle in order. He made Odčigin Noyan[35] to set the led horses in order. The Naiman, withdrawing themselves from Čakirma'ud, stood along the front of Naqu Qun and the skirt of the mountains. And so, our watchmen, having driven before them the watchmen of the Naiman, having driven them before them so that they united themselves at their great middle at the front of Naqu Qun, arrived. Tayang Qan seeing that they were thus driving his watchmen before them and were arriving, as to Jamuɣa, then, with the Naiman, his army setting forth, being come with them, being there, Tayang Qan asked of Jamuɣa. He asked, saying, "Those are what? Even as the wolves pursue the many sheep and come, pursuing them unto the folds, these what people, so pursuing, draw nigh?" When Jamuɣa spake, he said, "Mine *anda*,[36] Temüjin, hath been wont to nourish 'four dogs'[37] with the flesh of men and to bind them, using

29. An oath.
30. I.e., in disgust.
31. I.e., "A mortal life and a passible body."
32. A mountain range.
33. This seems to mean, "It is all or nothing," i.e., "We shall risk all."
34. This is the only passage in *The Secret History* in which these three types of tactics are specifically mentioned by name: 1. "To march the 'qaraɣana' march" means to march with the troops massed in close order in the manner of the qaraɣana, a thorny shrub that grows in thick clumps on the steppe. 2. "To array oneself in the 'lake' array" means to deploy with the troops widely scattered in the manner of the water of a lake spreading over a large area. 3. "To fight the 'chisel' fight" means to engage the enemy with a thrust at his center in the manner of a chisel thrust into a piece of wood.
35. Temüge, the youngest brother of Temüjin.
36. "Tally-friendship/union," i.e., "friendship or union as close as two matching tallies; a sworn brother."
37. Jebe, Qubilai, Jelme, and Sübe'etei. Also see notes 38 and 39.

chains of iron. Those who draw nigh, pursuing those our watchmen, are they. Those 'four dogs,'

> Having helmets which are copper,
> Having snouts which are chisels,
> Having tongues which are awls,
> Having hearts which are iron,
> Having whips which are swords,

march, eating the dew and riding the wind—those.

> On the days when they and the enemy kill one another
> They eat the flesh of men—those.
> On the days when they and the enemy encounter one another,
> They take the flesh of human beings as their provision—those.

Have they, their chains being put off, now not been restrained? Rejoicing, they draw nigh, so drivelling—those." When he said, "Those 'four dogs,' who are those?" he said, "Both Ĵebe and Qubilai and both Ĵelme[38] and Sübe'etei[39] are those four." When Tayang Qan spake, saying, "Let us stand far from those lowly creatures," moving backward, he stood, straddling the mountain and the plain. Seeing those who, skipping for joy and making circles, were drawing nigh behind them, again Tayang Qan asked of Ĵamuɣa. He asked, saying, "Those are what? How so draw those nigh, making circles as foals which one hath loosed early in the morning, foals which, sucking the milk of their mothers, run merrily round about their mothers?" When Ĵamuɣa spake, he said, "Those are called the Uru'ud[40] and the Mangɣud,[41]

> Which, driving before them
> The men with lances,
> Strip them of their bloody clothing;
> Which, pushing before them,
> The men with swords, cutting them down and killing them,
> Take from them their treasure and clothing.

Those now, rejoicing and skipping for joy, so draw those not nigh?" Then, when Tayang Qan spake, saying, "If it be so, let us stand far from those lowly creatures," again, to the rearward, ascending the mountain, he stood. Saying, "Those who, pushing a point before the others, draw nigh behind them.

> Driveling
> Like falcons

38. Of the Uriangqad; elder brother of Sübe'etei; a captain of a thousand.
39. Also a captain of a thousand.
40. A clan.
41. A clan.

which are become greedy of food, who are they who draw nigh?," Tayang Qan asked of Jamuɣa. When Jamuɣa spake, he said, "This is mine *anda*, Temüjin, which draweth nigh. In the armor on his whole body

> There is no space betwixt to pierce for an awl
> Which hath been cast
> Of unwrought copper.
> There is no space betwixt to pierce for a great needle
> Which hath been hammered
> Of iron.

Mine *anda*, Temüjin, draweth nigh like a falcon which is become greedy of food and driveling. Have ye seen him? The Naiman companions were doing nothing other than saying that, if they ever saw the Mongɣol, they would not leave them even the skin of the foot of a kid.[42] See ye them now." At this word, when Tayang Qan spake, saying, "It is fearful! Let us, ascending the mountain, stand there," he ascended the mountain and stood there. Again, when Tayang Qan asked of Jamuɣa, again he asked, saying, "Who are they who thickly draw nigh behind him?"[43] When Jamuɣa spake, he said, "Mother Hö'elün[44] was wont to nourish one of her sons with the flesh of men.

> Having a body three *alda*[45] in height,
> Having as food cattle of three years old,
> Wearing a breast-plate
> Of three layers,
> He draweth nigh, making three bulls to draw his cart.
> If he swallow
> A man with a quiver—the whole man—
> He will not be obstructed in his gullet.
> If he swallow a whole man,
> It satisfieth not his heart.[46]
> If he be wroth,
> If, drawing his bow, he release his *angɣu'a*[47] arrow,
> He shooteth so as to pierce
> Ten or twenty
> People
> Which are

42. The goat is the animal which, with the Mongols, has the least value. Of the five kinds of livestock, i.e., the horse, camel, ox, sheep, and goat, it is the last in order. Consequently, the skin from the extremity of the foot of a kid is almost less than nothing.

43. I.e., Temüjin.

44. Bride of Čiledü of the Merkid; wife of Yesügei; mother of Temüjin.

45. An *alda*, properly, the span of the arms, is a measure of approximately six feet.

46. I.e., "It does not satisfy his appetite."

47. This word is glossed "name of [a kind of] arrow." It is an arrow with a forked tip.

Beyond
A mountain.
If, drawing his bow, he release his *keyibür*[48] arrow,
He shooteth so as to join[49] and so as to pierce
The companions[50] with which he hath quarreled—
Those who are beyond
The steppe.
If, drawing his bow, in a great manner, he shoot,
He shooteth at a place at a distance of nine hundred *alda*.
If, pulling and drawing his bow, he shoot,
He shooteth at a place at a distance of five hundred *alda*.
He is other in countenance than all other men.
He is called J̌oči Qasar[51] which was born a *gürelgü*[52] python.

He is that one." Then, when Tayang Qan spake, saying, "If it be so, let us strive for the height of the mountain. Ascend ye upward!," ascending the mountain, he stood there. Again, when Tayang Qan asked of J̌amuγa, he said, "Who are those who draw nigh behind him?" When J̌amuγa spake, he said, "That is Odčigin, the youngest son of Mother Hö'elün. He is said to be one which hath a sluggish liver.[53] He is one which sleepeth early and one which ariseth late.

Yet even he remaineth not behind from the multitude.
Yet even he remaineth not behind from the battle array."

When Tayang Qan spake, he said, "If it be so, let us go up on the top of the mountain."

J̌amuγa having thus spoken these words unto Tayang Qan, separating himself from the Naiman, going out, being alone, when he sent, letting a message go in unto Činggis Qahan, when he sent, speaking, saying, "Speak unto the *anda*," he sent, saying, "Tayang Qan,

At my word,
Losing his head,
Striving for the heights,
Being terrified, is gone up.
Being killed
By my mouth,
Being afraid,

48. This word is glossed "name of [a kind of] arrow."
49. To transfix, as on a spit.
50. I.e., enemies.
51. Second son of Yesügei Ba'atur (father of Temüjin).
52. This word is glossed "name of a [kind of] python."
53. I.e., "which is a sluggard."

He is gone up,
Ascending
The mountain.

Anda, be thou prudent! The same are gone up into the mountain. These do not have the countenance of daring to set face against thee. As for me, I have separated myself from the Naiman." Činggis Qahan, the sun becoming evening, halted and passed the night compassing the mountain of Naqu Qun. That night, as the Naiman began to escape and to remove, tumbling down from on Naqu Qun, heaping themselves up the one on top of the other, their bones falling to pieces, they crushed one another so that they stood like rotten trees and thus they died. On the morrow they made an end of Tayang Qan. Whereas Güčülüg Qan was elsewhere, when, removing, revolting, being but few persons in number, he was overtaken, he made a *güre'en*[54] at the Tamir River. Not being able to stand in that his *güre'en*, removing, fleeing away, he went out and departed. They assembled the nation of the Naiman people, making an end of it, at the front of the Altai. The Ĵadaran, the Qatagin, the Salĵi'ud, the Dörben, the Tayiči'ud, the Unggirad,[55] and others which had been with Ĵamuɣa also submitted themselves there. When Činggis Qahan, making one to bring Gürbesü, the mother of Tayang, spake, saying, "Wast thou not saying, 'The scent of the Mongɣol is bad?' Why art thou now come?" Činggis Qahan took her to wife.

Adapted from the translation of Francis Woodman Cleaves

54. "Circle," i.e., "an encampment around which the carts are drawn up in the form of a circle for protection."
55. Various clans and tribes that had been allied with the Naiman tribe.

Moral Lessons

193
Exemplary Sayings

Chapter 2

Yang Hsiung (53 B.C.E.−18 C.E.)

Someone asked, "Sir, when young, were you fond of the rhapsody?" I answered, "Yes, young lads carve worm characters and engrave seal script."[1] After a moment I said, "But a grown man does not engage in such activities."

Someone asked, "Can a rhapsody be used for admonition?" I answered, "Admonish? If it admonishes, it should stop there. If not, I am afraid it cannot avoid being anything but an encouragement."

Someone asked, "But does it not have the elegant beauty of misty gauze?" I responded, "It is only a defect in a seamstress' work."

The *Swordsman's Disquisition* says, "A sword can be used to protect the body." I responded, "Does prison make a person more mannerly?"

The author was born in Ch'eng-tu (in present-day Szechwan). A great admirer of Ch'ü Yüan (see selection 148) and Ssu-ma Hsiang-ju (see selection 151), Yang Hsiung mined their works for fine phrases and stylistic devices. Yang was himself one of the most distinguished practitioners of the rhapsody, so it is ironic that he is at pains to disparage the genre so thoroughly in this piece. He was a major thinker and had composed his own transformed version of the *Classic of Changes*, entitled *Classic of the Grand Mystery (T'ai-hsüan ching)*. His deep interest in the languages and topolects of the various regions of China was hampered by the lack of a phonetic script with which to record them accurately and unambiguously.

1. Yang Hsiung is saying here that the writing of *fu* or rhapsody (see selections 148–156) is a puerile exercise comparable to the calligraphic exercises of young boys, who were expected to master six types of script, including the worm and seal script.

Someone asked, "Were the rhapsodies of Ching Ts'o, T'ang Le, and Mei Ch'eng beneficial?"[2] I answered, "What is certain is that their writing was immoderate." "What do you mean by immoderate?" "The rhapsodies of the *Songs* poets were beautiful but regulated. The rhapsodies of the epideictic writers are beautiful but immoderate. If the school of Confucius had used the rhapsody, Chia Yi would have mounted the hall and Ssu-ma Hsiang-ju would have entered the inner compartments. But they did not use the rhapsody, so what of it?"

Someone asked, "What about flies, red, and purple?"[3] I said, "Look sharply." Someone asked, "What about such semblances as the music of Cheng and Wei?"[4] I said, "Listen carefully." Someone asked, "When the five tones and the twelve pitches are combined, why is it that sometimes one hears classical music, and sometimes the music of Cheng?" I responded, "When the sounds are moderate and proper, one produces classical music. When the sounds are lewd and lascivious, we have the music of Cheng." "I beg to ask about the basis of classical music." I responded, "It begins with the Yellow Bell,[5] and is harmonized with moderation and propriety. Thus, we can be certain that the music of Cheng and Wei does not intrude."

Someone asked, "Women have a physical attraction. Does writing also have a similar attraction?" I responded, "Yes. But, in women one detests the powder and rouge spoiling their modesty and grace, and in writing, one detests extravagant verbiage that detracts from the moral code."

Someone asked, "Was Ch'ü Yüan wise?" I said, "At first he was like jade, like a lustrous gem, but then he changed to vermeil and green pigment. Such was his wisdom! Such was his wisdom!"

Someone asked, "Does a gentleman admire rhetoric?" I responded, "What a gentleman admires are the facts. But when factual detail overpowers style and rhetoric, one has a dry discourse. When rhetoric and style overpower a factual presentation, one has a rhapsody. When facts and rhetoric are in balance, one has a classic. Verbosity and excessive posturing are mere ornaments on virtue."

Someone asked, "Kung-sun Lung thought his ten thousand paradoxes could serve as standards. Are they standards?" I responded. "There are standards to be followed even in cutting wood to make a game board or to turn

2. Ching Ts'o and T'ang Le (both late third century B.C.E.) were poets from the Ch'u region. Except for a few pieces of dubious authenticity, none of their writings survive. Mei Ch'eng (or Sheng) was a prominent rhapsody writer of the Former Han.

3. Blue flies, thought to contaminate the pure colors of black and white, are the traditional symbol of petty men and slanderers. Red and purple are the impure "intermediate" colors that detract from the "proper" pure colors of vermilion and black respectively.

4. Confucius reputedly said that he "detested things that seemed to be proper but were not." One of the semblances he detested was the "licentious" music of Cheng and Wei, which could be confused with the proper, orthodox music.

5. The fundamental pitch of the five-tone scale.

leather into a ball. But whatever does not conform to the standards of the former kings a gentleman will not follow.

"Reading books is like viewing mountains and rivers. By climbing the Eastern Peak one may understand the smallness of other mountains, not to mention the tiny hillocks. Having floated the azure sea, one may understand the shallowness of the Yangtze and the Yellow River, not to mention a dried-up swamp. Abandoning the Five Classics and trying to reach the Way—it simply cannot be done. He who abandons common fare and craves strange delicacies—how can one say he has good taste? He who abandons the great sage and shows a preference for other philosophers—how can one say he knows the Way?"

A path leading into mountain defiles cannot be followed. A door that leads into a wall cannot be entered. Someone said, "By what means does one enter?" My response: "Through Confucius. Confucius is the door." He asked, "Have you entered his door?" I responded, "I have indeed entered his door! Indeed I have! How could I have not entered his door?"

Someone wished to study the *Ts'ang Chieh* and *Shih p'ien*.[6] I said, "What fine scribal works! What fine scribal works! Studying them is preferable to making reckless guesses or leaving lacunae in the text."

Someone asked, "Suppose there were a man who said his surname was K'ung and his sobriquet was Chung-ni, that he entered Confucius' door, mounted his hall, leaned on his armrest, and wore his clothes. Could one call him Confucius?" I responded, "His outer form is that of Confucius, but his essence is not." "I venture to ask what you mean by essence." I responded, "Suppose there is an animal with the essence of a goat dressed in a tiger skin. Upon seeing grass it would rejoice, but if it saw a dhole, it would tremble. This is because it would forget it was dressed in a tiger's skin. A sage has the distinction of a tiger: his outer adornment is brilliant. A gentleman has the distinction of a leopard: his outer adornment is elegant. A sophist has the distinction of a racoon-dog: his outer adornment is thick. If a racoon-dog changes, it can become a leopard; if a leopard changes, it can become a tiger."[7]

To be fond of books but not seek the essentials in Confucius is to be a book-stall. To be fond of disquisition but not seek the essentials in Confucius is to be storyteller's clapper. There is nothing hurtful in a gentleman's speech, and nothing immoderate in what he hears. Hurtfulness leads to disorder, and immoderation leads to depravity. There are cases of those who followed the proper way yet had a little iniquity, but there has never been a man of iniquity who even slightly followed the proper way.

6. Early dictionaries that contained standard forms for the lesser and greater seal script respectively.

7. That is to say, with effort, a sophist can become a gentleman, and a gentleman can become a sage.

The way of Confucius is clear and easy! Someone asked, "Although one practices it from his youth, he is still befuddled when he becomes old and gray. How can it be clear and easy?" I responded, "This means that he did not treat the wicked as wicked and did not treat falsehood with falsehood. If he had treated the wicked as wicked and falsehood with falsehood, even if they saw him with their own eyes and heard him with their ears, how could he have rectified them?"

When one hears many things, he holds only to the essentials; when one sees many things, he holds only to the distinctive. If one hears little, he has no essentials; if he hears little, he has nothing distinctive.[8]

Three hundred green robes—but what about the color?[9] Three thousand grass-cloth remnants—but what about the cold?[10]

There are four easy aspects to the way of the gentleman: it is simple and easy to use, it is focused on the essentials and is easy to grasp, it is brilliant and easy to see, and it follows the norms and is easy to speak about.

It is only after a raging wind and a pounding rain that we begin to appreciate the cover provided by a great house; it is only after a cruel government has oppressed the age that we begin to appreciate the protection provided by a sage.

In ancient times Yang Chu and Mo Ti blocked the road, but Mencius opened it with his eloquent speech, and all was clear and open again. In later times there were others who have blocked the road. I compare myself with Mencius.

Someone asked, "Each person approves of what he considers right and condemns what he considers wrong. Who can determine what is correct?" I answered, "The myriad things are manifoldly complex and thus their disposition depends upon Heaven. The words of the many thinkers are confused and chaotic, and must be judged by a sage." Someone asked, "But how can one find a sage to evaluate them?" I answered, "When he is living, one may consult the man; after his death, one may consult his books. The principle to be obtained in either case is the same."

Translated by David Knechtges

8. Partly following Mencius, Yang Hsiung is saying here that a man may acquire broad learning, but the most important thing is to discern what is essential among the many things he has learned.

9. Green is one of the intermediate or impure colors. Yang Hsiung is probably alluding to the following lines from the *Classic of Odes* (poem 27): "Green is the robe, /A green robe with yellow lining." Yellow is one of the five correct colors. According to the Confucian interpretation current in Yang's time, using an intermediate color such as green for the outer part of the garment and a correct color for the lining shows a reversal of what is proper. Yang Hsiung is saying here that anything that is improper, regardless of number, cannot be used.

10. Yang Hsiung is saying here that anything of inferior quality, even in great numbers, is of no use.

194

Lessons for Women

Instructions in Seven Chapters for a Woman's Ordinary Way of Life in the First Century C.E.

Pan Chao (45–120?)

Introduction

I, the unworthy writer, am unsophisticated, unenlightened, and by nature unintelligent, but I am fortunate both to have received not a little favor from my scholarly father, and to have had a cultured mother and instructresses upon whom to rely for a literary education as well as for training in good manners. More than forty years have passed since at the age of fourteen I took up the dustpan and the broom[1] in the Ts'ao family. During this time with trembling heart I feared constantly that I might disgrace my parents, and that I might multiply difficulties for both the women and the men of my husband's family. Day and night I was distressed in heart, but I labored without confessing weariness. Now and hereafter, however, I know how to escape from such faults.

Being careless, and by nature stupid, I taught and trained my children without system. Consequently I fear that my son Ku may bring disgrace upon the Imperial Dynasty by whose Holy Grace he has unprecedentedly received the extraordinary privilege of wearing the Gold and the Purple,[2] a privilege for the attainment of which by my son, I a humble subject never even hoped. Nevertheless, now that he is a man and able to plan his own life, I need not again have concern for him. But I do grieve that you, my daughters,[3] just now at the age for marriage, have not at this time had gradual training and advice; that you still have not learned the proper customs for married women. I fear that by failure in good manners in other families you will humiliate both your ancestors and your clan. I am now seriously ill, life is uncertain. As I have thought of you all in so untrained a state, I have been uneasy many a time for

These admonitions for women, particularly as reformulated and popularized by later writers, had a tremendous impact on the way women were expected to behave in ancient China. The author was undoubtedly the most celebrated female writer of early China. She was the sister of Pan Ku (32–92), whose *History of the Han Dynasty (Han shu)* she completed (see selection 227), the daughter of Pan Piao (3–54), a famous poet who had begun the compilation of the *History of the Han,* and grandniece of Pan Chieh-yü (c. 45–5 B.C.E.), who also had a great literary reputation.

1. A conventional expression for the inferior position of the daughter-in-law in relation to her parents-in-law.

2. Gold seal and purple robe (symbols of high nobility).

3. Not necessarily her own daughters only, but girls of her family as a whole.

you. At hours of leisure I have composed in seven chapters these instructions under the title *Lessons for Women*. In order that you may have something wherewith to benefit your persons, I wish every one of you, my daughters, each to write out a copy for yourself.

From this time on, every one of you strive to practice these lessons.

Chapter 1: Humility

On the third day after the birth of a girl the ancients observed three customs: first to place the baby below[4] the bed; second to give her a potsherd with which to play;[5] and third to announce her birth to her ancestors by an offering. Now to lay the baby below the bed plainly indicated that she is lowly and weak, and should regard it as her primary duty to humble herself before others. To give her potsherds with which to play indubitably signified that she should practice labor and consider it her primary duty to be industrious. To announce her birth before her ancestors clearly meant that she ought to esteem as her primary duty the continuation of the observance of worship in the home.

These three ancient customs epitomize a woman's ordinary way of life and the teachings of the traditional ceremonial rites and regulations. Let a woman modestly yield to others; let her respect others; let her put others first, herself last. Should she do something good, let her not mention it; should she do something bad, let her not deny it. Let her bear disgrace; let her even endure[6] when others speak or do evil to her. Always let her seem to tremble and to fear. When a woman follows such maxims as these, then she may be said to humble herself before others.

Let a woman retire late to bed, but rise early to duties; let her not dread tasks by day or by night. Let her not refuse to perform domestic duties whether easy or difficult. That which must be done, let her finish completely, tidily, and systematically. When a woman follows such rules as these, then she may be said to be industrious.

Let a woman be correct in manner and upright in character in order to serve her husband. Let her live in purity and quietness of spirit, and attend to her own affairs. Let her love not gossip and silly laughter. Let her cleanse and purify and arrange in order the wine and the food for the offerings to the ancestors. When a woman observes such principles as these, then she may be said to continue ancestral worship.

No woman who observes these three fundamentals of life has ever had a

4. On the floor or the ground.

5. In the *Classic of Odes*, it is written that "daughters . . . shall have tiles to play with." Since potsherds were used as spindle weights, they served both as toys for little girls and as an early introduction to domesticity.

6. Literally, "let her hold filth in her mouth," i.e., let her swallow insult.

bad reputation or has fallen into disgrace. If a woman fail to observe them, how can her name be honored; how can she but bring disgrace upon herself?

Chapter 2: Husband and Wife

The Way of husband and wife is intimately connected with yin and yang, and relates the individual to gods and ancestors. Truly it is the great principle of Heaven and Earth, and the great basis of human relationships. Therefore the *Rites* honor union of man and woman; and in the *Classic Book of Poetry*, the "First Ode" manifests the principle of marriage. For these reasons the relationship cannot but be an important one.

If a husband be unworthy, then he possesses nothing by which to control his wife. If a wife be unworthy, then she possesses nothing with which to serve her husband. If a husband does not control his wife, then the rules of conduct manifesting his authority are abandoned and broken. If a wife does not serve her husband, then the proper relationship between men and women and the natural order of things are neglected and destroyed. As a matter of fact, the purpose of these two, the controlling of women by men and the serving of men by women, is the same.

Now examine the gentlemen of the present age. They only know that wives must be controlled and that the husband's rules of conduct manifesting his authority must be established. They therefore teach their boys to read books and study histories. But they do not in the least understand that husbands and masters must also be served, and that the proper relationship and the rites should be maintained.

Yet only to teach men and not to teach women—is that not ignoring the essential relation between them? According to the *Rites*, it is the rule to begin to teach children to read at the age of eight years, and by the age of fifteen years they ought then to be ready for cultural training.[7] Only why should it not be that girls' education as well as boys' be according to this principle?

Chapter 3: Respect and Caution

As yin and yang are not of the same nature, so man and woman have different characteristics. The distinctive quality of the yang is rigidity; the function of the yin is yielding. Man is honored for strength; a woman is beautiful on account of her gentleness. Hence there arose the common saying: "A man though born like a wolf may, it is feared, become a weak monstrosity; a woman though born like a mouse may, it is feared, become a tiger."

Now for self-culture nothing equals respect for others. To counteract firmness nothing equals compliance. Consequently it can be said that the Way of

---

7. Not merely literary studies, but all the accomplishments of a gentleman: ceremonies, music, archery, horsemanship, writing, and numbers.

respect and acquiescence is woman's most important principle of conduct. So respect may be defined as nothing other than holding on to that which is permanent; and acquiescence nothing other than being liberal and generous. Those who are steadfast in devotion know that they should stay in their proper places; those who are liberal and generous esteem others, and honor and serve them.

If husband and wife have the habit of staying together, never leaving one another, and following each other around within the limited space of their own rooms, then they will lust after and take liberties with one another. From such action improper language will arise between the two. This kind of discussion may lead to licentiousness. Out of licentiousness will be born a heart of disrespect to the husband. Such a result comes from not knowing that one should stay in one's proper place.

Furthermore, affairs may be either crooked or straight; words may be either right or wrong. Straightforwardness cannot but lead to quarreling; crookedness cannot but lead to accusation. If there are really accusations and quarrels, then undoubtedly there will be angry affairs. Such a result comes from not esteeming others, and not honoring and serving them.

If wives suppress not contempt for husbands, then it follows that such wives rebuke and scold their husbands. If husbands stop not short of anger, then they are certain to beat their wives. The correct relationship between husband and wife is based upon harmony and intimacy, and conjugal love is grounded in proper union. Should actual blows be dealt, how could matrimonial relationship be preserved? Should sharp words be spoken, how could conjugal love exist? If love and proper relationship both be destroyed, then husband and wife are divided.

Chapter 4: Womanly Qualifications

A woman ought to have four qualifications: 1. womanly virtue, 2. womanly words, 3. womanly bearing, and 4. womanly work. Now what is called womanly virtue need not be brilliant ability, exceptionally different from others. Womanly words need be neither clever in debate nor keen in conversation. Womanly appearance requires neither a pretty nor a perfect face and form. Womanly work need not be work done more skillfully than that of others.

To guard carefully her chastity, to control circumspectly her behavior, in every motion to exhibit modesty, and to model each act on the best usage—this is womanly virtue.

To choose her words with care, to avoid vulgar language, to speak at appropriate times, and not to weary others with much conversation may be called the characteristics of womanly words.

To wash and scrub filth away, to keep clothes and ornaments fresh and clean, to wash the head and bathe the body regularly, and to keep the person free from disgraceful filth may be called the characteristics of womanly bearing.

With wholehearted devotion to sew and to weave, to love not gossip and silly laughter, in cleanliness and order to prepare the wine and food for serving guests may be called the characteristics of womanly work.

These four qualifications characterize the greatest virtue of a woman. No woman can afford to be without them. In fact they are very easy to possess if a woman only treasure them in her heart. The ancients had a saying: "Is Love far off? If I desire love, then love is at hand!"[8] So can it be said of these qualifications.

Chapter 5: Wholehearted Devotion

Now in the *Rites* is written the principle that a husband may marry again, but there is no canon that authorizes a woman to be married the second time. Therefore it is said of husbands as of Heaven, that as certainly as people cannot run away from Heaven, so surely a wife cannot leave a husband's home.[9]

If people in action or character disobey the spirits of Heaven and of Earth, then Heaven punishes them. Likewise if a woman errs in the rites and in the proper mode of conduct, then her husband esteems her lightly. The ancient book, *A Pattern for Women*, says: "To obtain the love of one man is the crown of a woman's life; to lose the love of one man is to miss the aim in woman's life."[10] For these reasons a woman cannot but seek to win her husband's heart. Nevertheless, the beseeching wife need not use flattery, coaxing words, and cheap methods to gain intimacy.

Decidedly nothing is better to gain the heart of a husband than wholehearted devotion and correct manners. In accordance with the rites and the proper mode of conduct, let a woman live a pure life. Let her have ears that hear not licentiousness and eyes that see not depravity. When she goes outside her own home, let her not be conspicuous in dress and manners. When at home let her not neglect her dress. Women should not assemble in groups, not gather together, for gossip and silly laughter. They should not stand watching in the gateways. If a woman follows these rules, she may be said to have wholehearted devotion and correct manners.

---

8. This is a direct quotation from the *Analects* (7.29) of Confucius. The word translated here as "love" is usually rendered as "benevolence" but is more accurately represented by "humaneness."

9. Even after the death of her husband, the worthy wife does not leave the home of his extended family.

10. More literally, this may be rendered as: "To become of like mind with one man may be said to be the final end; to fail to become of like mind with one man may be said to be the eternal end."

If, in all her actions, she is frivolous, she sees and hears only that which pleases herself. At home her hair is disheveled and her dress is slovenly. Outside the home she emphasizes her femininity to attract attention; she says what ought not to be said; and she looks at what ought not to be seen. If a woman does such as these, she may be said to be without wholehearted devotion and correct manners.

Chapter 6: Implicit Obedience

Now "to win the love of one man is the crown of a woman's life; to lose the love of one man is her eternal disgrace." This saying advises a fixed will and a wholehearted devotion for a woman. Ought she then to lose the hearts of her father- and mother-in-law?

There are times when love may lead to differences of opinion between individuals; there are times when duty may lead to disagreement. Even should the husband say that he loves something, when the parents-in-law say "no," this is called a case of duty leading to disagreement. This being so, then what about the hearts of the parents-in-law? Nothing is better than an obedience that sacrifices personal opinion.

Whenever the mother-in-law says, "Do not do that," and if what she says is right, unquestionably the daughter-in-law obeys. Whenever the mother-in-law says, "Do that," even if what she says is wrong, still the daughter-in-law submits unfailingly to the command.

Let a woman not act contrary to the wishes and opinions of parents-in-law about right and wrong; let her not dispute with them what is straight and what is crooked. Such docility may be called obedience that sacrifices personal opinion. Therefore the ancient book, A *Pattern for Women*, says: "If a daughter-in-law who follows the wishes of her parents-in-law is like an echo and a shadow, how could she not be praised?"

Chapter 7: Harmony with Younger Brothers- and Sisters-in-Law

In order for a wife to gain the love of her husband, she must win for herself the love of her parents-in-law. To win for herself the love of her parents-in-law, she must secure for herself the good will of younger brothers- and sisters-in-law. For these reasons the right and the wrong, the praise and the blame of a woman alike depend upon younger brothers- and sisters-in-law. Consequently it will not do for a woman to lose their affection.

They are stupid both who know not that they must not lose the hearts of younger brothers- and sisters-in-law, and who cannot be in harmony with them in order to be intimate with them. Excepting only the Holy Men, few are able to be faultless. Now Yen Tzu's[11] greatest virtue was that he was able to reform. Confucius praised him for not committing a misdeed the second time. In comparison with him a woman is the more likely to make mistakes.

Although a woman possesses a worthy woman's qualifications and is wise and discerning by nature, is she able to be perfect? Yet if a woman lives in harmony with her immediate family, unfavorable criticism will be silenced within the home. But if a man and woman disagree, then this evil will be noised abroad. Such consequences are inevitable. The *Classic of Changes* says:

> Should two hearts harmonize,
> The united strength can cut gold.
> Words from hearts which agree,
> Give forth fragrance like the orchid.

This saying may be applied to harmony in the home.

Though a daughter-in-law and her younger sisters-in-law are equal in rank, nevertheless they should respect each other; though love between them may be sparse, their proper relationship should be intimate. Only the virtuous, the beautiful, the modest, and the respectful young women can accordingly rely upon the sense of duty to make their affection sincere, and magnify love to bind their relationships firmly.

Then the excellence and the beauty of such a daughter-in-law becomes generally known. Moreover, any flaws and mistakes are hidden and unrevealed. Parents-in-law boast of her good deeds; her husband is satisfied with her. Praise of her radiates, making her illustrious in district and in neighborhood; and her brightness reaches to her own father and mother.

But a stupid and foolish person as an elder sister-in-law uses her rank[12] to exalt herself; as a younger sister-in-law, because of parents' favor, she becomes filled with arrogance. If arrogant, how can a woman live in harmony with others? If love and proper relationships be perverted, how can praise be secured? In such instances the wife's good is hidden and her faults are declared. The mother-in-law will be angry, and the husband will be indignant. Blame will reverberate and spread in and outside the home. Disgrace will gather upon the daughter-in-law's person, on the one hand to add humiliation to her own father and mother, and on the other to increase the difficulties of her husband.

Such then is the basis for both honor and disgrace, the foundation for reputation or for ill-repute. Can a woman be too cautious? Consequently, to seek the hearts of young brothers- and sisters-in-law decidedly nothing can be esteemed better than modesty and acquiescence.

11. Yen Hui, the favorite disciple of Confucius.

12. In the *Record of Rites* (*Li chi*), the power of control over the other sons' wives is accorded to the eldest daughter-in-law.

Modesty is virtue's handle; acquiescence is the wife's most refined characteristic. All who possess these two have sufficiency for harmony with others. In the *Classic of Poetry* it is written that "Here is no evil; there is no dart." So it may be said of these two, modesty and acquiescence.

Translated by Nancy Lee Swann

Parallel Prose

195
Memorial of Indictment Against Liu Cheng

Jen Fang (460–508)

As Palace Aide to the Censor-in Chief, your subject, Jen Fang, bows his head to the ground and declares:

> Your subject has heard that
> Ma Yüan[1] honored his widowed sister-in-law;
> Unless he were wearing official garb, he would never approach her.
> Fan Yü[2] was kind to the orphans of his clan;

This text is a literary curiosity. The basic structure is that of highly mannered parallel prose. However, the euphuistic, allusive quality of this genre contrasts sharply with the quoted depositions of the witnesses which contain a number of vernacular elements. These extremely rare passages constitute one of the earliest examples of written vernacular in China outside of a Buddhist context. It is interesting to observe that Hsiao T'ung (501–531), the compiler of the *Literary Selections (Wen hsüan)*, in which this text was first anthologized, removed the vernacular passages, probably due to his belief that, while "content should derive from deep thought, form should be expressed in an elegant style." We must be grateful to Li Shan, the early T'ang commentator of the *Literary Selections*, who restored the vernacular passages to their rightful place.

The author was an official who served ably under three of the southern dynasties—Sung, Ch'i, and Liang—during the division between the north and south. Toward the end of his career, he was viewed as the chief arbiter in matters of prose writing.

For another example of parallel prose, see selection 18.

1. A general of the early Eastern Han period.
2. A man from the early Western Chin period who refused office and was content to live in poverty.

He treated them no differently from his own children.
Thus,

The righteous sire and the man of mettle,
Hearing these examples, strive to emulate them.
As felicitous accounts of the last millennium,
These two must be placed at the forefront.

Your subject, Jen Fang, kowtows repeatedly and begs your mercy over and over. Respectfully do I submit that the widow Fan of the last Chamberlain Administrator of Hsi-yang under the Ch'i dynasty, Liu Yin, came before the censorate to make a complaint. Her testimony was as follows:

"I was married to Liu Yin for twenty some years. After his death, the care and upbringing of his orphaned children fell to me. Liu Yin's younger brother, Cheng, was constantly trying to do me harm. Before the division of the family property, he snatched away the slaves Docile Lad and Nunky, making them part of the clan's common holdings. Then he proceeded to compensate his sisters and younger brother Wen with cash, but kept the two slaves for his personal use. He then appropriated the maid, Green Grass, who belonged to Yin's son, Chün, and surreptitiously sold her for cash without even sharing any of it with Chün. Last year in the tenth month, Śrī ("Good Fortune"), Yin's second son by a concubine, betook himself to Cheng's fields where he stayed for twelve days, whereupon Cheng charged me six pecks of rice for feeding him. Before I had sent him the rice, he suddenly appeared at my door, shaking his fist at me through the curtain and cursing mightily. Abruptly, he barged into the room and seized the canopy for our cart that was hanging on the movable door-screen, taking it away as surety for the rice.

"On the night of the ninth day of the second month, his maid Pretty Voice stole the railings, shafts, and harness for our cart. When I asked about the missing objects, Cheng gave my son Chün a beating. Cheng, his mother, and four servants came into my room and began cursing mightily with loud voices. The maid Pretty Voice raised her hand and grabbed me by the arm. I request that you apprehend them and investigate the matter in accordance with the complaint I have made."

I forthwith had the old slave, Ocean Frog, who had been owned by Liu Cheng's deceased father, apprehended and brought before the bench for interrogation. His testimony was as follows:

"Cheng's deceased father Hsing-tao, who was the former general of Ling-ling commandery, had acquired four male and female slaves. When his property was divided up, the slave Docile Lad was given to his eldest son, Yin. After Yin died, his second son, Cheng, appropriated Docile Lad, saying: 'He should become part of the clan's common holdings.' Yet he kept him for his personal use, compensating his sisters and younger brother to the amount of five thousand cash,[3] without sharing any of it with Chün. As for Yin's slave, Nunky, he had formerly been part of the clan's common holdings. Before Cheng and his brothers divided up the family property,[4] Cheng's older brother Yin mortgaged him for seven thousand cash so that he could work in the clan's fields.[5] When Yin gave up his position in Hsiyang and returned, although the brothers had not yet broken up their households into separate eating units, he redeemed Nunky for seven thousand cash from his private funds and took him along to serve him in his new post at Canton. Later, when Yin died, Cheng divided up the male and female slaves with his brother and sisters, leaving only the maid Green Grass to become part of the clan's common holdings. Moreover, Cheng said that Yin had never paid for the redemption of Nunky, so he should revert to the clan's common holdings. Cheng's greedy intention was to get Nunky for himself and push Green Grass off on Chün. Cheng reckoned that when Nunky returned from Canton he would take him for his own purposes. Seven years passed, however, and Nunky did not come back, so Cheng thought he had already died and would never be back again. Consequently, he appropriated the maid Green Grass and sold her for seven thousand cash. Cheng divided up this money with his brother and sisters, once more not sharing any of it with Chün. Cheng's wife Fan said, 'Nunky was privately redeemed by my late husband, so he should belong to our son Chün.' In the sixth month of the second year of the Heavenly Supervision reign period [503], Nunky returned from Canton. When he arrived, Cheng appropriated the slave for himself, saying, 'He should become part of the clan's common holdings as recompense for four years of wages[6] when he was employed by Yin in Canton.' Nunky is now working at Cheng's place."

I then had Cheng's maid Pretty Voice brought in for questioning. Her testimony was as follows.

"Last year on the twelfth day of the tenth month, Liu Cheng's older brother Yin's second son, Śrī, suddenly went off to the cottage of Cheng's where he stayed for twelve days. Cheng requested six pecks of rice from his brother's wife, Fan, for feeding him. Before Fan was able to return the rice,

3. A "cash" (< Portuguese *caixa* < Tamil *kācu* < Sanskrit *karṣa*) is a coin of small denomination, especially one with a perforated center through which a string may be passed for ease of carrying.

4. After their father's death.

5. It would have been Cheng's right to take Nunky with him when he assumed his position in Hsi-yang.

6. Being a slave, the value of Nunky's labor belonged to the clan as a whole, not to himself. Cheng refused to admit that Yin had ever paid the clan for the right to use Nunky for his own purposes in Canton.

Cheng got angry and barged into Fan's dwelling place, taking away a cart canopy that was hanging on her movable door-screen as security. Fan then sent Cheng the six pecks of rice, which he accepted at once.[7] This year on the night of the ninth of the second month, Fan lost the railings, shafts, harness, and so forth for her cart. She and her son Chün thought that they must have been stolen by Pretty Voice. When Cheng heard about their suspicions, he gave Chün a beating. Fan called out to him, asking, 'What do you mean by beating my son?' At that moment, Cheng and his mother came out from the central courtyard and argued with Fan through the curtain. The maid Pretty Voice and the slaves Docile Boy, Ch'u Jade, and Dharmacārin, four of them all together, were standing to the left and right of Cheng and his mother at the time. Cheng told Pretty Voice, 'She said that you stole her cart furnishings. Why don't you go inside and bawl her out?', upon which Pretty Voice went in and wrangled with Fan. As she was raising her hand, she grabbed Fan by mistake. The cart railings, shafts, and harness were not stolen by Pretty Voice."

I then had Slovenly Slave, the slave of Yin's wife Fan, brought in for questioning. His testimony was as follows:

"The mistress said that on the night of the ninth of the second month, she lost the railings, shafts, and harness for her cart. She suspected that they were stolen by Cheng's maid Pretty Voice. The young master Chün and I went to the Chin-yang gate to sell rice and happened to see Pretty Voice there selling the railings and shafts for a cart. I wanted to catch her right away and take back the cart furnishings, but Chün said to me, 'Let it be! Don't try to take them back!' I lingered there stealthily for a little while and observed someone buy the harness for a price of five thousand cash. As I had to follow Chün home, I didn't see the money being handed over."

The testimonies of Pretty Voice, Slovenly Slave, and the others roughly corresponded with Fan's complaint. I then reexamined Nunky and Docile Lad, who testified: "We were appropriated from the mistress and are now working at Cheng's place." Since this was completely in agreement with the testimony of Ocean Frog, I turned the case over to the law. The director of the court, P'an Seng-shang ("Saṃgha-Respecter"), deliberated as follows:

"For summarily snatching away the maid of his brother's son Chün and selling her off before the division of the family property, and for using the slave Docile Lad and others for his own purposes, as if there were no official regulations, he should be forthwith detained in a nearby prison while his punishment is being determined. All those who have been implicated should be handed over to the penal officials while they are being

7. The implication being that Cheng never thought of returning the cart canopy.

cleared of the responsibility for what happened. Everything should be carried out in accordance with the institutions of the law. It is the opinion of the court that Cheng is the chief culprit."

Your servant respectfully states:

The recently appointed Adjutant of the Middle Army, Liu Cheng,

> Is nothing but a vulgar villain,
> Who flouts the doctrine of the sages.

Simply because

> He married the descendant of an erstwhile empress,
> He associated in office with the silk-stocking crowd.
> His evil deeds and violent offenses have long accumulated,
> So that even his family and friends look at him askance.
> In defiance of principle he directly confronted his sister-in-law,

And

> Recklessly gave vent to the most vile expressions.
> For his own child he would stay awake the whole night,

But

> He wantonly gave his nephew a sound thrashing.

> When Hsüeh Pao[8] divided up his property,
> He kept the old and weak slaves for himself;
> Kao Feng[9] besmirched himself to keep out of office,
> Fraudulently brought suit against his widowed sister-in-law.

Cheng did not observe

> The profound generosity of Hsüeh Pao;

He only emulated

> The mendacious precedent of Kao Feng.

> The ancient paragons regarded their relatives so magnanimously
> That not even clothing was considered a constant possession;
> While Cheng's niggardly treatment of his nephew
> Was like Kung-sun Hung's[10] feeding an old friend brown rice.[11]

Why could he not

> Tear up the debts for the bushels his sister-in-law owed,

But instead

> Seized her fringed cart canopy for security?

8. A man of the Eastern Han period who, when faced with the demands of the younger members of his family to live separately, kept the worst of slaves, maids, fields, utensils, clothes, and so forth, for himself.

9. Another man of the Eastern Han period who, desperately desirous of keeping out of officialdom, defamed himself by claiming that he was originally a wizard and by pretending that he was engaged in a suit brought against the widow of his older brother.

10. A typical tightwad.

11. To serve someone imperfectly hulled rice was regarded as an insult in old China.

To think that human unkindness
Could reach such a degree as this!
Truly, this is
Something that can not be tolerated by the doctrine of righteousness,
Something that all men of stature must unanimously reject!

After consultation and deliberation, we request that Cheng be removed
from office for his role in the present affair and that instructions forthwith be
used for him to be detained externally [12] by the Chamberlain for Law Enforcement who will administer punishment according to legal and penal regulations. All those who have been involved should be handed over to the penal
authorities while they are being cleared of responsibility for what happened.
Everything should be carried out in accord with the institutions of the law.
The maid Pretty Voice does not admit that she stole the cart railings, shafts,
and harness, so we request that she be detained by the penal authorities while
the truth is being determined. As for the clan elders and local authorities who
did not intercede at the beginning and all others who are involved, we request
that further investigation be suspended on the grounds of insufficient evidence.
In sincere fear and trembling, your subject kowtows repeatedly and begs your
mercy over and over. I bow my head to the ground as I inform you.

Translated by Victor H. Mair

12. That is to say, Liu Cheng is now to be tried and sentenced in the criminal courts,
outside of the special disciplinary proceedings reserved for officials.

196

Preface to "Ascending the Pavilion of King T'eng in Hung-chou on an Autumn Day for a Parting Feast"

Wang Po (648–675)

The pavilion is in the ancient prefecture of Yü-chang
Which is now the administrative center of Hung-chou. [1]

Li Yuan-ying (enfeoffed as King T'eng in 639) was the twenty-second son of the first T'ang
emperor, Kao Tsu. He built the celebrated pavilion in 659 after he was appointed Military
Governor of Hung-chou. It was a very fancy specimen of architecture and was considered to be
the tourist spot *par excellence* in the south. After Li left this post, the pavilion seems to have
fallen into disrepair, but it was renovated by 675 when Wang Po passed through Hung-chou on
the way to see his father in distant Vietnam.

> Its astronomical field is determined by Wing and Axletree;
> The land it is on adjoins the mountains Heng[2] and Lu.[3]

On the day of the Double Ninth Festival, Wang ascended the pavilion of King T'eng with the current Military Governor Yen and other guests for a farewell feast. Legend has it that the Military Governor first requested his son-in-law to compose a suitable piece in commemoration of the event and that he had a rough draft already prepared on the day of the feast. Out of courtesy, paper and brush were passed around to the guests, but they politely and sensibly declined to write the proposed commemorative piece. When the materials reached Wang, however, he impulsively accepted. The Military Governor brushed his clothes in indignation, stood up, and stepped outside to relieve himself. During his absence, his underlings were ordered to watch Wang closely as the latter wrote. As the preface came from Wang's brush, it was reported to the Military Governor line by line. The first report was:

> The pavilion is in the ancient prefecture of Yü-chang
> Which is now the administrative center of Hung-chou.

Upon hearing this, the Military Governor smiled and said, "This is the commonplace talk of old pedants." The next report was:

> Its astronomical field is determined by Wing and Axletree;
> The land it is on adjoins the mountains Heng and Lu.

To which His Honor commented, "Old hat!" A further report came:

> It is girdled by the three rivers and belted by the five lakes,
> Controls the way to barbarous Ch'u, is the gateway to the southeast.

The Military Governor muttered to himself but said nothing. Then, in rapid succession, a number of underlings came to announce what Wang Po had written. He could do no more than flap his jowls in grudging approval. When these famous lines (lines 41–42) were reported,

> Evening clouds descend and fly along together with a lonely wild duck;
> Autumn's waters coalesce in a single shade with the outstretched heavens.

the Military Governor, completely taken aback, was forced to admit: "This is true genius! It will last through the ages without tarnishing." In no time at all, the preface was completed and the Military Governor was greatly pleased with it. The feast was a joyous event, and Wang was presented with five hundred pieces of silk. Unfortunately, the poet died at the tender age of twenty-eight of complications from a near-drowning while on his journey to the remote south.

The Preface to "Ascending the Pavilion of King T'eng . . . ," deemed more important than the poem that it was ostensibly meant to accompany, is a fine model of parallel prose. Like nearly all such pieces it is ornately euphuistic and highly mannered. Wang Po, recognized as one of the "Four Distinguished Poets of the Early T'ang," was about twenty-five years old when he wrote this enduring work of art.

1. Yü-chang and Hung-chou are two different names for the same place that was located in north central Kiangsi, not far south of P'o-yang Lake.

2. Southernmost of the five sacred mountains of China, it would have been to the southwest of the pavilion in Hunan.

3. South of Chiu-chiang in Kiangsi, it would have been to the north of the pavilion.

5   It is girdled by the three rivers and belted by the five lakes,
     Controls the way to barbarous Ch'u,[4] is the gateway to the southeast.

     The richness of its material culture is a heavenly treasure—
          the aura of swords transformed into dragons shoots up into
               space between the Dipper and the Herdboy;[5]
     The excellence of its human resources is an earthly wonder—
          the Prefect, Ch'en Fan, put down a couch for a commoner, Hsü Ju-
          tzu.[6]

     Grand cities spread out in a misty blur;
10   Brilliant men rush about like shooting stars.

     Its walls and dry moats are a buffer at the nexus between central China
          and the southern barbarians;
     The host and his guests are one and all the finest people of the
          southeast.

     His Honor the Military Governor Yen has a reputation for
          refinement—
          preceded by a silk-covered spear for an insignia, he has made the
          long journey hither;
     The Governor of Hsin-chou, Yü-wen, is a model of perfection—
          he has stopped his curtained carriage here to join us for a while.
15   The Military Governor is enjoying his fortnightly vacation—
          his bosom friends gather like clouds;
     From hundreds of miles away they arrive to be welcomed—
          his illustrious companions fill all of the places.

     Their writing is replete with dragon flourishes and phoenix flights—
          'tis the skill of the literatus Meng;[7]
     Electric blue lightning and steely frost—
          here is an arsenal of military sagacity to match that of General
          Wang.

     My father is now a district magistrate—
          on my way to see him, I have come to this famous place;
20   I am but a young man and have little knowledge—
          yet I have been fortunate enough to attend this sumptuous feast.

                         ~   ~   ~

4. A powerful southern kingdom during the Warring States period.
5. Constellations.
6. Ch'en (?–168 C.E.) was serving as Prefect of Yü-chang when this incident supposedly occurred.
7. Literatus Meng and General Wang are contrasting paradigms of talent.

Today is the ninth of the month;
The season is late autumn.[8]

Summer's rain puddles have all dried up, the water in the ponds is cold
 and clear;
A misty glimmer precipitates in a purple glow over the sunset hills.

25 Three abreast and heads held high, my chariot horses race along the
 high road,
There I visit scenic spots on lofty crests;
I look down on the long island of the imperial son, King T'eng,
And attain at last the venerable hall of that ethereal being.

Storied terraces raise their halcyon-colored roofs—
 above, the pavilion penetrates the layered clouds;
30 Soaring balconies seem a whirl of scarlet—
 below, they are suspended over empty space.

Spits for cranes and islets for wild ducks
 extend the length of the sinuous and islanded shores;
Cassia courts and magnolia mansions
 match the topography of the ridges and peaks.

~   ~   ~

The embroidered door-screens are thrown open;
We look down upon sculptured ridge-poles.

35 The vast breadth of the mountains and plains fills one's vision;
The tortuous turnings of the streams and marshes startles the eye.

Village gates and ward gates cover the ground—
 inside them are families that ring gongs for dinner and cook in huge
 bronze tripods;
Junks and barges obscure the ferry-crossings—
 their sterns are decorated with blue birds and yellow dragons.

The clouds clear, the rain stops;
40 The setting sun cuts a swath of light across the land.

Evening clouds descend and fly along together with a lonely wild duck;
Autumn's waters coalesce in a single shade with the outstretched
 heavens.

On the fishing boats, they are singing songs of evening—
 the echoes carry to the shores of P'o-yang Lake;

8. This would date the farewell feast on the ninth of the ninth month which would be the
Double Ninth Festival.

A formation of wild geese is startled by the cold—
    their cries cut across the banks of Heng-yang[9]

~   ~   ~

45 Distant thoughts begin to unfurl;
    Surpassing fancies begin to take flight.

Nature's brisk pipes are vented, causing a soothing breeze to spring up;
Lilting songs linger in the air, bringing the white clouds to a halt.

As it did 'neath the green bamboos of King Hsiao's park by the Sui
    River,[10]
    the convivial atmosphere here, too, exceeds that of T'ao Ch'ien's
        solitary cup.[11]
As it did by the pink lotuses in the ponds of Ts'ao P'i's garden at Yeh,[12]
    the literary brilliance here, too, could illuminate Hsieh Ling-yün's[13]
    talented brush.

50 Here we have complete the four fortunes—a nice day, beautiful
      scenery,
                         appreciative hearts, and pleasant entertainment;
And, equally difficult to come by, both excellent guests and a worthy
    host.

They give full scope to the play of their vision which scans the mid-
    heavens;
Allow free rein to the pursuit of pleasure on this, their day of leisure.
The skies are high, the land is broad—
    one is made aware of the boundlessness of the universe;
55 Pleasure passes and sadness arrives—
    one is made to recognize that waxing and waning are fated.

I gaze toward Ch'ang-an[14] which seems to be beyond the sun,
    Then point at Kuei-chi Mountain[15] amidst the clouds;
The latter's lay of land runs far—far to the deep South Sea,

9. Southwest of Hung-chou in Hunan.

10. King Hsiao of Liang, the second son of Emperor Wen of the Han dynasty, built a pleasure garden at Sui-yang in Honan where a coterie of the most famous rhapsody writers of the day gathered. One of them was Mei Ch'eng (see selection 152).

11. T'ao Ch'ien (see selection 29) was magistrate of P'eng-tse in Kiangsi and a famous toper.

12. The famous general Ts'ao Ts'ao (see selection 170) was enfeoffed here. Toward the end of the Chien-an reign period (196–219) of the Han dynasty, his sons, Ts'ao P'i (see selection 17, unnumbered note) and Ts'ao Chih (see selection 26) and other illustrious poets of the age would enjoy themselves in the Yen-hsi garden there.

13. See selection 30.

14. The capital of the T'ang dynasty, which was far to the north.

15. A reference to Shao-hsing, the intellectual and political seat of power in the south.

Above the former, the Pillar of Heaven towers high—high as the distant
North Star.

60   Frontier passes and mountain peaks are difficult to cross—
who mourns for the man who loses his way?
Duckweed drifting on the water's surface, we meet—
we are one and all sojourners from another land.

I yearn for My Lord's gate but it is lost to my view;
When will I ever be summoned to his hall of audience?

~   ~   ~

Alas!

65   Fortunes differ,
Fate is often perverse;
Feng T'ang grew old without recognition,[16]
Li Kuang fought valiantly sans reward.[17]

Chia Yi was sent to Ch'ang-sha under duress,[18]
yet the reigning emperor was not unenlightened;
70   Liang Hung felt compelled to scurry away to a corner of the sea,[19]
but can one say that the age was lacking in sagacity?

Depend upon it:

The gentleman is unruffled by poverty;
The man of intelligence understands fate.

As we grow old, we ought to become stronger—
shall our hearts waver simply because our heads turn white?
75   In extremity, we should remain firm
and not allow our high and noble ambitions to flag.

Even when we drink from the fountain of avarice, we may still feel
generous;
Even if we be as fish in a dried-up rut[20] we may yet remain joyful.

16. Feng T'ang's true virtue and ability were recognized only very late in his life, at an age
when such recognition was of little practical value to him.
17. Li Kuang (?–119 B.C.E.) was an illustrious general who, through ill fortune, did not
receive the recognition he deserved.
18. A brilliant scholar who was slandered by jealous officials and banished to the south as
tutor of the king of Ch'ang-sha (see selection 150).
19. A farmer-recluse and poet sought by Emperor Chang (r. 76–88) who preferred to hire
himself out as a huller of rice rather than enter public life.
20. A reference to a well-known parable in the *Chuang Tzu* (see selection 9) about the
immediate urgency of a desperate request.

Though the North Sea is far away,
  one could reach it by riding a cyclone;
The sun may leave its bed in the east,
  but it is not too late even when it is resting in the treetops of the
    west.

80 Meng Ch'ang was a man of lofty ideals[21]—
  in vain did he cherish the desire to exert himself for the empire;
Juan Chi was wildly unrestrained[22]—
  one should not emulate him by crying when the road comes to an
    end.

        ~   ~   ~

I, Wang Po,

Am but a minor official who wears a short sash;
A mere student and a rather bookish one at that.

        ~   ~   ~

85 The way is not open for me to request the tokens of an important
      mission
  as Chung Chün[23] did, though I am still in my twenties as he
    was;
I yearn to throw aside my writing-brush
  in admiration of Tsung Ch'üeh's far-ranging aspiration.[24]

I renounce official hatpin and tablet for the rest of my life,
So that I may wait on my father, morning and night, in a distant
    place;
I am not so praiseworthy a son as the "jade trees" of the Hsieh
    family,[25]
90 But am pleased to find myself in virtuous company that Mencius'
      mother[26] would have approved of.

21. An upright official of the later Han dynasty.
22. Juan Chi (see selection 27) was a man given to strange behavior. Among other eccentrici-
ties, he would get in a chariot and drive off by himself when the urge took him. Leaving the
beaten track, he would go on and on until he could go no farther, upon which he would
cry pitifully.
23. Chung Chün (140–113 B.C.E.) was a precocious official who volunteered to go on a
difficult mission to Annam.
24. As a youth, Tsung Ch'üeh was asked by his uncle what his ambition was. He replied
that he wanted to mount a far-ranging wind to subdue a thousand miles of waves.
25. Hsieh Hsüan (343–388) declared as a youth that people desire worthy descendants
because they are like "iris and orchid or a jade tree" growing in one's courtyard.
26. An allusion to the oft-repeated story of Mencius' mother moving thrice in order to find
the ideal neighborhood for the benefit of her son.

Before long, I shall be hurrying across my father's courtyard
   respectfully to attend him and comply with his instructions as
      Confucius' son did;[27]
Today, however, I present myself to Your Lordship here,
   happy for this chance to entrust myself to your good graces.

Not having met a Yang Te-yi[28] who could introduce my work to an
   appreciative audience,
      I can but coddle my cloud-transcending artistry in self-
      commiseration:
Since I have already chanced upon an auditor as discerning as
   Chung Tzu-ch'i,
      why should I blush to perform my rills and trills?

～   ～   ～

95   Alack!

Places of scenic beauty do not last long,
Sumptuous feasts such as this are seldom repeated;
The Orchid Pavilion[29] is, alas, no more,
The Catalpa Marsh[30] has become a wasteland.

100   It is customary, on the eve of departure, to make a gift of words,
         Fortunate are we for having received from the Military Governor
                              this splendid farewell dinner;
      To climb to a height and compose poetry
         is what he hopes from you, honorable gentlemen.

I have been so bold as to exert myself in all humility and sincerity
By respectfully inditing this brief introduction.
One word shall be assigned as the rhyme for all,

27. "Once Confucius was standing alone when his son, Li, came hurrying across the courtyard. Confucius asked him: 'Have you learned *The Classic of Odes* yet?' Li replied that he had not. 'If you do not study *The Classic of Odes*, you'll have nothing to talk about.' Li withdrew to study *The Classic of Odes*. Sometime later, Confucius was again standing alone when Li came hurrying across the courtyard. Confucius asked him: 'Have you learned the *Rites*?' Li replied that he had not. 'If you do not study the *Rites*, you will have nothing to stand on.' Li withdrew to study the *Rites*" (from the *Analects*).

28. Emperor Wu of the Han dynasty, on reading Ssu-ma Hsiang-ju's "Mr. Nonentity Rhapsody" (see selection 151), lamented that he had not been fortunate enough to live at the same time as the author of such a marvelous piece of writing. Yang Te-yi, director of the palace kennels, informed him that the author was a native of his hometown in Szechwan and still quite alive. The emperor, of course, made much of Ssu-ma Hsiang-ju. The name Yang Te-yi, as an allusion, thus came to stand for an individual who could introduce a talented young writer to an appreciative and influential audience, particularly the emperor himself.

29. Site of the famous drinking party celebrated in selection 20.

30. A fabulous park owned by the inordinately wealthy Shih Ch'ung (249–300).

105   And four couplets will be required to complete the stanza;
    Be so kind as to let your rivers of poetic talent flow freely like that of
        P'an Yüeh,
    Each of you, pour out your oceans of genius as Lu Chi[31] did,
                                if you please.[32]

~ ~ ~   ~ ~ ~

    The high pavilion of King T'eng looks down upon the islets in the river,
    The jade pendants and tinkling carriage bells of visiting officials, the
        songs and dances of old are all silent now;

    In the morning, painted beams soar like the clouds over South Bank,
IV In the evening, beaded curtains are rolled up like the rain above West
        Mountain.

    Lazy clouds are reflected in deep pools, the days pass leisurely by,
    The landscape changes, the stars shift—how many autumns have there
        been?

    Inside the pavilion, where is the royal scion today?
VIII Outside the balustrade, the long river flows on—expressionless and
        unheeding.

Translated by Victor H. Mair

---

31. P'an and Lu, often linked together, were poets of the Western Chin period.
32. The parallel prose preface ends here with an invitation to the assembled worthies jointly
to compose the poem which follows.

Letters

197
Letter to Han Ching-chou

Li Po (701–762)

I have heard that, when the empire's chatty scholars gather together, they say to each other, "During one's lifetime, it is not necessary to be a marquis with the income from ten thousand households, if one could hope but once to make the acquaintance of Han, the Governor of Ching-chou."[1] How is it that you have caused men to lionize you to such a degree? Is it not because you have the spirit of the Duke of Chou who, in his anxiety not to miss any callers, would interrupt his meals by spitting out his food and his bath by wringing his half-washed hair?[2] The result is that all the elite within the realm rush to you and give you their allegiance. Once having passed the hurdle of gaining your recommendation,[3] their credit increases tenfold. Thus, those gentlemen who are hidden away in retirement like coiled dragons and reclusive phoenixes are all desirous of receiving a good name and establishing their worth with Your Honor. I pray that Your Honor does not pride yourself on

This is one of a series of letters which the famous T'ang poet, Li Po (see selection 45), wrote in search of political patronage. It has been dated to the year 734.

1. Han Ch'ao-tsung's (686–750) checkered official career included a drastic demotion late in life for cowardice in the face of rumors that rebels were on the verge of insurrection.

2. The mention of the Duke of Chou seems to have been a common technique in letters such as these.

3. The famous "dragon gate" through which aspiring candidates for preferment had to pass in order to become transformed from small fry into adult fish (i.e., officials).

association with the rich and noble,[4] nor scorn the poor and lowly. Then, if among your many guests there would be a Mao Sui,[5] should I but get a chance to show the tip of my head, I shall be that man.

I am a commoner from Lung-hsi[6] and have drifted here to Ching-chou.[7] At fifteen, I was fond of swordsmanship and ranged broadly in search of employment with various lords. At thirty, I became an accomplished litterateur and contacted successively a number of high officers. Although I am not quite a six footer,[8] I am braver than ten thousand men. Princes, dukes, and high ministers admit that I have moral courage and high principles. This, then, has been my past spiritual biography. How could I venture not to explain it fully to Your Lordship?

Your writings are worthy of the gods and your virtuous conduct moves Heaven and Earth. Your pen is imbued with creative energy and your scholarship plumbs heavenly principles and human affairs. I hope, because of your open-mindedness and good nature, that I shall have the good fortune not to meet with a refusal in making this low bow before you.[9] If you receive me with grand feasts, give free rein to my untrammeled discourse,[10] and then request that I attempt to indite ten thousand words a day, just wait! I'll dash

4. "Not to pride yourself on the rich and noble" is from the ninth chapter of the *Tao Te Ching* (see selection 10).

5. Li Po, in asking for a chance to show his talents, cannot avoid comparing himself to Mao Sui, a follower of the Lord of P'ing-yüan of the Chao kingdom during the Warring States period. Mao, though occupying an obscure position in his lord's entourage, volunteered to go to Ch'u in search of aid for the relief of the Chao capital, Han-tan, which had been surrounded by Ch'in. The Lord of P'ing-yüan was at first reluctant to allow Mao the privilege of the mission because he had not distinguished himself in the three years he had dwelt with his lord. The situation, said the lord, was similar to an awl being placed in a bag. If it were at all sharp, surely it would show its tip at once. To this Mao replied that were he really placed in the bag of opportunity, his sharpness would allow him to come completely out. The expression "Mao Sui introduces himself" has come to be used as an epithet to describe one who volunteers for a task that others may have thought him less than qualified to perform. We may note that, although Mao Sui did indeed "introduce himself," the metaphor of an awl in a bag was originally suggested by the Lord of P'ing-yüan. Mao but elaborated upon it.

6. Not so. For Li Po to say that he was from Lung-hsi (the southeast corner of Kansu) is to make the same sort of claim of aristocratic connections that someone with the surname Wang makes when he says that he comes from Lang-yeh (the eastern portion of Shantung). Li is known to have spent his early years at Ch'ing-lien village of Ch'ang-ming district in Szechwan, but his ancestry is also generally acknowledged to include certain Central Asian connections. The scholarly consensus now would appear to be that Li Po was of at least partially Turkic extraction.

7. Li Po uses the ancient appellation, Ch'u Han.

8. A rough approximation from the "seven (Chinese) feet" in the text.

9. That is, "in paying this formal call."

10. The "untrammeled discourse" ("pure talk" or "unsullied discourse") is a carryover from the epoch of division between the north and the south.

them off on the spur of the moment.[11] Today, the whole empire holds you to be the life-and-death arbiter in literary matters and the scales upon which men are weighed. Once having been adjudged worthy by you, one can then be a superb scholar. So why should you begrudge me a modest space before your stairs, thus neither allowing me a feeling of pride and self-fulfillment nor stimulating me to rise up to the cloudy blue?[12]

Of old, when Wang Tzu-shih[13] was serving as Governor of Yü-chou, he summoned Hsün Tz'u-ming[14] even before he had assumed office.[15] And, when he did assume office, he summoned K'ung Wen-chü.[16] When Shan T'ao was acting as Governor of Chi-chou, he picked out more than thirty individuals who became either court attendants or state secretaries, for which he was admired by previous generations.[17] Your Lordship, as well, had but to recommend Harmonizer of the Scales Yen and he was admitted to the court as Secretary in the Imperial Library. Among others, there are people like Ts'ui Tsung-chih,[18] Fang Hsi-tsu, Li Hsin, and Hsü Jung, some of whom made your acquaintance because of their reputation for brilliance and some of whom were appreciated by you because of their unimpeachable character. I have often observed their introspective devotion and the way they exert themselves in acts of loyalty. As a result, I am deeply impressed and realize the empathy which you extend to worthy individuals. Therefore, I shall not give my allegiance to anyone else but willingly entrust myself to you who are without peer in our land. Should you ever get into difficulty such that I might be of use to you, may I be so bold as to offer, in gratitude, my humble services? Yet none of us is a Yao or a Shun.[19] Who can be perfect? How could

11. This allusion is from *A New Account of Tales of the World* (see selection 241): "Huan Hsüan-wu (312–373) was engaged in a northward expedition. Yüan Hu (328–376), at this time, was in attendance. He was reprimanded and relieved of his office. But when there was a necessity for spreading abroad a proclamation, Yüan was called forward and ordered to write while leaning against his horse. The pen in his hand did not stop once and, before long, seven pages were produced. It was decidedly something worth seeing. Wang Tung-t'ing (350–401) was standing nearby and exclaimed at length on Yüan's genius, to which Yüan Hu replied, 'It ought to gain some advantage for us in a war of words.' "

12. A euphemism for "official employment."

13. Wang Yün (137–192), a precocious official of the Later Han period.

14. Hsün Shuang (128–190), another noted official from the latter part of the Later Han.

15. Literally, "even before he had descended from his carriage."

16. K'ung Jung (153–208), a descendant of Confucius in the twentieth generation and an active proponent of the sage's teaching.

17. Shan T'ao (205–283). In his biography in the *Chin History*, we read, "When Shan T'ao was serving as the governor of Chi-chou, he discerned and elevated men who dwelt in obscurity or who had been wronged. He sought out and visited men of virtue and talent."

18. His name was Ch'eng-fu but he went by his style. Ts'ui held the hereditary title of Duke of Ch'i as well as several posts in the T'ang government. He was also a drinking companion of Li Po. Little is known of the following three individuals.

19. Two legendary emperors.

I be so presumptuous as to boast of my counsels and plans? As for my own writings, I have accumulated a large number of scrolls. Although I flatter myself that you will deign to look at them, I fear that these "insect carvings" and trivial exercises will not suit Your Honor's taste. If you would do me the favor of reading my rustic pieces, please provide me with paper and ink along with a copyist. Then I shall retreat to a vacant room and, having tidied it up, will have a copy of them made to present to you. This is similar to the increased value which would accrue to the sword, Cyan Duckweed, by placing it at the door of Hsüeh Chu and to the gem, Congealed Greenness, by placing it at the door of Pien Ho.[20]

May you extend your blessings to me in my lowly station, greatly encouraging and rewarding me. It all depends on how Your Lordship views[21] the matter.

Translated by Victor H. Mair

20. Hsüeh Chu, an expert at identifying swords, was from Viet, and Pien Ho was a man who knew the value of gems—one in particular (see selection 20, note 4). Both men lived during the Spring and Autumn period of antiquity. The translation assumes a pair of hypothetical situations—not that Hsüeh Chu actually saw Cyan Duckweed or that Pien Ho really knew of Congealed Greenness. Li Po does not associate the two conoisseurs with the objects normally linked with them (namely, the swords Ch'un-kou and Chan-lu on the one hand, and the gem Ho-shih Pi on the other), probably because he thought it would leave a flat taste and because of the faint, but pleasant, echo between the two types of greenness in the names that he does use.

21. To be more blunt, how you "plan" for me, i.e., "the matter is now in your hands—it's up to you!"

198
Letter in Reply to Liu Yi-chang

Tsung Ch'en (1525–1560)

From several thousand tricents away, I occasionally receive a letter from you, which satisfies my constant sense of yearning. This, indeed, makes me feel already very fortunate. Why need you have further troubled yourself by favoring me with gifts? This leaves me wondering all the more how I shall repay you. The cordiality of your letter is evidence of your not forgetting my father and your awareness that his regard for you is profound. And, when you speak

In this well-known description of literati toadying during the Ming dynasty, the sycophant is mercilessly satirized. The blatant ills of parasitism described here were fostered by the ruthlessness and corruption of the prime minister, Yen Sung (d. 1562), and his son, Yen Shih-fan.

Tsung Ch'en was a member of a group of writers and critics active during the mid-sixteenth century who were known as the later Seven Masters and who were advocates of archaism.

to me of "superior and inferior persons having mutual trust" and "ability and good character corresponding to position," I am deeply moved.

That my ability and character are not in keeping with my position is something of which I am keenly aware; and I am especially to be faulted when it comes to the question of trust. But nowadays when we speak of mutual trust what do we mean? Here is one who whips up his horse day and night to wait at the gates of the powerful. The gatekeeper, on purpose, does not admit him. Then, with sweet words and seductive phrases, and putting on the airs of a woman, he takes some money from his sleeve and presses it upon the gateman. Even if the gateman does take in his calling card, the host does not come out to see him at once. Standing in the stable amidst the grooms, noxious fumes permeating his clothing, even if the hunger and cold or the cruel summer heat are unbearable, he does not leave.

When evening comes, the one who had earlier received the money comes out and announces to the guest, "His Lordship is weary and cannot see any more guests. You are requested to come back tomorrow." So the next day, he dares not refrain from coming. At night, he sits up with a robe thrown over his shoulders. As soon as he hears the cock crow, he rises and performs his morning toilet. As he races his horse up to the gate, the gatekeeper angrily asks, "Who are you?" to which he responds, "The guest who came yesterday." Whereupon the gatekeeper angrily counters, "You're very persistent, aren't you? Do you think that His Lordship receives guests at such an hour?"

The guest feels shamed yet forces himself to forbear.

"But I'm desperate! You'll just have to let me in."

The gatekeeper again collects his gift of money, gets up, and goes in. Again, the guest stands in the stable where he previously stood.

Fortunately, the host comes out and, facing the south, beckons him. Whereupon he runs timorously and crawls on hands and knees to the foot of the steps.

"Enter!" the host says. He prostrates himself twice and purposely is slow about rising. When he does rise, he offers up his gifts of gold and silk. The host purposely refuses them but the guest is firm in insisting that he take them. The host purposely persists in his refusal and the guest persists with his offer. At last, the host orders an underling to take them for him, upon which the guest again prostrates himself twice and is again purposely slow about rising. When he does rise, he bows five or six times before finally going out. As he leaves, he bows to the gatekeeper and says, "It was so kind of you to be considerate of me. When I come again some day, I hope that you'll not hinder me." The gatekeeper bows in reply.

Overjoyed, he goes rushing off. Riding along on his horse, when he meets someone he knows, he at once flourishes his whip and informs him, "I'm just coming from His Lordship's house. His Lordship is so good to me! Oh, he's so good to me!" And he makes up a lot of stories describing his visit. Even those with whom he is well acquainted are awed by His Lordship's liberal reception. His Lordship, too, voices it about here and there, "So-and-so is a man of virtue. He really is!" And those who hear this approve and praise him to one another. This, then, is what people call "the superior and the inferior having mutual trust." Do you believe that I am capable of this?

As for the powerful families mentioned, I never visit them the whole year long except to hand in a calling card at New Year's and on the summer and winter holidays. If, on occasion, my path takes me by one of their gates, then I stop up my ears, close my eyes, and gallop away on my horse as fast as though there were someone in pursuit. It is on account of this narrow-mindedness of mine that I have never been liked by the senior officials. But, increasingly, I pay no heed to all this and am always making such grandiose statements as: "Human life is fated; the only thing for me to do is to be content with my own lot." When you hear this, can you not but be exasperated by my noncomformity?

Translated by Victor H. Mair

Prefaces and Postfaces

199
Postface to *Explanation of Simple and Compound Graphs*

Hsü Shen (fl. 100–121)

In ancient times, P'ao-hsi[1] came to rule the world. Looking up, he contemplated the phenomena in the sky, and looking down, the markings on the

The *Explanation of Simple and Compound Graphs (Shuo wen chieh tzu)* is the oldest extant comprehensive dictionary of the sinographs or Chinese characters. The *Shuo wen* (as it is usually styled for short) was preceded—probably by a couple of centuries—by a small lexicon entitled *Elegance (Erh-ya)*, which was a listing of synonyms arranged according to categories together with occasional short definitions. It cannot be emphasized too strongly, however, that the *Shuo wen* itself is not a true dictionary of words but rather one of graphs. That is to say, the *Shuo wen* does not explain either the semantic or the true etymological properties of words in the spoken language. Rather, it analyzes the forms, sounds, and meanings of the graphs used to write individual syllables, which are usually—but by no means always—equivalent to monosyllabic words. Recent phonological and etymological researches have shown that the explanations of the graphs in the *Shuo wen* are often mistaken or irrelevant for an understanding of the words of the living language that they are meant to represent, a significant proportion of which were bisyllabic even at the time of the writing of the *Shuo wen*. It is essential when conceptualizing the nature of the sinographs and trying to comprehend how they function that a clear distinction be made between a given language and a particular script (which is one possible vehicle among many that might be used to record the language).

Regardless of its classification, the *Shuo wen* has been enormously influential in shaping Chinese conceptions of the nature of writing. The opening and closing sections of its postface are included here to afford the reader some idea of how sinographs are constructed and,

earth. He observed the patterns on birds and animals and their adaptations to the earth. From nearby, he took some hints from his own body, and elsewhere from other things. Then he began to make the eight trigrams of the *Changes*,[2] to pass on to others the regular patterns in the world.

Later, when the Divine Farmer[3] made knots in rope[4] to direct and regularize activities, all kinds of trades and professions were multiplied, and then artificial and refined things sprouted and grew.

Ts'ang Chieh, scribe for the Yellow Emperor, on looking at the tracks of the feet of birds and animals, realizing that the principles and forms were distinguishable, started to create graphs,[5] so that all kinds of professions could be regulated, and all categories of people could be kept under scrutiny. This he probably took from the hexagram *Kuai*. "*Kuai*: exhibit in the royal court"— means the patterns show education and enlightenment to the king's court. "Thus the ideal man bestows benefits on his subordinates. If one is virtuous, one is cautious."[6]

When Ts'ang Chieh first created writing (*shu*), he probably imitated the forms according to their categories; so the figures were called "patterns" (*wen*). Later, when the writings were increased by combining the forms and phonetics, the results were called "compound graphs" (*tzu*). "Compound graph" means reproduction and gradual increase. When they are written on bamboo and silk, they are called "records" (*shu*). "Records" means likeness.

During the time of the Five Emperors and Three Kings,[7] the writing

---

moreover, to provide a sense of the mythological awe in which writing was held by the early Chinese.

The compiler of the *Shuo wen* was Hsü Shen, who came from the present Yen-ch'eng district, Honan province. His activities were centered on the study of the Five Classics: *Changes, Documents, Odes, Rites,* and *Spring and Autumn Annals.* Hsü belonged to the ancient text school of textual critics, who often differed on points of interpretation with the modern text school (it is actually ancient now, of course, but was considered "modern" to Hsü Shen and his contemporaries). According to the biographical information in the *History of the Han Dynasty,* Hsü was considered to be without peer in the study of the Five Classics. Indeed, his motivation in compiling the *Shuo wen* was to counter the ideas on the interpretations of the Classics espoused by a rival school of textual critics.

Hsü held several official posts, but retired to carry on his studies. He probably finished the *Shuo wen* in 100 C.E., but it was not until 121 that Hsü's son presented it to the throne, while the compiler was ill.

1. Alternate name Fu-hsi, the mythological emperor and first man.
2. See selection 3.
3. The mythological emperor and supposed inventor of agriculture.
4. Compare with the Peruvian quipu.
5. This could be interpreted as "graphs" or "carving of graphs."
6. With minor differences, these quotations may be found in the *Classic of Changes* (see selection 3).
7. Mythological rulers of hoary antiquity.

changed into various styles. Of the seventy-two[8] eras in which altars were made on Mount T'ai, all used different styles.

In the *Rites of Chou* it says:[9] "When children reached the age of eight *sui*,[10] they began the study of language arts under the Protector, who started teaching the children of the nobles the six types of graphs."

The first is called "indicate-things." When one sees a graph of this type it may be understood on seeing it; by inspection one sees the meaning.[11] The graphs "up" (*shang* 上) and "down" (*hsia* 下) are of this sort.

The second is called "imitate-form." For this type one draws a picture of an object; thus the lines follow the natural shape. "Sun" (*jih* 日) and "moon" (*yüeh* 月) are of this sort.

The third is called "form-and-sound." For this type, a name is made after considering a relation of things, i.e., a comparison is made by combination of phonetic and classifier. "Stream" (*chiang* 江) and "river" (*ho* 河) are of this sort.

The fourth is called "join-meaning." For this type, suitable figures are compared and suitably combined, whereby appears what is indicated. "Warrior" (*wu* 武) and "trust" (*hsin* 信) are of this sort.

The fifth is called "interchangeable notation." For this type, one establishes a category, then puts other graphs with similar meanings under that category. The two graphs for "aged" (*k'ao* 考 and *lao* 老) are of this sort.

The sixth is called "loan-borrowing." These are for words which originally had no graph of their own and depend on the sounds to stand for something else. "Command" and "honorable" (*ling* 令) and "grow" or "long" (*chǎng* and *ch'áng* 長) are of this sort.[12]

~ ~ ~   ~ ~ ~

The *Documents* says: "I wish to contemplate the designs of the ancients."[13] This means one must follow the old writings and not make distortions.[14] Confucius said: "I can remember when a scribe left a blank in his text. Now this is no longer done, alas."[15] It is not because men do not know and do not ask, but because if they all used their own private judgement, right and wrong would have had no standard, and clever opinions and heterodox pronouncements would have caused confusion among all the scholars under heaven.

8. Eurasian mystical number not to be taken literally.

9. There is no such statement in the *Rites of Chou* (*Chou li*) as the text now exists, although it mentions the six types of graphs taught by the Protector.

10. I.e., having passed the seventh lunar new year after birth.

11. These characterizations of the six types of graphs are all in the form of two rhymed lines of four syllables each, as though a mnemonic device. The meanings are subject to speculation.

12. Here the translation skips from the opening section of the postface to its final section.

13. Quoted from the *Classic of Documents* (see selection 188).

14. Literally, "to bore through," hence "to give a farfetched or strained interpretation," "to read too much into something," "to overinterpret."

15. Quoted from the *Analects* (see selection 7).

Now the written language is the foundation of classical learning, the source of kingly government. It is what the former generations relied on to transmit culture to later ages and what men of later times rely on to understand antiquity. Therefore it is said: "When the foundation is established, the Way grows;"[16] and "When you know all under heaven that is extremely obscure, you cannot be confused."[17]

Now I have arranged the small seal graphs together with ancient Chou graphs. I have broadly adopted from those who understand the small and the great, from those who are believable and have proof, and I preserve and explain their opinions.

In order to classify all kinds of things and correct mistakes, and to state clearly to wise scholars the subtle meanings, I have divided the graphs into groups, so as not to confuse them with each other. The myriad things can be found here, and nothing has been omitted. If some meanings are not clear, then I explain with examples.

I follow the interpretations in the text of the *Changes* preserved by Meng Hsi, the *Documents* by K'ung An-kuo, and the *Odes* by Mao Kung. As to texts on ritual, I have used that of the Chou officials, and I took Tso's commentary on the *Spring and Autumn Annals*. I also used the *Analects* and the *Classic of Filial Piety*. In each case I used the ancient text.[18] That with which I am not familiar I omitted.

Translated by K. L. Thern

16. Quoted from the *Analects*.
17. A similar line occurs in the *Classic of Changes*.
18. However, in the dictionary Hsü actually cites texts from both ancient and modern texts.

200
Preface to *Collected Poems from the Orchid Pavilion*

Wang Hsi-chih (c. 303–c. 361)

In the ninth year of the Eternal Harmony era in the beginning of the last month of spring when the calendar was in *kuei-ch'ou*,[1] we met at the Orchid

Wang Hsi-chih, from Kuei-chi (modern Shao-hsing, Chekiang), was an influential official, writer and, above all, calligrapher during the Eastern Chin dynasty. He wrote this preface to commemorate a festive springtime gathering of forty-one notable figures, who made an excursion outside Kuei-chi to a spot about ten miles southwest of modern Shao-hsing on April 22, 353. As part of the entertainment, wine-cups were floated down a winding stream, and the guests were asked to write a poem before the cups passed their seats or else drink a forfeit. Only twenty-six

Pavilion in Shan-yin, Kuei-chi to celebrate the Bathing Festival.[2] All the worthy men assembled; the young and the senior gathered together. Here were lofty mountains and towering hills, thick groves and tall bamboo. And, there was a clear, rapid stream reflecting everything around that had been diverted to play the game of floating wine-cups along a winding course. We sat down in order of precedence. Though we had none of the magnificent sounds of strings and flutes, a cup of wine and then a poem was enough to stir our innermost feelings.

This was a day when the sky was bright and the air was pure. A gentle breeze warmed us. Upwards we gazed to contemplate the immensity of the universe; downwards we peered to scrutinize the abundance of living things. In this way, we let our eyes roam and our emotions become aroused so that we enjoyed to the fullest these sights and sounds. This was happiness, indeed!

Men associate with each other but for the brief span of their lives. Some are content to control their innermost feelings as they converse inside a room. Some are prompted to give rein to their ambitions and lead wild, unfettered lives. There is all the difference between controlled and abandoned natures, just as the quiescent and the frenzied are unalike. Yet, both take pleasure from whatever they encounter, possessing it but for a while. Happy and content, they remain unaware that old age is fast approaching. And, when they tire of something, they let their feelings change along with events as they experience a deep melancholy. What they had taken pleasure in has now passed away in an instant, so how could their hearts not give rise to longing? Furthermore, a long or short life depends on the transformation of all things: everything must come to an end. An ancient said, "Life and death are the greatest of matters, indeed!"[3] Isn't this reason enough to be sad?

Whenever I read of the causes of melancholy felt by men of the past, it is

---

guests were able to comply, and their efforts were gathered in a volume to which Wang wrote this short introduction. Despite its brevity, few examples of Chinese prose have had such widespread influence on subsequent literati culture. Wang was canonized as the "sage" of calligraphy, and the original text in his hand became a model of the "running mode." The image of the gathering generated a veritable cult of the Orchid Pavilion celebrated in poetry, painting, and the decorative arts while the area of the original event became a literary shrine.

1. April 22, 353.

2. The Bathing Festival was originally an ancient festival of purification held in the first ten days of the third lunar month when the people would go to sacrifice and bathe in a nearby river or lake. During the Six Dynasties period, its early religious significance was lost, and it became a social occasion for the literati to gather and write poetry.

3. See *Chuang Tzu*, chapter 12: "Confucius said, 'Life and death are the greatest of matters, indeed, but he [Wang T'ai] is unaffected by them. Although Heaven may overturn and the Earth might sink, it is no loss to him. He carefully observes whatever is pure and does not let things influence him. He recognizes as fate the transformation of things and holds fast to their guiding principles.' " Here, Confucius is ironically made to espouse Chuang Tzu's philosophy by praising a cripple, Wang T'ai, who had his foot cut off as a penalty yet gathered as many disciples as Confucius himself.

like joining together two halves of a tally. I always feel sad when I read them, yet I cannot quite understand why. But I know that it is meaningless to say life and death are the same; and to equate the longevity of P'eng-tsu with that of Shang-tzu is simply wrong. [4] Future readers will look back upon today just as we look back at the past. How sad it all is! Therefore, I have recorded my contemporaries and transcribed what they have written. Over distant generations and changing events, what gives rise to melancholy will be the same. Future readers will also feel moved by these writings.

Translated by Richard Strassberg

4. See *Chuang Tzu*, chapter 5: "No one has lived longer than Shang-tzu and P'eng-tsu died young." Chuang Tzu paradoxically reverses the common belief that P'eng-tsu lived for eight hundred years, longer than any other man, and that Shang-tzu died in his youth.

201
Preface to the "Foolish Brook Poems"

Liu Tsung-yüan (773–819)

To the north of the Kuan River, there is a brook. It flows eastward into the Hsiao River. Some say that a Mr. Jan once lived there and hence named it Jan Brook. Some say that the water in the brook can be used for dye [*jan*] and that it was named "Dye Brook" because of this property. I have transgressed through my foolishness and consequently have been banished to the bank of the Hsiao River. I am fond of this brook. I went upstream one day for two or three tricents and came upon an especially exquisite place, and I made my home there. In ancient times, there was a Valley of the Foolish Old Man.[1] Now, having made the brook the site of my home, I could not decide on a name for it. Every day, people passing by argued continually over its name, so

This preface, written in 810, also functions as a landscape essay. The author, Liu Tsung-yüan (see selection 55), was one of the most brilliant practitioners of that genre. In this very peculiar landscape essay, Liu dwells on the theme of "foolishness" (*yü*) and expresses not so much his love of nature, but his obsession with the recent change in his fortunes and his own role in his disgrace. Because of his association with the Wang Shu-wen faction at court, he lost favor after Emperor Shun-tsung (reigned 805) was forced to abdicate on account of severe illness. It was during his banishment to a minor post in remote Yung-chou (Hunan province) that he wrote the "Foolish Brook Poems" and their preface.

The preface was an important place for a Chinese author to make a statement about the purpose of his own literary work or about the nature of literature in general. Beyond that, however, the prefaces themselves often have literary significance. Other prefaces collected in this anthology are found in selections 16, 18, 196, 245, and 250.

1. Lin-chih district in Shantung.

that the name could not remain unchanged. Therefore I changed its name to Foolish Brook.

Along Foolish Brook I purchased a small hill and called it Foolish Hill. Sixty paces to the northeast of Foolish Hill, there is a spring. I purchased it for my dwelling place and called it Foolish Spring. The spring has six mouths out of which water gushes up from under the hill. Flowing together, the water from the six openings meanders southward to form Foolish Ditch. I had earth carried there and stones piled up to dam the water where the passage is narrow, and thereby made Foolish Pond. East of Foolish Pond, I built Foolish Hall, and south of the hall, I built Foolish Pavilion. In the pond is Foolish Island. Beautiful trees and rare stones are placed there. They are all remarkable sights in this landscape, but because of me, they suffer the mortification of carrying the name "foolish." Water is a substance in which the wise man takes delight. Why must this brook alone suffer the mortifying name "foolish"?

Its water level is so low that it cannot be used for irrigation. Moreover, its currents are too rapid, and there are too many islets and rocks in it, so large boats cannot enter it. Besides, it is too secluded and too recessed, too shallow and too narrow; no dragon would ever deign to live in it because there is not enough water with which to make clouds and rain. It has nothing to offer to the world. In that respect it is exactly like me. This being the case, it might as well tolerate the humiliation of being called "foolish."

Ning-wu Tzu acted as if he were foolish when his country was in disorder.[2] He was a wise man, but he acted in an apparently foolish way. Master Yen Hui never disagreed with any of Confucius' teachings as if he were a foolish man.[3] He was someone who was intelligent but appeared to be foolish. In my case, I live under an orderly government, but I have gone against the inherent principle of things and mishandled state affairs. hence no one who has acted foolishly is as foolish as I am. This being so, then no one in the world can rival my claim to this brook. I have the sole right to name it "foolish."

The brook has nothing to offer to the world, but it serves well as a mirror to all creation. It is limpid, lustrous, graceful, and pure. It jingles like the ancient bells and lithostones. It delights the foolish one so much that he, laughing merrily, is totally infatuated with it and cannot bear to leave.

Although I am out of tune with the times, yet I still take considerable comfort in writing. I can immerse the myriad creatures in my works and

---

2. An allusion to *Analects*, 5.20: "The Master said, 'When good order prevailed in his country, Ning Wu acted the part of a wise man. When his country was in disorder, he acted the part of a stupid man. Others may equal his wisdom, but they cannot equal his stupidity.' " (Translated by James Legge)

3. *Analects*, 2.9: "I have talked with Hui for a whole day and he has not made any objection to anything I said; as if he were stupid. He was retired, and I have examined his conduct when away from me and found him able to illustrate my teachings. Hui! He is not stupid." (Translated by James Legge)

capture all their forms and poses, letting nothing escape. I sing about Foolish Brook with my foolish verses; they go surprisingly well together in their common obscurity. Overtaking the undifferentiated state of the primordial world, and submerging myself in its insentience, vacuous and inane, I will thus be recognized by no one. Therefore, I have written eight foolish poems and have recorded them on rocks by Foolish Brook.

Translated by Yu-shih Chen

202

Postface to a Catalog on a Collection of Bronze and Stone Inscriptions

Li Ch'ing-chao (1084–c.1151)

I married into the Chao family in 1101. My father-in-law[1] was the minister of civil service, but the family did not live extravagantly. Te-fu (my husband) was at that time a student at the Imperial University. On the first and fifteenth of every month, he could leave college. He would pawn his clothing and with 500 cash[2] in his pocket go to Hsiang-kuo Temple in search of old prints and come home with some fruit. We would enjoy examining what he had bought while munching fruit together. Two years later, when he got a post in the government, he started to make as complete as possible a collection of rubbings or prints from bronze or stone inscriptions and other ancient scripts. When a print was not available, he would have a copy made and thus our collection of famous calligraphy and antiques began. Once a man tried to sell us Hsü Hsi's painting of "Peony" for 200,000 cash, and Te-fu asked permission to take it home and keep it for a few days and consider. We found no means to buy it and reluctantly returned it to the owner. Te-fu and I were upset about it for days. When he served as magistrate at two posts, he spent his entire salary over the care and preservation of rare editions. Every time we obtained a rare book, we would examine it critically and see about its repair and rebinding, or if it was a painting or antique vessel, we would spend the evening pawing over it and looking for imperfections. Because of this, our collection was considered the best among all the collectors in regard to mount-

---

The famous poet Li Ch'ing-chao (Li Yi-an, see selection 125) and her husband fled south during the fall of the Northern Sung dynasty to the Chin (Jürchen) invaders in 1126. She survived her collector-husband and had an unhappy second marriage.

1. A former premier.
2. One thousand cash equals one "dollar."

ing and care and condition of the scripts. Whenever we found in bookstalls a volume which was complete and had no bad errors, we would purchase it for the purpose of comparison with other texts.

I have a power for memory, and sometimes after supper, sitting quietly in the Homecoming Hall, we would boil a pot of tea and, pointing to the piles of books on the shelves, make a guess as to which line of which page in which volume of a book contained a certain passage and see who was right, the one making the correct guess having the privilege of drinking his cup of tea first. When a guess was correct, we would lift up the cup and break out into a loud laughter, so much so that sometimes the tea was spilled on our dress and we were not able to drink at all. We were then content to live and grow old in the world! Therefore, we held our heads high, although we were living in poverty and sorrow. . . . [3] In time our collection grew bigger and bigger and the books and art objects were piled up on tables and desks and beds, and we enjoyed them with our eyes and with our minds and planned and discussed the collection, tasting a happiness above those enjoying the horse races and music and dance.

In the year 1126, Te-fu was magistrate at Tsechuan [4] when the northern invaders threatened the national capital. [5] He had a presentiment that we were not going to be able to keep the collection intact during the ensuing chaos. The following year, we came down south on the occasion of the funeral for his mother. [6] We realized that a part of the collection had to be sacrificed. First we discarded the heavy, bulky volumes, the less important works of a painter, and vessels that bore no inscriptions. Next we threw out books of which standard editions existed, paintings of no extraordinary merit, and bronze that was too heavy for transportation. Even then, the collection filled fifteen cartloads and was carried in a fleet of boats when we came down the Huai River. We had planned on moving things kept at our old house at

3. The translator has omitted a passage of more than a hundred sinographs giving details of how Li Ch'ing-chao economized on food and jewelry, etc., to get their treasured volumes into fine shape on the shelves of the Homecoming Hall. He has also omitted a brief introduction of approximately the same length and simplified the ending. In general, Lin Yutang's translations, tremendously popular in the United States about half a century ago, are much freer and looser than the standard required by sinological scholarship today. Still, his renderings have a flair and charm all their own.

4. Or Tzu-ch'uan, in Shantung province.

5. Kaifeng.

6. Of course they fled for another more imperious reason, the fall of North China. But to ascribe it to the occasion of a mother's funeral is accepted as the correct way of saying it. Likewise, it is highly improbable that her husband, the son of a minister, had to "pawn clothing" to buy odd curios, as said at the beginning, but this is the generally accepted euphemism. It has become the tradition for scholars to say that one's wife took off a gold bodkin from her hair to sell for money with which to buy wine to entertain a friend for the night. Cf. p. 735.

Chingchow[7] the following year, but the house, we found later, was burned down with its dozen roomfuls of objects.

In 1129,[8] we were living at Chihyang.[9] Te-fu had to go to the temporary capital.[10] As he stood on the bank to say good-bye, I felt sick at heart and asked, "What shall I do in case of trouble?" He replied from the bank, "Do as the others. If necessary, abandon the food supplies first, then the clothing; books next, the scrolls after that, and the bronze last of all. But never part with the Sung ware no matter what happens. And take good care of it!" Then he left on horseback.

In August, Te-fu died of an illness. At that time, the imperial court was fleeing to Kiangsi. I asked two employees to bring more than 20,000 volumes of books and over 2,000 prints of inscriptions to Hungchow[11] first. In winter of that year, the town fell and all was lost. What we had brought down the river in a fleet of boats was all gone. What was saved were a few small scrolls, the works of Li Po, Tu Fu, Han Yü, and Liu Tsung-yüan,[12] the *Shih Shuo*,[13] the *Debate on Iron and Salt*,[14] several dozens of rubbings, over a dozen pieces of bronze, and several boxes of *Southern T'ang History*, which happened to be with me in my personal luggage. As I could not have gone upriver, I came down south and moved from Taichow, to Wenchow, to Chuchow, to Yuehchow, finally to Hangchow, and had the collection stored at Cheng-hsien.[15] In 1130, rebel troops came to the town and raided it, and all that passed into the ownership of old General Li. About 50 or 60 per cent of what had been saved was again gone. I had still six or seven baskets which I brought with me when I moved to Yüehcheng.[16] One night, a burglar came and got away with five baskets. What I have left now are only a few odd volumes of several incomplete books.

I suddenly came upon this Catalog (compiled by my husband) and the feeling was like that of meeting an old friend. I remember when we were living at Tunglai[17] at our house called "Tsingchiht'ang,"[18] Te-fu was working every day on the volumes, giving each ten volumes a protecting cloth case

---

7. In Shantung province.
8. When the enemy came down to Nanking.
9. In Anhwei province.
10. Then at Nanking.
11. Present-day Nan-ch'ang city in Kiangsi province.
12. Famous T'ang authors, all of whom are represented in this volume.
13. See selection 55.
14. A book by Huan Kuan (fl. 73 B.C.E.) about an important government monopoly.
15. All of these cities are located in Chekiang province. Hangchow was where the Southern Sung capital was finally established.
16. Modern Kuei-chi in Chekiang province.
17. In Shantung.
18. Hall of Quiet Governance.

with silk fastenings. Usually, he checked over two volumes per day and wrote a postscript note on one volume. Among the 2,000 volumes of prints from stone and bronze, only 502 now bear his signature and notes. The ink is as fresh as the day he wrote them, but the tree over his grave has shot up to a considerable height already. I realize that this is the common fate of things: they come and go, or change ownership or are destroyed. There is nothing surprising in it. I merely write this story down, that collectors may take warning from it.

The fourth year of Shaohsing (1134)
Translated by Lin Yutang

Discourses, Essays, and Sketches

203
Discourse on Nourishing Life

Hsi K'ang (223–262)

There are people nowadays who say that immortal sagehood can be attained though study, that immortality can with effort be reached. There are also those who put the longest life at one hundred and twenty years and claim it has always been so. They say all accounts of people living longer than this are nothing but lies. Both of these positions miss the way things are, so permit me to try, in my coarse way, to explain.

It is true that immortals cannot be seen with your eyes, but if we examine clearly and weigh all that has been written in the records and documents and all that has been transmitted by the former historians, their true existence is a certainty. They seem to be the special recipients of a unique *ch'i* (vital breath), the receiving of which comes about spontaneously. It is not something one

Hsi K'ang was one of the celebrated Seven Worthies (or Sages) of the Bamboo Grove, a group of literati who chose to avoid the normal course of government service during politically troubled times and retire to a life of estheticism and indulgence (compare with selection 27). Though admired in a caricatured form for their antiestablishment stand, self-indulgences, humor, and explorations of intoxication by alcohol and other drugs, Hsi and his colleagues contributed a wealth of serious prose and poetry to subsequent ages.

Hsi was an acknowledged master of the *lun* ("essay"), and the "Essay on Nourishing Life" was one of nine he wrote on themes of personal cultivation, longevity, feelings, and the arts. This essay illustrates the tide of interest in practices associated with Taoism, artistic expression and individual emotions, and the obligations of the individual to himself and society that typified Hsi's era, one that witnessed a basic shift in views on life and art after the collapse of the Han dynasty.

can reach with an accumulation of learning. But if we talk about the proper care of oneself, according to the principles, in order to maximize one's allotted span of life, then it is certainly possible for a person to get, at the best, more than a thousand years, at the very least, several hundred. Nowadays, no one is skilled in this care, and therefore no one can achieve such longevity. How can I explain this?

If you take some drug to make yourself perspire, it will perhaps in some cases have no effect. But should you suffer some terrible embarrassment, sweat will literally pour forth. If you skip eating all morning, your mouth will water and you'll dream of eating. Yet Tseng Tzu,[1] choked with grief, went seven foodless days without feeling hunger. If you sit up half the night, you'll begin to nod off and dream of bed. But if inside you're stirred with a great anxiety, the dawn will come before you fall asleep. You can brush energetically to get your hair to stand up or drink a strong wine to redden your face, but the results will only be marginal. Yet a young fellow when angry will redden with a fearsome face and his hair will push up against his hat. From these examples, I assert that the relationship of a person's spirit to his body is like that of a country and its ruler. When the spirit is rash within, the body decays without, just as when the ruler on top is muddled, the country below falls to chaos.

Now, for those growing grain during the drought of Emperor T'ang,[2] there was from time to time the contribution of an isolated rainfall. When that was over, things returned to being parched and dried, and what depended on that single rain would later wither up; nonetheless, the benefits of that single rainfall can certainly not be gainsaid. Nowadays people often say that a single burst of rage is not sufficient to do violence to one's innate nature or that a single bout of grief to harm one's body. Treating these things lightly, they indulge themselves often, as if they did not recognize the benefits of a single rainfall, but looked forward to getting good grain from desiccated sprouts.

By this, the gentleman knows that form can stand only by relying on spirit, and that spirit in turn needs form for its existence. When one grasps how easily the system of life is unbalanced, one realizes the harm to life of even one such excess. Therefore, one's innate nature is cultivated in order to preserve the spirit, and the mind is kept peaceful to keep whole the body. Love and hate must not come to rest in one's feelings, nor must grief and joy be harbored in one's thoughts. Drifting, insensate, the bodily *ch'i* is level and

---

1. Also called Tseng San, he was a disciple of Confucius renowned for his filiality and extreme attendance on his parents. Upon their death, Tseng Tzu did not even taste water for seven days.

2. King T'ang, also called Ch'eng T'ang, is credited in traditional accounts with defeating the Hsia dynasty and founding the Shang dynasty in 1766 B.C.E. A ruler of great virtue, he expanded a small, seventy-tricent state to one that stretched across the Yellow River plain through a series of eleven conquests.

quiet. Then inhale and exhale in a rigorously controlled manner, and ingest the things which will nourish your body. This will bring form and spirit closer together, and will benefit you inside and out.

Now, if a field when planted yields ten measures of grain, it's called a "prime" field, and it will be so named throughout the underheaven. No one realizes that under close and intense cultivation, it could yield more than one hundred measures. Planting a field is one thing, and arboriculture is quite another. With trees, successful planting lies in spreading them apart. It is said that a merchant can never make a thousand percent profit, and a farmer has no prospects for a hundred measure yield. These are cases of clinging to the status quo and not changing. Beans make a person gain weight; elm seeds make one sleepy. The acacia relieves anger; the day-lily helps one forget sorrow. The wise and the foolish alike know these things.

Garlic and onion harm the eyes, and pork and fish are not life-prolonging foods. These facts too are common knowledge today. If lice live in your hair, they absorb the black, and a musk-deer that eats cypress leaves becomes cedar fragrant. The necks of people who live in high places develop goiters, and the people of Chin[3] have yellow teeth. Deducing from this, it is clear that the *ch'i* of everything you eat permeates the innate nature and pervades the body. There is nothing that does not elicit some reaction. Is it possible there is only steaming to make things heavy but none to make them light, injury to make things dark but none to make them bright, smoking to make things yellow but none to make things firm, perfuming to make things fragrant but none to make things endure? Thus Shen Nung's[4] maxim, "Superior medicines nourish one's life; middle medicines nourish one's nature," truly recognizes the interrelation of innate nature and life, perfected through a course of support and nourishment.

But people nowadays do not look into these things. Nothing more than the five grains is seen, blinded as people are by addiction to glaring sights and sounds. Their eyes are blunted by deep red and yellow, and their ears are enslaved to raucous music. The spicy flavors they consume fry their vital organs; the wines stew their stomachs and entrails; the spices and aromatics rot their bones and marrow; and alternating passions of joy and anger pervert their proper *ch'i*; dwelling on worries dissipates their spirit essence; suffering and pleasures wreak havoc on their equilibrium. The attacks on their petty persons come from all sides. The body so easily exhausted must meet enemies from inside and out. Not being made of wood or stone, can we last long under these conditions?

People today both laugh at and pity those who go to extremes with themselves, those who eat and drink without measure and then fall victim to a

3. Shansi.
4. The Divine Farmer was one of China's cultural heroes of high antiquity to whom is credited the organization and presentation of agricultural and herbal skills to the Chinese people.

myriad of illnesses, those who indulge tirelessly in sex until their vitality comes to a weary end. The banes of the wind and the cold, the injuries of the hundred toxins will plague them with a host of obstacles only halfway along life's allotted span.

We say they are not skilled at maintaining life. Where do they lose touch with the basic principles in caring for themselves? They perish by the most subtle points. The subtle points compound to become harm, and the compounding of harm adds up to decline. From decline comes whiteness, and from whiteness comes agedness, and agedness brings on the end. Enclosed in this syndrome, a person has no way out. People of only average understanding or less refer to this as "natural." Even though victims come to a minor realization of things, it is invariably expressed as remorse as soon as the disaster is actually encountered. Never are people aware and cautious about the many dangers before symptoms manifest themselves. For this reason, Lord Huan was already gripped by fatal illness before he realized it, and yet he cursed the physician Pien Ch'üeh's early diagnosis.[5] He mistakenly thought that the day one first feels the pain is the day an illness begins. What harmed him had its trivial origins, but he sought help only after the ailment was obvious, and the cure, therefore, was unsuccessful.

Travel around the world of ordinary men and you will find they all have the same slice of longevity. Look up, look down; there are no exceptions. This span of life is said to be all that nature's principles allow. The numbers alone make it self-evident, and the company makes for each one's solace. Even when someone has heard stories about "nourishing life," he will say they're untrue, basing his judgment on what he can see around him. Slightly better than this person is someone who approaches, wary as a fox, and although he gets a wee bit closer, does not know where to begin. Slightly better than this is someone who energetically consumes elixirs, then decides after six months or a year that there is no visible effect and he is wasting his efforts, and thus gives up along the way. Perhaps such people feel their attempts are like a trickle into the oceans, while water leaks in torrents out the other side. They want to sit down and watch for obvious rewards. Perhaps they are people who have suppressed their feelings or held their desires in check, lopped off and discarded their worldly ambitions. But the objects of temptations are always directly before their eyes and ears, and the goal of their nobler aspirations lies several dozen years away. So fearing that they'll lose both, they lack inner resolve; inside the heart is fighting with itself and outside things are luring them from the path. The forces combine to drag them from the Way, and they too fall in defeat.

5. The story is told by the philosopher Han Fei Tzu. Lord Huan refers to Duke Huan of Chin. The physician Pien Ch'üeh (see selection 228, note 3) visited Duke Huan several times, at ten-day intervals, charting the course of Huan's illness at its early stages. Feeling no symptoms, Huan refused to listen until he was beyond curing.

Only by reason can we know the subtlety of esoteric things, not by perception with our eyes. This may be likened to the Yü-chang tree, growing for seven years before it is recognizable. Now with hasty and tempestuous hearts, we climb on the path of stillness and quietude. Our idea is for hasty progress, but events come slowly; our expectations focus on the near future, but responses to our efforts are far-off, and thus no one is able to reach to the end. Those who push anxiously do not seek on, because they see no immediate results, and those who do seek on fail in the endeavor for lack of concentration. Those who incline toward one side or the other achieve nothing for lack of breadth, and those who pursue occult practices become quagmired in the byways. In all efforts of this sort, of ten thousand people who seek long life, not a single one can succeed.

Those truly skilled at nourishing life are not at all this way. Clear, empty, quiet, expansive, they reduce the selfish and minimize desires. Knowing the harm that fame and status do to virtue, they simply ignore them, leave them beyond the confines of their lives. It is not a case of wanting these things and forcibly forestalling them. They recognize the harm that the rich-flavored does one's innate nature and discard it, pay it no heed. It is not that they hunger for such things and then control themselves. External things entangle the heart, so they have no presence. Spirit *ch'i* alone is manifest, by virtue of its purity. Those skilled at nourishing life are open wide, without worry or grief, at peace without thoughts and ponderings. They preserve this state with oneness, nourish it with harmony. Harmony with the principles brings daily advance, becoming one with the great flow. Afterward one is infused with the numinous nutrient, imbued with the ambrosial spring waters, basked in the dawning sun, and made tranquil with the *ch'in* zither's five strings. So with nonaction, it comes in and of itself, the body subtle and the heart profound, forgetting pleasure so that joy is complete, abandoning the trappings of life so that the person may be preserved. Proceeding in this manner, one's life span could compare with Hsien Men's;[6] one could compete in years with Wang Ch'iao.[7] How could anyone think that such people do not exist!

Translated by Kenneth J. DeWoskin

6. An ancient who achieved transcendence and longevity. Living atop the remote Mount Chieh-shih, he was pursued for his secrets of long life by China's first emperor, Ch'in Shih-huang.

7. Also called Wang-tzu Ch'iao, he was an immortal transcendent who lived atop Mount Sung-kao during the time of the Chou king Ling (571–544 B.C.E.).

204

The Peach Blossom Spring

T'ao Ch'ien (365–427)

During the T'ai-yüan period[1] of the Chin dynasty, a fisherman of Wu-ling[2] once rowed upstream, unmindful of the distance he had gone, when he suddenly came to a grove of peach trees in bloom. For several hundred paces on both banks of the steam there was no other kind of tree. The wild flowers growing under them were fresh and lovely, and fallen petals covered the ground—it made a great impression on the fisherman. He went on for a way with the idea of finding out how far the grove extended. It came to an end at the foot of a mountain whence issued the spring that supplied the stream. There was a small opening in the mountain and it seemed as though light was coming through it. The fisherman left his boat and entered the cave, which at first was extremely narrow, barely admitting his body; after a few dozen steps it suddenly opened out onto a broad and level plain where well-built houses were surrounded by rich fields and pretty ponds. Mulberry, bamboo, and other trees and plants grew there, and crisscross paths skirted the fields. The sounds of cocks crowing and dogs barking could be heard from one courtyard to the next. Men and women were coming and going about their work in the fields. The clothes they wore were like those of ordinary people.[3] Old men and boys were carefree and happy.

When they caught sight of the fisherman, they asked in surprise how he had got there. The fisherman told the whole story, and was invited to go to their house, where he was served wine while they killed a chicken for a feast. When the other villagers heard about the fisherman's arrival, they all came to pay him a visit. They told him that their ancestors had fled the disorders of Ch'in times and, having taken refuge here with wives and children and neighbors, had never ventured out again; consequently they had lost all

This is the most important and most quoted description of a utopia in the whole of Chinese literature. Note that the prose preface is actually far more famous than the poem to which it is attached. The poem, indeed, is usually taken to be little more than a perfunctory versification of the story.

For information on T'ao Ch'ien, see selection 29.

1. 376–396.

2. Modern Ch'eng-te in Hunan. It is not far from the town of T'ao-yüan ("Peach Spring") on the Yüan river.

3. This line is probably intended to convey the idea that these were not immortals or other-worldly beings clad in shining raiment or covered with feathers, but people just like any other. The term translated here by "ordinary people" (literally, "outside people") occurs later as "outsiders," those who live outside this hidden retreat. This second occurrence makes it unlikely that it means "foreigners" here—that they were wearing a garb not familiar in fourth-century China, as might be the case if they were actually dressed in the style of the Ch'in dynasty.

contact with the outside world. They asked what the present ruling dynasty was, for they had never heard of the Han, let alone the Wei and the Chin. They sighed unhappily as the fisherman enumerated the dynasties one by one and recounted the vicissitudes of each. The visitors all asked him to come to their houses in turn, and at every house he had wine and food. He stayed several days. As he was about to go away, the people said, "There's no need to mention our existence to outsiders."

After the fisherman had gone out and recovered his boat, he carefully marked the route. On reaching the city, he reported what he had found to the magistrate, who at once sent a man to follow him back to the place. They proceeded according to the marks he had made, but went astray and were unable to find the cave again.

A high-minded gentleman of Nan-yang named Liu Tzu-chi[4] heard the story and happily made preparations to go there, but before he could leave he fell sick and died. Since then there has been no one interested in trying to find such a place.[5]

> The Ying[6] clan disrupted Heaven's ordinance[7]
> And good men withdrew from such a world.[8]
> Huang and Ch'i went off to Shang Mountain[9]
> And these people too fled into hiding.
> 5 Little by little their tracks were obliterated,
> The paths they followed overgrown at last.
> By agreement they set about farming the land
> When the sun went down each rested from his toil.
> Bamboo and mulberry provided shade enough,
> 10 They planted beans and millet, each in season.[10]
> From spring silkworms came the long silk thread,
> On the fall harvest no king's tax was paid.

4. An individual whose devotion to principle and whose refusal to accept office must have excited T'ao Ch'ien's admiration. He surely would have been one to appreciate the advantages of such a retreat.

5. The concluding line of the story more literally reads, "Since then no one has asked about the ford," an allusion to the *Analects* (selection 7, passage 18.6) upon which T'ao Ch'ien so often drew.

6. The first Emperor of the Ch'in is here referred to by his clan name.

7. This refers to a passage in the *Classic of Documents* (selection 188) where Hsi and Ho are blamed for throwing heaven into disorder. There it is the regular progression of the heavenly bodies; here it is the order of nature generally that has been upset by bad rule.

8. This line versifies a phrase from the *Analects* (14.37): "The worthy man withdraws from the world."

9. Hsia Huang-kung and Ch'i Li-chi, two of the Four White-head recluses who withdrew from society to the isolation of Shang Mountain.

10. This line is constructed with components from two odes in the *Classic of Odes* (selection 22).

No sign of traffic on overgrown roads,
Cockcrow and dogsbark within each other's earshot.
15   Their ritual vessels were of old design,
And no new fashions in the clothes they wore.
Children wandered about singing songs,
Graybeards went paying one another calls.
When grass grew thick they saw the time was mild,
20   As trees went bare they knew the wind was sharp.
Although they had no calendar to tell,
The four seasons still filled out a year.
Joyous in their ample happiness
They had no need of clever contrivance.[11]
25   Five hundred years[12] this rare deed stayed hid,
Then one fine day the fay retreat[13] was found.
The pure and the shallow belong to separate worlds:
In a little while they were hidden again.
Let me ask you who are convention-bound,
30   Can you fathom those outside the dirt and noise?
I want to tread upon the thin, thin air
And rise up high to find my own kind.

Translated by James Robert Hightower

11. Based on *Tao Te Ching* (selection 10), chapter 18: "When cleverness appears, then we have the Great Imposture."

12. It was more like six hundred years from 220 B.C.E. to 380 C.E., but "five hundred" is a good, round number.

13. The retreat is hyperbolically called "spiritual" in the sense of "not of this world."

205

An Explication of "Progress in Learning"

Han Yü (768–824)

One morning a professor at the Imperial University entered his college and called all the students to line up in front of the school. He then instructed them as follows:

"Progress in Learning" is defined by the following paragraph from the "Record of Studies" chapter of the *Record of Rites* (*Li chi*):

A good student, even though his teacher be lax, will outperform others, but ultimately attribute the merit to his teacher. The bad student, even though his teacher be strict, will do

"Hard work will perfect your studies,
 which can be lost through play;
hard thought will achieve right conduct,
 which sloth may then undo.
5 At this moment,
  our Sage-king[1] has met
  his men of worth,[2]
  and tools of good rule
  have covered the earth.
10 They have rooted up, destroyed
  the evil and cruel,
 have raised and honored
  the perfect and true.
Even those with the smallest skill
15 are all enrolled,
those known for a single art
  are all employed.
They dig, they unearth, they comb, they screen,[3]
they rub out blemishes, they polish to a sheen.
20 Some, indeed, are perhaps
  by chance selected,
but none can say he was
  worthy and unaccepted.
So all you students—
25 beware lest your studies
  go unperfected,

---

only half as well as others, and in the end will ultimately put the blame on his teacher. Those who are good at asking questions are like a woodsman who trims a great tree: first he cuts the easy parts, then later the joints and knots. After a long while, teacher and student enjoy solving problems through mutual discussion. Those who are not good at asking questions are the opposite of this. Those who are good at being questioned are like a bell when struck: when that which strikes it is small, the sound is small; when that which strikes it is large, the sound is large. When the bell is struck consistently and with force, then it gives forth its full sound. Those who are not good at answering questions are the opposite of this. And this is the way of making progress in learning.

It is important to observe that this inimitable piece is a comic attempt at the "explication" (a genre of commentary) of the classical idea of "progress in learning." In other words, this is a mimicry of commentarial writing at the same time that it is a self-satire of intellectuals like the author himself.

For Han Yü, see selection 53.

1. "Sage-king" refers to emperor Hsien Tsung of the T'ang period, who was on the throne during Han Yü's active years.

2. The sage-king's prime ministers.

3. Describing the work of the prime ministers.

and worry not that our officials
   may be unaware;
beware your conduct
30   is not yet true,
and worry not that our officials
   may be unfair."

Before this lecture was over, someone in the ranks laughed and said,

   "You would deceive us, Sir!
We pupils have served you now
35   these many years,
and your mouth has not ceased
   to intone the texts
   of the Six Classics,
and your hands not ceased
40   to unroll the scrolls
   of the hundred persuasions;
you have extracted the essence
   of historical accounts
and plumbed the mysteries
45   of abstruse compilations.
Yet still you strove
   and worked for more,
and big or small
   did all belong;
50 you burned your oil
   to stretch the sun's shadow,
tired and weary
   year after year.
Truly, Sir, of your own studies,
55   it must be said,
   you've worked hard and long.

"You refute, resist
   false doctrines,
repel, reject
60   Buddhist and Taoist,
you patch and mortar
   crack and leak,
fill out and expand
   the dark and oblique.
65 Alone you search the far
   maze of fallen threads,

and everywhere seek to join them
    across time's gap.
You have channeled and brought home
70   the hundred streams,
have turned back a raging wave,
    already crested.
Truly, Sir, it must be said,
    your labors for Confucian teaching
75   are uncontested.

"You have immersed, submerged
    yourself in ambrosial essence,
taking flowers to your mouth
    to savor their blooms;
80 and these you have worked
    to your own literary art,
these writings that now
    fill your rooms.
Your earliest models
85 are the 'Books of Yüh'[4]
and the 'Books of Hsia,'[5]
    without end vast and profound;
the 'Pronouncements of Chou,'[6]
the 'Proclamations of Yin,'[7]
90   tortuous and hard to construe;
the *Spring and Autumn*,
    strict and severe;
the *Chronicle of Tso*,
    verbose and inflated;
95 the *Changes*,
    prodigious yet ordered;
the *Odes*,
    refined yet true.
Your later models
100   are *Chuang Tzu*[8]

4. "Books of Yüh" refers to the early chapters of the *Classic of Documents* (see selection 188), traditionally ascribed to Emperor Shun, whose dynastic name was Yüh.

5. "Books of Hsia" refers to the following chapters of the *Classic of Documents* attributed to Yü the Great, founder of the Hsia dynasty.

6. "Pronouncements of Chou" refers loosely to the latter chapters of the *Classic of Documents*, supposedly dating from the Chou dynasty, such as the "Grand Pronouncement."

7. "Proclamations of Yin" refers to the *P'an keng* chapters of the *Classic of Documents*, allegedly dating from Shang times.

8. See selection 9.

and 'Encountering Sorrows'[9]
and what the Grand
  Historian[10] recorded;
then Yang Hsiung[11]
105   and Ssu-ma Hsiang-ju,[12]
all skilled alike, yet
  each in a separate norm.
Truly, Sir, it can be said,
  your labors at literature
110 have enlarged its core,
  set free its form.

"Ever since you were young
  and began to study,
you've been strong in
115   your courage to act.
Now grown, and versed
  in the social arts,
you've made all around you
  into what it should be.
120 Truly, Sir, it can be said,
  your behavior as a man
is perfect in all its parts.

"Yet in spite of all this
  in public no one
125   will trust you;
  in private no one
  will help you.
Stumbling ahead,
  falling behind,
130 whenever you move
  there's ruin anew.
For a short time, you
  served as censor,
but then were exiled
135   to the southern wilds.
For three years, you
  held the doctorate,[13]

9. See selection 148.
10. See selection 225.
11. See selection 193.
12. See selection 151.
13. This actually happened to Han Yü (806–809).

a useless post, no merits
at all to come by.
140   You are fated always
to fight with your foes,
and another reverse could
come at any time.
Even in a warm winter,
145   *your* children cry of cold;
even after a good harvest,
your wife weeps in hunger.
Your head's gone bald,
your teeth are gapped;
150   and things'll never get better
till the day you die.
But you yourself refuse to reflect
on any of this,
Preferring instead to teach
155   to others what you deem apt."

The master replied,[14]

"You, there, stand to the front!
Great timber is
turned into beams,
the smaller logs
160   become rafters,
columns, batten,
and shorter stays,[15]
doorjambs, pivots,
posts and seams;
165   that each of these
works as it will

14. The metaphors in the ensuing lines derive from the following passage in the *Huai-nan Tzu*:

A wise lord uses men like a skilled craftsman works his lumber. The large pieces he uses for boats and barges, for beams and rafters; the smaller ones he uses for poles and wedges. Long ones become planks and eaves; short ones become stays and cornices. Thus for him no piece is too large, small, long, or short; but each functions as best it will. He measures their shapes, and so each is used and placed.

No substance under Heaven is more lethal than wolf's-bane; and yet a good physician collects and stores it, for it does have some use. Therefore no tree or shrub from the forest should be discarded. How much truer is this of men!

15. "Shorter stays" may also be translated as "dwarf, a man of small stature." This and most of the other architectural terms in this passage derive from the *Record of Rites*.

and is used and placed
    to complete a house
is all the master
170   craftsman's skill.

"Shavings of jade,[16]
    red cinnabar,
'Scarlet arrow,'[17]
    brown mushrooms,
175 bull's urine,
    and puffballs,
and old leather
    drum skins,
all these he searches out
180   then stores apart,
awaiting the time
    and use for each—
such is the master
    physician's art.

185 "With wise promotions
    and fair selections,
he uses alike
    both able and inept,
so the devious are refined,
190   the outstanding enshrined:
he examines for failings,
    weighs for strengths
so that each to his measure
    is staffed—
195 such is the prime
    minister's craft.

"In ancient times,
because Mencius was fond of dispute,
    the way of Confucius was brought to light:
200 but the tracks of his wagon
    encircled the world,
and he ended
    old in his travels.

16. The substances in this and the following lines are all important in traditional Chinese medicine.

17. "Scarlet arrow" is the root of *Gastrodia elata*, a plant belonging to the orchid family, used as a restorative.

Hsün Tzu embraced
205   what was right,
    his great teachings
        towered over everything,
    yet he fled to Ch'u
        to escape slander
210 and died an exile
        in Lan-ling.
    These were two scholars
        who brought forth words
        that became our classics,
215   who trod the steps
        that became our models.
    They surpassed by far
        the ranks of their peers
    and entered deep
220   in the realm of the Sage.
    Yet how were they
        met by their age?

"Now although your professor has worked hard at his studies,
    he could not trace their lineage;
225 although he has spoken much,
    he could not strike their heart;
    his literary style is outstanding,
        but could not succeed at real use;
    his conduct has been exemplary
230   but has not marked him as one apart.
    And yet in spite of all this,
        every month [18] he
        receives a salary,
    and every year
235   consumes his rice and wheat;
    his children do not hoe,
    his wife does not sew;
    he travels by horse,
        is attended by pages,
240 and sits in comfort
        and ease to eat;
    he earnestly treads the narrow,
        common lanes,

---

18. T'ang officials received a monthly salary in cash and a yearly allotment of grain.

pores over old pages
245   to rob and to plunder.
And yet our Sagacious Lord
    imposes no wrath upon him,
nor have ministers rebuked
    him for blunder.
250 How fortunate indeed has he been!

"If his every action
    has drawn slander,
so renown too
    has followed him.
255 To be thrown this idle
    empty post
is thus for him
    a proper fate.
And so, were he now
260 to argue the extent
    or not of his wealth,
to reckon the status
    of his rank and estate,
to forget what best befits
265   his own gifts,
and to mark his elders
    as evils incarnate,
all such were to query a master craftsman
    who would not use a pear-tree stake
270   for a column head,
or to malign a master physician
    who prescribed sweet flag for long life
    and then take chinaroot instead." [19]

Translated by Charles Hartman

19. The root of "sweet flag" or calamus (*Acorus calamus*) was commonly ingested for longevity. Chinaroot, on the other hand, a variety of tuckahoe, was an ancient purgative.

206
The Three Zithers

Ou-yang Hsiu (1007–1072)

My family owns three zithers, one of which is said to have been made by Chang Yüeh, one by Lou Tse, and one by the Lei clan. They all show exquisite craftsmanship and are constructed in accordance with ancient standards. Still, it is impossible to be sure about their provenance. But the important thing about a zither, after all, is how it sounds, not who made it. The upper boards of these instruments have transverse cracks like the markings on a snake's belly, and those who know zithers tell me that these are antique instruments. It seems that the lacquer used on zithers only develops such cracks after a hundred years, hence they are generally considered proof of an instrument's age.

One of the zithers has gold studs, one has stone studs, and one has jade studs. The one with gold studs is the Chang Yüeh zither, the one with stone studs is the Lou Tse zither, and the one with jade studs is the Lei clan zither. The tone of the one with gold studs is rich and penetrating, that of the one with stone studs is pure and gentle, and that of the one with jade studs is harmonious and resonant. At the present, anybody who possessed a single one of these would treasure it, and now I own all three.

However, it is really only the zither with stone studs that is suitable for an old man like me. Contemporaries like to play zithers with studs of gold, jade, pearl-mussel shell, or lapis-lazuli, because when such instruments are placed beside a candle at night, the studs shimmer in the light. But it is hard for an old man whose eyesight is failing to place his fingers squarely on those studs. It is only the stone studs that do not reflect light, and so even when they are placed beside a candle, the white studs can be readily distinguished from the dark wood. That is why stone-studded zithers are best for old men.

Ever since I was young I never liked popular music. Zither music is the only kind I like, and I am particularly fond of the zither piece, "Flowing Waters." During my many difficult years, when duties kept me running north

The author was one of the dominant figures of Northern Sung literature and politics. He was noted as a leader of a group of literary stylists who revived the ideals of ancient-style writing. Later recognized as one of the "Eight Masters of T'ang and Sung Prose," Ou-yang Hsiu was a prolific author in a number of genres. As editor of the *New T'ang History*, he insured that it was compiled on the model of ancient-style prose and, as Chief Examiner in 1057, required the use of the ancient style in essays, failing those who used a more elaborate and florid style. It was through this examination that he discovered Su Shih (see selection 156) and his brother Su Ch'e (1039–1112). Twice falsely accused of incest, he experienced several setbacks to his political career. He had a fondness for singers and was given to writing romantic poetry. Unlike Su Shih, he was not very interested in metaphysics, but was more concerned with the practical questions of quotidian life.

and south, I forgot all the zither pieces I once learned. But "Flowing Waters," that one piece, never went out of my head, even in my dreams. Nowadays, although I have already grown old, I can play it from time to time. Otherwise, all I can play are a few short melodies, yet these too suffice to give me pleasure.

One need not learn many zither pieces. The important thing is to enjoy playing. Likewise, one need not own many zithers. But since I have already come into possession of this many, it would be foolish for me now to start worrying about having a surplus and to get rid of some. On the day after the Double Third Festival in the seventh year of the Chia-yu period (1062), having asked for a leave of absence because of illness, I was practicing calligraphy and, letting my brush write what it would, I composed this account of the three zithers of the Ou-yang family.

Translated by Ronald Egan

A Record of the Pavilion of an Intoxicated Old Man

Ou-yang Hsiu

All around Ch'u[1] there are mountains, but the forests and valleys of that assemblage of peaks to the southwest are the finest. There is one that appears from afar most luxuriant and deepest in verdure—that is Lang-ya. After you have walked six or seven tricents into the mountains, there you will gradually notice the sound of water gurgling. Where it drains out between the two peaks, this is Brewer's Spring. Rounding the peak the road winds; there a pavilion hangs, like a wing, out over the spring. This is the Intoxicated Old Man's pavilion. Who was it that built this pavilion? A monk of these mountains, Chih-hsien. And who named it? The prefect, who called it after himself. When prefect and guests come to drink here, because he becomes intoxicated after only drinking a little and because he is the oldest in years, that is why he nicknamed himself the Intoxicated Old Man. But what he means by Intoxicated Old Man has nothing to do with the wine; it has to do instead with being in the mountains by the water. This joy from the mountains and the water he feels within his mind; he merely ascribes it to the wine.

Now the sun rises and the forest mists dissipate, the clouds return and the caves in ravines grow gloomy—these alternations of dusk and light mark mornings and evenings amid the mountains. Wild flowers bloom with their

This playful self-portrait is the most celebrated of Ou-yang Hsiu's many fine essays.

1. Ch'u prefecture was located in modern Ch'u district of Anhwei province.

hidden scents, beautiful trees leaf out with deepening shade, then winds rise and pure frost appears, the water level drops and the rocks protrude—such are the four seasons amid the mountains. In the morning he goes there, in the evening he returns; the scenery of the four seasons is never the same, hence his joy knows no bounds.

Those who carry loads on their backs sing along the path; sojourners rest beneath the trees. The ones in front call out and those behind respond. Some are bent over with age and others so young that they must be led by the hand. They come and go without cease—such are the travelers around Ch'u. One may lean over this stream and fish; the stream being deep, the fish are fat. Or one may brew wine with the spring water; the spring being fragrant, the wine is crystal clear. Sliced meats from the mountains and wild vegetables arrayed in profusion before the guests—such are the prefect's banquets. The joys of the feast are not from strings or winds; they are from winning at pitch-pot, from victory in chess. Passing goblets and mugs back and forth, shouting with abandon, now sitting, now on their feet—such is the happy abandon of the guests. And the one who, ruddy-faced and white of hair, lies sprawled in their midst—that is the prefect intoxicated.

When the merriment is over and the evening sun sets among the mountains, the prefect goes home with his guests in tow, their shadows jumbled together. The forest gloom deepens; birds call high and low. The revelers all gone, the birds are joyful. Yet, though birds may know the joy of mountain forests, they know not the joy of mankind; men may know the joy of revels with the prefect and yet never know the prefect's enjoyment of their joy.

Intoxicated yet able to share their joy, able when sober to describe it in writing—such is the prefect. And what is this prefect's name? Ou-yang Hsiu of Lu-ling.

Translated by Robert E. Hegel

207

Brush Talks from Dream Brook

Shen Kua (1030–1094)

[On Possession by a Spirit] [1]

By old custom, on the night of the full moon of the first month, one would welcome the Spirit of the Toilet, called "The Purple Maiden." Nor did it

Shen Kua served in a number of governmental positions in the capital and in the provinces. His duties concerned river control, compilation of the imperial diary, border fortifications against

necessarily have to be in the first month, for she could be summoned at any time. When I was little I would occasionally see children summon her just for fun.

Among my relatives there were cases in which she was summoned and would not depart; twice I saw such things, after which no one dared summon her. In the midst of the Ching-yü period,[2] it happened in the family of the learned doctor Wang Lun that a spirit haunted one of his unmarried daughters when "The Purple Maiden" was summoned. It called itself a "Maiden of the Lord-on-High's Palace." It composed elegantly, and its work, the *Immortal Lady's Anthology*, is still in circulation. It had several styles of calligraphy, full of vigor, yet none of which were the "seal" or "clerkly" scripts familiar to the world. Altogether there were over ten styles. . . .[3]

Wang Lun and my father were old friends, and I would play with his children, so I saw its writings with my own eyes. In his family, they would occasionally see its form. If you saw it only from the waist up, it was a fine woman, while below it was constantly shrouded in mist. It was skilled at playing the zither, the sounds of which were sad and beautiful and could make one forget tiredness.

It once asked his daughter: "Will you ride the clouds and travel with me?" When the girl agreed, the courtyard filled with clouds like steam, but when the girl stepped on them, the clouds could not support her. The spirit said: "There is some dirt on the bottom of your slippers; you can take them off and then ride on the clouds." The girl took off her slippers, got on as if walking on silk threads, gracefully reached the ceiling, and then came down. The spirit said: "You are unable to go as yet, but perhaps there will be another time."

Afterwards the girl married, and the spirit no longer came. Her family was entirely unaffected by either good luck or bad. Those who recorded these things for her did so in great detail. This was something I saw with my own eyes, which I have roughly set down here.

In recent years, there have been many cases of people summoning the "Purple Maiden Immortal," and on the whole they are all able at composition, songs, and poetry. Some are very skilled, and I have frequently seen them.

---

the Tanguts (Hsi-hsia), and diplomatic missions to the Khitans (Liao). Wherever he went, he was always a keen observer and wrote voluminously about all manner of things that he encountered. Possessed of a polymathic mind, Shen jotted down his diverse data and thoughts in the form of random notes—*pi-chi*, "brush talks." His extremely broad interests in science, technology, language, and literature are evident in the celebrated collection known as *Sketches from Dream Brook (Meng hsi pi-t'an*, named after the place where his estate was located), from which the present selections have been taken.

1. Section title provided by the translator.
2. 1034–1037.
3. The list of styles is omitted.

Many call themselves "Immortals in exile from P'eng-lai."[4] In medicine and divination, there is nothing they cannot do, and in the game of *go*[5] they are on a par with our national champions. Nevertheless, there was never one so unusual and striking as the one in Wang Lun's family.

Translated by Richard W. Bodman

4. A mythical isle in the eastern sea on which immortals are said to dwell. Immortals are frequently banished to the human world for bad behavior.

5. *Wei-ch'i*, China's native form of chess, is better known to Western readers by the Japanese name *go*.

[On a UFO][1]

In the Chia-yü period,[2] a "pearl"[3] appeared in Yang-chou. It was very large and frequently appeared at night. At first it emerged from the swamps of T'ien-ch'ang county; later it moved to Pi-she Lake; and finally it was at Hsin-k'ai Lake. For more than ten years, residents and travelers would constantly see it.

My friend had a study by the lakeside and one night saw that the "pearl" was very near. At first it opened its door very slightly, and light shot out from the crack like a golden ray. After a moment, it opened wider to the space of half a mat; within there was white light like silver. The "pearl" was as big as a fist and so bright you couldn't look at it directly. For over ten tricents, the trees cast shadows, exactly as when the sun has just come up. In the distance you saw only a sky reddened as if by a forest fire. All of a sudden it went far off, moving as if in flight, floating over the waves, shining like the sun.

In the past there was a "moongem," but its color was unlike the moon; shimmering with sharp flames, it rather resembled the sun. Ts'ui Po-yi once wrote a "Rhapsody on the Bright Gem." Ts'ui was from Kao-yin[4] and so must have seen it often.

In recent years, it hasn't appeared again; no one knows where it has gone. Fan-liang-chen is where the "pearl" used to appear, and when travelers reach there, they usually tie up their boats for a few nights to watch for its appearance. The pavilion there is called "The Playful Pearl."

Translated by Richard W. Bodman

1. Section title provided by the translator.

2. 1056–1063.

3. In Chinese folklore, pearls are endowed with the magic power to give off their own light, to protect their owner from sickness, and to repel water (when their owner is swimming).

4. Kao-yin is in Kiangsu province near Yang-chou.

208

The Relic of King Aśoka Temple

Chang Tai (1597–1679)

King Aśoka Temple[1] is a Buddhist monastery remote and tranquil. Before the front steps are eight or nine old pines, all quite majestic with an air of antiquity. The main hall is located at some distance from the outer gate. A misty light among the shady trees shines through the gate so that one can look up to the sky and perceive a brilliance which is icy, cold, crystal clear, and penetrating. To the right, one winds toward the gate to the abbot's quarters where there are two *śāla*[2] trees so high that they pierce the empyrean. A hall to the side contains a sandalwood Buddha and, in the middle, a bronze stūpa whose patina is quite old. It is a reliquary donated by the Empress Dowager Tz'u-sheng during the Wan-li era.[3] The relic often emits a light, glassy and multicolored, radiating in all directions through the openings in the stūpa.[4] Every year, this is witnessed on three or four occasions. Whenever someone prays to the relic, it produces all kinds of visions according to the person's karma; but if it remains dark as ink and nothing is seen, the person will certainly die. In the past, the monk Chan visited the temple. He did not see

Chang Tai was the scion of a prominent family of Shan-yin (modern Shao-hsing, Chekiang). Like a number of wealthy literati during the late Ming, he did not pursue an official career. Instead, during the first half of his life, he led an idyllic existence as a talented esthete and socialite. During the final four decades of the Ming, he was able to travel extensively in comfort and observe many of the fashionable scenes of the time. At some point, he took the artistic name "Studio of Contentment (T'ao-an)." After the collapse of the dynasty in 1644, his fortunes declined and he withdrew from society. During the remaining forty years or so of his life, he lived in reduced circumstances as a recluse, writing his memoirs in the form of miscellanies. *Dreamy Memories from the Studio of Contentment*, his best-known collection, contains short, epigraphic narratives of the travels of his youth as well as vignettes of personalities, customs, and various cultural pursuits.

1. King Aśoka (reigned c. 268–232 B.C.E) was an Indian king who united most of the South Asian subcontinent and converted the region to Buddhism, becoming its first important royal patron. He is believed to have encouraged missionary work throughout much of Asia, including to the borders of China. The Aśoka Temple described in this essay is located in modern Yin district, Chekiang, near the city of Ningpo and was first built in 425.

2. *Shorea* (or *Valeria*) *robusta*, sometimes identified as the teak tree. It has a particularly close association with Śākyamuni Buddha because of the twin *śāla* trees in the grove where he entered nirvana.

3. The Wan-li emperor of the Ming dynasty reigned from 1572 to 1620.

4. This would be the reliquary dome-shaped shrine within the temple grounds. It was thought to contain a part of the remains of the historical Buddha. The stūpa (from Sanskrit *stūpaḥ*) or tope (from Prakrit *thūpo*) is both linguistically and architecturally the source of the Chinese pagoda (*t'a*, from [*su-*]*t'ou-p'o* or *t'a*[*-p'o*], etc., which are transcriptions of Indian words).

any visions from the relic and died later that year. There have been numerous confirmations of this power.

The morning after my arrival when the sun had just begun to shine, a monk escorted me to it where I offered prayers to the Buddha. He opened the bronze stūpa. A purple sandalwood shrine contained a smaller stūpa shaped like a hexagonal brush-holder, though of neither wood, nor mulberry bark, nor leather, nor lacquer. Its top and bottom were covered with hide. It was pierced all around with ornamental designs and the corners were decorated with Sanskrit letters. The relic was suspended from the top of the stūpa and hung down, swaying back and forth. One stared intently through the open-work, then turned one's eyes upward to look at the relic to discern its shape. At first glance, I saw three pearls strung together like Śākyamuni's Chain shining brilliantly.[5] I bowed down again and sought a vision. When I looked at it once more, I saw a small image of White-robed Kuan-yin,[6] whose eyebrows and eyes were clearly defined and whose side-locks were clearly visible. Ch'in Yi-sheng looked at it again and again but, in the end, saw nothing. He trembled with fright, turned red, and left weeping. Indeed, Ch'in Yi-sheng died in the eighth month of that year. What an amazing confirmation of its power!

Translated by Richard Strassberg.

5. Śākyamuni's Chain was a string of pearls believed to have been manufactured by Śākyamuni, the historical Buddha. Such a relic was worshipped in Shantung province.

6. The Bodhisattva Kuan-yin (from Sanskrit Avalokiteśvara, "Hearer of the Cries of the World") is frequently depicted seated on a white lotus.

Liu Ching-t'ing[1] the Storyteller

Chang Tai

Pockmarked Liu from Nanking had a swarthy face that was covered all over with bumpy scars. He was relaxed and at ease, but his body looked as though it were made out of wood or clay. Liu was good at telling stories.[2] Each day he would tell one chapter of a story, for which he charged an ounce of silver. Whoever wanted to invite Liu for a storytelling session had to send him the program and earnest money ten days in advance. Even then he was often too busy to come. In those days there were two extremely popular performers

1. Born in 1587.
2. The word used here is *shuo-shu* (literally, "say/explain book") which refers to a specific genre of Chinese oral performing arts.

in Nanking; one was the songstress, Moonbeam Wang, and the other was Pockmarked Liu.

I once heard Liu tell the plain text[3] of "Wu Sung Beats the Tiger on Ching-yang Ridge."[4] It was quite different from what was written in the book.[5] His descriptions were graphic and went into the tiniest details, yet he was very clear-cut about when to be expansive and when to stop short and was by no means garrulous. Liu's full voice was like a giant bell and, as the story reached a climax, his stentorian exclamations were so awesome that they shook the house. When Liu told how Wu Sung went into the wine-shop to order a drink and found no one there, he gave a mighty roar that made all of the empty jugs and jars in the shop reverberate. Even when there was a lull in the plot, he would spruce it up, so particular was he about minutiae.

The sponsors of a performance by Liu had to sit quietly with bated breath and listen attentively before he would begin to wag his tongue. If he saw anybody in the audience murmuring or whispering, or if one of the auditors yawned or stretched, he would stop speaking immediately and no one could force him to continue. Often it would be the middle of the night, when his table had been wiped clean, the lampwick trimmed, and he was sipping tea from a white porcelain cup, before Liu would begin slowly to tell his story. The pace and emphasis of Liu's narrative, the quality and amplitude of his delivery—all were perfectly in accord with sentiment and reason, and all struck a deep chord in the fiber of every listener's being. If you could grab all of the storytellers in the world by the ear and make them listen carefully to him, rest assured that even they would gasp in wonderment.

Pockmarked Liu's face was unusually ugly, but his enunciation was precise, his eyes were expressive, and his clothes were spotless. Thus he was as handsome as Moonbeam Wang was beautiful, and his standing in the enter-tainment world was equally high.

Translated by Victor H. Mair

3. "Plain" refers to the spoken language as opposed to singing. In other contexts, it refers to the classical book language (in which verse was most likely to be composed).
4. See selection 261.
5. *River Banks* (*Shui-hu chuan*, also translated as *Water Margins* and *All Men Are Brothers*).

Professional Matchmakers

from *Dream Memories of West Lake*

Chang Tai

At Yangchow, there were hundreds of people making a living from activities connected with the "lean horses." One should never let it be known that one was looking for a concubine. Once this leaked out, the professional agents and go-betweens, both men and women, would swarm about his house or hotel like flies, and there was no way of keeping them off. The next morning, he would find many of them waiting for him, and the matchmaker who arrived first would hustle him off, while the rest followed behind and waited for their chance.

Arriving at the house of the "lean horse," the person would be served tea as soon as he was seated. At once the woman agent would come out with a girl and announce, "*Ku-niang,*[1] curtsy!" The girl curtsied. Next was said, "*Ku-niang,* walk forward!" She walked forward. "*Ku-niang,* turn around!" She turned around, facing the light, and her face was shown. "Pardon, can we have a look at your hand?" The woman rolled up her sleeve and exposed her entire arm. Her skin was shown. "*Ku-niang,* look at the gentleman." She looked from the corner of her eyes. Her eyes were shown. "How old is *Ku-niang?*" She replied. Her voice was shown. "Please walk again a bit." This time the woman lifted her skirts. Her feet were shown. There is a secret about judging women's feet. When you hear the rustle of her skirts when she comes out, you may guess that she has big feet, but if she wears her skirts relatively high and reveals her feet as she takes a step forward, you already know that she has a pair of small feet that she is proud of. "*Ku-niang,* you can go back."

As soon as the girl went in, another came out, and the same thing was repeated. Usually there were five or six girls in a house. If the gentleman decided he would take a certain girl, he would put a gold hairpin or ornament on her hair; this was called *tsatai.* If no one was satisfactory, a tip of several hundred cash was given the woman agent or the maids of the house, and one was shown another house. When one woman agent had completed the round of the houses she operated with, other women agents came around. Thus it continued for one, two, perhaps four or five days. There was no end to it and the agents were

The original title is "Lean Horses," a local name for matchmakers. The author describes the practice of Yangchow, nationally famed as the center of luxury and the place where regular houses trained girls to be singsong artists or concubines. The time was the early seventeenth century.

This piece describes what may be called the "concubine market" and its efficiency. It is the most unromantic way of securing a mistress; only coarse businessmen would buy a concubine this way.

1. Mademoiselle.

never tired. But after one had seen fifty or sixty of them, they were all just about alike, with a painted face and a red dress. It is like writing characters; by the time you have made the same sign a hundred times or a thousand times, you cannot recognize it any more. One does not know what to decide or which one to take, and eventually makes his choice on one of them.

After the choice was made, signaled by *tsatai*, the owner came out with a red sheet of paper and a writing brush. On the paper were written the items: silks, gold flowers, cash present, and pieces of cloth. The owner would dip the brush in ink and hold it ready for the customer to fill in the number of pieces and the cash present he was prepared to give for the girl. If this was satisfactory, the deal was concluded and the customer took his leave.

Before he arrived at his own place, drummers and musicians and carrier-loads of lamb and red and green wines were already there. In a moment, ceremonial papers, fruit, and pastry also arrived, and the senders went back accompanied by the musicians. Before they had gone a quarter mile, there came back with the band floral sedan chairs, floral lanterns, torches, handled torches, sedan chair carriers, bridesmaids, candles, more fruit, and roasts. The cook arrived with a carrier-load of vegetables and meats, sweets, followed by awnings, tablecloths, chair cushions, table service, longevity stars, bed curtains and stringed instruments. Without notice and even without asking for approval, the floral sedan chair and another chair supposed to accompany the bride started off to welcome the bride with a procession of bridal lanterns and handled torches. Before you knew it, the bride had arrived. The bride came up and performed the wedding ceremony,[2] and she was ushered to take her place at the dinner table already laid. Music and song began, and there was much ado about the house. Everything was efficient and fast. Before noon, the agent asked for her tip, said good-bye, and rushed off to look for other customers.

Translated by Lin Yutang

2. By bowing to the groom and guests.

209
Account of a Peach-Stone Boat

Wei Hsüeh-yi (c. 1606–c. 1625)

During the Ming period there was an ingeniously skilled craftsman named Wang Shu-yüan who could make houses, implements, human figures, and

Late Ming society displayed a particular fondness for such minor arts as inside-painted snuff bottles, decorated incense burners, detailed ivory figurines, elaborately carved buckles, and even birds, beasts, trees, and rocks from a piece of wood an inch in diameter. He never failed to image the shape of an object in accord with the configuration of his raw material, and each of his creations possessed its own sentiment and mood.

Wang bequeathed to me a peach-stone boat that might well be entitled "The Elder Su Drifting on the River at Red Cliff." From stem to stem the boat was approximately eight tenths plus a fraction of an inch long, and its height was roughly that of a bit more than two millet grains. In the center was a lofty, spacious part which served as the cabin. This was covered by a mat made of broad-leaved bamboo. Small windows were inserted on the sides, four each to the left and the right for a total of eight shutters. When the windows were thrown open and you looked in, you could see across to the carved railings on the opposite side. If you closed them, on the right was engraved "MOUNTAINS HIGH MOON SMALL; WATER RECEDES STONES EMERGE," and on the left was engraved PURE WIND SLOWLY COMES; WATERY WAVES NOT RISE." The characters were filled in with azurite pigment.

Seated in the prow were three men. In the center, with a high-peaked cap, was East Slope (Su Tung-p'o).[1] To his right was Buddha Imprint[2] and to his left was Simple Straight (Huang T'ing-chien).[3] Su and Huang were reading a handscroll together. East Slope held the beginning of the scroll with his right hand and was patting Simple Straight's back with his left hand. Simple Straight held the end of the scroll with his left hand and was pointing to the scroll with his right hand, as though he were saying something. East Slope's right foot was showing and Simple Straight's left foot was showing. Both of their bodies were leaning slightly. Their two knees that were next to each other were hidden beneath the bottom of the scroll and in the folds of their clothing. Buddha Imprint bore an extremely close resemblance to Maitreya.[4] His chest was bare and his breasts were revealed. Head raised, he was looking upward in a spirit quite unlike that of Su and Huang. His right knee was stretched out horizontally, and his bent right arm was supported by the boat

---

engraved seals. This sort of kitschy craftsmanship, which fueled European chinoiserie in the following centuries, was mirrored in literature by a taste for intricately descriptive essays. Art and literature come together in this famous piece inspired by an actual object, the likes of which may still be seen—with the aid of a magnifying glass—in the National Palace Museum (Taipei, Taiwan). The boat made of a kernel was, in turn, inspired by Su Shih's celebrated "Red Cliff Rhapsody" (selection 156 in this volume), which is quoted directly by Wei Hsüeh-yi.

The author, a brilliant young student, died of grief over the death of his father at the hands of the notorious eunuch faction of the Ming court.

1. Su Shih, the famous Sung period scholar-official and author of the "Red Cliff Rhapsody."

2. Fo-yin, a monkish friend of Su Tung-p'o.

3. A celebrated calligrapher and poet who was also a close associate of Su Tung-p'o (see selection 73).

4. The Buddha of the future. Popularly referred to as the "Laughing Buddha," he is usually depicted with an exposed fat belly.

while he dangled a rosary from his left arm, which rested on his perpendicular left knee. The rosary beads could be counted one by one.

A scull was lying horizontally across the stern. To the left and right of the scull there were two boatmen. The one on the right side had his hair tied up in the shape of a mallet. His left hand was braced against a horizontal board and his right hand was grabbing his right toes. He looked as though he were shouting. The one on the left held a fan made of palm leaves in his right hand and was touching a stove with his left hand. On top of the stove was a kettle. The man had a fixed gaze and a quiet expression, as though he were listening to the tea-water.

The back of the boat was rather even and the craftsman had written an inscription on its surface. The inscription read: "Carved by Wang Yi, styled Shu-yüan, of Yü-shan,[5] on an autumn day in the *jen-hsü* year[6] of the Heavenly Revelation." The characters, black in color, were fine as the legs of a spider, yet each of the strokes was clearly distinct. There was also a seal, red in color, written in an archaic script. It read: "Hermit of Ch'u-p'ing."[7]

If we calculate for the whole boat, there were five men, eight windows, one broad-leaved bamboo mat, one scull, one stove, one kettle, one handscroll, and one rosary. All together, there were thirty-four characters in the matching couplets, the inscription, and seal. Yet, when we calculate the length of the boat, it was not even a full inch. As a matter of fact, the craftsman had made it from a long, narrow peach-stone that he had selected. After I had finished scrutinizing the boat in detail, I marveled, "Ah! that skill could be so preternatural! There are a good many stories recorded in the *Chuang Tzu*[8] and the *Lieh Tzu*[9] in which beholders are startled by those who possess supernatural skills, yet who among them could let a knife play freely in a piece of material less than an inch in size while producing figures with beards and eyebrows that are clearly visible? If someone were to repeat my own words to me, I would certainly suspect that they were exaggerating. But now I have seen the peach-stone boat with my own eyes. Judging from what I have observed, it is not necessarily impossible to carve a female monkey on the tip of a jujube thorn.[10] Ah! that skill could be so preternatural!"

Translated by Victor H. Mair

5. In the province of Kiangsu.

6. I.e., 1622.

7. Ch'u-p'ing is the soubriquet of Wang Yi (Shu-yüan). It is likely that he adopted this fancy name from the legend of Huang Ch'u-p'ing, a Taoist recluse for more than forty years and said to have been able to metamorphose rocks into goats.

8. See selection 9.

9. See selection 12.

10. A feat falsely claimed by a couple of tricksters in the book attributed to Master Han Fei (d. 233 B.C.E).

210
The Vocal Mimic

Lin Ssu-huan (fl. c. 1644–1661)

In the capital,[1] there was a man who was good at vocal mimicry. On the occasion of a great banquet to which many guests were invited, a screen eight feet in height was set up in the northeast corner of the hall. The vocal mimic was seated behind the screen. His only properties were a table, a chair, a fan, and a ruler that he used as a clapper. The assembled guests were seated around the front of the screen. After a short while, they heard from behind the screen the sound of the ruler being struck against the table once, whereupon the entire audience grew quiet. No one dared to make any more noise.

Far off, they heard a dog barking in a deep alley, then a woman who was startled awake stretched and yawned while her husband mumbled in his sleep. Before long, her baby woke up and started bawling loudly, causing the husband to wake up too. He told the woman to soothe the baby by letting it nurse, but the baby continued to cry while sucking on her teat, so she patted it and cooed to it. The husband got up to urinate, and the wife got up to urinate while still holding the baby. Then an older child who was on the bed also woke up and began to jabber unceasingly. By this time, the sounds of the wife patting her baby and cooing to it, the baby sucking on her teat, the older child as he was waking up, and the husband scolding the older child were all issuing simultaneously, and each sound was performed to marvelous perfection. All of the guests who were seated in the audience craned their necks, strained their eyes sideways, smiled, and sighed in silent admiration, thinking to themselves how utterly wonderful it all was.

Before long, the husband got back in bed and went to sleep. The wife told the older child to go pee and, when he had finished, they got back in bed and went to sleep too. Gradually, even the baby began to fall asleep. As the husband started to snore, the sounds of the wife patting her baby gradually became intermittent. Then there were the faint sounds of a rat scrabbling about, a bowl being knocked over, and the woman coughing while she dreamed. The guests felt a bit more relaxed and sat up a little more straight.

Suddenly, somebody loudly shouted, "Fire!" The husband got up and started shouting loudly too and the wife did likewise. Both of the children were crying and soon there was a multitude of people shouting, children crying, and dogs barking. Amidst this commotion were the multitudinous sounds of houses collapsing with a thud, fire crackling, and wind howling all

Next to nothing is known of the author other than that he hailed from Chin-chiang in the province of Fukien and that he passed the Presented Scholar examination sometime between 1644 and 1661.

1. Peking.

at once. And interspersed among all the rest were the multitudinous sounds of people calling for help or coming to the rescue, of people pulling down houses[2] with a heave and a ho, of saving things from the fire, and of splashing water. Whatever sounds would be expected of a conflagration were all to be heard. Even if you had a hundred hands and every hand had a hundred fingers, you wouldn't be able to point out each of them. And if you had a hundred mouths and every mouth had a hundred tongues, you wouldn't be able to name each of them.

The result was that all of the guests got up from their seats with ashen faces, rolled-up sleeves, and wobbly legs. Just as they were on the verge of scrambling to get out ahead of the others, the ruler struck against the table once and the myriad echoing sounds came to a halt. When the screen was removed, all that could be seen were a man, a table, a chair, a fan, and a ruler.

Translated by Victor H. Mair

2. This would have been done for one of two reasons: to stop the path of the fire or for safety's sake if a building was already tottering.

211

The Arts of Sleeping, Walking, Sitting, and Standing

from *The Arts of Living*

Li Yü (1610/11–1680)

There are many ways of enjoying life that are hard to hold down to any one theory. There are the joys of sleeping, of sitting, of walking, and of standing up. There is the pleasure in eating, washing up, hairdressing, and even in such lowly activities as going about naked and barefooted, or going to the toilet. In its proper place, each can be enjoyable. If one can enter into the spirit of fun and take things in his stride anywhere any time, one can enjoy

Li Yü was a most original and versatile writer who was not so much a scholar as an artist of living. Aside from writing the preface for the well-known *Guide to Painting from the Mustard Seed Garden*, he was also the author of a number of popular works, including one on making couplets. The book entitled *The Arts of Living* or *Sketches of Idle Pleasure* gives his always original thoughts on musical plays, acting, houses and their interiors, food and drink, horticulture, and sundry other subjects. For additional information on Li, see selection 257.

some things over which others may weep. On the other hand, if one is a crude person and awkward in meeting life or taking care of one's health, he can be the saddest person amidst song and dance. I speak here only of the joys of daily living and of the ways in which advantage may be taken of the commonest occupations.

1. The Art of Sleeping

There was a yogi who traveled about, teaching the secrets of conservation of life force and of prolonging life, and he wanted me to be his pupil. I asked him what he could do to attain longevity and where such blessings were to be found. I thought it would be fine if his methods agreed with my way of thinking, and if not, I could at least befriend him.

This man told me that the secret of longevity lay in controlled breathing, and peace of mind was to be sought through séance. I said to him, "Your ways are hard and forced, and only people like you can practice it. I am lazy and like motion. I seek joy in everything. I am afraid it is not for me."

"What is your way then?" he asked. "I should like to hear it, and we can compare notes."

And this is what I said to him:

In the natural scheme of things, it is meant for man to spend half his time in activity and half at rest. In the day, he sits, moves, or stands, and at night, he rests. If a man labors by day and does not rest by night and continues this day after day, you can get ready and wait for his funeral to pass by. I try to keep my health by dividing half my time in rest and half my time in activity. If something troubles me and prevents me from sleep, there's the danger signal! I should count my remaining years on my fingers!

In other words, the secret of good health lies in a good and restful sleep. One who sleeps well restores his energy, revitalizes his inner system, and tones up his muscles. If you do not believe me, compare a sick man with a healthy person. A man who is not permitted to rest will get sick; his eyes become sunken, and all kinds of symptoms appear. A sick man becomes worse without sleep. But after a good sleep, he wakes up full of eagerness for life again. Is not sleep the infallible miracle drug, not just a cure for one illness but for a hundred, a cure that saves a thousand lives? To seek health by controlled breathing and the hard exercises of sitting in meditation would only involve great concentration and effort to keep awake instead! Would I throw away the best medicine in the world for an untested formula?

The man left abruptly, considering me not worth his time. And, indeed, I am not worth his teaching: I merely presented what I myself had achieved, sincerely for the sake of discussion, to see clearly which way is better.

An ancient poem goes, "After a long, sound sleep in bamboo-shaded quiet,

I feel so far removed from the day's turmoil. If the hermit of Huashan comes to visit me, I shall not ask for the secret of becoming an immortal, but of sleeping well." A modern saying goes, "First rest your mind, then rest your eyes."

There is a proper time and a proper place for sleep, and there are certain sleeping habits which should be avoided. To be specific, one should rest between 9 P.M. and 8 A.M. To go to bed before nine is too early; it is a bad sign to be craving for sleep like a sick person. To sleep after eight in the morning is bad for health, like all oversleeping. Where would be the time left for other pleasures?

I know a friend who never gets up before noon, and anyone visiting him before noon is kept waiting. One day I sat miserably in his parlor waiting, and with ink and brush ready, I playfully parodied an ancient poem and wrote as follows

> I am busy sleeping,
> Throughout the whole morn.
> If I live to seventy,
> Five and thirty are gone.

Although it was done in fun, it is close to the truth. One should only sleep at night as a rule. The pleasure of an afternoon nap is understandable, but it should be reserved only for summer when the day is long and the night is short. It is natural that one tires easily in the heat, and it is as good for a man to sleep when tired as to drink when thirsty. This is common sense. The best time is after lunch. One should wait a while until the food is partly digested and then leisurely stroll toward the couch. Do not tell yourself that you are determined to get a nap. In that way, the mind is tense and the sleep will not be sound. Occupy yourself with something first and before it is finished, you are overcome with a sense of fatigue and the sandman calls. The never-never land cannot be chased down. I love that line in a poem which says, "Dozing off, the book slips out of my hand." Thus sleep comes without his artifice or knowledge. This is the secret of the art of sleeping.

Next, one must consider the place, which should be cool and quiet. If it is not quiet, the eyes rest but not the ears. If it is too hot, the soul rests but not the body, and body and soul are at loggerheads. This goes against the principle of good health.

Lastly, we will consider the sleeper himself. Some people are busy, and others have plenty of time. Logically, the man of leisure needs little sleep; it is the busy man who needs it most of all. But often the busy man cannot sleep well. He rests his eyes in sleep but not his mind. In fact, he gets no rest from sleep at all. The worst of it is to think of something during the half-awake hours of the morning and suddenly remember something he hasn't done or someone he hasn't seen. It is very, very important! He must not sleep another wink or something will be spoiled! That very thought drives away all sleep. He becomes tense and gets up more keyed up than before. Such is the rest of the busy man. The man of leisure rests his mind before his eyes are shut, and his mind wakes up refreshed before his eyes are open, happy to slumber and happier to wake up. Such is the sleep of the man of leisure.

Yet in this world how many such idle men are there? All men cannot lead a life with nothing to do. Therefore a method must be found. It is best to dispose of the urgent business of the day in the morning, and delegate to others those things that are not finished. Then one knows that everything is in order and under control. He can afford to seek the pillow and go for that slumber which is described as the "dark, sweet village." He will then sleep as well as the man of leisure.

Another thing: to enjoy a perfect sleep requires a peaceful conscience. Such a man will not be "frightened when there is a knock on the door at midnight," as the saying goes. He will not mistake the peckings of chickens in the barnyard for policemen's footsteps!

2. The Art of Walking

The rich man will go out only in a horse and carriage. It may be called a comfort and a luxury, but it can hardly be said that it fulfills the intention of the Creator in giving man a pair of legs. He who does not use his legs is by that very fact deprived of the use of his legs. On the other hand, a man who uses his legs is giving exercise to his entire body. That is why an ancient poor scholar[1] boasted that "a leisurely stroll is as good as a drive." Now to drive or to go on foot are both methods of transportation or locomotion. A man who is used to driving or riding on horseback can learn to enjoy the pleasures of a walk. Perhaps he comes upon a beautiful view or beautiful flowers on the way, or stops to talk with a peasant in his palm hat or meets a recluse philosopher-turned-woodcutter in the deep mountains. Sometimes one might enjoy a drive, and sometimes a walk. Surely this is better than the obstinacy of that proud scholar of ancient days!

What the poor man can be truly proud of is not the fact that he uses his legs, but that he does not depend on others for going anywhere. If he is not in a hurry, he can go slowly, and if he is, he breaks into a run. He does not have to wait for someone else, and he is not dependent on the carriage, unlike the rich man who is helpless when the driver is not there. The poor man has fulfilled the intentions of the Creator in giving him legs to walk with. It makes me happy just to think of this.

1. Yen Cho, of the third century B.C.E., was a Diogenes who refused gifts of money and power from a king.

3. The Art of Sitting

No one knew the art of living better than Confucius. I know this from the statement that he "did not sleep like a corpse[2] and did not sit like a statue." If the Master had been completely absorbed in keeping decorum, intent on appearing like a gentleman at all hours and being seen as a sage at all times, then he would have had to lie down like a corpse and sit like a statue. His four limbs and his internal system would never have been able to relax. How could such a stiff wooden statue expect to live a long life? Because Confucius did not do this, the statement describes the ease of the Master in his private life, which makes him worthy of worship as the father of all cultured gentlemen. We should follow Confucius' example when at home. Do not sit erect and look severe as if you were chained or glued to the chair. Hug your knee and sing, or sit chin in hand, without honoring it with the phrase of "losing oneself in thought."[3] On the other hand, if a person sits stiffly for a long time, head high and chest out, this is a premonition that he is heading for the grave. He is sitting for his memorial portrait!

4. The Art of Standing

Stand straight, but do not do it for long. Otherwise, all leg muscles will become stiff and circulation will be blocked up. Lean on something!—on an old pine or a quaint rock, or on a balcony or on a bamboo cane. It makes one look like one is in a painting. But do *not* lean on a lady! The foundation is not solid and the roof may come down!

Translated by Lin Yutang

2. With straight legs.
3. As Chuang Tzu said (see selection 9).

212

Thoughts upon Student Huang's Borrowing of Books

Yüan Mei (1716–1797)

The student, Huang Yün-hsiu, asked to borrow some books from me and I, the master of Sui Garden,[1] gave them to him with the following admonition:

For information on the author, see selection 106.
1. The name of Yüan Mei's estate north of Nanking, the ostensible meaning of which is "Follow Garden" (see the second item in selection 106).

If you don't borrow books, you can't read them. Have you not heard about those who collect books? The "Seven Categories"[2] and the "Four Divisions"[3] were imperial collections, but how many emperors actually read them? Books fill the homes of the rich and the honored to the very rafters, but how many of the rich and the honored actually read them? As for all the fathers and grandfathers who have amassed books only to see their sons and grandsons throw them away, there's no need to discuss it.

But it's not just books that are treated like this; everything under heaven is treated the same way. If we manage to borrow something that is not our own, we worry that someone will force us to give it back and so we fondle it fearfully without end, saying, "Today I have it; tomorrow it may be gone and then I won't see it any more!" If it's something that already belongs to us, then we wrap it up and put it on a high shelf, storing it away and saying, "I'll leave it there for the time being and take a peek at it later on."

When I was young, I loved books but my father was poor, so it was hard to get hold of them. There was a Mr. Chang who had a rich collection of books; I went to borrow some from him but he wouldn't give me any. When I returned home, I had a dream about my unsuccessful attempt to borrow books, which shows how eager my desire was. Thus, when I did get to read something, I invariably remembered it. After I became an official and was established in my own residence, as I spent out my salary the books came pouring in till they were piled up everywhere in great profusion and the scrolls and tomes were covered with silverfish and cobwebs. Later I would sigh with admiration at the attentiveness with which those who borrowed books read them and think how precious the months and years of one's youth are.

Now, Student Huang, you are poor like I used to be and you borrow books like I used to. It would seem that the only difference is that I share my books with you whereas Mr. Chang was stingy with his books to me. But was I unfortunate to have encountered Mr. Chang? And are you fortunate to have encountered me? To know whether someone is fortunate or not, it depends on how diligently he reads the books he has borrowed and how swiftly he returns them. To explain my thoughts on borrowing, I am sending this note[4] along with the books.

Translated by Victor H. Mair

2. Divisions of the Imperial Library assembled by Liu Hsiang (77–6 B.C.E.) and his son, Liu Hsin (c. 50 B.C.E.–23 C.E.) for the Han emperor Ch'eng Ti. Compare selections 238, 242, and especially 243, note 4.

3. Probably short for "Complete Library in Four Divisions" (*Ssu-k'u ch'üan-shu*), an enormous project initiated by the Ch'ien-lung emperor in 1772, although the bibliographical term "Four Divisions" goes back well over a thousand years before that time (see selection 248, introductory note).

4. Here and in the title, this piece is actually called a *shuo* ("explanation") by the author.

213

Mr. Jan Cooks His Dog

Ts'ui Shu (1740–1816)

There was a man in our district surnamed Jan who had a fierce dog. Whenever it saw a passerby, the dog would immediately lunge and bite at him. Often people would be injured, and the owner of the dog would have to go and make apologies himself. Many were the occasions on which he had to pay for medical treatment. Jan was much troubled by his dog on account of this but, because it was such a fierce watchdog, he could not bear to put it to death, so he tried to ignore the situation.

Liu Li-tung said to me, "Once I was returning late at night and was about a tricent away from the gate to my house. All the dogs in the village were barking loudly, and Jan's dog also came rushing forward to bark at me. I fended the other dogs off with a willow switch and they kept their distance, only Jan's dog kept lunging at me and almost bit me several times. Trembling as I went, I finally got past Jan's gate and continued east. It was only after I had gone several dozen paces that the dog finally stopped. By that time, I was extremely exhausted. Fortunately, however, I gradually put enough distance between the dog and me that I could rest by the side of the road. After quite a while, I began to walk again, but the dog was still looking at me and barking. After I reached home, I thought what a fine dog Jan had. If a robber or an enemy of his came during the night to steal something, the dog would bar the doorway and snarl at them so that, even if there were a couple of dozen men, they wouldn't be able to make an inch of headway into the room.

"I've heard that Jan was so troubled by his dog that if perchance you met him with it in the market, he would have to keep commanding it not to kill. This was a dog that you couldn't buy even if you scraped together a thousand pieces of gold!

"Several days later, Jan's neighbor came to visit me and I asked him about the dog. 'He cooked it,' the neighbor said. Surprised, I asked the neighbor why he had done so. 'A few days ago, Jan was awakened by thieves and he called out to his two sons who drove them off with staves. Frightened, the thieves ran away. Jan thought it strange that the dog hadn't barked at them and, when he called to it, the dog didn't respond. He looked all around for the dog but couldn't find it. As he was getting ready to go back to sleep, he heard a faint breathing sound beneath his bed. When he shone a candle there, it turned out to be the dog. It was crouching in a curled-up position and dared

---

The author was a serious and critical evidential scholar who, among other significant achievements, proved that the final five chapters of the *Analects* of Confucius (see selection 7) were dated later than the rest of the text. He was not at all above collecting strange tales and jotting down curious anecdotes, though he often strove to draw some moral lessons from them.

not make the slightest movement. It hung its head and had its eyes closed, as though it were afraid someone might hear its breathing. 'Damn!' said the owner. 'I've tolerated it all along and didn't put it to death because I thought that it might be of some use in an emergency. Who would have thought that it's only brave when it lunges at passersby, but when it sees a thief it shrinks back cowardly?' That's why he cooked it."

Alas! Under heaven, is it only this dog that is brave in lunging at people but cowardly when it sees a robber? The scoundrels who hang around the markets and wells these days commonly cause disturbances by behaving like tyrants in the villages and hamlets. Some of them find irregular employment as district yamen[1] runners while others sponge off the army. They insult those who are civil or young, abuse those who are good or weak. When they pass through the market, everybody stays far away from them. If they get angry at someone, they call their gang together and circle around the person to club him with their staves. No one dares say a word, as though they were warriors. But if perchance there's a band of petty thieves, it takes no less than a hundred and several dozen of these scoundrels armed with weapons to protect the government offices. If a horse suddenly gets spooked in the night, they think that thieves have arrived and their hands begin to shake so badly that they can't pull their swords out of their scabbards. If by luck they do manage to get them out, then they make a big racket by striking them together. When they have to ignite a rocket or other gunpowder device, they could try half a dozen times and it still would not light. When they hear that they're about to be sent to an outpost, even though it be several hundred tricents from the bandits and only a couple of marches from their homes, they immediately begin to wail tearfully as they take leave of their parents, wife, and children, fearful that they'll never see them again. This is how pusillanimous they are! Therefore, I ask, when it comes to those who are brave in private quarrels but cowardly in public battles, why should we merely take exception to dogs and cook them? Ai! this is really too much.

Those who raise cats do so because they want them to catch rats; those who raise dogs do so because they want them to guard against thieves. But if they cannot fulfill those duties, then truly they're not of much use. This is all the more so if they go around biting people. If such be the case, why keep them? Shih Lo wanted to kill Shih Hu,[2] but his mother said to him, "A fast ox is bound to wreck a few carts while it's still young. Just try to put up with him for a little while." Afterward, the royal line of the Shih family in the end was destroyed by Hu. One should not be heedless of the ox that wrecks carts

1. District government office.
2. Shih Lo (reigned 319–330) was the non-Chinese founder of the Later Chao kingdom in the area of modern Shansi and Honan. Shih Hu, his nephew, was a murderous ruffian appointed to the prime ministership by Shih Hung, the son of Shih Lo, after the death of the latter. It was not long before Shih Hu killed Shih Hung and founded his own dynasty.

simply because one likes to go fast; still less should one be heedless of the ox that wrecks carts but doesn't even go fast. But the humanitarian impulse of women has ever and always been the same. Viewed from this perspective, Jan's wisdom far exceeds that of other people.

People's talents may be great in some respects, but they will necessarily be lacking in others; only the superior man is different. When Chung Yü[3] had archery contests with his advisers and assistants, Wei Shu[4] would keep score. Once, it happened that there were not enough contestants, so they asked Wei Shu to fill in. Each of his shots hit the target, startling all those who were present. When Yü Ta-yu[5] spoke to people, he was as polite as any Confucian literatus. But when the war drums were beating and he was standing beside the garrison gate, his courage multiplied a hundredfold, so that no one could overcome him in battle. Men such as these are indeed few and far between. Next are those who are honest and circumspect, but who are not capable of great achievements. Next after that are those who are careless and incompetent, but who can work together on things. If someone is only capable of harming others but cannot help get things done, he's no better than a dog! Nevertheless, I have heard of a certain person who has a dog that normally never barks the whole night long, but when it does bark, its owner knows that there are thieves about. In this case, we have a dog that is better than some people. However, if a dog only lunges and snarls at passersby but does not protect against thieves, then it is an inferior specimen among its own kind.

Translated by Victor H. Mair

3. A high-ranking official of the kingdom of Wei during the Three Kingdoms period.

4. Senior Subaltern to Chung Yü, he had a reputation for being somewhat of a slow simpleton, so no one paid much attention to him.

5. A general of the Ming dynasty famous for suppressing pirates.

Travelogues and Scenic Descriptions

214

A Poem on Wandering at the Stone Gate, with Introduction

Laymen of Mount Lu Associated with Hui-yüan (344–416/17)

The Stone Gate is over ten tricents south of the *vihāra*,[1] and is also known as Screen Mountain. Its base joins the great range of Mount Lu, and its form

The preface and accompanying poem on wandering at the Stone Gate Gorge of Mount Lu in 400 C.E. have long been associated with the charismatic Buddhist monk Hui-yüan and his community of monks and laymen who studied and practiced Buddhism on Mount Lu (Kiangsi province). Hui-yüan himself is referred to in the preface as "the Master of the Doctrine," and hence is unlikely to be the author. Among his influential literary lay disciples were two avid mountain-climbers who mention in their writings a Stone Gate that may be the Mount Lu Gorge. One was Tsung Ping (375–443), a Buddhist apologist, musician, and landscapist, who defended Hui-yüan's doctrine of the immortal spirit and believed in the direct experience of a limitless universe newly conceived from the reading of Buddhist texts. The other was the poet Hsieh Ling-yün (385–433, see selection 30), a rugged individualist who nonetheless felt the need of an understanding mind to share his "landscape Buddhism," a mystical insight into the natural order.

Like other sacred sites where spectacular scenery and fantastic rock formations were taken as a sign of the supernatural, Mount Lu had been hallowed by popular Taoism before it became a center of Buddhist learning, and appreciations of its views were already being written in Han times. Although the preface on the Stone Gate expedition offers an explicit definition of the experience of nature in a Buddhist context, it was evidently influenced by the famous "Preface to the Festival at the Orchid Pavilion," written by Wang Hsi-chih (303–379) at the gathering of 353 C.E. in the Kuei-chi district (Chekiang province) (see selection 200). Like the poetry-writing contest during the spring purification festival at the Orchid Pavilion, the "landscape Buddhism" rises above the clustered hills. It constitutes the juncture of three streams; standing close together, it initiates their currents. The inclining cliffs darkly gleam from above; they receive their external shapes from Nature. On this account it was named the Stone Gate. Although this spot is but one corner of the Lu range, nonetheless it is the most extraordinary view of the region. All this was known through earlier accounts, but there were many who had never seen it themselves. This was perhaps due to the fact that the waterfall was so precipitous that trails for men and beasts were cut off, and, since paths wind about twisting hills, access was blocked and walking difficult. Hence few people have visited it.

In the second month of spring in the fourth year of Lung-an (400 C.E.), Shih Hui-yüan, the Master of the Doctrine, who had been hymning the landscape, accordingly took up his ringed abbot's staff and wandered off. On this occasion there were some thirty men of like mind among his companions. Together we donned our robes and set off at dawn in low spirits but increasingly exhilarated. Although the forests were gloomy and valleys deep, we still broke a path through and vied to push forward. And ascending the heights and treading on rock we were wholly at ease through what gave us pleasure. On reaching the gorge, we pulled ourselves up by trees and grasped for

---

of Mount Lu was a communal experience of emotional release in a setting of great natural beauty. Esthetic impressions served to stimulate meditation or focus the mind in a manner similar to Hui-yüan's devotional practice of visualizing the Buddha's body. Hui-yüan also fostered a strong feeling of community among his lay disciples. In a collective vow made during the year 402 for rebirth in the Western Paradise, all present were to help one another ascend to the supernatural realm of the mountain paradise, "mindful of the principle of marching together!" The smaller group of men who climbed the Stone Gate two years earlier were moved to express their shared joy in a communal hymn.

The occasion described in the introduction to "A Poem on Wandering at the Stone Gate" requires little explanation. Interestingly enough, Hui-yüan and his companions are inspired to climb by poems on landscape. Through their efforts they gain a view, which is initially characterized in general terms; then they note the layout of mountain and rock formations that seem to indicate the palace grounds of the immortals. Illusory qualities of shapes are underlined by shifting light and atmospheric effects, and a feeling of spatial disorientation is given by the blurring of sense impressions. These accidental perceptions arouse a selfless delight, which is then analyzed by the group as the correct response to phenomena. At sunset the view from on high suggests the vast scale of the universe; in turn this stimulates thoughts of eternal time and the remoteness of the Buddha. After meditating on him for a while, the group is moved by a shared emotion to compose a poem on their experience. Despite a few Taoist references, it treats the climb up the cliffs of the Stone Gate as a stage in a spiritual ascent that leads through meditation to nirvana. In the preface, purification of the mind through the perception of emptiness allows it to respond correctly without emotion and to seek the merging with the universal spirit that was the aim of Hui-yüan's teaching. A gradual detachment from illusory forms and an enlarging perspective that diminishes personal concerns are the qualities valued in the landscape experience.

1. The Tung-lin monastery. The Stone Gate Gorge is "the ravine with the waterfall" located on the western side of Mount Lu near the Tung-lin monastery.

creepers, traversing the perilous and plumbing the precipitous; only when arms, stretched apelike, were extended to each other did we advance to a summit. Thereupon, leaning against the cliff, we seized the view and clearly saw what was below, experiencing for the first time the beauty of the seven ridges and the gathering of exceptional sights in the spot.

The twin gate-towers soared up in opposition before us, while layered precipices gleamed about behind; peaks and hills twisted and turned to form a screen, and high cliffs built up on all sides to support the roof of heaven. Within there was a stone tower and a rocky pond, semblances of palace halls and representational shapes; it was all most pleasing.

Limpid brooks ran separately and poured together; pellucid depths were of a mirrorlike translucency in the Heavenly Pond. Patterned rocks displayed their colors, tangibly present in their glory, while tamarisks, pines, plants, and herbs dazzled the eyes with their luxuriance; all that constitutes spirited beauty was present.

On this day, various emotions hastened our enjoyment and we gazed at length without tiring. We had not looked about for long before the weather changed several times. In the dusty gathering of mist and fog, all things concealed their forms; in the reflected illumination of radiating light, the myriad peaks were inverted as mirrored scenery. At intervals of clearing, appearances had a numinous quality yet could not be fathomed.

When we went on to climb, hovering birds fluttered pinions and crying apes harshly clamored. Homing clouds, driving back, called to mind the visitations of feathered men;[2] mournful cries blended in harmony like the lodging of mysterious tones. Even though they were heard only faintly, one's spirit felt expansive. And, although in enjoying one did not expect delight, nonetheless happiness lasted throughout the day. At that time, this experience of empty pleasure truly had subtleness yet was not easy to define.

We then withdrew to seek an explanation. For, as the assembled beings in these cliffs and valleys lacked conscious selves, response was not through emotions. Yet they awakened an exhilaration that drew us onward to such an extent. Could it not be that emptiness and luminosity clarify reflections, and quietness and distance solidify the emotions? Altogether we repeated this discussion several times, and its subtlety was still inexhaustible.

Suddenly the sun announced evening, and this world was gone. We then became aware of the mysterious perception of world-renouncers and comprehended the true nature of enduring things: could it be merely the landscape that caused such divine pleasure? Thereupon, as we roamed on cliffs and precipices, shifting our gaze to scan all sides, the nine rivers[3] were like a belt and foothills formed low mounds. From this one could deduce that as in forms there are large and small, so knowledge is also proportionate.

2. The "feathered men" are Taoist transcendents.
3. Of Kiukiang, i.e., Chiu-chiang.

We then sighed deeply, lamenting that though the universe is of long duration, ancient and modern are of a piece. The Vulture Peak is far away, and the overgrown path is daily more impassable. Without the Sage,[4] even though His influence and traces of His teaching still remain, His profound enlightenment must necessarily be remote. With feeling we reflected for a long while. As each of us was enjoying the shared happiness of a rare time, moved by an auspicious moment that would be hard to recreate, emotions burst forth from our midst, and we accordingly hymned them together:

> Supermundane exhilaration is without root cause;
> When one is moved by insight, exhilaration comes of itself.
> Suddenly, as we heard of roaming at the Stone Gate,
> These unusual lays brought forth our hidden feelings.
> Plucking up our robes, we thought of cloud-charioteering immortals;
> And gazing at precipices, we envisaged the tiered city of K'un-lun.
> Spurring forward, we climbed up the great cliffs
> Without perceiving the diminishing of substantial being.
> Lifting up our heads, we ascended the cloudy gate-tower
> As remote as if it reached to the Great Purity of heaven.
> Seated upright, we turned the empty wheel of the mind,
> Setting in motion the Norm from within Profundity.
> Spirits and immortals share in the changes of all beings;
> It is better that both self and others be altogether darkened in oblivion.

Translated by Susan Bush

4. Śākyamuni Buddha.

215

The Establishment of the White Horse Temple

from *The Record of the Monasteries of Loyang*

Yang Hsüan-chih (fl. 555)

The establishment of the Pai-ma Temple (Temple of the White Horse) by Emperor Ming[1] of the Han marked the introduction of Buddhism into China.

This is the "official" version of the introduction of Buddhism to China. In all likelihood, the powerful Indian religion must have begun to filter into China in an unrecognized and inchoate fashion long before emperor Ming's dream, although the early history of the religion is very difficult to document. This account of the White Horse Temple, the title of which has been supplied by the editor, is taken from a book dedicated to the description of the Buddhist

The temple was located on the south side of the Imperial Drive, three tricents outside the Hsi-yang Gate.

The emperor dreamed of the golden man sixteen Chinese feet tall, with the aureole of sun and moon radiating from his head and his neck. A "golden god," he was known as Buddha. The emperor dispatched envoys to the Western Regions in search of the god, and, as a result, acquired Buddhist scriptures and images. At the time, because the scriptures were carried into China on the backs of white horses, White Horse was adopted as the name of the temple.

After the emperor's death, a hall for meditation[2] was built on his tomb. Thereafter stūpas were sometimes constructed even on the graves of the common people.

The scripture cases housed in the temple have survived until this day; to them incense was often burned and good care was given. At times, the scripture cases gave off light that illuminated the room and hall. As a result, both laymen and Buddhist devotees reverently worshiped as if they were facing the real Buddha.

In front of the stūpa were pomegranate trees and grapevines that were different from those grown elsewhere: they had luxuriant foliage and huge fruits. The pomegranates each weighed seven catties, and the grapes were bigger than dates. The taste of both was especially delicious, superior to all others in the capital.[3] At harvest time the emperor often came in person to pick them. Sometimes he would give some to ladies in the harem, who in turn would present them as gifts to their relatives. They were considered rare delicacies. The recipients often hesitated to eat them; instead, the fruits would be passed on and on to several households. In the capital there was a saying:

> Sweet pomegranates of the White Horse,
> Each fruit is as valuable as an ox.

Translated by Yi-t'ung Wang

---

monasteries of Loyang in the early sixth century. The city, with all its grandeur, was destroyed in 534. Noted for its superb literary quality as well as for the wealth of valuable historical, social, and cultural data that it preserves, *The Record of the Monasteries of Loyang* (*Loyang ch'ieh-lan chi*) was written by Yang Hsüan-chih, an official of the Northern Wei (Tabgatch) dynasty.

1. Reigned 58–75 C.E.

2. *Jetavana*—a term that derives from a garden donated by Prince Jeta for the orphaned and helpless, literally "Jeta's Grove."

3. Loyang.

216

A Climb up Mount Omei

from *Diary of a Boat Trip to Wu*

Fan Ch'eng-ta (1126–1193)

[*Sixth lunar month*] *twenty-fifth day* (22 July 1177): Set out from Omei town. Leaving by the West Gate, we began climbing the mountain and passed the two monasteries of Benevolent Fortune and Universal Security, White River Manor, and Shu Village Way-Stop. After twelve tricents came to Dragon Spirit Hall. From here on, mountain torrents ripped and roared; shady forests stood mighty and deep. Took a brief rest at Avataṁsaka Monastery. Then crossed Green Bamboo Bridge, Omei's New Abbey Crossroad, Plum Tree Bank, West Dragon Hall, and reached Central Peak Monastery. The monastery has a Samantabhadra Gallery wreathed by a circle of seventeen peaks. It nestles against White Cliff Peak. The highest of the peaks rising prominently on the right is called Shout-and-Response Peak. Below is the retreat of Mao Chen the Venerated One — a place rarely visited by man.[1] Sun Ssu-miao lived in seclusion on Mount Omei. When Mao Chen was here he often

---

This selection is an excerpt from a well-known travel diary titled *Wu-ch'uan lu* (*Diary of a Boat Trip to Wu*). Written in 1177 by the famous Sung dynasty statesman and poet Fan Ch'eng-ta, this text describes a boat journey from Ch'eng-tu (in modern Szechwan), where the author had just finished serving as governor, to his home in Wu township (near modern Soochow, Kiangsu). After an initial sightseeing trip that took Fan to several scenic and historic sites situated to the north and west of Ch'eng-tu, his custom-made riverboat carried him, his family, and attendants down the Yangtze River all the way to Chen-chiang (modern Kiangsu). From there they proceeded south on the Grand Canal directly to Soochow. In all, the trip took a hundred and twenty-two days (from 27 June to 26 October), and covered a distance of almost two thousand English miles.

During the journey, Fan Ch'eng-ta kept detailed records in the *Wu-ch'uan lu* of his many visits to local places of interest. Among these, his account of a ten-day trip to Mount Omei (Omei shan) in Szechwan is the most widely acclaimed, not only because it is the earliest detailed account of the mountain known, but also because of Fan's lively prose style and eye for fascinating details. The excerpts translated here describe his ascent to the mountain's summit. Without a doubt, his observation of the "Buddha Light" (Fo-kuang), an optical phenomenon that the devout believed to be a manifestation of Omei's "resident" Bodhisattva, P'u-hsien (Samantabhadra in Sanskrit), is the highlight of Fan's experience on Mount Omei. We join Fan and his traveling party (which did not include his family; they were sent earlier to a town downriver to wait for him) just as they depart from the town at the base of the mountain and begin their ascent into the clouds.

1. Mao Chen was a Taoist adept of the Sui dynasty who supposedly gained immortality during his stay on Mount Omei. Sun Ssu-miao, mentioned in the next sentence, is also reported to have sought eternal life during his residence on Omei in the Sui and T'ang periods. He had a strong interest in alchemy and is well known for having authored several important medical treatises.

shouted and responded back and forth with Sun Ssu-miao from this spot, or so it is said.

Left the monastery and passed the two precipices of Camphor-Wood and the Ox Heart Monastery Crossroad. Then we reached the Twin Stream Bridges. The jumbled mountains hereabout huddle together like standing screens. There are two mountains opposite one another, each of which produces a stream. Side by side they flow to the base of the bridge. Their rocky channels are several tens of fathoms deep. With dark waters of deep green hue, the soaring torrents spurt foamy snowcaps as they race beyond the bridges and then pass into a high thicket. Several tens of paces from there the two streams form into one and then plunge into a great ravine. The waters in the abyss, still and deep, clear and pure, disperse to form stream rapids. All the small stones in the rapids are either multicolored or have patterns of green on a white background. The pale yellow hue of the water complements the colors of the stones, making the rapids look like an outstretched piece of emerald-colored brocade. This scene is not something that could be captured in a sketch. When the sunlight of dawn shines on the water and rocks, a shimmering brilliance emits from the surface of the stream that reflects off the cliffs and ravines. Tradition says this is a "Minor Manifestation" of the Noble Master (or Samantabhadra). As for Ox Heart Monastery, when Chi-yeh,[2] Master of the Tripiṭaka, was returning home from the Western Regions he was going to found a sect here. He came upon two rocks poised against one another on the bank of the stream. He picked up one of them, in which there was an eyelike hole that ran straight through to its base. Chi-yeh regarded it as something precious and auspicious. To this day it still is housed in the monastery. The river here is thus named "Precious Manifestation Stream."

From here we climbed some precipitous stone steps and passed the Bodhisattva Gallery. On the road there was a sign that read: "The Empire's Great Mount Omei." Then we reached the White River Samantabhadra Monastery. Every step along the way from the town to here is nothing but steep hillsides for more than forty tricents. Only now are we beginning to climb the foothills of the crested peaks.

Twenty-sixth day (23 July): Spent the night at White River Monastery. It was raining heavily, so we could not ascend the mountain. Paid a visit to the bronze statue of the Noble Master Samantabhadra. It was cast in Ch'eng-tu by imperial decree at the beginning of the dynasty. Among the gifts conferred on the statue by the courts of the emperors T'ai-tsung,[3] Chen-tsung,[4] and Jen-tsung[5] are more than one hundred scrolls of texts of imperial authorship, a

---

2. Chi-yeh was a famous Buddhist monk from Kaifeng who, under imperial auspices, traveled with three hundred other monks to India in 964 in order to get copies of various sūtras. He did not return to China until 976.

3. Reigned 976–997.

4. Reigned 997–1022.

5. Reigned 1022–1063.

seven-jeweled headdress, a gemmy necklace of gold and pearls, a Buddhist's cassock, a gold and silver urn, an alms bowl, a makeup case, a censer, an incense spoon, joss sticks, a fruit plate, a bronze bell, a drum, a gong, a stone chime, "foamy" tea,[6] a pagoda, and a *chih*-mushroom.[7] There are also many other items conferred on the state by the Empress during the Ch'ung-ning reign,[8] such as pennants embroidered with gold coins and pennants woven with red silk. Among these treasures is a Buddhist cassock of red silk with purple embroidery conferred by the emperor Jen-tsung. On it are proclamations written in the emperor's own hand that read: " 'Buddha's Dharma is enduring and exalted'; 'The Dharma Wheel is forever turning'; 'May the Empire be mighty, the people secure, winds favorable, and rains opportune'; 'May spears and pikes be forever at rest'; 'May the people know peace and joy'; 'May sons and grandsons be abundant'; 'May all living beings reach to the opposite shore of salvation.' Recorded and signed by the emperor in the Hall of Prosperity and Peace on the seventh day of the tenth month in the seventh year of the Chia-yu reign (20 November 1062)."

Next we reached the monastery's Sūtra Depository, which is a treasure-depository built by artisans from the Directorate of Manufacturing dispatched here by the Imperial Court. The front of the depository is a gate-tower. Smaller towers flank it on both sides. The gate-tower's nails and hinges are all made of jade-stone, and are extremely well crafted and amazingly extravagant. Tradition says they are modeled exactly after the style of the main gate in the National Capital.[9] The sūtras here were produced in Ch'eng-tu. They use blue, weighty paper with characters written in liquid silver. At the head of each scroll is a picture painted in liquid gold. Each picture covers the events in one scroll. A wheel sign[10] and objects such as small bells and pestles are embroidered on the outside covers of the sūtras, as well as expressions such as "Peace in the Empire!" and "Long Live the Emperor!" which are placed amid patterns of dense flowers and elaborate foliage. Today one no longer sees this type of embroidery pattern.

Next we reached the Hall of the Three Thousand Iron Buddhas. We were told that Samantabhadra resides on this mountain, and that a company of three thousand disciples live with him. Thus, they built these Buddhas. The casting is very plain and simple. On this day we set out offerings and prayed to the Noble Master (or Samantabhadra), begging for three days of fine, clear skies so we could climb the mountain.

6. Fan is probably referring to a special variety of tea from Fukien which, when brought to a boil, produces a waxlike film on the surface of the water. It is also possible, however, to read this as "candles, tea. . . ."

7. A *chih* is a wood-fungus believed by some to confer longevity.

8. 1102–1107.

9. That is to say, the gate is styled after the main access gate to the Forbidden City in Kaifeng (modern Kaifeng, Honan), the capital of the Northern Sung dynasty.

10. Referring to the nine-leveled wheel or karma sign placed on top of a pagoda.

Twenty-seventh day (24 July): It was a clear, beautiful day and so we began our ascent to the upper peak. From here to the Luminous Form Monastery and Seven Treasure Cliff on the peak's crest is another sixty tricents. The distance there from the level terrain in the town is probably no less than one hundred tricents. Moreover, no longer do we find any stone-step paths. Timbers have been cut and made into a long ladder, which is fastened into the cliff wall. One ascends the mountain by crawling up it. I submit that of all the mountains to climb in the empire, none matches this one in danger and height. As strong yeomen supported my sedan-chair in its forced ascent, thirty mountain lads drew it upward while they advanced pulling on a huge rope. My fellow travelers made use of the "ladder sedan-chairs" on the mountain.[11]

We left the White River Monastery through a side gate and then ascended to Touching Heart Mountain. It is said to be so steep that it makes climbers' feet and knees touch their hearts and bosoms. Passed Thatch Pavilion Point, Small Stone Thunder, the Greater and Lesser Deep Gullies, Camel Precipice, and the Clustered Bamboo Way-stop. Generally, when one speaks of a way-stop, they mean a one-room wooden structure facing the road. If there are travelers about to climb the mountain, monks at the monastery first dispatch men ahead to boil water at a way-stop so that a hot, steamy meal will await the travelers.

Next we passed Peak Gate, Arhat Way-stop, the Greater and Lesser Supports and Lifts, Illusory Joy and Delight, Tree Bark Village, Monkey's Ladder, and Thunder Cavern Flat. Generally, when one speaks of a flat, they mean a place where one can more or less find a foothold. As for Thunder Cavern, the path here is on a steep cliff ten thousand rods high. There is a breach in the stone steps. If you spy down through it into the murky, black depths, it seems like a cavern. Tradition says that a divine dragon lives in a deep pool down there. In all, there are seventy-two caverns here. If there is a drought, people pray for rain at the third cavern. At first, they cast down perfumes and silks. If the dragon does not respond with rain, they then cast down dead swine and worn-out women's shoes, which are meant to excite and arouse him. Often, thunder and wind then suddenly burst forth. Most of the so-called fleecy clouds above the Luminous and Bright Cliff on the peak's summit are produced in this cavern.

Passed New Way-stop, Eighty-Four Switchbacks, and Teak Tree Flat. As for the teak tree, its frame and leaves are similar to those of the *tobira* shrub. They also resemble the red bayberry tree. Their blossoms are red and white, and they bloom between spring and summer. Teak trees are found only on this mountain. I first saw them when we had reached halfway up the mountain. But when you get here, they are everywhere. For the most part, the

---

11. The term "ladder sedan-chairs" probably refers to wooden litters for one person that are tied on a bearer's back.

plants, trees, birds, and insects on Mount Omei are not found anywhere else in the world. I certainly heard about this long ago. Today I personally verified it.

I came here during the last month of summer. A few days ago there was a heavy snowfall. The tree leaves were still marked with mottled patterns of snow. As for the extraordinary vegetation, examples would be the eight immortals, which here is deep purple, the herdboy, which here is several times the usual size, and the knotweed, which here is pale green. I heard that in springtime the extraordinary flowers are especially numerous. But in that season the mountain is cold, so few people are able to become acquainted with them. As for the extraordinary plants and leaves, their numbers are also beyond calculation. The mountain is high and windy. Trees do not grow well here. Their branches all droop down. Ancient mosses, like disheveled hair, hang loosely and laxly from treetops, drooping to the ground, several yards long. There are, as well, pagoda pines that resemble conifers in shape, but their needles are round and slender. They are also unable to grow tall. Layer upon layer, they turn and twist upward like a pagoda. When you get to the mountain's summit they are especially numerous. Furthermore, there are absolutely no birds here, probably because the mountain is so lofty that they cannot fly up this high.

From Teak Tree Flat we went on to pass Longing-for-the-Buddha Pavilion, Tender Grass Flat, and Foot-washing Stream. Then we reached our destination, the Luminous Form Monastery on the peak's summit. This monastery is also a wooden structure with several tens of rooms. No one was staying there. Inside there is a Minor Hall of Samantabhadra. We had begun our ascent in the *mao* double-hour (5:00–7:00 A.M.). When we reached here it was already past the *shen* double-hour (3:00–5:00 P.M.). At first, I wore my summer garments, but it gradually got colder as we climbed higher. When we reached the Eighty-Four Switchbacks, it quickly turned cold. By the time we got to the summit of the mountain, I hastily put on two layers of wadded jackets, over which I added a fur cloak and a fur robe. This exhausted all the clothes stored in my trunk. I wrapped my head with a double-layered scarf and put on some felt boots. Still, I couldn't stop shivering and trembling. Then we burned some coals and sat stiffly as we pressed against the brazier.

On the summit of the mountain there is a spring. If you boil rice in the spring water it will not cook. It just disintegrates into something like fine sand. One cannot cook things in the icy, snowy juices of ten thousand antiquities! I knew about this before. I had some water in an earthenware pot brought up from the lower reaches of the mountain, which was barely enough for myself.

A short time later we braved the cold and climbed to the Heavenly Immortal Bridge. Reached the Luminous and Bright Cliff. We burned incense in a small hall covered with a roof made of tree bark. Wang Chan-shu,[12] the Vice

12. Or Wang Chih-wang (1103–1170).

Grand Councilor, once put tiles on the roof but they were worn away by snow and frost. Without fail, the tiles crumble to pieces within a year. Later he changed the roof back to tree bark, which on the contrary can last two or three years.

Someone told us that "Buddha's Manifestation" (or "Buddha Light") only comes out during the *wu* double-hour (11:00 A.M.–1:00 P.M.). Since it was already past the *shen* double-hour, we thought it might be best to return to our lodgings and come back the next day. Just as we pondered our decision, clouds suddenly emerged from the gorge to the side and below the cliff, which is Thunder Cavern Mountain. The clouds marched in columns like the Imperial Honor Guard. When they met with the cliff, the clouds halted for a short while. On top of the clouds there appeared a great globe of light with concentric coronas of various colors in several layers positioned opposite one another. In the middle was a watery, inky reflection that looked like the Immortal Sage (or Samantabhadra) riding an elephant. After the time it takes to drink a cup of tea, the light disappeared. But off to the side appeared yet another light just like the first one. In an instant it too disappeared. In the clouds there were two shafts of golden light that shot across into the belly of the cliff. People also call this a "Minor Manifestation." At sunset all the cloud forms scattered. The mountains in the four directions fell silent. At the *yi* night-watch (9:00–11:00 P.M.) the lamps came out.[13] They teemed everywhere below the cliff — tens of thousands of them filling our gaze. The night was so cold that we couldn't stay outside for too long.

Twenty-eighth day (25 July): Again we climbed up to the cliff to view and gaze at the sights. Behind the cliff are the ten thousand folds of the Min Mountains. Not far to the north is [Little] Tile-roof Mountain, which is in Ya county. Not far to the south is Big Tile-roof Mountain, which is near Nan-chao.[14] In shape it looks just like a single tile-roofed house. On Little Tile-roof Mountain there is also a luminous form called the Pratyeka-Buddha Manifestation. Behind all these mountains are the Snow Mountains[15] of the

13. Earlier in his journey Fan Ch'eng-ta had observed similar "lamps" on Mount Green Wall in Szechwan and commented on their possible origins: "Some people say they are the glow of cinnabar drugs hidden away by the ancients. Others say they are the essence of plants and trees, which has a glow. And still others say they are made by dragon spirits and mountain demons. The explanation most people believe is that they have been devised by immortals and sages." Others in traditional China identify these same lights as "flitting fires," which, they explain, emit from long-standing concentrations of blood found in places such as old battlefields. Western scholars have also offered possible explanations of these "lamps." Some equate them with *ignis fatuus* (or "will-o' the-wisp"), the spontaneous combustion of an inflammable gas derived from decaying organic matter. Others say they might be the result of sparks of static electricity or a kind of electroluminescence known as *ignis lambens*. All these explanations, however, are tentative at best. For now at least, the precise origin of Mount Omei's "lamps" remains a mystery.

14. An ancient Buddhist kingdom situated in what is now Yunnan province.

15. The Himalayas and their associated ranges.

Western Regions. Their jagged and cragged peaks, which seem carved and pared, in all number in the tens and hundreds. When the first light of day shines on them, their snowy hue is piercing and bright, like glistening silver amid the dazzling and resplendent light of dawn. From ancient times down to today, these snows have never melted. The mountains stretch and sweep into India and other alien lands, for who knows how many thousands of tricents. Gazing at them now, they seem spread out on a little tea-table right before my eyes. This magnificent, surpassing view tops everything I have seen in my life.

We paid a second visit to the hall on the cliff and offered prayers. Suddenly a dense fog arose in the four directions, turning everything completely white. A monk said: "This is the Silver World." A short time later, there was a heavy downpour and the dense fog retreated. The monk said: "This is the rain that cleanses the cliff. Buddha is about to make a Great Manifestation." The fleecy clouds again spread out below the cliff, gathered thickly, and mounted upward to within a few yards of the cliff edge, where they abruptly halted. The cloud tops were as smooth as a jade floor. From time to time raindrops flew by. I looked down into the cliff's belly, and there was a great globe of light lying outstretched on a flat cloud. The outer corona was in three layers, each of which had blue, yellow, red, and green hues. In the very center of the globe was a hollow of concentrated brightness. Each of us onlookers saw our forms in the hollow and bright spot, without the slightest detail hidden, just as if we were looking in a mirror. If you raise a hand or move a foot, the reflection does likewise. And yet you will not see the reflection of the person standing right next to you. The monk said: "This is the Body-absorbing Light." When the light disappeared, winds arose from the mountains in front and the clouds scurried about. In the wind and clouds there again appeared a huge, globular form of light. It spanned several mountains, exhausting every possible color and blending them into a beautiful array. The plants and trees on the peaks and ridges were so fresh and alluring, so gorgeous and striking, that you could not look at them directly.

When the clouds and fogs have scattered and only this light remains shining, people call it a "Clear-Sky Manifestation." Generally, when the Buddha Light is about to appear it must first spread out some clouds — this is the so-called Fleecy-Cotton World. The light-form depends on the clouds to make its appearance. If it docs not depend on the clouds, it is called a "Clear-Sky Manifestation," which is extremely rare. After the time it takes to eat a meal, the light gradually moves off, traversing the mountains and heading off westward. If you look back to the left, on Thunder Cavern Mountain another light appears like the first one but a little smaller. After a short while, it too flies off and beyond the mountains. When the light reaches the level countryside, it makes a special point of circling back into direct alignment with the cliff. Its color and shape change completely, turning into a golden bridge that some-

16. This famous bridge was near Fan Ch'eng-ta's home in Kiangsu.

what resembles Suspended Rainbow Bridge on the Wu River.[16] But the ends of this bridge have purple clouds holding them up. In general, the cloud forms clear away between the *wu* and *wei* double-hours (11:00 A.M.–3:00 P.M.). This is called "Closing the Cliff." Only the "Golden Bridge Manifestation" waits until after the *yu* double-hour before it disappears.

Those accompanying me to the peak's summit included the Aide-de-Camp Chien Shih-chieh, style Po-chün; Yang Kuang, style Shang-ch'ing; Chou Chieh-te, style Chün-wan; the Presented Scholar Yü Chih, style Tzu-chien; as well as my younger brother Fan Ch'eng-chi. Today we were also joined by my fellow graduate Yang Sun, style Po-mien, and the Aide-de-Camp Li Chia-mou, style Liang-chung, both of whom had come from Chia-chiang town to join us. The light appeared just when they arrived.

Twenty-ninth day (26 July): Started down the mountain. When we first made our ascent, although we clambered upward with difficulty and had ropes pulling us in front, it was dangerous but not perilous. When we started down the mountain, although ropes were again tied to our sedan-chairs to lower us down the rungs of the ladder, the bearers found it difficult to keep their footing, and it was both dangerous and perilous. As we went down the mountain, gradually I began to feel the hot summer air, and so I peeled off my heavy winter garments one by one. During the *wu* double-hour, when we reached the White Water Monastery, I put on the light summer linens I had on before. . . .

Translated by James M. Hargett

217
Observing the Tidal Bore

from *Reminiscences of Wu-lin*

Chou Mi (1232–1298)

The tidal bore on the Che River[1] is one of the great sights of the world. It reaches its full force from the sixteenth to the eighteenth of the month. When

Many writers and poets since the T'ang period have mentioned the tidal bore along the Ch'ien-t'ang River as an awesome phenomenon. Known to foreigners during the last century and a half as the "Hangchow Bore," it is a series of high waves which occurs near the first and middle of each month and crests at a height of five to six feet. The two occurrences nearest the spring and autumn equinoxes, however, often reached a height of eighteen to twenty-five feet. These used to be occasions for festivities and Chou Mi vividly recalled the autumnal one in the eighth lunar month around 1280.

Following the establishment of the Yüan in 1279, Chou Mi remained a Sung loyalist and moved to Hangchow when his family business burned down in Wu-hsing (in modern Chekiang). His later years were spent preserving Sung literature and culture, and he wrote several unofficial

it begins to arise far away at Ocean Gate,[2] it appears but a silver thread; but, as it gradually approaches, it becomes a wall of jade, a snow-laden ridge, bordering the sky on its way. Its gigantic roar is like thunder as it convulses, shakes, dashes, and shoots forth, swallowing up the sky and inundating the sun, for its force is supremely vigorous. Yang Wan-li described this in a poem:

> The ocean surges silver to form a wall;
> The river spreads jade to gird the waist.[3]

As in every year, the governor of the capital appeared at the Che River Pavilion[4] to inspect the navy. Warships in the hundreds were arrayed along both banks. Suddenly, they all rushed to divide into "quintuple formation." Moreover, there was equitation, banner waving, spear juggling, and sword dancing while afloat, just as on land. In an instant, yellow smoke arose on all sides, and people could barely see each other. The explosions on the water were deafening and earth-shaking; the sounds were like those of mountains collapsing. When the smoke dispersed and the waves calmed, there was not a trace of a hull: all the "enemy ships" had been burned by fire and had disappeared under the waves.

There were several hundred youths of Wu who were expert at swimming. They had loosened their hair and had tatoos on their bodies. In their hands, they held ten colored banners some twenty feet long and raced each other with the utmost exertion, swimming against the current, floating and sinking in the leviathan waves a myriad yards[5] high. Their leaping bodies executed a

---

histories including *Reminiscences of Wu-lin*, completed c. 1280. The latter is one of the most extensive and detailed records of life in the Southern Sung capital. It contains a variety of short descriptions such as this one, in addition to poems, lists of things, and selections from other sources covering not only court life, but popular culture, scenic places, and daily life of the common people.

Today, the height of the tidal bore along the Ch'ien-t'ang River, diminished because of modern dams, can no longer be seen from the city as in the past. One must travel forty miles away to Hai-ning on Hangchow Bay for the best view, where the sixty-mile wide bay narrows to two miles and the incoming tide confronts the outgoing flow of the Ch'ien-t'ang River.

This prose description of a tidal bore may be compared with the rhapsodic treatment of another one from a much earlier period by Mei Ch'eng in selection 152, pages 411–28, and a later poetic description by Cheng Hsieh in selection 105.

1. The Che River (Che-chiang) is another name for the Ch'ien-t'ang River.

2. Ocean Gate (Hai-men) is located on the northeast coast at the juncture of the Che River and Hangchow Bay.

3. Yang Wan-li (1127–1206) was considered one of the major poets of the early Southern Sung (see selection 74). The author of over 4,200 poems, he espoused a literary theory influenced by Zen Buddhist ideals of enlightenment and often employed illusionistic imagery. These lines, however, do not appear in his collected works.

4. The Southern Sung capital of Lin-an (modern Hangchow). The Che River Pavilion was located south of the city on the northern bank of the river.

5. The word translated as "yards" actually signifies a measurement eight feet in length. The description, in any event, is hyperbolic.

hundred different movements without getting the tail of the banners even slightly wet — this was how they showed off their skill. Prominent commoners and high officials competed to bestow silver prizes.

Up and down along the river banks for more than ten tricents, pearls, jade, gauze, and silk flooded the eyes; horses and carriages clogged the roads. Every kind of food and drink cost double the normal price and yet, where viewing tents were rented out, not a bit of ground was left for even a mat. The palace viewed the scene, as customary, from Nature's Picture.[6] From this high terrace, the bird's-eye view made it all appear as if in the palm of one's hand. The people of the capital gazed up at the yellow canopies and feathery fans above the empyrean, just as if it were the Flute Terrace or the Island of P'eng-lai.[7]

Translated by Richard Strassberg

6. A terrace located within the imperial palace at Lin-an.

7. According to legend, the Flute Terrace was built by Duke Mu of Ch'in (reigned 659–621 B.C.E.) for his daughter Nung-yü and her husband, Hsiao-shih, an excellent flutist. Hsiao-shih summoned phoenixes with his flute, and he and Nung-yü flew off to become transcendents. P'eng-lai was one of the mythological islands where transcendents were said to dwell, located in the sea off the northeastern coast.

Miscellanea

218
Fan Sheng-chih's Book

Chapter 1: Basic Principles of Farming

Fan Sheng-chih (1st century B.C.E.)

The basic principles of farming are: choose the right time, break up the soil, see to its fertility and moisture, hoe early, and harvest early.

With the choice of appropriate time and favorable conditions of the soil, a harvest of ten piculs per sixth-acre[1] is obtainable even from very poor land.

This selection shows that even something so seemingly mundane as a treatise on farming might be written in an expressive, almost lyrical fashion. The original text, an agricultural treatise of the first century B.C.E., was lost long ago, but portions of it were preserved in *Essential Arts for the Common People (Ch'i min yao shu)*, a comprehensive and authoritative handbook completed about 535 by Chia Ssu-hsieh, who was a government official in Shantung. *Fan Sheng-chih's Book* is the earliest Chinese book of individual authorship devoted wholly to agriculture to which we still have access.

1. The approximate equivalents of measures used in Fan's book are as follows:

Length

one *ts'un* ("inch") = 22 millimeters
one *ch'ih* ("foot") = ten *ts'un* = 22 centimeters
one *chang* ("decafoot") = ten *ch'ih* = one hundred *ts'un* = 2.2 meters

Volume

one *sheng* ("pint") = 167 millimeters

In springtime, after thawing, the breath of the earth[2] comes through, so the soil breaks up for the first time. With the summer solstice, the weather begins to become hot and the yin breath strengthens, so the soil breaks up again. Ninety days after the summer solstice, the duration of the day equals to that of the night, and the breath of heaven harmonizes with that of the earth. To plow in these proper seasons, one operation is worth five. Such conditions are denoted as "fecund moisture"; therein lies the benefit of appropriate timing.

In the spring, when the breath of the earth comes through, hard heavy lands and black soils may be plowed first. Then harrow to level down the clods, and let the grasses sprout. After the sprouting of the grasses, plow again. Then plow again after a drizzle. Always break up any clod, and wait for the proper time to sow. This is what is denoted by "making the heavy soils light."

In the springtime, watch for the coming through of the breath of the earth: sharpen a wooden stake one foot and two inches long, bury one foot of it below and let the remaining two inches appear above the ground level. After "Setting of Spring,"[3] the clods begin to disintegrate, hence the soil will heap up and cover the top of the stake, then old stumps of the previous year can be lightly pulled out. This is the proper time to plow.

Twenty days later, the mellow breath of the earth is gone and the soil hardens. One plowing in proper time is worth four, but four plowings will not equal to one after the mellow breath is gone.

Light soils are to be plowed when apricot trees come in blossom.[4] Plow again when the blossoms fade, and roll down[5] every time after plowing. After the grasses sprout, plow and roll down again when it rains and the soil is moist. With soils which are too light, drive cattle over them to tread them

---

one *tou* ("peck") = ten *sheng* = 1.67 liters
one *tan* ("picul") = one *hu* = ten *tou* = one hundred *sheng* = 16.7 liters

Area

one *mou* ("sixth-acre") = 5.078 ars [one ar = one hundred square meters]

Weight

one *chin* ("catty") = 177.8 grams
one *tan* ("picul") = one hundred and twenty *chin* = 21.336 kilograms

This is basically a decimal system already in use in China over two thousand years ago.

2. "Breath of the earth" or "yin breath" means the complex conditions of low temperature and high humidity of the soil and the reverse conditions of the air. "Breath of heaven," on the other hand, indicates warm and dry conditions prevailing under sunshine (yang).

3. The first of the twenty-four subseasons of a year.

4. About the time of the first ten days in April.

5. This calls for pulling a weighted roller across the field.

down. The soils will then become hard. This is what is denoted by "to make the light soils heavier."

In the spring, when the breath of the earth has not come through, the soil will be lumpy when plowed, it will be unable to retain moisture, and thus will not support the growth of crop plants for the whole year to come unless heavily manured.

Never plow too early. Wait till the grasses sprout. Plow only when the time for sowing comes and it rains, so that the seeds and the soil will be in good contact; seedlings alone grow well, while sprouted weeds now rot beneath the clods and a good field results. This is what "one plowing worth five" means.

If a field is plowed too early, the clods will be hard, and seedlings will come out of the same crevices with weeds. No hoeing can be done and a bad field will result.

If one plows in the autumn when it does not rain, the breath of the earth is cut off and the soil will be hard and cloddy. This is called "bacony field." If one plows in a severe winter, the yin breath of the earth is broached and the soil will be dry and parched. This is called "jerked[6] field." Both bacony and jerked fields are damaged.

If a field gives a poor crop in the second year, fallow it for one year.

Fields intended for wheat should always be plowed in the fifth month. Plow again in the sixth month. Don't plow in the seventh month, but diligently harrow it level and wait for sowing. One plowing in the fifth month is worth three; one in the sixth month, two; but five in the seventh is not worth one.

Upon every pause of snowfall, roll down so as to catch any snow on the ground surface and stop its drifting away by wind. Roll down the later snowfalls in the same way. The moisture of the soil is thus secured for the spring to come, insects will be killed by the freezing of the soil water, and good crops for the harvest will thus be warranted.

Translated by Shih Sheng-Han

6. From the verb "to jerk" (to cut meat into long strips and dry in the sun or cure by exposing to smoke).

219

Miscellanies, Secret H

A *Fragment*

Anonymous (2nd century C.E.)

In the first year of Chien-ho (147 C.E.), the fourth moon, the *ting-hai* day, Maid Wu of the Court of Serving Women went with the edict of the *ping-shu* day[1] to the house of Chamberlain Chao. The edict says, "We hear that the first poem of the *Classic of Odes* celebrated a royal marriage, and that the choice of a good royal spouse has ever been the concern of good rulers of the past. The chaste reputation of the bereaved young daughter of the late General Cheng Shang has reached our ears. Let the Chamberlain go with Maid Wu to the late general's house, and examine her deportment and all intimate details and report faithfully. We intend to select her for the palace."

Bringing the letter of authorization, I [Maid Wu] and Chao went to the house of the late General Shang and found the family just having dinner. Our arrival created a great excitement in the house. The girl, named Nuying, left the hall and went to her inside quarters. Chao and I followed the instructions of the edict and studied her deportment carefully and were satisfied. Chao then went out and I went with Ying [the girl] to her private room, where I sent away all attendants and closed the door. At that time, the sunlight came through the shell windows and shone upon Ying's face, which radiated a brightness like the morning cloud or snow, so that I instinctively avoided looking at her directly. Ripples of light came from her eyes and her eyebrows were curved. She had red lips and white teeth, a long pair of ears, and a pointed nose. Her cheeks were full and her chin well-formed, all in proper proportion. I then took off her long, bending hair ornament[2] and let down

This is one of the most curious fragments to have survived the ages. The title of the document, "Miscellanies, Secret H" (*Tsa-shih mi hsin*), seems to indicate that it came from the secret archives of the Han palace, the word *hsin* having no meaning unless it serves as a symbol in the Chinese cycle for labeling a series, like the letter H in the alphabet standing for "Number 8." This is a court record of the queen of Emperor Huan (reigned 147–167 C.E.) of the Later Han dynasty, beginning with a report of the physical examination of her when she was a girl of sixteen, given by a woman servant of the palace. The rest deals with the formal six ceremonies of engagement (first set of presents; asking for the name of the girl, her age, and her ancestors; divination; second set of formal gifts, which signified the formal engagement; asking for the date of the marriage; and finally the wedding itself), and ends with her "coronation" as empress. The woman's report is full of realistic details. The phrases she used, not found in literary language, are part of her spoken language. Here only the woman's report is given.

1. The day before. The designations *ting-hai* and *ping-shu* are based on a cycle of sixty.

2. A hairpin several inches long, made of light, soft metal so that it bobbed as the girl walked. Hence the name used here, *pu-yao*, which means "shaking at every step."

her hair, which was jet-black. I felt it in the palm of my hand, and it reached the ground, with more to spare.

   This done, I asked her to loosen her underclothes. Ying blushed all over and refused, and I said to Ying, "It is a palace rule, which must be complied with. Please let a poor old woman see it. Loosen the belt knot and I shall be very careful." Ying's tears came to her eyes and she turned her face away and closed her eyes. I then loosened her belt knot, and turned her toward the light. I smelled an exquisite smell. Her skin was white and fine and so smooth that my hand slipped as it touched it. Her belly was round and her hips square. Her body was like congealed lard[3] and carved jade. Her breasts bulged out, and her navel had enough depth to permit a half-inch pearl to go in. Her *mons veneris* rose gently. I opened her thighs and saw that the vulva was bright red, while the labia minora slightly protruded. I was satisfied that she was a chaste virgin. In general about Ying's body, her blood well nourished her skin, her skin well covered her muscles, and her muscles well concealed her bones. Her dimensions were right. She stood seven feet one inch,[4] her shoulders were one foot six wide, her hips three inches less [*sic*] than her shoulders. She measured two feet seven inches from her shoulders to the tips of her fingers, and her fingers were four inches from the tips to the palm, looking like ten pointed bamboo sticks. The length of her legs from the thighs to the feet was three feet two inches, and her feet measured eight inches. Her ankles and arches were round and full, her soles smooth, and her toes small.[5] The tight silk and close-fitting socks were gathered in as with ladies in the palace. For a long time she stood speechless. I urged her quickly to thank His Imperial Majesty, and she bowed and said, "Long Live[6] the Emperor!" Her voice was like a wind moving through a bamboo grove, very pleasant to the ear. She had no piles, no bad marks, no moles, and no sores, or defects in the mouth, the nose, the armpit, the private parts, or the feet.

   I am a stupid humble woman and cannot express properly what I saw or felt. I make this secret report, properly sealed, knowing that my life depends upon Your Imperial pleasure.

Translated by Lin Yutang

   3. Literally, "constructed fat." Such phrases are evidently from the woman's patois.
   4. The foot in Han days was probably about seven tenths of a modern English foot, which means that the girl was just under five feet tall.
   5. This line contains evidence that her feet were not bound. Bound feet cannot have smooth soles, for the soles are bent and folded over. Footbinding did not become a custom in China till nearly a thousand years later.
   6. Literally, *wan-sui* (= Japanese *banzai*), which means "ten thousand years."

220
Li Shang-yin's Miscellany

Li Shang-yin (c. 813–c. 858)

1. Definitely Won't Come!

1. An intoxicated guest deserting the feast (won't come to take farewell).
2. A guest making off with the spoons.
3. Noblemen's servants when sent for.
4. A dog whistled by one holding a stick.
5. Singing-girls invited by a hard-up scholar.

2. Incongruities

1. A poor Persian.
2. A sick physician.
3. A (Buddhist) disciple not addicted to drink.
4. Keepers of granaries coming to blows.[1]
5. A great fat bride.
6. An illiterate teacher.
7. A pork-butcher reciting sūtras.
8. A village elder riding in an open chair.
9. A grandfather visiting courtesans.

3. Shameful

1. A new wife careless of the proprieties.
2. A pregnant nun.
3. Wrestlers with swollen faces.
4. A rich man suddenly poor.[2]
5. A maid offending public opinion.
6. A son in mourning getting drunk.

Li Shang-yin is best known for his imagistic, recondite poetry (see selection 65). This *Miscellany (Yi-shan tsa tsuan)*, which is not included in his collected works, reveals Li as capable of writing blunt, earthy prose as well (if, indeed, he is the actual author; the attribution is doubtful). The four hundred sayings are grouped under forty-two heads. Although they vividly reflect the manners and morals of the period in which the book was written, many of them are still applicable to life in all Chinese communities today. The language, too, is astonishingly modern.

1. Too well fed to fight. Another version is "Lean men fighting," Chinese wrestlers and boxers being always fat and heavy.
2. The wealthy are respected and loss of wealth involves loss of respect.

4. Guilty Secrets

1. Kidnapping another's children.
2. Seducing another's concubine.
3. Dodging the Customs.
4. A robber's cache.

5. Not to be Despised

1. Coarse food when hungry.
2. A poor steed when traveling afoot.
3. A second-class seat after a long walk.
4. Cold broth to drink when thirsty.
5. A small boat when traveling in haste.
6. A small house in a storm.

6. Reluctant

1. A new wife to see strangers.
2. A poor devil to contribute to a feast.
3. A poor family to make marriages.
4. To visit retired officials.
5. A pregnant woman to go afoot.

7. No Alternative[3]

1. Drinking wine when ill.
2. Attending meetings in hot weather.
3. Beating children without explanation.
4. Being ceremonious when sweating.
5. Being cauterized when in pain.
6. Abusing one's concubine at the behest of one's wife.
7. Receiving visitors in hot weather.
8. Applying to resign on account of old age.
9. Entertaining guests in a miserable temple.

8. Resemblances

1. A metropolitan official, like a winter melon, grows in the dark.
2. A raven, like a hard-up scholar, croaks[4] when hungry and cold.

3. I.e., things done only if there is no alternative.
4. *Yin*, to croak, also to hum over verses when composing.

3. A seal, like an infant, always hangs about one.
4. A magistrate, like a tiger, is vicious when disturbed.
5. Nuns, like rats, go into deep holes.
6. Swallows, like nuns, always go in pairs.
7. A slave, like a cat, finding any warm corner, stays.

9. " 'Tis Folly to be Wise"

1. A hard-up scholar who knows about music spoils his career.
2. A woman who knows about poetry gets herself talked about.
3. A priest who knows about drink breaks his vows.
4. A wretched slave who knows about reading makes mistakes.
5. A young man who knows about alchemy invites poverty.
6. A scholar who knows about manual work demeans himself.

10. Passing Hates

1. Squabbles between man and wife.
2. Finding fault with a concubine.
3. Bad temper shown by underlings of a high official.
4. Abuse of his staff by a corrupt official.
5. Debauched monks and nuns maligning a novice.

11. Vexations

1. Happening upon a tasty dish when one's liver is out of order.
2. Making a night of it and the drinks giving out.
3. For one's back to itch when calling upon a superior.
4. For the lights to fail just when the luck begins to favor one at cards.
5. Inability to get rid of a worthless poor relation.
6. A man cleaning out a well who has to go to the toilet in a hurry.

12. The Name Without the Reality

1. A student who does not study the appointed themes is not a real student.
2. A mourner who feels no grief when condoling with the bereaved is not a real mourner.
3. An old servant who neither tidies things away nor chatters about family affairs is not a real old servant.
4. A host who escorts a guest no farther than the door is not a real host.
5. A cook without an apron or a knife and chopping-block is not a real cook.

6. A teacher who does not correct his pupil's exercises and studies is not a real teacher.
7. Underlings who do not squabble and curse are not real underlings.
8. A head of a family who does not check his possessions regularly is not a real head.
9. A servant who is slovenly in his dress is not a real servant.
10. A guest who sends his host no word of thanks after a feast is not a real guest.
11. An officer who mutters replies and marches lazily is not a real officer.

13. Ambiguity

1. Only of a poor gift does one say, "Can it be repaid?"
2. Only of an ugly bride does one say, "She is my fate!"
3. Only of a nobody does one say, "T'ai Kung met King Wen at eighty."[5]
4. Only of a poor appointment does one say, "It's a place to make a living."
5. Only to be rude to a guest does one say, "Make yourself at home."
6. Only of a poor dwelling does one say, "It's quite all right to live in."
7. Only those incapable of making a living for themselves rail at their ancestors.

14. Indications of Prosperity

1. Horses neighing.
2. Candles guttering.
3. Chestnut husks.
4. Lichee shells.[6]
5. Flower petals flying about.
6. The twittering of orioles and swallows.[7]
7. The sound of reading aloud.[8]
8. Dropped hair ornaments.
9. A flute being played in a lofty belvedere.
10. The sound of pounding drugs and rolling tea.

5. T'ai Kung ("Grand Duke"), a high state official, retired into exile to avoid the tyranny of Chow Hsin, last ruler of the Yin (i.e., Shang) dynasty. Years later King Wen, founder of the Chou dynasty which overthrew the Yin in 1122 B.C.E., saw T'ai Kung (who was then eighty years old) fishing and invited him to become his chief adviser.
6. Chestnuts and lichees are luxuries.
7. This refers to the birdlike sound of women's voices.
8. Leisure to enjoy literature and music.

15. *Misleading Statements*

1. To say that a courtesan feels affection.
2. To say that alchemy brings wealth.
3. To say that official work gets its reward.
4. To say that one is on intimate terms with one's master.
5. To say what income one derives from one's land.
6. To say that one's concubine is young.
7. A needy magistrate prating about official probity.
8. To say of oneself that one studies hard.
9. To boast of the cost of one's possessions.[9]

16. *Humors of Low Life*

1. A rural magistrate transferred to the city.
2. The way being cleared for a village magistrate.[10]
3. A village magistrate entertaining guests.
4. A mule braying in the village.
5. A country lout calling chickens.
6. A rustic with new clothes.
7. Playing the flute on cowback.
8. A beggar driving out the demon of pestilence.
9. Unofficial performers on the "single-stick" drum.

17. *Disheartening*

1. Cutting with a blunt knife.
2. Catching the wind in a torn sail.
3. Trees shutting out the view.
4. Building a wall that hides the mountains.
5. No wine at blossom time.
6. A summer feast spread out of the breeze.

18. *Dismaying*

1. To infringe on another's taboo.
2. To meet an enemy.
3. To meet a creditor.
4. To blunder at a reception.
5. To hear one's drunken remarks when sober.

9. Literally, "vessels, dishes."

10. It is not a prerogative of the village magistrate to have the road cleared for his sedan-chair, as it is for higher ranking officials.

19. Desecration (spoiling the scenery)

1. To be "moved on" when enjoying flowers.
2. To weep when looking at flowers.
3. To spread a mat on moss.
4. To cut down a weeping poplar.
5. To dry small clothes amid flowers.
6. To carry a load on a spring jaunt.
7. To tether a horse to a decorative stone pillar.
8. To bring a lamp into moonlight.
9. To talk banalities at a musical banquet.
10. To plant cabbages in a fruit garden.
11. To build a pavilion that shuts out the mountains.
12. To keep poultry under a flower-stand.

20. Unbearable

1. A lonely house and gibbons crying.
2. The coarse talk of the marketplace.
3. Sounds from the threshing floor at a wayside inn in autumn.
4. A young wife mourning her husband.
5. An old man mourning his son.
6. A magpie[11] after "flunking."
7. Beggars calling at night.
8. The sound of music when in mourning.
9. To hear one has graduated among the first three and die forthwith.

21. A Waste

1. Being ill at blossom time.
2. Being harassed in fine weather.
3. A eunuch with a handsome wife.
4. A festival day in a poor home.
5. A well-to-do family at loggerheads.
6. A poverty-stricken family with a taste for flowers.
7. Seeing a beautiful view and not making a poem.
8. A fine house and no entertaining.

22. Unendurable

1. The hot season by a fat man.
2. To go home to an ill-tempered wife.

11. The call of the magpie denotes good luck.

3. To come across greedy and tyrannical superiors.
4. Colleagues with bad habits.
5. A long journey in the hot season.
6. Long contact with a coarse person.
7. A wet day in a boat with leaky awnings.
8. Dirt and damp in a poor cottage.
9. An officious official.

23. Hard to Bear

1. Priests joking with courtesans.
2. Servants imitating the behavior of scholars.
3. Juniors behaving arrogantly to their betters.
4. Servants and concubines cutting into the conversation.
5. Soldiers and rustics trying to talk like scholars.

24. The Power of Suggestion

1. Wearing green in winter makes one feel cold.
2. Seeing red in summer makes one feel hot.
3. Entering the shrine of a good spirit suggests seeing a bad one.
4. A nun with a big belly makes one think of pregnancy.
5. Heavy curtains suggest someone lurking.
6. Passing a butcher's gives a frowzy feeling.
7. Seeing water cools one.
8. Seeing plum trees makes one's mouth water.

25. Bad Form

1. To wrangle with one's fellow guests.
2. To fall from one's polo pony.
3. To smoke in the presence of superiors.
4. Priests and nuns lately returned to ordinary life.
5. To vociferate orders at a banquet.
6. To cut into the conversation.
7. To fall asleep in somebody's bed with one's boots on.
8. To preface remarks with a giggle.
9. To kick over the table when a guest.
10. To sing love songs in the presence of one's father- or mother-in-law.
11. To reject distasteful food and put it back on the dish.
12. To lay chopsticks across a soup-bowl.

26. Inopportune

1. To talk books in the presence of a nobody.
2. To recite poems to a courtesan.
3. To claim relationship with an exalted person.
4. To be hospitable at the expense of one's master.
5. To return half-eaten food to the host.
6. To take children to a banquet.
7. To boast of the cleverness of one's children.
8. To encourage children to be silly and spoiled.
9. To find fault with the dishes at a banquet.
10. To insist upon the latest fashion.
11. To hinder one's host by sitting on after a meal.
12. To ask one's host the price of his food.
13. To be on friendly terms with a widow.
14. To eat another's food and not defer to him.
15. To make the lender come for a borrowed article.
16. To pick up things and examine them in another person's rooms.
17. To be ungrateful to a benefactor.
18. To pick fruit in another's garden.
19. To talk big when hard up.
20. To play the rich man when poor.
21. To be a visitor and call oneself a guest. [12]
22. To stay overly long when invited to a summer banquet.

27. Mortifications

1. Failure of an honored guest to accept one's invitation.
2. The arrival of a hated person [13] uninvited.
3. To be unable to rid oneself of a drunken man.
4. To be penniless when things are cheap.
5. To go for a stroll and run across a creditor.
6. To find oneself seated next to an enemy.
7. To meet a disliked person on a hot day.
8. To have a lovely concubine and a jealous wife.

28. Stupidities

1. To have money and not pay off debts.
2. To recognize one's faults and be unable to reform.

12. I.e., claim the privileges of a guest.
13. Literally, "a bad guest."

3. To listen to another's conversation and contradict him sharply.
4. To read another's essay and assail it violently.
5. To be blind to one's own failings but violently disapprove of another's.
6. To guess wrongly in a drinking game but refuse to pay the forfeit.[14]
7. Trying hard to pose as wealthy when poor.

29. Foolishness

1. To discuss a man's faults behind his back.
2. To love betraying secrets.
3. To destroy one's family for love of wine.
4. To be a suborned witness.
5. Deceitfully to hasten to flatter.
6. To blab abroad the shortcomings of one's relatives.
7. To demand division of property while parents are alive.
8. To be ignorant of the order of precedence in an assembly or a wedding.
9. To cherish resentment and yet expect forgiveness.
10. To be kind to a man and expect gratitude.

30. Contemporary Crazes

1. Unreasoning jealousy.
2. Invoking the Spirits in one's cups.
3. A son in mourning reciting ditties.
4. A son in mourning for his parents going to cock-fights and dog-races.
5. Enemies remembering those who were kind.
6. Adults flying kites.
7. Supporting idlers.
8. Women cursing in public.
9. Selling property to defray wedding or funeral expenses.
10. Mortgaging one's house and lands.

31. Improper

1. To call upon sons and grandsons to testify to one's virtue.
2. To hail a maternal uncle as an "unc" during one's mother's lifetime.
3. To call wife or younger brother in the presence of one's parents.
4. To uphold one's wife and blame one's elders.
5. To sacrifice to the dead and yet play music.
6. To walk straight into another's private rooms.

14. Guessing games to encourage drinking were (and are) common in many forms, the penalty for an error being to drink a cup of wine.

32. *Things Gone Awry*

1. Good parents lacking good sons.
2. A good son lacking a good wife.
3. A good daughter lacking a good husband.
4. Having money and not being able to use it.
5. Having fine clothes and not being able to wear them.
6. A fine dwelling left unswept.
7. Having silk and not making clothes.
8. Having a beautiful color and not knowing how to match it.
9. Being obliged to set a beloved concubine to do menial tasks.
10. Grudging the money to get treatment when sick.
11. Letting children grow up untaught.
12. Having a library and not knowing how to read.
13. Going to bed early on moonlit nights.
14. Looking at beautiful flowers and neither reciting poetry nor drinking wine.
15. Failing to enjoy fine scenery when near it.
16. Having delicately flavored food and yet being stingy enough to hoard rancid bean-curd.
17. An official demanding probity in others and himself breaking the law against bribes.
18. Wasting one's talents in idling.
19. Having power and not using it to do good.
20. In youth loving ease and learning nothing.

33. *Unlucky*

1. To eat lying down.
2. To sigh for nothing.
3. To sing in bed.
4. To eat bareheaded.
5. To write bareheaded.
6. To swear an oath involving one's parents.
7. To beat one's breast while cursing another.[15]
8. To sit on matting on which a corpse has lain.
9. To go to the toilet or let down one's hair in the light of the sun or moon.
10. To dip spoon or chopsticks in the bowl before the meal begins.

---

15. Curses are apt to light upon the person pointed at, and an angry man beating his own breast inadvertently indicates himself as the object of his curses.

34. *Poverty is Inevitable When One —*

1. Has a lazy wife.
2. Lies long abed.
3. Brings up a boy to be inferior to his father.
4. Runs into debt.
5. Does not check storehouse lists.
6. Neglects one's farm.
7. Throws away food or wine.
8. Likes gambling or drinking.
9. Fills storerooms with useless objects.
10. Is careless about grain.
11. Wastes one's estate in the pursuit of pleasure.
12. Is not thrifty.
13. Maintains many concubines.
14. Is always changing one's residence.
15. Frequents the company of the powerful and rich.
16. Is economical to the point of meanness.
17. Insists on buying when things are dear.
18. Does not buy when things are cheap.
19. Tries too many smart tricks.
20. Screens the members of one's family when they do wrong.

35. *Wealth Is Assured When One —*

1. Seeks diligently and uses sparingly.
2. Widens knowledge by practical experience.
3. Frequently takes stock of family affairs.
4. Is not infatuated with wine and women.
5. Does not fail to collect debts.
6. Has slaves who understand plowing and maids who understand weaving.
7. Sleeps by night and rises early.
8. Rears stock.
9. Tills in proper season.
10. Stores up when the season arrives.
11. Has apprentices who work in harmony.
12. Has a wife who does not believe in Buddha.
13. Has womenfolk who all agree.
14. Can put up with hardships.
15. Keeps an inventory of one's valuables.
16. Gathers the "mites" that make the "muckle."

17. Catches the market.
18. Does not damage his possessions.

36. *They Are Wise and Capable Who—*

1. Keep their natures within moderate bounds.
2. Are discreet in secret matters.
3. Associate with the wise.
4. Are wide awake in a crisis.
5. Do not babble in their cups.
6. Respect other people's taboos.
7. Are acquainted with things ancient and modern.
8. Do not practice meannesses.
9. Boast not unbecomingly.
10. Esteem the virtuous.
11. Join not themselves to the meaner sort.
12. Credit not blindly the words of servants.
13. When they enter a house inquire its tabooed words.
14. Inquire about the customs of any state they enter.
15. Are on the alert at night.
16. Ask when in doubt.
17. Do not argue with fools.
18. Do not speak much after drinking.

37. *Train a Son to—*

1. Learn the ancestral business.
2. Keep faith.
3. Be ceremonious, just, moderate, modest.
4. Be thoroughly versed in the six arts.[16]
5. Converse intelligently.
6. Be dignified in social intercourse.
7. Be loyal, true, respectful, economical.
8. Be filial, reverent, kindly, gracious.
9. Read widely and hold liberal views.
10. Make friends with the worthy.
11. Avoid becoming a slave to amusement.
12. Practice restraint.
13. Be resourceful.

16. Propriety, music, archery, charioteering, writing, and mathematics, i.e., the sum of education.

38. *Train a Daughter to—*

1. Learn women's duties.
2. Discuss food and drink.
3. Be meek, true, respectful, thrifty.
4. Be attractive in person and manner.
5. Learn writing and reckoning.
6. Be careful to speak softly.
7. Remain pure and chaste in the inner apartments.
8. Sing no ditties.
9. Avoid gossip.
10. Serve her elders well.

39. *Lapses*

1. Talking to people with one's hat off.
2. Scolding another's servants.
3. Boring a hole in the wall to spy upon neighbors.
4. Entering a house without knocking.
5. Being careless about dripping snot or spitting on the mat.
6. Going into the room and sitting down uninvited.
7. Opening other people's boxes and letters.
8. Lifting chopsticks before the host's signal.
9. Laying down chopsticks before all have finished eating.
10. Stretching across the table to reach things.

40. *Presumption*

1. Seeing another man's dispatches and insisting on opening and reading them.
2. Seeing another man's saddled horse and insisting on riding it.
3. Seeing another man's bow and arrows and insisting on trying them.
4. Seeing another man's possessions and insisting on appraising them.
5. Criticizing another's composition.
6. Settling another's domestic affairs.
7. Taking part in another's quarrel.
8. Deciding in a dispute.

41. *Want of Judgment*

1. To abuse another without saying why.
2. To join in a scheme without investigation.

3. For a layman to imitate the ways of the priesthood.
4. Not to discriminate between right and wrong in a matter.
5. To allow a son to take up music.
6. To allow a son to cage animals.
7. For a man to learn women's work.
8. To be on the lookout for petty advantages.

42. *Some Don'ts*

1. Don't drink to intoxication.
2. Don't enter a widow's house alone.
3. Don't go alone in the dark.
4. Don't consort with rogues.
5. Don't take things for fun and say nothing about it.
6. Don't open another's private letters.
7. Don't borrow without returning promptly.

Translated by E. D. Edwards

221
Lay Student Notations from Tun-huang

Anonymous (third quarter of the 9th century)

Pitee the poor lay stoodent
Whose horse has gone up to the stebul in haven.
[Which] family haz a nice girl
That can be married off to a lay student?

When copying, do not drink wine,
Lest the whole day, the tip of your brush be drie;
Just doo what seems appropriate.
This morning I was at a boring meeting,

These random jottings appear in the margins and in the unused spaces of a scroll from Tun-huang (see selection 266) that consists of a commentary on chapter five of the Confucian *Analects* (see selection 7). They were written by two or three lay students enrolled in a school attached to one of the Buddhist monasteries at Tun-huang. Although such lay students obviously did not possess full literacy, they were of enormous importance in the creation of written vernacular narrative in China. The overwhelming majority of the earliest written vernacular texts in China, dating to approximately a thousand years ago, were copied by just such lay students. This translation attempts to replicate in English the orthographically erroneous quality of their writing, here apparently exacerbated by drunkenness.

It brought my worries home to me all the more;
I bought five pints of good wine,
And sent my worries a thousand miles away.

One scroll of corrected copying by two students Li.

The smoke which has been spit out settles to form a vapor.
At the tip of the mountain, the fifth month's moon is bright;
Having received a summons, I anchor my boat 'midst the islets at night,
The peach trees come out to pay their respects to the wal sity.

When copying, do not drink wine,
Lest the whole day the tip of your brush be drae;
Just doo what seems appropriate,
If there are mistakes, later people will see them.

If there are mistakes, people will. . . .

Pity the poor lay stodent
Whose horse has gone up to haven;
Which family has a nice girl
To marry off to a lay stodent?
Which family have a Lady's Finger
To marry of too thish bu givup two mush. . . .
Pity the poor lay student
Whose horse has gone up to haven.
Whose family has a nice girl
To merry off to a stud-. . . ?

Translated by Victor H. Mair

222

That Which Is Mandated by Heaven Is Called Nature

Ch'ü Ching-ch'un (d. 1569)

A. Breaking Open the Topic
   1. It has been said: "Heaven is the origin of the Way,"

The practice of selecting topics for civil service examinations from one of the four Confucian classics (the *Analects*, the *Mencius*, the *Great Learning*, or the *Doctrine of the Mean*) began during the Yüan dynasty and continued into the Ming and Ch'ing. The topic of Ch'ü Ching-

2. And: "The Superior Man embodies It and thereby provides Heaven with assistance."
3. By following the Way, the singularity of the principles of things can be seen.

B. Carrying the Topic Forward
   1. The principles of Heaven and Man are one and the same, not two.
   2. In the beginning the Way is mandated by Heaven.
   3. In the end It becomes an ability of one's own.
   4. Such being the case, how could it be permissible for the Superior Man
   5. To excuse himself from making an effort to embody the Way?

C. Opening Statement
   1. Formerly, Tzu-ssu[1] worried about the Way not being clear,
   2. And about many people burdening their minds with selfishness.
   3. Thus, he discussed these matters in order to instruct people, saying that
   4. Originally our human mind circulates through Heaven, Earth, and the Ten Thousand Things.
   5. When trying to embody the Way,
   6. If our minds are not used to exhaust completely the measure of Heaven, Earth, and the Ten Thousand Things,
   7. But are instead shackled by their appearance,
   8. Then we split Heaven and Man into two things.

D. Taking up the Topic
   1. Do we not see the source from which the Way arises, and the end toward which It is heading?
   2. Now, just what is the action of the Way?

E. Opening Limb
   a 1. The Way guides our human Nature which is mandated by Heaven;
   b 2. It is not an embellishment external to ourselves.
   a 3. The Way is practiced in accord with Teachings which are cultivated through the Way;

---

ch'un's essay is the opening line of Tzu-ssu's *Doctrine of the Mean*. To be successful, a candidate had to develop philosophical themes according to Chu Hsi's Neo-Confucian commentaries. The essay had to follow rigid rules of composition requiring grammatical as well as thematic parallelism developed in specific rhetorical segments. Skill in this so-called "eight-legged essay" composition remained a prescription for success in the civil service examinations until their abolition early in this century.

Many scholars were hesitant to accept the eight-legged essay, a product of the examination hall, as a genre of prose literature. Others distinguished themselves as eight-legged essay stylists. During the late Ming and early Ch'ing, exemplary essays were anthologized, widely discussed, and evaluated. By the end of the Ch'ing, however, the eight-legged essay had become a fashionable target of criticism and a scapegoat for the ills of a declining empire.

1. Confucius' grandson (483–402 B.C.E.?), to whom the *Doctrine of the Mean* has traditionally been attributed.

b   4. The self originally possesses It.

c   5. Since nothing under Heaven is not the Way,

c   6. There is nothing which is not also the self.

      7. The Way truly should not be left even for a moment.

      8. For can one leave the Way yet suppose that one is studying It?

      9. Hence, one who enters the Way out of instruction never relaxes his effort.

F.   Empty Limb

a   1. Sometimes the Way is invisible and inaudible,

b   2. As though one could get away from it.

c   3. But, whether one is active or at rest, there is no departing from the Heavenly Principle.

d   4. Therefore, how should the Superior Man be wary and vigilant in order to preserve the Nature mandated by Heaven?

e   5. Must he wait to verify Its color and sound?

a   6. Sometimes the Way is neither evident nor manifest,

b   7. As though one could get away from It.

c   8. But, with regard to the minute and the obscure, the human mind should allow no lacunae.

d   9. Therefore, how should the Superior Man be careful when alone to practice the Way of following his Nature?

e   10. Must he wait for what is most evident and most manifest?

    11. It is not that the Way originally is separate from man,

    12. And that the merit of the Superior Man therefore consists in making It inseparable.

    13. Rather, it is that the spirit of the Way permeates Heaven, Earth, and the Ten Thousand Things,

    14. And actually fills our single mind.

G.   Middle Parallel

a   1. That is to say, the mind that is not yet aroused

b   2. Is at rest and simply unmoved.

c   3. Thus, when our mind breaks away from the prejudices of bias and inclination,

d   4. One word, "impartiality," suffices to characterize the Way of all under Heaven.

e   5. The embodiment of the Way is within our mind;

f   6. Can we stop at being watchful and wary?

a   7. That is to say, the mind that is already aroused

b   8. Responds simply by opening to the Way.

c   9. Thus, by following guidelines of appropriate cooperation,

d   8. A single word, "harmony," suffices to encompass the situation of the Ten Thousand Things.

e   9. The function of the Way is within our mind;

f 10. Can we stop at being cautious when alone?

11. Although some people have not yet completely embodied It,

12. That

g 13. Has nothing to do with Heaven and Earth

g 14. And is unrelated to the Ten Thousand Things.

H. Back Parallel

1. If one really can,

a 2. By being watchful and wary, achieve impartiality,

b 3. Thereby daily strengthening one's preservation of the heavenly mandate;

a 4. And, by being cautious when alone, achieve harmony,

b 5. Thereby daily broadening behavior which follows our Nature,

6. Then

c 7. Heaven, Earth, and oneself will all have the same body,

d 8. So that by using mind to respond to mind,

e 9. Heaven and Earth will not be destroyed

f 10. But will stay fixed,

c 11. And moreover, the Ten Thousand Things will function like oneself,

d 12. So that compliance will attract compliance;

e 13. All categories of being will prosper,

f 14. And will fulfill their lives.

I. Concluding Parallel

1. Hence,

a 2. In the beginning Heaven endowed us with this principle;

a 3. In the end we use this principle to assist Heaven and Earth.

b 4. The Way does not exceed the capacity of our mind.

b 5. The mind is not inadequate for conforming to the Way.

J. Postlude

1. If someone cannot fully actualize the Way with his mind,

2. Just because his mind is small,

3. That is not the fault of the Way.

4. Tzu-ssu, being the first to speak of this,

5. Revealed his concern for the Way.

Translated by Wayne Alt

223

Three Customs and Ten Sins

A Fragment on Fashions in Cuisine

Anonymous (probably 17th century)

In the *Yang-ku man-lu* by Hung Shun of the Sung dynasty (c. twelfth century), there is a story about a female cook. It says that in the capital, the middle and lower classes preferred to have daughters rather than sons. Every time a girl was born, she was carefully brought up and protected like a jewel. When she began to grow up, she was given training in some special line according to her talent, so that her service would be wanted by the rich families. These young women for household service were classified into several kinds, such as "personal maids," "skilled women," "sewing women," "housekeepers," "actresses," "washing women," "musicians," "cooks," etc. These were all sharply divided professions, and among these the lowest was that of a female cook. But, even so, only the wealthiest families could afford to keep them.

The story is told of the experience of one official who employed such a female cook. There was a certain magistrate who came from a poor family and who had filled posts in several districts. His habits were frugal, and when he was back home on account of his parents' mourning period,[1] he was short of servants and his food was badly prepared. He remembered that once in the capital he had tasted an extraordinary supper at the home of a friend, prepared by a female cook. There happened to be someone going to the capital and he sent a letter to the friend asking that he look for one for him. Most of them would not leave the capital, but some time later his friend wrote him that he had secured a female cook. She was just over twenty and had recently left a high official's home, had great skill and was quite pretty, and understood writing and arithmetic. He was sending the girl down south immediately. In less than a month's time she arrived. At the suburban station, she sent her husband[2] ahead with a note in her own handwriting. Her calligraphy was very

The above is one of the two surviving fragments of *Three Customs and Ten Sins (San feng shih chien chi)*, a book presumably found in Soochow. It is a record of changing social customs—mostly wicked—of the Soochow-Changshu region. The other fragment, which is not translated here, deals with a woman of notorious morals, who ruined almost all the families in the village and who, even in her sixties, bewitched young men with her charms.

1. Every official, including a prime minister, had to resign for three years during the period of mourning for a parent's death. Concealment of such a funeral and continuing in office, when exposed, would be a very serious crime in the eyes of the law. Nothing of importance to the state could excuse breaking the Confucian custom of loyalty to one's parents.

2. In the other fragment, the author notes that when the Yüan dynasty collapsed, the Mongol soldiers were segregated. Their women soon earned more money than their husbands, who waited outside rich men's residences to take them home.

good and well formed. It began with the usual polite phrases about how happy she was to come to serve him and to begin service that very day, etc., and at the end begged him to send a soft sedan-chair to receive her so as to keep up proper form. It was couched in a very refined language, not what a common woman would be able to write. The magistrate was greatly delighted.

When she entered the house, her deportment and manners were perfect. She was in a red jacket and green skirts, and bowed to the others and retired. This was more than the magistrate had expected, and all his friends proposed that they should have a dinner to celebrate. On her part, the woman was anxious to show her skill. The magistrate told her that he would give a formal dinner later, but for the present he would like to have a small household dinner with five courses of "five-inch"[3] dishes. The woman asked for his orders in the way of meat and vegetables, and the magistrate wrote them down and gave the list to her, asking among other things for lamb's head and *pâté d'ail*.[4]

The cook took the order, then opened her writing case and wrote down the things to be bought.[5] In this list she put down ten lambs' heads and five catties of garlic, the other things in proportion. The owner thought that that was a great deal but did not want to make her think that he was stingy. When the foodstuff was all bought, the cook opened her baggage and took out her kitchenware, consisting of various pans, spoons big and small, soup plates, etc., and asked a maid to show them to the master. They were beautiful and shining, consisting all of "white copper,"[6] each vessel worth about twenty taels[7] of silver. The other kitchen utensils, like knives and chopping boards, were also of a very fine quality. Everybody was impressed. Then she put on her apron, with silver chains around her upper arms. With a sweeping gesture, she entered the kitchen and sat on a large hardwood settee. Slowly she got up to prepare her food, handling her knife most expertly. In preparing the lambs' heads, she had them rinsed and put on a table, then began to pick the meat from the jowls and threw all the rest away. On being asked, she said, "Gentlemen don't eat those things." The others picked up the thrown-away parts and put them away, and she laughed and said, "Are you people going to eat dog's food?" In preparing her garlic paste, she scalded the garlic with boiling water once, took off all the leafy parts, leaving the stem, which she cut up into lengths according to the diameter of the dish to be used. Again she peeled the outer layers and took only the yellowish, tender middle part. This she soaked in wine and salt, and threw all the rest away without stint. But her food was something of a dream, tasty and crisp and fragrant, and extremely neat in

3. Small.
4. Garlic paste.
5. By other servants.
6. Copper alloy with nickel in it, as mined in Yunnan.
7. Roughly equal to 1⅓ ounces each.

appearance. The friends cleaned up the plates and looked at each other in admiration. After dinner, the female cook came in, made a double bow, and said, "I am glad that my food meets with your approval. Please give the regular gratuity." The magistrate was embarrassed and did not know what to say. The female cook suggested, "Why don't you follow the usual practice?" Then she took out several slips of paper from her coat pocket and presented them, saying, "This is what I used to get." The magistrate looked at them, and found that for a formal dinner she was given ten thousand cash and twenty pieces of silk, and half of that amount for a small dinner. The magistrate thought he was trapped and could only do what was demanded of him. In private he told his friends, "How can I afford to give such dinners and keep such a cook?" In about ten days, he dismissed her on some pretext.

This was the custom prevailing at the time of the Northern Sung when people were willing to spend money on food. Even thrifty people were sometimes forced to follow the custom. How much more so is it today? I have already recorded all the customs of keeping actresses and the song and dance entertainments under the head of "Customs of Professional Women." But even in worship of the dead, sacrifices of animals are made before the priests start to chant their prayers. In places of amusement, lavish and choice dinners are given before the songs and dances start. So a good dinner is the usual preliminary to song and dance. That is why I have included the matter of food under the category of "Customs of Professional Women."

The attention to good food began in the city[8] with the pawnbroker Fang Shih-mou. He gave extravagant dinners. In place of Sung porcelain dishes, which were considered too small, he used large bowls for keeping fish and, in place of three-inch dishes, he used big ones such as are used for holding Buddha's hands.[9] His "golden lacquer leg of pork" consisted of an entire leg which had been prepared with brown sugar and sweet sauce, served whole on the table. His "crystal leg of mutton," prepared with white sugar and white wine, was also served entire on the table. Roast chicken and duck were always served in pairs, also entire. Most of his other dishes were like that, and the rich families began to copy him. In the Ming dynasty the regular custom was to serve only six courses, or even five, using small dishes, and sometimes there was a wooden dish, shaped like a fish with scales and all, containing some beans.[10] Now the custom has greatly changed.

Assistant Commissioner Chien was a rich man before he became an official and grew richer still. He loved to give dinners when he was at home. His wife

8. Soochow or Changshu.
9. *Hsiang-yüan*, a variety of citron, with one end shaped like fingers.
10. The custom is based upon a pun. The word for "fish" is *yü*, which also means "enough to spare" or "extra." It was considered good luck to have more than necessary, and guests, on coming to the end of the dinner, would raise their chopsticks and say, "We have enough to spare."

was an expert cook, her dishes being distinguished by three qualities: novelty, delicacy,[11] and choiceness. Some of her famous dishes are the following:

Lamb Kidney

First take the raw kidney and cook it lightly with the skin on. Then take it out, skin it, and cut it into thin slices. Sauté it with crushed walnut until the walnut oil has penetrated the kidney. Add spices, old wine, and grade A soy sauce. Fry in deep oil. Its taste is better even than bear's paw.[12] When lamb kidney cannot be obtained, pig kidney can be prepared in the same way.

Turtle Skirt

Take only turtle found in creeks, and not those from Kiangpei.[13] Cook a little and cut the "skirt"[14] and peel off the black skin with a pair of pincers, leaving an absolutely clean white meat. Fry in crackling pork fat with ginger and cinnamon powder. It melts in the mouth and has a piquant aroma. The guests would not know that it was turtle meat. Therefore it was given a special name of *hun fenp'i.*[15]

Steamed Wild Duck

Domestic-fed duck which is fat and juicy is not uncommon. One must take wild duck caught with a net. Feather it clean. Take out the entrails and stuff it with sweet sauce,[16] soy sauce, and old wine. Sew up and wrap it on the outside with a freshly made *fu-yi.*[17] Steam until thoroughly soft. Then skin it from neck to leg and open up the joints and bone it, leaving only the head and the legs. Cook this entire over a slow fire with spices, sweet sauce, soy sauce, and old wine along with its own juice until the sauce is almost dry. Then serve.

Other animals which are greasy, like the guinea hen, *ts'e-mao* [porcupine?], and eagle, should be steamed with a wrapping of *fu-yi*, so that the meat will taste moist with the natural fat kept in.

11. Nongreasiness.

12. Bear's paw is as old as Mencius (see selection 8) and is still a delicacy in the Manchurian provinces. It is a cartilaginous substance, cooked until gluey like Provençal tripe, but is distinctly nongreasy.

13. North of the Yangtze, in Kiangsu.

14. Fleshy part with black skin.

15. A gluey paté, but made with meat.

16. *T'ien-chiang*, sweet and sour, made with the juice of shellfish.

17. Hardened sheet of bean-curd. This is always done for wrapping roasts to prevent escape of juice while in the oven or being steamed.

Duck's Tongue

A large quantity must be collected from cooks or restaurants. After cooking, take out the thin cartilage in the center. Slice in half lengthwise, and stir-fry [or sauté] with the tender part of bamboo shoot and champignon in sesame oil. Sprinkle in a little sweet white wine. The guests will think it is a kind of prepared champignon but the taste is different. This ranks first among the hors d'oeuvres.

Pickled Coxcomb

The pickled coxcomb comes next among the delicacies. It is also collected from various restaurants or cooks. Wrap in *chuan* silk and marinate in *tsao*[18] overnight. Sesame oil and sweet white wine dregs can also be used. Sauté it with tips of bamboo shoot and champignon. The guests will like its flavor without knowing what it is.

Chicken and Duck Gizzards

Next among the delicacies comes the gizzard. It is also collected from restaurants and cooks and soaked in sediment of wine. Cook it with good spring water to make a delicious soup, with fresh tips of bamboo shoot or fresh, tender *sung-hua* mushroom.[19]

Pigeon Egg Soup

Make reservations for eggs with breeders of pigeons, paying down an advance. One needs about twenty of these to make a bowl of soup. Boil them in water and take off the shell. There will remain white, translucent lovely balls to put in soup. At the same time, make flour balls with flour from lotus root, with stuffing of crushed pine seeds made into a paste with the finest foreign sugar. These white flour balls can go with the pigeon eggs in the same soup. Sometimes the guests will take home a few of these white flour balls, smelling their subtle fragrance all the way. This is a most distinguished, exotic soup.

Carp's Tongue Soup

The tongue will also have to be collected. It is drenched with white wine and cooked with good spring water to make soup, with a pinch of fine onion. Served at the end of a wine dinner, it is most delicate.

18. Grains from a distillery, the dregs or sediment of wine casks, regularly used in marinating foodstuff.
19. This grows under pines and is prized for its flavor.

Blackfish Tail Soup

Choose a large blackfish and cut off its tail to use for soup. Boil it in plain water. Take out of the water and cut into thin threads, after removing the tail bone. Mix with bamboo shoot, mushroom, and seaweed in the soup. Or add a little lotus root flour[20] and a few drops of rice vinegar. Taken after a wine dinner, it cools one's spirits and has a flavor that stays in the mouth. This is also a recherché recipe.

The above tend toward the exotic. The usual rich food seems to be ignored. Perhaps these things are prized for their special nutritive value, or perhaps the Assistant Commissioner did not like rich food. A competitive spirit developed among families to outdo him by more fancy dishes, but he seemed to stick to his principles of novelty, delicacy, and choiceness. Thus there was another change in cuisine fashions.

Then followed Mr. Chao of Taiyuan with his steamed eel, and Mr. Chen of Yingchuan tried to better Mr. Chao with his boneless mullet. The cook Shu made a name with his stewed shad in spring; then Mr. Shao Sheng-shih tried to better Mr. Shu with his shad in all seasons.

Chao's Steamed Eel

Choose a big fat eel with a full belly. Throw away its head and tail and innards. Chop into one-inch sections, and rub them with natural salt. Arrange the pieces in a pewter heater[21] packed with sweet white *niang*[22] and place the heater inside a boiling pan of soup. After a while, add the best quality soy sauce. When the spine shows through the flesh, pinch off the bone right inside the heater. Then cover the sections with a thick coating of chopped onion, pepper, and good white pork fat. Keep them in the heater surrounded with boiling water until the pork fat has melted at the bottom and serve. This food is extremely rich in flavor. It makes a gourmet's mouth water just to mention it.

Chen's Steamed Boneless Mullet

Mr. Chen gave money to the wholesale fish dealers with an order to reserve big mullets exclusively for him. He wanted to outdo Mr. Chao, and chose the mullet instead of eel, and he also cooked it by means of a heater. The fish is slashed in two from the back, leaving the belly connected. The head is kept.

20. Like cornstarch.
21. A pewter jar used to keep spirits warm by being held suspended in boiling water. Functions like a double boiler.
22. Fermented rice, like *tsao*, a regular substance for marinating food.

Pack white fermented rice at the bottom of the heater and place the fish over it, and steam without direct contact with boiling water until it is done. Then take off the spine and nip off all the bones clean. Close the two halves again, with head and tail intact. Again cover it with chopped onion, pepper, salt, and pork fat, and steam again until it is thoroughly soft. It is served in the heater. It is boneless and tender and soft with a very delicate flavor. The guests can hardly wait for the host's invitation to eat by raising his chopsticks.

Shu's Steamed Shad

Shad is a tasty fish, considered among the best seafood in the south. It used to be steamed or boiled. Mr. Shu in general copied the method of the above two in preparing eel and mullet, but added only white foreign sugar and did not chop the fish into sections. The scales are not removed.[23] The result is a very tasty and clean piece of fish, rich in flavor, different from shad prepared in other ways. His shad became very much sought after.

Shao's Shad in All Seasons

Mr. Shu could provide shad only in spring, but Mr. Shao was able to provide it in all seasons. When asked how he did it, he explained that it was not easy. In late spring, he asked his servants who understood how to preserve fish to go to the river port provided with cash and the preservatives, like foreign sugar, pepper, and salt, and the best kind of *tsao*, or fermented rice. They went to the fishermen's homes, and as soon as fish came in, the entrails were taken out but the scales were kept. Foreign sugar was rubbed into the inside and over the scales. They packed a jar at the bottom with a heavy layer of *tsao*, adding some pepper and natural salt. The fish was placed above the *tsao* and again covered with *tsao* and pepper and salt. This was continued until the jar was almost full, when the contents were pressed firm with the hand and the mouth sealed with fine clay. After reaching home, the jars were buried underground to keep them cool. This was what Mr. Shao told his friends.

Sautéed Porcupine

But this is nothing compared with the trouble in preparing porcupine. Yu-shan[24] is close to the sea[25] where river porcupines come in large quantities in the spring. Everybody knows that it is poisonous, and there were few who dared to eat it until Mr. Li Tse-ning came along. He was a wholesale dealer, grew rich, and took an interest in food. The first thing was the careful

23. Much of the flavor comes from the fat contained in the skin of shad.
24. In Kiangsu, north of Soochow.
25. The Yangtze River estuary.

preparation of the "porcupine paste" made of yellow beans a year before. Only the best yellow beans were used. First the brown and black beans were removed, then the yellow ones with small black dots or purple grains on them, until the mass consisted entirely of pure yellow. Every piece had to be scrutinized. This was cooked until it was soft and made into a yellow paste with the addition of Huai wheat flour. In June this was mixed with a little white salt and exposed in the hot sun, with a veil to keep out dust. When this was done, it was put in a jar, which was covered with an earthen basin and sealed with lime. This was the "porcupine paste." It is said that in the making of the paste the slightest presence of black or brown beans, or those with black or purple markings, when eaten with porcupine would kill a person. Or when dust got mixed in during the preparation, it would also be harmful. That is why so much care had to be taken. Men were then sent to a clear river, where boats carried several jars of the river water. All washing and cooking of porcupine was done with this river water.

Take several pairs of porcupine, gouge out their eyes and embryos in the stomachs. Slash out their spines and clean out all blood. Use a silver pin to pick out all remaining clots of blood on the fat. Cut out the meat and boil it in water with the skin on. Then take it out, place it on a wooden board, and pick out all bristles without exception with fine pincers. Then cut the flesh and skin into squares, with bone and skin and flesh and all, and sauté with pork fat. After this, fry the meat in hot oil, mixing in the yellow bean paste prepared a year ago. Whenever the pot is opened, the cover should be held over it to prevent dust from falling in. Take a paper roll, dip it in the sauce, and light it with a match. If the paper roll lights, the meat is done; if not, it is not done yet. Usually a large quantity is prepared,[26] but when prepared it must be eaten and must not be kept over. It was found that thus prepared, it was absolutely harmless, and for this reason, Li's porcupine became famous and very popular. Every year, about March or April, friends would collect money to have a dinner at his place, and everybody was excited and busy, as if the porcupine feast was a great event of the year. And they ate and ate almost every day until the arrival of the beginning of summer.

Broiled Crabs

Crabs are best produced in lakes. The yellow kind with big claws are called "Golden Claws." Crabs used to be boiled. Later someone thought that, in boiling, some of the flavor was lost. By tying up the claws and putting them in baskets for steaming, the flavor was better preserved. Then there came Pockmark Chou who introduced a new method of broiling them when he returned from the capital. He opened a wineshop in West City, and it was a roaring

26. Because of so much trouble.

success. He first boiled the crabs, then, dipping them in sweet wine and sesame oil, put them on an iron grill to broil. In a short while, the shell rose as if it was ready to burst, and the shell of the two claws and eight feet was all cracked by the heat and the joints at the belly fell open. It was only necessary to prick the shell lightly with one's fingers and the shell fell off, leaving only the meat and the roe. Each man was given a portion on a small dish, which he ate after dipping it in vinegar prepared with sliced ginger. It was delicious and very simple without the usual trouble in getting at the meat. But he would not reveal the secret. Others tried to copy it, but the crab was scorched black and still the shell remained as before. Then someone circulated the story that this Pockmark Chou used to hire beggars to catch hundreds of snakes in spring. When the snakes were cooked, there floated on top a coat of oil. This snake oil was collected and secretly applied. When he told people that he used sesame oil, it was really snake oil. The story was believed, and the people stopped going to the shop, which after three or four years was closed. Then the custom of eating steamed crabs came back to the town. At first it started with the clerks and officers connected with water transportation. Each person was provided with a set of special tools for eating them—a small hammer, a small knife, and a pair of small crackers, for breaking, cutting, and picking the crabs. This became a popular custom, in which even the cultured gentlemen joined.

Shark's Fin and Swallow's Nest

At this time, sea trade was still forbidden. Seafood that came from Fukien and Kwangtung was as expensive as gold, and people were satisfied with their local products. Soon the ban on overseas trade was lifted, and overseas food began to arrive. It was then the custom never to give a formal dinner without a delicacy from overseas, and first among these was the "big" dish, by which was meant the edible swallow's nest. It cost five or six dollars a catty in Canton and double that amount in Soochow. Then there was shark's fin of various qualities. People liked these novelties and soon forgot the taste of fish and meat.

Table Service

Modern extravagances extended to the table service. Certain kinds of food had to be served in Ko-yao[27] plates, and certain others, although quite ordinary, had to be served in Hsüan-yao[28] ware. Food had to come from a great distance, and the utensils used had to be period pieces. Thus just attention to

27. Twelfth century.
28. Or Hsüan-te; fifteenth century.

food itself was not enough, and once more the fashion in eating changed. Therefore Sun Feng-kung wrote his *Tung-shu lu,* and Lu Pi-pu wrote his *Shih-ching chu.* [29] These were a literary man's pastimes, but still they showed the popular love of good food. I have no idea what future readers of this book will think of the whole subject.

Translated by Lin Yutang

29. Treatises on food.

224
Jokes

The Man Who Bit off His Own Nose
from *Grove of Laughter (Hsiao-lin)* [1]

Han-tan Ch'un [2] (fl. early 3rd century).

While A and B were having a fight, A bit off B's nose. When a government official wished to prosecute him, A claimed that B had bitten off his own nose. "A person's nose is higher than his mouth," said the official, "so how could he have reached his nose to bite it off?" "He stepped up on a bed and bit it off." was A's reply.

The Frog That Was Afraid of Being Executed
from *Master Mugwort's Miscellany (Ai Tzu tsa-shuo)*

Compiled by Su Tung-p'o (1037–1101)

Master Mugwort was floating his boat on a lake and stopped one evening to moor it on an islet. At night, he heard the sound of crying beneath the water.

Contrary to the view of China as a humorless country devoid of wit, the Middle Kingdom has a long and rich heritage of jokes and funny stories, some of them by well-known authors. The usual subjects of Chinese humor are physical deformities, bodily functions, stupidity, sons-in-law, blindness, illiteracy, misreading characters (i.e., sinographs), greedy officials, rich landlords, poverty, and other conditions that are highly revealing of social mores and customs. There are also more subtle types of humor, examples of which are included in this selection of jokes from collections made throughout the centuries.

1. The original work is lost, but twenty items from it are preserved in *Extensive Records from the Reign of Great Peace (T'ai-p'ing kuang-chi).*

2. The compiler had another name, Chu, which usually means "India."

Since it also seemed as though someone were talking, he listened more closely. This is what he heard: "Yesterday the dragon king issued an order that all members of the watery tribe who have tails should be beheaded. I'm a water-lizard, so I'm crying because I'm afraid of being executed. But you're a frog who has no tail. Why should you cry?" Then he heard another voice say, "I'm lucky that I don't have any tail now, but I'm worried that I'll be treated for what I was as a tadpole."

The Same Sickness
from A *Collection of Witticisms* (*Ying hsieh lu*)

Liu Yüan-ch'ing (Ming period)

Chang Hsü-tzu made a fancy couch for himself that he kept in his bedroom. Since no one could see it there, however, he feigned illness and lay down on the couch after notifying his friends and relatives so that they would come to pay their regards. There was a relative of his, Yu Yang-tzu, who had just knitted a new pair of socks for himself and wanted to show them off too. So he hiked up his skirts and sat down, crossing one leg on top of his other knee. Then he asked, "What illness do you have, sir?" Observing the way Yu Yang-tzu was sitting, Chang Hsü-tzu looked at him and said with a smile, "I have the same sickness as you!"

Flattery Will Get You Everywhere
from A *Collection of Witticisms*

Liu Yüan-ch'ing

The magistrate of Canton, by nature, enjoyed being flattered. Whenever he issued a directive, his underlings would join in unanimous praise, which would make the magistrate happy. A retainer who wished to curry favor with him calculatingly said to the person standing next to him, "Almost everyone who occupies a position of power over the people enjoys being flattered by others. Only our host is different—he despises those who praise him." When the magistrate heard these words, he immediately called the retainer forward. Patting his chest with satisfaction and prancing with glee, he commended the retainer endlessly, saying, "Splendid! You're the only one who understands my heart! What an excellent retainer!" From that time on, the magistrate increased his intimacy with the retainer.

Monkey Business
from *Grove of Laughter (Hsiao-lin)*

Master Bottoms Up (Fu-pai Chu-jen) (Ming period)

A monkey who had died went before the king of the underworld and requested that he be reborn as a human being. "If you want to be a human being," said the king, "then you must pull out all of the hairs on your body." Whereupon he called his *yakṣa*-guards to start pulling out the monkey's hairs. The monkey, unable to endure the pain, cried out. "You're not even willing to part with a single hair," said the king with a laugh. "How could you be a man?"

A Quick Bow
from *Grove of Laughter*

Master Bottoms Up

A man who performed his bows much too quickly often offended other people. Someone instructed him, saying, "When you bow, recite the names of the months from the first to the second and all the way to the twelfth before you finish. That way you will naturally bow slowly."

One day, the man met a friend of his on the street and bowed to him very slowly as he had been told. By the time he finished his bow, the friend had already gone off. Whereupon the man asked a bystander, "Which month did he leave?"

Tofu
from *Grove of Laughter*

Master Bottoms Up

A man who had a guest for dinner served him only various dishes made with tofu. As he did so, he said out loud to himself, "Tofu is my life! In my estimation, no other flavor can match it."

On another day, the man went to the home of his former guest and the latter, remembering his culinary preferences, added tofu to the meat and fish dishes. But the man picked out only the meat and fish, gorging himself on them.

"I once heard you say, 'Tofu is my life!' How come you're not eating any of it today?" asked the former guest.

"When I get a glimpse of meat and fish," replied the man, "I'd even give up my life!"

Geomancy
from *Grove of Laughter*

Master Bottoms Up

There was a firm believer in geomancy who would always consult a yin-yang diviner before he made the slightest move. One day, just as he happened to be seated at the base of an earthen wall, the wall toppled over upon him. Pinned beneath it, the man frantically called out for someone to come save his life.

When his family heard him crying out and saw him pinned beneath the wall, they wanted to rescue him. At the same time, however, they immediately remembered that he was ordinarily such an ardent believer in geomancy, so they dared not act rashly. Instead, they consoled him, saying, "Just be patient for a while until we can go ask the yin-yang master whether today's a good day for moving earth."

Borrowing an Ox
from *Grove of Laughter*

Master Bottoms Up

A person came bearing a note asking to borrow a plow-ox from a rich old man. The rich man was just at that moment entertaining guests and didn't want to let them know that he was illiterate. So he opened the seal on the note and, pretending to read it, said, "I understand. I'll come over in a few minutes and do it myself."

A Seven for Elocution
from *Jests* (T'iao-nüeh)

compiled by Wang Shih-chen (1526–1590)

The following story was told by Li Hsiao-chang.

When Kuo Kung-fu was passing through Hangchow, he brought out a scroll of his poems which he showed to Su Tung-p'o and then proceeded to recite them himself. The sound of his voice reverberated in every corner of the room.

When he was finished, he said to Tung-p'o, "How would you rate my poems?"

"I'd give 'em a ten," said Tung-p'o.

Delighted, Kung-fu asked, "On what basis did you rate them?"

"I gave them a seven for elocution," said Tung-p'o, "and a three for the poetry. Doesn't that add up to a ten?"

The Wife Who Was Born Under the Sign of the Ox
from *Treasury of Laughs (Hsiao-fu)*

Master of the Ink Idiot's Studio (Mo-han-chai chu-jen),
Feng Meng-lung (1574–1645)

The subordinates of a prefect who was having a birthday heard that he was born under the sign of the rat, so they each contributed some gold from which a full-scale rat was cast to celebrate his longevity. Much pleased, the prefect said, "Did you know that my bosom mate's birthday is coming up soon? She was born under the sign of the ox."

Dreaming of the Duke of Chou [3]
from *Treasury of Laughs*

Feng Meng-lung

A teacher who had fallen asleep during the daytime woke up and fibbed, saying, "I was dreaming of the Duke of Chou." The next day, his pupil emulated him, but the teacher woke him up with the swat of a paddle and said, "How could you do such a thing?" "I, too, dreamed that I went to see the Duke of Chou," said the pupil. "What did the Duke of Chou say to you?" asked the teacher. The pupil answered, "The Duke of Chou said, 'I did *not* see your respected teacher yesterday.' "

The God of the Archery Target Helps Win the War
from *Expanded Treasury of Laughs (Kuang hsiao-fu)*

Feng Meng-lung

A military officer engaged in a campaign was on the verge of being defeated when suddenly a superhuman warrior joined his formation so that he ended up achieving a great victory instead. The officer kowtowed before the warrior and asked to know his name. "I am the spirit of the archery target," said the superhuman warrior. "What virtue does a humble general like me have that

3. An important figure in the founding and early rule of the Chou dynasty. "Dreaming of the Duke of Chou" is a conventional expression in Chinese that means approximately the same as "went to the Land of Nod," except that it sounds as though something more important than mere sleep were taking place.

would induce you, O honored spirit, to trouble yourself to come to my aid?" To which the spirit replied, "I was moved by the fact that, in the past, when you practiced on the archery range, you never once wounded me with an arrow."

Vegetables, Wine, et nihil alter[4]
from *Expanded Treasury of Laughs*

Feng Meng-lung

A Confucian official who had to go to meet a superior of his had just gotten on his horse and was ready to leave when a fellow villager dropped in for a visit. Not having leisure to give detailed instructions to his wife, he told her curtly, "Offer him vegetables, wine, *et nihil alter.*"

His wife, who couldn't understand literary language, had no idea that *et nihil alter* meant "and nothing else." After consulting with the maids and servants, she believed that when her husband said **alter,** he must have meant **tail.** By "tail," she guessed that he must have been referring to the long-tailed goat that they kept, so she butchered the goat and prepared a rich feast for the visitor who ate it and then left.

The Confucian official returned and asked his wife why she had butchered the goat. When he found out, he sighed and lamented that she had been needlessly extravagant. His chagrin over the loss of the goat was endless. Later on, whenever the official would go out, he would invariably order his wife, saying, "From now on, if guests come when I'm away, just give them 'vegetables and wine.' Be sure not to give them any '*et nihil alter.*' "

Comparing Ages
from *Expanded Treasury of Laughs*

Feng Meng-lung

A man with a newborn daughter was visited by another man who had a boy two years old and who wished to make a match between the two children.[5] The first man was indignant, saying, "My daughter's in her first year[6] and

4. The proper Latin should be *et nihil aliud* or, better still, *et neque aliud*. But since the Confucian official who is the main character in this joke displays a rather shaky command of the classical language, it is not inappropriate to use a bit of inferior Latin to convey his errant pedantry.

5. Marriage alliances in traditional China were often contracted by parents while children were still in their infancy.

6. A Chinese baby was considered to be one *sui* ("year") old at birth.

your son's in his second year. When my daughter turns ten, your son will be twenty. It wouldn't be right for her to be married to such an old husband!"

When the first man's wife heard what had happened, she said, "You fool! Our daughter's one now, but next year she'll be as old as their boy. What's wrong with a match like that?"

That's Preposterous!
from *In Praise of Laughter* (*Hsiao tsan*)

Chao Nan-hsing (Ming period)

A man who was trying to improve his vocabulary heard someone say "That's preposterous!"[7] and, falling in love with the expression, he practiced using it from time to time. It so happened, however, that once when he was busily concerned with crossing a river in a ferryboat he suddenly forgot it, so he kept walking around the boat trying to recover it. A boatman asked whether he had lost something, to which he replied, "Yes, a sentence."

"Whoever heard of losing a sentence?" said the boatman. "That's preposterous!"

"You found it for me," said the man. "Why didn't you say so earlier?"

Severe Amnesia
from *Further Tales of Master Mugwort* (*Ai Tzu hou yü*)

Lu Shao (Ming period)

There was a man from Ch'i who suffered from amnesia. If he were walking, he would forget to stop, and if he lay down, he would forget to get up. His wife was worried about him and so she said, "I've heard that Master Mugwort is a humorous and wise man and that he can cure diseases that other doctors consider to be hopeless. Why don't you go and make him your teacher?" "All right," said the man, whereupon he got on his horse and went off with his bow and arrow tucked under his arm. Before he had completed the first stage[8] of his journey, his bowels felt distended so he got off his horse to relieve himself. He stuck his arrow in the ground and tied his horse to a tree. After he had finished his bowel movement, he turned to the left and saw his arrow. "Boy, was that close!" he said. "I wonder where that came from? It almost struck me!" Then he turned to the right and exclaimed with delight, "Al-

7. The original text has *ch'i yu tz'u li*, a Classical Chinese expression borrowed into Mandarin. Since this expression is actually a whole question sentence in Classical Chinese ("How can there be such a principle?") and is completely based on Classical Chinese vocabulary and grammar, it can be learned by Mandarin speakers only through rote memory.

8. Thirty tricents (about ten miles).

though that whizzing arrow gave me quite a fright, I've found myself a horse!"
As he grabbed the reins and started to turn the horse around, he stepped in his
own mess. Stomping his foot, he said, "Drat! I would have to step in a pile of
dog-do and get my shoe all dirty!"

He whipped up the horse and headed it for home. When he reached there,
he paced back and forth outside the gate, saying, "Whose place is this? Could
it be Master Mugwort's residence?" Just at that moment, his wife caught sight
of him and, realizing that he was experiencing another bout of forgetfulness,
she scolded him. Annoyed, the man said to his wife, "Look, lady, I've never
met you before. So why are you chewing me out?"

The Provincial Education Commissioner in the World of the Dead and in the World of the Living
from *Ticklish Tales (Hsi-t'an lu)*

Compiled by Man of the Way from Smallstone (Hsiao-shih Tao-jen)
Edited by Guffawing Gaffer (Ts'an-jan Sou) (Ch'ing period)

A family in the eastern part of a village wanted to hire a teacher to hold classes
for their children. Afraid that they would end up with someone whose learning
was inferior, they discussed the matter with the local government schoolmaster.

"It's true that there are quite a few Cultivated Talents[9] under my jurisdiction who have already passed their examinations, but very few of them are
well versed. If you want to hire a qualified Cultivated Talent, unless you set
up some sort of procedure to test the applicants, you can't tell how much
learning they actually have under their belts."

"May I ask how I should test them?" said the man who wanted to hire
a teacher.

"You must prepare a banquet to which you invite several of the better
qualified candidates," replied the schoolmaster. "Wait until they are all seated,
then just when they have all drunk to the full, secretly signal someone
to announce, 'The Provincial Education Commissioner is arriving tomorrow!' This will certainly startle all of the Cultivated Talents who are
present. If, however, there happens to be one among them who is not
frightened, his learning must be of superior quality. You may invite him to
hold classes for your children and he will definitely be able to fulfill his
responsibilities."

The man who wanted to hire a teacher followed the schoolmaster's plan.
He selected four or five Cultivated Talents whom he invited to a banquet
where they were warmly entertained. After the wine had made several rounds,

9. *Hsiu-ts'ai*, comparable to the Bachelor of Arts degree in the West.

suddenly someone came in and announced, "The Provincial Education Commissioner is arriving tomorrow!" Immediately, the assembled Cultivated Talents were either visibly shaken and lost composure or they were left dumbstruck and staring catatonically—with the exception of one fellow who retained his composure in all respects and sat there quietly and immobilely.

"This surely must be the teacher for me!" said the host. Upon approaching the man and looking at him more closely, he realized that the fellow had already expired. When the relatives of the dead man heard what had happened, they wished to bring a suit against the host for having fatally startled him. The man who wanted to hire a teacher was greatly troubled by this and so he sought help from the schoolmaster.

"No matter what," said the schoolmaster, "don't move the body! I have a technique for bringing him back to life." Whereupon he quickly ordered someone to shout loudly in the face of the dead man, "The Provincial Education Commissioner is going to make an inspection tour of hell!" The dead candidate forthwith came back to life.

Dying for Money
from *Sequel to Ticklish Tales (Hsi-t'an hsü lu)*

Man of the Way from Smallstone

A traveler who was returning to his village with all of his luggage passed through Shantung on his way home. The province was experiencing a great famine and the number of poor people who had died was incalculable. All the inns had been deserted and were no longer accepting guests. The traveler was forced to put up in a temple. In the east wing of the temple he saw several dozen coffins, but in the western wing there was only one coffin that stood all by alone in magnificent isolation. After the third watch, around midnight, a hand extended from each of the coffins. The hands were all sallow and skinny, except for the hand that reached out of the coffin in the western wing, which was fat and fair. The traveler, being a bold fellow by nature, looked about him to the left and the right, then with a laugh, "I suppose you bunch of poor ghosts are all dead broke and want some money from me, right?"

Thereupon he opened his purse and put a big coin in each of the extended hands. All of the ghosts' hands in the eastern wing withdrew into their coffins, but the hand of the ghost in the western wing remained extended as before.

"It looks like a single coin won't satisfy you," said the traveler, "so I'd better give you some more."

The traveler added an additional hundred coins for the ghost in the western wing, but its hand still did not move. Becoming angry, the traveler said,

"What an insolent wretch! Your greed is insatiable!" In the end, however, he took out two strings of cash with a thousand coins in each which he placed in the outstretched palm, whereupon the ghost withdrew its hand instantly.

Surprised by what happened, the traveler picked up a lamp and shone it around on all sides of the temple. What he discovered was that all of the coffins in the eastern wing had written on them "So-and-so Who Died of Starvation." Only the single coffin in the western wing had written on it "Casket of His Honor So-and-So, the Jailor of Such-and-Such a District."

Conversation Between a Senior Official and His Subordinate
from *Sequel to Ticklish Tales*

Man of the Way from Smallstone

A district duty officer who had obtained his position through purchase did not understand Mandarin.[10] After he took office, he paid a courtesy call upon a regional official who asked him, "What are the **customs** like in your honorable district?"

"People don't **cuss** much there and there aren't many **toms** either."

"How are the **fingerlings** this year?"

"**Finger rings** cost two hundred and eighty cash."

"Are there many contributions of **gentry grain?**"

"Your servant's teeth **gently gleam.**"

"How are the **commoners** getting on?"

"We only have a couple of **cum**min bushes, but there are lots of cinna**mon** trees."

"I was asking about the **populace.**"

"We've got lots of **poplars,** but they don't produce much timber."

"I wasn't asking you about trees and such. What I am trying to find out about is the condition of the **citizens.**"

Standing up hurriedly, the duty officer replied, "I regret to inform you, sir, that I have a face full of **zits** and an arse full of **wens.**"

---

10. Mandarin (< Sanskrit *mantrin* ["counselor"]) quite literally means "language of the officials." The Mandarin equivalent of this word is *kuan-hua* ("official speech"). Mandarin was the vernacular language employed by members of the Chinese bureaucracy who hailed from different parts of the country and, as such, spoke a variety of more or less mutually unintelligible native languages and topolects. Mandarin was based upon—but not entirely equivalent to—the language of the capital, being a somewhat refined version of the latter. This joke, which is very difficult to render into English, reveals the difficulties inherent in forging a national bureaucracy from a multilingual constituency.

How to Get Rid of Robbers
from *Bowled over with Laughter (Hsiao-tao)*

Ch'en Kao-mo (Ch'ing period)

A fool who heard that robbers had entered his courtyard gate quickly wrote the four words, "Off Limits, Keep Out," on a piece of paper and stuck it on the door to the main hall of his house. When he heard that the robbers had already stepped into his main hall, he wrote "Road Closed" on another piece of paper and stuck it on the door to his inner chambers. When he heard that the robbers had already reached his inner chambers, he fled to the toilet. The robbers, hot on his trail, pursued him to the toilet, so he closed the door and coughed, saying, "Occupied."

Moving the Statues of Lao Tzu and the Buddha
from *Have a Good Laugh (Hsiao te hao)*

Stone Becomes Gold (Shih Ch'eng-chin) (Ch'ing period)

There was a certain temple that had a clay image of Lao Tzu on the left side and a clay image of the Buddha on the right side. Upon seeing this arrangement, a Buddhist monk said, "The dharma of our Buddha is profound. How can he be placed to the right of Lao Tzu?" So he moved the statue of the Buddha to the left of Lao Tzu.

Some later time, upon seeing this new arrangement, a Taoist priest said, "The Taoist doctrine deserves the utmost respect. How can Lao Tzu be placed to the right of the Buddha?" So he moved the statue of Lao Tzu to the left of the Buddha.

This moving back and forth went on relentlessly until, before they knew what had happened, the monk and the priest has caused the statues made of mud to crumble.

"You and I were getting along all right," said Lao Tzu with a laugh to the Buddha, "until those two scoundrels destroyed us with their constant moving."

Blaming the Farter
from *Have a Good Laugh*

Shih Ch'eng-chin

Somebody farted in a group of people who were sitting around. Although they didn't know for sure who it was, they all suspected a certain person, so they pointed at him and started to blame him. As a matter of fact, it wasn't he who had left the fart. Instead of defending himself, however, the accused began to laugh.

"What's so funny?" asked all the others.

To which he replied, "I'm having a good laugh at the guy who really left the fart but who is blaming me for it along with all the others."

A Method for Taking a Nap
from *Have a Good Laugh*

Shih Ch'eng-chin

A nursemaid became exasperated when the little child she had just finished feeding kept crying and wouldn't be quiet and go to sleep. All of a sudden, she called out to the child's father to bring her a book quickly. When the father asked what for, she replied, "I've noticed that you always fall asleep when you start to read a book."

The Odor's Even Worse over Here
from *Have a Good Laugh*

Shih Ch'eng-chin

There was a wealthy old man who would from time to time leave an occasional fart in the presence of his guests. Once when he did so, two guests were sitting right next to him.

"Although your fart was loud," said the first guest, "I can't smell the slightest odor."

"Not only is there no bad odor," said the second guest, "on the contrary, there is a sort of extraordinary fragrance."

Knitting his brows, the wealthy old man said, "I've heard that if someone's farts don't stink, his five viscera are internally damaged and that the time of his death is not far off. Do you suppose I'm about to die?"

The first guest fanned the air with his hand and went sniffing about with his nose. "Phew!" he said. "The odor's finally hit me."

The second guest wrinkled his nose and inhaled deeply through it. Then, covering his nose with his hands and furrowing his forehead, he said, "The odor's even worse over here where I am!"

Goldfinger
from *Have a Good Laugh*

Shih Ch'eng-chin

A transcendent spirit who could transmute stone into gold appeared among mankind. He went about testing people, trying to find someone whose heart was not avaricious so that he could convert that person into a transcendent like himself. Though he searched the whole land over and transformed big rocks into gold at the touch of his finger, all whom he encountered complained that they were too tiny.

Finally, the transcendent met a person to whom he said as he pointed at a stone, "How would you like it if I touched this stone and turned it into gold for you?" The man shook his head to indicate that he didn't want it. The transcendent suspected that the man had rejected the offer because the stone was too small, so he pointed at a big rock and said, "How would you like it if I touched this great big rock and turned it into gold for you?" Again the man shook his head to indicate that he didn't want it. The old transcendent began to think that this man was completely without avariciousness, a rare person indeed, and someone who ought to be converted to transcendenthood. Consequently, he asked the man, "Since you want neither big nor little pieces of gold, what is it you'd like?"

The man extended his finger and said, "I don't want anything at all. Just exchange for mine the tip of your finger which can transmute stone into gold at a touch, oh old transcendent. That way I can go about everywhere transmuting gold as I please and won't even have to keep track of the amount."

Translated by Victor H. Mair

Biographies, Autobiographies, and Memoirs

225
The Biography of Ching K'o

Ssu-ma Ch'ien (145–90? B.C.E.)

Ching K'o was a native of Wey.[1] His forebears had been natives of Ch'i who had moved to Wey. The people of Wey called him Master Ch'ing,[2] but when he went to Yen,[3] the people called him Master Ching.

Ssu-ma Ch'ien's place in the development of Chinese historiography is comparable to that of Herodotus in the Western tradition. His *Records of the Grand Historian* (*Shih chi*, also rendered in English as *Records of the Scribe*) provided the pattern for all later official dynastic histories of China. Begun by his father Ssu-ma T'an, Grand Astrologer of the Han court during the early years of Emperor Wu's reign, the bulk of the *Records of the Grand Historian* was researched and written by Ssu-ma Ch'ien himself. Much of the finest writing in this enormous work occurs in the "Memoirs" (sometimes referred to as "Biographies of Hereditary Houses") section. The present selection is a good example of how exciting such historical prose can be. It comes from chapter 86 of the "Biographies/Memoirs of Assassins" and describes in electrifying detail an attempt on the life of the First Emperor of the Ch'in dynasty. This is the same First Emperor who ruthlessly reunified China at the close of the Warring States period and whose tomb is guarded by a vast terra-cotta army, one of the most sensational archeological finds of this century, which lies just east of present-day Sian in Shensi province.

The translation has been undertaken with close consultation of the account of Ching K'o as given in the *Intrigues of the Warring States* (see selection 238), which was apparently one of Ssu-ma Ch'ien's primary sources for this biography. For a later poetic version of Ching K'o's attempted assassination of the First Emperor of the Ch'in dynasty, see the third item in selection 29.

1. A petty state near the present P'u-yang district at the south end of Hopei, to be carefully distinguished from the larger state of Wei, which was one of the seven important states of the Warring States period.

Master Ching liked to read books and to handle the sword. He once used his arts to try to influence Prince Yüan of Wei,[4] but Prince Yüan would not employ him. Later on Ch'in attacked Wei,[5] established the commandery of Tung[6] out of the territory it captured, and moved a relative of Prince Yüan to Yeh-wang.[7]

Once when Ching K'o was traveling through Yü-tz'u,[8] he held a conversation with one Ko Nieh about swords. Ko Nieh became angry and gave him a fierce look, and Ching K'o went away. Someone said that they should call Master Ching back. Ko Nieh said: "In the past, if I talked with someone about swords and he did not suit me, I would give him a fierce look. If this has caused him to leave, it is quite proper that he has left, and I shall not venture to detain him." However, he sent a messenger to his master, but Ching K'o had then already harnessed his horse and departed from Yü-tz'u. The messenger returned and reported this. Ko Nieh said: "He has indeed gone. I have given him a fierce look and frightened him."

When Ching K'o was traveling to Han-tan,[9] one Lu Kou-chien disputed with him for the right of way. Lu Kou-chien became angry and reviled him, but Ching K'o escaped without saying anything, and did not again confront him.[10]

On arriving in Yen, Ching K'o became fond of a certain "dog butcher" of Yen and of Kao Chien-li, who was an excellent lute player.[11] Ching K'o liked wine, and every day he drank with the dog butcher and with Kao Chien-li in the marketplace of the Yen capital, becoming drunk before he departed. While Kao Chien-li strummed his lute, Ching K'o would sing along and make merry with him in the midst of the marketplace. Afterward they would weep together, as if there were no one around them.

Yet, though Ching K'o mixed with drunkards, he was a serious man who

2. "Master" is used here and below as a term of respect. Ssu-ma Chen (fl. 720) points out in his commentary that there was a family in Ch'i (modern Shantung) which had borne the name of Ch'ing given here. During his travels, however, Ching K'o's name became changed from Ch'ing to Ching.

3. A state in Hopei, near the present Peking.

4. Reigned 251–230 B.C.E.

5. An important state occupying northern Honan and southwestern Shansi, which at this time dominated the lesser state of Wey mentioned in the first sentence.

6. A large region south of the present P'uyang district, Hopei.

7. This event took place in 241 B.C.E., although it was not a relative of Prince Yüan, but Prince Yüan himself, who was thus shifted. Ssu-ma Ch'ien implies by this anecdote that if Prince Yüan had employed Ching K'o, he would have escaped this disaster. Yeh-wang was in what is now Ch'inyang district in Honan.

8. Near the modern Taiyuanfu, the capital of Shansi; it was then part of the state of Chao.

9. Capital of the state of Chao, ten tricents southwest of the present Hantan district in Hopei.

10. These incidents are given by Ssu-ma Ch'ien to show that Ching K'o, though brave in a righteous cause (as will be seen below), was by nature of a conciliatory and gentle disposition.

11. The kind of lute mentioned here was, according to Ssu-ma Chen, strummed with a piece of bamboo. Dog meat was eaten in ancient China, and a dog butcher was a very lowly

loved books, and the persons with whom he associated during his travels among the feudal lords were all of superior worth and excellence. When he came to Yen, a Mr. T'ien Kuang, who was a retired gentleman in Yen, also received him well, and knowing that he was not an ordinary man, had him live with him for some time. It was just at this period that Tan, Crown Prince of Yen, who had been a hostage in Ch'in, returned in flight to Yen.[12]

Crown Prince Tan of Yen had at one time been a hostage in Chao, and Cheng, the king of Ch'in, had been born in Chao.[13] In his youth he had been friendly with Tan, but when Cheng became king of Ch'in and Tan was a hostage in Ch'in, the king of Ch'in did not treat Crown Prince Tan of Yen well. Therefore Tan became angry and fled back to Yen. On his return, he looked for someone who would take vengeance on the king of Ch'in, but his state was small and its power inadequate.

Later on Ch'in was constantly sending forth its soldiers east of the mountains[14] to attack Ch'i, Ch'u, and the three Chin.[15] Gradually it made encroachments upon the feudal lords, even unto Yen. The lords and ministers of Yen all feared that disaster would befall it, and Crown Prince Tan, being worried, asked his tutor, Chü Wu, about the matter.

Chü Wu replied: "The territory of Ch'in spreads through the world, and it has intimidated the houses of Han, Wei, and Chao. In the north it possesses the fortifications of Sweet Springs and Valley Mouth.[16] In the south it has the irrigation of the Ching and the Wei.[17] It has seized for itself the riches of Pa and Han.[18] On its right are the mountains of Lung and Shu,[19] and on its left are the defiles of Kuan and Yao.[20] Its people are numerous and its gentry are

---

man. In later times the expression "dog butcher" has come to be used generally to denote any mean person of lowly origin.

12. This event took place in 232 B.C.E. It was a custom in ancient China to send hostages to different states.

13. The later unifier of China, the famous First Emperor of Ch'in (246–210 B.C.E.). He was born in Chao in 259 B.C.E.

14. I.e., east of the strategic Han-ku Pass which separated Ch'in from the other feudal states on the east and which was located south of the present Lingpao district in Honan.

15. The three states of Han, Chao, and Wei, into which the state of Chin had been divided in 403 B.C.E.

16. There are several places called Sweet Springs (Kan-ch'üan) in Shensi, but this is probably the one in the district of the same name toward the north of Shansi. The mention of Valley Mouth (Ku-k'ou) here is decidedly strange, as its location northwest of Chingyang district, Shensi, puts it almost in the same latitude as the Ching and the Wei, mentioned immediately below as being to the south.

17. The Ching River meets the Wei River very near the present city of Sian in Shensi; the Wei joins the Yellow River at the place where the latter makes its right-angled bend to the north.

18. Pa was a wild region in what is now Szechwan, conquered by Ch'in in 316 B.C.E. The Han River flows through southern Shensi and joins the Yangtze at Hankow.

19. Lung was in a district of the same name in Shensi. Shu was in Szechwan, close to Pa.

20. Kuan, meaning "the Pass," was the Han-ku Pass, for which see note 14. The Yao Pass

fearsome. It has an overabundance of military supplies. Once it has the idea of sallying forth, then south of the Long Wall and north of the Yi River there can be no security.[21] How, with the hatred that comes of oppression, can you wish to oppose it?"[22]

"Well, then," said Tan, "what is to be done?"

He replied: "I beg to retire and think the matter over."

After some period of time had elapsed, Fan Yü-ch'i, a Ch'in general who had fallen into disgrace with the king of Ch'in, fled as a fugitive to Yen, where the Crown Prince received and sheltered him. Chü Wu remonstrated, saying: "You cannot do this. When, with all his harshness, the king of Ch'in heaps up hatred against Yen, it is enough to chill one's heart. How much more so when he hears of the whereabouts of General Fan! This is called throwing meat in the path of a hungry tiger. The resulting disaster is inescapable. Even if you had Kuan or Yen, they could not plan successfully against it.[23]

"I should like the Crown Prince to send off General Fan quickly to the Huns[24] in order to do away with him. I beg you to ally yourself with the three Chin on the west, link yourself with Ch'i and Ch'u on the south, and put yourself on good terms with the *Shan-yü*[25] on the north. After this you can make plans."

The Crown Prince said: "The Grand Tutor's plan is something for a long period. But I am perplexed and fear I cannot wait even a moment. Yet this is not the only point. For General Fan was in great straits in the world when he gave himself to me, and never, to the end of my life, could I, because of pressure from a powerful Ch'in, cast aside the bonds of pity and compassion and put him away among the Huns. If I did such a thing, it would certainly be time for me to die. Let the Grand Tutor reconsider the matter."

---

was fifty tricents north of Yungning district in Honan. Left and right for a Chinese would mean east and west respectively, as the Chinese cardinal direction is the south.

21. The Long Wall here was not the famous so-called Great Wall linked together by the state of Ch'in, but one of several walls built by different states at various times and later consolidated by Ch'in into one system. The reference here is to the state of Yen, which occupied the area between the Long Wall and the Yi River.

There were three Yi rivers in ancient times, all near each other in Hopei. The one here was probably that which flowed from the district of the same name in western Hopei down to the southeast of Tinghsing district on the Peking-Hankow railway, where it joined the Chüma river.

22. Literally, "to rub against its resisting scales." The figure occurs in the *Han Fei Tzu*, end of chapter 12, where it refers to the resisting scales of the dragon. It means opposing oneself to one's superior or to a superior force.

23. These were Kuan Chung (d. 645 B.C.E.) and Yen Ying (d. 500 B.C.E.), who were prime ministers in the state of Ch'i and among the most famous statesmen of antiquity.

24. Hsiung-nu, nomadic tribes to the northwest of China, who some centuries later were driven out by the Chinese and migrated to the west, where they have been identified with the famous Huns.

25. *Shan-yü* was the title by which the Huns addressed their leader.

Chü Wu said: "To move into danger thereby wishing to gain peace; to create calamities thereby to obtain good fortune; to hold to shallow plans for requiting deep hatreds; to bind oneself in lasting bonds to a single man, without regard for the great harm therefrom to the nation: such is what is called encouraging enmities and inviting disaster. When wild duck feathers are burned on a stove's charcoal, there can be nothing to bother about.[26] All the more so, then, when eaglelike Ch'in carries out its cruel hates. What is there then to talk about?[27] In Yen there is a Mr. T'ien Kuang who is a man of deep wisdom and great bravery. You can plan with him."

The Crown Prince said: "I should like through you to make the acquaintance of Mr. T'ien. Can it be done?"

Chü Wu replied: "I respectfully obey." He went to see Mr. T'ien and told him that the Crown Prince wished to discuss affairs of state with him. T'ien Kuang said: "I respectfully receive his command," and thereupon went to him. The Crown Prince welcomed him, led him inside, knelt, and dusted off the mat for him to sit on.

T'ien Kuang sat down and settled himself, and there was nobody around them. The Crown Prince moved from his mat toward his visitor and requested him, saying: "Yen and Ch'in cannot both stand. I should like you, sir, to put your mind on this fact."

T'ien Kuang replied: "Your servant has heard that when the unicorn is in its prime, it can traverse one thousand tricents.[28] But when it has become weak and old, a broken-down nag can outstrip it. The Crown Prince has heard falsely that I am in my prime, and does not know that I have already lost my vitality. Nevertheless, I dare not on that account slight affairs of state. A good person who could be employed would be Master Ching."

The Crown Prince said: "I should like through you to make the acquaintance of Master Ching. Can it be done?"

T'ien Kuang replied: "I respectfully obey." He then arose and hastened to depart. The Crown Prince escorted him to the gate, and warned him, saying: "What I have told you and what you have said are important state matters. I wish you, sir, not to disclose them."

T'ien Kuang nodded and smiled, saying: "I obey." With body stooped by age he departed to see Master Ching, to whom he said: "There is no one in the state of Yen who does not know that we are on good terms with each other. The Crown Prince heard today that I was in my prime, but he did not know that my body is already failing. He graciously told me: 'Yen and Ch'in

26. I.e., Yen will be consumed by Ch'in as easily as the wild duck's feathers will burn in the stove.

27. I.e., no one can withstand such a cruel force as Ch'in.

28. The unicorn is the Chinese mythical animal, the *ch'i-lin*, which, like the unicorn, has a single horn on its forehead.

cannot both stand. I should like you, sir, to put your mind on this fact.' I was careful not to alienate myself from this matter, and I spoke of you to the Crown Prince, sir. I should like you to go to the Crown Prince at his palace."

Ching K'o said: "I respectfully receive your instructions."

T'ien Kuang continued: "I have heard that an old man, when he acts, does not cause people to doubt him. But now the Crown Prince has said to me: 'What we have spoken about are important state matters. I wish you, sir, not to disclose them.' This means that the Crown Prince doubts me. One who acts so as to make people doubt him is not an honorable knight."

In order to inspire Master Ching with feelings of heroism, he wished to kill himself as an example of uprightness, and continued: "I want you to go quickly to the Crown Prince, sir, and tell him that I have already died, so as to show him that I have not spoken." With this, he cut his throat and died.

Ching K'o then went to see the Crown Prince. He told him that T'ien Kuang was already dead, and reported what T'ien Kuang had said. The Crown Prince bowed twice, knelt, moved about on his knees,[29] and wept. Some moments passed and then he said: "The reason why I warned Mr. T'ien not to speak was that I wished to bring the plans for an important matter to fruition. But now Mr. T'ien has used death to show that he did not speak. Alas! How could I have meant that?"

Ching K'o sat down and settled himself. The Crown Prince moved from his mat toward his visitor, bowed his head, and said: "Not knowing of my unworthiness, Mr. T'ien has done what you have just dared to relate. Heaven has afflicted Yen in this, yet it has not abandoned its Orphan.[30]

"Ch'in has an avaricious heart and its desires are insatiable. It will remain unsatisfied until it has made subject the kings of all the lands in the world within the seas. Ch'in has now already taken the king of Han captive and has annexed all his territory.[31] It has furthermore raised soldiers to attack Ch'u in the south and overlook Chao in the north. Wang Chien,[32] commanding a host of several hundreds of thousands, has reached Chang and Yeh,[33] while Li Hsin[34] has gone to T'ai-yüan and Yün-chung.[35]

"Chao cannot withstand Ch'in and must become its vassal. If it becomes its vassal, disaster will then overtake Yen. Yen is small and weak, and has often

29. An expression of grief.

30. The ruler of a state often referred to himself as "orphan," because it is characteristic of a ruler that his father is dead. As Ssu-ma Chen points out, however, the expression is an anachronism here, because Crown Prince Tan was not yet ruling, and his father was still alive.

31. This happened in 230 B.C.E.

32. One of the best known of the Ch'in generals.

33. Places close to each other in the present Linchang district in Honan, and forty tricents west of this district, respectively.

34. Another well-known Ch'in general.

35. T'ai-yüan was at modern Taiyuanfu, the capital of Shansi. Yün-chung was a large region occupying modern northern Shansi, Suiyuan, and part of Mongolia.

suffered from war. Were I now to plan to conscript the entire country, the result would be insufficient to oppose Ch'in. The feudal lords are submissive to Ch'in, and none of them dare to join in a north-to-south alliance.[36]

"My own simple plan would be to secure one of the world's brave men and send him to Ch'in, where he could attract the king of Ch'in's cupidity by the promise of great profit. With his strength,[37] he would certainly obtain for us what we desire. If we could actually succeed in carrying off the king of Ch'in and force him to return all the territory of the feudal lords that has been invaded, as Ts'ao Mo did with Duke Huan of Ch'i, it would be splendid.[38] But if this were not possible, he could use the opportunity to stab and kill him. If, while the great Ch'in generals were holding their troops outside the borders, there were to be trouble within, then ruler and ministers would mutually distrust each other. And if at this juncture the feudal lords could succeed in forming a north-to-south alliance, their defeat of Ch'in would be assured. This is my highest desire, but I know not to whom to entrust my mission. Do you, Master Ching, put your mind on this."

After some time Ching K'o said: "This is an important state matter. Your servant is an inferior nag, and fears that his capacities are inadequate for the trust."

The Crown Prince bowed before him and pressed him not to give up the trust, after which he finally consented. He then honored Master Ching by making him a High Dignitary and lodging him in a superior house. Every day the Crown Prince went to his door, offering him the Great Sacrifice of sheep, pig, and ox, giving him rare objects, at intervals bringing him carriages, horsemen, and beautiful women, and freely granting Ching K'o whatever he desired, so as to satisfy his inclinations.

After this had continued for some time, Ching K'o still had no idea of going away to Ch'in. The Ch'in general Wang Chien defeated Chao, took its king captive, and annexed his entire territory.[39] He advanced his army northward, seizing territory as far as Yen's southern boundary. Crown Prince Tan was alarmed and begged Ching K'o, saying: "Once the Ch'in soldiers are in a position freely to cross the river Yi,[40] though I should then wish to support you, sir, how could it be done?"

Ching K'o replied: "I had intended to ask about this if you had not spoken

36. Literally, "vertical" alliance, often attempted by the other states as a defense against Ch'in, which on its part tried to form horizontal alliances extending from west to east.

37. The *Intrigues of the Warring States* reads "gifts" instead of "strength."

38. The biography of Ts'ao Mo heads chapter 86 of the *Records of the Grand Historian*, which is devoted to noted assassins, and of which Ching K'o's biography forms a part. At a diplomatic meeting between the states of Ch'i and Lu in 681 B.C.E., Ts'ao Mo, a native of Lu, threatened physical violence to Duke Huan and thus forced him to give back to Lu what he had won in three battles.

39. This happened in 228 B.C.E.

40. Yen's southern boundary (see note 21).

of it. But were I to go now without having the confidence of the state of Ch'in, then the king of Ch'in could still not be approached. The king of Ch'in has offered one thousand catties of gold and a city of ten thousand families for the capture of General Fan. Now if we could actually get hold of the head of General Fan and present it to the king of Ch'in, together with a map of Tu-k'ang in Yen,[41] then the king of Ch'in would certainly be pleased to see your servant, who would thus have the opportunity of avenging the Crown Prince."[42]

The Crown Prince replied: "General Fan came to me in poverty and distress. I could not permit myself, for my own selfish aim, to violate a higher ideal. I should like you, sir, to reconsider the matter."

Ching K'o realized that the Crown Prince would not consent, so he privately visited Fan Yü-ch'i and said to him: "Ch'in's treatment of you, General, can indeed be called far-reaching! Your father, mother, and kindred have all been executed, and now I hear that a reward of one thousand catties of gold and a city of ten thousand families have been offered for your head. What are you going to do?"

Fan Yü-ch'i looked up to Heaven, heaved a great sigh, shed some tears, and said: "Each day I think about this and suffer constantly unto my very bones and marrow. But whatever plan I consider, I know not where it will lead me."

Ching K'o said: "Now, suppose a single statement could free the state of Yen from its tribulations and avenge you of your hatred. How would you feel?"

Fan Yü-ch'i came forward and asked: "What is it?"

Ching K'o replied: "I should like to have your head to present to the king of Ch'in. Then the king of Ch'in would certainly be delighted to see me. With my left hand I would seize his sleeve, and with my right I would stab his breast. In this way your hatred of Ch'in would be avenged and the shame of Yen's oppression would be wiped out. What do you think of this?"

Fan Yü-ch'i bared his arm, grasped his wrist,[43] and drew nearer, saying: "Day and night I have been grinding my teeth and beating my breast on this account. But now I have heard my instructions." And with this he cut his throat.

When the Crown Prince heard of it, he hastened to the recumbent corpse and mourned with deep grief. But the deed was already accomplished and there was nothing to be done, so he placed the head of Fan Yü-ch'i in a container and closed it. After this the Crown Prince set about to look for one

---

41. A fertile region situated south of the present Yi district, Hopei. The giving of the map would symbolize the actual cession of the territory. This appears to be the earliest reference to the existence of maps in China.

42. The words "Crown Prince" are added from the *Intrigues* version.

43. A gesture of determination.

of the world's sharp daggers,[44] and obtained one belonging to a man of Chao, Hsü Fu-jen. He gave him one hundred catties of gold for it and had a workman impregnate it with poisonous drugs, so that anybody whose clothing it caused to be stained with blood would immediately die. He then put this in a bag and had it sent to Master Ching.

In the state of Yen there was a bravo, Ch'in Wu-yang, who at the age of thirteen[45] had already killed a man, so that no one dared to eye him contrarily. Ch'in Wu-yang was then commanded to be assistant to Ching K'o.

There was someone whom Ching K'o was waiting for, wishing to be with him before starting off, and as this man lived far away and had not yet arrived, he delayed his going. When after some time he had still not gone, the Crown Prince felt that Ching K'o was procrastinating, and suspected that he regretted his decision, so he again requested him, saying: "The day is already done, and what are your intentions? I beg to be allowed to send Ch'in Wu-yang in advance."

Ching K'o became angry, and upbraided the Crown Prince, saying: "Who is this you would send! This one who will go, never to return, is a mere boy. And he will be entering an immeasurably powerful Ch'in, carrying only a single dagger. I have delayed in order to await my visitor and be with him. But now that you say I am procrastinating, I beg to bid farewell."

With this he departed. The Crown Prince and those of his pensioners who knew about the affair all put on white clothes and caps, so as to see him off as far as the bank of the river Yi.[46] Having offered a sacrifice to the god of the roads, they took the highway. While Kao Chien-li played the lute, Ching K'o joined with him in a song in the key of I♯,[47] and all the gentlemen shed tears and wept.

Once more moving forward, he sang a song which said:

"The wind sighs softly;
On the river Yi 'tis cold.
Once our young hero has gone,
He will never return."

44. Literally, "spoon head," a kind of dagger supposedly one foot eight inches long, with its tip or "head" shaped like a spoon.

45. The *Intrigues* gives the age as twelve instead of thirteen. About Ch'in Wu-yang, we are told in the *Records of the Grand Historian*, chapter 110 (On the Huns): "Yen had a good general, Ch'in K'ai, who was a hostage among the Hu tribes. When he returned to Yen, he made a surprise attack on the Eastern Hu and put them to flight. The Eastern Hu lost more than one thousand tricents of territory. Ch'in Wu-yang, who with Ching K'o tried to stab the king of Ch'in, was his grandson."

46. White is the Chinese mourning color. The river Yi constituted Yen's southern boundary.

47. *Pien-chih*, the fourth note in the ancient Chinese seven-note scale, which was derived from the earlier five-note scale by adding two intermediate notes.

Then he sang again, a stirring song in the key of A.[48] All the gentlemen assumed a stern gaze and their hair bristled up against their caps. At this point Ching K'o went to his carriage and departed; unto the end he did not look back.

When he arrived in Ch'in,[49] he took goods worth one thousand catties of gold, and made lavish presents of them to Meng Chia, who was one of the favored ministers of the king of Ch'in, and an attendant of the heir apparent.[50] Meng Chia went on his behalf to speak first to the king of Ch'in, saying: "Verily, the king of Yen trembles with terror before the majesty of the Great King. He dares not raise soldiers to oppose your military officers, but wishes, taking his kingdom, to become your inner vassal; to set an example to the other feudal lords; to send in tribute like one of your own commanderies or prefectures; and so be allowed to sacrifice to and preserve the temple of his ancestor kings. Being fearful, he dares not present himself, but has cut off the head of Fan Yü-ch'i and placed it in a closed box, together with a map of the territory of Tu-k'ang in Yen, which he respectfully presents. The king of Yen, making obeisance, has sent these to the court, and has dispatched an emissary to give news of them to the Great King. May the Great King but command him."

On hearing this, the king of Ch'in was greatly delighted. He put on court clothing as for a great state occasion,[51] and gave the Yen emissary an audience in the palace at Hsien-yang.

Ching K'o approached to present the box with the head of Fan Yü-ch'i, followed by Ch'in Wu-yang, presenting the container with the map. When they came to the steps of the throne, Ch'in Wu-yang changed color and shook with fear. The courtiers wondered at this. Ching K'o looked at Wu-yang with a smile and went forward to excuse him, saying: "He is a common man of the northern barbarians, and has never seen the Son of Heaven. Therefore he shakes with fear. May it please the Great King to excuse him for a little while and allow me, a mere humble emissary, to come forward."

The king of Ch'in said to Ching K'o: "Bring the map carried by Ch'in Wu-yang." Ching K'o thereupon brought the map and presented it. The king of Ch'in took out the map, and when it was entirely exposed the dagger appeared. At this moment Ching K'o seized the sleeve of the king of Ch'in with his left hand, while with his right hand he grasped the dagger and struck at him. But it did not reach his body. The king of Ch'in, alarmed, drew himself back and leaped up, so that his sleeve tore off. He pulled at his sword, but the sword

48. Yü, the sixth note in the seven-note scale.
49. Which was in 227 B.C.E.
50. Though not mentioned elsewhere, Meng Chia was no doubt a member of the Meng family, which played an important role in Ch'in.
51. Literally, for the "nine guests," originally the nine classes of nobles and officers who assembled at special times at the court of the Chou dynasty.

was long and clung to its scabbard. By this time he was completely terrified. The sword hung vertically, and therefore he could not draw it out immediately. Ching K'o pursued the king of Ch'in, who ran around a pillar. All the courtiers, thunderstruck, hurriedly jumped up without thinking what they were doing and completely lost their ranks.

According to the Ch'in laws, none of the courtiers who attended court in the hall above was allowed to bear any weapon whatsoever.[52] The officers of the guard in charge of the soldiers were all ranged in the hall below, and unless there was a summons they were not allowed to come up. At this moment of emergency, there was no time to call for the soldiers below. Thus Ching K'o pursued the king of Ch'in, while the latter, in a state of complete panic, having nothing with which to strike Ching K'o, warded him off with his two joined hands.

At this moment an attendant physician, Hsia Wu-chü, struck Ching K'o a blow with his bag of medicine which he was to have presented. The king of Ch'in was running around and around the pillar, and had completely lost his wits, so that he did not know what he was doing. The bystanders then cried out: "Put your sword behind you, king!"

The king did so, and thus had room to pull it out. He struck Ching K'o with it and cut his left thigh. Ching K'o, being disabled, then raised his dagger and hurled it at the king of Ch'in. It missed him and hit the bronze pillar. The king of Ch'in struck at Ching K'o repeatedly, so that the latter received eight wounds.

Ching K'o realized that his attempt had failed. He leaned against the pillar and laughed; then squatting down, he cursed the king, saying: "The reason why my attempt did not succeed was that I wished to carry him off alive. Someone else must be found to carry out the pledge to avenge the Crown Prince." At this point those about him rushed forward and killed Ching K'o.[53]

The king of Ch'in was not at ease after this for a long time. Later he decided which of the courtiers should be rewarded for their merit, and which punished, each according to his degree. Hsia Wu-chü he rewarded with two hundred *yi* of yellow gold,[54] saying: "Wu-chü loves me. With his bag of medicine he struck Ching K'o."

Then the king of Ch'in was greatly enraged. He sent more soldiers to advance on Chao, and commanded the army of Wang Chien to attack Yen. In the tenth month it seized the city of Chi.[55] King Hsi of Yen, Crown Prince Tan, and their followers all led their best soldiers eastward to defend

---

52. Literally, "a foot or an inch of weapon."

53. These last words of Ching K'o seem rather inconsequential. Moreover, it is peculiar that nothing is said of what happened to Ch'in Wu-yang. As he had not been armed, he must have been seized by someone during the commotion and thus prevented from helping Ching K'o.

54. An *yi* is equal to twenty-four ounces.

55. North of the present Wanp'ing district which is a little southwest of Peking.

themselves at Liaotung.[56] The Ch'in general, Li Hsin, pursued and attacked the king of Yen impetuously.

King Chia of Tai[57] then sent King Hsi of Yen a letter that said: "The reason why Ch'in continues to press Yen so impetuously is Crown Prince Tan. If now the king would actually kill Tan and give him up to the king of Ch'in, the king of Ch'in would surely desist and your spirits of the soil and grain would happily have their sacrifices."[58]

Li Hsin later pursued Tan, who concealed himself at the river Yen.[59] The king of Yen then sent an official who beheaded Crown Prince Tan, wishing to give him up to Ch'in.[60]

Ch'in again sent in soldiers to attack him, and five years later Ch'in completely wiped out Yen and made King Hsi of Yen captive.[61] The next year the king of Ch'in unified the world and established for himself the title of Sovereign Emperor.[62]

After this, Ch'in pursued the followers of Crown Prince Tan and of Ching K'o, so that they all disappeared. Kao Chien-li changed his personal name and his surname, and became a servant. He lived in concealment at Sung-tzu[63] and for a long time endured much hardship. Once he heard the honored guests of the household playing the lute. He moved about irresolutely and could not go away, and about each of them he expressed his opinion, saying that such and such a person was good or not good. The servants told their master, saying: "That fellow knows music. He takes the liberty of saying what is right and what is wrong." The master of the house summoned him and had him come forward and play the lute. The entire gathering acclaimed his excellence, and rewarded him with wine.

Kao Chien-li, reflecting that he had long been in retirement, and fearing lest his straitened circumstances might continue for an interminable time, withdrew himself and took out from his luggage box his lute and his good clothes. Then, having changed his appearance, he came forward. The entire assemblage of guests was surprised. They descended to give him the honors of

---

56. At the present promontory of the same name, a little west of Korea.

57. The son of the last king of Chao. The latter was captured by Ch'in in 228. His son then fled to Tai, where he ruled from 227 until he was in his turn wiped out by Ch'in in 222. Tai was a small territory in the modern Yü district in southern Chahar.

58. Each state in ancient China was presided over by its own deities of the soil and grain, to which only the ruling house could offer sacrifice. Thus the cessation of such sacrifice was synonymous with the extinction of the state.

59. A river that flows from near Mukden, in Manchuria, into the gulf of Liaotung and is now known, probably after this event, as the T'ai-tzu or Crown Prince River.

60. All these events took place in 226 b.c.e.

61. In 222 b.c.e.

62. *Huang-ti.*

63. Twenty-five tricents north of the present Chao district, Hopei, west of the Peking-Hankow railway.

an equal, made him an honored guest, and had him play the lute and sing. Then among the guests there was not one who did not shed tears on departing. After this the people of Sung-tzu one after another received him as a guest.

The report of this came to the First Emperor of Ch'in, who summoned him for an audience. Someone who was there recognized him and said that he was Kao Chien-li. But the First Emperor of Ch'in pitied him for his excellent playing of the lute, and found it difficult to kill him. So he had him blinded and employed him to play the lute. Never was there a time when he did not acclaim his excellence, and little by little he became more familiar with him. Kao Chien-li then put some lead inside his lute, and when next he entered and came close, he raised the lute and struck at the First Emperor of Ch'in. But he missed. Thereupon the Emperor had Kao Chien-li put to death, and for the rest of his life he did not again allow followers of the feudal lords to come close to him.

Lu Kou-chien, having heard of Ching K'o's attempt to stab the king of Ch'in, privately exclaimed: "Alas! What a pity that I did not discuss with him the arts of swordsmanship. How little do I know men! Once I reviled him, and now he has made a mere nobody out of me."

The Grand Historian says:

People of the world say that when Ching K'o undertook the mission of Crown Prince Tan, Heaven rained grain and horses sprouted horns. These are great errors. They also say that Ching K'o wounded the king of Ch'in. This is all wrong. Kung-sun Chi-kung and Tung Sheng were at one time associates of Hsia Wu-chü,[64] and they both knew about the matter. They have told it to me as it is here. As for the five men from Ts'ao Mo down to Ching K'o,[65] sometimes they succeeded in their intentions and sometimes they did not, but the ideas which they based themselves on are clear. They did not betray their resolve, and their names have come down to later generations. How can they have been in vain!

Translated by Derk Bodde

64. The physician who struck Ching K'o with his medicine bag. Kung-sun Chi-kung and Tung Sheng appear to be unknown elsewhere.

65. The five men treated in the chapter on assassins in the *Records of the Grand Historian*, from which this account of Ching K'o is taken. For Ts'ao Mo, the first of them, see note 38 above.

226

The Biography of a Wandering Knight: Kuo Hsieh

from *History of the Former Han*

Pan Ku (32–92)

Kuo Hsieh was a native of Chih in Ho-nei.[1] He was a grandson on his mother's side of the famous physiognomist Hsü Fu, who was skilled at reading faces. Kuo Hsieh's father was executed in the time of Emperor Wen because of his activities as a knight.

Kuo Hsieh was keen and quick-tempered; he did not drink wine. In his youth he was sullen, vindictive, and quick to anger when crossed in his will, and this led him to kill a great many people. In addition, he would take it upon himself to avenge the wrongs of his friends and conceal men who were fleeing from the law. When he was not engaged in some kind of violence, robbing or assaulting people, he was counterfeiting money or looting graves— it would be impossible to say how many times he was guilty of such actions. But he met with extraordinary luck, and no matter what difficulties he found

---

The *History of the Former Han* was started by Pan Piao (3–54), largely written by his son Pan Ku, and completed by the latter's sister Pan Chao (see selections 23 and 194). It deals with the period from 206 B.C.E. to 23 C.E. and is one of the most renowned and influential of all Chinese historical works. Admired for the rich detail of its narrative and the purity and economy of its style, along with the *Records of the Grand Historian* (see selection 225), the *History of the Former Han* served as a model for the official histories compiled in later centuries to cover all the Chinese imperial dynasties. From the time they were written until the end of the period of traditional culture, no one in China could consider himself truly educated who was not thoroughly familiar with their pages.

It has often been remarked that in ancient China historical works such as the *Records of the Grand Historian* and the *History of the Former Han* appealed to tastes that in other literary traditions were satisfied by works of fiction. The present selection will give an idea of why this might be so. It is taken from chapter 92, "The Biographies of Wandering Knights," one of the so-called collective biographies in Pan Ku's history, that is, chapters devoted to men of a particular profession, temperament, or life-style. The wandering knights were adventurers or local bosses who often assisted persons in trouble or offered their services in the carrying out of private vendettas. While acknowledging the faults of the wandering knights in his preface to the chapter containing their collective biographies in his *Records of the Grand Historian*, Ssu-ma Ch'ien praised them for their willingness to aid the oppressed and to abide by their word. Pan Ku, however, disapproved of such a sympathetic attitude and wrote a preface for his chapter on wandering knights that condemned them and took a strong "law and order" position in regard to their activities. Here Pan Ku appears as a Confucian-minded revisionist, correcting what he considered to be errors of judgment and opinion in the work of his illustrious predecessor.

1. Kuo Hsieh's precise dates are unavailable, but he was active in the period 150–127 B.C.E.

himself in, he always managed to escape or was pardoned by a general amnesty.

When he grew older, he had a change of heart and became much more upright in his conduct, repaying hatred with kindness, giving generously, and expecting little in return. In spite of this, he took more and more delight in daring and chivalrous actions. Whenever he had saved someone's life, he would never boast of his achievements. At heart he was still as ill-tempered as ever, however, and his meanness would often flare forth in a sudden angry look. The young men of the time emulated his actions and would often take it upon themselves to avenge his wrongs without telling him.

The son of Kuo Hsieh's elder sister, relying upon Hsieh's power and position, was once drinking with a man and tried to make him drink up all the wine. Though the man protested that it was more than he could manage, Hsieh's nephew threatened him and forced him to drain the cup. In anger the man stabbed and killed the nephew and then ran away.

Hsieh's sister was furious. "In my brother's own lifetime someone murders my son and gets away with it!" she exclaimed. Then she threw her son's corpse into the street and refused to bury it, hoping to shame Hsieh into action.

Kuo Hsieh sent men to discover where the murderer was hiding, and the latter, fearful of the consequences, returned of his own accord and reported to Hsieh exactly what had happened. "You were quite right to kill my nephew," said Hsieh. "He was at fault!" Then he let the murderer go and, laying the blame for the incident entirely on his nephew, took the corpse away and buried it. When men heard of this, they all admired Hsieh's righteousness and flocked about him in increasing numbers.

Whenever Kuo Hsieh came or went, people were careful to get out of his way. Once, however, there was a man who, instead of moving aside, merely sat sprawled by the road and stared at Hsieh. Hsieh sent someone to ask the man's name. Hsieh's retainers wanted to kill the man on the spot, but Hsieh told them, "If I am not respected in the village where I live, it must be that my virtue is insufficient to command respect. What fault has this man committed?" Then he sent secret instructions to the military officials of the district, saying, "This man is very important to me. Whenever his turn comes for military service, see that he is let off!"

As a result, the man was let off from military service every time his turn came, and the officials made no attempt to look for him. The man was baffled by this and asked the reason, whereupon he discovered that Hsieh had instructed that he be excused. The man then went to Hsieh and, baring his arms, humbly apologized for his former disrespect. When the young men of the district heard of this, they admired Hsieh's conduct even more.

In Loyang there were two men who were carrying on a feud and although ten or more of the worthy residents and "strong men" of the city tried to act as mediators between them, they refused to listen to talk of a settlement. Someone came to ask Kuo Hsieh to help in the matter and he went at night to visit the hostile families, who finally gave in and agreed to listen to Hsieh's arguments. Then he told them, "I have heard that the gentlemen of Loyang have attempted to act as mediators, but that you have refused to listen to any of them. Now, fortunately, you have consented to pay attention to me. However, I would certainly not want it to appear that I came here from another district and tried to steal authority from the virtuous men of your own city!" He therefore went away the same night so that people would not know of his visit, telling the feuding families, "Pay no attention to my advice for a while and wait until I have gone. Then let the 'strong men' of Loyang act as your mediators and do as they say!"

Kuo Hsieh was short in stature and respectful and frugal in his ways. When he went abroad, he never had horsemen attending him, and he would not venture to ride in a carriage when entering the office of his district. He would often journey to neighboring provinces or kingdoms in answer to some request for aid. In such cases, if he thought he could accomplish what had been asked of him, he would undertake to do so, but if he thought the request was impossible, he would go to pains to explain the reasons to the satisfaction of the other party, and only then would he consent to accept food and wine. As a result, people regarded him with great awe and respect and vied with each other in offering him their services. Every night ten or more carriages would arrive at his gate bearing young men of the town or "strong men" of the neighboring districts who had come begging to be allowed to take some of Hsieh's guests and retainers into their own homes.

When the order went out for the "strong men" in the provinces to be moved to the city of Mou-ling, Kuo Hsieh's family was exempted, since his wealth did not come up to the specified amount.[2] He was so well known, however, that the officials were afraid they would get into trouble if they did not order him to move. General Wei Ch'ing spoke to the emperor on his behalf, explaining that Kuo Hsieh's wealth was not sufficient to require him to move. But the emperor replied, "If this commoner has enough influence to get you to speak for him, General, he cannot be so very poor!" So in the end Kuo Hsieh's family was ordered to move, and the people who came to see him off presented him with over ten million cash as a farewell gift.

A district official named Yang, the son of one Yang Chi-chu of Chih, tried to prevent Kuo Hsieh from receiving the gift, whereupon the son of Hsieh's elder brother cut off the head of the Yang official.

2. Emperor Wu had established his mausoleum at Mou-ling, and in 127 B.C.E. he ordered that rich and powerful families be moved there from other parts of the empire. The purpose was to populate the town, and at the same time to break the power of the big provincial families and settle them near the capital where they could be more easily watched.

After Kuo Hsieh entered the Pass,[3] the "strong men" and persons of worth within the Pass, both those who had known him before and those who had not, soon learned of his reputation and vied with each other in making friends with him.

Meanwhile, someone in the city of Chih murdered Yang Chi-chu, the father of the official who had tried to interfere with Kuo Hsieh. The Yang family sent a letter of protest to the throne, but someone murdered the bearer of the letter of protest outside the gate of the imperial palace. When the emperor learned of this, he sent out the law officials to arrest Kuo Hsieh. Hsieh fled and, leaving his mother and other members of his family at Hsia-yang, escaped to Lin-chin.

Chi Shao-weng, who had charge of the pass at Lin-chin, had never known Kuo Hsieh and therefore allowed him to go through the pass. After having received permission to leave from Chi Shao-weng, Hsieh turned and entered the region of T'ai-yüan. Whenever Hsieh stopped anywhere in his flight, he would make his destination known to his host, so that the law officials were able to trail him without difficulty. When his trail led to Chi Shao-weng, the latter committed suicide to keep from having to give any information.

After some time, Kuo Hsieh was captured, and a thorough investigation made of all his crimes. It was found, however, that all the murders he had committed had taken place before the last amnesty.

There was a certain Confucian scholar from Chih who was sitting with the imperial envoys at Kuo Hsieh's investigation. When one of Hsieh's retainers praised Hsieh, the Confucian scholar remarked. "Kuo Hsieh does nothing but commit crimes and break the law! How can anyone call him a worthy man?" The retainer happened to overhear the remark and later killed the Confucian scholar and cut out his tongue. The law officials tried to lay the blame on Hsieh, though as a matter of fact he did not know who had committed the murder. The murderer disappeared, and in the end no one ever found out who he was.

The officials finally submitted a report to the throne stating that Hsieh was innocent of the charges brought against him, but the imperial secretary Kung-sun Hung objected, saying, "Hsieh, although a commoner, has taken the authority of the government into his own hands in his activities as a knight, killing anyone who gave him so much as a cross look. If he did not know the man who murdered the Confucian scholar, his guilt is greater than if the crime had been committed by someone he knew. He should be condemned as a treasonable and unprincipled criminal!" In the end Kuo Hsieh and all the members of his family were executed.

Translated by Burton Watson

3. See notes 14 and 20 of selection 225.

227

The Biography of Hua-t'o [1]

from *History of the Three Kingdoms*

Ch'en Shou (233–297)

Hua-t'o, whose style was Yüan-hua ("Primal Evolution"), was a man of the district of Ch'iao[2] in the kingdom of P'ei. Another name of his was Fu. As a peripatetic student in the area of Hsü-chou,[3] he became familiar with a number of the classics. The senior administrator of P'ei, Ch'en Kuei, recommended him as a high-level candidate for appointment and the defender-in-chief, Huang Wan, offered him employment, but he did not accept either position. Hua-t'o had mastered the technique for nourishing one's nature. Although his contemporaries thought that he must have been a hundred years old, he still looked hale and hardy.

Hua-t'o was also highly skilled in prescribing medicines. In curing illnesses, the decoctions that he prepared required only a few ingredients. His mind was so adept at dividing up and compounding according to the right proportions that he did not have to weigh the different components of his medicines with a balance. Once the decoction was boiled thoroughly it could be drunk. Hua-t'o would tell the patient how to take the medicine and then he would go away, after which the patient's condition would promptly improve.

If Hua-t'o employed moxibustion, he would only burn punk in one or two places and in each place he only made seven or eight separate cauterizations, to which the disease would rapidly respond during the course of its elimination. If he employed acupuncture, it was also only in one or two places. As he inserted the needle, he would instruct the patient, "I am going to guide the

The *History of the Three Kingdoms* is the official history of the three states—Wei, Shu, and Wu—that resulted from the breakup of the Later Han dynasty and that jockeyed for power in the perennial quest to [re]unite China. Among its biographies is to be found some of the most interesting writing in the dynastic histories. The material of the *History of the Three Kingdoms* was fictionalized in the popular novel, *Romance of the Three Kingdoms* (see selection 258).

1. The reconstructed ancient Sinitic pronunciation of this phenomenal physician's name was roughtly *ghwa-thā. It is quite likely that this name derives from an Indian source (Sanskrit *agada* [with the initial syllable lopped off] = "medicine"), as do a number of the stories recounted in this biography which have a suspiciously Ayurvedic character to them. Hua-t'o was many hundreds of years ahead of his time in medical knowledge and practice. The precise sources of his remarkable expertise remain to be investigated. It is perhaps significant, however, that the cities and towns in which Hua-t'o was active lay precisely in the area where the first Buddhist communities were established in China. Hua-t'o's dates are traditionally given as 110–207. These, too, are compatible with the period of early Buddhist activity in China.

2. Corresponding to the modern district of Po in Anhwei province.

3. The area in Kiangsu north of the Yangtze and the southeast part of Shantung.

point to such-and-such a spot. When you feel it reach there, tell me." As soon as the patient told him that the point had already reached the designated spot, he would withdraw the needle and the sickness would likewise be virtually alleviated.

If a sickness were concentrated internally where the effect of acupuncture needles and medicines could not reach it, Hua-t'o would recognize that it was necessary to operate. In such cases, he would have his patients drink a solution of morphean[4] powder[5] whereupon they would immediately become intoxicated as though dead and completely insensate. Then he could make an incision and remove the diseased tissues. If the disease were in the intestines, he would sever them and wash them out, after which he would stitch the abdomen together and rub on an ointment.[6] After a period of about four or five days, there would be no more pain. The patient would gradually regain full consciousness and within a month he would return to normal.

When the late wife of the senior administrator of Kan-ling[7] was six months pregnant, a pain in her abdomen caused her disquietude. Hua-t'o examined her pulse and said, "The fetus is already dead." He had someone[8] manipulate her abdomen to discover the position of the fetus, saying that it would be a boy if it were on the left and a girl if it were on the right. The person reported that it was on the left. Thereupon a solution was used to cause an abortion and, indeed, the dead fetus was a male. After that, the lady swiftly recovered.

4. The Chinese text has *ma-fei* (literally, "hemp-boil," hitherto unidentified) which appears to be a transcription of some Indo-European word related to "morphine," which in turn is derived from "Morpheus," the name of the god of sleep. Although morphine was not chemically isolated and identified until about 1805 by the German scientist, Friedrich W. A. Sertürner, it is a naturally occurring substance, being the principal alkaloid of opium. It is conceivable that some such name as morphine was already in use before Sertürner as a designation for the anesthetic properties of this opium derivative or some other naturally occurring substance. If this is so, it would have enormous implications not only for the history of Chinese medicine, but also for the history of Indian and Western medicine. There are ancient Indian records which describe doctors traveling to the area of Bactria where they learned acupuncture, cauterization, surgery, and external medicine.

5. The corresponding passage of Hua-to's biography in the *History of the Later Han*, written over a hundred years after that by Ch'en Shou translated here, states that *ma-fei* powder was administered in an alcohol solution.

6. The corresponding passage in the *History of the Later Han* reads: "He would sever them and wash them out. Then he would remove the diseased portion[s] and, after that, he would sew [them/it] back up and apply a miraculous ointment."

7. Modern Lin-ch'ing in Shantung.

8. Note that, due to strict rules of decorum, Hua-t'o took the woman's pulse but could not touch her abdomen. Chinese physicians even later in history would "examine" female patients by pointing to a model rather than by an actual contact with their bodies.

The district subofficial functionary, Yin Shih, was tormented by discomfort in his limbs. His mouth was parched, he could not abide the sound of other people's voices, and it was not easy for him to pass urine. "Let us try giving him hot food," said Hua-t'o. "If we can get him to break into a sweat, he'll recover. If he does not sweat, he'll die after three days." So hot food was prepared for him to eat but he did not produce any sweat. "The vital breath of his viscera has already been extinguished within." Indeed, the result was as Hua-t'o predicted.

The commandery subofficial functionaries Ni Hsün and Li Yen came together to see Hua-t'o. Both had headaches and felt feverish; their complaints were exactly the same. Hua-t'o declared, "Hsün should receive a purgative and Yen should receive a febrifacient." Someone called Hua-t'o's prescription into question, to which he responded, "Hsün's firmness is external and Yen's firmness is internal, so it is fitting that their treatment should be dissimilar." Whereupon he gave each of them the appropriate medicine. By dawn the next day they had both improved.

Yen Hsin of Salt Sluice[9] and several others were waiting for Hua-t'o. No sooner had he arrived than he said to Hsin, "Are you feeling all right?"

"Just as usual," replied Hsin.

"You have a severe illness which I can see in your face," said Hua-t'o. "You had better not drink so much wine."

After they had sat together for a while, everybody returned to their own places. When he had gone several tricents, Hsin suddenly became dizzy and fell out of his cart. Someone helped him get up and took him back to his home. He died that night.

The late local inspector, Tun Tzu-hsien, had been ill but was already convalescing. He paid a visit to Hua-t'o, who felt his pulse and said, "You're still depleted and won't be able to recover. Don't overexert yourself. If you engage in intercourse, you will die soon and, at the moment of death, your tongue will hang out several inches."

When Tun's wife heard that he had gotten over his illness, she came from a distance of more than a hundred tricents to look in on him. That night they had sex and, within three days, Tun suffered a relapse that was in all particulars just as Hua-t'o had said it would be.

9. Yen-tu, the equivalent of modern Yen-ch'eng ("Salt City") in Kiangsu.

The local inspector, Hsü Yi, fell ill and Hua-t'o went to look in on him. "Last night, after I had the subaltern in the medical section treat me by the insertion of acupuncture needles in the stomachic duct,[10] I suffered a bitter fit of coughing. I felt as though I wanted to go to sleep, but couldn't relax."

"The needles should not have been inserted in the stomachic duct because they have mistakenly affected the liver. Your appetite will decrease from today and within five days you will be beyond saving."

The illness progressed as Hua-t'o had said it would.

The two-year-old baby boy of Ch'en Shu-shan, who was from Tung-yang,[11] became ill and was experiencing diarrhea. At first he cried a lot but, with each day, the baby was becoming thinner and more listless. Ch'en asked Hua-t'o what the problem was and Hua-t'o replied, "His mother is pregnant and her vital yang breath is being directed inward toward the nourishment of the fetus, leaving her milk coldly devoid. Since the baby acquired this coldness from his mother, it will be impossible to cure him right away." Hua-t'o gave him a pill made of *Aster fastigiatus* and three other ingredients. After ten days, the child's illness was eliminated.

A woman of P'eng-ch'eng[12] went to the toilet in the middle of the night and was stung on the hand by a scorpion. The pain was so unbearable that all she could do was groan. Hua-t'o had the woman soak her hand in a tepid decoction with the result that she was finally able to fall asleep, but several attendants had to keep changing the decoction to ensure that a constant warmth was maintained. She recovered completely by dawn.

The army subaltern, Mei P'ing, having fallen ill, disenrolled and returned home, which was in Kuang-ling.[13] While he was still two hundred tricents away, he stopped off at the home of a relative. Before long, Hua-t'o also happened to visit the owner of the house who requested that he examine P'ing. Hua-t'o did so and told him, "If you had seen me earlier, sir, you could have avoided coming here. Your sickness has already solidified, so you had better go home quickly to see your family, for in five days it will all be finished." P'ing went back to his home immediately and everything transpired as Hua-t'o had predicted.

10. An acupuncture point located four inches above the navel.
11. Northwest of modern T'ien-ch'ang district in Anhwei province.
12. Modern Hsü-chou in Kiangsu province.
13. The area around the modern city of Yang-chou in Kiangsu province.

Hua-t'o was walking along the road when he saw someone suffering from a blocked pharynx. He was fond of eating, but could not get anything down. The members of his family had put him in a cart with the intention of taking him to a doctor. When Hua-t'o heard the man's moaning, he stopped the cart and went over to examine him, saying, "Just now I passed a biscuit seller by the side of the road who had some vinegar with mashed garlic. If you procure three pints from him and drink it, the sickness will go away of its own."

They proceeded to do as Hua-t'o had directed and the man immediately vomited a snakelike parasite. He hung it from the side of his cart and went off to visit Hua-t'o to thank him. Hua-t'o had not yet returned, but his children who were playing outside the gate saw the man coming toward them and said to each other, "He must have met our old man. You can tell by the sickness-causing thing that is hanging from the side of his cart." The patient went inside to sit down and saw hanging on the north wall of Hua-t'o's house some ten-odd snakelike parasites the same as his own.

Then there was a commandery governor who was sick. Hua-t'o suspected that the man would be healed if he really got angry, so he accepted many payments-in-kind from the man but did nothing to cure him. Before long, Hua-t'o abandoned the man and went away, leaving behind a letter in which he cursed the man. As expected, the governor flew into a great rage and ordered his men to catch up with Hua-t'o and kill him. The governor's son understood what was going on and told the functionaries not to pursue Hua-t'o. Because the governor became so tremendously angry, he vomited several pints of black blood, upon which he recovered.

Then there was a high official who was feeling uncomfortable and to whom Hua-t'o said, "Your sickness is deep-rooted, sir, so I would have to cut open your abdomen to remove it. But you won't live more than ten years longer in any event and the sickness will not kill you. If you can endure the sickness for ten more years, by that time you will also have achieved the peak of your longevity, so it's not worth undergoing an operation on account of this sickness." But the official could not bear the pain, so he insisted that it be removed, whereupon Hua-t'o did the operation. The official's complaints were promptly alleviated, but he died in ten years after all.

The governor of Kuang-ling, Li Teng, had an illness which caused him to be distressed by a feeling of stuffiness in his chest. He also had a red face and no desire for food. Hua-t'o took his pulse and said, "Your honor, there are several pints of parasitic bugs in your stomach and you are on the verge of developing an ulcer. This was caused by eating raw fish." Whereupon he prepared two pints of a decoction for the governor. Hua-t'o had him drink one pint first and then after a little while had him finish the remainder. In the space of time that it takes to eat a meal, the governor vomited up three pints or so of parasites. They had red heads and were all wriggling; half of their bodies looked like sashimi.[14] The discomfort that he had experienced was immediately relieved. "This sickness will erupt after three years. If you are attended by a good doctor, he will be able to save you." The sickness did indeed erupt after the specified period. At the time, Hua-t'o was not in the area and the governor died as Hua-t'o had said he would if he did not have a good doctor.

Ts'ao Ts'ao[15] heard about Hua-t'o and summoned him to court where he henceforth was often in attendance. Ts'ao Ts'ao suffered from blustery headaches. Whenever an attack came on, he would become dizzy and confused. Hua-t'o would employ acupuncture treatment at the diaphragmatic transport insertion point and the condition would be alleviated as soon as the procedure was carried out.

The wife of General Li was quite sick and Hua-t'o was called to examine her pulse. "She was injured during pregnancy," said Hua-t'o, "but the fetus did not miscarry."

"I was informed not only that she had truly been injured during pregnancy," said the general, "but that the fetus had also miscarried."

"My reading of her pulse is that the fetus has not yet miscarried," said Hua-t'o.

The general believed that Hua-t'o's diagnosis was incorrect. After Hua-t'o went away, the lady improved slightly. A hundred days later, however, she was again beset by sickness. When they called Hua-t'o once more, he said, "The indications of her pulse are that there is still a fetus. Initially, she had conceived twins, but one of them came out first during the miscarriage. She must have lost a lot of blood then, so that the second child was not born on time. The mother herself was unaware of this and other people did not realize it either. Since there was no longer any movement toward parturition, the child could not be born. The fetus then died, but the pulse did not return to normalcy because the dead fetus desiccated and stuck to the mother's spinal column and it is this which caused her much pain along the spine. Now she

14. Raw fish strips.
15. The text here and below has T'ai Tsu ("Grand Progenitor"), a posthumous title conferred upon Ts'ao Ts'ao (155–220, the tyrannical founder of the Wei dynasty) for use in sacrificial ceremonies held in the ancestral temple.

ought to be given a decoction and I will insert acupuncture needles in one spot, then the dead fetus will come out." After the decoction was given and the acupuncture treatment carried out, the woman experienced sharp pain as though she were going into labor. "This dead fetus has already been dried up for a long time and cannot come out by itself. It is necessary for someone to probe for it and pull it out." And, indeed, they found a dead baby boy with hands and feet that were completely formed. Its color was blackish and it was about a foot or so in length.

Examples of Hua-t'o's superlative skills are in general of this sort. However, since he was originally a scholar, he often regretted that he was looked upon as a physician by profession. Later, when Ts'ao Ts'ao took personal control of the affairs of state, his sickness intensified and he had Hua-t'o attend him exclusively. "It will be difficult to heal you in the near term, but if we maintain a program of treatment over a longer period, it will be possible to extend your life-span."

Hua-t'o had been far away from home for a long time and wished to return, so he said, "I just received a letter from home and would like to go back temporarily." After he reached home, excusing himself on the grounds of his wife's illness, he requested several extensions of his leave and did not come back. Ts'ao Ts'ao repeatedly wrote letters to Hua-t'o calling him back, and he issued imperial orders to the commandery and district authorities to send Hua-t'o back. Proud of his ability and finding it distasteful to wait upon others for a living, Hua-t'o continued to procrastinate in setting off on the journey.

Ts'ao Ts'ao became very angry and dispatched men to go and investigate. If Hua-t'o's wife were really sick, Ts'ao Ts'ao would present him with forty bushels of lentils and be lenient in setting a date when his leave would expire. But if Hua-t'o were prevaricating, then he was to be apprehended and escorted back. Consequently, Hua-t'o was handed over to the prison at Hsü[16] where, after interrogation, he confessed his guilt. Interceding on behalf of Hua-t'o, Hsün Yü[17] said, "Hua-t'o's techniques are truly effective and people's lives are dependent upon them. It is fitting that you be clement toward him."

"Don't worry," said Ts'ao Ts'ao. "Do you think there aren't any other rats like him under heaven?"

Whereupon the investigation against Hua-t'o was concluded with the announcement of the death penalty. When Hua-t'o was about to be executed, he brought out a scroll with writing on it and handed it over to the jailer, saying, "This can preserve people's lives." Fearful of the law, the prison subaltern would not accept it, nor did Hua-t'o force it upon him. Instead, he asked for a fire in which he burned the scroll.

16. Modern Hsü-chang in Honan.
17. Ts'ao Ts'ao's adviser.

After Hua-t'o's death, Ts'ao Ts'ao's blustery headaches did not go away. "Hua-t'o could have cured me," said Ts'ao Ts'ao, "but the scoundrel prolonged my illness, wishing thereby to enhance his own position. Thus, even if I hadn't put the knave to death, he never would have eradicated the source of my sickness." Later on, when his beloved son Ts'ang-shu was critically ill, Ts'ao Ts'ao said with a sigh, "I regret having put Hua-t'o to death and causing my son to die in vain."

Formerly, the army subaltern Li Ch'eng suffered from a cough that prevented him from sleeping day and night. Occasionally he would vomit bloody pus. When he asked Hua-t'o about this, Hua-t'o said, "Your illness is an intestinal ulcer. What you're spitting up when you cough does not come from the lungs. I will give you two tenths of an ounce of a powder that should make you vomit a little over two pints of bloody pus. When that's over, you'll feel better and, if you nurse yourself, in a month there will be some small improvement. If you take good care of yourself for a year, you'll return to full health. After eighteen years, you'll have a minor recurrence, but if you take this powder it will be alleviated again. If you cannot obtain this medicine, you'll surely die." Hua-t'o gave Ch'eng an additional two tenths of an ounce of the powder and he went away with the medicine.

Five or six years later, one of Ch'eng's relatives developed the same sickness that he had. "You're strong and healthy now," he said to Ch'eng. "I'm on the verge of death. How can you bear to hide your medicine away, waiting for something unfortunate to happen, when your situation is not critical? Lend me the medicine now and when I get better I'll ask Hua-t'o for some more for you." Ch'eng gave the medicine to his relative and made a special trip to Ch'iao, but by that time Hua-t'o was already incarcerated and Ch'eng was so flustered that he could not bear to request the medicine. After the eighteen years were up, Ch'eng's sickness did flare up and, since there was no medicine for him to take, it progressed till he died.

Wu P'u of Kuang-ling and Fan Ah[18] of P'eng-ch'eng[19] both studied with Hua-t'o. Using Hua-t'o's methods of treatment, many people were completely cured by Wu P'u. "The human body needs exertion," Hua-t'o told Wu P'u, "but it shouldn't be pushed to the limit. Movement of the limbs facilitates the absorption of nutrients in food and enables the blood in the arteries to flow freely, preventing sickness from occurring. It's like a door-pivot that never

18. This is an unusual name and may indicate that the individual in question was a foreigner.

19. The area around modern T'ung-shan ("Copper Mountain") in Kiangsu, location of the first known Buddhist community in China.

decays from bugs or worms because of the constant opening and closing. That's why, when the ancient transcendents[20] practiced duction,[21] they strode like a bear and turned their head backward like an owl. They elongated their waist and limbs and moved all of their joints, seeking to stave off old age. I have a technique called 'the exercise of the five animals.'[22] The first is the tiger, the second is the deer, the third is the bear, the fourth is the ape, the fifth is the bird.[23] They may also be used to get rid of illness and are beneficial for the legs and feet because they are a type of duction. If there is discomfort somewhere in your body, get up and do one of my animal exercises until you're soaking with sweat, then sprinkle powder on yourself. Your body will feel relaxed and you'll have a good appetite."

Wu P'u followed this regimen and lived to be more than ninety. His sight and hearing were still sharp and all of his teeth remained solidly in place. Fan Ah was good at acupuncture. Whereas ordinary doctors would say that on the back and in the area between the chest and the viscera one should not carelessly insert acupuncture needles, and that if one did insert them they should not go in more than four tenths of an inch, Fan Ah would insert needles in the back up to one or two inches and in the area of the solar plexus, the chest, and the viscera, he would insert them up to five or six inches, bringing about an immediate cure of the patient's ailment. Fan Ah requested from Hua-t'o the recipe for an orally ingested medicine that would be beneficial to one's health, and Hua-t'o instructed him how to make a powder of varnish tree leaves and herbe de flacq. The proportions are fourteen ounces of shredded herbe de flacq for each pint of shredded varnish tree leaves. Hua-t'o said that if one takes a long course of this medicine, it will get rid of the three worms,[24] benefit the five viscera, make the body feel nimble, and prevent your hair from turning white. Fan Ah followed his words and lived to be more than a hundred years old. Varnish tree leaves are available everywhere, and herbe de flacq grows in Feng, P'ei, P'eng-ch'eng,[25] and Ch'ao-ko.[26]

Translated by Victor H. Mair

20. The word used here may refer to ancient Indian rishis ("holy men").
21. Guiding of the vital breath through the channels of the body.
22. These postures are clearly related to the *āsanas* that are well known from Yoga.
23. This passage is extremely important for understanding the Yogic basis of Taoist physical regimens. It is discussed in detail in Victor H. Mair, "[The] **File** [on the Cosmic] **Track** [and Individual] **Dough**[tiness]: Introduction and Notes for a Translation of the Ma-wang-tui Manuscripts of the *Lao Tzu* [Old Master]," *Sino-Platonic Papers* (October, 1990), 20: 38.
24. Different types of parasites that can eat away the five viscera.
25. Places around Hsü-chou in modern Kiangsu.
26. Southwest of modern T'ang-yang in Honan.

228
Physicians Cannot Raise the Dead

Yeh Meng-te (12th century)

Hua-t'o was certainly a miraculous physician, but both Fan Yeh and Ch'en Shou, in their accounts of how he treated illness, stated that if it were actively concentrated internally where the effect of acupuncture needles and medicines could not reach it, he would first order the patient to take some morphean powder in wine, whereupon the patient would become intoxicated to the point of unconsciousness, and then he would make an incision into the abdomen or the back, enabling him to pull out the diseased tissue that had accumulated and cut it away. If the illness were in the intestines or the stomach, he would dissect them, then wash and rinse them, before removing the diseased portions, after which he would sew them back together and apply a miraculous ointment. In four or five days the wound would heal, and within a month the patient would completely return to normal.

There is absolutely no principle whereby to account for this. That which makes a human being a human being is his physical form, and that which enlivens the physical form is the vital breath. I have no way of knowing whether Hua-t'o's medicine could make a person intoxicated to the point of unconsciousness so that he could endure being cut open and could fully recuperate, causing the damaged portions to grow back together again. However, once the abdomen, back, intestines, or stomach have been cut open and dissected, how can they again be infused with vital breath? Being in such a condition, how could they be brought back to life again? If Hua-t'o could do this, then whoever was subjected to the punishment of dismemberment could be brought back to life again and there would no longer be any reason for carrying out royal punishments.[1]

The discourses of the tutor of the heir apparent of the state of Kuo are recorded in the Grand Historian's[2] biography of Pien-ch'üeh.[3] He believed that sickness could be treated without decoctions, fluids, brandies, wines,

This text, included here out of chronological sequence and genre category, is a critique of the biography of Hua-t'o as presented in Fan Yeh's *History of the Later Han* and Ch'en Shou's (233–297) *History of the Three Kingdoms* (see selection 227, especially notes 5 and 6). It is noteworthy that, more than a thousand years after Hua-t'o's time, conventional wisdom still could not comprehend his methods and achievements. Yeh Meng-te was a high-ranking scholar-official of the late Sung period. He represents Confucian rationalism as against imaginative Buddho-Taoist/Indian medical theorizing.

1. Because punishments involving physical mutilation required the consent of the ruler, they were referred to as "royal punishments."

2. Ssu-ma Ch'ien, author of the *Records of the Grand Historian* (see selection 225).

3. A renowned physician from the period of the Warring States. His precise dates unknown, he is thought to have lived during the fifth century B.C.E.

pointed stones, or bending and extending.[4] Instead, incisions were to be made in the skin, the flesh separated, the blood vessels plucked out, the sinews tied up, the intestines and stomach washed and rinsed, and the five viscera irrigated and cleansed. In antiquity, Yü Fu[5] possessed these techniques. The biography does not claim that Pien-ch'üeh could do these things, but later generations attributed them to Hua-t'o. How could it be that a single medical practitioner could increase or decrease a person's allotted life-span or determine whether he lives or dies? Unfortunately, there are those whose illness would not necessarily be fatal yet who are nevertheless killed by common physicians. But there has never been a case of someone with an incurable illness who was restored to life by a physician.

The fundamental purpose of medical books is to help the physician be prepared for curable illnesses and prevent him from harming the patient—that is all. Even Pien-ch'üeh himself said, "I, Yüeh-jen,[6] cannot bring dead people back to life. If a patient is supposed to live, I can bring him back to health." Therefore, it is better for someone in the course of an illness to know a little bit about how to cure the body himself rather than to be harmed by the fraudulent practices of a common physician with a fondness for strange but untested remedies. That way, they could conserve their health in happy, uneventful times so as to maintain themselves during the years allotted to them by heaven.

Translated by Victor H. Mair

4. These are all traditional methods for the treatment of disease in China. The last named was apparently similar to osteopathic or chiropractic manipulations. "Pointed stones" is a traditional way of referring to acupuncture and suggests that this technique goes back to the Stone Age.

5. A legendary physician said to have lived in the time of the Yellow Emperor. He clearly subscribed to the same tradition of medicine as Hua-t'o, a tradition that seems to have disappeared in China for a couple of millennia during the interval between these two famous physicians and was lost again until more than a thousand years after the latter. The descriptions of their surgical techniques detailed by both Ssu-ma Ch'ien and Ch'en Shou are astonishingly similar to surgical techniques developed in the West. No adequate explanation of these similarities has yet been given. Pien-ch'üeh belongs in the mainstream of traditional Chinese medicine; Yü Fu and Hua-t'o are almost preternaturally mysterious aberrations.

6. Pien-ch'üeh's personal name. It could mean either "Viet Man" (i.e., man of Viet) or "Surpasses Others."

229

The Autobiography of Instructor Lu

Lu Yü (733–804)

Master Lu's name was Yü and his style was Hung-chien. It is not known where he was from. Some say that his style was Yü and that his name was Hung-chien, but it is impossible to know who is right. His appearance was as ugly as that of Wang Ts'an[1] or Chang Tsai[2] and he stammered like Ssu-ma Hsiang-ju[3] or Yang Hsiung,[4] but he was talented and persuasive and had a sincere and trustworthy character. He was narrow-minded and irritable, showing a great deal of subjectivity in his opinions. When his friends reproved him, however, he could be more open-minded and less suspicious. If he were living with another person and got the inclination to go somewhere else, he would leave without saying anything, causing others to suspect that he was born full of anger. But if he had an agreement with another person, he would never fail to keep his word, even if it meant traveling a thousand tricents through ice and snow over roads infested by wolves and tigers.

At the beginning of the Superior Origin reign period (760–761), Lu Yü built a hut by the bank of Grandiflora Stream.[5] He closed his door and read books, refusing to mix with rogues, though he would spend whole days chatting and convivializing with eminent monks and lofty scholars. Often, he would travel back and forth between various mountains and monasteries in his little slip of a boat, clad only in a gauze kerchief, vine sandals, a short shirt of coarse wool, and a pair of underpants. He would frequently walk alone in the wilderness reciting Buddhist scriptures or chanting ancient poems. Striking the forest trees with his staff or dabbling in the flowing water with his hand, Lu Yü might dilly-dally hesitantly from morning until evening and on into the darkness of night after the sun had gone completely down, whereupon he would return home wailing and weeping. So the southerners would say to each other, "Master Lu must be today's Madman of Ch'u."[6]

An abandoned waif at the age of three, Lu Yü was taken in and raised in the Ching-ling meditation[7] monastery by the great teacher Chi-kung. From the age of nine he learned how to write and Chi-kung revealed to him the

This is the extraordinary self-account of the enormously influential founder of the tea cult.

1. A famous writer (177–217) from the kingdom of Wei during the Three Kingdoms period.
2. Another famous writer of the kingdom of Wei (third century).
3. See selection 151.
4. See selection 193.
5. In the northern part of Chekiang, it rises in the vicinity of Celestial Eye mountain (T'ien-mu shan) and flows into Lake T'ai.
6. Chieh-ÿu, an eccentric of the Spring and Autumn period who is noted for having taunted Confucius with a wild song about the phoenix.
7. Sanskrit *dhyāna* = Japanese Zen, Chinese Ch'an.

occupation of escaping from the world that was described in the Buddhist books. In reply, the lad said to him, "To be cut off from one's brothers, to have no further descendants, to wear a cassock and shave one's head, to call oneself an adherent of Śākyamuni[8]—if the Confucians were to hear of this, would they proclaim it to be filial behavior? Would it be all right if I request that you teach me the writings of the Confucian sages?"

"It's excellent," said the elder, "that you wish to show your filial devotion, but you have no idea at all how great is the meaning of the Way of the tonsure and cassock from the West." The elder obdurately insisted that Lu Yü study the Buddhist canon, and Lu Yü obdurately insisted that he study the Confucian canon. Consequently, the elder feigned not to love the youngster any longer and tested him with a series of demeaning tasks. He had him sweep the monastery grounds, clean out the monks' toilet, mix mud with his feet to plaster on walls, carry tiles on his back and build rooms, and herd thirty head of cattle. At Ching-ling and around West Lake, there was no paper for the lad to practice writing, so he would trace characters on the backs of the cattle with a piece of bamboo.

One day, Lu Yü asked a learned person about some characters and the person gave him a copy of Chang Heng's[9] "Rhapsody on the Southern Capital." The lad could not recognize the characters of the rhapsody, but there in the pasture he imitated the little boys who were students. He would sit up straight with the scroll unrolled before him and move his mouth, but that was all. When the elder learned of this, he was afraid that the lad was gradually becoming infected by heretical texts and thus daily growing more distant from the Way. So he confined him to the monastery and ordered him to cut away the overgrown bushes and weeds under the supervision of the head gateman.

From time to time, a character would come to mind, and then Lu Yü would fall into a stupor as though he were lost. He might spend a whole day standing there disheartened like a wooden post and doing nothing. The supervisor thought he was lazy and struck him with a whip. The result was that the lad sighed over the passing of the months and years, fearing that he would never acquire the knowledge that was in books, which caused him to sob uncontrollably. The supervisor thought that he harbored resentment and whipped him on the back until his cane broke. Because he was weary of these labors, the lad escaped from the supervisor and ran away. With only a few extra items of clothing rolled up in a bundle, he joined a variety troupe. While with them, he wrote "Jests" in three chapters. As an actor, he played the role of the phony blockhead clerk who hides a pearl.

Upon finding him, the elder said, "When I think how you have become

8. The Buddha.

9. A famous writer, especially of rhapsodies (see selections 149 ff.), and inventor of the Eastern Han period. His dates are 78–139.

lost to the Way, how sad it is! Our founding teacher had a saying that, in a twenty-four hour day, a disciple was only permitted to study two hours of non-Buddhist subjects so that heretical teachings might be overcome. Since there are so many people in our monastery, I'll let you do as you wish now. You may also study miscellaneous subjects and practice your calligraphy."

During the Heavenly Jewel reign period (742–755), some people from Ch'u held a feast in the circuit of Ts'ang-lang.[10] The district subofficial functionary invited Lu Yü to be the director of the entertainers who were hired for the occasion. At the time, Li Ch'i-wu, administrator of Honan, had been appointed governor of Ts'ang-lang and was in attendance at the feast. He considered Lu Yü to be someone of extraordinary talent, so he shook his hand and patted him on the back, then personally presented him with his own poetry collection. Thereupon the common people of the Han and Min valleys also considered Lu Yü to be extraordinary.

After that, Lu Yü carried his books to the villa of Master Tsou on Firegate Mountain. This happened to be just when the director of the ministry of rites, Ts'ui Kuo-fu,[11] was appointed adjutant of Ching-ling commandery. Altogether, Lu Yü and he enjoyed each other's company for three years. During this period, Lu Yü was presented with a white donkey, a jet-black pack ox, and a bookcase made of patterned pagoda tree wood. The white donkey and pack ox were given to him by Li Ch'eng, the governor of Hsiang-yang;[12] the bookcase of patterned pagoda tree wood was a present from the late vice-director of the chancellery, Lu. These three things were all much cherished by the recipient himself. Realizing that they are well suited for riding and storing by rural folk, that is why they gave me these items in particular.

At the beginning of the Highest Virtue reign period (756–757), refugees[13] from Shensi fled south of the Yangtze and Lu Yü also went south at that time. There he developed a friendship with the monk Chiao-jan[14] that ignored their difference in age and religious status.

From the time he was young, Lu Yü enjoyed writing, mostly in a satirical vein. If he saw people do something good, he would feel as though he himself had done it; but if he saw people do something bad, he would feel as though he were ashamed of himself. "Bitter medicine is hard to swallow; bitter words are hard to hear"—since there was nothing that he would shy away from saying, the average person kept out of his way. In response to An Lu-shan's[15] rebellion in the Central Plains, he wrote a poem entitled "Quadruple Sorrow"

10. In the modern province of Hupei.
11. A T'ang poet and official.
12. In Hupei.
13. Escaping from the An-Shih rebellion (see selection 180).
14. A well-known Buddhist poet (730–799).
15. Roxsan the Arsacid, of Sogdian-Turkish ancestry, had been a favorite of the T'ang emperor, Hsüan Tsung, and his "precious consort," Yang Kuei-fei (see selections 180 and 181).

and, in response to Liu Chan's insurrection[16] in the region west of the Huai River, he wrote "Rhapsody on the Unclarity of Heaven." All these pieces were inspired by his passionate reaction to current events which caused him to weep and snivel. His other writings include *The Contract Between Ruler and Subject* in three scrolls, *Genealogy of Four Surnames from South of the Yangtze* in eight scrolls, *An Account of Men of Distinction from North and South* in ten scrolls, *A Record of Successive Officials in Wu-hsing* in three scrolls, *A Historical Record of the Prefecture of Ch'ao-chou* in one scroll, *Tea Classic* in one scroll, and *The Divination of Dreams* in three scrolls (A, B, C), all of which he keeps in a coarse cloth sack.

> Composed during the second year of the
> Superior Origin reign period (761),
> when Lu Yü was twenty-nine years of age.
> *Translated by Victor H. Mair*

16. This occurred in 760.

230
Biography of the Child Ou Chi

Liu Tsung-yüan (773–819)

Mr. Liu[1] says that the people of Viet[2] are lacking in kindness. When they give birth to a child, whether boy or girl, they look upon it as a commodity. From the time children lose their baby teeth, their fathers and older brothers sell them off out of a desire for profit. If they do not earn enough from their own children, they snatch them away, bound and manacled, from other families. If they do not have the strength to resist, even those who are old enough to grow a beard are invariably forced to become slaves. It is common for such mutual depredations to occur right out on the main thoroughfares. Those children who are fortunate enough to grow up turn around and capture others who are smaller and weaker than they. Because the Han[3] officials themselves consider this trade profitable if they illicitly obtain a slave child through it, they let it go on freely and ask no questions. Consequently, the fertility of the Viet population is being squandered.

For a brief note on the author, see selection 55.
1. The author himself.
2. The area of modern Fukien and Chekiang. Vietnam means "south of Viet."
3. Chinese.

Few of the children manage to escape by themselves. That child Ou Chi was able to do so when he was only eleven years old is most extraordinary. Tu Chou-shih,[4] a retainer in the Kweichow surveillance commissioner's office, told me how it happened.

Child Chi was a herd-boy and woodcutter from Liu-chou.[5] Once when he was out herding and cutting firewood, a couple of ruffians kidnapped him. They tied his hands behind his back and gagged him with a piece of cloth, then took him to a market forty tricents away to sell him. Chi pretended to cry like a boy and trembled with fear, putting on the customary appearance of a little boy. The ruffians, thinking he would be easy to handle, drank together until they were tipsy. Then one of them went off to do some business and the other lay down after sticking his knife in the ground by the side of the road.

When child Chi stealthily noticed that the ruffian had fallen asleep, he backed up against the knife blade with his bound hands and moved them up and down vigorously until the rope broke, whereupon he grabbed the knife and killed the sleeping ruffian. Before the child was able to run very far away, however, the ruffian who had gone off to do some business returned and caught him. Greatly startled by what had happened to his partner, he was all set to kill the child when the latter spoke hastily, "How can being the servant of two masters compare with being the servant of one master? He was unkind to me. If you can honestly preserve my life and be kind to me, I'll do anything for you."

The ruffian who had come back from doing business thought about it for quite a while then said, "Rather than kill this slave, wouldn't it be better to sell him? And rather than sell him and then have to divide up the profits, wouldn't it be better for me to get them all for myself? So it's fortunate that the kid killed him after all. Excellent!" Thereupon the ruffian buried his partner's corpse and took the child along with him to the place where he was staying, making sure to tie his bonds still tighter.

In the middle of the night, the child rolled over by himself and burned through his bonds by getting close to the fire in the stove. Even though the fire singed his hands, he did not shrink from it. Once again, he grabbed a knife and killed the second ruffian. Then he began to yell so loudly that the whole town was alarmed. "I am the son of a man named Ou," said the child, "and should not have to be a slave. These two ruffians captured me, but luckily I was able to kill both of them! I request that you inform the courts of this matter."

The town subofficial functionary reported what had happened to the prefect and the prefect reported what had happened to the superior prefect. When the

---

4. Received his Advanced Scholar's degree in 801.
5. In modern Hunan province.

superior prefect summoned the boy, he saw before him an earnest young lad. The prefect Yen Cheng[6] marveled at Ou Chi and wished to retain him as a minor subofficial functionary, but the child was unwilling. The prefect gave him a set of clothing and sent a subofficial functionary to escort him back to his village.

All those in the village who were engaged in abduction looked at Ou Chi warily and dared not pass by his gate. "This boy is two years younger than Ch'in Wu-yang,"[7] they said, "but he's already put two ruffians to death. We'd better stay clear of him!"

Translated by Victor H. Mair

6. Appointed as prefect of Kweichow in present-day Kwangsi, a remote southern province.

7. A courageous youth of the state of Yen during the Warring States period who at age thirteen killed some thugs (see selection 225, note 45).

231

Biography of a Girl Surnamed Chao

P'i Jih-hsiu (c. 833–c. 883)

She was a young girl with the surname Chao who was from Salt Hill in Shan-yang commandery.[1] Her father was a salt merchant who stole some government salt for personal profit and failed to pay the statutory taxes on it.[2] He was arrested by officials and, according to the law, was to be put to death. He had already confessed and the execution date was imminent. His daughter, whom we will call the Chao girl, sought an audience with the commissioner for the salt and iron monopoly and told her tearful tale before the court.

"When I was seven, my mother died. Thanks to my father's salt-running, he was able to make enough money to provide me with food and clothing. Father's kindness in keeping me alive is truly immeasurable. Now that his crime has been exposed, I should be adjudged together with him. If the law cannot permit that, would your honor please forgive him? Please allow me to be adjudged together with him." The judge, Ts'ui Chü of Ch'ing-ho district, swayed by her righteousness, declared, "It is only fitting that I reduce the sentence."

For information on the author, see selection 66.

1. In modern Kiangsu province.

2. The T'ang government strove to exercise total monopoly on the production and sale of salt. Naturally, this was achieved only through ruthless control over the sources of salt and those who actually extracted the salt from the land.

The Chao girl burst into tears and said, "My life was previously preserved by my father. Now, sir, it has been saved by you. I swear that I shall shave my hair and become a Buddhist in order to repay your virtue." Concerned that others might not believe the words of a girl, she took out a stiletto that she carried in her bosom and forthwith cut off her ear to demonstrate that she would certainly keep her oath. Ts'ui Chü was all the more impressed by her and, in the end, preserved her father's life intact. After nursing her father back to health from the punishment he had received when he was arrested, the Chao girl bid him adieu and entered a Buddhist nunnery.

P'i Jih-hsiu comments: "In times of danger or disaster, many were the ancients who would make a show of their trustworthiness, but after their family or nation had been preserved whole, they would go back on their oath. Yet the Chao girl, who was still wet behind the ears, declared herself willing to die together with her father to plead for his life—such was her filial devotion. And she mutilated herself to seal her oath—such was her trustworthiness. Having a firm grasp both of filial devotion and trustworthiness, she strode loftily above the world. Not even fabled gems are adequate to describe her spotless purity; not even redolent orchids are adequate to describe her luxuriant fragrance. She was far superior to those ancients who rescued their families or countries from disaster and danger, but then went back on their oaths.

"The gentleman of today, when faced with adversity, does not maintain his high moral principles and, when enjoying security, does not fulfill his pledge of trustworthiness. Let him take the Chao girl as his model! May those in the future who compile women's history not forget the Chao girl!"

Translated by Victor H. Mair

232

The Biography of A-liu [1]

Lu Jung (1436–1494)

A-liu was a servant boy in the house of Chou Yüan-su of T'ai-ts'ang.[2] By nature, he was doltish and unruly, but Yüan-su kept him around anyway.

The author became a Presented Scholar in 1466 and filled a succession of middle-level posts in the bureaucracy. He was known more for his erudition than for his literary ability, but wrote a number of perceptive and charming essays.

1. The name of the main character in this sketch probably means something like "hang around" or "stick around." The prefix "a" indicates that he is most likely of low birth.

2. Located in the modern province of Kiangsu.

Once Yüan-su asked him to do the sweeping and he spent the whole morning moving the broom but couldn't even finish a single room. When his master upbraided him, A-liu threw the broom on the floor and said, "If you're so good at sweeping, why bother me with it?"

Occasionally Yüan-su would go somewhere else and he'd have A-liu watch the gate. But he couldn't even remember the names of those visitors with whom he was familiar. If Yüan-su asked who had come, he'd invariably say, "One of 'em was short and fat; one of 'em was skinny and bearded; one of 'em was pretty good-looking; one of 'em was so old and crippled he had to lean on a cane." Later, he realized that it was too hard to remember what everybody looked like, so he closed the gate and refused to greet guests any longer.

Yüan-su's family had a collection of ancient bronze vessels.[3] Once when some guests came, he put them out on display. A-liu waited until the guests left and then secretly went up and tapped on the vessels. "This stuff is bronze, isn't it?" he asked himself. "How come it's so black and tarnished?" So he went outside and got some sand and pebbles that he used along with water to give the vessels a good scrubbing.

Yüan-su had a couch with short legs that was missing one of them. He asked A-liu to cut off the branch of a tree to fix it. Grasping an ax and a saw, A-liu traipsed around the garden for an entire day. When he returned, A-liu held up two fingers like a forked branch and said, "All tree branches grow upward. I couldn't find any that point downward." The whole family burst into laughter when they heard him say this.

Once Yüan-su planted several new willows in front of his house. Afraid that the neighbor's children would tug at them, he asked A-liu to guard them. When the time came for A-liu to eat, he pulled up the willows and brought them into the house for safekeeping. The ridiculous things that A-liu did were mostly of this sort.

Yüan-su had an excellent calligraphic hand in the regular script and was a particularly good painter. One day as he was preparing his inks, he said playfully to A-liu, "Can you do this?" "What's so hard about that?" answered A-liu. Whereupon Yüan-su asked him to paint something. The density and consistency with which A-liu applied the inks were like those of someone who was long practiced in painting. Yüan-su tested him repeatedly, and everything he produced met with people's approval.

From that time on, Yüan-su employed A-liu especially as a painter, never abandoning him to the end of his life.

Translated by Victor H. Mair

---

3. These are specified as *tsun* (for wine), *yi* (also for wine), *ting* (tripot for cooking), and *tui* (for serving food).

233
The Biography of Actor Ma

Hou Fang-yü (1618–1654)

Actor Ma was a member of the theater world[1] in Chin-ling,[2] the former capital of the Ming dynasty. The altars to the earth and grain were still there as were various government offices. Furthermore, since it was a time of great peace and prosperity, it was easy for people to make merry. The men and women who visited Peach Leaf Ferry and made excursions to Rain Flower Terrace[3] were so numerous that they stepped on each other's toes. In the theater world, there were roughly several dozen troupes that were famous for their skilled actors, but the two most outstanding troupes were called Reformation and Flower Grove.

One day, some Cantonese merchants from Hsin-an jointly hired the two troupes for a large party to which they invited all the leading men of letters and beautiful ladies of Chin-ling, none of whom refused. They had Reformation set up in East Market and Flower Grove in West Market; both troupes were to perform "Cry of the Phoenixes,"[4] which tells the story of Yang Chi-sheng's accusation of Yen Sung.[5]

As the opera reached the halfway mark, the notes were being played to perfection and the rhythms varied exquisitely, so that everyone exclaimed how good both troupes were. At the point where the two ministers, Hsia Yen and Yen Sung, were discussing whether or not to take back Ho-t'ao[6] from the Tartars, the role of the minister Yen was being played by Actor Li in West Market and by Actor Ma in East Market. The audience turned toward the West and sighed with appreciation. Some of them shouted loudly as they ordered more wine or they moved in closer, till they no longer turned their heads toward East Market at all. Before long, the situation reached a point where the troupe in East Market could not go on with its performance. When

The author was a Ch'ing period advocate of the ancient-style prose movement, especially as conceived by Han Yü (see selection 53) and Ou-yang Hsiu (see selection 206). He is the hero of the famous romance portrayed in K'ung Shang-jen's drama, "The Peach Blossom Fan" (see selection 277).

1. The text has "Pear Garden," an old name for the acting profession that dates back to the T'ang dynasty.
2. Chin-ling is an old name for Nanking.
3. Popular tourist attractions in Nanking.
4. *Ming feng chi*, attributed to Wang Shih-chen (1526–1590), a dominant poet and critic during the late sixteenth century (not the same person as the author of selection 103, whose name is similar and who played a similar literary role during the seventeenth century).
5. Two Ming dynasty officials involved in a power struggle.
6. The bend of the Yellow River as it passes through the Ordos Desert.

they were asked why, they said that Actor Ma was so ashamed by his inferiority to Actor Li that he changed out of his costume and ran away.

Actor Ma was one of the best singers in Chin-ling. With him gone and the Reformation troupe unwilling to replace him immediately, they finally stopped performing and disbanded. Thus the Flower Grove troupe had the stage all to itself.

After he had been away for three years, Actor Ma returned. He went around to contact his old associates and then made the following request to the Cantonese merchants: "Please be so kind as to have another banquet today and invite all the guests who came that day three years ago. We'd like to perform 'Cry of the Phoenix' with the Flower Grove troupe once again for a day of enjoyment."

The performance was arranged and before long they came to the scene where the discussion over Ho-t'ao takes place. Actor Ma again appeared as the minister Yen Sung. Actor Li suddenly lost his voice and came crawling to declare himself the disciple of Actor Ma. That day the Reformation troupe far surpassed the Flower Grove troupe.

In the evening, the Flower Grove troupe went to call on Actor Ma, saying, "Sir, there are many fine performers under heaven, but none who can take the place of Actor Li. Actor Li's performance of minister Yen is the height of perfection. From whom did you learn how to overtake him?"

"Admittedly," said Actor Ma, "there's no one under heaven who can take the place of Actor Li, and Actor Li was unwilling to accept me as his student. But I heard that the current minister, Ku Ping-ch'ien of K'un-shan, bears a striking resemblance to minister Yen. So I traveled to the capital where I begged to serve as his doorman for three years. Every day I waited upon the minister from K'un-shan in his offices at court. I observed his movements and listened to his speech habits. After a long time, I finally mastered them. This is how I taught myself." The members of the Flower Grove troupe arrayed themselves around Actor Ma and did obeisance to him, then left.

Actor Ma's name was Chin and his style was Yün-chiang ("Cloud General"). His ancestors came from the Western Regions[7] and his contemporaries also called him "Moslem Ma."

Hou Fang-yü comments: How extraordinary was Actor Ma's manner of finding a teacher for himself! Because Actor Li's skill was unparalleled, there was no one whom he could ask to teach it to him. So he went to wait upon the minister from K'un-shan. Watching the minister from K'un-shan was just like watching minister Yen Sung who was from Fen-yi. To use the living likeness of the minister from Fen-yi to instruct himself how to act the role of the minister from Fen-yi, how could he not succeed? Amazing! Ashamed that his skill was inferior, he journeyed several thousand tricents and served as a

---

7. Central Asia and beyond, hence Ma was not of Chinese ancestry.

doorman for three years. If three years had not been enough, he still would not have returned. With such determination, one need not ask how refined his skills must have been.

Translated by Victor H. Mair

234

Six Chapters of a Floating Life

Chapters 1 and 3

Shen Fu (1763–1808?)

Chapter 1: Wedded Bliss

I was born in 1763, under the reign of Ch'ienlung, on the twenty-second day of November. The country was then in the heyday of peace and, moreover, I was born in a scholars' family, living by the side of Ts'anglang Pavilion in Soochow. So altogether I may say the gods have been unusually kind to me. Su Tungp'o said: "Life is like a spring dream which vanishes without a trace." I should be ungrateful to the gods if I did not try to put my life down on record.

Since the *Classic of Odes* begins with a poem on wedded love, I thought I would begin this book by speaking of my marital relations and then let other matters follow. My only regret is that I was not properly educated in childhood; all I know is a simple language and I shall try only to record the real facts and real sentiments. I hope the reader will be kind enough not to scrutinize my grammar, which would be like looking for brilliance in a tarnished mirror.

I was engaged in my childhood to one Miss Yü, of Chinsha, who died in her eighth year, and eventually I married a girl of the Ch'en clan. Her name was Yün and her literary name Suchen. She was my cousin, being the daughter of my maternal uncle, Hsinyü. Even in her childhood, she was a very clever girl, for while she was learning to speak, she was taught Po Chüyi's poem, "The P'ip'a Player," and could at once repeat it. Her father died when she was four years old, and in the family there were only her mother (of the Chin clan) and her younger brother K'ech'ang and herself, being then practi-

Of the six original chapters of this book, only the first four have survived. *Six Chapters* is an extraordinarily frank autobiographical document that is totally unprecedented and unparalleled in the history of Chinese literature. It describes the life of the author Shen Fu and his beloved wife, Ch'en Yün (1763–1803), in extremely revealing detail. The intimacy and joy shared by the couple are as unusual by normal standards of Chinese married life as is the author's daringness in revealing them to others. Their close, playful relationship stands in defiant opposition to the staid decorum of married life expected by Confucian ideology.

Except for the information contained in these fragmentary memoirs, which were only discovered in the mid-nineteenth century, next to nothing is known about the author.

cally destitute. When Yün grew up and had learned needlework, she was providing for the family of three, and contrived always to pay K'ech'ang's tuition fees punctually. One day, she picked up a copy of the poem "The P'ip'a Player" from a paper basket, and from that, with the help of her memory of the lines, she learned to read. Between her needlework, she gradually learned to write poetry. One of her poems contained the two lines:

> Soaked in autumn, one's figure becomes thin,
> Touched by frost, the chrysanthemum grows fat.

When I was thirteen years old, I went with my mother to her maiden home and there we met. As we were two young innocent children, she allowed me to read her poems. I was quite struck by her talent, but feared she was too clever to be happy. Still I could not help thinking of her all the time, and once I told my mother, "If you choose a girl for me, I won't marry any one except cousin Su." My mother also liked her for being so gentle, and gave her her gold ring as a token for the betrothal.

This was on July 16 in the year 1775. In the winter of this year one of my girl cousins was going to get married and I again accompanied my mother to her maiden home. Yün was of the same age as myself, but ten months older, and as we had been accustomed to calling each other "elder sister" and "younger brother" from childhood, I continued to call her "Sister Su."

At this time the guests in the house all wore bright dresses, but Yün alone was clad in a dress of quiet color, and had on a new pair of shoes. I noticed that the embroidery on her shoes was very fine, and learned that it was her own work, so that I began to realize that she was gifted at other things, too, besides reading and writing.

Of a slender figure, she had drooping shoulders, and a rather long neck, slim but not to the point of being skinny. Her eyebrows were arched and in her eyes there was a look of quick intelligence and soft refinement. The only defect was that her two front teeth were slightly inclined forward, which was not a mark of good omen. There was an air of tenderness about her which completely fascinated me.

I asked for the manuscripts of her poems and found that they consisted mainly of couplets and three or four lines, being unfinished poems, and I asked her the reason. She smiled and said, "I have had no teacher in poetry, and wish to have a good teacher-friend who could help me to finish these poems." I wrote playfully on the label of this book of poems the words: "Beautiful Lines in an Embroidered Case," and did not realize that in this case lay the cause of her short life.

That night, when I came home from my relatives' place in the country, whither I had accompanied my female cousin the bride, it was already midnight, and I felt very hungry and asked for something to eat. A maid-servant gave me some dried dates, which were too sweet for me. Yün secretly pulled me by the sleeve into her room, and I saw that she had hidden away a bowl of warm congee and some dishes to go with it. I was beginning to take up the chopsticks and eat it with great gusto when Yün's cousin Yüheng called out, "Sister Su, come quickly!" Yün quickly shut the door and said, "I am very tired and going to bed." Yüheng forced the door open and seeing the situation, said with a malicious smile at Yün, "So, that's it! A while ago I asked for congee and you said there was no more, but you really meant to keep it for your future husband." Yün was greatly embarrassed and everybody laughed at her, including the servants. On my part, I rushed away home with an old servant in a state of excitement.

Since the affair of the congee happened, she always avoided me when I went to her home afterward, and I knew that she was only trying to avoid being made a subject of ridicule.

On the twenty-second of January in 1780, I saw her on our wedding night, and found that she had the same slender figure as before. When her bridal veil was lifted, we looked at each other and smiled. After the drinking of the customary twin cups between groom and bride, we sat down together at dinner and I secretly held her hand under the table, which was warm and smooth, and my heart was palpitating. I asked her to eat and learned that she had been keeping fast for several years already. I found that the time when she began her fast coincided with my smallpox illness, and said to her laughingly, "Now that my face is clean and smooth without pockmarks, my dear sister, will you break your fast?" Yün looked at me with a smile and nodded her head.

This was on the twenty-second, my wedding night. On the twenty-fourth, my own sister was going to get married, and as there was to be a national mourning and no music was to be allowed on the twenty-third, we gave my sister a sendoff dinner on the night of the twenty-second, and Yün was present at the table. I was playing the finger-guessing game with the bridesmaids in the bridal chamber and, being a loser all the time, fell asleep drunk like a fish.[1] When I woke up the next morning, Yün had not quite finished her morning toilet.

That day, we were kept busy entertaining guests and toward evening, music was played. After midnight, on the morning of the twenty-fourth, I, as the bride's brother, sent my sister away and came back toward three o'clock. The room was then pervaded with quietness, bathed in the silent glow of the candlelights. I went in and saw Yün's woman-servant taking a nap behind the bed, while Yün had taken off her bridal costume, but had not yet gone to bed. Her beautiful white neck was bent before the bright candles, and she was absorbed reading a book. I patted her on the shoulder and said, "Sister, why are you still working so hard? You must be quite tired with the full day we've had."

1. The loser in Chinese finger-guessing games must drink a glass of alcoholic beverage as penalty.

Quickly Yün turned her head and stood up, saying, "I was going to bed when I opened the bookcase and saw this book and have not been able to leave it since. Now my sleepiness is all gone. I have heard of the name of *Western Chamber* for a long time, but today I see it for the first time. It is really the work of a genius, only I feel that its style is a little bit too biting."

"Only geniuses can write a biting style," I smiled and said.

The woman-servant asked us to go to bed and left us and shut the door. I began to sit down by her side and we joked together like old friends after a long separation. I touched her breast in fun and felt that her heart was palpitating too. "Why is Sister's heart palpitating like that?" I bent down and whispered in her ear. Yün looked back at me with a smile and our souls were carried away in a mist of passion. Then we went to bed, when all too soon the dawn came.

As a bride, Yün was very quiet at first. She was never sullen or displeased, and when people spoke to her, she merely smiled. She was respectful toward her superiors and kindly toward those under her. Whatever she did was done well, and it was difficult to find fault with her. When she saw the gray dawn shining through the window, she would get up and dress herself as if she had been commanded to do so. "Why?" I asked. "You don't have to be afraid of gossip, like the days when you gave me that warm congee." "I was made a laughingstock on account of that bowl of congee," she replied, "but now I am not afraid of people's talk; I only fear that our parents might think their daughter-in-law lazy."

Although I wanted her to lie in bed longer, I could not help admiring her virtue, and so got up myself, too, at the same time with her. And so every day we rubbed shoulders together and clung to each other like an object and its shadow, and the love between us was something that surpassed the language of words.

So the time passed happily and the honeymoon was too soon over. At this time, my father Chiafu was in the service of the Kueich'i district government, and he sent a special messenger to bring me there, for, it should be noted that, during this time, I was under the tutorship of Chao Shengtsai of Wulin. Chao was a very kindly teacher and today the fact that I can write at all is due entirely to his credit.

Now, when I came home for the wedding, it had been agreed that I could go back any time. So when I got this news, I did not know what to do. I was afraid Yün might break into tears, but on the contrary she tried to look cheerful and comforted me and urged me to go, and packed up things for me. Only that night I noticed that she did not look quite her usual self. At the time of parting, she whispered to me, "Take good care of yourself, for there will be no one to look after you."

When I went up on board the boat, the peach and pear trees on the banks were in full bloom, but I felt like a lonely bird that had lost its companions and as if the world was going to collapse around me. As soon as I arrived, my father left the place and crossed the river for an eastward destination.

Thus three months passed, which seemed to me like ten insufferable long years. Although Yün wrote to me regularly, still for two letters that I sent her, I received only one in reply, and these letters contained only words of exhortation and the rest was filled with airy, conventional nothings, and I felt very unhappy. Whenever the breeze blew past my bamboo courtyard, or the moon shone upon my window behind the green banana leaves, I thought of her and was carried away into a region of dreams.

My teacher noticed this, and sent word to my father, saying that he would give me ten subjects for composition and let me go home. I felt like an exiled prisoner receiving his pardon.

Strange to say, when I got onto the boat and was on my way home, I felt that a quarter of an hour was like a long year. When I arrived home, I went to pay my respects to my mother and then entered my room. Yün stood up to welcome me, and we held each other's hands in silence, and it seemed then that our souls had melted away or evaporated like a mist. My ears tingled and I did not know where I was.

It was June then and the rooms were very hot. 'Luckily, we were next door to the Lotus Lover's Lodge of the Ts'anglang Pavilion on the east. Over the bridge, there was an open hall overlooking the water, called "After My Heart"—the reference was to an old poem:

> When the water is clear, I will wash the tassels of my hat,
> And when the water is muddy, I will wash my feet.

By the side of the eaves, there was an old tree which spread its green shade over the window and made the people's faces look green with it; and across the creek, you could see people passing to and fro. This was where my father used to entertain his guests. I asked permission from my mother to bring Yün and stay there for the summer. She stopped embroidery during the summer months because of the heat, and the whole day long we were either reading together, or discussing the ancient things, or else enjoying the moon and passing judgments on the flowers. Yün could not drink, but could take at most three cups when compelled to, and I taught her literary games in which the loser had to drink. We thought there could not be a more happy life on earth than this.

One day Yün asked me, "Of all the ancient authors, which one should we regard as the master?" And I replied, *Intrigues of the Warring States* and *Chuang Tzu* are noted for their agility of thought and expressiveness of style, K'uang Heng and Liu Hsiang are known for their classic severity, Ssuma Ch'ien and Pan Ku are known for their breadth of knowledge, Han Yü is known for his mellow qualities, Liu Tsungyüan for his rugged beauty, Ouyang Hsiu for his romantic abandon, and the Sus, father and sons, are known for their sustained eloquence. There are, besides, writings like the political essays of Chia Yi and Tung Chungshu, the euphuistic prose of Hsü Ling and Yü Hsin, the memorandums of Lu Chih, and others more than one can enumerate. True appreciation, however, must come from the reader himself."

"The ancient literature," Yün said, "depends for its appeal on depth of thought and greatness of spirit, which I am afraid it is difficult for a woman to attain. I believe, however, that I do understand something of poetry."

"Poetry was used," I said, "as a literary test in the imperial examinations of the T'ang Dynasty, and people acknowledge Li Po and Tu Fu as the master poets. Which of the two do you like better?"

"Tu's poems," she said, "are known for their workmanship and artistic refinement, while Li's poems are known for their freedom and naturalness of expression. I prefer the vivacity of Li Po to the severity of Tu Fu."

"Tu Fu is the acknowledged king of poets," said I, "and he is taken by most people as their model. Why do you prefer Li Po?"

"Of course," said she, "as for perfection of form and maturity of thought, Tu is the undisputed master, but Li Po's poems have the wayward charm of a nymph. His lines come naturally like falling flowers and flowing water, and are so much lovelier for their spontaneity. I am not saying that Tu is second to Li; only personally I feel, not that I love Tu less, but that I love Li more."

"I say, I didn't know that you are a bosom friend of Li Po!"

"I have still in my heart another poet, Po Chüyi, who is my first tutor, as it were, and I have not been able to forget him."

"What do you mean?" I asked.

"Isn't he the one who wrote the poem on 'The P'ip'a Player'?"

"This is very strange," I laughed and said. "So Li Po is your bosom friend, Po Chüyi is your first tutor, and your husband's literary name is Sanpo. It seems that your life is always bound up with the Pos."

"It is all right," Yün smiled and replied, "to have one's life bound up with the Pos, only I am afraid I shall be writing Po characters all my life." (For in Soochow we call misspelled words "po characters.") And we both laughed.

"Now that you know poetry," I said, "I should like also to know your taste for fu poems."

"The Ch'utz'u is, of course, the fountainhead of fu[2] poetry, but I find it difficult to understand. It seems to me that among the Han and Chin fu poets, Ssuma Hsiangju is most sublime in point of style and diction."

"Perhaps," I said, "Wenchün was tempted to elope with Hsiangju not because of his ch'in[3] music, but rather because of his fu poetry," and we laughed again.

---

2. Rhapsody. Most of the works and authors mentioned in this and the preceding paragraphs are either included or discussed in this anthology.
3. Zither.

I am by nature unconventional and straightforward, but Yün was a stickler for forms, like the Confucian schoolmasters. Whenever I put on a dress for her or tidied up her sleeves, she would say "So much obliged" again and again, and when I passed her a towel or a fan, she must receive it standing up. At first I disliked this and said to her, "Do you mean to tie me down with all this ceremony? There is a proverb which says, 'One who is overcourteous is crafty.' " Yün blushed all over and said, "I am merely trying to be polite and respectful; why do you charge me with craftiness?" "True respect is in the heart, and does not require such empty forms," said I, but Yün said, "There is no more intimate relationship than that between children and their parents. Do you mean to say that children should behave freely toward their parents and keep their respect only in their heart?" "Oh! I was only joking," I said. "The trouble is," said Yün, "most marital troubles begin with joking. Don't you accuse me of disrespect later, for then I shall die of grief without being able to defend myself." Then I held her close to my breast and caressed her, and then she smiled. From then on our conversations were full of "I'm sorry's" and "I beg your pardon's." And so were remained courteous to each other for twenty-three years of our married life like Liang Hung and Meng Kuang of old, and the longer we stayed together, the more passionately attached we became to each other. Whenever we met each other in the house, whether it be in a dark room or in a narrow corridor, we used to hold each other's hands and ask "Where are you going?" and we did this on the sly as if afraid that people might see us. As a matter of fact, we tried at first to avoid being seen sitting or walking together, but after a while, we did not mind it anymore. When Yün was sitting and talking with somebody and saw me come, she would rise and move sideways for me to sit down together with her. All this was done naturally, almost without any consciousness, and although at first we felt uneasy about it, later on it became a matter of habit. I cannot understand why all old couples must hate each other like enemies. Some people say, "If they weren't enemies, they would not be able to live together until old age." Well, I wonder!

On the seventh night of the seventh moon of that year [1780], Yün prepared incense, candles, and some melons and fruits so that we might together worship the Granddaughter of Heaven[4] in the hall called "After My Heart." I had carved two seals with the inscription: "That we might remain husband and wife from incarnation to incarnation." I kept the seal with positive characters, while she kept the one with negative characters, to be used in our correspondence. That night, the moon was shining beautifully and when I looked down at the creek, the ripples shone like golden chains. We were wearing light silk dresses and sitting together with a small fan in our hands

4. The seventh day of the seventh moon is the only day in the year when the heavenly lovers, the Cowherd and the Spinning Maid (also called Weaver Girl and the "Granddaughter of Heaven") are allowed to meet each other across the Milky Way.

before the window overlooking the creek. Looking up at the sky, we saw the clouds sailing through the heavens, changing at every moment into myriad forms, and Yün said: "This moon is common to the whole universe. I wonder if there is another pair of lovers quite as passionate as ourselves looking at the same moon tonight?" And I said, "Oh there are plenty of people who will be sitting in the cool evening and looking at the moon, and perhaps also many women criticizing or enjoying the clouds in their chambers; but when a husband and wife are looking at the moon together, I hardly think that the clouds will form the subject of their conversation." By and by, the candlelights went out, the moon sank in the sky, and we removed the fruits and went to bed.

The fifteenth of the seventh moon was All Souls' Day. Yün prepared a little dinner so that we could drink together with the moon as our company, but when night came, the sky was suddenly overcast with dark clouds. Yün knitted her brow and said, "If it be the wish of God that we two should live together until there are silver threads in our hair, then the moon must come out again tonight." On my part I felt disheartened also. As we looked across the creek, we saw will-o'-the-wisps flitting in crowds hither and thither like ten thousand candlelights, threading their way through the willows and smartweeds. And then we began to compose a poem together, each saying two lines at a time, the first completing the couplet which the other had begun, and the second beginning another couplet for the other to finish, and after a few rhymes, the longer we kept on, the more nonsensical it became, until it was a jumble of slapdash doggerel. By this time, Yün was buried amidst tears and laughter and choking on my breast, while I felt the fragrance of the jasmine in her hair assail my nostrils. I patted her on the shoulder and said jokingly, "I thought that the jasmine was used for decoration in women's hair because it was round like a pearl; I did not know that it is because its fragrance is so much finer when it is mixed with the smell of women's hair and powder. When it smells like that, even the citron cannot remotely compare with it." Then Yün stopped laughing and said, "The citron is the gentleman among the different fragrant plants because its fragrance is so slight that you can hardly detect it; on the other hand, the jasmine is a common fellow because it borrows its fragrance partly from others. Therefore, the fragrance of the jasmine is like that of a smiling sycophant." "Why, then," I said, "do you keep away from the gentleman and associate with the common fellow?" And Yün replied, "I am amused at the gentleman that loves the common fellow." While we were thus bandying words about, it was already midnight, and we saw the wind had blown away the clouds in the sky and there appeared the full moon, round like a chariot wheel, and we were greatly delighted. And so we began to drink by the side of the window, but before we had tasted three cups, we heard suddenly the noise of a splash under the bridge, as if some one had fallen into the water. We looked out through the window and saw there was not a thing, for the water was as smooth as a mirror, except that we heard the noise of a duck scampering in the marshes. I knew that there was a ghost of someone who had been drowned by the side of the Ts'anglang Pavilion, but knowing that Yün was very timid, dared not mention it to her. And Yün sighed and said, "Alas! Whence cometh this noise?" and we shuddered all over. Quickly we shut the window and carried the wine-pot back into the room. A lamplight was then burning as small as a pea, and the curtains moved in the dark, and we were shaking all over. We then put out the light and went inside the bed-curtain, and Yün had already run up a high fever. Soon I had a high temperature myself, and our illness dragged on for about twenty days. True it is that when the cup of happiness overflows, disaster follows, as the saying goes, and this was also an omen that we should not be able to live together until old age.

On the fifteenth of the eighth moon, or the Mid-Autumn Festival, I had just recovered from my illness. Yün had now been a bride in my home for over a year, but still had never been to the Ts'anglang Pavilion itself next door. So I first ordered an old servant to tell the watchman not to let any visitors enter the place. Toward evening, I went with Yün and my younger sister, supported by an amah and a maid-servant and led by an old attendant. We passed a bridge, entered a gate, turned eastward and followed a zigzag path into the place, where we saw huge grottoes and abundant green trees. The pavilion was situated on the top of a hill. Going up by the steps to the top, one could look around for miles, where in the distance chimney smoke arose from the cottages against the background of clouds of rainbow hues. Over the bank, there was a grove called the "Forest by the Hill" where the great officials used to entertain their guests. Later on, the Chengyi College was erected on this spot, but it wasn't there yet. We brought a blanket which we spread on the pavilion floor and then sat around together while the watchman served us tea. After a while, the moon had already arisen from behind the forest, and the breeze was playing about my sleeves, while the moon's image sparkled in the rippling water, and all worldly cares were banished from our breasts. "This is the end of a perfect day," said Yün. "Wouldn't it be fine if we could get a boat and row around the pavilion!" At this time, the lights were already shining from people's homes, and thinking of the incident on the fifteenth night of the seventh moon, we left the pavilion and hurried home. According to the custom at Soochow, the women of all families, big and small, came out in groups on the Mid-Autumn night, a custom which was called "pacing the moonlight." Strange to say, no one came to such a beautiful neighborhood as the Ts'anglang Pavilion.

My father Chiafu was very fond of adopting children; hence I had twenty-six adopted brothers. My mother, too, had nine adopted daughters, of whom Miss Wang, the second, and Miss Yü, the sixth, were Yün's best friends. Wang was a kind of a tomboy and a great drinker while Yü was straightforward and very fond of talking. When they came together, they used to chase me out so that the three of them could sleep in the same bed. I knew Miss Yü was responsible for this, and once I said to her in fun, "When you get married, I am going to invite your husband to come and keep him for ten days." "I'll come here, too, then," said Miss Yü, "and sleep in the same bed with Yün. Won't that be fun?" At this Yün and Wang merely smiled.

At this time, my younger brother Ch'it'ang was going to get married, and we moved to Ts'angmi Alley by the Bridge of Drinking Horses. The house was quite big, but not so secluded and refined as the one by the Ts'anglang Pavilion. On the birthday of my mother, we had theatrical performances at home, and Yün at first thought them quite wonderful. Scorning all taboos, my father asked for the performance of a scene called "Sad Parting," and the actors played so realistically that the audience were quite touched. I noticed across the screen that Yün suddenly got up and disappeared inside for a long time. I went in to see her, and the Misses Yü and Wang also followed suit. There I saw Yün sitting alone before her dressing table, resting her head on an arm. "Why are you so sad?" I asked. "One sees a play for diversion," Yün said, "but today's play only breaks my heart." Both Wang and Yü were laughing at her, but I defended her. "She is touched because hers is a profoundly emotional soul." "Are you going to sit here all day long?" asked Miss Yü. "I'll stay here until some better selection is being played," Yün replied. Hearing this, Miss Wang left first and asked my mother to select more cheerful plays like *Ch'ihliang* and *Househ*. Then Yün was persuaded to come out and watch the play, which made her happy again.

My uncle Such'un died early without an heir, and my father made me succeed his line. His tomb was situated on Longevity Hill in Hsik'uatang by the side of our ancestral tombs, and it was our custom to go and visit the grave every spring. As there was a beautiful garden called Koyüan in its neighborhood, Miss Wang begged to come with us. Yün saw that the pebbles on this hill had beautiful grains of different colors, and said to me, "If we were to collect these pebbles and make them into a grotto, it would be even more artistic than one made of Hsüanchow stones." I expressed the fear that there might not be enough of this kind. "If Yün really likes them, I'll pick them for you," said Miss Wang. So we borrowed a bag from the watchman, and went along collecting them. Whenever she saw one, she would ask for my opinion. If I said "good," she would pick it; and if I said "no," she would discard it. Very soon we had a fairly full bag and Miss Wang was perspiring all over. "If we get any more, we shan't be able to carry them home," she said. "I have been told," said Yün, as we were going along, "that mountain fruits must be gathered by monkeys, which seems quite true." Miss Wang was furious and stretched both hands as if to scratch her. I stopped her and said to Yün by way of reproof, "You cannot blame her for being angry, because she is doing all the work and you stand by and say such unkind things." Then on our way back, we visited the Koyüan Garden, in which we saw a profusion of flowers of all colors. Wang was very childish; she would break a flower branch for no reason, and Yün scolded her, saying, "You are not going to put it in a vase or in your hair. Why destroy flowers like that?" "Oh! what's the harm? These flowers don't feel anything." "All right," I said "you will be punished for this one day by marrying a pockmarked, bearded fellow for your husband to avenge the flowers." Wang looked at me in anger, threw the flowers to the ground, and kicked them into the pond. "Why do you all bully me?" she said. However, Yün made it up with her, and she was finally pacified.

Yün was at first very quiet and loved to hear me talk, but I gradually taught her the art of conversation as one leads a cricket with a blade of grass. She then gradually learned the art of conversation. For instance, at meals, she always mixed her rice with tea, and loved to eat stale pickled bean-curd, called "stinking bean-curd" in Soochow. Another thing she liked to eat was a kind of small pickled cucumber. I hated both of these things, and said to her in fun one day, "The dog, which has no stomach, eats human refuse because it doesn't know that refuse stinks, while the beetle rolls in dunghills and is changed into a cicada because it wants to fly up to heaven. Now are you a dog or a beetle?" To this Yün replied, "One eats bean-curd because it is so cheap and it goes with dry rice as well as with congee. I am used to this from childhood. Now I am married into your home, like a beetle that has been transformed into a cicada, but I am still eating it because one should not forget old friends. As for pickled cucumber, I tasted it for the first time in your home." "Oh, then, my home is a dog's kennel, isn't it?" Yün was embarrassed and tried to explain it away by saying, "Of course there is refuse in every home; the only difference is whether one eats it or not. You yourself eat garlic, for instance, and I have tried to eat it with you. I won't compel you to eat stinking bean-curd, but cucumber is really very nice, if you hold your breath while eating. You will see when you have tasted it yourself. It is like Wuyien, an ugly but virtuous woman." "Are you going to make me a dog?" I asked. "Well, I have been a dog for a long time, why don't you try to be one?" So she picked one with her chopsticks and pushed it into my mouth. I held my breath and ate it and found it indeed delicious. Then I ate it in the usual way and found it to have a marvelous flavor. And from that time on, I loved the cucumber also. Yün also prepared pickled bean-curd mixed with sesame seed oil and sugar, which I found also to be a delicacy. We then mixed pickled cucumber with pickled bean-curd and called the mixture "the double-flavored gravy." I said I could not understand why I disliked it at first and began to love it so now. "If you are in love with a thing, you will forget its ugliness," said Yün.

My younger brother Ch'it'ang married the daughter of Wang Hsüchou. It happened that on the wedding day, she wanted some pearls. Yün took her own pearls, which she had received as her bridal gift, and gave them to my mother. The maid-servant thought it a pity, but Yün said, "A woman is an incarnation of the female principle, and so are pearls. For a woman to wear pearls would be to leave no room for the male principle. For that reason I don't prize them." She had, however, a peculiar fondness for old books and broken slips of painting. Whenever she saw odd volumes of books, she would try to sort them out, arrange them in order, and have them rebound properly. These were collected and labeled "Ancient Relics." When she saw scrolls of calligraphy or painting that were partly spoiled, she would find some old paper and paste them up nicely, and ask me to fill up the broken spaces.[5] These were kept rolled up properly and called "Beautiful Gleanings." This was what she was busy about the whole day when she was not attending to the kitchen or needlework. When she found in old trunks or piles of musty volumes any writing or painting that pleased her, she felt as if she had discovered some precious relic, and an old woman neighbor of ours, by the name of Feng, used to buy up old scraps and sell them to her. She had the same tastes and habits as myself, and besides had the talent of anticipating my wishes, doing things without being told and doing them to my perfect satisfaction.

Once I said to her, "It is a pity that you were born a woman. If you were a man, we could travel together and visit all the famous places of the world."

"Oh! This is not so very difficult," said Yün. "Wait till I am middle-aged. Even if I cannot accompany you to the five sacred mountains then, we can travel to the nearer places, like Huch'iu and Lingyen, as far south as the West Lake and as far north as P'ingshan."[6]

"Of course this is all right, except that I am afraid when you are middle-aged, you will be too old to travel."

"If I can't do it in this life, then I shall do it in the next."

"In the next life, you must be born a man and I will be your wife."

"It will be quite beautiful if we can then still remember what has happened in this life."

"That's all very well, but even a bowl of congee has provided material for so much conversation. We shan't be able to sleep a wink the whole wedding night, but shall be discussing what we have done in the previous existence, if we can still remember what's happened in this life then."

"It is said that the Old Man under the Moon is in charge of matrimony," said Yün. "He was good enough to make us husband and wife in this life, and we shall still depend on his favor in the affair of marriage in the next incarnation. Why don't we make a painting of him and worship him in our home?"

So we asked a Mr. Ch'i Liut'i, who specialized in portraiture, to make a painting of the Old Man under the Moon, which he did. It was a picture of the Old Man holding a red silk thread in one hand and a walking-stick with

5. The author was a painter and for a time painted for a living. Some of his paintings still remain.
6. In Yangchow.

the *Book of Matrimony* suspended from it in the other. He had white hair and a ruddy complexion, apparently bustling about in a cloudy region. Altogether it was a very excellent painting of Ch'i's. My friend Shih Chot'ang wrote some words on it and we hung the picture in our chamber. On the first and fifteenth of every month, we burned incense and prayed together before him. I do not know where this picture is now, after all the changes and upsets in our family life. "Ended is the present life and uncertain the next," as the poet says. I wonder if God will listen to the prayer of us two silly lovers.

After we had moved to Ts'angmi Alley, I called our bedroom the "Tower of Guests' Fragrance," with a reference to Yün's name,[7] and to the story of Liang Hung and Meng Kuang who as husband and wife were always courteous to each other "like guests." We rather disliked the house because the walls were too high and the courtyard was too small. At the back, there was another house, leading to the library. Looking out of the window at the back, one could see the old garden of Mr. Lu, then in a dilapidated condition. Yün's thoughts still hovered about the beautiful scenery of the Ts'anglang Pavilion.

At this time, there was an old peasant woman living on the east of Mother Gold's Bridge and the north of Kenghsiang. Her little cottage was surrounded on all sides by vegetable fields and had a wicker gate. Outside the gate, there was a pond about thirty yards across, and on both sides of the gate was a wilderness of trees and flowers. This was the old site of the home of Chang Shihch'eng of the Yüan dynasty. A few paces to the west of the cottage, there was a mound filled with broken bricks, from the top of which one could command a view of the surrounding territory, which was open country with a stretch of wild vegetation. Once the old woman happened to mention the place, and Yün kept on thinking about it. So she said to me one day, "Since leaving the Ts'anglang Pavilion, I have been dreaming about it all the time. As we cannot live there, we must put up with the second best." "I have been thinking, too," I said, "of a place to go to and spend the long summer days. If you think you'll like the place, I'll go ahead and take a look. If it is satisfactory, we can carry our bedding along and go and stay there for a month. How about it?" "I'm afraid Mother won't allow us." "Oh! I'll see to that," I told her. So the next day, I went there and found that the cottage consisted of only two rooms, which could be partitioned into four. With paper windows and bamboo beds, the house would be quite a delightfully cool place to stay in. The old woman knew what I wanted and gladly rented me her bedroom, which looked quite new after I had the walls repapered. I then informed my mother of it and went to stay there with Yün.

Our only neighbors were an old couple who raised vegetables for the market. They knew that we were going to stay there for the summer, and came and called on us, bringing us some fish from the pond and vegetables from their own fields. We offered to pay for them, but as they wouldn't take

7. "Yün" in Mandarin means a type of fragrant weed.

any money, Yün made a pair of shoes for them, which they were finally persuaded to accept. This was in July when the trees cast a green shade over the place. The summer breeze blew over the water of the pond, and cicadas filled the air with their singing the whole day. Our old neighbor also made a fishing line for us, and we used to angle together under the shade. Late in the afternoons, we would go up on the mound to look at the evening glow and compose lines of poetry when we felt so inclined. Two of the lines were:

> Beast-clouds swallow the sinking sun,
> And the bow-moon shoots the falling stars.

After a while, the moon cut her image in the water, insects began to cry all around, and we placed a bamboo bed near the hedgerow to sit or lie upon. The old woman then would inform us that wine had been warmed up and dinner prepared, and we would sit down to have a little drink under the moon. After we had a bath, we would put on our slippers and carry a fan, and lie or sit there, listening to old tales of retribution told by our neighbor. When we came in to sleep about midnight, we felt our whole bodies nice and cool, almost forgetting that we were living in a city.

There along the hedgerow, we asked the gardener to plant chrysanthemums. The flowers bloomed in the ninth moon, and we continued to stay there for another ten days. My mother was also quite delighted and came to see us there. So we ate crabs in the midst of the chrysanthemums and whiled away the whole day. Yün was quite enchanted with all this and said, "Some day we must build a cottage here. We'll buy ten sixth-acres of ground, and around it we'll have the servants plant vegetables and melons for our food. You will paint and I will do embroidery, from which we could make enough money to buy wine and compose poems over dinners. Thus, clad in simple gowns and eating simple meals, we could live a very happy life together without going anywhere." I fully agreed with her. Now the place is still there, while the one who knows my heart is dead. Alas! Such is life!

About half a tricent from my home, there was a temple to the God of Tungt'ing Lake, popularly known as the Narcissus Temple, situated in the Ch'uk'u Alley. It had many winding corridors and a small garden with pavilions. On the birthday of the god, every clan would be assigned a corner in the temple, where they would hang beautiful glass lamps of a kind, with a table in the center, on which were placed vases on wooden stands. These vases were decorated with flowers for competition. In the daytime, there would be theatrical performances, while at night the flower-vases were brilliantly illuminated with candlelights, a custom which was called "Illuminated Flowers." With the flowers and the lanterns and the smell of incense, the whole place resembled a night feast in the Palace of the Dragon King. The people there would sing or play music, or gossip over their teacups. The audience stood around in crowds to look at the show and there was a railing at the curb to keep them within a certain limit.

I was asked by my friend to help in the decorations and so had the pleasure of taking part in it. When Yün heard me speaking about it at home, she remarked, "It is a pity that I am not a man and cannot go to see it." "Why, you could put on my cap and gown and disguise yourself as a man," I suggested. Accordingly she changed her coiffure into a queue, painted her eyebrows, and put on my cap. Although her hair showed slightly round the temples, it passed off tolerably well. As my gown was found to be an inch and a half too long, she tucked it around the waist and put on a *makua*[8] on top. "What am I going to do about my feet?" she asked. I told her there was a kind of shoes called "butterfly shoes," which could fit any size of feet and were very easy to obtain at the shops, and suggested buying a pair for her, which she could also use as slippers later on at home. Yün was delighted with the idea, and after supper, when she had finished her makeup, she paced about the room, imitating the gestures and gait of a man for a long time, when all of a sudden she changed her mind and said, "I am not going! It would be so embarrassing if somebody should discover me, and besides, our parents would object." Still I urged her to go. "Who doesn't know me at the temple?" I said. "Even if they should find it out, they would laugh it off as a joke. Mother is at present in the home of the ninth sister. We could steal away and back without letting anyone know about it."

Yün then had such fun looking at herself in the mirror. I dragged her along and we stole away together to the temple. For a long time nobody in the temple could detect it. When people asked, I simply said she was my boy-cousin, and people would merely curtsy with their hands together and pass on. Finally, we came to a place where there were some young women and girls sitting behind the flower show. They were the family of the owner of the show, by the name of Yang. Yün suddenly went over to talk with them, and while talking, she casually leaned over and touched the shoulder of a young woman. The maid-servants near by shouted angrily, "How dare the rascal!" I attempted to explain and smooth the matter over, but the servants still scowled ominously at us and, seeing that the situation was desperate, Yün took off her cap and showed her feet, saying, "Look here, I am a woman, too!" They all stared at each other in surprise, and then, instead of being angry, began to laugh. We were then asked to sit down and have some tea. Soon afterward we got sedan-chairs and came home.

When Mr. Ch'ien Shihcho of Wukiang died of an illness, my father wrote a letter to me, asking me to go and attend the funeral. Yün secretly expressed her desire to come along since, on our way to Wukiang, we would pass the

---

8. A riding-jacket with wide sleeves.

Taihu Lake, which she wished very much to see. I told her that I was just thinking it would be too lonely for me to go alone, and that it would be excellent, indeed, if she could come along, except that I could not think of a pretext for her going. "Oh! I could say that I am going to see my mother," Yün said. "You can go ahead, and I shall come along to meet you." "If so," I said, "we can tie up our boat beneath the Bridge of Ten Thousand Years on our way home, where we shall be able to look at the moon again as we did at the Ts'anglang Pavilion."

This was on the eighteenth day of the sixth moon. That day, I brought a servant and arrived first at Hsükiang Ferry, where I waited for her in the boat. By and by, Yün arrived in a sedan-chair, and we started off, passing by the Tiger's Roar Bridge, where the view opened up and I saw sailing boats and birds on the sandbanks. The water was a white stretch, joining the sky at the horizon. "So this is Taihu!" Yün exclaimed. "I know now how big the universe is, and I have not lived in vain! I think a good many ladies never see such a view in their whole lifetime." As we were occupied in conversation, it wasn't very long before we saw swaying willows on the banks, and we knew we had arrived at Wukiang.

I went up to attend the funeral ceremony, but when I came back, Yün was not in the boat. I asked the boatman and he said, "Don't you see someone under the willow trees by the bridge, watching the cormorants catching fish?" Yün, then, had gone up with the boatman's daughter. I followed her there, and saw that she was perspiring all over, still leaning on the boatman's daughter and standing there absorbed, looking at the cormorants. I patted her shoulder and said, "You are wet through." Yün turned her head and said, "I was afraid that your friend Ch'ien might come to the boat, so I left to avoid him. Why did you come back so early?" "In order to catch the renegade!" I replied.

We then came back hand-in-hand to the boat, and when we stopped at the Bridge of Ten Thousand Years, the sun had not yet gone down. And we let down all the windows to allow the river breeze to come in, and there, dressed in light silk and holding a fan, we sliced a melon to cool ourselves. Soon the evening glow was casting a red hue over the bridge, and the distant haze enveloped the willow trees in darkness. The moon then came up, and all along the river we saw a stretch of lights coming from the fishing boats. I asked my servant to go astern and have a drink with the boatman.

The boatman's daughter was called Suyün. She was quite a likable girl, and I had known her before. I beckoned her to come and sit together with Yün on the bow of the boat. We did not put on any light, so that we could the better enjoy the moon, and there we sat drinking and playing literary games with wine as forfeit. Suyün just stared at us, listening for a long time before she said, "Now I am quite familiar with all sorts of wine-games, but have never heard of this one. Will you explain it to me?" Yün tried to explain it by all sorts of analogies to her, but still she failed to understand. Then I laughed and said, "Will the lady teacher please stop a moment? I have a parable for explaining it, and she will understand at once." "You try it, then!" "The stork," I said, "can dance, but cannot plow, while the buffalo can plow, but cannot dance. That lies in the nature of things. You are making a fool of yourself by trying to teach the impossible to her." Suyün pummeled my shoulder playfully, and Yün said, "Hereafter let's make a rule: let's have it out with our mouths, but no hands! One who breaks the rule will have to drink a big cup." As Suyün was a great drinker, she filled a cup full and drank it up at a draft. "I suggest that one may be allowed to use one's hands for caressing, but not for striking," I said. Yün then playfully pushed Suyün into my lap, saying, "Now you can caress her to your full." "How stupid of you!" I laughed in reply. "The beauty of caressing lies in doing it naturally and half-unconsciously. Only a country bumpkin will hug and caress a woman roughly." I noticed that the jasmine in her hair gave out a strange fragrance, mixed with the flavor of wine, powder, and hair lotion, and remarked to her, "The 'mean little fellow' stinks all over the place. It makes me sick." Hearing this, Suyün struck me with her fist in a rage, saying,

"Who told you to smell it?"

"She breaks the rule! Two cups!" Yün shouted.

"He called me 'mean little fellow.' Why shouldn't I strike him?" explained Suyün.

"He really means by the 'mean little fellow' something which you don't understand. You finish these two cups first and I'll tell you."

When Suyün had finished the two cups, Yün told her of our discussion about the jasmine at the Ts'anglang Pavilion.

"Then the mistake is mine. I must be penalized again," said Suyün. And she drank a third cup.

Yün said then that she had long heard of her reputation as a singer and would like to hear her sing. This Suyün did beautifully, beating time with her ivory chopsticks on a little plate. Yün drank merrily until she was quite drunk, when she took a sedan-chair and went home first, while I remained chatting with Suyün for a moment, and then walked home under the moonlight.

At this time, we were staying in the home of our friend Lu Panfang, in a house called Hsiaoshuanglou. A few days afterward, Mrs. Lu heard of the story from someone, and secretly told Yün, "Do you know that your husband was drinking a few days ago at the Bridge of Ten Thousand Years with two sing-song girls?" "Yes, I do," replied Yün, "and one of the sing-song girls was myself." Then she told her the whole story and Mrs. Lu had a good laugh at herself.

When I came back from eastern Kwangtung in July, 1794, there was a cousin of mine, by the name of Hsü Hsiufeng, who had brought home with him a concubine. He was crazy about her beauty and asked Yün to go and see her. After seeing her, Yün remarked to Hsiufeng one day, "She has beauty, but no charm." "Do you mean to say that when your husband takes a concubine, she must have both beauty and charm?" answered Hsiufeng. Yün replied in the affirmative. So from that time on, she was quite bent on finding a concubine for me, but was short of cash.

At this time there was a Chekiang sing-song girl by the name of Wen Lenghsiang, who was staying at Soochow. She had composed four poems on the willow catkins which were talked about all over the city, and many scholars wrote poems in reply, using the same rhyme-words as her originals, as was the custom. There was a friend of mine, Hsienhan of Wukiang, who was a good friend of Lenghsiang and brought her poems to me, asking me to write some in reply. Yün wasn't interested because she did not think much of her, but I was intrigued and composed one on the flying willow catkins which filled the air in May. Two lines which Yün liked very much were:

> They softly touch the spring sorrow in my bosom,
> And gently stir the longings in her heart.

On the fifth day of the eighth moon in the following year, my mother was going to see Huch'iu with Yün, when Hsienhan suddenly appeared and said, "I am going to Huch'iu, too. Will you come along with me and see a beautiful sing-song girl?" I told my mother to go ahead and agreed to meet her at Pant'ang near Huch'iu. My friend then dragged me to Lenghsiang's place. I saw that Lenghsiang was already in her middleage, but she had a girl by the name of Hanyüan, who was a very sweet young maiden, still in her 'teens. Her eyes looked like an autumn lake that cooled one by its cold splendor. After talking with her for a while, I learned that she knew how to read and write. There was also a younger sister of hers, by the name of Wenyüan, who was still a mere child. I had then no thought of going with a sing-song girl, fully realizing that, as a poor scholar, I could not afford to give a feast in return. But since I was there already, I tried to get along as best I could.

"Are you trying to seduce me?" I said to Hsienhan secretly.

"No," he replied, "someone had invited me today to a dinner in Hanyüan's place in return for a previous dinner. It happened that the host himself was invited by an important person, and I am acting in his place. Don't you worry!"

I felt then quite relieved. Arriving at Pant'ang, we met my mother's boat, and I asked Hanyüan to go over to her boat and meet Yün. When Yün and Han met each other, they instinctively took to each other like old friends, and later they went hand-in-hand to see the famous hill. Yün was especially fond of a place called "A Thousand Acres of Clouds," and she remained there for a long time, lost in admiration of the scenery. We returned to the Bank of Rural Fragrance where we tied up the boats and had a jolly drinking party together.

When we started on our way home, Yün said, "Will you please go over to the other boat with your friend, while I share this one with Han?" We did as she suggested, and I did not return to my boat until we had passed the Tut'ing Bridge, where we parted from my friend and Hanyüan. It was midnight by the time we returned home.

"Now I have found a girl who has both beauty and charm," Yün said to me. "I have already asked Hanyüan to come and see us tomorrow, and I'll arrange it for you." I was taken by surprise.

"You know we are not a wealthy family. We can't afford to keep a girl like that, and we are so happily married. Why do you want to find somebody else?"

"But I love her," said Yün smilingly. "You just leave it to me."

The following afternoon, Hanyüan actually came. Yün was very cordial to her and prepared a feast, and we played the finger-guessing game and drank, but during the whole dinner, not a word was mentioned about securing her for me. When Hanyüan had gone, Yün said, "I have secretly made another appointment with her to come on the eighteenth, when we will pledge ourselves as sisters. You must prepare a sacrificial offering for the occasion." And pointing to the bracelet on her arm, she continued, "If you see this bracelet appear on Hanyüan's arm, you'll understand that she has consented. I have already hinted at it to her, but we haven't got to know each other as thoroughly as I should like to yet." I had to let her have her own way.

On the eighteenth, Hanyüan turned up in spite of a pouring rain. She disappeared in the bedroom for a long time before she came out hand-in-hand with Yün. When she saw me, she felt a little shy, for the bracelet was already on her arm. After we had burned incense and pledged an oath, we continued to drink again. It happened that Hanyüan had an engagement to go and visit Shih-hu Lake, and soon she left.

Yün came to me all smiles and said, "Now that I have found a beauty for you, how are you going to reward the go-between?" I asked her for the details.

"I had to broach the topic delicately to her," she said, "because I was afraid that she might have someone else in mind. Now I have learned that there isn't anyone, and I asked her, 'Do you understand why we have this dinner today?' 'I should feel greatly honored if I could come to your home, but my mother is expecting a lot of me and I can't decide by myself. We will watch and see,' she replied. As I was putting on the bracelet, I told her again, 'The jade is chosen for its hardness as a token of fidelity and the bracelet's roundness is a symbol of everlasting faithfulness. Meanwhile, please put it on as a token of our pledge.' She replied that everything depended on her mother. So it seems that she is willing herself. The only difficulty is her mother, Lenghsiang. We will wait and see how it turns out."

"Are you going to enact the comedy *Linhsiangpan* of Li Liweng right in our home?"

"Yes!" Yün replied.

From that time on, not a day passed without her mentioning Hanyüan's name. Eventually Hanyüan was married by force to some influential person, and our arrangements did not come off. And Yün actually died of grief on this account.

Chapter 3: Sorrow

Why is it that there are sorrows and hardships in this life? Usually they are due to one's own fault, but this was not the case with me. I was fond of friendship, proud of keeping my word, and by nature frank and straightforward, for which I eventually suffered. My father Chiafu, too, was a very generous man; he used to help people in trouble, bring up other people's sons and marry off other people's daughters in innumerable instances, spending money like dirt, all for the sake of other people. My wife and I often had to pawn things when we were in need of money, and while at first we managed to make both ends meet, gradually our purse became thinner and thinner. As the proverb says, "To run a family and mix socially, money is the first essential." At first we incurred the criticism of the busybodies, and then even people of our own family began to make sarcastic remarks. Indeed, "absence of talent in a woman is synonymous with virtue," as the ancient proverb says.

I was born the third son of my family, although the eldest; hence they used to call Yün "*san niang*" at home, but this was later suddenly changed into "*san t'ait'ai*." This began at first in fun, but later became a general practice, and even relatives of all ranks, high and low, addressed her as "*san t'ait'ai*." I wonder if this was a sign of the beginning of family dissension.[9]

When I was staying with my father at the Haining yamen[10] in 1785, Yün used to enclose personal letters of hers along with the regular family correspondence. Seeing this, my father said that, since Yün could write letters, she should be entrusted with the duty of writing letters for my mother. It happened that there was a little family gossip and my mother suspected that it had leaked out through Yün's letters, and stopped her writing. When my father saw that it was not Yün's handwriting, he asked me, "Is your wife sick?" I then wrote to inquire from her, but got no reply. After some time had elapsed, my father was angry with her and spoke to me, "Your wife seems to think it beneath her to write letters for your mother!" Afterward when I came home, I found out the reason and proposed to explain the matter, but Yün stopped me, saying, "I would rather be blamed by Father than incur the displeasure of Mother." And the matter was not cleared up at all.

In the spring of 1790, I again accompanied my father to the magistrate's

---

9. *San* means "number three." The meanings of *niang* and *t'ait'ai* vary with local usage, but generally the former refers to a young married woman in a big household, while the latter suggests the mistress of an independent home.

10. District magistrate's headquarters.

office at Hankiang.[11] There was a colleague by the name of Yü Fout'ing, who was staying with his family there. One day, my father said to Fout'ing, "I have been living all my life away from home, and have found it very difficult to find someone to look after my personal comforts. If my son would sympathize with me, he should try to look for one from my home district, so that there will be no dialect[12] difficulty." Fout'ing passed on the word to me, and I secretly wrote to Yün, asking her to look round for a girl. She did, and found one of the Yao clan. As Yün was not quite sure whether my father would take her or not, she did not tell Mother about it. When the girl was leaving, she merely referred to her as a girl in the neighborhood who was going for a pleasure trip. After learning, however, that my father had instructed me to bring the girl to his quarters for good, she listened to someone's advice and invented the story that this was the girl my father had had in mind for a long time. "But you said she was going for a pleasure trip! Now why does he marry her?" remarked my mother. And so Yün incurred my mother's displeasure, too.

I was staying at Chenchow in 1792. My father happened to be ill at Yangchow, so I went there to see him, and fell ill myself. At that time, my younger brother Ch'it'ang was with my father, too. In her letter to me, Yün mentioned that Ch'it'ang had borrowed some money from a woman neighbor, for which she was the guarantor, and that now the creditor was pressing for repayment. I asked Ch'it'ang about it, and he was rather displeased, thinking that Yün was meddling with his affairs. So I merely wrote a postscript at the end of a letter with the words: "Both father and son are sick and we have no money to pay the loan. Wait till younger brother comes home, and let him take care of it himself." Soon my father and I got well and I left for Chenchow again. Yün's reply came when I was away and was opened by my father. The letter spoke of Ch'it'ang's loan from the neighboring woman, and besides contained the words: "Your mother thinks that old man's illness is all due to that Yao girl. When he is improving, you should secretly suggest to Yao to say that she is homesick, and I'll ask her parents to come to Yangchow to take her home. In this way we could wash our hands of the matter." When my father saw this, he was furious. He asked Ch'it'ang about the loan and Ch'it'ang declared that he knew nothing about it. So my father wrote a note to me: "Your wife borrowed a loan behind your back and spread scandals about your brother. Moreover, she called her mother-in-law 'your mother' and called her father-in-law 'old man.'[13] This is the height of impudence. I have already sent

11. Yangchow.

12. "Dialect," as used loosely in reference to Sinitic tongues, often signifies separate and mutually unintelligible languages according to usual linguistic standards.

13. Forms of address are extremely important in Chinese society and, when improperly used, can lead to serious consequences.

a letter home by a special messenger, ordering her dismissal from home. If you have any conscience at all, you should realize your own fault!" I received this letter like a bolt from the blue, and immediately wrote a letter of apology to him, hired a horse, and hurried home, afraid that Yün might commit suicide. I was explaining the whole matter at home when the family servant arrived with my father's letter which detailed her various points of misconduct in a most drastic tone. Yün wept and said, "Of course I was wrong to write like that, but Father-in-Law ought to forgive a woman's ignorance." After a few days, we received another letter from Father; "I won't be too harsh on you. You take Yün along and stay away from home, and do not let me see your face again."

It was proposed then that Yün might stay at her maiden home, but her mother was dead and her younger brother had run away from home, and she was not willing to go and be a dependent on her kinfolk. Fortunately, my friend Lu Panfang heard of the matter and took pity on us, and asked us to go and stay in his home at Hsiaoshuanglou. After two years had passed, my father began to know the whole truth. It happened that shortly after I returned from Lingnan,[14] my father personally came to the Hsiaoshuanglou and said to Yün, "Now I understand everything. Why not come home?" Accordingly we returned happily to the old home and the family was reunited. Who would suspect that the affair of Hanyüan was still brewing!

Yün used to have woman's troubles, with discharges of blood. The ailment developed as a consequence of her brother K'ehch'ang running away from home and her mother dying of grief over it, which affected Yün's health very much. Since coming to know Hanyüan, however, the trouble had left her for over a year and I was congratulating myself that this friendship proved better than all medicine. Then Han was married to an influential person, who had offered a thousand dollars for her and, furthermore, undertook to support her mother. "The beauty had therefore fallen into the hands of a barbarian." I had known of this for some time, but dared not mention it to Yün. However, she went to to see her one day and learned the news for herself. On coming back, she told me amid sobs, "I did not think that Han could be so heartless!"

"You yourself are crazy," I said. "What do you expect of a sing-song girl? Besides, one who is used to beautiful dresses and nice food like her would hardly be satisfied with the lot of a poor housewife. It were better like this than to marry her and find it to one's cost afterward."

I tried my best to comfort her, but Yün could never quite recover from the shock of being betrayed and her troubles came again. She was confined to bed and no medicine was of any avail. The illness then became chronic and she grew greatly emaciated. After a few years, our debts piled up higher and higher, and people began to make unpleasant remarks. My father also began

14. In Kwangtung (Canton) province.

to dislike her more and more on account of the fact that she had been a sworn sister to a sing-song girl. I was placed in an embarrassing position between father and wife, and from that time on, I did not know what human happiness was.

Yün had given birth to a daughter, named Ch'ingchün, who was then fourteen years old. She knew how to read, and being a very understanding child, quietly went through the hardships with us, often undertaking the pawning of jewelry and clothing. We had also a son named Fengsen, who was then twelve and was studying with a private tutor. I was out of a job for many years, and had set up a shop for selling books and paintings in my own home. The income of the shop for three days was hardly sufficient to meet one day's expenses, and I was hard pressed for money and worried all the time. I went through the severe winter without a padded gown and Ch'ingchün too was often shivering in her thin dress, but insisted on saying that she did not feel cold at all. For this reason, Yün swore that she would never see any doctor or take any medicine.

It happened once that she could get up from bed, when my friend Chou Ch'unhsü, who had just returned from the yamen of Prince Fu, wanted to pay for someone to embroider[15] a Buddhist book, the *Prajñāpāramitā Sūtra*. Yün undertook to do it, being attracted by the handsome remuneration and besides believing that embroidering the text of a Buddhist sūtra might help to bring good luck and ward off calamities. My friend, however, was in a hurry to depart and could not wait, and Yün finished it in ten days. Such work was naturally too much of a strain for a person in her condition, and she began to complain of dizziness and backache. How did I know that even Buddha would not show mercy to a person born under an evil star! Her illness then became very much aggravated after embroidering the Buddhist sūtra. She needed more attention and wanted now tea and now medicine, and the people in the family began to feel weary of her.

There was a Shansi man who had rented a house to the left of my art shop, and used to lend money at high interest for his living. He often asked me to do some painting for him, and in this way came to know me. There was a friend of mine who wanted to borrow fifty dollars from him and asked me to guarantee the loan. I could not refuse him and consented, but my friend eventually ran away with the money. The creditor, of course, came to me as the guarantor for the money, and made a lot of fuss about it. At first, I tried to pay back a part of the loan with my painting, but finally I just had nothing left to offer him in place of cash. At the end of the year, my father came home, and one day the creditor was creating a lot of noise in the house, demanding repayment of the loan. He called me to him and scolded me, saying, "We

---

15. Presumably the cover of the book, although some short texts, such as the *Heart Sūtra* (which was extracted from the *Prajñāpāramitā Sūtra*), were sometimes embroidered.

belong to a scholars' family; how could we fail to repay a loan from such common people?" While I was trying to explain the matter, there appeared a messenger from Mrs. Hua, a childhood friend of Yün's, who had heard about her illness and had sent him to inquire after her health. My father thought that this messenger was from the sing-song girl Han, and became still more infuriated. "Your wife does not cultivate the feminine virtues, but has become sworn sister to a sing-song girl. You yourself do not associate with good friends, but go about with low-class people. I cannot bear to put you to death, but will allow you three days. Make up your own mind what you are going to do in the meantime, or else I will prosecute you at court for filial impiety!" When Yün heard of this, she wept and said, "It is all my fault that we have displeased our parents. I know that if I die, you will not be able to bear my death, and if we separate, you will not be able to bear the parting. Let's ask Mrs. Hua's servant to come in, and I will try to get up from bed and have a talk with him."

I then asked Ch'ingchün to assist her mother to get up and escort her outside her bedroom, where we asked the messenger from Mrs. Hua whether his mistress had sent him specially to enquire after her illness, or he was merely taking a message on his way. "My mistress has long heard of your illness," replied the servant, "and was thinking of coming personally to see you, but refrained because she thought she had never been here before. When I was leaving, she told me to say that if madame didn't mind living in a poor country home, she would like her to come to her place for a rest, in order to fulfill a pledge of their childhood days." The messenger was referring to a girlhood pledge between Yün and Mrs. Hua, when they were doing embroidery work together under the same lamplight, that they should assist each other in sickness or trouble.

"You go back quickly then, and tell your mistress to send a boat secretly for us within two days," she instructed the servant.

When the man had retired from the interview with her, he said to me, "You know that Mrs. Hua is as good to your wife as to her own sister and she won't at all mind your coming along, too. As for the children, I am afraid that it will be inconvenient for you either to bring them along or to leave them here to trouble your parents. I should suggest that you make some arrangements for them within these two days."

There was a cousin of mine by the name of Wang Chinch'en who had a son called Yünshih, for whom he wished to secure the hand of my daughter. "I hear," said Yün, "that this son of Wang's is rather weak and useless. At best, he would be good only for carrying on, but not for building up a family fortune, but there is no fortune in the family for him to carry on. However, they are a scholars' family and he is the only son. I don't mind giving Ch'ingchün to him." So I said to Chinch'en, "We are cousins and, of course, I should be glad to give Ch'ingchün to your son, but I am afraid it is difficult under the circumstances for us to keep her until she should grow up. I propose, therefore, that you bring the matter up to my parents after we have gone to Hsishan, and take her over as your 'child daughter-in-law.' I wonder what you think of it?" Chinch'en was very pleased and agreed to my suggestion. As for my son Fengsen, I also asked a friend of mine by the name of Hsia Yishan to place him in a shop as an apprentice.

As soon as these arrangements had been made, Mrs. Hua's boat arrived. This was on the twenty-fifth of December, 1800. "If we should leave like this," said Yün, "I am afraid the neighbors will laugh at us, and besides, we haven't repaid the loan due to the Shansi man. I don't think he will let us off. We must leave quietly before dawn tomorrow."

"But can you stand the early damp of the morning in your present state of health?" I asked.

"Oh! I wouldn't worry about that," she said. "It's all a matter of fate how long one is going to live!"

I secretly informed my father about this arrangement, which he also thought best. That night, I first brought a little bag down to the boat and asked Fengsen to go to bed first. Ch'ingchün was weeping by her mother's side, and this was Yün's parting instruction to her: "Mamma was born under an evil star and is, besides, sentimentally passionate. That is why we've come to this. However, your father is very kind to me and you have nothing to worry about on my account. I am sure that, in two or three years, we shall be able to manage so that we can be reunited. When you go to your new home, you must try to be a better daughter-in-law than your mother. I know that your parents-in-law will be very kind to you because they are very proud of this match. Whatever we have left behind in the trunks and bags are yours, and you can bring them along. Your younger brother is still young, and therefore we have not let him know. At the time of parting, we are going to say that Mamma is going away to see a doctor and will return in a few days. You can explain the whole thing to him when we have gone a long distance, and just let Grandfather take care of him."

There was with us at this time an old woman who was the one that had let us her country house, as mentioned in the first chapter. She was going to accompany us to the country, and was now sitting in the room, silently and continually wiping her tears. In the small hours of the morning, we warmed up some congee and ate it together. Yün forced herself to smile and joke, saying, "We first met around a bowl of congee and now we are parting also around a bowl of congee. If someone were to write a play about it, it should be entitled, 'The Romance of the Congee.'"

Fengsen heard these words in his sleep, woke up and asked, while yawning, "What is mamma doing?"

"Mamma is going to see a doctor," Yün replied.

"But why so early?"

"Because the place is so far away. You stay at home with Sister and be a good boy and don't annoy grandmother. I am going away with papa and shall be home within a few days."

When the cock had crowed three times, Yün, buried in tears and supported by the old woman, was going out by the back door, when Fengsen suddenly wept aloud and cried, "I know Mamma is not coming back!"

Ch'ingchün hushed him up, afraid that the noise might wake up other people, and patted him. All this time, I felt as if my bowels were torn to shreds and I could not say a single word except to ask him to stop crying. After Ch'ingchün had closed the door on us, Yün walked along for just about a dozen paces and found she could no more, and I carried her on my back, while the old woman carried the lantern before us. We were almost arrested by a night sentinel when coming near the river, but luckily through the old woman's ruse, Yün passed off as her sick daughter, and I her son-in-law. The boatmen, who were all servants of the Hua family, came to the rescue and helped us down to the boat. When the boat was untied and we were moving, Yün broke down completely and wept bitterly aloud. Actually, mother and son never saw each other again.

Mr. Hua, whose name was Tach'eng, was living on the Tungkao Hill at Wusih, in a house facing the hillside. He tilled the field himself and was a very simple, honest soul. Mrs. Hua, whose family name was Hsia, was, as I have mentioned, Yün's sworn sister. We arrived that day at their home about one o'clock. Mrs. Hua came with her two little daughters to the boat to meet us, and we were all very happy to see each other. She supported Yün up the riverbank to her home and gave us a most cordial welcome. The neighboring women and children all came crowding into the house to look at Yün, some inquiring for news and some expressing their sympathy with her, so that the whole house was full of their twitter.

"Now I really feel like the fisherman who went up to the Peach Blossom Spring,"[16] said Yün to Mrs. Hua.

"I hope Sister won't mind these people. The country folk are merely curious."

And so we lived at the place very happily and passed the New Year there. Hardly twenty days had passed since our arrival when the festival of the fifteenth day of the first moon came and Yün was already able to leave her bed. That night we watched a dragon lantern show in a big yard for threshing wheat, and I noticed that Yün was gradually becoming her normal self again. I felt very happy and secretly discussed our future plans with her.

"I don't think we ought to be staying here forever, but, on the other hand, we have no money to go elsewhere. What shall we do?" I said.

"Your wife has thought about it, too," said Yün. "I have an idea. You know the husband of your sister, Mr. Fan Hueilai, is now serving as treasurer in the

---

16. Refers to an idyllic retreat mentioned in an essay by T'ao Yüan-ming (see selection 204).

Salt Bureau of Chingkiang. Do you remember that, ten years ago, we lent him ten dollars, and it happened that we did not have sufficient money and I sold my hairbrooch to make up the amount?"

"Why, I'd forgotten all about it!" I replied.

"Why don't you go and see him? I hear Chingkiang is only a short way from here," said Yün.

I took her advice and started off on the sixteenth of the first moon, in 1801. The weather was quite mild, and one felt too warm even in a velvet gown and a serge *makua*. That night I stayed at an inn at Hsishan, and rented some bedding for my bed. Next morning I took a sailing boat for Kiangyin. The wind was against us and there was a slight rain. At night, we arrived at the mouth of the river by Kiangyin. I felt chilled to the bone and bought some wine to warm myself up, in that way spending the last cash I had with me. I lay there the whole night thinking what I should do, rotating in my mind the idea of perhaps pawning my inside jacket in order to get money for the ferry.[17]

On the nineteenth, the north wind becoming severer, the snow still came down in great quantity and I shed tears. I calculated the expenses for the room and the ferry-boat and dared not buy another drink. While I was shivering both in my body and my heart, suddenly I saw an old man in sandals and a felt hat enter the shop, carrying a yellow bag on his back. He looked at me and seemed to know me.

"Aren't you Mr. Ts'ao of Taichow?" I asked.

"Yes," replied the old man. "Were it not for you, I should have died long ago in the gutter. Now my little daughter is still living and well, and she remembers you with gratitude all the time. What a pleasant surprise for us to meet here! What has brought you to this place?"

It should be explained that when I was working in the yamen of Taichow some years ago, there was a Mr. Ts'ao of a humble family who had a beautiful daughter already betrothed to someone, and an influential person had lent him money with the object of obtaining his daughter. In this way he was involved in a lawsuit. I helped him in the affair and managed to return his daughter to the family of the betrothed. Old Ts'ao came to offer his services at the yamen as a token of his gratitude and kowtowed to thank me. That was how I came to know him. I told him how I was on my way to see my brother-in-law and how I had run into the snow.

"If it clears up tomorrow," said Ts'ao, "I shall accompany you, for I am passing that way myself." And he took out some money to buy wine, showing the greatest cordiality toward me.

On the twentieth, as soon as the morning temple bell had struck, I already heard the ferryman crying at the bank for passengers to come aboard. I got up in a hurry and asked Ts'ao to go with me. "No hurry. We must eat something

17. Kiangyin is on the south bank of the Yangtze.

before going down to the boat," said Ts'ao. Then he paid the room and board for me and asked me to come out for a drink. As I had been delayed so long on my way and was anxious to start off, I was in no mood for eating, but merely chewed two pieces of sesame-seed cake. When I got to the boat, there was a piercing wind blowing over the river, and I was shivering all over.

"I am told there is a native of Kiangyin who hanged himself at Chingkiang, and his wife has engaged this boat to go there," said Ts'ao. "We have to wait till she comes before we can cross the river."

So I waited there, hungry and cold, till noon before we started off. When we arrived at Chingkiang, there was already an evening haze lying over the countryside.

"There are two yamen at Chingkiang, one inside the city and the other outside. Which one is your relative working in?"

"I really don't know," I said, walking dismally behind him.

"In that case we might just as well stop here and call on him tomorrow," said Ts'ao.

When I entered the inn, my shoes and socks were already drenched through and covered with mud, and I had them dried before the fire. I was all in, hurried through my meal, and dropped into a sound sleep. Next morning when I got up, my socks were half burned by fire. Ts'ao again paid for my room and board. When I arrived at Hueilai's home in the city, he had not got up yet, but hurriedly put on his gown and came out to see me. When he saw the state I was in, he was quite astonished and said, "Why, what's the matter with brother-in-law? You look so shabby!"

"Don't ask me questions. Lend me two dollars first, if you have any with you. I want to pay back a friend who came along with me."

Hueilai gave me two Mexican dollars which I gave to Ts'ao, but Ts'ao would not take them; only after my insistence did he receive one dollar before going away. I then told Hueilai about all that had happened, as well as the purpose of my visit.

"You know we are brothers-in-law," said Hueilai, "I should help you even if I did not owe you the debt. The trouble is, our salt boats on the sea were recently captured by pirates, and we are still trying to straighten up the accounts, and I am afraid I shan't be able to help you much. Would it be all right if I tried to provide twenty dollars in repayment of the old debt?" As I was not expecting much anyway, I consented. After staying there for two days, the sky had cleared up and the weather became milder and I came home, arriving at Mrs. Hua's house on the twenty-fifth.

"Did you run into the snow on the way?" inquired Yün. I told her what had happened on the way and she remarked sadly, "When it snowed, I thought you had already arrived at Chingkiang, but you were then still on the river! It was very lucky of you to have met old Ts'ao. Really, Heaven always provides for good people."

After a few days, we received a letter from Ch'ingchün informing us that her younger brother had already found a job as apprentice through the good offices of my friend Yishan. Ch'ingchün herself was also brought to Chinch'en's home on the twenty-fourth of January, with the permission of my father. Thus my children's affairs were all settled, but it was hard for parents and children to part like this.

The weather was clear and mild in the beginning of February. With the money I had obtained from my brother-in-law, I made arrangements for a trip to Yangchow, where my old friend Hu K'engt'ang was working at the Salt Bureau. I obtained a post there as secretary at the imperial tax bureau and felt more settled. In the eighth moon of the following year, 1802, I received a letter from Yün that said: "I have completely recovered now. I don't think it is right for us to be staying at a friend's place forever, and wish very much to come to Yangchow, and see the famous P'ingshan." I then rented a two-room house on a river outside the First-in-Spring Gate of Yangchow City, and went personally to bring Yün to our new home. Mrs. Hua presented us with a little boy-servant, called Ah Shuang, who was to help us in cooking and general housework. She also made an agreement with us that someday we should live together as neighbors. As it was already in the tenth moon and it was too cold at P'ingshan, I asked her to come next spring for a visit.

I was fully hoping, then, that we were going to have a quiet life and Yün's health would steadily recover and that eventually we might be reunited with our family. In less than a month, however, the yamen was reducing its staff and cut off fifteen persons. As I was only indirectly recommended by a friend, naturally I was among those sent away. Yün at first thought of different plans for me; she tried to be cheerful and comforted me, and never said a word of complaint. Thus we dragged on till the second moon of 1803, when she had a severe relapse, with profuse discharges of blood. I wanted to go again to Chingkiang for help, but Yün said, "It is better to go to a friend than to a relative for help."

"You are quite right," I said, "but all my friends are themselves in trouble and won't be able to help us, however kind they are."

"All right, then," she said. "The weather is quite mild now and I don't think there will be any snow. Go quickly and come back quickly, but don't worry on my account. Take good care of yourself and increase not the burden of my sins."

At this time, we were already unable to meet our daily expenses, but in order to ease her mind, I pretended to her that I was going to hire a donkey. As a matter of fact, I took the journey on foot, merely eating some wheat cakes in my pocket whenever I felt hungry. I went in a southeasterly direction and crossed two creeks. After going eighty or ninety tricents, I found a deserted country without any houses around. As night came, I saw only a stretch of yellow sands under the starry sky. There I found a little shrine of the God of

Earth, about five feet high, enclosed by a low wall, with two little cypress trees in front. Then I kowtowed to the god and prayed, "I am Mr. Shen of Soochow on my way to a relative's. I've lost my bearings and intend to borrow thy temple to pass a night here. Protect me, I pray!" I then put away the little stone incense tripod and tried to crawl in. The shrine, however, was too small for my body by half and I managed to sit on the ground, leaving my legs outside. I turned my traveling cap around, using the back to cover my face, and thus sat there listening with my eyes closed, but all I could hear was the whistling of winds blowing by. My feet were sore and my spirit was tired and soon I dozed off.

When I woke up, it was already broad daylight and suddenly I heard people's footsteps and sounds of talking outside the low enclosure. Immediately I peeped out and saw that it was the peasants, who were going to a fair, passing by. I asked them for directions and they told me that I was to go straight south for ten tricents until I should reach Taihsing City, and after going through the city, to go southeast for ten tricents until I should come across an earthen mound; after passing eight such mounds, I would then arrive at Chingkiang. All I had to do was to follow the main road. I turned back then, put the incense tripod back in its original place, thanked the god for the night's rest and started off. After passing Taihsing, I took a wheelbarrow [18] and arrived at Chingkiang about four o'clock in the afternoon.

I sent in my card and waited for a long time before the watchman came out and said, "Mr. Fan is away on official business to Ch'angchow." From the way he talked, I thought this was merely a pretext for not seeing me. I asked him when his master was coming home.

"I don't know," replied the servant.

"Then I am going to stay here until he returns, even if I have to wait a year."

The watchman guessed the purpose of my visit and secretly asked me, "Is Mrs. Fan really your own sister by the same mother?"

"If she weren't my own sister, I wouldn't have decided to wait until Mr. Fan's return."

The watchman then asked me to stay. After three days, I was told that Mr. Fan had returned and was given twenty-five dollars, with which I hurriedly hired a donkey and returned home.

I found Yün very sad and sobbing at home. When she saw me, she said rather abruptly, "Do you know that Ah Shuang ran away yesterday with our things? I have asked people to go about looking for him, but so far with no results. I don't mind losing the things, but the boy was given to me by his own mother, who told me repeatedly on parting to take good care of him. If he is running home, he will have to cross the Yangtze River, and I don't know what

---

18. A primitive form of transportation in some parts of China.

may happen to him. Or if his partners should hide him away and ask me for their son, what are we to do? And how am I going to face my sworn sister?"

"Please calm yourself," I said. "I think there is no ground for such anxiety. One who hides away his own son must do it for blackmail, but they know perfectly well that we haven't got any money. Besides, since the boy's coming here half a year ago, we have given him food and clothing, and have never struck him or been harsh to him, as everybody around here knows. I think the real fact is that the boy was a rascal and, seeing that we were in a bad way, stole our things and ran away. As for Mrs. Hua, it is she, rather than you, that should feel uneasy—for sending you such a scamp. The thing to do is for us to report the matter immediately to the magistrate, and prevent any future complications."

Yün felt a little easier after hearing my view of the situation, but from then on she often cried out in her sleep "Ah Shuang has run away!" or "How could Han be so heartless!" and her illness became worse and worse every day. I wanted to send for a doctor, but Yün stopped me, saying, "You know my illness started in consequence of deep grief over my mother's death following upon K'ehch'ang's running away, then it was aggravated through my passion for Han and finally made worse by my chagrin at this recent affair. Besides, I was often too cautious and afraid of making mistakes. I have tried my best to be a good daughter-in-law, and have failed, and have consequently developed dizziness and palpitation of the heart. The illness is now deep in my system and no doctor will be of any avail, and you may just as well spare yourself the expense. As I look back upon the twenty-three years of our married life, I know that you have loved me and been most considerate to me, in spite of all my faults. I am happy to die with a husband and understanding friend like you and I have no regrets. Yes, I have been as happy as a fairy at times, with my warm cotton clothing and frugal but full meals and the happy home we had. Do you remember how we used to enjoy ourselves among springs and rocks, as at the Ts'anglang Pavilion and the Hsiaoshuanglou? But who are we to enjoy the good luck of a fairy, for which only those are worthy who have lived a virtuous life from incarnation to incarnation? We had, therefore, offended God by trying to snatch a happiness that was above our lot; hence our various earthly troubles. It all comes of your too great love, bestowed upon one who is ill-fated and unworthy of this happiness."

After a while she spoke again amid sobs, "Everyone has to die once. My only regret is, we have to part halfway from each other forever, and I am not able to be your wife until the end of your days and see with my own eyes the wedding of Fengsen." After saying this, tears rolled down her eyes as big as peas. I tried to comfort her by saying," You have been ill for eight years, and this is not the first time that you are in a critical condition. Why do you suddenly say such heartbreaking words?"

"I have been dreaming lately," she said, "of my parents who have sent a boat to welcome me home. Whenever I close my eyes, I feel my body is so light, so light, like one walking among the clouds. It seems that my spirit has already departed and only my body remains."

"This is the effect of your extreme weakness," I said. "If you will take some tonic and rest yourself properly, I am sure you will get well."

Then Yün sighed again and said, "If there were the slightest ray of hope, I would not have told you all these things. But now death is approaching and it is high time I spoke my mind. I know you have displeased your parents all on my account; therefore when I die, your parents' attitude will change around, and you yourself will feel more at ease toward your parents. You know they are already very old, and when I die, you should return to them as soon as possible. If you cannot bring my remains back to the native district for burial, you can temporarily keep my coffin here and then see to its removal afterward. I hope you will find another one who is both beautiful and good to take my place and serve our parents and bring up my children, and then I shall die content." At this point, I broke down completely and fell to weeping as if my bowels had been cut through.

"Even if you should leave me halfway like this," I said, "I shall never marry again. Besides, 'it is difficult to be water for one who has seen the great seas, and difficult to be clouds for one who has seen the Yangtze Gorges.' " Then Yün held my hand and was going to say something again, but she could only mumble the words "Next incarnation!" half audibly again and again. Suddenly she began to feel short of breath, her chin was set, her eyes stared wide open, and however I called her name, she could not utter a single word. Two lines of tears began to roll down her face. After a while, her breath became weaker, her tears gradually dried up and her spirit departed from this life forever. This was on the thirtieth of the third moon, 1803. A solitary lamp was shining then in the room, and a sense of utter forlornness overcame me. In my heart opened a wound that shall be healed nevermore!

My friend Hu K'engt'ang kindly helped me with ten dollars, and together with this and what I could obtain by selling what I had in the house, I saw to her proper burial.

Alas! Yün was a woman with the heart and talent of a man. From the time she was married into my home, I had been forced to run about abroad for a living, while she was left without sufficient money, and she never said a word of complaint. When I could stay at home, our sole occupation was the discussion of books and literature. She died in poverty and sickness without being able to see her own children, and who was to blame but myself? How could I ever express the debt I owe to a good chamber companion? I should like to urge upon all married couples in the world neither to hate nor to be too passionately attached to each other. As the proverb says, "A loving couple can never reach grand old age together." Mine is a case in point.

According to custom, the spirit of the deceased is supposed to return to the house on a certain day after his death, and people used to arrange the room exactly as the deceased had left it, putting his old clothes on the bed and his old shoes by the bedside for the returning spirit to take a farewell look. We called this in Soochow "closing the spirit's eyes." People also used to invite Taoist monks to recite incantations, calling to the spirit to visit the deathbed and then sending it away. This was called "welcoming the spirit." At Yangchow the custom was to prepare wine and dishes and leave them in the dead man's chamber, while the whole family would run away, in order to "avoid the spirit." It often happened that things were stolen while the house was thus deserted. On this day, my landlord, who was staying with me, left the house, and my neighbors urged me to leave the offerings at home and get away also. To this I gave a cold, indifferent reply, for I was hoping to see the spirit of Yün again. There was a certain Chang Yümen of the same district who warned me saying, "One may be very well possessed by the evil spirit, when one's mind dwells on the uncanny. I should not advise you to try it, for I rather believe in the existence of ghosts."

"This is the very reason I am going to stay—because I believe that ghosts do exist," I replied.

"To encounter the spirit of the deceased on its return home has an evil influence on living men," Chang replied. "Even if your wife's spirit should return, she is living in a world different from ours. I am afraid you won't be able to see her form, but will, on the other hand, be affected by her evil influence."

I was so madly in love with her that I did not care. "I don't care a bit about it," I said to him. "If you are so concerned about me, why not stay on and keep me company?"

"I'll stay outside the door. If you should see anything strange, just call for me."

I then went in with a lamp in my hand and saw the room was exactly as she had left it, only my beloved was not there, and tears welled up in my eyes in spite of myself. I was afraid then that with my wet eyes, I should not be able to see her form clearly, and I held back my tears and sat on the bed, waiting for her appearance with wide-open eyes. Softly I touched her old dress and smelled the odor of her body which still remained, and was so affected by it that I fainted off. Then I thought to myself, how could I let myself doze off since I was waiting for the return of her spirit? I opened my eyes and looked around and saw the two candlelights burning low on the table as small as little peas. It gave me gooseflesh and I shuddered all over. Then I rubbed my hands and my forehead and looked carefully and saw that the pair of candlelights leaped higher and higher till they were over a foot long and the papered wooden frame of the ceiling was going to catch fire. The sudden glow of the lights illuminated the whole room and enabled me to look around clearly, when suddenly they grew small and dark as before. At this time I was in a state of excitement and wanted to call in my companion, when I thought that her gentle female spirit might be scared away by the presence of another living man. Secretly and in a quiet tone, I called her name and prayed to her, but the whole room was buried in silence and I could not see a thing. Then the candlelights grew bright again, but did not shoot high up as before. I went out and told Yümen about it, and he thought me very brave, but did not know that I was merely in love.

After Yün's death, I thought of the poet Lin Hoching who "took the plum trees for his wives and a stork for his son," and I called myself "Meiyi," meaning "one bereaved of the plum tree." I provisionally buried Yün on the Golden Cassia Hill outside the West Gate of Yangchow, at the place which was commonly known as "The Precious Pagoda of the Ho Family." I bought a lot and buried her there, according to her dying wish, bringing home with me the wooden tablet for worship. My mother was also deeply touched by the news of her death. Ch'ingchün and Fengsen came home, wept bitterly, and went into mourning.

"You know father is still angry with you," said my brother Ch'it'ang. "You'd better stay away at Yangchow for some time and wait till Father returns home, when I shall speak for you and then write for you to come home."

I then kowtowed to my mother and parted from my daughter and son and wept aloud for a while, before I departed again for Yangchow, where I painted for my living. Thus I was often enabled to loiter round and weep over Yün's grave, forlorn soul that I was! And whenever I passed our old house, the sight was too much for me to bear. On the festival of the ninth day of the ninth moon, while all the other graves were yellow, hers was still green. The graveyard keeper said to me, "This is a propitious place for burial, that is why the spirit of the earth is so strong." And I secretly prayed to her, "O Yün! The autumn wind is blowing high, and my gowns are still thin. If you have any influence, protect me and arrange that I may have a job to pass the old year, while waiting abroad for news from home."

Soon afterward one Mr. Chang Yü-an, who had a post as secretary at the Kiangtu yamen, was going to bury his parents at home in Chekiang, and asked me to take his place for three months. And thus I was provided against the winter. After I left that place, Chang Yümen asked me to stay at his home. He was out of a job too, and told me that he was finding it hard to meet the expenses at the end of the year. I gave him all of the twenty dollars I had in my pocket, and told him that this was the money I had reserved for bringing Yün's coffin home and that he could pay me back when I heard word from my family.

So that year I passed the New Year at Chang's home. I was waiting for mail from home morning and night, but no news came at all. In March of 1804, I received a letter from my daughter Ch'ingchün, informing me of my father's illness. I wanted very much to go home to Soochow, but was afraid of Father's anger. While I was still hesitating, I received a second letter from her, telling me that father had died. Sorrow went into my heart and pierced my bones, and I cried to heaven in vain, for I knew it was too late. Brushing aside all considerations, I dashed home under the starry sky. I knocked my head against the coffin until I bled and wailed bitterly. Alas! My father had a hard time all his life working away from home, and he begot such an unfilial son as I, who was neither able to minister to his pleasure while he was alive, nor able to serve him at his deathbed. Great, indeed, is my sin!

"Why didn't you come home earlier then?" said my mother, seeing me weeping so bitterly.

"Had it not been for Ch'ingchün's letter," I said, "I would not even have heard of it at all." My mother cast a look at my brother's wife and kept silent.

I then kept watch over the coffin in the hall, but for seven days and seven nights not one in the whole family spoke to me about family affairs or discussed the funeral arrangements with me. I was ashamed of myself for not fulfilling a son's duties and would not ask them questions, either.

One day some men suddenly appeared at our house to ask for repayment of a loan, and made a lot of noise in the hall. I came out and said to them, "I don't blame you for pressing for repayment of the debt. But isn't it rather mean of you to create such a turmoil while my father's remains are scarcely cold yet?" One among them then secretly explained to me, "Please understand we have been sent here by somebody. You just get away for a moment, and we will ask for repayment directly from the man who told us to come here."

"I'll return myself what I owe! You had better all go away!"

My wish was immediately obeyed, and the people having left, I called Ch'it'ang to my presence and remonstrated with him, "Although elder brother is stupid, I have never committed any great wrongs. If you are thinking of my being made heir to uncle, remember that I did not receive a single cent of the family fortune. Do you suppose I came home to divide property with you instead of for the funeral? A man ought to stand on his own feet; I have come empty-handed, and empty-handed I will go!" After saying this, I left him and went behind the curtain again and cried bitterly before the coffin.

I then said good-bye to my mother and went to tell Ch'ingchün that I was going to a mountain to become a Taoist monk. While Ch'ingchün was just trying to persuade me not to do so, some friends of mine arrived. They were the brothers Hsia Nanhsün, literary name Tan-an, and Hsia Fengt'ai, literary name Yishan. They remonstrated with me in a very severe tone, and thus began, "We don't blame you for being angry with this kind of a family, but although your father is dead, your mother is still living, and although your wife has died, your son is not independent yet. Have you really the heart to become a monk?"

"What am I going to do then?" I replied.

"For the time being," said Tan-an, "you could put up at our home. I hear that his honor Shih Chot'ang is coming home on leave from his office. Why don't you wait till he comes and see him about it? I am sure he will be able to give you a position."

"This is hardly proper," I said. "I am still in the hundred days of my mourning, and your parents are still living."

"Don't worry on that account," said Yishan, "for our father, too, joins us in the invitation. If you think it's not quite proper to do so, then there is a temple on the west of our home where the abbot is a good friend of mine. How about putting up there?" To this I agreed.

Then Ch'ingchün said to me, "Grandfather has left us a family property certainly not less than three or four thousand dollars. If you will not have a share of the property, will you not even take along your traveling bag? I'll fetch it myself and bring it to the temple for you." In this way not only did I get my traveling bag, but also found ingeniously stuck in it some books, paintings, ink slabs, and pots for holding writing brushes left behind by father. The monk put me up at the Tower of Great Mercy. The tower faced south and on its east was a Buddha. I occupied the western room which had a moon window exactly opposite the Buddha, this being the room where pilgrims used to have their meals. At the door, there was a most imposing standing figure, representing the God of War holding a huge knife in his hand. A big maidenhair tree stood in the yard, three fathoms in circumference, and cast a heavy shade over the whole tower. At night the wind would blow past the tree, making a roaring noise. Yishan often brought some wine and fruit to the place to have a drink between ourselves.

"Are you not afraid of staying here alone on a dark night?" he asked.

"No," I replied. "I have lived a straight life and have a free conscience. Why should I be afraid?"

It happened that shortly after I moved in, there was a pouring rain that continued day and night for over a month. I was always afraid that some branch of the maidenhair tree might break off and crash onto the roof, but, thanks to the protection of the gods, nothing happened. In the country around us, however, a great number of houses had fallen down and all the rice fields were flooded. I spent the days painting with the monk as if nothing had happened.

In the beginning of July, the sky cleared up and I went to the Ts'ungming Island as a personal secretary of Yishan's father, whose name was Shunhsiang and who was going there on business. For this I received twenty dollars as remuneration. When I returned, they were making my father's grave, and Ch'it'ang asked Fengsen to tell me that he was in need of money for the burial expenses and would I lend him ten or twenty dollars? I was going to turn over the money I had to him, but Yishan would not allow it and insisted on contributing half of the amount. I then went ahead to my father's grave, accompanied by Ch'ingchün.

After the burial, I returned to the Tower of Great Mercy. At the end of September, Yishan had some rent to collect from his crops at Yungt'ai Beach in Tunghai and I accompanied him there, where I stayed for two months. When I returned, it was already late winter and I moved to his home at the Snow-and-Wild-Goose Hut to pass the New Year. He was better to me than my own kin.

In July, 1805, Chot'ang returned home from the capital. This was his "fancy name," while his real name was Yünyü and his literary name Chihju. He was a childhood chum of mine, took the first place in the imperial examinations in 1790 during the reign of Ch'ienlung, and then became magistrate of Chungking in Szechwan. During the rebellion of the White Lily Secret Society, he won great merit for himself fighting the rebels for three years. When he returned, we were very glad to see each other. On the ninth day of the ninth moon, he was going again to his office at Chungking with his family and asked me to accompany him. I then said good-bye to my mother at the home of Lu Shangwu, the husband of my ninth sister, for by this time my father's home had already been sold. My mother gave me parting instructions as follows: "You should try your best to glorify the name of the family, for your younger brother will never amount to anything. Remember, I depend entirely on you." Fengsen was seeing me off, but on the way he suddenly began to cry pitifully, and I bade him go home.

When our boat arrived at Kingk'ou,[19] Chot'ang said he wanted to see an old friend of his, Wang T'ifu, who was a *chüjen*[20] and was working at the Salt Bureau in Yangchow. He was going out of his way to call on him and I accompanied him there, and thus had another chance to look at Yün's grave. Then we turned back and went up the Yangtze River and enjoyed all the scenery on the way. When we arrived at Kingchow we learned that my friend had been promoted a *taot'ai*[21] at Tungkuan.[22] He, therefore, asked me to stay at Kingchow with his son Tunfu and family, while he went to pass the New Year at Chungking with just a small entourage and went directly to his new office via Chengtu. In February of the following year, his family at Szechwan then followed him there by boat up the river as far as Fanch'eng. From that point on, we had to travel by land. The way was very long and the expenses very heavy; with the heavy load of men and luggage, horses died and cart-wheels were often broken on the road, and it was altogether a tortuous journey. It was March when we arrived at Tungkuan, when Chot'ang was again transferred to Shantung as inspector. As he was out of money and his family could not follow him there, we remained temporarily at the T'ungch'uan College. Only at the end of October did he receive his salary

19. Chinkiang.
20. Provincial graduate.
21. Circuit intendant.
22. In Honan.

from his Shantung office, which enabled him to send for his family. In his letter he enclosed a note from Ch'ingchün, which informed me that Fengsen had died in April. Then I began to understand that the tears he shed when sending me off from home were tears of farewell. Alas! Yün had only one son and must even he be taken away and not allowed to continue her line! Chot'ang was also greatly touched at the news, and presented me with a concubine. From that time on, I was again thrown into life's mad turmoil, a floating dream from which I do not know when I shall wake up!

Translated by Lin Yutang

Fictional and Fictionalized Biographies and Autobiographies

235
The Biography of Fur Point

Han Yü (768–824)

Fur Point was a native of Central Mountain. His patriarch, Bright Sight,[1] aided Yü in bringing order to the lands of the East, and he had some success in nourishing nature, thus he was enfeoffed with the lands of Mao.[2] When he died, he became one of the twelve spirits. He once said, "My descendants will be the posterity of a spirit-illuminate and shall not be the same as normal beings. They will be born by being vomited."[3] And, indeed, that is how it was!

This is a humorous essay on a writing brush, couched in the form of a traditional biography in the standard histories as established by Ssu-ma Ch'ien (see selection 225). The first level of the narrative camouflages a satirical statement on the nature of the relationship between the ruler and his ministers—which may refer directly to Han Yü's own career. This work and others of a similar nature fostered the relationship between the reformed "ancient-style prose" of the early ninth century and the then fledgling fictional genre known as ch'uan-ch'i ("transmission of the strange"; see selections 249ff.).

For a note on the author, arguably the greatest essayist in Chinese literary history, see selection 53.

1. "Bright Sight", like many names in this piece, is taken from a classical, metonymic reference to the rabbit (here from the Records of Ritual [Li chi]).

2. A fairly common surname in China, as in Mao Tse-tung, which also happens to mean "fur," as translated in the title.

3. A traditional notion of how rabbits are born.

The eighth-generation descendant of Bright Sight was Bunny, who, so popular tradition has maintained for ages, lived in Central Mountain during the Yin dynasty and learned the artifices of the spirit-immortals so that he was able to hide in bright light and bring about alchemical changes in things. He had secret relations with Heng Ŏ and rode a toad to the moon.[4] His descendants, therefore, withdrew from government service.

One of them named Wiley, who lived near the eastern city-wall, was crafty and a skilled runner. He put his talents to a test against Blackie of Han, who could not catch him. Since he was angry, he plotted with Sung Ch'üeh to kill Wiley and then tore his family to ribbons.

During the time of the First Emperor of Ch'in,[5] General Meng T'ien[6] led an expedition south against Ch'u and camped at Central Mountain, intending to undertake a great hunt to intimidate Ch'u.

He summoned his stewards of the left and right and his staff to divine concerning the prospect of the hunt with the *Lien-shan*.[7] He obtained the oracles "heaven" and "human culture," and the diviner congratulated him:

> In today's catch,
> no horns or fangs to match,
> but one dressed in coarse clothes,
> with a harelip and long whiskers 'neath his nose.
> with eight orifices and his legs tucked in flat,
> you'll only take the hair from his head,
> and with it, on bamboo and wooden slat,
> unify the empire's scripts to be read;
> thus Ch'in will unite the feudal lords instead.

Then the hunt began. They surrounded all of Mao's clan, pulled out their best, and, taking up Point, returned. Meng T'ien presented him as a captive at the Patterned Platform Palace, along with his clansmen, gathered and bound. The Emperor of Ch'in ordered that he be granted a hot cleansing bath, and invested him in Tube City, naming him "Baron of Tube City." Daily he gained favor and was employed in more affairs.

Point was the sort of man who had a strong memory and an easy understanding of things. From the "era of rope knots"[8] down to the events of Ch'in's rise to power, there was nothing he did not compile. The works of the yin-yang school, of the diviners, of the physiognomists, of physicians and

4. Heng (later Ch'ang) Ŏ in ancient Chinese lore stole an elixir of immortality from her husband, the archer Yi, and fled to the moon. The story as Han Yü tells it is different from all classical text versions and may well be intended to refer allegorically to a contemporary set of events.

5. 246–210 B.C.E.

6. The supposed inventor of the writing brush (d. 210 B.C.E.).

7. One of the early divination works.

8. A system of notation similar to the quipu of the ancient Peruvians.

pharmacists, genealogists, geographers, local historians, calligraphers, painters, of the nine schools, the one hundred philosophers, the gods, and even the theories of Buddha, Lao Tzu, and other foreigners, were all among those things he knew in detail. He was also versed in contemporary affairs, administrative records, accounts and records of market transactions, and whenever the emperor wanted to take note of something, he always stood at his service. Everyone from the emperor himself to the Crown Prince Fu-su and his son Hu-hai, the Grand Councilor Li Ssu, the Keeper of the Chariots Chao Kao, on down to the people, loved and respected him. He was, moreover, expert at following his master's intent and in demonstrating uprightness or crookedness, skill or clumsiness, always taking his cue from the other person. Even if forsaken by someone, he would not allow an inkling of anything to leak out. Soldiers alone he did not like; but, if invited, he would also go to them from time to time.

His rank rose until he was made "Officer Fit for Composition." He became even more intimate with the emperor, so that the latter took to calling him "Lord Fit for Composition." The emperor personally decided all matters, going through one hundred pounds of documents each day. Not even his personal staff was permitted to stand in attendance. Only Fur Point and Candle Holder served him always, put out only when the emperor retired.

Fur Point was a close friend of Spread-out Black[9] from Chiang, Porcelain Pool[10] from Hung-nung, and Mulberry Tree[11] from Kuei-chi. They recommended one another, and when one would go out or stay in, the others had to go along. If the emperor summoned Fur Point, the other three did not wait for a command, but came directly together and the emperor never reprimanded them for it.

Later during an audience, since the emperor had a task he wanted Fur Point to undertake and tried to rub up to him, Point removed his cap to express his gratitude. The emperor saw his bald spot, and, since in his copying of paintings he was no longer able to reach the standard desired by the emperor, the latter chided him: "Lord Fit for Composition, you are old and balding and can no longer perform useful service. I have called you 'Fit for Composition.' Can it be that you are now 'Not Fit?' " Fur Point replied, "I am one who has 'Worn out His Heart' for you." Thus he was called for no more, but returned to the city of his fief and came to his end there in Tube City.

His descendants were very numerous. They spread out through the empire and into barbarian lands. All lay claim to the title of Tube City for themselves, but only those who lived in Central Mountain were able to continue their ancestor's profession.

9. Ink.
10. Ink reservoir.
11. Paper.

The Grand Historian comments: In the Mao clan there were two lineages. The first took the surname Chi and were the sons of King Wen. They were enfeoffed in Mao and were the ones referred to in the expression "Lu, Wei, Mao, and Tan." During the Warring States period their lineage included Mao Kung and Mao Sui.[12] Although the origin of the Central Mountain lineage is unknown, its descendants were most numerous. But upon the completion of *The Spring and Autumn Annals* they all came to an end with Confucius, through no fault of their own. Since General Meng pulled out their heir on Central Mountain and the First Emperor installed him in Tube City, each generation has had someone well known. But as to the lineage surnamed Chi, nothing can be learned.

Fur Point was first presented as a captive and finally became a trusted servant. When Ch'in annihilated the feudal lords, he played a role in the success. But his rewards did not requite his toil and, because of his age, he was estranged. Ch'in was truly wanting of gratitude!

Translated by William H. Nienhauser, Jr.

12. Historical personages who happened to bear the surname Mao ("Fur").

236
Biography of the Vagrant of Rivers and Lakes

Lu Kuei-meng (?–c. 881)

A vagrant is someone who is dissolute. His mind wanders, his ideas wander, his form wanders, and his spirit wanders. Being completely unbridled, he is looked askance at by his contemporaries. People who are constrained by decorum distance themselves from him by saying, "This man is a vagrant." The vagrant does not consider this shameful, but goes right along with them in calling himself what they do.

People may ridicule him, saying, "Those who look upon you as a vagrant mean to fault you, yet you take this word as your own sobriquet. Why is this?"

The vagrant would reply, "Heaven and earth are quite large, but they are just a speck within Great Vacuity. They labor themselves in covering and supporting the myriad objects; they labor themselves with the constant revolu-

Lu Kuei-meng was born into a family of moderate means from a town near Soochow. He was a learned student of the Confucian classics but had closer ties with Taoism. In fact, he was something of an alchemist and a fancier of mushrooms and herbs. An eccentric character, he wandered about the countryside visiting temples and monasteries while hunting for all sorts of oddities and observing local phenomena. Lu was a fervent devotee of the then newly popular beverage, tea (see selection 229), and a friend of the poet and essayist, P'i Jih-hsiu (see selections 66 and 231).

tion of the spheres. If the inclination of the gnomon gets out of kilter, the seasons will be jumbled. Thus heaven and earth cannot hope for even a moment's vagrancy.

"Let us examine, however, whether the vagaries of water and soil are of any use. Water in its vagrancy becomes rain, dew, frost, and snow. When confined, it appears as ponds, rivers, puddles, or droughts. Soil in its vagrancy may be piled up to become high hills, may be dug out to become deep pits, may give life when things are planted in it, may harbor death when corpses are buried in it. When confined in the form of an ocarina, it can no longer be made into a pottery mold; when confined in the form of a brick, it can no longer be made into a basin. Is this not because when soil and water are in a vagrant state they are open to transformation, whereas when they are confined they are not?

"If a person does not adopt an attitude of vagrancy when he withdraws from public life, then he will still cling to those expedient devices which enable him to gain fame; if a person does not adopt an attitude of vagrancy when he enters public life, then he will strive to grasp ephemeral power. But can he cling to such devices forever and can he grasp such power forever?"

Therefore, I have composed some vagrant's songs and this vagrant's biography to celebrate the vagrancy of the man of the rivers and lakes.

Translated by Victor H. Mair

237

Biography of the Gentleman With No Name

Shao Yung (1012–1077)

The Gentleman With No Name was born in the Chi[1] area and grew old in the Yü[2] area. When he was ten he sought to learn from the people of his

Shao Yung was born just south of modern Peking and died in Loyang, his home for fifty years, surrounded by his family, friends, and followers. All of Loyang mourned his demise. Known today as a philosopher and the paterfamilias of the fortune-telling tradition, he was recognized as one of the most learned men alive and a highly accomplished poet during his own time. Shao lived as a gentleman in retirement (a man in reclusion in Chinese parlance), disengaged from worldly and political pursuits: he never took the examinations that provided entrée to official position, and eschewed all offers of official employ. Although he was materially wanting, he was treated with reverential respect by officials and commoners alike on account of his humility.

Shao formulated his philosophical ideas in a masterwork entitled *Supreme Principles Traverse the Ages*. They center upon an exposition of the universe—and its history—in terms of cosmic cycles, and focus on the Way (not on human interaction) and an objective mode of perception

village, and subsequently exhausted the insights of the villagers. When he left them behind, of his dregs he had cast out one or two parts in ten. At twenty he sought to learn from the people of the district, and subsequently exhausted the insights of the district's people. When he left them behind, of his dregs he had cast out three or four parts in ten. At thirty he sought to learn from the people of the state, and subsequently exhausted the insights of the state's people. When he left them behind, of his dregs he had cast out five or six parts in ten. At forty he sought to learn from the past and the present, and subsequently exhausted the insights of the past and the present. When he left them behind, of his dregs he had cast out eight or nine parts in ten. At fifty he sought to learn from Heaven and Earth, and subsequently exhausted the insights of Heaven and Earth. When he wished to leave them behind, of his dregs there was nothing he could cast out.

At the beginning, the villagers wondered whether he was peculiar and asked the people of the district, who said, "This man is adept at keeping company with others; how can you call him peculiar?" Later, the people of the district wondered whether he was superficial and asked the people of the state, who said, "This man does not indiscriminately have relations with others; how can you call him superficial?" Later, the people of the state wondered whether he was inferior and asked people of all four directions, who said, "This man cannot be typed and put to use;[3] how can you consider him inferior?" Later, the people of all four directions further wondered about him and sought for an explanation of him from among the people of the past and the present. But of the people of the past and the present, there was not a single one among them who could be considered the same as him. They further took their investigation of him to Heaven and Earth, but Heaven and Earth did not respond. At that time, the people of all four directions were bewildered and in confusion, and as they could gain no further information they accordingly gave him the sobriquet of the Gentleman With No Name. "With No Name" signifies that he was unnamable.

---

of the phenomenal world whereby one "views things from the vantage of things," that is, freed of the limitations of subjectivity.

Shao was well versed in Buddhism and Taoism, but he considered himself purely Confucian. While this is borne out in his philosophical writings, much of his poetry has a distinctive Ch'an (Zen) flavor and his "Dialogue Between a Fisherman and a Woodcutter" has a Taoist bent. "Biography of the Gentleman With No Name," moreover, portrays an inimitable Confucian individual with strong Taoist overtones.

Shao composed "Biography of the Gentleman With No Name" late in life as an unmistakable laudatory exposition of himself. The poetic interludes in it are extracted from pieces in his collection of poetry.

1. Hopei province, north of the Yellow River.

2. Honan province, south of the Yellow River.

3. Referring to *Analects*, 2.12, where we are told that the Princely Man is not to be considered a utensil.

Whenever things have a form, they then can be typed and put to use. When something can be typed and put to use, it can be named. This being so, then did this man have no body? It is said that he had a body; he was one who had a body but left no traces. Did this man have no usefulness? It is said that he was useful; he was one who was useful but had no animus. As for those who leave traces and have an animus, they can be found out about. As for those who leave no traces and have no animus, whereas even ghosts and spirits cannot be fathomed, nor can they be named, how much more is the case for men? Therefore his poem says:

> Before reflection and contemplation arose,
> Ghosts and spirits were known to none.
> If not coming from among us,
> Then from whom do they come instead?

What is capable of creating the myriad things is Heaven and Earth. What is capable of creating Heaven and Earth is the Non-Plus-Ultra.[4] As to the Non-Plus-Ultra, could it possibly be fathomed? Therefore when forced to name it, we call it the Non-Plus-Ultra. "Non-Plus-Ultra"—is that not a designation for its lack of a name? Thus, he himself once composed for it a panegyric, which says:

> I borrow from you face and appearance,
> And appropriate from you body and form.
> I calmly juggle[5] with leisure to spare,
> Coming and going in idlesse.

When others accused him of cultivating prosperity, he replied, "I have never once not practiced goodness." When others accused him of sacrificing to avert disaster, he replied, "I have never once indiscriminately made oblation." Thus he wrote in a poem:

> If calamity permitted exemptions,
>   people would have to flatter.
> If prosperity awaited being sought,
>   Heaven could be outguessed.

He also wrote:

> "Inner Sincerity" brings about trust,
>   so whether in peace or annoyance I pray.

4. T'ai-chi, also called the Supreme Ultimate.
5. "Calmly juggling" implies insouciance and imperturbability. See, for instance, the example referred to in the *Chuang Tzu* (selection 9), ch. 24.

"Innocence" generates disaster,
so I never alter my sacrifices.[6]

By nature he enjoyed drinking wine, and often called it "The Great Harmonizing Liquid." He did not drink much of it, and when slightly tipsy he would stop; he did not like to surpass his capacity. Therefore a poem of his says:

By nature he enjoys drinking wine;
Drinking, he enjoys being slightly flushed.
When drinking and not yet slightly flushed,
His mouth first chants and intones.
When chanting and intoning is insufficient,
He then presses into exuberant song.
When exuberant song is insufficient,
Then what is he left to do?

He called the house where he slept "Nest of Peace and Joy." He did not seek excessively beautiful things, he but sought to be warm in the winter and cool in the summer. If it happened that he had thoughts of dozing, then he would go to his pillow. Thus a poem of his says:

His walls are higher than his windows,
His room larger than a bushel container.
His cloth coverings are warm aplenty,
And after his coarse pottage has filled him,
The breath and life-blood within his breast
Fill up full the universe.

As to his relations with others, even if they were lowly, he certainly was on good terms. To the end of his life there was nothing he longed for, and he never once engaged in any affair that would cause one to knit one's brows. Thus others all were the recipients of his joyful heart. When he encountered an honored person, he never once was obsequious. When he encountered a person of bad character, he never once hurried away. When he encountered a good person whom he did not yet know, he never once hurried to ally with him. Thus a poem of his says:

A free and easy "wind and moon" state of mind,
A liberated "rivers and lakes" disposition;
In a startling flight he rises up,
After soaring about he then arrives.
He is without poverty, without wealth,
Without baseness, without nobility.

6. "Inner Sincerity" and "Innocence" are hexagrams from the *Classic of Changes* (nos. 61 and 25), to which these lines refer.

> There is nothing he resists, nothing he welcomes;
> He is without restraints, without cares.

When he heard of slander by others, he never once became angry. When he heard of praise by others, he never once was glad. When he heard others speak of another's evils, he never once joined in. But when he heard others speak of another's goodness, then he went forward and joined them, and moreover found joy in doing this. Thus a poem of his says:

> He delights in meeting good people,
> He delights in hearing of good doings.
> He delights in speaking good words,
> He delights in carrying out good intentions.
> He hears the evil of others
> As though toting prickly grass.
> He hears the goodness of others
> As though girding sweet blooms.

Although his household was poor, he never once begged from others. When others offered him food, though it be little he would be certain to accept. Thus a poem of his says:

> Though distressed, he never has been grieved.
> When drinking, he doesn't reach drunkenness.
> Reaping the "springtide of the world,"
> He brings it home to his vital organs.

When the court conferred official positions on him, even though he did not vigorously decline, neither was he compelled to accede. Late in life he had two sons;[7] he instructed them in humaneness and righteousness, and imparted to them the Six Classics. Though the entire world esteemed empty talk, he never once hung onto a single word. Though the entire world esteemed strange affairs, he never once adopted strange conduct. Thus his poem says:

> He doesn't toady to Buddhist elders,
> He doesn't flatter men of arcane arts.
> Without leaving his courtyard,
> He straightaway conjoins with Heaven and Earth.

His family's longstanding calling was Confucianism, and in word and deed he never practiced anything but Confucian conduct. Thus a poem of his says:

---

7. Shao Yung had only one son, Shao Po-wen (1057–1134). His other "son" was actually a brother by a different mother, Shao Mu, who treated Shao Yung, older by twenty years, as a father.

His mind has no reckless thoughts,
His feet no reckless steps.
He has no indiscriminate relations with others,
And no indiscriminate acceptance of goods.
When there is hot debate about something,
He willfully keeps to his humble manner.
But when there is calm discussion,
None can excel him.
The writings of Fu-hsi and the Yellow Emperor[8]
Never have left his hands;
The words of Yao and Shun[9]
Never have been gone from his mouth.
Keeping to the center, harmonizing with Heaven,
He shares his joy and easily makes friends.
He intones "free from trammels" poems
And drinks "pleasing and joyous" wine.
One hundred years of soaring peace
Cannot be but unexpected;
But with seventy years of health and vigor,
He cannot be but longlived.

Would not this be the conduct of the Gentleman With No Name?

Translated by Alan J. Berkowitz

8. Mythical culture heroes of the ancient past.
9. Legendary rulers of prehistoric times.

PART IV

Fiction

Rhetorical Persuasions, Parables, and Allegories

238
Intrigues of the Warring States

Compiled by Liu Hsiang (77–6 B.C.E.)

Pien-ch'iao and the King's Carbuncle

The great physician Pien-ch'iao[1] visited King Wu of Ch'in and the king showed him the carbuncle on his face. Pien-ch'iao offered to remove it.

The *Intrigues of the Warring States (Chan-kuo ts'e)* consists of material from the Warring States period that was compiled by Liu Hsiang (77–6 B.C.E.) and reorganized by Kao Yu (fl. 200 C.E.). While it is generally agreed that the *Intrigues* is the largest pre-Han collection of historical anecdotes, fables, snippets of romances, and tales of famous persons, the uses to which it has been put by the Chinese are as varied as the ages through which it has passed. Their persistent view has been that the book is a piece of bad history, and from time to time it has joined that group of alluring, if slightly sinister, "secret books of the ancients" which, if studied diligently enough, would never make one a "True King" but might lead one to great secular power and wealth. An equally persistent, but very sound, conviction is that the *Intrigues* contains many of the finest examples of "ancient prose" extant. Hence avid readers have condemned its morality while praising its style ever since Han times. On a less subjective level, it appears in fact to be a heterogeneous collection of rhetorical pieces, which may have been used as grist by the wandering political persuaders of the times and may actually record some of their happier inspirations.

The fictionality of much of the *Intrigues* was long ago demonstrated by Henri Maspero. Thus, while the *Intrigues* itself may not be classified as fiction per se, with it begins the impulse toward fictionalization which achieves full bloom during the T'ang period, partly under the influence of Buddhism. The dividing line between fiction and nonfiction is, of course, notoriously difficult to draw. In general, however, the fictional component of those texts earlier in the prose section of this anthology is less than that of those which follow below.

For a note on the compiler, see selection 242.

1. A famous physician of antiquity (see selection 228, note 3). His name is also spelled as Pien-ch'üeh.

"Your majesty's carbuncle is forward of the ear and below the eye," cried the king's attendants. "If the physician should not cease soon enough while removing it he might cause your majesty to lose his hearing or the sight of an eye."

As a result the king excused Pien-ch'iao. Pien-ch'iao was furious and threw down his flint lancet.

"Your majesty planned this by consulting with one who had knowledge, but now he revokes it on the advice of those who know nothing! If the government of Ch'in were run in the same fashion, the country would perish with your first action."

The Queen of Ch'in and Her Lover

The widowed Queen Hsüan of Ch'in had had one Wei Ch'ou as her lover. Ill and on her deathbed, she issued an order that he was to be buried with her when she died. This troubled Wei Ch'ou. A certain Yung Jui went to the queen on Wei Ch'ou's behalf to dissuade her from her plan.

"Does your highness believe that there is sentience after death?" he asked.

"No, I do not," replied the queen.

"Ah! Your highness's godlike intelligence clearly perceives that the dead feel nothing. Why then would you have one whom you loved alive buried with the dead who feel nothing? If the dead are sentient, your highness, then your husband, the deceased king, will have been harboring his anger against you for a long time now, and you will scarce have time to make amends to him and certainly no time left for further dalliance with Wei Ch'ou."

"True," said the queen and desisted.

A Dialect[1] Word

Marquis Ying[2] said, "In Cheng they call jade which has not been worked 'pure'; in Chou they call fresh-dressed rats which have not yet been preserved 'pure.'

"A man of Chou carrying fresh-dressed rats passed a Cheng merchant and asked him if he wanted to buy some 'pures.' The merchant replied that he did. But when he was shown dressed rats he declined them.

"Now Lord P'ing-yüan[3] is busy getting himself a name for virtue throughout the empire. It was he who banished his own ruler, the former king of Chao, to Sha-ch'iu in order to become minister, yet rulers everywhere still respect him. This merely proves that rulers are less intelligent than the Cheng merchant. They are so dazzled by the word 'pure' that they do not trouble to discover what reality lies behind it."

1. On the special meaning of "dialect" in China, see selection 234, note 12; also see selection 224, note 10.
2. Minister of Ch'in.
3. Kung-tzu Sheng.

The Handsome Man

Tsou Chi was tall and fair of face and figure. He put on his court robes and cap and looked in the mirror.

"Am I more handsome than Mr. Tardy of Northwall?" he asked his wife.

"You are much more so," replied his wife. "How can Mr. Tardy even be compared with you?"

Now, Mr. Tardy was a man known in Ch'i for his beauty, and Tsou Chi was not content, so he asked his concubine:

"Am I more handsome than Mr. Tardy?"

"How can there be any comparison?" she replied.

Next morning when guests, not members of his family, came and he sat with them and talked, he asked them:

"Who is the more handsome, Mr. Tardy or I?"

"Mr. Tardy is not as handsome as you are, sir," they replied.

The day after that Mr. Tardy himself came. Tsou Chi examined him closely and decided he was not as handsome as Mr. Tardy. Then he looked in the mirror at himself and decided he was much less well favored than was Mr. Tardy. When he went to bed that night he thought about it:

"My wife thinks me handsome because she is close to me, my concubine because she fears me, and my guests because they want something of me."

He then went to the court, had audience with King Wei, and said:

"Your servant knows he is really not as handsome as Mr. Tardy. My wife is close to me, my concubine fears me, and my guests want something of me, so they all say I am more handsome than he. Now in the thousand square tricents of our country and in its one hundred and twenty cities there is no woman of the king or attendant who is not close to him. In the court there is no minister who does not fear him, and within the borders of the land there is no one who does not seek something of the king. If one looks at it this way, the king has been monstrously hoodwinked!"

"It is so," said the king, and he sent down an order:

"To all ministers, officers, and citizens who will criticize the king's faults to his face will go the highest reward; those who will remonstrate with the king in writing will be given the next highest reward; and to those who overhear criticism of the king and convey it to his ears will go the least reward."

As soon as the order had been given, ministers came in with remonstrations; the doorway to the chamber looked like a marketplace. In a few months there were occasional petitioners, and after a year none who spoke to the king had petitions to present.

When Yen, Chao, Han, and Wei heard of this, they all came to court at Ch'i. This is what is meant by "winning a battle from the throne room."

Feng Hsüan Sings Three Songs to His Longsword and Burns the Tallies

A man of Ch'i, one Feng Hsüan, being in a most impoverished condition, sent a mediary to Lord Meng-ch'ang to inform him that he wished to become his retainer.

"What is the gentleman partial to?" asked Lord Meng-ch'ang.

"He has no partiality," was the reply.

"What is he especially capable of?"

"Nothing."

Lord Meng-ch'ang laughed. "So be it," he said, and admitted him.

From this, Lord Meng-ch'ang's attendants assumed that their lord held the new retainer in low esteem and supplied him with only coarse fare. After a time he appeared, leaning against a pillar, tapping on his unsheathed longsword and singing: "Longsword, let us return! We find no fish on our plate." When his attendants reported this to Lord Meng-ch'ang, he told them to make Feng Hsüan's fare that of his other retainers.

Shortly thereafter, Feng Hsüan again sang his sword song: "Longsword, let us return! No carriage to ride in state!" The attendants laughed at him and reported it to Lord Meng-ch'ang.

"Have a conveyance made, the equal of those who have carriages," he replied.

Thereafter Feng Hsüan would ride in his carriage with his sword over his shoulder and, passing his friends, would say: "Lord Meng-ch'ang honors me as a guest."

Still later Feng Hsüan sang his sword song again: "Longsword, let us return. No support, can my family wait?"

The attendants all disliked him then, for they thought him covetous and malcontent.

"Does he have a family?" asked Lord Meng-ch'ang.

"His mother," they replied.

So Lord Meng-ch'ang dispatched a man to supply her needs so that she might not suffer want. Feng Hsüan never sang his song again.

Afterwards, Lord Meng-ch'ang inscribed a notice asking his retainers, "Who among you can keep accounts and will collect the monies owed me in my fief of Hsüeh?"

Feng Hsüan sent in his reply, "I can."

Lord Meng-ch'ang was curious and asked who he was. His attendants told him it was he who sang the song of the longsword.

"So he has his capabilities after all!" laughed Lord Meng-ch'ang. "But I have neglected him and never given him audience."

When Lord Meng-ch'ang received Feng Hsüan, he apologized and said: "I have been much busied by affairs and vexed with troubles so that my feelings are blunted. Deep in affairs of state, I have wronged you; yet you, sir, take no offence and are willing to collect debts for me in Hsüeh?"

"I am."

When Feng Hsüan had made ready his attire and loaded the wagons with debt-tallies, he took leave of Lord Meng-ch'ang.

"When the debts have been collected, is there anything I may buy for you when I return?" he asked.

"If you have seen something that my house lacks, buy it," replied Lord Meng-ch'ang.

Feng Hsüan hastened to Hsüeh and sent out an officer summoning all those who owed debts to come forth and match their tallies. When all had been matched, Feng Hsüan feigned an order from Lord Meng-ch'ang that all debts were to be forgiven the people. The tallies were burned and the people cheered.

Feng Hsüan returned to Ch'i without a halt and arrived in the early morning asking audience. Lord Meng-ch'ang, surprised at his haste, donned his formal robes and admitted him.

"Why do you return so speedily? Have the debts been collected?"

"They have already been collected," was the reply.

"What did you purchase on your return?"

"My lord, you asked me to see if there was anything your house lacked," answered Feng Hsüan. "It was my humble opinion that your castle was filled with precious objects, that your stables and kennels abounded in steeds and coursers, and the lower palaces with beauties. It seemed that one thing only was lacking and that was fealty. This I bought, my lord."

"How can one buy fealty?" exclaimed Lord Meng-ch'ang.

"At the moment you hold the little fief of Hsüeh; you do not cherish the people there as your own children, but look on them as a source of profit," replied Feng Hsüan. "Your servant took it upon himself to feign an order from you that all debts should be forgiven the people of Hsüeh. The tallies were burned and the citizens cheered you. This is how your servant purchased fealty."

Lord Meng-ch'ang was displeased. "So be it! You may now rest, sir."

A full year later, the new king of Ch'i informed Lord Meng-ch'ang that he dared no longer use a minister of the former king. Lord Meng-ch'ang had to return and govern his own fief of Hsüeh. When he was still one hundred tricents from the city, its people, supporting the old ones and holding their children by the hand, welcomed their lord in midjourney. Lord Meng-ch'ang turned and looked at Feng Hsüan.

"Your purchase of fealty on my behalf, sir, is apparent to me today."

"My lord," replied Feng Hsüan, "the wiliest rabbit must have three burrows before he can even preserve his life. At the moment you can scarcely rest secure with only one. I beg my lord allow me to dig him two more."

Fifty carts and five hundred catties of gold were given Feng, and he made his way westward to speak to King Hui of Liang.

"Ch'i has released its great minister Lord Meng-ch'ang," said Feng Hsüan, "and he is now free among the feudal lords. The first state to welcome him will enrich itself and make its soldiery powerful."

The king of Liang vacated his highest post by making his former minister a Marshal. He then sent emissaries, one hundred chariots, and a thousand catties of gold to engage Lord Meng-ch'ang. Feng Hsüan hurried ahead of them to caution him.

"A thousand in gold is great wealth and a hundred chariots a visible entourage. We must let Ch'i hear of them!"

Thrice the emissaries of Liang came to Hsüeh, but Lord Meng-ch'ang firmly refused to accompany them. Ch'i heard of it; ruler and ministers were sore afraid, and the Grand Tutor was dispatched with gifts of a thousand catties of gold, two ornamented chariots, and a ceremonial sword in its case. The king wrote a letter of apology to Lord Meng-ch'ang:

> We are truly unfortunate! We are given ill omen in the ancestral temples; we are surrounded by sycophants; and we have offended you, sir. Truly we are not worthy to rule! We beg you, sir, for the sake of the ancestral temples, come back now to unite the people!

Feng Hsüan again cautioned Lord Meng-ch'ang: "I must ask you to request him to send the ancestors' sacrificial objects here so that the ancestral temple may remain in Hsüeh!"

When the temple was erected, Feng Hsüan returned to Lord Meng-ch'ang and said, "The three burrows are complete, my lord. You may now rest secure and happy."

That Lord Meng-ch'ang could be minister for several decades without the slightest misfortune was due to the planning of Feng Hsüan.

The Tiger and the Fox

"I hear that the North fears Chao Hsi-hsü," said King Hsüan to his ministers. "What say you to this?"

None of them replied, except Chiang Yi, who said, "The tiger hunts all the animals of the forest and devours them, but once when he caught a fox, the fox said, 'You dare not eat me. The Lord of Heaven ordained me chief among beasts; if you now kill me you will be disobeying the will of Heaven. If you doubt it, follow behind me through the forest and watch the animals flee when they see me.' The tiger did indeed doubt the fox and therefore followed him. Animals saw them and fled, but the tiger did not know that the animals ran because they feared him. He thought they were afraid of the fox.

"Now your majesty's country is five thousand tricents square and in it are a million first-class troops, all of whom are under Chao Hsi-hsü. Therefore when the North fears Hsi-hsü, in reality it fears your majesty's arms, just as the animals of the forest feared the tiger."

Translated by James I. Crump

239

Discourse on a Thoroughbred[1]

Liu Yü-hsi (772–842)

When a certain Mr. Po assisted with military affairs on the northern frontier, he obtained a well-bred horse to give me. Not knowing of its high breeding, I fed it with grass and chaff and gave it stagnant pond water to drink. As for its stable, it was dank and damp below. For its halter I just knotted up some rope and joined a few thongs of leather together. In this way I treated the horse as insignificant.

I did not care much for it and even tried repeatedly to sell it in the marketplace. The horse-broker in the marketplace also did not recognize it as a well-bred steed, and took issue with my asking price of sixty strings of cash, which I was in fact just about to adjust when there appeared a certain Mr. P'ei who sought to buy the horse by offering to give twenty more strings of cash. I considered this an excellent price and ended up selling it to Mr. P'ei.

P'ei was on good terms with a certain Mr. Li, who was both discriminating and shrewd and was trained in the art of appraising horses. He was especially meticulous in examining this horse from teeth to tail, after which he gleefully looked at it, smiled, and laughed. Then he clapped his hands and said, "It has

Allegories have a long tradition in China. They were originally linked to persuasive rhetoric and sometimes found in philosophical writings such as *Chuang Tzu, Lieh Tzu,* and *Han Fei Tzu.* By the T'ang dynasty, a number of writers, who were involved to varying degrees with the literary reforms known as the *ku-wen* ("old-style prose") movement, experimented with different types of allegories. These works, written either in prose or in verse, often featured animals rather than people. Through descriptions of situations in the animal world with direct counterparts in the human sphere, writers were able to offer indirect criticism or moral instruction about general philosophical principles. Animal allegories were also used to illustrate the possible dangers of a given political situation or to express the author's dissatisfaction with events in his own life. Since the analogies in these works were often fairly subtle, authors had more freedom of expression than they did in more narrowly defined, constraining genres. T'ang animal allegories also present a fascinating look at how writers of this era envisioned the natural world and the role of man within it.

For a note on the author, see selection 110.

1. The translation of *chi* as "thoroughbred" should not be confused with the breed of English horse of that name.

been a long time indeed since I have seen a horse such as this! Oh! what total culmination of a gentle heart, vigorous frame, unusual spirit, and elegant deportment. Oh! the curve of his lines, the music of his neighing, the way he glistens, the way he soars! Now the virtue of this horse has already reached perfection. Yet he is only a colt; his potential lies hidden. But he has been fed according to perverse methods, thus to the average eye he appears unhappy. Wait until all of his teeth have grown in and his spirit has been fully actualized, then his abundant beauty will be manifest. Optimally he could be offered to the imperial stables; at the very least he could be sold for a thousand pieces of gold."

When Mr. P'ei heard this, he became alarmed and he subsequently admonished his groom to clean the stable, to use a bamboo basket for the horse's dung and a sacrificial vessel for his urine, and to let him munch fine grain and feed on fragrant fodder. He also instructed him not to be idle for even a second when it came to getting the horse up, bedding him down, washing him down, and drying him off.

Thus it was that he applied the most advanced methods of equine husbandry to the raising of this horse. Before long, it was indeed deemed to have the virtue of a thoroughbred horse.

A visitor consoled me on the loss of this treasure and also chided me for having sold it so cheaply. Indifferently I said to him, "At first when I had this horse, I treated him as an ordinary horse; now I have traded him and the new owner raises him as if he were a valuable horse. This is merely the difference between treating something either as valuable or as ordinary. Furthermore, when he pranced and jumped in the past, I thought he was going to kick or bite me, so I would strike him with a whip, not knowing he was trying to ascend to the clouds. As for the way he breathed and snorted in the past, I thought he was sick and diseased, so I merely threw him some pellets or herbs, not knowing he was trying to spout jade.[2] If one were to continue to treat him like this, although it might take days or even months, eventually he would reach the point where he grows feeble and stumbles. Thus how could he ever be valuable? Now, if I were to extend this idea and apply it to a gentleman, then isn't eighty strings of cash better than five sheepskins?"[3]

My guest was taken aback in surprise. I then told him that the virtue of this horse was stored within his external shape and was readily apparent to the eye,

2. This expression is frequently used in descriptions of exceptional horses.
3. The reference is to the famous Five Sheepskins grandee. This phrase is an allusion to Pai-li Hsi (fl. c.664 B.C.E.), an official whose freedom, when he was held captive by the state of Ch'u, was effected by his admirer Duke Mu of Ch'in for a mere five sheepskins. After this was done, Pai-li Hsi agreed to serve as an adviser to Duke Mu, becoming known as the "Five Sheepskins grandee." Liu Yü-hsi is thus stating that the eighty strings of cash he received for his thoroughbred, even though not equal to its true value, comes closer to the worth of the horse than the five sheepskins did to the worth of Pai-li Hsi.

but still people could not see that this was so. How much more is this true when one's virtue is hidden within one's heart?

This is a plaint that has existed ever since days of old; it is not something I myself dare sigh over.

Translated by Madeline K. Spring

240

The Donkey of Ch'ien

Liu Tsung-yüan (773–819)

There were no donkeys in Ch'ien [1] until someone who was fond of curiosities brought one in by boat. After the man got it there, he found the donkey was useless, so he let it loose near the hills. A tiger, upon seeing it, thought it was such a large beast that it took it for a god. So the tiger hid in the forest to spy on it. Bit by bit the tiger came closer to it, but carefully so that it wouldn't know.

One day the donkey brayed, and the tiger was so terrified that he ran far off. He thought that the donkey was going to eat him and was extremely frightened. Yet as the tiger kept observing it time and again, he realized there wasn't anything unusual about the donkey. The tiger had gotten increasingly used to hearing the braying. He now came out near the donkey circling it, but still dared not pounce. In a little while, he pressed even closer to it, and he nudged it unconcernedly. Overcome with rage, the donkey kicked out at the tiger.

Now the tiger happily reckoned to himself, "So this is the extent of its talents." Thereupon he leaped, roaring loudly, and ripped open the donkey's throat. He ate his fill and then left.

Alas! The donkey's larger size made it seem to be a creature of virtue; its loud voice made it seem to be a creature of ability. If it had never revealed the limit of its talents, the tiger, despite his own ferociousness, would still have been suspicious and fearful and in the end would not have dared attack it. Now, instead, things have come to this — how disheartening!

Translated by Madeline K. Spring

The first of a group of "Three Admonitions."
For a brief note on the author, see selection 55.
1. An old name for Kweichow.

Anecdotal Fiction

241
A New Account of Tales of the World

Liu Yi-ch'ing (403–444)

When K'ung Jung[1] was in his tenth year, he accompanied his father to Loyang. At the time Li Ying[2] was at the height of his reputation there as commandant of the Capital Province. Those who came to his gate gained

A *New Account of Tales of the World* (*Shih-shuo hsin-yü*) consists of stories, conversations, and short characterizations. It covers the period from the second through the fourth centuries. In contrast to formal historical writing on this period, *Tales of the World* was written closer to the time when the events depicted actually occurred, hence it is likely to be more reliable; certainly it is more vivid. Nearly all six hundred and twenty-six characters appearing in the pages of the *Tales of the World* are attested in the histories and other sources. Furthermore, for most incidents and remarks recorded therein, allowing for literary embellishment and dramatic exaggeration, there is no compelling reason to doubt their veracity. Only a small minority pose problems of anachronism, contradiction of known facts, gross supernatural intrusions, or apparent internal inconsistencies. And yet, the *Tales of the World* was never considered by Chinese bibliographers as a work of history. Rather, it was always classed as "minor talk" (*hsiao-shuo*, i.e., "fiction"). Its main purpose was considered to be that of an aid to conversation and another of its aims, so it was said, was to provide enjoyment. The bias against *Tales of the World* as a legitimate work of history undoubtedly stemmed from its failure to subscribe to the sanctioned conventions of historiography enshrined in the dynastic histories, and from its inclusion of colorful dialogues and details normally not considered appropriate in the pages of a historical text. All of this, furthermore, is expressed in lively language that occasionally flirted with bits of colloquial, making it all the more unseemly to the staid Confucian arbiters of "proper" history-writing.

1. K'ung Jung (153–208) was a descendant of Confucius in the twentieth generation.
2. Li Ying (110–169) was an implacable foe of eunuchs in government, but lost in his struggles against them.

admittance only if they were men of exceptional talent and unblemished reputation, or if they were relatives on their father's or mother's side. Jung arrived at Li's gate and announced to the gatekeeper, "I'm a relative of Commandant Li." After he was let in and seated before his host, Li Ying asked him, "And what relationship have you with me?"

He answered, "Long ago my ancestor K'ung Chung-ni (Confucius) had the respectful relationship of student to teacher with your ancestor Li Po-yang (Lao Tzu),[3] which means that you and I have carried on friendly relations for generations."

Li Ying and all the guests marveled at him.

The Great Officer of the Center, Ch'en Wei,[4] arrived later. Someone reported what Jung had said, and Wei remarked, "If a lad is clever when he's small it doesn't necessarily mean he'll be superior when he grows up."

Jung retorted, "I suppose when you were small you must have been clever?"

Wei was greatly discomfited.

3. Confucius's surname was K'ung and Lao Tzu's surname was supposedly Li. There are many apocryphal stories about Confucius receiving instruction from Lao Tzu, the ostensible founder of Taoism and the alleged author of the *Tao Te Ching* (see selection 10).

4. Active during the late second century.

Hsü Yün's wife was the daughter of Juan Kung and the younger sister of Juan K'an. She was extraordinarily homely. After the marriage ceremony was over, Yün had no intention of ever entering her apartment again. The members of her family were very upset over this. It happened once that Yün was having a guest come, and his wife had a female slave look to see who it was. She returned and reported, "It's Master Huan." Now "Master Huan" was Huan Fen.

The wife said, "Then there's nothing to worry about. Huan will surely urge him to come to my apartment."

As expected, Huan said to Hsü, "Since the Juan family gave you a homely daughter in marriage, they obviously did so with some purpose in mind. You would do well to look into it."

Accordingly, Hsü had a change of heart and entered his wife's apartment. But the moment he saw her he immediately wanted to leave again. His wife foresaw that if he went out this time there would be no further chance of his returning, so she seized his robe in an effort to detain him. Hsü took the occasion to say to his wife, "A wife should have four virtues.[1] How many of them do *you* have?"

1. According to the *Rituals of Chou* (*Chou li*, 1.48), the nine preceptresses were in charge of the methods of womanly instruction by training the nine imperial concubines in proper womanly behavior, speech, appearance, and work. These later became known as the four womanly virtues.

His wife answered, "Where your bride is deficient is only in her appearance. But a *gentleman* should have a hundred deeds. How many have *you?*"

"I have them all."

"Of those hundred deeds, virtue is the first. If you love sensual beauty, but don't love virtue,[2] how can you say you have them all?"

Yün looked ashamed, and thereafter held her in respect and honor.

---

2. In the *Analects* (see selection 7), 9.16, Confucius declares, "I have not seen any who love virtue as they love sensual beauty."

Tales of the Strange

242
Biographies of Transcendents

Attributed to Liu Hsiang (77–6 B.C.E.)

T'ao An-kung held the post of Superintendent of the Foundry at Liu-an,[1] where he kept many furnaces in full blast. From them one day flames shot forth and mounted upward to the sky in sheets of purple fire, whereupon T'ao An-kung cast himself prostrate upon the ground beside his smelting crucibles and begged for mercy. Hardly had he done so when the Scarlet Bird[2] alighted

The author was a Han polymath and statesman who was also a sort of magician. He was a distinguished bibliographer and ubiquitous editor-redactor of ancient texts, a compiler of anecdotal literature, and a poet and author in his own right, particularly of lamentations (see selection 238). The *Biographies of Transcendents* (*Lieh hsien chuan*) is the earliest extant Taoist hagiographical work and inspired many similar later collections (see, for example, selection 246). In all, it includes seventy brief accounts of Taoist adepts thought to have achieved immortality in one form or another.

Dragons are often depicted as aerial steeds of the transcendents. The short account above gives the legend connected with one such incident and also embodies several ancient religious beliefs.

1. In Anhwei.

2. One of the Four Supernatural Creatures that symbolize the four quadrants of heaven. It is also a group of constellations in the southern sky and a position in geomantic fields. As such, it stands for the south and, according to the notions of ancient Chinese philosophy, is associated with the element fire and with the numeral 7. It is to be noted that T'ao An-kung was carried off toward the southeast which, together with the south, is that point of the compass where the element fire is located. Modern scholarship has attempted to identify the Scarlet Bird with the quail, but archaic representations show a crested bird with prominent tail feathers—a figure that

upon a crucible and thus spake: "An-kung! An-kung! Thy flames have reached unto Heaven. On the seventh day of the seventh month I will send a red dragon to fetch thee."

When the appointed day arrived, the red dragon came in a deluge of rain, and An-kung rode off on its back toward the southeast. Thousands of the inhabitants of Liu-an had collected on one of the city walls to make votive offerings for a propitious journey; and all bade T'ao An-kung farewell.

Translated by W. Perceval Yetts

---

might well be meant for a peacock or one of the pheasants, and, indeed, is not unlike the traditional Chinese phoenix.

243
Search for the Supernatural

Kan Pao (fl. 318)

Preface

Even though we examine ancient fragments in the written documents and collect bits and pieces which have come down to the present time, these things are not what has been heard or seen by one person's own ears and eyes. How could one dare say that there are no inaccurate places? Note Wei Shuo's[1] losing the country. The two commentaries are at odds in what they have heard. Note Lü Wang's[2] serving Chou. In the *Shih chi* there exist two stories.[3]

Search for the Supernatural (Sou-shen chi) is a collection of over four hundred stories gathered by the Eastern Chin court historian Kan Pao. It is the best example of a genre of literary tale that contemporaries called "leftover history," and later scholars identified as the beginnings of Chinese fiction. The tales borrow an austere documentary style of official history writing, but their subjects reach beyond that range. Mixed together in the collection are tales of avenging ghosts, fox spirits, Taoist adepts, diviners and doctors, dreams and transformations, strange creatures of distant places, and odd customs of non-Han peoples. They demonstrate the profound interest of medieval literati in matters that were curious, bizarre, and remote.

The influence of Kan Pao's collection on later fiction and drama is tremendous. Many of the characters introduced so briefly here reappear as the protagonists of complete plays and short stories in later dynasties. And the genre of collecting brief tales of the supernatural continues as well, culminating in huge collections of thousands of stories, many in later times highly crafted and literary.

1. This refers to Duke Hui of Wei, a noble of the Spring and Autumn period. Kan Pao's point is that historical works are often at odds with each other about the interpretation of events.

2. I.e., Lü Shang, a minister to King Wen of the Chou dynasty.

3. The *Shih chi* is the *Records of the Grand Historian* by Ssu-ma Ch'ien (see selection 225). In addition to better known historical records about Lü Shang, the *Shih chi* includes a hearsay

Things like this occur time and time again. From this standpoint we can observe that the difficulties of hearing and seeing have come down from ancient times.

Even in writing the set words of a funerary announcement or following the manuals of the official historians, one finds places where it is difficult to write accurately. How much more difficult then is looking back to narrate events of a past one thousand years ago, writing down the characteristics of distant and peculiar ways of life, stringing together word fragments between textual faults and fissures, questioning the old people about things in former times! If one must have historical events without any discrepancies, have the words in every text agree, and only then regard them as veritable, then this point will surely seem a defect of previous historians.

Nonetheless, the state does not eliminate the office charged with writing commentaries on historical documents, and scholars do not cease in their recitations of the texts. Is this not because what is lost is inconsequential and what is preserved is vital?

As for what I am putting together now, when they are items gotten from previous accounts, then the fault is not mine. In the event they are recent happenings which I have collected or found out, should there be errors or omissions, I would hope to share the ridicule and condemnation with scholars and worthies of the past.

Coming now to what these records contain, it is enough to make clear that the spirit world is not a lie. On this subject, the countless words and hundred differing schools are too much even to scan. And what one perceives with his own eyes and ears is too much to write down. So I have lumped records together that are just adequate to express the main points of the eight categories[4] and provide some trivial accounts; that is all.

I will count myself fortunate if in the future curious scholars come along, note the basis of these stories, and find things within them to enlighten their hearts and fill their eyes. And I will be fortunate as well to escape reproach for this book.

Translated by James I. Crump and Kenneth DeWoskin

---

story about his chance meeting with the king. Kan Pao's point here is that even the classic histories like the *Shih chi* saw fit to include information that was suspect but conveniently ready at hand.

4. The precise meaning of "categories" is not known. One possibility is that it refers to the addition of *chih-kuai* ("tales of anomalies"), such as those in the *Search for the Supernatural*, to the traditional seven categories of Liu Hsin's (?–23 C.E., son of Liu Hsiang, for whom see selection 242) seminal bibliographical scheme. In this case, it would imply "satisfying the needs of this [maverick] genre." Alternatively, and perhaps more likely, it refers to the classes of spiritual phenomena, meaning roughly "satisfying my purpose of displaying all eight types of spiritual phenomena."

Wang Tao-p'ing's Wife Restored to Life

In the days of the First Emperor of the Ch'in dynasty, Wang Tao-p'ing of Ch'ang-an and the beautiful daughter of his fellow townsman, T'ang Shu-chieh (whose childhood name was Fu-yü), swore they would be husband and wife though they were quite young.

In time, however, Tao-p'ing was conscripted for the southern expeditionary forces and disappeared in the lands of the south. Nine years passed, Fu-yü was full-grown, and her parents engaged her to Liu Hsiang.

Now, the girl took her oath with Tao-p'ing very seriously and was completely unwilling to serve another. Her parents pressed her, however, until finally she left her home to become the wife of Liu Hsiang. Three years passed, and in all that time Fu-yü was miserable — yearning constantly for Tao-p'ing. Grief and resentment deepened until finally she died from anxiety and unrest.

Another three years passed and Tao-p'ing returned home. He immediately inquired the whereabouts of Fu-yü from his neighbors and they told him: "The girl thought only of you, but her parents married her off to Liu Hsiang, and now she is dead!"

"Then where is her grave?" he asked, and the neighbors led him to the tomb.

Tao-p'ing sobbed with grief; thrice he called out the girl's name as he walked around the tomb in bitter sadness, unable to contain himself.

"You and I swore an oath before heaven and earth that we would forever be true, each to the other," cried Tao-p'ing. "Who could have foreseen that official orders were to keep us apart for so long that your parents gave you to Liu Hsiang? This done, we can never realize our original intention. The quick and the dead are parted forever; but if your spirit still resides here, grant me one more vision of your face as I knew it in life. If your spirit has vanished, then we must here and now take our leave forever."

Having spoken these words, Tao-p'ing continued weeping and pacing around her tomb. But then the girl's ghost came forth from the tomb and questioned Tao-p'ing: "Where have you been?" she asked. "We swore we would be with one another to the end of our days, but my parents forced me to go to Liu Hsiang. For three years with him I longed for you day and night until I finally died from the weight of anger and grief and went on my shadowy journey. But my thoughts of you and my longing for you in the past were never forgotten, and so strong was my wish to further comfort you that my body did not corrupt: it can again be brought back to life, and we can yet be husband and wife. Make haste to uncover the tomb, break open my coffin, and restore me to life!"

Taking her words to heart, Tao-p'ing opened the doors of the tomb and her coffin to find that she was indeed alive. And as a result of all this, they returned home together.

Liu Hsiang heard of the events and, finding them surpassing strange, put the case before the district magistrate. That official examined the events and could find no law which applied. So he memorialized the king, who passed judgment that the woman should be given to Tao-p'ing to wife.

The couple lived to the age of one hundred and thirty years. In truth, this all came about because of their deep sincerity of spirit which penetrated both heaven and earth and brought forth from them this response.

Translated by James I. Crump and Kenneth DeWoskin

Treasure Recovered Through the Classic of Changes

Huai Shao was a citizen of the Hung-shou relay station settlement well versed in the *Classic of Changes*. As he drew near death, he presented his copy of the *Changes* to his wife, saying, "When I am gone, there will be a great famine. Though this be so, I enjoin you never to sell the house. In the spring of the fifth year after my passing, an emissary surnamed Hung will stop at the relay station. This man owes me a debt; take the book to him and demand payment. You must give me your word and honor it."

After he died, there were in fact great troubles. Several times Huai's wife was tempted to sell off the house, but she remembered her husband's words and stopped herself. When the time came, a certain Hung did indeed stay at the relay station, whereupon Huai's wife presented him her copy of the *Changes* and taxed him with the debt. He accepted the book but was puzzled by her words.

"Never in my life did I contract such a debt," said he. "I wonder what is behind this?"

"As my husband neared death, he put his hand to his very book and saw what was to be. Truly, I would not deceive you," insisted the woman.

The emissary pondered and muttered to himself for some time until finally he understood. He ordered milfoil stalks to be brought so that a divination might be made. A while later, he clapped his hands together and sighed.

"Most wonderful, Mr. Huai," he exclaimed. "You have concealed your brilliance and hidden your tracks so that none of us had heard of you. But obviously you were one who could hold a mirror up to failure and success and fathom felicity and ill-fortune."

The emissary then turned to Huai's wife and said, "I never did incur such a debt. Your husband had the money. He knew that after his death you would temporarily find yourself in straitened circumstances so he hid the gold that it might wait upon better times. He deliberately told neither wife nor child about it for fear the money would disappear before the bad times had. He knew I was skilled in the *Changes* and therefore left this copy so that his intentions might become known. Now, five hundred catties of gold are buried in a black jar capped with a sheet of copper near the east wall of your house. It is exactly one rod from the wall and is buried nine feet deep."

The wife went home and dug. She recovered the gold and all was as had been divined.

Translated by James I. Crump and Kenneth DeWoskin

The Origins of the Man[1] Barbarians

In the times of Kao-hsin, an elderly woman attached to the palace had been suffering from an earache for some time. The physician treated her and removed an insect the size of a silkworm cocoon. When the woman had left, the physician placed the insect in a gourd pot (*hu*) and covered it with a dish (*p'an*). In no time it turned into a dog mottled with colorful patches. This dog was called P'an-hu and was reared by the physician.

At that time, the Wu barbarians had become numerous and strong and several times penetrated the borders. Generals were sent against them but could not gain victories. A declaration was sent throughout the kingdom: "Anyone bringing in the head of the Wu leader will be rewarded with a thousand catties of gold, an appanage of ten thousand households, and the hand of the emperor's youngest daughter."

Sometime later P'an-hu appeared carrying a head in its mouth and went straight to the king's palace. The king examined the head and concluded that it belonged to the Wu leader. What was he to do?

His officers all said "P'an-hu is a domestic animal; he cannot be allowed to join the ranks of officials and certainly cannot be given your daughter to wed! Though he has acquired merit for the deed, he cannot be given the reward."

When his younger daughter heard of this, she addressed the king: "Since Your Majesty promised me to anyone in the world and P'an-hu brought you the head, ridding your kingdom of danger, we have here the will of Heaven. This is not something P'an-hu's intelligence could have contrived. Kings must keep promises, rulers must be believed. You cannot repudiate your word, clearly given to the world, for the sake of my humble person; that would result in calamity for your kingdom."

The king feared she was right and ordered her given to P'an-hu.

The dog took the girl into the southern hills where the undergrowth was so dense that the feet of men never trod. There she discarded her court robes,

---

1. The tribal name "Man" is completely unrelated to the English word designating a human being. The Man people lived in the southeast reaches of the Chinese empire.

donned those of a common freeman, and bound herself to P'an-hu as his servant. He then led her over mountains and through valleys until they reached a cave in the rocks.

Now, the king sorely missed his daughter and he often sent men forth to search for her. However, the heavens would always rain, the mountain peaks would shake, and clouds would so darken the sky that they could not reach where she was.

Nearly three years passed. The princess had given birth to six boys and six girls when P'an-hu died. Their offspring married one another; they wove cloth from the bark of trees dyed with the juices of berries and fruits — for they loved colorful garments — and they cut the cloth to fit their tails.

Later, their mother returned to the palace and the king sent envoys to welcome the children — this time the heavens did not rain. But their clothes were outlandish, their speech barbaric; they squatted on their haunches to eat and drink, and preferred mountain wilds to cities. The king acceded to their wishes and gave them famed mountains and broad swamps for their home. They were called Man barbarians.

The Man barbarians appear stupid but are in fact crafty. They are contented in the lands they inhabit and set store by their old ways. They believe they were given strange capacities by the will of Heaven and therefore they act under laws not common to others. They farm and they trade but have no documents to show at borders, no identifications or tallies, nor do they have rents or taxes of any sort. They live in small villages where the headmen are given tallies and wear crowns of otter-skin, for the Man secure their food from the waters.

Presently the commanderies of Liang, Han, Pa, Shu, Wu-ling, Ch'ang-sha, and Lu-chiang are all inhabited by Man barbarians. They eat rice-gruel mixed with the flesh of various fish; they pound on containers and howl to honor P'an-hu with sacrifices of gourds. This custom has lasted until the present day. These are the reasons for the saying:

> Red buttocks, yellow trousers do
> Reveal descendants of P'an-hu.
>
> *Translated by James I. Crump and Kenneth DeWoskin*

The Spirit of Young Mrs. Ting

There was in Huai-nan in the district of Ch'üan-chiao a certain newly married Miss Ting. She was of the Tan-yang Ting family. Her mother-in-law was strict and cruel, forcing her to work constantly and, if her tasks were not finished in time, she was beaten beyond bearing. Finally, on the ninth of the ninth month she hanged herself, and thereafter her spirit was heard among the citizens and she spoke through a medium, saying, "I have pity for young wives who labor without respite. Let the ninth of the ninth month be set aside as a day of rest for them."

She appeared to humans in bright green robes with a black head-covering, followed by a maid-servant. Once she came to Oxenford and sought passage across from two young men who were fishing from a boat. They laughed at her and trifled with her, saying, "When you let us take you to wife, we will ferry you over."

"I took you to be good men," she cried, "but little did I know! If you are men at all, may you perish in the mud; if you are ghosts, may you drown!"

Having said this, she made her way through the undergrowth on the shore and came upon an old fisherman in a boat with a full load of grass for fodder. When she asked him to ferry her, the old man responded, "My craft has no sunshade, and I fear this is no way for a lady to cross the river."

She told him not to worry about that, so he removed half his load of grass. When he seated her, the boat did not move, and he sculled her slowly across. Having gained the south shore, she was about to depart when she addressed the old fisher, "I am not human, but a ghost. I could have crossed by myself, but thought it best to let local people know of me. I was much moved by your leaving half your cargo to ferry me. If you speedily return now, you will see something and you will gain something."

"I fear that I could only give you clumsy help — how am I to expect thanks for that?" asked the fisher.

Nevertheless, the old man retraced his journey and discovered two young men under the water. A bit farther on he found that thousands of fish had leaped up in the river and been blown onto the bank by the wind. The old man discarded his load of fodder and went home instead with a whole boatload of fish.

Thereafter, Ting's ghost returned to Tan-yang and the people of Chiang-nan still speak of her as "Auntie Ting." The ninth of the ninth month is considered by all a day of rest on which women do no work. There are shrines to Auntie Ting everywhere now.

Translated by James I. Crump and Kenneth DeWoskin

Liang Wen and Lord Kao-shan

During the Han, Liang Wen from the Ch'i area was given to Taoist practices. He added a room three or four beams wide onto his house as an offertory. His altar was covered with a large, dark drape and he spent much time in there.

This is how things went for more than a decade. Then, because of the numerous sacrifices directed to the shrine, one day the sound of a voice suddenly issued from beneath the altar cloth.

"I am the Lord Kao-shan,"[1] it said. The god had quite an appetite for food and drink and was efficacious in curing illness. Liang Wen was very attentive and respectful toward it.

And so things went for several more years until one day the god invited Liang Wen to come under the altar drapes. There Wen found the god very drunk, but he respectfully asked if he could reverently look upon the sacred countenance.

"Stretch thy hand forth," said Kao-shan, and Liang Wen did as the god bade him. He was then allowed to finger the god's chin. His hand came in contact with quite a long beard. Gradually and carefully Wen wrapped the beard around his fingers — and suddenly gave a great tug!

There was the sound of a loud goat bleat. Wen's congregation all jumped to their feet in surprise and helped him drag the god forth. It was a goat belonging to the house of Yüan Shu! Seven or eight years before, the family goat had disappeared and the Yüan family had no idea where it had gone.

They slaughtered the goat and there were no manifestations after that.

Translated by James I. Crump and Kenneth DeWoskin

1. Meaning "high hill," where goats are most often pastured.

The Archers Yu-chi and Keng-lei

The king of Ch'u was enjoying his park when he came upon a white gibbon. The king ordered his best archers to shoot it. They launched many arrows, but the gibbon simply laughed and brushed them aside. Then the king ordered Yang Yu-chi to shoot. Yu-chi only touched his bow, and the gibbon clutched a tree trunk and cried aloud. During Six States times, Keng-lei said to the king of Wei, "I am able to release my bow with no arrow on the string and bring down a bird."

"Can archery reach such perfection?" exclaimed the king.

"It can," replied Lei. A moment later they heard geese coming over from the east. Keng-lei shot his bow with no arrow and a bird dropped for him.

Translated by James I. Crump and Kenneth DeWoskin

Compare this tale with its source in *Intrigues of the Warring States* (see selection 238), "The Wounded Bird and the Archer":

> When the empire had joined the Alliance, Chao's envoy Wei Chia had audience with Lord Ch'un-shen of Ch'u and said:
>
> "Have you already got a general, my lord?"
>
> "I have," replied Lord Ch'un-shen, "I am going to make Lord Lin-wu my commander."
>
> "When I was young," said Wei Chia, "I used to be enamored of archery, so with your indulgence I should like to use a comparison from archery."
>
> "You may."

"One day Skinbone accompanied the king of Wei to the foot of the High Terrace where they watched the birds flying.

" 'Your Majesty,' said Skinbone, 'I can draw my bow, fire it with no arrow on the string, and bring down a bird for you.'

" 'Can archery reach such perfection?' exclaimed the king.

"A little while later a wild goose came from the east, and Skinbone discharged his bow with no arrow on the string and brought it down.

" 'How can archery reach such perfection?' exclaimed the king.

" 'Oh,' replied Skinbone, 'this bird was already weakened.'

" 'How do you know that?'

" 'His flight was labored and his call was sad,' replied Skinbone. 'The slow flight was the result of a wound and his call was sad because he had been long away from his flock: therefore, his wound had not mended and his fright had not left him. When he heard the twang of a bowstring he tried to climb, strained open his wound, and fell.' "

Translated by James Crump

As always, the point in *Intrigues* is persuasion, whereas in *Search* the same material is twisted to seem supernatural because that, after all, is what Kan Pao is after. *Intrigues* goes out of its way to give a rational explanation.

244
Ou Ching-chih and the Corpse Eater

Attributed to Tsu Ch'ung-chih (429–500)

Ou Ching-chih, a "camp man"[1] of Nan-k'ang prefecture,[2] took a boat trip with his son one day during the first year of the Yüan-chia reign period.[3] They started from the prefectural seat and proceeded far upstream to a secluded branch of the river. The place was remote and desolate, completely cut off from the outside world; no human being had ever set foot there before. They went ashore in the evening to camp for the night. There Ching-chih had a stroke and died unexpectedly.

Tsu Ch'ung-chih was a mathematician and astronomer. His interest in "records of anomalies" (*chih-kuai*), of which this is a typical specimen, seems to suggest that such stories attracted scientifically oriented minds, whether as entertainment or as material for investigation.

This story is an example of the type of "records of anomalies" that feature evil creatures inhabiting the wild terrain beyond the pale of human civilization. Here narrative purpose is subservient to that of description and portrayal.

1. In the Six Dynasties, commoners of a defeated state were sometimes kept as bond peasants to work the land of their captors. They were called "camp people," and were accorded a status lower than that of ordinary peasants.

2. Modern Kan district in Kiangsi.

3. The dates of this reign period are 424–453.

His son built a fire to keep vigil over the body. Suddenly he heard someone wailing mournfully in the distance, calling out, "Uncle!" Ou's son was mystified and frightened. Presently the mourner came into sight. It was a creature the size of a man, with long hair reaching down to its feet and completely covering the features of its face. As it came closer, it called Ou's son by name and tried to console him. Seized with fear, the son threw all the wood in to kindle the fire, so that it might shine on the creature. The creature said, "I have come to offer my condolences and to comfort you. Why are you frightened and make the fire blaze up like that?"

It then sat down by the head of the corpse to mourn. Stealing a look at the creature, the son saw it bend over and cover the face of the corpse with its own. In an instant, the corpse's face was clean of flesh, the skull exposed. The son was terrified, and sought to drive the creature away, but there was nothing at hand he could use as a weapon. By the time he turned to look again, only the bones of the body were left; and in another moment, even the skin and bones had been consumed.

It was never known what kind of monster or evil spirit that creature was.

Translated by Karl S. Y. Kao

245
The Office of the Record-Keeper in Hsiu-chou

from *The Record of the Listener*

Hung Mai (1123–1202)

Of the many strange apparitions in the office of the record-keeper in Hsiu-chou,[1] one always wore a green kerchief and cloth robe, had a short and broad shape, and walked with slow and heavy steps. A woman also went out abruptly every night and bewitched the office runners on night duty.

At the time my father occupied this post, my older brother, the future grand councilor, was just nine. In broad daylight he opened his eyes wide as

Hung Mai was the son of a prominent official in Kiangsi. A prolific essayist, storyteller, memorialist, and collector and critic of T'ang poetry, he developed an eclectic taste for Buddhism, Taoism, and Confucianism, and read widely in the histories. After becoming a Presented Scholar in 1145, he had a long but fitful career as an official.

The Record of the Listener (Yi-chien chih) originally consisted of almost 2,700 tales of the bizarre and supernatural, about half of which are lost. All of the tales were written by Hung Mai himself between the years 1161 and 1198. *The Record*, a sort of *Ripley's Believe It or Not* from the twelfth century, is the largest Chinese collection of stories after the celebrated *Extensive Records from the Reign of Great Tranquility (T'ai-p'ing kuang-chi)*, which preserved many

if he had seen something and said, "Water, water." Only after the passage of quite some time did he regain consciousness.

Two days later, my father came home late from the office. A concubine grabbed his robe from behind, suddenly called out, and fell to the ground. My father had heard that ghosts feared leather belts, so he took one to bind the concubine and carried her to bed. After a long while, the ghost speaking through her said, "This person has previously insulted ghosts and gods. Just now she is carrying something [the belt] in her right hand that's really frightening. I don't dare to get close. Still, she didn't know I was coming from her left. Just as I was congratulating myself on capturing her, I was detained by an official who uses the Chung K'uei[2] demon-quelling method. I would prefer to go now without causing any mutual inconvenience."

He was asked, "Who are you?"

The ghost was unwilling to answer.

After several repetitions he said, "I am farmer Stem Nine from Chia-hsing county. With my fellow canton resident Water Three, we had nine mouths to our two households. During the flood two years ago we all began to wander about begging for food. We died just before the officials began famine relief. Now I live on top of the big tree behind your house. Several days ago, the one the little official, your son, saw was Water Three."

My father said, "I worship the star god Chen-wu because he is very efficacious, and I also have images of the Buddha, and of the earth and stove gods. How is it that you come here so insistently?"

The ghost said, "The Buddha is a benevolent deity who does not concern himself with such trivial matters; every night the star god Chen-wu unbinds his hair, grasps his sword, and flies from the roof. I carefully avoid him, that's all. The earth god behind your house is not easily aroused to his duties. Only at the small temple to the stove god in front of your house am I reprimanded every time I'm seen. I just entered the kitchen, and His Lordship asked, 'Where are you going?'

"I answered, 'I'm just strolling around.'

"He upbraided me, 'You're not allowed to do wrong.'

"I said, 'I wouldn't dare,' and came here."

---

important T'ang period classical-language short stories. Hung was also a master of the genre known as *pi-chi* ("notes," literally "brush [i.e., pen]-records"), a brief type of casual, anecdotal essay that enables the author to discuss virtually any subject or object under the sun or in the netherworld. Hung prided himself on taking careful notes when someone told him an anecdote, and he often included the names of his informants. The anecdote selected here, one of the few in *The Record* about Hung's own family, took place in 1124, when he was one year old, and reveals much about the religious beliefs of one official's family.

1. Chia-hsing county, Chekiang province.
2. A famous demon-destroyer.

My father said, "What are the two things that always come out?"

The ghost said, "The one with the kerchief is the spirit of a rock who's called Gentleman Shih (Rock). He's just under the hedge outside the study window, about three feet under the ground. The woman is Second Woman of the Ch'in family. She's lived here a long time."

My father said, "I give paper money to the earth god on the first and fifteenth day of every month. How can he allow ghosts from outside to come in? You go and ask him for me. Tomorrow I shall destroy his shrine."

The ghost said, "Do you mean to say you don't understand? Even though he has money, how can he go without food? When I enter your house, if I get something, I must give him a share to placate him, and that is why he has always permitted me to come." He ate silently for a while and then he spoke again, "I have told the earth god about your warning. He was angry that I was so loquacious and used a stick to drive me out."

My father said, "Have you seen my family's ancestors or not?"

He said, "Every time there is a holiday and you make offerings, I definitely come to observe. I smell the fragrant food and want to eat it but do not get any. Among the places at the mat a few are empty, but if a yellow-clothed woman sees me, she gets angry."

My father asked him to go see the ancestors again. After a moment, the ghost gasped and became pale. Eventually he spoke, saying, "Just as I reached the door, I was chased by a woman carrying a stick. I quickly ran in the other direction and barely escaped."

The woman he spoke of was my great-grandmother Chi-kuo.

My father asked what the ancestors wanted. The ghost said, "They're consumed by suffering and hunger, and would like a meal with some good wine and a fat goose for everyone—not the usual skinny chicken you give them."

When my father had finished speaking, the ghost cocked his ear timorously as if someone had called him and said, "The earth god is very angry and has expelled our two households. Now we'll briefly go to the top of the city wall. We have no home to return to. Please free me quickly. I won't dare to come again."

My father undid his belt. The concubine slept in a daze for a whole day and then woke up.

Translated by Valerie Hansen

246

Biographies of Transcendents

Huan-ch'u (late Yüan period)

Po-shih Sheng

Po-shih Sheng was a pupil of the Venerable Chung Huang. In the days of P'eng Tsu[1] he was then more than two thousand years of age. Instead of wishing to ascend on high to the celestial abode of the transcendents, he preferred a long life on earth and regarded that as the acme of bliss. The Elixir of Gold was the most efficacious drug for his purpose, but, being poor, he could not obtain it. So he kept pigs and sheep, and after some ten years had amassed considerable wealth, which enabled him to buy the nostrum and drink it.

His habit was to boil white stones and use them as food. Later on, he made his abode on the White Stone Mountain, and thus acquired the name of Po-shih Sheng ("Mr. Whitestone"). Sometimes he would eat dried meat, at other times nothing at all.

He was able to walk as far as three or four hundred tricents in one day. His appearance was that of a man of thirty. When anyone asked him why he did not wish to fly up into the sky, he answered, "I'm not at all sure that one would have in heaven a better time than in this world."

Pictures of this transcendent show him seated beside a caldron in which bubbles a stew of stones. The tale illustrates one of the countless directions in which Taoist adepts were thought to be able to transcend the weaknesses of ordinary mortal flesh. It is taken from a book that bears the identical title of the *Biographies of Transcendents* attributed to Liu Hsiang (see selection 242). This namesake of the Han period classic was compiled by a Taoist called Huan-ch'u ("Return to the Beginning"), probably toward the end of the Yüan period. Unlike the older work, it is illustrated, the fifty-five transcendents whose lives it contains being portrayed in a corresponding number of woodcuts. It is a careless compilation: many passages that can be traced to their origin are misquoted or mutilated and textual errors are frequent. Perhaps these facts explain its exclusion from the official Taoist canon. However, its convenient size, low price, frequent editions, and many illustrations led to wide circulation, and it was the most popular handbook of Taoist legends in late imperial China. In many ways it offers a striking parallel to eighteenth-century chapbooks in England. The *Biographies* may justly be regarded as a repository of folklore valuable to the student, and especially so with regard to the identification of Taoist themes represented in works of art.

1. The mythological Chinese equivalent of Methuseleh.

Ch'en Nan

Ch'en Nan (also called Nan Mu and Ts'ui Hsü), a native of the district town of Po-lo,[1] was originally a cooper and basket-maker by trade.

1. Not far from Hui-chou, on the East River.

Later in life he obtained from a Buddhist priest of P'i-ling a pinch of the Great Monad together with instructions for making the Philosopher's Stone; also from a divine being on Mount Li-mu[2] he gained possession of a treatise called "The Cornelian Book of Thunder in Cloudless Skies."

Ch'en Nan had the power of curing diseases with some medicine which he made by kneading earth and charmed water together into a bolus, and in consequence was nicknamed "Mud-pill Ch'en" by his contemporaries.

With hair disheveled, clothes tattered like a quail's tail and patched all over, and his person covered with filth, Ch'en Nan used at times to travel four or five hundred tricents in one day. He liked eating dog's flesh, and not a day passed but he got dead drunk.

Once it happened that when he was at Ts'ang Wu,[3] the prefect was offering up prayers on account of the drought. Ch'en Nan seized an iron rod and cast it into a pool to drive out the dragon that inhabited it; and in an instant there came a storm of thunder and rain.

Both at San-shan[4] and at Ta-yi,[5] which he visited in the course of his travels, he found the river too swollen and turbulent for a boat to venture on, so he just launched his wide-brimmed hat and passed over standing on that.

Once when traveling in the circuit of Ch'in-kuan, he encountered on the road a band of robbers, who seized and killed him. After he had lain buried for three days and the robbers had scattered and gone, Ch'en Nan came to life again and rose from his grave.

On another occasion, while wandering about at Ch'ang-sha,[6] he came into collision with the retinue of the general commanding the troops, who in consequence had him arrested and sent under escort to a prison at Yung-chou.[7] However, after a few days he managed to escape and returned to Ch'ang-sha.

At nighttime Ch'en Nan used to sit up instead of lying down. Things which he put into a bath of mercury were by next morning transformed into solid silver. It was he who imparted to Po Yü-ch'an[8] the method of making the Philosopher's Stone. During the *chia-ting* period of the reign of Ning Tsung [c. 1215], Ch'en Nan jumped into the River Chang,[9] and thus departed this world and gained release from the trammels of the flesh.

Translated by W. Perceval Yetts

2. Near his native town.
3. The prefectural city of Wu-chou in Kwangsi.
4. A town on the south bank of the Yangtze near Wu-hu.
5. Near Lu-an in Shansi.
6. In Hunan.
7. The present Nan-ning in Kwangsi.
8. Another transcendent in Huan-ch'u's book.
9. A river in Chihli and Honan.

247

Strange Tales from Make-Do Studio

P'u Sung-ling (1640–1715)

The Mural

While staying in the capital, Meng Lung-t'an of Kiangsi and Master of Letters Chu once happened upon a monastery. Neither the shrine-hall nor the meditation room was very spacious, and only one old monk was found putting up within. Seeing the guests enter, the monk straightened up his clothes, went to greet them, and showed them around the place. An image of Zen Master Pao-chih[1] stood in the shrine-hall. On either side-wall were painted fine murals with lifelike human figures. The east wall depicted the Buddhist legend of "Heavenly Maidens Scattering Flowers." Among the figures was a young girl with flowing hair[2] with a flower in her hand and a faint smile on her face. Her cherry-red lips were on the verge of moving, and the liquid pools of her eyes seemed to stir with wavelike glances. After gazing intently for some time, Chu's self-possession began to waver, and his thoughts grew so abstracted that he fell into a trance. His body went adrift as if floating on mist; suddenly he was inside the mural. Peak upon peak of palaces and pavilions made him feel as if he was beyond this earth. An old monk was preaching the Dharma on a dais, around which stood a large crowd of viewers in robes with their right shoulders bared out of respect. Chu mingled in among them.

Before long, he felt someone tugging furtively at his sleeve. He turned to

P'u Sung-ling, possibly of distant Persian, Turkic, or Arabic ancestry, passed the regional examinations for the Bachelor of Letters degree at age nineteen, but was repeatedly rejected in numerous subsequent provincial examinations, well into his seventies. P'u spent most of his life teaching in a country schoolroom. Through poverty and austerity, he learned to identify closely with the common people.

Most of the stories in *Strange Tales from Make-Do Studio* (*Liao chai chih yi*) were collected from various sources, while others were made up by the author himself. All of them were exquisitely created and elegantly constructed. Although the collection is extremely well known, few Chinese could read it in the original because of the difficulty of the elegant, allusive classical book language in which it was written. Instead, the recondite tales were made known to the wider public through dramatic presentations, oral storytelling, vernacular paraphrases, and other types of popularizations. Ironically, P'u was also the author of earthy, colloquial arias and plays of his own that were quite opposite in character to the highly classical *Strange Tales*. Indeed, so dissimilar are these two types of writing that it is hard to imagine they are from the same hand.

The comments by the Chronicler of the Tales that occur at the conclusion of most of the stories are by the author himself. These are modeled after the comments at the end of each chapter by the Grand Historian, Ssu-ma Ch'ien, in his *Shih chi* (see selection 225) and often give a wry twist to the narrative or offer bitter social criticism without being overtly and offensively didactic.

1. A monk who lived during the Northern and Southern dynasties (420–589).
2. Her hair was not bound up, signifying that she was unmarried.

look, and there was the girl with flowing hair giving him a dazzling smile. She tripped abruptly away, and he lost no time following her along a winding walkway into a small chamber. Once there, he hesitated to approach any farther. When she turned her head and raised the flower with a beckoning motion, he went across to her in the quiet, deserted chamber. Swiftly he embraced her and, as she did not put up much resistance, they grew intimate. When it was over she told him not to make a sound and left, closing the door behind her. That night she came again. After two days of this, the girl's companions realized what was happening and searched together until they found the scholar.

"A little gentleman is already growing in your belly, but still you wear those flowing tresses, pretending to be a maiden," they said teasingly. Holding out hairpins and earrings, they pressured her to put her hair up in the coiled knot of a married woman, which she did in silent embarrassment. One of the girls said, "Sisters, let's not outstay our welcome." At this the group left all in a titter.

Looking at the soft, cloudlike chignon piled atop her head and her phoenix ringlets curved low before her ears, the scholar was more struck by her charms than when she had worn her hair long. Seeing that no one was around, he began to make free with her. His heart throbbed at her musky fragrance but, before they had quite finished their pleasure, the heavy tread of leather boots was heard. A clanking of chains and manacles was followed by clamorous, arguing voices. The girl got up in alarm. Peering out, they saw an officer dressed in armor, his face black as lacquer, with chains in one hand and a mace in the other. Standing around him were all the maidens. "Is this all of you?" asked the officer. "We're all here," they answered. "Report if any of you are concealing a man from the lower world. Don't bring trouble on yourselves." "We aren't," said the maidens in unison. The officer turned around and looked malevolently in the direction of the chamber, giving every appearance of an intention to search it. The girl's face turned pale as ashes in fear. "Quick, hide under the bed," she told Chu in panic. She opened a little door in the wall and was gone in an instant. Chu lay prostrate, hardly daring to take a little breath. Soon he heard the sound of boots stumping into, then back out of, the room. Before long, the din of voices gradually receded. He regained some composure, though the sound of passersby discussing the matter could be heard frequently outside the door. After cringing there for quite some time, he heard ringing in his ears and felt a burning ache in his eyes. Though the intensity of these sensations threatened to overwhelm him, there was no choice but to listen quietly for the girl's return. He was reduced to the point that he no longer recalled where he had been before coming here.

Just then his friend Meng Lung-t'an, who had been standing in the shrine-hall, found that Chu had disappeared in the blink of an eye. Perplexed, he asked the monk what had happened. "He has gone to hear a sermon on the

Dharma," said the monk laughingly. "Where?" asked Meng. "Not far," was the answer. After a moment, the monk tapped on the wall with his finger and called, "Why do you tarry so long, my good patron?" Presently there appeared on the wall an image of Chu standing motionless with his head cocked to one side as if listening to something. "You have kept your traveling companion waiting a long time," called the monk again. Thereupon he drifted out of the mural and down to the floor. He stood woodenly, his mind like burned-out ashes, with eyes staring straight ahead and legs wobbling. Meng was terribly frightened, but in time calmed down enough to ask what had happened. It turned out that Chu had been hiding under the bed when he heard a thunderous knocking, so he came out of the room to listen for the source of the sound.

They looked at the girl holding the flower and saw, instead of flowing hair, a high coiled chignon on her head. Chu bowed down to the old monk in amazement and asked the reason for this. "Illusion is born in the mind. How can a poor mendicant like myself explain it?" laughed the monk. Chu was dispirited and cast down; Meng was shaken and confused. Together they walked down the shrine-hall steps and left.

The Chronicler of the Tales comments: " 'Illusion is born in the mind.' These sound like the words of one who has found the truth. A wanton mind gives rise to visions of lustfulness. The mind dominated by lust gives rise to a state of fear. The Bodhisattva made it possible for ignorant persons to attain realization for themselves. All the myriad transformations of illusion are nothing but the movements of the human mind itself. The old monk spoke in earnest solicitude, but regrettably there is no sign that the youth found enlightenment in his words and entered the mountains with hair unbound to seek the truth."

Translated by Denis C. Mair and Victor H. Mair

The Taoist of Lao Mountain [1]

In our district lived scholar Wang, the seventh son of an old family. From youth onward he was attracted to Taoist arts. Hearing that immortals abounded on Lao Mountain, he packed his books on his back and set out there on an adventure. Climbing to the top of a peak, Wang came to a Taoist temple set in a wild, secluded spot. A Taoist with white hair hanging past his collar was sitting on a bast mat. He had about him an otherworldly air that was graceful and lofty. Scholar Wang made obeisance to him and struck up a conversation. The Taoist's talk impressed him as quite mysterious and subtle. Wang asked to be accepted as his disciple, to which he replied, "I am afraid you are too soft and lazy to work hard."

1. An old sacred spot for Taoists on the Shantung coast of Chiao-chou Bay.

"Oh, but I can," answered Wang. The Taoist had a crowd of acolytes, all of whom came together at dusk. Having saluted each of them, Wang settled down in the hermitage.

At the crack of dawn the Taoist woke Wang, gave him an ax, and made him go to gather firewood with the others. Wang did exactly as he was told. After more than a month of this, his hands and feet had calluses on top of calluses. Unable to bear the toil, he nursed secret intentions of returning home. One evening on his return he saw two men drinking with his master. The sun had already set but no lamps or candles had yet been lit, so the master cut paper in the shape of a mirror and pasted it on the wall. Suddenly a light as bright as the moon's flooded the room, making the tiniest hairs visible. The acolytes in attendance ran back and forth at the guests' bidding. One of the guests said, "It's a beautiful night for good times. We ought to share them with everyone here." The Taoist picked up a pitcher of wine from the table and began to pour some for each acolyte, urging them to drink their fill. Wang thought to himself, "How can a pitcher of wine suffice for seven or eight people?" Each of them hunted up a drinking vessel. They vied to see who would be first to drain his cup. Their only fear was that the pitcher was empty, but when they went to pour from it again they were astonished to find that the wine had not gone down in the slightest. Soon another guest said, "You have been nice enough to give us moonlight to drink by, but there is still no entertainment. Why don't you call the goddess of the moon to come?" At this the Taoist tossed a chopstick into the moon and a beautiful woman appeared out of the circle of light. At first she was not even a foot tall, but she grew to normal size as she descended to the floor. Her slender waist and graceful neck moved through the fluttering gyrations of the Dance of the Rainbow Skirt and Feathered Blouse.[2] To the tempo of the dance she sang,

> Immortal of the mountains,
> Is it true you're bound for home?
> Will you leave me all alone
> In this icy crystal dome?

Her silvery voice was as piercing as a flute. At the end of the song she arose with a sweeping motion, jumped up on the table and, in the space of an astonished glance, was already a chopstick again. The three men laughed boisterously.

The other guest spoke up, "This evening has been wonderful, but the wine is getting the better of me. Would it be all right if we had a farewell drink in the palace of the moon?" The three men moved their mats and slowly floated into the moon. The acolytes saw the three seated in the moon drinking, their features distinct as reflections in a mirror. After a time the moon gradually dimmed. When the acolytes brought a lighted candle, they found the Taoist

2. A famous dance which flourished in palaces during the T'ang dynasty (618–907).

sitting alone, his guests nowhere to be seen. The delicacies on the table were just as before, and the moon on the wall was nothing more than a disk of paper.

"Did you have enough to drink?" the Taoist asked the acolytes.

"Enough," they said.

"Then you ought to go right to bed. Don't let this interfere with gathering wood and kindling."

The acolytes said "yes" and retired.

Wang's intention of leaving subsided out of heartfelt admiration. But after another month had passed the grinding toil became too much for him, and the Taoist would not pass on even a single magical technique. Unable to wait any longer, Wang took his leave, saying, "I came a hundred miles to study under such an immortal master as yourself. Even though I cannot learn the art of everlasting life, there may perhaps be some small skill you could impart that would appease my wish for learning. For the past two or three months all I have done is go out to gather wood in the morning and return in the evening. When I was at home, I was not used to this kind of hard work."

The Taoist answered with a laugh, "I said from the start that you would not be able to stand hard work, and you have proven me right. I will send you off tomorrow morning."

"I have labored for many days. If you could just impart some insignificant part of your art, my coming would not be in vain." The Taoist asked what art he hoped to learn.

Wang answered, "I have often noticed that walls are no hindrance to your free motion. I would be satisfied to learn the method of such magic."

The Taoist gave his assent with a laugh. Then he taught Wang the words of a spell and told him to chant it through by himself, at which he cried, "Go through." Wang faced the wall, not daring to walk into it. Again the Taoist cried, "Try to go through it!" Doing as he was told, Wang gingerly approached the wall, but it proved unyielding to his forward movement.

"Lower your head and go through quickly. Don't hold back," instructed the Taoist. So Wang backed several steps away from the wall and ran toward it. When he came to the wall it seemed not be there at all. Turning around to look, he found that he was already outside the building. Overjoyed, he went back in to thank his master. The Taoist said, "You must live chastely after your return, or the spell will not work." Then he gave Wang money for the trip home and sent him off.

Upon reaching home Wang boasted that he had met with an immortal and that now his power was such that no solid wall could stop him. His wife found this hard to believe. Wang stood several feet from a wall and ran headlong against it as he had done before, but this time his head smacked against the hard wall and he tumbled backward. His wife helped him up and looked at the goose egg rising moundlike on his forehead. Shamed but incited by her ridicule into a fury, he raved that the old Taoist was nothing but a reprobate.

The Chronicler of the Tales comments: "No one who hears of this incident can keep from laughing out loud, but those who laugh do not realize that the Scholar Wangs of this world are by no means few and far between. Take the case of a worthless official who would 'rather swallow poison than medicines.' A 'boil-sucking, hemorrhoid-licking' sort of person might cater to his wishes by advocating brutal, self-aggrandizing policies and inveigle him, saying, 'You need only adhere to such and such a policy—nothing will stand in your way.' The first time he tries, it might yield some small measure of success, thus giving him the idea that such policy can be applied to all cases under heaven. Those who are taken in by this will not stop until they run headlong into a solid wall and topple over backward."

Translated by Denis C. Mair and Victor H. Mair

The Cricket

During the Hsüan-te reign period (1426–1435) of the Ming dynasty, cricket-keeping was a popular amusement in the palace. The insects were levied annually from the populace. Live crickets were not originally a Shensi product until a magistrate in Hua-yin county who was anxious to win favor with his superiors presented one, which was tried in the ring and found to be an outstanding fighter. From then on Hua-yin county was charged with providing crickets to the court regularly. The magistrate delegated the responsibility to the headman in each ward. Young idlers in the marketplace kept the best of them in cages, forcing prices up by cornering the market. Cunning ward administrators used this as an excuse to impose a head tax on the peasants. For every cricket that was requisitioned, several families were driven into bankruptcy.

In the district there was a man named Ch'eng Ming, a long unsuccessful candidate for the Bachelor of Letters degree. The crafty ward administrator, seeing that Ch'eng was impractical and slow of speech, recommended him for the position of headman. Ch'eng made numerous futile attempts to free himself from the obligations of this office. Before a year had passed his meager resources were used up. Then came the cricket levy. Ch'eng did not dare collect money from the households, nor could he fulfill the duty out of his own funds. He was so despondent he wanted to kill himself.

"What good would killing yourself do?" said his wife. "It would be better to look for a cricket yourself. There is a slight chance you might find one."

This made sense to Ch'eng. He went out in the mornings, and returned at nightfall, bamboo pail and wire cage in hand, poking under stones and opening burrows amid crumbling walls and thick growths of grass. There was nothing he did not try, but it was no use. The few that he did manage to catch were too puny to fit the regulations. The magistrate's deadline was rigorously enforced, and he was given a total of a hundred strokes with a cane over a period of ten days. Blood and pus oozed from his buttocks and, what was worse, he was unable to go looking for the insects at all. He tossed and turned on his bed, his mind filled with thoughts of suicide.

It was then that a hunchbacked shamaness who performed divinations with the help of a spirit-familiar came to the village. Ch'eng's wife scraped up a sum of money and went to call on her. Smartly dressed young women and white-haired old ladies were milling around the door. Inside the house was a curtained-off sanctum, with an altar standing outside the curtain. Petitioners lit incense in the censer and kowtowed twice, while the shamaness stood to one side looking off into space and pronouncing an invocation for them, her lips contorted with unintelligible mutterings. Everyone stood stiffly listening until shortly a piece of paper, bearing a message that dealt with the petitioner's troubles, was thrown out from within the curtain. The messages were never off by a hair.

Ch'eng's wife placed her money on the table, lit incense, and kowtowed like those before. After the time it takes to eat a meal passed by, the curtain moved and a slip of paper was tossed out onto the ground. Picking it up, she saw not words but a drawing depicting a group of buildings, apparently those of a monastery. Behind it at the foot of a hill was a jumble of odd-looking boulders. There, at the edge of a dense bramble thicket, couched a shiny black cricket. Beside it was a toad that seemed to be on the point of leaping. She spread the drawing out and pored over it, unable to make out its meaning. Still, the cricket was just what she had been looking for. She folded the paper up, tucked it away, and took it back to show Ch'eng who, after much reflection, wondered if the picture were not telling him where to hunt for a cricket. Careful scrutiny of the scene in the drawing revealed a close resemblance to the Great Buddha Abbey east of the village.

Ch'eng dragged himself out of bed, propped himself up with a cane and proceeded, drawing in hand, to the rear of the monastery. The overgrown ruins of an ancient tomb stood before him. Following the edge of the tomb, he saw boulders squatting one on top of the other like fish scales, precisely as in the drawing. He walked slowly through a jungle of weeds, cocking his head to catch the slightest sound and looking for all the world as if he were searching for a needle or a mustard seed. He could no longer maintain the intentness of eyes, ears, and mind, but he had not yet seen or heard a cricket. He was still groping about, when suddenly to his great amazement a wart-headed toad leaped from underfoot. He stayed close behind it as it ducked into a dense growth of grass. He stepped gingerly into the grass, spreading the blades apart with his hands to get a better look. There, crouching at the base of a bramble-bush was an insect. He hurriedly grabbed for it, but it ducked into a hole in the stones. He poked at it with a sharp blade of grass, but it

would not come out. Finally, by pouring water from his bucket into the hole, he was able to flush the robust-looking cricket out. He gave chase and caught it. A closer look showed it to have a thick torso, a long tail, a blue-green neck, and metallic wings. Great was Ch'eng's joy as he put it in the cage and returned home.

The whole family rejoiced as if he had found a treasure more precious than the legendary piece of jade worth fifteen cities.[1] They put it in a basin and nourished it on crabmeat and chestnuts, going to every extreme to give it the best of care. They planned to keep it until the deadline, when Ch'eng would use it to discharge his official duty.

But one day Ch'eng's nine-year-old son, seeing that his father was out, furtively lifted the lid off the basin. The cricket hopped straight out, so quickly that the boy could not grab it. He jumped and caught it in his hand, breaking off a leg and cracking its abdomen. In a few short moments it was dead. The terrified boy ran crying to tell his mother. Her face paled to the hue of ashes at what she heard.

"A bad seed, that's what you are!" she cursed him loudly. "Your day of doom will not be long now! When your father comes home he'll settle accounts with you." The boy ran out sniveling. Ch'eng soon returned. When his wife told him what had happened, it was as if a heap of freezing snow had been dumped on his head. He called angrily for his son but the boy was nowhere to be seen. Soon afterward, they found his body in a well. Ch'eng's rage turned to sorrow. Stricken half-dead with grief, he struck his head on the ground and cried out to heaven. Husband and wife went inside and each turned their sobbing faces toward separate corners. No cooking fire was lit in their thatched hut that night. They had come to their wit's end and could only stare dumbly at one another. As the day drew to an end, they prepared to wrap their son in a grass mat for burial. Touching him, they found that he was now breathing haltingly. Joyfully they placed him on the bed. In the middle of the night he regained consciousness, which relieved his parents somewhat, but his breath came in gasps and he had the vacant look of a sleepwalker. Looking at the empty cricket cage was enough to rob them of breath and make their voices die in their throats, but they dared not question their son again. Their eyes did not close for the whole night. When the sun in the east began its course through the heavens they lay down stiffly, brooding sleeplessly.

Suddenly there was a chirping outside their door. They got up in amaze-

---

1. An allusion to Pien Ho of the state of Ch'u during the Spring and Autumn period, who presented two kings successively with jade enclosed in an uncut stone, and each time was accused of trying to pass off sham jade as genuine and punished by the loss of one of his feet. When the third king came to the throne, he summoned Pien, had the stone carved up, and found the jade inside. The jade was later claimed by a king to be worth the price of fifteen cities.

ment to observe; there was the cricket looking as sound as ever. Jumping for joy, they ran to catch it, but it gave a chirp and hopped rapidly away. Ch'eng covered it with a cupped hand, but he seemed to have grasped nothing but thin air. As soon as he lifted his hand, the cricket leaped swiftly out from under it. He followed it closely, but lost it when it rounded the corner of a wall. As he walked about distractedly, looking all around him, he saw a cricket crouching on the wall. A careful look showed that it was short, small, and reddish-black in color—certainly not the one he had been chasing. It was worthless to him because of its small size. He went on walking aimlessly and staring in all directions for the one he had been chasing. All of a sudden the little cricket jumped off the wall and landed on the side of his robe. It was built like a mole cricket, with finely veined wings, a square head, and long neck. It impressed him as a good specimen, so he was glad to keep it. His plan was to present it at the yamen, but the thought that it might not meet the magistrate's expectations made him shudder, so he decided to observe how it would perform in a fight.

A young man known as a busybody in the village was keeping a cricket which he had named Crabshell Blue. He matched it daily with the crickets of other young men, and it always emerged victorious. He was holding onto it until he could turn a nice profit, but nobody would pay the high price he asked. One day this young man went to Ch'eng's house for a visit. Seeing the cricket Ch'eng was keeping, he had to stifle a laugh with his hand. He took out his cricket and put it into the cage. Ch'eng was discomfited at the sight of its huge build. He dared not pick up the gauntlet, but the young man insisted. It occurred to Ch'eng that keeping an inferior specimen would be useless anyway, and that he might as well set his cricket against the other for a laugh. Both insects were placed in a fighting basin. The small one crouched motionless, looking as foolish as a wooden chicken.[2] The young man guffawed once more as he used a boar bristle to poke at the cricket's antennae. Still it did not move, provoking the young man into another burst of laughter. He prodded it repeatedly. The insect exploded with rage and ran at its opponent. They attacked one another with flying leaps, rousing themselves to battle with defiant chirps. In an instant the small cricket jumped up, its antennae and tail stiffly erect, and bit down on its opponent's neck. The frightened young man pulled them apart and put an end to the fight. The small cricket drew itself up and chirped proudly, as if it were reporting victory to its master.

Ch'eng was overjoyed. As he and his guests were admiring the winner, a chicken caught sight of it, ran over, and delivered a peck at the small cricket. Ch'eng stood there numb with dread and cried out in alarm. Luckily the chicken's beak had missed its mark; the cricket leaped a foot and some inches away. The chicken lunged forward and bore down upon it. Before Ch'eng

---

2. A fable in the *Chuang Tzu* (see selection 9) describes a superb gamecock as having such a placid exterior that it seemed to be made of wood.

could come to its rescue, the insect was under the chicken's claws; he turned pale and stamped his feet helplessly. But in the next moment he saw the chicken stretching its neck and fluttering about. Much to his amazed delight, upon closer inspection he found the cricket hanging tenaciously onto the fowl's comb. He picked it up, put it in its cage, and presented it to the magistrate the next day.

The magistrate berated Ch'eng angrily for bringing such a puny cricket, nor was he convinced by Ch'eng's account of the cricket's extraordinary prowess. The cricket was tried in the ring against others of its kind: all were vanquished. When it was tried against a chicken, the outcome confirmed Ch'eng's story.[3] The magistrate thereupon rewarded him and presented the cricket to the provincial governor. The governor, greatly delighted, presented it to the emperor in a golden cage along with a memorial detailing its abilities.

After the champion was taken into the palace, all sorts of unusual crickets, such as "butterflies," "mantises," "oily beaters," and "silky green foreheads" were tried against it, but none could get the better of it. When it heard the music of lutes and zithers it hopped to the beat, which made people marvel at it all the more. The emperor was so pleased that he called for the provincial governor and gave him thoroughbred horses and satins for clothing. The governor did not forget the source of his good fortune; before long word was going around that the magistrate was an "outstanding" official. The delighted magistrate released Ch'eng from his duties as headman and instructed the civil examiner to grant him admission to the district academy.

A little more than a year later Ch'eng's son regained his faculties, claiming that he had been transformed into an agile, combative cricket and that today his soul had finally reentered his body. The provincial governor rewarded Ch'eng generously. Within a few years Ch'eng possessed fifteen hundred acres of fields; pavilions and storied buildings in such number that thousands of rafters had been used to roof them over; and sheep and horses numbering in the hundreds. The furs he wore and the horses he rode when he went out could not have been equaled by an aristocratic family.

The Chronicler of the Tales comments: "The emperor may use something once on a whim and give it no more thought, but for the people who carry out his wishes it becomes a fixed article of tribute. With the greed of officials and the cruelty of administrators on top of this, there is no end to hardships which make peasants give up their wives and sell their children. Thus, every time the emperor takes a step, the lives of the people are affected. There is no room for carelessness. Ch'eng's case was unique: after being reduced to poverty by the depredations of corrupt officials, a cricket brought him wealth enough to go about flaunting furs and fine horses. Back in the days when he was beaten for failing to fulfill his duties as headman, how could he have foreseen

3. Cockfighting was a popular betting sport in China from a very early period (see selection 25, second poem).

that such a fortune was in store for him? Heaven made the provincial governor and magistrate enjoy the benefits of the cricket's favor as a means of rewarding one man's honesty. When the Taoist master in the old story perfected the elixir and rose to heaven, immortality redounded even to his dogs and chickens. There is much truth in this!"

Translated by Denis C. Mair and Victor H. Mair

Rouge

Old Pien of Tung-ch'ang,[1] a veterinarian by profession, had an intelligent, beautiful daughter whose childhood name was Rouge. Her father intended to find a mate from an esteemed family for his beloved, precious girl, but noblemen were too proud to connect themselves with him, for they despised his low rank and lack of means. Thus the girl reached hairpin age without being spoken for.

The wife of the Kung family across the street, née Wang, was a capricious, madcap sort who often spent time conversing in the girl's chamber. One day, while seeing her friend to the door, the girl caught sight of a passing young man, commandingly handsome in his white gown and hat. She must have found him distracting, judging from the way the rippling glances of her eyes lingered after him. The young man lowered his head and hastened away. The girl's gaze remained fixed on him as he dwindled in the distance. Wang saw what was on her mind and poked fun at her: "With ability and looks like yours, young lady, I am sure there would be no regrets if you could be matched with such a man." A tinge of red spread over the girl's cheeks. She said nothing, but her pulse quickened.

"Do you know that gentleman?" asked Wang.

"No, I don't," she answered.

"That's Bachelor of Letters Ĕ Autumn-Falcon from South Lane, son of the late Exemplar. I used to live in his neighborhood, so I know him. No man in this world is as kind and gentle as he is. He's in plain dress now because the mourning period for his wife is not yet over. If you are willing I will carry a message telling him to send a matchmaker."

The girl did not speak. Wang went away laughing. Several days passed with no news. She surmised that Wang had not yet found time to pay a visit, and she also doubted if the son of an official would care to stoop and pick up what was left in his way. She whiled way her time despondently, suffering from thoughts that would not go away, till melancholy deprived her of appetite and rest. It was then that Wang came to see her and demanded to know the reason for her illness.

"I don't know myself," was her answer. "But since the last day you saw me,

---

1. A district in Shantung province.

I've been restless and depressed. I'm living from breath to breath. It will be all over any day now."

Wang lowered her voice: "My husband hasn't gotten back from his selling trip yet: there is nobody to get the word to young Ĕ. Is that what is making you ill?"

The girl's face was crimson for a good while. Wang joked: "So that's what it's about. Now that you are in this condition, why bother about scruples? Have him come spend a night with you first. You don't think he'll turn you down, do you?"

"Things have gotten to the point that I can't play coy," said the girl. "If only he could see far enough past my poverty and low rank to send a matchmaker over, my illness would be cured. But if it takes having a rendezvous with him, I simply won't do it!"

Wang nodded and left. In her younger days she had been involved with a young man named Su Chieh who lived next door. Now that she was married, Su continued relations with her, watching for times when her husband was elsewhere. Su happened to come this same night, so Wang amused him by repeating what the girl had said, and jokingly instructed him to relay the message to young Ĕ. Su, who had known of the girl's beauty long before, was glad to hear this, because of the opportunity it left open to him. He thought of discussing his plans with Wang but then reconsidered, fearing her jealousy. And so he plied her with seemingly disinterested questions to learn exactly where the girl's chamber was in the house.

The next night he climbed in over the wall, went right to the girl's room, and tapped on a window with his finger.

"Who is it?" came a voice from inside.

"It's Ĕ," he replied.

"I want you for a lifetime, not for a single night. If you really love me, the only right thing to do is send a matchmaker soon. If you're talking about a secret affair I am afraid I can't satisfy your wishes."

Su pretended to agree and beseeched her to let him hold her delicate wrist as a pledge of trust. The girl felt too sorry for him to overdo her refusal, and so used all her strength to push the door open. Su darted in, embraced her, and begged for joy. Lacking the strength to resist him, she fell to the ground, her breath coming in unconnected gasps. Su pulled her arm impatiently.

"What corner did you crawl out of, you scum? You couldn't be Master Ĕ. If you were Ĕ and knew the cause of my illness, you would be kind and considerate like him and feel pity for me, instead of acting like a brute. If you keep behaving this way I'll be forced to scream. It won't do either of us any good to have our good names ruined!"

Fearing that his deception would be uncovered, Su dared not force himself on her any further, so he only asked to meet her again. The girl set the bride-welcoming as the time for their next meeting. Su thought that was too long to wait and asked again. The girl, fed up with his clinging, asked him to wait for her recovery. Su begged her to give him a token of remembrance, but she would not, and so he grabbed her by the leg, pulled off her embroidered slipper, and left.

The girl called him back, saying: "I've already promised myself to you: why should I grudge you anything? My only fear is that 'the tiger might be painted to look like a god.' We could become the objects of vile slander because of this. Now you are holding part of my intimate wardrobe in your hand. I see no hope of getting it back. If you betray me, death is my only way out."

After Su left he went to stay the night at Wang's place. He lay down in bed, but he could not stop thinking of the slipper. He furtively fumbled in his robe and was shocked to find that it was not there. He jumped up, turned the lampshade, then shook his clothes and felt around on the floor. He turned to ask Wang, who wouldn't answer his questions, so he began to wonder if she had hidden it. She laughed deliberately to heighten his suspicions. Su could not keep it to himself any longer; he told her the truth. When his story was finished he went over every inch of ground outside the gate, candle in hand, but still it did not turn up. He went back to bed greatly annoyed, cheering himself with the thought that nobody was out this late at night and if he had dropped the slipper it would still be in the street. He got up early in the morning and searched for it, but it was still nowhere to be found.

Now there lived on the same street a shiftless vagrant named Mao the Elder, who had once made futile advances to Wang. Knowing that Su was having an affair with her, he had the notion to catch them in a compromising situation so that he could make demands. Walking by her gate this same night, he found it unlocked and slipped inside. Just outside the window he stepped on something soft and cottony. He picked it up to look: it was a woman's slipper wrapped in a handkerchief. Eavesdropping at the window, he heard Su give a complete account of his evening. Mao congratulated himself on his good luck as he crept away.

Several evenings later he climbed the wall and entered the girl's house. Being unfamiliar with the layout, he blundered into the old man's quarters. The old man looked out the window and saw a man who, judging from the sounds and movements he made, had evidently come for his daughter. Rage swelled in the old man's heart as he rushed out, knife in hand. Mao turned in great fright and ran. He was about to climb the wall, but old Pien was close behind. In desperation at having nowhere to run, he turned around and wrenched the blade away. Behind them the old woman let out a loud scream. Unable to free himself from the old man's grip, Mao put an end to him. The girl, who by this time had recovered somewhat from her illness, was roused up by the noise. Everyone went to the scene with candles; the old man's skull was split and he had lost the power of speech. In a short while he was no longer of this world. An embroidered slipper was found beneath the wall, and the old woman could see that it belonged to Rouge. When force was applied the girl sobbed out the truth. Not being hardhearted enough to implicate Wang, she claimed that young Ě had come on his own.

At daybreak charges were brought before the district court. The magistrate had Ě taken into custody. Ě was a quiet, reserved person, nineteen years of age, who got flustered like a child in the presence of strangers. Being arrested frightened him out of his wits. He lacked the presence of mind to defend himself in the courtroom. All he did was tremble, which gave the magistrate all the more reason to accept the truth of the accusations. He put the finger-vise and cane to brutal use: the pain was more than a bookishly inclined person could stand, and in this way a confession was wrung out of Ě. Afterward he was transported to the prefectural court, where he received as many floggings as he had in the district.

Young Ě was consumed with outrage. Over and over he wished for the chance to confront Rouge and demand the truth, but when they did meet she vilified him with such fury he was tongue-tied and could not state his own case, with the result that he was sentenced to death. None of the numerous officials he was sent back and forth to for further hearings opposed the sentence.

Finally the case was referred to Tsinan[2] prefecture for a confirmatory decision. At that time Master Wu Nan-tai was the prefect of Tsinan. One look at young Ě was enough to make him doubt that this man was a murderer. Wu secretly sent a person to question him informally and considerately so that he could say his piece. The result convinced Wu that Ě had been unjustly accused. He spent a few days before the hearing devising a strategy.

First he asked Rouge: "Was anyone aware that you had agreed to a meeting?"

"No one," was the answer.

"Was anyone else present when you first saw young Ě?"

"No one."

Wu then called Ě to the stand and reassured him in kind tones. The scholar testified without being asked: "Once, when I was walking past her gate, I noticed my former neighbor Wang coming out of the doorway with this young woman. I quickened my steps right away to get past them. Since then I have not spoken so much as a word to her."

Master Wu roared at the girl: "You just said that nobody was with you. What was the neighbor woman doing there?" He ordered his men to prepare the instruments of interrogation.

"Wang was there," said the girl in fright. "But she really had nothing to do with him."

Master Wu adjourned the hearing and gave an order to arrest Wang. She

2. Now provincial capital of Shantung.

was brought in a few days later and forbidden any communication with the girl. Wu resumed the hearing immediately.

"Who is the killer?" he asked Wang.

"I don't know."

Then Master Wu laid a trap for her, saying: "Rouge has testified that you were familiar with the man who killed old Pien. Are you trying to conceal that fact?"

"It's a lie," wailed the woman. "The cheap chambermaid got all worked up over this man. I may have said something about acting as matchmaker, but I was only joking with her. How was I to know that she would lure a lover onto her property?"

Master Wu had to question her in detail before she would repeat what she had said jokingly on that and later occasions. He called Rouge to the stand and thundered: "You claimed she did not know a thing. Now she testifies that she was going to have you two introduced. Why is that?"

"My foolishness caused my father's cruel death," the girl wailed tearfully. "Who knows how many years it will take before this case is concluded? On top of that, I have involved other people. I just can't bear it."

Master Wu asked Wang: "After you had made those jokes, did you tell anyone about them?"

"I did not," Wang testified.

"There is nothing that a husband and wife don't talk about in bed," thundered Master Wu. "How can you say that you didn't?"

"My husband was away on a long trip," Wang testified.

"That may well be, but playing a joke on someone is invariably a matter of mocking another's dullness in order to show off one's own intelligence. Who do you think you can fool by claiming that you didn't tell anyone?" He ordered the use of finger-vises on all ten fingers.

The woman had no choice. "I told Su about it," she admitted.

Then Master Wu released Ě and had Su arrested. When Su was brought into court he testified: "I don't know."

"Anyone who sues for the favor of a whore is not a proper gentleman!"

A severe beating was all it took to make Su admit. "It's true that I tricked the girl, but after I lost the slipper I didn't dare go back. I swear that I know nothing of the murder."

"A man who would climb over a wall is capable of anything!" Again Master Wu had Su beaten. Unable to stand up to the torture, Su finally accepted the blame.

The confession was written up and reported to Wu's superiors. There was not one who did not praise Master Wu's perspicuity. It was an irrevocable case—as settled as a mountain—so there was nothing left for Su but to crane his neck and watch as the day of execution drew near. Still, even though Su was reckless and ill-behaved, he was a widely known intellectual in the eastern region.[3] He had heard of the civil examiner Master Shih Yü-shan's superior ability as well as his fondness and solicitude for scholars of talent, so he complained of the wrong done to him in a touching and sorrowful petition. Master Shih reviewed his confession, poring over it again and again, and struck his desk, saying: "This young man has been wronged!"

Then Master Shih applied to the administrative and judicial authorities of the province for permission to hold another hearing.

He asked Su: "Where did you lose the shoe?"

"I don't remember," answered Su. "But it was still in my sleeve when I knocked on Wang's gate."

Shih then proceeded to question Wang: "How many lovers do you have besides Su Chieh?"

"I have none."

"Why should a promiscuous woman restrict herself to one man?" asked Master Shih.

"I was involved with Su Chieh since childhood," she testified. "That is why I could not break it off. It wasn't that no one made advances to me after that, but I really didn't care to accept them."

Shih told her to name such a man in order to substantiate her claim.

"Mao the Elder of my neighborhood made repeated advances; I refused him every time," she testified.

"How is it that you've become so chaste and pure all of a sudden?" asked Master Shih. He ordered his men to beat her. The woman bumped her forehead on the floor until blood ran to protest her innocence, so he let her go. Then he resumed his questioning: "When your husband was far away, weren't there men who came claiming to have business with him?"

"There were. I let So-and-so A and So-and-so B into my house a few times to borrow money or leave gifts."

Actually A and B were idlers living in the same alley who had designs on Wang without being able to realize them. Master Shih had their names entered in the record and ordered them into court. When they were rounded up, Master Shih had them taken to the temple of the city god [along with Mao the Elder], where they were [all] made to kneel before the altar. Then he told them: "A short while ago a spirit came to me in a dream and told me that one of you is the murderer. There can be no lying now that you are before the all-knowing god. If you give yourself up, there is still the possibility of forgiveness. If you speak falsely, there will be no pardon once the truth is out."

All of them claimed with one voice that they had not committed murder. The judge had wooden cangues, manacles, and fetters laid out on the ground and was about to have them put on the suspects. Their hair was to be knotted atop their heads and they were to be stripped naked. All howled at the injustice

3. Shantung.

of this harsh treatment. The judge ordered them untied and said, "Since you won't confess, I will have ghosts and spirits point out the murderer."

He had his men screen off all the windows in the main hall with blankets of felt, making sure that there was not the slightest crack of light. Then he had the suspects' shirts pulled down to expose their backs and drove them into the dark, where they were given a basin of water to wash their hands. That done, he had them tied near the wall and warned them: "Keep your face toward the wall and do not move. The god will write a sign on the back of whichever one of you is the murderer."

Before long he called them out for inspection, then pointed at Mao, saying: "This is the murderer!"

Actually the judge had told his men to smear ashes on the wall beforehand and put soot into the water in which they washed their hands. The murderer, afraid that the god would come to write on him, got ashes on his back by pressing it against the wall. On the way out he tried to protect his back with his hands, thus smearing it with soot. Master Shih's previous suspicions of Mao the Elder were confirmed. With the application of ruthless torture, Mao spat out the whole truth.

Master Shih's verdict was as follows:

Regarding Su Chieh: This man flirted with death like P'en-ch'eng K'uo, and he nearly rivals Teng T'u-tzu for lechery. On the strength of a childish infatuation, he made a wild duck out of a household fowl. When the uttering of a few ill-placed words moved the conqueror of Lung to hanker after Shu, he climbed unwanted over a garden wall and swooped down like a falcon. Fancying himself an irresistible magnet to fairy maidens, he proceeded to the mouth of Rouge's grotto and finally wheedled her door open. By disturbing a lady's girdle sash, he aroused a shaggy dog. Even a rat has skin on its face, but this man had no idea of shame. He clambered after flowers, snapping off branches on the way. A man of such low conduct does not deserve the name of scholar. It was a saving grace that he heeded the feeble sparrow's cries; he had the heart to spare this piece of unblemished jade. Out of pity for her willowy frailness, he did not go wild like a March-mad oriole, but released the fledgling phoenix from his grasp, as any man of learning should. Regrettably, he wrested a fragrant token from beneath her petticoat, proving how truly worthless he was! That same night a different butterfly flitted over his lover's wall. A pair of ears lurked outside the bedroom window. The petal torn from the lotus was dropped on the ground and lost, and so it was that falsehood sprang up within falsehood. Who could imagine that a second injustice would lie beyond the first! Heaven sent calamity down upon our Su Chieh—a vicious beating to the edge of death. His own wrongdoing caught up with him, and his head and body nearly ended up in different places. Climbing walls and tunneling through cracks is a strain on a scholar's cap, but when a peach-boring insect tries to infect a plum tree, the fumes of injustice are not easily blown clean. Thus it is proper to show some leniency: we will spare Su Chieh the rod, to make up for the cruel pain he has already suffered, and open for him the road to self-renewal by demoting him to black robes.[4]

Now as for Mao the Elder, that idle, weaselly ruffian of the marketplace: Though he met with a refusal from his neighbor girl as curt as a shuttle thrown in his face, his lustful intentions would still not die. He bided his time until a flippant young man slipped into the alley, and then a bright idea occurred to his devious mind. Later, outside an open sliding door, another wind blew his way, and he imagined himself going to meet his beloved. He was looking for home-brew, and caught the scent of fine wine. His delusions were like the heady fumes of an aphrodisiac perfume. How was he to know that his strength would be sapped by heaven, and his spirit would be carried off by ghosts? He got his log raft and rode the silvery waters straight toward the Moon Palace. He floated along in his fisherman's boat, thinking he knew the way to Peach-blossom Spring. In the end his passionate flames were doused by a tidal wave in the sea of desire. With an unlooked-for knife coming straight at him, he lashed out, as robbers often do when backed against a wall. Even a cornered rabbit will use its teeth in desperation. He landed in this fix because he thought jumping the wall into someone else's courtyard would be as easy as "Mr. Li wearing Mr. Chang's hat." Because he dropped the slipper while wrenching away the weapon, the fish swam through the net while a goose was caught. It hardly seems possible that an event so demonic should arise on the path of romance. How could a banshee like this exist in the land of warmth and softness? Mao the Elder's head shall be severed from his neck for the gratification of all.

Now as for Rouge: This girl has not yet been spoken for, though she is already of hairpin age. A fairy maiden straight from the Moon Palace should naturally have a bridegroom like jade. A member of the Rainbow Skirt Dancers can rest assured that a golden house awaits her. Now the mating cry of the osprey arouses her longing for a perfect mate; the time has come for Mistress Spring to wrap her up in dreams. Thinking of a likely gentleman, she resents the falling plum-blossoms, and her soul goes out of her body in search of love. However beautiful other women may be, they cannot be compared to Rouge. No matter how fierce the other taloned birds may be, they all take wing at the sight of Autumn-Falcon.

A single entangling thread caused a horde of demons to converge upon this lovely girl. Once the lotus slipper was plucked away, the petal's fragrance was hard to keep. Intruders at the iron threshold nearly smashed a precious gem.

Just as the red dots inlaid in dice are etched by tears of disappointment, a love that is felt to the bone can be a gateway to disaster. An upright tree

4. Black robes were worn by licentiates of the lowest rank.

succumbed to the ax, and a sweet young thing became a "swamp of perdition." But she guarded her dignity, and luckily her white jade remains unflawed. She writhed in his grasp, glad for the brocade quilt that covered her. She is admirable for refusing an intruder who was already in her room. By remaining pure and clean, she has proven herself to be a person of character. Fulfilling her wish to throw her bouquet would be an elegant closing chapter to this romance. I trust the district magistrate will play the part of matchmaker.

After the case was settled, this verdict was spread and recited far and wide.

The girl did not know that she had wrongfully blamed Young Ĕ until after Master Wu's hearing. When they met outside the hall, she sniffled guiltily, as if she had words of remorse in mind but could not yet speak out. The young man, touched by her regard, began to feel strongly toward her. But the thought of her humble origins, along with her daily appearances in court where a thousand people had pointed and leered at her, made him fear he would be ridiculed for marrying her. He brooded night and day, but could not make up his mind. The words of the verdict when it was finally delivered put him at his ease. The district magistrate had the betrothal gifts sent to the girl's house on his behalf and furnished music for the wedding procession.

The Chronicler of the Tales comments: "How great the need for caution is in hearing legal cases! Even if one could know that the plum tree was damaged wrongfully, who would think that the peach as well was decimated by mistake? Still, even the most obscure matter must have openings that let light through. Without careful thought and shrewd observation these cannot be traced. What a regret it is that people admire the wise man's brilliant resolution of a court case, while they fail to recognize the painstaking efforts of a master mind. In this world people who hold positions of authority fritter away whole days playing chess and cancel their morning audiences so as to stay beneath silken covers, never bothering their heads about the sentiments or hardships of the people. When the drums sound the opening of magisterial sessions, they sit high and mighty on the bench, silencing those who cry out for justice by slapping them into irons. Small wonder that so many injustices are hidden from the light of day!"

Translated by Denis C. Mair and Victor H. Mair

248

A Chi Yün Sampler
Sketches from the Cottage for the Contemplation of Subtleties

Chi Yün (1724–1805)

Preface to A Record of Whiling away the Summer at Luan-yang

In the summer of 1789, I went to Luan-yang[1] for the purpose of putting in order the imperial library[2] there. At the time, the editing had long since been completed, and it remained only to supervise the officials who were writing

These prefaces and stories are taken from a large collection of approximately twelve hundred stories, tales, anecdotes, and notes brought together by Chi Yün at the end of the eighteenth century. Its author was one of the three chief editors of the famous Ch'ing imperial library known as the "Complete Library in Four Branches [classics, histories, thinkers, and collected works] of Literature." The catalog of this library, for which Chi Yün was largely responsible, is still recognized as the most complete and important bibliographical work on traditional Chinese literature.

The Sketches (Yüeh-wei ts'ao-t'ang pi-chi) originally appeared between 1789 and 1798 in a series of five parts (hence the five prefaces) which were assembled in their present form by one of Chi's students, Sheng Shih-yen, in 1800. The titles of the five parts convey the deceptively casual manner in which the sketches were composed, yet behind the facade of entertaining stories and anecdotes lies a serious moral purpose.

The sketches are brief, seldom running to more than a page of Chinese text. The subject usually has ostensibly to do with the supernatural, but a hint of satire is almost always present. Virtually without exception, the supernatural forces in these tales adopt a favorable attitude toward virtuous people, genuine scholars, filial sons, and exemplary officials. On the other hand, these supernatural forces take a negative attitude toward immoral individuals, pedants, disrespectful youth, and evil officials. In effect, the supernatural agents ironically represent normative social values. It should be emphasized that this is accomplished without heavy-handed didacticism, a fatal error to which Chi's many imitators succumbed. These sketches conspicuously bear the mark of rich creativity and make for delightful reading. Such a relatively large sampling of Chi Yün's work is given here because it is virtually unknown outside of China except by a few specialists. Even within China, Sketches is inadequately known, perhaps because it has long been overshadowed by the brilliantly allusive Strange Tales from Make-Do Studio by P'u Sung-ling (see selection 247) and the acerbically witty What the Master [Confucius] Would Not Discuss (Tzu pu yü) by Yüan Mei (see selection 106).

1. Ch'eng-te district in Hopei.

2. This refers to the "Complete Library in Four Divisions" (Ssu-k'u ch'üan-shu) completed in 1782. The original was installed in the "Pavilion of the Pool of Literature" (Wen-yüan ko). Six copies were distributed to various parts of the empire, one of these being placed in the "Pavilion of the Ford to Literature" (Wen-chin ko) at Luan-yang where the Ch'ing court maintained a summer retreat. The magnitude of the task of setting up these copies can be appreciated from the fact that the "Complete Library in Four Divisions" was composed of nearly eighty thousand fascicles.

title slips and placing the books on the shelves. The days being long and uneventful, I would record things that I had seen and heard in the past. Since I wrote them down as they came to mind, there is neither form nor arrangement to these materials. They are but "small talk" and "anecdotes collected by 'tare-gathering officials.' "[3] I realize that they have nothing to do with "genuine composition." But even "street gossip and alley discussions" may be of benefit in exhorting people to goodness and dissuading them from evil. For the time being, I have handed these materials over to a scribe for safekeeping and have entitled them "Whiling away the Summer at Luan-yang." Et cetera.

Preface to *That's the Way I Heard It*[4]

Some time ago, I wrote *Whiling away the Summer at Luan-yang*. Though still an unfinished, rough draft, it was hurriedly and clandestinely printed by a book-shop. This was not in accord with my wishes. And yet, there are some gentlemen of learning and refinement who do not consider this a blunder and, indeed, who have continued to inform me of new items of interest. Therefore, supplementing them with some tales that I had heard before, once again, I have completed four scrolls.

Ou-yang Hsiu said: "Things often accumulate where they are liked."[5] How very true this is! Accordingly, I realize that, once we become partial to something, we necessarily become so absorbed in it that we cannot stop on our own. That affairs under heaven are invariably like this is worth pondering deep and long.

Inscribed on the twenty-first day of the seventh month in the year 1791.

---

3. This expression was used in the "Treatise on Bibliography" in the *History of the Han* to designate those officials who were dispatched throughout the empire to gather stories common among the people that would presumably reveal their sentiments to the central government.

For the editor of the "Complete Library" and the author of the *Résumé* of its catalog to make such a statement is a severe condemnation of the literary worth of his own sketches. Chi Yün must have been fully aware of the pejorative connotations of "small talk" and "anecdotes collected by tare-gathering (i.e., petty) officials." Indeed, it was probably he himself who wrote in the catalog of the imperial library in the section dealing with these types of writings: "For the present, we have selectively recorded those which are somewhat refined in order to broaden our knowledge. But we have excluded those which are unpolished and absurd and would serve only to confound the senses."

4. *Ju shih wo wen*, a standard Chinese translation of the Sanskrit *evaṃ mayā śrutam* ("Thus have I heard [from the Buddha]").

5. From the preface to the *Record of Collecting Antiquities* (*Chi ku lu*). For a brief note on Ou-yang Hsiu, see selection 206.

Preface to *Miscellany from the Old House West of the Scholar Tree*

When I was again put in charge of the Censorate,[6] because I often had to meet jointly with the other High Courts[7] to judge criminal cases, I spent many days at West Park.[8] There I borrowed several rooms from my son-in-law, Yüan Hsü.[9] Above them, a wooden tablet read "Old House West of the Scholar Tree."[10] Whenever I was at leisure from my official duties, I would rest there. As it was several tens of tricents distant from the city, there were very few visitors except for my subordinates who would come to make reports. The days were long and I had much free time. All was peace and quiet.

Previously, my two books, *Whiling away the Summer at Luan-yang* and *That's the Way I Heard It*, were published by a book-shop. Consequently, when my friends would gather together, they would often tell me extraordinary tales. So I put a notebook there and, when it was my turn to be on duty, I would write them out just as they came to mind. When it was not a day for me to be there on duty, I would not write anything and, likewise, when I could not recall a tale in its entirety. The months and years passed quickly and, before I knew it, once again I had finished four fascicles. My grandson, Shu-hsin, has recorded them as a single book, the title of which is *Miscellany from the Old House West of the Scholar Tree*. Its form and arrangement are the same as those of the earlier two books.

Perhaps in the future I shall grow tired of this and put down my brush. If so, this collection may be compared to the third and last part of Wang Ming-ch'ing's *Records of Conversations Prompted by Waving a Whisk*.[11] But perhaps I won't be able to remain inactive in my old age and will have something more to add. If so, this collection may also be compared to the third part in the continuing series of Hung Mai's *Record of the Listener*.[12]

Recorded in the sixth month of the year 1792 by the Man of the Way Who Kibitzes at Go.[13]

---

6. The expression used in the original is "Raven Terrace," a fancy designation for the President of the Censorate.

7. The Board of Punishment, the Censorate, and the Court of Judicature and Revision met together as a kind of Supreme Criminal Court to supervise the administration of criminal law.

8. An imperial garden in Peking located on the western side of the Forbidden City.

9. Son of the Governor-General of Chihli, Yüan Shou-t'ung.

10. During the T'ang dynasty, *huai* (*Sophora japonica*) trees were planted on the grounds of the Censorate. Thus "west of the scholar tree" means "west of the Censorate."

11. Wang Ming-ch'ing (b. 1127) actually issued an additional fourth part of his *Records* (*Hui chu lu*).

12. *Yi-chien chih.* Hung Mai's dates are 1123–1202 (see selection 245).

13. *Kuan-yi tao-jen,* Chi Yün's sobriquet.

Preface to *Listen if You Will*

By nature, I like being alone, but I cannot stay idle. From my boyhood up to today, scroll, brush, and inkstone have never been out of my hands for more than several tens of days. Before I was thirty, I studied textual criticism. Like an otter sacrificing fish,[14] I would encircle the place where I sat with reference books. After I was thirty, I vied with all under heaven in literature. I would "isolate the word 'yellow' and pair it with 'white'."[15] Invariably, I would stay up the whole night racking my brains. After I was fifty, because I was commanded to edit the palace library, once more I applied myself to textual criticism. Now I am old. No more do I feel the enthusiasm of the years gone by. Just to while away the months and years, from time to time I simply take paper and ink to record tales that I had heard in the past. Thus I completed the three books, *Whiling away the Summer at Luan-yang*, etc., as well as the present collection.

I think back to ancient authors, such as Wang Ch'ung[16] and Ying Shao,[17] who demonstrated their erudition and profound knowledge by citing the classics and referring to antiquity. T'ao Yüan-ming,[18] Liu Ching-shu,[19] and Liu Yi-ch'ing[20] wrote simply and sparely, yet naturally achieved a wondrous depth. Truly, I dare not recklessly imitate my illustrious predecessors, but my main purpose is a desire not to go against their precepts. If one harbors his own likes and dislikes, he thereby subverts right and wrong as did Wei T'ai[21] and Ch'en Shan.[22] I am confident that I have not done so.

It happens that my pupil, Sheng Shih-yen, wishes to have blocks engraved for printing this collection of tales. So I have hastily written these few lines to serve as a foreword. Because most of the materials herein were learned by hearsay, using Chuang Tzu's expression, I have entitled this book *Listen If You Will*.

Inscribed on the twenty-fifth day of the seventh month of the year 1793 by the Man of the Way Who Kibitzes at Go.

14. An old simile for a scholar with his books spread out in front of him.

15. This expression, which indicates the painstaking care employed in writing parallel prose (see selections 195-6), is from Liu Tsung-yüan's (see selection 55) essay on the testing of feminine skills on the seventh day of the seventh month (the festival of the Weaver Girl and the Herd-boy).

16. Author of *Balanced Discussions* (see selection 11).

17. Author of *A General Interpretation of Social Customs* (*Feng-su t'ung-yi*). Ying Shao flourished around 178 C.E.

18. T'ao Ch'ien (see selection 29), poet and author of *Sequel to Search for the Supernatural* (*Sou-shen hou chi*; compare with selection 243).

19. Compiler of *Florilegium of Extraordinary Events* (*Yi-yüan*). He died c. 468 C.E.

20. Compiler of *A New Account of Tales of the World* (see selection 241).

21. Author of *Recorded Notes from the Eastern Studio* (*Tung hsüan pi-lu*). He flourished around 1082 C.E.

22. Author of *New Stories Told While Catching Cooties* (*Men shih hsin hua*). He flourished around 1147 C.E.

Preface to A *Sequel to the Record of Whiling away the Summer at Luan-yang*

In the sunset of life, my spirit daily declines. No more do I have any ambition to write seriously.[23] But once in a while I do make some miscellaneous notes just to pass the time away. The four books, *Record of Whiling away the Summer at Luan-yang*, etc., were so much toying with my brush to beguile the days. In recent years, even this has become wearisome. Occasionally, when I hear of some extraordinary happening, I will jot it down on a piece of paper. Or if I suddenly recall something from the past, I will attempt to supplement my previous works. Then again, none of it is very tidy, being rather more like clouds or smoke drifting before the eyes, so that for a long time I have not completed a book.

In the fifth month of this year, I was a member of the imperial retinue that went to Luan-yang. In my spare time when I was off duty, the days were long and I had much leisure, so I pieced together these materials to make a book which I have entitled *Sequel to the Record of Whiling away the Summer at Luan-yang*. Having finished a fair copy of the book, I have inscribed these few words to explain how it came into being. As for what I hope to bequeath to posterity through these writings, the prefaces to the four previous books discuss it in sufficient detail that I need not repeat myself here.

Written on the third day after the festival of the reunion of the Herd-boy and the Weaver Girl (seventh day of the seventh month) in the year 1798 by the Man of the Way Who Kibitzes at Go in his seventy-fifth year at his lodgings while on duty in the Ministry of Rites.

I

The following was told to me by Wu Hui-shu, a member of the Royal Academy.

There was a certain doctor whose nature it was to be earnest. One night, an old lady brought him a pair of gold bracelets with which she wished to buy an abortifacient. The doctor was appalled by the request and so steadfastly refused it. The next evening, she came again bringing an additional two pearl hairpins. The doctor was all the more appalled and so forcibly sent her away.

More than half a year later, he suddenly dreamed that he was arrested by an officer from the nether world. The officer stated that someone had accused him of killing a person. When they arrived in the nether world, a young woman with disheveled hair and a red strip of cloth bound about her neck tearfully made her plaint of being denied medicine that she had sought.

"Medicine," said the doctor, "is for the preservation of human life. How could I have dared to kill a person for personal gain? You ruined yourself through adultery. How am I at fault?"

23. The original text only says "to write" (*chu-shu*), but it is clear from the context and from Chi Yün's accustomed usage elsewhere that this expression refers specifically to proper writing.

"When I begged you for the medicine," said the woman, "the fetus had not yet developed. If I had been able to abort it, I would not have died. It was a matter of breaking up an unconscious clot of blood to preserve a life that was on the verge of extinction. Since I could not obtain the medicine, there was no way I could avoid childbirth. In the end, the fate of the baby was to suffer horribly by being strangled. And I was so beset that all I could do was hang myself. In wishing to preserve one life, you ended up destroying two lives! If the responsibility for this crime does not fall upon you, then upon whom does it fall?"

"What you have stated is a consideration of the particular circumstances of this case," the judge of the nether world declared with a deep sigh. "What he, the doctor, insists upon is the principle of the matter. Since the Sung dynasty, there has been a stubborn insistence upon a single principle without estimating the advantages and disadvantages of actual situations. It's not just this man alone! Case dismissed!"

The judge banged the table and the doctor awoke with a start.

II

The following was told to me by Wang Hsiao-yüan, a member of the Royal Academy.

There was an old monk whose tears began to fall freely as he was passing by a butchery. A bystander who was surprised by this asked him why he did so.

"It's a long story," replied the monk. "I can remember events from two other lives. In my first life, I was a butcher and I died when I was a little over thirty. My celestial soul was trussed up and pulled away by several persons. The judge in the nether world rebuked me for the enormity of my murderous karma and had me sent away in custody to the universal spiritual king[24] to receive retribution for my evil. My senses were blurred and confused, as though I were drunk or dreaming. And my brain was so hot that I could not endure it. Suddenly, it seemed to be cool and I found myself in a pigpen.

"After I had been weaned, I noticed that humans were unclean and realized that the food they were giving me was contaminated.[25] But my hunger pains were excruciating and my inwards felt as though they were being torn in shreds. There was nothing I could do but eat what they gave me.

"Later, I gradually learned pig language and often asked questions of my fellow creatures, many of whom could remember events from former incarnations. But we were quite incapable of talking to human beings. For the most

24. *Chuan-lun* (Shanskrit *cakravartī*). I suspect that this is an error for *lun-chuan* (Sanskrit *saṃsāra*), "transmigration," hence "to undergo transmigratory retribution for my evils."

25. *Hui* is an adjective which refers to the impurity of the world in contrast to the Pure Land of Mahāyāna Buddhism. It also refers to leftover food or food with has been touched by someone with an illness.

part, we were aware that we would be slaughtered. At such times, we would grunt and groan with worry. Feeling sorry for ourselves, we would constantly have traces of tears on our eyelashes.

"The body of a pig is stiff and heavy so that, at the peak of summer, we suffered from the heat. Only by wallowing in the muddy water could we obtain a measure of relief, but we seldom got the chance to do that. A pig's bristles are sparse and stubby so that, in the dead of winter, we suffered from the cold. Compared to ours, the fur of dogs and sheep is as soft and thick as that of a mythical beast.

"When the time came for me to be seized, I knew that I couldn't escape. Nevertheless, I hopped about and ran away, hoping that I could delay for a while. After my pursuers caught up with me, they trampled upon my neck and head; they tore at my shanks and pettitoes. They tied up my legs with a rope which cut deeply into my bones. It was as painful as if I were being sliced with a knife.

"Sometimes we were transported by boat or cart and then, layer after layer, we'd press upon each other. My ribs were nearly broken; my veins and arteries surged and choked; my belly nearly burst. Sometimes they carried me by sticking a pole between my legs, which was even more painful than being shackled and fettered. When I arrived at the butchery, I was thrown upon the ground, which shook my heart and spleen so that they almost shattered. I might have died that very day or remained tied up for several days.

"What was even harder to endure was to see the cleaver and chopping board to the left, the pot full of water for scalding to the right—without knowing what pain they would cause when they touched my body. Whereupon I would be seized with paroxysms of uncontrollable fear. Then, again, I often looked at my own body and wondered into how many unknowable pieces I would one day be sundered and in whose cup I would serve for a soup. I was so despondent that I nearly expired.

"When the time came for me to be slaughtered, my eyes went dim with fright as soon as the butcher tugged at me and all of my legs went limp. It felt as though my heart were surging wildly to left and right and that my soul flew right up out of my head and then fell back down. When I saw the gleaming light of the blade, I dared not look at it directly but only closed my eyes and waited for the cutting and cleaving. The butcher began by stabbing his knife-blade into my throat and then shook and twisted it, allowing my blood to drain into a basin. The pain was such that words cannot describe it. I hoped for death but it would not come, so all I could do was utter a long squeal. After the blood was emptied, the butcher pierced my heart which caused me to suffer so greatly that I could no longer make any sound.

"Gradually, my senses blurred and I became confused as though drunk or in a dream. It was as though I were in the early stages of transmigration. A considerable time passed before I awoke sufficiently to see that I had taken on human form. The judge in the nether world allowed me to be a man again since I still had some good karma from previous lives.

"That is why in the present life, when I just now saw this pig, I lamented its suffering. So I thought of the past when I had undergone such suffering. I also felt sorry for this man who is wielding the knife and who in the future will undergo such suffering. I was so enwrapped by these thoughts of the past, present, and future that, before I knew what was happening, my tears began to fall."

Upon hearing this, the butcher threw his knife on the ground at once and changed his occupation to that of vegetable seller.

III

The following was told to me by Sung Meng-ch'üan.

A Mister Sun O-shan once fell ill aboard a boat at Kao-yu.[26] Suddenly, it seemed as if he had strolled over to the river bank and that his feelings had become exceedingly invigorated. Soon there was a man who led him as he walked along. Trancelike, he was not fully aware of what was happening to him nor did he ask any questions. He followed along until they came to a house, the gateway to which was neat and tidy. Gradually, they made their way into an inner chamber where he saw a young woman who was at that moment sitting on a mat of rushes used in childbirth. He wanted to retreat but a hand was pressing him from behind so that he fell into a dazed unconsciousness.

After a long while, he gradually revived but his body had shrunk to a small size. Nestled amidst the soft swaddling-clothes, he realized that he had been reborn and there was nothing he could do about it. He wished to speak but he felt a cold air enter through his fontanel which abruptly silenced him so that he could not utter a word. He looked around at the tables, couches, and furnishings and saw clearly all the hanging couplets, calligraphy, and paintings.

On the third day, a maid picked up the baby to give him a bath, but her hand slipped and he fell to the floor. Again he fell into a dazed unconsciousness. When he revived, he was still lying in the middle of the boat. A member of his household told him, "You'd stopped breathing for three days but, since your limbs were flexible and the area around your heart was still warm, we didn't dare to prepare you for the coffin."

Mr. Sun hurriedly took a piece of paper and made a written statement on it of all that he had seen and heard. He dispatched a messenger who was to carry this, by way of a certain road, to such-and-such a house and who was to tell them not to be unduly harsh in punishing the maid. Thereupon, he leisurely related to his family all of the particulars.

26. In Kiangsu province.

He recovered from his illness that very day and went directly to the same house. When he saw the maids and serving-women, they were all like old acquaintances. The head of the house was old and childless. Face to face with Mr. Sun, all he could do was sigh with regret and exclaim how strange it was.

Recently, the same sort of thing happened to the Executive Agent, Meng Chien-hsi. He too recalled the road to the gate of a certain house and, sure enough, when he visited it, he found that a baby boy had been born there that day but that the baby had died immediately. When I was on duty in the palace not long ago, T'u Shih-ch'üan of the Royal Academy told me all the circumstances in great detail. For the most part, it was similar to what Mr. Sun O-shan had said, except that Sun recalled going but not returning whereas Meng Chien-hsi was quite clear about both going and returning. But there was the slight difference that Meng met his deceased wife on the way and that, when he reached the house and went inside, he saw his wife and the woman who was to be his new mother seated together.

Comment: The doctrine of transmigration of souls is disputed by the Confucians. But the fact is that it happens all of the time. The principle of cause and effect is, of course, not to be falsified. It is just that these two gentlemen momentarily entered the process of transmigration and then rapidly returned to their original bodies. For no apparent reason, this illusory realm had been made manifest. Thus it cannot be explained on the basis of principle alone. "The sages set aside without discussion what lies beyond the world."[27] It is advisable to reserve judgment on that whereof one is uncertain.

IV

The following was told to me by the Redactor, Wang Shih-t'ing.

There was a student surnamed Ts'ui who was garrisoned in Kwangtung[28] as punishment for a crime which he had committed. Fearful that something unexpected might happen if he took along his children,[29] he left them with his wife and concubine so that he could travel alone. After he reached the garrison, he became exceedingly disconsolate and depressed, completely unable to distract himself. While thinking of his young wives, he climbed a tower to look toward his hometown, but this only increased his sorrow all the more.

By chance, he happened to meet an old man who said that his surname was Tung and that his style was "Oblivious." As they talked, the two of them

27. From the second chapter of the *Chuang Tzu* (selection 9).

28. Since Kwangtung (Canton) province was in the far south of the empire, away from the center of Chinese civilization, it was considered a form of punishment to be sent there.

29. This is clearly an error on the part of Chi Yün, since it is apparent below that Ts'ui had no children. Here the author probably meant to say "family" instead of "children." The next sentence would then be interpreted to mean that, leaving his wife and concubine behind, he traveled alone.

got along quite well. Taking pity on the student's vagabondage, Tung invited him to be his son's tutor. And so they came to be on very good terms with each other.

One evening, host and guest were having a soirée on a high tower beneath the full moonlight. Suddenly, Ts'ui was stirred to feelings of estrangement. Holding his wine-cup and leaning against the railing, he forgot all about exchanging toasts with his companion.

"Might it be that you are thinking of 'billowy chignon and jade-white arms'?"[30] the old man asked with a smile. "Because of our close friendship, I had long ago made arrangements. But, since I haven't yet been able to learn whether they will arrive or not, I didn't inform you beforehand. After ten months, there ought to be some news."

When another half-year had passed, the old man suddenly instructed his servant-boys and maids to make ready an extra room. He seemed to be in a great hurry. Before long, three small sedan-chairs arrived. Ts'ui's wife and concubine together with one of their maids raised the curtains and got out. Surprised and happy, Ts'ui asked his wives how such an uncanny thing could have happened.

"We received your letter calling us to come," they replied. "You directed us to travel in the company of the family of a certain official. But we were in such a hurry that we could not wait that long. So we came like this in all haste. The family affairs have been entrusted to one of our brothers to manage in our absence. It has been agreed that, each year, he will exchange the yearly rent rice from our tenants for cash and send it to us."

"Where has the maid come from?" Ts'ui asked.

"She's the concubine of a certain official," they said. "His first wife wouldn't accept her. We bought her cheaply while we were on the boat that brought us part of the way here."

The student was so grateful to the old man that he bowed before him and even began to weep. Thus was the whole family brought back together again and Ts'ui no longer had dreams of his old estate.

After several months had passed, the old man spoke to the student: "Your wives met this maid on the way by chance, yet she has followed them through thick and thin. This surely must have been predestined. It would seem that she, too, ought to wait upon you in the bed-chamber and not be left out in the cold alone."

After another few years, there was an amnesty and they were allowed to return home. The student was so delighted that he was unable to sleep. But his wives and the maid were all sad, appearing as though they were about to say goodbye to someone they loved. Ts'ui comforted them and asked, "Are

30. The T'ang poet Tu Fu (see selection 48), in similar circumstances, wrote of his wife in "Moonlit Night": "Her billowy chignon must be dampened by the fragrant mist, / And her jade-white arms chilled by the cold glimmer."

you reluctant to leave the master who has been so kind to us? If death does not intervene, there will come a day when I shall repay him." None of them answered, hurrying only to pack the student's baggage.

When he was about to leave, the old gentleman poured wine and prepared a farewell dinner. At the same time, he called out the three women and said to them, "Today this matter must be clearly explained."

Turning to the student, he folded his hands in a bow and said, "I am an earth fairy. In a previous life, I was a colleague of yours. After I died, you made numerous plans and appeals to assist my wife and children in returning to their hometown. I have never forgotten that vivid recollection. This time it was you who was separated from your mates; naturally it was right for me to take care of things for you. But the way was long and there were many mountains and rivers to cross. How could the two delicate ladies have made it? So I summoned two flower sprites, sending them first to your home for half a year. There they observed the appearance and speech of your noble wives until they were able to imitate them perfectly. Furthermore, the flower sprites investigated the past affairs of your household in order to have proofs which would forestall your doubts. They were originally three sisters so I added a maid. They are all illusions; do not think about them any longer. When you get home and face the wives you so fondly recall, it will be no different from being here."

The student requested permission to return with the three women.

"Each ghost and spirit has its earthly limitations," the old man said. "They can appear for a brief spell but cannot spend too long a time."

The three women grasped Ts'ui's hand as they bid him farewell, tears falling so profusely that it dampened their clothes. In the twinkling of an eye, they were no more to be seen. When Ts'ui boarded his boat, he saw them in the distance, standing on the bank. He beckoned them, but they did not come.

After he had returned home, his wives said that the family had fallen on hard times and that they had relied on the money which he sent them every year to survive to that day. This too, was no doubt the work of the old man.

If all the people of the world who are separated from their loved ones were to meet this old man, there would be no more "yearning of Herd-boy and Weaver Girl across the Milky Way."[31]

"True enough," declared Wang Shih-t'ing. "However, if Kwangtung has its earth fairy, surely there must be earth fairies in other places too. If the old fairy Tung has such magic, surely other fairies must have it too. The reason why no one else has met Tung again must be because, in past lives, he had not received any kindnesses from them. Therefore he is unwilling to exert himself on their behalf by working wonders."

31. This refers to the stars Altair and Vega, around which a charming fairy tale developed. It tells how, though separated by the Milky Way, a bridge of stars enables the two lovers to cross it once each year on the seventh day of the seventh moon.

V

In the village of Li, there was a farmer's wife who would invariably see a woman following beside her every morning and evening when she took food to her husband in the fields. She asked her companions about it but they saw nothing. This terrified her greatly. Later, the woman gradually followed her all the way home, remaining in the courtyard or at a corner of the wall without entering the living quarters. When the wife pressed forward to get a look at her, she would retreat at once. And, when the wife turned away, she would come forward again at once. The wife knew that she must be an enemy with a grievance. So she asked her across the distance what it was.

"In a former life," answered the woman, "you and I were both concubines of a man of high position. You were jealous of the favor in which I was held and so you falsely accused me of adultery, which caused me to die in solitary confinement. Now I have come to take my revenge. Unexpectedly, you have waited upon your mother-in-law so attentively in this life that a beneficent spirit always protects you and prevents me from getting near. That is why, day after day, I follow you. When one considers what the situation is, my chances of paying you back are one in a million. If you sponsor a mass to save my soul,[32] it will enable me to be reborn and the grudge will be absolved."[33]

The wife declined on the grounds of poverty.

"You speak not in vain when you say you are poor," the woman replied. "But if you could yourself recite the name of the Buddha ten thousand times, that too would save me."

"How can that save a ghost?" asked the farmer's wife.

"When the average person recites the name of the Buddha," said the woman, "the Buddha does not hear it. Even when he repeats it over and over expressly as though he were facing the Buddha, it serves only to collect the mind. But whenever a loyal official or a devoted son, whose sincerity is such that it moves the spirits, recites the name of the Buddha, the sound is heard throughout the Three Realms.[34] Therefore, its power is equivalent to reading aloud the sūtras and making of confessions. You are a devoted daughter-in-law; I feel certain that it would be efficacious."

Resolved to undertake the recitation of the Buddha's name, the wife did as she was told. Each time that she recited his name, she would see the woman make a bow. Upon reaching the full measure of ten thousand, the woman was no more to be seen.

32. Literally, "if you make a Taoist or Buddhist ceremonial site" (compare with Sanskrit *bodhimaṇḍala*). This would, of course, involve the expenditure of considerable funds.

33. A disembodied soul that bears a grudge is unable to be reborn until that grudge is either worked out or sufficient merit to offset the wrong done is transferred to it by a concerned person.

34. Sanskrit *trailokya*, the Buddhist metaphysical conception of the worlds of desire, form, and spirit.

When the wife was old, she recounted this incident and was convinced that serving one's parents and parents-in-law with a firm determination is even more important than faithfully worshipping the Buddha.

VI

In the year 1784, there were many disastrous fires in the city of Tsinan.[35] At the end of the fourth month of that year, a fire broke out again inside the south gate on West Cross Street. Spreading from east to west, the fire burned fiercely in the narrow alleys and raged violently through the cramped lanes.

There was a certain Mr. Chang who had a three-pillar hut on the north side of the road. He would have had time to get his family out before the flames reached it but, because his mother's coffin was inside, he tried first to think of a way to move it to safety. Soon, the situation was such that he, his wife, and their four children could not get out. They embraced the coffin and wept sorrowfully, swearing that they would perish with it.

At that very moment, a lieutenant-colonel of the governor's army was directing his troops in rescue operations. When he heard the faint sound of crying, he ordered his troops to climb up on the roofs in the alley behind. They followed the sound to its source and let down a strap with which to haul them out. But Chang and his wife called out together: "Our mother's coffin is here. How can we abandon it?"

The children called out likewise: "Our parents are willing to die for their parent. Shouldn't we be willing to die for our parents too?" Nor would they consent to go up.

Suddenly, the fire was upon them. The troops leaped over the roofs to flee from it and barely escaped with their lives. Imagining that the entire family had been reduced to ashes, all they could do was sigh in sympathy as they watched from a distance.

When the fire was extinguished and the inspectors came to their hut, amidst all the other houses, it alone remained unscathed. Most likely, a whirlwind had suddenly arisen and caused the fire to veer off to the north. It went around behind their hut and burned down a pawnshop belonging to their neighbor before it finally turned toward the west again. Were it not for some ghost or spirit protecting them, how could this have happened?

This matter was recorded and sent to me in the seventh month of 1793 by Mr. Chang Ch'ing-yüan who is the principal of an academy in Te-chou.[36] It is similar to the matter about the widow which I included in the "Records of Whiling away the Summer at Luan-yang." But that a husband, his wife, and their children would all be of the same mind and will is even more so the rarest of the rare. For, "when two people are of the same mind, they have the

35. The capital of Shantung province.
36. Also in Shantung province.

strength to overcome the hardest obstacles."[37] How much more so with six people! "No sooner does the ordinary woman call out than thunder strikes down."[38] How much more so when there are six people, all of them truly devoted! "When the highest sincerity is attained, heaven, earth, and man are moved with sympathy."[39] Although one's life is fated, he cannot but try to reverse the tide of misfortune. "Human determination can transcend destiny."[40] This, too, is one way of putting it. Although the matter here related is "unusual news," one may aver that it bespeaks a common principle.

I am not acquainted with Chang Ch'ing-yüan and yet he has taken the pains to send me this account through the mails. Inasmuch as he made certain that it was transmitted, one can get an idea of Chang's purpose. Consequently, I have edited what he wrote and recorded it here.

VII

A man from Wu-yi[41] had gone flower-viewing with some of his friends and relatives at a Buddhist temple. Though the ground in front of the hall for storing the Tripiṭaka[42] was quite spacious and open, strange things often happened inside the hall. When night came, no one dared to sit next to the hall. But the man from Wu-yi, who was a self-appointed neo-Confucian, calmly expressed his disbelief. In a state of drunken exhilaration, he was holding forth on the notion in Chang Tsai's "Western Inscription"[43] that all creation partakes of the same substance. While everyone present listened intently, night imperceptibly fell.

Suddenly, a stern voice railed at him from inside the hall: "At this very moment, many people are dying because of famine and pestilence. You are a local official. Since you have not considered advocating timely measures on behalf of the public such as distributing food and dispensing medicine, you should have availed yourself of this fine night to have a pleasant sleep behind the doors of your own house. At least that would not be out of character for the self-centered person that you are. Instead, here you prattle and twaddle away, lecturing on 'brotherhood with the people and identification with all creation.'[44] I wonder, even if you lecture straight on to daybreak, whether that

37. From section eight of the first chapter of "The Great Appendix" in the *Classic of Changes*.

38. This sentence differs significantly from the sentence in the *Huai-nan Tzu*, whence it was borrowed, in having "calls out" instead of "invokes Heaven."

39. This is one variation of a frequently pronounced idea that, in part, goes back as early as the *Chuang Tzu*.

40. From the *Treatise on Reclusion* (*Kuei-ch'ien chih*).

41. In Hopei.

42. The Buddhist canon.

43. Perhaps the most succinct and authoritative statement of basic neo-Confucian principles. Chang's dates are 1020–1077.

44. From the "Western Inscription" (see note 43).

can make any food for the people to eat or medicine for them to take? I'll just toss a brick at you and then we'll see if you lecture again on 'heresy not overcoming the truth'!"

Suddenly, a brick from the city wall came flying down with a crash like thunder, breaking the cups, plates, and the long, low table.

Startled, the man from Wu-yi went running out as he said: "May it not be that this apparition is an apparition simply because it does not believe in the theories of Ch'eng and Chu?"[45]

Slackening his pace, he sighed heavily and left.

VIII

One summer night, Ma Ta-huan ("Great Return")[46] of Tung-kuang[47] had fallen asleep naked in the hall for storing the Tripiṭaka[48] of the Tzu-sheng ("Surpassing Aid") Temple when he felt someone tugging at his arm and saying: "Get up! Get up! Don't sully the Buddhist scriptures!"

When he awoke, he saw an old man at his side and asked, "Who are you?"

"I am the guardian spirit of the Tripiṭaka."

By nature, Ta-huan was both uninhibited and fearless. At the time, the light of the moon made it bright as day. So Ta-huan called the spirit to sit down and have a chat with him.

"Why, sir, are you protecting this canon?"

"Because I was so ordered by Heaven."

"The Confucian books are so numerous that they reach to the rafters and would spill out of an ox-cart, but I've never heard there's a spirit to protect them. May it be that Heaven is partial to the Buddhist scriptures?"

"Buddhism establishes its doctrine through the way of gods[49] in whom living beings either believe or not. Therefore it is protected by the gods. Confucianism establishes its doctrine through the way of men and all men ought to respect and protect it. This is also the reason why all men know they are to respect and protect it. There is no need to bother with spiritual powers. It is not because Heaven is partial to the Buddhist scriptures."

"Then does Heaven view the three doctrines as one?"

"Confucianism has as its substance the cultivation of self and, for its function, the government of men. Taoism has as its substance quietude and, for its function, flexibility. Buddhism has as its basis meditation[50] and, for its

45. The founders of neo-Confucianism.

46. The usual understanding of this expression is that it is a reference to Taoist alchemical refining of cinnabar. Given the remarks which Mr. Ma makes about Taoism, it is ironic that he chose such a name for himself.

47. A district in Hopei.

48. See note 42.

49. This is a rather unusual application of a clause that occurs in commentaries to Hexagram 20 of the *Classic of Changes* (see selection 3).

50. *Ting* (Sanskrit *samādhi*).

function, compassion.[51] Their fundamental purposes are each distinct and cannot be considered as one. But there is no difference with reference to their teaching men to do good, nor is there any difference in the assistance they afford to all creation. Since their ultimate aims are more or less the same, Heaven surely cannot but preserve them side by side. Yet the Confucian takes the people as the fulfillment of his Heaven-ordained being and exercises this basic principle in his own person. Buddhism and Taoism are both teachings that concentrate on the self and devote whatever energy remains to other beings. Therefore elucidation of the way of man is taken to be primary and elucidation of the way of spirits is taken to be supportive of that. Nor may all under heaven be ruled exclusively by Buddhism and Taoism. This is how they are not the same and yet the same, how they are the same and yet not the same. We may say that Confucianism is like the five staple grains; if one does not eat them for a single day, he will starve. If he goes several days without eating them, he will certainly die. Buddhism and Taoism are like medicines; one takes them at a crisis of life and death or when he is feeling overly strong emotions. They may be used to free one of grievance and grief or to dissipate melancholia. For these purposes, they are far more effective than Confucianism. Their concepts of calamity and good fortune, of cause and effect, may be used to incite the ignorant masses to goodness. For this purpose, too, they penetrate more readily than Confucianism. But once the illness has been treated, they should be discontinued. They are not to be used exclusively nor administered frequently for that would result in the misfortune of partiality.

"Some Confucians may idly talk of 'mind' and 'nature,'[52] thus confusing Confucius with Gautama[53] and Lao Tzu. Others may attack the latter two worthies, as though they were defending against their mortal enemies. But these are both limited viewpoints."

"The Taoist priests in their yellow caps and the Buddhist monks in their black robes indulge in supernatural foolishness. If we do not strenuously attack them, would this not beget trouble for manners and morals?"

"What I was talking about were the basic premises of these doctrines. If we focus on their decadent aspects, it's not Buddhism and Taoism alone that beget trouble for manners and morals. The trouble begot by Confucianism is by no means inconsequential. For example, sir, your getting drunk and falling

---

51. *Tz'u* (Sanskrit *maitra* or *karuṇā*).

52. There are numerous possible interpretations of *hsin-hsing*, Buddhist and otherwise. That given in the translation might actually be construed as Mencian. The usual Buddhist understanding of the expression is "the immutable mind-nature" (*citta-dharmatā*). While it is difficult to identify precisely what Chi Yün intended here, it would seem that he is criticizing those Confucians who have adulterated the doctrine of the sages with concepts that are fundamentally Buddhist.

53. The Buddha.

asleep naked here, I suspect, is not necessarily in conformity with the rites and regulations of the Duke of Chou and Confucius."

After apologizing, Ta-huan freely carried on his conversation with the spirit until dawn, whereupon he departed. He never did find out which spirit it was. Some say it was a fox.

IX

The following was told to me by a criminal named Kang Ch'ao-jung who had been banished to Urumchi.[54]

There were two men on a business trip to Tibet.[55] Each of them was mounted on a mule. As they were passing through the mountains, they lost their way and could not tell east from west. Suddenly, more than ten people jumped down from an overhanging cliff. The merchants suspected that they were bandits.[56] As they came closer, the merchants saw that they were all seven to eight feet fall.[57] Their bodies were covered with fine hair of a yellowish green color and their faces seemed human but not yet fully so. Their speech was so croaky that it was impossible to understand. Believing the approaching figures to be demons, the merchants thought that they would surely die, so they fell to the ground trembling. But the ten-odd people looked at each other and laughed, giving no indication that they would seize the merchants and devour them.

Instead, they clasped the merchants under their arms and went off driving

54. Chi Yün himself had been banished to this remote city for one year (1770–1771). Many of his sketches are set in and around Urumchi or were told to him by people from that city. Urumchi is located in Sinkiang ("New Territory"), the westernmost region of modern China. The original inhabitants of this area were Indo-European peoples such as the Tocharians, Yüeh-chih (Ju-chih), and Sakas (Scyths). These were Caucasoid and Europoid peoples, many of whom had long noses, blond or reddish hair, and deep-set blue or greenish eyes. In further contrast to the people of the Middle Kingdom, they were also tall, dolichocephalic, and hirsute. Their existence has been proven by wall-paintings from this area dating to over a thousand years ago and by numerous extremely well-preserved, fully clothed corpses dating to approximately 4,000–2,300 years ago. In spite of the understandable amazement of the two merchants in this story, it would appear that Chi Yün is basically reporting reliable facts that are of great importance for history, linguistics, and anthropology. The data presented in this story have been repeatedly corroborated by other travelers in the Kunlun and Pamir ranges who have encountered such fantastic creatures. They could be the descendants of the original Indo-European inhabitants of the Tarim basin and surrounding areas who have retreated into the mountains to evade more recently arrived groups such as the Altaic Uighurs, Kirghiz, and Kazakhs and the Sinitic Han peoples.

55. Trade between Tibet and what is now Sinkiang has flourished for thousands of years, the enormous difficulties of the terrain notwithstanding.

56. The text has *chia-pa*, said to be the Mandarin transcription of a Tibetan word (perhaps *kampa*).

57. About six feet according to the U.S. system of measurement.

the mules before them. When they reached a hollow in the mountains, they put the two merchants on the ground. Then they pushed one of the mules into a pit and butchered the other with a sharp knife. They built a fire and, having roasted the mule meat over it, sat down in a circle and began to gorge themselves. They picked up the two merchants and gave them places as well, putting meat before each of them. Perceiving that the men had no evil intentions and beset by hunger and exhaustion, the merchants decided they might as well just go ahead and eat it. After they had eaten their fill, the ten-odd men patted their stomachs, raised their heads, and wheezed, making a sound like the whinny of a horse.

Two of the men then each clasped one of the merchants under their arms as before and sped off over three or four ridges as swiftly as a gibbon or a bird. After sending the merchants to the side of a main road, they gave each of them a stone and disappeared in a flash. The stones were as large as melons and were both turquoise. The merchants carried the stones back and sold them for a price worth double their losses.

This incident occurred sometime between 1765 and 1766. Ch'ao-jung had met one of the merchants who had told him about it in great detail.

One does not know whether these creatures were mountain specters or tree spirits. Judging from their actions, however, they were not demons. Perhaps they are simply a kind of feral human being that has always lived in isolated mountain valleys and has been cut off from communication with the rest of the world.

X

There was a neo-Confucian scholar who claimed that there were no ghosts. A group of people [including me] challenged him, saying, "It just so happens that today it's exceedingly hot. Do you think you can go to the old cemetery and spend a night there alone enjoying the cool air?" In the end, the old gentleman went resolutely and, sure enough, there was nothing to be seen. When he came back, he was even more self-assured and said, "Would Master Chu Hsi [58] have cheated me?"

"Supposing one journeys a thousand tricents with a rich supply of provisions," I replied, "and he encounters no robbers on the road. It cannot therefore be declared that the road has no robbers. Or supposing that one goes off hunting for a whole day and meets no animals in the wild. It cannot therefore be declared that the wild has no animals. To conclude that there are no ghosts anywhere under heaven because a single place is without them, or to conclude that throughout all eternity there have been no ghosts because a single night was without them—this is to instance a particular to refute the general. As for

58. Chu Hsi (1130–1200), canonized as Wen-kung ("Duke of Letters"), is the most famous of the Sung period neo-Confucian philosophers. The old gentleman is under the (mistaken, according to Chi Yün) impression that Master Chu disbelieved in ghosts.

the theory that there are no ghosts, it began with Juan Chan[59] and not with Master Chu. Master Chu held that the usual principle[60] is for the celestial element of the soul[61] to ascend and for the terrestrial element[62] to descend, while all wonders and prodigies are indicative of an unusual principle. He did not say that there were none. Therefore, he is reported[63] by Chin Ch'ü-wei[64] to have said: 'In the first place, the Ch'eng brothers[65] did not say that there were no ghosts nor spirits, but that there were no ghosts nor spirits such as are spoken of by the world today.'

"Chu Hsi is reported by Yang Tao-fu to have said: 'Wind, rain, dew, and thunder; the sun, the moon, day, and night—these are traces of ghosts and spirits. These are upright ghosts and spirits which operate openly in broad daylight. As for those which are said to shout amidst the rafters or bump into one's chest, they are the so-called "depraved spectres." Sometimes they are present and sometimes not, sometimes they come and sometimes go, sometimes they gather and sometimes disperse.[66] Then there is what is known as "prayers that are answered, supplications that are granted." This, too, reflects the same principle as that of the so-called "ghosts and spirits." '

"Chu Hsi is reported by Pao Yang to have said: 'The principle of ghosts and spirits and of life and death is certainly not as the Buddhists claim[67] nor as the

59. Juan Chan (fl. 307–312) was the son of Juan Hsien (234–263) and the grandnephew of Juan Chi (210–263, see selection 27), both of whom were among the Seven Sages of the Bamboo Grove. In fascicle 49 of the *History of the Chin Dynasty* (*Chin shu*), there is an interesting anecdote which probably accounts for Chi Yün's remark here: "He held the belief that there are no such things as bogies, and was one day arguing the point rather warmly with a stranger, when the latter jumped up in a rage and cried out 'I am a bogy myself!' The stranger then assumed a hideous shape, and finally vanished. Yüan [i.e., Juan] Chan was greatly upset by this, and died within the year." (Translation by Herbert Giles)

60. *Li* is a technical term with the neo-Confucians meaning "order" or "principle."

61. *Hun.* Chinese metaphysics posits a dual animus which consists of a celestial (yang) and a terrestrial (yin) component, the former called *hun* and the latter *p'o.* We may think of these two types of soul as animus and anima. It is popularly held that a person has three *hun* and two *p'o.*

62. *P'o.*

63. The formula "X *lu yüeh*" which occurs so frequently in the following pages means "X (a given student or friend of Chu Hsi) has recorded [that the Master] said." All of these citations may be found, often with a slight variation in wording, in the *Classified Conversations of Master Chu* (*Chu Tzu yü-lei*), fascicle 3, and the *Complete Works of Master Chu* (*Chu Tzu ch'üan-shu*), fascicle 51.

64. The individuals whose names occur in the formula "Chu Hsi is reported by X to have said" are friends or students of the Master. A list of their names and the dates of the recorded conversations may be found in the Prefatory Catalog of the *Classified Conversations.*

65. Ch'eng Hao (1032–1085) and Ch'eng Yi (1033–1107), famous neo-Confucian philosophers who preceded Chu Hsi.

66. "Gather" and "disperse" refer to the agglomeration and diffusion of energy which constitutes a given spectra.

67. Transmigration of souls.

common people see it.[68] However, there are also clear incidents about which we cannot reason on the basis of principle. In such cases, do not try to comprehend.'[69]

"Again, Chu Hsi said of Nan-hsüan,[70] 'It was only a matter of stubborn disbelief. There are such things as the monsters and goblins cast on Yü's tripods.[71] Deep mountains and great swamps are where they dwell. When men go and occupy these places, how could there not be hauntings? The Taoist Liu from Yü-chang[72] dwelled on a mountain top in a hut which he had built. One day a bunch of lizards came and drank up all the water in his hut. After a while, hailstones were piled up everywhere outside of the hut. The next day it actually hailed at the foot of the mountain. My wife's uncle "Eldest Liu,"[73] who was quite simple and honest and who was incapable of wild talk, said that he was passing a ridge when he heard a sound in the woods beside a brook. It turned out to be a multitude of lizards, each holding an object that looked like a crystal. Before he had gone several miles, it started to hail. Here again, one doesn't know what sort of principle is involved.

" 'Of old, there was a town that had a large Buddha modeled out of clay which was revered and believed in by the entire area. Later, its head was broken off by an ill-mannered youth of the clan. When the people assembled and wept over this, a miraculous substance[74] came forth from the wood and clay of the Buddha's neck. How could wood and clay have contained such a material? It simply was brought about by the minds of men.'

"It is reported by Wu Pi-ta[75] that, while discussing the sighting of a ghost in Hsüeh Shih-lung's[76] house, Chu Hsi said: 'Those in the world who believe in ghosts and spirits all say that they actually exist between heaven and earth. Those who do not believe in them firmly maintain that there are none. On the other hand, there are people who really have seen them. Cheng Ching-wang[77] therefore took the sighting at Hsüeh's to be a reality. He didn't realize that this was just something on the order of a rainbow.' Question: 'Is a rainbow simply energy[78] or has it also form and substance?' Chu Hsi said: 'Since it can sup water, it must necessarily have a stomach and intestines. It's only that,

68. The dead continuing to live on as spirits.
69. More literally, "comprehend [through] principle."
70. Chang Shih (1133–1180), son of Chang Chün (see note 91).
71. The bronze tripods of state of the legendary emperor Yü.
72. In Kiangsi.
73. Chu Hsi's wife was, indeed, surnamed Liu.
74. Sanskrit *śarīra* ("relic").
75. Flourished 1188–1196.
76. 1134–1173, a student of Ch'eng Yi (see note 65).
77. Born 1128.
78. *Ch'i.* Also rendered in English as "subtle matter," "matter-energy," "material force," and so forth. May be compared to Sanskrit *prāṇa* and Greek *pneuma*.

once it disperses, it is no more. Spirits like those in the class of Thunder and Storm [79] are also of this type.'

"Question by Lin Tz'u: 'Those in the world who have seen ghosts and spirits are quite numerous. But I cannot determine whether there are any or not. What is your opinion?' Chu Hsi's answer: 'Since the people in the world who have seen them are extremely numerous, how can one claim that there are none? It is only a matter of abnormal principle. As with Po-yu [80] becoming an ogre, Ch'eng Yi claimed that it was owing to a different principle. It must have been that the time had not yet come for his human energy to be exhausted when he died a violent death. The celestial and terrestrial souls having nowhere to revert to, naturally the result would be like this.

" 'There was once a man who was walking along the Huai River at night. He saw numberless shapes which seemed like men but were not quite men appearing and disappearing in the rain. [81] The man knew full well that they were ghosts so he had no choice but to rush at them and pass by. Later, he asked around and found out that this place was an ancient battleground. All those ghosts had died unnatural deaths. It made sense that, bearing grudges and harboring resentment, they hadn't dispersed.'

"They sat for a while and then someone said, 'In a certain village, there was a Li the Third who became an ogre when he died. In this isolated village, whenever there was a sacrifice or Buddhist ceremony, they would invariably set aside a portion for this man. Afterward, because someone exploded firecrackers and burned down the tree where it was lodged, the ogre was thereupon exterminated.' Chu Hsi said that this happened because the man had died an unjust death and so his energy had not dispersed, but that it had been startled into dispersing by the firecrackers.

"Chu Hsi is reported by Shen Hsien to have said: 'When people do not submit to their deaths, though they have already died, their energy does not disperse but becomes phantoms and prodigies. As for those who die horrible deaths as well as Buddhist monks and Taoist priests, though they have already died, in most cases their energy does not disperse. (Original note: [82] Buddhist monks and Taoist priest strive to nourish their spirits which, as a result, cohere and do not disperse.)'

"Chu Hsi is reported by Wan Jen-chieh to have said: 'When someone dies and his energy disperses, there is utterly no trace of him. This is the usual

79. See E.T.C. Werner, *A Dictionary of Chinese Mythology* (Shanghai: Kelly and Welsh, 1932), p. 244.

80. Liang Hsiao of the state of Cheng during the Spring and Autumn period. For this very early Chinese ghost story, see the seventh year of Duke Chao in the *Chronicle of Tso* (*Tso chuan*).

81. Emending *liang* ("two") to *yü* ("rain")—the two graphs are very close in appearance. Without the emendation, we may, with effort, read "between the two channels."

82. This is the "original note" as it appears in the *Complete Works*.

principle of things. So, in the case of reincarnation, it aberrantly happens that the energy collects together, does not disperse, and thus goes to encounter some enlivening energy; then it is reborn.'

"Chu Hsi is reported by Yeh Ho-sun to have said: 'There was a court case in T'an-chou[83] in which a wife had murdered her husband and secretly buried him. Later he began to haunt the place but, when the affair was uncovered, he immediately ceased haunting it. From this we know that in criminal proceedings, should the guilty not be convicted in such cases, then the grievance of the one who has died will necessarily remain unrelieved.'

"Chu Hsi is reported by Li Chuang-tsu to have had the following conversation. Someone asked, 'There are spirits in the world who receive sacrificial food in temples continuously for several hundred years. Now, what principle is this?' Chu Hsi replied: 'Over a long period of time, they too will gradually dissipate. Once, when I was serving as prefect of Nan-k'ang,[84] there was a long drought. I couldn't avoid going about everywhere to pray to the spirits. It happened that I came to one particular temple which had but three rooms without walls[85] and was in an advanced stage of disrepair. The people there said that, thirty or forty years before, the spirit had been as quick in its response as an echo. When someone came, the spirit would speak to him from within the curtains. Its responsiveness in the past had been effective to such a degree but its responsiveness today is such that it can't even keep its own temple in repair. Naturally, one can see that spirits, too, over a long period of time will gradually dissipate.'

"In discussing the matter of ghosts and spirits, Chu Hsi is reported by Yeh Ho-sun to have said: 'The "Second Son"[86] Temple at Kuan-k'ou in Szechwan was established by Li Ping[87] in connection with his opening of the "Separated Hill" irrigation channel.[88] Recently, a number of wonders and prodigies have appeared there. These are none other than the manifestations of his second son. At first, he had been dubbed a "Prince." Later, the Emperor Hui Tsung,[89] who was fond of Taoism, changed his title to "Perfect Man."[90]

83. In the province of Honan.

84. In Kiangsi. Chu Hsi was appointed to the post of prefect of the military prefecture of Nan-k'ang in 1178, took up his post the following year, and was faced with a severe drought in 1180.

85. One suspects that this is rather intended to be "ramshackle rooms" (pi shih).

86. Erh-lang (see note 88).

87. Flourished 250 B.C.E.

88. The reference is to the large-scale irrigation system outside Ch'eng-tu (in Szechwan) and the temples to Li Ping and his son, Erh-lang, who were responsible for its construction. Erh-lang developed into an extremely powerful deity in folk religion.

89. Reigned 1101–1125.

90. Taoist term for an individual who has attained the highest degree of spiritual purification.

When Chang Chün, the duke of Wei,[91] sent his troops into battle,[92] he prayed in this temple. That night, he dreamed of the spirit of the temple which said to him, "All along, I had been dubbed 'Prince' and received offerings of sacrificial meat. Therefore my awesome, beneficial powers could be exercised. Now I have been styled a 'Perfect Man.' Although I am venerated by men who present vegetarian sacrifices to me, there is no longer any nourishment from meat sacrifices. Therefore the efficacy of my awesome, beneficial powers is no more. Now it is necessary that my title be changed back to 'Prince' whereupon my awesome powers will be restored." The duke of Wei thereupon requested that he be given back his former title. I don't know whether the duke of Wei had such a dream or whether he made up this story on the spur of the moment when he was sending his troops into battle. Then, again, there is the God of Literature of Tzu-t'ung[93] who is exceedingly powerful. These two spirits, it would seem, have divided up for themselves the two halves of Szechwan.

" 'For the most part, ghosts and spirits use all of the living things which are sacrificed to them as a source of enlivening energy which they rely on for their power. When the ancients consecrated a bell or a tortoise shell[94] with blood, it was with this idea in mind.

" 'Han-ch'ing[95] said that Li T'ung told of a man who shot at a tiger. He saw several men following along behind the tiger. This was the undispersed enlivening energy of the people who had been killed by the tiger which had, therefore, coalesced to form their shapes.'

"Chu Hsi is reported by Huang Yi-kang to have said, in a discussion of the matter of inviting the Violet Lady Spirit[96] to chant poetry: 'There has even been a case when someone was successful in inviting her to appear in her own actual person. A little girl of the household saw her but didn't know what sort of thing she was.

" 'And then there was the man of Ch'ü-chou[97] who was worshiping a spirit. All he did was set down a list of recorded queries on a piece of paper and seal it up in front of the shrine. After a short period of time, he broke open the seal. On the paper were the answers which had appeared of themselves. One doesn't know what to make of this.'

---

91. Died 1164.

92. Chu Hsi wrote a lengthy biographical account of this "Second Tutor to the Crown Prince" entitled "Shao-shih Wei kuo Chang kung hsing-chuang."

93. A place in Szechwan where a scholar of the T'ang dynasty named Chang Ya lived, who was later canonized as the God of Literature.

94. Used for purposes of divination.

95. Han-ch'ing is the sobriquet of Fu Kuang, a disciple of Chu Hsi.

96. Goddess of Latrines.

97. In Chekiang.

"All of these stories are recorded, in great profusion, in the *Classified Conversations* compiled by Li Ching-te. May it not be you, sir, who has maligned Master Chu?"

The old gentleman asked for the book and began to read it. After quite a while, he unhappily remarked, "So Master Chu has written this sort of thing too?" Disappointed and silent, he left.

But I still have my doubts. Master Chu's main point is that when man is born, he is endowed with the energy of heaven and earth; when he dies, it dissipates and returns to heaven and earth. Master Chu is reported by Yeh Ho-sun to have declared that "The case is like a fish in water. The water outside is the same as the water inside its stomach. The water inside the stomach of a perch is the very same stuff as the water inside the stomach of a carp." His reasoning is excellent!

Yet what about the reasons for the sacrifices which were instituted by the sages and recorded in the classics? On their account, Master Chu is found to admit that descendants are constituted of the same energy as their ancestors and interact with them.[98] When the ancestors' energy is reconstituted, they receive sacrifice; when they have ceased receiving sacrifices, they disperse into emptiness. But I am unsure whether, after this energy has dissipated, it coalesces and becomes one with the primordial energy or it is interspersed within the primordial energy. If it coalesces and becomes one, then it is like the many rivers which return to the sea and join together to make a single body of water. The Yangtze, the Huai, the Yellow River, and the Han cannot then be made to reconstitute themselves individually in a given place. Or it is like a soup blended from various seasonings that combine to make a single flavor. The ginger, salt, vinegar, and soy sauce cannot be made to reconstitute themselves individually in a given place. Furthermore, how can so-and-so's material energy be differentiated from the whole and be caused individually to communicate with its descendants? If it is interspersed in the primordial energy, then, like flying dust, it will scatter in the four directions. One does not know into how many millions and billions of places they will separate— like drifting silk threads flying chaotically with the wind. One does not know how many millions and billions of tricents apart they will travel. When the time comes for the descendants to present their sacrificial offerings, does it not seem far from the principle of things that the bits and specks of dust, the wisps and tufts of thread would be reunited as one? Even though it be granted that they can get back together, it would seem that this energy would be without consciousness. How, then, could it respond to the earnestness of the sacrificer? And how could it enjoy the offerings? If it be assumed that this energy have consciousness, whence does the consciousness arise? It must be assumed that

---

98. The following long paragraph is Chi Yün's critique of the principal arguments put forward in the section on Ghosts and Spirits of Chu Hsi's *Classified Conversations*.

there is a mind. To what, then, does the mind adhere? It must be assumed that there is a body. Now, given that there is a body, what we are left with is only a ghost. Moreover, before they got back together again—these billions of tiny dust particles, these billions of wisps—each particle and each wisp would have possessed its own consciousness. Thus, there would not be just one single ghost.

Nevertheless, there are Buddhist ghosts lurking beneath the ground and Confucian ghosts whirling about in midair. The Buddhist ghosts are present every day and the Confucian ghosts amass extemporarily. How can they be borne? This is, indeed, not something which such an unlearned person as myself is capable of understanding.

Translated by Victor H. Mair

Classical-Language Short Stories

249
Tu Tzu-ch'un

Anonymous (8th century?)

Tu Tzu-ch'un lived, apparently, around the time of the Chou[1] and Sui dynasties. As a young man he was extravagant and unmindful of his patrimony. Being a man of free and easy spirit, he gave himself over to drinking and dissipation until he had squandered all his wealth. When he appealed to his relatives, they disowned him, one and all, as irresponsible.

Winter was coming on, his clothing was in rags, and his belly was empty. As he walked about Ch'ang-an, the sun set and he still had had nothing to eat. He found himself at the west gate of the East Market, uncertain where to turn. His hunger and chill were obvious, and he looked up to heaven and sighed.

An old man there leaning on a staff asked him, "What are you sighing about, sir?"

Tzu-ch'un said what was on his mind. As he grew eloquent over the shabby treatment he had received from his relatives, his indignation showed on his face.

"How many strings of cash would you need to feel well off?" the old man asked.

This is a typical example of the Tang classical-language short story (ch'uan-ch'i, literally "transmission of the strange"). Its origins are explained in the notes to selection 250.

1. This is the Northern Chou dynasty (557–581), the last of the non-Chinese regimes that occupied North China during the Northern and Southern Dynasties period.

"With thirty or fifty thousand I could get along."

"That's not enough."

"A hundred thousand."

"Still not enough."

"A million."

"Still not enough."

"Three million."

"That should do," the old man said at last, and drew from his sleeve a single string of cash, saying, "This is for tonight. Tomorrow at noon be waiting for me at the Persian Hostel in the West Market. Don't be late!"

Tzu-ch'un went at the appointed time, and the old man actually delivered the three million, leaving without telling his name.

Now that he was rich, Tzu-ch'un's profligate nature flared up again; he was convinced that he would never again be a pauper. He rode sleek horses and dressed in light furs; he assembled drinking companions, hired musicians, singers, and dancers in the gay quarter with never a thought for the future. Within a year or two he had gradually exhausted his resources. Fine clothes and carriage were replaced by cheap ones, he surrendered his horse for a donkey, and then gave up the donkey and walked. In no time he was as destitute as before.

At his wit's end, he stood at the gate to the market, bemoaning his lot. As if in response to his sighs, the old man appeared. Seizing Tzu-ch'un's hand, he exclaimed, "Amazing, that this should happen again! I will help you again—how much do you need?"

Tzu-ch'un was too embarrassed to reply and, to the old man's urgings, he could only shake his head in shame.

"Come again at noon tomorrow, the same place," the old man said.

Swallowing his shame, Tzu-ch'un went, and was given ten million strings of cash. Before receiving them, he was filled with determination to invest his money wisely in the future, putting Shih Chi-lun and Yi Tun[2] quite in the shade. But once the money came into his hands, his resolve grew unstable and his irresponsible character reasserted itself. Within a couple of years he was poorer than ever.

Again he ran into the old man in the same old place. Humiliated past endurance, he covered his face and fled. The old man seized the skirt of his robe and stopped him. "Too bad!" he said. "You have had bad luck." And he offered him thirty million, with the warning, "If this does not cure you, poverty is in your blood."

Tzu-ch'un thought, "When I lost all I had through extravagance and dissipation, my relatives and high connections spared me not a glance. Yet

2. Shih Ch'ung, styled Chi-lun, was a legendary rich man of the Chin dynasty. Yi Tun was an exceptionally rich salt merchant of the Spring and Autumn period.

this old man has come to my aid three times—how can I repay him?" And to the old man he said, "With what you have given me I can put my affairs in order. It enables me to provide for widows and orphans and restore my name as a man of honor. I am deeply touched by your great generosity, and when I have accomplished this task, I will be at your disposal."

"It is what I had hoped. When you have taken care of your affairs, meet me next year on the fifteenth of the seventh month[3] by the twin junipers at the Temple of Lao Tzu."

Reckoning that most widows and orphans of his clan were to be found in the area to the south of River Huai, he transferred his capital to Yang-chow, where he bought some fifteen hundred acres of good land. Within the city he built a large house, and on the main roads he erected over a hundred hostels, in which he lodged the widows and orphans of the whole region. He married off his nieces and nephews and had the unburied remains of his relatives moved to the clan cemetery. He requited those who had been kind to him and avenged his wrongs. When this was all done, the date was approaching, and he went to the appointed place, where he found the old man whistling in the shade of the twin junipers.

Together they climbed the Cloud Terrace Peak in the Hua Mountains. When they had gone forty tricents or so, they came upon an imposing edifice, not the dwelling of any ordinary person. High overhead were colored clouds, and wary cranes were soaring about. The main hall stood out; inside was an alchemist's furnace over nine feet high emitting purple flames that lit up the door and windows.

Nine jade damsels[4] stood around the furnace, which rested on a green dragon in front and a white tiger behind. Just before sunset the old man appeared, no longer in ordinary dress, but now wearing the yellow cap and red robe of a Taoist priest. In his hands he held three pills of hornblende and a cup of wine, which he gave to Tzu-ch'un, instructing him to swallow them. Then he spread a tiger skin against the inner wall on the west side and seated him on it, facing east.

"Be careful not to speak," he warned. "Though you see imposing spirits or fearful demons, or yakshas,[5] or fierce wild beasts or hell itself—even though your dearest relatives are bound and tortured, none of it will be real. Through it all you must neither move nor speak; quiet your heart and fear not, and in the end you will suffer no harm. Just put your mind on what I have said." And he went out.

3. The popular Taoist term *chung-yüan*, literally the "middle principal," refers to the fifteenth of the seventh month. This day is also the Buddhist Avalamba[na] or Ullambana ("All Souls' Day") Festival. The complementary terms are *shang-yüan* ("upper principal"), which refers to the fifteenth of the first month, and *hsia-yüan* ("lower principal"), which refers to the fifteenth of the tenth month.

4. The Taoist fairies.

5. Monsters.

Tzu-ch'un looked around in the hall. There was only a large earthen jar filled to the brim with water, and nothing else. No sooner had the Taoist departed than the slopes of the hillside were covered with armed men carrying flags and banners, a thousand chariots, and ten thousand horsemen. The roar of their shouts shook heaven and earth. One of them they addressed as "Great General"; he was over ten feet tall, clad, as was his horse all in golden armor of a dazzling radiance. His bodyguard of several hundred men, all holding swords or drawn bows, dashed into the hall shouting, "Who are you that dare face the Great General?"

On both sides they raised their swords and advanced, demanding to know Tzu-ch'un's name and what sort of person he was, to which he made no response. Enraged, they made a great uproar as if they were about to slash him and shoot arrows into him, but he paid them no attention. The general left in a fury.

All at once there were all sorts of creatures—fierce tigers and poisonous dragons, griffins and lions, cobras and scorpions—roaring and snatching as they rushed forward to seize and bite, even leaping into the air over his head. Tzu-ch'un remained unperturbed, and in a little while they were all gone.

Then a great rain fell in torrents, with thunder and lightning in the murky air, and fire wheels racing by to the left and the right, the lightning striking in front and behind, until he could not open his eyes. In a moment the water in the hall was over ten feet deep, lightning came in an unbroken stream, and the thunder roared, as though the very hills and rivers were split open. In no time the waves had reached the place where Tzu-ch'un sat, but he did not budge at all and paid no attention to anything around him.

Before long, the general appeared again, leading a troop of ox-headed jailers and demons of extraordinary appearance. They carried a huge caldron which they placed in front of Tzu-ch'un. They surrounded him on all sides with long, forked spears. He was given an ultimatum: if willing to tell his name, he would be set free; if not, he would be impaled through the heart and thrust into the boiling caldron. He made no response.

Next they brought in his wife and dragged her to the foot of the steps. Pointing to her, the general said, "Tell your name and we will let her go."

When he did not respond, she was whipped until the blood flowed. They shot her with arrows, cut her with knives, poured boiling water on her, and seared her flesh with irons until she could not endure it and screamed and wept, "I am of no account, a disgrace to a gentleman like you. But I have after all had the good fortune to serve you more than ten years as your wife. Now I am tormented past endurance by these demons. I would never expect you to get down on your knees and beg favors of them, but all it would take to save my life is just one single word!" Her tears rained down as she alternately prayed and cursed.

When Tzu-ch'un persisted in paying no attention, the general shouted,

"You think we can't hurt your wife?" And he ordered them to bring the knife and block and slice her, inch by inch, beginning with her feet. She screamed and wept even more desperately, but to the end Tzu-ch'un never once paid her the slightest attention.

The general then announced, "This villain has perfected his black magic and cannot be allowed on earth any longer." He ordered the attendants to behead him, and when it was done, they led his ghost before the Yama King, who said, "Is this the sorcerer of the Cloud Terrace Peak? Deliver him to the tortures of hell."

There he experienced in complete form all the tortures—swallowing molten bronze, being beaten with an iron cudgel, pounded in a mortar, ground in a mill, buried in a fiery pit, boiled in a caldron; he climbed the mountain of knives and the tree of swords. Through it all he remembered the Taoist master's injunction and it all seemed bearable, so never a sigh escaped him. The torturers reported that he had suffered all the punishments, and the Yama King said, "This man is a secret villain. It is not fitting that he should be reborn a man; we will have him born a daughter in the family of Wang Ch'üan, the deputy magistrate of Shan-fu county in Sung-chou."[6]

From birth the little girl was sickly, and hardly a day passed without acupuncture or moxa-burning or some nasty medicine. And she was always falling out of bed or into the fire, but whatever the pain she never made a sound. Soon she was grown into an extraordinarily beautiful girl, but because she never spoke, she was thought by her family to be dumb. Her relatives would take liberties with her and offer her all sorts of insults, but she would not respond.

In the same town was a *chin-shih*[7] named Lu Kuei who, hearing of her beauty, sought her through an intermediary for his wife. The family declined on the grounds that she was dumb, but Lu said, "If my wife is worthy, what need has she for speech? She will serve as a reproach to sharp-tongued women." They agreed to the match, and Lu married her as his wife, with all the six rites.

For several years their love was very deep. She bore him a son, who at two years was unusually bright and clever. His father held the child in his arms and talked to her, but she did not respond. He tried all sorts of ways to get her to talk, but never a word would she say. In a fury he exclaimed, "Minister Chia's wife[8] despised her husband and would never smile, until he shot a pheasant, which made her feel better about him. I cannot do as well as he did, though I should think my accomplishments as a man of education were

6. In modern Kiangsu province.
7. "Presented Scholar," the highest degree in the civil service examination system and the gateway to high office in the imperial bureaucracy.
8. Of the Spring and Autumn period.

better than any mere archery. If you are not ever going to speak, what use to a man of honor is the child of a wife who despises him?"

And he took the child by its two feet and dashed its head against a stone, spattering blood for several paces around. In Tzu-ch'un's heart love welled up, and for an instant he forgot his vow, inadvertently letting slip a sound of distress: "No—"

The sound was still in the air as he found himself sitting in his old place, the Taoist standing in front of him. It was just the beginning of the fifth watch. He saw the purple flames shoot up through the roof and all at once they were surrounded by a fire. Roof and walls were all in flames.

"You have failed me!" the Taoist said with a sigh.

He seized Tzu-ch'un's hair and threw him in the water jar, and the flames subsided.

"My son, your heart was purged of joy and anger, grief and fear, loathing and desire," the Taoist said to him. "It is only love that binds you still. If you had not uttered that cry, my elixir would have been ready, and you, too, could have become an immortal with me. It is hard, alas, to find someone with the capacity for immortality. I can smelt my elixir again, but your body must remain earthbound. Take heed!"

Pointing out the distant road back, he sent Tzu-ch'un on his way. Tzu-ch'un climbed up on the platform to look. The furnace split apart and inside was an iron rod thick as a man's forearm and several feet long. The Taoist had put off his robe and was cutting at the rod with a knife.

When Tzu-ch'un got back home, he was filled with shame that he had forgotten his vow, and resolved to go back and try to make amends. He went to the Cloud Terrace Peak, but there was no sign of anyone, and he returned home again, sighing and chagrined.

Translated by James R. Hightower

250

The Vigil of the Champion

from *Records of the Western Regions*

Hsüan-tsang (600–664)

To the east of the Deer Forest two or three tricents, we come to a *stūpa* by the side of which is a dry pool about eighty paces in circuit, one name of

This text is included here out of strict chronological sequence and genre category because of its close relationship to the story of Tu Tzu-ch'un (selection 249).

which is "Saving Life," another being "Ardent Master." The old traditions explain it thus: Many hundred years ago there was a solitary sage[1] who built by the side of this pool a hut to live in, away from the world. He practiced the arts of magic, and by the extremest exercise of his spiritual power he could change broken fragments of bricks into precious stones, and could also metamorphose both men and animals into other shapes, but he was not yet able to ride upon the winds and the clouds, and to follow the Rishis[2] in mounting upward. By inspecting figures and names that had come down from of old, he further sought into the secret arts of the Rishis. From these he learned the following: "The spirit-Rishis are they who possess the art of lengthening life.[3] If you wish to acquire this knowledge, first of all you must fix your mind on this—namely, to build up an altar enclosure ten feet around; then command an 'ardent master,'[4] faithful and brave, and with clear intent, to hold in his hand a long sword and take his seat at the corner of the altar, to cover his breath, and remain silent from evening till dawn. He who seeks to be a Rishi must sit in the middle of the altar, and, grasping a long knife, must repeat the magic formulas and keep watch. At morning light, attaining the condition of a Rishi, the sharp knife he holds will change into a sword of diamond, and he will mount into the air and march through space, and rule over the band of Rishis. Waving the sword he holds, he will accomplish everything he wishes, and he will know neither decay nor old age, nor disease nor death." The man,

---

Many early Chinese short stories were derived from Indian tales, although the exact source is often difficult to pinpoint because of uncertainties surrounding the dating of Indian texts and because so many Indian tales were either only transmitted orally or, if written down, are no longer extant. "Tu Tzu-ch'un" is one Chinese short story for which we can probably identify the exact Indian source and even the precise means by which it was brought to China.

It is revealing that a tale clearly of Indian origin is passed off as an ostensibly Taoist piece. This tells us much about the nature of the assimilation of foreign cultural elements in China. The extent to which the story has been transformed during the process of adaptation is remarkable, yet the Indian substratum is retrievable because of the documentation available from an intermediary Chinese text.

"The Vigil of the Champion" is actually taken from the celebrated Buddhist pilgrim Hsüan-tsang's account of his journey through Central Asia and India. Altogether the pilgrimage lasted eighteen years (627–645) and covered 16,000 miles. After leaving the area of modern Turfan (then called Kōchō), he passed through 110 countries and heard of 28 others. His main purpose in making this arduous journey was to bring back Buddhist sūtras which he and his associates would translate into Chinese. The trip was a great success for, although he broke the law by leaving the country without permission, he returned a hero with 657 scriptures. He spent the remaining years of his life rendering 74 of these into Chinese.

Hsüan-tsang was born Ch'en Wei, the youngest son of a Sui dynasty local official, and became a monk at the age of thirteen.

1. A sorrowful or obscure master.
2. Ancient Indian holy men or seers who possessed supernatural powers. The technical transcription of this word is ṛṣi.
3. The magic art of lengthening life, or of a long life.
4. A hero.

having thus obtained the method of becoming a Rishi, went in search of such an "ardent master." Diligently he searched for many years, but as yet he found not the object of his desires. At length, in a certain town he encountered a man piteously wailing as he went along the way. The solitary master, seeing his marks,[5] rejoiced at heart, and forthwith approaching him, he inquired, "Why do you go thus lamenting, and why are you so distressed?" He said, "I was a poor and needy man, and had to labor hard to support myself. A certain master seeing this, and knowing me to be entirely trustworthy, engaged me for his work during five years, promising to pay me well for my pains. On this I patiently wrought in spite of weariness and difficulties. Just as the five years were done, one morning for some little fault I was cruelly whipped and driven away without a penny. For this cause I am sad at heart and afflicted. Oh, who will pity me?"

The solitary master ordered him to accompany him, and coming to his cabin, by his magic power he caused to appear some choice food, and ordered him to enter the pool and wash. Then he clothed him in new garments, and giving him five hundred gold pieces, he dismissed him, saying, "When this is done, come and ask for more without fear." After this he frequently bestowed on him more gifts, and in secret did him other good, so that his heart was filled with gratitude. Then the "ardent master" was ready to lay down his life in return for all the kindness he had received. Knowing this, the other said to him, "I am in need of an enthusiastic person. During a succession of years I sought for one, till I was fortunate enough to meet with you, possessed of rare beauty and a becoming presence, different from others. Now, therefore, I pray you, during one night to watch without speaking a word."

The champion said, "I am ready to die for you, much more to sit with my breath covered." Whereupon he constructed an altar and undertook the rules for becoming a Rishi, according to the prescribed form. Sitting down, he awaited the night. At the approach of night, each attended to his particular duties. The "solitary master" recited his magic prayers; the champion held his sharp sword in his hand. About dawn suddenly he uttered a short cry, and at the same time fire descended from heaven, and flames and smoke arose on every side like clouds. The "solitary master" at once drew the champion into the lake,[6] and having saved him from his danger, he said, "I bound you to silence; why then did you cry out?"

The champion said, "After receiving your orders, toward the middle of the night, darkly, as in a dream, the scene changed, and I saw rise before me all my past history. My master[7] in his own person came to me, and in consolatory words addressed me; overcome with gratitude, I yet restrained myself and spoke not. Then that other man came before me; towering with rage, he slew

5. The marks on his person indicating his noble character.
6. I.e., to escape the fire.
7. I.e., "my lord or master, whom I now serve"—the solitary master or Rishi.

me, and I received my ghostly body. I beheld myself dead, and I sighed with pain, but yet I vowed through endless ages not to speak, in gratitude to you. Next I saw myself destined to be born in a great Brahman's house in southern India, and I felt my time come to be conceived and to be brought forth. Though all along enduring anguish, yet from gratitude to you no sound escaped me. After a while I entered on my studies, took the cap,[8] and I married; my parents dead, I had a child. Each day I thought of all your kindness, and endured in silence, uttering no word. My household connections and clan relatives all seeing this, were filled with shame. For more than sixty years and five I lived. At length my wife addressed me, 'You must speak; if not, I slay your son!' And then I thought, 'I can beget no other child, for I am old and feeble; this is my only tender son.' It was to stop my wife from killing him I raised the cry."

The "solitary master" said, "All was my fault; 'twas the fascination of the devil." The champion, moved with gratitude, and sad because the thing had failed, fretted himself and died. Because he escaped the calamity of fire, the lake is called "Saving the Life," and because he died overpowered by gratitude, it has its other name, "The Champion's Lake."

Translated by Samuel Beal

8. Of manhood.

251
Liu Yi; or, Tale of the Transcendent Marriage of Tung-t'ing Lake

Li Ch'ao-wei (fl. c. 790)

In the Yi-feng period,[1] a young scholar named Liu Yi was presented as a provincial candidate but failed to be classed in the examination. As he prepared to go home to the banks of the Hsiang[2] he recalled that a man from his part of the country was staying in Ching-yang[3] and went over to bid him

Another classical-language short story from the T'ang period. It is preserved in two of the major sources for this genre, *Extensive Records from the Reign of Grand Tranquility* (*T'ai-p'ing kuang chi*) and *Classified Stories* (*Lei shuo*). Little is known about the author.

1. 676–678 C.E.

2. The Hsiang River flows north through the heart of modern Hunan province to empty into Tung-t'ing Lake.

3. Ching-yang was and is a few miles northwest from the site of the T'ang western capital, Ch'ang-an, situated on the southern bank of the Ching River.

farewell. But six or seven tricents along the way a bird flew up, and his horse took fright. It left the road and bolted, covering six or seven more tricents before coming to a stop.

Liu now caught sight of a woman tending sheep by the wayside, and finding this strange he took a closer look. She was remarkably pretty, yet her delicate brows were knit, her clothes badly weathered. She stood listening intently, poised there as though expecting someone.

Liu Yi asked her: "Why do you demean yourself so with this hard work?"

At first, in her distress, she refused to speak, but finally made a tearful reply: "Poor, unfortunate maid that I am, today I receive a gentleman's kind attention! But I am so full of bitterness that I cannot hold modestly back—I hope I may put my case to you! I am the youngest daughter of the Dragon Lord of Lake Tung-t'ing. My parents married me to the second son of the River Ching, but my husband is a playboy, infatuated with servant girls, and each day has brought new contempt and neglect from him. So I complained to my husband's parents, but they were too fond of their son to be able to control him. And as I complained more often and more urgently, they became displeased, put blame on me, and cast me out into this plight!"

With these words she sobbed and the tears flowed in uncontrolled grief. Then she went on: "Who knows how far this place is from Tung-t'ing? Over that vast tract of space no letter can get through. And with those closest to my heart so utterly cut off from me, they have no way to know my woes. But I hear that you are going back to Wu,[4] sir, and will pass close by Tung-t'ing. If perhaps I entrusted a letter to your care, I wonder if you might be willing to consent?"

Liu Yi said: "I am a man of chivalry, and hearing your tale has so stirred my system and roused my blood that I curse the lack of wings that stops me flying straight there. How can I possibly say no? However, Lake Tung-t'ing is deep water, and I live on dry land. So how could I deliver your message? My one fear is that, since no communication links this bright world with that dark one, I should fail your deeply felt request and frustrate my own strong desire. What magic do you have that could take me there?"

Weeping bitterly she thanked him and said: "The burden you are taking on is of such value that I shall say no more than this: if I receive a message in reply I'll repay you even though it costs my life! I would not have ventured to speak if you had not said yes, but since you have agreed and put the question— there is no difference worth mentioning between Tung-t'ing and the capital city."

Liu Yi asked to hear more.

She said: "On Tung-t'ing's southern shore is a large orange tree, known to

4. This is puzzling. If Liu Yi's home is on the banks of the Hsiang River, in central southern China, it cannot be associated with Wu, a region far away on the east coast. But the actual site of his home is never stated, and he moves to other parts of China later in the story.

the local people as the Orange Tree Soil God.[5] You must take off this belt you are wearing and strap on something else. Next, knock three times on the tree, and someone will come in response. You then go with him, and nothing will stand in your way. I hope, sir, that apart from what is set out in the letter, you will convey all the heartfelt things I have said. On no account break your trust!"

Liu Yi said: "I am humbly at your service."

She then took out a letter from inside her jacket and handed it to him, bowing repeatedly. And as she gazed eastward she wept tears of sadness that she seemed unable to control. Liu Yi felt deeply distressed for her.

He now put the letter in his bag and asked another question: "I don't know what purpose you are tending sheep for—surely the gods do not slaughter them?"

She said: "These are not sheep, but rain-makers."

"And what are rain-makers?"

"The same kind of things as peals of thunder."

When Liu Yi looked around at them they glanced with pride and trod with vigor, seeming most remarkable as they browsed and drank, although in their size, their coat, and horns there was nothing to distinguish them from other sheep.

Liu Yi spoke again: "If I act as your messenger I hope you will not avoid my presence when one day you go back to Tung-t'ing!"

She answered: "Not only shall I not avoid you—I shall treat you as a very kinsman!"

With these words they made their farewells, and he set off to the east. When he glanced back after a few dozen steps the woman and her sheep were all lost to sight.

That night he came to the county town and took leave of his friend. And after a month or more he reached his own district and went back home.

He now made a search of Lake Tung-t'ing, and sure enough there was the Orange Tree Soil God on its southern shore, upon which he changed his belt, faced the tree, and struck it just three times. Presently a warrior emerged from the waves, bowed twice, and invited him in, asking: "Where have you come from, noble guest?"

But Liu Yi would not divulge the truth. He said: "I have just come to have audience with the king."

The warrior parted the water and, pointing the way, led Liu Yi forward with the instruction: "Close your eyes and count your breaths,[6] and you will be able to get through."

---

5. There is a clear link in popular Taoist lore between trees (especially the orange or tangerine), the soil god, prayers for rain, and the dragon who controls rainfall.

6. Counting breaths was part of Zen Buddhist meditation practice. But Ko Hung's *Master Who Embraces Simplicity* (*Pao-p'u Tzu*) refers to a technique of one Lord Cheng: "If you simply

Liu Yi did as he said, and they arrived at the palace. Only now did he see terraces and towers in facing ranks, gateways in their countless thousands, every single known kind of rare herb and precious tree. The warrior made Liu Yi stop in the corner of a great chamber, saying: "Our guest must wait for him here."

Liu Yi asked: "What place is this?"

He answered: "The Hall of Transcendent Void."

On close inspection every precious substance known to man proved to be there: the pillars were of white jade, the steps of green jade; the couches were of coral, the blinds of rock crystal. Carved colored glass studded the nephrite eaves, decorative amber adorned the rainbow ridge-beam. Words could do no justice to this scene of dim splendor.

Time went by, yet the king did not come. Liu Yi asked the warrior: "Where is the Lord of Tung-t'ing?"

He said: "My Lord has graced with his presence the Tower of the Dark Pearl, where he is debating *The Book of Fire* with the Taoist Master of the Sun Principle. He will finish in a moment."

Liu Yi asked: "What is *The Book of Fire?*"

The warrior replied: "My Lord is a dragon, and dragons use water as their divine element. By wielding a single drop they are able to engulf valleys and hills. The Taoist master is a human, the race that uses fire as its sacred element. A man could burn down the O-p'ang Palace,[7] by putting a single lamp to it. Yet, with those distinct transcendent functions they have different occult processes. The Taoist Master of the Sun Principle is expert in the ways of man, and my Lord has invited him here to hear him speak."

As they finished talking the palace gates opened and they saw, thronged about with a great concourse of followers, a man robed in purple and bearing a green jade tablet.[8] Leaping up, the warrior said: "This is my Lord!" and went forward to announce Liu Yi.

The Lord surveyed him, then asked: "You must surely come from the world of men?"

Liu Yi replied: "That is so," and proceeded to bow repeatedly. The Lord bowed too, and bade him sit at the lower end of the Hall of Transcendent Void.

He said: "In the deep obscurity of my watery realm I lack the blessings of

---

practice holding your breath for as long as a thousand inhalations, then in the long run you will be able to stay underwater for a day or more." The passage goes on to describe the use of rhinoceros horn to enable humans to function underwater, in one case to "breathe underwater."

7. The royal palace at the Ch'in capital Hsien-yang, built in 212 B.C.E. and burned down in 206 by the usurper Hsiang Yü.

8. The jade tablet (*kuei*) was an ancient emblem of imperial sovereignty. The green jade tablet was identified specifically in the *Chou Rituals* (*Chou li*) with worship of the East.

enlightenment. But you, sir, have 'seen fit to travel a thousand tricents': do you 'have some purpose'?"[9]

Liu Yi said: "I am a fellow countryman of yours, Great King. I grew up in Ch'u, my studies took me to Ch'in. But lately, when I failed to gain a class, I made a passing visit to the right bank of the Ching, where I saw your daughter tending sheep in the country. It was unbearable to watch her lovely hair being tossed in the wind and rain. So I questioned her, and she told me she was mistreated by her husband, ignored by her parents-in-law, and thus reduced to this plight. Her tears of woe streaming down truly cut to the heart. She then entrusted a letter to me, I gave her my promise, and now here I am with it."

He took out the letter and offered it up. When the Lord of Tung-t'ing had read it he covered his face with his sleeve and wept. "It was her father's fault," he said. "I failed to pay close attention, idly turned a blind eye and a deaf ear, causing a frail child from my ladies' chambers to come to violent harm far from her home! Yet you, sir, a mere passerby, were able to recognize her distress. As long as I am blessed with health and strength I shall never dare forget your goodness."

Uttering these words he broke into long lament, and all around him shed tears. The Lord now handed the letter to a eunuch in close attendance on him, with instructions to take it into the inner palace. Moments later the inner palace filled with anguished weeping. In alarm the Lord told his attendants: "Quickly tell them to be silent in the palace, in case Ch'ien-t'ang finds out!"

Liu Yi asked: "Who is Ch'ien-t'ang?"

"He is my dear younger brother, once master of the Ch'ien-t'ang River, but now in retirement."

Liu Yi asked: "Why must he not be allowed to find out?"

"Simply because his valor surpasses other men's. When, long ago, Yao suffered nine years of flooding, that was a single outburst from this young man! And when he quarreled recently with a general in heaven, the Five Peaks all quaked. The Monarch on High was lenient with my brother's crime because I had performed various small services over the years. But he is still tethered up here, and for that reason the people of Ch'ien-t'ang await him day by day."[10]

He was still speaking when a mighty roar broke out, the sky split apart, the earth burst open, the palace halls heaved turbulently about, while clouds and

---

9. A simple allusion to the *Mencius*, IA.1, in which King Hui of Liang greets Mencius in these terms.

10. A reference to the great tidal bore which sweeps up the Ch'ien-t'ang River from its estuary in Hangchow Bay at certain times of the year, often causing serious flooding (see selection 217).

mist seethed and boiled. Before long a crimson dragon appeared, over a thousand feet long, with flashing eyes and gory tongue, ruddy scales and fiery whiskers. It trailed a golden chain from its neck, and dangling from the chain was a pillar of jade. Thunderbolts in their thousands whirled about its body; sleet, snow, rain, and hail all came down at once. It flew off, ripping the blue sky asunder.

In his terror Liu Yi stumbled and collapsed on the ground. The Lord rose personally to help him up, saying: "Don't be afraid! You will come to no harm, for sure!"

It was some time before he settled a little and was able to regain his self-control. He then took leave, saying: "I want to go home alive, so as not to be there when he returns."

The Lord said: "He'll certainly not come like that! Though he set off in this style, he will not come back the same way. Now I hope we can do the honors for you as best we may." And he ordered drink to be served. They toasted one another in hospitable fellowship.

Presently, as happy breeze and cloud of bliss blew mild and warm, as banners and staffs of ceremony displayed their delicate crafting and music created by Emperor Shun moved along in company, huge thousands of lovely girls crowded in with gay chatter and bright laughter. In their midst was one whose gossamer brows were in repose, who wore shining jewels all over, whose gown of crepe silk rippled out around her. A close look revealed that this was she who had earlier sent the message. Both joy and grief showed through as her tears flowed in streams. And moments later, with one side veiled in red mist and the other wrapped in purple haze, circled about by scented airs, she moved into the inner palace. The Lord said smiling to Liu Yi: "The Prisoner from the River Ching is back!" And he took leave to go into the palace. A moment more brought sounds of bitter grief which lasted on and on.

Some time later the Lord came out again and joined Liu Yi in eating and drinking. Another man—robed in purple and bearing the green jade, with buoyant looks and bursting pride—now took his place beside the Lord, who said to Liu Yi: "This is Ch'ien-t'ang!"

Liu Yi rose and made haste to bow to him. Ch'ien-t'ang likewise received him with all due courtesy. He said: "My niece had the ill luck to be shamefully used by a young lout. She owes it to you, a gentleman of shining chivalry and good faith, that news of her distant sufferings came through to us. If not, she would now be dust in a grave by the River Ching. Words cannot express how grateful and indebted we feel for your goodness and favor!"

Modestly Liu Yi drew back and declined all this with courteous bows and polite murmurs. Then the man turned to report to his brother:

"Just now I set out from Transcendent Void at morning prime and came to

Ching-yang by midmorning; I fought there at noon, and was back here by midafternoon. Between times I sped up to the highest heaven to report the affair to the Monarch on High. And he, learning of our grievance, pardoned my crime. In this way I have been let off my earlier sentence. But in that violent surge of dauntless spirit I had not time to spare for due leavetaking. I have alarmed and disturbed the inner palace, and what is more I have insulted our guest. In fear and shame, I cannot imagine what offense I have given!"

He drew back and bowed repeatedly.

The Lord asked: "How many were killed?"

"Six hundred thousand."

"Crops damaged?"

"Eight hundred tricents."

"And where is that unfeeling husband?"

"I have eaten him."

In dismay the Lord said: "True, the young lout's attitude was not to be endured. But you were still too hasty. The Monarch on High has displayed his sage wisdom in understanding our profound grievance. If he had not, what case could I have made? But from now on, do not behave like that again!"

Ch'ien-t'ang bowed some more.

That night Liu Yi was lodged in the Hall of Unwavering Light. And next day they feasted him anew in the Palace of Blue Cloud. Friends and kin were invited in, grand ballets were staged; sweet wines were served, good food and fine tableware were set before him.

First, to the sound of reed pipes and military drums, wielding banners and pennons, swords and halberds, ten thousand men danced out on the right. One of their number stepped forward to say: "This is the ballet *Ch'ien-t'ang Breaks the Ranks*."[11] The banners and weapons showed such superior style, the wheeling and charging struck such terror, that the guests' hair bristled up as they watched.

Then, to music of bells and chimes, of strings and wind, costumed in gauze and patterned silk, in pearls and jade, a thousand girls danced out on the left. One of their number stepped forward to say: "This is the ballet *A Princess Returns to the Palace*." The pure notes curved in such sweet cadence, spoke with such yearning, that the seated guests found themselves shedding tears as they listened.

At the end of these two ballets the Dragon Lord in great delight bestowed gifts of fine silks to distribute among the dancers. And then they all drew their seats together in a close line to enjoy the full pleasure of hearty drinking.

---

11. This made-up title mimics the standard court ballet *The Prince of Ch'in Breaks the Ranks*, which originally celebrated the military exploits of the future T'ai Tsung and served T'ang China as a kind of national anthem in dance.

Once they were warmed up with drink, the Lord of Tung-t'ing sang this song, beating time on his mat:

"The vast sky is deep blue/the great earth stretches broad.
Each man has his aim/but how can this be gauged?
Fox sprites and rat saints/ may cling to Soil Altars, hug close to walls,
But when the thunderbolt shoots forth/which of them dares hold its own?
Thanks to this good man/so strong in chivalry and troth,
Our flesh and blood/can return to her home.
With one voice we speak our gratitude:/never shall we forget!"

When the Lord of Tung-t'ing finished his song, the Lord of Ch'ien-t'ang bowed twice and sang:

"High heaven matched them together,/but life and death go separate ways.
Hers was not to be his wife,/nor his to be her husband.
Our dear heart suffered hard times/beside the stream of Ching:
Frost and wind all over her hair,/rain and snow on her jacket.
But thanks to you, noble sir,/who brought over her letter,
Our flesh and blood was enabled/to come back to her old home.
Forever shall we voice our high esteem,/and never fall silent!"

As Ch'ien-t'ang's song came to its close the Lord of Tung-t'ing rose together with him, and they offered a tankard to Liu Yi. With due deference he accepted it, drank it up, then offered two more to the two lords. And he sang:

"As the pale blue clouds drifted by/and the River Ching flowed east,
I grieved for the lovely girl/with pouring tears and blossoming sorrow.
But her letter brought from far away/has served to clear my Lord's distress:
The woeful grudge now duly purged,/she comes back to dwell in repose.
I am obliged for this cordial and refined entertainment,/I thank you for the
    excellent food.
But my rustic home is deserted:/I cannot stay longer.
As I prepare to take my leave/sadness binds me about."

At the end of his song they all cheered.

The Lord of Tung-t'ing now produced a box of blue jade containing rhinoceros horn[12] that could part the waters, and in turn the Lord of Ch'ien-t'ang produced a tray of red amber containing a luminescent jewel. They both rose to present them to Liu Yi. Politely declining at first, he accepted them. Then the ladies of the inner palace all cast silk festoons, pearls, and jade disks down at Liu Yi's side. These piled up in dazzling heaps, and moments later

12. The horn of the rhinoceros was reputed to have this property: "If a horn is obtained at least three inches [variant one foot] long, carved in the form of a fish and placed in the mouth as the water is entered, the water will often be opened up to man." Compare with note 6 above.

he had vanished in the midst of them. Liu Yi looked all around, exclaiming and laughing, and scarcely had time to make his bows of gratitude.

When they had drunk their fill, Liu Yi rose and lodged once more in the Hall of Unwavering Light.

The next day they feasted him again in the Tower of Pure Light. Ch'ien-t'ang, flushed with wine, unceremoniously squatted down and said to Liu Yi: "You must have heard the saying 'a tough rock may be split but not bent, a chivalrous knight may be killed but not shamed'? Now I have a thought that I wish to put to you, sir. If you approve, then we shall soar together to the highest heaven; if not, we shall all be groveling in the muck. What do you say?"

Liu Yi asked to hear more.

Ch'ien-t'ang said: "The wife from Ching-yang is the Lord of Tung-t'ing's beloved daughter, and her sweet nature and fine disposition are prized by all her kin. She had the ill luck to suffer shame from a scoundrel. But now that is all finished, and we are hoping to entrust her to a man of lofty principle, to be kin of ours for generations to come so that she who received your kindness will know the man she is joining, and we who hold her dear will know the man we are giving her to. That surely is the way for a true gentleman to see through his work to the end!"

Liu Yi gravely rose to his feet and gave a sharp laugh: "Truly I never knew that the Lord of Ch'ien-t'ang was as wretched as this! When I first heard of your bestriding the Nine Provinces and enfolding the Five Peaks as you gave vent to your fury, and when later I saw you snap the golden chain and drag along the jade pillar as you rushed to an emergency, I thought that your firm resolution and clear integrity could have no rivals. For to face up to death when another affronts you, to risk your very life when your affections are stirred—this must show a true man's sense of purpose! But what now!—while flutes and pipes are serenading a peaceful gathering of relatives and guests, you spurn all principles to impose your might on another man! Not what I would once have expected! If I had met you among mighty waves or amid gloomy mountains, flourishing whiskers and scales and robed in clouds and rain as you pressed me to the point of death, then I would have regarded you as a mere beast and would have no grounds for complaint! But now you are clothed in cap and gown, you sit talking of ritual decorum and moral right, you have a commitment to the Five Relationships,[13] a command of the nuances of conduct that would surpass some of the best in the world of men, let alone the deities of the rivers! Yet with hulking body and violent temper, fortified by strong drink, you want to put pressure on another man. Is that anything like honest behavior? Now my substance is scarcely big enough to

---

13. The five Confucian social relations, those between prince and minister, father and son, older and younger brothers, husband and wife, and friends.

conceal inside one of your scales. Yet even so, with unyielding spirit I dare defy your unprincipled passion! Pray consider that, Prince!"

Ch'ien-t'ang falteringly made apology: "Born and bred in palace chambers, we never received correct instruction. The words said just now were wild and reckless: they have rudely offended a man of wisdom and insight. When I step back to examine myself, my fault brooks no excuse. I hope, respected sir, that you will not let this come between us!"

That night they held another convivial banquet, enjoying the same pleasure as before, and Liu Yi and Ch'ien-t'ang now became the closest of friends.

Next day Liu Yi took leave to go home. The Lady of Tung-t'ing held a separate feast for him in the Hall of Hidden Vista. All the children, servants, and concubines came out to join in the party. The Lady said, weeping, to Liu Yi: "My flesh and blood, who received such great kindness from you, good sir, only wishes she could demonstrate her gratitude—yet now you have come to the moment of parting and separation." And she made that one-time woman of Ching-yang bow before Liu Yi, there at the banquet, in token of thanks.

The Lady went on: "Now that you two are parting, will the day ever come when you meet again?"

Although in the first place he had rejected Ch'ien-t'ang's proposal, on the occasion of this feast Liu Yi bore a look of deep regret. And when at the end he bade farewell, the whole palace grieved. The treasure presented to him was wondrous beyond description.

He now followed the route back, and as he emerged upon the riverbank he saw some dozen attendants escorting him with sacks on their shoulders. They came as far as his home, then took leave and departed.

Liu Yi went to the jewelers' shops in Kuang-ling[14] to sell what he had gained, and before a hundredth part of it was gone his wealth amounted to millions. The richest families of the region felt that he outstripped them all.

He now married a Chang, who died.[15] Again he married a Han, who also died within a few months. He moved house to Chin-ling where, saddened by his single state, he took some steps to find a new mate.

A marriage-broker reported: "There is a woman of the Lu family from Fan-yang, whose father is named Hao and was once magistrate of Ch'ing-liu.[16] In

14. An ancient name for Yang-chou that was revived in 742. This canal port at the center of an important salt-producing area saw a great concentration of merchant wealth following migrations caused by the An Lu-shan Rebellion (see selection 180) and was a major center of international trade. It is clear why Liu Yi should choose to market his jewelry here.

15. The words "who died" do not appear in the text but are clearly implied by the context.

16. The name Hao suggests the vastness of a body of water—here by implication the Tung-t'ing Lake. The administration of Ch'ing-liu ("Clear Stream") district perhaps has a similar allusive intention, although the place (now Ch'u district) does actually lie only a few miles northwest of Chin-ling (now Nanking), where Liu Yi is residing. The Lu of Fan-yang were among the leading clans of the T'ang aristocracy.

the evening of life he devoted himself to the Way and went roaming the wilderness alone. By now there is no news of his whereabouts. The girl's mother, called Cheng, married her a year ago to a Chang of Ch'ing-ho,[17] but unfortunately Chang died early. The mother is now seeking a new husband to match her with, for she pities the girl's youth and sees her intelligence and beauty as precious assets. I wonder what you think?"

So Liu Yi fixed a day and went through the ceremony. Since both bride and groom were from great families, the ritual goods and gifts were of the utmost splendor. The whole of Chin-ling society was much impressed.

One evening a month or so later Liu Yi came home and, as he looked at his wife, had the strong sense that she resembled the dragon woman, though appearing even more lovely, buxom, and bonny. So he spoke to her of those past events.

She said to him: "Surely nothing like that could happen in the world of men! But you and I are expecting a child!"

Liu Yi showed her more affection than ever. Once the child was born and the first month seen out, she changed her clothes and adorned herself richly to invite in all their kin.[18] In the course of that reunion she said smiling to Liu Yi: "Don't you remember me from the past?"

He said: "I once delivered a letter for the Lord of Tung-t'ing's daughter, and she stays in my memory to this day!"

His wife said: "I am the daughter of Lord Tung-t'ing. Through you, sir, I was able to declare the wrongs I bore by the river Ching. I felt such gratitude for your kindness that I vowed in my heart to find a way to repay you. But when my uncle Ch'ien-t'ang proposed a marriage you refused, and we then moved apart to far ends of the earth. Unable to keep in touch, I made myself ill with pining and fretting. My parents wanted to wed me to the youngest son of Cho-chin,[19] but I closed my door and cut off my hair to show how unwilling I was. The point was this: my private vow could not be set aside, yet neither could my parents' bidding be defied; I had been rejected by you, sir, without hope of reunion; yet, although able to report that first grievance to my parents, I had failed to see through my vow to repay you. Then, just when I hoped to come and declare myself before you, you were marrying one woman after another. You married Chang, and when that was over you married Han. Once those ladies had each died in turn you made your home here, and my parents were pleased that I had the chance to carry out my aim of repaying

17. This family was one of the recognized clans in the T'ang middle aristocracy, but its choice here must again reflect a play on the place Ch'ing-ho ("Clear River") and the river home of the dragon who was actually the girl's last husband.

18. The reference is to the family celebration at the end of the traditional one-month ritual seclusion for the mother and newborn child.

19. Name of a river flowing through Szechwan.

you. Today I am able to serve as your wife, and we can spend the rest of our days in happiness together. I shall die without regrets!"

She sobbed, and the tears flowed down. Then she faced him and said: "I would not speak out at first because I knew you were not disposed to be swayed by woman's beauty. I speak now because I know you are minded to love your son. As a woman I am of small consequence, not able to create lifelong commitment through bonds of affection. So I entrust my humble self into your hands on the strength of your love for our son. I wonder what view you will take? Fear and sadness both possess my mind, and I'm not able to dispel them. That day when you accepted the letter you laughed and said to me: 'Be sure not to avoid my presence when one day you go back to Tung-t'ing!' Truly I wonder whether at that point you could have had today's situation in mind? And later, when Uncle put the proposal to you and you firmly refused, were you genuinely saying no, or was it just a fit of anger? Please tell me, sir!"

Liu Yi said: "It all seems fated. When I saw you first by the side of the Ching, crushed by your wrongs and stricken by your sufferings, I was moved by a true sense of injustice. Yet I kept my own feelings in check, because nothing was a concern of mine but bearing the news of your complaint. What I said at first about not avoiding my presence was no more than a chance remark—certainly not a considered one! And when Ch'ien-t'ang put pressure on me there was something in the principle of the thing that could not be put straight—that alone provoked me to anger. You see, my intention from the start had been to act with chivalry—so how could I possibly get a husband put to death and then accept his wife in marriage? That was one thing wrong with it. And I have always given highest priority to maintaining my integrity. How could I compromise myself to surrender to my heart? That was the second thing wrong with it. What is more, with my blunt, frank nature in the thick of drinks plied to and fro, plain speaking was my only thought. I had none to spare for avoiding harm. Yet, on the day I was going to depart, I saw you look so longingly that I felt deep regret at heart. And in the end, tied up with worldly affairs, I had no way to respond with thanks. Ah!—now you are one of the Lu family and married into human society—so my early feelings were no mere daydream! From now on I shall always love you. Not the slightest trace of care shall trouble our hearts."

Deeply moved, his wife wept sweetly. It took her some time to recover, then after a pause she said to him: "Don't think that being another kind of creature deprives me of right feelings: I shall most certainly repay you. Dragons, you know, live ten thousand years. I will share this with you now, and you can go anywhere on water or land. Don't think I am being fanciful!"

Liu Yi was impressed. He said: "I never realized that this matchless beauty would also be a prescription for eternal life!"

They now went together to pay their respects to Tung-t'ing, and the lavish ceremonies of hospitality there were beyond description.

Afterward they moved their home to Nan-hai.[20] Within a mere forty years Liu Yi's residences, carriages, horses, treasures, equipment, and adornment were such that no household of marquis or earl could have bettered them. Liu Yi's entire lineage shared in his bounty. And, to the amazement of all Nan-hai, his looks showed no decline with the mounting years.

When the K'ai-yüan period[21] came the emperor fixed his mind on matters of transcendence and immortality and diligently sought out Taoist techniques. Liu Yi had no peace, and so retired in company with his wife to Tung-t'ing. No one saw a trace of him for more than ten years.

Then, at the end of K'ai-yüan, a maternal cousin of his called Hsüeh Ku,[22] serving as a magistrate in the Western Metropolitan province, was demoted to a post in the southeast. As he sailed over Lake Tung-t'ing one clear day he gazed into the distance and presently saw a blue hill emerge far out among the waves. The sailors crowded to the side, saying: "There was no hill there before—surely it can only be a monster of the waters!"

In a brief moment the hill had come up close to the vessel, and a festooned boat sped over to welcome Hsüeh Ku. A man on board hailed him: "Master Liu is here to wait upon you!" In a flash Hsüeh Ku remembered him, and he hastened over to the foot of the hill, hitched up his gown, and climbed quickly upward.

At the top of the hill was a palace just like one in the human world. He saw Liu Yi standing in a chamber of the palace with an orchestra of wind and strings formed up in front of him and a company of bejeweled girls behind. The ornamental objects were many times more splendid than those in the human world. Liu Yi's discourse was more esoteric than ever, and his complexion more youthful.

He welcomed Hsüeh Ku at the palace steps, seizing his hand with the words: "It is no time since we last met, yet your hair is already going gray!"

Hsüeh Ku laughed: "Cousin, you are a divine being, I am dry bones. Such is fate!"

Liu Yi now produced fifty medicinal pills and gave them to Hsüeh Ku, saying: "Each one of these pills can add just one year to your life. When those years are up, come back here. Don't make trouble for yourself by lingering on in the world of men."

After a merry feast Hsüeh Ku took leave and went on his way. From that

---

20. An old name for the administrative area around modern Canton.

21. Second reign period (713–741) of the emperor Hsüan Tsung.

22. This known individual, who is credited with the transmission of the story in the author's comment below, may be its one firm point of historical reference. The official appointment noted for him in the genealogical tables of the *New T'ang History* is consistent with that given here.

moment on there was neither sight nor sound of Liu Yi again. Hsüeh Ku often told this story to others, but after some forty or fifty years he too vanished from sight.

Li Ch'ao-wei of the Lung-hsi clan, who has written this account, offers an admiring comment: "Here we can see how, among creatures of the five breeds,[23] preeminence always comes from spiritual power. Man is the naked breed, but he can communicate his good faith to the scaly breed. Tung-t'ing's forbearance and uprightness, Ch'ien-t'ang's impetuosity and frank openness— these should be handed down. Hsüeh Ku, whose poems on the subject were never recorded, was the only man able to come near that other region. I have written this piece because I see true chivalry in it."

Translated by Glen Dudbridge

23. Five classes of living creatures, distinguished as feathered, hairy, shelled, scaly, and naked—the human race belonging to and being preeminent in the last, just as the dragon belonged to and was preeminent in the fourth class.

252
The Story of Ying-ying

Yüan Chen (?) (779–831)

During the Chen-yüan period[1] there lived a young man named Chang. He was agreeable and refined, and good-looking, but firm and self-contained, and

"The Story of Ying-ying" (the name of the heroine means "Oriole") is perhaps the most celebrated of all classical-language short stories. It is also probably the best known of all Chinese love stories, regardless of genre or language. Extremely well crafted, this beautiful and moving story formed the basis for the medley entitled "Master Tung's Western Chamber Romance" (see selection 269) and the splendid Yüan drama, *Record of the Western Chamber* (recently translated in full into English as *The West Wing*) by Wang Shih-fu (fl. 1234).

The writing of fiction, even in the classical language, was traditionally considered by Confucian purists to be a trivial pursuit, and literati would seldom publicly admit that they indulged in it (this was, of course, particularly the case with vernacular-language fiction). Nonetheless, there are good grounds for attributing the story of Ying-ying to the famous poet and statesman, Yüan Chen. Among these is the long, stuffy poem by him that appears near the end of the story. Yüan was descended from Tabgatch royalty (the non-Han rulers of the Northern Wei dynasty). At the age of fourteen, he was already well versed in the classics and had passed the first of several competitive examinations. In 822 he was appointed to one of the highest bureaucratic offices in the empire but was removed from it shortly thereafter due to factional infighting at court. Yüan was a close friend of the renowned poet-official Po Chü-yi (see selection 180).

1. Chen-yüan (785–804) was the last of the three reign periods of Emperor Te Tsung of the T'ang dynasty.

capable of no improper act. When his companions included him in one of
their parties, the others could all be brawling as though they would never get
enough, but Chang would just watch tolerantly without ever taking part. In
this way he had gotten to be twenty-three years old without ever having had
relations with a woman. When asked by his friends, he explained, "Teng-t'u
tzu[2] was no lover, but a lecher. I am the true lover—I just never happened to
meet the right girl. How do I know that? It's because things of outstanding
beauty never fail to make a permanent impression on me. That shows I am
not without feelings." His friends took note of what he said.

Not long afterward Chang was traveling in P'u,[3] where he lodged some ten
tricents east of the city in a monastery called the Temple of Universal Salvation. It happened that a widowed Mrs. Ts'ui had also stopped there on her
way back to Ch'ang-an. She had been born a Cheng; Chang's mother had
been a Cheng, and when they worked out their common ancestry, this
Mrs. Ts'ui turned out to be a rather distant cousin once removed on his
mother's side.

This year Hun Chen[4] died in P'u, and the eunuch Ting Wen-ya proved
unpopular with the troops, who took advantage of the mourning period to
mutiny. They plundered the citizens of P'u, and Mrs. Ts'ui, in a strange place
with all her wealth and servants, was terrified, having no one to turn to.
Before the mutiny Chang had made friends with some of the officers in P'u,
and now he requested a detachment of soldiers to protect the Ts'ui family. As
a result all escaped harm. In about ten days the imperial commissioner of
inquiry, Tu Ch'üeh,[5] came with full power from the throne and restored order
among the troops.

Out of gratitude to Chang for the favor he had done them, Mrs. Ts'ui
invited him to a banquet in the central hall. She addressed him: "Your
widowed aunt with her helpless children would never have been able to escape
alive from these rioting soldiers. It is no ordinary favor you have done us; it is
rather as though you had given my son and daughter their lives, and I want to
introduce them to you as their elder brother so that they can express their
thanks." She summoned her son Huan-lang, a very attractive child of ten or
so. Then she called her daughter, "Come out and pay your respects to your
brother, who saved your life." There was a delay; then word was brought that
she was indisposed and asked to be excused. Her mother exclaimed in anger,

2. Teng-t'u was an archetypal lecher. This allusion originates from the character ridiculed
in Sung Yü's (fl. 3rd century B.C.E., see selection 149) rhapsody, "The Lechery of Master
Teng-t'u."

3. P'u-chou, also known as Ho-chung in T'ang times, was under the jurisdiction of Chiang-
chou. It is modern Yung-chi district in Shansi province, located east-northeast of Ch'ang-an.

4. Hun Chen, the regional commander of Chiang-chou, died in P'u-chou in 799.

5. Tu Ch'üeh, originally prefect of T'ung-chou (in modern Shensi), was appointed, after the
death of Hun chen, the prefect of Ho-chung as well as the imperial commissioner of inquiry of
Chiang-chou.

"Your brother Chang saved your life. You would have been abducted if it were not for him—how can you give yourself airs?"

After a while she appeared, wearing an everyday dress and no make-up on her smooth face, except for a remaining spot of rouge. Her hair coils straggled down to touch her eyebrows. Her beauty was extraordinary, so radiant it took the breath away. Startled, Chang made her a deep bow as she sat down beside her mother. Because she had been forced to come out against her will, she looked angrily straight ahead, as though unable to endure the company. Chang asked her age. Mrs. Ts'ui said, "From the seventh month of the fifth year of the reigning emperor to the present twenty-first year, it is just seventeen years."

Chang tried to make conversation with her, but she would not respond, and he had to leave after the meal was over. From this time on Chang was infatuated but had no way to make his feelings known to her. She had a maid named Hung-niang with whom Chang had managed to exchange greetings several times, and finally he took the occasion to tell her how he felt. Not surprisingly, the maid was alarmed and fled in embarrassment. Chang was sorry he had said anything, and when she returned the next day he made shame-faced apologies without repeating his request. The maid said, "Sir, what you said is something I would not dare repeat to my mistress or let anyone else know about. But you know very well who Miss Ts'ui's relatives are; why don't you ask for her hand in marriage, as you are entitled to do because of the favor you did them?"

"From my earliest years I have never been one to make any improper connections," Chang said. "Whenever I have found myself in the company of young women, I would not even look at them, and it never occurred to me that I would be trapped in any such way. But the other day at the dinner I was hardly able to control myself, and in the days since, I walk without knowing where I am going and eat without hunger—I am afraid I cannot last another day. If I were to go through a regular matchmaker, taking three months and more for the exchange of betrothal presents and names and birthdates[6]—you might just as well look for me among the dried fish in the shop.[7] Can't you tell me what to do?"

"Miss Ts'ui is so very strict that not even her elders could suggest anything improper to her," the maid replied. "It would be hard for someone in my position to say such a thing. But I have noticed she writes a lot. She is always reciting poetry to herself and is moved by it for a long time after. You might see if you can seduce her with a love poem. That is the only way I can think of."

Chang was delighted and on the spot composed two stanzas of spring verses

6. To determine an astrologically suitable date for a wedding.

7. An allusion to the parable of help that comes too late in chapter 9 of the pre-Ch'in philosophical work *Chuang Tzu* (see selection 9).

which he handed over to her. That evening Hung-niang came back with a note on colored paper for him, saying, "By Miss Ts'ui's instructions."

The title of her poem was "Bright Moon on the Night of the Fifteenth":

> I await the moon in the western chamber
> Where the breeze comes through the half-opened door.
> Sweeping the wall the flower shadows move:
> I imagine it is my lover who comes.

Chang understood the message: that day was the fourteenth of the second month, and an apricot tree was next to the wall east of the Ts'uis' courtyard. It would be possible to climb it.

On the night of the fifteenth Chang used the tree as a ladder to get over the wall. When he came to the western chamber, the door was ajar. Inside, Hung-niang was asleep on a bed. He awakened her, and she asked, frightened, "How did you get here?"

"Miss Ts'ui's letter told me to come," he said, not quite accurately. "You go tell her I am here."

In a minute Hung-niang was back. "She's coming! She's coming!"

Chang was both happy and nervous, convinced that success was his. Then Miss Ts'ui appeared in formal dress, with a serious face, and began to upbraid him: "You did us a great kindness when you saved our lives, and that is why my mother entrusted my young brother and myself to you. Why then did you get my silly maid to bring me that filthy poem? You began by doing a good deed in preserving me from the hands of ravishers, and you end by seeking to ravish me. You substitute seduction for rape—is there any great difference? My first impulse was to keep quiet about it, but that would have been to condone your wrongdoing, and not right. If I told my mother, it would amount to ingratitude, and the consequences would be unfortunate. I thought of having a servant convey my disapproval, but feared she would not get it right. Then I thought of writing a short message to state my case, but was afraid it would only put you on your guard. So finally I composed those vulgar lines to make sure you would come here. It was an improper thing to do, and of course I feel ashamed. But I hope that you will keep within the bounds of decency and commit no outrage."

As she finished speaking, she turned on her heel and left him. For some time Chang stood, dumbfounded. Then he went back over the wall to his quarters, all hope gone.

A few nights later Chang was sleeping alone by the veranda when someone shook him awake. Startled, he rose up to see Hung-niang standing there, a coverlet and pillow in her arms. She patted him and said, "She is coming! She is coming! Why are you sleeping?" And she spread the quilt and put the pillow beside his. As she left, Chang sat up straight and rubbed his eyes. For some time it seemed as though he were still dreaming, but nonetheless he waited dutifully. Then there was Hung-niang again, with Miss Ts'ui leaning on her arm. She was shy and yielding, and appeared almost not to have the strength to move her limbs. The contrast with her stiff formality at their last encounter was complete.

This evening was the night of the eighteenth, and the slanting rays of the moon cast a soft light over half the bed. Chang felt a kind of floating lightness and wondered whether this was an immortal who visited him, not someone from the world of men. After a while the temple bell sounded. Daybreak was near. As Hung-niang urged her to leave, she wept softly and clung to him. Hung-niang helped her up, and they left. The whole time she had not spoken a single word. With the first light of dawn Chang got up, wondering, was it a dream? But the perfume still lingered, and as it got lighter he could see on his arm traces of her makeup and the teardrops sparkling still on the mat.

For some ten days afterward there was no word from her. Chang composed a poem of sixty lines on "An Encounter with an Immortal" which he had not yet completed when Hung-niang happened by, and he gave it to her for her mistress. After that she let him see her again, and for nearly a month he would join her in what her poem called the "western chamber," slipping out at dawn and returning stealthily at night. Chang once asked what her mother thought about the situation. She said, "She knows there is nothing she can do about it, and so she hopes you will regularize things."

Before long Chang was about to go to Ch'ang-an, and he let her know his intentions in a poem. Miss Ts'ui made no objections at all, but the look of pain on her face was very touching. On the eve of his departure he was unable to see her again. Then Chang went off to the west. A few months later he again made a trip to P'u and stayed several months with Miss Ts'ui.

She was a very good calligrapher and wrote poetry, but for all that he kept begging to see her work, she would never show it. Chang wrote poems for her, challenging her to match them, but she paid them little attention. The thing that made her unusual was that, while she excelled in the arts, she always acted as though she were ignorant, and although she was quick and clever in speaking, she would seldom indulge in repartee. She loved Chang very much, but would never say so in words. At the time she was subject to moods of profound melancholy, but she never let on. She seldom showed on her face the emotions she felt. On one occasion she was playing her zither alone at night. She did not know Chang was listening, and the music was full of sadness. As soon as he spoke, she stopped and would play no more. This made him all the more infatuated with her.

Some time later Chang had to go west again for the scheduled examinations. It was the eve of his departure, and though he had said nothing about what it involved, he sat sighing unhappily at her side. Miss Ts'ui had guessed that he was going to leave for good. Her manner was respectful, but she spoke deliberately and in a low voice: "To seduce someone and then abandon her is perfectly natural, and it would be presumptuous of me to resent it. It would be an act of charity on your part if, having first seduced me, you were to go through with it and fulfill your oath of lifelong devotion. But in either case, what is there to be so upset about in this trip? However, I see you are not happy and I have no way to cheer you up. You have praised my zither-playing, and in the past I have been embarrassed to play for you. Now that you are going away, I shall do what you so often requested."

She had them prepare her zither and started to play the prelude to the "Rainbow Robe and Feather Skirt."[8] After a few notes, her playing grew wild with grief until the piece was no longer recognizable. Everyone was reduced to tears, and Miss Ts'ui abruptly stopped playing, put down the zither, and ran back to her mother's room with tears streaming down her face. She did not come back.

The next morning Chang went away. The following year he stayed on in the capital, having failed the examinations. He wrote a letter to Miss Ts'ui to reassure her, and her reply read roughly as follows:

I have read your letter with its message of consolation, and it filled my childish heart with mingled grief and joy. In addition you sent me a box of ornaments to adorn my hair and a stick of pomade to make my lips smooth. It was most kind of you; but for whom am I to make myself attractive? As I look at these presents my breast is filled with sorrow.

Your letter said that you will stay on in the capital to pursue your studies, and of course you need quiet and the facilities there to make progress. Still, it is hard on the person left alone in this far-off place. But such is my fate, and I should not complain. Since last fall I have been listless and without hope. In company I can force myself to talk and smile, but come evening I always shed tears in the solitude of my own room. Even in my sleep I often sob, yearning for the absent one. Or I am in your arms for a moment as it used to be, but before the secret meeting is done I am awake and heartbroken. The bed seems still warm beside me, but the one I love is far away.

Since you said good-bye the new year has come. Ch'ang-an is a city of pleasure with chances for love everywhere. I am truly fortunate that you have not forgotten me and that your affection is not worn out. Loving you as I do, I have no way of repaying you, except to be true to our vow of lifelong fidelity.

Our first meeting was at the banquet, as cousins. Then you persuaded my maid to inform me of your love; and I was unable to keep my childish heart firm. You made advances, like that other poet, Ssu-ma Hsiang-ju.[9] I

8. After this Brahman music was introduced into China, it was dignified by the elegant name given to it by Emperor Hsüan Tsung of the T'ang dynasty and by the performance of his favorite consort Yang Kuei-fei (see selection 180).

9. An allusion to the story of the Han poet, Ssu-ma Hsiang-ju (179–117 B.C.E.), who enticed the young widow Cho Wen-chün to elope by his zither-playing (see selection 158).

failed to repulse them as the girl did who threw her shuttle.[10] When I offered myself in your bed, you treated me with the greatest kindness, and I supposed, in my innocence, that I could always depend on you. How could I have foreseen that our encounter could not possibly lead to something definite, that having disgraced myself by coming to you, there was no further chance of serving you openly as a wife? To the end of my days this will be a lasting regret—I must hide my sighs and be silent. If you, out of kindness, would condescend to fulfill my selfish wish, though it came on my dying day it would seem to be a new lease on life. But if, as a man of the world, you curtail your feelings, sacrificing the lesser to the more important, and look on this connection as shameful, so that your solemn vow can be dispensed with, still my true love will not vanish though my bones decay and my frame dissolve; in wind and dew it will seek out the ground you walk on. My love in life and death is told in this. I weep as I write, for feelings I cannot express. Take care of yourself; a thousand times over, take care of your dear self.

This bracelet of jade is something I wore as a child; I send it to serve as a gentleman's belt pendant. Like jade may you be invariably firm and tender; like a bracelet may there be no break between what came before and what is to follow. Here are also a skein of multicolored thread and a tea roller of mottled bamboo. These things have no intrinsic value, but they are to signify that I want you to be true as jade, and your love to endure unbroken as a bracelet. The spots on the bamboo are like the marks of my tears,[11] and my unhappy thoughts are as tangled as the thread: these objects are symbols of my feelings and tokens for all time of my love. Our hearts are close, though our bodies are far apart and there is no time I can expect to see you. But where the hidden desires are strong enough, there will be a meeting of spirits. Take care of yourself, a thousand times over. The springtime wind is often chill; eat well for your health's sake. Be circumspect and careful, and do not think too often of my unworthy person.

Chang showed her letter to his friends, and in this way word of the affair got around. One of them, Yang Chü-yüan,[12] a skillful poet, wrote a quatrain on "Young Miss Ts'ui":

> For clear purity jade cannot equal his complexion;
> On the iris in the inner court snow begins to melt.

10. A neighboring girl, named Kao, repulsed Hsieh K'un's (280–322) advances by throwing her shuttle in his face. He lost two teeth.

11. Alluding to the legend of the two wives of the sage ruler Shun, who stained the bamboo with their tears.

12. The poet Yang Chü-yüan (fl. 800) was a contemporary of Yüan Chen.

> A romantic young man filled with thoughts of love,
> A letter from the Hsiao girl,[13] brokenhearted.

Yüan Chen[14] of Honan[15] wrote a continuation of Chang's poem "Encounter with an Immortal," also in thirty couplets:

> Faint moonbeams pierce the curtained window;
> Fireflies glimmer across the blue sky.
> The far horizon begins now to pale;
> Dwarf trees gradually turn darker green.
> A dragon song crosses the court bamboo;
> A phoenix air brushes the well-side tree.
> The silken robe trails through the thin mist;
> The pendant circles tinkle in the light breeze.
> The accredited envoy accompanies Hsi Wang-mu;[16]
> From the clouds' center comes Jade Boy.[17]
> Late at night everyone is quiet;
> At daybreak the rain drizzles.
> Pearl radiance shines on her decorated sandals;
> Flower glow shows off the embroidered skirt.
> Jasper hairpin: a walking colored phoenix;
> Gauze shawl; embracing vermilion rainbow.
> She says she comes from Jasper Flower Bank
> And is going to pay court at Green Jade Palace.
> On an outing north of Loyang's[18] wall,
> By chance he came to the house east of Sung Yü's.[19]
> His dalliance she rejects a bit at first,
> But her yielding love already is disclosed.
> Lowered locks put in motion cicada shadows;[20]

13. In T'ang times the term "Hsiao-niang" referred to young women in general. Here it means Ying-ying.

14. Yüan Chen was a key literary figure in the middle of the T'ang period.

15. The Honan Circuit in T'ang times covered the area to the south of the Yellow River in both the present provinces of Shantung and Honan, up to the north of the Huai River in modern Kiangsu and Anhwei.

16. Hsi Wang-mu, the Queen Mother of the West, is a mythological figure supposedly dwelling in the K'un-lun Mountains in China's far west. In early accounts she is sometimes described as part human and part beast, but since early post-Han times she has usually been described as a beautiful immortal. Her huge palace is inhabited by other immortals. Within its precincts grow the magic peach trees which bear the fruits of immortality once every three thousand years. This might be an allusion to Ying-ying's mother.

17. The Jade Boy might allude to Ying-ying's brother.

18. Possibly a reference to the goddess of the Lo River. This river, in modern Honan, is made famous by the rhapsody of Ts'ao Chih (192–232, see selection 26), "The Goddess of Lo."

19. In "The Lechery of Master Teng-t'u" (see note 2 above), Sung Yü tells about the beautiful girl next door to the east who climbed up on the wall to flirt with him.

20. Referring to her hairdo in the cicada style.

Returning steps raise jade dust.
Her face turns to let flow flower snow
As she climbs into bed, silk covers in her arms.
Love birds in a neck-entwining dance;
Kingfishers in a conjugal cage.
Eyebrows, out of shyness, contracted;
Lip rouge, from the warmth, melted.
Her breath is pure: fragrance of orchid buds;
Her skin is smooth: richness of jade flesh.
No strength, too limp to lift a wrist;
Many charms, she likes to draw herself together.
Sweat runs: pearls drop by drop;
Hair in disorder: black luxuriance.
Just as they rejoice in the meeting of a lifetime
They suddenly hear the night is over.
There is no time for lingering;
It is hard to give up the wish to embrace.
Her comely face shows the sorrow she feels;
With fragrant words they swear eternal love.
She gives him a bracelet to plight their troth;
He ties a lovers' knot as sign their hearts are one.
Tear-borne powder runs before the clear mirror;
Around the flickering lamp are nighttime insects.
Moonlight is still softly shining
As the rising sun gradually dawns.
Riding on a wild goose she returns to the Lo River,[21]
Blowing a flute he ascends Mount Sung.[22]
His clothes are fragrant still with musk perfume;
The pillow is slippery yet with red traces.
Thick, thick, the grass grows on the dike;
Floating, floating, the tumbleweed yearns for the isle.
Her plain zither plays the "Resentful Crane Song";
In the clear Milky Way she looks for the returning wild goose.[23]
The sea is broad and truly hard to cross;
The sky is high and not easy to traverse.
The moving cloud is nowhere to be found—
Hsiao Shih stays in his chamber.[24]

21. Again the theme of the goddess of the Lo River.
22. Also known as the Central Mountain, it is located to the north of Teng-feng county in Honan province. Here the one ascending the mountain may refer to Chang.
23. Which might be carrying a message.
24. Hsiao Shih was a well-known flute-playing immortal of the Spring and Autumn period.

All of Chang's friends who heard of the affair marveled at it, but Chang had determined on his own course of action. Yüan Chen was especially close to him and so was in a position to ask him for an explanation. Chang said, "It is a general rule that those women endowed by Heaven with great beauty invariably either destroy themselves or destroy someone else. If this Ts'ui woman were to meet someone with wealth and position, she would use the favor her charms gain her to be cloud and rain or dragon or monster—I can't imagine what she might turn into. Of old, King Hsin of the Shang and King Yu of the Chou [25] were brought low by women, in spite of the size of their kingdoms and the extent of their power; their armies were scattered, their persons butchered, and down to the present day their names are objects of ridicule. I have no inner strength to withstand this evil influence. That is why I have resolutely suppressed my love."

At this statement everyone present sighed deeply.

Over a year later Ts'ui was married, and Chang for his part had taken a wife. Happening to pass through the town where she was living, he asked permission of her husband to see her, as a cousin. The husband spoke to her, but Ts'ui refused to appear. Chang's feelings of hurt showed on his face, and she was told about it. She secretly sent him a poem:

> Emaciated, I have lost my looks,
> Tossing and turning, too weary to leave my bed.
> It's not because of others I am ashamed to rise;
> For you I am haggard and before you ashamed.

She never did appear. Some days later when Chang was about to leave, she sent another poem of farewell:

> Cast off and abandoned, what can I say now,
> Whom you loved so briefly long ago?
> Any love you had then for me
> Will do for the one you have now.

After this he never heard any more about her. His contemporaries for the most part conceded that Chang had done well to rectify his mistake. I have often mentioned this among friends so that, forewarned, they might avoid doing such a thing, or if they did, that they might not be led astray by it. In the ninth month of a year in the Chen-yüan period, when an official, Li Kung-ch'ui, [26] was passing the night in my house at the Pacification Quarter,

---

25. Hsin Chow was the infamous last ruler of the Shang dynasty, whose misrule and fall are attributed to the influence of his favorite concubine, Ta-chi. King Yu (reigned 781–771 B.C.E.), last ruler of the Western Chou, was misled by his consort Pao-ssu. The behavior of both rulers is traditionally attributed to their infatuation with the women they loved.

26. Kung-ch'ui was the style of the T'ang poet Li Shen (780–846; see selection 60).

the conversation touched on the subject. He found it most extraordinary and composed a "Song of Ying-ying" to commemorate the affair. Ts'ui's child-name was Ying-ying, and Kung-ch'ui used it for his poem.

Translated by James R. Hightower

253

An Account of the Governor of the Southern Branch

Li Kung-tso (c. 778–848)

Ch'un-yü Fen of Tung-p'ing was a man who wandered about the lower Yangtze region avenging wrongs as he saw fit. He was too fond of drinking and given to impulse, paying little attention to the finer points of convention. He had amassed a great deal of property and supported a retinue of gallant men like himself. Once, because of his military skills, he had been appointed

"An Account of the Governor of the Southern Branch" belongs to a subgenre of dream stories in which the dreamer is allowed to see how his own life would develop if he could achieve his worldly goals. The form may originally have come from India in the collections of allegories which were translated into Chinese during the Period of Disunion (180–589 C.E.), and it certainly has strong Buddhist and Taoist overtones during the T'ang dynasty (618–907 C.E.).

Irrespective of the story's origins, its resonances are purely Chinese in the hands of its author, Li Kung-tso. The story may be based on a local legend in the Yangchow region where Li served for a time. But the unusual surname Ch'un-yü would likely call to mind Ch'un-yü K'un, a tippler who, a millennium earlier, depended on his wife's family for support. Some scholars read the story as a topical allegory, intended to mock the practice of marrying royal princesses to local satraps to hold their loyalty, a practice particularly popular around the turn of the ninth century. The motif of messengers clad in hues of blue or purple coming to take an unsuspecting mortal to another realm for instruction is a hoary Taoist one. Other features of the story, such as the women of the court being so attracted to our protagonist, are familiar. In fact, their names identify them as Taoist "nuns" who oft-times plied the world's oldest trade in the T'ang demimonde and who were especially active on holidays (such as those mentioned in the story) when men and women encountered each other on the streets (these encounters were not normal at other times).

The tree translated as "locust" is actually the *Sophora japonica*. It is written with a sinograph which, when broken into its basic components, means "tree of ghosts." (The "ghost" component is actually only a phonetic element.) Like its Western cousin, the acacia, the tree is often host to ants.

Li Kung-tso was one of the main authors of classical-language short stories during the T'ang period. Information concerning him is vague and scanty, but it is known that he successfully passed the Presented Scholar examination, perhaps sometimes around the mid-790's, after which he received several low-level administrative positions in the far southern regions.

a general in the Huai-nan Army. But he drank too much, gave rein to his passions, and offended his commander. Thus he was dismissed and drifted about with nothing to do, spending all his time in unrestrained drinking.

His family lived a few miles east of Kuang-ling commandery. To the south of the house in which they lived was a grand, old locust tree, its branches and trunk long and interwoven, its cool shade spreading for nearly an acre. Ch'un-yü and his hearties would drink profusely beneath it every day.

In the ninth month of the seventh year of the Chen-yüan reign period[1] Ch'un-yü drank so heavily that he became ill. The two friends who were seated with him at the time carried him into his house and laid him in a room to the east of the main hall.

"You should get some sleep," they said to him. "We'll feed the horses, wash our feet, and wait for you to recover before we go."

When Ch'un-yü took off his headband and put his head on the pillow, everything went dark and seemed to spin about, as if in a dream. He saw two envoys clad in purple, kneeling before him, who said: "The king of the Nation of Locust Tranquility has sent us to deliver his message of invitation to you."

Ch'un-yü got down off the couch unconsciously, straightened his clothing, and followed the two envoys toward the gate. There he saw a black-lacquered carriage driven by four steeds and seven or eight attendants. They helped him up into the carriage and departed, pointing to an opening under the old locust tree as they went out the main gate. Then they sped into the opening. Ch'un-yü found this most strange, but he didn't dare to ask any questions.

Suddenly he saw that the landscape, climate, vegetation, and roadways were all markedly different from those of the world he knew. After they had gone a dozen or so miles they came to the suburbs and ramparts of a city. Here, vehicles and people both flowed along the road. To the left and right of him were runners who called out orders very sternly so that passersby on either side struggled to give way. Farther on they entered a great city wall with red gates and a high tower. On the tower "The Great Nation of Locust Tranquility" was written in golden letters. The gate guards made haste to pay their respects and perform their attendant duties. After a short period of time a rider called out, "Because the future royal son-in-law has traveled far, the king has ordered that you rest a while in the Eastern Flowery Lodge." Then he went ahead to clear the way. All of a sudden Ch'un-yü saw an open door and he descended from the carriage and went in. There were many-colored railings next to carved columns, flowering trees with rare fruits, row upon row beneath a dais. Benches and tables, cushions and mats, curtains and a feast were all arranged on the dais. He was most pleased. Again someone called out, "The Chief Minister of the Right is about to arrive." Ch'un-yü then descended the stairs to meet him properly. A man wearing purple and holding an ivory court-

1. 791 C:E.

tablet came forward quickly, and they greeted each other according to all the rules of propriety.

"My Liege has not considered our humble land too far out of the way to welcome Milord," the Chief Minister began, "He is hoping to contract a formal marriage with you."

"How could this humble person dare to hope for such a thing?" Ch'un-yü replied.

The Chief Minister thereupon asked that Ch'un-yü accompany him to where the king was. After they had gone about one hundred paces, they entered a red gate. Guards with spears, shields, axes, and halberds standing in formation to the left and the right stepped back to let them pass. Chou Pien, a lifelong drinking companion of Ch'un-yü, was among them. Ch'un-yü was secretly pleased to see him, but didn't dare to step forward and greet him. The Chief Minister led the way up into a spacious hall, heavily guarded as if it were the king's. There he saw a man, large and imposing, sitting on the throne, dressed in a white silken gown and wearing a crimson-flowered crown. Ch'un-yü Fen trembled and didn't dare to look up. The attendants to the left and right told him to kneel down and do homage.

Then the king said, "Sometime before, I received your father's word that he wouldn't reject our small nation out of hand and he agreed to allow my second daughter, Jade Fragrance, to serve you respectfully as your wife."

Ch'un-yü could only continue staring at the ground. He didn't dare to say anything.

The king went on, "Take him back to the guest lodge first, we will carry out the ceremony later!" There was also a formal edict stating that the Chief Minister should also go back with him to the guest lodge.

Ch'un-yü thought this over. As far as he knew, his father had been a general on the border and because of that had fallen captive to the enemy, so that it wasn't known whether he was still alive. Had the king meant to say that after communicating with his father, who was among the northern barbarians, this matter had been concluded? His mind was very confused and he didn't really know how it had come about.

That evening everything for the ceremony was in complete readiness: the gifts of lambs, geese, monies, and silk, awe-inspiring attendants standing tall, female singers and musicians, wines and savory foods, lamps and candles, carriages and riding horses. There was a group of women, one calling herself Lady Flowery Slope, another Ms. Green Stream, another Higher Transcendent, and yet another Lower Transcendent. There seemed to be a large number of them, each with several thousand attendants. They wore kingfisher- and phoenix-feather hats, golden-cloud cloaks, gems of all colors, and golden jewelry, so that they overwhelmed the eye. Roaming about and enjoying themselves, they stopped by his door, competing to trifle with Master Ch'un-yü. Their manner was very bewitching, their speech seductive, so that he was unable to respond. There was another girl who said to him, "Once on the third day of the third month I went along with Madame Mithridate to the Wisdom of Zen Temple. In the India Hall we saw Shih-yen[2] dance the Brahman Dance. I sat on the stone bench under the north window with some of my companions. At that time you were still young, but you also dismounted and came to watch. You alone tried to force us closer, teasing and flirting. My little sister Hortensia Flower and I knotted a red scarf and put it on a bamboo pole.[3] How could you have forgotten? Another time on the sixteenth of the seventh month I was in the Filial Feelings Temple attending Lady Higher Purity and listening to the monk, Bound to Mystery, lecture on the *Lotus Sūtra*. I left a pair of golden-phoenix hairpins as an offering beneath the podium and Higher Purity left a box made of water-buffalo horn. At the time you were also on the lecture mat and you asked the monk for the hairpins and the box to examine them, sighing repeatedly with appreciation and uttering cries of admiration for some time. Turning to look at us you said, 'Both you and your things are not the sort we have in this world.' Then whether you asked about my family or where I lived, I refused to respond. Your heart was filled with love and you were loath to take your eyes off us. Can it be you don't remember?"

"I treasure the memory in my heart," Ch'un-yü replied. "How could I have forgotten it?"

The women in one voice said, "Who would have imagined that today you would become our relative?"

Three men, very grand in their official hats and sashes, also came forward to pay their respects. "We have received a command to serve the royal son-in-law as best men." Among them was a man who seemed to be an old friend of Ch'un-yü Fen. Fen pointed to him and said, "Aren't you T'ien Tzu-hua of P'ing-yi?" "Yes, I am," T'ien replied. Fen came forward, took his hands, and talked over old times for long while. Then he asked, "Why are you living here?"

"I was wandering about at large, when the Chief Minister of the right, Mr. Tuan, the Marquis of Wu-ch'eng, recognized my abilities. Because of this I've joined up with him."

"Chou Pien is here. Did you know?" Fen went on to ask.

"Mr. Chou," Tzu-hua replied, "is a notable person. He is serving as Metropolitan Commandant, and great are his power and influence. Several times I have benefited from his protection." And so they chatted and laughed happily.

In a short time a messenger called out, "The Royal Son-in-law may go in now!" The three men then outfitted him in a sword, a belt, a cap, and clothes.

2. A general from Sogdiana in Central Asia.
3. This is similar to dropping a handkerchief for a gentleman to pick up in Western society.

"I never thought the day would come when I could personally witness such a marriage," said Tzu-hua. "Don't forget about me once you're married!"

Then several dozen of those transcendent beauties played the most extraordinary music for them, sweet and pure, but with a melancholy melody, such that no mortal had ever heard. There were also several dozen of them holding candles and leading the way for him. To the left and right appeared cloth partitions of various hues and lusters, embroidered with kingfisher feathers and golden thread, which ran on for over a mile. Fen sat upright in the carriage, very agitated, unable to settle down. T'ien Tzu-hua often said something or smiled to help him dispel the tension. Those women he had just spoken with each rode in phoenix-wing carriages and were also coming and going in the palace. They came to a gate on which was written "Cultivation Palace." Those transcendent women all gathered on either side of the gate, telling him to get out of his carriage and bowing and making way, ascending and descending— all just as it is in the world of men. They removed the partitions and took away the screens and he saw a woman who was called "Princess of the Golden Branch." She was about fourteen or fifteen and was just like an immortal. Preparations for the rites of the wedding night were also evident.

From this time on, with each day Ch'un-yü Fen's affection for her grew deeper as his star shined brighter at court. The carriages and vestments in which he went about, on excursions or at banquets, were always inferior only to those of the king. The king ordered Ch'un-yü Fen and his fellow officials to ready the palace guard to go on a grand hunt at Efficacious Tortoise Mountain in the western part of the nation. There were mountains and hills steep and lofty, streams and marshes far and wide, forests of trees in abundance and luxuriance, and of the birds that fly and the beasts that run, there were none which were not bred there. The soldiers had a huge catch, and only when night fell did they go home.

One day Ch'un-yü Fen asked the king for instruction. "On that day when I got married, Your Majesty said he was following my father's orders. My father had served as a general on the northern frontier, but he was defeated in battle and fell into Tartar hands. Since then I haven't had a letter from him in nearly twenty years. As Your Majesty knows his whereabouts, I beg to be allowed to visit him."

"Your honorable father," the king quickly replied, "is serving guard over the northern lands. We haven't lost contact with him. You need only prepare a letter stating your news. There's no need to go to see him immediately!"

Then Ch'un-yü Fen ordered his wife to prepare presents to send with the letter to his father. In a few days a reply arrived. As Ch'un-yü Fen read over the general ideas in this letter, he found that they followed closely those his father had held all his life. In the letter instructions were recalled and emotions expressed indirectly, all as in the past. He also asked whether their relatives were still alive and about the prosperity of their village. And he said that the road between them was lengthy and blocked by winds and mists. The tone of his letter was sad and there was distress in his writing. Further, he would not allow Ch'un-yü Fen to come to visit him, explaining, "In the Ting-ch'ou year,[4] I will meet you again." Fen clasped the letter and choked back a sob, overcome with emotion.

Sometime later his wife said to him, "Why don't you ever think about politics?"

"I am a reckless sort who has no experience in politics," Fen replied.

"But if you were to pursue a political goal, I would support you," she said. Then she reported this conversation to the king. After some time had passed, he said to Fen, "Our province of Southern Branch is not well governed. The governor has been dismissed and I'd like to engage your talents. If you would condescend to take such a limited position, you could go there with our young daughter!"

Fen took these instructions to heart. The king then ordered those in charge of such things to outfit the new governor for his journey. For this reason they arrayed gold and jade, brocades and silks, baskets and boxes, servants and maids, carriages and horses along a broad thoroughfare for the princess to take with her.

As a youth, Ch'un-yü Fen had been a knight-errant and had never dared to have such hopes, so when he achieved this postion he was greatly pleased. Thereupon he submitted a memorial, saying:

> Your subject is the descendant of generals, just an ordinary man with no cultural refinement or administrative talent. He is too coarse to serve in such an important position and would certainly disrupt the regulations of the court. It would be like a common cart-puller changing places with his noble passenger, or like sitting idly while a caldron overturns. Now I want to search far and wide for the worthy and the sagacious to assist me in areas I am unable to manage. Your Subject has found that the Metropolitan Commandant, Chou Pien from Ying-ch'uan, is loyal, upright, law-abiding, and has the talents to assist me. T'ien Tzu-hua from P'ing-yi, who is currently living in retirement, is honest, prudent, and understands government thoroughly. He would enable me to improve the effectiveness of my administration. I have been friends with these two for ten years. I understand fully their talents and can rely on them in political matters. I'd like to request that Chou be appointed Minister of Justice of Southern Branch and T'ien be appointed Minister of Agriculture. This would allow my administration to achieve merit and fame and our legal system to maintain order.

The king made the appointments completely in accordance with the memorial.

That night, the king and his wife gave them a farewell banquet in the

4. 797 C.E.

southern part of the capital. The king said to Fen, "Southern Branch is the largest commandery in the nation. Its lands are fertile and rich, its people numerous and hearty. Without a gracious political policy, you won't be able to govern it. Moreover, you have your two assistants, Chou and T'ien, so we hope you will do your utmost to meet the nation's expectations."

Then his wife admonished the princess, "Mr. Ch'un-yü is by nature inflexible and intemperate, and besides he is young. You must act as is proper for a wife, valuing most compliance and obedience. If you can serve him well, I won't be concerned. Although the border to Southern Branch is not that far, mornings and nights we'll be separated.[5] Thus today since we must part, how could I hold back my tears?"

Ch'un-yü Fen and his wife paid their respects and left for the South, mounting their carriage and urging on their horses, all the while talking and joking in great happiness. After a few days they reached the commandery. Officials, clerks, Buddhists, Taoists, local elders, musicians, carriages, military guards, and horses with bells pressed forward to welcome them. People crushed around them and the sounds of bells and drums clamored for several miles. They could see parapets, towers, and lookouts. The place exuded an abundance of good auras.

As they entered the city-gate, it also had a large plaque written in golden characters which read: "The Seat of Southern Branch Commandery." The homes with red windows and ornamented halberds before their doors were as thick as trees in a forest.[6]

Ch'un-yü Fen "got out of his carriage"[7] and began to examine the local customs, to heal disease, and end suffering. Political matters he entrusted to Chou and T'ien, so that throughout the commandery things were gradually put in order. Twenty years after he took the position of governor, the people throughout the commandery had been reformed by his teachings and they all sang his praises. They erected a Meritorious Virtue Tablet in a shrine they set up for him.

The king greatly valued him and bestowed upon him further emoluments and land, also conferring him with rank and position, so that he became Prime Minister.

Chou and T'ien both became famous because they governed well and were steadily promoted to higher positions. Ch'un-yü Fen had five sons and two daughters. The sons received official positions through the hereditary rank system and the daughters were all married to members of the royal family.

5. Children were expected to call on their parents every morning and evening.

6. Red windows and ornamented halberds arranged before the door were indications of wealth.

7. A figurative expression indicating an official arriving to take up a new post. One of the first duties of such officials was to look into "local customs" to determine that the moral influence of the government was in force.

His fame and glory were the highest of the era, beyond that of all his contemporaries.

In that year the Nation of Sandalwood Creepers came to attack this commandery. The king ordered Ch'un-yü Fen to train his officers and exhort his troops so that they could attack the invaders. Fen submitted a memorial asking that Chou Pien be put in command of thirty thousand foot soldiers to defend against the bandit host at Jade Tower City. Chou was too reckless and underestimated the enemy, so his troops were defeated. Under the cover of night he returned alone on horseback, having cast off his armor to flee the enemy. The rebels also collected the provisions and armor his troops had abandoned and withdrew. Ch'un-yü Fen for these reasons imprisoned Chou Pien and asked that he be punished as well, but the king pardoned them both.

In the same month the Minister of Justice, Chou Pien, got an ulcer on his back and died. Ch'un-yü Fen's wife, the princess, suddenly became ill and after ten days she also passed away. Ch'un-yü Fen therefore asked to be relieved of his governorship to escort her body back to the capital; the king granted his request. Then he entrusted the Minister of Agriculture, T'ien Tzu-hua, with the duties of Governor of Southern Branch. Ch'un-yü Fen set out, sadly accompanying her hearse. As they moved in a dignified manner along the road men and women wailed, people set out offerings of food, and those who obstructed the carriage or blocked the road were too numerous to count. When their procession reached the capital city, the king and his wife, weeping and clothed in white, were in the suburbs, awaiting the arrival of the hearse. The princess received the posthumous title of "The Princess of Mild Bearing." An honor-guard carrying feathered umbrellas and beating drums had been prepared, and she was buried a few miles east of the capital city at Coiled Dragon Tumulus. The same month the son of the former Minister of Justice, Chou Jung-hsin, also escorted his father's remains back to the capital city.

While Ch'un-yü Fen was stationed in Southern Branch, he got to know many personalities in the capital, so that all the noble and prominent families were on good terms with him. Since he had resigned from his position as governor and returned to the capital city, he went out constantly, numbering friends and retainers in his company, so that his prestige and fortune increased daily. The king began to suspect and fear him. At that time someone from the capital city submitted a memorial, which read:

> In the signs from heaven an error is evident, suggesting a great threat to the nation. The capital will be moved, and the ancestral temple will collapse. The cause of this strife came from another people, but the matter lies within Your Majesty's walls.

At the time it was agreed that this was an omen caused by Fen's extravagance. Then Fen's bodyguard was taken away, he was forbidden to see his band of friends, and he was placed under house arrest. Fen, certain that in his many years as governor of the commandery he had not failed in his policies and that rumors unjustly found fault with him, was melancholy and unhappy. The king knew this and said to Fen, "You have been related to us by marriage for more than twenty years. Unfortunately, my daughter died young and wasn't able to be with you in your old age. This is really hard to bear!"

For this reason his wife, the queen, kept her grandchildren in her charge to care for and to educate. A little later the king said to Fen, "You have been separated from your family for a long time. You ought to go home to your village for a time and see your relatives. You can leave your children here. They will want for nothing. After three years[8] we shall send them to you."

"But this is my home," Fen replied. "Where else would I go?"

The king laughed and said, "You come from the world of men—your home is not here!"

Suddenly Fen grew groggy with sleep and his sight was hazy for a while until he became aware of his former life again. Then he wept and asked to return there. The king turned to his attendants indicating they should see him off. Bowing repeatedly, Fen left, and again saw the two purple-clad envoys from before following him.

When they had walked through the main palace gate, he was astonished to see that the carriage he was to ride was dilapidated and there were no diligent envoys or palace servants as when he had come. He got into the carriage and after a few miles they came out of the great city. It seemed to be the eastern road along which he had come to the capital in the past. The mountains, streams, plains, and fields on either side were all the same as before. But his two attendants were not as awe-inspiring, leaving him even less pleased. He asked them, "When will we arrive at Kuang-ling commandery?" But the two went on singing and paid him no heed, until one of them, after a long time, answered, "We will be there soon."

Not long after, they emerged from a hole and he saw the lane through his village which had not changed from former days. Deeply moved, he could not hold back his tears. The two envoys helped Fen out of the carriage, into his gate, and up his stairs, where he saw his own body lying underneath the veranda east of the main hall. Fen was in great dread and didn't dare to advance farther. The two envoys for this reason called out his name in a loud voice a few times and Fen then came back to his senses as before. He saw one of the household servants sweeping the courtyard with a broom and one of his retainers sitting on a bench washing his feet. The setting sun had not yet sunk behind the western wall of his compound and the wine left in their goblets

8. I.e., in the Ting-ch'ou year.

was still glistening by the eastern window. In the dream which flashed by him it was as if he had passed an entire lifetime.

As Fen recalled his dream, he was moved to sigh. Then he called his two friends to him and recounted what had happened. Amazed, they then went out with him to search for the hole beneath the locust tree. Fen pointed to it and said, "This is where I entered in my dreams." The two friends supposed he must have been struck by a fox spirit or a tree elf.

Subsequently they ordered servants to take axes to the knotted roots and newly sprouted secondary trunks and locate the mouth of the opening. Nearby the road running north to south was a large hole, cavernous but well lit, which was large enough to have accommodated a bench. The soil piled on the roots made it seem they were city walls, escarpments, towers, and palaces in which several bushels of ants were hiding. In their midst was a raised platform, its color a kind of crimson. Two large ants about three inches in length with white wings and red heads sat upon it. Several dozen large ants assisted them there, and all the other ants cowered before them. This was their king and it was none other than the capital city of Locust Tranquility.

Farther on they followed another hole which ran straight up nearly two rods into a southern branch. Winding about within the hole were earthen walls and small towers. A swarm of ants was also there, which was none other than the Southern Branch Commandery which Fen had directed.

Farther on was another hole. It went west for over a rod, broad and expansive with tightly packed walls and a deep pit of strange shape. In it was a rotting turtle-shell as big as a peck measure. It was immersed in rainwater that had accumulated there. Small plants grew thick, providing shadows of luxuriance and overlapping each other as they swayed up and down in the wind. This was the Efficacious Tortoise Mountain where Fen had hunted.

They discovered another hole which ran east about a rod: old roots twisted about, shaped like dragons and snakes. In its midst there was a small earthen mound, a little over a foot tall. This, then, was the grave at Coiled Dragon Tumulus where Fen had buried his wife.

When he thought back to those former affairs he sighed and was moved, as those places they had discovered by opening the base of the tree all fit closely with those of which he had dreamed. Not wanting his two friends to destroy them, he quickly ordered them covered up as before.

That night there was a violent storm. In the morning, when he went to look into the hole, the ants had disappeared without a trace. Therefore the prediction made earlier—"When great disaster threatens the nation, the capital city must be moved away"—had its fulfillment.

Now Ch'un-yü Fen recalled the events of the campaign against Sandalwood

Creepers, and again asked his two friends to go out and look for traces of it. Not half a mile to the east of his home was an old dried-up brook. On its bank was a huge sandalwood tree covered with vines and creepers so that if you looked up you couldn't see the sun. There was a small hole in the side of the trunk in which indeed swarms of ants were concealed. Could the Nation of Sandalwood Creepers be anywhere else than here?!

Ah! If even the spiritual mystery of ants is unfathomable, how much more are the transformations of those who hide in the mountains or conceal themselves in forests.[9]

At the time Fen's drinking companions Chou Pien and T'ien Tzu-hua both lived in Six Harmonies county, but had not been by to visit for ten days. Fen anxiously sent his servant-boy to hurry and ask after them. Mr. Chou had suddenly taken ill and passed away, and Mr. T'ien was also bedridden with a disease. Feeling even more the transience of the Southern Branch and understanding man's life was only a sudden moment, Fen then rested his mind in the gate of the Tao, giving up wine and women. Three years later in the Ting-ch'ou year[10] Fen also died in his home at the age of forty-seven, just as predicted.

In the eighth month—the fall—of the eighteenth year of the Chen-yüan reign era,[11] the author of this piece, having sailed from Wu to Loyang and moored my boat for a short time at Huai-p'u, chanced to meet Master Ch'un-yü. I inquired about these events and visited the places involved so that we went over them a number of times. As the events were all verifiable, I recorded and edited them into this account as matter for those fond of such things. Although it is all searching after spirits and speaking of the strange rather than matters involved with the classics, I hope it will be a warning to those young men who wish to steal their way into an official position. May you later gentlemen be fortunate to take the Southern Branch as an accident of life and may you not act so haughtily in this world because of fame or position!

The former Military Adviser of Hua prefecture, Li Chao, composed a coda:

> The noblest emolument and position,
> Power to overthrow cities and lands—
> The wise man regards these things
> As nothing different from swarming ants.

Translated by William H. Nienhauser, Jr.

9. Hermits and ascetics.

10. 797 C.E.

11. This is the equivalent of 802 C.E., an obvious inconsistency in the original. On the basis of material presented by Wang Meng-ou in his annotated version of the text, it should probably be emended to 795 C.E.

Vernacular Short Stories

254
The Shrew: Sharp-Tongued Ts'ui-lien

Anonymous (late 14th or early 15th century)

The Storyteller's Preamble:

> She declaims whole chapters extempore—
> > let no one despise her gift!
> Each speech brings her fresh enemies;
> > her fate moves men to pity.
> Though she lacks the persuasion of the wise Tzu-lu [1]
> May her tale yet win a laugh from you.

This highly colloquial short story harks back to the T'ang transformation texts (*pien-wen*) as preserved in tenth-century manuscripts at Tun-huang, in which verse and prose alternate in both narrative and dialogue (see selection 266). The form of its verse, in which heptasyllabic lines predominate, interspersed with trisyllabic lines and punctuated by a rough and ready rhyme (not reproduced in the translation), is similar to that of the Tun-huang stories, which it also resembles in its mixing of the serious with the grotesque, in its naive tone and incoherence, and in its homeliness of language and infelicitous allusions. When it is further remembered that the heroine ends up as a nun, the ultimate monastic origins of the story would seem to be beyond doubt.

Although the present text of "The Shrew" probably dates to the early fifteenth century, it must have assumed more or less its present shape around the end of the thirteenth century, and many of the customs and motifs it portrays date back at least a century earlier. It is likely that the oral precursor of the present written text derives from Buddhist recitations held in fairgrounds during the eleventh century after monastic performances were forbidden by the government.

1. The disciple of Confucius noted more for fortitude than for wisdom or eloquence.

These lines refer to former days in the Eastern Capital,[2] where dwelled a gentleman by the name of Chang Eminent, who had in his house much gold and silver. Of his two grown-up sons,[3] the older was called Tiger, the younger Wolf. The older son had already taken a wife, the younger was not yet married. In the same city was another gentleman, Li Lucky, who had a daughter named Ts'ui-lien,[4] aged sixteen and uncommonly pretty, accomplished in the art of the needle and conversant even with the Classics, Histories and Hundred Philosophers. She was, however, somewhat too ready with her tongue. In speaking to others, she composed whole essays, and the flow of her speech became a flood. Questioned about one matter, she answered about ten, and when questioned about ten, she answered about a hundred. There is a poem to prove it:

> Asked about one thing, she tells about ten—indeed a feat!
> Ask her ten things, she'll tell you a hundred—rare talent!
> Her speech is ready, her words come swift—truly a marvel!
> Regard her not as common; she is no ordinary maid.

The story went that in the same city was a Madam Wang who went to and fro between the two families to arrange about a marriage. The family stations corresponding, a match was agreed upon, and a propitious day and hour chosen for the wedding. Three days before the event, Li Lucky said to his wife, "Our daughter is faultless in most respects; only her tongue is quick and you and I cannot be easy about it. Should her father-in-law prove hard to please, it were no trifling matter. Besides, the mother-in-law is certain to be fussy, and they are a large family with older brother, sister-in-law, and numerous others. What shall we do?" And his wife said, "You and I will need to caution her against it." With this, they saw Ts'ui-lien come before them, and when she found that the faces of both her parents were clouded with grief, and their eyebrows closely knit, she said:

> "Dad as bounteous as heaven, Ma as bounteous as earth,
> To arrange this match for me today!
> The man finds a wife, the maid a mate,
> It's a time for rejoicing: be gay for luck!
> A fine husband, people all say,
> Possessed of riches and many precious things, and well connected,
> Clever and nimble,
> Good at Double-Six,[5] chess, and all the gentle arts.

2. I.e., the Northern Sung capital Pien, or Kaifeng.
3. The original merely says "two sons," but Wolf's younger brother is later mentioned.
4. The name means "Blue Lotus," and thus has Buddhist associations.
5. A dice game. Skill in the game was rated an accomplishment, certainly in the Yüan and Ming. In *Chin P'ing Mei* (late sixteenth century, see selection 260), go-betweens cataloging the

He composes verse, and antithetical couplets[6] on demand;
He even knows trade and commerce, selling and buying.
How do you like him for a son-in-law
That bitter tears should fall in drops?"

When Li Lucky and his wife had heard her to the end, they were exceedingly angry. They said, "We were grieving even because your tongue is as sharp as a blade. We feared that when you entered your husband's house you might talk too much and offend against the proprieties, and thus incur the displeasure of your parents-in-law and everyone else, and become a laughing-stock. So we called you to caution you to talk as little as possible. But higgledy-piggledy, you come out again with a long discourse! What a bitter lot is ours!" Ts'ui-lien, however, said in reply:

"Dad, ease your mind; Ma, be consoled;
Brother, rest assured; sister-in-law, stop worrying;
It is not that your daughter would boast of her cleverness
But from childhood she has been on her mettle:
She can spin, she can weave,
She makes dresses, does patching and embroidery;
Light chores and heavy duties she takes in her stride,
Has ready the teas and meals in a trice;
She can work the hand-mill and pound with the pestle;
She endures hardship gladly, she is not easily tired,
Thinks nothing of making dumplings and cookies,
Prepares any soup or broth, does to a turn some cutlet or chop.
At night she is vigilant,
Fastens the back door and bolts the gate,
Scrubs the frying pan, shuts the cupboard,
Tidies up the rooms both in front and behind,
Makes ready the beds, unrolls the quilts,
Lights the lamp, asks the mother-in-law to retire,
Then calls out 'Rest well' and returns to her room:
Thus shall I serve my parents-in-law,
And would they be dissatisfied?
Dear Dad and Ma, let your minds be at rest—
Besides these set tasks, nought matters more than a fart."

When Ts'ui-lien had finished, her father rose from his chair to beat her. But the mother pleaded with him, and loudly reproved her, saying, "Child, your father and I were worried just because of your sharp tongue. From now on,

---

virtues of prospective lovers and bridegrooms invariably mention a knowledge of chess and Double-Six.

6. Making up such couplets was part of the schoolboy's exercise in composition.

talk less. The ancients say, 'Loquacity earns the hatred of many.' When you enter your husband's house, be wary of speaking. A thousand times remember this!" Ts'ui-lien thereupon said, "I know now. From this time onward I will keep my mouth shut."

On the eve of the wedding,[7] Mrs. Li said to Ts'ui-lien, "Old grandfather Chang next door is a neighbor of long standing, and you grew up, as it were, under his very eyes. You should go over and bid him farewell." And Mr. Li also said, "That would be right." Ts'ui-lien then went over to the neighbors', crossed their threshold, and spoke in a loud voice:

> "Grandpa Chang, hearken; Grandma Chang, hearken;
> Hearken to my speech, you two old ones.
> Tomorrow at dawn I mount my bridal sedan;
> Today I am come to make the announcement.
> My parents are frail, they have no support;
> Pray keep an eye on them morning and night.
> If my brother and his wife offend you in any way,
> Forgive them for my parents' sake.
> When I return a month after the event,
> I shall myself come to ask your pardon."

Grandfather Chang replied, "Little lady, set your mind at rest. Your father and I are dear old friends. I shall certainly look after him morning and evening. And I shall ask my aged spouse to keep your mother company. On no account let it trouble you."

When Ts'ui-lien returned from bidding Grandfather Chang farewell, Li Lucky and his wife said to her, "Child, you should now tidy up and go to bed early. Tomorrow you have to rise before daybreak to attend to things." Ts'ui-lien then said:

> "Dad, retire first; Ma, retire first;
> You are not like us young ones.
> Sister-in-law and brother can keep me company
> While each part of the house I tidy up.
> The young can watch all through the night;
> Older folk, when they try it, fall a-dozing."

When Ts'ui-lien had spoken, the father and mother were greatly vexed. They cried, "Have done! Have done! As we were saying, you would never change. We will now retire. You can tidy up with your brother and sister-in-law, and then 'Early to bed and early to rise.' "

When Ts'ui-lien saw that her parents had gone to rest, she hurriedly went to the door of her brother's room and shouted aloud:

7. The time, not mentioned in the original, is inserted by the translator.

"Do not pretend to be drunk, sister-in-law and brother—
How distressing even to think of you two!
I am your own dear little sister
And shall be home just one more night.
However could you two act in this way,
Leaving all the chores to me,
Shutting your door, ready to fall asleep?
Sister-in-law, how ungracious of you!
I am at home but this short while—
Would it matter so much if you lent a hand?
You cannot wait to send me away
That the two of you may be free and easy."

Ts'ui-lien finished speaking, and the brother remonstrated with her, saying, "How could you still behave like this? With Dad and Ma there, I am not in a position to scold you. Go and rest now, and get up early tomorrow. Your sister-in-law and I will attend to whatever has to be done." So Ts'ui-lien went back to her room to sleep. In a little while the brother and sister-in-law had tidied up each part of the house, and the entire family retired for the night.

Li Lucky and his wife woke up after a good sleep. They called out to Ts'ui-lien, saying, "Child, what time is it now? Is it fine or rainy?" Then Ts'ui-lien broke into speech:

"Dad, do not rise yet; Ma, do not rise yet;
I do not know if it be rainy or fine;
I do not hear the watch being sounded—or the cock crow.
The streets are quiet, none are conversing;
I only hear Mrs. Pai next door
    making ready to grind her bean-curd,
And old father Huang opposite pounding his sticky rice.
If not still the fourth watch,
Certainly it would be the fifth.
Let me rise first,
Start the fire, chop the wood, and fetch the water.
Next let me scrub the pot,
Boil water with which to wash my face,
And comb my hair till it is smooth and shining.
Let everyone else rise early too,
Lest the bridal procession find us all in a flurry."

Then father, mother, brother, and sister-in-law all rose from their beds. And the father and mother said in an outburst of rage, "All too soon it will be bright in the east. Yet instead of attending to your toilet, you are busy wagging your tongue." But Ts'ui-lien said in reply:

"Dad, do not scold; Ma, do not scold;
See how cleverly I adorn myself in my room.
My raven-black hair I flatten around each temple,
Mix powder and rouge and rub them on my cheeks,
Then paint my red lips and pencil my eyebrows.
A golden earring I wear in each lobe,
Silver and gold, jade and pearl I pin all over my head,
Pendants of gems and tinkling bells I attach to my sides.
You arc marrying me off today,
But, oh! my Dad and Ma, how could I leave you?
I bethink me of the favors of giving suck and rearing
And teardrops wet through my scented silk handkerchief.
Hark, I hear voices outside the house—
Despite myself I grow alarmed.
But today is my lucky day:
Why go on tattling and prattling like this?"

Ts'ui-lien stopped. However, when her toilet was done, she went straight into her parents' presence and said:

"Dad, hear my report; Ma, hear my report;
The dumplings are steamed, the noodles are cut,
The viands and box of delicacies are laid out.
I have them all ready, and now wait patiently
Even while the drumbeats give out the fifth watch.
Mark how our own rooster crows right on the hour!
We must send for the relatives who planned to see me off.
It would matter little if Ma's sister and Uncle's wife stayed away,
But how wicked of Dad's own sister!
She sets no store by her words.
She promised to be here by the fifth watch only yesterday;
The cock has crowed, yet there is no trace of her.
When, later, she enters our gate, I must just—
Instead of a final invitation—
Offer her a resounding slap with all five fingers outstretched."[8]

Angry though they were at her words, Li Lucky and his wife forbore to speak out. Mrs. Li said, "Child, go and ask your brother and sister-in-law to rise now and attend to things. The bridal procession will soon be here." When Ts'ui-lien heard her mother say this, she hurriedly went to the door of the brother and sister-in-law and shouted aloud:

"Dear sister-in-law, dear brother, you are no longer children.
From now on I shall seldom be home;

8. Presumably to give a harder smack.

You could at least have risen early today—
Will you sleep until broad daylight?
It's time to unbolt the gate and open the windows;
Next, you might light the candles and aromatic incense;
Then give the ground, within and without, a sweeping:
The bridal sedan is expected any moment,
And if the hour[9] be missed and my parents-in-law annoyed,
The pair of you shall hear from me!"

The brother and sister-in-law swallowed the affront and kept silent, and they attended to various tasks in the house. Then Li Lucky said to Ts'ui-lien, "Child, you should go before the family shrine, make obeisance to your ancestors, and bid them farewell. I have already lit the candles and incense; so do it while we wait for the bridal procession. May the ancestors protect you and you be at peace in your husband's home." Thus instructed, Ts'ui-lien took a bunch of lighted incense sticks and went before the shrine, and even as she made obeisance, she prayed aloud:

"Shrine that guides the household,
You sages that were our ancestors,
This day I take a husband,
Yet shall not dare keep my own counsel:
At the solstices and equinoxes and the beginning of each season,
I still will offer up the smoke of incense.
I pray to your divine wisdom
Ten thousand times that you pity and hearken!
The man takes a wife, the maid a mate—
This is in the nature of things—
May there be good fortune and rejoicing!
May husband and wife both remain sound and whole,
Without hardship, without calamity,
Even for a hundred years!
May they be merry as fish in water
And their union prove sweeter than honey,
Blessed with five sons and two daughters—
A complete family of seven children—
Matched with two worthy sons-in-law,
Wise and versed in etiquette,
And five daughters-in-law too,
Paragons of filial piety.
May there be grandsons and granddaughters numerous
To flourish generation after generation.

9. The lucky hour fixed upon by the astrologer for the wedding ceremony.

May there be gold and pearls in heaps,
And rice and wheat to fill a granary,
Abundance of silkworms and mulberry trees,
And cattle and horses drawn up neck to neck,
Chickens, geese, ducks, and other fowl,
And a pond teeming with fish.
May my husband obey me,
Yet his parents love and pity me;
May the sister-in-law and I live in harmony,
And the older and the younger brother be both easy to please;
May the servants show full respect,
And the younger sister take a fancy to me.
And, within a space of three years,
Let them die, the whole lot,
And all the property be left in my hands:
Then Ts'ui-lien would be happy for some years!"

When Ts'ui-lien had finished her prayer, there was a din outside the gate. It was a confused noise of many musical instruments, above which rose the shrill notes of pipes and singing. The procession from the bridegroom's family, carriage, horsemen and all, was at the gate. And the astrologer accompanying the procession chanted in verse:

"Roll up your bead curtain and fasten it with jade hooks;
A perfumed carriage, followed by noble horses,
    has reached your gate.
Be liberal in your happy-omened tips on this auspicious occasion
And in wealth, honor, and splendor pass a hundred autumns."

Li Lucky then asked his wife to fetch money to reward the astrologer, the matchmaker, the grooms, and other attendants. But when Mrs. Li came out with the banknotes, Ts'ui-lien snatched them from her, saying, "Let me distribute these notes—

Dad, you are not used to this; Ma, you are not used to this;
Brother and sister-in-law, you too are not used to this dealing.
Hey, all of you there, come and stand before me!
Be it less or more, it is as I shall apportion.
To the sedan-bearers, five thousand copper cash;
Mr. Astrologer and the matchmaker each get two and a half.
Keep your money well, do not start a row;
If any of you lose it, you have but yourself to blame.
Look, there's another thousand cash note remaining—
Take it, matchmaker, and buy a cake
To comfort your dotard of a husband at home."

The astrologer, the sedan-bearers, and the others were all aghast when they heard this. They said, "We have seen thousands of brides but never one so quick in speech." They gaped and put their tongues out and, swallowing their anger, crowded around Ts'ui-lien and helped her onto the bridal sedan.

While they were on their way, the matchmaker kept on admonishing Ts'ui-lien, "Little lady, when you reach the gate of the house of your parents-in-law, on no account open your mouth." Before long, the procession reached the gate of the Chang home and the sedan-chair was let down. The astrologer chanted:

> "The sound of nuptial music is heard all over the capital;
> The Weaving Maid this day weds the Divine Cowherd.[10]
> The relatives of this house come forth to receive the treasure;
> The bride in her finery accepts her mouthful of rice—
>   a custom from time immemorial."

To go on with the story, the matchmaker held up a bowl of rice and shouted loudly, "Little lady, open your mouth to receive the rice."[11] Upon this, Ts'ui-lien in her bridal sedan burst out in rage:

> "Shameless old bitch! Shameless old bitch!
> One moment you tell me to shut my mouth,
>   and the next you ask me to *open* it!
> Oh! the unfathomable glibness of matchmakers!
> However could you change your don'ts at once into do's?
> Are you drunk already so early in the day
> That foolishly you open *your* mouth,
>   lying and wagging your tongue?
> Just then while you walked by my sedan
> You warned me on no account to open my mouth.
> I have only now been set down before the gate—
> Why then do you ask me to open my mouth?
> Blame me not for calling you names—
> Really you are but a painted old bitch."

The astrologer then said, "Bride, cease your anger. She is the matchmaker. You go too far in your words. There is no precedent for such behavior in a bride." But Ts'ui-lien replied:

> "Mr. Astrologer, you are a man of learning;
> How then could you be so dull of apprehension?
> Not to speak when one ought to is, by definition, slow-witted.
> This bawd of a matchmaker will be the death of me!

10. The lovers who were transformed into two stars separated by the Milky Way, to meet only on the night of the seventh of the seventh moon each year.

11. The custom is not recorded in the accounts of Sung city life.

She says the bridegroom's family is wealthy and high-ranking,
Possessed of riches and precious things, much silver and gold;
A calf or horse they would kill for their table;
Their gate is made of sandal and sapanwood;
They have silks, gauzes, brocades in numberless rolls,
And pigs, goats, cattle, and horses all in droves.
Yet even before I enter the house, they dish up this cold rice:
Better be poor than wealthy and high-ranking in *this* fashion.
Hard indeed to endure a family so uncouth
As would serve up cold rice and expect me to swallow it!
Had I no regard for the faces of both parents-in-law,
I could beat you till you saw stars!"

Ts'ui-lien having had her say, the matchmaker was so incensed that she tasted not a drop of wine but, like a whiff of smoke, vanished into the house, neither minding Ts'ui-lien's descent from the bridal sedan [12] nor the ensuing ceremony at the altar.

But the relatives of the bridegroom's family crowded around Ts'ui-lien and escorted her into the ceremonial hall, where they made her stand with her face to the west. [13] The astrologer, however, announced, "The bride will turn and face the east. The stars of good luck are all in the east today." At this, Ts'ui-lien again burst out:

"Just then it was west, and now I must face east.
Will you drag the bride about as you would lead a beast?
Having turned around and around, tending in no fixed direction,
I am so vexed, my heart is afire:
I cannot tell who my mother-in-law
Or who my father-in-law is
Amidst this noisy crowd of relatives even to the ninth degree,
With the younger brother and sister adding to the confusion.
The red paper tablet is placed in the center
And red silken lanterns, several pairs of them, are lit.
But, wait, my father-in-law and mother-in-law are not yet deceased.
Why then should there be a lamp for the dead?"

Old Chang Eminent and his wife were furious when they heard this. They exclaimed, "It was earlier agreed that our son would marry the daughter of a respectable family. Who would have known it would turn out to be this ill-mannered, ill-bred, long-tongued wayward peasant girl?" And all the relatives of the nine degrees gaped, utterly confounded.

12. This involved much ceremony.
13. The customary position. The altar is in the north, and as seen by the guests, the bride would be on the right and the groom on the left.

Finally the astrologer said, "This child has been spoiled at home. She has only just arrived today. You will need to train her gradually. Let us proceed with the ceremony of bowing before the altar, to be followed by the bowing to the relatives." And when the ceremony was over and all the relatives, old and young, had been introduced, the astrologer, chanting in verse, requested the bride and groom to enter the nuptial chamber for the strewing of the bed-curtains:

"The newly wed move their steps across the lofty hall;
Nymph and god together enter the nuptial chamber.
Be liberal in your happy-omened tips
    on this auspicious occasion—
Scatter the grain in all directions,
    that yin and yang mingling may increase."

Wolf went in front, with Ts'ui-lien behind him. The astrologer, holding before him a peck containing a mixture of the five grains, followed them into the nuptial chamber.

The newly wedded couple sat on the bed while the astrologer chanted with the grain in his hand:

"Scatter the grain east of the bed-curtains—
Red candles cast their shadows where thick screens enfold.
Long may youthful charms bloom, not fade;
Eternal spring prevail in the painted hall!

Scatter the grain west of the bed-curtains—
Pennants and ribbons stream down the corners of the bed.
Lift the veil and you will see the goddess's face;
The godlike bridegroom attains his laurel branch.[14]

Scatter the grains south of the bed-curtains—
Nuptial bliss long to linger over!
A gentle breeze in moonlight cools hall and bower,
Flapping two belts adorned with the 'heir-bearing' plant.[15]

Scatter the grain north of the bed-curtains—
That overflowing beauty between her eyebrows!

14. The goddess Ch'ang-o dwells alone with a white rabbit and a laurel tree in the moon, where her earthbound husband, Yi, eventually joins her. In other versions, she is visited by the woodcutter Wu Kang, who is, however, condemned to hack eternally at the laurel branches, which heal at once. Thus mythology. T'ang examination candidates spoke of "breaking off a laurel branch" when they were successful. Since successful examination candidates were readily accepted as bridegrooms, "attainer of the laurel branch" and "moon-goddess's guest" came to be applied to both successful examinees and bridegrooms.
15. The day lily.

In the warmth of the embroidered curtains on a night in spring
The moon goddess detains her favored guest.

> Scatter the grain above the bed-curtains—
> A pair of intertwining mandarin ducks!
> May you dream tonight of the bear[16]
> And the pearl-oyster falling onto your palm!

> Scatter the grain within the bed-curtains—
> A pair of jade hibiscus under the moon!
> It's as if one encountered a fair immortal,
> Wrapped in crimson clouds, alighting from Mount Wu.[17]

> Scatter the grain under the bed-curtains—
> Some say a golden light will shine in the room.
> Share now the lucky dreams of this night:
> Bring forth next year a man-child and win enhanced standing.

> Scatter the grain in front of the bed-curtains—
> Hovering in the air is neither mist nor smoke,
> It is the coiled-dragon incense fume:
> The student at last meets his fairy bride.[18]

> Scatter the grain behind the bed-curtains—
> Man and wife agreeing, long cherish each other.
> From of old 'Wife chimes in when husband sings';
> Do not then roar like the proverbial lioness."[19]

To go on with the story, the astrologer had not yet completed the ceremony of
strewing the bed-curtains, when Ts'ui-lien sprang up and, groping about,
found a rolling-pin, with which she dealt him two smart blows in the sides,
and roundly abused him, "You skunk of a windbag. It's your own wife who
would be the lioness." And without further ado she drove him out of the
bridal chamber, shouting after him:

> "Scatter the grain indeed! I ask you, to what purpose?
> Having littered that way, again to litter this way—
> Beans, rice, wheat, barley all over the bed.
> Just pause to think: Ain't it a pretty sight?
> The parents-in-law are rude and rash,
> The bride's untidy and careless, they'll say.

16. Omen of the birth of a son. The pearl-oyster is the symbol of pregnancy.

17. Mount Wu, whose goddess came to the Ch'u king, Huai, in a dream. Her presence, she
told him, was to be felt in the morning clouds and evening rain. Hence the expression "clouds
and rain" for a love encounter.

18. The legendary student Wen Hsiao met his fairy bride Wu Ts'ai-luan in the mountains.

19. Euphemism for wife's scolding.

> And if the husband should pretend to be vexed,
> He would say the wife was slatternly.
> Off with you at once—out of the gate.
> And spare yourself more blows from my rolling-pin."

The astrologer took his beating and went out through the gate. The bridegroom, Wolf, was now roused and exclaimed, "Of the thousands of misfortunes, to have married this peasant woman! Strewing the bed-curtains is an ancient ceremony." To this Ts'ui-lien said in reply:

> "Husband, husband, be not angry,
> Hear me and judge the right and wrong for yourself.
> The mere thought of that man tries my patience,
> Littering beans and barley all over the place.
> Yet you ask no one to sweep them away;
> Instead you say, I lack womanly obedience.
> If you vex me any further,
> You too I will drive out with him,
> Shut my door, sleep by myself.
> 'Early to bed and early to rise' as I please,
> And 'Amitābha'[20] chant my prayers
> With my ears undisturbed in careless solitude."

And Wolf, at a loss what to do with her, went out to join in the feasting and toast his guests.

By nightfall the feast broke up and the relatives all went home. Sitting alone in the nuptial chamber, Ts'ui-lien thought to herself, "Soon my husband will come into the room and his hands are certain to rove in some wild ecstatic dance. I have to be prepared." So she stood up, removed her jewelry, undressed and, getting into bed, rolled herself tightly in a quilt and slept. Now, to go on with the story, Wolf came in and undressed, and was about to go to bed, when Ts'ui-lien stunned him with a thundering cry:

> "Wretch, how ridiculously mistaken in your designs!
> Of a truth, what an uncouth rustic!
> You are a man, I a woman;
> You go your way, I go mine.
> You say I am your own bride—
> Well, do not call me your old woman yet.
> Who was the matchmaker? Who the chief witness?
> What were the betrothal presents? How was the gift of tea?
> How many pigs, sheep, fowl, and geese? How many vats of wine?
> What floral decorations embellished the gifts?

20. The Buddha of immeasurability who is associated with the paradise called Sukhāvati, or the Western Pure Land. Perhaps ultimately of Iranian origin.

How many gems? How many golden head ornaments?
How many rolls of silk gauze, thick and thin?
How many pairs of bracelets, hatpins, hairpins?
With what should I adorn myself?
At the third watch late at night,
What mean you to come before my bed?
At once depart, and hurry away,
Lest you annoy my folk at home.
But if you provoke my fiery temper,
I will seize you by the ears and pull your hair,
Tear your clothes and scratch your face;
My heavy hand with outstretched fingers shall fall pat on your cheek.
If I rip your hairnet, don't say I did not warn you,
Nor complain if your neatly coiled hair gets disheveled.
This is no bawd's lane.
Nor the dwelling of some servile courtesan.
What do I care about silly rules like 'Two and two make four'?
With a sudden laying about of my fist
I'll send you sprawling all over the room."

When Wolf heard his bride declaim this chapter, he dared not approach her, nor uttered even a groan, but sat in a far-off corner of the room.

To go on with the story, soon it was indeed almost the third watch, and Ts'ui-lien thought to herself, "I have now married into his family. Alive, I shall remain one of their household; dead, I shall dwell among their ghosts. If we do not sleep in the same bed tonight, when tomorrow my parents-in-law learn about it, they will certainly blame me. Let it be, then! I will ask him to come to bed." So she said to Wolf:

"Dumb wretch, do not say you are drunk!
Come over, I will share the bed with you.
Draw near me and hear my command:
Fold your hands respectfully before you;
    tread on your toes; do not chatter.
Remove your hairnet and off with your cap;
Gather up your garments, socks, and boots;
Shut the door, lower the curtain,
And add some oil to the lamp grown dim.
Come to bed, and ever so softly;
We'll pretend to be mandarin ducks or intertwining trees.
Make no noise, be careful of what you say;
When our conjugal rites are completed,
    you'll curl up next to my feet,
Crooking your knee-joints, drawing in your heels.

> If by chance you give even one kick,
> Then know it's *death* for you!"

And the story went that the whole night through Wolf indeed dared not make the least noise. They slept until dawn, when the mother-in-law called out, "Wolf, you should ask your bride to rise early, finish her toilet, and come out to tidy up." So Ts'ui-lien spoke out:

> "Do not hurry, do not rush;
> Wait till I have donned my everyday clothes.
> Now—vegetables with vegetables, ginger with ginger,
> Each variety of nuts into a separate pack.
> Pork on one side, mutton on the other;
> We'll sort out the fresh fish from boiled tripe.
> Wine by itself, away from the broth;
> Salt chicken and smoked venison should not be mixed.
> In the cool of this time of year
> They will keep yet a good five days.
> Let me set apart some neat slices
> To serve on the third morn with tea for the aunts.
> And if the relatives do not eat them all,
> The parents-in-law can have the leftovers as a treat."

When the mother-in-law had heard this, she was a long while speechless. She wanted to scold Ts'ui-lien but was afraid she would only make herself a laughing-stock. So she swallowed her anger and endured in silence until the third morn,[21] when the bride's mother called in to present her gifts. And when the two mothers-in-law had met, Mrs. Chang could no longer contain herself: she recounted from beginning to end how Ts'ui-lien had inflicted blows on the astrologer and how she had abused the matchmaker, how she had insulted her husband and how she had slighted her parents-in-law. Upon hearing this account, Mrs. Li grew exceedingly ashamed. She went straight to her daughter's room and said to Ts'ui-lien, "What did I warn you against when you were still at home? I told you not to jabber and chatter when you entered your husband's house, but you never listened to me. It is only the third day, yet your mother-in-law made many complaints about you just then, causing me to be in fear and trepidation, and unable to utter a word in reply." Ts'ui-lien, however, said:

> "Mother, don't start a row yet;
> Listen while I relate it in each particular.

---

21. It was customary during the Sung period for the bride's family to send gifts of colored silks and honey cake or to call themselves, which was known as "comforting the daughter."

Your daughter is no untaught peasant woman;
There are some matters you little know about.
On the third morn the new daughter-in-law enters the kitchen[22]
(Ha ha, to relate this would but earn me ridicule!)
Two bowls of thin rice porridge with salt was all they provided
And, to serve with the meal, not even tea but plain boiling water!
Now you, their new relation, make your first call,
   At once they start their tittle-tattle:
Regardless of white or black, true or false,
Harassing me is all they are bent on.
My mother-in-law is by nature too impetuous,
The things she says are none too proper.
Let her beware—lest driven to my last resource,
With a bit of cord and swing from the noose
I leave her to answer for my corpse."

When the mother found Ts'ui-lien talking in this way, she could not very well
scold her. And without drinking her tea or tasting the wine, Mrs. Li instantly
took leave of her new relations, mounted her sedan-chair, and returned home.

To go on with the story, Wolf's older brother, Tiger, now began to shout
in the house, "What kind of a family are we now? It was said at first that
brother would be marrying a well-behaved young woman. Who would have
expected it to be this tavern waitress who chatters the whole day, wagging her
tongue and declaiming sentences and maxims? It is quite outrageous!" Ts'ui-
lien heard him and said in reply:

"Brother-in-law, you err against ritual;
I did not in the least provoke you.
A full-grown, manly pillar of society
To call his sister-in-law a glib tavern-waitress!"

Tiger then called to Wolf and said, "Haven't you heard the old saying: 'Teach
a wife when she first comes to you'? Though you need not go so far as to beat
her, you might at least lecture her now and then; or else go and tell her old
bawd of a mother." At this, Ts'ui-lien exclaimed:

"Busybody of a brother-in-law!
I did not dip my fingers in your bowl of rice.
Though I may be a bit loquacious,
There's husband and mother-in-law, to keep me in order.
Your new relations did not provoke you—
Why then do you call my mother a bawd?

22. In accordance with custom, to prepare her first meal for the family.

> Wait till I go back when the month is over;[23]
> I will tell my own dear brother at home.
> My brother is a hotheaded firebrand;
> You will perhaps know me better
> When his fist and hand shall both at once hit out,
> And like a tortoise in a drought you'll crawl in vain for shelter."

Tiger was enraged by her speech and, laying hands upon Wolf, thought to give the brother a thrashing. But his wife, Mistress Ssu, ran out from her room and said, "To each his own; how should brother's wife concern you? It was said of old: 'Don't wear your clean shoes to tread on a dunghill.' " At once Ts'ui-lien burst out again:

> "Sister-in-law, don't start trouble;
> This kind of conduct would never do.
> Was it not enough for brother-in-law to shout at me
> But you must step forward to scold some more?
> It ever has been: when the wife is dutiful, the man shuns all ills
> And succeeds in the highest enterprise.
> Go off then quickly, back to your room,
> And sit in hiding in some secure corner.
> Sister-in-law, I did not provoke you—
> Why then do you liken me to dung?
> Since we must die even if we lived to a hundred,
> Shall you and I now fight it out?
> And if any mishap befell me,
> Before Yama, King of the Underworld, I would not let you off."

The daughter of the house, Wolf's younger sister, heard this. She went into her mother's room and said, "You are her mother-in-law. Why don't you keep her under control? How very unseemly it would be if she carried on like this unchecked! People would only laugh at us." But when Ts'ui-lien saw the younger sister thus engaged, she called out after her:

> "Younger sister, how wicked of you
> To sneak within to incite your mother!
> If my mother-in-law should beat me to death,
> I would carry you off with me to the king of hell.
> My father is by nature pugnacious—
> He's not one to endure wrongs meekly—
> He would insist on a hundred priests, Taoist and Buddhist,
> To conduct services seven nights and seven days,

---

23. A month after the wedding, the bride visits her own home.

And a pine-wood coffin with a solid block for base,
And mother-in-law and father-in-law to burn paper-money for me.
You, younger sister, and sister-in-law,
    would wear mourning headscarves,
And brother-in-law could prostrate himself as my heir,
And the relatives of the nine degrees would carry the bier.
The funeral ended, our troubles would start afresh:
Accusations would have sped to the local and high courts,
Whose judges with all your silver you would bribe in vain.
Even had you millions upon millions of strings of cash,
You would spend them all and still forfeit your lives."

The mother-in-law now came out and said to Ts'ui-lien, "Luckily you have been my daughter-in-law only these three days; had you been these three years, would any of us in this family, old ones and young ones, ever get to speak at all?" Ts'ui-lien replied:

"You are too easily swayed, my mother-in-law;
When older folk grow slack, they lose the respect of the young.
Dear younger sister, do not tempt fortune too far;
Must you splutter all before your mama,
Exaggerating heavily the lightest rumors?
To which the old fool, listening and readily believing,
Stings me to the quick with this remark or that
In words unfit for the ear.
If any mishap befell me,
Rest assured the old one would pay with her life."

When the mother-in-law heard this, she went straight back to her room. And she said to the old gentleman, "Just look at that new daughter-in-law of ours. Her tongue is as sharp as a blade, and she has insulted each member of the family in turn. You are her father-in-law. Don't be afraid to summon and reprimand her." The old gentleman said, "I am the father-in-law, and so hardly in a position to reprimand her. However, let me ask her for some tea to drink, and we can then see what happens." His wife then said, "When she sees you, she will not dare wag her tongue."

Thereupon Mr. Chang gave the order, "Ask Wolf's wife to brew some midday tea." When Ts'ui-lien heard the father-in-law calling for tea, she hurriedly went into the kitchen, scrubbed the pot, and boiled the water. She then went to her own room and took out a variety of nuts, and, returning to the kitchen, made bowls of tea, which she placed on a tray. Holding the tray before her, she went into the ceremonial hall, where she arranged the chairs. She then went before her parents-in-law, saying, "Pa and Ma will please have their tea in the hall." And she also went to the sister-in-law's room and said, "Brother and sister-in-law will please have tea in the hall." Mr. Chang then remarked, "You were all saying the new daughter-in-law had a sharp tongue. Now when I order her to do something, she dare not raise her voice." His wife rejoined, "Since this is so, you shall give her all the orders."

In a little while, the entire family were gathered in the ceremonial hall and sat down in order of seniority. And they saw Ts'ui-lien come forward with her tray to address them:

> "Pa, have tea; Ma, have tea;
> Brother and sister-in-law, come and have your tea.
> If younger sister and younger brother would like tea,
> They can help themselves to the two bowls on the oven.
> But hold your bowls well, the pair of you, and tread with care
> Lest the hot tea scald your hands and you cry 'Oh! oh!'
> This tea we call Granny's Tea;
> The name is homely, the taste delicious.
> Here are two chestnuts freshly roasted brown,
> Half a pinch of fried white sesame seeds,
> Olives from south of the Yangtze, and mixed nut kernels,
> And walnuts from beyond the Great Wall, and shelled haws.
> You two venerable ones will eat them slowly
> Lest all unwares you lose a tooth or two."

When the father-in-law found her speaking in this manner, he said in a rage, "A female person should be gentle and staid, and sober in speech: only then is she fit to be a daughter-in-law. Was there ever a long-tongued woman like this one!" But Ts'ui-lien again spoke out:

> "Venerable Pa, venerable Ma,
> And brother and sister-in-law too, sit you down,
> You two old ones, do not scold me
> But listen to your daughter-in-law's account:
> She is not stupid nor is she sly;
> From childhood on, she was straight and blunt,
> And unkind words, once uttered, slip clean out of her mind.
> Pa and Ma, do not detest her overmuch;
> But if you really disapprove, then—repudiate her:
> She will not grieve nor be afraid;
> She will mount her sedan and return home.
> No new husband shall she think of—
>   neither one who would dwell with her parents
> Nor one who would take her to his own house.
> She will not put on powder and rouge, nor adorn herself,

But, as in mourning, wear white from top to toe,
And so wait on her parents and end her days.
I remember many ancient men of wisdom:
Chang Liang[24] and K'uai Ch'e were skilled in argumentation,
Lu Chia and Hsiao Ho ever ready with some learned allusion;
Ts'ao Chih and Yang Hsiu were no less ready in wit;
The eloquence of Chang Yi and Su Ch'in swayed the Warring States,
And Yen Tzu and Kuan Chung overcame mighty princes
    through persuasion;
And there were Ch'en P'ing with his six stratagems, and Li Tso-chü,
And the twelve-year-old official Kan Lo,
    and the disciple Tzu-hsia himself:
These ancients all excelled in making speeches;
They regulated their households, governed their kingdoms,
    and pacified the Empire.
If Pa would stop me from speaking,
Then you must stitch up my mouth."

Mr. Chang cried, "Have done! Have done! Such a daughter-in-law would one day bring down the family name and be a reproach to the ancestors." And he called Wolf before him and said, "Son, put your wife away. I will find you another, a better wife." Though Wolf assented to this, he could not find it in his heart to cast her off. And Tiger and his wife both pleaded with the father saying, "Let her be taught gradually." But Ts'ui-lien, having heard them, once more spoke up:

"Pa, do not complain; Ma, do not complain;
Brother and sister-in-law, do you not complain.
Husband, you need not persist in clinging to me;
From now on, each will do as he pleases.
At once bring paper, ink, slab, and brush,
Write out the certificate of repudiation and set me free.
But note:[25] I did not strike my parents-in-law
    nor abuse the relatives;
I did not deceive my husband nor beat the humble and meek;
I did not go visiting neighbors, west or east;

24. Chang Liang, etc. All were eloquent and persuasive speakers, including the twelve-year-old Kan Lo, who belonged to the Warring States period, as also Chang Yi and Su Ch'in; still earlier, Yen Tzu and Kuan Chung were ministers of the Ch'i state, and Tzu-hsia, the disciple of Confucius. Chang Liang, K'uai Ch'e, Lu Chia, Hsiao Ho, Ch'en P'ing (see selection 257), and Li Tso-chü were of early Han; and Ts'ao Chih and Yang Hsiu were of the Three Kingdoms period.

25. According to the *Record of Ritual* (*Li chi*), a wife may be repudiated on any one of seven grounds: if she refused to obey her parents-in-law; if she produced no heir; if she was lewd; if she was jealous; if she suffered from foul disease; if she talked too much; or if she thieved or robbed.

I did not steal nor was I cozened;
I did not gossip about this person nor start trouble with that one;
I was not thievish nor jealous nor lewd;
I suffer from no foul disease; I can write and reckon;
I fetched the water from the well, hulled the rice,
    and minded the cooking;
I spun and wove and sewed.
Today, then, draw up the certificate as you please,
And when I carry away my dowry, do you not resent it.
In between our thumbprints add these words:
'Never to meet again, never to see each other.'
Conjugal affection is ended,
All feelings dead;
Set down on paper many binding oaths:
If we chance upon each other at the gate of hell,
We shall turn our heads away and not meet."

Wolf, because his parents had decided for him, wrote out the document with tears in his eyes, and the two of them affixed their thumbprints. The family called for a sedan-chair, loaded the trousseau on it, and sent Ts'ui-lien home with the certificate of repudiation.

In the Li family, Ts'ui-lien's father, mother, brother, and sister-in-law all blamed her for her sharp tongue. But she said to them:

"Dad, do not shout; Ma, do not shout;
Brother and sister-in-law, do you not shout.
It is not that your lassie would sing her own praises,
But from childhood she has been of high mettle.
This day I left their household,
And the rights and wrongs of the affair I will leave off.
It is not that my teeth are itching to speak,
But tracing patterns and embroidering, spinning, and weaving,
Cutting and trimming garments, in all these I am skilled.
True it is, moreover, I can wash and starch, stitch and sew,
Chop wood, carry water, and prepare choice dishes;
And if there are silkworms, I can keep them too.
Now I am young and in my prime,
My eyes are quick, my hand steady, my spirits bold;
Should idlers come to peep at me,
I would give them a hearty, resounding slap."

A wife may not, however, be repudiated if she no longer had her own family to return to; if she had mourned her parents-in-law for three years; or if her husband had been poor at the time of their marriage but since grown rich and important. In Ts'ui-lien's list of faults of which she is innocent there occurs one important omission.

Mr. Li and his wife cried, "Have done! Have done! The two of us are now old; we can no longer keep you under our control. What we are afraid of is that some indiscretion or other would make you simply an object of ridicule. Poor, pitiful one!" But Ts'ui-lien went on:

"Your daughter was destined at birth to a lonely, wretched life—
She married an ignorant, foolish husband!
Though I might have endured the severity of his father and mother,
How could I have borne those sisters-in-law?
If I but moved my lips,
Off they went and stirred up the old ones.
Besides, such venom lay behind their scolding,
It soon led to blows and kicks,
From which began an incessant to-do;
Then all at once they wrote the certificate of dissolution.
My one hope was to find contentment and peace at home—
How should I expect even Dad and Ma would blame me?
Abandoned by the husband's family and my own,
I will cut off my hair and become a nun,
Wear a straight-seamed gown and dangle a gourd from a pole,
And carry in my hands a huge "wooden fish."[26]
In the daytime from door to door I shall beg for alms;
By night within the temple I shall praise the Buddha,
Chant my 'Namaḥ,'[27]
Observe my fasts and attend to my exercises.
My head will be shaven and quite, quite bald;
Who then will not hail the little priestess?"

And having spoken, she removed her ornaments and changed out of her gay garments into a suit of cotton clothes. She then went before her parents, joined the palms of her hands to perform a Buddhist salute, and bade them farewell. And she turned and bade her brother and sister-in-law farewell. And the brother and sister-in-law said to her, "Since you have chosen to take the vows, let us accompany you to the Clear Voice Temple in the street in front." Ts'ui-lien however, replied:

"Brother and sister-in-law, do not accompany me; I will go by myself;
And when I am gone, you can be easy and free.
As the ancients put it well:

26. Skull-shaped block on which Buddhist priests beat time when chanting. As a religious recitation, "Sharp-Tongued Ts'ui-lien" was probably accompanied by the "wooden fish" in the first instance. Such performances eventually may have evolved into Cantonese *mukyu* (literally, "wooden fish"), a popular type of prosimetric storytelling.

27. Expression of submission or reverence.

'Though here not welcome, elsewhere I shall be.'[28]
Since I am renouncing the world
And shall have my head shaven,
All places may be my home—
Why only the Clear Voice Temple?
Unencumbered and without a care,
I too shall be free and easy."

She would not cling to wealth and rank;
Wholeheartedly she embraced her vows.
She donned her nun's brocade robes
And constantly fingered her beads.
Each month she kept her fasts;
Daily she offered up fresh flowers,
A Bodhisattva[29] she might not become:
To be Buddha's least handmaid would still content her!

Translated by H. C. Chang

28. A fairly common saying.
29. Characteristic savior figure of Mahāyāna Buddhism.

255

The Canary Murders

Feng Meng-lung (1574–1645)

A bird it was at the root of the trouble;
Seven lives lost—what a lamentable case!
Note, all of you, this tragic lesson:
Do not let your sons and daughters neglect their home.

It is told how in the year 1121, the third year of the period Hsüan-ho in the reign of the Emperor Hui Tsung of the great Sung dynasty, a master-weaver

This gripping tale was included in a collection entitled *Stories Old and New* or *Illustrious Words to Instruct the World*, edited by the indefatigable Feng Meng-lung (see selections 185 and 224). The story commemorates a series of incidents alleged to have taken place in the vicinity of Lin-an (modern Hangchow in Chekiang province) in 1121, six years before the city was made the capital of the Southern Sung court. Although there is no means of establishing the authenticity of the events recorded or the personages concerned, there is equally no reason to doubt that the story was based on an actual crime of local and contemporary notoriety, and written down while the public memory was fresh.

named Shen Yü had his home in the prefecture of Hai-ning, near Hangchow. He lived below the New North Bridge, outside the Wu-lin Gate. This Shen Yü, styled Pi-hsien, was in a prosperous way of business, and he and his wife, Madam Yen, were devoted to each other. They had an only son, Shen Hsiu, who had reached the age of sixteen but had not yet married. The father made his living solely from weaving silk cloth, but to everyone's surprise Shen Hsiu took no heed of his duty to earn his keep. He devoted himself to pleasure and amusement and spent all his time breeding canaries,[1] and his parents doted on their only child and had no control over him. The neighbors gave him the nickname "Birdie" Shen. Every day at dawn he would take up one of his canaries and hurry off to match it against others in the park of willows inside the city.

This went on day after day, until it came to the end of spring, when the weather is neither too hot nor too cold, when the flowers bloom red and the willows are green. One morning at this time Shen Hsiu got up at the crack of dawn, washed and dressed and ate his breakfast, and made ready a cage, into which he put one matchless canary. This creature was the sort that is found only in heaven and not here below. He took it all over the place to fight, and it had never been defeated. It had won him over a hundred strings of cash, and he doted on it and held it dearer than life itself. He had made a cage for it of gold lacquer, with a brass hook, a green gauze cover, and a seed-pot and water-pot of Ko-yao porcelain.[2] This particular morning Shen Hsiu took up the cage and proudly hurried off through the city-gate to match his bird in the

---

Our story is a forerunner of the detective story, which had its greatest vogue in the nineteenth century. Perhaps "detective" is a misnomer; more properly, these are stories of clever magistrates. Although the magistrate makes only a brief appearance in "The Canary Murders," he is the central figure in many other stories. The reason is that, as the highest civil authority in the district, the magistrate shouldered the manifold responsibilities for the maintenance of law and order. It was his duty in a criminal case to bring the offender to book, to conduct the trial, and to pronounce sentence. Since he alone was responsible for ascertaining the true facts of the case, it followed that where there was any element of mystery he must function as his own detective. He could rely on his runners to make inquiries, detain witnesses, and arrest suspects, contenting himself with making deductions from the statements he heard or extracted in court; or, as often happens in such stories, he could leave his court incognito to conduct his own investigations. One of the most famous magistrate-detectives in Chinese history, Ti Jen-chieh (607–700), was the model for the main character in Robert van Gulik's popular "Judge Dee Mysteries."

1. "Canary" is used purely for the sake of familiarity to represent the bird *hua-mei*. There are, in fact, several points of resemblance. The *hua-mei* is a member of the oriole family: it is known to ornithologists as *Oreocinola dauma aurea*. It is 4–5 inches in length. Its plumage is grayish-yellow, speckled with black, the breast being yellowish-white. White markings above its eyes give rise to the name *hua-mei* (literally "painted eyebrows"). The male bird is both a singer and a fighter. The *hua-mei* is commonly found in North China, both wild and as a pet.

2. Ko-yao means "the elder brother's kiln," a term used to describe the work of the Sung potter Chang Sheng-yi, whose kiln was at Lung-ch'üan in Chekiang.

willow park. And who would have thought that Shen Hsiu, off on this jaunt of his, was going to his death? Just like

> A pig or a lamb to the slaughter,
> Seeking with every step the road to death.

Shen Hsiu took his bird into the willow park, but he was later than he had thought and the bird-fanciers had dispersed. The place was silent and gloomy, with not a soul about. Shen Hsiu, finding himself alone, hung the bird in its cage on a willow-branch, where it sang for a while. Then, disappointed, he took the cage down again and was just about to go back, when suddenly a bout of pain came surging up from his belly and forced him to his knees.

The fact was that Shen Hsiu was a sufferer from what is known as "dumplings of the heart," or hernia. Every attack sent him into a dead faint. It must have been that he had risen earlier than usual that morning, and then, arriving late to find no one there, he felt disappointed and miserable, so that this time the attack was particularly severe. He collapsed on the ground at the foot of a willow tree, where he lay unconscious for four whole hours.

Now, wouldn't you agree that "there is such a thing as coincidence"? This very day a cooper called Chang came walking through the park, his pack on his back, on the way to a job at the Ch'u household. He saw from a distance that there was someone lying at the foot of this tree, and so he came bounding up to the spot, set down his load, and had a look. Shen Hsiu's face was a waxy yellow, and he was still in a coma. There was nothing of any value on him, but at one side was the canary in its cage; and the canary chose just this moment to sing away more beautifully than ever. It was a case of "the sight of the treasure provides the motive," and "the plan is born when the man is poorest." Chang thought, "I might work all day for a couple of silver cents. What good would that do me?"

Shen Hsiu must have been doomed to die, for at the sight of Chang the canary began to sing harder than ever. Chang said to himself, "The rest doesn't matter, but this canary alone is worth two or three silver taels at least." So he picked up the cage and was just making off, when to his surprise Shen Hsiu came round. Shen opened his eyes to see Chang picking up the cage. He tried to get up but couldn't. All he could do was cry out, "Where are you off to with my canary, you old blackguard?"

"This little fool has too quick a tongue," Chang thought to himself. "Suppose I take it, and he manages to get up and comes after me—he'll make trouble for me. There's only one thing for it, one way or the other I'm in a mess." So he went to the barrel he had been carrying and took out a curved paring-knife, then turned to Shen Hsiu and struck at him. The knife was sharp and he used all his strength, and Shen Hsiu's head rolled away to one side.

Chang cast panic-stricken glances to left and right, fearful lest someone should have seen him. Then, looking up, he saw that to one side stood a hollow tree. Hurriedly he picked up the head and dropped it into the hollow trunk, returned the knife to the barrel, and hung the bird-cage from his pack. He did not go on to the job at the Ch'u house, but went off like a puff of smoke, through the streets and alleys of the town, looking for somewhere to hide.

Now, how many lives do you think were lost on account of this one live bird? Indeed,

> Private words among men,
> Heard in Heaven like thunder;
> A misdeed in a dark room,
> But the gods have eyes like lightning.

As Chang walked along, the thought came to him, "There is a traveling merchant who stays in an inn at Huchou-shu, and I have often seen him buying pets. Why not go there and sell the bird to him?" And he made straight for the suburb past the Wu-lin Gate.

The evil fate in store must have been determined from a previous existence, for there he saw three merchants with two youths at their heels, five persons all told. They had just packed up their goods to go back, and he met them coming in through the gate. The merchants were all men of the Eastern Capital, Pien-liang.[3] One of them was called Li Chi, a trader in herbs. He had always had a fancy for canaries, and seeing this lovely bird on the cooper's back, he called to Chang to let him see it. Chang set down his pack. The merchant examined the canary's plumage and eyes, and saw that it was a fine bird. It had a lovely singing voice, too, and he was delighted with it. "Would you like to sell him?" he asked Chang.

By this time Chang's only concern was to be rid of the evidence. So he said, "How much will you give me, sir?"

The longer Li Chi looked at the bird the more he liked it. "I'll give you a tael of silver," he said.

Chang realized the deal was on. "I don't want to haggle," he said. "It's just that this bird's very precious to me. But give me a little more and you can have him."

Li Chi took out three pieces of silver and weighed them: there was one tael and a fifth. "That's the lot," he said, handing it to Chang.

Chang took the silver, examined it, and put it in his wallet. He gave the canary to the merchant and took his leave. "That's a good deed done, getting rid of the evidence," he told himself. He did not go back to his work, but hurried straight home. But still he felt certain misgivings at heart. Indeed,

3. Kaifeng.

> The evil-doer fears the wrath of Heaven and Earth,
> The swindler dreads discovery by gods and demons.

Chang's home was in fact against the city-wall by the Yung-chin Gate. There was only himself and his wife; they had no children. When his wife saw him coming back, she said, "You haven't used a single splint. Why have you come home so early? What's the trouble?"

Chang said not a word until he had entered the house, taken off his pack, and turned back to bolt the door. Then he said, "Come here, wife, I've something to tell you. Today I've been to such-and-such and done such-and-such, and I've come by this ounce and a fifth of silver. I'm giving it to you so that you can enjoy yourself for a while." And the two of them gloated over the money.

But this does not concern us. Let us rather go on to tell how there was no one about in the willow park until late morning, when two peasants carrying loads of manure happened to pass through. The headless corpse blocking their path gave them a fright, and they began to kick up a fuss, quickly rousing the ward headman and all the citizens of the neighborhood. The ward submitted the matter to the district and the district to the prefecture, and the next day a coroner and other officers were sent to the willow park to investigate. They found no mark on the body: the only thing wrong was that the head was missing; nor had anyone come forward as plaintiff. The officers made their report to the authorities at the prefecture, who dispatched runners to arrest the criminal. Within the city and out in the suburbs, all was thrown into an uproar.

Let us now rather tell how Shen Hsiu's parents, when evening came and he still had not returned, sent people out in every direction to search for him, but without success. When again at dawn searchers were sent into the city, in the vicinity of the inn at Hu-chou-shu they heard a commotion about the headless corpse of a murdered man being found in the willow park. When Shen Hsiu's mother heard of this, she thought, "My boy went into the city yesterday to show his canary, and there's still no sign of him. Can it be him?" And at once she cried to her husband, "You must go into the city yourself and make inquiries."

Shen Yü gave a jump when he heard this and, filled with alarm, he hurried off to the willow park. There he saw the headless corpse, which, after a careful look at the clothing, he recognized as his own son. He began to wail in a loud voice. "Here is the plaintiff," said the ward headman. "Now all that is missing is the criminal."

Shen Yü went at once to make accusations before the prefect of Lin-an. "It is my son," he said. "Early yesterday morning he went into the city to show his canary, and he has been murdered, no one knows how or why. Your Highness, I demand justice!"

Runners and detectives were sent from the prefecture throughout the area, with orders to arrest the criminal within ten days. Shen Yü was ordered to prepare a coffin in the willow park to contain the corpse. He went straight home and said to his wife, "It's our son; he's been murdered. But no one knows where the head has been taken. I have made accusation at the prefecture, and they have sent runners out everywhere to arrest the criminal. I've been told to buy a coffin for him. What is best for us to do about it all?"

At this news, Madam Yen began to wail aloud and collapsed to the floor. "If you don't know how she felt inside, first see how she lies there motionless." Indeed,

> Body like the waning moon at cockcrow, half-hidden behind the hills;
> Spirit like a dying lamp at the third watch, the oil already gone.

They proceeded to revive her by forcing hot soup down her throat, and when she came to, she said through her tears, "My boy would never listen to good advice, and now he is dead and we cannot bury him.[4] O my son, so young, and dead in such a grievous manner. Who could have told that in my old age I should be left without support?" All the time she was speaking her tears flowed ceaselessly. She would take neither food nor drink, although her husband used every effort to console her. Somehow or other they got through the next fortnight, without any news. Then Shen Yü and his wife began to discuss the matter. "Our boy would never heed our words, and now this terrible thing has happened and he has been murdered. Nor can the murderer be found. There is nothing we can do about it. But at least it would be something if his corpse could be made whole. Our best plan is to write out a notice and inform people everywhere that if they find the head, so that the corpse can be made whole, they will be rewarded for it."

When the two had come to this decision, they promptly wrote out copies of a notice and went out to paste them up all over the city. The notice ran:

> To all citizens: One thousand strings of cash reward to anyone discovering the whereabouts of the head of Shen Hsiu. Two thousand strings of cash reward to anyone apprehending the murderer.

They informed the prefecture of this, and the authorities issued fresh orders to the runners to arrest the criminal within so many days, and put out an official notice, as follows:

> Official reward of five hundred strings of cash to anyone discovering the whereabouts of the head of Shen Hsiu. One thousand strings of cash reward to anyone apprehending the murderer.

---

4. It would be the gravest of misfortunes for Shen Hsiu in the next world if his corpse were buried while still incomplete. His parents were anxious to postpone the funeral for as long as possible in the hope that the head might be found.

We will leave the town in its ferment of excitement over the notices, and go on to tell how at the foot of the Southern Peak there lived an old pauper whose name was Huang and who was known by the nickname "Old Dog." He was an ignorant man who had spent his life as a chair-coolie. With old age he had lost his sight, and he depended entirely on the support of his two sons, Big Pao and Little Pao. The three of them, father and sons, had neither enough clothes to wear nor enough food to eat. They lived from hand to mouth and their bellies were never full. One day Old Dog Huang called Big Pao and Little Pao to him and said, "I hear talk of some rich man or other called Shen Hsiu, who's been murdered, and his head is missing. And now they're offering a reward, and they say if anyone finds this head, the family will give them a thousand strings of cash and the authorities will give them another five hundred. I've called you together now just to say this: I'm an old man now anyway, and I'm no use, I can't see and I've no money. So I've decided to give you two a chance to make something and enjoy yourselves. Tonight you must cut off my head. Hide it in the water at the edge of the Western Lake, and in a few days it will be unrecognizable. Then you must take it to the prefecture and claim the reward, and altogether you'll get one thousand five hundred strings of cash. It's better than staying on here in misery. It's a very clever scheme, and you mustn't waste any time, because if somebody else gets in first, I'll have lost my life for nothing."

This "Old Dog" made this speech because he had given up in despair; moreover, his two sons were very stupid men and understood nothing of the law. Indeed,

> The mouth is the gateway of disaster,
> The tongue is an executioner's knife.
> Keep your mouth shut and your tongue well hidden,
> And you will live at peace and secure.

The two went outside to discuss the matter. "This is a brilliant idea of our father's," said Little Pao. "Not even a Commander-in-Chief or a Field Marshal could have thought up a plan like this. It's a very good one, although it's a pity we have to lose Dad."

Big Pao was by nature both cruel and stupid. He said, "He's got to die sooner or later anyway. Why shouldn't we seize this opportunity and do him in? We can dig a pit at the foot of the mountain and bury him, and there'll be no trace, so how can we be found out? This is what they call 'doing it while the water's hot,' and 'leaving no trace.' Men's hearts are governed by Heaven: it wasn't ourselves who forced him to it, he told us to do this of his own accord."

"All right then," said Little Pao, "only we'll not set to work until he's fast asleep."

Having laid their plans, the brothers went bustling off and bought two bottles of wine on credit. They came back to their father, and the three of them got good and drunk and sprawled about all over the place. The two brothers slept right through to the early hours of the morning, when they crept out of bed to watch the old man lying there, snoring. Then Big Pao took a kitchen-knife from in front of the stove, and with one powerful stroke at his father's neck cut his head clean off. Hurriedly they wrapped it in an old garment and hid it in the bed. Then they went off to the foot of the mountain and dug a deep pit. They carried the body there and buried it, and before it was daylight they had hidden the head in the shallow water at the edge of the lake, near the Lotus House at the foot of the Nan-p'ing Hills.

A fortnight later they went into the city and looked at the notice. First of all they went to Shen Yü's house to make their report, "The two of us were shrimping yesterday when we saw a human head by the edge of the lake near the Lotus House. We thought it must be your son's head."

"If it really is," said Shen Yü at this, "there is a reward of a thousand strings of cash for you, not a copper short." Then he prepared food and wine for them, and presently they took him straight to the point by the Lotus House at the foot of the Nan-p'ing Hills. There they found the head, lightly buried in the mud. When they picked it up and examined it, they found it had been under water so long that the features were bloated and past recognition. But Shen Yü thought, "It must be my son's head. If it isn't, how does another head come to be here?"

Shen Yü wrapped the head in a kerchief and accompanied the two of them straight to the prefecture, where they reported the discovery of Shen Hsiu's head. The prefect repeatedly questioned the two brothers, who replied, "We saw it when we were shrimping. We don't know anything else about it." Their word was accepted, and they were given the five hundred strings of cash. Then, taking the head with them, they accompanied Shen Yü to the willow park. They opened the coffin, set the head on the shoulders of the corpse, and nailed the coffin up again. Then Shen Yü took the brothers back to his home. When Madam Yen heard that her son's head had been found she was much happier, and at once set out food and wine to feast the brothers. They received the thousand strings of cash as their reward, and took their leave and returned home. There, they built a house, and bought farming implements and household goods. "We are not going to work as chair-coolies any longer," they said to each other. "We'll work hard at our farming, and we can make a bit extra by gathering firewood from the hillside and selling that."

But this does not concern us. Indeed, "time flew like an arrow" and "days and months passed like a weaver's shuttle." Several months passed unnoticed, and the authorities grew lax and concerned themselves less every day with the affair.

We will say no more of all this, but go on to tell how the time came for Shen Yü, who was a master-weaver for the Eastern Capital, to make a journey there to deliver a consignment of cloth. When all his weavers had completed their quotas, he went to the prefecture for the delivery permit, returned home to order his affairs there, and then started out. This journey, just because Shen Yü chanced to see a bird which had belonged to his own family, resulted in the forfeiture of another life. Indeed,

> Take no illegal goods,
> Commit no illegal acts.
> Here above the law will catch you,
> Down below the demons pursue you.

Let us now tell how Shen Yü, on his journey, ate when hungry and drank when thirsty, rested each night and set out again each morning, and after more than one day like this arrived in the Eastern Capital. He delivered each and every bolt of cloth, and collected his permit to return. Then he thought, "I have heard that the sights of the Eastern Capital are unique. Why shouldn't I stroll about for a while? This is an opportunity which doesn't come often." He visited all the historic sites and beauty spots, the monasteries both Taoist and Buddhist, and all the other celebrated sights. Then he chanced to pass by the gate of the Imperial Aviary. Now, Shen Yü was very fond of pets and he felt he would like to have a look inside. On distributing a dozen or so cash at the gate he was allowed in to have a look round. All at once he heard a canary singing beautifully. Taking a careful look at it, he realized it was his son's canary which had disappeared. When the canary saw Shen Yü's familiar face, it sang louder than ever and hopped about its cage jerking its head toward him. The sight of the bird reminded Shen Yü of his son. Tears streamed down his face and his heart filled with sorrow. Without reflecting where he was, he began to cry out and make an uproar, shouting, "Could such a thing come to pass?"

The guard who was keeper of the aviary shouted, "Here's a fool who doesn't know the regulations. Where do you think you are, making such a fuss?"

Shen Yü, unable to contain his grief, began to yell louder still, and the guard, fearful of bringing trouble on his own head, found nothing for it but to arrest Shen Yü and have him brought before the Grand Court. The officer of the Grand Court shouted, "Where do you come from, that you dare to enter a part of the palace itself and make a disturbance like this? If you have some grievance, come straight out with it like an honest fellow, and you'll be let off."

So Shen Yü told how his son had gone off to match his canary and had been murdered, the whole story from beginning to end. The officer of the Grand Court was dumbfounded by the story. Then he reflected that the bird had been presented as tribute by a man of the capital, Li Chi; but whoever had dreamed there could be all this business behind it? He sent off runners to arrest Li Chi and bring him to court on the instant. The questioning commenced, "What was your reason for murdering this man's son in Hai-ning, and bringing his canary here as tribute? Make a full and open statement, or you will be punished."

"I went to Hangchow on business," said Li Chi, "and as I was going through the Wu-lin Gate I chanced to see a cooper who had this canary in a cage hanging from his pack. When I heard it singing and saw that it was a fine bird I bought it, for an ounce and a fifth of silver. I brought it back with me; but I did not dare to keep it for myself, because it was such a fine specimen, and so I presented it as tribute for the emperor's use. I know nothing about any murder."

"Who are you trying to implicate?" said his interrogator. "This canary is concrete evidence. Tell the truth!"

Li Chi pleaded again and again, "It is the truth that I bought it from an old cooper. I know nothing about a murder. How would I dare to make a false statement?"

"This old man you bought it from," went on the interrogating officer, "what was his name and where did he come from? Give me the true facts and I will have him brought in. Then we shall get at the truth, and you will be released."

"I simply bought it from him when I ran into him on the street," said Li Chi. "I really don't know what his name is or where he lives."

The interrogating officer began to abuse him, "You're only trying to confuse the issue. Are you hoping to make someone else pay for this man's life? We must go by the concrete evidence, this canary. This rascal won't confess until he's beaten."

Li Chi was flogged over and over until his flesh was ripped open. He could not bear the pain and had no alternative but to make up a story that, when he saw what a fine bird this canary was, he had killed Shen Hsiu and cast his head away. Thereupon Li Chi was committed to the main jail, while the officer of the Grand Court prepared his report for submission to the emperor. The imperial rescript ran: "Li Chi was beyond doubt the murderer of Shen Hsiu, the canary being evidence of this. The law requires that he shall be executed." The canary was returned to Shen Yü, who was also given a permit and allowed to return to his home; while Li Chi was sent under escort to the execution-ground, and there beheaded. Indeed,

> When the old turtle won't turn tender,
> You shift the blame onto the firewood.

At this time, the two merchants who had accompanied Li Chi to Hai-ning on business could hardly keep still for indignation. "How could such an injustice be done," they complained, "when it was plain for all to see that he had bought the canary. We would have pleaded for him, but what could we do? Although we would recognize the man who sold Li Chi the canary, we don't know his name any more than Li did. Moreover, he is in Hangchow. We would not have been able to clear Li Chi, and we would have implicated ourselves. How can the truth be brought to light? A man has been executed when he was obviously innocent, and all because of one single bird. The only thing is for us to go to Hangchow and, when we get there, to wring the truth out of this fellow."

Let us say no more of this, but rather tell how Shen Yü packed his baggage, picked up his canary, and hurried home, traveling day and night. He reported to his wife, "When I was in the Eastern Capital, I succeeded in avenging our son."

"How did that come about?" asked Madam Yen. Shen Yü told her the whole story right through, beginning with his seeing the canary in the Imperial Aviary. When Madam Yen saw the canary she burst out weeping, for the sight of things brings back sad memories; but we will say no more of this. The next day Shen Yü took up the canary again and went to the prefecture to have his permit canceled, and there he reported all that had happened. "What a lucky coincidence," cried the delighted prefect. Indeed,

> Do nothing of which you need feel ashamed:
> Who, throughout time, has been allowed to escape?

And murder, needless to say, is the concern of Heaven, not to be taken lightly. The prefect dismissed Shen Yü with the words, "Since the criminal has been caught and executed, you may have the coffin cremated." Shen Yü had the coffin cremated and the remains scattered, and we will say no more of this, but go on to tell how of the two merchants who had accompanied Li Chi to Hangchow on that former occasion to sell herbs, one was called Ho and the other Chu. These two got some more herbs together and went straight to Hangchow, to stay in the inn at Hu-chou-shu. They quickly sold up their herbs, then, their hearts filled with a sense of injustice, they went into the city to look for the cooper. They searched all day without finding a trace of him, and returned, weary and dispirited, to the inn to sleep. The next morning they returned to the city, and as luck would have it, they chanced to see a man with a cooper's pack. "Tell us, brother," they said, calling to him to stay, "is there another cooper here, an old man who looks like this?" And they described him. "We don't know his name, but perhaps you know him?"

"Gentlemen," said the cooper, "there are only two old men here in the cooper's trade. One is called Li, and he lives in Pomegranate Garden Street; the other is called Chang, and he lives by the city-wall on the west side. I don't know which one it is that you want."

The two merchants thanked him and carried their search straight to Pomegranate Garden Street. As it happened, the man named Li was sitting there cutting splints. The two took a look at him, but he was not their man. Then they found the house by the western wall and, coming up to the door, they asked if Chang was at home. "No, he isn't," replied Chang's wife. "He's gone out to a job."

The two men turned away again without more ado. It was now early afternoon. They had gone no more than a few hundred yards when they saw in the distance a man carrying a cooper's pack. And this man's fate it was to pay for the life of Shen Hsiu and to clear the name of Li Chi. Indeed,

> Let mercy and righteousness everywhere prevail,
> And you will meet with them at every turn of your life;
> Never make an enemy,
> For when you meet him in a narrow path it is not easy to turn back.

Chang was walking south toward his home, and the two men were walking toward the north, so that they met face to face. Chang did not recognize the pair, but they recognized him. They stopped him and asked his name, "My name is Chang," he replied.

"It must be you who lives by the western wall," they continued. "That is so," replied Chang. "What do you want of me?"

"We have some things at the inn that need repairing," said the merchants, "and we are looking for an experienced man to do the job. That's why we want you. Where are you going now?"

"I'm on my way home," said Chang. The three of them talked as they went along, until they came to Chang's door. "Please sit down and have some tea," said Chang.

But the others replied, "It is getting late. We'll come again tomorrow."

"Then I won't go out tomorrow, but will wait for you here," said Chang.

The two men took their leave of him, but they did not return to the inn: they went straight to the prefecture to inform on him. The court had just begun its evening session, and the two men went straight in and knelt down. They told the whole story of Shen Yü's recognition of the canary and Li Chi's execution, and of Li's earlier meeting with Chang when he bought the canary. "We two are filled with a sense of injustice, and with the desire to avenge Li Chi. We entreat your honor to question Chang thoroughly and to find out how he came by the canary."

"The Shen Hsiu case has been wrapped up," said the prefect. "The criminal has been executed—what more remains to be done?"

So the two merchants made accusation, "The officer of the Grand Court was misled. He took the canary as evidence, but did not look carefully into the details of the case. It is plain for all to see that Li Chi was wrongfully executed. We have 'found injustice in our path,' and are determined to avenge Li Chi. If we were not speaking the truth, how would we dare to make a nuisance of ourselves with this accusation? We beg your honor in your mercy to intervene in this matter."

Observing how earnestly they pleaded, the prefect at once sent out runners to arrest Chang that very night. It was just like

Vultures chasing a purple swallow,
Fierce tigers slavering over a lamb.

That night the men from the court hurried to the western wall. They tied Chang's arms behind his back and delivered him up to the prefecture, where he was committed to the main jail. When court opened the next day, Chang was brought from the jail and forced to his knees. The prefect said, "What was your reason for murdering Shen Hsiu and making Li Chi pay for it with his life? Today the facts have come to light, and the right must prevail." The prefect shouted to his men to flog the prisoner, and Chang received thirty strokes to begin with, till his flesh was ripped open and the blood came soaking out. Over and over again he was flogged, but he would not confess.

The merchants and the two youths who had been with them shouted at him, "Although Li Chi is dead, we four are still here, and we were with him when he bought your canary for an ounce and a fifth of silver. Who are you going to put the blame on now? If you say it wasn't you who did it, then tell us where the canary came from. Tell the truth: you can't lie your way out of this, and it's no use trying to make excuses."

But Chang continued to defy them, and at last the prefect roared at him, "The canary is genuine evidence of the theft, and these four are eyewitnesses. If you still refuse to confess, we'll have the finger-press out and torture you." Terrified, Chang had no choice but to confess everything, how he had stolen the canary and cut off Shen Hsiu's head.

"When you had killed him, where did you put the head?" asked the prefect.

"I was seized by panic," Chang answered, "and seeing a hollow tree nearby I dropped the head into the hole. Then I picked up the bird and went straight to the Wu-lin Gate. There I happened to come across three merchants with two youths. They wanted to buy the canary, and I got an ounce and a fifth of silver for it. I took the money home and spent it, and this is the truth."

The prefect ordered Chang to make his mark on his deposition, and sent men to summon Shen Yü. Then they all proceeded, with Chang under escort, to the willow park to search for the head. Hundreds of people on the streets, all agog, gathered round and followed them to the willow park to look for it. They found that there was indeed a hollow tree, and when they had sawn it down they gave a shout of excitement, for there inside the trunk was a human head. When they examined it, they saw it to be completely unaffected by the passage of time.[5] When Shen Yü saw the head, he took a close look

---

5. The religious explanation for this is that corruption would not set in until the spirit had departed. The spirit of the murdered boy was waiting for the murderer to be brought to justice. In actuality, the head was probably preserved by the resins of the hollow tree.

and recognized it as that of his son. He cried out in a loud voice and fainted to the ground, remaining unconscious for a long time. Then they wrapped the head in a cloth and returned to the prefecture, with Chang still under escort.

"Now that the head has been found," said the prefect, "the facts are clear and the guilt established." They put a large wooden cangue round Chang's neck, fettered his hands and feet, and dragged him off to the condemned cells, where he was put under close guard. The prefect then put a question to Shen Yü. "Those two Huang brothers, Big Pao and Little Pao: where did they get that human head when they came to claim the reward? There is some mystery here. Your son's head has been found now: whose head was that?"

Runners were immediately ordered to bring in the Huang brothers for interrogation. Shen Yü led the runners to the Huangs' house in the southern hills. The two brothers were arrested and brought to court, where they were forced to kneel.

"The murderer of Shen Hsiu has been arrested," the prefect told them, "and Shen Hsiu's head has been recovered. Who was it that you two conspired together to murder, so that you could claim the reward for his head? Confess or you will be tortured!"

Big Pao and Little Pao were dumbfounded and bewildered and could make no reply. The prefect, enraged, ordered them to be strung up and flogged, but for a long time they refused to confess. But then they were branded with red-hot irons. This was more than they could bear, and they fainted away. When water was spurted over them and they revived, they saw there was nothing for it but to blurt out the truth. "Seeing that our father was old and sick and miserable," they said, "on an evil impulse we got him drunk and cut off his head. We hid it at the edge of the Western Lake near the Lotus House, and then made up a story to claim the reward."

"Where did you bury your father's body?" asked the prefect. "At the foot of the Southern Peak," they replied. When the brothers were taken there under escort and the ground was dug, there did indeed prove to be a headless corpse buried at the spot. The two men were taken back to the prefecture and the guards reported, "There is indeed a headless corpse, in a shallow grave in the southern hills."

"That such a thing should happen!" said the prefect. "It is a most abominable crime. If there really are such evil men in this world, I want neither to speak nor hear nor write of them. Let them be flogged to death here and now, and we shall be rid of them; how can this evil deed ever be expiated?" He shouted to his men to flog them without keeping count of the strokes. The two brothers were flogged unconscious and revived again many times, then large cangues were placed on them and they were taken off to the condemned cells to be closely guarded.

Shen Yü and the original plaintiffs returned to their homes to await events, while a report on the wrongful execution of Li Chi was at once submitted in the form of a memorial. The imperial rescript ordered the Board of Punishments and the Censorate to investigate the conduct of the officer of the Grand Court who had originally questioned Li Chi, and to reduce him to the status of commoner and banish him to Ling-nan.[6] Li Chi was declared to have been innocent and wrongfully convicted. The imperial sympathy was expressed, and his family was granted one thousand strings of cash in compensation and his descendants exempted from compulsory service. Chang, for premeditated murder for gain and for wronging an innocent man, was to be executed in accordance with the law. In view of the seriousness of the crime, the execution was to be performed by the slow process, with two hundred and forty cuts, and his corpse dismembered. The Huang brothers, convicted of patricide for gain, were both without distinction to be executed by the slow process, with two hundred and forty cuts, their corpses dismembered, and their heads publicly exposed as a warning. Indeed,

> Heaven, clear and profound, is not to be deceived,
> Before the design appears to you it is already known.
> Do nothing of which you need feel ashamed:
> Who, throughout time, has been allowed to escape?

When the rescript reached the prefecture, officers and executioners and the rest mounted the three criminals on "wooden mules," and it was broadcast throughout the city that in three days' time they were to be executed by the slow process, their corpses dismembered, and their heads publicly exposed as a warning.

When Chang's wife heard that her husband was to be sliced to death, she went to the execution-ground in the hope of catching a glimpse of him. Who would have thought it possible?—when the executioners were given the signal to start, they all began to slice their victims, and it was indeed a frightful sight: Chang's wife was frightened out of her wits, and she turned to go, her body bent with grief. But by accident she tripped and fell heavily, injuring her whole body, and when she reached home she died. Indeed,

> Store up good deeds and you will meet with good,
> Store up evil and you will meet with evil.
> If you think about it carefully,
> Things usually turn out right.

Translated by Cyril Birch

6. In the southernmost province of Kwangtung.

256

Wine Within Wine:
Old Nun Chao Plucks a Frail Flower;
Craft Within Craft:
The Scholar Chia Gains Sweet Revenge

Ling Meng-ch'u (1580–1644)

In the words of the poem:

>A hungry lustful devil is the monk,
>The ways of those in nun's garb are the same;
>For they can pass forbidden chamber doors,
>And with one swoop destroy a woman's name.

It is often said that good people should be most wary of dealings with the three old sisters and the six hags.[1] For such folk are both idle of occupation and sharp of mind. And what is more, having passed the portals of countless homes, they have come to know much of the world and to be well versed in its ways. Not to mention those faithless women who can be taken almost at will, nine out of ten times, even among those who show not the slightest chink in their armor, they can exercise any number of wiles to produce an opening; their cleverness rivals that of Chang Liang and Ch'en P'ing,[2] their

Ling Meng-ch'u published two volumes of vernacular stories known collectively as *Tales to [Make One] Strike the Table in Amazement.* These collections, together with three similar volumes by Feng Meng-lung (see selections 185 and 255) entitled with variations on the phrase *Illustrious Words to Instruct the World,* came to be known jointly as "the three *Words* and the two *Strikes.*" Together they comprise the central corpus of the remarkable flowering of prose fiction in the late-Ming colloquial short-story form. Like Feng, Ling was a man of the theater, a noted publisher of plays, and an urbane and versatile representative of the early seventeenth-century literary world in China. In the hands of people like Feng and Ling, the colloquial short story was transformed from a vehicle of popular culture into a highly sophisticated medium of literary expression. Ling's contributions to this cultural achievement may be even more noteworthy than Feng's, since Ling did not base his compositions on earlier materials from popular storytelling and historical narratives, as Feng had done, but instead produced a set of stories of great variety and depth that represent primarily his own imagination. As a result, his tales rely less on the conventions of oral storytelling imitated and adapted in many contemporary pieces, and more on projecting a sense of the author's own personality. At times this takes the form of light exercises in wit and satire, but often it takes us in the direction of glimpsing one seventeenth-century Chinese author's deepest convictions on questions of morality and human nature.

1. "Three sisters and six hags": a general reference to women of various mystical occupations.
2. Chang Liang and Ch'en P'ing (see selection 256) were famed strategists of the early Han.

nimble wits equal those of Sui Ho and Lu Chia;[3] they can instigate an incident where there has been no cause for trouble. That is why respectable families of high position are wont to post explicit notice that such are forbidden to enter their gates.

Among their ranks, perhaps the most malignant is the nun. Using the Heavens of Buddha as a leaven and the sacred cloisters as a store of grain, she can induce women of good family to come to light incense, while she invites young men to come to take their pleasure. If she is questioned or addressed by a man, her forms of greeting are exactly like those of a monk; she may receive them directly with no embarrassment. Proceeding inside she will always invoke the name of the Buddha and look roughly through the sūtras. But since she is, after all, a woman, she is all the more free to achieve her designs. No doubt in nine out of ten of all the affairs of procuresses and bawds, it is actually a nun who brings the affair to its conclusion, and a nunnery that is the scene of the tryst.

But let us turn now to the story of a woman of the house of Ti in T'ang times. Born of the family of an illustrious minister, her husband was also a high official, and so she was addressed as "your grace."[4] Now this lady was of a radiant beauty that defied equal; her reputation shook the capital. Indeed, the very noblest ladies of the capital, when vying with one another for someone's favor, were given to berating each other with the words, "You may claim to be elegant, but no matter what you say you will never compare to Madame Ti. And yet you dare to speak ill of me!" Moreover, though her celebrity was without equal in her time, she remained chaste of disposition, sparing of frivolous words, a woman of uncommon virtue.

Now in those days it was the custom every year for the ladies and gentlemen of the capital to throng to the West Lake for spring outings. Even the most noble families joined the procession, their curtained carriages forming an unbroken train as they went. And so Madame Ti as well could scarce help but observe the custom and join the procession.

It happened that on this one occasion there was a certain young man among the company at the lake, a dashing youth by the name of T'eng, who had come to the capital to await official appointment. When he set his eyes upon this vision of loveliness, he was so stricken that his three spiritual souls[5] and seven corporeal essences[6] were sundered from his body and whirled away into space, as he followed her about unable to tear his eyes from her. Madame Ti also lifted her eyes now and then and noticed his engaging manner, but since she had no mind for such things, she thought no more of him. But the

3. Sui Ho and Lu Chia were famed orators of the early Han.
4. An official title of respect assigned to wives and mothers of officials of the third rank and higher in the T'ang administrative system.
5. The life-principle, the senses, and the soul.
6. The spirits residing in the body.

young man had already become infatuated with her; so taken that he would fain have found a drink of water and swallowed her down clothes and all. Questioning someone nearby, he learned that she was the Madame Ti so famed for her beauty. After the carriages and mounts of the procession had all gone their separate ways, the young man made his way home in despair, and passed the night in uneasy thought. From that day on, he walked about in a daze, forgetting even to eat, as one who has lost some favorite object and is anxious for it every hour and every minute of the day. Unable to subdue his kindled passions, he hovered about her house seeking some tidings of her, only to learn that her purity was constant and that there could be no avenues by which to approach her. "Certainly it cannot be that she has not one confidante among the women of her kin," he thought to himself. "If I can only get a chance to question one of them, perhaps I may find some excuse to inquire about her in more detail." And so it happened that one day a nun came walking out from the gates of the house. T'eng followed behind her for a distance, before learning from someone by the way that she was Hui-ch'eng, the abbess of the Cloister of Calm Delight, a frequent guest at the home of Madame Ti. At this T'eng cried aloud, "That is fine! Fine!" and sped straight-away to his lodgings. There he prepared a packet of twenty ounces of silver and dashed off in great haste toward the Cloister of Calm Delight, where he inquired, "Might the Abbess be in?" Hui-ch'eng soon appeared, and seeing that it was a young man of the official class, invited him in for tea. After bowing respectfully, she asked him, "Tell me, my lord, your worthy name and that of your noble clan. What has turned your steps toward our humble convent?" T'eng made known his name and replied, "I have no other business but that I have long esteemed the purity and virtue of your honored sanctuary. And so I have gathered together a small pittance to provide for some incense and have come to pay my respects before the Joy of the Law."[7] And with this he produced the silver from within his sleeve and presented it to her. Now Hui-ch'eng was quite versed in the ways of the world, and, gauging its weight with one quick glance, realized that there had to be some matter for which he wished to solicit her aid. "This is not right," she said by way of polite refusal, but by now she was already holding it in her hands and could only thank him, "I humbly accept your bounteous gift; have you no further words for me?" But T'eng insisted that he had no intention other than to express his good will, and saying thus he took his leave and returned to his lodging.

"Now if this is not strange!" thought the old nun to herself, "Such a handsome young man, what does he want with an old nun like me? To give me such a kind gift with no special request." But for the time being she was at a loss to grasp his intent. Meanwhile, he was coming every day without fail to the convent, and every time they met he was even more respectful, so they

---

7. To pay a visit to a Buddhist temple.

gradually grew fairly intimate with one another. One day, Hui-ch'eng asked him, "My lord seems to be troubled by something; there must be something the matter. You know, if you would only bid me, there is nothing in which I would not do my utmost for you." "By rights I should not even speak of it," replied T'eng, "for I expect it cannot be done; but since my very life hangs in the balance, perhaps I may have hope that my reverend teacher will expend the slight bit of effort necessary to save me. If it is, after all, impossible, then let me take sick and die and be done with it!" Hui-ch'eng saw that he was hesitant about speaking and coaxed him, "What possible? What impossible? Out with it." And so T'eng related how he had met Madame Ti at the West Lake, and so on and so forth, and how if only she could bring this predestined match to fruition he would spare no amount of gold to thank her. After he had finished his story, Hui-ch'eng replied with a laugh, "Yes, this certainly is a difficult matter. This person with whom I am acquainted is, it is true, lovely beyond description, but since she has not the slightest flaw in her character, how do you propose to approach her?" T'eng thought a moment and inquired, "Since my reverend teacher is so well acquainted with her, you must know what it is that she is most fond of in her life." "She does not seem to be especially fond of any material objects," replied Hui-ch'eng. "Has she never requested you to do anything for her?" pressed T'eng; and she replied, "Several days ago she did ask me to find for her some pearls of superior quality. In fact she repeated this two or three times. But this is the only thing of the kind." At this T'eng laughed aloud, "That is perfect! Perfect! Our union was surely ordained by Heaven. It happens that I have a relative who is a pearl dealer; he has plenty of fine pearls and it just happens that I am presently lodging in his house. I can ask for as many as you say, and I am certain that he will be willing to give them to me." And with this he bounded out the door and sped away, returning to the convent shortly with two bags of large pearls. He showed these to Hui-ch'eng and said, "These pearls are worth twenty thousand strings of cash, but taking her great beauty into consideration I will meet her halfway and sell them to her for ten thousand strings." "But her husband is in the north on an official mission," replied Hui-ch'eng. "How can she, a woman, raise such a large sum of money?" T'eng laughed, "Well, even if it is only four or five thousand strings, that would be all right, or else one thousand and several hundred would be sufficient. If she is only willing to consummate our fated union, I will be satisfied with no money at all." Hui-ch'eng also laughed, "What foolishness! Well, since you have these pearls, I will use the tongue of Su Ch'in and Chang Yi,[8] I will exercise the six extraordinary tactics,[9] I will do anything, but no matter what, I will find some way to get her to come here to the convent. When that time comes, I will look for an

8. Famed orators of the Warring States period.
9. From the "Annals of the Hereditary House of Prime Minister Ch'en P'ing" in the *Records of the Grand Historian* (*Shih chi*) by Ssu-ma Ch'ien (see selection 225).

opportunity to arrange it so that she will meet you face to face. Then you can put your own methods to the test. Whether you succeed or not depends on your own fortune; that is no longer my affair." "I put myself entirely in your masterful hands," begged T'eng. "Deliver me!"

And so Hui-ch'eng picked up the two bags of pearls and, tittering to herself, made her way to the house of Madame Ti. After she had paid her respects, Madame Ti inquired of her, "What might you have in those bags?" to which she replied, "It is the pearls your grace requested me to find for you the other day. I have here two sacks of superior quality, which I respectfully present for your grace's inspection." And with this she loosened one of the bags, and Madame Ti reached in and drew out a handful, crying aloud, "These certainly are fine pearls!" She scrutinized them a while, too fond of them to put them down, and asked, "What is their price?" "They are asking ten thousand strings," replied Hui-ch'eng. Madame Ti was perplexed, "Yes, just this one would be worth half of that amount. It is certainly unusually reasonable. But my lord is presently away and I could never get together such a sum on such short notice. What shall I do?" At this, Hui-ch'eng took Madame Ti by the hand, saying, "Your grace, let us take a stroll as we talk." And so she accompanied her to her inner chambers, where she disclosed to her, "If your grace is really so fond of these pearls, there is no need for cash; for there is a certain official who desires a certain matter of you." Storyteller! Do you mean to say that one could actually broach such a subject directly before a lady of good family, saying, "I will give you these pearls, and you must consent to a certain matter." Can this be so? Worthy reader! Be not impatient; you shall see the mastery of our nun, with her own subtle persuasion.

And so it was that, when Madame Ti demanded, "To what matter must I consent?" Hui-ch'eng replied, "There is a certain young official who has fallen from his position due to the calumny of an enemy, and begs of you this one kindness, that you plead on his behalf before the Bureau of Personnel, and request a restoration of his post, for which he will gladly part with these pearls. Considering that your grace's worthy brothers and husband are all men of eminent rank, I am confident that your grace may be able to find an avenue to press his suit, and so these pearls may be yours for no money." "In that case," replied Madame Ti, "return the pearls to him for the time being and allow me time to consider the matter thoroughly. When I have found such an avenue as you mention, we can then make further arrangements." "But his affair is at a critical moment," warned Hui-ch'eng. "If I were to return them to him he would surely look for someone else, and then how will you ever retrieve the pearls? I believe it would be better to keep them here with your grace and say to him that you do have such an avenue, while I will come tomorrow for further information, and leave it at that." "That sounds reasonable," answered Madame Ti. And at this, Hui-ch'eng took her leave and proceeded directly to T'eng to recount fully what had transpired. "How shall we proceed from here?" asked T'eng. Hui-ch'eng replied, "Since she has already taken a liking to the pearls and has taken them into her keeping, I am certain that I will be able to find a way, no matter what happens, to get her to come to the convent tomorrow. Then you can observe my skill." T'eng then presented her with another twenty ounces of silver with the enjoinder, "Go at an early hour tomorrow!"

Meanwhile, after the departure of Hui-ch'eng, Madame Ti had once again scrutinized the pearls, growing more and more attached to them, and thought to herself, "For me to entreat my brothers to appeal on his behalf is no difficult matter; these pearls are as good as mine already." Thus it is that good people should banish all cupidity from their minds, for as soon as one harbors covetous desires and these are espied by others, then one is certain to fall prey to their snares. If Madame Ti had never requested that the nun find pearls for her, there would be no ground from which trouble might spring. And even if she had seen the pearls, if she had the money she should have bought them, and if not, let the matter end at that, the one or the other, so that, be you the very finest man alive, she would not have been budged an inch. But since she took a liking to the pearls, while yet unable to raise the money, she had already fallen into someone's clutches, and one as clear as crystal and pure as jade was brought to an inexcusable pass.

But let us return to Madame Ti, who the following morning was wrapped in thoughts of this matter when Hui-ch'eng appeared and asked, "Does your grace find that this matter can be accomplished?" to which she replied, "Last night I investigated that matter thoroughly and have found that there are such avenues; I need only set things in order." "However, there is one difficulty," responded Hui-ch'eng. "A transaction of ten thousand strings is no mean matter. If you leave everything up to me, a poor humble nun whose very flesh would weigh not more than a few pounds, I can talk up and talk down, but when the two parties involved are not acquainted with one another, even though I say, 'It shall be done,' wherefore should this person be willing to take my word?" "What you say is certainly so," replied Madame Ti, "but what do you propose to do about it?" "In my humble view," said Hui-ch'eng, "your grace might come to the convent as if to make a fast and wait there for this official. Then you could encounter him as if it were completely without forethought, and both parties could scrutinize one another. Might this be acceptable?" But Madame Ti was a woman of honor, and so, upon hearing that one would have her meet a stranger face to face, she reddened to the tips of her ears and exclaimed with a wave of the hand, "How could I do such a thing?" Hui-ch'eng changed her expression and continued, "What is so difficult? You need only let him relate his purposes and acknowledge to his face that you can do his bidding, so that he need have no further misgivings, and the matter will then be absolutely settled. But if your grace says 'to meet him personally is unthinkable,' then this matter will be impossible, and you might as well forget about it, for I dare not press him." Madame Ti thought another moment and replied, "Seeing that the judgment of my reverend teacher is so, I fancy there can be no great harm in it. The day after tomorrow happens to be the anniversary of my brother's passing, so I can come to the convent to make a fast. But by all means instruct him to say his piece briefly and be gone, for we must avoid any appearance of coarseness." Hui-ch'eng reassured her, "My own wishes are precisely the same; once he has stated his case, for what would I detain him? You need not be anxious on that account." And so, the engagement thus settled, Hui-ch'eng returned to the convent, where she recounted the preceding, point by point, to T'eng, who was already there waiting for her. Upon hearing this he exclaimed in grateful obeisance, "Even the fabled genius of Chang Yi and Su Ch'in cannot surpass this!"

On the appointed morning, Hui-ch'eng rose at an early hour, set the fasting mats in their proper places, and secreted T'eng away in a quiet room far from prying eyes, where she had set out a table of the finest wines and delicacies. Pulling the door to, she came to the outer chambers, where she took charge of final preparations for Madame Ti's arrival. It was precisely a case of

> "Setting out a bait of pungent fragrance,
> And lying in wait for a whale to take the hook."

Shortly after noon that day, Madame Ti appeared as planned, dressed in full array. Fearing to attract unwanted attention, she had dismissed all of her servants and entered the convent with only one young maid. Upon meeting Hui-ch'eng, she inquired, "Has this person arrived already?" to which Hui-ch'eng replied, "Not as yet." "That is excellent," said Madame Ti, "for I can complete the matter of my fast in the meantime." Whereupon Hui-ch'eng recited a formal declaration of her guest's pious intentions, and chanted through several devotional hymns, before bidding a young nun lead the maid away to another spot for refreshment. And saying to Madame Ti, "Let us sit a while in my quarters," she led her back down several narrow winding passages to a small chamber. When she lifted the blinds to enter, behold! a handsome young man sat alone within, beside a table spread richly with wines and delicacies. She was startled and hastened to withdraw, but Hui-ch'eng called the man forth, "You wish to have a word with her grace, my lord; and yet you hesitate to greet her." At this, T'eng hastened forward with a flourish of elegance and fell to his knees in obeisance. Madame Ti, at a loss for what to do, could only return the compliment. At this point, Hui-ch'eng urged, "My lord, in gratitude for your grace's beneficence, has expressly prepared a bit of wine to thank your grace. Let your grace take notice of his token of sincerity and not refuse to share his cup." As Madame Ti was about to rise, she lifted her eyes and saw that it was none other than he whom she had met at the West Lake. Seeing that he was in the bloom of youth and delightfully well mannered, her feelings had already softened toward him. With a pleased yet coy expression, she asked, "Tell me, what is this matter? Speak straight out, I beg of you." At this point, Hui-ch'eng pulled Madame Ti by the sleeve and said, "Let your grace be seated and continue the conversation in comfort; wherefore do you remain standing?" T'eng then poured a brimming cup of wine, bowed with a laugh, and with both hands bore it to her, whereupon they took their places at the table. Madame Ti, unable to decline, could not but accept it, and drained it at one draught. Hui-ch'eng then took the wine vessel and poured out another cup, whereupon Madame Ti, sensing her intention, took the cup and returned the compliment to T'eng. As intimate glances passed back and forth between them, Madame Ti quickly lost sight of the solemn demeanor she had borne earlier. When she finally inquired, "Pray tell, what office is it that my lord wishes to fill?" T'eng cast a look at Hui-ch'eng and said, "With our reverend teacher here I cannot speak straight out," whereupon Hui-ch'eng offered, "I will withdraw a moment." And jumping to her feet, she hastened out and thrust the door shut behind her. Quicker than the telling of it, T'eng shifted his seat across the room, drew beside Madame Ti, and took her in his arms with the entreaty, "Since the day I first saw your grace at the lake I have longed for you day and night. Unless my lady will take pity and deliver this miserable life of mine, I will surely waste away to my death. If only, perchance, your grace will deign to fulfill these desires that possess me, I will be yours body and soul. What care have I whether I get this post or not? How could I even put such a thing in my desperate mind?" And with this he fell to his knees in supplication. Madame Ti perceived his handsome features, his piteous expressions, and his mournful plaint, replete with a hundred "your grace's," a thousand "my lady's," and was overcome with alarm and affection. She wanted to cry out, but realized that it was of no avail. She wanted to refuse him, but how could she resist his two arms clasped tightly about her? From his kneeling position, he lifted her straight up off the ground and carried her to the bed, where, laying her down upon it, he proceeded to tear frantically at her garments. She, in her turn, aroused to passion in the heat of the moment and scarcely able to suppress her desire, could do nothing. Though she vainly attempted to conceal her exposure, in the end she could not long resist and could only let him thrash about. Now T'eng was a sturdy youth who was well versed in this business. With his consummate skill, he soon brought Madame Ti to such a state that her whole body was limp with desire, her womanly juices already set aflow. Though Madame Ti, for her part, was not unfamiliar with conjugal matters, she had never known this realm of experience, so her delight was without limit. When the clouds and the rain had finally dispersed, she took his hand in hers and said, "Who are you, and what is your clan? Were it not for this day, I might have lived my entire life in vain. From this day forth I must see you every night." And so, T'eng revealed to her his name, amid paeans of gratitude. Just then, Hui-ch'eng opened the door and entered the room. Madam Ti could not speak for shame, but Hui-ch'eng spoke up, "Pray, your grace, do not think ill of me. This gentle sir was about to die on your account, so I, a poor nun acting from the roots of compassion, sought a way that your grace might deliver him, and thus gain merit surpassing that to be gained through the construction of a seven-tiered pagoda." "You certainly did play me false!" protested Madame Ti, "and now it will be up to you to conduct him to my home every night; that is all there is to it." "This I can do," replied Hui-ch'eng.

And so they parted that night, and thenceforth every evening a side door to her house was opened to receive him within; so that not a night did she spend in solitude. Madame Ti nourished a deep love for him within her breast, and fearing only that she would lose his favor, spared no efforts to do his bidding; while he, in his turn, did all he could to be worthy of her. Several months later, after her husband had returned from the capital, he was gradually seen less and less. Still, when her husband was away, she would always bid someone call him to her. Another year passed and more, before her husband, hearing some faint report, placed her under strict surveillance, forbidding any visits to her. Madame Ti, unable to bear her longing, took sick and died. And so, a lady of fine character, her body beguiled through the work of a nun, was sent to her grave. But this was still due to the essential femininity of Madame Ti herself, such that when she was slightly aroused she lost her self-control and could thus be taken in this way.

And now we have another honorable lady who is stung by the venomous wiles of a nun, but to the end remains unswayed. United with her husband in common will and common plan, she brings the nun to a dishonorable death, without even a grave for her rotting corpse, and so finds deep satisfaction at last. It is truly a story such as is rarely heard and rarely seen in our times. Just as it is said in the *Tractate of the Universal Gate:*[10]

> "Put a curse upon all venom,
> All desires are a bane to the flesh;
> Call upon the power of Kuan-yin,[11]
> Returning to your original self."

The story is told that there lived in Wu-chou a young degree-holder by the name of Chia, who though still a youth, was rich in learning, gifted with talents far beyond those of his peers. His wife, born of the Wu clan, was fair beyond all praise, though chaste of disposition. The two lived in perfect harmony, taken to one another like fish to water, bound by ties of mutual respect and love such that never a harsh word passed between them. Now this young scholar was employed as a tutor in the private academy of a great house far away, so that a period of several months often passed in which he could not return home. And so Lady Wu would remain behind, passing the time in

10. A section of the *Lotus Sūtra* (see selection 13) that often circulated separately.
11. Avalokiteśvara, the bodhisattva (enlightened being who functions as a savior).

domestic pursuits, accompanied by her maid named Spring Blossom. Now
this lady, having a fine hand for embroidery, had once fashioned a tapestry of
Kuan-yin, the Goddess of Mercy, both imposing in design and strikingly
lifelike in its rich detail. Profoundly pleased with her handiwork, she bid her
husband take it to the mounting shop to be mounted, where no one who set
eyes on it failed to acclaim its beauty. Once it had been mounted upon a
scroll, she had it brought back home and hung it up in an immaculate room
in a quiet corner of the house, where she burned incense before it each
morning and evening. Now since her homage was devoted exclusively to the
goddess Kuan-yin, an old nun by the name of Chao, who inhabited a temple
of Kuan-yin on that very street, was in the habit of visiting her house regularly.
When the scholar was away from home, the lady would keep her there for
several days at a time for companionship. And the old nun Chao would in her
turn at times invite her to come visit her at the convent, though Lady Wu,
conscious of her place and unwilling ordinarily to idly leave the confines of
her gates, was not in the habit of going more than once or twice in a year.

One fine spring day when the scholar was away, the old nun came to visit.
After chattering for a while, the lady rose to escort her to the door, when the
nun remarked, "What fine weather! Will my lady come along with me outside
to enjoy the view!" And so, just as if it had been planned, she sauntered off
after the old nun out to the threshhold of her gates and, putting her head
tentatively outside the gates to take a look, behold! a young man with all the
trappings of a rogue came barreling down the street and ran full tilt into her.
Lady Wu lost no time in retreating inside and hiding behind the gate, but
Sister Chao remained standing where she was. For it happened that this man
was well acquainted with the old nun and hailed her, "Well, well. If it is not
my reverend teacher, Sister Chao, I was just now looking for you at your place
but you were not in. And here you are now. There is a small matter I wish to
discuss with you." The nun replied, "I will take leave of the lady of this house
and then come to speak with you," whereupon she turned back within and
took her leave of Lady Wu. Lady Wu, on her part, shut the door and returned
to her chambers.

But let us now turn to the roguish gent who has hailed the old nun Chao:
named Liang of the house of Pu,[12] he was a notorious libertine and ne'er-do-
well of the city of Wu-chou. Once he set eyes on a lady of some beauty and
determined to possess her, he would not rest until she was in his clutches.
Moreover, his lustful nature knew no bounds; he desired every woman that he
met, be she fair or foul. And thus it was that such nuns as this were on
intimate terms with him, serving him now as panderer, now taking a share in
his diversion. Now this old nun Chao had at the time a disciple by the
monastic name of Original Void, who was just over twenty years old and quite

---

12. Pu Liang, a pun on "ne'er-do-well."

charming. But to tell the truth, who could consider her as having actually taken vows? It was just as if the old nun were harboring a fille de joie who would share one's couch for money, and was playing the nun only to deceive the world and nothing more. And this Pu Liang was one of the nun's leading patrons.

And so on this day, after taking leave of Lady Wu, the old nun hastily overtook him and inquired, "What matter might it be that my lord Pu wishes to speak of to me?" "This house from which you have just come," returned Pu Liang, "might it be none other than that of the scholar Chia?" "Precisely," replied the nun. "I have long heard," continued Pu Liang, "that the lady of this house is quite charming. This woman that just came out with you and then hid behind the gate: I warrant she must be the one?" "Heaven be praised for your cleverness!" rejoined the nun. "There is none other like her in this house, and not only in this house, but on this entire street there is none other as lovely as she." "Yes, she certainly is lovely," returned Pu Liang, "Her reputation is certainly not unfounded. When may I have a chance to see her once again and regard her more fully?" The nun replied, "What is difficult about this? The nineteenth day of the second month will be the name-day of the Bodhisattva Kuan-yin and a veritable deluge of people will pour out to view the processions in the streets. Go to the house directly across from the gate of her house, rent a room, and move in in the meantime. On that morning I will go and invite her to come outside her gate to witness the spectacle since she is all alone in the house; and she is certain to stand outside for quite a while. During that time you can strain your prying eyes to your heart's content; will that not satisfy you?" "Excellent! That is excellent!" answered Pu Liang.

On the appointed day, Pu Liang occupied a second-story room across the street according to plan, and fixed his gaze upon the gates of the Chia house. Sure enough, the old nun Chao soon appeared on the scene, entered the house, and led the lady out. Lady Wu, being completely unsuspecting and fearing only that someone on the street would spy her, since she was, after all, at the gates of her own house, could hardly be expected to guard against someone eying her furtively from an upper-story window on the opposite side of the street. And so Pu Liang was able to view her meticulously from head to toe. Only when she had reentered the house did he finally descend from the upper floor, just as the nun was also coming out from the gates of the Chia house. As the two met, the nun asked with a laugh, "Did you get a close look?" to which Pu Liang replied, "Yes, I did view her rather thoroughly, as far as that may go, but, you know, empty musing is completely worthless. The sight of her has fired my blood and I must have her somehow." "Oh, yes!" scoffed the old nun. "The toad in the ditch fancies himself partaking of the flesh of the wild swan. Why, she is the lady of a degree-holder. She will not even leave her house ordinarily; and you are neither kith nor kin, without the slightest connection to her house. From where do you propose to gain her confidence? You had better just take your look and be gone." As they talked, they walked back toward the nunnery, where, upon entering within the gates, Pu Liang fell to his knees and implored the nun, "You are in and out of her house constantly. Surely you can think of some scheme to deliver her to me." The old nun shook her head, "That is hard! Hard! Hard!" "If I might only have one slight taste of this savor, I would face death with a glad heart," returned Pu Liang. "But this lady," replied the nun, "cannot be compared to the others. Even in speaking to her one must guard his words with care. If you are thinking of trying to arouse her natural desires, and thus establish relations with her, you will not be successful in a million years. Yet, if you wish only a taste of her, and are willing, right or wrong, to use coercion on her, that is no great task. Only, do not be impatient." "Do you mean rape her?" cried Pu Liang. "You need not actually force her," replied the nun, "you need only make it so that she is unable to refuse you." "Yes, yes," urged Pu Liang, "but where is your infallible strategy? If it does succeed, I will build you an altar and bow down before you as a general of the faith!" "Since ancient times it has been said," continued the nun, " 'Row your boat with an easy stroke and catch a drunken fish.' And so we have only to get her drunk, and you may do your will with her. What do you say to that?" "Yes, that is fine," replied Pu Liang, "but what sort of trick do you propose to use to get her drunk?" The old nun replied, "This lady has never so much as sniffed a drop of wine; she will be determined not to drink, and I, of course, would be hard put actually to force her to. For if I did coax her too insistently, she would become suspicious and perhaps become angry with me. And then she would, after all, drink nothing, and we would be able to do nothing. And then again, even granted I could make her drink a cup or two, she would be quick to fall drunk and quick to recover, and so you could never take her with impunity." "Well then," pressed Pu Liang, "what do you propose to do?" The nun hesitated, "I have my ways to make her fall; you need not concern yourself." But Pu Liang demanded that she explain herself, and so she bent close to his ear and whispered, "We will do so and so, thus and such. . . . Do you approve?" Pu Liang stamped his foot and laughed aloud, "An excellent plan! An excellent plan! Never in all history was there such a fine plan!" "But there is one thing," continued the nun. "If I do this for you and play her so false, after she has recovered her senses and realized her plight she will surely condemn me and refuse to see me again. What have you to say about that?" "You need only worry about delivering her to me," Pu Liang reassured her. "Once she is mine, what plight is there for her to realize? How can she turn her back on you? I am confident I can use sweet words and flattery to win her over. And who knows, perhaps I may be able to establish a permanent relationship with her after all. If she bears any ill feelings toward you, I will personally make it up to you royally, that is all. And if, perchance, we do become intimate, I will certainly plead your case for you." "Hold your tongue," retorted the nun in jest, and the two continued to banter for a while before going their separate ways.

From this time on, Pu Liang would come to the convent every day to inquire as to how the matter was progressing, and nun Chao was occupied day in and day out with calculating just how to ensnare Lady Wu. After a space of several days, the old nun prepared a few boxes of pastries and made her way to the Chia house, where she was kept by Lady Wu for dinner. The nun seized this opportunity to cajole her, "My lady and her lord the degree-holder are both in the springtime of their youth, and have joined together for quite a long time. By now there ought to have been heard the glad tidings that you will bear a young master." "Yes, that is quite true," agreed Lady Wu. "Well then," continued the nun, "why not take a vow of devotion and beseech the goddess on your behalf?" "But I am lighting incense morning and night before the portrait of Kuan-yin that I embroidered myself, and I have already offered quite a few prayers, though there has been no response that I can see," complained Lady Wu. "My lady is still very young," the nun went on, "and is not aware of the proper ways to beseech the goddess for children. In such supplications, one must beseech the Kuan-yin of the White Robe, for which there is a special scroll known as the *Sūtra of the White Robe*. Now this is neither the ordinary Goddess of Mercy, nor the Kuan-yin *Sūtra of the Tractate of the Universal Gate*. This *Sūtra of the White Robe*, as it is called, possesses a remarkable efficacy. A complete record of its use has been inscribed on the copy we have commissioned for our convent. It is a pity I did not bring it with me to show to my lady. Not to mention any other places, within the area of our city of Wu-chou alone, both within and without the city walls, no one who has but printed and distributed it, and then chanted it aloud, has failed to bear a son. Truly, it is unfailing in its power; one thousand incantations will bring one thousand fulfillments, ten thousand will bring ten thousand." "If it is as unfailing as you say," enjoined Lady Wu, "may I humbly beg to trouble my reverend teacher to bring a copy here to my house, that I may recite it." "But my lady does not know the proper way to recite it," returned the nun, "and this is not something that I can teach you to recite straight off. I fear I must bid my lady come to the convent and personally pledge a certain number of recitations before the holy image of the Great Bodhisattva of the White Robe. If you will allow me to pronounce your sincerity and initiate the reading of the scroll myself, as well as recite it through several times for you, then when you return to your home later you will have become familiar with the method of reciting and will be able to recite it yourself every day thereafter." "That will be fine," agreed Lady Wu. "I will first make a partial fast for two days, and then come to the convent to declare my sincerity and begin the reading of the sūtra." "That you will fast for two days beforehand is sufficient evidence of my lady's earnestness," encouraged the nun. "After we have initiated the reading of the scroll, you should still eat only a light meatless breakfast in the mornings before reading the sūtra, but after the reading there will be no harm in eating meat as usual." "Certainly, certainly!" replied Lady Wu. "That will be easily managed." And so Lady Wu appointed the day with her to come to the convent, and offered her five pieces of silver in advance to cover the expenses of the reading of the sūtra and the preparation of a chamber. The old nun then left her house, and hastened to convey the news to Pu Liang.

True to her vow, Lady Wu kept a fast for two days, and on the third day arose before the fifth watch,[13] completed her toilette and, leading her maid Spring Blossom, set out early for the Kuan-yin convent, while there were as yet few people about on the streets. Take heed, worthy reader! Be it even to a nun's cloister or a monk's sanctuary, the sons and daughters of good families should not venture out lightly. Yes, storyteller, if I had been born in the same year and grown up alongside her, and had overheard what was about to befall her, I would certainly have held her back or barred her way, so that not only would the fine name of Lady Wu have remained unsullied, but even the old nun Chao might have preserved her life and limb intact. But because of this one misstep, the inevitable consequence was that

> "A vision of loveliness from an ancient house—a jade-tree soiled by the muddy stream,
> The karmic essence of the Gate of the Void—a scarlet maple stained with blood."

But of this we shall speak anon. Let us hear now the sequel to what has gone before.

The old nun welcomed Lady Wu with a thousand expressions of joy at her coming and bid her come within and be seated. After tea had been served, she led her in to worship before the Bodhisattva Kuan-yin of the White Robe. Lady Wu prayed softly to herself, while the nun went forward to pronounce her sincerity, saying, "Lady Wu, a faithful daughter of the house of Chia, respectfully requests to personally recite the *Sūtra of the Kuan-yin of the White Robe,* in the hope that she may soon bear a young master. May all her wishes be auspiciously fulfilled!" The ceremony of pronouncing her sincerity thus complete, the nun tapped a wooden resounding-block and began to recite, beginning with: "Oh, true word of the karma of pure speech!" and continuing: "Oh, true word of the land of peace!" And having opened the ceremony thus, she invoked the name of the Buddha for a long while, before proceeding to recite the sūtra itself, which she recited twenty or more times without a pause. Now was this old nun not cunning? She was fully aware that Lady Wu had come at an early hour and, what is more, had kept a fast for the past two days

---

13. Between three and five in the morning.

and had certainly not eaten breakfast at home that morning. Yet she intentionally let this slip her mind, neither bringing out anything to eat nor asking
her, "Has my lady eaten yet?" Instead, she applied herself to prolonging the
proceedings, hoping that Lady Wu would suffer from hunger and be laid open
to her devices. Now Lady Wu, frail and nervous of disposition, had risen early
that morning and come on an empty stomach to the convent,where she was
forced to sit quietly through the nun's unending incantations. But though she
felt both fatigue and hunger, she was in no position to speak openly of it, and
so calling her maid Spring Blossom to her, she whispered in her ear, "Go and
see if there is any hot soup in the kitchen and fetch me a bowl." The old nun
noticed this and asked with design, "Forgive me, I have been so involved in
reading the sūtras and finishing our main concern that I had completely
forgotten to ask whether my lady has eaten breakfast or not." Lady Wu replied,
"I came very early, and so have actually not yet eaten." "What an old
muddlehead I am," returned the nun. "I prepared no breakfast for you, and
now I fear it is too late. What shall we do? Perhaps we can just take our
midday meal somewhat earlier." "I need not deceive my teacher," assented
Lady Wu. "I do feel hungry, indeed. If you would just bring a small dish of
anything at all to eat in the meantime, it would be fine." The old nun
intentionally hesitated a while, disappeared into her quarters for a time, and
then stopped by the kitchen for a spell, before finally sending the young novice
Original Void out with a platter of things to eat and a pot of tea. Now by this
time, Lady Wu was so hungry her stomach was rumbling and her intestines
joining the chorus. On the table were spread quite a number of fresh candies
and sweetmeats, but none there could have relieved her hunger save a large
plate of steaming hot cakes. Lady Wu took one of these and found it both soft
and sweet, and without realizing it due to her hunger, ate several of them in
quick succession. Meanwhile the young novice poured out a cup of hot tea
and she took a few swallows, ate several more pieces of cake, and then poured
out another cup of tea. But before she had drunk a few mouthfuls of this tea,
suddenly her face flushed red, the heavens whirled, and the earth spun
beneath her feet; yawning with a shudder, she sank down limp in her chair.
The old nun cried out in mock alarm, "My goodness! What is this? I warrant
she has risen too early and her head has become dizzy. Let us carry her to the
bed and let her sleep for a while." And so Original Void together with her
mistress picked her up, chair and all, and carried her to the bedside, where
they laid her on the bed, lowered her head, and left her to sleep. Now why,
do you suppose, was this cake so potent? You see, the old nun knew all along
that Lady Wu would not take wine, and so she had expressly devised this cake
as follows: first she ground glutinous rice to a fine powder and mixed it with
wine spirits, then baked this mixture very dry. Then she ground it again,
added more wine, and repeated the process two or three times,mixing in
several kinds of various and sundry drugs, before making it into a cake. Once

this cake was touched by the hot water, the force of the drugs and of the wine both came issuing forth, as when yeast is used to ferment wine. Now if even other people could not withstand this powerful brew, certainly Lady Wu, who could have become drunk eating wine lees, and what is more, had risen early that morning, feeling empty inside, and then in her hunger had both eaten a good deal and washed it down with hot tea, could never have withstood the potent reaction. It was truly a case of

> "Be you as vicious as a devil,
> Try and drink the slops from an old woman's feet."

And so the old nun had used this calculated plan to bring Lady Wu to her knees. When the maid Spring Blossom saw that her mistress was asleep, she seized upon this fleeting chance for a half-day's freedom and went off with the young novice to eat, drink, and take her pleasure. What reason was there to stand by and wait upon her mistress? At this point the old nun hastened to the hiding spot of Pu Liang and called him out saying, "The bitch sleeps upon the bed; do with her as you will. But how will you ever thank me for this?" Pu Liang entered the room, pulled the door shut behind him, and lifted up the bed curtains. Before him lay Lady Wu, her two cheeks appealingly red, enveloped in a thick fragrance of wine, just like a drunken begonia, lovelier than ever. His passions kindled, Pu Liang first kissed her, and then, seeing that she was aware of nothing, stealthily slipped off her trousers, exposing her snow-white nether parts. With a bound Pu Liang clambered up on top of her. Hurriedly spreading her legs apart, he inserted his member and thrust wildly, all the while congratulating himself, "I don't deserve this! My day has finally come!" Lady Wu lay limp, her body offering no resistance, as if in a vague, misty dream. Although she did have some slight consciousness, she mistakenly imagined that she was at home with her husband, and so, unable to distinguish white from black, she submitted to this indignity, for a time abandoning all restraint. As matters reached their climax, Lady Wu, in her state of dreamlike intoxication, began to moan uncontrollably. This pushed Pu Liang's delight to the limit. He held her in a tight embrace and with a cry, "Oh, my heart's desire, I'm dying of pleasure!" he poured forth a torrent of release. After he was done with her, Lady Wu lay there, her troubled sleep unbroken, while Pu Liang lay face to face with her, his arms draped about her. Before long the force of the drugs began to be dispelled, and coming to herself somewhat, Lady Wu saw that a strange man lay beside her. A cold sweat sprang from her pores as she cried out in horror, "Oh, no! Oh, no!" As she scrambled to her feet, the drunkenness which had caused her ruin was completely dispelled from fright. "Who are you?" she bawled, "that you dare soil a woman of good family?" Pu Liang, quite startled at this, fell to his knees and begged forgiveness, "In the name of compassion, my lady, pray forgive this discourtesy." Lady Wu now noticed that she had been deprived of her trousers, and realizing that she had been taken, could say nothing in reply but pull her trousers on and jump down from the bed, shouting, "Spring Blossom!" Pu Liang, fearing lest he be discovered, did not dare to pursue her, instead remained hidden in the room. Lady Wu opened the door and marched out, shouting again, "Spring Blossom?" Now Spring Blossom, having risen equally early that morning, had dozed off in the young novice's room. When she heard her mistress shouting her name, she gave out an enormous yawn and came out front to see what the matter was. "Worthless creature," cursed Lady Wu, "I was sleeping in that room; who told you to leave me unattended?" Choked with rage, she was about to beat her when the old nun appeared and tried to calm her. When Lady Wu set her eyes upon the nun, her bitterness and anger welled up to a peak, and she slapped Spring Blossom several times, saying, "Quickly! Get our things together and let us be gone!" "But you have not yet read the sūtra," wailed the maid. "Shameless creature!" Lady Wu snapped back. "Who told you to concern yourself with that?" And so, her face purple and swollen with rage, she made her way straight out of the convent, pausing neither to take notice of the old nun, nor to inquire further into the matter, and arrived home in an instant. Opening the gate and proceeding within, she shut the door at once behind her and sat a long while disconsolate. When her wrath had calmed down somewhat, she questioned Spring Blossom, "I remember being hungry and eating some cakes, but how did I come to be lying on that bed?" Spring Blossom replied, "After you ate the cakes and took several swallows of tea, you collapsed in your chair. It was the old teacher and young novice who then together carried you to bed." "And where were you?" pressed Lady Wu. "When my lady fell asleep," replied Spring Blossom, "I was also hungry, so I first ate the cakes you left over, and then went to the novice's quarters for a cup of tea. I felt rather sleepy and I must have dozed off until my lady called me and I came to you." "Did you see anyone go into the room?" "I saw no one; no doubt it was the nuns." Lady Wu made no reply, but tried to recall the visions she had seen in her dreams, remembering in a vague way what had happened. Passing her hand over the font of her womanhood, she found it damp and sticky, and sighed to herself, "Enough! Enough! Who would have guessed that this whore of a nun could be so deadly as to hand my chaste body over to some infernal wretch and stain it with his filth. How can I go on living?" And so she held back her tears and brooded in silence. She would fain have ended her miserable existence, but she could not bear the thought of never again seeing her lord. Going before the portrait of the Bodhisattva she had embroidered, she lamented tearfully, "Your disciple bears a mortal hatred in her breast and looks to the power of the Bodhisattva for vengeance." Her prayer thus ended, she thought mournfully of her husband and her sobs broke into tears before she retired in utter despair. Spring

Blossom, meanwhile, had not the slightest notion of what had occurred. But let us speak no more of the grief of Lady Wu.

Nun Chao, in the meantime, seeing Lady Wu stalk out with such a look of rage, knew that Pu Liang had taken his prize. Going into the chamber, she saw him still resting on the bed, his finger in his mouth, dreaming blankly of what had transpired. Seeing this state of affairs, the nun began to feel neglected, and, scrambling up on top of him, said, "Will you not show your gratitude to the matchmaker?" Literally throwing herself on top of him, she stretched out her hand to touch his member, but as he had ejaculated there was no way she could make it rise again. Beside herself, the old nun gave Pu Liang a bite and complained; "You are getting off easy this time. You've gotten me so worked up, you'll be the death of me." "My gratitude to you is boundless. I will attend to you untiringly this evening," promised Pu Liang. "For I also wish to discuss with you our further plans." "But you said you wished only one taste," retorted the nun. "What further plans do you have?" "When one has conquered Lung[14] he looks toward Shu.[15] That is a constant fact of human nature. Now that I have savored the taste of her, how can I be content to leave it at that? Just now it was under duress. I will only be truly satisfied when she herself finally enjoys it and comes to me of her own accord." "You certainly are an insatiable wretch," scolded the nun. "You just raped her and she ran out in a fit of anger, without even saying good-bye; who knows what her disposition is now? How can you even think of ever meeting her again? You had better just wait until I can find another opportunity; if she has not actually cut off all relations with me, perhaps there will be something to discuss after all." "Yes, you are right," agreed Pu Liang. "I leave myself completely in the hands of your superior genius." That night, wishing, from gratitude, to attend to the nun's every pleasure, Pu Liang remained behind at the convent, abandoning himself to her debauchery. But let us speak no more of this.

Let us turn instead to the scholar Chia away in a far-off academy. It happened that that night he had a dream, in which he saw himself back at home. A woman clad in white came walking in through the gates and, just as he went forward to question her, disappeared into his chambers. The scholar was pursuing her with long strides when, behold! she entered into the very tapestry itself of the Kuan-yin which hung upon the wall. As he lifted his head in wonder, he saw several lines of writing on it. When he took a closer look, and read it from the beginning, it said:

> "What comes from the mouth shall pass to the mouth;
> Vengeance and purgation lie with the disciple."

14. Kansu province.

15. Szechwan province. Together, these terms comprise a proverbial expression for insatiably rising expectations.

After he had finished reading, he turned about and saw his wife kneeling on the ground before him. Just as he took hold of her to lift her up, the dream dispersed and he awoke with a start. "This dream is truly puzzling," he thought to himself. "It must be that my wife suffers from some accident or disease, and the goddess has communicated with me in this way that I may be informed of it." And so, the very next day he took leave of his employer and left the academy, puzzling all the way home about the precise meaning of the dream. Feeling extremely uneasy, he finally reached his house and knocked on the door. When Spring Blossom came out to open it for him, he questioned her, "Where is my wife?" to which she answered, "My mistress has not yet risen; she is still resting in bed." "How is it that she is not up at this hour of the day?" inquired the scholar. "My mistress is greatly distressed," reported the maid. "She is constantly calling for her lord and weeping." Hearing this, the scholar hastened into her chambers where, seeing that her lord had come, she practically cartwheeled to her feet. As he looked closer, he saw that her face was unwashed and her hair disheveled, while her two eyes were darkly bloodshot. She approached him and, weeping profusely, fell to the floor in supplication. The scholar was startled. "Wherefore do you act this way?" he asked, pulling her to her feet. And she replied, "Let my lord decide my wretched fate." "Who is it that has thus dishonored you?" asked the scholar. Sending the maid off to the kitchen to warm some tea and prepare a meal, she reported tearfully, "Since the day your slave was wed to you, my lord, not a harsh word has passed between us, not one iota have I strayed from the path. But now a grievous guilt weighs upon me. Truly, I deserve to die, but I have waited for you to come, so that I may reveal the truth to you and you may decide my wretched fate. Then I can die with a clean heart." "What is it that has happened?" asked the scholar, "that you speak such confusing words?" And so Lady Wu told him how the old nun had deceived her into coming to the convent, and how she had tricked her into eating the cakes and falling drunk, and how she had allowed someone to rape her while she was yet unconscious. And telling this, she fell weeping to the ground. By the time the scholar had heard the full story, his hair was practically standing on end with rage, and he howled, "This is outrageous!" "Do you know who this man is?" he questioned further. "How could I know?" replied Lady Wu. At this the scholar drew the sword at the head of the bed and struck the table. "If I do not put this wretch to death, how can I call myself a man! But since we do not know his identity, if we are not prudent he will surely slip from our grasp. We must plan our actions with care." "I have reported the matter to my lord," broke in his wife, "and my own business is now done. Let me use the sword in my lord's hand to end my life here and now, and there will be no need for further discussion." "Do not be so hasty," warned the scholar. "This is no case of a wife willingly losing her virtue. This is a misfortune you have suffered; your good faith is evident. And moreover, if you are to rashly take your life in this way, there will be a good deal of unpleasantness for me." "What sort of unpleasantness?" asked the wife. "I cannot foresee any such." "If you were to die," explained the scholar, "your family, as well as others, would of course ask for the reason. Now, if I were to reveal the entire story, you could scarce avoid ill fame even in death, while my official career would be finished. And if I did not tell the whole story, your family and clansmen would have nothing more to do with me. And how could I ever set things straight alone; how could I ever avenge this grievous wrong?" "If it is your wish that I do not die, this whore of a nun and this sneaking scoundrel must both die before my eyes, else how can I go on living with this shame upon me?" The scholar thought awhile before asking, "That day when you were deceived, what did you say when you saw the nun?" "I was so furious I came straight home," answered the lady. "I did not exchange a word with her." "Since it is so," continued the scholar, "this wrong cannot be avenged in the open. If I were to act openly there would certainly be talk in the courts, and it would be impossible, eventually, to conceal the truth. Then there would be a noisy dispute and your name would be stained. Let me try now to think of a perfect plan such that we can gain our revenge without the slightest trace, yet such that neither of them can slip away." And with this, he lowered his head in thought. Suddenly he exclaimed, "I have it! I have it! This plan fits precisely the words of the Kuan-yin in my dream. Perfect! Perfect!" "What might this plan be?" asked the lady. "My wife," exhorted the scholar, "if you wish to clear your soul of this matter and avenge this wrong, you must agree to everything I say. If you are unwilling to obey me, this wrong cannot be avenged, and this mental anguish can never be cleared up." "How could I dare disobey the judgment of my lord?" replied Lady Wu. "I wish only that you bring everything to a satisfactory conclusion." The scholar continued, "Since you did not speak further to the old nun, and did not come to blows with her, she may assume that you were ashamed at the moment, but that, being a weak, sensual woman, you may not have been entirely unmoved. Now you, for your part, must go deceive the old nun, and then you will see my ingenious plan." And bending close to her ear, he whispered, "So and so, thus and such. . . . This is an utterly invincible plan." "This plan may be excellent," replied Lady Wu, "but it is certainly humiliating. Yet, in order to avenge this evil, I will not speak of that."

And so the husband and wife having determined their course of action, the next morning the scholar hid in a secluded spot behind the rear gate, and Lady Wu bade Spring Blossom go to the convent and invite the nun to come and speak with her. When the nun saw Spring Blossom and heard this invitation, she thought to herself, "I fancy this bitch has tasted a little honey and is now so burning with desire that she has changed her tune." And so she as much as flew with Spring Blossom back to the house, swaggering as she came. When the nun saw Lady Wu, she apologized, "The other day I did you ill, my lady. It was certainly inhospitable of me. Pray do not judge me too harshly." Lady Wu sent Spring Blossom away, and taking the nun's hand in hers asked casually, "Who was that man the other day?" The old nun, seeing her intent, lowered her voice and said, "He is master Pu Liang, a well-known gallant in this area. He is so amiable and high-spirited that he delights any girl that chances to see him. He was sorely vexed with longing for your beauty and was coming to beseech me day and night, so I took pity on his earnestness, for I could not, in any event, turn him away. Moreover, seeing that my lady was living in solitude and most likely feeling rather desolate, I felt that it would be far better for you in the time of your youth to have companionship and not let the springtime of your life pass by in vain. That is why I did this thing. For whose cat does not eat meat? These old eyes of mine miss nothing. Pray, my lady, do not take this matter too seriously, and you will find great bliss; for he will worship you like a bodhisattva and keep you like a treasure. What could be amiss?" "Yes," assented Lady Wu, "but you should have discussed the matter fully with me first and not taken advantage of me so. But now that the state of affairs is such, we need speak no further of it." "Anyway," continued the nun, "he was a stranger to you, and if I had disclosed the matter to you, how could you have consented? But having now had this one experience, you might well look toward a lasting relationship." Lady Wu replied, "I felt so humiliated at the time that I could not see clearly. What sort of a man is he? What is his disposition? If he does love me as you say, I'll bid him come to my house for another interview. If I find that he is to my taste, then it will be possible to allow him to come regularly in secret." "Here is the opportunity," thought the nun to herself, scarcely able to control her delight and not the slightest bit suspicious. "If it is as you say, my lady," she continued, "I can bid him come to you this very evening. I am confident you will find him a man of fine mettle in every respect." "I will await him within the gates at the hour of the lighting of the lamps. When I give a cough as a signal, I will let him enter my chambers."

And so the old nun returned to the convent beside herself with joy and conveyed the news to Pu Liang. As soon as Pu Liang heard this, he fell into a flurry of impatience, longing for the golden crow[16] to quickly sink and the jade hare[17] to soar on high. By nightfall he was already to be found by the gates of the Chia house, poking his head impatiently about. By now he would gladly have drawn out the "old story" then and there and hurled it through the gates of the house. Presently it was nighttime and, seeing that the door had been shut fast, he began to suspect uneasily that perhaps the nun was playing him for the fool. Just then, as he wavered there uncertain of what to do, a cough resounded from behind the gate. He responded with a cough of

16. The sun.
17. The moon.

his own from the outside, and the gate was opened slightly. He gave another cough, which was again answered, and slipped through the opening in the gate. Proceeding several paces within, he found himself in a courtyard. By the light of the moon and stars, he could perceive the form of Lady Wu in the distance, whereupon he approached and embraced her at once, saying, "The goodness and mercy of my lady are truly bounteous as the hills." A veritable universe of indignation welled up in Lady Wu's breast, but she compelled herself to offer no resistance and took a firm hold of him with both her hands, submitting to his embrace. Pu Liang hastily brought his mouth to hers and thrust his tongue within, thrashing it about, while she clasped him tighter than ever in her arms and sucked at his tongue vigorously. By now, Pu Liang was in a state of frenzy, his member thrusting upward, and he poked his tongue even farther within her mouth, when suddenly she gave vent to her dammed-up wrath and lunged forward, clamping her teeth deep into his tongue. Pu Liang released his grip in agony and struggled wildly, but Lady Wu had already bitten off about half an inch of his tongue. In complete panic, he dashed madly outside, whereupon Lady Wu spit the piece of his tongue into her hand, hastily barred the door, and went to the rear gate. There she found the scholar and said, "I have bitten off the villain's tongue as you bade me." The scholar took the tongue with great pleasure and wrapped it in his handkerchief, whereupon he buckled on his sword and, by the pale light of the moon and stars, made his way to the Kuan-yin convent.

Now the old nun, assuming that Pu Liang would surely gain his ends and spend the night in the Chia house, had barred the door and retired for the night. The novice was quite young and would be asleep as soon as she lowered her head, so she could not be awakened even if one had pounded the door in. But the nun had this matter in her thoughts, and as she mused about Pu Liang and Lady Wu together, her lust blazed within her so that she could not even attempt to fall asleep. And so, when she heard a knock at the door, she suspected that Pu Liang had done his will and returned for the night. Calling the novice and receiving no reply, she had scrambled to her feet and gone to open the door when, the moment she opened the gate, she met the scholar's sword head-on as it came slashing down into her skull. The nun collapsed backward, a torrent of warm blood pouring forth, and went the way of all flesh. The scholar barred the door behind him, raised his sword, and went inside to look for any others, thinking to himself, "If perchance that Pu Liang is in the convent, I can finish him off as well." Spying a crystal lantern burning before the image of the Buddha, he cast its light in every direction, but saw no one save the young novice sleeping within the chamber. Dispatching her with one blow, he quickly turned up the lantern and by its light undid his handkerchief, whereupon he took out the tongue and, prying open her mouth with his sword blade, placed it inside. And with this, he snuffed out the lantern, pulled the door shut, and made his way back home, where he announced to his wife, "Both teacher and disciple lie slain, the wrong has been avenged!" "But this wretch has lost only a tongue," cried Lady Wu. "He has not been slain!" "Have no fear!" the scholar reassured her. "He will certainly be killed by someone. But meanwhile we must feign complete ignorance. Let us not mention the matter again."

But let us tell now how the next morning the neighbors living adjacent to the Kuan-yin convent saw the sun rise to its midday post, while the door of the convent remained shut and not a soul could be seen to stir within. Their suspicions aroused, they went up and tried the door, and finding it unbarred, pushed it right open. Seeing the murdered nun just inside the gate, they stood a moment aghast, and then proceeded within, where they found the murdered novice in the chamber: the one her head cleft in two, the second her throat severed. Bursting into a fever of activity, they called the local ward headmen who came to view what had happened in order to report it to the magistrate's office. When the local constables appeared en masse to investigate the proceedings, they noticed the jaw of the novice tightly shut about some object, which, when they drew it out, turned out to be a human tongue. "Needless to say," pronounced the constable, "this is a case of assault with intent to rape. But how can we determine who is the culprit? We had better refer the matter to the district magistrate for appropriate action." Whereupon he made out a brief official report and, proceeding to the official chambers just as the magistrate was opening the day's session, submitted it directly to him. "It will not be difficult to discover the felon in this matter," remarked the magistrate. "As soon as someone with a severed tongue is found in or around the city, it will be certain that it was he that did this deed. Quickly dispatch a party to every ward of the city and every village to conduct an inquest in cooperation with the local guarantors of every five or ten families, and the matter will soon come to light." And not very long after the order had been issued, sure enough a constable appeared with the man in his charge.

Now at the time that Pu Liang's tongue was so unexpectedly bitten off, he was already quite aware of the fact that he had been hoodwinked and, beside himself in panic, had scampered madly away, only to lose all sense of direction, unable to tell east from west, north from south, in his fear of being pursued. Choosing a secluded alley, he ducked in and found a spot beneath the eaves of someone's house, where he sat crouched the remainder of the night, hoping to find his way home when it had become light again. But the will of Heaven was surely conspiring for his fall, for though he scampered back and forth, searching vainly in every direction for some familiar street, he was unable, in his agitation, to find a main thoroughfare and could not, of course, open his mouth to ask someone. When the people on the street noticed his suspicious behavior, they divined at once that there had been some foul play; and when, presently, rumors of the incident at the convent reached their ears, and the magistrate's official proclamation was posted, a number of the more officious among them approached and put him to questioning, though he could only jabber unintelligibly in reply, his entire jaw stained with blood. Shortly, the constable's men came dashing up to the crowd and surrounded him, saying, "Who else but this man could be the murderer?" And giving him no chance for disputation, they bound him with a cord and dragged him to the official court. Many people at the court recognized him at once, saying, "This man has always been incorrigibly depraved. It is no surprise that he has committed this act." When the magistrate took his seat at the bench, the crowd brought Pu Liang forward and the magistrate questioned him, but all he could utter was "Oo-li, Oo-la" in reply; not a single word could be made out. The magistrate ordered someone to slap his face several times and demanded that he show his tongue, whereupon they saw that it was without its tip, the bloody wound still fresh. "This filthy cur!" the magistrate questioned the constable, "what are his name and surname?" Now among the crowd assembled, there were some people who had despised him for some time, and so they disclosed everything to the magistrate: his name, his thieving and fraudulent activities in the past, every story they knew about him, both good and bad. "It is self-evident," declared the magistrate, "that this filthy cur must have been planning to rape the young novice and, when the old nun opened the door, cut her down first and then went to attack the other. The novice must have been infuriated with disgust and bitten off the end of his tongue; and he then must have flown into a rage and murdered her. What is there to discuss further?" When he heard this, Pu Liang waved his arms and stamped his feet trying to say something in his defense, but there was not even half a word that was intelligible. "For a scoundrel like this," stormed the magistrate, "why should we waste paper and ink? Besides, he cannot even speak in his defense and the murder weapon has not been found, so it will be difficult to make a formal case against him. So pick out a large-sized rod and beat him until he is dead, here and now, and we shall be done with him." And so the cry rang out, "One hundred blows!"

Now Pu Liang was a decadent pleasure-seeker; how could he ever endure such a punishment? By the time fifty strokes and more had rained down upon him, he had already expired. The magistrates entrusted the constables to order the family of the deceased to reclaim his corpse, and bade the constables cremate the bodies of the nuns and store their ashes. Finally, he issued a proclamation, on which he personally inscribed the following:

> "Pu Liang, Pu Liang! Where is thy tongue? 'Tis, for sure,
>   the destiny of a severed tongue,
> Oh worthy nun! Who has deserved thy fine neck, that
>   he make the covenant of the slit throat?
> His death is fitting and proper; who can doubt the facts?
> I hereby establish this file for future reference."

And so the magistrate closed the case, we need speak of it no more.

When the reports of this affair came buzzing through the streets to the ears of the scholar Chia and Lady Wu, the husband and wife secretly shared a rewarding flush of happiness. Neither the deception of days past nor the affair carried out that day ever came to the knowledge of anyone else. This was due both to the superior wisdom of the scholar and to the intervention of the goddess Kuan-yin, who saw his sincerity of purpose, granted him a divine message, and laid bare to him the means by which he could avenge this bitter wrong and thus restore the integrity of his name. As Lady Wu witnessed the resolute action of her husband, and the scholar Chia saw the faithfulness and unwavering virtue of his wife, their mutual respect grew ever deeper.

In later times, someone commented on this story to the effect that, though revenge and exoneration from shame, especially when wrought under a veil of secrecy, may be considered quite worthy of praise, still the chaste body of Lady Wu had been, after all, soiled. Although this was known to no one but them, still it was a source of sorrow to her. And so, it was because of idle acquaintance with a nun that she was brought to this pass. Take heed, women of good faith! Fail not to take this example to heart!

In the words of the poem:

> "The fragrance of a fallen blossom fades,
> For in the spring it bared its weakness sore.
> Take heed, these words I offer you this day:
> 'A lady should not pass her chamber door!' "

Translated by Andrew H. Plaks

257

The Female Ch'en P'ing[1] Saves Her Life with Seven Ruses

Li Yü (1610/11–1680)

Lyric:

> Women have always been fickle and weak,
> Flinging their affections about.

Li Yü (see also selection 211) is the comic specialist of Chinese literature—in drama, fiction, and the essay. To an unprecedented degree, he emphasized originality and invention in litera-

So tempered let your censure be,
And chide not those who stand out.[2]

In peacetime chastity is easy to swear,
But in war it's hard to uphold.
Silk that comes white from an indigo jar
Will be worth a thousand in gold.

Loyalty, filial piety, chastity, and fidelity are terms of general approbation that everyone rejoices in. The trouble is that loyalty is regularly found on the lips of traitorous officers and filial piety in the mouths of incorrigible sons, while adulterous husbands are constantly holding forth about fidelity and wanton wives about chastity. As a result it is almost impossible to distinguish true virtue from false. However, as the proverb has it: "Fierce winds reveal the sturdy plant and troubled times the loyal subject." Generally, if you want to tell whether something is true or false, you subject it to a test. The trouble is that in this case there is no test applicable. When metals are tested in a furnace, for example, the false are destroyed and the true survive. But if the people who claim to possess these four virtues are put to the test, the false will survive and only the true will perish.

But let me put loyalty, filial piety, and fidelity aside, and address myself solely to the subject of chastity.

During the final two decades of the Ming dynasty, from the time the roving bandits fomented their rebellions and the Dashing Brigand[3] seized his chance right up until the change of mandate, countless women were abducted. Their reactions varied widely. Some kept their vows and either killed themselves or submitted to execution; these, numbering less than one in a thousand, belong in the very highest category. Some were raped by the bandits at the outset and later felt so ashamed that they committed suicide; they should be placed near the top of the middle category. Others went willingly with the stranger but still

---

ture; he usually presents himself in his work as challenging some accepted belief. His plays were written throughout the 1650s and 1660s, but his fiction was confined to a brief period from about 1655 to 1658. *Silent Operas* (*Wu-sheng hsi*), his first collection of stories, appeared probably in 1655 or 1656. It was soon followed by *Silent Operas, Second Collection*, by a novel, *The Carnal Prayer Mat* (*Jou-p'u t'uan*), which is a sexual comedy, and by a third collection of stories, *Twelve Towers* (*Shih-erh lou*). "The Female Ch'en P'ing," which is drawn from *Silent Operas*, is entirely characteristic of Li Yü. Its heroine, an illiterate peasant woman, is offered to the audience as a genius who rivals the great strategists of history; the story deals in comic detail with risqué or bawdy subject matter; and it maintains a mockingly humorous tone throughout.

1. A tactician of legendary ingenuity who advised the first emperor of the Han dynasty.

2. The poem contains a reference to *The Spring and Autumn Annals* and its technique of censure.

3. The rebel Li Tzu-ch'eng, who helped topple the Ming dynasty, was known as "The Dashing Prince," of which "Dashing Brigand" is a sardonic variation. The change of mandate refers to the founding of the Ch'ing (Manchu) dynasty.

longed for home and wrote letters begging their husbands to come and ransom them; shameful as their conduct was, it is still understandable, and we have no choice but to put them near the bottom of the middle category. The most despicable of all were those who lived off the fat of the land and dressed in fine raiment, who delighted in singing the alien tunes and spurned their native accents. They even refused to acknowledge their husbands after they had traveled great distances to ransom them. Sluts like these belong in the lowest category of all, and even to mention them is enough to make us gnash our teeth. True, I have heard tell of one righteous commander who actually beheaded such a slut on the spot to avenge her husband, but heart-warming actions like that are only hearsay. I have never witnessed one myself.

Gentle reader, is it not tragic that so many women spoke about chastity and martyrdom before the rebellions, but then, once they were cast into the furnace of sexual lust and the true were separated from the false, only the false ones survived?

I shall now tell of a jewel of a woman who did survive the test and whose actions will be spoken of for generations to come. Although her case cannot be regarded as the norm, she still ranks higher than those who endured disgrace in order to avenge themselves later. Gentle reader, to follow the criteria by which *The Spring and Autumn Annals* criticized the virtuous and to demand perfection of such a woman—that is no fair or proper way to judge people at the end of an epoch.

During the Ch'ung-chen period, there was a certain woman living in the countryside outside Wu-kung county of Sian prefecture of Shensi. Her husband, surnamed Keng, was the second in his generation, so she was known as Secunda Keng. She was, we need hardly say, a woman of personable looks and graceful figure. But in addition to these qualities, she was also exceptionally intelligent. Although she could neither read nor write, she was naturally perceptive. If you were troubled by some insoluble problem, you had only to tell her about it and she would manage, by some imaginative inference, to come up with a brilliant solution that no one else would have thought of, and proceed to solve your problem. While she was applying it, everyone would say it was pointless, but when they thought about the matter afterwards, they were forced to conclude that hers was the ideal solution.

Once, while she was still a girl in her mother's household, there was a neighbor fishing by the river who chanced to be holding a fishhook in his mouth while talking. He swallowed the hook, which then lodged in his throat. He had the line in his hand, but he was afraid to pull on it, lest the hook catch in his throat, and he was equally afraid to swallow the hook, lest it puncture his intestines. He couldn't cry, any more than he could laugh. The doctors he consulted all told him that there was nothing on that topic in any of the medical treatises and that therefore there was no cure. In a state of panic, he rushed about asking everyone he met for a solution.

Secunda was at home when she heard the news. "I know a solution," she told her brother. "Do such-and-such and such-and-such, then pull it out."

Her brother went off to the man's house. "If you've got an old beaded lantern in the house, bring it out," he said. The man at once brought out such a lantern, and her brother tore it apart and began threading the beads one by one onto the line and pushing them down the man's throat. When they would go no farther, he knew that they had reached the hook. Then, forcing the beads down with one hand while holding the line in the other, he gave a sharp tug. The hook straightened out and came up through the beads without damaging the man's throat. Everyone was vastly impressed with Secunda's ingenuity.

On another occasion, after her marriage, her sister-in-law was lifting a trunk down from its shelf to get out some clothes. When she came to replace it, however, she found the shelf too high and the trunk too heavy. She heaved the trunk over her head—and her arms promptly locked into her shoulder sockets. The trunk was back in its place, but her arms remained over her head and she could not bring them down. The slightest movement was sheer agony. Her husband was at his wits' end. He raced about consulting the best doctors and asking the village elders, but no one had a suggestion to offer.

He turned to Secunda. "*You're* awfully clever, sister-in-law. Please think of something I can do."

"It's quite easy to get her arms down," she replied. "Just take off all her clothes and have someone give her a rubdown. The only problem is that you'll have to get a few men to stand beside her, so that she can absorb their yang force and bring her muscles and arteries back into harmony. I'm only afraid she'll be too embarrassed to allow it."

"So long as she gets better," said her husband, "she won't mind at all." He invited his brothers and cousins to stand around her in a ring while he stripped off her upper garments and gave her a vigorous rubdown. It produced no effect whatsoever.

He returned to Secunda for advice. "All four limbs are interconnected," she said, "and it's no use just rubbing her arms. You'll have to take off the rest of her clothes and rub her legs as well. I guarantee you it will work."

He returned to his wife and took off her skirt. But when he came to undo her trousers, she suddenly screamed, "No! You mustn't!" And in trying to protect herself, she automatically brought down her hands and clutched at her trousers.

All this while Secunda had been outside the window and now she came in. "Congratulations!" she said. "You're cured. There's no need to take off your clothes." All her talk about rubdowns and yang forces had been nothing but a ruse. She had calculated that her sister-in-law would be so embarrassed in front of men that she would ignore the pain and that her arms would snap back into place when she tried to protect herself. This is what is meant by "The cure is all in the mind."

Everyone roared with laughter. "What a great idea!" they said, bestowing on her a new nickname: "The Female Ch'en P'ing." Whenever a problem arose in the village, people would turn to her for a solution.

Secunda and her husband were deeply in love. Poor as they were, they managed to make a living because she was accustomed to cooking without rice and to weaving hemp and straw.

Then, all of a sudden, the bandits arose in rebellion and wreaked havoc throughout the land, massacring the men and raping their womenfolk. Ugly women would be cast aside as soon as the bandits had satisfied their lust, but any women who were at all attractive would be taken away with them.

One day the bandits reached a place close to Wu-kung county, and the village women flocked to Secunda for advice.

"We are in the midst of a thousand-year cycle of history," she told them. "This is not the sort of situation we can scheme our way out of." The women returned weeping and wailing to take a final farewell of their husbands. Some sought out razors, while others bought arsenic and hid it on their persons. They all said that they would kill themselves as soon as the bandits arrived. They would never let their virtue be sullied.

"The time has come for us to part forever," Secunda's husband said to her.

"At this point there is nothing we can do," she said. "If they seize me and take me off, I'll certainly not live a life of shame, but I'm not going to sacrifice myself lightly either. I'll call on all the strength and ingenuity I possess and see what I can do. Only if I absolutely cannot escape will I take the other course. If I see the slightest chance, I shall certainly escape and join you. As soon as the bandits come, you must run for your life, not be so concerned about me that we are both destroyed. If they take me off and you don't think you have the money to pay the ransom, you needn't come after me. Just wait for me here."

She shed a few tears, then went to the bed and found some rags which she tucked up her sleeves. She also produced ten copper cash and told her husband to go to the herbalist's and buy her some croton-oil beans.

"What do you want them for?" he asked.

"Never you mind. I have my uses for them."

As her husband left the house, he was stopped by a crowd of people. "What precautions is your wife taking?" they asked. He repeated what she had told him, adding, "She found a few rags which she tucked away in her clothes, and she told me to go and buy croton-oil beans, I don't know why." No one could guess what she had in mind.

When he returned with the beans, she shelled them and sewed the kernels into the lining of her clothes. She then urged her husband to flee from the bandits, while she combed her hair, powdered her face, and dressed up to await their arrival.

Before long the vanguard arrived. No sooner had the troops set eyes on Secunda than they began a tug-of-war over her, whereupon another bandit came up, a handsome man in his early thirties. The troops left the scene as soon as they saw him, and Secunda knew that he must be a chieftain. Sinking to her knees, she pleaded, "General, take me as your maid or concubine, I beg you." The chieftain quickly raised her to her feet. "I've captured many a woman in my time," he said, "but never one as beautiful as you. If you are willing to join me, I'll make you my wife, not a mere concubine. There is just one danger, though. There's a leader in the main force who outranks me. When he sees how beautiful you are, he'll want you for himself, and you won't end up with me."

"Simple!" she said. "Let me muss my hair and rub blacking on my face. When he sees me looking so ugly, he won't want me."

The chieftain embraced and patted her. "We've only just met and you show me such affection! I can only imagine how loving you'll be once we are husband and wife!"

By the time Secunda was ready, the main force had arrived. The bandit leader inspected all the women in the camps, but failed to notice her. Relieved, the chieftain then locked her up in an empty room while he went out and seized four or five other women, neighbors of Secunda's, whom he handed over to her. "These will do for your maid-servants," he said.

That evening he had them prepare dinner. When he and Secunda had eaten, they washed themselves, and then she blithely stripped off her clothes and got into bed. At the sight of her snow-white flesh, the chieftain was like

> A greedy cat spotting a sleek little mouse,
> A hungry hawk spying a tender chick.

Far too impatient to undo his clothes, he simply tore off belt and sash. Before he had even lain on her, that erect member of his, poised before the cavity, gave a mighty thrust—and thrust straight into a rag!

"What is *this?*" he asked.

"To tell you the truth," she replied in a calm voice, "today happens to be that time of the month. My period has just begun." Skeptical, the chieftain picked up the rag and sniffed it. It reeked of stale blood.

"If a woman has sex during her period," she said, "she is sure to get ill. If you don't want to marry me, I can't stop you. But if you do, and you want to have children some day, you'd better put it off for a couple of nights. Besides, there are plenty of substitutes available. You don't need to risk *my* life in order to enjoy yourself."

"You're right," he said. "I'll go and sleep with them."

She embraced him again. "You're so young and handsome, I just adore you! The only pity is that I can't do as I'd like. But as soon as you're finished with them, come back to my bed. Just lying beside you and touching you will be enough to make me happy."

"Of course I will," he replied.

Her nauseating little speech had conquered a heart hardened against the government's surrender appeals as well as a soul that had long eluded the King of Hell. The chieftain, reluctant to part from her, had to force himself out of bed.

Gentle reader, why do you suppose her period occurred at such an opportune moment? Actually, this was her first ruse since leaving the cottage. It was also the reason she had provided herself with the rags, which, since she had used them before for her periods, naturally smelled of stale blood. Having bluffed her way through the first night, she was now in a position to meet the next challenge.

The other women were sleeping on the floor. As the chieftain took them on in single combat, he deployed all of his battlefield skills, partly because he thought of them as substitutes for Secunda and wanted to work off the day's passion, and partly because he wanted her to overhear and be impressed with his prowess. The women received him warmly and made no resistance. The razors and arsenic that they had prepared for just such a contingency were never put to use. In fact, while battling for his favor, each would have dearly loved to poison the others with her arsenic or slit their throats with her razor, so as to have him all to herself.

From her bed Secunda listened intently to everything the chieftain said. She noticed how, after the sex, he would rest until he caught his breath and ask them, "Do you have any money hidden away anywhere? Did you leave any jewelry with anyone?" Some admitted it, others didn't.

"I see," said Secunda, nodding to herself.

The chieftain returned to her bed and clasped her tightly in his arms. "And how did your husband's ability compare with mine?" he asked.

"He wasn't a thousandth part of the man you are," she said. "But it's not just his ability I'm talking about. He wasn't as handsome as you either, or as kind and considerate. This disaster has turned out to be a stroke of fortune for me. But there's one thing I don't understand. With a face like yours,[4] you'd have no trouble earning a living. Why do you have to lead this dangerous life in the saddle?"

"I know that what I'm doing isn't right," said the chieftain, "but these days money's not so easy to come by. As soon as I have enough loot to set myself up in business, I intend to go straight."

"I see. And how much have you got so far?"

"Including gold, pearls, and jewelry, over two thousand taels. If I can get

4. A reference to the practice of fortune-telling by physiognomy.

as much again, I'll have in the neighborhood of five thousand, and then I'll be a man of means and you'll be a lady of means."

"I'm afraid you're just saying that to deceive me. If you were really willing to reform, you could have ten thousand, not a mere five."

His heart skipped a beat. "Where is it?"

"Three pairs of ears are one pair too many. This is not the time to talk, with everyone present. Let's discuss it tomorrow night." The chieftain had to curb his impatience for the rest of that night.

The next day they followed the bandit leader to a new place. The chieftain installed the other women in separate quarters so that he could talk freely with Secunda.

"Now, what about that ten thousand?" he asked, climbing into bed.

"Oh, you men are all so fickle," she said. "You say you're going to marry me, but I'm afraid that once you've got your hands on the money, you'll go off and look for someone better to be your lady of means. If you really want to be my lifelong husband, you'll have to swear a solemn vow."

The chieftain somersaulted out of bed and, kneeling down, addressed the heavens, "If I ever change, may I die beneath ten thousand swords!"

"To tell you the truth," said Secunda, helping him to his feet, "my father-in-law, who died a few years ago, was famous for his wealth. The present situation seemed so dangerous to my husband, what with rebellions breaking out all over the country, that he gathered up all the money, which, including the jewelry and wine things, came to ten thousand taels,[5] and dug a pit and buried it. If you dig it up, you and I will have more money than we will ever be able to spend."

"Perhaps someone has dug it up already?"

"My husband and I were the only ones who knew about it, and he was killed by your men yesterday. I saw that with my own eyes. So who knows the secret now, apart from me? What's more, it's buried out in the wilds, where not even a god would think of looking for it. But I can't very well go there myself, because I might be recognized. Leave me behind with one of your relatives, and I'll tell you where it is and you can go."

"A roving bandit like me doesn't have any relatives to leave his family with! Besides, I'm totally unfamiliar with the area. Where would I start digging? No, we'll have to go together."

"If we're going together, we'd better dress up as beggars and beg our way there, lest we be recognized."

"Good idea! But if we're going as beggars, we won't be able to take all of my gear with us. Where shall we leave it?"

"I have an idea," said Secunda. "Pack it up, and at night, when everyone's asleep, we'll carry it over to the river and throw it in. So long as we make a

5. The weight of a tael varies with time and place, but may be considered roughly equivalent to two ounces.

note of the place, we can come back this way after digging up the money and fish it out again."

"Sweetheart! Dearest!" he cried over and over, clasping her in his arms and praising her looks, intelligence, and loving nature. "I don't know how many good deeds I must have done in my last existence to deserve such a splendid helpmeet in this one. That would be blessing enough, but now I'm going to get a big dowry as well!"

That night he and Secunda slept in each other's arms. Assuming that her period would be over by the following day, he conserved his energies in anticipation, the better to serve his lady of means, and did not go off and sleep with the other women.

The third day, while following the bandit leader to yet another place, they came upon a husband and wife begging by the wayside. The chieftain stripped them of their clothes, which he handed to Secunda. "A gift from the gods," he said. "Is your period over yet?"

"Yes."

His eyes sparkled with delight and he rubbed his hands together in anticipation. He could hardly wait for nightfall to indulge his desires.

But that afternoon Secunda suddenly collapsed on her bed and began moaning prettily while complaining of severe pain. The chieftain asked her where it hurt.

"I don't know why," she said, "but I have a swelling down there the size of a bowl, and I feel hot and cold all over. It's un*bear*able!"

"Where does it hurt, exactly?"

She raised a slender, jadelike finger and pointed beneath her skirt.

"But that's my gate of life!" exclaimed the chieftain in alarm. "How could you get an infection there?" He pulled up her skirt, tore open her silk drawers, and looked at her gate of life. This is what he saw:

> Jade-white flesh that has risen high,
> Held in a purple glow.
> Deep cleft swollen to a shallow slit,
> With no gate left to enter.
> Two parts forming a single whole,
> With a crack that is hard to open.
> Like a bun left steaming three whole nights,
> Or a dried mussel soaked for ten days.

The chieftain was fearfully upset. He rubbed it for a while, then rushed off to a doctor for some ointment. But strangely enough, the more ointment he applied, the more it swelled up. Little did he realize that this was another of Secunda's ruses. Well aware that she would not be spared again, she had taken one of the croton-oil beans from her clothes, squeezed the oil out of it, and smeared it around her vagina. This substance has the most drastic effects—the healthiest skin will swell up immediately on contact with it. Secunda had seen it tried out at home, and that was why she had purchased the beans and brought them with her.

That night the chieftain lay beside her and held her in his arms. "I managed to endure two nights without you," he said, "and tonight I was looking forward to enjoying myself freely. But now there's *this* setback, and I really don't know how I'm going to bear it. I'll simply have to do it eunuch-fashion and rub myself against you." He proceeded to do so.

"You're *hurting!*" she screamed. "I can't *stand* it!" With a kerchief wrapped around her hand, she squeezed his member. The ploy by which she now fended him off was the following: she first smeared some croton oil onto the kerchief, then held his member while squeezing oil onto it. Before long it flared up angrily.

"That's strange!" said the chieftain. "Now *I'm* starting to feel all hot and cold down there. Surely I can't have caught that infection just by rubbing myself against you?" He got out of bed, lit the lamp, and found that his member was so badly swollen that it looked like a laundry beater made of crystal.

From that point on, Secunda had no need to fend him off; he did not dare come near her.

All of Secunda's ruses and ploys were devoted to preserving her "insignia of rank,"[6] which she refused to yield to anyone. Everything else she possessed— rosy lips, crimson tongue, soft breasts, tiny feet, and jadelike fingers—she looked upon as inanimate things external to her, and she let him clip, suck, fondle, and pinch them as if unaware of what he was doing. Hers was the expedient of "saving root and trunk at the expense of branches and leaves."

At midnight the chieftain said, "This would be a good time to get started, now that everyone's asleep." They got up and carried the bundle that they had packed up that day to the river, where they dropped it off a bridge, carefully noting the bridge's location and the trees along the bank. Then they returned and changed into beggars' clothes, taking with them only a few ounces of loose silver and leaving the rest of their clothes and other belongings behind. Without a word to the other women, they sped swiftly away through the night.

They walked until dawn, by which time they had traveled a good ten miles from the camp, and then stopped at an inn to eat. While the chieftain was not watching, Secunda took out another bean, crushed it, and mixed it with his food. Within two hours he had a severe attack of diarrhea; in walking a single mile he had to relieve himself at least a dozen times. All that night he was in and out of bed as his diarrhea continued. At breakfast the next morning, she added another half bean to his diet. What an absurd figure he cut, this tiger of a bandit chief whom it took only one and a half croton-oil beans just a

6. See the *Tso chuan* (selection 190), Duke Chao, year 23.

couple of days to turn into a sallow, emaciated creature incapable of walking or speaking, let alone of any nighttime activity.

His thoughts, however, ran like this: "When a woman goes with a man, she is merely looking for a little bedroom pleasure. Those first two nights we were prevented by her period and the next two nights by her infection. Now that her period is over and the infection has cleared up, just when I should be giving her something to enjoy, I have to come down with diarrhea! If I try to force myself, I'll only be let down by this gutless thing of mine! I'll never be able to make it stand up." He genuinely pitied her.

Precisely in order to prevent that outcome, Secunda had been especially solicitous from the time he fell ill. During the day she took his arm as they walked, and at night she helped him onto the heated bed. There were occasions when he could not get out of bed in time and filthied the mat, and she would wipe up the mess without a trace of revulsion.

"We're husband and wife in name only; we've never enjoyed the reality," he said, weeping. "But since I caught this filthy disease, you've not only shown no disgust, you've been more loving than ever. Even if I die, I'll never be able to repay your kindness." Secunda consoled him with fond words.

Next day they arrived in the vicinity of her home and put up at an old temple scarcely a mile away. At dinner, she mixed in one more bean, whereupon he had such a severe attack of diarrhea that he collapsed and could not get up.

"All my vital energy has drained away," he said, "and I feel more dead than alive. If you love me as a wife, get me some medicine or I'll die before your eyes."

"I'll get you some first thing tomorrow," said Secunda. Before it was light, on the pretext of getting the medicine, she went back to her cottage. When her husband opened the door, there before him stood his wife, as if she had dropped down from heaven. His joy was unbounded.

"What method of escape did you use?" he asked. Secunda told him in broad outline how she had deceived the bandit with her story of buried treasure. At this stage all Keng knew was that she had gotten away by means of a ruse. He did not realize that she had escaped with her seal intact.

"Since he's so close by, let me go and kill him."

"Not so fast!" she said. "I still have a use for him. Without telling a soul, you must hurry off tonight to a bridge in such-and-such a place. In the channel under the bridge, you'll find a bundle of things that are worth over ten thousand taels. When you've brought them back, I'll tell you my idea."

He did as she asked, rushing off without a word to anyone.

She then went to the herbalist's, as she had promised, and brought the chieftain a powder made of ginseng, china-root, and paichu. After he took it, his diarrhea lessened and, following three or four days' recuperation, he was ready to get up and dig for treasure.

"You'll need a hoe to dig with," she said. "Let me go to the blacksmith's and get you one." On the pretext of buying a hoe, she went home and found that her husband had returned with the articles from under the bridge.

"Now we can see to him," she said. "But we mustn't be too hasty. You'll have to do thus-and-thus.[7] Be careful you don't leave out a single step." Then, changing her clothes, she sat down at home and did not go back to the temple.

Following her plan, Keng fetched a chain and got two other men to assist him. Together they went to the temple and shouted inside, "Bandit! Where do you think *you're* going?"

The chieftain was startled out of his wits. Keng chained him up and brought him to a public place, where he struck the gong and shouted, "Neighbors! Relations! Come and see a bandit put to death!" The villagers quickly gathered. Keng bound the chieftain, hung him up, and then took a large stick and began beating him, shouting with each blow, "You seized my wife and raped her!"

"I've seized many women," said the chieftain. "Which one was your wife?"

"Secunda Keng, the one you came back with."

"But she told me she had seen her husband die before her eyes! How is it you're still alive? In that case, *everything* she told me must have been a lie! There's just one thing I want to say. I did seize her, and I did come back with her, but I never had anything to do with her. Sir, you mustn't beat me for something I did not do."

"You smooth-tongued rascal! You slept with her for over ten nights and yet you still claim you had nothing to do with her! Who's going to believe anything *you* say?" Raising his stick, he began beating again.

"I can explain," said the chieftain. "Let me make a full confession."

"I don't want to hear it."

"Let him confess," said the crowd. "There'll be plenty of time afterwards to beat him."

Keng put down the stick, and the crowd fell silent in anticipation.

"When I saw how pretty she looked," began the chieftain, "I wanted her as my wife. I was deeply in love with her. But that first night we spent together, I noticed a rag between her legs, and she told me she was having her period. So I went and slept with the other women and never touched her. I endured the next night too. On the third night, I was just about to sleep with her when I found she had an infection right on the crucial spot and I still couldn't do anything. By the fourth night we were on the road, but just as her infection got better, I had an attack of diarrhea that hit me hundreds of times the following day and night. I didn't have the energy to walk or talk, let alone do *that*. I've been suffering from diarrhea ever since we left camp, and although

7. The narrator is hiding the plan from his readers.

we've been traveling together and spending each night in each other's company, the truth is that we've been apart the whole time. Sir, if you don't believe me, go and ask your wife."

A few of the sharper bystanders broke in at this point, *"That's it!* That explains why you told us she was collecting rags and buying croton-oil beans. We asked you what she wanted them for. This is what they were for! In that case, she never was dishonored."

Some of those in the crowd whose wives had been seized along with Secunda then asked, "Well, then, how many of the women you took that day kept their chastity?"

"Not one, apart from her," said the chieftain. "Some of them brought razors and arsenic with them, but they weren't prepared to give up their lives, and they all slept with me." When his questioners heard this answer, they knew that their own wives had been dishonored, and although they couldn't say anything, their faces went livid.

Keng raised his stick and began beating the chieftain again.

"Sir!" he shrieked. "I have more than two thousand taels for you. Spare my life!"

"Where's the money?" called the people in the crowd.

"Underneath the bridge at such-and-such a place. Why not go and get it?"

"It's money you've looted, every penny of it," said Keng, "and I don't want your ill-gotten gains. I'm going to rid us of this menace once and for all!"

The men in the crowd who had asked questions of the chieftain were consumed with hatred. "Yes, let's get rid of the menace!" they responded. Keng had no need to join in; they punched and beat the chieftain until, within minutes, he lay there dead.

Some of the bystanders were overcome by avarice and coveted the two thousand taels. Letting no one else know, they rushed there through the night to look for the money. But all their efforts came to nought; they were "fishing for the moon."

Gentle reader, wouldn't you agree that Secunda's ruses were amazing? Wouldn't you agree they were ingenious? I shan't speak of the many other brilliant schemes she pulled off between her departure and return, but let me just point out how marvelous this last stroke was. Had she wanted to put the chieftain to death along the road, it would have taken only a few more croton-oil beans. Simple! Instead she persisted in keeping him alive until they got home, so as to use his testimony in vindicating her own conduct. *That* is what makes it so amazing! Had she done him to death along the road and then returned home alone denying she had lost her honor, no one would have believed her. Even her own husband would have considered her a little disingenuous, for who has ever seen a piece of white cloth pulled from an indigo jar? But once the accolade had been bestowed on her by the enemy, everyone accepted it as fact. This is why she was known as "The Female Ch'en P'ing," even though Ch'en brought off only six amazing ruses and she managed seven.

Later someone turned her seven exploits into the following jingle:

> Ruse One: As she left home, rags were her seal;
> Ruse Two: A bun-sized swelling needn't heal;
> Ruse Three: Pure yang to a crystal beater turned;
> Ruse Four: One magic pill, and his insides churned;
> Ruse Five: A ten-thousand tael lie ends her captivity;
> Ruse Six: Underwater money spells prosperity;
> Ruse Seven: An enemy's gallows confession brings credibility.

Critique:

Wives who preserve their chastity have always qualified as sages amongst women. Those who vow martyrdom and keep their vows are the pure sages. Those who endure disgrace to gain revenge are the responsible sages. The kind to which Secunda Keng belongs is that of the accommodating sages. Not only was she called "The Female Ch'en P'ing," she should also have been dubbed "The Distaff Liu-hsia Hui."[8]

Translated by Patrick Hanan

---

8. The whole passage is based on *Mencius*. See D.C. Lau, trans., *Mencius* (London: Penguin Books, 1970), p. 150. Liu-hsia Hui is the nickname of Chan Ch'in, a minister of the Lu state in the Warring States period and a paragon known for his staunch resistance to sexual temptation.

Novels

258
Romance of the Three Kingdoms

Anonymous (mid-Ming?)

Chapter 45

Ts'ao Ts'ao suffers casualties at Three Rivers;
Chiang Kan springs a trap at the Congregation of Heroes.

In the Confucian tradition, history and literature are not by and large separate "fields" or "disciplines" but rather interrelated and interacting parts of the culture. Thus, the historical novel *Three Kingdoms* (*San-kuo-chih yen-yi*) has shaped the thinking of the Chinese people about the issues of war, politics, and history perhaps more than any other single work. It is also a major literary masterpiece that influenced the development of drama as well as the novel in China.

Originally written in the early Ming and attributed to Lo Kuan-chung (c. 1330–c. 1400), but extensively revised by later hands, *Three Kingdoms* portrays in unsparing detail the fall of the Han empire (220 C.E.), the forced abdication of the last Han emperor, and the emergence of three warring kingdoms from the ruins. In this historical process, no event was more determinative than the Battle at Red Cliffs (see selection 156), fought in the autumn of 208 C.E. Throughout that year, Prime Minister Ts'ao Ts'ao (see selection 170), the power behind the Han court, had been marshaling a vast invasion force on the northern shore of the Yangtze River: he was determined to reassert the court's authority over the quasi-independent Southland, the Chiang-nan or region below the Yangtze. Would the Southland resist or surrender? How could the Southland, a land smaller and less populous than the north, mobilize the forces to throw back the invaders? In the first forty-eight chapters of the novel, all events march as if directed by destiny toward the moment when these questions are answered. In chapter 49 the historic battle is joined; the remaining seventy-one chapters of the novel track the consequences—immediate and remote—of the battle.

Chu-ke Chin recounted his conversation with K'ung-ming. As Chou Yü listened, his hostility deepened, and he made up his mind that he would have to dispose of K'ung-ming.

The following day, after reviewing his commanders, Chou Yü went to take leave of Sun Ch'üan. "You proceed," said Ch'üan, "I will bring up the rear with another force." Chou Yü withdrew and, together with Ch'eng P'u and Lu Su, commenced the expedition. He also invited K'ung-ming, who accepted eagerly. With the four on board, the ship hoisted sail and began tacking toward Hsia-k'ou. Some fifty tricents from Three Rivers the convoy halted. Chou Yü, commanding the center, established his headquarters and ordered a ring of camps built along the shore around the Western Hills. K'ung-ming betook himself to a little boat of his own.

His arrangements completed, Chou Yü called K'ung-ming to his tent. After the formalities, Chou Yü said, "In an earlier campaign Ts'ao had far fewer troops than Yüan Shao; but he won all the same by following Hsü Yu's advice and cutting off Shao's food supply at Wu-ch'ao. Now Ts'ao has eight hundred and thirty thousand men to our fifty or sixty thousand. How can we resist? Only by cutting off his supplies. According to information I have already gathered, everything is stored at Iron Pile Mountain. Since you have lived on the River Han and are familiar with the terrain, I wonder if I could prevail upon you, together with Lord Kuan, Chang Fei, and Chao Tzu-lung—as well as the thousand men that I will give you—to go at once to the mountain and sever their supply line. This would be in the interest of both our lords. I hope you will accept." K'ung-ming mused, "He is scheming to murder me because I will not agree to leave Lord Liu. Rather than look foolish, I'll go along and figure out later what to do." And so, to Chou Yü's satisfaction, K'ung-ming accepted the assignment enthusiastically.

After K'ung-ming had left, Lu Su said privately to Chou Yü, "What's

---

This reading selection consists of the whole of chapters 45 and 46. In chapters 43 and 44, one of the novel's heroes, Chu-ke Liang (K'ung-ming), enters the Southland on behalf of his lord Liu Pei (Hsüan-te) to argue down the faction advocating surrender to Ts'ao and to convince the Southland leader, Sun Ch'üan, to resist Ts'ao Ts'ao militarily. To this end K'ung-ming urges Sun Ch'üan to form a united front with Liu Hsüan-te (better known as Liu Pei, the leader of Shu [modern Szechwan] in the southwest), another adversary of Ts'ao Ts'ao's. K'ung-ming's mission requires him to work with the leaders of the pro-war faction in the Southland, First Field Marshal Chou Yü, the chief commander for Sun Ch'üan, and Lu Su, a high-level adviser and emissary. All the while K'ung-ming remains well aware of the dangers he faces from these same allies.

In the following selection, we can observe how the northern and southern camps maneuver against each other as they prepare for the showdown; we can also observe some of the intrigues unfolding inside the southern and northern camps, as well as the articulation between these internal intrigues and the main conflict. The selection also affords a glimpse of Liu Hsüan-te, the novel's protagonist, and his sworn brother Lord Kuan, another major figure on the novel's stage.

behind this sending K'ung-ming to steal their grain?" "Killing K'ung-ming would only invite ridicule," Chou Yü explained. "Let Ts'ao Ts'ao be the one to save us future trouble." Lu Su then went to K'ung-ming to find out what he knew. But K'ung-ming, betraying no anxiety, was gathering his forces for roll call, preparing to set out. The kindhearted Lu Su said pointedly, "What chance does this mission have, good sir?" With a smile K'ung-ming replied, "I have mastered the fine points of every form of warfare, naval, foot, horse, and chariot. I fear no failure—unlike Southland leaders like you, sir, or Chou Yü, who have only one specialty." "What do you mean?" asked Lu Su. K'ung-ming replied, "Isn't there a children's rhyme going around the south, 'To ambush a trail or hold a pass, Lu Su's the man to trust; / for marine war, Commander Chou Yü's a must'? So it seems that you're not good for more than a roadside ambush or guarding a pass and that Chou Yü can fight on water but not on land."

Lu Su reported this conversation to Chou Yü, who exclaimed angrily, "So he thinks I can't fight on land! Fine. Let him stay here. I'll raid Ts'ao's supplies myself with ten thousand men." Lu Su carried this new development back to K'ung-ming, who smiled as he said, "All Chou Yü really wanted was for Ts'ao Ts'ao to kill me. So I teased him with that remark. He is touchy, though. This is a critical moment. My only wish is for Lord Sun and Lord Liu to work together, for then we may succeed. Plotting against one another will undo our cause. The traitor Ts'ao has plenty of tricks. In his career as a general he's made a specialty of severing enemy supply lines; his own storage is sure to be well prepared for raids: if Chou Yü goes they'll only capture him. What is called for now is a decisive engagement on the river to blunt the enemy's mettle while we try to work out a plan for their defeat. It's up to you to explain this to Chou Yü in a reasonable way."

As Lu Su recounted K'ung-ming's words that night, Chou Yü shook his head and stamped his feet, crying, "He is ten times my better. If we don't destroy him now, he will destroy this land of ours." "At this critical time," Lu Su argued, "I hope you will consider the Southland above all. There will be time enough for such schemes after Ts'ao Ts'ao is defeated." Chou Yü had to agree.

Liu Hsüan-te charged Liu Ch'i with the defense of Chiang-hsia, while he and his commanders moved ahead to Hsia-k'ou. In the distance they saw flags and banners shadowing the river's southern shore, and row upon row of spears. Surmising that the Southland had already mobilized, Hsüan-te shifted all the Chiang-hsia troops across the Great River and east to Fan-k'ou. He then addressed his followers: "We have had no word from K'ung-ming since he went south, and no one knows how things stand. Who will find out for us and report back?" Mi Chu volunteered, and Hsüan-te, having provided him with sheep, wine, and other gifts, instructed him to go to the Southland and learn what he could while pretending to feast the southern troops.

Mi Chu piloted a small boat downriver and arrived in front of Chou Yü's camp. After being received, Mi Chu prostrated himself, conveyed Hsüan-te's respects, and presented the articles he had brought. Chou Yü accepted the gifts and called a banquet to welcome Mi Chu. "K'ung-ming has been here too long," Mi Chu declared. "I would like to bring him back with me." "But he is consulting with us on the campaign against Ts'ao Ts'ao," said Chou Yü. "He can't simply leave. I, for my part, desire to see Lord Liu in order to confer with him. But, alas, I am personally directing the army and cannot leave the scene. How gratifying it would be, though, if Lord Liu would consider traveling here to visit me." Mi Chu assented and returned to Hsüan-te.

Lu Su said to Chou Yü, "Why do you want to see Hsüan-te?" "He's the craftiest owl on earth," responded Chou Yü. "I must be rid of him. This is my chance to lure him here and kill him, and save our house future grief." Lu Su argued over and over against such measures—to no avail. Chou Yü issued a secret order: "If Hsüan-te comes, I want fifty armed men hidden behind the curtains. I'll throw a cup to the ground as the signal to strike."

Mi Chu returned to Hsüan-te and relayed Chou Yü's invitation. Hsüan-te called for a swift boat and set out. Lord Kuan objected, "Chou Yü is a schemer; moreover, we have no letter from K'ung-ming. I see treachery in this. Let's think it over some more." "But they are our allies in the struggle against Ts'ao Ts'ao," said Hsüan-te. "Not to go when they call violates the spirit of the alliance. Constant mutual suspicion will ruin our cause." "If you insist on going, brother," said Lord Kuan, "I shall join you." "And I too," added Chang Fei. "No. Let Lord Kuan accompany me," Hsüan-te replied. "You and Chao Tzu-lung can guard the camp, and Chien Yung can guard Ŏ-hsien. I will return soon."

Hsüan-te and Lord Kuan boarded a light craft and, with a small guard of some twenty men, sped downriver to the Southland. Hsüan-te viewed the cutters and war-boats of his ally, their flags and armored men, their orderly array, with mounting excitement. His arrival was swiftly reported to Chou Yü, who asked, "With how many boats?" "Just one," he was informed, "and about twenty men." "His life is mine," said Chou Yü, smiling. He deployed his men and went forth to greet his guest. Hsüan-te, with Lord Kuan and his guards, followed his host to the main tent. Salutations exchanged, Chou Yü saw Hsüan-te to the seat of honor. "General," Hsüan-te protested, "you are renowned throughout the empire. I am a man of no talent. Do not trouble so much over ceremony." They partook of a banquet as host and guest.

At the riverside K'ung-ming discovered that Hsüan-te and Chou Yü were having a meeting. Anxiously entering the main tent to see what was afoot, he noted a murderous look in Chou Yü's eye and the armed guards behind the wall curtains. "What am I to do about this?" he said to himself in alarm. He turned and observed Hsüan-te chatting and laughing, completely at ease, while Lord Kuan stood behind him, hand on his sword. "He is safe," K'ung-ming thought and left to return to the river.

Host and guest had savored several rounds of wine when Chou Yü stood up, cup in hand. Observing Lord Kuan, hand on sword, Yü inquired who he was. "My younger brother, Kuan Yün-ch'ang," replied Hsüan-te. "Not the one who cut down generals Yen Liang and Wen Ch'ou?" Chou Yü asked nervously. "The same," Hsüan-te answered. Chou Yü, alarmed, broke into a sweat. He poured a cup for Lord Kuan and drank with him. Moments later Lu Su came in. "Where's K'ung-ming?" Hsüan-te asked him. "Could you bring him here?" "There'll be time enough for meeting when Ts'ao Ts'ao is defeated," said Chou Yü, closing the subject. Lord Kuan eyed Hsüan-te, who sensed his brother's intent and rose. "I shall bid you farewell for now," Hsüan-te told Chou Yü, "but I will return expressly to celebrate with you the defeat of Ts'ao Ts'ao." Chou Yü made no effort to detain his guest and escorted him out the main gate.

Hsüan-te and Lord Kuan reached the edge of the river, where they found K'ung-ming in his boat. Hsüan-te was elated. "My lord," said K'ung-ming, "you were in more danger than you knew!" Aghast, Hsüan-te said, "No!" "He would have killed you but for Lord Kuan," K'ung-ming remarked. Hsüan-te, only then realizing the actual situation in the Southland, begged K'ung-ming to return with him to Fan-k'ou. But K'ung-ming said, "Here in the tiger's mouth I am as secure as Mount T'ai. What you have to do is prepare your forces for action. On the twentieth day, first of the cycle, of the eleventh month, send Chao Tzu-lung in a small boat to wait for me at the south shore. There must be no slip-up." Hsüan-te asked what he was planning, but K'ung-ming simply replied, "Look for a southeast wind. That's when I'll come back." Hsüan-te wanted to know more, but K'ung-ming hurried him aboard and returned to his own boat.

Hsüan-te, Lord Kuan, and their followers had sailed but a few tricents when they saw fifty or sixty boats speeding downriver toward them; in the lead was General Chang Fei, spear at the ready. Fearing some mishap to Hsüan-te, he had come to back up Lord Kuan. And so the three brothers returned to their camp together.

Chou Yü, having seen Hsüan-te off, returned to camp. Lu Su asked, "You lured Hsüan-te here. Why didn't you strike?" "Lord Kuan is the fiercest of generals. He never leaves Hsüan-te's side. If I had acted, he would have slain me," Chou Yü explained. Lu Su was astounded at the awe Lord Kuan had inspired.

At that moment an emissary from Ts'ao Ts'ao arrived, bearing an envelope with the words: "The prime minister of the Han authorizes Field Marshal

Chou to open this." Chou Yü angrily tore the envelope, unopened, into pieces and threw them to the ground. He then ordered the bearer put to death. "Two kingdoms at war don't kill each other's envoys," Lu Su urged. "I do so to show my confidence in our strength," answered Chou Yü. The envoy was executed, and his head was given to his attendants to carry back to Ts'ao Ts'ao. Chou Yü then commanded Kan Ning to lead the van, Han Tang to lead the left wing, and Chiang Ch'in to lead the right, reserving for himself the task of relief and reinforcement. The next day they breakfasted at the fourth watch and sailed out at the fifth, drums and battle cries heralding their advance.

The news that Chou Yü had destroyed his letter and beheaded his messenger infuriated Ts'ao Ts'ao. At once he organized a vanguard led by Ts'ai Mao, Chang Yün, and other Ching-chou commanders who had submitted to him. Ts'ao Ts'ao himself took command of the rear and supervised the transfer of the fleet to Three Rivers. Soon he saw the approaching war-boats of the southerners spread across the length and breadth of the river. Their lead general, seated in the prow of one boat, shouted out, "Kan Ning comes! Who dares oppose?" Ts'ai Mao sent his younger brother, Hsün, to meet him. The two boats drew near. Kan Ning steadied his bow and toppled Hsün with one shot. Kan Ning pressed ahead, his archers massing their bolts; Ts'ao Ts'ao's forces reeled before the assault. Following up, Chiang Ch'in sailed from the right and Han Tang from the left, straight into the center of the northerners' position. Most of Ts'ao's soldiers, coming from the provinces of Ch'ing and Hsü, were unused to naval warfare and lost their balance on the rolling ships. This gave the southerners—now augmented by Chou Yü's force—control of the waterway. Thousands of Ts'ao Ts'ao's men fell by bombard or arrow in a battle that lasted from mid-morning to early afternoon. But despite his advantage, Chou Yü, still wary of Ts'ao Ts'ao's greater numbers, beat the gong recalling his boats.

After his defeated troops had returned, Ts'ao Ts'ao appeared in his land headquarters and directed the reordering of his forces. He rebuked Ts'ai Mao and Chang Yün, "The troops of the Southland, though few, have defeated us—because you lack commitment." Ts'ai Mao protested, "We were defeated because the Ching-chou sailors have been off their training and because the Ch'ing-chou and Hsü-chou troops have no experience in naval warfare. The thing to do now is to establish a naval camp, placing the Ch'ing-chou and Hsü-chou troops inside, the Ching-chou troops outside, and train them every day until they are fit for combat." To this Ts'ao replied, "You are already the chief naval commander and can perform your duties at your discretion. There's no need to petition me."

Ts'ai Mao and Chang Yün undertook the training of a navy. Along the river they set up a row of twenty-four water lanes for communication; the larger boats formed the outer rim, enclosing the smaller like a city wall. At night the torches lit up the sky and river, while on land the camps, which stretched for three hundred tricents, sent up smoke and fire day and night.

The triumphant Chou Yü had returned to camp, rewarded his troops, and sent news of the victory to Sun Ch'üan. After nightfall Chou Yü surveyed the scene from a height: the glow in the west reached the horizon. "The fires and torches of the northern army," his aides said. Shocked, Chou Yü decided to investigate Ts'ao's naval encampment himself the following day. He ordered a two-tiered boat outfitted with drums and other instruments. Accompanied by his ablest commanders, all armed with long bows or crossbows, he boarded and set out.

The craft threaded its way upriver. When it reached the edge of Ts'ao Ts'ao's camp, Chou Yü dropped anchor. The instruments began playing, and Chou Yü observed how the camp responded. "They have mastered the finest points of naval warfare," he exclaimed. "Who's in general command?" "Ts'ai Mao and Chang Yün," his assistants reported. "Longtime residents of the Southland, they're skilled in naval tactics," Chou Yü mused. "I'll have to put them out of the way before I can defeat Ts'ao." At that moment Ts'ao Ts'ao was informed of the spy ship's presence and ordered it captured. Chou Yü saw Ts'ao Ts'ao's signal flags in motion and had the anchor raised; the oarsmen had pulled the two-tiered vessel more than ten tricents into open water by the time Ts'ao Ts'ao's boats came forth. Finding the Southland vessel out of range, the captains returned and reported to Ts'ao Ts'ao.

Ts'ao Ts'ao conferred with his commanders. "Yesterday," he said, "we lost a battle and our momentum. Now they've sailed in again, close enough to spy on our camp. How can we defeat them?" As he spoke, one man stepped forward and said, "Chou Yü and I have been close since childhood when we were students together. Let me try my powers of persuasion on him and see if I can get him to surrender." Ts'ao Ts'ao turned a grateful eye on the man. It was Chiang Kan (Tzu-yi) of Chiu-chiang, a member of his council. "You are on good terms with Chou Yü?" Ts'ao Ts'ao asked. "Your troubles are over, Your Excellency," said Chiang Kan. "When I go south, I shall not fail." "What will you need?" asked Ts'ao. "A page to accompany me, two servants to row me across." Ts'ao Ts'ao, immensely pleased, regaled Chiang Kan with wine and saw him off. The envoy, dressed in hempen scarf and plain-weave robe, sped downriver, straight to Chou Yü's camp. His arrival was announced—"An old friend comes to pay a call"—just when Chou Yü was in conference. Delighted by the news, he turned to his commanders and said, "The 'persuader' has come." Then he told each of them what to do, and they left to perform their duties.

Chou Yü adjusted his cap and garb and, surrounded by several hundred in brocade clothes and decorated hats, came forth. Chiang Kan approached boldly and alone, save for his one young attendant who was dressed in plain black. Chou Yü received him with low bows. "You have been well since we parted, I trust," said the visitor. "My friend, you have taken great trouble, coming so far to serve as Ts'ao Ts'ao's spokesman," Chou Yü responded.[1] Taken aback, Chiang Kan said, "We have been apart so long, I came especially to reminisce. How could you suspect me of such a thing?" With a smile Chou Yü answered, "My ear may not be so fine as the great musician Shih K'uang's, but I can discern good music and good intentions too."[2] "Dear friend," Chiang Kan replied, "if this is how you treat an old friend, I must beg my leave." Still smiling, Chou Yü took Chiang Kan by the arm and said, "I was afraid, brother, that you were working for Ts'ao; that's all. If you have no such purpose, there is no need to rush. Please stay." And so the two of them went into the tent. After the ritual greetings they seated themselves, and Chou Yü summoned the notables of the south to meet his friend.

Chief officials and generals in formal dress and subordinate officers and commanders clad in silvered armor entered shortly in two columns. Chou Yü had each dignitary introduced to Chiang Kan and seated in one of two rows to the side. A great feast was spread and victory music performed. Wine came too, round after round. Chou Yü addressed the assembly: "Here is one of my schoolmates, a close friend. Although he has come from north of the river, he is not serving as a spokesman of Ts'ao Ts'ao's cause. Set your minds at ease on that score." He then removed the sword at his side and handed it to T'ai-shih Tz'u, saying, "Wear the sword and supervise the banquet. We will speak of friendship today and nothing else. If anyone so much as mentions the hostilities between Ts'ao Ts'ao and the lord of the Southland, take off his head!" T'ai-shih Tz'u acknowledged the order and sat at the feast, his hand resting on the sword. Terror-stricken, Chiang Kan said little.

"Since taking command of the army," Chou Yü declared, "I have drunk no wine. But today, in the company of an old friend, with no lack of trust, let us have our fill and then some." With that, he laughed loudly and drank deeply. The toasts came thick and fast. When they had grown flushed and mellow, Chou Yü took Chiang Kan by the hand, and the two friends strolled outside the tent. To the left and right of them stood soldiers in complete outfit, armed with dagger and halberd. "Formidable, are they not?" Chou Yü asked. "Ferocious as bears, fierce as tigers," Chiang Kan agreed. Then Chou Yü led his guest around behind the headquarters where hills of grain and fodder were stored. "Enough for any eventuality, don't you think?" Chou Yü asked his

1. Chiang Kan has appeared in the guise of a hermit.
2. Shih K'uang was a musician of the state of Chin during the Spring and Autumn period; he was skilled at distinguishing differences in pitch.

guest. " 'Crack troops and full bins.' Your high reputation is not for nothing," Chiang Kan agreed again.

Feigning intoxication, Chou Yü laughed heartily. "To think we were once students together!" he said. "Who would have foreseen a day like today?" "Brother," said Chiang Kan, "with your supreme abilities, such accomplishment is only too fitting." Gripping Chiang Kan's hand, Chou Yü said, "As a man of honor all my life and one having the good fortune to serve a lord who appreciates me, I am as obligated to that honored bond between liege and liege man as I am by my kinsmen's love. What I say, he does. What I propose, he approves. His misfortunes and his blessings are mine as much as his. Were the great rhetoricians of old—Su Ch'in, Chang Yi, Lu Chia, Li Yi-chi[3]—to walk the earth again, delivering speeches like cascading streams and wielding their tongues like sharp swords, they could not move me!" Having spoken, Chou Yü burst into laughter. Chiang Kan's face was ashen. Chou Yü led his guest back into the tent, and the general carousing resumed. Chou Yü pointed to his commanders and said, "These are the flower of the Southland. And this gathering today shall be known as the Congregation of the Heroes." The company kept on drinking until it was time to light the lamps. Then Chou Yü rose and performed a sword dance, singing:

> In this life a man must make his name:
> A good name is a comfort all life long.
> A lifelong comfort: Oh, let me feel the wine,
> And flushed with wine, I'll sing my wildest song.

When he finished, the whole table laughed gaily. As the night advanced, Chiang Kan prepared to take his leave. "The wine was too much for me," he said. Chou Yü dismissed the guests, and the commanders departed. "We have not shared a couch for many a year, my friend," Chou Yü said. "Tonight we share a bed foot-to-foot." Again feigning intoxication, he led Chiang Kan arm-in-arm into his bedchamber and there collapsed, sprawling into bed fully dressed and vomiting copiously. How could Chiang Kan sleep? He lay on his pillow, listening. The drum sounded the second watch. Lifting his head, he saw the wasted candle still giving light. Chou Yü was snoring heavily. On the table Chiang Kan noticed a sheaf of documents. He rose and stealthily looked through them: among the correspondence was a letter from Ts'ao Ts'ao's two naval commanders, Ts'ai Mao and Chang Yün. He peeked at the contents:

We surrendered to Ts'ao by dint of circumstance, not for wealth or rank. We have tricked the northern army by enclosing it inside the large ships. The moment we have the chance, we will deliver the traitor Ts'ao's head

---

3. Lu Chia and Li Yi-chi were two diplomats of the early Han dynasty.

to you. Someone will come with further information. Have no doubts. Herein our respectful reply.

Chiang Kan said to himself, "So Ts'ai Mao and Chang Yün are in league with the Southland!" and stowed the letter in his clothes. He was going to look at some of the other papers, but Chou Yü turned over in bed. Chiang Kan extinguished the lamp and lay down. Chou Yü began to mumble, "My friend, wait a few days and you'll see the head of that traitor Ts'ao!" Chiang Kan managed a reply. Again Chou Yü said, "Do stay a while . . . you'll see Ts'ao Ts'ao's head. . . ." Chiang Kan tried to question him, but he saw that he had fallen fast asleep.

Chiang Kan lay on the bed. The fourth watch was near. He heard someone come into the tent and call out, "Is the marshal awake yet?" Chou Yü, giving the appearance of a man startled from his dreams, asked the man, "Who is this sleeping on my bed?" "Marshal," was the reply, "you invited Chiang Kan to share your bed. Can you have forgotten?" In a repentant tone, Chou Yü said, "I never allow myself to get drunk. I was not myself yesterday. I don't remember if I said anything." "Someone came from the north," said the man. "Lower your voice!" said Chou Yü urgently. He then called Chiang Kan, but Kan feigned sleep. Chou Yü slipped out of the tent. Kan listened intently. Outside someone was saying, "Chang Yün and Ts'ai Mao said, 'We are not able to take quick action. . . .' " The remainder was spoken too low for Chiang Kan to make out.

Moments later Chou Yü reentered the tent and called his friend again. Chiang Kan continued the pretense by pulling the blanket over his head and making no response. Chou Yü took off his clothes and lay down. Chiang Kan thought, "Chou Yü is a shrewd man. He is sure to kill me in the morning when he discovers the letter is gone." Chiang Kan rested until the fifth watch, then rose and called Chou Yü. No answer. He put on his hood and slipped out of the tent, called his young companion, and headed for the main gate. "Where to, sir?" the guard asked. "I'm afraid I have been keeping the field marshal from his work, so I am saying good-bye for now." The guard made no attempt to stop them.

Chiang Kan boarded his boat and sped back to see Ts'ao Ts'ao. "How did it go?" the prime minister asked. Chiang Kan said, "Chou Yü is too high-minded to be swayed by speeches." Angrily Ts'ao replied, "The mission failed. And we end up looking like fools!" "Though I could not persuade him to join us, I did manage to find out something of interest for Your Excellency. Would you ask the attendants to go out?" So saying, Chiang Kan produced the stolen letter and related point by point all that had happened in the bedchamber. "That's how the villains repay my kindness!" roared Ts'ao Ts'ao, and he summoned Ts'ai Mao and Chang Yün to his quarters at once. "I want you two to begin the attack," Ts'ao Ts'ao said to them. "The training is still unfinished. It would be risky," they replied. "And when the training is completed, will my head be delivered to Chou Yü?" said Ts'ao. Ts'ai Mao and Chang Yün could make no sense of this and were too confused to respond. Ts'ao Ts'ao called for his armed guards to put them to death. But the moment the two heads were brought in, Ts'ao Ts'ao realized he had been tricked.[4] A poet of later times left these lines:

> Ts'ao Ts'ao, a master of intrigue,
> Fell for Chou Yü's cunning ruse.
> Ts'ai and Chang betrayed their lord
> And fell to Ts'ao Ts'ao's bloody sword.[5]

Ts'ao Ts'ao's commanders wanted to know the reason for the executions. But Ts'ao Ts'ao was unable to admit his mistake. "They flouted military rules; therefore, I had them killed," he said. The stunned commanders groaned and sighed. Ts'ao Ts'ao chose Mao Chieh and Yü Chin to serve as the new chief naval commanders.

Meanwhile, spies reported the execution to Chou Yü. "I feared those two the most," he said with satisfaction. "With them out of the way, I have no problems." "Commander," said Lu Su, "if you can wage war this well, we will have nothing to worry about. Ts'ao will be beaten." "My guess is that none of our commanders knows what happened," said Chou Yü, "except for K'ung-ming, who knows more than I do. I doubt if even this plan fooled him. Try to sound him out for me. Find out if he knew. And tell me right away." Indeed,

> His success in dividing his rivals would not be complete
> Until he knew what the stony-eyed observer on the side was thinking.

Once again Lu Su went to see K'ung-ming for Chou Yü. Could he keep the alliance from breaking up?
Read on.

Chapter 46

> K'ung-ming borrows Ts'ao Ts'ao's arrows through a ruse;
> Huang Kai is flogged following a secret plan.

Chou Yü sent Lu Su to find out if K'ung-ming had detected the subterfuge. K'ung-ming welcomed Lu Su aboard his little boat, and the two men sat face-to-face. "Every day I am taken up with military concerns and miss your advice," Lu Su began. "Rather, I am the tardy one, having yet to convey my

4. It has been suggested that Ts'ao Ts'ao might not have killed the commanders had they defended themselves instead of allowing their confusion to lend them a guilty appearance.
5. After Liu Piao died, Ts'ai Mao and Chang Yün conspired to do away with Piao's heir, Liu Tsung, and deliver his province, Ching-chou, to Ts'ao Ts'ao. This occurs in chapter 40.

felicitations to the chief commander," answered K'ung-ming. "What felicitations?" asked Lu Su. "Why," replied K'ung-ming, "for that very matter about which he sent you here to see if I knew." The color left Lu Su's face. "But how did you know, master?" he asked. K'ung-ming went on, "The trick was good enough to take in Chiang Kan. Ts'ao Ts'ao, though hoodwinked for the present, will realize what happened quickly enough—he just won't admit the mistake. But with those naval commanders dead, the Southland has no major worry, so congratulations are certainly in order. I hear that Ts'ao Ts'ao has replaced them with Mao Chieh and Yü Chin. One way or another, those two will do in their navy!"

Lu Su, unable to respond sensibly, temporized as best he could before he rose to leave. "I trust you will say nothing about this in front of Chou Yü," K'ung-ming urged Lu Su, "lest he again be moved to do me harm." Lu Su agreed but finally divulged the truth when he saw the field marshal. Astounded, Chou Yü said, "The man must die. I am determined." "If you kill him," Lu Su argued, "Ts'ao Ts'ao will have the last laugh." "I will have justification," answered Chou Yü. "And he will not feel wronged." "How will you do it?" asked Lu Su. "No more questions now. You'll see soon enough," Chou Yü replied.

The next day Chou Yü gathered his generals together and summoned K'ung-ming, who came eagerly. At the assembly Chou Yü asked him, "When we engage Ts'ao Ts'ao in battle on the river routes, what should be the weapon of choice?" "On the Great River, bow and arrow," K'ung-ming replied. "My view precisely, sir," Chou Yü said. "But we happen to be short of arrows. Dare I trouble you, sir, to undertake the production of one hundred thousand arrows to use against the enemy? Please favor us with your cooperation in this official matter." "Whatever task the chief commander assigns, I shall strive to complete," replied K'ung-ming. "But may I ask by what time you will require them?" "Can you finish in ten days?" asked Chou Yü. "Ts'ao's army is due at any moment," said K'ung-ming. "If we must wait ten days, it will spoil everything." "How many days do you estimate you need, sir?" said Chou Yü. "With all respect, I will deliver the arrows in three days," K'ung-ming answered. "There is no room for levity in the army," Chou Yü snapped. "Dare I trifle with the chief commander?" countered K'ung-ming. "I beg to submit my pledge under martial law: if I fail to finish in three days' time, I will gladly suffer the maximum punishment."

Elated, Chou Yü had his administrative officer publicly accept the document. He then offered K'ung-ming wine, saying, "You will be well rewarded when your mission is accomplished." "It's too late to begin today," said K'ung-ming. "Production begins tomorrow. On the third day, send five hundred men to the river for the arrows." After a few more cups, he left. Lu Su said to Chou Yü, "This man has to be deceiving us." "He is delivering himself into our hands!" replied Chou Yü. "We did not force him. Now that he has publicly undertaken this task in writing, he couldn't escape if he sprouted wings. Just have the artisans delay delivery of whatever he needs. He will miss the appointed time; and when we fix his punishment, what defense will he be able to make? Now go to him again and bring me back news."

Lu Su went to see K'ung-ming. "Didn't I tell you not to say anything?" K'ung-ming began. "He is determined to kill me. I never dreamed you would expose me. And now today he actually pulled this trick on me! How am I supposed to produce one hundred thousand arrows in three days? You have to save me!" "You brought this on yourself," said Lu Su. "How can I save you?" "You must lend me twenty vessels," K'ung-ming went on, "with a crew of thirty on each. Lined up on either side of each vessel I want a thousand bundles of straw wrapped in black cloth. I have good use for them. I'm sure we can have the arrows on the third day. But if you tell Chou Yü this time, my plan will fail." Lu Su agreed, though he had no idea what K'ung-ming was up to, and reported back to Chou Yü without mentioning the boats, "K'ung-ming doesn't seem to need bamboo, feathers, glue, or other materials. He seems to have something else in mind." Puzzled, Chou Yü said, "Let's see what he has to say after three days have gone by."

Lu Su quietly placed at K'ung-ming's disposal all he had requested. But neither on the first day nor on the second did K'ung-ming make any move. On the third day at the fourth watch, he secretly sent for Lu Su. "Why have you called me here?" Su asked. "Why else? To go with me to fetch the arrows," K'ung-ming replied. "From where?" inquired Lu Su. "Ask no questions," said K'ung-ming. "Let's go; you'll see." He ordered the boats linked by long ropes and set out for the north shore.

That night tremendous fogs spread across the heavens, and the river mists were so thick that even face-to-face people could not see each other. K'ung-ming urged his boats on into the deep fog. The rhapsody "Heavy Mists Mantling the Yangtze" describes it well:

> Vast the river! Wide and far-flung! West, it laps the mountains Mang and Ŏ. South, it grips the southern shires. North, it girdles the nine rivers, gathers their waters, and carries them into the sea, its surging waves rolling through eternity.
>
> Its depths hold monsters and strange forms: the Lord of the Dragons, the Sea Thing, the river goddesses, the Ocean Mother, ten-thousand-span whales, and the nine-headed centipede. This redoubt of gods and spirits, heroes fight to hold.
>
> At times the forces of yin and yang that govern nature fail, and day and darkness seem as one, turning the vast space into a fearful monochrome. Everywhere the fog, stock-still. Not even a cartload can be spotted. But the sound of gong or drum carries far.
>
> At first, a visible gloom, time for the wise leopard of the southern hills

to seclude itself. Gradually darkness fills the expanse. Does it want the North Sea leviathan itself to lose its way? At last it reaches the very sky and mantles the all-upbearing earth. Gray gloomy vastness. A shoreless ocean. Whales hurtle on the waves. Dragons plunge and spew mist.

It is like the end of early rains, when the cold of latent spring takes hold: everywhere, vague, watery desert and darkness that flows and spreads. East, it blankets the shore of Ch'ai-sang. South, it blocks the hills of Hsia-kou. A thousand war-junks, swallowed between the river's rocky steeps, while a single fishing boat boldly bobs on the swells.

In so deep a fog, the deep-domed heavens have gone dark. The countenance of dawn is dull: the day becomes a murky twilight; the reddish hills, aquamarine jade. Great Yü, who first controlled the floods, could not with all his wisdom sound its depths. Even clear-eyed Li Lou[1] could not use his measures, despite his keen vision.

Let the water god calm these waves. Let the god of elements put away his art. Let the sea creatures and those of land and air be gone. For now the magic isle of P'eng-lai[2] is cut off, and the gates of the polar stars are shrouded.

The roiling, restless fog is like the chaos before a storm, swirling streaks resembling wintry clouds. Serpents lurking there can spread its pestilence, and evil spirits can havoc wreak, sending pain and woe to the world of men, and the storms of wind and sand that plague the border wastes. Common souls meeting it fall dead. Great men observe it and despair. Are we returning to the primal state that preceded form itself—to undivided heaven and earth?

By the fifth watch, K'ung-ming's little convoy was nearing Ts'ao Ts'ao's river base. The vessels advanced in single file, their prows pointed west. The crew began to roar and pound their drums. Lu Su was alarmed. "What if they make a sally?" he asked. K'ung-ming smiled and replied, "I'd be very surprised if Ts'ao Ts'ao plunged into this fog. Let's pour the wine and enjoy ourselves. We'll go back when the fog lifts."

As the clamor reached Ts'ao Ts'ao's camp, the new naval advisers Mao Chieh and Yü Chin sent reports at once. Ts'ao Ts'ao issued an order: "The fog has made the river invisible. This sudden arrival of enemy forces must mean an ambush. I want absolutely no reckless movements. Let the archers and crossbowmen, however, fire upon the enemy at random." He also sent a man to his land headquarters calling for Chang Liao and Hsü Huang to rush an extra three thousand crossbowmen to the shore. By the time Ts'ao's order reached Mao Chieh and Yü Chin, their men had already begun shooting for

1. A legendary figure possessed of extraordinarily good eyesight.
2. The islands of immortality that lie in the ocean east of China.

fear the southerners would penetrate their camp. Soon, once the marksmen from the land camp had joined the battle, ten thousand men were concentrating their shots toward the river. The shafts came down like rain.

K'ung-ming ordered the boats to reverse direction and press closer to shore to receive arrows while the crews continued drumming and shouting. When the sun climbed, dispersing the fog, K'ung-ming ordered the boats to hurry homeward. The straw bundles bristled with arrow shafts, for which K'ung-ming had each crew shout in unison, "Thanks to the prime minister for the arrows!" By the time this was reported to Ts'ao Ts'ao, the light craft, borne on swift currents, were twenty tricents downriver, beyond overtaking. Ts'ao Ts'ao was left with the agony of having played the fool.

K'ung-ming said to Lu Su, "Each boat has some five or six thousand arrows. So without costing the Southland the slightest effort, we have gained over one hundred thousand arrows, which tomorrow we can return to Ts'ao's troops—a decided convenience to us!" "Master, you are indeed supernatural," Lu Su said. "How did you know there would be such a fog today?" "A military commander is a mediocrity," K'ung-ming explained, "unless he is versed in the patterns of the heavens, recognizes the advantages of the terrain, knows the interaction of prognostic signs, understands the changes in weather, examines the maps of deployment, and is clear about the balance of forces. Three days ago I calculated today's fog. That's why I took a chance on the three-day limit. Chou Yü gave me ten days to finish the job, but neither materials nor workmen. He plainly meant to kill me for laxity. But my fate is linked to Heaven. How could Chou Yü have succeeded?" Respectfully, Lu Su acknowledged K'ung-ming's superior powers.

When the boats reached shore, five hundred men sent by Chou Yü had already arrived to transport the arrows. K'ung-ming directed them to take the arrows—upward of one hundred thousand of them—from the boats and to deliver them to the chief commander's tent. Meanwhile, Lu Su explained in detail to Chou Yü how K'ung-ming had acquired them. Chou Yü was astounded. Then, with a long sigh of mingled admiration and despair, he said, "K'ung-ming's godlike machinations and magical powers of reckoning are utterly beyond me!" A poet of later times left these lines in admiration:

> That day thick fog covering the river
> Dissolved all distance in a watery blur.
> Like driving rain or locusts Ts'ao's arrows came:
> K'ung-ming had humbled the Southland's commander!

K'ung-ming entered the camp. Chou Yü came out of his tent and greeted him with cordial praise, "Master, we must defer to your superhuman powers of reckoning." "A petty subterfuge of common cunning," K'ung-ming replied, "not worth your compliments." Chou Yü invited K'ung-ming into his tent to drink. "Yesterday," Chou Yü said, "Lord Sun urged us to advance. But I still lack that unexpected stroke that wins the battle. I appeal to you for instruction." "I am a run-of-the-mill mediocrity," replied K'ung-ming. "What kind of unique stratagem could I offer you?" "Yesterday I surveyed Ts'ao's naval stations," Chou Yü continued. "They are the epitome of strict order, all according to the book, invulnerable to any routine attack. I have one idea, but it may not be workable. Master, could you help me to decide?"

"Refrain from speaking for a moment, chief commander," K'ung-ming said. "We'll write on our palms to see whether we agree or not." Chou Yü was delighted to oblige. He called for brush and ink, and, after writing on his own masked hand, passed the brush to K'ung-ming, who wrote on his own. Then the two men shifted closer to one another, opened their hands, and laughed. The same word was on each: fire. "Since our views coincide," said Chou Yü, "my doubts are resolved. Protect our secret." "This is our common cause," answered K'ung-ming. "Disclosure is unthinkable. My guess is that even though Ts'ao Ts'ao has twice fallen victim to my fires, he will not be prepared for this. It may be your ultimate weapon, chief commander." After drinking, they parted. None of the commanders knew of their plan.

Ts'ao Ts'ao had lost a hundred and fifty or sixty thousand arrows with nothing to show for it, and a surly temper ruled his mind. Hsün Yu put forward a plan: "With Chou Yü and Chu-ke Liang framing strategy for the Southland, there is little hope of defeating them in a quick strike. Rather, send a man to the Southland claiming to surrender, one who can serve as our spy in their camp. Then we will have a chance." "I was thinking much the same thing," said Ts'ao. "Whom would you choose for the mission?" "We've executed Ts'ai Mao. His clansmen are all in the army: Ts'ai Chung and Ts'ai Ho are now lieutenant commanders. Bind those two to you, Your Excellency, with suitable favors, and then send them to declare their submission to the Southland. They will not be suspected." Ts'ao Ts'ao agreed.

That night the prime minister secretly called the two into his tent and gave them their instructions: "I want you to take a few soldiers south and pretend to surrender. Send covert reports of all you observe. When your mission is done, you will be enfeoffed and amply rewarded. Do not waver in your loyalties." "Our families are in Ching-chou," they replied. "How could our loyalties be divided? Rest assured, Your Excellency. We will secure the heads of Chou Yü and Chu-ke Liang and place them before you." Ts'ao Ts'ao paid them handsomely. The next day Ts'ai Chung and Ts'ai Ho sailed south in several boats, accompanied by five hundred men and headed for the southern shore on a favorable wind.

Chou Yü was working on preparations for his attack when it was reported that the ships approaching from the north shore were bringing two defectors, kinsmen of Ts'ai Mao's, Ts'ai Ho and Ts'ai Chung. Chou Yü summoned them into his presence, and the two men prostrated themselves, weeping as they spoke, "Ts'ao Ts'ao has murdered our elder brother, an innocent man. We want to avenge him. So we have come to surrender in the hope that you will grant us a place. We want to serve in the front line." Delighted, Chou Yü rewarded them handsomely and ordered them to join Kan Ning in the vanguard. The two men gave their respectful thanks, believing their plan had worked.

Chou Yü, however, secretly instructed Kan Ning: "This is a false surrender. They have not brought their families. Ts'ao Ts'ao has sent them here to spy. I want to give him a taste of his own medicine by giving them certain information to send back. Be as solicitous of them as possible, but on your guard. The day we march, we will sacrifice them to our banners. Take the strictest precautions against any slip-up." Kan Ning left with his orders.

Lu Su said to the chief commander, "The surrender of Ts'ai Chung and Ts'ai Ho is undoubtedly a pretense. We should not accept it." Chou Yü rebuked him, "They have come to avenge their brother whom Ts'ao Ts'ao murdered. What 'pretense' are you talking about? If you are so full of suspicions, how are we going to open our arms to the talents of the realm?" Silently, Lu Su withdrew and went to inform K'ung-ming, who smiled but said nothing. "What are you smiling at?" Lu Su demanded. "At your failure to detect Chou Yü's plan. Spies cannot cross the river so easily. Ts'ao Ts'ao sent them to defect so that he could probe our situation. Chou Yü is fighting fire with fire and wants them to transmit certain information. 'There is no end of deception in warfare'—Chou Yü's plan exemplifies the adage." And so Lu Su left enlightened.

Once night Chou Yü was sitting in his tent, when Huang Kai stole in. "You must have a fine plan to show me, coming in the night like this," said Chou Yü. "The enemy is too numerous," said Huang Kai, "for us to maintain this standoff long. Why don't we attack with fire?" "Who told you to offer this plan?" Chou Yü asked. "No one," he replied. "It's my own idea." "Well, it's exactly what I mean to do," said Chou Yü. "That's why I'm keeping those two false defectors: to convey false information to Ts'ao's camp. But I need a man to play the same game for us." "I am willing to do it," Huang Kai answered. "What credibility will you have," said Chou Yü, "if you show no sign of having suffered?" "To requite the favor and generosity that the house of Sun has bestowed on me," Huang Kai answered, "I would freely and willingly strew my innards on the ground." Bowing low, Chou Yü thanked him, saying, "If you are willing to carry out this trick of being flogged to win the enemy's confidence, it will be a manifold blessing to the Southland." "Even if I die, I will die content," was Huang Kai's reply. He took leave of Chou Yü and departed.

The next day Chou Yü sounded the drums, convening a general assembly of his commanders outside his tent. K'ung-ming too was in attendance. Chou Yü began, "Ts'ao Ts'ao's million-strong horde, deployed along a three-hundred-tricent stretch of land and shore, will not be defeated in a single day. I am ordering the commanders to take three months' rations and prepare to defend our line." Huang Kai came forward, interrupting him. "Never mind three months'—thirty months' rations won't do the job," he said. "If we can beat them this month, then let's do it. If not, what choice have we but to go along with Chang Chao's advice, throw down our weapons, face north, and sue for peace?"

Chou Yü exploded in fury. "I bear our lord's mandate," he cried, "to lead our troops to destroy Ts'ao Ts'ao. The next man to advocate surrender dies! Now at the very moment of confrontation between the two armies, how dare you weaken our morale? If I spare you, how will I hold my men?" Roughly, he barked orders to his guards to remove Huang Kai, execute him, and report back when done. Huang Kai turned to denounce him, "My service to Lord Sun's father, General Sun Chien, has taken me the length and breadth of the Southland through three successive reigns. Where do the likes of you come from?" Chou Yü ordered immediate execution.

Kan Ning rushed forward and made an appeal: "Huang Kai is one of the Southland's elder leaders. I beg you to be lenient." "What are you trying to do, destroy the rules of the army?" Chou Yü shouted back and barked orders to his guards to drive Kan Ning from the assembly with their clubs. At this point the entire assembly got on their knees, attempting to intercede: "No doubt Huang Kai deserves to die for this offense, but that would not be in the interests of the army. Let the chief commander be lenient and simply make note of his act for the present time. There will be time enough to dispose of him after we have beaten Ts'ao Ts'ao." Chou Yü would not relent, but in the face of the strenuous protests of his commanders, he said, "If not for my consideration for your views, he would lose his head. But I shall spare him for now." Then, turning to his attendants, he added, "Throw him to the ground. One hundred strokes across the back should teach him a proper lesson." The commanders renewed their appeals for Huang Kai, but Chou Yü overturned his table, silenced them with a gesture, and ordered the whipping carried out.

Huang Kai was stripped and forced face down to the ground. After fifty blows of the rod the officers once again appealed for mercy. Chou Yü jumped to his feet and, pointing at Huang Kai, said, "You have dared to show your disrespect! The other fifty will be held in reserve. Any further insults will be doubly punished." Still muttering angrily, he reentered his tent. The officers helped Huang Kai to his feet. His skin was broken everywhere and his oozing flesh was crossed with welts. Returning to his camp, he fainted several times. All who came to express their sympathy wept freely. Among the callers was Lu Su.

Afterward Lu Su went to K'ung-ming's boat. "Chou Yü made Huang Kai pay for it today," Lu Su said. "As his subordinates, we couldn't plead too hard and incur Chou Yü's displeasure. But you, sir, are a guest. Why did you stand by so apparently unconcerned?" K'ung-ming smiled and answered, "Don't mock me, Lu Su." "Since crossing the river together," Lu Su protested, "when have I mocked you? Do not say such things!" "Don't tell me, my friend," K'ung-ming went on, "you didn't know today's beating was all a trick. What would be the point of having me oppose it?" These words awakened Lu Su to the meaning of what had happened. "Without the 'battered-body trick,' " K'ung-ming remarked, "how could Ts'ao Ts'ao be taken in? Chou Yü will be sending Huang Kai over to 'defect,' so he wants Ts'ai Chung and Ts'ai Ho to report today's events to Ts'ao Ts'ao. But it is imperative that Chou Yü not know that I know. Tell him simply that I too resented the beating."

After leaving K'ung-ming, Lu Su went to Chou Yü, and the two men conferred privately. "Why did you condemn Huang Kai so bitterly today?" Lu Su asked. "Did the commanders resent it?" responded Chou Yü. "Most of them were disturbed," answered Lu Su. "And K'ung-ming?" Chou Yü asked. "He too expressed unhappiness at your extreme intolerance," replied Lu Su. "This time around I have deceived him," said Chou Yü. "What?" Lu Su asked. "The beating was a ruse," Chou Yü explained. "I wanted Huang Kai to feign defection, and his body had to be badly bruised to make it convincing. While Huang Kai is in their camp, we will attack with fire; victory will be ours." Lu Su marveled to himself at K'ung-ming's insight but dared not breathe a word.

Huang Kai lay in his tent. All the commanders came to sympathize. Kai moaned but did not speak. When the military counselor K'an Tse arrived to pay his respects, Huang Kai dismissed his attendants. "I can't believe you have made an enemy of the chief commander," K'an Tse said. "I haven't," Huang Kai replied. "Then your punishment must be a trick to win the enemy's confidence," K'an Tse said. "How did you know?" asked Huang Kai. "I was watching Chou Yü's every move," K'an Tse responded, "and guessed the truth pretty much." "The house of Sun has been my benefactor under three masters," said Huang Kai. "I proposed this plan for destroying Ts'ao because of my appreciation and I submitted to this beating willingly. But there is no one in the army I could trust to help me, except for you, who have a loyal and honorable mind and the courage to serve our lord without question." "Do you

mean," K'an Tse said, "that you want me to deliver the letter of surrender?"
"That is my wish. Are you willing?" Huang Kai asked. Eagerly, K'an Tse
accepted. Indeed,

> A brave general requites his lord without a thought for his own safety;
> A counselor serves his land with the selfsame devotion.

What would K'an Tse say next?
Read on.

Translated by Moss Roberts

259
The Journey to the West

Chapter 7

Attributed to Wu Ch'eng-en (c. 1506–1582)

From the Brazier of Eight Trigrams the Great Sage escapes;
Beneath the Five Phases Mountain the Monkey of the Mind[1] is stilled.

The Journey to the West is a comic fantasy based on the pilgrimage of the monk Hsüan-tsang (596–664), also known as Tripiṭaka ("Three Baskets," i.e., the Buddhist Canon), to India for the purpose of collecting Buddhist scriptures. His journey lasted seventeen years altogether in real life, although the novel only has him spending fourteen years on the road. From the factual travelog written by the monk himself and a biography of him written by his disciples, the story of Hsüan-tsang's passage to India underwent a long period of development through various forms of popular literature (see, for example, selection 270) culminating in the one-hundred chapter novel of which the present selection is the seventh.

As portrayed in the novel, Hsüan-tsang is accompanied by four disciples of superhuman ability. Foremost among them is Sun Wu-k'ung whose name may quite literally be interpreted as "The Monkey Who is Enlightened to Vacuity." In many ways, the novel may be said to be more about Sun Wu-k'ung than about Hsüan-tsang, ostensibly the main character. Next comes Chu Pa-chieh whose revealing name may be rendered as "The Pig of Eight Prohibitions." He is the epitome of sensuality, slothfulness, and gargantuan appetite. Sha Ho-shang ("Sand Monk"), a cannibalistic monster symbolizing the dangers of the desert, is converted by Kuan-yin (Avalo-kiteśvara), the salvific Bodhisattva of Compassion. Lastly, there is the faithful white horse who was originally a dragon prince.

On their way, the pilgrims encounter all sorts of demons and monsters who are determined to devour Tripiṭaka, in part because it was thought that consuming his flesh would make them immortal. Tripiṭaka is repeatedly captured and in danger of being eaten or otherwise destroyed, but he is invariably rescued by his disciples, especially by Sun Wu-k'ung, who are assisted by various protective deities.

Fame and fortune,
All predestined;
One must ever shun a guileful heart.
Rectitude and truth.
The fruits of virtue grow both long and deep.
A little presumption brings on Heaven's wrath;
Though yet unseen, it will surely come in time.
If we ask the Lord of the East[2] for reasons why
Such pains and perils now appear,
It's because pride has sought to scale the limits,
Confounding the world's order and perverting the law.

We were telling you about the Great Sage, Equal to Heaven, who was taken by the celestial guardians to the monster-execution block, where he was bound to the monster-subduing pillar. They then slashed him with a scimitar, hewed him with an ax, stabbed him with a spear, and hacked him with a sword, but they could not hurt his body in any way. Next, the Star Spirit of the South Pole ordered the various deities of the Fire Department to burn him with fire, but that, too, had little effect. The gods of the Thunder Department were then ordered to strike him with thunderbolts, but not a single one of his hairs was destroyed. The demon king Mahābāli and the others therefore went back to report to the Throne, saying, "Your Majesty, we don't know where

---

The first seven chapters of the novel tell of the birth and acquisition of magical powers of Sun Wu-k'ung. He represents the human mind and, as such, is resourceful and intelligent, but at the same time is unbridled and wild unless controlled. In the novel, we see Sun Wu-k'ung being tamed by the powerful discipline of Buddhism. This selection is one of the chapters dealing specifically with Sun Wu-k'ung and his subjugation. He is hatched from a stone egg that for eons had absorbed the essences of Heaven and Earth and the Sun and the Moon. In this connection, we should note the cosmogonic symbolism of stone in Chinese mythology. The Monkey King raises turmoil in Heaven until the Jade Emperor entitles him Great Sage Equal of Heaven. Eventually, Sun Wu-k'ung becomes possessed of formidible powers of transformation and a magic rod with which he can conquer any opponents. He is kept in check, however, by the tight fillet which has been fastened around his head and which ensures that his awesome powers are harnessed for Buddhism. The chapters dealing with Sun Wu-k'ung could well stand alone as an independent story cycle, but they are essential underpinning for the rest of the novel.

Readers of the *Journey to the West* who are familiar with the *Rāmāyaṇa* will note many striking correspondences between Sun Wu-k'ung and Hanumat, the famous monkey-chief of that great Indian epic.

1. This is the first of several instances in the chapter (e.g., the first poem on p. 970) and in the book (e.g., the titles of chapters 14, 30, 35, 36, and 41) where reference is made to the phrase "Monkey of the Mind and Horse of the Will." Bridling these symbols of restless human intelligence and impetuous self-assertiveness is a theme central to the entire narrative. Sun Wu-k'ung is the very embodiment of the Monkey of the Mind; it is necessary for Tripiṭaka to control this wayward and forceful creature if he is to achieve his religious and spiritual goals.

2. Possibly a reference to the sun god.

this Great Sage had acquired such power to protect his body. Your subjects slashed him with a scimitar and hewed him with an ax; we also struck him with thunder and burned him with fire. Not a single one of his hairs was destroyed. What shall we do?" When the Jade Emperor heard these words, he said, "What indeed can we do to a fellow like that, a creature of that sort?" Lao Tzu[3] then came forward and said, "That monkey ate the immortal peaches and drank the imperial wine. Moreover, he stole the divine elixir and ate five gourdfuls of it, both raw and cooked. All this was probably refined in the stomach by the Samādhi fire[4] to form a single solid mass. The union with his constitution gave him a diamond body which cannot be quickly destroyed. It would be better, therefore, if this Taoist takes him away and places him in the Brazier of Eight Trigrams, where he will be smelted by high and low heat. When he is finally separated from my elixir, his body will certainly be reduced to ashes." When the Jade Emperor heard these words, he told the Six Guardians of Darkness and the Six Guardians of Light to release the prisoner and hand him over to Lao Tzu, who left in obedience to the divine decree. Meanwhile, the illustrious Sage Erh-lang[5] was rewarded with a hundred gold blossoms, a hundred bottles of imperial wine, a hundred pellets of elixir, together with rare treasures, lustrous pearls, and brocades, which he was told to share with his brothers. After expressing his gratitude, the Immortal Master returned to the mouth of the River of Libations, and for the time being we shall speak of him no further.

Arriving at the Tushita Palace,[6] Lao Tzu loosened the ropes on the Great Sage, pulled out the weapon from his breastbone, and pushed him into the Brazier of Eight Trigrams. He then ordered the Taoist who watched over the brazier and the page-boy in charge of the fire to blow up a strong flame for the smelting process. The brazier, you see, was of eight compartments corresponding to the eight trigrams of Ch'ien, K'an, Ken, Chen, Sun, Li, K'un, and Tui.[7] The Great Sage crawled into the space beneath the compartment which corresponded to the Sun[8] trigram. Now Sun symbolizes wind; where there is wind, there is no fire. However, wind could churn up smoke, which at that moment reddened his eyes, giving them a permanently inflamed condition. Hence they were sometimes called Fiery Eyes and Diamond Pupils.

3. The legendary founder of Taoism (see selection 10).
4. The fire that is said to consume the body of Buddha when he enters Nirvāṇa. But in the Buddhism of popular fiction, this fire, possessed by many fighters or warriors who have attained immortality, is often used as a weapon.
5. The supernatural creature who was able to subdue the not yet fully developed Sun Wu-k'ung in a fantastic battle of transformations (see selection 248, notes 86 and 88 for the prototype of this figure).
6. A heaven ruled over by Maitreya, the Buddha of the future.
7. See selection 3.
8. Pronounced *soon*, this is the name of a trigram and has nothing whatsoever to do with the English word "sun" or the surname of Wu-k'ung, which means "monkey."

Truly time passed by swiftly, and the forty-ninth day[9] arrived imperceptibly. The alchemical process of Lao Tzu was perfected, and on that same day he came to open the brazier to take out his elixir. The Great Sage at the time was covering his eyes with both hands, rubbing his face, and shedding tears. He heard noises on top of the brazier and, opening his eyes, suddenly saw light. Unable to restrain himself, he leaped out of the brazier and kicked it over with a loud crash. He began to walk straight out of the room, while a group of startled fire tenders and guardians tried desperately to grab hold of him. Every one of them was overthrown; he was as wild as a white-brow tiger in a fit, a one-horn dragon with a fever. Lao Tzu rushed up to clutch at him, only to be greeted by such a violent shove that he fell head over heels while the Great Sage escaped. Whipping the compliant rod out from his ear, he waved it once in the wind, and it had the thickness of a rice bowl. Holding it in his hands, without regard for good or ill, he once more careened through the Heavenly Palace, fighting so fiercely that the Nine Luminaries[10] all shut themselves in and the Four Devarājas[11] disappeared from sight. Dear Monkey Monster! Here is a testimonial poem for him. The poem says:

> This cosmic being perfectly fused with nature's gifts
> Passes with ease through ten thousand toils and tests.
> Vast and motionless like the One Great Void,
> Perfect and quiescent, he's named The Primal Depth.
> Refined a long while in the brazier, though not of mercurial stuff,[12]
> He's the very immortal, living ever above all things.
> Knowing boundless transformations, he changes still;
> The three refuges and five commandments[13] he all rejects.

Here is another poem:

> Just as light supernal fills the boundless space,
> So does that cudgel serve his master's hand.
> It lengthens or shortens according to the wish of man;
> Upright or recumbent, it grows or shrinks at will.

9. The time is calculated according to the sacred number 7. In popular Buddhism, forty-nine days is the usual amount of time it takes for a soul to be reincarnated after death. This accounts for the customary length of a complete cycle of funeral services.

10. The sun, moon, Mars, Mercury, Jupiter, Venus, Saturn, the spirit that causes eclipses, and the comet Ketu.

11. Guardian generals of the god Indra who dwell on the four sides of Mount Meru (the *axis mundi*) and who ward off the attacks of evil spirits.

12. Mercury is one of the crucial elements in alchemy.

13. The "three refuges," or Triśaraṇa, refer to three kinds of surrender: to surrender to the Buddha as master, to the Law (*Dharma*) as medicine, and to the community of monks (*Saṅgha*) as friends. The "five commandments" (*pañca veramaṇī*) are prohibitions against killing, stealing, adultery, lying, and intoxicating beverages.

And another:

> A monkey's transformed body weds the human mind.
> Mind is a monkey—this, the truth profound.
> The Great Sage, Equal to Heaven, is no idle thought.
> For how could the post of pi-ma [14] justly show his gifts?
> The Horse works with the Monkey—this means both Mind and Will
> Must firmly be harnessed and not be ruled without.
> All things return to Nirvāṇa, taking this one course:
> In union with Tathāgata [15] to live beneath twin trees. [16]

This time our Monkey King had no respect for persons great or small; he lashed out this way and that with his iron rod, and not a single deity could withstand him. He fought all the way into the Hall of Perfect Light and was approaching the Hall of Divine Mists, where fortunately Wang Ling-kuan, aide to the Immortal Master of Adjuvant Holiness, was on duty. He saw the Great Sage advancing recklessly and went forward to bar his way, holding high his golden whip. "Wanton monkey," he cried, "where are you going? I am here, so don't you dare be insolent!" The Great Sage did not wait for further utterance; he raised his rod and struck at once, while the Ling-kuan met him also with brandished whip. The two of them charged into each other in front of the Hall of Divine Mists. What a fight that was between

> A red-blooded patriot with reputation great,
> And a defier of Heaven with notorious name!
> The saint and the sinner gladly do this fight,
> To test the skills of two warriors brave.
> Though the rod is brutal
> And the whip is fleet,
> How can the hero, upright and just, forbear?
> This one is a supreme god of vengeance with thunderous voice;
> The other, the Great Sage, Equal to Heaven, a monstrous ape.
> The golden whip and the iron rod used by the two
> Are both weapons divine from the House of God.
> At the Treasure Hall of Divine Mists this day they show their might,
> Displaying each his prowess most admirably.
> This one brashly seeks to take the Big Dipper Palace.
> The other with all his strength defends the sacred realm.

14. A minor position in the stables of Heaven to which Sun Wu-k'ung had been appointed and which he found terribly insulting.

15. Tathāgata ("Thus Come/Gone"): one of the highest titles of Buddha. It may be defined as: "He who comes as do all other Buddhas"; or, "He who took the absolute way of cause and effect, and attained perfect wisdom."

16. The twin Sāl trees in the grove in which Śākyamuni entered Nirvāṇa.

In bitter strife relentless they show their power;
Moving back and forth, whip or rod has yet to score.

The two of them fought for some time, and neither victory nor defeat could yet be determined. The Immortal Master of Adjuvant Holiness, however, had already sent word to the Thunder Department, and thirty-six thunder deities were summoned to the scene. They surrounded the Great Sage and plunged into a fierce battle. The Great Sage was not in the least intimidated; wielding his compliant rod, he parried left and right and met his attackers to the front and to the rear. In a moment he saw that the scimitars, lances, swords, halberds, whips, maces, hammers, axes, gilt bludgeons, sickles, and spades of the thunder deities were coming thick and fast. So, with one shake of his body, he changed into a creature with six arms and three heads. One wave of the compliant rod, and it turned into three; his six arms wielded the three rods like a spinning wheel, whirling and dancing in their midst. The various thunder deities could not approach him at all. Truly his form was

> Tumbling round and round,
> Bright and luminous;
> A form everlasting, how imitated by men?
> He cannot be burned by fire.
> Can he ever be drowned in water?
> A lustrous pearl of maṇi [17] he is indeed,
> Immune to all the spears and the swords.
> He could be good;
> He could be bad;
> Present good and evil he could do at will.
> Immortal he'll be in goodness or a Buddha,
> But working ill, he's covered by hair and horn. [18]
> Endlessly changing he runs amok in Heaven,
> Not to be seized by fighting lords or thunder gods.

At the time the various deities had the Great Sage surrounded, but they could not close in on him. All the hustle and bustle soon disturbed the Jade Emperor, [19] who at once sent the Wandering Minister of Inspection and the Immortal Master of Blessed Wings to go to the Western Region and invite the aged Buddha to come and subdue the monster.

The two sages received the decree and went straight to the Spirit Mountain.

17. The maṇi pearl, said to give sight to the blind, is known for its luster.
18. I.e., he is reduced to an animal.
19. It is interesting to observe that the chief deity in the Taoist pantheon here invites the Buddha to restore order to his own heaven.

After they had greeted the Four Vajra-Buddhas[20] and the Eight Bodhisattvas[21] in front of the Treasure Temple of Thunderclap, they asked them to announce their arrival. The deities therefore went before the Treasure Lotus Platform and made their report. Tathāgata at once invited them to appear before him, and the two sages made obeisance to the Buddha three times before standing in attendance beneath the platform. Tathāgata asked, "What causes the Jade Emperor to trouble the two sages to come here?"

The two sages explained as follows: "Some time ago there was born on the Flower-Fruit Mountain a monkey who exercised his magic powers and gathered to himself a troop of monkeys to disturb the world. The Jade Emperor threw down a decree of pacification and appointed him a pi-ma-wen,[22] but he despised the lowliness of that position and left in rebellion. Devarāja Li and Prince Naṭa were sent to capture him, but they were unsuccessful, and another proclamation of amnesty was given to him. He was then made the Great Sage, Equal to Heaven, a rank without compensation. After a while he was given the temporary job of looking after the Garden of Immortal Peaches, where almost immediately he stole the peaches. He also went to the Jasper Pool and made off with the food and wine, devastating the Grand Festival. Half-drunk, he went secretly into the Tushita Palace, stole the elixir of Lao Tzu, and then left the Celestial Palace in revolt. Again the Jade Emperor sent a hundred thousand heavenly soldiers, but he was not to be subdued. Therefore Kuan-yin[23] sent for the Immortal Master Erh-lang and his sworn brothers, who fought and pursued him. Even then he knew many tricks of transformation, and only after he was hit by Lao Tzu's diamond snare could Erh-lang finally capture him. Taken before the Throne, he was condemned to be executed; but, though slashed by a scimitar and hewn by an ax, burned by fire and struck by thunder, he was not hurt at all. After Lao Tzu had received royal permission to take him away, he was refined by fire, and the brazier was not opened until the forty-ninth day. Immediately he jumped out of the Brazier of Eight Trigrams and beat back the celestial guardians. He penetrated into the Hall of Perfect Light and was approaching the Hall of Divine Mists when Wang Ling-kuan, aide to the Immortal Master of Adjuvant Holiness, met and fought with him bitterly. Thirty-six thunder generals were ordered to encircle him completely, but they could never get near him. The situation is desperate, and for this reason, the Jade Emperor sent a special request for you to defend the Throne."

When Tathāgata heard this, he said to the various bodhisattvas, "All of you

20. Diamond Buddhas, the same as the Four Heavenly Kings (Devarājas), for which see note 11.

21. Eight saviors.

22. See note 14.

23. Avalokiteśvara, the all-seeing, all-hearing Bodhisattva (savior) of compassion.

remain steadfast here in the chief temple, and let no one relax his meditative posture. I have to go exorcise a demon and defend the Throne."

Tathāgata then called Ānanda and Kāśyapa, his two venerable disciples, to follow him. They left the Thunderclap Temple and arrived at the gate of the Hall of Divine Mists, where they were met by deafening shouts and yells. There the Great Sage was being beset by the thirty-six thunder deities. The Buddhist Patriarch gave the dharma[24] order: "Let the thunder deities lower their arms and break up their encirclement. Ask the Great Sage to come out here and let me inquire of him what sort of divine power he has." The various warriors retreated immediately, and the Great Sage also threw off his magical appearance. Changing back into his true form, he approached angrily and shouted with ill humor, "What region are you from, monk, that you dare stop the battle and question me?" Tathāgata laughed and said, "I am Śākyamuni, the Venerable One from the Western Region of Ultimate Bliss. I have heard just now about your audacity, your wildness, and your repeated acts of rebellion against Heaven. Where were you born? When did you learn the Great Art? Why are you so violent and unruly?"

The Great Sage said, "I was

> Born of Earth and Heaven, immortal magically fused,
> An old monkey hailed from the Flower-Fruit Mount.
> I made my home in the Water-Curtain Cave;
> I sought friend and teacher to gain the Mystery Great.
> Perfected in the many arts of ageless life,
> I learned to change in ways boundless and vast.
> Too narrow the space I found on that mortal earth;
> I set my mind to live in the Green Jade Sky.
> In Divine Mists Hall none should long reside,
> For king may follow king in the reign of man.
> If might is honor, let them yield to me.
> Only he is hero who dares to fight and win!"

When the Buddhist Patriarch heard these words, he laughed aloud in scorn. "A fellow like you," he said, "is only a monkey who happened to become a spirit. How dare you be so presumptuous as to want to seize the honored throne of the Exalted Jade Emperor? He began practicing religion when he was very young, and he has gone through the bitter experience of one thousand, seven hundred and fifty kalpas, with each kalpa lasting a hundred and twenty-nine thousand, six hundred years. Figure out yourself how many years it took him to rise to the enjoyment of his great and limitless position! You are merely a beast who has just attained human form in this incarnation. How

24. The Buddhist law or doctrine.

dare you make such a boast? Blasphemy! This is sheer blasphemy, and it will surely shorten your allotted age. Repent while there's still time and cease your idle talk! Be wary that you don't encounter such peril that you will be cut down in an instant, and all your original gifts will be wasted."

"Even if the Jade Emperor has practiced religion from childhood," said the Great Sage, "he should not be allowed to remain here forever. The proverb says, 'Many are the turns of kingship, and next year the turn will be mine!' Tell him to move out at once and hand over the Celestial Palace to me. That'll be the end of the matter. If not, I shall continue to cause disturbances and there'll never be peace!" "Besides your immortality and your transformations," said the Buddhist Patriarch, "what other powers do you have that you dare to usurp this hallowed region of Heaven?" "I've plenty of them!" said the Great Sage. "Indeed, I know seventy-two transformations and a life that does not grow old through ten thousand kalpas. I know also how to cloud-somersault, and one leap will take me a hundred and eight thousand miles.[25] Why can't I sit on the Heavenly throne?"

The Buddhist Patriarch said, "Let me make a wager with you. If you have the ability to somersault clear of this right palm of mine, I shall consider you the winner. You need not raise your weapon in battle then, for I shall ask the Jade Emperor to go live with me in the West and let you have the Celestial Palace. If you cannot somersault out of my hand, you can go back to the Region Below and be a monster. Work through a few more kalpas before you return to cause more trouble."

When the Great Sage heard this, he said to himself, snickering, "What a fool this Tathāgata is! A single somersault of mine can carry old Monkey a hundred and eight thousand miles, yet his palm is not even one foot across. How could I possibly not jump clear of it?" He asked quickly, "You're certain that your decision will stand?" "Certainly it will," said Tathāgata. He stretched out his right hand, which was about the size of a lotus leaf. Our Great Sage put away his compliant rod and, summoning his power, leaped up and stood right in the center of the Patriarch's hand. He said simply, "I'm off!" and he was gone—all but invisible like a streak of light in the clouds. Training the eye of wisdom on him, the Buddhist Patriarch saw that the Monkey King was hurtling along relentlessly like a whirligig.

As the Great Sage advanced, he suddenly saw five flesh-pink pillars supporting a mass of bluish air. "This must be the end of the road." he said. "When I go back presently, Tathāgata will be my witness and I shall certainly take up residence in the Palace of Divine Mists." But he thought to himself, "Wait a moment! I'd better leave some kind of memento if I'm going to negotiate with Tathāgata." He plucked a hair and blew a mouthful of magic breath onto it, crying, "Change!" It changed into a writing brush with extra thick hair soaked

25. Seventy-two and one hundred and eight thousand are both sacred Buddhist numbers.

in heavy ink. On the middle pillar he then wrote in large letters the following line: "The Great Sage, Equal to Heaven, has made a tour of this place." When he had finished writing, he retrieved his hair, and with a total lack of respect he left a bubbling pool of monkey urine at the base of the first pillar. He reversed his cloud-somersault and went back to where he had started. Standing on Tathāgata's palm, he said, "I left, and now I'm back. Tell the Jade Emperor to give me the Celestial Palace." "You stinking, urinous ape!" scolded Tathāgata. "Since when did you ever leave the palm of my hand?" The Great Sage said, "You are just ignorant! I went to the edge of Heaven, and I found five flesh-pink pillars supporting a mass of bluish air. I left a memento there. Do you dare go with me to have a look at the place?" "No need to go there," said Tathāgata. "Just lower your head and take a look." When the Great Sage stared down with his fiery eyes and diamond pupils, he found written on the middle finger of the Buddhist Patriarch's right hand this sentence: "The Great Sage, Equal to Heaven, has made a tour of this place." A pungent whiff of monkey urine came from the fork between the thumb and first finger. Astonished, the Great Sage said, "Could this really happen? Could this really happen? I wrote those words on the pillars supporting the sky. How is it that they now appear on his finger? Could it be that he is exercising the magic power of foreknowledge without divination? I won't believe it! I won't believe it! Let me go there once more!"

Dear Great Sage! Quickly he crouched and was about to jump up again, when the Buddhist Patriarch flipped his hand over, and tossed the Monkey King out of the West Heavenly Gate. The five fingers were transformed into the Five Phases of metal, wood, water, fire, and earth. They became, in fact, five connected mountains, named Five-Phases Mountain, which pinned him down with just enough pressure to keep him there. The thunder deities, Ānanda, and Kāśyapa all folded their hands and cried in acclamation: "Wonderful! Wonderful!"

> Taught to be manlike since hatching from an egg that year,
> He set his aim to learn and walk the Way of Truth.
> He lived in a lovely region by ten thousand kalpas unmoved.
> But one day he changed, dissipating vigor and strength.
> Craving high place, he flouted Heaven's dominion;
> Mocking sages, he stole pills and upset the great relations.
> Evil, full to the brim, now meets its retribution.
> We know not when he may hope to find release.

After the Buddhist Patriarch Tathāgata had vanquished the monstrous monkey, he at once called Ānanda and Kāśyapa to return with him to the Western Paradise. At that moment, however, T'ien-p'eng and T'ien-yu, two heavenly messengers, came running out of the Treasure Hall of Divine Mists and said, "We beg Tathāgata to wait a moment, please! Our Lord's grand carriage will arrive momentarily." When the Buddhist Patriarch heard these words, he turned around and waited with reverence. In a moment he did indeed see a chariot drawn by eight colorful phoenixes and covered by a canopy adorned with nine luminous jewels. The entire cortege was accompanied by the sound of wondrous songs and melodies, chanted by a vast celestial choir. Scattering precious blossoms and diffusing fragrant incense, it came up to the Buddha, and the Jade Emperor offered his thanks, saying, "We are truly indebted to your mighty dharma for vanquishing that monster. We beseech Tathāgata to remain for one brief day, so that we may invite the immortals to join us in giving you a banquet of thanks." Not daring to refuse, Tathāgata folded his hands to thank the Jade Emperor, saying, "Your old monk came here at your command, Most Honorable Deva. Of what power may I boast, really? I owe my success entirely to the excellent fortune of Your Majesty and the various deities. How can I be worthy of your thanks?" The Jade Emperor then ordered the various deities from the Thunder Department to send invitations abroad to the Three Pure Ones, the Four Ministers, the Five Elders, the Six Women Officials,[26] the Seven Stars, the Eight Poles, the Nine Luminaries, and the Ten Capitals. Together with a thousand immortals and ten thousand sages, they were to come to the thanksgiving banquet given for the Buddhist Patriarch. The Four Great Imperial Preceptors and the Divine Maidens of Nine Heavens were told to open wide the golden gates of the Jade Capital, the Treasure Palace of Primal Secret, and the Five Lodges of Penetrating Brightness. Tathāgata was asked to be seated high on the the Spirit Platform of Seven Treasures, and the rest of the deities were then seated according to rank and age before a banquet of dragon livers, phoenix marrow, juices of jade, and immortal peaches.

In a little while, the Jade-Pure Honorable Divine of the Origin, the Exalted-Pure Honorable Divine of Spiritual Treasures, the Primal-Pure Honorable Divine of Moral Virtue, the Immortal Masters of Five Influences, the Star Spirits of Five Constellations, the Three Ministers, the Four Sages, the Nine Luminaries, the Left and Right Assistants, the Devarāja, and Prince Naṭa all marched in leading a train of flags and canopies in pairs. They were all holding rare treasures and lustrous pearls, fruits of longevity and exotic flowers to be presented to the Buddha. As they bowed before him, they said, "We are most grateful for the unfathomable power of Tathāgata, who has subdued the monstrous monkey. We are grateful, too, to the Most Honorable Deva, who is having this banquet and asked us to come here to offer our thanks. May we beseech Tathāgata to give this banquet a name?" Responding to the petition of the various deities, Tathāgata said, "If a name is desired, let

26. According to the *History of the Sui*, the Six Women Officials were established in the Han dynasty. They were in charge of palace upkeep, palatial protocol, court attire, food and medicine, banquets, and the various artisans of the court.

this be called 'The Great Banquet for Peace in Heaven.'" "What a magnificent name!" the various immortals cried in unison. "Indeed, it shall be the Great Banquet for Peace in Heaven." When they finished speaking, they took their seats separately, and there was the pouring of wine and exchanging of cups, pinning of corsages[27] and playing of zithers. It was indeed a magnificent banquet, for which we have a testimonial poem. The poem says:

> That Feast of Peaches Immortal disturbed by the ape
> Is now surpassed by this Banquet for Peace in Heaven.
> Dragon flags and phoenix chariots stand glowing in halos bright,
> As standards and blazing banners whirl in hallowed light.
> Sweet are the tunes of immortal airs and songs,
> Noble the sounds of panpipes and double flutes of jade.
> Incense ambrosial surrounds this assembly of saints.
> The world is tranquil. May the Holy Court be praised!

As all of them were feasting happily, the Lady Queen Mother also led a host of divine maidens and immortal singing-girls to come before the Buddha, dancing with light feet. They bowed to him, and she said, "Our Festival of Immortal Peaches was ruined by that monstrous monkey. We are beholden to the mighty power of Tathāgata for the enchainment of the mischievous ape. In the celebration during this Great Banquet for Peace in Heaven, we have little to offer as a token of our thanks. Please accept, however, these few immortal peaches plucked from the large trees by our own hands." They were truly

> Half red, half green, and spouting aroma sweet,
> Of luscious roots immortal, and ten thousand years old.
> Pity those fruits planted at the Wu-ling Spring![28]
> How do they equal the marvels of Heaven's home:
> Those tender ones of purple veins so rare in the world,
> And those of matchless sweetness with pale yellow pits?
> They lengthen your age and prolong your life by changing your frame.
> He who has the luck to eat them will never be the same.

After the Buddhist Patriarch had pressed together his hands to thank the Queen Mother, she ordered the immortal singing-girls and the divine maidens to sing and dance. All the immortals at the banquet applauded enthusiastically. Truly there were

27. Supposedly a custom of the Sung dynasty. After offering sacrifices at the ancestral temple of the imperial family, the emperor and his subjects would pin flowers on their clothes or on their caps.

28. Wu-ling is the prefecture in which is located the town of Ch'ang-te, in Hunan province. Its fame rests on the utopian "Peach-Blossom Spring," poems written by T'ao Ch'ien (365–427) and later by Wang Wei (701–761). The spring is said to be near the town (see selection 204).

Whorls of heavenly incense filling the seats.
And profuse array of divine petals and stems.
Jade capital and gold arches in what great splendor!
How priceless, too, the strange goods and rare treasures!
Every pair had the same age as Heaven.
Every set increased through ten thousand kalpas.
Mulberry fields or vast oceans, let them shift and change.
He who lives here has neither grief nor fear.

The Queen Mother commanded the immortal maidens to sing and dance, as wine-cups and goblets clinked together steadily. After a little while, suddenly

A wondrous fragrance came to meet the nose,
Rousing Stars and Planets in that great hall.
The gods and the Buddha put down their cups.
Raising his head, each waited with his eyes.
There in the air appeared an aged man,
Holding a most luxuriant long-life plant.
His gourd had elixir of ten thousand years;
His book listed names twelve millennia old.
Sky and earth in his cave knew no constraint;
Sun and moon were perfected in his vase.[29]
He roamed the Four Seas in joy serene,
And made the Ten Islets[30] his tranquil home.
Getting drunk often at the Peaches Feast
He woke; the moon shone brightly as of old.
He had a long head, short frame, and large ears.
His name: Star of Long Life from South Pole.

After the Star of Long Life had arrived and had greeted the Jade Emperor, he also went up to thank Tathāgata, saying, "When I first heard that the baneful monkey was being led by Lao Tzu to the Tushita Palace to be refined by alchemical fire, I thought peace was surely secured. I never suspected that he could still escape, and it was fortunate that Tathāgata in his goodness had subdued this monster. When I got word of the thanksgiving banquet, I came at once. I have no other gifts to present to you but these purple agaric, jasper plant, jade-green lotus root, and golden elixir." The poem says:

Jade-green lotus and golden drug are given to Śākya.
Like the sands of Ganges is the age of Tathāgata.
The brocade of the three wains[31] is calm, eternal bliss.

29. A metaphoric expression for the alchemical process.
30. Legendary home of the immortals.
31. The three vehicles (*triyāna*), drawn by a goat, a deer, and an ox to convey the living across the cycles of births and deaths (*saṁsāra*) to the shores of Nirvāṇa.

> The nine-grade[32] garland is a wholesome, endless life.
> In the School Mādhyamika[33] he's the true master,
> Whose home is the Heaven both of form and emptiness.[34]
> The great Earth and cosmos all call him Lord.
> His sixteen-foot[35] diamond body abounds in blessing and life.

Tathāgata accepted the thanks cheerfully, and the Star of Long Life went to his seat. Again there was pouring of wine and exchanging of cups. The Great Immortal of Naked Feet also arrived. After prostrating himself before the Jade Emperor, he too went to thank the Buddhist Patriarch, saying, "I am profoundly grateful for your dharma which subdued the baneful monkey. I have no other things to convey my respect but two magic pears and some fire dates,[36] which I now present to you." The poem says:

> Fragrant are the pears and dates of the Naked-Feet Immortal,
> Presented to Amitābha, whose count of years is long.
> Firm as a hill is his Lotus Platform of Seven Treasures;
> Brocadelike is his Flower Seat of Thousand Gold adorned.
> No false speech is this—his age equals Heaven and Earth;
> Nor is this a lie—his luck is great as the sea.
> Blessing and long life reach in him their fullest scope,
> Dwelling in that Western Region of calm, eternal bliss.

Tathāgata again thanked him and asked Ānanda and Kāśyapa to put away the gifts one by one before approaching the Jade Emperor to express his gratitude for the banquet. By now, everyone was somewhat tipsy. A Spirit Minister of Inspection then arrived to make the report, "The Great Sage is sticking out his head!" "No need to worry," said the Buddhist Patriarch. He took from his sleeve a tag on which were written in gold letters the words *Oṁ maṇi padme hūṁ*.[37] Handing it over to Ānanda, he told him to stick it on the top of the mountain. This deva[38] received the tag, took it out of the Heavenly Gate, and stuck it tightly on a square piece of rock at the top of the Mountain of Five Phases.[39] The mountain immediately struck root and grew together at the

32. The nine classes or grades of rewards in the Pure Land.

33. The Mādhyamika or San-lun School advocates the doctrine of formlessness or nothingness (*animitta, nirābhāsa*).

34. "Form is emptiness and the very emptiness is form" is the famous statement of the *Heart Sūtra* (the *Prajñāpāramitāhṛdaya*).

35. Buddha's transformed body is said to be sixteen feet, the same height as his earthly body.

36. Pears and dates are the traditional fruits of religious Taoism.

37. Said to be a prayer to Padmapāṇi (Kuan-yin/Avalokiteśvara holding a lotus flower), this Lamaistic charm begins with the universal sacred syllable *Oṁ*. Each syllable is supposed to have its own mystic power of salvation, but the prayer is often translated as meaning "Oh, jewel in the Lotus."

38. Divine being.

39. The five elements of Chinese cosmology: earth, wood, fire, metal, water.

seams, though there was enough space for breathing and for the prisoner's hands to crawl out and move around a bit. Ānanda then returned to report, "The tag is tightly attached."

Tathāgata then took leave of the Jade Emperor and the deities, and went with the two devas out of the Heavenly Gate. Moved by compassion, he recited a divine spell and called together a local spirit and the Fearless Guards of Five Quarters to stand watch over the Five-Phases Mountain. They were told to feed the prisoner with iron pellets when he was hungry and to give him melted copper to drink when he was thirsty. When the time of his chastisement was fulfilled, they were told, someone would be coming to deliver him. So it is that

> The brash, baneful monkey in revolt against Heaven
> Is brought to submission by Tathāgata.
> He drinks melted copper to endure the seasons,
> And feeds on iron pellets to pass the time.
> Tried by this bitter misfortune sent from the Sky.
> He's glad to be living, though in a piteous lot.
> If this hero is allowed to struggle anew,
> He'll serve Buddha in future and go to the West.

Another poem says:

> Prideful of his power once the time was ripe,
> He tamed dragon and tiger, exploiting wily might.
> Stealing peaches and wine, he roamed the House of Heaven.
> He found trust and favor in the Capital of Jade.
> He's now imprisoned, for his evil's full to the brim.
> By the good stock[40] unfailing his spirit will rise again.
> If he's indeed to escape Tathāgata's hands.
> He must await the holy monk from T'ang court.

We do not know in what month or year hereafter the days of his penance will be fulfilled, and you must listen to the explanation in the next chapter.

Translated by Anthony C. Yu

---

40. Good stock (Sanskrit *kuśala-mula*): the Buddhist idea of the good seeds sown by a virtuous life which will bring future rewards.

260
Gold Vase Plum

Chapter 12: Golden Lotus Narrowly Escapes Disaster

Anonymous (late 16th century)

The tree is pitiful that stands alone
Its branches fragile and its roots uncertain.
The dew may give it moisture, but the wind
Blows it to one side and the other.
There is none to raise the silken coverlet
I must sit and keep my watch from night to morning.
Sorrow has made me thin
No loving wish of yours has given me
This slender waist.

Hsi-men Ch'ing was so delighted with Cassia's beauty that he stayed at the bawdy house for several days. Many times the Moon Lady sent servants with horses to bring him back, but Cassia's family hid his hat and clothes, and would not let him go. The ladies of his own household were for once at a loss for something to do. Most of them were quite content, but Golden Lotus was still not thirty years old, and her passions were by no means under control. Day after day, she made herself look as pretty as a jade carving, and stood at

Although other works may be more sexually explicit (e.g., *The Carnal Prayer Mat* [*Jou-p'u t'uan*], see introductory note to selection 257), *The Golden Lotus* or *Gold Vase Plum* (*Chin p'ing mei*; the title is made up of the names of the three main female characters) is generally recognized as China's greatest pornographic novel. But it offers more than erotica, of which there is plenty enough in the novel. *Gold Vase Plum* also affords a vivid description of the corrupt life and customs of society and proffers a subtle, but extended, lesson in Buddhist ethics. First published around 1617, *Gold Vase Plum* is much indebted to the earlier popular novel, *Water Margin* (see selection 261), which evolved between the fourteenth and early sixteenth century, even borrowing several of its characters for central roles. Like *Water Margin, Gold Vase Plum* is set around the collapse of the Northern Sung dynasty and there are many other resonances between the two novels. The borrowed material, however, has been skillfully and thoroughly assimilated by the author of *Gold Vase Plum*, who created the most tightly knit Chinese novel before this century.

The author disguised his identity by using the pseudonym Scoffing Scholar of Lan-ling (see selection 187, note 1). It is almost certain, however, that he was from Shantung because the earthy language of this hundred-chapter novel includes many distinctive elements of the colloquial topolect of that province.

In this selection from the early part of the novel, we find the (anti-)hero, Hsi-men Ch'ing, engaged with some debauched cronies in one of his countless escapades. The clever, sometimes vicious, competition among the many women who vie for Hsi-men's attention is vividly described.

the main gate with gleaming teeth and scarlet lips, leaning upon the door and waiting for her husband to return. Not until evening did she go to her room, and there the pillow seemed deserted and the curtains forlorn, and there was none to share the joys of her dressing-table. Sleep would not come to her, and she went to the garden, walking delicately upon the flowers and moss and, when she saw the moon reflected in the water, she thought of the uncertainty of Hsi-men's nature, and as she watched the tortoise-shell cats enjoying each other's company, it brought only disturbance to her own sweet heart.

Ch'in T'ung, the boy who had accompanied Tower of Jade when she married Hsi-men Ch'ing, was now sixteen years old, and for the first time took his place in the household as a full-grown youth. He had finely arched eyebrows and eyes full of intelligence, and was indeed both clever and attractive. Hsi-men Ch'ing had entrusted him with the care of the garden, and he slept every night in a small room there. Golden Lotus and Tower of Jade sometimes sewed or played chess in an arbor in the garden. At such times, Ch'in T'ung waited upon them attentively and, whenever Hsi-men Ch'ing was about, would come to give them warning. Golden Lotus liked him, and often summoned him to her room and gave him wine. So morning after morning and evening after evening, they exchanged understanding glances, and were not entirely indifferent to one another.

It was now about the seventh month and Hsi-men's birthday was drawing near. The Moon Lady was well aware of her husband's doings, and once again told Tai An to take a horse and go for him. Golden Lotus privately wrote a note, and told the boy to give it to Hsi-men Ch'ing in secret. "Tell him," she said, "that I hope it will not be long before he comes back." Tai An rode off to the bawdy house, and there found all Hsi-men's boon companions keeping company with him, kissing the girls, and being very merry.

"What has brought you here?" Hsi-men Ch'ing said, when he saw Tai An. "Is there anything wrong at home?" "No," said Tai An. "Well, tell your uncle Fu to collect the money that is owing, and, when I come back, I'll settle up with him."

"He has been collecting some during the last few days," the boy said, "and he is only waiting for you to come home to go through the accounts."

"Did you bring clothes for your Aunt Cassia?"

"Yes," the boy replied, "here they are." He took a red vest and a blue skirt from a parcel, and gave them to the girl. She made a reverence to him, and called for food and wine to be given him. When he had finished, he came over to Hsi-men and whispered in his ear, "The Fifth Lady has given me a note for you, asking you to go home soon."

Hsi-men Ch'ing was just about to take the note when Cassia saw it. She thought it was a love-letter from some other girl, and made a dash for it. When she opened it, she found a sheet of patterned paper with several columns of writing in black ink and handed it to Chu Shih-nien, asking him to read it for her.

> I think of him as evening falls; I think of him when the sky is bright.
> I think about my lover till my thoughts o'erwhelm me, and I faint
> Yet still he does not come.
> For him I am wounded; for him my spirit faints
> Oh, it is sad.
> I lie alone under the figured coverlets; the flickering lamp is nearly out
> The world is sleeping, and the moonbeams creep across the window.
> That heart is unrelenting, like a wolf's;
> How can I bear this agony another night?

Cassia listened to this, then left them and went to her room, where she threw herself face downwards on the bed. Hsi-men Ch'ing saw that she was upset, tore the note to pieces, and kicked Tai An. Twice he implored Cassia to come back, but she paid no heed. Finally, getting more and more excited, he went to her room and carried her out.

"Get on your horse and go home," he said to Tai An; "as for the strumpet who told you to come, when I get home, I'll beat her till she comes to a disgusting end."

Tai An went home with tears in his eyes.

"Please don't be so angry," Hsi-men said, "it is only from my fifth wife. She wants me to go home to talk about something or other. There is nothing else."

Chu Shih-nien teased them. "Don't believe him, Cassia; he is deceiving you. Golden Lotus is his latest flame, a very pretty girl too. Don't let him go."

Hsi-men Ch'ing slapped him. "You ruffian! You'll be the death of somebody with these silly jokes of yours. She is angry enough without your talking rubbish."

"Brother," Cinnamon said, "you are not fair. If you were a good husband, you would not run about teaching singing-girls the arts of love. You should stay at home. Then all would be well. Why, you've only been here a few hours, and now you're getting ready to go away again."

"That's quite true," Po-chüeh said. "You had better take my advice, both of you. Your Lordship must stay here, and you, Cassia, must not lose your temper. The first person to leave will have to spend a couple of taels and treat the rest of us."

Hsi-men Ch'ing took Cassia on his knee, and they drank together happily. Soon afterwards seven cups of the most delicious tea were brought and handed around.

"Now we'll have a song from everyone who can sing," Hsieh Hsi-ta said. "He who can't sing must tell a funny story, and we'll persuade Cassia to take a little more wine with us. I'll begin.

"Once, a bricklayer was doing some paving in a house, and the lady of the house treated him shabbily. So he quietly took a brick or two and stopped up the drain. Not very long afterwards it began to rain and, of course, the water flooded the whole place. The woman didn't know what on earth to do, and ran to find the bricklayer. This time she gave him a meal and offered him some money, and got him to make the water flow again. When he had eaten his fill, he went to the gutter, took the bricks out, and the water flowed away at once. 'What was the matter with it?' the lady of the house asked him. 'Just what the matter is with you,' the bricklayer replied. 'If there is any money about, the water gate will open; but, if not, there will be no admission.' "

Cassia thought that this story was aimed at her, and she lost no time before retaliating.

"I should like to tell you a story," she said. "Once upon a time, Sun, the Immortal, thought he would give a banquet to his friends, and sent his tiger around to invite them. As ill luck would have it, the tiger gobbled them all up on the way. The Immortal waited until it was dark, but nobody came. At last the tiger came back. 'Where are my guests?' the Immortal said. 'Master,' said the tiger, 'I fear I am not a success at inviting people. Somehow I seem much better at eating them up.' "

This did not please the brothers at all. "Oh, indeed," Ying Po-chüeh said, "so we are always sponging, are we?" He took a small silver pin from his hair. Hsieh Hsi-ta found in his hat a pair of gilt rings of no great value. Chu Shih-nien took from his sleeve a tattered old handkerchief worth a couple of hundred coppers. Sun Kua-tsui took a white apron from around his waist. Ch'ang Chih-chieh had nothing, so he borrowed a small piece of silver from Hsi-men Ch'ing. They handed all these things to Cinnamon, and asked her to provide a feast in honor of Hsi-men Ch'ing and Cassia. She turned them over to a servant to buy some pork and chicken, but all the rest she had to pay for herself. Soon everything was brought in, and they sat down. The order was given: "Chopsticks into action." Our description must take time, but there was nothing slow about the movements we describe.

> Then every mouth was opened wide and every head was bent.
> No sun or sky was to be seen; it was like a cloud of locusts.
> They blinked their eyes, their shoulders heaved;
> Starvelings they might have been, from some dark dungeon.
> One quickly snatched a piece of leg, as though no food
> Had passed his lips for years.
> One waved his chopsticks thrice, it was as though for years and years
> He had not seen a meal.
> Sweat trickled down the cheeks of one, he carved a chicken bone
> As though inspired by hatred.
> Gravy adorned his comrade's lips. With copious drafts of spittle

He gobbled down the pork, with hair and skin.
They ate, and in a flash, the cups and plates were clean;
It might have been a den of wolves.
They ate, and in a flash again, the flying chopsticks
Crossed and recrossed the table.
This is the marshal of the King of Gluttons;
This the general of the Lickers-up.
Though it has long been empty, from the wine-jar
They try to fill their cups.
Though all the food has gone long since,
They search and search again.
The luscious meal, with all its hundred flavors,
Has vanished in a moment.
To worship has it gone,
To worship in the temple of the belly.

They cleared up everything till the plates and dishes looked like the head of a shining bald-pated Buddha. Hsi-men Ch'ing and Cassia could get nothing but a cup of wine each. They did indeed pick out a few pieces of food, but the others snatched them away. Two of the chairs were broken. The boys, who were looking after their horses, could not get in to share in the repast, and contented themselves by pulling down the statue of the divinity of the place and piddling upon it. When the time came for them to go away, Sun Kua-tsui took a gilded image of Buddha, which was venerated in an inner room, and slipped it inside his trousers. Ying Po-chüeh pretended to kiss Cassia, and stole a gold pin from her hair. Hsieh Hsi-ta went off with Hsi-men's fan. Chu Shih-nien went secretly to Cinnamon's room and stole her mirror. As for Ch'ang Chih-chieh, he did not hand over the money he had borrowed from Hsi-men Ch'ing, but had the sum put down to his account. They were all in the highest spirits.

When Tai An reached home, he found the Moon Lady, Tower of Jade, and Golden Lotus sitting together. They asked him if his master was coming. "Father kicked me and cursed me," the boy said, his eyes still red. "He says that anyone who tries to get him away will find herself in trouble."

"What an outrageous fellow he is," the Moon Lady cried. "It is quite bad enough that he refuses to come, without ill-treating this poor boy."

"It was bad enough for him to kick the boy, but why should he threaten us?" Tower of Jade said.

"The affection of a dozen of these strumpets wouldn't amount to anything," Golden Lotus said. "There is an old saying that a shipload of gold and silver would never satisfy people of their sort."

Picture of Grace had seen Tai An return, and, as Golden Lotus was speaking, she came to the window and listened. They could not see her. She heard Golden Lotus speak of her family as a host of strumpets. After that, she hated Golden Lotus from the bottom of her heart, and there was always enmity between them.

Golden Lotus, while Hsi-men was away, found that the days passed very slowly. When she realized that he did not mean to return, she waited till her two maids had gone to bed and then, making believe to go and walk in the garden, called Ch'in T'ung to her room and made him drunk. Then she shut her door, undressed, and the pair made love together.

After this, she called the boy to her room every night and kept him there until daybreak. She gave him two or three of her golden pins, and put them in his hair. On another occasion she gave him a perfume-box which she wore on her skirt. Unfortunately, the boy was not very discreet and, as he frequently went drinking and gambling with his fellow-servants, it was not long before the affair became known. As the proverb says, "If you would have none to know your secret, you must do no evil." One day the rumor came to the ears of Beauty of the Snow and Picture of Grace.

"That thievish strumpet has been high and mighty for a long time," they said, "but now we have her." They went and told the Moon Lady. She would not believe a word they said.

"You only wish to make things unpleasant for her," she said, "but you will annoy the Third Lady, and she will say you are slandering her boy." They said no more, and went away.

That evening Golden Lotus and the boy were amusing themselves. The woman had forgotten to shut the kitchen door. The maid Chrysanthemum chanced to use that door on her way to the privy, and saw everything that was going on. The next morning, she told Tiny Jade, and Tiny Jade told Beauty of Snow.

Once again Beauty of Snow and Picture of Grace went to tell the Moon Lady. They gave her all the details, and added, "Her own maid told us about it; it is not something we have invented to get her into trouble. If you will not do anything in the matter, we will tell Father ourselves. If he can forgive a whore like this, he can forgive a scorpion."

It was the twenty-seventh day of the seventh month when Hsi-men Ch'ing came back from the bawdy house to celebrate his birthday.

"He has just come back," the Moon Lady said to the two women, "and this should be a happy day for him. If you will not listen to me, and are still determined to tell him, I will not be responsible for the consequences."

They paid no attention to her, and, as soon as Hsi-men came in, they both ran up and told him that Golden Lotus was carrying on with one of the boys. Hsi-men Ch'ing had been in an amiable mood, but at this he flew into a towering rage. He went to the front court, and called, "Ch'in T'ung! Ch'in T'ung!" over and over again. Golden Lotus had heard what was happening, and, with trembling hands and feet, she told Plum Blossom to call the boy to her room. She begged him not to say a word to his master, and took the pins out of his hair, but she was so excited that she forgot the perfume-box.

Hsi-men Ch'ing ordered the boy to the hall and made him kneel down. Then he told some of the other servants to get a large bamboo and make it ready for use.

"You rascally slave," he cried, "do you confess your guilt?" Ch'in T'ung made no reply.

"Take out his pins and let me see them," Hsi-men said to the boys. They looked but could not find any.

"What have you done with the silver pin with a golden head?"

"I have no silver pin," Ch'in T'ung said.

"Ah, you slave, you think you will deceive me, do you?" Hsi-men said, and ordered the boys to take down his trousers. Three or four of them stripped Ch'in T'ung. On his jade-colored short trousers he was wearing, the perfume-box hung. As soon as Hsi-men caught sight of it, he made the boys show it to him, and recognized at once that it was the same one that used to hang on Golden Lotus's skirt.

"Where did you get this?" he cried in a fury. "Tell me the truth. Who gave it to you?"

The boy was so terrified that it was a long time before he could speak, but at last he said, "I was tidying the garden one day and picked it up. Nobody gave it to me."

This reply made Hsi-men still more angry. He bit his lips and told his servants to beat the boy with all their strength. Ch'in T'ung was bound and given thirty terrible stripes till his flesh was torn and the blood ran down his legs. Then Hsi-men told Lai Pao to cut the boy's hair at the temples and turn him out, and on no account to allow him to return. Ch'in T'ung kotowed, wept, and went away.

Golden Lotus soon heard all that had happened and felt as though a stream of icy water had been poured over her. It was not long before Hsi-men Ch'ing arrived. She was so frightened that she trembled, and the blood in her veins seemed to freeze. She went forward to take his clothes, but Hsi-men Ch'ing boxed her ears so hard that he knocked her down. Then he told Plum Blossom to shut all the doors and keep everybody out. He took a small chair, went out, and sat in the courtyard in a shady place. Then he took a horse-whip and made the woman take off her clothes and kneel before him. She bowed her white face, but did not dare to make a sound.

"You rascally whore," Hsi-men cried, "don't pretend you are dreaming. I have questioned that slave and he has confessed everything. You had better tell me the truth. When I was away, how many times did you play your games with that boy?"

"Oh, Heavens! Heavens!" Golden Lotus said, sobbing, "somebody has been telling lies about me, and I shall die if you believe them. All these days you've been away, I have spent my whole time sewing with Tower of Jade. As soon as it was dark, I locked my door and went to bed. Unless there was something very urgent, I never ventured to go beyond the corner door. If you don't believe me, ask Plum Blossom. There was nothing I could do without her seeing." She called to Plum Blossom, "Sister, come here and tell your Father all about it."

"You rascally whore," Hsi-men said again, "I know you gave the boy two or three gold pins. Why don't you admit it?"

"These suspicions will be the death of me," Golden Lotus cried. "Some nasty-minded strumpet who will come to a foul end has been telling you lies. I suppose she was jealous because she saw you always coming to sleep in my room. You know how many pins there were; there is not one missing. Count them yourself and see. How can you suspect me of being so base as to carry on with a slave? If he were a full-grown slave, they would probably tell the same story, but this short-haired lad is hardly out of his cradle. There is not a word of truth in the story. They have made up the whole chapter of scandal."

"We will leave the pins out of it," Hsi-men said, taking the perfume-box from his sleeve. "This, I think, belongs to you. How do I come to find it on that boy's person? Now perhaps you will not have so much to say." And, with these words, Crash! fell the whip on her delicate white body. The pain was so great that she burst into tears.

"Oh, dear good Father," she cried, "you mustn't treat me like this. If you will only give me a chance, I can explain everything. If you won't give me the chance but beat me to death, you'll make a very nasty mess here. As for that perfume-box, one day when you were away, Tower of Jade and I were doing some needlework in the garden. It wasn't firmly attached, and it must have fallen down as I was going through the flower arbor. I looked everywhere for it, but the boy must have picked it up. I am sure I did not give it to him."

This certainly seemed to agree with what Ch'in T'ung had said. Hsi-men looked again at the woman. Her flower-like body, unclothed, was kneeling as she uttered these softening words and wept so touchingly. His anger flew to Java, and he began to cool down. He called Plum Blossom and kissed her.

"Did she play heads and tails with that boy? If you tell me I ought to forgive the little strumpet, I will do so."

Plum Blossom sat on his knee and made herself most charming and affectionate. "Father," she said, "you are making a fool of yourself. Mother and I never left one another the whole time. How can you possibly imagine that she would have anything to do with that slave? No, the whole thing is a plot made up by somebody who is jealous. You must deal with the matter yourself, Father. If the story gets about, and you make yourself a laughing-stock, that won't be very pleasant."

Hsi-men Ch'ing could say no more. He told Golden Lotus to stand up and dress, and bade Chrysanthemum prepare a meal. Golden Lotus poured out a full cup of wine and, offering it to him with both hands, knelt to wait for its return.

"This time I forgive you," Hsi-men said. "Whenever I am away, you must keep your mind pure and your ways clean. Shut your door early, and be on your guard against thoughts of evil. If I ever hear of anything of this sort again, there will be no more forgiveness."

"Your word is my law," Golden Lotus said meekly. She kotowed four times, and sat down to drink with him.

So Golden Lotus, despite the high favor in which she was held by her husband, brought shame upon herself.

Hsi-men Ch'ing was drinking wine in Golden Lotus's room when a boy knocked at the door and told him that the Moon Lady's two brothers, Fu, the manager of his shop, Hsi-men's daughter Orchid and her husband, and several other relatives had called to congratulate him on his birthday. He left Golden Lotus and went to receive his guests. Ying Po-chüeh, Hsieh Hsi-ta, and the other brothers had also brought presents. Even Cassia had sent a servant with a gift. Hsi-men Ch'ing was soon very busy receiving all his presents and sending out letters of invitation in return.

Meanwhile Tower of Jade, who had heard all about Golden Lotus's trouble, seized the opportunity while Hsi-men was not there, and went to see her without the others knowing anything about it. When she came, Golden Lotus was lying on the bed.

"Do tell me what it is all about, Sister," she said.

Golden Lotus cried bitterly. "That little strumpet has been telling tales about me. She made our husband so angry that he thrashed me. I hate those two whores with a hate as deep as the ocean."

"If you had to play tricks with the boy," Tower of Jade said, "you might at least have made sure that I shouldn't lose him. But don't be unhappy. Our husband is bound to look at things from our point of view. If he comes to see me tomorrow, I shall tell him what I think about him."

"It is good of you to trouble about me," Golden Lotus said. She called Plum Blossom and told her to serve tea. They chatted for a while, and Tower of Jade went back to her own rooms. That night, Mistress Wu was staying with the Moon Lady and Hsi-men Ch'ing went to sleep with Tower of Jade.

"It was very wrong of you to distress Golden Lotus so unreasonably," Tower of Jade said. "She did not do anything. This trouble has all come from her quarrel with Beauty of the Snow and Picture of Grace. Without taking the trouble to make any inquiries, you had my boy beaten. You have certainly been most unjust, and it makes things very awkward for the poor woman. Do you imagine our mistress would not have told you, if there had been any truth in the story?"

"I did ask Plum Blossom," Hsi-men Ch'ing said, "and she said exactly what you say."

"The Fifth Lady is very much upset," Tower of Jade said. "Why don't you go and see her?"

"I will go and see her tomorrow," Hsi-men promised.

The next day was Hsi-men's birthday, and many visitors came to take wine with him, Major Chou, the magistrate Hsia, Captain Chang, and Uncle Wu, the Moon Lady's brother. Hsi-men Ch'ing sent a sedan-chair for Cassia, and engaged two singing-girls, who performed throughout the day.

As soon as her niece arrived, Picture of Grace took her to visit the Moon Lady and the others, and she drank tea with them. They asked Golden Lotus to come and see her, and twice a maid went to her room to invite her, but she said she was not very well and refused to come. Later in the evening, when Cassia was about to go home, the Moon Lady gave her a silk handkerchief and some artificial flowers, and went with Picture of Grace to see her off. Cassia was anxious to go to the garden and pay her respects to Golden Lotus, but as soon as Golden Lotus heard she was coming, she told Plum Blossom to bolt and bar the corner door. When Cassia got there, Plum Blossom said, "My Mistress's orders. I dare not open the door." Cassia had to go away, greatly abashed.

That evening Hsi-men Ch'ing went to see Golden Lotus. Her beautiful tresses were all in disorder, and she seemed very weary and faded. But when he came, she took his clothes, served him tea, brought hot water to wash his feet, and showed him a hundred signs of affection. That night, as they played together, she did for him whatever he asked of her.

"Brother," she said, "who in all this household really cares about you? They are all just stale married women, nothing more. I am the only one who understands you, and you understand me. The others see that you show me favor and spend most of your time here; it makes them jealous, and they try to vent their spite on me. How could you be caught by such talk, and treat me so unkindly? There is an old saying, 'When a farmyard chicken is beaten, it turns round and round; a wild one flies away.' You may beat me to death, but I shall never run away. The other day, when you were at the bawdy house and kicked Tai An, I never complained. The Great Lady and Tower of Jade know that quite well. I said I was afraid the girls there would do you no good. I said singing-girls in places like that care for nothing but money. What is true love to them? Is there a single one of them who really loves you? That is all I said. Somebody came slyly up and secretly listened, and then they plotted together to get me in disgrace. Fortunately, while people may injure others, they cannot kill them; it is only those whom Heaven wishes to destroy who die. In the future you will realize that I am speaking the truth, and you will know what to do if such a thing happens again."

Hsi-men Ch'ing was completely won over, and his delight in her was greater than ever.

Some days afterwards he mounted his horse and went off to the bawdy house, attended by Tai An and P'ing An. Cassia had other visitors, but as soon as she heard he was coming, she went to her room, washed off her powder, removed her rings and ornaments, lay down on the bed, and pulled the bedclothes over her. Hsi-men Ch'ing came in. He waited for a long time before the old woman appeared and made a reverence to him.

"Why is it so long since you were here?" the old lady said. She asked him to take a seat.

"I was very busy on my birthday," Hsi-men Ch'ing said, "and there is no one at home who seems able to attend to things."

"I am afraid my daughter must have been a trouble to you," the old lady said.

Hsi-men asked why Cinnamon did not come to see him on his birthday. The old woman told him that she had been away; a traveler had taken her to stay with him at the inn, and she was still there. They talked for a while, and the old woman offered him tea.

"Where is Cassia?" Hsi-men said at length.

"Don't you know, Sir!" the old woman said. "Ever since the child came back from your house, she has been terribly overwrought. She is not at all well. I can't tell you what the matter is with her, but she has stayed in bed all the time and refused to leave her room. You must have a heart like a wolf's not to have been to see her before."

"This is the first I have heard of it," Hsi-men said. "Where is she? I will go and see her."

"She is lying down in her bedroom," the old lady said. She told a maid to go and raise the lattice. Hsi-men Ch'ing went into the room. Cassia, covered with the bedclothes, was sitting on the bed, her face turned to the wall; her hair was in disorder and she seemed in a sad way. She did not move when Hsi-men came in.

"Why have you been ill since you were at my place?" Hsi-men said. The girl did not reply.

"What has made you so angry? Tell me."

He questioned her for a long time, and at last she said, "It is all your Fifth Lady's doing. Since you have someone in your own home who is as good as any strumpet, I can't imagine why you come here and make love to a wicked girl like me. I may have been brought up in this house, but I don't believe I'm any worse than some in other houses I could mention. I did not go as a singing-girl that day; I came to give you a present. Your great lady was very kind and gave me flowers and clothes, and when I heard you had a fifth lady, I asked to be allowed to pay my respects to her. If I hadn't done so, she would have said that the girls from the bawdy house are very ill-mannered, but I *did* ask, and she refused to see me. When I was leaving your house, I asked once more, and she ordered her maid to shut the door in my face. Really she is lacking in the very elements of politeness."

"You mustn't blame her too much," Hsi-men Ch'ing said. "She wasn't very well that day. If she had been, I'm sure she wouldn't have refused to come and see you. But I've often felt like giving that little strumpet a beating. She's always hurting somebody with that sharp tongue of hers."

Cassia slapped him lightly on the face. "Why haven't you beaten her, then, you shameless fellow?"

"You don't know how severe I can be," Hsi-men Ch'ing said. "I have punished most unmercifully all the women and maids in my house, except, of course, my first wife. Sometimes I use a whip upon them twenty or thirty times or even more, and sometimes I cut their hair off."

"Oh," said Cassia, "I've met men before who talk about cutting the hair off their womenfolk, but never one who did more than brag about it. You may have bowed three times and made reverence twice to them for all anybody could prove. If you mean what you say, go home and cut off a single tress, bring it here, and show it to me. If you do that, I'll believe you are the greatest hero there is in this part of the world."

"Your hand upon it," Hsi-men cried.

"A hundred times, if it pleases you."

Hsi-men Ch'ing spent the night with Cassia, and the next day, as he was mounting his horse to go home, she called after him, "If you don't bring it to me, don't dare to show your face here again."

This made Hsi-men very excited, especially as he was already half drunk. As soon as he got home, he went straight to Golden Lotus's room. She saw that he had had some wine, and was most careful in her attentions. She offered him something to eat, but he would have none of it. He told Plum Blossom to make the bed, then sent her away and shut the door. He sat on the bed and ordered the woman to take off his shoes. She took them off. Then he got onto the bed, but he would not go to sleep, and sat on a pillow. He bade Golden Lotus undress and kneel down. She was so terrified that the sweat rolled down her body. She had not the faintest notion what was amiss, and could only kneel down sobbing quietly.

"Father," she said, "tell me what is wrong, even if it kills me. I have been so careful all day, and still I don't seem to satisfy you. You are just sawing me asunder with a blunt knife. How can I bear it?"

"You rascally little whore," Hsi-men cried, "if you don't take your clothes off, I will show you no mercy." He called to Plum Blossom, "Bring me the whip that is hanging behind the door."

Plum Blossom would not go into the room, and he had to call for a long time before she slowly pushed the door open and went in. Golden Lotus was on her knees, and the lamp had fallen down beside the table. In spite of Hsi-men's orders, the maid did not obey him.

"Plum Blossom, Sister, please help me," Golden Lotus cried, "he is going to beat me again."

"Don't worry about her, little oily mouth," Hsi-men said. "Give me the whip. I am going to beat the strumpet."

"How can you be so shameless, Father?" Plum Blossom cried. "What has Mother done wrong? You seem to listen to anything any bad woman likes to tell you, making a storm in a teacup all the time. Mother is one heart and mind with you. What makes you so changeable? I shall not do what you say." She shut the door and went out. Hsi-men Ch'ing could only burst out laughing.

"I won't beat you this time," he said to Golden Lotus. "Come here, I want you to give me something. Will you give it me or not?"

"My precious darling," Golden Lotus said, "I belong to you, heart and soul. Whatever you ask, it is yours. What do you want?"

"I want some of your hair," Hsi-men said.

"Heavens!" Golden Lotus cried, "if you had asked me to set myself on fire, I would have done it. But to cut off my hair . . . that is too much. You must wish to frighten me to death. From the day of birth, twenty-six years until this very day, I have never done such a thing. And lately my hair has been falling out of its own accord. Do, please, spare me that indignity."

"You are always complaining about my bad temper," Hsi-men Ch'ing said, "yet you won't do a single thing I ask you."

"If I don't obey you, I don't obey anybody. But tell me, why do you want my hair?"

"I am thinking of having a hairnet made," Hsi-men said.

"If you want a net, I will make one for you, but you must not take my hair to that strumpet to lay a spell on me."

"I won't give it to anybody," Hsi-men said, "but I must have your hair to make the foundation for a net."

"Very well," Golden Lotus said, "in that case I will let you cut some off." She parted her hair. Hsi-men took a pair of scissors and cut a large tress from the crown of her head. He wrapped it in paper and put it in his sleeve. Golden Lotus pressed close to him and wept quietly.

"I will do anything you wish," she said. "The only thing I ask is that you love me always. You may play with others as much as you please, but you must not forget me."

That night their joy in each other seemed more glorious than ever. The next morning, when Hsi-men Ch'ing got up, she served him with tea; then he mounted his horse and rode to the bawdy house.

"Where is the hair you were going to cut off?" Cassia cried.

"Here you are," said Hsi-men. He took the hair from his sleeve and handed it to her. She opened the packet. It contained a tress of beautiful hair, as black as the blackest coal. She put it into her sleeve.

"You have seen it now," Hsi-men said. "Give it back to me. She was terribly upset because I insisted on cutting off that hair, and, until I changed countenance and frightened her, she wouldn't hear of my cutting it off. I told her I wanted it to make a net. You see, I have brought it to you. Perhaps now you will believe that I always do what I say."

"I don't see why you should be so alarmed," Cassia said. "There is nothing so very extraordinary about it. I'll let you have it before you go. You shouldn't have taken it if you are so frightened of her."

"What makes you think I'm afraid of her?" Hsi-men Ch'ing said, laughing. "If I were I shouldn't tell anybody."

Cassia asked her sister to take wine with Hsi-men Ch'ing, and, going to a quiet place, put some of the hair into her shoe, that she might tread it underfoot every day. She kept Hsi-men a prisoner for several days and would not allow him to go home.

Golden Lotus was very unhappy for several days after her hair had been cut. She refused to leave her room, and seemed too languid to take food or tea. The Moon Lady sent one of the boys to bring old woman Liu, an old favorite of hers, to see what the matter was.

"The lady is suffering from some secret grief," the old woman said, "and because the trouble is insistent and she can't free herself from it, she has headaches and gnawing pains at the heart, and does not feel inclined to take her food."

She opened her medicine-box, and, taking out two black pills, told Golden Lotus to take them in the evening with some ginger-water. "I will bring my husband tomorrow," she said. "He will tell your fortune for the coming year and see whether there is any bad luck in store."

"Can your husband really see what is in one's life?" Golden Lotus asked.

"He is blind," the old woman said, "but there are three things he can do. He can tell fortunes and read the yin-yang, and so save people from misadventure. He can bleed the sick, cauterize, and cure cysts. The third thing is only to be mentioned with discretion, but, as a matter of fact, he can make philtres to change people's hearts."

"What are these philtres for?" Golden Lotus said.

"Well," old woman Liu said, "suppose father and son do not agree as well as they might, or there is a slight misunderstanding between brothers, or a quarrel between wives. If my husband is told the true state of affairs, he will make a spell and write a charm. This is put in water, and the people concerned are given it to drink. Three days after drinking this water, father and son will love one another again, brothers will reach a perfect understanding, and wives will live in harmony together.

"Again, when a man is unsuccessful in business, or his lands and family are not doing very well, my husband can produce the necessary money and increase profits. And when it comes to curing illnesses and making people immune, praying to the stars and invoking the planets, my husband is absolutely a master. People call him Liu the Master of the Stars. I remember the case of a household where there was a new wife who came from a family which was none too well-off. She was inclined to be light-fingered, and was always stealing things from her mother-in-law to give to her own people. When her husband found her out, he beat her. My husband exercised his art on her behalf, made a charm, and when it had been burned to ashes, the ashes were put into the cistern. The whole family drank the water from this cistern, and afterwards, even if they actually saw her stealing, they didn't seem to realize what she was about. He also put another charm under her pillow, and when her husband had once slept on that pillow, his hands might have been tied, for he could not beat her any more."

Golden Lotus listened to this and stored it away in her mind. She told the maid to give the old woman some tea and cakes, and, when she was about to take her departure, she gave her not only three small pieces of silver for her fee, but five more to buy the materials needed for making a charm. She told her to bring the blind man early the next day so that he could burn the charm. The old woman went home, and the next morning very early she brought the blind old rascal to the gate and was about to go to the inner court. Hsi-men Ch'ing was standing in the courtyard, and the gatekeeper asked the blind man what his business was.

"We have come to burn some papers for the Fifth Lady," the old woman said.

"Very well, in you go," the boy said, "but mind the dog doesn't bite you."

The old woman led her husband to Golden Lotus's apartments, and they waited some time for her. When she came, the blind man made a reverence to her; then they sat down, and Golden Lotus told him the eight characters of her destiny. The blind rascal reckoned for a while on his fingers and said, "Lady, I will now interpret the eight characters of your destiny. They are *Keng Ch'en* for the year, *Keng Yin* for the month, *Yi Hai* for the day, and *Chi Ch'ou* for the hour of your birth. The eighth of the month is the Spring Day, we must reckon your fate as from the first month. According to the admirable doctrine of Tzu P'ing, though your eight characters are indeed both clear and remarkable, you will never have the husband-star in a favorable conjunction. The question of children, too, does not seem to be decided in your favor. The *Yi* tree grows in the first month and, though this would seem to show that you will enjoy good health, you must be careful lest you overdo things. *Keng* gold appears twice, and the *Yang Jen* star is unduly prominent, while the husband-star is very troublesome. I should say that you will only reach contentment when you have outlived two husbands."

"I have already outlived one," Golden Lotus said.

"I beg you to excuse me, Lady," the blind rascal went on, "but though your life appears to be of the type known as *Sha Yin,* you are handicapped by the fact that there is the water of *Kuei* in the *Hai* as well as in the *Ch'ou.* This is decidedly a superabundance of water, and it rushes out of a single *Chi* earth. The stars *Kuan* and *Sha* are confused. In the case of a man, if the influence of the *Sha* star is predominant, he will attain to dignity and prominence, but, in the case of a woman, such a state of affairs indicates that she will be dangerous to her husbands. The fact that you belong to this class shows that you know very well what you're about and that you attract men.

"With regard to your fortune for the present year, this year is *Chia Ch'en* in the cycle, and this is a sign of coming calamity. The two stars *Hsiao Hao* and *Kou Chiao* are influencing you, and, though this does not indicate any real catastrophe, you will have trouble from friends and relations, and backbiters will prove a nuisance."

"It is kind of you to have gone so carefully into all this for me," Golden Lotus said, "and now I should like you to make a spell for me. Here is a tael of silver to spend on a cup of tea. All I want is that backbiters shall leave me in peace, and that my husband shall have a high esteem for me." She went to her room, found a couple of hair ornaments, and gave them to the blind man. He put them in his sleeve.

"If you would like me to make a spell," he said, "I shall take a piece of willow-wood and fashion it into two figures, one male and the other female. On one I shall write your husband's eight characters and on the other your own. Then I shall bind them together with forty-nine red threads. I shall cover the man's eyes with a piece of red cloth and stuff him with the leaves of artemisia. I shall put a needle through his hands and stick the feet with gum. You must put the figures under his pillow, secretly. I shall also write a charm in red ink, and the ashes of this you must put into his tea. Then providing he sleeps on this pillow, you will see the result in three days at the utmost."

"What is the meaning of all this?" Golden Lotus said.

"I will explain," the old rogue replied. "The covering of the eyes with cloth will make you appear to him as beautiful as Hsi Shih. Stuffing the figure with artemisia will make him love you. If I put a needle through his hands, that will ensure that, whatever your faults, he will not be able to raise his hand against you. Finally, the sticking of the feet with gum will prevent his wandering away from you."

Golden Lotus found this extremely satisfactory, and she wasted no time in getting candles and paper to burn the charms. The next day old woman Liu brought them, with water and the spell-figures. Golden Lotus did with them as she had been told. She burned the charm to ashes, and prepared some of the best tea. When Hsi-men Ch'ing came back, she told Plum Blossom to give him some of the tea. That night they slept on the same pillow. Two or three days passed, and their happiness was as great as that of fishes sporting in the water.

Readers, every household, no matter whether it be great or small, should make a rule that nuns, priests, nurses, and procuresses like these should always be kept at a distance.

Translated by Clement Egerton

261
Wu Sung Fights the Tiger

from *Water Margin*

Anonymous
Commentary by Chin Sheng-t'an (1610?–1661)

Now we'll divide the story and tell of how Wu Sung, after he left Sung Chiang, put up at an inn that evening. The next morning he lit up the fire and had breakfast, and after settling the account he packed, carried his club [*Club: the fifth time.*] and set out again. He thought to himself, "I have heard much about the Opportune Rain, Sung Kung-ming,[1] among men of rivers and lakes. It is really not false talk. To become a sworn brother with such a person is not in vain." [*Flowers in the mirror and the moon in water. An ordinary writer wouldn't be able to paint such a picture. This is truly a piece of writing concocted out of thin air.*]

After traveling on the road for a few days, Wu Sung came to the district of

---

This famous and exciting episode involving a life-and-death struggle between man and beast is taken from *Water Margin* (*Shui-hu chuan*), one of the earliest Chinese novels written in the vernacular language. Greatly indebted to a rich oral tradition, the novel came into existence probably during the fourteenth century and is attributed variously to Shih Nai-an (late Yüan–early Ming) and Lo Kuan-chung (see selection 258, introductory note). It celebrates the exploits of a band of a hundred and eight colorful, daredevil bandit-heroes who dare to rob the wealthy and powerful and fight against government troops. In this excerpt, the hero, Wu Sung, fights with the tiger in the days before he joined the band.

Most of the old editions of the novel were printed with comments made by later readers. Of all the running commentaries for the novel, the one by Chin Sheng-t'an is the most widely known. As can be seen in the episode here, Chin's comments (italicized and enclosed in brackets) are lively and idiosyncratic, and at their best they enhance the reader's appreciation of the dazzling narrative skill demonstrated by the author. The celebrated modern essayist Chou Tso-jen (1885–1967) put it best when he explained why he liked to read the novel together with Chin's commentary: "Of all commentaries on fiction, Chin Sheng-t'an's are of course the best. . . . When I read *Water Margin*, I pay equal attention to the main text and to the comments. It is like eating white fungus (*pai mu-erh,* a Chinese delicacy); they taste even better eaten with soup."

1. I.e., Sung Chiang.

Yang-ku. There was still some distance to the district town. That day, toward noon, Wu Sung walked until he was both hungry and thirsty. He saw in the distance a wine-shop with a pennant sticking out in front of the door. On the pennant were written five characters: No Crossing After Three Bowls. [*Extraordinary writing.*] [Comments on upper margin: *The next few chapters from here on all describe Wu Sung's supernatural valor. The wine drinking here should be read as one section, the fight with the tiger as another.*]

Wu Sung entered the wine-shop and sat down; leaning the club to the side [*Club: the sixth time.*], he called, "Shop owner, bring out your wine right away so I can drink." [*Wu Number Two was fond of wine all his life. From this very first sentence spoken by him, it is as though we can hear his voice and see his person.*] Then we see the shop owner bring three bowls [*Extraordinary writing.*], a pair of chopsticks, and a plate of freshly cooked vegetables and set them out in front of Wu Sung. He then poured wine to fill one bowl to the brim. [*The first bowl. In this, the first segment, the author describes the action bowl by bowl. In the second, third, and fourth segments, he writes segment by segment. In the fifth and sixth segments, he writes both at once.*] Wu Sung took up the bowl and downed it at one gulp. "What potent wine!" he cried out. [*We know what the wine is like.*] "Shop owner, if you have anything that's filling, I want to buy some to go with the wine." [*He calls for wine first and then meat. So we can understand which one is more important to him. I have heard that meat-eaters are despicable. As for wine, no person of an unconventional bent doesn't like it.*] "There is only cooked beef," said the owner. "Bring me two or three catties[2] of the best part to eat," said Wu Sung.

The shop owner went inside to cut up two catties of cooked beef. Putting everything on a big platter, he brought it out and placed it before Wu Sung. At the same time he poured another bowl of wine. [*The second bowl.*] "Excellent wine," said Wu Sung after finishing it. [*Again he praises the wine. We know therefore it is good wine.*] The shop owner again poured a bowl. [*The third bowl.*] After Wu Sung finished drinking the third bowl of wine, the shop owner never came out again. [*Extraordinary writing.*] Knocking on the table, Wu Sung cried out, "Shop owner, why aren't you coming to pour more wine?" The owner replied, "If you want more meat, sir, I will bring some." [*The reply doesn't match the question. Hilarious!*] "I also want wine," said Wu Sung, "and cut more meat too." "I will cut the meat and bring it to you," said the owner. "As for wine, I will not add any more."

"What is the meaning of all this?" said Wu Sung, perplexed, and he proceeded to ask the shop owner, "Why don't you want to sell wine to me?" "Sir," said the owner, "surely you can see the pennant in front of the door. On it is clearly written 'No Crossing After Three Bowls.' " "What do you mean by 'No Crossing After Three Bowls'?" asked Wu Sung. "Although my

2. A catty is equal to about 1⅓ pounds.

wine is the rustic kind," said the owner, "it is as tasty as the old brews. All the guests who come to my shop get drunk after three bowls and are not able to cross the mountain ridge ahead. Hence, we say 'No Crossing After Three Bowls.' Traveling guests who pass by here never ask for more after three bowls." [*Ordinary folks are not worth mentioning.*]

Wu Sung laughed and said, "So that's what you mean. I have had three bowls; how come I am not drunk?" "This wine of mine is called 'Bottle Penetrating Fragrance' [*Good name.*]. It is also known as 'Fall Down Outside the Door' [*Good name.*]. It tastes rich and mellow when you first sip it, but in a short while you will fall down." "Don't talk nonsense," said Wu Sung. "It is not like I am not paying. Pour me three more bowls."

Seeing that Wu Sung was not affected at all, the owner poured three more bowls. [*The fourth bowl, fifth bowl, and sixth bowl.*] "Truly fine wine," said Wu Sung after finishing. [*Again he praises the wine profusely. We know it is good wine.*] "Shop owner, every time I finish one bowl I will give you money for it. So just keep pouring." "Sir," said the owner, "please don't keep drinking. This wine will really make you drunk and there is no antidote for it." "Stop your cursed talk," said Wu Sung. "I'll be able to smell it even if you put a narcotic in the wine." Unable to gainsay him, the shop owner again poured three bowls in a row. [*The seventh bowl, eighth bowl, and ninth bowl.*]

"Bring me two more catties of meat," Wu Sung demanded. [*The author writes about Wu Sung's capacity for food while writing about his drinking ability. All this is to show his valor.*] After cutting two more catties of cooked beef, the owner again poured three bowls of wine. [*The tenth bowl, eleventh bowl, and twelfth bowl.*] His appetite now fully activated, Wu Sung kept asking for more. Fishing out some loose silver that he carried with him, he called, "Shop owner, come and look at my silver. Is it enough to pay for the wine and meat?" [*The author switches to another way of writing. I cannot help roaring with laughter in reading this.*] Taking a look, the owner said, "More than enough. You should get some change back." [*Marvelous thought and marvelous writing. We can see that the wine-shop owner doesn't want to sell any more wine.*] "I don't want your change," said Wu Sung. "Just keep the wine coming." "Sir," said the owner, "if you want more wine, there are only five or six bowls left. But I am afraid you cannot take any more." "If you still have as many as five or six bowls," Wu Sung demanded, "pour them all out for me." "If a tall fellow like you falls down drunk," said the owner, "who can prop you up?" [*All of a sudden, as though out of nowhere, Wu Sung's features are revealed through the eyes and mouth of the wine-shop owner. How can an ordinary writer describe this?*] "I am no brave man if I need you to prop me up," replied Wu Sung. But the owner refused to bring the wine out.

Agitated, Wu Sung said, "I am not drinking for nothing. Don't get your old Daddy upset, or I will smash up everything in this room and turn your cursed shop upside down." The owner said to himself, "This fellow is drunk.

I'd better not provoke him." He poured six more bowls for Wu Sung. [*The thirteenth bowl, fourteenth bowl, fifteenth bowl, sixteenth bowl, seventeenth bowl, and eighteenth bowl.*] Altogether Wu Sung drank eighteen bowls of wine. [*A concluding sentence.*]

Picking up his club, Wu Sung stood up [*Club: the seventh time. Throughout this episode the author singles out the club for special description at every turn. His intention is to make the reader feel that when later on Wu Sung suddenly confronts the tiger he can rely on this thing completely without any fear. Who could anticipate that something unexpected is going to happen that would frighten the reader to death? Picking up his club—the first posture he assumes with the club.*] [Comments on upper margin: *In writing about the club, the author has Wu Sung assume countless postures.*] and said, "I am not drunk." Walking out the door, he laughed and said, "Who says 'No Crossing After Three Bowls'?!" [*Amusing.*] Carrying his club, he walked away. [*Club: the eighth time. Carrying his club—the second posture he assumes with the club.*]

The wine-shop owner ran after him and called out, "Where are you going, sir?" [*Extraordinary writing.*] Wu Sung halted and asked, "What are you calling me for? I don't owe you any wine money. Why do you beckon me?" [*The author again creates waves.*] "I mean well," the owner called out. "Please come back to my house and see an official proclamation copied on a piece of paper." [*Extraordinary writing.*] "What proclamation?" Wu Sung asked. "Nowadays," said the owner, "there is a tiger with slanting eyes and a white forehead on the Ching-yang Ridge ahead. At night it comes out to harm people. It has already killed twenty or thirty big, stout fellows. The authorities now have given a deadline to the hunters to capture the tiger on pain of flogging. The proclamation is posted on every road near the ridge instructing passing travelers to cross the ridge in groups and during the hours from mid-morning to mid-afternoon. They are not allowed to cross the ridge during hours immediately before and after. Single travelers especially must wait to form groups before they can cross. It's going to be late afternoon pretty soon. Seeing you leave without asking people, I am afraid you might lose your life in vain. Why don't you put up at my place for now? Tomorrow, when twenty or thirty people have gathered, you may cross the ridge together."

Upon hearing this, Wu Sung laughed and said, "I am a resident of nearby Ch'ing-ho district. I must have crossed this Ching-yang Ridge at least ten or twenty times. Whoever has heard of a tiger? Don't scare me with this cursed talk of yours. I am not afraid even if there is a tiger." "I am trying to save you out of compassion," said the wine-shop owner. "If you don't believe me, come in and read the official proclamation." "You are just making some cursed noise," said Wu Sung. "Your old Daddy is not afraid even if there is really a tiger. You want me to put up at your place—could it be because you want to rob and kill me in the middle of the night and therefore scare me with this cursed tiger?" "Look, you," said the owner. "I do this completely out of compassion and yet you think I harbor evil intentions. If you don't believe me, just go as you please." While saying this, he shook his head and went back into his shop. [*The owner's change of countenance is described as vividly as a painting.*]

Wu Sung carried his club [*Club: the ninth time. Carried his club—the third posture he assumes with the club.*], and in big strides went toward the Ching-yang Ridge. After having gone about four or five tricents, he came to the foot of the ridge. There he saw a huge tree, the bark of which had been scraped away, so that there was a patch of white wood. On the white patch were written two columns of characters. Wu Sung could recognize quite a few characters, so when he raised his head to look, he saw there written: "Because of the tiger on the Ching-yang Ridge that has been inflicting harm on the people recently, if there are travelers passing, they should cross the ridge in groups and between the hours from mid-morning to mid-afternoon. Please do not endanger yourselves." [*Extraordinary writing.*]

After having read the notice, Wu Sung laughed and said, "This is a trick played by the innkeeper to frighten the travelers so that they will stay in his inn. What cursed thing should I be afraid of?" Holding his club sideways [*Club: the tenth time. Holding his club sideways—the fourth posture he assumes with the club.*], he walked up the ridge.

At that time it was already late in the afternoon, and the red sun, like a wheel, was slowly rolling down the side of the mountain. [*Frightening scenery.*]

Wu Sung walked up the ridge heedlessly on the strength of the wine. In less than half a tricent, he came upon an abandoned shrine to the mountain spirit. [*Extraordinary writing. Were it not for this shrine, there would be almost no place for pasting the proclamation.*] Approaching the front of the shrine, he saw pasted on the door a proclamation with an official seal. When Wu Sung stopped to read, he saw there written: "A Proclamation from the district of Yang-ku: On Ching-yang Ridge, recently a tiger has taken the lives of people. At present, the heads of various villages as well as hunters have been given a deadline for capturing the tiger on pain of flogging. They have not yet succeeded. For this reason, if there are any passing travelers, they are instructed to cross the ridge in groups and during the hours from mid-morning to mid-afternoon. No one is allowed to cross the ridge by himself, or at other times, lest he lose his life. Everyone should take note of this. Proclaimed on such a day in such a month of such a year in the reign period Cheng-ho." [*Extraordinary writing.*]

After finishing the proclamation, Wu Sung began to realize that truly there was a tiger. He was about to turn around to go back to the wine-shop [*With this sign of weakness, Wu Sung's valor is brought out even more clearly. Otherwise, it would mean that things happened too suddenly, and Wu Sung simply could not avoid meeting the tiger, and that he was lucky to have escaped from the mouth of the tiger*],[3] when he thought to himself, "If I go back, I shall be ridiculed by him for not being a brave man. I will not turn back." [*Is it not extraordinary to stake one's life for the sake of fame?*] After debating with himself for a while, he said, "What cursed thing am I afraid of? Let me just go up and see what will happen." [*Wu Sung's valor is vividly portrayed.*]

As Wu Sung walked, the fumes of the wine rose up in his head. [*See how methodically the author writes about drunkenness!*] So he whisked away his felt hat to hang on his back [*This is wintertime, but the author insists on describing the great heat felt by Wu Sung. Later when the tiger jumps at him, he is so scared as to shed cold sweat. A superb writer!*], tucked the club underneath his arm [*Club: the eleventh time. Tucked the club underneath his arm—the fifth posture he assumes with the club*], and step by step went up the ridge. He turned his head around to look at the sun, and saw that it was gradually going down. [*Frightening scenery. If I were there at that time, even if there were no tiger coming out, I would cry aloud.*] This was right in the midst of the tenth month. The days were short and the nights long, and it grew dark very quickly. [*This is the author's own explanatory note.*] Wu Sung mumbled to himself, "What tiger is there? People just scare themselves and dare not climb the hill." [*Again the author lets Wu Sung comfort himself.*] After Wu Sung had walked for a while, the strength of the wine became apparent. [*Drunk.*] He began to feel scorchingly hot inside. [*Hot.*] With one hand carrying the club [*Club: the twelfth time. Again he carries the club—the sixth posture he assumes with the club*] and the other opening up his coat at the chest [*A superb picture.*], he stumbled and staggered, and blundered straight through a forest of tangled trees. [*Frightening scenery. We know it is a forest for tigers.*] He saw a high, smooth, bluish rock. [*After having Wu Sung pass the tangled trees, the author might be expected to let the tiger jump out. Instead, he conjures up a piece of blue rock, and almost lets Wu Sung fall asleep on it. After having caused the reader to be worried to death, he then brings out the tiger. How incorrigible is the man of genius!*] He leaned his club against the side of the rock [*The club was leaned to the side—the seventh posture Wu Sung assumes with the club. Club: the thirteenth time.*] and was just about to lay himself down upon the rock to sleep [*The reader is frightened to death.*], when there rose a violent gust of wind. After the gust of wind had passed, Wu Sung heard a great crash behind the tangled trees, and out leaped a tiger with slanting eyes and white forehead. [*The tiger came out with force and power.*] Seeing it, Wu Sung cried, "Ah-ya!" and rolled down from the blue rock. [*With this sign of weakness, Wu Sung's valor is brought out even more clearly. Otherwise, it would be like the story of Tzu-lu[4] told in a small village, extremely untrue to life.*] Grasping the club in his hand [*Club: the*

---

3. Wu Sung, after hesitating, deliberately chose to confront the tiger rather than simply being forced to meet it. This shows his courage and valor.

4. One of Confucius' disciples, known for his physical strength and impetuosity.

fourteenth time. Grasping the club—the eighth posture he assumes with the club.], he dodged to the side of the blue rock. [The first dodging. From here on the man becomes a superman and the tiger a live tiger. The reader must pay very close attention from paragraph to paragraph. I have often thought that there are places to see a painted tiger, but none to see a genuine one; one can see a genuine tiger that is dead, but not one that is living; a living tiger walking can probably be seen occasionally, but a living tiger battling with a man—there are never places to see such a thing. Now suddenly in an almost casual way, Nai-an[5] with his playful pen has painted a complete picture of a living tiger battling with a man. From now on those who want to see a tiger can all come to the Ching-yang Ridge in Water Margin to stare to their satisfaction. Moreover, they need not be frightened. What a great kindness Nai-an has rendered to his readers! It is said that Chao Sung-hsüeh[6] was fond of painting horses. In his latter years, his technique became even more penetrating. Whenever he wished to meditate on how to paint a new picture, he would loosen his clothes in a secluded room and crouch on the floor. He would learn first how to be a horse, and then order a brush. One day Lady Kuan[7] came upon him in this process, and Chao even appeared to be a horse. Now when Nai-an was writing this passage, could it be that he too had loosened his clothes, and while crouching on the ground, assumed the postures of a pounce, a kick, and a cut?[8] Su Tung-p'o in a poem on a painting of geese wrote:

> *When wild geese see the approach of a man,*
> *They appear startled even before taking off.*
> *From what hidden place have you observed them,*
> *To catch this natural pose of theirs so oblivious of man?*

I really don't know where in his mind Nai-an obtained this method of painting a tiger eating a man. When I say that of all writers of the past three thousand years he alone is a genius, is this mere empty praise?]

The tiger was both hungry and thirsty. With just a light touch on the ground with its two front paws, it gathered itself and sprang through the air. [*The tiger.*] Wu Sung was frightened and the wine in him came out in a cold sweat. [*Subtle and marvelous writing. As I was reading this under the lamp, the light seemed to shrink into the shape of a bean, and its color became*

---

5. The putative author of the novel.

6. 1254–1322. A famous painter of the Yüan period whose given name was Meng-fu (see selection 78).

7. Chao's wife.

8. As will soon be seen in the following narrative description, these are the three things the tiger did in its efforts to seize Wu Sung. Chin's claim about Chao Meng-fu's emulation of the horse and Shih Nai-an's complete success in bringing to life Wu Sung's fight with the tiger is what we today would call "empathy."

green.]⁹ In less time than it takes to tell it, when Wu Sung saw that the tiger was coming down upon him, with one quick move he dodged behind it. [*The man. The second dodging.*] Now it is most difficult for a tiger to see someone behind its back. [*In the midst of this turmoil the author takes time out to provide an explanatory note.*] It therefore dug its front paws into the ground, and with one sweep lifted up its back and rear parts to kick. [*The tiger.*] With a single quick move Wu Sung dodged to one side. [*The man. The third dodging.*] Seeing that it could not kick Wu Sung, the tiger let out a tremendous roar which, like a thunderclap in the sky, shook the whole mountain ridge. It then erected its tail like an iron staff and slashed down. [*The tiger.*] But Wu Sung again dodged to one side. [*The man. The fourth dodging.*] Ordinarily when a tiger tries to seize a man, it does so only with a pounce, a kick, and a cut. If after these three maneuvers it cannot seize a man, half of its heart and temper desert it. [*In the midst of this turmoil the author takes time out to provide an explanatory note. A genius, commanding a wide acquaintance with things, certainly does not speak falsely. However, there is no place to verify this statement of his. This passage brings all the previous action to an end. In what has gone above, Wu Sung only used the method of dodging four times. In what follows he will apply his strength.*]

Unable to cut Wu Sung with its tail, the tiger roared again and swiftly circled round. [*The tiger.*] Seeing that the tiger had again turned, Wu Sung whirled his club with both hands [*Whirled his club—the ninth posture he assumes with the club. Club: the fifteenth time.*] and with all his strength brought it down from mid-air in one swift blow. [*The man. After this blow, who would not think that the tiger will be done away with? And yet unexpected things are going to take place.*] There was a crashing sound, and leaves and branches scattered down over his face. When he fixed his eyes to see, Wu Sung found that he had not hit the tiger [*He had marshaled all his strength and yet he did not hit the tiger. What a hair-raising sentence!*]; instead in his haste he had hit a withered tree. [*In this turmoil the author again takes time out to provide this explanatory note.*] The club broke in two, and he was only holding half of it in his hand. [*Club: the sixteenth time. The author has been busy writing about the club for a long while. We all thought that Wu Sung could rely on it to strike the tiger, but all of a sudden it comes to nought here: we are absolutely stunned and hardly dare read on. After the club is broken, Wu Sung's extraordinary power of fighting the tiger with his bare hands can be revealed. However, the reader is so frightened that his heart and liver have jumped out of his mouth.*]

The tiger roared, its wrath fully aroused. Turning its body around, it again leaped toward Wu Sung. [*The tiger.*] Wu Sung again jumped away and

---

9. A sure sign of the presence of a powerful ghost or spirit.

retreated ten steps. [*The man.*] No sooner had he done so than the tiger planted its two forepaws right in front of him. [*The tiger.*] Seizing the opportunity, Wu Sung threw away the broken club [*The club is gotten rid of. Club: the seventeenth time.*], and with the same motion both his hands clutched the tiger's spotted neck and pressed the head down. [*The man.*] The tiger in desperation attempted to struggle loose [*The tiger.*], but Wu Sung forced it down with all his strength, unwilling to relax his grip even for a moment. [*The man.*] Then he kicked the tiger's face and eyes wildly. [*Kicking with a foot— marvelous. For he cannot loosen his hands. Kicking the eyes—marvelous. For it would be hard to kick any other spot.*] The tiger began to roar, and clawed up two heaps of yellow mud underneath its body, forming a mud pit. [*The tiger. How did Nai-an know that the man who kicks at a tiger must kick its eyes, and that when a tiger is being kicked at, it will make a mud pit? All this is improbable writing, and yet the matter must be a certainty. How absolutely extraordinary! How absolutely marvelous!*][10] Wu Sung pressed the tiger's mouth straight into the pit. [*The man.*] Being so mauled by Wu Sung, the tiger became completely worn out. [*The tiger.*]

Wu Sung then used his left hand to grasp tightly the tiger's spotted neck, and freeing the right hand, lifted up his hammerlike fist and bludgeoned the tiger with all his strength. [*The man.*] After fifty or seventy blows, blood began to gush out from the tiger's eyes, mouth, nose, and ears. The tiger, unable to stir any more, could barely gasp for breath. [*The tiger.*] Wu Sung let go of the beast, and went among the pine trees in search of his broken club. Grasping the broken club in his hand and fearing lest the tiger was not yet dead, he struck it again. [*Club: the eighteenth time. This is the last mention of the club.*] Only after he saw the tiger's breathing cease did he finally throw down the club. [*The club ends here.*] He then thought to himself, "I'll just pick up the tiger and drag it down the ridge." [*His first thought is to take it away. Marvelous.*] But when he tried to pull the tiger from its pool of blood with both his hands, he couldn't! The truth was he had completely used up his strength, and all his limbs were weak and powerless. [*With this sign of weakness his powers of a moment ago become even more evident.*]

Wu Sung returned to the blue rock and sat there for a while. [*Wu Sung's extreme weariness depicted here brings out more clearly through contrast his great prowess of a moment ago. The narrative comes back to the blue rock again. Absolutely marvelous!*] He thought to himself, "It is getting dark. Suppose another tiger leaps out, how will I subdue it? I'd better get down the ridge somehow, and come back tomorrow morning to take care of the beast." [*The sentence is specially designed so as to make what follows appear surpris-*

10. What Chin seems to mean here is that the account is more convincing *because* it departs from literal truth—an indication of Chin's love of paradox. Or perhaps he is saying that, unlikely as it would be to invent or observe such details, they really must be true.

ing.]¹¹ He then found his felt hat by the side of the rock [*With a cry "Ah-ya!"* *he rolled down from the blue rock. At that moment he was so frightened out of* *his wits that he hadn't noticed where his hat had dropped. Penetrating writ-* *ing.*], went through the tangled trees [*The author comes back to the tangled* *trees*], and dragged himself down the ridge a step at a time.

Wu Sung had not traveled more than half a tricent when two tigers leaped out of the withered grass. [*Extraordinary writing that will frighten people to* *death.*] "Ah-ya!" he cried. "This is the end of me." [*Extraordinary writing that* *will frighten people to death.*] But suddenly the two tigers stood upright in darkness. [*Extraordinary writing that will frighten people to death.*] When Wu Sung looked closely at them, he saw that they were none other than two people wrapped tightly in clothes sewn together from tiger skins. They each had a five-pronged pitchfork. [*Extraordinary writing.*] Seeing Wu Sung, they were startled and said, "You . . . you, have you eaten a crocodile's heart, or a leopard's gall, or a lion's leg, that you are not afraid of anything? How dare you walk over the ridge alone in the darkness of the approaching night without any weapon? You . . . you, are you a man or a ghost?" [*Although the fight* *with the tiger is over, the author comments on the event through the mouths of* *the hunters.*] "Who are you two?" asked Wu Sung. "We are local hunters," replied one of them. "What are you doing on the ridge?" asked Wu Sung. [*These are words that will make people split their sides. I am on the ridge to kill* *the tiger, but what are you up here for? Absolutely marvelous!*]

Greatly surprised, the two hunters said, "So you still don't know. Nowa- days, there is a huge tiger on the Ching-yang Ridge. It comes out every night to harm people. Even we hunters have lost seven or eight of our own. Countless passing travelers have been eaten by this beast. The district magis- trate has instructed the village leaders and us hunters to capture it. But the evil beast is powerful and hard to get near. [*We know therefore that a pounce,* *a kick, and a cut were unusual things.*] Who dares approach it? Because of it we don't know how many floggings we have received for our failures in our mission. Still we cannot capture it. Tonight is our turn again to try. We are here with a dozen or so villagers. Spring-bows and poisoned arrows are set up all over the place to await its arrival. We were waiting in ambush when we saw you nonchalantly [*Four characters (in the original). Wu Sung's valor is* *described unintentionally.*] walking down the ridge. You gave us a start. But who are you? Have you seen the tiger?"

"I am from Ch'ing-ho district, surnamed Wu and number two among siblings. [*In the midst of this turmoil the author fixes our attention on the case* *of Wu Sung's going to see his elder brother. Therefore these four characters*

---

11. As we shall see shortly, Wu Sung runs into two hunters disguised as tigers when he is going down the ridge, which creates another moment of high suspense. What Chin means here is probably that when Wu Sung's fear (the possibility of encountering another tiger) seemingly comes true later in the story, the surprise felt by the reader is even greater.

('number two among siblings') are planted everywhere.] A while ago, I bumped into that tiger by the tangled trees up on the ridge and killed it by punching and kicking." [*His first recapitulation.*] The two hunters looked stunned upon hearing this and said, "You are making it up!" "If you don't believe me," said Wu Sung, "look at the bloodstains on my clothes." [*Too bad he is wearing a red jacket.*] "How did you kill it?" asked the two. Wu Sung repeated his story of killing the tiger. [*His second recapitulation. Actually, it is something he is most proud of. Therefore he cannot help saying it over and over again. I too want to say it over and over again, but unfortunately there isn't anything I have to say that is worth speaking about.*]

Upon hearing this, the two hunters were both joyous and astonished. They called out to gather the ten villagers. The ten villagers, all carrying pitchforks, crossbows, knives, and spears, gathered around right away. "Why didn't they come up the hill with you?" Wu Sung asked. "That beast was just too ferocious," said the hunters. "How dared they come up?"

The dozen or so villagers now all stood in front. The two hunters asked Wu Sung to tell the crowd how he killed the tiger. [*His third recapitulation. It is also marvelous that the hunters should ask Wu Number Two to speak. Even others felt proud, let alone Wu Sung himself.*] None of the group believed it. "If you don't believe me," said Wu Sung, "come with me and see for yourselves." They all carried steel and flint with them, so they struck fire and lit five or six torches. [*Fine. Like a picture.*] Tagging after Wu Sung [*These four characters read like a picture.*], they again ascended the ridge. Seeing that the tiger was dead there in a heap, they were all overjoyed. They dispatched someone ahead to report to the village leader and the responsible prominent family. Meanwhile five or six villagers tied up the tiger and carried it down the ridge.

Translated by John Wang

262
The Scholars

Wu Ching-tzu (1701–1754)

Chapter 3

Examiner Chou picks out true talent.
Butcher Hu cuts up rough after good news.

The Scholars or The Unofficial History of the Grove of Literati (*Ju-lin wai-shih*) was completed around 1750 and first published two or three decades later. Consisting of fifty-five chapters, the work takes the form of a series of loosely linked stories—a structure dubbed "architectonic"—and

When Chou Chin fell senseless to the ground, his friends were greatly taken aback, thinking he must be ill.

"I suppose this place has been shut up so long that the air is bad," said the guild head. "That must be why he has collapsed."

"I'll hold him up," said Chin to the guild head, "while you go and get some hot water from the workmen over there to bring him to."

When the guild head brought back the water, three or four of the others raised Chou Chin up and poured water down his throat till he gave a gurgle and spat out some phlegm. "That's better," they said, and helped him to his feet. But when Chou Chin saw the desk he beat his head against it again. Only, instead of falling unconscious, this time he burst into loud sobbing. Not all their entreaties could stop him.

"Are you out of your mind?" demanded Chin. "We came to the examination school to enjoy a bit of sightseeing. Nobody has died in your family. Why take on like this?" But Chou Chin paid no attention. He just leaned his head against the desk and went on crying. After crying in the first room, he rushed over to cry in the second and then the third, rolling over and over on the floor till all his friends felt sorry for him. Seeing the state he was in, Chin and the guild head tried to lift him up, one on each side; but he refused to budge. He cried and cried, until he spat blood. Then all the others lent a hand to carry him out and set him down in a tea-house in front of the examination school. They urged him to drink a bowl of tea. But he just went on sniffing and blinking away his tears, looking quite broken-hearted.

---

is thus not a novel in the most narrow and conventional sense. The prologue gives the idealized biography of a historic painter, Wang Mien, who is not directly related to the business of the novel, but his appearance sets the tone for what follows and may be said to point the moral for the whole book. Aside from Wang Mien, *The Grove of Literati* is the first long fictional work in Chinese literature that borrows no characters from history or legend. Hence it is one of the most creative and imaginative works of Chinese fiction. In a sophisticated narrative dripping with bitter satire, the author is merciless in his denunciation of the hypocritical and corrupt scholarly class. He uses autobiographical materials extensively and models many of his characters on friends and acquaintances. The innovative structure of the novel may also be seen in the limited use of songs and verses, although some of the traditional storyteller's formulaic expressions are retained.

The chapter selected here is a good example of the loosely structured narrative of *The Grove of Literati*. In the entire chapter, only a couple of the seventy or so principal characters who drift in and out of the nebulous plot even appear at all, and their role is poorly defined. This structural diffuseness, however, in no way diminishes the effectiveness of the novel as a critique of bureaucratic mores and social turpitude.

Chou Chin is a humble village schoolmaster who has lost his job for failure to curry favor with the local elite. On the verge of starvation, he is fortunate enough to be hired as an accountant by a group of merchants who are on their way to the provincial capital to buy some goods. While in the capital, Chou is permitted to take a look at one of the cells of the examination hall and is overcome by the sight of the hallowed desk inside. The third chapter of the novel begins with his friends trying to revive him. The man named Chin in this selection is his brother-in-law Chin Yin-yu.

"What's your trouble, Mr. Chou?" asked one of them. "What made you cry so bitterly in there?"

"I don't think you realize, gentlemen," said Chin, "that my brother-in-law is not really a merchant. He has studied hard for scores of years, but never even passed the prefectural examination. That's why the sight of the provincial examination school today upset him."

Touched on the raw like this, Chou Chin let himself go and sobbed even more noisily.

"It seems to me you're the one to blame, Old Chin," said another merchant. "If Mr. Chou is a scholar, why did you bring him on such business?"

"Because he was so hard up," said Chin. "He had lost his job as a teacher; there was no other way out for him."

"Judging by your brother-in-law's appearance," said another, "he must be a very learned man. It's because nobody recognizes his worth that he feels so wronged."

"He's learned all right," said Chin, "but he's been unlucky."

"Anybody who buys the rank of scholar of the Imperial College can go in for the examination," said the man who had just spoken. "Since Mr. Chou is so learned, why not buy him a rank so that he can take the examination? If he passes, that will make up for his unhappiness today."

"I agree with you," rejoined Chin. "But where's the money to come from?"

By now Chou Chin had stopped crying.

"That's not difficult," said the same merchant. "We're all friends here. Let's raise some money among us and lend it to Mr. Chou, so that he can go in for the examination. If he passes and becomes an official, a few taels of silver will mean nothing to him—he can easily repay us. Even if he doesn't pay us back, we merchants always fritter away a few taels one way or another, and this is in a good cause. What do you all say?"

The others responded heartily, "A friend in need is a friend indeed!"

"A man who knows the right thing to do, but doesn't do it, is a coward!"

"Of course we'll help. We only wonder if Mr. Chou will condescend to accept."

"If you do this," cried Chou Chin, "I shall look on you as my foster-parents. Even if I become a mule or a horse in my next life,[1] I shall repay your kindness." Then he knelt down and kowtowed to them all, and they bowed to him in return. Chin thanked them too. They drank a few more bowls of tea, and Chou Chin no longer cried, but talked and laughed with the others until it was time to return to the guild.

The next day, sure enough, the four merchants raised two hundred taels of silver among them. This they gave to Chin, who promised to be responsible for any expenses over and above that sum. Chou Chin thanked them again;

1. This refers to the Buddhist belief in transmigration, and men's fear that in their next life they might not be human beings again.

and the guild head prepared a feast for the merchants on Chou Chin's behalf. Meantime Chin had taken the silver to the provincial treasury. As luck would have it, it was just the time for the preliminary test for the provincial examination. Chou Chin took the test and came first of all the candidates from the Imperial College. On the eighth of the eighth month he went to the examination school for the provincial examination, and the sight of the place where he had cried made him unexpectedly happy. As the proverb says, "Joy puts heart into a man." Thus he wrote seven excellent examination papers, then went back to the guild, for Chin and the others had not yet completed their purchases. When the results were published, Chou Chin had passed with distinction, and all the merchants were delighted.

They went back together to Wenchang county, where Chou Chin paid his respects to the magistrate and the local examiner, and officials sent in their cards and called to congratulate him. Local people who were no relations of his claimed relationship, and perfect strangers claimed acquaintanceship. This kept him busy for over a month. When Shen Hsiang-fu heard the news, he got the villagers in Hsueh Market to contribute to buy four chickens, fifty eggs, and some rice balls, then went to the county-seat to congratulate Chou Chin, who kept him to a feast. Mr. Hsun, it goes without saying, came to pay his respects too.

Soon it was time to go to the examination in the capital. Chou Chin's traveling expenses and clothes were provided by Chin. He passed the metropolitan examination too; and after the palace examination he was given an official post. In three years he rose to the rank of censor and was appointed commissioner of education for Kwangtung province.

Now though Chou Chin engaged several secretaries, he thought, "I had bad luck myself for so long; now that I'm in office I mean to read all the papers carefully. I mustn't leave everything to my secretaries and suppress real talent." Having come to this decision, he went to Canton to take up his post. The day after his arrival he burned incense, posted up placards, and held two examinations.

The third examination was for candidates from Nanhai and Panyu counties. Commissioner Chou sat in the hall and watched the candidates crowding in. There were young and old, handsome and homely, smart and shabby men among them. The last candidate to enter was thin and sallow, had a grizzled beard, and was wearing an old felt hat. Kwangtung has a warm climate; still, this was the twelfth month, and yet this candidate had on a linen gown only, so he was shivering with cold as he took his paper and went to his cell. Chou Chin made a mental note of this before sealing up their doors. During the first interval, from his seat at the head of the hall he watched this candidate in the linen gown come up to hand in his paper. The man's clothes were so threadbare that a few more holes had appeared since he went into the cell. Commissioner Chou looked at his own garments—his magnificent crimson robe and gilt belt—then he referred to the register of names, and asked, "You are Fan Chin, aren't you?"

Kneeling, Fan Chin answered, "Yes, Your Excellency."

"How old are you this year?"

"I gave my age as thirty. Actually I am fifty-four."

"How many times have you taken the examination?"

"I first went for it when I was twenty, and I have taken it over twenty times since then."

"How is it you have never passed!"

"My essays are too poor," replied Fan Chin, "so none of the honorable examiners will pass me."

"That may not be the only reason," said Commissioner Chou. "Leave your paper here, and I will read it through carefully."

Fan Chin kowtowed and left.

It was still early, and no other candidates were coming to hand in their papers, so Commissioner Chou picked up Fan Chin's essay and read it through. But he was disappointed. "Whatever is the fellow driving at in this essay?" he wondered. "I see now why he never passed." He put it aside. However, when no other candidates appeared, he thought, "I might as well have another look at Fan Chin's paper. If he shows the least talent, I'll pass him to reward his perseverance." He read it through again, and this time felt there was something in it. He was just going to read it through once more, when another candidate came up to hand in his paper.

This man knelt down, and said, "Sir, I beg for an oral test."

"I have your paper here," said Commissioner Chou kindly. "What need is there for an oral test?"

"I can compose poems in all the ancient styles. I beg you to set a subject to test me."

The commissioner frowned and said, "Since the emperor attaches importance to essays, why should you bring up the poems of the Han and T'ang dynasties? A candidate like you should devote all his energy to writing compositions, instead of wasting time on heterodox studies. I have come here at the imperial command to examine essays, not to discuss miscellaneous literary forms with you. This devotion to superficial things means that your real work must be neglected. No doubt your essay is nothing but flashy talk, not worth the reading. Attendants! Drive him out!" At the word of command, attendants ran in from both sides to seize the candidate and push him outside the gate.

But although Commissioner Chou had had this man driven out, he still read his paper. This candidate was called Wei Hao-ku, and he wrote in a tolerably clear and straightforward style. "I will pass him lowest on the list," Chou Chin decided. And, taking up his brush, he made a mark at the end of the paper as a reminder.

Then he read Fan Chin's paper again. This time he gave a gasp of amazement. "Even I failed to understand this paper the first two times I read it!" he exclaimed. "But, after reading it for the third time, I realize it is the most wonderful essay in the world—every word a pearl. This shows how often bad examiners must have suppressed real genius." Hastily taking up his brush, he carefully drew three circles on Fan Chin's paper, marking it as first. He then picked up Wei Hao-ku's paper again, and marked it as twentieth. After this he collected all the other essays and took them away with him.

Soon the results were published, and Fan Chin's name was first on the list. When he went in to see the commissioner, Chou Chin commended him warmly. And when the last successful candidate, Wei Hao-ku, went in, Commissioner Chou gave him some encouragement and advised him to work hard and stop studying miscellaneous works. Then, to the sound of drums and trumpets, the successful candidates left.

The next day, Commissioner Chou set off for the capital. Fan Chin alone escorted him for ten miles of the way, doing reverence before his chair. Then the commissioner called him to his side. "First-class honors go to the mature," he said "Your essay showed real maturity, and you are certain to do well in the provincial examination too. After I have made my report to the authorities, I will wait for you in the capital."

Fan Chin kowtowed again in thanks, then stood to one side of the road as the examiner's chair was carried swiftly off. Only when the banners had passed out of sight behind the next hill did he turn back to his lodgings to settle his bill. His home was about fifteen miles from the city, and he had to travel all night to reach it. He bowed to his mother, who lived with him in a thatched cottage with a thatched shed outside, his mother occupying the front room and his wife the back one. His wife was the daughter of Butcher Hu of the market.

Fan Chin's mother and wife were delighted by his success. They were preparing a meal when his father-in-law arrived, bringing pork sausages and a bottle of wine. Fan Chin greeted him, and they sat down together.

"Since I had the bad luck to marry my daughter to a scarecrow like you," said Butcher Hu, "Heaven knows how much you have cost me. Now I must have done some good deed to make you pass the examination. I've brought this wine to celebrate."

Fan Chin assented meekly, and called his wife to cook the sausages and warm the wine. He and his father-in-law sat in the thatched shed, while his mother and wife prepared food in the kitchen.

"Now that you have become a gentleman," went on Butcher Hu, "you must do things in proper style. Of course, men in my profession are decent, high-class people; and I am your elder too—you mustn't put on any airs before me. But these peasants round here, dung-carriers and the like, are low people. If you greet them and treat them as equals, that will be a breach of etiquette and will make me lose face too. You're such an easy-going, good-for-nothing fellow; I'm telling you this for your own good, so that you won't make a laughing-stock of yourself."

"Your advice is quite right, father," replied Fan Chin.

"Let your mother eat with us too," went on Butcher Hu. "She has only vegetables usually—it's a shame! Let my daughter join us too. She can't have tasted lard more than two or three times since she married you a dozen years ago, poor thing!"

So Fan Chin's mother and wife sat down to share the meal with them. They ate until sunset, by which time Butcher Hu was tipsy. Mother and son thanked him profusely; then, throwing his jacket over his shoulders, the butcher staggered home bloated. The next day Fan Chin had to call on relatives and friends.

Wei Hao-ku invited him to meet some other fellow candidates, and since it was the year for the provincial examination, they held a number of literary meetings. Soon it was the end of the sixth month. Fan Chin's fellow candidates asked him to go with them to the provincial capital for the examination, but he had no money for the journey. He went to ask his father-in-law to help.

Butcher Hu spat in his face, and poured out a torrent of abuse. "Don't be a fool!" he roared. "Just passing one examination has turned your head completely—you're like a toad trying to swallow a swan! And I hear that you scraped through not because of your essay, but because the examiner pitied you for being so old. Now, like a fool, you want to pass the higher examination and become an official. But do you know who those officials are? They are all stars in heaven! Look at the Chang family in the city. All those officials have pots of money, dignified faces, and big ears. But your mouth sticks out and you've a chin like an ape's. You should piss on the ground and look at your face in the puddle! You look like a monkey, yet you want to become an official. Come off it! Next year I shall find a teaching job for you with one of my friends so that you can made a few taels of silver to support that old, never-dying mother of yours and your wife—and it's high time you did! Yet you ask me for traveling expenses! I kill just one pig a day, and only make ten cents per pig. If I give you all my silver to play ducks and drakes with, my family will have to live on air." The butcher went on cursing at full blast, till Fan Chin's head spun.

When he got home again, he thought to himself, "Commissioner Chou said that I showed maturity. And, from ancient times till now, who ever passed the first examination without going in for the second? I shan't rest easy till I've taken it." So he asked his fellow candidates to help him, and went to the city, without telling his father-in-law, to take the examination. When the examination was over he returned home, only to find that his family had had no food for two days. And Butcher Hu cursed him again.

The day the results came out there was nothing to eat in the house, and

Fan Chin's mother told him, "Take that hen of mine to the market and sell it; then buy a few measures of rice to make gruel. I'm faint with hunger."

Fan Chin tucked the hen under his arm and hurried out.

He had only been gone an hour or so, when gongs sounded and three horsemen galloped up. They alighted, tethered their horses to the shed, and called out, "Where is the honorable Mr. Fan? We have come to congratulate him on passing the provincial examination."

Not knowing what had happened, Fan Chin's mother had hidden herself in the house for fear. But when she heard that he had passed, she plucked up courage to poke her head out and say, "Please come in and sit down. My son has gone out."

"So this is the old lady," said the heralds. And they pressed forward to demand a tip.

In the midst of this excitement two more batches of horsemen arrived. Some squeezed inside while the others packed themselves into the shed, where they had to sit on the ground. Neighbors gathered round, too, to watch; and the flustered old lady asked one of them to go to look for her son. The neighbor ran to the marketplace, but Fan Chin was nowhere to be seen. Only when he reached the east end of the market did he discover the scholar, clutching the hen tightly against his chest and holding a sales sign in one hand. Fan Chin was pacing slowly along, looking right and left for a customer.

"Go home quickly, Mr. Fan!" cried the neighbor. "Congratulations! You have passed the provincial examination. Your house is full of heralds."

Thinking this fellow was making fun of him, Fan Chin pretended not to hear and walked forward with lowered head. Seeing that he paid no attention, the neighbor went up to him and tried to grab the hen.

"Why are you taking my hen?" protested Fan Chin. "You don't want to buy it."

"You have passed," insisted the neighbor. "They want you to go home to send off the heralds."

"Good neighbor," said Fan Chin, "we have no rice left at home, so I have to sell this hen. It's a matter of life and death. This is no time for jokes! Do go away, so as not to spoil my chance of a sale."

When the neighbor saw that Fan Chin did not believe him, he seized the hen, threw it to the ground, and dragged the scholar back by main force to his home.

The heralds cried, "Good! The newly honored one is back." They pressed forward to congratulate him. But Fan Chin brushed past them into the house to look at the official announcement, already hung up, which read: "This is to announce that the master of your honorable mansion, Fan Chin, has passed the provincial examination in Kwangtung, coming seventh in the list. May better news follow in rapid succession!"

Fan Chin feasted his eyes on this announcement, and, after reading it through once to himself, read it once more aloud. Clapping his hands, he laughed and exclaimed. "Ha! Good! I have passed." Then, stepping back, he fell down in a dead faint. His mother hastily poured some boiled water between his lips, whereupon he recovered consciousness and struggled to his feet. Clapping his hands again, he let out a peal of laughter and shouted, "Aha! I've passed! I've passed!" Laughing wildly he ran outside, giving the heralds and the neighbors the fright of their lives. Not far from the front door he slipped and fell into a pond. When he clambered out, his hair was disheveled, his hands muddied, and his whole body dripping with slime. But nobody could stop him. Still clapping his hands and laughing, he headed straight for the market.

They all looked at each other in consternation, and said, "The new honor has sent him off his head!"

His mother wailed, "Aren't we out of luck! Why should passing an examination do this to him? Now he's mad, goodness knows when he'll get better."

"He was all right this morning when he went out," said his wife. "What could have brought on this attack? What *shall* we do?"

The neighbors consoled them. "Don't be upset," they said. "We will send a couple of men to keep an eye on Mr. Fan. And we'll all bring wine and eggs and rice for these heralds. Then we can discuss what's to be done."

The neighbors brought eggs or wine, lugged along sacks of rice or carried over chickens. Fan Chin's wife wailed as she prepared the food in the kitchen. Then she took it to the shed, neighbors brought tables and stools, and they asked the heralds to sit down to a meal while they discussed what to do.

"I have an idea," said one of the heralds. "But I don't know whether it will work or not."

"What idea?" they asked.

"There must be someone the honorable Mr. Fan usually stands in awe of," said the herald. "He's only been thrown off his balance because sudden joy made him choke on his phlegm. If you can get someone he's afraid of to slap him in the face and say, 'It's all a joke. You haven't passed any examination!'—then the fright will make him cough up his phlegm, and he'll come to his senses again."

They all clapped their hands and said, "That's a fine idea. Mr. Fan is more afraid of Butcher Hu than of anyone else. Let's hurry up and fetch him. He's probably still in the market and hasn't yet heard the news."

"If he were selling meat in the market, he would have heard the news by now," said a neighbor. "He went out at dawn to the east market to fetch pigs, and he can't have come back yet. Someone had better go quickly to find him."

One of the neighbors hurried off in search of the butcher and presently met him on the road, followed by an assistant who was carrying seven or eight catties of meat and four or five strings of cash. Butcher Hu was coming to offer his congratulations. Fan Chin's mother, crying bitterly, told him what had happened.

"How could he be so unlucky!" exclaimed the butcher. They were calling for him outside, so he gave the meat and the money to his daughter, and went out. The heralds put their plan before him, but Butcher Hu demurred.

"He may be my son-in-law," he said, "but he's an official[2] now—one of the stars in heaven. How can you hit one of the stars in heaven? I've heard that whoever hits the stars in heaven will be carried away by the King of Hell, given a hundred strokes with an iron rod, and shut up in the eighteenth hell, never to become a human being again. I daren't do a thing like that."

"Mr. Hu!" cried a sarcastic neighbor. "You make your living by killing pigs. Every day the blade goes in white and comes out red. After all the blood you've shed, the King of Hell must have marked you down for several thousand strokes by iron rods, so what does it matter if he adds a hundred more? Quite likely he will have used up all his iron rods before getting round to beating you for this, anyway. Or maybe, if you cure your son-in-law, the King of Hell may consider that as a good deed and promote you from the eighteenth hell to the seventeenth."

"This is no time for joking," protested one of the heralds. "This is the only way to handle it, Mr. Hu. There's nothing else for it, so please don't make difficulties."

Butcher Hu had to give in. Two bowls of wine bolstered up his courage, making him lose his scruples and start his usual rampaging. Rolling up his greasy sleeves, he strode off toward the market, followed by small groups of neighbors.

Fan Chin's mother ran out and called after him, "Just frighten him a little! Mind you don't hurt him!"

"Of course," the neighbors reassured her. "That goes without saying."

When they reached the market, they found Fan Chin standing in the doorway of a temple. His hair was tousled, his face streaked with mud, and one of his shoes had come off. But he was still clapping his hands and crowing, "Aha! I've passed! I've passed!"

Butcher Hu bore down on him like an avenging fury, roaring. "You blasted idiot! What have you passed?" and fetched him a blow. The bystanders and neighbors could hardly suppress their laughter. But although Butcher Hu had screwed up his courage to strike once, he was still afraid at heart, and his hand was trembling too much to strike a second time. The one blow, however, had been enough to knock Fan Chin out.

The neighbors pressed around to rub Fan Chin's chest and massage his back, until presently he gave a sigh and came to. His eyes were clear and his

---

2. A scholar who passed the provincial examination was sometimes eligible for such posts as that of a county magistrate.

madness had passed! They helped him up and borrowed a bench from Apothecary Chen, a hunchback who lived by the temple, so that Fan Chin might sit down.

Butcher Hu, who was standing a little way off, felt his hand begin to ache; when he raised his palm, he found to his dismay that he could not bend it. "It's true, then, that you mustn't strike the stars in heaven," he thought. "Now Buddha is punishing me!" The more he thought about it, the worse his hand hurt, and he asked the apothecary to give him some ointment for it.

Meanwhile Fan Chin was looking around and asking, "How do I come to be sitting here? My mind has been a whirl, as if in a dream."

The neighbors said, "Congratulations, sir, on having passed the examination! A short time ago, in your happiness, you brought up some phlegm; but just now you spat out several mouthfuls and recovered. Please go home quickly to send away the heralds."

"That's right," said Fan Chin. "And I seem to remember coming seventh in the list." As he was speaking, he fastened up his hair and asked the apothecary for a basin of water to wash his face, while one of the neighbors found his shoe and helped him put it on.

The sight of his father-in-law made Fan Chin afraid that he was in for another cursing. But Butcher Hu stepped forward and said, "Worthy son-in-law, I would never have presumed to slap you just now if not for your mother. She sent me to help you."

"That was what I call a friendly slap," said one of the neighbors. "Wait till Mr. Fan finishes washing his face. I bet he can easily wash off half a basin of lard!"

"Mr. Hu!" said another. "This hand of yours will be too good to kill pigs any more."

"No indeed," replied the butcher. "Why should I go on killing pigs? My worthy son-in-law will be able to support me in style for the rest of my life. I always said that this worthy son-in-law of mine was very learned and handsome, and that not one of those Chang and Chou family officials in the city looked so much the fine gentleman. I have always been a good judge of character, I don't mind telling you. My daughter stayed at home till she was more than thirty, although many rich families wanted to marry her to their sons; but I saw signs of good fortune in her face and knew that she would end up by marrying an official. You see today how right I was." He gave a great guffaw, and they all started to laugh.

When Fan Chin had washed and drunk the tea brought him by the apothecary, they all started back, Fan Chin in front, Butcher Hu and the neighbors behind. The butcher, noticing that the seat of his son-in-law's gown was crumpled, kept bending forward all the way home to tug the creases for him.

When they reached Fan Chin's house, Butcher Hu shouted, "The master is back!" The old lady came out to greet them and was overjoyed to find her son no longer mad. The heralds, she told them, had already been sent off with the money that Butcher Hu had brought. Fan Chin bowed to his mother and thanked his father-in-law, making Butcher Hu so embarrassed that he muttered, "That bit of money was nothing."

After thanking his neighbors too, Fan Chin was just going to sit down when a smart-looking retainer hurried in, holding a big red card, and announced, "Mr. Chang has come to pay his respects to the newly successful Mr. Fan."

By this time the sedan-chair was already at the door. Butcher Hu dived into his daughter's room and dared not come out, while the neighbors scattered in all directions. Fan Chin went out to welcome the visitor, who was one of the local gentry, and Mr. Chang alighted from the chair and came in. He was wearing an official's gauze cap, sunflower-colored gown, gilt belt, and black shoes. He was a provincial graduate and had served as a magistrate in his time. His name was Chang Chin-chai. He and Fan Chin made way for each other ceremoniously, and once inside the house bowed to each other as equals and sat down in the places of guest and host. Mr. Chang began the conversation.

"Sir," he said, "although we live in the same district, I have never been able to call on you."

"I have long respected you," replied Fan Chin, "but have never had the chance to pay you a visit."

"Just now I saw the list of successful candidates. Your patron, Mr. Tang, was a pupil of my grandfather; so I feel very close to you."

"I did not deserve to pass, I am afraid," said Fan Chin. "But I am delighted to be the pupil of one of your family."

After a glance round the room, Mr. Chang remarked, "Sir, you are certainly frugal." He took from his servant a packet of silver, and stated, "I have brought nothing to show my respect except these fifty taels of silver, which I beg you to accept. Your honorable home is not good enough for you, and it will not be very convenient when you have many callers. I have an empty house on the main street by the east gate, which has three courtyards with three rooms in each. Although it is not big, it is quite clean. Allow me to present it to you. When you move there, I can profit by your instruction more easily."

Fan Chin declined many times, but Mr. Chang pressed him. "With all we have in common, we should be like brothers," he said. "But if you refuse, you are treating me like a stranger." Then Fan Chin accepted the silver and expressed his thanks. After some more conversation they bowed and parted. Not until the visitor was in his chair did Butcher Hu dare to emerge.

Fan Chin gave the silver to his wife. When she opened it and they saw the white ingots with their fine markings, he asked Butcher Hu to come in and gave him two ingots, saying, "Just now I troubled you for five thousand coppers. Please accept these six taels of silver."

Butcher Hu gripped the silver tight, but thrust out his clenched fist, saying, "You keep this. I gave you that money to congratulate you, so how can I take it back?"

"I have some more silver here," said Fan Chin. "When it is spent, I will ask you for more."

Butcher Hu immediately drew back his fist, stuffed the silver into his pocket and said, "All right. Now that you are on good terms with that Mr. Chang, you needn't be afraid of going short. His family has more silver than the emperor, and they are my best customers. Every year, even if they have no particular occasions to celebrate, they still buy four or five thousand catties of meat. Silver is nothing to him."

Then he turned to his daughter and said, "Your rascally brother didn't want me to bring that money this morning. I told him, 'Now my honorable son-in-law is not the man he was. There will be lots of people sending him presents of money. I am only afraid he may refuse my gift.' Wasn't I right? Now I shall take this silver home and curse that dirty scoundrel." After a thousand thanks he made off, his head thrust forward and a broad grin on his face.

True enough, many people came to Fan Chin after that and made him presents of land and shops; while some poor couples came to serve him in return for protection. In two or three months he had men-servants and maid-servants, to say nothing of money and rice. When Mr. Chang came again to urge him, he moved into the new house; and for three days he entertained guests with feasts and operas. On the morning of the fourth day, after Fan Chin's mother had got up and had breakfast, she went to the rooms in the back courtyard. There she found Fan Chin's wife with a silver pin in her hair. Although this was the middle of the tenth month, it was still warm, and she was wearing a sky-blue silk tunic and a green silk skirt. She was supervising the maids as they washed bowls, cups, plates, and chopsticks.

"You must be very careful," the old lady warned them. "These things don't belong to us, so don't break them."

"How can you say they don't belong to you, madam?" they asked. "They are all yours."

"No, no these aren't ours," she protested with a smile.

"Oh yes, they are," the maids cried. "Not only these things, but all of us servants and this house belong to you."

When the old lady heard this, she picked up the fine porcelain and the cups and chopsticks inlaid with silver, and examined them carefully one by one. Then she went into a fit of laughter. "All mine!" she crowed. Screaming with laughter she fell backwards, choked, and lost consciousness.

But to know what became of the old lady, you must read the next chapter.

Translated by Hsien-yi Yang and Gladys Yang

263

A Burial Mound for Flowers

from *Dream of Red Towers*

Ts'ao Hsüeh-ch'in (1718?–1764)

To return now to Queen Yüan-ch'un in the Palace,[1] when she had read over the poems written on the occasion of her visit to the Garden of Pomp and State[2] and rearranged them as a collection with her own comments on their

"A Burial Mound for Flowers" is taken from chapter 23 of *Dream of Red Towers* (*Hung-lou meng*), originally called A *Record of the Stone* (*Shih-t'ou chi*). Generally recognized as China's greatest novel, *Dream* was left unfinished in eighty chapters by its young author, Ts'ao Hsüeh-ch'in. The novel was continued for another forty chapters by Kao Ŏ (fl. 1792).

Ts'ao Hsüeh-ch'in was the descendant of a once fabulously wealthy family that had its roots in Sung dynasty officialdom and had ably served the Manchus for nearly a century. By the time the author had achieved maturity, however, the family had suffered serious financial setbacks due to dramatic political changes at court. As a consequence, he was forced to live in much reduced circumstances. Brooding melancholily over the lost grandeur of the family, he poured his soul into the writing and rewriting of his masterwork.

The novel is so complex and is peopled with such a vast number of major and minor characters that it would be futile to attempt to summarize it in a paragraph or two. It is the story about the decay of an aristocratic family affiliated with the Manchus and gives an intimate picture of upper-class life as in no other Chinese work. The external world, however, is seen as reflected in the hero's heart, and the book has a symbolic scheme. The stone of the original title is as old as the world itself and for one brief lifespan it was transformed—with the help of a mangy Buddhist monk and a crazy Taoist priest—into a young man and lover, and tasted the joys and sorrows of the human lot before reverting to its stone-hearted existence. The young man, who is the hero, was born with a piece of jade in his mouth and named Pao-yü ("Precious Jade"), jade being stone carved, polished, and rendered artificial. His family, among the noblest in the land, bears the surname Chia (punningly interpreted as "Unreal").

The present episode is one of the most memorable of the novel. It is highly symbolic in that the beautiful and flowerlike Tai-yü ("Lustrous Jade"), who laments the fallen petals and prepares a burial mound for them, may seem to be tending her own grave. The passage also shows something of the love tradition under which novelists and romancers labored. Upon looking into the famous Yüan drama, *The West Chamber* (see selections 252 and 269, unnumbered notes), Pao-yü is suddenly emboldened in his love prattle; and the stray lines from *The Peony Pavilion* (selection 276), overheard by Tai-yü while the tunes were being rehearsed on the other side of the garden wall, define and give shape to her own feelings. In the context of this book, the passage also reveals the reading habits of the young in rich households and the insidious influence—so greatly dreaded by their elders—of novels and plays.

1. Yüan-ch'un, i.e., Prime of Spring, was born on New Year's Day; hence her name. She is the daughter of Chia Cheng (Pao-yü's father) and is one of the emperor's consorts. To enable her to visit her parents in comfort and seclusion, the family built for her sole use the Garden of Pomp and State adjoining their residence. Yüan-ch'un is a dozen or more years older than her brother Pao-yü, whom as a child she taught to read.

2. Ta-kuan-yüan, by which is meant "world in a nutshell," including, as it does, buildings in various styles, an artificial village, and a temple in a varied landscape setting. The name has also been rendered as "Grand Prospect Garden."

respective merits, it occurred to her that the Garden with its arbors and rockeries would be utterly desolate if, after her own visit, her father, Secretary of the Board of Works Chia Cheng,[3] as he was in duty bound, had the gates locked and sealed, thus hiding it from the view of all. Besides, there were all her literary female cousins at home, and who better than they to inhabit a place so delightful? They need never feel their inspiration dry up; nor could the flowers and willows languish in such lovely company. She then thought of her own younger brother, Pao-yü,[4] who, unlike her male cousins, had been brought up with the girls—how that, if he should be left out, he would certainly feel lonely and neglected, which in turn might affect the spirits of her own mother and grandmother, the Dowager Duchess: she therefore considered it best to allow Pao-yü to move into the Garden with the female cousins.

Having thus decided, Yüan-ch'un sent the Steward of the Palace, the eunuch Hsia Chung, to the Jung Residence[5] with the order that Pao-ch'ai and the other female cousins[6] should take up their abode in the Garden, which was on no account to be locked up with entry debarred to all, and that Pao-yü was also to move in, to pursue his studies along with the cousins. Secretary Chia and his lady respectfully received the Queen's command and, when the eunuch had made his departure, reported the matter to the Dowager Duchess before ordering the servants to enter the Garden and sweep and tidy up each corner of it, and outfit the various buildings with curtains, screens, beds, and hangings.

While all who heard the news rejoiced, Pao-yü alone was in raptures: he began at once to demand this or that piece of her furniture from the Dowager. But his animated conference with his grandmother was interrupted by a servant girl entering to announce: "The master wants Pao-yü." The effect of this upon Pao-yü was like a thunderbolt[7]—his countenance fell, almost as if his face was charred; all his newly raised hopes seemed dashed; and like a stick of gum he attached himself to the Dowager, turning and twisting in every direction and refusing to come unstuck. The Dowager, however, said soothingly, "My precious! Go to your father, who won't eat you! Remember, there's always Grandmamma behind you. Besides, you've just written that good essay for him! Since the Queen would have you and the girls housed in the Garden,

3. Chia Cheng, grandson of Duke Jung and son of the Dowager Duchess, is only Junior Secretary in chapter 2, but is made Senior Secretary of the Board of Works in chapter 85.

4. In this part of the story, he is about thirteen years of age.

5. Residence of Duke Jung, now inhabited by his descendants. The residence of Jung's brother, Duke Ning, is similarly referred to as the Ning residence.

6. Pao-ch'ai ("Precious Hairpin") is the daughter of Aunt Hsüeh, sister of Mrs. Secretary Chia; she is aged fifteen and a rival to the heroine, Tai-yü, who is mentioned below with the other female cousins. As a relative rather than one of the Dowager Duchess's granddaughters, Pao-ch'ai is given precedence over the others.

7. The strange antipathy between Pao-yü and his father is a recurrent theme in the novel.

I suppose your father will have a few things to say to you, only so as to keep you out of mischief. Be a good boy and agree with whatever he might say." And even as she calmed Pao-yü, she called two of her own serving women and told them to accompany Pao-yü and not let the master scare him.

Pao-yü was now obliged to obey his father's summons and came away with the old women, though advancing no more than a few inches with each step he took. Eventually, however, he reached his mother's apartments[8] where, a family council being in progress, the servant girls Gold Bangle, Rainbow Cloud, Sunset, Bird of Paradise, and Embroidered Phoenix stood waiting outside, under the eaves. At the sight of Pao-yü crawling along, they puckered up their mouths and sniggered. Suddenly Gold Bangle pulled Pao-yü toward her and announced with a chuckle, "I've just smeared my lips with rouge soaked in fragrant oil. Lick me! Now's best!"[9] Rainbow Cloud hurriedly pushed Gold Bangle aside and, herself giggling, said below her breath, "We aren't in the mood. No teasing!" And turning to Pao-yü, she continued, "You'll find the master in a good temper—better go in at once!"

Pao-yü dragged himself into the room, only to learn that his parents were in the inner room. Madam Chao, the concubine,[10] who had remained in the outer room, now lifted the door curtain for Pao-yü, who entered the bedroom and made his bow. Secretary Chia and his lady were seated opposite each other on the heated brick-bed, talking. A row of chairs facing the brick-bed was occupied by the girls, Ying-ch'un, T'an-ch'un, and Hsi-ch'un,[11] and Pao-yü's half-brother Huan;[12] the three last, being all younger than Pao-yü, stood up upon his entering. Secretary Chia raising his head, saw before him Pao-yü with his lofty and graceful air and his strikingly handsome appearance, which showed up all the more the drooping hangdog look and ill-bred, clownish manners of the son of the concubine—Huan, who stood beside him. Secretary Chia then remembered his eldest boy,[13] Chu, now dead, and realized with a twinge of remorse how deeply his wife loved and cherished her sole surviving son. He himself, too, was aging, his beard already turned gray. All these

8. As the lady of the house, Mrs. Secretary Chia occupies the center courtyard with a main suite of five stately rooms, but lives for the most part in three smaller rooms constituting the east wing. The center courtyard is connected by a rear passage to the Dowager Duchess's courtyard, situated to its west.

9. It is Pao-yü's habit to lick the rouge off the lips of the servant girls.

10. Secretary Chia's concubine, being regarded as an inferior, is kept out of the family council, though her two children are not.

11. Ying-ch'un ("Welcome Spring") is the daughter of Pao-yü's uncle, the Duke, noted below; Hsi-ch'un ("Pity Spring") is descended from Duke Ning and not one of the Dowager's granddaughters; T'an-ch'un ("Seek Spring") is Pao-yü's half sister, i.e., the daughter of the concubine, but unlike her brother, Huan, she is in no way handicapped by her birth.

12. Huan, Pao-yü's half brother, is the son of the concubine.

13. Chu, Pao-yü's older brother, does not appear in the story but leaves a widow, Li Wan, mentioned below, and a son.

considerations combined to militate against his aversion for his son and his inclination to chastise him. After indulging for some time in this musing, which left him nine tenths mollified, Secretary Chia said, not unkindly, "It is the Queen's wish that you, who are in the habit of following your idle whims day after day outside the house, should now be confined to the Garden, where you will carry out your reading and writing in the company of your sister and cousins. Ply well at your books, my lad. If you persist in your dawdling, rest assured that you will hear about this."

Pao-yü responded with a whole string of yeses, and his mother pulled him on to the brick-bed beside her. The others, too, sat down again. Gently rubbing her hand against Pao-yü's neck,[14] Mrs. Secretary Chia asked, "Have you finished the pills, my boy?" Pao-yü said, "There is one left still." His mother continued, "I'll send for another ten tomorrow, and remind Bombarding Scent[15] to make you take it at bedtime." Pao-yü protested, "Why, Bombarding Scent does give it to me every night! She has not once forgotten ever since you, Mother, told her to." At this point, Secretary Chia broke in with some impatience, "Who is this Bombarding Scent?" Mrs. Chia replied blandly: "Oh, one of the maids." The head of the family went on contemptuously, "A servant girl might of course be called anything. But why such a name? Whose farfetched conceit was this?" His manner alarmed his lady, who, to shield Pao-yü, declared: "It was our gracious mother who gave the girl the name." Secretary Chia sneered, "Mother? Would Mother even dream of such an expression? It could only be Pao-yü." Pao-yü saw that concealment no longer availed; slipping off the brick-bed, he justified himself thus before his father: "In reading the old poets, I chanced upon the line—'The flowers' bombarding scent proclaims a sultry morn'[16] which came pat when I learned that the girl's surname was Flower; so I gave her that name." Mrs. Chia hurriedly added, "You had better hunt out another name for her, Pao-yü, as soon as you get back to Grandmamma."[17] Then, turning to Secretary Chia, she said, "I should not have thought it necessary, my lord, to lose one's temper over a thing like that." Secretary Chia conceded, "There is no real harm in that name and certainly no need to change it now. But it does serve to show that Pao-yü wastes all his time on precious verse compositions to the detriment of his proper studies." And suddenly rounding upon his son, he barked, "Wretch! Be off with you!" Mrs. Chia, anxious for Pao-yü to be gone,

14. To detect any glandular swellings the pills were expected to cure.

15. A demure and level-headed girl who was one of the Dowager's own maids before she is assigned to Pao-yü, whom she jealously guards and protects. Her surname is Hua (Flower). Pao-yü alters her own name, Pearl, to Bombarding Scent. She is a few years older than Pao-yü.

16. The line is derived from Lu Yu, "Joys of Village Life" (see selection 75).

17. Pao-yü, being the Dowager Duchess's favorite grandchild, lives in his grandmother's courtyard, as does Tai-yü, who, at least in the earlier part of the story, enjoys a position of privilege.

also said, "Go now. Don't let Grandmamma keep waiting for you to come to dinner."

Pao-yü assented gravely and slowly withdrew from his father's presence. But when he found himself among the servant girls outside, he remembered their joke and stuck his tongue out at Gold Bangle before scurrying off, followed by the two old women. At the end of the corridor leading to the Dowager's courtyard, he noticed Bombarding Scent herself leaning against the door, waiting for him. When Bombarding Scent saw Pao-yü return, safe and unscathed, she asked, beaming, "What was it about?" Pao-yü said, "Oh, hardly anything at all. Merely that I was to keep out of scrapes in the Garden, the usual words to that effect." As he spoke, he started for the room of his grandmother, to whom he reported the interview with his father. His cousin Tai-yü[18] happening also to be there, he now asked her, "Which house would you rather have?" Tai-yü, whose mind had been engaged on the same subject, responded to his question with a smile; she said, "I was thinking of Hsiao-Hsiang Hermitage. I love those bamboos screening the curved railing—it's so much quieter there than anywhere else." Upon hearing this, Pao-yü grinned and clapped his hands in glee, crying, "Just as I thought! And it's just where I wanted you to stay! I'll live in Crab Red Court, where we shall be near each other and both in secluded spots."

As the two of them went on planning in this fashion, a woman-servant entered with a message from the head of the household to the Dowager: "The cousins are to move on the twenty-second of the second month, an auspicious day, into the Garden, which is being swept. The houses will be got ready in the few intervening days." Pao-ch'ai chose for her abode Aromatic Herb Rockery; Tai-yü, Hsiao-Hsiang Hermitage; Ying-ch'un, Tapestry Tower; T'an-ch'un, Autumn's Breath Studio; Hsi-ch'un, Smartweed Bank Loggia; Li Wan,[19] Sweet Paddy Village; and Pao-yü himself, Crab Red Court. At each of the dwellings, two older women and four girls were to be in attendance, not counting the wet nurse and the personal maid, cleaners and gardeners being additionally provided. Thus on the twenty-second, the entire company took possession of the Garden of Pomp and State: embroidered waistbands now brushed against the flowers, and perfumed breezes intoxicated the willows, so that the place was no longer desolate.

Pao-yü dwelt in the Garden and found everything to his heart's content and longed for no other happiness than that of spending each day in the company of the female cousins in reading or practicing calligraphy, in playing the guitar

18. Tai-yü is the daughter of Aunt Lin, the Dowager's daughter. When Aunt Lin dies, Tai-yü is taken, at the age of six, from her father's official residence in Yangchow to live with her grandmother in the capital. In chapter 3, Tai-yü describes herself as being a year younger than Pao-yü, whose favorite cousin she fast becomes.

19. Li Wan, the widow of Chu, Pao-yü's older brother. She is the only adult among the seven, her son Lan being only two or three years younger than Pao-yü.

or games of chess, in painting or composing verse. And in such pastimes of
theirs as the tracing of embroidery patterns, perhaps of some phoenix or bird
of paradise, and the embroidery itself, or the hunting out of rare plants[20] and
the arranging of flowers as part of their headdress, or singing or humming
tunes, or word-games and riddles, he too joined with zest. And Pao-yü wrote
some poems in which he described scenes in the Gardens at various times of
year, of which four are quoted below, not, to be sure, for their excellence, but
because they were based on his actual experience:

Night in Spring

Shut in by rainbow-colored silk bed-curtains,
I fancy I hear frogs croaking beyond the wall.
A chill creeps up my pillow; rain taps at the window.
Before my eyes, lo, she whom I wooed in my dream—
"The candle drips tears—tears shed for whom?
The flowers in the vase seem a cluster of griefs—my griefs!"
"Let alone a simple nurse-maid, poor sleepyhead me!
When lying abed, I can't abide jesting and teasing."[21]

Night in Summer

The girl has fallen asleep at her embroidery;
The parrot in its gold cage[22] renews its call for "tea";
The full moon shines through the open window—a rounded mirror;
Sandalwood fumes from rival censers circle about the room.
Amber cups overflow with sparkling "Dew on Lotus";
Breezes rustling the willows spread cool through the glass verandah.
Silk fans now wave all over the water pavilion:
Roll up the curtain—my lady's evening toilet is done.

Night in Autumn

A breathless hush reigns within the Crimson Library,[23]
But shimmering moonlight *will* peep through gauze curtains.

20. A competitive game in which each participant produces an unusual plant or flower, or a
branch or shoot notable for its shape or color, and sets forth the claims of his/her particular
specimen in poetical or horticultural terms.
21. Personalities are deliberately vague in Chinese verse, and the apportioning of the lines
to two speakers is the translator's own. The more favored servant girls slept in the same beds as
the children, often even when they ceased to be children.
22. The cloistered part of Crab Red Court is filled with exotic birds in cages of various
colors, thus further adding to the "maze" and "trap" symbolism; and Tai-yü has a parrot that
recites verses.

Sheltered by the moss-grown rockery, the cranes curl up in sleep;
Crows perch on the well-curb wet with dew.
A drowsy maid brings a quilt, unrolling a golden phoenix;[24]
The beloved one returns from the window, her hairpin undone.
Awake in the still night, athirst with too much wine,
I poke at the smoldering embers and infuse fresh tea.

Night in Winter

Flowering plums[25] and bamboos engulf each other's dreams at the
    third watch:
But embroidered coverlet and kingfisher-down would still induce no
      sleep.
Amidst shadows of pines in the courtyard, a lonely crane flaps;
Frost, like pear blossoms, bestrews the ground, though no oriole sings.
The girl with the green sleeves tosses off verses about the cold;
His golden sable pledged for wine,[26]
    the gay young lord declares it insipid.
Luckily my lord's page is thoroughly adept in blending tea—
Sweeping up the new snow, he makes an instant brew.[27]

It being then known that these verses were by a scion of the Jung branch of
the Chia ducal house, aged but twelve or thirteen, the crowd of sycophants
made copies of them and took every opportunity of reading them aloud and
praising them. Flippant young men, attracted by the showy, amatory diction,
wrote them on their fans and on the walls of their rooms, reciting them
repeatedly with undiminished pleasure. It thus came about that, through
intermediaries, strangers would approach Pao-yü with requests for a poem or
a piece of calligraphy or an inscription on some picture, which he, being
much flattered, willingly obliged, spending days on end upon such extramu-
ral activities.

Nevertheless, the very tranquility of the Garden became a source of vexation. One day, Pao-yü suddenly felt out of sorts and declared himself dissatis-

23. Crimson Library is used as an alternative name for Crab Red Court. It is to be regarded
as the name of Pao-yü's study rather than any specific part of Crab Red Court.

24. A golden phoenix embroidered on the quilt.

25. The Chinese plum (*mei-hua*) with its five-petaled flower blooms in winter and early
spring. The plum, the bamboo, and the pine are designated the "Three Friends of Winter,"
symbolizing hardiness and purity.

26. Yüan Fu (279–327) exchanged his official cap of golden sable for wine, for which he
was impeached, though later pardoned.

27. In chapter 41, the nun Miao-yü makes a special brew of tea with snow gathered from
plum blossoms five winters previously and sealed in a jar buried in the ground.

fied with one thing after another, and wandered in and out of the place, moody and dispirited. For the Garden was inhabited mostly by young ladies in a state of primordial innocence, given over to childish candor and oblivious as yet of the proprieties, neither shunning one another while sitting or lying down nor intending by a smile or laugh more than the spontaneous expression of gladness or merriment. How indeed could they divine what went on in Pao-yü's mind? For his part, being continually in an ill humor, he would no longer remain within the Garden but loafed away his time outside its precinct, looking all the while blank and abstracted.

When the library page, Tea-Tobacco,[28] saw his young master thus preoccupied, he took it upon himself to devise some means of diverting him. Tea-Tobacco considered one expedient after another, but Pao-yü seemed already familiar with them all, and tired of them all, unlikely to be amused by any of them. There remained, however, a source of delight not yet known to Pao-yü, which having at last hit upon, Tea-Tobacco went straight to the booksellers and bought many volumes of stories old and new,[29] and the Intimate and Revealing Histories of Chao Fei-yen and her sister Ho-te,[30] and of the Empress Wu,[31] and of the beauteous Yang Kuei-fei,[32] and the texts of numerous plays, and showed them to Pao-yü, who never having read such books before, rejoiced exceedingly in the new discovery. Tea-Tobacco then warned Pao-yü not to take the books into the Garden,[33] for if they should be seen, the wrath that would descend upon him, Tea-Tobacco, would be great and terrible. Pao-yü, however, would not now hear of being deprived of their company. After prolonged debate with himself, he picked out a few sets of elegant diction and refined sentiment, and these he brought with him into Crab Red Court,

---

28. Tea-Tobacco (Ming-yen), whose duty it is to accompany Pao-yü to school during the fitful periods of the latter's attendance and generally to wait upon his young master in and about the library. He would be a few years older than Pao-yü.

29. Light reading was anathema to Confucian orthodoxy and regarded as a source of corruption, which it often was. *Stories Old and New* was the title of Feng Meng-lung's first collection of colloquial stories of about 1621, and a general title to all his three collections, but the reference here would seem to be to stories generally rather than specifically Feng's collections (see selection 255).

30. Chao Fei-yen and her equally beautiful sister Ho-te were ladies in the harem of Emperor Ch'eng-ti of the Han dynasty. In such "intimate histories" (*wai-chuan*), the secrets of the harem are recounted with undisguised relish.

31. A fictional narrative bearing the title *Tse-t'ien wai-shih* (*Intimate History of Wu Tse-t'ien*) seems not to have survived, but the intrigues of the Empress Wu are part of traditional lore. Wu Tse-t'ien (624–705) was the only woman in Chinese history to found her own dynasty (see selection 45, note 11 and selection 264, introductory note).

32. The celebrated favorite of Emperor Hsüan-tsung of the T'ang dynasty (see selection 180).

33. In spite of the fourth poem, "Night in Winter," Tea-Tobacco is not allowed into the Garden.

where he hid them above his bed[34] and read them when no one was about. But the ones that were low and coarse he kept in the library outside.

It being now the middle of the third month,[35] Pao-yü took with him after breakfast one day a copy of *The Meeting with Fay*, otherwise known as *The West Chamber*, and sat on a stone under the peach tree by the bridge above Soaking Fragrance Weir.[36] Opening the book, he read slowly from the beginning, drinking in each line. When he reached the lines:

> "A fresh shower of red petals descending,
> Ten thousand flakes of melancholy!"[37]

a sudden gust shook the boughs and robbed the peach tree of a good half of its blossoms, the falling petals alighting all over Pao-yü and the pages of his open book and the surrounding earth. Pao-yü was on the point of dusting himself off but, at the thought of the flowers being scattered and trodden upon, he desisted; instead he lifted the skirt of his robe and, moving forward a few steps, emptied the blossoms into the pond. The red petals floated and whirled on the water until, drifting with the current, they disappeared down the weir. Returning to the spot where he had sat before, he now noticed the blossoms on the ground, and when he paused to consider what to do with them, a voice from behind called to him—"And what business brings *you* here?"

Pao-yü turned round: it was Tai-yü, who came up, shouldering a small hoe, from which hung a dainty silk bag, and holding a besom[38] in her hand. Pao-yü shouted with joy, "Well met! The very thing I wanted! Come and sweep up the blossoms so that we may throw them into the pond! I have already thrown a whole lot in." Tai-yü, however, said, "It would be a pity to do that! The water is clear enough here, but once it leaves the Garden and flows through the crowded part of town, it will be polluted and the poor blossoms themselves outraged. Over there, in that corner, I have prepared a tomb for the flowers. I shall sweep up these petals and put them in my silk bag and consign the whole to earth so that the flowers may return to dust, a clean and proper end for them." Struck by the idea,[39] Pao-yü was in transports; he agreed eagerly and then added: "Let me put down my book first. Then I can help you to gather them up." Tai-yü asked, "What book?" At the recollection of which, Pao-yü tried hastily to conceal the book he had been reading and

34. I.e., above his four-poster bed, concealed by the bed-curtains.

35. About the middle of April.

36. The bridge is directly above Soaking Fragrance Weir, below which the stream flows into a river outside the garden.

37. Only the first line is quoted in the original, but the full force of the allusion is lost without the second line (itself taken from a poem by Tu Fu), which has therefore been supplied in the translation.

38. Broom made of twigs.

39. The sanctity of earth does not readily occur to Pao-yü, who places his trust in the purity of water.

stammered, "Ah, well, only *The Doctrine of the Mean and The Great Learning*.[40] Why, what else could it be?" Tai-yü laughed, saying, "I know your tricks! Now surrender that book at once!" Pao-yü then said sheepishly, "Dearest cousin! It's not that I am afraid of your seeing the book, but don't—for heaven's sake!—tell anyone. In truth, its style is inimitable! I wager you'll be forgetting your meals when you're reading it." And with that he handed over the text of the plays.

Tai-yü laid down her gardening tools and took the book. Reading from the beginning, she became more and more absorbed in it as she went on, so that within a short while she had read through all sixteen scenes.[41] Being herself enthralled by its arresting tropes and frothy eloquence, she laid the book aside and, looking vacant and pensive, repeated in her mind many of its lines and phrases. Pao-yü ventured to smile; he asked, "Did you like it, cousin?" And when Tai-yü returned his smile and said, "Yes, I really have enjoyed it," Pao-yü suddenly giggled and started to quote from the plays: "'The melancholy and sickly lover'—*that* I am assuredly! And yours—yours, 'the face that overthrew cities and kingdoms'!" Tai-yü instantly flushed, her cheeks, neck, and ears turned a furious crimson; she frowned, then half raised her eyebrows;[42] her sparkling eyes narrowed to two slits, then opened wide again in a disdainful stare: her exquisite features were now the picture of anger and reproach. Pointing her finger accusingly at Pao-yü, she exclaimed, "How dare you! It's death that you deserve for this! Foisting lewd verses upon me and using such rude language too! What an affront! I'll tell my uncle and aunt."

At the word "affront," two red rings showed around her eyes, and she turned abruptly to go. Pao-yü started up in a panic and barred her way, pleading: "Forgive me this once, dearest cousin! I was at fault in giving utterance to such absurdities, but if I really had intended any affront, then let me fall into the pond tomorrow and be swallowed by a monstrous turtle, and so be reborn as a large turtle myself that I might bear the stone tablet on your tomb[43] when one day you die, the lady of some great minister or other!" This grotesque protestation caused Tai-yü to burst out laughing again. Hurriedly rubbing her eyes, she cried triumphantly, "That scared the daylights out of you, didn't it? I won't stand any more nonsense from you:

40. Forming, with the *Analects* and *The Book of Mencius*, the Confucian "Four Books" studied by every schoolboy.

41. Strictly speaking, sixteen acts (*che*). The term "scene" (*ch'ü*) is taken over from the Southern drama, and the four plays regarded as one long play.

42. Tai-yü is noted for her frown, which is regarded as a sign of her poor health and for which she is nicknamed "Miss Eyebrows." Here Pao-yü has already had more than his share of her smiles and laughter.

43. Stone steles often had for their pedestal the figure of a tortoise; "turtle" and "tortoise" are words of abuse which readily occur in oaths. Pao-yü's momentary fancy of himself as a stone tortoise at Tai-yü's tomb is, however, the foreboding of an unhappy end for both.

'Tut! A weak sapling—
A spearhead of tinfoil—that you are!' "[44]

The allusion did not escape Pao-yü, who broke into hilarious laughter, saying, "What about yourself then? I'll go and tell on you too!" Tai-yü, however, refused to be intimidated. She answered playfully, "But it did come out of *your* book. If—like the prodigy you are—you can memorize and recite whole essays after a single reading, will you not allow that I may be able to take in ten lines at a glance?"

Pao-yü now put away the book and, with a happy grin, declared, "To our task! Let us bury the flowers and forget the other part." So the two of them swept up the fallen petals, which they placed in the silk bag and solemnly deposited in a hollow in the earth. When finally they had covered up the hollow with a tiny mound,[45] Bombarding Scent rushed up and said reproachfully to Pao-yü: "Here of all places! As if I haven't looked all over the Garden for you! The cousins have gone across to ask after your uncle, the Duke,[46] who is indisposed, and the old mistress has ordered you to go, too. Come back now for a change of clothes." Pao-yü thereupon picked up his book and, having excused himself to Tai-yü, returned with Bombarding Scent to Crab Red Court to dress for the visit to his uncle, which forms no part of our story.

Being now left alone and having heard that the female cousins were all away, Tai-yü turned her steps sadly toward the Hermitage.[47] As she reached the corner of Pear Courtyard, from across the wall came the sweet notes of pipes, now loud, now muted, blending with the melodious voices of singers, and it occurred to her that the troupe of twelve girls from Soochow were rehearsing the airs of their Southern repertory.[48] Only Tai-yü had never cared much for the Southern drama and, paying no regard to the music, she walked

44. A quotation from near the end of *The West Chamber* which alludes to a line from the *Analects* about a plant that does not blossom.

45. "Which they placed . . . tiny mound" is the translator's own version. The original merely reads: "So the two swept up the fallen petals, and just when they had buried them, Bombarding Scent . . . ."

46. The Duke is Chia She, elder brother to Secretary Chia, who lives in a separate part of the Jung residence, entered through its own street gate. Being neither learned nor a man of affairs, he is content with a role secondary to his more ambitious younger brother.

47. The Hsiao-Hsiang Hermitage, which is her own residence. The Hsiao and Hsiang, two rivers of Hunan province, are the subject of numerous misty landscapes by painters and are redolent of tragic, suicidal poets and ethereal goddesses. These and other evocative aspects of the Hermitage make it perfectly suited for Tai-yü.

48. The twelve girls were brought to the capital from Soochow to give musical and dramatic performances on the occasion of the Queen's visit. They are appropriately housed in Pear Courtyard adjoining the Garden, Emperor Hsüan Tsung of T'ang having trained his three hundred musicians in a pear orchard.

on.[49] But borne by the breezes, two lines of a song assailed her ears, each word falling clear and distinct:

"Gay purple and exquisite red abloom everywhere,
But all abandoned to a dried-up well and crumbled walls."[50]

The words filled Tai-yü with a deep melancholy and longing. She stopped and, inclining her head, listened intently. The song now went:

"That glorious moments amidst this splendid scene
    should enshroud despair!
In whose courtyard do hearts still rejoice in the present?"

These last two lines caused her to sigh and nod inadvertently in agreement. She thought to herself: "It is true, then, that one may come across fine verse even in the theater, but I suppose most people simply follow the action and do not pause to savor the language."

The next moment, however, she blamed herself for letting her mind wander instead of attending to the song. And when she listened again, she heard:

"Because of your flowerlike beauty
And tender years like a rushing stream,"[51]

and almost trembled with excitement. She then heard the lines that followed:

"I sought you in each nook and corner
But find you dejected in your chamber."

Being now quite overcome with emotion, she could hardly remain on her feet but sank on to a rock to brood over the words,

"Because of your flowerlike beauty
And tender years like a rushing stream,"

alert to their every nuance and suggestion. Suddenly she recalled a line she had read in the T'ang poets only the other day:

"Faded blossoms borne on a plaintive stream: lovelorn both";[52]

and also from among the lyric compositions:

"The water rushing, the blossoms falling: Spring is gone forever!

49. Tai-yü's native place is Soochow and, in spite of her lack of interest, her ear would be attuned to Southern melodies. For Southern drama, see selections 274 and 277.
50. The song is from *Peony Pavilion*, scene 10: it is sung by the heroine, Bridal Tu; see selection 276.
51. *Peony Pavilion*, scene 10; sung by the hero, Willow.
52. From Ts'ui T'u (late ninth century), "Evening in Spring."

Alas, heaven above and man's despair!"[53]

and the lines, too, she had just read in *The West Chamber*:

> "The stream speckled with red petals falling,
> Each speck a grain of sorrow."[54]

Buoyed up from the depths of memory, all these lines floated in her mind, juxtaposed as in some conspiracy. She pondered over each passage and her heart was touched to the quick; her crowding fancies raced one another; and tears dropped from her eyes. While Tai-yü was thus enveloped in her thoughts, she felt a sudden pat on her back, and when she turned to look . . . .[55]

Translated by H. C. Chang

53. Being the last two lines of Li Yü, "Lang t'ao sha." Li Yü (937–978, see selection 115) was the last ruler of the Southern T'ang kingdom, and the poem, written after he was deposed by the Sung in 976, contrasts his state of captivity with his regal past. The two concluding lines, which point the contrast, lend themselves to a variety of interpretations. An alternative version reads:
"The water rushing, the blossoms falling—gone forever!
Alas, heaven above and man's despair!"
54. These lines are from the introduction.
55. This is followed by "but as to who it was that she saw, it shall be told in the next chapter" and two lines of verse which end chapter 23.

One Smear Wang

from *Dream of Red Towers*

Ts'ao Hsüeh-ch'in

The next day, Pao-yü arose at the crack of dawn. After he had finished washing his face and combing his hair, he got dressed. Then, following a few old nannies, he got in a carriage which drove out through the West Gate of the city wall to the Level with Heaven Temple. There he was to burn incense in repayment of a vow his grandmother had made for his recovery. The temple had already spent the previous day making elaborate preparations for his visit. Being timid by nature, Pao-yü dared not approach the terrifying images of

This episode is taken from the last few pages of the original final chapter (the eightieth) of *Dream of Red Towers*, the novel featured in the previous portion of this selection. In the present episode, we find the young hero of the novel, Pao-yü ("Precious Jade"), just as he is emerging from a long convalescence.

spirits and demons. So he hastily burned his offering of paper money and grain, then withdrew to the courtyard to take a breather.

After a short while, when the meal was finished, the troop of nannies along with Li Kuei and the others formed a circle around Pao-yü and followed him as he went about disporting himself. But he soon became tired and returned once again to a quiet room where he rested peacefully. The troop of nannies were quite afraid that he would fall asleep so they asked the abbot of the place, the old Taoist priest, Wang, to come and keep him company by engaging him in conversation. Now, this old priest specialized in selling specious medicines and concocting exotic remedies for the purpose of turning a profit. Outside of the monastery, he had hung up a sign which advertised that he sold all types of pills, powders, and medicinal ointments. He also came and went in the Peace and Glory palaces[1] so frequently that he became a familiar figure there. Everyone called him by his nickname, which was "One Smear Wang." It was said that his medicated ointments were marvelously efficacious. All you had to do was smear them on and your illness would vanish.

When One Smear Wang came in, Pao-yü was lying crosswise on the bed. Seeing One Smear Wang enter, Pao-yü said to him with a smile, "You've come just at the right time. I've heard it said that you're extremely good at telling jokes. How about telling us one now?"

"Oh, really? Careful you don't fall asleep, little brother, and 'let that gluten in your tummy start tootin,' " said One Smear Wang with a smile. As he spoke, everyone in the room laughed, including Pao-yü who sat up and straightened his clothing. Wang ordered his disciples to be quick with steeping some good tea and bringing it to Pao-yü.

"Our master is not about to drink your tea," said Tea Scent.[2] "Simply sitting here in this room, he feels the medicinal odors offensive."

"Stuff and nonsense!" said One Smear Wang with a smile. "I've never brought medicine into this room. If I had known that Young Master were coming for sure today, I'd have fumigated the place with fragrant herbs three or four days beforehand."

"But day after day all I hear is how good your ointment is," said Pao-yü. "What illnesses, after all, can it cure?"

"If you're asking about my ointment," replied One Smear Wang, "it's a long story and it would be hard to tell you all the details in a few words. Altogether, it's got one hundred and twenty ingredients. It'll cure lord and servant, and can be used both by the choleric and the phlegmatic. As for internal medicine applications, it can regulate the constitution and build up the spirit, nourish the blood and vital essences, stimulate the appetite, calm the nerves and settle the soul, banish chills and fevers, comfort indigestion and dissolve phlegm. As for surgical medical applications, it can harmonize

1. Where Pao-yü lives and where most of the action of the novel takes place.
2. One of Pao-yü's maids.

the pulse, relax the muscles and the blood vessels, break up dead tissue and promote the growth of new tissue, counteract apoplexy and break down poisons. It is divinely efficacious; those who have smeared it on know."

"I don't believe that one ointment could cure so many diseases," said Pao-yü. "But let me just ask you if it is of any value in curing one certain disease which I am thinking of?"

"There is no disease nor ailment whatsoever for which it is ineffective," replied One Smear Wang. "If it is not effective, it wouldn't matter to me if the Young Master plucked out my beard, slapped this old face of mine, and tore down this temple of mine. Just tell me how the disease came about."

"Guess," said Pao-yü. "If you guess correctly, you are indeed an adept smearer of ointments."

One Smear Wang listened, thought for a moment, and then said with a laugh, "This is really hard to guess. I suspect that the ointment will be, shall we say, not too 'esthetic'." Pao-yü told One Smear Wang to sit down beside him. One Smear Wang's heart began to beat a little faster and then, laughing quietly, he said to Pao-yü. "I've guessed it! It must be that the Young Master is engaged in a chamber affair these days and is in need of a tonic or philtre. Am I right?"

Before he had finished speaking, Tea Scent cut in sharply, "Scoundrel! You deserve a good slap on the mouth!" Pao-yü hadn't yet caught on and was busy asking Wang what he had said. "Don't believe this nonsense," said Tea Scent.

One Smear Wang was so frightened that he didn't give Pao-yü a chance to inquire further about what he had said. "Would the Young Master please be more explicit?" he asked.

"I ask you whether there is any prescription which can cure the disease of jealousy[3] in a woman?" was Pao-yü's rejoinder.

When One Smear Wang heard this, he clapped his hands and said with a laugh, "That's too much! Not only must I admit that I don't have a prescription for that, I've never even heard of one."

"If this is what your art is like, it's not worth very much," said Pao-yü with a smile.

"I've never had any experience with an ointment that could be used to cure jealousy," and One Smear Wang hurriedly. "But there is a decoction that might work, only it would be rather slow. You couldn't expect to see an effect right away."

"Which decoction is that?" asked Pao-yü. "How should it be taken?"

"It's called an Antijealously Draft," said One Smear Wang. "You use one exceptionally fine autumn pear, two maces of crystal-sugar, one mace of bitter tangerine peel, and three bowls of water. Boil the ingredients in the water

3. An issue that is at the core of Pao-yü's tortured, metaphysical love relationship with his cousin, Tai-yü ("Lustrous Jade"), and that runs through the entire novel.

until the pear is thoroughly cooked. The patient takes one pear every day early in the morning and, if she just keeps eating them, she'll get better."

"That's not worth very much either," said Pao-yü. "I'm afraid that it wouldn't necessarily be effective."

"If a single dose is not effective," said One Smear Wang, "then the patient should take ten doses. If it's not effective one day, take it again the next day. If it's not effective this year, take it again next year. Anyway, all three of the ingredients in this medicine serve as demulcents for the lungs and stimulants for the appetite without any injurious side effects. This decoction is syrupy sweet and also acts as a cough suppressant. What's more, it tastes good. The patient could take this medicine for a hundred years, but sooner or later she'll have to die. Once she's dead, could she still be jealous? That's when you'll see how effective this medicine is."

While he was talking, Pao-yü and Tea Scent couldn't stop laughing loudly. "Glib-tongued ox-head!" they scolded him.

"I was merely jesting to help dispel your noontime drowsiness," said One Smear Wang. "What does it matter? I should charge just for making you two laugh. Let me tell you something. Even my ointments are phony. If I had a true medicine, I would take it myself and become a transcendent! If I had the real thing, do you think I would run around trying to make ends meet?"

As he was talking, the auspicious hour for sacrifice had arrived, and Pao-yü was invited to go make his libations, to burn more paper money and grain, and to distribute blessings to the Taoists and to the poor. Only after he had completed all of his assigned tasks that were part of the ritual did Pao-yü go back to the city and return home.

Translated by Victor H. Mair

264
The Women's Kingdom

from *The Romance of the Flowers in the Mirror*
Li Ju-chen (c. 1763–1830)

After several days, they reached the Women's Kingdom. Having anchored the ship, the coxswain, old Tuo,[1] came within and invited T'ang Ao[2] to go ashore

This selection is taken from chapters 32–37 of *The Romance of the Flowers in the Mirror* (*Ching hua yüan*), an inimitable blend of mythology and adventure story, fantasy and allegory, satire and straightforward instruction. The one-hundred-chapter novel is informed throughout with learning and sustained by wit, with an admixture of games and puzzles for the unhurried reader.

The book opens with a quotation from the Grand Instructress Ts'ao, Pan Chao, who was

with him to see the sights. Now T'ang Ao had heard about the monk Tripiṭaka's sojourn in the Women's Country[3] during his journey to the Western
Paradise to fetch sūtras at the command of the Emperor T'ai Tsung, how that
the monk had there been detained by the queen, from whose enticements
he had with difficulty extricated himself; T'ang Ao, therefore, was wary of
disembarking. The old helmsman, however, laughed hilariously, saying, "You
are, of course, right to be circumspect, Master T'ang, but this Women's
Kingdom is quite unlike the other! If this had been the same Women's
Country that Tripiṭaka journeyed through, then not only had you to remain
on board; for all the profit his merchandise could bring him, even Master
Lin[4] durst not venture forth. This Women's Kingdom is another sort. There
was never any lack of males among them, and men and women mate as we
do, but with this difference, that the men wear skirts and tunics and call
themselves women and run the household, whereas the women wear boots
and tall hats, call themselves men, and preside over public affairs. Thus

---

sister of the historian Pan Ku (32–92) and wife of Ts'ao Shou. She was summoned to the palace
to teach the empress and other court ladies; hence her title (see selection 194). The quotation is
about the four aspects of feminine conduct—virtue, speech, appearance, and accomplishment—
in justification of the book's professed aim: the praise of womanhood. But its three chief
characters are, in fact, men: the inspired and resourceful T'ang Ao ("Wandering Chinese"), an
almost preternatural scholar; the ingenuous and down-to-earth Lin Chih-yang ("Ocean-faring
Lin"), a merchant; and the wise and experienced Tuo Chiu-kung ("Old Man Long at the
Helm"), a mariner.

The story is set in the reign (684–705) of the usurping Empress Wu—an era of the
ascendancy of women, or rather, of one woman—which interrupted the continuity of the great
T'ang dynasty. Being of indomitable will, the empress commanded the hundred flowers in the
imperial Shang-lin Park to blossom on a winter's day: they obeyed, thus disrupting the harmony
of the seasons. For their pains, the hundred fairies in charge of the flowers were banished from
heaven, to be born as girls in families all over the empire and even in lands across the seas
(chapters 3–6; chapters 1 and 2 take place in heaven). T'ang Ao, a graduate recently deprived of
his hard-won title of t'an-hua (literally, Seeker of Flowers) because of his earlier association with
the empress's political enemies, decides to join his brother-in-law, Lin Chih-yang, on a voyage.
Being advised by a temple god in a dream to search for twelve famous flowers and transplant
them back to China, T'ang sets off, armed with flowerpots and, for merchandise, tons of cast
iron "useful as ballast should they prove unsalable," to the amusement and disgust of the
commercially astute Lin (chapters 7–8).

While on their voyage (chapters 8–40), T'ang and Lin and their coxswain Tuo visit many
strange kingdoms, in various degrees also allegorical. The parallels with Jonathan Swift's (1667–
1745) famous satirical novel of the previous century, *Gulliver's Travels*, are striking and merit
close investigation.

1. Tuo Chiu-kung, i.e., old man long at the rudder.
2. T'ang Ao, i.e., the Chinese on a journey.
3. Tripiṭaka in the Women's Country (see selection 270, chapter 10). The story being set in
the T'ang dynasty, Tripiṭaka's journey to India to seek Buddhist scriptures is alluded to as a
recent event.
4. Lin Chih-yang, i.e., Lin who traversed the ocean. Lim, i.e., Lin, is probably the
commonest surname among the Chinese inhabitants of Malaysia and Singapore.

though men and women are connubial partners as in other places, the roles of domestic and external affairs are reversed."

Upon this, T'ang Ao cried, "If their men call themselves women and look after the house, must they daub their faces with powder and rouge? Do they bind their feet?" His brother-in-law, the merchant Lin Chih-yang, now joining them, said, "Bound feet are a fetish among these people—so I have been told—and the small foot is prized in families great and humble alike. As for powder and rouge, they could never do without those. I congratulate myself that I was born in the Celestial Country.[5] Had I been born here, I too should have had to bind my feet, and what mortification and shame that would have been!" Then, producing from his bosom an inventory, he unfolded it and continued, "Look, brother-in-law. The goods listed are all intended for this place." T'ang Ao took the paper and saw that the items consisted entirely of powder, rouge, combs, fine-toothed combs, etc., every one of them some toilet or cosmetic article. Handing it back to Lin, he said, "I remember, when the freight was being checked just before our departure from Ling-nan,[6] I did wonder at the large quantity of these things, but I now see why you brought them along. Having so carefully listed the goods, why have you not included the prices?"

The merchant Lin replied, "When you engage in trade abroad, you never fix the price beforehand; instead you try to discover what they are short of, and raise the price of that commodity accordingly. For us who traverse the seas, the very secret of success is readiness to clinch a deal on the spur of the moment." T'ang Ao then asked, "If, in spite of its name, 'Women's Kingdom,' the country is not in fact inhabited only by women, why should there be such a demand for cosmetics?" The old coxswain said in reply, "It is the custom of the land. They are otherwise thrifty enough, from the ruler down to the populace; but their sole indulgence is the adorning and beautifying of their women. When they speak of female attire and ornaments, rich and poor alike start raving, and even those who could ill afford them would try to purchase powder and rouge and trinkets from abroad. Being acquainted with their customs, Master Lin deliberately chose his merchandise; once his inventory has gone round the richer households, the whole lot will be bought up within two or three days, and when the goods are delivered and the silver collected, his profit could easily be two or threefold or more, even if not quite the windfall of his transactions in the Lands of Giants and Pygmies."[7]

T'ang Ao now observed, "I had always regarded the words of the ancients,

5. The exact translation is "Celestial Court," to which lesser nations send bearers of tribute. "Celestial Country" and "Celestial Land" are used indiscriminately as the name for China recognized by the travelers and the foreign countries alike.

6. Ling-nan, where they started on their journey, is roughly Kwangtung province.

7. In the Land of Giants, the inhabitants were eighty feet tall; in the Land of Pygmies, they were under a foot in height.

'Men's place was in the home, but women's in the sphere of public affairs,' read in my youth, as pure invention, little imagining I should really be visiting such a land today. An unusual country, to say the least, one that I must go ashore and see for myself! But my brother-in-law's flushed cheeks seem to augur some event of great felicity. Very likely he now goes to meet his best customer yet, and their brisk commerce would be the occasion of feasting and merrymaking." Lin himself also said, "Two magpies kept up a loud chatter before me this morning, and a pair of black spiders landed upon my feet. Perhaps there will be stroke of luck, as when those birds' nests came to me unsought!"[8] And grinning all over, he started out with his inventory.

T'ang Ao then went ashore with Tuo, the coxswain, and they entered the city, determined to take a close look at the inhabitants. They found old and young alike to be beardless and, though dressed like men, speaking with high-pitched feminine voices, and, furthermore, not only slight in build but possessing a certain elegance and charm. T'ang Ao remarked, "Have you noticed, Tuo, my friend? They are really women, but perversely disguised as men. Is not this the height of affectation?" The mariner said, laughing, "That is what *you* maintain, Master T'ang. But if *they* saw us, would they not regard us as women dissatisfied with our natural lot and, in our folly and affectation, masquerading as men?" T'ang Ao nodded in agreement and continued, "You are right! There was the saying: 'Habit is nature's strongest propensity.' We may find them extraordinary, but since this is how they always ordered their affairs, we too must seem odd to them. If the 'men' here are like this, what about the 'women'?"

Slyly the old helmsman pointed to one side and whispered, "Look! There's a middle-aged person with needle and thread in hand, making a pair of slippers. If that is not a woman—" T'ang Ao turned and saw a humble dwelling, in the doorway of which a middle-aged woman was seated. Her hair was jet black and, being liberally sprinkled with some fragrant oil, presented a surface so smooth and glossy as a passing fly might have slid on; it was carefully braided and coiled in the shape of an elaborate crown. At her temples, pearls and jade hairpins dazzled in their profusion, and from her ears hung golden earrings. She wore a purple-rose tunic over an onion green skirt, from under which protruded the tiniest feet encased in scarlet embroidered slippers just three inches in length. Her white hands were held up before her, their ten dainty fingers busy at a piece of embroidery. Her almond-shaped eyes were clear and sparkling, matched by eyebrows coquettishly arched, and her face was heavily painted with powder and rouge. Agreeably surprised, T'ang

8. The magpie (*hsi-ch'üeh*) and black spider (*hsi-chu*) both have the character *hsi* (i.e., joy) and were omens of joyful occasions, especially of weddings. In chapter 12, at the end of their visit to the Gentlemen's Country, the crew received ten piculs (roughly, hundredweights) of edible birds' nests as a present from the Wu brothers. Finding the birds' nests tasteless, the sailors sold them to Lin for a few strings of cash. On that occasion, too, the magpies made a chatter.

Ao slowly directed his gaze toward her mouth, and it was then that he noticed thick bristles, in truth, bushy side-whiskers, at which sight he could no longer contain himself and burst into a titter. The woman laid aside her embroidery, gave T'ang Ao one look, and said imperiously, "Young woman! How dare you snigger at me?" Her voice boomed and twanged like a cracked gong, hearing which T'ang Ao beat a hasty retreat, dragging Tuo after him.

From where she sat, however, the woman railed at them in a loud voice, "Don't tell me, with that beard on you, you are not a woman! And yet you go about in a long robe and a high hat and pass yourself off for a man! Have you never heard of such a thing as the segregation of the sexes? Now while you pretend to be spying upon women, your real purpose is of course to peep at the men. Take a good look at yourself in the mirror, trollop, and see if you remember what you are! Have you no sense of shame?—The minx! She should be thankful, too, it was I who caught her out.—Hey, you could really have been mistaken for a man peeping at the women! And the blows that might have rained upon you!" T'ang Ao heard it all but, being now safely distant, he turned to the old helmsman, saying, "Well, at least their speech is readily intelligible! Judging from the way she spoke, she really took us for women. Minx and trollop indeed! Was ever a man called such names? I wager it is the strangest insult on record. My poor brother-in-law! Let us hope that in his dealings in this place he is at least treated like a man."

The coxswain wondering at his words, T'ang Ao explained, "With his fair complexion my brother-in-law always gave the impression of having painted his face. Besides, during our recent visit to the Land of Flames, his beard caught fire, with the loss of which he seems younger than ever.[9] If these people should look upon him as a woman, surely there is cause for alarm." Old Tuo then said, "They have always been on the most amicable terms with their neighboring states. Coming, moreover, from the Celestial Country, we shall be treated with the utmost respect. You need scarcely worry on that score, Master T'ang." Observing a crowd gathered round a roadside placard, reading aloud, T'ang Ao suggested finding out what was happening. As they drew near, however, they could hear, from what was being said, that a certain river channel was blocked. T'ang Ao was suddenly impelled to break through the crowd and read the placard for himself. But Tuo protested, "Must you read it? What have the rivers here to do with us? Surely you do not mean to dredge their rivers and claim a reward, Master T'ang."

T'ang Ao said, "Do not tease me, Master Coxswain. What do I know about river channels? But I *am* interested in the vulgar forms of characters, of which this placard reminds me, such as certain local forms in the southern provinces: $^{\text{'LARGE'}}_{\text{SEAT}}$ for 'secure'; and $^{\text{'NO'}}_{\text{LIFE}}$ for 'end'; and others with equally

---

9. In chapter 26, Lin Chih-yang having nearly lost his beard in the flames, Tuo the coxswain himself thus describes him, "Master Lin is a man of forty years and over, but with his beard perished in the fire and his fair complexion, he would seem no more than twenty."

obvious meanings.[10] And that is sufficient reason for my wanting to read any proclamation, to discover the language of the country. To be sure, it would not qualify as scholarship, but the odd character picked up here and there comes in useful at times." Thus pushing his way through the crowd, he studied the placard and reemerged, saying, "The style is clear enough and the calligraphy passable; moreover, I did find a character, NOT/HIGH, which was new to me." Old Tuo said, "It is read 'low,' as far as I remember, in the southern provinces and refers to height." T'ang Ao cried, "It occurred in the phrase 'high and NOT/HIGH dikes,' and 'low' would certainly be correct! So from my visit to the Women's Kingdom I have actually learned a new word!"

As they went on, they saw some women walking about, who seemed no different from women elsewhere: their skirt tails revealed the tiniest feet and their slender waists swayed sinuously and, where there was a crowd, they shunned the public gaze and sought to hide themselves, the bashfulness itself awakening much admiration. Some carried infants in their arms; others held on to their children. Some were middle-aged women with beards of varying thickness; others, also in their middle years, had no beard at all. Upon closer inspection, however, the beardless ones turned out to be those unwilling to grow old, who had removed the evidence of their age by plucking every hair off their chin. T'ang Ao remarked, "Look, my friend! There are pores where the stubs were, and the cheeks seem indeed somewhat improved, but to pluck the hair from the chin and upper lip and denude the whole surface like a mower rooting out every blade of grass would seem too drastic an alteration of the contours, and the face should consequently acquire a new name." The old helmsman, too, quipped, "I recall that phrase in *The Analects*, 'hides of tigers and leopards.'[11] Since the chin and upper lip of these persons have been plucked clean, why not call their faces 'dressed human hides'?"[12]

Thus joking and punning, they moved to other parts of the city, where after lingering for some time, they went back on board the ship, to learn that Lin Chih-yang had not yet returned. After supper, they sat up waiting for him till the second watch. When Mistress Lin expressing much anxiety about the merchant's safety, T'ang Ao and the old coxswain set off again with lanterns to look for him; but the city gates were shut and they had to turn back. The next day, the search was resumed, but there was not a shadow of the man. On the third day, they took some of the crew with them and made a thorough search in several directions without success. They continued their inquiries in

10. Local forms of characters, mainly coinages, such as are still common in Cantonese and Hokkien. Without such nonce forms, it is impossible to write Sinitic languages other than Mandarin and Classical Chinese in characters.

11. *The Analects*, XII. viii. 3 (Legge): "Ornament is as substance; substance is as ornament. The hide of a tiger or a leopard stripped of its hair is like the hide of a dog or a goat stripped of its hair." Prejudice against the razor has tended to persist.

12. Some more facetious exchanges that follow have been omitted in the translation.

the ensuing days: the man seemed, however, to have vanished like a millstone dropped into the ocean. Mistress Lin and her daughter Wan-ju[13] now spent their days in weeping and wailing, while T'ang Ao and the coxswain combed the city's streets and environs.

They could hardly have known that when, on that first day Lin Chih-yang ventured into the city and called at various warehouses with his inventory, he found that, though there was a scarcity of the commodities he had to offer, the prices were well below his expectations. This led him to try a rich household, where, an order having been placed, he was further directed to "the residence of the Royal Brother-in-law, with a very large domestic establishment taking up vast supplies, where, if you ask, you shall secure abundant profit." Lin inquired the way and came to an imposing mansion with a high gate and an air of unusual splendor.[14] Taking out his inventory, he begged the gatekeeper to hand it up for inspection. Presently a reply came from within, "The articles listed are required for use at the Royal Palace, where His Majesty the King has for the past twelve-month[15] been exercised in the choice of a royal consort as well as ladies of the Inner Palace. The inventory is being forwarded to the Palace, whither the trader should hasten in the company of our messenger, there to await further instructions." Shortly afterwards, the house-steward appeared with the inventory and conducted Lin through a succession of golden gates into the Palace grounds, where, walking along jade-paved paths, Lin was chilled by the sight of armed guards stationed at every turning.

When they reached the gate leading to the Inner Palace, the house-steward stopped and said to Lin, "Wait here, my good woman. I must now attend upon His Majesty and will let you know presently the requirements of the Palace." The steward then went through the gate but soon came out to say, "My good woman, how may one figure out the prices, which are not listed with the goods?" Lin replied, "I carry them in my head. When you have made up your order, I will quote you the prices of those goods required." The steward went in again, but was back before long to ask, "What is the price in silver of a hundred-weight[16] of rouge, my good woman? And of a hundred-weight of fragrant powder? And of hair oil? And of hair cord?" Lin gave his answer, and the steward returned within. A little while later the steward again appeared and said, "My good woman, how much for a box of flowers worked

13. Wan-ju, see note 47.

14. This is the end of chapter 32, and the narrative is followed by the formula, "As to what happened next, it shall be told in the following chapter," here omitted. Chapter 33 begins with: "The story goes that when Lin Chih-yang came to the Royal Brother-in-law's residence," which is also omitted in the translation.

15. In the original, "the past few years." Since, however, the Queen died only the year before, the change seems desirable.

16. A picul (*tan*), which is a hundred catties.

with kingfisher's feathers? How much for a box of silk embroidered flowers? And for a box of sandalwood beads? And of combs, ordinary and fine-toothed?" Lin gave his answer, and the steward went in, but came out yet once more, and this time he said, "His Majesty is graciously pleased to place an order for every available item on your list, though in varying quantities. As regards price, my running back and forth can but lead to error, and the commerce must be between yourself and His Majesty. My good woman, since you are from the Celestial Country, a land acknowledged as our superior, His Majesty commands you to enter the Inner Palace. But I warn you—take heed lest you incur royal displeasure."

Lin Chih-yang replied, "I shall be discretion itself." And he followed the steward into the Inner Audience Chamber, where, after making his obeisance to the King, he stood to one side. Now though the King was already over thirty, his pale cheeks and bloodred lips presented an appearance of youth and beauty which was highly attractive. His Majesty, who was surrounded by a great many maids of honor, held up the inventory with the tips of ten delicate royal fingers and demanded in a melodious voice the price of each article. During question and answer, however, His Majesty's piercing eyes scanned the merchant from top to toe, at which, Lin growing uneasy, said to himself, "What does this King want of me that he should look me over in this fashion? I suppose he has never met a Chinese trader." A maid of honor then entering to announce dinner, His Majesty dismissed the house-steward with compliments to the Royal Brother-in-law, intimating that the inventory was to be left at the Palace. And commanding the maids of honor[17] to entertain "the woman from the Celestial Court" at dinner, the King retired to the Royal Apartments.

There was but a moment's delay before several maids of honor brought Lin Chih-yang up the staircase of another building, where a sumptuous meal with wine was spread in an upper-story room.[18] Before they had risen from table, a clamor broke out below and court ladies swarmed up the stairs hailing Lin as their Queen and sovereign, kowtowing to him and offering him their congratulations. More maids of honor followed, and these held in their hands the phoenix bridal crown and ceremonial collar, the jade girdle and ceremonial dragon robes, as well as skirt and undergarments, hairpins and earrings, and other ornaments. Despite his protests, their several pairs of hands now fell upon Lin, undoing all his garments and underclothing; for these maids of honor were of prodigious strength and they laid hold of him as a hawk might pounce upon a swallow, without the least fuss. When Lin had been unclad and his shoes removed, they deposited him in a perfumed bath

17. "Maid of honor," "waiting woman," etc. are used indiscriminately, the distinction not being made in the original.

18. In the "Country of Eastern Women," according to the accounts in the official T'ang histories, the inhabitants lived in multistoried houses, buildings in the Palace rising to nine stories.

and, having washed and scrubbed him, dressed him in blouse and underpants, over which he was made to wear a skirt and the dragon robes. His large feet were afforded the protection of stiff silk socks; his hair was carefully braided and copiously sprinkled with hair oil, after which they laid the phoenix crown on his head; scented powder was daubed all over his face; his lips were painted scarlet; and rings were placed on his fingers and a gold bangle on each wrist.

A curtained bed was now set up, which Lin was invited to sit on. Poor Lin Chih-yang! He thought of himself as being in a dream or in a drunken stupor. Staring about him in blank astonishment, he at last resolved to ask one of the maids of honor, who explained that His Majesty had chosen him, Lin Chih-yang, as a Royal Concubine and that they awaited only an auspicious day for his installation in the Royal Apartments. Though now in a state of extreme agitation, Lin noticed more waiting women enter: these were middle-aged and fully bearded, tall and thickset. One of them, whose beard was turned steel gray, came up with needle and thread in her hand and knelt before the bed, saying, "By my lady's leave. His Majesty commands the piercing of my lady's ears." Upon this, four waiting women sprang forward, their arms gripping Lin like so many clamps. The gray-bearded one herself then rising, pinched and twirled Lin's right ear-lobe with her practiced fingers and suddenly sent her needle through the flesh. Lin gave a loud shriek, "That stab! It's the death of me!" And he threw his head back, but the waiting women held him tightly, and the gray-bearded one then pinched and twirled the left ear-lobe and, with one thrust of the needle, pierced it too. Lin howled with the pain.

The ears having been pierced, the wounds were smeared with powder, the ear-lobes gently massaged, and a pair of gold earrings affixed. Her task dispatched, the gray-bearded waiting woman retired. Immediately afterwards, however, a black-bearded waiting woman came up with a roll of white silk gauze in her hand and knelt before the bed, saying, "By my lady's leave. His Majesty commands the binding of my lady's feet." Two others also came forward and, kneeling down, grasped Lin's legs, removing the stiff silk socks. The black-bearded waiting woman then placed a low stool near the bed, sat down on it, and tore off a good length of the silk gauze. Then, pulling Lin's right foot onto her knees, she sprayed the chinks between the toes with alum; next, she doubled up the toes and pressed them down by main force so as to accentuate the curvature of the arch; finally, she wrapped the crushed foot in tight layers of silk gauze. Another waiting woman came up with needle and thread and, as soon as the second layer of bandage was done, sewed up the hem in close stitches; and even as the cruel bandaging progressed, so the relentless stitching followed. All this while, Lin had been wedged in by the four waiting women; the two others kept his legs firmly in place so that he could not move them an inch. When at last the binding came to an end, his feet were in searing pain as if he was treading on red-hot charcoal. He felt suddenly sick at heart and burst out sobbing, "Oh, mortification and shame!"

Both feet having been bound, a pair of soft scarlet slippers were quickly sewn and put on for him. Lin Chih-yang now stopped crying and, having racked his brains in vain for a better plan, proceeded to implore the mercy of those present, saying, "Gentlemen, intercede on my behalf, I beg of you, with His Majesty. I am a *man*, with a wife of my own. How, then, could I be turned into a Royal Concubine? As for my man-sized feet, they never knew restraint till this moment; they are like reluctant students who, having played truant from the beginning, would not now submit to the tyranny of the examinations.[19] I only beg for my early release. Be assured that my wife, too, would be grateful to you." But the waiting women only said, "His Majesty has commanded that my lady be installed in the Palace as soon as her feet are properly bound. Who are we to say otherwise?"

Before long, lamps were brought and supper laid out. Though it was a veritable feast, Lin had lost all desire for food, and left it to the maids of honor and waiting women to enjoy the splendid repast. Presently, however, feeling the need to discharge water, he spoke to one of the waiting women, "My dear fellow, kindly help me downstairs. I must make water." The waiting women nodded and soon brought out a night-commode, at the sight of which Lin squirmed. But struggle was useless; for his feet had been so tightly bound that he could not walk. He resigned himself to leaning on the arms of the waiting women, with whose help he climbed down from the bed and sat on the commode. Then, when his hands had been washed, a further basin of hot water was brought by a waiting woman, who said, "Water for my lady's ablutions." Lin exclaimed, "But I have already washed my hands! Why should I wash again?" The woman replied demurely, "Not the hands, my lady; the privates." Lin cried in exasperation, "The privates? Where? I have never heard of such a thing." The waiting woman persisted—"Whence the water issued, my lady, there wash with water. But if my lady is not accustomed to doing so, we will carry out our duty." Instantly two other fat waiting women came forward; one of them undid Lin's underpants, and the other soaked a red silk handkerchief in the water and began wiping and cleansing. Lin Chih-yang screamed, "Stop, gentlemen! The joke is getting out of hand. I am a *man*, and this will give me a terrible itch. Stop it, I say. The more you wipe, the itchier it gets." The waiting woman, however, only muttered, "That may well be. You say, the more I wipe, the itchier you are; but, of course, the itchier you get, the more I'll wipe!"

These ablutions being over, he was again placed on the bed. His feet were now in excruciating pain and, being unable to sit up any longer, he lay down in his clothes. The foot-binder came forward once more and said, "Since my

19. This is topical and the exact translation should be: "like licentiates who had wandered far from their home districts and had taken no revision examinations for many years, and who, having been left alone, would not submit to such restraints again."

lady is tired, we beg to commence the bedtime toilet." The others now crowded round the bed, bustling confusedly, one of them holding a candlestick, another a hand spittoon, a third a basin, still others a dressing case, jars of oil and cream, a face cloth, and silk handkerchiefs, to all whose attentions he politely submitted. His face having been washed and carefully dried, a maid of honor offered to apply the face powder, which Lin resolutely refused. Thereupon the gray-bearded waiting woman who had pierced his ears came forward to deliver a grave discourse, "The preparation of a powder mask at bedtime is a practice conferring inestimable benefit. Being mixed in the right proportion with unctuous musk, powder renders the skin smooth and white. To be sure, my lady has an excellently fair complexion, but her skin is at present not deeply imbued with sweet fragrance, and she must therefore invoke the aid of powder, with prolonged application of which not only will her face seem carved out of white jade, but a warm, delicious fragrance will ooze from the very pores. In short, the whiter the skin, the more sweet-smelling; and the more sweet-smelling, the more spotlessly white. Its effect upon the beholder is indeed irresistible—a single sniff leads to enslavement and, being thus enslaved, one longs to touch and smell again. But the full benefit is felt only with regular application over an extended period." And she went on earnestly, though unheeded by Lin.[20] The others now cried, "What a contrary new Concubine! We shall have to memorialize the throne without omission or concealment, and request the presence of the Mother of Correction!" Thus they dispersed for the night.

Fits of pain caused Lin Chih-yang to start from his sleep. He tugged and tore at the silk bandage and succeeded, after endless exertion, in unripping the gauze and removing the wrapping. Freed from their bondage, his ten toes were again spread out, each delighting in its newly won freedom—like licentiates exempted from their revision examinations! With this feeling of release, he sank into a deep sleep. Sitting up in bed the next morning, having washed his face and rinsed his mouth, he was confronted by the black-bearded waiting woman, whose province was his feet. Discovering, all of a sudden, both her charges shorn of their elaborate covering, she at once reported to the King, who straightway commanded the Mother of Correction to administer twenty heavy strokes to the new Concubine and, furthermore, to station herself within the courtyard for strict enforcement of the household regulations. The Mother of Correction received the command and, leading her four attendants who carried the bamboo for her, marched up the stairs and knelt before the bed, saying, "The Concubine has flouted the household regulations. His Majesty commands the use of the bamboo of correction." Lin stared. The Mother of Correction, a long-bearded woman, then rose and took the bam-

20. Lin being himself a dealer in cosmetics and hence unimpressed by her patter.

boo, a heavy rod eight feet in length and three inches wide at the thick end, at which sight Lin trembled, protesting feebly, "The bamboo! What do you mean?" The four attendants, strapping women with small beards and brawny arms, rushed up and, ignoring his protests, laid him prostrate on the bed and removed his lower garments; and the Mother of Correction, herself briskly wielding the bamboo, smote hip and thigh. Lin set up a howl, finding the pain more than he could endure; for, by the end of the fifth stroke, the flesh was lacerated and blood came gushing out onto the bed. The Mother of Correction paused and, turning to the foot-binder, said, "Talk of a bath of blood! And it's only five strokes, too! The new Concubine has indeed a delicate behind, and to administer the full twenty might inflict real injury. Besides, her wound taking too long to heal would delay the wedding. Before I start again, go, my good sister, and report to His Majesty on my behalf, and beg for fresh instructions." The foot-binder assented and left immediately.

The Mother of Correction, still clutching her heavy bamboo, began muttering to herself, "It is skin and flesh same as anybody has got, but so soft and white! And such a shape too! One would have to admit that this precious bottom is worth every bit of the handsome faces of P'an An and Sung Yü."[21] But correcting herself, she added hastily, "P'an An and Sung Yü—theirs were, of course, faces. A bottom's only a bottom, not to be spoken of in the same breath." The foot-binder now returning, announced, "His Majesty has sent to ask if the Concubine will from this moment abide by the household regulations, and has commanded that, if the Concubine repents of her past misdeed, further punishment be waived." Being in dread of more beating, Lin hastily cried, "I have thoroughly reformed!" The Mother of Correction and her attendants then desisting, the maids of honor wiped away the blood with silk handkerchiefs. The King presently sent a dressing for the wound and a potion compounded of the ginseng root and various soothing herbs. The dressing being then applied and the potion taken, Lin fell back on the bed and found the pain suddenly eased.

The foot-binder now reasserted her authority and bandaged the feet anew with great care. She insisted that Lin descend from his bed and walk about the room, and he took a few steps, leaning on the arms of the waiting women; though the hip wounds no longer bothered him, the feet were still in pain, and he longed to rest. The foot-binder, however, was bent on keeping to her schedule and became implacably strict, so that, whenever he made as if to sit down, she threatened to report to the King. Thus Lin remained on his feet as best he could, and continued walking back and forth as if his life depended on it. And night brought no remission: for pain interrupted his sleep and kept

21. Sung Yü (about third century B.C.E., see selection 149), the rhapsody writer, was noted for his beauty. P'an An is P'an Yüeh (247–300), much admired by women, who pelted him with fruit as he drove along in his cart so that he would return loaded with provisions.

him in a state of vigil, and waiting women sat by his bed day and night, watching him by turns and noting his every movement. Having reached such a pass, Lin Chih-yang, he who traversed the ocean, felt his manly courage and resolution ebb and dissolve in womanly sighs and tears.[22]

The story goes that Lin's "lily feet" having daily been first dipped in a solution of alum and then even more tightly bandaged by the waiting women, within a fortnight the arch of each foot was crushed into two halves; and all the ten toes had turned septic and were dripping blood. One day as he, in his agony, was being walked by the maids of honor, he felt anger and vexation mounting within him. He said to himself, "I, Lin Chih-yang, have held my temper in check until this moment, submitting to a hundred tortures and indignities in the hope of my brother-in-law and coxswain coming to my rescue. Yet there has not been one word from them and I am clearly abandoned! Rather than go on suffering piecemeal in this fashion, far better die at once and so get it over and done with!" Still leaning on the arms of the others, he took a few more steps, but his aggrieved feet now smarted with the slightest motion. He made a dash for the bed, where he planted himself and, to the pleas of all present, gave one reply only, which he addressed repeatedly to the Mother of Correction: Would the good gentleman inform the King that he, Lin Chih-yang, preferred instant death to the binding of his feet, which he would resist to the bitter end. And as he spoke, he kicked off his embroidered slippers and tore at the white silk bandages. The waiting women all rushing up to restrain him and repair the damage, the ensuing struggle resulted in endless confusion. The Mother of Correction having sized up the situation for herself, left forthwith to report to the King, but returned before long, fortified by a fresh mandate, which she announced without kneeling, "His Majesty has ruled that, in refusing to comply with custom in the binding of the feet, the Concubine did violate the household regulations. His Majesty commands that the Concubine's feet be tied to the beam, her body to hang upside down."

Lin, who looked to death for his release, heard the word "hang" and appealed aloud to the maids of honor, "Make haste—I beg of you, gentlemen! The sooner I die, the better! And the more grateful I shall be. Therefore, hurry!" And he cooperated eagerly in their latest maneuvers. But as soon as they had tied his feet together with a rope, a new pain brought out the old again; and when they had actually hung him from the beam, feet up, body suspended in midair, stars seemed to pop out of his eyes as his head swung round in a dizzy spin. Cold sweat flowed all the way up his spine, and his two legs were, in turn, sore and numb. With manly fortitude, Lin clenched his teeth, bit his lip and shut his eyes, expecting at any moment to expire and thus contract out of the unending installments of punishment. A long while he held out, but death failed to come to his relief. Instead a heightened

22. The end of chapter 33, the concluding formula ("As to what happened next, it shall be told in the following chapter") being omitted in the translation.

consciousness descended upon him, intensifying every sensation of pain and discomfort. One moment he felt his feet pricked by hundreds of needles; the next, a knife blade seemed to be cleaving bone and tendon. As a last resort, he set his jaw, but this no more warded off the pain, which soon getting the better of him, all of a sudden Lin squealed like a pig in the slaughterhouse and entreated the King's mercy.

The Mother of Correction again reporting to the King, His Majesty commanded that the Concubine be set down. From then on, Lin endured all his troubles uncomplainingly, not daring to show the least intransigence. Knowing that he had been thoroughly cowed, the waiting women now sought the quickest returns from his feet, which, dead or alive, they would bind and constrict in their desire to please the King. Though time and again Lin looked for some opportunity to do away with himself, yet, since he was under constant watch day and night, even as liberty was denied him, so death, too, was beyond his reach. Imperceptibly the flesh on his feet and toes putrefied and decomposed; the wounds dried up and healed; only the bare bones remained. His feet had shrunk beyond recognition. Moreover, his raven locks, having been rubbed with every variety of hair oil, shone with a new gloss; daily immersion in a fragrant bath had rendered his skin smooth and soft; and plucking and trimming had transformed his thick eyebrows into two crescents. In addition, his lips were coated with a bloodred rouge, which set off his powder-masked face, topped by pearl and jade ornaments all over his head—a splendiferous sight!

Several times a day the King sent to inquire about the progress of the ticklish business. When, at last, the Mother of Correction reported one day that the feet had been bound, His Majesty ascended the stairs to inspect the new Concubine. And the King found a face as fair as the peach blossoms; and a waist that swayed like the weeping willow; and a pair of eyes clear as autumn rivers; and eyebrows arched like distant hills. [23] Each gaze awakened yet greater admiration in His Majesty, who could not help musing, "Quite a gem! And to think she was actually disguised as a man! Had not our observant eyes picked her out, such a rose would have been left to blush on the high seas!" And the King took out a bracelet, which was a string of real pearls, and with his own delicate fingers slipped it on Lin's wrist. The maids of honor having made him bow low to give thanks to His Majesty, the King pulled him up and, still holding him by the hand, bade him sit down, so that they sat shoulder to shoulder. The King then contemplated the newly bound feet with unconcealed delight, after which His Majesty sniffed and kissed and stroked and cuddled him all over, displaying a love full to overflowing.

On his part, Lin was already flushed with shame upon the King's arrival,

---

23. A parody of the stereotyped Chinese heroine, especially in novels.

and he found it mortifying to sit like a concubine shoulder to shoulder with that obviously female King; but when his feet were then subjected to the monarch's amorous scrutiny, and his hands to fond caressing, and his forehead and cheeks and neck and arms to rapturous kissing, he blushed scarlet and was covered with confusion. The doting King returned to the Royal Apartments, all the better pleased with the new favorite. On the instant His Majesty fixed upon the morrow as the happy day on which the Concubine was to be installed; and, to mark the joyful occasion, the warders of the King's prisons were commanded to set their inmates free. Lin Chih-yang, who until that moment had still retained hope of T'ang Ao and Tuo the coxswain coming to rescue him, was now resigned to the certainty of his removal on the next day to the Royal Apartments. With sharp pangs he remembered his wife, and tears all but drenched him. What was worse, the binding of his "lily feet"—the bones weakened, the muscles tender—had so emasculated him that he was too weak to stand or be capable of moving about without the support of the waiting women. Ruminating on his present distress, he recalled happy days of the past and concluded ruefully that one could live in two different worlds. Thus assailed by a thousand bitter sorrows, he felt every inch of his entrails crack, and he wept all through that night.

The next morning—it being the day appointed for the wedding—the maids of honor and waiting women rose at an unearthly hour. Some of them came to "pluck the bride's face,"[24] others to comb the new Concubine's hair, still others to apply the powder and rouge, all with redoubled solicitude. The "lily feet" were indeed still somewhat long; yet, being well arched under their bandages and cushioned by a high insole, they appeared suitably tiny in their scarlet phoenix slippers. Lin was now arrayed in his ceremonial dragon robes with the phoenix bridal crown firmly placed on his head; for ornament, he wore a dozen or more tinkling jade pendants; and his sweetly scented face perfumed the air:

> Though, in truth, not of transcendent beauty,
> This bride was, at least, comely and charming.

Breakfast being over, the other Royal Concubines called to offer their congratulations. All morning, the staircase was lined with visitors; and in the afternoon, the maids of honor bustled about in great excitement, rearranging each detail of Lin's dress and adornments in preparation for the grand event, which was heralded by the ceremonial entry of a number of court attendants holding lanterns in their hands. The new arrivals knelt in a row before Lin and announced, "The lucky hour has struck. My lady will now proceed to the

24. To remove the fine hair on a girl's face on her wedding day and thus declare her a woman. The ceremony should precede the plucking and trimming of the eyebrows, but Lin's beauticians had already transformed his eyebrows into crescent-shaped curves many days before.

main audience chamber, where, His Majesty having dismissed court, the
nuptial rites will be celebrated, to be followed by installation in the Royal
Apartments. The sedan waits below."

The announcement descended upon Lin Chih-yang like a thunderbolt.
There was a confused buzzing in his ears, and his soul was temporarily
dislodged from its seat. His protests went unheard; the women in attendance
rushed up and kept him supported all the way down the stairs until they
deposited him in the phoenix sedan, which was then carried to the main
audience chamber, followed by hundreds of maids and women in waiting.
His Majesty had already dismissed court, and the audience hall was resplendent with hundreds of candles and lanterns. Leaning on the arms of the maids
of honor, Lin advanced, swaying and trembling like a full-blown flower, until
he reached the King's presence, when, guided by firm, controlling fingers, he
bent with a jerk and, pulling his sleeves over his hands, made a bride's low
bow. The other Royal Concubines, too, came forward to bow to the King and
offer their felicitations. The bowing over, it was time to retire to the Royal
Apartments, but a sudden commotion was heard from outside the Palace: men
were shouting and screaming, and their shrill cries startled the King, whose
composure soon gave way to fear and doubt.

It turned out that the shouting in the street was a ruse of T'ang Ao's. For
ever since that first evening, he had continued to search with the old coxswain
high and low for his missing brother-in-law, though without the least result.
One day, the two men had gone ashore as usual to look for Lin Chih-yang,
each taking a separate route. After a fruitless morning's search, T'ang Ao had
returned to the ship, where, sitting down to his midday meal, he found
Mistress Lin and her daughter both weeping. While he was trying to comfort
them, old Tuo rushed on board, his forehead covered in sweat, shouting,
"There's news of Master Lin! It was worth all my efforts—at last I have got
news of him!" Mistress Lin asked anxiously, "Where is my husband? Is he
dead or alive?" The old helmsman, however, went on, "As I made my
inquiries, by chance I came across a steward of the Royal Brother-in-law's
household, from whom I learned that Master Lin had been detained at the
Royal Palace. It would seem that the King of this land of women had expressed
an interest in Master Lin's commodities, then taken a great liking to Master
Lin himself, and eventually decided to make him, Master Lin, a Royal
Concubine. Master Lin's large feet proved an impediment and, at the King's
command, the wedding was postponed until the feet could be bound. According to the steward, the foot-binding is now completed and the King has
chosen tomorrow as the day for the installation of the new Concubine."

Before he could proceed further, Mistress Lin, who had been crying piteously, swooned in her grief. Her daughter Wan-ju, herself bitterly weeping,
revived her, whereupon that afflicted lady went on her knees before T'ang Ao
and the coxswain, solemnly invoking their help in saving her husband. T'ang

Ao having ordered Wan-ju and her companion to help Mistress Lin up, old Tuo finally resumed, "I then persuaded the steward to request his master to intercede on our behalf with the throne, offering our entire cargo as ransom for Master Lin. The steward most obligingly transmitted my message, but the Royal Brother-in-law, regarding intercession at this late stage to be futile, the wedding being imminent, would have nothing to do with the matter, and I could make no headway. Thus I have returned in the hope that Master T'ang might know of a better plan." Being, however, struck dumb by the intelligence, T'ang Ao was slow to answer. At last, he said, "Since it is already the eve of the wedding, our hope is but slender. Under these circumstances, we should draw up a petition for clemency, pleading extreme hardship, and hand up copies at the various ministries and departments, trusting that some upright minister of the King's would take up our cause and argue the case before the throne so as to secure my brother-in-law's release. No other course remains to us."

Mistress Lin thereupon cried, "My brother-in-law has certainly thought up a good plan! They are a great kingdom; there must be no end of ministers, among whom some doubtless will be upright. An eloquent petition, placed in the hands of one such minister, will surely restore me my husband! Please, then, good brother-in-law, have as many copies transcribed as you can, and see that they are handed up soon!" T'ang Ao at once drafted the petition, of which the coxswain approving, the two each made several copies and, leaving their dinner untouched, departed in great haste for the city. At every government department or office they could find, they presented a copy of the petition: invariably the paper was taken within, studied, and thrown out again with a cheerless "It is no concern of ours. Try another department." By the end of the day, they had called at several score government offices, all with the same result. At dusk, famished and exhausted, they returned to the ship, and when Mistress Lin learned what had happened, she broke into a loud wailing. And she and her daughter lay awake all through that night, sobbing.

The next morning, T'ang Ao and the coxswain again went into the city for news. . . . .[25] There was a crowd in the distance, and men were walking in procession toward them. As they hurried forward, they found the procession to be formed by scores of porters, shouldering pole-loads of splendid gifts. Old Tuo observed in a whisper, "The courier bringing up the rear is the house-

25. Snatches of conversation between T'ang Ao and Tuo, in the leisurely manner of Chinese novels, forming the last page or so of chapter 34, have here been omitted. The two overhear reports of a new Concubine being installed in the Palace, of an amnesty, and of government offices being closed for the day to enable officials to attend at the Palace and offer their congratulations to the King. At noon, T'ang Ao and Tuo stop for tea and dumplings at a teahouse and, at the beginning of chapter 35, they consult a fortune-teller, whose cryptic reply—that a wedding will lead to but a brittle union and that a certain person now in trouble will be freed after ten days—buoys them up for the moment.

steward of the King's brother-in-law I was telling you about. What would he be doing with all those gifts?" T'ang Ao said, "Just look at their embroidered wrapping! They are certainly gifts for the King." The coxswain now approaching the steward for news, returned presently, looking even more downcast; jesting bitterly, he cried, "Gifts for the King, did you say, Master T'ang? They are for our good Master Lin!" To T'ang Ao's question—"What do you mean?"—Tuo replied, "The courier tells me that the gifts have been prepared by the Royal Brother-in-law for distribution among the ladies at court by the new Concubine on the occasion of her installation. And you maintain they are not for Master Lin?"

T'ang Ao scratched his ears in sullen silence. Overhead, the afternoon sun was slowly sinking. The officials who had converged upon the Palace to offer the King their congratulations now began to disperse, seated in their sedans or riding on horseback. The released prisoners, too, were trooping past, smiling happily as they made their way home. Before long, the porters reappeared, their loads now empty. It was almost dusk, and there was nothing left that the two of them could still try; so they hung their heads and took the road back. . . .[26] As they walked on, they again reached the spot where they had read the proclamation. T'ang Ao sighed, "On the day we sailed into this port, while my brother-in-law went about his business, you and I came ashore and stood before this placard. But we never foresaw our long stay nor the grievous misfortune. My poor brother-in-law! I wonder how he has fared and what strange torments have been his! What longings, too, for our rescue, all in vain!" As he spoke, tears rolled down T'ang Ao's cheeks. In a flash, however, a thought struck him; it took him but a few more moments, with his head lowered pensively, to follow it through. Striding up to the notice board, he carefully detached the placard and lifted it up.[27]

The guards stationed by the placard rushed forward to cross-question T'ang Ao, "Where are you from, woman? Do you realize what you are doing? You are absolutely certain you have understood the King's proclamation?" A large crowd had meanwhile gathered. For when word went round that a stranger had intimated acceptance of the King's commission by lifting the placard, the sensation it created was electric. From the city and its environs, old and young trooped in greater numbers to the notice board. When T'ang Ao saw that there was a crowd, he addressed those present in a loud voice, declaring, "My name is T'ang. I have journeyed across the seas from the Celestial Land, where every man or woman knows the art of taming floods. Passing through your esteemed country, I find this placard containing your King's proclamation, from which I quote: 'The floods have devastated our land for years in succession and caused our people extreme hardship, in view of which we

26. A further short exchange between T'ang Ao and Tuo has been omitted.
27. Thus indicating his acceptance of the undertaking advertised.

solemnly proclaim that, in the event of the sovereign of a neighboring kingdom succeeding in confining our rivers and averting disaster for our people, we would willingly acknowledge ourselves a vassal state and tender tribute. If the subject of a neighboring state effected the same, we would freely offer in reward riches, rank, and honors. . . .' The desire, thus expressed, of bringing this great evil to an end seems to me most sincere and admirable, and I have therefore come forward to offer you my services in the assuaging of the floods, in which cause I shall not spare myself. . . ."

The beginning of this speech found a number of people in the crowd kneeling confusedly and chanting aloud, "We beg the distinguished visitor from the Celestial Land to be compassionate and save us and our homes." T'ang Ao now went on, "Pray, rise, my friends, and let me resume. Though I am able to regulate your rivers, I am unmoved by the proffered reward of riches and high rank, which our Celestial Country offers in abundance. No, my friends, grant me but one thing, and I commence my labors without delay." Those who were kneeling rose and cried, "What would our distinguished visitor have us do?" T'ang Ao then said, "I have a brother-in-law, who, on being admitted to the Royal Palace to sell his goods, was against his will detained there and made a Concubine-elect. The wedding, I now learn, takes place this very evening. If you wish me to assuage your floods, then go before the Palace and, with weeping and wailing, plead with your King for this person to be released, so that I may start work on the rivers. But if your King should spurn your lives and welfare by refusing to restore my relative, then not for the greatest treasure in the world would I tame your floods, but must instead return to my homeland."

As he spoke, the crowd grew ever thicker until a great multitude was assembled. And when the people heard T'ang Ao threaten to leave for home, they made a thunderous outcry, and all rushed headlong toward the Palace gates. The guards having earlier marched off to report to their superiors the stranger's answering of the Proclamation, T'ang Ao and the coxswain found themselves alone. Tuo broke into an urgent whisper, "Master T'ang, you do, of course, know something about river conservancy?" T'ang Ao said, "Was I ever an officer in the River Conservancy? No, my dear sir, never. Frankly I know nothing about inundations and flood control." The mariner cried, "You know nothing about them! I hope you knew what you were doing when you took down that placard. If you bungle the job and spend their public funds to no purpose, why, we all exchange rudder and sail for the distaff!" T'ang Ao persisted, "It was rash of me, I admit, to remove that placard, but my brother-in-law's plight is desperate; he has to be saved somehow and, there being no alternative, I took a leap in the dark. However, now that we have set the people on to worry their rulers, it seems not unlikely that the King might give in to public opinion and postpone the wedding. As for that river, something must be done, but not until I have examined the flooded area in the next day or so. Let us hope that my brother-in-law's ruling planet is now in the ascendant; for there is no telling what luck may do, even to a river channel! But if the situation really got out of hand, Master Coxswain, I entreat you: depart for some neighboring kingdom, offer them our shipload, and beg for their intervention. We could do worse than follow such a course."

Old Tuo shook his head, frowning hard at T'ang Ao's sudden eloquence. The guards now returned with a sedan-chair and a horse, and T'ang Ao was escorted like a great personage to the Government Guest House; Tuo, adopting perforce the role of servant, trailed behind on foot. The Warden of the Guest House had dinner and wine laid out for T'ang Ao, Tuo being served separately at a lower table, but since both were hungry, the seating arrangements did not prevent either of them from enjoying a hearty meal. After dinner, the coxswain returned to the ship to give Mistress Lin the news and what cheer he could, before rejoining T'ang Ao at the Government Guest House, where they calmly awaited an official summons.

In its noisy progress toward the Royal Palace, the crowd that had heard T'ang Ao's harangue attracted a host of others, so that eventually tens of thousands were gathered outside the Palace gates, where, shouting and hallooing, they made a great clamor. In the audience chamber within, the King was receiving the final ceremonial bows from the Royal Concubines, when shattering cries reached the royal ears, causing surprise and consternation. An usher presently entered to announce that the Royal Brother-in-law craved leave to confer with His Majesty on urgent affairs of state. The King now dismissed the Concubines and others, and summoned the Brother-in-law, who, having made his salute, reported at length how a woman from the Celestial Country had answered the Proclamation, claiming to be able to confine the rivers but stipulating, as prior condition, the freeing and restoration of her relative, a female vendor of cosmetics from that same country upon whom His Majesty had been graciously pleased to confer the rank of Royal Concubine; and how tens of thousands were assembled at that moment outside the gates, crying out for a clear sign of their King's solicitous regard for their welfare and the welfare of half a million others, all His Majesty's loyal subjects, whose homes were all threatened by the rising floods—even the immediate release of the said person in order that work on the flooded areas might begin and their dwellings and means of livelihood be preserved.

The King replied shrilly but regally, "The custom of our land has ever been that no wife, even among the humblest, is ever cast out or permitted remarriage. Shall we then, the country's sovereign, so far forget ourselves as to act against age-old custom in regard to a Royal Concubine?" The Royal Brother-in-law persisted nevertheless, "The point was indeed made perfectly plain in a carefully worded statement, which Your Majesty's servant himself read out repeatedly to the people, 'Let all hear and comprehend: inasmuch as among the subjects of this land a wife is never granted a dispensation from the marriage bond, so His Majesty the King would under no circumstances deign to forgo a Royal Concubine.' The people, however, argue thus: that this being the day fixed for the wedding, the Concubine is not yet installed in the Royal Apartments and the Royal marriage therefore not yet been consummated; that the case is thus to be differentiated from that of a Royal Concubine already so installed, on which ground they beg Your Majesty to take pity on them and grant their plea." The King was a long while silent. At last, making as if to rise from the throne, His Majesty snorted, "Is this what they say? Then tell the people: 'The King has retired and is not to be disturbed until the morning audience.' In the morning, we confront them with a fait accompli: our action thus legitimized, their demand falls to the ground."

The King proving adamant to all further entreaties, the Royal Brother-in-law returned to the gate-tower, where, as commanded, he made the announcement. When the people heard it, they feared that by morning their battle would have been lost: there was instant uproar, with thousands of voices simultaneously raised in protest. Their piercing cries reverberated through the audience chambers and the King was stricken with horror, being conscious of his own blame in the matter; yet, as to relinquishing his new favorite, he was no more willing than before. While thus he debated with himself, the cries came nearer and nearer, and men seemed to have broken through the Palace gates. Suddenly roused, the King exclaimed, "My craven scruples! It's neck or nothing now!" At once His Majesty called the Colonel of the Guards on duty and placed a hundred thousand troops under his command with orders to march immediately on the rabble and crush the revolt. The Colonel of the Guards having received his command and mustered his men, reports of cannon and musket fire soon rocked the Palace walls.

The besiegers, however, would not be dislodged. They shouted, "Kill us! We would sooner be blown up by the King's gunpowder than swept away by the floods and devoured by fish and sea monsters!" Thus the swarming multitude howled and wailed, their thunderous roar seeming to shake the heavens. The Royal Brother-in-law, sensing the reckless mood of the crowd and fearing a full-scale rebellion, had earlier instructed the guards on no account to aim their guns at His Majesty's good subjects. He now stepped forward once more to pacify them, and addressed them thus, "Good people, return to your homes. Be assured that I will transmit your request to the throne and secure the services of the person who answered the King's proclamation in the relieving of the floods. You may safely entrust this matter to me. Tomorrow, at my home, I shall have further news for you all." His speech, repeated a number of times, by degrees took effect. The crowd dispersed, and the Colonel of the Guards also recalled his men.

It being then reported that the mob had scattered, the King retired to the Royal Apartments, where Lin Chih-yang was commanded to sit shoulder to shoulder with His Majesty. Under the lamplight, the royal eyes flashed and twinkled as they renewed their measured survey of the new Concubine. What a slim figure—undoubtedly supple and lithe! Bashful, too, every bit the blushing bride! Eyebrows knit in an enticing melancholy! Perfect, indeed, in each particular! Having reveled in so vital a scrutiny, the King took a swift glance at the chiming clock[28] and declared in a shrilly musical voice, "You are now our consort. Such melancholy does not become this gay occasion. It is of course a misfortune to be born female; that conceded, you have risen as high as any in the world. Just think! You are now a First Lady of our realm. What more could a woman ask for? For the future, if you bring forth children, your days of happiness will be lasting. Rather than go about pretending to be a man and so contravene the laws of nature, is it not far better thus to resume the feminine role and share our throne like a queen? Let us drink on that thought!" And the King commanded that the banquet be spread and that gifts of jewelry, gold, and silver be bestowed upon the new Concubine.

The banquet being presently ready, the maids of honor filled a goblet for Lin to offer to the King. Now Lin, who at the mere thought of his wife and daughter felt his heart pierced by a thousand wounding arrows, was left without the least spark of animation; beside, he was faint with hunger, having tasted neither tea nor rice for the few preceding days, so that he could find no strength in his limbs. When, therefore, he reached for the goblet, he was trembling all over, and his unsteady hand found the drinking-cup the weight of a millstone; his knees grew cold, his fingers lost their grip, and the goblet fell on the table with a loud clink. A maid of honor picked it up and filled another goblet, at the touch of which Lin was affected with a worse panic than before, and he again spilled the wine. The nuptial cup had, therefore, to be presented to the King by the others. And the King commanded that a goblet also be filled for Lin and held up to his lips. This, with an effort, he drank, and a second cup was immediately poured out, it being deemed lucky to have two of everything, two denoting a happy couple. At other times Lin Chih-yang held his liquor as well as any man but, his inside having been many days empty, he was caught unawares, after his second cup, by the floor and ceiling slowly gyrating, and barely managed to keep his seat. The King drank a few more cups and asked for the time. His Majesty's pocket watch having been brought, after one glance the King declared the feast at an end.

A smile now lit up the King's flushed cheeks; his misty eyes leered; he said merrily, "It is late, my love. Time for bed." Servants of the bedchamber came forward to undress the bridal pair; they removed Lin's jewelry and ceremonial garments, and the King, too, divested himself of his outer robes. Then stretch-

---

28. Being of foreign origin and associated with exotic palaces, the chiming clock has found its way into the Royal Palace of the Women's Kingdom, as has also the pocket watch. In *Dream of Red Towers* (see selection 263), chapter 92, an elaborate chiming clock of over three feet is mentioned as suitable for presentation to the Emperor; the price demanded for the clock together with an intricate inlaid screen was five thousand silver taels (compare with selection 104).

ing out both hands with their jadelike fingers, the King firmly held Lin's wrists and dragged the new Concubine after him into the bedchamber, where they ascended the royal couch and, the sharkskin bed-curtain[29] having been lowered, reposed for the night.

Thus did the King celebrate the royal wedding. In the Government Guest House, T'ang Ao gave rein to his imagination, reckoning a postponement of the happy event as a certainty. As the evening wore on, however, and he waited anxiously for news, some old men returning from the Palace called at the Guest House and told how the army had been called out to crush the revolt. Their story sent a shock through T'ang Ao, who turned ashen pale. Tuo the coxswain, on the contrary, now found his tongue. "The wedding deferred in deference to the people's wishes? What has happened to your confident prediction, Master T'ang? Eh, quite the opposite, do you now say? Mind you, the guards actually opened fire, and the King's army is to stamp out any further revolt. From what we have just heard, the King is a real lecher, utterly indifferent to the welfare of his people. So from tomorrow we draw our pay as river dredgers and clean out their river channels for them? A sailor must try his fortune, but we deceive ourselves if we expect Master Lin back." To hide his confusion, T'ang Ao resorted to scratching his head. In the meantime, the Royal Brother-in-law had sent his steward with bedding for T'ang Ao and Tuo, together with a team of servants, who were placed at the disposal of the two visitors. The steward made a speech; "My master, the Royal Brother-in-law, sends his best compliments. It being late tonight, my master is unable to call, but will himself attend upon our honored guests after the morning audience to discuss the repairing of the river channel. Our guests will kindly overlook any unintended negligence, for which my master will apologize in person." With this, the steward departed, followed by the old men who had brought the news.

The next day, T'ang Ao and his companion waited in the Guest House for the Royal Brother-in-law, who failed, however, to appear. Late at night, the old helmsman set out to make inquiries and only then learned that the Royal Brother-in-law's residence was completely hemmed in by the people, who had swarmed there, impatient for news. The report caused T'ang Ao a sleepless night. When they rose at dawn on the third day, Tuo remarked, "Well, Master T'ang, one more day in the land of women! Don't take it amiss, but at this rate we shan't sail for home until they've presented us with red eggs."[30] T'ang Ao cried, "What do you mean?" The helmsman then said, "It's two

---

29. As described in *Dream of Red Towers*, chapter 92, such curtains were made of a fabulously thin and light fabric manufactured from the skin of the shark. It was of foreign origin and a large piece of it was priced at five thousand silver taels, hence it was customarily to be found only in the imperial palace.

30. Hen's eggs with shells dyed red, distributed among relations and friends after the birth of a child.

days they've been married, good Master Lin and the female King. Let a few more days elapse and we may expect to hear of an heir on the way. Next comes the birth of the infant prince, at which red eggs are certain to be distributed, a large share falling to yourself as brother-in-law to the King's concubine." Annoyed and perplexed, T'ang Ao did not answer but continued to wait for the Royal Brother-in-law.

The latter, after pacifying the crowd on the evening of the wedding, duly attended at the Palace in the morning. His Majesty was, however, now reported to be indisposed: no audiences were to be held that day. Debarred from the King's presence, the Royal Brother-in-law paced the audience chamber and courtyards, tormented by anxiety yet powerless to act. Word was meanwhile brought that his own house had been surrounded many times over by the people, who were clamoring for the King's reply, and not being ready with the promised reply, he could not face them. He was afraid, too, of T'ang Ao escaping and ordered a strong guard to be posted at the city gates; and he sent men at intervals with food and wine to the Government Guest House, and others with pole-loads of fish and meat, and chickens and ducks, to T'ang Ao's ship as a gesture of goodwill, while he himself watched his time. And that night he slept in the main audience chamber in the Palace.

On the third day, the King rose before dawn, highly displeased. The Royal Brother-in-law having been summoned, His Majesty asked abruptly, "Where is the woman now who answered our Proclamation?" The Royal Brother-in-law replied, "That person is lodged in the Government Guest House but, having waited in vain for Your Majesty's commission, is understood to be on the point of leaving for her homeland." The King then said, "We must have some assurance that the woman knows what she is about. If she proves indeed capable of regulating our rivers and watercourses, considerations for the lives of our people are naturally nearest our heart, and we shall be prepared even to relinquish our Royal Concubine. To be sure, so momentous a sacrifice is contingent upon the woman successfully carrying out her task. Our plan, therefore, is to keep the new Concubine in the Palace until such time as the flooding has been relieved. Thus in the event of the repairs not proceeding according to plan or yielding no results and our treasury depleted to no purpose, we would hold the Concubine hostage and the woman may redeem her—if need be, at some later date—with silver to the amount wasted in the venture. What does our Brother-in-law say to the plan?" Overjoyed, the courtier cried eagerly, "An excellent one, Your Majesty! With the guaranty for any potential losses to Your Majesty's treasury, it would curb extravagant spending. It would calm and comfort the people. And if the regulating of the rivers should indeed succeed, a great evil would have been removed from our land. A masterstroke of statecraft, Your Majesty!" Upon which, the King dismissed him, saying, "Then act upon it, good Brother-in-law!"

The Royal Brother-in-law now went straight to the Government Guest

House, where he met T'ang Ao, with whom he exchanged civilities. For the King's relative was a nobleman with the surname She,[31] under fifty years of age, with a smooth chin and a high-pitched voice reminiscent of a eunuch. When tea had been served, the courtier began in earnest, "The people of our land congregated yesterday outside the gates of the Royal Palace and gave a full and moving account of how our honored guest, deeply affected by reports of persistent flooding of our fields and valleys, has come forward to deliver them from danger and destruction. Being at the time engaged with other business at court, I was unable to attend upon our guest, for which omission I crave our guest's indulgence. In regard, Sir, to your honorable relative, who was suddenly taken ill while displaying her wares and has since lain on a sickbed in the Palace, be assured that, as soon as she regains her health, she will be safely escorted back to the ship. As for the preposterous story of her having been made a Royal Concubine, we rely on our guest's good sense for his lending no credence to such idle rumors. Now to the relief of the floods— I stand ready to be instructed in the subject."

T'ang Ao then held forth, "The exact cause of the inundation in this most remarkable country is, of course, still to be ascertained. Not having inspected the flooded areas, I would not hazard an opinion. But, in general, the mitigation of floods may be traced back to the great Yü,[32] who, we learn, dredged the nine great rivers. Now 'dredge' is the key word in river engineering: so to dredge the various streams as to cause them all to flow freely, each leading to some other stream or, alternatively, to a lake or the sea. Thus the water should be traced to its source and conducted to its outlet. Once the source is kept clear of sand and gravel, and the middle section unobstructed, the river can no longer cause devastation. These, however, are but ill-considered views, rashly expressed. The Royal Brother-in-law must instruct me further when we have examined the river itself." And the nobleman repeatedly nodded his head in assent.[33]

The story goes that when the Royal Brother-in-law had heard T'ang Ao's learned exposition, he nodded with approval and cried, "My honored guest, you have suddenly made it all clear to me with that one word 'dredge'! And I bow before your superior wisdom. It would seem, then, that we might expect a speedy end to all flooding in our land. For the present, I must take my leave in order to report to the throne, but tomorrow I will accompany you on a tour of the inundated region." And having ordered the servants to prepare a sumptuous dinner for their distinguished guest and to serve him with the

31. K'un, the female, as opposed to Ch'ien, the male (see selection 3).

32. Yü, who according to the legendary account in the Classic of Documents (Shu ching), brought the floods under control in the reign of the emperor Shun and, himself succeeding to the throne, founded the Hsia dynasty.

33. The end of chapter 35, the formula "As to what happened next, it shall be told in the following chapter" being omitted in the translation.

utmost care and diligence, the Royal Brother-in-law mounted his sedan-chair and departed with his train of attendants.

The old coxswain now remarked, "It is curious how Master Lin, who appeared irrevocably lost to us when the army was called out night before last, would seem now to be on the point of joining us again. Perhaps the wedding ceremony never took place—I wonder!" T'ang Ao, too, said thoughtfully, "It would certainly be the influence of the populace then. For fear of the people breaking out in revolt, the King might have postponed the whole affair." Tuo continued, "Time enough to find that out. But to come back to that river, I hope you will agree it requires careful handling. The slightest mishap and not only must Master Lin remain forever in the harem, but we ourselves would be doomed to perpetual servitude to these women. It is not as if a sailor worries easily either. What plan are you putting forward when we have looked over the floods tomorrow?" T'ang Ao replied, "The inspection need only be a formality: my plan has been ready for some time. After all, when a river overflows its banks, either its channel is choked or it has no proper outlet or it is turbid at the source. When we have actually seen where the flooding occurs, I shall start by deepening the channel there, then widen the river's surface along the whole of that stretch, and finally check the flow of the stream into its outlet. Once the river has been both deepened and widened, its capacity is greatly increased; and with the increased capacity and unobstructed current, there would be no flooding."

The helmsman exclaimed with barely concealed impatience, "Nothing could be simpler! Would they not have thought of these expedients before?" T'ang Ao said, "When you went back on board the ship yesterday to give them the news, I called two of the servants before me, and it became clear in the course of my conversation with them that little in the way of copper and iron is produced in this land. Furthermore, to prevent crime and armed uprisings, the possession of weapons and even edge-tools is prohibited, most families possessing only bamboo knives; only the rich occasionally use silver knives, which are considered a rarity. As for digging and dredging, the very implements are unknown to them. But, as luck would have it, we have tons of cast iron laid up in the hold![34] Tomorrow, therefore, I will prepare sketches of the implements needed, and teach them how to make them. The situation, my friend, is by no means irretrievable."[35]

The following day, the Royal Brother-in-law took T'ang Ao outside the city to inspect the offending river, and again on the day after. Upon their return, T'ang Ao said, "It is clear from our careful inspection of the past two days that the flooding is due precisely to the omission of dredging, the subject of my

34. The tons of cast iron were brought along as merchandise by T'ang Ao and accepted with great reluctance by Lin.

35. Some facetious comments by Tuo that follow are here omitted.

previous discourse. To take the level of the river in relation to its banks—the dikes on either side are as high as hillocks [36] and the river, too, is almost as high; yet its channel is of no great depth so that it holds no more water than a shallow dish of that size and is ready to overspill at any moment. Such a state of affairs first came about through the setting up of dikes and embankments at a time when the river was already rising and threatening to overflow its banks. But once the danger was averted and the water had receded, no further thought was given to the preventive measure of deepening the channel through dredging; instead, more and higher dikes were built whenever the river rose again. The depositing of silt year after year, however, kept on raising the riverbed until now it is as if you had a bathtub placed on the ridge tiles: if the tub overflows, the water rushes down a slope to drench a whole area and turn it into a lake. To protect the surrounding area, you must sink the tub in the earth so that its bottom is much lower than the level of the ground, thus reducing the risk of violent outbreaks, and this may be accomplished by thorough digging and dredging. Your shallow dish would then be transformed into a caldron with ample capacity for the current even at its greatest, and you need have no fear of any inundation."

The Royal Brother-in-law readily agreeing with the diagnosis, proceeded to ask about tools for dredging. T'ang Ao gave a further discourse on the need for labor and the futility of half-hearted measures such as reliance on the force of the current itself for the removal of silt, finally offering the iron in the hold of their vessel for the making of dredging tools. The noble courtier, having repeatedly nodded his head in approval, promised the entire national labor force; [37] he also gave orders for craftsmen from all over the city to be in attendance early the next day, and large numbers of laborers also, to carry out whatever tasks were required of them. The Royal Brother-in-law then taking his leave, T'ang Ao drew sketches of various dredging tools, while Tuo was entrusted with the unloading of the iron. In the morning, the craftsmen having been assembled, T'ang Ao showed them the designs and, after giving detailed instructions, made them light their furnaces and forge the metal parts of the implements. Now, though these artisans were dressed like men, they were really women and, therefore, clever and adroit, unlike your clumsy louts who looked blank even when you had talked yourself hoarse; these, on the

36. An unmistakable reference to the dangerous flood-control methods used to tame the Yellow River. Contained within dikes and levees, the silt-laden river gradually rose high above the surrounding countryside. When the dikes and levees would periodically break, the floodwaters that poured through them would wreak enormous devastation on the land and its people. Much of the novel in selection 265 deals with the problem of how to control the Yellow River.

37. "The Royal Brother-in-law readily agreeing with the diagnosis . . . promised the entire national labor force" being the translator's summary of the rest of the conversation between the nobleman and T'ang Ao.

contrary, needed but the merest hint to see what was expected of them, so that within two or three days they had all the tools ready, whereupon an auspicious day was chosen for work on the river itself to begin.

On the appointed day, the Royal Brother-in-law went to the flooded area with T'ang Ao, who directed that a series of mud embankments be erected across the river, thus breaking it up into many sections. Next, through the use of chain pumps worked by waterwheels, every other section was drained and the water emptied into its adjoining section. The drained section having then been dug and the channel much deepened, the embankment dividing it from its adjoining section was removed and the water allowed to flow back into the first section with its vastly increased capacity; the adjoining section itself was now dug and a deeper channel formed. All along the inundated part of the river, men were digging with might and main. It was at first found difficult to remove the mud scooped up from the riverbed; large baskets were then lowered into the pits and, when they were filled, hoisted up by means of a windlass with unstinted exertion. For the people of that land had for years been harassed by the floods, so that directly work on the river was begun, the whole country joined in, digging and dredging and building dikes. Thus within ten days the task set by T'ang Ao was completed. And they further checked the flow of the current, continuing to dig and dredge as they went along. And the people observed that T'ang Ao was at the river from dawn to dusk,[38] utterly unsparing of himself as he superintended the progress of the work, and their gratitude and admiration knew no bounds. The elders of the land made a collection, commissioned his portrait, and set up a shrine with huge characters inscribed in gold on an overhanging horizontal tablet: "Overflowing Benevolence."[39]

Reports of T'ang Ao's success in subjugating the river reached the Palace and, before long, were conveyed to Lin Chih-yang by one of the royal princes. For when, after the wedding, Lin ascended the royal couch hand in hand with the monarch of the Women's Kingdom, he suddenly recalled how, after their visit to the Black Teeth Country with its learned women,[40] T'ang Ao had teased him about having to be rescued from the hordes of females in the Women's Kingdom. And he thought to himself, "Why, this has indeed come to pass! What a strange premonition on my brother-in-law's part! At the time,

38. T'ang Ao's tireless exertion is true to the type of the Chinese "tamer of waters" beginning with the great Yü, the latest example being the author's own father, Li Chieh-t'ing.

39. More prosaically, "His benevolence shall last for as long as the river itself." This is reminiscent of the temples dedicated to the great river engineer, Li Ping, and his son, Li Erh-lang, builders of the immense irrigation system on the Chengtu plain in Szechwan in the third century B.C.E. (see selection 248, note 88).

40. The Black Teeth Country was a country of bluestockings, whose learning so overawed T'ang Ao and his companions that they trembled at the prospect of further disputations in the Women's Kingdom (chapter 19). The translation has been expanded to allow room for the allusions.

old Tuo had actually said, 'And supposing you really were detained in the Women's Country, what would you do?' And without a moment's hesitation I had replied, 'Why, if they did detain me, feigning ignorance would be my best defense.'[41] That, too, having been spoken in jest, might be an omen! Yes, since this female king is determined to have me, why don't I act the insensate statue and, like a clay figure or block of wood, feign ignorance of warmth and animation? Precious time could be gained, perhaps even the siege raised!"

Being thus resolved, he yearned all the more for home, and the thought of his wife awakened sharp pangs and sent tears rushing down his cheeks. And he remembered the countless indignities and tortures he had endured from the time of his arrival at the Palace, how his feet had been bound and his earlobes pierced, and how he had been savagely beaten and hung with his aching feet tied to the beam, all at the command of this female king—a cruel and vicious virago, his declared enemy, to be shunned at all costs! How, then, could one entertain the notion of intimacy with such a creature! In this frame of mind, he studied the monarch's face under the lamplight and perceived that, though the female ruler was young and attractive, yet the air of a murderess lurked in her handsome features: he had not, to be sure, seen her in the act of killing, but her every amorous gesture now suggested to him the knife or dagger. The more he looked at her, the greater his fear of losing his life at her hands. His blood was chilled, his heart froze, and his body grew limp like cotton wool. For two nights in succession, therefore, the royal spouse coaxed and cajoled, and exercised all manner of blandishments, but the sweet expectations came to nothing.

Bitterly disappointed as the King was, His Majesty was not unmindful of the devastation caused by the overflowing river, and judged it prudent to inflict no further punishment upon Lin. After consulting the Royal Brother-in-law about measures for flood control, His Majesty made prolonged deliberation and at last decided that there would be no satisfaction in keeping Lin, who was forthwith banished to his upstairs apartment with the regimen of foot-binding, powder application, and other such exercises no longer insisted upon. Being thus mercifully spared, Lin, though still held a prisoner, was consoled to find his feet at large again. As to whether he would eventually be freed and why there had been a riot some days before, he could obtain no answers to the questions he put to the maids of honor.

One day as he, shedding tears, thought of his native land, a young Prince[42]

41. Defense from being drawn into learned arguments.

42. The Crown Prince of the Women's Kingdom, the reincarnation of the Fairy of the Peony, the peony being regarded as the king of flowers. The peony was the Empress Wu's favorite flower; but being the slowest among the hundred flowers to obey her command to blossom in midwinter, it was banished from the capital (chapters 4–5). Its reincarnation is thus the furthest removed from the Celestial Land.

entered and, kowtowing, said, "I have come specially to bring you news, my royal mother. I am told that a distinguished personage of the name T'ang has arrived from the Celestial Country and has undertaken to relieve our floods, and that as soon as the river is reduced to its normal level, my royal father will send you back to your home. Therefore, do not worry, royal mother." Lin helped the Prince up and asked to be further enlightened, and only then heard about T'ang Ao's acceptance of the King's commission. His eyes flowing with tears, he said, "I am filled with gratitude toward you, young Prince, for bringing me news in my captivity. If I, Lin Chih-yang, should one day be reunited with my family, I would burn incense and pray to your memory. Please send me word again as soon as my brother-in-law has completed his great task on the river, and intercede with His Majesty on my behalf that I might be released the sooner. Then, indeed, you would be my savior!" The Prince wiped away Lin's tears, saying, "Do not distress yourself, royal mother. I will make further inquiries and bring you news again." The Prince then took his leave.

Now from the time of Lin Chih-yang's relegation to the upper story, the maids of honor, regarding him no longer as the royal consort but as any common stranger awaiting deportation, ceased to pay attention to him. At meals the fare was meager; there was never any tea; and the service generally grew exceedingly slack. But the daily visit of the Prince brought the food and tea rations back to normal again and for that, too, the famished Lin was thankful. A fortnight had soon elapsed. Lin's feet were back to their original shape, but felt thin and small in his man-sized shoes. One day, the Prince entered in haste and announced, "The distinguished personage T'ang has completed his river scheme! This morning, His Majesty my royal father inspected the river and, being thoroughly pleased, ordered the entire court assemblage to form a procession and escort the illustrious visitor from the Celestial Land back to his ship. The procession included a band that played all the way, and a gift of ten thousand ounces of silver in recognition of the outstanding service rendered. I am, moreover, reliably informed that my royal mother will herself be sent back to the ship tomorrow, and with this news I have hurried here."

Jubilant with relief, Lin cried, "What have I not owed to you, my dear Prince, ever since His Majesty consigned me to these upstairs rooms? But if I leave tomorrow, shall I ever see you again? At least I hope to return your great kindness at some future date." Observing no one to be near them, the Prince suddenly knelt before Lin and, bursting into tears, confided, "Royal mother! I am in extreme danger. Help me! Remember what little filial piety I have shown you and throw open the gates of mercy in your heart, that I might yet be saved!" Lin helped the young Prince to his feet and asked, "What is this danger that you speak of, Prince? Tell me at once!" The Prince then told his story. "It was six years ago that, at the age of eight, I was chosen heir to the throne. Such, however, was my misfortune that my own mother, the Queen, died last year; and now, another—whom I must also call 'royal mother'—has become the favorite, whose sole purpose is for her own son to supplant me, in furtherance of which she sought on numerous occasions to destroy me, though without success. Lately her calumny has so wrought upon my father, the King, that he, too, has turned against me and appears eager to have me removed. Now, therefore, is the time to betake myself to flight; for if I remain, I should never escape her deadly clutches. My father sets out in ten days[43] to attend the birthday celebrations of the King of the Yellow Emperor's Descendants.[44] The vice-regent and other ministers who shall be left in charge, the palace servants, and the government officials are all of her faction. Being young and inexperienced and having, moreover, pored too long over my books, I am without even a confidant, far less a party of followers to keep a constant watch over my safety. One careless step and my life could be forfeit! Royal mother, have pity on me and, when you return to the ship tomorrow, take me with you! If I am delivered from this den of perils, believe me, even to my dying day I shall be grateful to you."

Lin Chih-yang almost screamed, "But you will have to dress like a woman if you go with me to the Celestial Country—so much do our customs at home differ from those of your Women's Kingdom! My Prince, you have always been accustomed to the freedom of a man's life. How could you possibly endure the ways of women? And don't forget the rigors of hairdressing and foot-binding!" The Crown Prince, however, declared, "I must just adopt your ways, then. For if I escape with my life, I should be content with even the humblest lot in the company of my royal mother." Lin then said, "But what if the maids of honor should discover us leaving the Palace together? Would it not be better if I went on board first and you, my Prince, then joined me secretly?" The Crown Prince shook his head[45] and replied, "I may not leave the Palace without good cause, and even then only under escort. There is not the least chance of my boarding the ship by myself! Since, however, the waiting women are seldom in attendance now, I shall hide in the sedan tomorrow before you are seated and, unnoticed, be carried to the ship with you. Do allow me to come with you, royal mother." To which Lin replied, "If you can contrive this in secret, my Prince, I shall naturally be at your service."

The next day, however, His Majesty sent a sedan-chair with bearers for Lin's return to the ship and commanded that the maids of honor all attend on

43. "Ten days" is taken from the Prince's speech in the next chapter.

44. The Hsien-yüan, a long-lived nation, whose king was celebrating his thousandth birthday. Hsien-yüan happens to be T'ang Ao and Lin's next port of call (chapters 38 and 39). The palace there being thrown open to all for the royal birthday celebrations, Lin Chih-yang finds himself, for a few embarrassing moments, face to face again with the monarch of the Women's Kingdom.

45. The end of chapter 36, the formula "As to what happened next . . ." being here omitted.

him as he changed into male garments and mounted the sedan. The Crown Prince stood apart from the crowd and, being almost in despair, shed many secret tears. As Lin was entering the sedan, the Prince rushed up and whispered urgently in his ear, "Our movements are watched and I cannot now leave with you; but my life is in your hands, good royal mother. Rescue me within ten days, or we may never see each other again. Remember, I live in the Peony Tower.[46] Remember!" And he followed the sedan a few steps until, suddenly breaking into sobs, he returned to his own apartments.

Thus Lin Chih-yang found himself once more on board his ship, where T'ang Ao and Tuo the coxswain had preceded him, having at the King's command been escorted there the previous day by a procession of courtiers and a band. When Lin saw T'ang Ao and Tuo, he thanked them again and again for his deliverance. Joy and grief intermingled in his reunion with his wife and his daughter, Wan-ju,[47] whose companion, Lan-yin,[48] he also rejoiced to see again. Then turning to T'ang Ao, he said, "When I took you, brother-in-law, as a passenger, all you wanted was to see the lands across the seas. But now you have saved my life and become my benefactor! I was often tempted in my state of captivity to do away with myself, but a dream about an immortal coming to my aid[49] made me endure it all in patience. It was surely no immortal that delivered me, but my own brother-in-law!" The coxswain, too, said, "It was no coincidence you had Master T'ang with you on this journey—it was Providence! I remember now that, after our visit to the Black Teeth Country, Master T'ang said that he would repay your kindness by rescuing you from all the women,[50] which has indeed come to pass. It would seem that, unknown to us, this strange mishap was presaged even then."

Suddenly T'ang Ao cried out, "My dear brother-in-law! Why are you shuffling along with such mincing steps? Don't tell me the King really had your feet bound!" Laughter getting the better of his shame and embarrassment, Lin said in a tone of disgust, "He might have contented himself with treating me like a woman and his concubine. But no! It had to be authentic down to the last detail—piercing the ears, foot-binding, and all. My poor feet felt as hedged in as a new bride and as sorely pressed as a new teacher taking his first class, so smothered they were all day and night! To cap it all, the waiting women boiled monkeys' bones and bathed my feet in the broth to hasten their contraction. A strange concoction indeed for one's foot-bath! So heady and

46. See note 42. The Crown Prince is the reincarnation of the Fairy of the Peony.

47. Wan-ju, Lin Chih-yang's daughter, reincarnation of the Fairy of the *Jasminum Grandiflorum*.

48. Lan-yin, Orchid Voice, daughter of the interpreter in the Forked Tongue Country. She joins the ship in search of a cure for her illness (chapter 30).

49. An immortal, etc., being a hint of the immortal existence T'ang Ao was later to attain.

50. See note 40 above. Here, too, the translation has been padded to bring out the point of the allusion.

potent it was that, though my feet have since been loosened, I am still like a man half-drunk, unsteady and weak-kneed. And to think that on the day I set off with my inventory of goods, a black spider actually landed on my feet! To judge by the amount of attention they received, my feet enjoyed more luck than was good for them!"

His daughter, Wan-ju, then exclaimed, "You've still got gold earrings on, father! Let me remove them for you." Thus reminded, Lin went on, "And the waiting woman who pierced my ear-lobes—I do believe she would have had her will of me, dead or alive! For she seized one ear at a time and gave a fierce stab, at the recollection of which my ear-lobes know the excruciating pain again. And it was all because those wretched apes in the Land of Flames had burned my beard,[51] so that, with my smooth chin, I appeared a far younger man to the King, which led to disaster! But I hear that, besides sending my brother-in-law back to the ship in state, the King also offered a reward of ten thousand ounces of silver. Has this money been paid?"

T'ang Ao replied, "It has been paid, but how did *you* know about it?" Lin then recounted in each particular how the Crown Prince had continually brought him news and looked after him throughout, and at the very last solemnly invoked his help in effecting his, the Prince's, own escape. When he had heard the story, T'ang Ao declared, "If the Prince is in danger, it is incumbent on us to rescue him; all the more so, since he has befriended you. Let us repay his kindness, too, by saving *him* from all those women![52] His plight must truly be desperate who would throw away a kingdom's inheritance to adopt a female disguise in a strange land, and we really cannot set sail without him. What says my friend Tuo?" The helmsman replied, "Repay his kindness and rescue him, too, from all the women—by all means! But how shall we do it? Without careful planning, such a venture could never succeed. You were a good many days in the Palace, Master Lin, and would be familiar with its layout; you might know of some means of effecting this." T'ang Ao then asked, "Is the Crown Prince at all like the Prince of the Forked Tongue Country?[53] If he is a good horseman and ready with his bows and arrows, we should soon have him with us." Lin replied, "The Prince is of course a girl in her teens, though dressed like a man. She is unlikely to be much of an archer or horsewoman. But, good brother-in-law, if you really mean to save the Prince, help from you alone will suffice; no others would avail." T'ang Ao cried, "Talk of taking up arms in a good cause! I am never among the tardiest. What is your plan then?"

Lin said, "It is simply this. Tonight, when it is dark, you will carry me on

51. See note 9 above.

52. "Repay his kindness," etc. takes up the joke from a couple of paragraphs above.

53. Forked Tongue Country, a land of phoneticians (chapters 28–31). The Prince of the Forked Tongue Country fell off his horse while hunting but was brought back to life by Tuo the coxswain.

your back and, with me as guide, scale the Palace walls,[54] find the Prince, and rescue him." T'ang Ao demurred, "The Palace is enormous. Do you know where the Crown Prince lives?" Lin replied, "At our parting this morning, the Prince whispered in my ear that he was staying in the Peony Tower. Their peonies grow to such a height that, to see them properly, you have to lean from a tower.[55] Once within the Palace, we shall look out for peonies: where they grow thick, we should find our Tower and Prince." T'ang Ao now expressed agreement, saying, "Let us at least sally forth tonight, make reconnaissance and decide on further action." But the old helmsman broke out in loud protest, "Hold, gentlemen! Master Lin is, to be sure, under a real obligation to the Crown Prince and Master T'ang zealous in a worthy cause, and in your selfless devotion you think to defy the sanctity of the Palace precincts. Pray consider. Are there no guards outside the walls? No watchmen patrolling the grounds? Supposing you gentlemen did enter the Palace and were then caught—have you allowed for that in your plan? Listen to me, an old man, and deliberate further. Rashness makes a poor beginning to so dangerous an enterprise." T'ang Ao, however, protested, "Not rashness, Master Coxswain! On the contrary, we shall exercise great caution, my brother-in-law and I, and watch our every step when we are near the Palace. Set your mind at rest, Master Tuo."

Having supped by late afternoon, T'ang Ao changed out of his scholar's robe into short garments. Lin Chih-yang also girded himself for the expedition; his old shoes being much too large for him, a sailor went ashore and obtained a pair—"men's size," Women's Kingdom—that fitted him. By the time their preparations were complete, it was already dusk, but Mistress Lin, fearful of further enterprise, began to remonstrate with her husband, who however was not to be dissuaded. Thus with a hurried "Adieu!" to the coxswain, Lin departed with T'ang Ao for the city, eventually reaching the Palace wall. There being no one about, T'ang Ao bore Lin on his back as planned, and leaped with ease onto the wall, where they paused to find their bearings. Within, the watchman's bell and rattle sounded from court after court. They passed over several more high walls, when at last the bell and rattle grew faint and distant. T'ang Ao said in a hushed voice, "Hark, brother-in-law! Not even the cawing of a crow or magpie! The stillness itself is forbidding. We must now be in the inner courts." Pointing with his finger, Lin said, "See where the high shrubs are? That structure should be the Peony Tower. Let us alight there."

As directed, T'ang Ao descended into the court. Lin slid down from his back, but no sooner were their feet upon the ground than two huge dogs

54. After swallowing a divine herb on East Mouth Mountain early in their voyage, T'ang Ao found that he could leap to a height of fifty or sixty feet (chapter 9).

55. The Chinese were actually able to graft peonies to mahogany trees (*Cedrela sinensis*) which enabled them to view the flowers from an upstairs window.

swooped upon them from behind a grotto, barking furiously and biting their clothes. The watchmen, being now alerted, converged swiftly upon the scene of the noise, lanterns in hand. Thus taken by surprise, T'ang Ao frantically shook off the dog and, with a sudden leap, regained the high wall. The watchmen rushed up to Lin, shone their lanterns upon him, and shouted, "Ah, a woman thief!" But a court attendant who had also appeared, cried, "Hush, you fools! It's the new Royal Concubine, yet dressed so queerly and alone in this court late at night! Still, it is not for us to ask questions. The King is at the Palace banquet, and I shall at once report to His Majesty." Forthwith Lin was escorted to Sunshine Pavilion, where the banquet was in progress. When the King's eyes once more alighted upon Lin's face, that former ardor, though for some little while cooled, revived in full blaze in the royal bosom. His Majesty spoke, "We did of course send you back to the ship, woman. Why, then, are you here again? Explain yourself." Lin could find no ready answer and remained dumb.

The King was pleased to be amused and said with a smirk, "We have understood you. When it came to the point, you were not prepared to forsake the splendor of these halls and have returned in the hope of gaining our favor anew. Since, then, you express yourself willing, for our part, we never dwell on past errors. Only, from tonight you really must have your feet bound properly, and we shall in due course install you in the Royal Apartments. Behave yourself, woman, and mend your stubborn ways: you shall be amply recompensed." The King then commanded that Lin be sent to his former upstairs apartment and dressed in feminine attire as before, and that the same maids of honor and women wait upon him; and further, that the successful completion of the foot-binding be immediately reported, to be followed by preparations for the installation.

The maids of honor and waiting women received their commands, helped Lin up the stairs and, having dipped him in a perfumed bath, arrayed him once more in embroidered garments. Before they could proceed to combing his hair and binding his feet, however, Lin thought to himself, "I am, alas, again trapped, but at least my brother-in-law is moving about freely on the high walls; he will know where I am and is certain to rescue me. At all costs, therefore, I must ward off these women from my regenerate feet!" So he said aloud to the waiting women, "I reentered the Palace of my own accord, and this time am fully as anxious as you to accomplish the foot-binding in order to hasten the blissful event. On no account would I allow any of you to tamper with my feet and delay the process of contraction. Besides, if I am kindly treated, when I am installed in the Royal Apartments yonder, I shall remember you all kindly; and if harshly treated?—I, too, shall remember the harshness and requite you accordingly! Tra-la-la, the King, my sun, will shine upon me! Heads will start rolling and the Royal Concubines themselves shall implore my mercy!"

The maids of honor and waiting women now recalled the occasion on which, following upon their complaints, Lin had been beaten; quaking at the thought of his revenge, they groveled and kowtowed, begging the new Concubine to forgive their past misdeeds and spare them for the future. Lin went on, "It is of the future that I speak, not the past. Rise now and banish all fear. If you will obey me in three things, I shall gladly be merciful." The women got up and shouted, "We shall obey you in a hundred, gracious lady. Tell us *which* three!" Lin then said, "First, I will look after the business of foot-binding and powder application and every detail of the toilet myself. It shall be none of your concern. Do you hear?" The women replied, "We hear and obey." Lin continued, "Next, when the Crown Prince and I are at conference, you will remove yourselves from our presence. Do you hear?" The women cried, "We shall obey you in this, too. What is the third thing?" Lin said, "There are many rooms on this upper floor; instead of crowding into my bedroom, you shall all sleep in another room. Do you hear?" The women heard but remained silent. Lin went on, "I suppose you are worried about my escaping if left alone in the night. Very well, I shall take the inner room and you can all stay in the outer one, adjoining the staircase; and you can have the windows of my room locked up every night and the keys removed. Not satisfied yet with these precautions? Would I have come back had I wished to escape?" The women, hearing this, cried in unison, "We shall obey you in all three!" And they busily set up beds while Lin made a show of binding his own feet with great vehemence, which soon allayed their suspicions. It being then the second watch, the maids of honor locked the windows, removed the keys, and went to sleep; before long, loud snoring[56] broke out from every corner of the room.

Toward the third watch, Lin Chih-yang, who lay awake expectantly, heard a tap at the window. Hurrying to it from his bed, he asked softly, "Are you there, brother-in-law?" T'ang Ao's answer came through clearly, "I had to shake off that dog, but from above the walls I followed your movements and remained up there when I saw them escorting you to this room. The others are sound asleep. Open the window now and come with me." Lin, however, replied, "The windows are fast and the keys hidden. Our plan would miscarry if we woke up the women. Go back now but return tomorrow evening, when I shall have seen the Prince again. We shall have a red lantern hanging outside the window: at the sign of a red lantern, come at once to our rescue. Leave me now!" T'ang Ao assenting, Lin then heard a whiz and knew he was gone.

The next day, the Crown Prince came to visit the new Concubine, having heard about her return. When Lin explained his presence in the Palace, the Prince was overcome with gratitude; but recovering himself, though still with

---

56. The waiting women were really men.

tears in his eyes, he said, "This is the eve of my birthday. Good royal mother, command your women to prepare a feast in my honor and have it sent to the Tower. I will attend to the rest." Lin nodded and presently gave orders to this effect. When it was almost dark, the Prince sent one of his own servants to invite the ladies from the upper story to join in the birthday eve feast. The Prince's invitation started a flutter; the maids of honor were impatient to be gone, and Lin readily granted permission to one and all.

Now when the Prince saw the maids of honor and waiting women all gathered at the Tower, and seated, he himself went across to Lin's apartments, opened the window, and hung out a red lantern in the dark. From high above, a figure suddenly descended and entered. Realizing it could only be T'ang Ao, the Prince knelt down, but T'ang Ao pulled him up, saying, "Do I see the Crown Prince?" Upon Lin nodding repeatedly in confirmation of this, T'ang Ao declared, "There's not a moment to lose. Let us go!" And he carried Lin, as before, on his back, but held the young Prince in his arms; then, with a bound, he regained the nearest wall. They crossed several more high walls before alighting outside the Palace, where the Prince was gently laid down and Lin also dismounted from T'ang Ao's shoulders. A faint moon having risen to guide their steps, the three walked toward the city wall, which they scaled in the same fashion. When at last they reached the ship, Tuo the coxswain welcomed them on board and immediately weighed anchor. Thus they sailed in the dark from the Women's Kingdom.

The Crown Prince changed out of his royal robes into the dress of a young Chinese woman and, kneeling before the merchant Lin Chih-yang, called him "father," and again before Mistress Lin, called her "mother"; the girls, Wan-ju and Lan-yin, being then introduced, they took to one another at once. But it was old Tuo, who, joining them later, asked the name of the Crown Prince, which turned out to be: Woman Like Flower.[57] When T'ang Ao heard the name "Flower," the dream that had appeared to him before he set out on the voyage flashed through his mind again. . . .[58]

Translated by H. C. Chang

57. Yin Jo-hua, i.e., Female Like Flower.
58. This is the end of chapter 37. The dream occurs in chapter 7: a temple god, who turns out to be the God of Dreams, tells T'ang Ao to seek out the twelve lost flowers across the seas and bring them back to China. At the beginning of chapter 38, T'ang Ao goes over the names of the young women they had met on the voyage and finds that each contains the name of a flower, e.g., Lan-yin (Orchid Voice). The Prince, Yin Jo-hua, being the twelfth, completes the list of "lost flowers."

265

The Travels of Lao Ts'an

Liu T'ieh-yün (1854–1909)

Chapter 1

The land does not hold back the water; every year comes disaster;
The wind beats up the waves; everywhere is danger.[1]

The story tells that outside the East Gate of Tengchoufu, in Shantung, there is a big hill called P'englai Hill,[2] and on this hill a pavilion called the P'englai Pavilion. It is most imposing with its "painted roof-tree flying into the clouds"

This novel in twenty chapters represents a transition between the traditional literary conventions in which it is grounded and the emerging consciousness of modernity that it adumbrates. It offers a critical look at Chinese officialdom and a revealing exposé of Chinese esotericism at the twilight of the imperial age.

The author, Liu È (or T'ieh-yün, his style), was in himself a fascinating mix of old and new. An authority on river conservancy, a mathematician, a medical practitioner, a poet, a musician, and much else, he seemed to be interested in nearly everything under the sun. For instance, Liu was the first person to realize the importance of the oracle shell and bone inscriptions (see selection 1), and was an advocate of the adoption of appropriate Western technology. Liu's almost schizophrenic character and tragic death in remote, desert Sinkiang, where he was banished shortly before the revolution that overthrew the imperial system forever, are fitting symbols of a dying nation struggling to be reborn and reinvigorated.

1. Following the form of traditional novels, each chapter is prefaced by a couplet consisting of two lines of six to eight sinographs, strictly parallel in form. The couplets are frequently unintelligible until the contents of the chapter are known. In this case, the first line refers to the illness of Mr. Huang (Yellow), which symbolizes the annual floods along the Yellow River, while the second line refers to the ship in danger of being wrecked, which symbolizes the precarious condition of the Chinese ship of state. Thus the first chapter introduces in allegorical form two of the main themes of the book, flood control and political reform. Note that control of the Yellow River also occupies an important place in selection 264.

2. Tengchoufu, now usually known as P'englai, is a city on the extreme north shore of the Shantung Peninsula. The P'englai Pavilion, originally built under the Sung dynasty, is said to be on the spot from which Ch'in Shih Huang-ti (reigned as emperor 221–209 B.C.E.) is reputed to have sent a Taoist sage, Hsü Fu, with three thousand men and women and a cargo of seeds to an island in the east. Tradition claims that the Japanese are the descendants of these people. The Han Emperor Wu (reigned 140–86 B.C.E.) is said to have seen the island of P'englai from here. The fame of the view is due to a mirage, probably caused by a group of rocky islands off the coast, which are thus the original of the Chinese Islands of the Blessed: P'englai, Fangchang, Yingchou, in which men and animals never die and where the palaces are of gold and silver. These islands, often referred to as the "Fairy Islands," are the eastern counterpart of Mount K'unlun, the home of the Western Queen Mother, another abode of immortals. Their names are still seen on banners at funerals.

and its "bead-screens rolled up against the rain."[3] To the west it overlooks the houses in the town, with mist hanging over ten thousand homes; to the east it overlooks the waves of the sea, undulating for a thousand tricents. It is a regular custom for the gentlemen of the town to take wine-cups and wine with them to the pavilion and spend the night there, to be ready the next morning before it is light to watch the sun come up out of the sea.

However, no more of this for the present.

It is further told that there was once a traveler called Lao Ts'an. His family name was T'ieh, his *ming* was of one character, Ying, and his *hao*, Pu-ts'an. He chose Ts'an as his *hao* because he liked the story of the monk Lan Ts'an roasting taros.[4] Since he was a pleasant sort of person, people deferred to his wish and began to call him Lao Ts'an, which eventually became a regular nickname. He was a Chiangnan[5] man. By the time he was thirty he had studied quite a lot of prose and poetry, but because he was not good at writing eight-legged essays,[6] he had taken no degrees and therefore nobody wanted him as a tutor. He was too old to learn a business and therefore did not

3. A good example of the allusiveness of Chinese writing. This is an abridged quotation from the poem at the end of Wang Po's famous "Preface to 'The Pavilion of King T'eng' " (see selection 197).

4. The Chinese have a multiplicity of names. The most common are: the *hsing*, family name or surname; the *ming*, personal name, given by the family, sometimes of two characters (one of which is frequently common to all of one generation in a family), sometimes, as here, of only one character; the *tzu*, a fancy name assumed on coming of age; and the *hao* or style, a fancy name chosen by the man himself or his friends. Besides this a man may have an additional *hao* or *pieh-hao*, a nickname. The author's *hsing* is Liu, his *ming*, Ě, and his *tzu*, T'ieh-yün. He has used one character of it, T'ieh, meaning Iron, as his hero's family name, and added Ying, meaning Heroic or Daring, as his personal name. Lan Ts'an was the nickname of a Buddhist priest of the T'ang period who started his career as a menial in a monastery on Hengshan, the sacred mountain of the south, in the T'ien-pao period (742–756). It is told of him that "he was lazy (*lan*) by nature, and fond of eating leftover scraps (*ts'an*), and was therefore called Lan Ts'an." When Li Pi, a famous statesman, visited the monastery, he went one night to see Lan Ts'an, who was poking a fire and roasting taros. Lan Ts'an pulled out half a taro and gave it to Li Pi saying, "Don't say much. Be prime minister for ten years." When he died the Emperor gave Lan Ts'an the title of Ta Ming Ch'an Shih (Illustrious Master of Meditation). The Pu in Pu-ts'an means "to mend or repair." The *hao* then means "he who mends broken things or leftovers," and probably refers to the profession of medicine.

5. Chiangnan (or Kiangnan), literally, "South of the River," is used sometimes for the territory south of the Yangtze River but here for the provinces of Kiangsu and Anhwei, which formed one province at the beginning of the Ch'ing period.

6. *Pa ku wen*, literally, "essays with eight thighs (or sections)," were essays written in the rigid, artificial style required for the official examinations. They were required to be written in eight *pi* (sections or paragraphs), and were usually limited to a total of 450, 550, or 600 characters (see selection 222).

attempt it. His father had been an official of the third or fourth rank but was too stubbornly honest to make money for himself, and after twenty years of office-holding he could only afford to travel home by selling his official clothes! How do you suppose he could have anything to give his son?

Since Lao Ts'an had nothing from his family and no definite occupation, he began to see cold and hunger staring him in the face. Just when he was at his wits' end, Heaven took pity on him, for along came a Taoist priest, shaking a string of bells, who said that he had been taught by a wonderful healer and could treat a hundred diseases. He said that when people met him and asked him to heal their diseases he had a hundred cures for every hundred treatments. So Lao Ts'an made obeisance to him as his teacher, learned the patter, and from that time on went about shaking a string of bells and filling his bowl of gruel by curing diseases. Thus he wandered about by river and lake for twenty years.

When our story begins, he had just come to an old Shantung town called Ch'iench'eng,[7] where there was a great house belonging to a man whose family name was Huang (Yellow) and whose *ming* was Jui-ho. This man suffered from a strange disease which caused his whole body to fester in such a way that every year several open sores appeared, and if one year these were healed, the next year several more would appear elsewhere. Now for many years no one had been found who could cure this disease. It broke out every summer and subsided after the autumn equinox.

Lao Ts'an arrived at this place in the spring, and the major-domo of the Huang household asked him if he had a cure for the disease. He said, "I have many cures; the only thing is that you may not do as I tell you. This year I will apply a mild treatment to try my skill. But if you want to prevent the disease from ever breaking out again, this too is not difficult; all we need do is to follow the ancients whose methods hit the target every time. For other diseases we follow the directions handed down from Shen Nung and Huang Ti, but in the case of this disease we need the method of the great Yü.[8] Later, in the Han period, there was a certain Wang Ching[9] who inherited his

---

7. Ch'iench'eng ("Thousand Chariots") was a Han-period city about one hundred miles northeast of the present Tsinanfu. Sufficient territory to support a thousand chariots was a theoretical unit in early Chinese administration.

8. Shen Nung, the Divine Husbandman, was a culture-hero, inventor of agriculture, and father of medicine. The connection between husbandry and herbal medicine is obvious. Huang Ti, the Yellow Ancestor, was the reputed author of the *Nei Ching* (*Classic on Internal Medicine*). Yü the Great was the first institutor of flood control and reputed to have been the successor of the mythical Emperor Shun.

9. Wang Ching was a Han-period official who was well versed in astronomy, mathematics, and the *Classic of Changes* and practiced various forms of meditation. In the time of Ming Ti (reigned 58–76), he had great success in controlling floods. He rose to be Prefect of Luchiang in the present province of Anhwei.

knowledge, but after that nobody seems to have known his method. Fortunately I now have some understanding of it."

The Huang household therefore pressed him to stay in the house and to give his treatment. Strange to say, although this year there was a certain amount of festering, not one open sore appeared, and this made the household very happy.

After the autumn equinox the state of the disease was no longer serious, and everybody was delighted because for the first time in more than ten years Mr. Huang had had no open sores. The family therefore engaged a theatrical company to sing operas for three days in thanksgiving to the spirits. They also built up an artificial hill of chrysanthemums in the courtyard of the west reception hall.[10] One day there was a feast, the next a banquet, all very gay and noisy.

On the day when our story begins, Lao Ts'an had finished his noon meal, and having drunk two cups of wine more than usual, felt tired and went to his room, where he lay down on the couch to rest. He had just closed his eyes when suddenly two men walked in, one called Wen Chang-po, the other Te Hui-sheng.[11] These two men were old friends of his. They said, "What are you doing at this time of day, hiding away in your room?" Lao Ts'an quickly got up and offered them seats saying, "I have been feasting so hard these two days that I needed a change." They said, "We are going to Tengchoufu to see the famous view from the P'englai Pavilion and have come especially to invite you. We have already hired a cart. Put your things together quickly and we will go right away."

Lao Ts'an's baggage did not amount to much—not more than a few old books and some instruments—so that packing was easy, and in a short time the three men were getting into the cart. After an uneventful journey[12] they soon reached Tengchou and there found lodging beside the P'englai Pavilion. Here they settled and prepared to enjoy the phantasmagoria of a "market in the sea" and the magic of "mirage towers."[13]

The next day Lao Ts'an said to his two friends Wen and Te, "Everyone says the sunrise is worth seeing. Why shouldn't we stay up to see it instead of sleeping? What do you say?" They answered, "If you are so inclined, we will certainly keep you company."

Although autumn is that time of year when day and night are about equal in length, the misty light that appears before sunrise and lingers after sunset makes the night seem shorter. The three friends opened two bottles of wine, took out the food they had brought with them, and, what with drinking and

10. Such a hall was a regular part of a large Chinese house.
11. Wen Chang-po means "Leader in Literary Composition." Te Hui-sheng means "Student of Morals and Wisdom."
12. Literally, "eating in the wind and sleeping in the dew," a conventional phrase.
13. This refers to the famous mirage to be seen from Tengchoufu (see note 2).

talking, before they were aware of it the east had gradually become bright. Actually it was still a long time before sunrise; the effect was due to the diffusion of the light through the air.

The three friends continued to talk for a while. Then Te Hui-sheng said, "It's nearly time now. Why don't we go and wait upstairs?" Wen Chang-po said, "The wind is whistling so, and there is such an expanse of windows upstairs that I'm afraid it will be much colder than this room. We'd better put on extra clothes."

They all followed this advice and taking telescopes and rugs went up the zigzag staircase at the back. When they entered the pavilion, they sat at a table by a window and looked out toward the east. All they could see were white waves like mountains stretching away without end. To the northeast were several flecks of blue mist. The nearest was Long Hill Island; farther off were Big Bamboo, Great Black, and other islands. Around the pavilion the wind rushed and roared until the whole building seemed to be shaking. The clouds in the sky were piled up, one layer upon another. In the north was one big bank of cloud that floated to the middle of the sky and pressed down upon the clouds that were already there, and then began to crowd more and more upon a layer of cloud in the east until the pressure seemed insufferable. The whole spectacle was most ominous. A little later the sky became a shining strip of red.

Hui-sheng said, "Brother Ts'an, judging from the look of things the actual rising of the sun will be invisible." Lao Ts'an said, "The winds of heaven and the waters of the sea are sufficient to move me; even if we do not see the sunrise the journey will not have been in vain."

Chang-po meanwhile had been looking through his telescope. Now he exclaimed, "Look! There is a black shadow in the east that keeps rising and falling with the waves; it must be a steamship passing." They all took their telescopes and looked in that direction. After a while they said, "Yes! Look! There is a fine black thread on the horizon. It must be a ship."

They all watched for a while until the ship had passed out of sight. Hui-sheng continued to hold up his telescope and looked intently to right and left. Suddenly he cried, "Ayah! Ayah! Look at that sailing boat among the great waves. It must be in danger." The others said, "Where?" Hui-sheng said, "Look toward the northeast. Isn't that line of snow-white foam Long Hill Island? The boat is on this side of the island and is gradually coming nearer." The other two looked through their telescopes and both exclaimed, "Ayah! Ayah! it certainly is in terrible danger. Luckily it's coming in this direction. It has only twenty or thirty tricents to go before it reaches the shore."

After about an hour the boat was so near that by looking closely through their telescopes the three men could see that it was a fairly large boat, about twenty-three or twenty-four chang long.[14] The captain was sitting on the poop,

14. A chang is a measure of length equivalent to ten feet. The whole description of the boat that follows is symbolic of the Chinese ship of state. The twenty-three or twenty-four chang

and below the poop were four men in charge of the helm. There were six masts with old sails and two new masts, one with a completely new sail and the other with a rather worn one, in all eight masts. The ship was very heavily loaded; the hold must have contained many kinds of cargo. Countless people, men and women, were sitting on the deck without any awning or other covering to protect them from the weather—just like the people in third-class cars on the railway from Tientsin to Peking.[15] The north wind blew in their faces; foam splashed over them; they were wet and cold, hungry and afraid. They all had the appearance of people with no means of livelihood. Beside each of the eight masts were two men to look after the rigging. At the prow and on the deck were a number of men dressed like sailors.

It was a great ship, twenty-three or twenty-four chang long, but there were many places in which it was damaged. On the east side was a gash about three chang long, into which the waves were pouring with nothing to stop them. Farther to the east was another bad place about a chang long through which the water was seeping more gradually.[16] No part of the ship was free from scars. The eight men looking after the sails were doing their duty faithfully, but each one looked after his own sail as though each of the eight was on a separate boat: they were not working together at all. The other seamen were running about aimlessly among the groups of men and women; it was impossible at first to tell what they were trying to do. Looking carefully through the telescope, you discovered that they were searching the men and women for any food they might be carrying and also stripping them of the clothes that they wore.

Chang-po looked intently and finally couldn't help crying out wildly, "The damnable blackguards! Just look, the boat is going to capsize any moment, and they don't even make a show of trying to reach the shore, but spend their time maltreating decent people. It's outrageous!" Hui-sheng said, "Brother Chang, don't get excited. The ship is not more than seven or eight tricents

---

represent the twenty-three or twenty-four provinces into which China was divided before the revolution of 1911. The captain is the Emperor. The four helmsmen are the four Grand Secretaries or perhaps the members of the Grand Council of State. The six masts with old sails are the six boards or government departments. Of the two new masts the one with slightly worn sails is probably the Foreign Office, created in 1861. Until the Western powers forced themselves on the Chinese there was no Foreign Office, as traditionally China was considered to be the only civilized state in the world, all other peoples being tributaries. The new mast with new sails is probably the Board of Admiralty, created in 1890. The men looking after each mast are the two presidents of each board, one a Chinese and the other a Manchu.

15. The Peking-Tientsin railway was opened for traffic in 1900. Liu T'ieh-yün was specially interested in the building of railways.

16. The gash three chang long represents Manchuria, usually referred to in China as the Three Eastern Provinces. At the beginning of the twentieth century these were already threatened by Japan and Russia. The other "bad place to the east" is Shantung, already threatened by Germany and Great Britain.

away from us. When it reaches land, we will go on board and try to make them stop—that's all."

While he was speaking, they saw several people on the boat killed and thrown into the sea. The helm was put about, and the ship went off toward the east. Chang-po was so angry that he stamped his feet and shouted, "A shipload of perfectly good people! All those lives! For no reason at all being killed at the hands of this crowd of navigators! What injustice!" He thought for a while and then said, "Fortunately there are lots of fishing boats at the bottom of our hill. Why don't we sail out in one of them, kill some of that crew, and replace the others? That would mean the salvation of a whole shipload of people. What a meritorious act! What satisfaction!" Hui-sheng said, "Although it might be satisfying to do this, still it would be very rash, and I'm afraid not safe. What does Brother Ts'an think?"

Lao Ts'an smiled at Chang-po and said, "Brother Chang, your plan is excellent: only I wonder how many companies of soldiers you are going to take with you." Chang-po answered angrily, "How can Brother Ts'an be so blind! At this very moment the lives of these people are in the balance. In this emergency we three should go to rescue them without delay. Where are there any companies of soldiers to take with us?" Lao Ts'an said, "In that case, since the crew of that ship is not less than two hundred men, if we three try to kill them won't we only go to our own deaths and accomplish nothing? What does your wisdom think of that?"

Chang-po thought for a while and decided that Lao Ts'an's reasoning was sound; then he said, "According to you, what should we do? Helplessly watch them die?"

Lao Ts'an answered, "As I see it, the crew have not done wrong intentionally; there are two reasons why they have brought the ship to this intolerable pass. What two reasons? The first is that they are accustomed to sailing on the 'Pacific' Ocean and can only live through 'pacific' days. When the wind is still and the waves are quiet, the conditions of navigation make it possible to take things easy. But they were not prepared for today's big wind and heavy sea, and therefore are bungling and botching everything. The second reason is that they do not have a compass. When the sky is clear, they can follow traditional methods, and when they can see the sun, moon, and stars, they don't make serious mistakes in their course. This might be called 'depending on heaven for your food.' Who could have told that they would run into this overcast weather with the sun, moon, and stars covered up by clouds, leaving them nothing to steer by? It is not that in their hearts they do not want to do the right thing, but since they cannot distinguish north, south, east, and west, the farther they go, the more mistakes they make. As to our present plan, if we take Brother Chang's suggestion to follow them in a fishing boat, we can certainly catch them, because their boat is heavy and ours will be light. If when we have reached them we give them a compass, they will then have a direction to follow and will be able to keep their course. If we also instruct the captain in the difference between navigation in calm and stormy weather and they follow our words, why shouldn't they quickly reach the shore?" Hui-sheng said, "What Lao Ts'an has suggested is the very thing! Let us carry it out quickly; otherwise the shipload of people will certainly be doomed."

The three men descended from the pavilion and told the servants to watch their baggage. They took nothing with them except a reliable compass, a sextant, and several other nautical instruments. At the foot of the hill they found the mooring place of the fishing boats. They chose a light, quick boat, hoisted the sail, and set out in pursuit of the ship. Luckily the wind was blowing from the north so that whether the boat went east or west there was a thwart wind and the sail could be used to the full.

After a short time they were not far from the big boat. The three men continued to watch carefully through their telescopes. When they were a little more than ten chang away, they could hear what the people on the boat were saying. They were surprised to find that, while the members of the crew were searching the passengers, another man was making an impassioned speech in a loud voice.

They only heard him say, "You have all paid your fares to travel on this boat. In fact, the boat is your own inherited property which has now been brought to the verge of destruction by the crew. All in your families, young and old, are on this boat. Are you all going to wait to be killed? Are you not going to find a way of saving the situation? You deserve to be killed, you herd of slaves!"

The passengers at whom he was railing said nothing at first. Then a number of men got up and said, "What you have said is what we all in our hearts want to say but cannot. Today we have been awakened by you and are truly ashamed of ourselves and truly grateful to you. We only ask you, 'What are we to do?' "

The man then said, "You must know that nowadays nothing can be done without money. If you will all contribute some money, we will give our energy and lifeblood for you and will lay the foundations of a freedom which is eternal and secure. What do you say to this?" The passengers all clapped their hands and shouted with satisfaction.

Chang-po, hearing this from a distance, said to his two companions, "We didn't know there was a splendid hero like this on the boat. If we had known earlier, we needn't have come." Hui-sheng said, "Let us lower part of our sails for the time being. We don't need to catch up with the ship. We'll just watch what he does. If he really has a sound scheme, then we can very well go back." Lao Ts'an said, "Brother Hui is right. In my poor opinion this man is probably not the sort who will really do anything. He will merely use a few fine-sounding phrases to cheat people of their money—that's all!"

The three then lowered their sails and slowly trailed after the big boat.

They saw the people on the boat collect quite a lot of money and hand it over to the speaker. Then they watched to see what he would do. Who could have known that when the speaker had taken the money he would seek out a place where the crowd could not touch him, stand there, and shout to them loudly, "You lot of spineless creatures! Cold-blooded animals! Are you still not going to attack those helmsmen?" And further, "Why don't you take those seamen and kill them one by one?"

Sure enough, some inexperienced young men, trusting his word, went to attack the helmsmen, while others went to upbraid the captain; they were all slaughtered by the sailors and thrown into the sea.

The speaker again began to shout down at them, "Why don't you organize yourselves? If all you passengers on the boat act together, won't you get the better of them?"

But an old and experienced man among the passengers cried out, "Good people! On no account act in this wild way! If you do this, the ship will sink while you are still struggling. I'm certain no good will come of it."

When Hui-sheng heard this, he said to Chang-po, "After all, this hero was out to make money for himself while telling others to shed their blood." Lao Ts'an said, "Fortunately there are still a few respectable and responsible men; otherwise the ship would founder even sooner."

When he had spoken, the three men put on full sail and very soon were close to the big boat. Their poleman pulled them alongside with his hook, and the three then climbed up and approached the poop. Bowing very low, they took out their compass and sextant and presented them. The helmsmen looked at them and asked them politely, "How do you use these things? What are they for?"

They were about to reply when suddenly among the lower ranks of seamen arose a howl, "Captain! Captain! Whatever you do, don't be tricked by these men. They've got a foreign compass. They must be traitors sent by the foreign devils! They must be Catholics! They have already sold our ship to the foreign devils, and that's why they have this compass. We beg you to bind these men and kill them to avoid further trouble. If you talk with them any more or use their compass, it will be like accepting a deposit from the foreign devils, and they will come to claim our ship."

This outburst aroused everybody on the ship. Even the great speechmaking hero cried out, "These are traitors who want to sell the ship! Kill them! Kill them!"

When the captain and the helmsmen heard the clamor, they hesitated. A helmsman who was the captain's uncle [17] said, "Your intentions are very honest, but it is difficult to go against the anger of the mob. You had better go away quickly."

17. Presumably one of the princes, uncles of the emperor.

With tears in their eyes, the three men hurriedly returned to their little boat. The anger of the crowd on the big ship did not abate, and when they saw the three men getting into their boat, they picked up broken timbers and planks damaged by the waves and hurled them at the small boat. Just think! How could a tiny fishing boat bear up against several hundred men using all their force to destroy it? In a short time the fishing boat was broken to bits and began to sink to the bottom of the sea.

If you don't know what happened to the three men, then hear the next chapter tell.

Chapter 2

At the foot of Mount Li the traces of an ancient emperor;
By the side of Lake Ming the song of a beautiful girl.

It has been told how the fishing boat Lao Ts'an was in was damaged by the mob and sank with him into the depths of the sea. He realized that there was no hope for his life. All he could do was to close his eyes and wait. He felt like a leaf falling from a tree, fluttering to and fro. In a short time he had sunk to the bottom. He could hear a voice at his side calling to him," Wake up, Sir! It is already dark. The food has been ready in the dining hall for quite a long time." Lao Ts'an opened his eyes in great confusion, stared around him, and said, "Ay! After all it was but a dream."

Some days later Lao Ts'an said to the major-domo, "The weather is now getting colder; your honorable master is no longer ill and the disease will not break out again. Next year if you need my advice I will come again to serve him. Now your humble servant wishes to go to Tsinanfu to enjoy the scenery of the Ta Ming Lake."[1] The major-domo repeatedly urged him to stay, but without success, so that night he prepared a farewell feast and presented Lao Ts'an with a packet containing a thousand ounces of silver as an honorarium.

Lao Ts'an said a few words of thanks and put it away in his baggage. Then he said good-bye, got into his cart, and started off. The road was among autumn hills covered with red leaves and gardens full of chrysanthemums so that he did not feel at all lonely. When he reached Tsinanfu and entered the city gate, the houses with their springs and the courtyards with their weeping willows seemed to him even more attractive than the scenery of Chiangnan. He found an inn called Promotion Inn on Treasury Street, took his baggage

1. Ta Ming Hu, the Great Clear Lake, fed by the numerous springs of Tsinan, occupies the whole of the north of the old city, covering about a quarter of the total area within the city walls.

off the cart, paid the carter his fare and wine money, had a hasty evening meal, and went to bed.

The next day he got up early, had a light breakfast, and then took a turn up and down the streets shaking his string of bells in pursuit of his calling. In the afternoon he walked over to the Magpie Bridge[2] and hired a small boat. After rowing north for a short distance, he reached the Lihsia Pavilion,[3] where he stopped the boat and went in. Entering the main gate, he found a pavilion from which most of the paint and lacquer had peeled. On the wall hung a pair of *tui-lien*[4] with the inscription:

> In Lihsia this pavilion is the oldest;
> In Tsinan there are many famous scholars.

In the upper right corner was written: "Composed by the *Kung Pu*, Tu."[5] In the lower left was, "Written by Ho Shao-chi of Taochou."[6] There were several buildings near the pavilion, none of any great interest. He returned to his boat and, rowing to the west, before very long reached the enclosure of the memorial temple to T'ieh Kung.[7]

Do you know who T'ieh Kung was? He was the T'ieh Hsüan who at the beginning of the Ming period caused a lot of trouble to the Prince of Yen. Later generations have honored him for his loyalty to the lawful emperor. For this reason even today at the spring and autumn festivals the inhabitants come to this place to burn incense.

When he reached the T'ieh Kung Temple, Lao Ts'an looked toward the south and saw facing him on the Thousand Buddha Hill[8] groups of monastic buildings among the gray-green pines and blue-green cypresses. The trees

2. Ch'üeh-hua Bridge. The magpie is a bird of good omen.

3. The city of Tsinan was formerly known as Lihsia, which means "Beneath Li." Lishan is the old name of the mountain about two miles south of the city.

4. Vertical plaques.

5. Tu, the *Kung Pu* ("Official of the Board of Works"), better known as Tu Fu (712–770), was one of the greatest poets of the T'ang period (see selection 48). The lines of the poem are misquoted. The first should be: "In the west of the lake this pavilion is the oldest." Tu Fu visited Tsinan in 745, and the poem from which these lines are quoted is said to have been written to commemorate a banquet at the Lihsia Pavilion to which the three poet friends, Tu Fu, Li Po, and Kao Shih, were invited by an important dignitary called Li Yung.

6. Ho Shao-chi (1799–1873), a distinguished calligrapher, was principal of the Lo-yüan Academy at Tsinan from 1858 to 1860.

7. T'ieh Kung was Governor of Shantung under the second Ming emperor, Hui Ti (reigned 1399–1403). Hui Ti was a minor when he came to the throne and antagonized his uncle, Chu Ti, who had been given control of a large area in the northeast with the title Prince of Yen. Chu Ti rebelled against his nephew, finally defeating him and becoming emperor with the reign title Yung Lo (reigned 1403–1425). T'ieh Hsüan was loyal to Hui Ti and opposed the Prince of Yen. He and his whole family were killed by the usurper.

8. Thousand Buddha Hill (Ch'ien Fo Shan) is another name for Lishan (see note 3). The mountain contains innumerable Buddhist grottoes.

were crowded together, some red with a fiery red, others white with the white of snow, some indigo blue, others jade green, a few patches of maple red showing among the rest. It was as though a great painting by the Sung artist Chao Ch'ien-li[9] had been made into a screen several tens of tricents long.

He sighed with sheer delight. Suddenly the sound of a fisherman's song reached him. He bent his head to see where the sound came from and found that the Ming Lake had become as smooth and clear as a mirror. The Thousand Buddha Hill was reflected in the lake and appeared with perfect clarity. The buildings, the terraces, and the trees down there were extraordinarily gay and varied and seemed even more beautiful and clear than the hill above. He knew that beyond the south shore of the lake was a busy street, but a bank of reeds completely concealed it. It was now their blossom time, and the stretch of white bloom reflecting the vapor-filled beams of the setting sun was like a rose-colored velvet carpet forming a cushion between the hill above and the hill below. It was indeed a fascinating sight.

Lao Ts'an thought to himself, "Such an enchanting scene! How is it there are no visitors to enjoy it?" He looked for a while longer and then turned round and read the *tui-lien* on the columns of the great gate. The inscriptions were:

> On four sides lotus blossoms, on three sides willows;
> A city of mountain scenery, half a city of lake.

He quietly bowed his head and said," It's absolutely true!" He then entered the great gate, and immediately opposite him was the ceremonial hall of T'ieh Kung. To the east was a lotus pond, around which went a zigzag gallery, and at the east end of the lotus pond was a circular gate. Beyond this was an old three-unit building with a weatherworn horizontal plaque on which were four characters forming the name "Ancient Water Spirit Shrine."[10] In front of the shrine were a pair of weatherworn *tui-lien* on which was written:

> A cup of cold spring water is offered to the autumn chrysanthemums;
> At midnight the painted boat pushes its way through the lotuses.

Leaving the Water Spirit Shrine, he went down to his boat and rowed to the back of the Lihsia Pavilion. On both sides the lotus leaves and lotus flowers crowded around the boat. The lotus leaves, which were beginning to shrivel, brushed against the boat with a sound, *ch'ih-ch'ih*. Water birds, startled by the coming of people, flew cawing into the air, *k'e-k'e*. The ripe lotus pods kept catching on the side of the boat and scattering through the windows.

9. A painting by this artist belonged to the author and was probably in his mind when he wrote this sentence.

10. This is one of the few places mentioned that the translator was unable to identify on a visit to Tsinan. The term "Water Spirit" is used to refer to several famous individuals in Chinese history who were drowned, usually for some righteous cause. It is also the name of the narcissus plant.

Lao Ts'an casually picked several pods, and while he was eating the seeds the boat reached the Magpie Bridge. Here he felt himself back in the press of human life. There were men carrying loads and men pushing small carts. There were a blue felt sedan-chair carried by two bearers and behind the chair a yamen runner wearing a hat with a red tassel and carrying a folder full of letters under his arm. He was running with his head down as though his life depended on it and mopped his brow with a handkerchief as he went. Several five- or six-year-old children in the road did not know how to keep out of people's way. One of them was accidentally knocked over by a chair-bearer and got up crying, "Wa, wa!" His mother quickly ran up asking, "Who knocked you down? Who knocked you down?" The child could only cry, "Wa, wa!" She asked him again and again. At last through his tears he got out the words, "The chair-bearer!" The mother raised her head and saw that the chair had already gone two or three tricents. She therefore took her child by the hand and muttering imprecations, *chi-chi, ku-ku*, went home.

As Lao Ts'an walked slowly south from the Magpie Bridge to Treasury Street, he happened to look up and saw pasted on a wall a strip of yellow paper about a foot long and seven or eight inches wide. In the middle of it were written three characters, "Recital of Drum Tales."[11] At the side was a line of small characters, "On the Twenty-Fourth at the Ming Lake House." The paper was not yet quite dry, so he guessed it had only just been put up. He did not know what it was about since he had never seen anywhere else an announcement of this kind. As he went along the road, he continued to puzzle over it. He heard two carriers talking, "Tomorrow the Fair Maid is telling stories. Let's leave our work and go to listen." And when he reached the main street he overheard a conversation behind a shop counter, "Last time you had a holiday to go and hear the Fair Maid sing; tomorrow it's my turn." Along his whole path the gossip was mostly on this subject. He wondered to himself, "What sort of person is this Fair Maid? What sort of tales are they? Why is the whole town so excited about this announcement?" He allowed his feet to lead him and very soon reached the door of Promotion Inn. He entered the inn and the servant asked him, "What will you have for supper, Sir?"

Lao Ts'an gave his order and then took the chance to ask, "What sort of

11. *Shuo Ku Shu* is a form of entertainment in which a story is sung to the accompaniment of one or more stringed instruments, the performer marking the rhythm by striking a small drum on a stand and clapping a pair of castanets. This art is still quite popular in Peking and other northern cities, most of the performers being women (attractive for their looks as well as their singing), though the best are men. The singing is accompanied by conventionalized gestures and a great variety of facial expressions. The subjects are drawn from the common store of Chinese legend and fiction. The life of these singers is the subject of Lau Shaw's (Lao She's) *The Drum Singers*.

local entertainment are these Drum Tales? Why is everyone so excited about them?" The servant replied, "You don't know, Sir! Drum Tales used to be a sort of popular country music in Shantung. Old stories were recited to the accompaniment of a drum and a pair of pear-blossom castanets, together called 'pear blossom and big drum.' There was nothing unusual about it. But recently Fair Maid and Dark Maid, two sisters from the Wang family, have appeared. The Fair Maid's personal name is Little Jade Wang. She is the most amazing creature you ever heard of. When she was twelve or thirteen years old she learned this art of storytelling, but she soon began to despise the country tunes and said they were dull. She started going to the theater, and as soon as she heard a tune, she could sing it, whether it was a *hsi-p'i* or an *erh-huang* or a *pang-tzu-ch'iang*. [12] When she heard Yü San-sheng's, Ch'eng Chang-keng's, or Chang Erh-k'uei's [13] tunes, she could sing them right off. When she sings, she can go as high as you like. She can hold a note as long as you want. She got hold of those southern—what-do-you-call-'em—*k'un ch'iang* [14] melodies as well. No matter what sort of style or melody, she puts them all into the singing of Drum Tales. In two or three years' time she created this kind of singing, and now, when people hear her sing, whether they are northerners or southerners, gentry or ordinary folk, there is nobody who is not stirred to the depths of his soul. The notices are up, so tomorrow she will sing. If you don't believe what I say, go and hear her, and then you will see. Only if you want to hear her, you'd better go early. Although the performance starts at one o'clock, if you go at ten o'clock there won't be any seats."

Lao Ts'an heard what he said but did not take it very seriously. The next day he got up at six o'clock and first went to see the Shun Well [15] inside the South Gate. Then he went out of the South Gate to the foot of Lishan to see the

12. *Hsi-p'i* and *erh-huang* are the two commonest types of melody used in the modern northern opera. When the two alternate in the same piece, the mixture is spoken of as *p'i-huang*. *Hsi-p'i* is generally sharp and shrill, and *erh-huang* is softer and more melodious. *Pang-tzu-ch'iang* is a style of operatic music characterized by the use of the *pang-tzu*, a piece of wood struck violently to emphasize the rhythm. These three types of opera music came into favor about 1800.

13. These three famous actors are still frequently referred to in discussions of opera in the present day.

14. *K'un-ch'iang* or *k'un-ch'ü*, is a southern style of singing, quieter and more refined than those already mentioned, but performed less nowadays. In the Ming dynasty reign period, Chia-ch'ing (1522–1566), Liang Ch'en-yü, a poet and musician of K'unshan in Kiangsu, learned a number of folk songs from Wei Liang-fu, a noted singer of his district, and converted them into art songs which were then used in drama.

15. Named after the legendary Emperor Shun who is supposed to have farmed the land at the foot of Lishan. See the couplet at the head of the chapter. There are several other mountains in China that claim to be the scene of Shun's activities (compare with selection 267).

place where, according to the tradition, the great Shun plowed the fields in ancient times. When he returned to his inn, it was already about nine o'clock, so he made a hasty breakfast and then went to the Ming Lake House, where he arrived before ten o'clock. It turned out to be a large theater. In front of the stage were more than a hundred tables, and to his surprise when he entered the gate he found all the seats taken, except for seven or eight empty tables in the middle section. These tables had red paper slips pasted on them which said, "Reserved by the Governor," "Reserved by the Director of Education," and so on.

Lao Ts'an looked for a long time but could not find a place. Finally he slipped two hundred cash to an attendant, who arranged a short bench for him in a gap between the tables. On the stage he saw an oblong table on which was placed a flat drum. On the drum were two pieces of iron and he knew that these must be the so-called pear-blossom castanets. Beside them was a three-stringed banjo. Two chairs stood behind the table, but no one was on the stage. When you saw this huge stage, quite bare except for these few things, you couldn't help wanting to laugh. Ten or twenty men were walking up and down among the audience with baskets on their heads, selling sesame-seed cakes and *yu-t'iao*[16] to those who had come to the theater without having breakfast.

By eleven o'clock sedan-chairs began to crowd at the door. Numerous officials in informal dress came in one after another, followed by their servants. Before twelve o'clock the empty tables in the front were all full. People still kept coming to see if there were seats, and short benches had to be wedged into the narrow spaces that were left. As this crowd of people arrived there were mutual greetings, many genuflections, and a few low bows.[17] Loud and animated conversation, free and easy talk, and laughter prevailed. Apart from those at the ten or so tables in front, the rest of the audience was made up of tradespeople, except for a few who looked like the scholars of the place. They all gossiped away, *ch'i-ch'i, ts'a-ts'a*, but since there were so many people, you couldn't hear clearly what they were saying. In any case, it was nobody's business.

At half-past twelve a man wearing a long blue cloth gown appeared through the curtained door at the back of the stage. He had a longish face, covered with lumps, like the skin of a Foochow orange dried by the wind. But ugly as he was, you felt that he was quiet and sober. He came out on the stage and said nothing but sat down on the chair to the left, behind the oblong table.

16. Fritters or crullers (literally, "oil-strips").
17. The genuflection (*ta-ch'ien-erh*) is the salutation of the Manchu: the left leg bent, the right stretched behind, the right knee and right hand almost touching the ground. The low bow is the common formal Chinese salutation consisting of a low bow with the hands hanging loosely below the knees and hidden by the sleeves, after which the clasped hands are raised to the level of the eyes.

Slowly he took up the three-stringed banjo, in a leisurely way tuned up the strings, and then played one or two little melodies, to which, however, the audience did not listen with much attention. After this he played a longer piece, but I don't know the name of the tune. I only remember that as it went on he began to pluck the strings in a circular motion, with all his fingers one after another, until the sounds, now high, now low, now simple, now intricate, entered the ears and stirred the hearts of the listeners so with their variety that there might have been several tens of strings and several hundreds of fingers playing on them. And now continuous shouts of approval were heard, not interfering, however, with the sound of the banjo. When he had finished this piece, he rested, and a man from the wings brought him a cup of tea.

After a pause of several minutes a girl came out from behind the curtains. She was about sixteen or seventeen years old with a long duck's egg face, hair done into a knot, and silver earrings in her ears. She wore a blue cotton jacket and a pair of blue cotton trousers with black piping. Although her clothes were of coarse material, they were spotlessly clean. She came to the back of the table and sat down on the chair to the right. The banjo-player then took up his instrument and began to pluck the strings, *chen-chen, ts'ung-ts'ung.* The girl stood up, took the pear-blossom castanets between the fingers of her left hand and began to clap them, *ting-ting, tang-tang,* in time with the banjo. With her right hand she took up the drumstick and then, after listening carefully to the rhythm of the banjo, struck the drum a sharp blow and began to sing. Every word was clear-cut and crisp; every note smooth-flowing like a young oriole flying out of a valley or a young swallow returning to the nest. Every phrase had seven words and every part several tens of phrases, now slow, now fast, sometimes high, sometimes low. There were endless changes of tune and style so that the listener felt that no song, tune, melody, or air ever invented could equal this one piece, that it was the peak of perfection in song.

There were two men sitting at Lao Ts'an's side, one of whom asked the other in a low voice, "I suppose this must be the Fair Maid?" The other man said, "No, this is the Dark Maid, the Fair Maid's younger sister. All her songs were taught her by the Fair Maid. If you compare her with the Fair Maid, it's impossible to estimate the distance that separates them! You can talk about her skill, but the Fair Maid's can't be put into words. The Dark Maid's skill can be learned by others, but the Fair Maid's can't possibly be learned. For several years now everybody has tried to sing like them. Even the singsong girls have tried! And the most anyone has done is to sing two or three phrases as well as the Dark Maid. As to the Fair Maid's merits, why, there's never been anybody who could do a tenth as well as she."

While they were talking, the Dark Maid had already finished singing and went out at the back. And now all the people in the theater began to talk and laugh. Sellers of melon seeds, peanuts, red fruit, and walnuts shouted their wares in a loud voice. The whole place was filled with the sound of human voices. Just when the uproar was at its height, another girl appeared at the back of the stage. She was about eighteen or nineteen years old, and her costume differed in no detail from that of the first. She had a melon-seed face and a clear white complexion. Her features were not particularly beautiful; she was attractive without being seductive, pure but not cold. She came out with her head slightly bent, stood behind the table, took up the pear-blossom castanets and clapped them together several times, *ting-tang*. It was most amazing! They were just two bits of iron, and yet in her hand they seemed to contain all the five notes and the twelve tones.[18] Then she took up the drumstick, lightly struck the drum twice, lifted her head, and cast one glance at the audience. When those two eyes, like autumn water, like winter stars, like pearls, like two beads of black in quicksilver, glanced left and right, even the men sitting in the most distant corners felt: Little Jade Wang is looking at me! As to those sitting nearer, nothing need be said. It was just one glance, but the whole theater was hushed, quieter than when the Emperor comes forth. Even a needle dropped on the ground could have been heard.

Little Jade Wang then opened her vermilion lips, displaying her sparkling white teeth, and sang several phrases. At first the sound was not very loud, but you felt an inexpressible magic enter your ears, and it was as though the stomach and bowels had been passed over by a smoothing iron, leaving no part unrelaxed. You seemed to absorb ambrosia through the thirty-six thousand pores of the skin until every single pore tingled with delight. After the first few phrases her song rose higher and louder till suddenly she drew her voice up to a sharp high-pitched note like a thread of steel wire thrown into the vault of the sky. You could not help secretly applauding. Still more amazing, she continued to move her voice up and down and in and out at that great height. After several turns her voice again began to rise, making three or four successive folds in the melody, each one higher than the last. It was like climbing T'aishan[19] from the western face of the Aolai Peak. First you see the thousand-fathom cleft wall of Aolai Peak and think that it reaches the sky. But when you have wound your way up to the top, you see Fan Peak far above you. And when you have got to the top of Fan Peak, again you see the South Gate of Heaven far above Fan Peak. The higher you climb, the more alarming it seems—the more alarming, the more wonderful.

After Little Jade Wang had sung her three or four highest flourishes,

---

18. The five notes are those of the traditional Chinese scale, and the twelve tones are those of the ancient bamboo pitch pipes.

19. This and what follows is an accurate description of T'aishan (Mount T'ai) in Shantung, the most famous sacred mountain in China. The South Gate of Heaven is a gateway at the head of the gorge up which the Pilgrim Way climbs, and passing through it the traveler reaches the various temples scattered over the top. It is clearly visible from the plain four thousand feet below when viewed from the south, but cannot be seen from the west approach which our author has in mind.

suddenly her voice dropped, and then at a powerful spirited gallop, in a short time, with a thousand twists and turns she described innumerable circles like a flying serpent writhing and turning among the thirty-six peaks of The Yellow Mountains.[20] After this the more she sang, the lower her voice became; the lower she sang, the more delicate it was, until at last the sound could be heard no more. Every person in the theater held his breath and sat intently, not daring to move. After two or three minutes it was as though a small sound came forth from under the ground. And then the voice again rose like a Japanese rocket which shoots into the sky, bursting and scattering with innumerable strands of multicolored fire. The voice soared aloft until endless sounds seemed to be coming and going. The banjo-player too plucked his strings with a circular movement of all his fingers, now loud, now soft, in perfect accompaniment to her voice. It was like the wanton singing of sweet birds in a spring morning in the garden. The ears were kept so busy that you couldn't decide which note to listen to. Just as it was becoming most intricate, one clear note sounded, and then voice and instrument both fell silent. The applause from the audience was like the rumbling of thunder.

After a while the uproar abated slightly and from the front row one could hear a young man of about thirty say with a Hunan accent, "When I was a student and came across that passage where the ancient writer describes the merits of good singing in the words 'The sound circles the beams and stops not for three days,'[21] I could not understand what was meant. If you think of it in the abstract, how can sound go round and round the beams? And how can it go on for three days? It was not until I heard Little Jade Wang sing that I realized how appropriate the words of the ancient writer are. Every time I hear her sing, her song echoes in my ears for many days. No matter what I'm doing my attention wanders. Rather I feel that the 'three days' of 'stops not for three days' is too short. The 'three months' of the saying about Confucius, 'For three months he knew not the taste of meat'[22] would describe it much more adequately." Those around him all said, "Mr. Meng Hsiang[23] expresses it so aptly that he arouses my envy."

While they were talking, the Dark Maid again came on to sing. After her the Fair Maid appeared again. Lao Ts'an heard a man near him say that this piece was called "The Black Donkey." It merely told the story of a scholar who saw a beautiful maiden riding by on a black donkey. Before describing the

20. In Anhwei province, two hundred miles west of Hangchow.

21. From *Lieh Tzu*, chapter 5 (see selection 12).

22. *Analects*, 7.13. The complete verse is: "When the Master was in Ch'i, he heard *Shao* (music in the style of the legendary Emperor Shun), and for three months he knew not the taste of meat. He said, 'I thought not that music could be made as excellent as this!' "

23. Meng-hsiang was the *hao* ("style") of Wang Yi-min of Wuling, Hunan, who in 1896 received an appointment to the Yellow River Conservancy under Governor Chang Yao. Wang Yi-min wrote a poem describing the singing of Little Jade Wang, and it must be this poem that the author had in mind when he wrote his description.

girl, it told all about the good parts of the black donkey, and when at last it came to tell about the maiden, in a few words it was finished. It was sung entirely in "rapid recitative"; the further it went, the faster it got. The poem by Po Hsiang-shan[24] expressed it perfectly,

Big pearls and little pearls fall into the jade platter.

The marvelous thing about it was that though she recited so quickly that you would have thought the listeners could not follow, every word was clear; not one was lost to their ears. Only she could obtain this clarity. But even this piece, it must be owned, was inferior to the preceding one.

It was not yet five o'clock, and everybody assumed that Little Jade Wang would sing once again. It would be interesting to see what her next piece would be like.

To learn what happened, hear the next chapter tell.

Translated by Harold Shadick

24. The famous T'ang poet, Po Chü-yi (see selection 180). The line quoted in the text comes from a long narrative poem called the "Song of the Guitar" (P'i-p'a hsing).

PART V

Oral and Performing Arts

Prosimetric Storytelling and Its Written Derivatives

266

Transformation Text on Mahāmaudgalyāyana Rescuing His Mother from the Underworld, with Pictures, One Scroll, with Preface

Anonymous (late 9th–early 10th century)

Now, on the fifteenth day of the seventh month, the heavens open their doors and the gates of the hells are flung wide. The three mires dissipate, the ten virtues increase. Because this is the day when the company of monks end their summer retreat, the deity who confers blessings and the eight classes of supernatural beings all come to convey blessings. Those who undertake to make offerings to them in the present world will have a supply of blessings and those who are dead will be reborn in a superlative place. Therefore, a purgato-

This tale is about the Buddhist saint, Mu-lien (the Chinese version of his Sankrit name which is given in the title), who saves his mother from the tortures of hell. It belongs to the popular genre called *pien-wen* ("transformation text"). This genre had a close relationship to pictures that were used as illustrations for oral storytelling, a trait evident even in the formula that occurs before the verse portions. Transformation texts constitute the earliest extended vernacular narratives in Chinese. The manuscript on which this translation is based was discovered around the turn of this century in a cave in the Chinese part of Central Asia at Tun-huang (far western Kansu province). The copying was completed on a date equivalent to May 26, 921, although the original composition occurred approximately 150 or more years before that date. Other manuscripts discovered at Tun-huang contain abbreviated versions of the tale, but this one offers the complete story.

Roughly 40,000 manuscripts were unearthed from one of the Caves of the Thousand

rian feast[1] is spread before the Three Honored Ones[2] who, through the grace of their welcoming the great assembly, put a priority upon saving those who are distressed by hanging in limbo.

Long ago, when the Buddha was in the world, he had a disciple who was styled Maudgalyāyana. When he was still a layman and had not yet left home to become a monk, his name was Turnip. He believed deeply in the Three Precious Ones,[3] and had a high regard for Salvationism.[4] Once he wanted to go to another country to engage in trade. So he disposed of his wealth, ordering his mother later on to arrange for vegetarian food to be provided for the many members of the Buddhist Trinity and the numerous beggars who would come. But after Turnip departed, his mother became stingy and hid away for herself all the riches which had been entrusted to her.

Before many months had elapsed, the son had completed his business and returned home. "As you had charged me," the mother said to her son, "I held vegetarian feasts which shall bring us blessings." Thus did she deceive commoners and saints so that, when her life came to an end, she fell into the Avīci Hell[5] where she endured much harsh suffering.

After Turnip finished observing the three full years of mourning, he immediately surrendered himself to the Buddha and left home to become a monk. Having inherited the good deeds of his former lives, he actualized these inherent causes by paying heed to the Law and attaining arhatship.[6] Whereupon he sought his mother in the six paths of transmigration with his unlimited vision, but nowhere did he see her.

Maudgalyāyana awoke from meditation full of sadness. "In which place is my dear mother enjoying happiness?" he inquired of the World-Honored.

The World-Honored then informed Maudgalyāyana: "Your mother has already dropped down into the Avīci hell, where she is now undergoing

---

Buddhas at Tun-huang where they had been sealed up sometime during the first half of the eleventh century. Written in a total of about twenty different languages, a number of which are now extinct, the Tun-huang manuscripts represent one of the most important archeological recoveries of written texts in history. Their reemergence in this century has revolutionized our understanding of medieval Chinese literature, religion, politics, institutions, economics, society, dance, music, art, and other areas of human endeavor.

The dots under some of the words in the translation indicate places where sinographs are missing on the manuscript and have had to be restored. Three dots equal roughly one sinograph.

1. The presumed source of the Yü-lan-p'en ("All Souls") festival.
2. Amitābha Buddha and his two attendant bodhisattvas (saviors).
3. The Three Precious Ones or the Buddhist Trinity are the Buddha, dharma (his doctrine), and *saṇgha* (Buddhist community).
4. Mahāyāna, the Greater Vehicle of Buddhism.
5. The deepest of the eight hot hells.
6. Sainthood.

much suffering. Although you have attained the fruit of the saintly life, your knowledge will be to no avail. You can save her only if you employ the might of the assembly on the day when the companies of monks in all directions disband at the end of the summer retreat." Therefore, the Buddha in his compassion instituted this expedient method. This, then, is the story of how the purgatorian offerings were founded.

From the time when Turnip's father and mother had passed away,
After three full years of ceremonial sorrow, the period of mourning
    came to an end;
Listening to music did not make him happy—his appearance became
    emaciated,
Eating fine foods gave him no pleasure—he wasted away to skin and
    bones.
But then he heard that the Tathāgata[7] was in the Deer Park,
Where he comforted and cared for all men and deities;
"Now I shall study the Way and seek the Tathāgata!"
And so he journeyed to the twin trees[8] to visit the Buddha.
At that time, the Buddha came immediately to receive him,
The monk prostrated himself before him who is most honored among
    men and deities;
To his right and left were the mighty Indra and Brahmā with their hosts,
To his east and west were the great generals and other sundry spirits.
The sauvastika[9] on the front of his breast had a crystalline glow,
The halo behind his neck was like the disc of the moon;
Don't you know, the hundreds of gems and the thousands of flowers on
    his throne,
Were just like the five-colored clouds at the edge of the horizon.
"I, your disciple, am a mediocre person who is limited by his desires,
Neither can I renounce nor free myself from desire and anger;
Just because the sinful karma of my whole life was of such enormity,
It extended to my dear mother, causing her to enter the gates of Hades.
I only fear that impermanence will press upon her,
And that she will sink in the ocean of misery beside the ford of births
    and deaths;
May you, oh Buddha, show compassion by saving your disciple,
Allowing me to concentrate on studying the Way so that I may repay
    my parents."
As soon as the World-Honored heard what Turnip was saying,
He knew that he was upright and was not being deceitful;

7. The "Thus-come/gone," an epithet of the Buddha.
8. The pair of *śāla* trees under which the Buddha entered nirvāṇa.
9. The Buddha's lucky mark, which is a reversed form of the swastika.

He began by enumerating and explaining the doctrine of the Four
Noble Truths,[10]
Then lectured him on the necessity of avoiding the seven rebellious
acts.[11]
Even though one amasses so much treasure that it towers to the Milky
Way,
This is not as good as urgently persuading others to leave home and
become monks;
It is precisely the same as a blind turtle bumping into a floating log,
Or yet like a lotus blossom issuing from a great expanse of water.[12]
It is difficult to escape from a house which is wrapped in flames,[13]
The raging sea of misery is so broad that it has no shores;
Just for the reason that all living beings are different,
The Tathāgata established three types of conveyances to nirvāṇa.
The Buddha summoned Ānanda to perform the tonsure,
And his clothing was then exchanged for a monk's cassock;
Instantaneously, Maudgalyāyana achieved sainthood,
And subsequently he received the commandments for monks.
During the time that Turnip was there in front of the Buddha,
Incense smoke curled up in wreaths from a golden censer;
The fabulous forest shaken by the six kinds of earthquakes[14] moved
heaven and earth,
The four divine flowers were wafted on the air and scattered through the
clear skies.
A thousand sorts of elegant brocades were spread on the couches and
seats,
Ten thousand styles of pearled banners hung in the air.
The Buddha himself proclaimed: "Now you are my disciple!"
And he styled him "Mighty Maudgalyāyana of Supernatural Power."

At that moment, Maudgalyāyana achieved sainthood beneath the twin
trees. How did it happen like this? It is just as in the *Lotus Sūtra:* "The
prodigal son first received his worth, then later was cleansed of his impurities."
This is precisely the same in that he first obtained the fruit of sainthood and
afterwards engaged in the study of the Way.

10. These are: 1. misery is a condition of life, 2. origination of misery, 3. stopping of misery,
and 4. the eightfold path that leads to the stopping of misery.

11. Shedding a Buddha's blood; killing one's father or mother, a monk, teacher, or arhat
(saint); disrupting religious organizations.

12. Both this and the preceding line are metaphorical expressions of the improbability of a
man being reborn as a man or meeting with a Buddha and his teaching. The implication is that
one should accumulate as much good karma as possible to better his chances of a happy rebirth.

13. This is the famous parable of the burning house in the *Lotus Sūtra* (see selection 13).

14. Auspicious signs of the Buddha's power.

Look at the place where Maudgalyāyana sits meditating deep in the mountains—how is it?

> After Maudgalyāyana's beard and hair had been shaved away,
> Right away he took himself into the depths of the mountains;
> It was a remote and quiet place where there was no one else,
> Right away, he contemplated unreality and sat in meditation.
> He sat in meditation and contemplated unreality, learning good and
>   evil,
> He subdued his mind, he settled his mind, until nothing more adhered
>   to it;
> Facing a mirror, its image was clear and unwavering,
> And all the while he pressed his right foot down upon his left foot.[15]
>> He sat with his body erect on a large rock,[16]
>> And with his tongue touching the roof of his mouth;
>> White bones became for him completely empty,[17]
>> His breathings no longer were intertwined.[18]
> Just at that time, a herd of deer stopped to drink in the woods,
> They drew near to the clear pool and looked across its waters;
> Beneath the bright moon in front of the courtyard, he listened to
>   religious discourses,
> Under the pines on the green hills, he sat meditating.
> The lake air on the horizon was like colored clouds,
> The watchtowers on the green hills outside the frontier were visible;
> The autumn wind soughed as it passed through the center of the forest,
> Yellow leaves drifted down and floated on the water.
> Maudgalyāyana sat reposefully in a state of incorporeality,
> Gradually he cultivated his internal and external experiential mind;
> By realizing discipleship, he occupied his hoped-for position,
> He entered and left the mountains[19] as free as he pleased.
>> Maudgalyāyana awoke from abstract meditation,
>> Then swiftly exercised his supernatural power;
>> His coming was quick as a thunderclap,
>> His going seemed like a gust of wind.
>> Wild geese honked at the hunter's darts,
>> Gray hawks escaped from nets and cages;
>> The mist in the center of the pond was greenish,
>> The sky was clear, the distant road was red.

15. The posture for overcoming evil spirits.
16. To symbolize solidity.
17. The ninth and final stage of meditation on the decomposition of a corpse for the purpose
of curbing desire.
18. He had achieved carefully controlled Yogic breathing.
19. In Buddhist parlance, "mountain" oftens stands for monastery.

With his supernatural power, he gained freedom,
So he hurled up his begging-bowl and leaped into space;
Thereupon, instantaneously,
He ascended to the heavenly palace of Brahmā.
In an instant, Maudgalyāyana arrived at the heavenly court,
All that he heard in his ears was the sound of music and drums;
Red towers[20] were faintly reflected on the golden halls,
A profusion of green lattices opened on white jade walls.
With his metal-ringed staff, he knocked at the gate three or four times,
Unaware of the tears which were crisscrossing his breast;
An elder came out from within to have a talk with him,
He brought his palms together[21] and began to speak of his sincere
    filiality.
"I wonder if you know me?" he inquired of the elder,
"I, a poor monk, am an inhabitant of Jambūdvīpa.
When I was still young, I was bereft of my father and mother;
Although our family was quite wealthy, it was lacking in sons and
    grandsons,
I was orphaned and, furthermore, had no future before me.
The dear mother of this poor monk was styled Nīladhi,
    My father's name was Śūlakṣaṇa;
All his life was spent in doing kind and charitable works,
After he died, it would have been fitting for him to be reborn in this
    heaven.
This is such a delightfully splendid and charming place,
Just gazing at it brings happiness to the hearts of men;
Bells and drums resound in harmony with elegant music,
The sound of harps being strummed is also loud and clear.

How sad it is that they never relaxed from their parental chores!
The affection she showed in nursing me is not easily forgotten;
I wonder whether they have been peaceful and well since leaving me,
And that is why I am now searching for them in this place."

When the elder heard these words, he seemed to be sympathetic,
But his mind was in a whirl and he spoke haltingly:
"I, your disciple, had a son in Jambūdvīpa,
But I wasn't aware that he had left home to become a monk.
Do not blame me, Your Reverence, if I question you closely,
There are so many different types of people in the world;
As I observed you speaking for the first time, I took you for a stranger,
But now that I reflect upon it, I am somewhat nonplussed.

20. Means "splendid mansions" (compare with selection 263).
21. In salutation.

> Among laymen, there are many people who have the same name and
>   surname,
> And there are hundreds of types of faces which are similar;
> Your appearance and disposition are familiar,
> But then when I think about it, I cannot place you.
> If, oh Teacher, you insist on seeking to be recognized,
> Please tell me some more about your family matters."

Maudgalyāyana went to the palaces of heaven in search of his father. He arrived at a gate where he met an elder. "When I was young," he informed the elder, "my name was Turnip. After my parents died, I surrendered myself to the Buddha and left home to become a monk. My whiskers and hair were shaved off and I was given the title 'Mahāmaudgalyāyana, Preeminent in Supernatural Power.' "

When the elder heard him say his childhood name, he knew right away that it was his son. "We have long been separated. Have you been well?"

After Turnip-Maudgalyāyana had been acknowledged by his dear father and had inquired about how he was getting along, he asked: "In what place is my dear mother enjoying happiness?"

The elder replied to Turnip: "Your mother's activities while she was alive were different from mine. I practiced the ten virtues and the five commandments, so that, after I died, my soul was reborn in heaven. Throughout her life, your mother committed a large number of sins and, at the end of her days, she fell into hell. If you search for mother along the infernal paths of Jambudvīpa, you'll soon find out where she has gone."

After hearing these words, Maudgalyāyana took leave of the elder. He vanished and descended to Jambūdvīpa. There he searched for his mother along the infernal paths but could not find her. However, he did see eight or nine men and women wandering about aimlessly with nothing to do.

This is the place where he goes forward and asks the reasons for this situation:

> "Please do not pay me any reverence.
> Who are you, my good friends,
> That have all gathered here in this place—
> Wandering about aimlessly with not a thing to do,
> Roaming around outside the walls of the city?
> I, who am a humble monk, only arrived here today,
> To my mind, it is really quite extraordinary."
> The men and women answered the reverend one with these words:
> "It's only because we had the same name and same surname as
>   someone else,
> Our names were mixed up with theirs and so we were escorted here;

The interrogation lasted just four or five days,
We were judged 'not guilty' and released to return to our homes.
Long since sent to the grave by our wives and sons,
Our solitary bodies were flung into the wilderness;
On all four sides, there were neither relatives nor companions,
Foxes, wolves, crows, and magpies competed to divide us up.
Our houses fell into disrepair leaving us with no place to take refuge,
We appealed to the King of the Underworld with plaintive voices;
His judgment was that we be released as wandering ghosts with nothing
   to do,
Having received this supplemental verdict, what more is there to say?
Today, we have already been cut off from the road of births and deaths,
Once the gates of Hades slam shut, they never open again.
Though there be a thousand kinds of food placed on our grave-mounds,
How can they alleviate the hunger in our stomachs?
All our wailing and weeping, in the end, will be to no avail,
In vain do they trouble themselves to make folded paper money. [22]
Take a message to the sons and daughters in our homes telling them:
'We entreat you to save us from infernal suffering by performing good
   deeds.' "

Maudgalyāyana waited a long while before speaking. "I wonder whether
you know of a Lady Nīladhi?"

"None of us know her," the men and women replied.

"Where does the Great King Yama dwell?" Maudgalyāyana continued with
his questioning.

"Reverend sir!" the men and women replied. "If you walk several steps
farther toward the north, you'll see in the distance a tower with triple gates
where there are thousands and ten thousands of stalwart soldiers, all holding
swords and cudgels. That is the gate of the Great King Yama."

Upon hearing these words, Maudgalyāyana walked several steps farther
toward the north. From there he could see the tower with its triple gates into
which stalwart soldiers were driving countless sinners. Maudgalyāyana went
forward and made inquiries but could not find his mother, so he sat by the
side of the road and cried loudly. When he had finished crying, he went
forward again and was taken in to see the King by functionaries.

This is the place where Maudgalyāyana is led in by the gatekeepers to see the
Great King who asks him his business:

When the Great King saw Maudgalyāyana enter,
He quickly joined his palms in salutation and was about to stand up:

22. Chinese still present such offerings to the dead (compare with selection 263, second
part).

"What is your reason for coming here, reverend sir?"
Hurriedly, he bowed respectfully from behind his table.
"Your coming here embarrasses me, oh Exemplar!
I, your disciple, am situated here in this infernal region,
    Where I flog sinners to determine whether they shall remain dead or
        be reborn;
    Although I do not recognize you, reverend sir,
    It was long ago that I had heard of your name.
It must be either that the Buddha has sent you here on a mission,
    Or that there is some private family business;
The Lord of Mount T'ai's[23] verdicts are, in the end, difficult to alter,
For all were sanctioned by heaven's bureaucrats and earth's pen-pushers.
A sinner's karmic retribution is in accord with conditional causation,
Who is there that could rescue them on the spur of the moment?
Fetid blood and congealed fats stink through the Long Night,[24]
Leaving an offensive stain on your clothing which is so pure.
These infernal paths are no place for you to spend much time,
It is my humble wish that you, oh Exemplar, make an early departure."
Maudgalyāyana replied to him as best as he could:
    "Perhaps you may be aware, oh Great King,
That I, poor monk, had a father and mother who, when alive,
Day and night observed the laws of abstinence, never eating after noon?
Based on their behavior while in the World of Mankind,
After their deaths, they should have been reborn in the Pure Land.
My father alone is dwelling in the mansions of heaven,
But I cannot locate my dear mother in any of the heavens;
In my estimation, she should not even have passed through hell,
My only fear is that she may have been unjustly punished by High
        Heaven.
I have followed her traces to the edges of heaven and earth,
Filled with sorrowful vexation, I heave a long sigh;
If she has come to this realm because of her karmic retribution,
Perhaps you, oh Great King, would have been made aware of it."

When Maudgalyāyana had finished speaking, the Great King then summoned him to the upper part of the hall. There he was given audience with
Kṣitigarbha Bodhisattva[25] to whom he quickly paid obeisance.
    "Have you come here in search of your mother?"
    "Yes," replied Maudgalyāyana, "I am searching for my mother."

23. T'ai-shan Lao-chün, the Taoist counterpart of Yama.
24. Of transmigration (saṃsāra).
25. Overlord of Yama, he is guardian of the earth.

"In the days when your mother was still alive, she committed a large number of sins. So limitless and boundless were they that she must have fallen into hell. Would you please come forward? My duty-officer will be here in just a moment."

The King then summoned his karma-watcher, fate-investigator, and book-keeper who came immediately.

"The name of this reverend monk's mother is Lady Nīladhi. How long has it been since she died?"

The karma-watcher replied to the Great King: "Three years have already passed since Lady Nīladhi died. The legal records of the criminal proceedings against her are all in the casebook of the Commandant of Mount T'ai, who is Recorder for the Bureau of the Underworld."

The King summoned the two Good and Evil Boys and told them to examine the books at Mount T'ai to find out which hell Lady Nīladhi was in.

"Reverend sir," the Great King said, "Follow along with the Boys. If you ask the General of the Five Ways, you should be able to find out where she has gone."

After Maudgalyāyana had heard these words, he took leave of the Great King and went out. He walked several steps and soon came to the banks of the Whathellwedo River.[26] There he saw numberless sinners taking off their clothes and hanging them on trees. There were many sounds of loud crying by those who wished to cross but could not. Distraught and apprehensive, they clustered in groups of threes and fours. They held their heads as they wept and wailed.

This is the place where Maudgalyāyana asks them the reason for this:

> The waters of the Whathellwedo River flow swiftly to the west,
> Broken stones and precipitous crags obstruct the road they walk on;
> They take off their clothes and hang them on the sides of tree branches,
> Pursued, they are not allowed to stand still for even a moment.
> At the edge of the river, when they hear their names being called out,
> They are unaware of the tears which are drenching their breasts;
> Today, at last, they know that their bodies have really died,
> They stand next to trees in pairs and weep sorrowfully for a long time.
> "When I was alive, I was in thrall to my prized possessions,
> I went out in a golden four-in-hand carriage with crimson wheels;
> Saying that it would never change in ten thousand ages,
> Who would have thought that it long ago was transformed into dust?
> Oh! Alas and alack! What pain there is inside my heart!
> In vain have my white bones been buried in a tall tumulus.
> My sons and grandsons ride the dragon-horses in the southern stables,

26. The Styx of the Chinese Buddhist underworld.

My wives and concubines use the scented carriage outside the
   northern window."
Their many mouths all said the same thing—"It is inexpressible!"
Long did they sigh but all their complaining went for nought;
Every person who commits sins will fall into hell,
He who does good will certainly be reborn in heaven.
Now each must follow his own circumstantial karma,
It is certain that it will be difficult to meet again later on;
They grasp each other's hands and repeatedly enjoin, "You must cheer up!"
Looking back, they wipe away their tears as they look longingly at
   one another.
In their ears, all they hear are cries of "Hurry along!"
As they are driven forward by the thousands and ten thousands;
On the river's southern bank, ox-head guards hold their truncheons,
At the water's northern edge, hell's jailers raise their pitchforks.
The eyes of the people in the water are filled with distress,
The tears of those who are on the banks flow copiously;
If only they had known earlier that they were to sink in a place of
   hardship,
Now all they can do is regret that they had not done good works while
   they were still alive.

Maudgalyāyana asked a man who was beneath a tree at the side of the
Whathellwedo River:

"Heaven's Mansions and Hell's Halls are not insubstantial;
It goes without saying that Heaven punishes those who do evil,
The minions of the underworld also promptly join in prosecution.
This poor monk's dear mother did not accumulate goodness,
So that her lost soul fell into the three mires leading to hell;
I have heard tell that she has been taken inside hell,
All I want to ask is whether or not you have any news of her?"
As all the sinners looked at Maudgalyāyana the teacher,
Together they wept mournfully and knitted their brows:
"It is only recently in time that we, your disciples, died,
Truly, we do not know of your dear mother, reverend sir.
While we were alive, we committed numerous sins,
Now, today, that we endure such suffering, we at last begin to feel
   regret;
Even though one has wives and concubines enough to fill the
   mountains and rivers,
Who among them would be willing to die in his place?
Whenever you are able to depart from the underworld gates,
Inform those sons and grandsons of ours who are still at home

That it is unnecessary to make coffins and caskets of white jade,
And that gold is spent in vain when it is buried in the grave.
Endless sorrow and sighs of resentment are ultimately to no avail,
For we hear not the sacred drum music and songs to string
    accompaniment;
If they wish to obliterate the suffering of the dead,
Nothing is better than cultivating blessedness to save these souls from
    darkness."

"When you go back, reverend sir, pass this news to all men. Instruct them to create blessings whereby they may save the dead. Except for the Buddha and him alone, there is no other way to be saved. We wish, reverend sir, that you achieve perfect wisdom and nirvāṇa which, even on ordinary occasions, is not concealed and that it will serve as a conveyance for all living beings. May your blade of knowledge be assiduously sharpened and not be obstructed by the forest of moral affliction. Thus will your awe-inspiring mind be active everywhere throughout the world and so realize the great vow of all the Buddhas. If we are to escape from this joyless place, it will be due to the universal bestowal of your compassionate regard, reverend sir."

After Maudgalyāyana heard this, he went forward once again and, within a short period of time, he arrived at the seat of the General of the Five Ways.

This is the place where he asks for news of his mother:

The General of the Five Ways had a frightful disposition,
The bright gleam of his golden armor intersected with the light from his
    sword;
      To his left and his right, there were more than a million men,
      And assistants who were continuously flying back and forth.
His yelling and shouting were like the terrifying rumble of thunder,
His angry eyes resembled the dazzling flash of lightning.
      There were some whose bellies were being rent and whose chests
        were being opened,
      And others whose faces were being skinned alive;
      Although Maudgalyāyana was a holy person,
      Even he was completely frightened out of his wits.
Maudgalyāyana wept mournfully as he thought of his dear mother,
He exercised his supernatural powers with the speed of the windborne
    clouds;
If you ask which is the most crucial place on the infernal paths,
None exceeds that of the great General of the Five Ways.
To the left and the right, a concentration of spears blocks the way,
To the east and west, there are more than ten thousand men with staves
    erect;

All together, they raise their eyes and gaze toward the southwest,
What they see is the imposing Spirit of the Five Ways.
He has been guarding this road for numerous aeons,
He fixes the type of punishment for thousands and ten thousands;
Starting with the very first one, each of them follows his own karmic
     conditions.
"The dear mother of this poor monk deviated from the practice of
     almsgiving
So that her souls were sent drifting along these infernal roads;
Whenever I ask which of the three mires leading to hell is the most
     painful place,
Everyone says that it is the devils' barrier of the Five Ways.
Men mill everywhere about the evil way to rebirth as an animal,
But the good way to the heavenly mansions is vacant morning and night;
All of those who are sinners must pass along this way,
It is my humble wish that you, General, will make a check of them."
The General brought his palms together in salutation and said to the ex-
     emplar,
"You must not weep so mournfully that you do harm to your ap-
     pearance.
The crowds on this road are usually as numberless as the sands of
     the Ganges,
But you have, on the spur of the moment, asked me if I know who
     Nīladhi is.
In Mount T'ai's regency, there are many sections dealing with names,
Investigations include heaven's bureaus and earth's offices;
Each of the overseers of documents also has these names,
And all warrants which come down pass through this place.
Today, it just so happens that I, your disciple, am the officer of names,
I shall spend a few moments trying to check up on this for you, oh
     Teacher;
If we are so fortunate as to come across her name,
It will not be very difficult to locate her whereabouts."

"Have you seen a Lady Nīladhi or not?" the General asked his attendants to
the left and right.
     On the left side there was an officer-in-charge who informed the General:
"Three years ago, there was a Lady Nīladhi who was summoned away by a
warrant sent up from the Avīci Hell. She is at this very moment in the Avīci
Hell undergoing torture."
     When Maudgalyāyana heard these words, he spoke to the General, who
replied to him: "Reverend sir, all sinners receive their sentences from the King
and only then do they descend farther into hell."

"Why didn't my mother see the King face to face?" Maudgalyāyana importuned him.

"Reverend sir," replied the General, "there are two kinds of people in the world who do not get to see the King's face. The first are those people who, during their lifetimes, cultivate the ten virtues and the five commandments. After they die, their souls are reborn in heaven. The second are those people who, during their lifetimes, do not cultivate good karma but commit a large number of sins. After their lives come to the end, they enter hell forthwith and they, too, do not get to see the King's face. Only those people who are half-good and half-bad are taken into the presence of the King to be sentenced. Then they are reincarnated, receiving their retribution in accordance with conditioning causes."

This is the place where Maudgalyāyana, when he hears these words, goes forthwith to the various hells in search of his mother:

> Maudgalyāyana's tears fell, his thoughts wandered aimlessly,
> The karmic retribution of sentient beings is like being tossed on the
>   wind;
> His dear mother had sunk into a realm of suffering,
> Her souls had already by that time long since dissipated.
> Iron discs continuously plunged into her body from out of the air,
> Fierce fires, at all times, were burning beneath her feet;
> Every place on her chest and belly had been stripped to shreds,
> Every inch of her bones and flesh had charred to a pulp.
> Bronze-colored crows pecked at her heart ten thousand times over,
> Molten iron poured on the top of her head a thousand repetitions;
> One might ask whether the tree of knives up ahead were the most
>   painful,
> But can it compare with the cleaving mill which chops men's waists in
>   two?
>   Beyond description
> Is the congealed fat and ground flesh so like a broad ferry-crossing;
> There are wild mountains all around for several hundred miles,
> Which, from their jagged peaks, plummet downwards for a league.
> Ten thousand iron lances are installed at the bottom,
> A thousand layers of smoke and fire obscure the four gates;
> Should one ask what sort of crimes are being punished herein,
> It is just for those who have killed others in the world of men.

After Maudgalyāyana had finished speaking, he went forward again. Before long, he came to another hell. "Is there a Lady Nīladhi in this hell?" he asked the warden. "It is because she is my mother that I have come hunting for her."

"Everyone in this hell is a man, reverend sir," replied the warden. "There are no women at all. If you go on ahead and ask whether she is in the hell with the hill made of knives, I am sure that, through your inquiry, you will get to see her."

Maudgalyāyana went forward and again he came to another hell. The left side of it was named Knife Hill and the right was named Sword Forest. Inside the hell, spear tips and swords were pointed from opposite sides and blood flowed copiously. He saw the warden driving countless sinners into this hell.

"What is the name of this hell?" Maudgalyāyana asked.

"This is the Knife Hill and Sword Forest Hell," answered an ogre.

"What sinful karma did the sinners who are in this hell produce that they should have fallen into *this* hell?" Maudgalyāyana asked.

"While they were alive," the warden informed him, "the sinners who are in this hell trespassed upon and damaged the perpetual property of the assembly of monks. They befouled the monastery gardens, were given to eating the fruit of the orchards held in perpetuity by the monasteries, and stole firewood from the forests held in perpetuity by the monasteries."

Here is the place where they are now being made to climb up the trees of swords with their hands, causing them to be stripped bare of every limb and joint.

> The white bones on Knife Hill were strewn chaotically every which way,
> The human heads in Sword Forest numbered in the thousands and ten
>   thousands;
> Those who wish to avoid clambering up the hill of knives,
> Should never pass by the monastery holdings without adding good
>   earth.
> Propagate fruit trees and present them to the monastery orchards,
> Contribute seeds to increase the crops from the fields held in perpetuity.
> Oh, you sinners! it is absolutely indescribable,
> How you will endure punishment through aeons as numerous as the
>   sands of the Ganges.
> Even when the Buddhas achieve nirvāṇa, you still will not get out.
> This hell stretches for hundreds of miles from the east to the west,
> The sinners race through it wildly, bumping against each others'
>   shoulders;
> The winds of karma blow upon the fire which advances as it burns,
> The jailers holding pitchforks jab at them from behind.
> Their bodies and heads are all like so many broken tiles,
> Their hands and feet immediately become like powder and froth;
> Boiling iron, light leaping from its surface, is poured into their mouths,
> Whomever it touches is pierced to the left and penetrated to the right.
> Bronze arrows fly beside them and shoot into their eyes,

Wheels of swords come straight down, cutting them in mid-air;
It is said that it will be a thousand years before they are reborn as men,
With iron rakes they are scraped together and revivified.[27]

When Maudgalyāyana heard these words, he wept mournfully and sighed with grief. He went forward and asked the warden: "Is there a Lady Nīladhi inside this hell?"

"What relationship has she to you, reverend sir?" the warden answered in reply.

"She is the dear mother of this poor monk," Maudgalyāyana informed him.

"Reverend sir, there is no Lady Nīladhi inside this hell," the warden told him. "Inside those hells which are on ahead, there are some which are all for women. You ought to be able to find her there."

After Maudgalyāyana had heard these words, he went forward again. He came to a hell which was about a league in depth. Great clouds of black smoke issued from it and malodorous vapors reeked to the heavens. He saw a horse-head ogre standing there arrogantly and holding a pitchfork in his hands.

"What is the name of this hell?" Maudgalyāyana asked him.

To which the ogre answered, "This is the Copper Pillar and Iron Bed Hell."

"Of the sinners who are in this hell," asked Maudgalyāyana, "what sinful karma did they create while they were alive that they should have fallen into this hell?"

To which the warden answered, "While they were alive, be it the woman who led on the man or the man who led on the woman, they indulged their sexual passions on their parents' beds. Those who were disciples did so on their masters' beds, and slaves did so on their owners' beds. Thus they were bound to fall into this hell."

The breadth from east to west was immeasurable and, in it, men and women complemented each other half-and-half.

Women lay on the iron beds with nails driven through their bodies,
Men embraced the hot copper pillars, causing their chests to rot away;
The iron drills and long scissors were sharp as lance-tips and sword-
edges,
The teeth of the plows with their sharp metal points were like awls.
When their intestines are empty, they are at once filled with hot iron
pellets,
If they cry out that they are thirsty, molten iron is used to irrigate them;
The metal thorns which enter their bellies rend them like knives,
Swords and halberds shoot by wildly like stars in mid-air.
Knives scrape the flesh from their bones, pound by pound it breaks,
Swords cut the liver and intestines, inch by inch they are severed;
                                                            Indescribable,

27. This does not constitute genuine rebirth. It is only part of the torture process.

How opposite to each other are heaven and hell!
In heaven's mansions, morning and night there is resounding music,
But there is not one who can beg his way out of hell.
Although parents in this present existence may have blessings created
    for them,
They receive only one seventh out of the total;[28]
Even though the eastern sea be transformed into mulberry orchards,[29]
Those who are suffering punishment will still not be released.

After Maudgalyāyana had finished speaking, he again went forward. Before long, he came to another hell. "Is there a Lady Nīladhi inside this hell or not?" he asked the warden.

To which the warden asked in reply, "Is Lady Nīladhi your mother, reverend sir?"

"Yes, she is my dear mother," Maudgalyāyana answered him.

"Three years ago," the warden informed the venerable monk, "there was a Lady Nīladhi who arrived in this hell. But she was summoned away by a warrant sent up from the Avīci Hell. She is at this very moment inside the Avīci Hell."

Stifled with sorrow, Maudgalyāyana collapsed. It was quite a long while before he revived.

This is the place where he slowly goes forward and soon happens upon an ogre who is guarding the road:

Maudgalyāyana was greatly distressed as he walked along,
The knives and swords by the side of the road were like wild grass;
He inclined his ear to listen for noises of the hells in the distance,
Abruptly, there was the howling sound of a strong wind.
For thinking of his dear mother, his heart was on the verge of breaking,
Walking without stopping along the road in front of him, he soon arrived;
Suddenly, he happened upon a prince of demons,
Hand resting on his sword, he sat there blocking the main way.

Maudgalyāyana addressed him, saying: "I am a poor monk,

A disciple of the Tathāgata, Śākyamuni Buddha,
I have witnessed the three insights[30] and have escaped from the cycle of
    birth and death.
How pathetic is my dear mother whose name was Nīladhi;

28. This reflects the folk-Buddhist concept that one who "pursues the departed with rites for their happiness" will receive a full complement of blessings while those for whom the ceremony is held will receive one seventh of the total.

29. I.e., "a long, long time."

30. Three types of knowledge of an arhat (saint): 1. memory of past lives, 2. supernatural insight into the future, and 3. knowledge of present mortal sufferings.

After she passed away, her souls descended into this place.
I have just now come from inspecting in order all the other hells,
Everyone whom I asked all said, 'No, this is the wrong place'—
But lately they've been saying that she was taken into Avīci,
Surely Great General, you are aware of this matter.
Do not hesitate to tell me truthfully whether she is here or not,
For the most profound human kindness is that of suckling one's child;
When I hear talk of my mother, it pains me to the marrow of my bones,
Yet there is no one who can readily understand this poor monk's heart."
Upon hearing these words, the demon's heart started to waver,
He spoke directly and, moreover, without mincing his words:
"Your filial devotion, reverend sir, is rare in all ages,
You have not shirked making a personal search along these infernal paths.
It seems as though there may be a Lady Nīladhi,
But I can't quite put my finger on what sort of appearance she has;
Poured steel has been used to make the outer walls, copper for the inner—
With a thunderous roar, the winds of karma abruptly begin to blow,
Turning the carcasses of those who enter to smithereens.
I advise you, oh Teacher, to return early to your own home,
In vain do you trouble yourself by seeking her in this place;
It would be better to leave early to see the Tathāgata—
What good is it for you to beat your chest in vexation?"

When Maudgalyāyana heard of the difficulties of this hell, he immediately turned around. Hurling up his begging-bowl, he leaped into space. Before very long, he had arrived at the Teak Tree Grove. Three times he circled around the Buddha, then withdrew and sat off to one side. He looked reverently upon the countenance of the Honored One, not averting his eyes for even a moment.

This is the place where he speaks to the World-Honored:

"For many days have I been negligent in my services to you, oh
    Tathāgata,
Because I was following my parents' traces to the ends of heaven and
    earth;
Only my father obtained rebirth in heaven above,
So I was unsuccessful in reuniting myself with my dear mother.
I have heard it said that she is suffering punishment in Avīci,
When I think of it, before I know what has happened, I become deeply
    aggrieved;
Due to the fierce fires, dragons, and snakes, it was difficult to go forward,
Nor was I able to come up with a suitable plan on the spur of the
    moment.

Your supernatural strength, oh Tathāgata, can move mountains and
    seas,
For which you are much admired by all living beings,
'Always has it been that a subject in distress unburdens himself to his
    lord'—
How will I be able to see my dear mother again?"
The World-Honored called out to him, saying, "Mahāmaudgalyāyana!
Do not be so mournful that you cry yourself heartbroken;
The sins of the world are tied to those who commit them like a string,
They are not stuck on clay-fashion by anyone else.
Quickly I take my metal-ringed staff and give it to you,
It can repel the eight difficulties[31] and the three disasters,[32]
If only you remember diligently to recite my name,
The hells will certainly open up their doors for you."

Having received the Buddha's awesome power, Maudgalyāyana flexed his
body and went downwards as swiftly as a winged arrow. In an instant, he had
arrived at the Avīci Hell. In mid-air, he met fifty ox-headed and horse-faced
guards. They were ogres and demons with teeth like knife-trees, mouths
similar to blood-basins,[33] voices like the peal of thunder, and eyes like the
flash of lightning. They were headed for duty in the Bureau of the Underworld. When they met Maudgalyāyana, they informed him from a distance:
"Don't come any farther, reverend sir! This is not a good way; it is the road to
hell. In the middle of the black smoke[34] on the western side are all the
poisonous vapors of hell. Should you be sucked up by them, reverend sir, you
will turn into ashes and dust."

This is the place:

"Haven't you heard tell, reverend sir, of the Avīci Hell?

Even iron and steel, should they pass through it, would be disastrously
    affected;
If you're wondering where this hell is situated,
It's over there on the west side in the midst of the black smoke."
Maudgalyāyana repeated the Buddha's name as often as there are sands
    in the Ganges,
And said to himself, "The hells are my original home—"

31. Situations in which it is difficult to see a Buddha or hear his dharma: in hell; as a hungry
ghost; as an animal; in the comfortable northern continent of *uttarakuru*; in the long-life
heavens; as someone deaf, blind, and dumb; as a worldly philosopher; in the interim between a
Buddha and his successor.
32. Major: fire, water, and wind. Minor: war, pestilence, and famine.
33. There is a hell in which women who die in childbirth are tortured by having to bathe in
an enormous pool of blood.
34. Similar black gasses are also mentioned by Dante in Canto V of the *Inferno*.

He wiped his tears in mid-air, and shook the metal-ringed staff,
Ghosts and spirits were mowed down on the spot like stalks of hemp.
Streams of cold sweat crisscrossed their bodies, dampening them like
    rain,
Dazed and unconscious, they groaned in self-pity;
They let go of the three-cornered clubs which were in their hands,
They threw far away the six-tined pitchforks which were on their
    shoulders.
"The Tathāgata has sent me to visit my mother,
And to rescue her from suffering in the Avīci Hell."
Not to be stayed, Maudgalyāyana passed by them with a leap,
The jailers just looked at each other, not daring to stand in his way.

Maudgalyāyana walked forward and came to a hell. When he was something over a hundred paces away from it, he was sucked in by the fiery gasses and nearly tumbled over. It was the Avīci Hell with lofty walls of iron which were so immense that they reached to the clouds. Swords and lances bristled in ranks, knives and spears clustered in rows. Sword-trees reached upward for a thousand fathoms with a clattering flourish as their needle-sharp points brushed together. Knife-mountains soared ten thousand rods in a chaotic jumble of interconnecting cliffs and crags. Fierce fires throbbed, seeming to leap about the entire sky with a thunderous roar. Sword-wheels whirled, seeming to brush the earth with the dust of starry brightness. Iron snakes belched fire, their scales bristling on all sides. Copper dogs breathed smoke, barking impetuously in every direction. Metal thorns descended chaotically from mid-air, piercing the chests of the men. Awls and augers flew by every which way, gouging the backs of the women. Iron rakes flailed at their eyes, causing red blood to flow to the west. Copper pitchforks jabbed at their loins until white fat oozed to the east. Thereupon, they were made to crawl up the knife-mountains and enter the furnace coals. Their skulls were smashed to bits, their bones and flesh decomposed; tendons and skin snapped, liver and gall broke. Ground flesh spurted and splattered beyond the four gates; congealed blood drenched and drooked the pathways which run through the black clods of hell. With wailing voices, they called out to heaven—moan, groan. The roar of thunder shakes the earth—rumble, bumble. Up above are clouds and smoke which tumble-jumble; down below are iron spears which jangle-tangle. Goblins with arrows for feathers chattered-scattered; birds with copper beaks wildly-widely called. There were more than several ten thousands of jailers and all were ox-headed and horse-faced.

This is the place where, though your heart be made of iron or stone, you too will lose your wits and tremble with fear:

Staff in hand, Maudgalyāyana went forward, listening,
As he thought about Avīci, he became more and more preoccupied;

Inside all of the other hells, there are periods of rest,
But within this Avīci, they never see a pause.
Crowds as numerous as the sands of the Ganges simultaneously enter,
Together their bodies are transformed into a single shape;
Supposing that, there being no one else, someone entered alone,
His body itself would fill up the surrounding iron walls.
Relentlessly, lamentlessly, iron weapons are flourished;
Querulous, perilous, the cloud-filled sky is turbulent,
Howling, growling, the wind which blasts the ground is terrifying.
There are long snakes which glisten and have three heads that are black,
There are large birds which glare and have pairs of wings that are dark-
    green;
In ten thousand red-hot ovens, heaped-up coals are fanned,
From a thousand tongues of crimson flames, shooting sparks explode.
On the east and the west, iron augers stab at the muscles of their chests,
To the left and the right, copper scissors puncture the pupils of their
    eyes;
Iron spears descend chaotically like the wind and the rain,
Molten iron from out of mid-air seems to be a baptismal sprinkling.
Lackaday! Welladay! How difficult it is to bear!
And to top it all off, long spikes are lowered into their bellies and backs.

When Maudgalyāyana saw this, he cried out "Horrors!"
Steadfastly he invoked the Buddha many thousands of times.
Though one breathe the poisonous vapors borne on the wind at a
    distance,
Right while you're watching, his body will become a pile of ashes.

With one shake of his staff, the bars and locks fell from the black walls,
On the second shake, the double leaves of the main gate flew open;
Before Maudgalyāyana there even had a chance to call out,
The jailers came right out, carrying pitchforks in their hands.
"About who, reverend sir, do you wish to find information?"
The gates in the walls of this hell were ten thousand leagues wide,
What sort of person could open and close them so easily?
Inside, knives and swords cluttered with a brilliant light,
The people undergoing punishment were remorsefully sad;
Great fires flamed and flared making the entire ground luminous,
Misty fog spread everywhere, filling the sky with blackness.
"Suddenly we saw an exemplar standing here in hell,
And furthermore, one with whom we have never been acquainted;
From the looks of things, it would appear that there is no one else,
It must be due to the compassionate power of the Three Jewels."

"For what reason," reverend sir, did you open the gates of this hell?" the warden asked him.

"If this poor monk didn't open them, who would?" he replied. "The World-Honored entrusted me with an object for opening them."

"What object did he entrust to you for opening them?" asked the warden.

"He entrusted me with his twelve-ringed metal staff to open them," Maudgalyāyana informed the warden.

"For what purpose have you come here, reverend sir?" a jailer asked again.

"The name of this poor monk's mother is Lady Nīladhi," Maudgalyāyana informed him. "I have come in order to see if I might find her."

Upon hearing this, the warden went back inside hell and climbed up on a tall tower from which he signaled with a white flag and beat a steel drum.

"Is there a Lady Nīladhi inside the first compartment?" he called out. There was none in the first compartment, so he went on to the second compartment. The warden signaled with a black flag and beat a steel drum.

"Is there a Lady Nīladhi inside the second compartment?" Neither was there any in the second compartment, so he went on to the third compartment. He signaled with a yellow flag and beat a steel drum.

"Is there a Lady Nīladhi inside the third compartment?" Again there was none. So he went on to the fourth compartment and again there was none When he reached the fifth compartment and asked, the answer there was also "none." He went on to the sixth compartment where again the answer was: "No Lady Nīladhi." The jailer walked to the seventh compartment where he signaled with a green flag and beat a steel drum.

"Is there a Lady Nīladhi inside the seventh compartment?"

At that very moment, Lady Nīladhi was inside the seventh compartment. All up and down her body, there were forty-nine[35] long spikes nailing her to a steel bed. She dared not respond.

The warden repeated the question: "Is there a Lady Nīladhi in the seventh compartment or not?"

"If you're hunting for Lady Nīladhi, this sinful body is she."

"Why didn't you speak up earlier?"

"I was afraid, warden, that you'd take me away to another place to receive punishment so I didn't dare to respond."

"There is a Buddhist monk outside the gate," the warden informed her. "His hair and beard have been shaved off and he wears a monastic robe. He claims to be your son and that is why he has come to visit you."

After Lady Nīladhi heard these words, she thought for quite a while and then replied: "Warden, I don't have any son who left home to become a monk. Isn't there some mistake?"

Upon hearing this, the warden turned around and walked back to the tall

35. This number was probably suggested by the length of the funeral service (forty-nine days).

tower. "Reverend sir!" he said. "Why do you pretend to recognize a sinner in hell as your mother? For what reason do you tell such a lie?"

When Maudgalyāyana heard these words, tears of sadness fell like rain. "Warden," he said, "when I explained things just now, my message was garbled. When I, poor monk, was a child, my name was Turnip. After my father and mother died, I surrendered myself to the Buddha and left home to become a monk. The title given me upon receiving the tonsure was Mahāmaudgalyāyana. Do not be angry, warden. Go and ask her once again."

After hearing these words, the warden turned around and went to the seventh compartment. "Sinner!" he announced. "As a child, the name of the monk outside the gate was Turnip. After his parents died, he surrendered himself to the Buddha and left home to become a monk. The title given him upon receiving the tonsure was Mahāmaudgalyāyana."

"If the name of the monk outside the gate as a child was Turnip, then he is my son," said Lady Nīladhi when she heard his words. "He is the precious darling of this sinful body."

When the warden heard Lady Nīladhi say this, he helped her up by pulling out the forty-nine long spikes. With steel chains locked about her waist and surrounded by gyves, she was driven outside of the gate.

This is the place where mother and son see each other:

> The interlocking links of the gyves were as numerous as gathering clouds;
> A thousand years of punishment is beyond comprehension,
> Trickles of blood flowed from the seven openings[36] of her head.
> Fierce flames issued from the inside of his mother's mouth,
> At every step, metal thorns out of space entered her body;
> She clanked and clattered like the sound of five hundred broken-down
>   chariots,
> How could her waist and backbone bear up under the strain?
> Jailers carrying pitchforks guarded her to the left and the right,
> Ox-headed guards holding chains stood on the east and the west;
> Stumbling at every other step, she came forward,
> Wailing and weeping, Maudgalyāyana embraced his mother.
> Crying, he said: "It was because I am unfilial,
> You, dear mother, were innocently caused to drop into the triple mire
>   of hell;
> Families which accumulate goodness have a surplus of blessings,
> High Heaven does not destroy in this manner those who are blameless.
> In the old days, mother, you were handsomer than P'an An,[37]
> But now you have suddenly become haggard and worn;

36. Eyes, ears, nose, and mouth.
37. P'an An-jen (P'an Yüeh). The story goes that the ladies of Loyang were so taken by his beauty that they tossed fruit at him when he went out on the street.

I have heard that in hell there is much suffering,
Now, today, I finally realize, 'Ain't it hard, ain't it hard.'[38]
Ever since I met with the misfortune of father's and your deaths,
I have not been remiss in sacrificing daily at your graves;
Mother, I wonder whether or not you have been getting any food to eat,
In such a short time, your appearance has become completely haggard."
Now that Maudgalyāyana's mother had heard his words,
"Alas!" she cried, her tears intertwining as she struck and grabbed
    at herself:
"Only yesterday, my son, I was separated from you by death,
Who could have known that today we would be reunited?
While your mother was alive, she did not cultivate blessings,
But she did commit plenty of all the ten evil crimes;
Because I didn't take your advice at that time, my son,
My reward is the vastness of this Avīci Hell.
In the old days, I used to live quite extravagantly,
Surrounded by fine silk draperies and embroidered screens;
How shall I be able to endure these hellish torments,
And then to become a hungry ghost for a thousand years?
A thousand times, they pluck the tongue from out of my mouth,
Hundreds of passes are made over my chest with a steel plow;
My bones, joints, tendons, and skin are everywhere broken,
They need not trouble with knives and swords since I fall to pieces
    by myself.
In the twinkling of an eye, I die a thousand deaths,
But, each time, they shout at me and I come back to life;
Those who enter this hell all suffer the same hardships,
It doesn't matter whether you are rich or poor, lord or servant.
Though you diligently sacrificed to me while you were at home,
It only got you a reputation in the village for being filial;
Granted that you did sprinkle libations of wine upon my grave,
But it would have been better for you to copy a single line of a sūtra."
Maudgalyāyana choked and sobbed, his tears fell like rain,
Right away, he turned around and petitioned the warden:
"Although I, poor monk, did leave home so that I could take orders,
How can I rescue my mother with my small strength?
One should cover up for the faults of those to whom he has
    mourning obligations,
This has been the teaching of sages and saints since ancient times;
My only wish, warden, is that you release my mother,
And I myself will bear the endless suffering for her."

---

38. The title of a popular ballad during the Six Dynasties and T'ang periods.

But the warden was a man of unyielding temperament,
He glared silently and vacantly at Maudgalyāyana;
"Although I, your disciple, do serve as a warden,
All of the decisions come from the Impartial King.
If your mother has sinned, she will receive the punishment for it,
And if you, oh Teacher, have sinned, you will bear the punishment for it;
The records of sins on the gold tablets and jade tokens cannot be wiped or
    washed away,
In the end, there is no one who can readily alter them.
It is simply that, today, the time has already arrived for her to be punished,
I must lead her back to the hall of punishments and apply the knife
    and spear;
If, reverend sir, you wish to obtain your mother's release,
You cannot do better than return home and burn precious incense."
The words of Maudgalyāyana's mother sounded plaintive,
But jailers holding pitchforks prodded her from both sides;
Just as she was about to reach the front of the hell, she nearly fell over,
Quickly she called out long and sad, "Take good care of yourself!"

With one of her hands, Lady Nīladhi held fast to the gate of hell and turned back to gaze at him. "Take good care of yourself!" she said. "Oh precious darling of this sinful body!"

"In the old days, your mother behaved avariciously.
I failed to provide myself with grace for the karmic retribution of the next
    life;
The things which I said deceived heaven and denied hell,
I slaughtered pigs and goats on a grand scale to sacrifice to ghosts
    and spirits.
My only concern was for the pleasures of the moment,
How could I have known that on these infernal paths they flog lost souls?
Now that I have already suffered the hardships of hell,
I finally learned to awaken to repentance of my own person.
But even though I do repent, what good does it do me?
'There's no use crying over spilt milk,' so says the well-known proverb;
When shall I be able to escape from this horrible suffering?
And how can I dare to hope that I'll ever again be a human being?
You, oh Teacher, are a disciple of the Buddha,
And are capable of understanding the kindness of your parents;
If, one day, you should attain the enlightenment of a sage,
Do not forget your mother who suffers so grievously here in hell."
After Maudgalyāyana had watched his mother depart,
He wished with all his heart that he could destroy himself;

Then, like Mount T'ai collapsing, he fell to the ground and
    pummeled himself,
Blood spattered from all the seven openings of his head.
"Mother, do not go back in for a while yet!" he said to her,
"Turn back and listen again to a word from your son;
The affection between a mother and her son is innate,
The kindness of her suckling him is a natural impulse.
Today, mother, you and I shall take leave of each other,
No one can tell for certain when we shall meet again;
How can I bear to listen to this horrible suffering?—
Sharp is the pain in my heart from the anxiety which weighs upon me.
Hell does not allow one to substitute for another,
All I can do is weep and wail and state my grievance loudly;
Since there is nothing at all I can do to save you,

"I too, will follow you, mother, and myself die before the gate of hell."

Maudgalyāyana watched his mother go back into hell. Grief-stricken and brokenhearted, he sobbed until his voice became hoarse. Then, as though he were five Mount T'ais collapsing, he fell to the ground and pummeled himself. Blood flowed with a gush from all of the seven openings of his head. After quite a long time, he died, and then he revived again. He got up by pressing against the ground with both hands.

This is the place where, having rearranged his clothing, he leaps into space and goes to the World-Honored.

Maudgalyāyana's consciousness was all hazy,
It seemed he could not hear people's voices, they were so indistinct;
After quite a long time, he moaned deeply and came to his senses,
Hurling up his begging-bowl, he leaped into space and called upon the
    World-Honored.
Facing the Buddha, Maudgalyāyana stated his bitter grievances,
He spoke both of the knife-mountains and of the sword-trees;
"I received supernatural strength from you, oh Buddha, and borrowed
    your surplus majesty,
Thus was I enabled to visit my dear mother in Avīci.
Smoke and flames flared up from the fires atop the iron walls,
The forests of sword blades were in ranks many ten thousands deep;
Human fat and ground flesh mixed together with molten copper,
The spattering flesh collected in pools of coagulated blood.
How can my dear mother's features endure such harsh treatment?
The whole night long she confronts the assault of knives and swords;
Her white bones climb the sword-trees ten thousand times over,
Her red face ascends the knife-mountains, making hundreds of passes.

In all the world, what is the most important thing?
It is the affection of one's parents and their kindness most profound;
You, oh Tathāgata, are the compassionate father and mother of all
　　living beings,
I beseech you to illuminate this ignorant and trifling heart of mine!"
The Tathāgata was by nature of great mercy and compassion,
When he heard these words, he knitted his brows with sorrow:
"All living beings emerge and disappear in the net of transmigration,
Just like chaff-gnats which have rushed against a spider's web.
In times past, many were the sins your mother committed,
As a result, her souls fell headlong into Avīci;
For these crimes of hers, an aeon will elapse before she can get out,
An ordinary person, one who is not a Buddha, cannot understand this."
The Buddha then summoned Ānanda and the company of his
　　followers:
"I will go to the infernal regions and save her myself!"

　The Tathāgata led the eight classes of supernatural beings who surrounded him, front and back.

This is the place where, radiating light and shaking the earth, they rescue the sufferers in hell:

The Tathāgata in his holy wisdom was, by nature, impartial,
Out of mercy and compassion, he rescued all the beings of hell;
A numberless host composed of spirits of the eight classes,
Following each other, they went forward as a group.
　　　　　Such pomp and circumstance!—
In heaven above and on earth below, it was an incomparable sight;
　Sinking on the left, disappearing on the right,
They were like mountains projecting high above the clouds.
　　　　　Precipitous—　　precarious—
Heaven's mansions and hell's halls opened their doors at once;
　Like driving rain—　　like rumbling thunder—
They made as full a circle as the moon rising over the ocean.
Commandingly, he walked by himself with a lion's pace,
Confidently, he moved alone with an elephant king's gait;
Amidst the clouds, there were strains of the "Willow Branch" tune,
In space, there fluttered "Plum Blossoms Falling."
Sovereign Śakra went forward carrying a jade token;
Brahmā followed behind holding a jade tablet;
It was a sight indescribably indescribable!—
The Tathāgata, with supernatural strength, rescued them from the gates
　　of Hades.

> To his left and right, there were deities and the host of the eight spirit
>   realms.
> To his east and west, there were attendant guards and the generals of
>   the four directions;
> Between his brows appeared a tiny hair that had a thousand different
>   forms,
> Behind his neck was a halo of five-colored clouds.
> Saturated by the light, hell dissolved completely,
> The sword-trees and knife-forests crumbled as though they were dust;
> Saturated by the light, all of the jailers fell to their knees,
> They joined their palms in heartfelt respect and prostrated themselves at
>   his feet.
> This day, the Buddha's mercy and compassion were aroused,
> He destroyed hell, leaving it completely in ruins;
> The steel pellets were transformed into luminous jewels,
> The knife-hills were transformed into sheets of lapis lazuli.
> Molten copper was changed into the water of merit and virtue;
> Meandering round pools and in currents, it was refreshing and clear,
> Mandarin ducks and other waterfowl nestled together like beads on a
>   necklace.
> Every night, emerald mists lifted from the red waves,
> Every morning, purple clouds rose above the green trees;
> All of the sinners obtained rebirth in heaven above,
> There was only Maudgalyāyana's mother who became a hungry ghost.
> Everything within hell was utterly transformed,
> And it was all because of the might of the holy Śākyamuni Buddha.

Having been granted the awesome power of the Buddha, Maudgalyāyana was enabled to visit his mother. But the roots of her sin were deep and fast; the karmic forces difficult to eliminate. Thus, although she was freed of the torments of hell, she fell upon the path of hungry ghosts. Here the sorrow and suffering were dissimilar, for misery and joy were completely polarized. When placed next to her previous existence, the difference was intensified hundreds, thousands, even ten thousands of times. Her throat was like the eye of a needle, through which a drop of water could not pass. Her head seemed to be Mount T'ai, which the three rivers could hardly fill. She never even heard the words "broth" or "water." Months would accumulate and years would pass while she endured the miseries of hunger and emaciation. She might see in the distance some clear, cool water but, when she came near, it would turn into a river of pus. Even though she obtained delicious food and tasty meals, they would immediately be transformed into fierce flames.

"Mother, now you are so distressed by hunger that your life is as though it were hanging by a thread. If your plight does not arouse in me compassion and mercy, how can I be called a filial son? Once we are separated by the road between life and death, it will be hard to expect that we shall meet again. If I wish to rescue you from this precarious danger, the urgency of the situation demands that I not delay. The way of those who have left home to become monks is to rely upon the donations of the faithful to maintain themselves. Even though you had a constant source of food and drink, I am afraid that it would be difficult for you to digest.

"I shall take leave of you now, mother, and go toward the center of Rājagṛha. There I will get some rice and then come to see you again."

Maudgalyāyana took leave of his mother. He hurled up his begging-bowl and leaped into the air. Within an instant, he had already arrived in the center of Rājagṛha. As he went from house to house begging for rice, he walked up to the gate of a householder.

This is the place where the householder detains and questions Maudgalyāyana when he sees that he is begging for food at the wrong time:

"The morning meal is already over, reverend sir. Since the time for eating has already past, for what purpose do you intend to use this food which you are begging?"

Maudgalyāyana replied to the householder:

"After this humble monk's mother had passed away,
Her souls[39] fell straightaway into the Avīci Hell;
Recently, I obtained her release with the help of the Tathāgata,
Her body was like a bunch of dried bones, her breath was wispy.
This poor monk's heart was rent in many tiny pieces,
How can anyone else understand the pain which afflicts me?—
Even though I realize that it is inappropriate, I am begging out of
 time.
Because it is to give to my dear mother to feed her."
When the householder heard these words, he was greatly startled,
Reflecting on the impermanence of things, he began to feel unhappy.
"Her golden countenance is forever deprived of being made up with
 rouge and mascara,"
Her jade-like appearance has no cause for entering the dressing-room.
 We sing for a while—   we are happy for a while—
Human life is frittered away like a sputtering candle.
We seek not the mansions of heaven where we could enjoy happiness,
Even though all we hear of is how numerous are the sinners in hell;
 Sometimes to eat—   sometimes to clothe ourselves—
We should not imitate those stupid people who accumulate much.
It would be better to create many good works for the future,

39. Celestial (yang) and terrestrial (yin).

For who can guarantee that his life will be preserved from morning to
  evening?
While two people are looking at each other, death steals upon them,
After which their riches are certainly no more to be grudged by their
  bodies.
When, one fine morning, we breathe our last and enter our eternal
  coffins,
Who knows what good are the libations sprinkled vainly upon our
  graves?
The wise man uses his money to create many blessings,
The fool spends his gold by purchasing fields and houses.
Throughout our lives, we search laboriously for riches,
But, after we die, it is all divided up by someone else."
When the householder heard these words, he was suddenly surprised,
It is not often that one has the opportunity to make offerings to a monk;
Hurriedly, he urged his assistants not to delay,
They brought rice from inside the house to give to the exemplar.
"From the sudden and complete dissolution of hell,
The ineffableness of the Buddhas is clearly perceived."
The householder held in his hand the rice which he had obtained,
And gave it over to the exemplar while making a grand vow:
"May this serve not only for you to present to your dear parent, reverend
  sir,"
But may it serve, as well, to fill all the sinners in the whole of hell!"
Maudgalyāyana was successful in begging for table-rice;
He picked up his begging-bowl and took it to present to his dear
  mother.
Thereupon, he walked as far as the deserted outskirts of the city;
Holding a golden spoon in his hand, he fed her himself.

Although she had undergone the hardships of hell, Lady Nīladhi's avarice
had, after all, not been eradicated. When she saw her son bringing the bowl
of rice, the mere expectation of his approach excited her greed.

"The monk who is coming is my own son! He has fetched rice for me from
the world of men. The whole lot of you others shouldn't get any ideas! I've got
to appease my own hunger right now. There won't be enough extra to help
anybody else!"

Maudgalyāyana offered up the rice which was in the begging-bowl. His
mother, afraid that it might be snatched away, raised her eyes and looked
about continuously on all four sides. She shielded the bowl with her left hand
and scooped up the food with her right. But, before it entered her mouth, the
food was transformed into a fierce fire. Although the householder's vow was a
solemn one, unfortunately the obstructiveness of her greed was even greater.

Seeing his mother like this, Maudgalyāyana felt as though his heart were being sliced with a knife. "The strength of my doctrinal understanding is still inferior. I am a wretched person of little wisdom. The only thing I can do is address my questions to the World-Honored. Then I shall surely learn the way to extricate her."

Look, now, at the place where he gives his mother the rice:

> When the Lady saw the rice, she went forward to receive it,
> Because of her avarice, she senselessly bickered before she began to eat:
> "My son brought this rice from far away in the world of men,
> I intend to take it to cure my own bottomless pit;
> If I eat it all by myself, it still looks like it won't be enough to satisfy me,
> All you others should give up your ideas of getting any—go slow with
>   your hopes!"
> The karmic force of Nīladhi's avarice was strong,
> As the food entered from her mouth into her throat, fierce flames
>   erupted.

When Maudgalyāyana

> Saw the rice his mother was eating become a fierce fire,
> He pummeled himself all over and fell to the ground like a mountain
>   collapsing;
> Blood began to flow from both his ears and his nostrils,
> Tearfully, he cried out to high heaven: "Oh, my mother!"
> This rice was given as charity in the world of mortal men,
> Above the rice, there was a spirit-light seven feet high;
> They took it to be a savory, flavorsome sustenance,
> But before the food entered her mouth, it had already turned into fire.
> Her appetite was avaricious and her heart had not changed,
> With the result that, year after year, she underwent punishment;
> Now he was painfully afflicted that he had no further means to save her,
> But karmic retribution did not allow that one substitute for another.
> The people of the world should not entertain jealous envy,
> For, once they fall into the three mircs of hell, the punishment is
>   endless;
> Before the savory rice had even entered her throat,
> Fiery flames began to issue from his mother's mouth.
> Though the sins of the mundane world fill the universe,
> It is this very sin of avarice which is most frequent;
> Unexpectedly, the flames issued from her mouth,
> Which shows clearly that karmic retribution does not devolve upon
>   others.

One should always exercise impartiality toward everything,
And should, furthermore, single-mindedly recite the name of
    Amitābha;
If only one can rid himself of his greedy heart,
The heavenly mansions of the Pure Land will be gained at his pleasure.
"My obedient son," Nīladhi called out to him,
"I cannot discard this sinful body by myself;
If I am not favored by *your* exercise of filiality, oh Teacher,
Who would be willing to exert themselves to save your mother?
I saw the rice but, before I could scoop it into my mouth,
It unexpectedly burst into flames and burned me;
Thinking over in my mind this display of avarice,
It simply must be due to the leftover ill effects of my past.
You, oh Teacher, who are your mother's obedient son,
Give me some cold water to relieve the hollowness in my stomach."

Maudgalyāyana listened to his mother's request for water, her breath catching and her voice harsh. While he was considering what to do, he suddenly recalled that, south of the city of Rājagṛha, there was a great river. Its waters were so wide as to be boundless and it was called by the name Ganges. Surely it would be sufficient to rescue his mother from the torment of her fiery calamity.

When the living beings of the mortal world saw the river, to them its waters were refreshing and cool. When the various deities saw the river, to them it was a precious pond of greenglass. When fish and turtles saw this river, to them it was either torrent or marsh. But when Nīladhi saw the river, to her it was a stream of pus and fiery flames. She walked up to the water's edge and, without waiting for her son to utter the requisite vows, immediately supported herself against the bank with her left hand in consequence of her selfishness and scooped up the water with her right hand in consequence of her greed. Her avaricious heart was simply not to be restrained. Before the water entered her mouth, it had already become fire.

Maudgalyāyana had seen how the rice his mother started to eat had become a fiery fire and how the water she was drinking became a fiery fire. He beat his chest and struck his breast, moaning sorrowfully and weeping. He came before the Buddha and circled three times around him. Then, standing off to one side, he addressed him with these words: "Your disciple's mother, oh World-Honored, did many things which were not good, and so she fell down into the three mires. Having been blessed by your mercy and compassion, I was able to rescue my mother from her suffering there. But now the rice which she eats becomes fire and the water she drinks becomes fire. How can I rescue my mother from the torment of her fiery calamity?"

"Maudgalyāyana!" the World-Honored called out to him, "it is true that your mother, up to now, has not been able to eat any food. She will obtain food to eat only if you observe annually, on the fifteenth day of the seventh month, the provision of a purgatorian feast on a large scale."

Maudgalyāyana looked at his starving mother and then spoke: "World-Honored, may it not be held monthly on the thirteenth and fourteenth? Must she wait each year for the fifteenth day of the seventh month before she gets any food to eat?"

"Not only is this the prescribed date on which to provide a purgatorian feast on a large scale for your mother," the World-Honored replied to him, "it is also the day on which those who have been sitting in meditation in the monasteries end their summer retreat, the day on which arhats achieve the fruit of their religious practice, the day on which Devadatta's[40] sins are annihilated, the day on which King Yama rejoices, and the day on which all hungry ghosts everywhere get to eat their fill."

Having received the Buddha's clear instructions, Maudgalyāyana went to the front of a temple which was near the city of Rājagṛha. There he read aloud the Mahāyana sūtras and performed the good deed of providing a purgatorian feast on a large scale. It was from these basins of food that his mother was finally able to eat a full meal. But after she received the food, he did not see his mother again.

Maudgalyāyana searched for his mother everywhere but could not find her. Tears of sorrow falling like rain, he came before the Buddha and circled three times around him. Then, standing off to one side, he joined his palms in reverent greeting and knelt respectfully. "World-Honored," he addressed him, "when my mother ate rice, it became fire; when she drank water, it became fire. Having been blessed by your compassion and mercy, I was able to rescue my mother from the torment of her fiery calamity. But, ever since the fifteenth day of the seventh month when she received the meal, we haven't seen each other again. Perhaps she has fallen into hell. Or perhaps she went toward the path of hungry ghosts?"

"Neither has your mother fallen into hell nor is she on the path of hungry ghosts," the World-Honored replied. "Having obtained the merit of your reading the sūtras and the good deed of providing a purgatorian feast, your mother's body as a hungry ghost has been transformed. She has gone into the center of Rājagṛha where she has taken on the body of a black dog. If you wish to see your mother, go from house to house begging for food, seeing that your mind and actions are impartial and that you do not question whether they are rich or poor. When you walk up to the gate of a certain very wealthy householder, a black dog will come out. It will tug at your cassock and,

40. The son of King Droṇodana and a cousin of Śākayamuni with whom he competed by cultivating supernatural powers. He was said to have been swallowed up in hell for his evil behavior toward the Buddha. Later, however, a tradition emerged which predicted that he would be a future Buddha known as Devarāja.

holding it in its mouth, will make human sounds. That will be your mother."

Having been granted the Buddha's clear instructions, Maudgalyāyana immediately took up his begging-bowl in one hand and a basin in the other and went in search of his mother. Without asking whether they were for the rich or the poor, he walked a complete circle through the city's wards and alleys, but nowhere did he see his mother. He walked up to the gate of a certain householder where he saw a black dog which came out from the house. It tugged at Maudgalyāyana's cassock and, holding it in its mouth, started to make human sounds.[41]

"Oh, obedient son of your mother!" it said, "if you could rescue your mother from the infernal paths of hell, why do you not rescue her from the torment of having the body of a dog?"

"My dear mother!" Maudgalyāyana addressed her, "because your son was unfilial, you met with misfortune and fell into the three mires. But wouldn't you prefer to be living here in the form of a dog rather than existing as a hungry ghost?"

"Obedient son!" his mother called out, "I have received this body of a dog and my dumbness as a due reward. I spend my life walking, standing, sitting, or lying. When I'm hungry, I eat human excrement in the latrines. When I'm thirsty, I drink the water which drips from the eaves to relieve the hollow feeling. In the morning, I hear the householder invoking the Three Treasures. In the evening, I hear his wife reciting the esteemed sūtras. I would rather have the body of a dog and endure the filth of the earth than hear in my ears the name of hell."

Maudgalyāyana led his mother away to the front of a Buddhist stupa in Rājagṛha. There, for seven days and seven nights, they read aloud the Mahā-yana sūtras, confessing and repenting, and reciting the prohibitions. Availing herself of this merit, she was transformed out of her dog-body. She sloughed off her dogskin and hung it on a tree. Then, getting back her body of a woman, she was once again in complete possession of a perfect human form.

"Mother," Maudgalyāyana said to her, "it is difficult to obtain a human body, difficult to be born in the Central Kingdom,[42] difficult to hear the Law of the Buddha, and difficult to manifest a good mind. I call upon you, mother, now that you have regained human form, swiftly to cultivate blessings."

Maudgalyāyana took his mother to the twin Sāl trees. He circled three times around the Buddha and then, standing off to one side, addressed him in these words: "Oh World-Honored! Would you look over for me the path of my mother's karma up to the present, examining it from the very beginning to see if she has any other sins?"

41. Dogs are, of course, normally dumb. That the dog is able to speak to Maudgalyāyana in this particular case is due to a special dispensation of the Buddha.

42. The "Central Kingdom" here refers to India, not China.

The World-Honored was not opposed to Maudgalyāyana's request. Observing her from the standpoint of the three types of karma, he found that there were no further individual sins.

Seeing that his mother's sins had been annihilated, Maudgalyāyana rejoiced greatly at heart. "Mother," he said to her,

"Let us go back!
The world of mortal men is not fit to remain in;
Birth, life, death—
It wasn't really a place to stay in anyway.
It is the Kingdom of Buddha in the West which is the finest!"

Deities and dragons were moved to lead the way in front and heavenly maidens came to welcome her. She was received forthwith into the Trayastriṁśa Heaven to enjoy happiness.

In the very beginning,[43] the Buddha uttered the stanzas with which he converted the first five disciples. At the time (the time this sūtra was preached) there were 84,000[44] bodhisattvas, 84,000 monks, 84,000 laymen, and 84,000 laywomen, all circling around the Buddha and making obeisance to him. They rejoiced in the receptivity and obedience of their faith.

Transformation Text on Mahāmaudgalyāyana, One Scroll
Written on the sixteenth day of the fourth month in the seventh year of the True Brightness reign-period by Hsüeh An-chün, lay student[45] at the Pure Land Monastery.

Chang Pao-ta's copy
Translated by Victor H. Mair

43. Of the transmission of the Law of the Buddha after his enlightenment.

44. The supposed number of atoms in the human body. As such, it was a frequently used figure for a large number of various phenomena or objects.

45. Lay students pursuing a largely secular curriculum under the auspices of various monasteries at Tun-huang were primarily responsible for the copying of transformation texts. They were thus extremely important in the creation of a written vernacular for China.

267

Transformation Text on the Boy Shun's Extreme Filial Piety

Anonymous (late 9th century–early 10th century?)

During the reign of King Yao, Heaven sent down countless good omens. Shun's own mother lived in the hall; she was Madame Lo-teng. Madame Lo-teng lay sick in bed and had not gotten up for three years. She called to her husband Ku-sou:[1] "Your wife leaves an orphan boy and girl in her husband's hands and begs him not to beat them." He replied to his wife: "They say everyone has an illness some time or other; my wife should try her best to get well." But as he spoke, she died. Shun observed mourning for three years, and for ten days lived alone in hempen clothes.

Ku-sou called his son Shun: "My son, while young you lost your mother, and there's no one at home to watch over you; if your Dad should take a second wife, how would you feel about it?" Shun folded his hands and replied to his father: "If you take a second wife, then she will be like my very own mother to me."

Ku-sou took a second wife, but within ten days he summoned his son: "Liaoyang city[2] is full of soldiers and horses; this year there will be good business. I will go to Liaoyang for a short while and try to look for some profit along the way. I will leave you, son, to look after things at home."

Though on leaving he spoke of being gone a single year, for three years he did not return home. Whenever his son would think of him, his heart would break, and he would take out his lute and put it on his knees. One day while Shun was strumming the lute, an old man came and stood by the gate. Shun hastened outside. "A thousand blessings on you, venerable sir; where do you come from?" The old man answered the young one: "Yesterday I came from Liaoyang and I bring you now a letter from your father."

Shun ran inside the house, knelt before his mother, and bowed four times.

As a boy, the legendary emperor Shun was considered to be the paragon of filiality. This hyperbolic tale about him, like so many other precious specimens of early popular literature, was preserved among the Tun-huang manuscripts (see selection 266). The transformation text on Shun as a boy is unusual for the genre in having verses only at the end instead of interspersed throughout and in having no overt references to visual aids. It is likely that the actual oral performance whence this written version was derived must have had the typical alternating prosimetric (prose plus verse) or chantefable (sung plus spoken) form and close relationship to illustrations of the overwhelming majority of other texts belonging to the genre and labeled on the manuscripts as such.

1. *Ku-sou* means "The Blind Man."
2. Probably in modern Liaoyang county, Liaoning province, near the Korean border; at one point capital of the Liao dynasty.

When his stepmother saw him bowing and kneeling four times, her heart was filled with venom. "It is neither a holiday nor a guest from afar, yet at high noon you kneel and bow four times—what kind of sorcery have you learned?"

Shun folded his hands and said to his mother: "Father went to Liaoyang for a short while, leaving me in charge of things at home. When he left, he was going to return within a year, but for three years he has not come home. I was thinking of him, heartbroken, and had my lute on my knees. While playing the lute, an old man came to the door. He came from Liaoyang yesterday and now bears a letter from Father. Two of my bows were to ask your health, and two were to wish you happiness."

When his stepmother heard that Ku-sou was coming, she immediately formed a plan in her mind and in a loud voice called Shun: "If truly Father is coming, then I fear our house is unprepared. I see that the fruit in the back garden is very fine and the red peaches are fresh and tasty. If we plucked the peaches, wouldn't that be doing our duty to the family?"

When Shun heard her mention picking peaches, he was very happy in his heart. Shun climbed the tree to pluck peaches and his mother also came to the base. She loosened her hair, pulled out a gold pin in her hand and pricked her own foot, calling out to Shun: "My son, you are a filial boy, why don't you come down the tree and look after your mother's hurt?" Shun heard what she said and believed her, and so he hurriedly climbed down the tree. [Gap in the text]

She lay in the room without getting up, but within two or three days, Ku-sou had arrived. Ku-sou entered the gate and went directly to his own room, where his second wife still lay in bed without rising. Ku-sou asked: "When you saw that I did not return for so long, how could you be happy? But now you see me come home and yet you lie flat in bed without getting up. Have you been fighting with the neighbors, or is it your time of the month?"

When his second wife heard these words, tears streamed down her face. "Ever since you went to Liaoyang and left me in charge of things at home, the child of your first wife has been unfilial. Seeing me pluck peaches in the backyard, he hid nasty thorns at the base of the tree which made sores all over my feet, and the pain pierces the marrow of my bones. At the time I thought of seeing the magistrate, but deferred on account of you. If you don't believe me, see how the soles of my feet are all swollen with pus. He saw my black hair and my white face and all of a sudden lusted for me like a dog or a pig."

Ku-sou called Shun: "I went to Liaoyang leaving you in charge of things at home, so why were you so unfilial at home? When your mother climbed the tree to pick peaches, who was it that buried lots of sharp thorns that cut her feet and made sores?" Shun knew the truth in his heart but feared to hurt his stepmother's feelings; and if he did not pardon her for her errors, he feared he would get his stepmother in trouble. "I am your son and have erred a thousand times; I alone will bear my father's punishment."

When Ku-sou heard these words he was angry yet could not be angry; he was pleased yet could not be pleased. In a loud voice he called: "Hsiang! Bring your father three thorn branches so that I can beat your stepbrother to death."

When Hsiang heard him say to get thorn branches, he ran into his mother's room and reported: "Father has told me to get branches to beat my stepbrother to death." Ku-sou's second wife said to her husband: "When children are naughty, they should be beaten, and not permitted to explain their reasons."

Hsiang went and got the thorn branches, and from them Ku-sou chose one that was coarse and thick, weighing three full ounces if it weighed a gram. He took Shun by the hair and hung him from a tree in the courtyard, and from the nape of his neck down to the backs of his knees, fresh blood flowed down and spattered the ground.

When Ku-sou beat Shun, he caused all birds to cry in sympathy, and the benevolent ravens cleaned up the blood without ceasing.

Shun was a filial and obedient son, and when Indra[3] in the upper world knew of his trouble, he changed himself into an old man, descended to the lower world, and gave such comfort to Shun that he felt as if he hadn't been beaten after all. Shun then returned to his study, recited first the *Analects* of Confucius and the *Classic of Filial Piety*, and then read the *Classic of Odes* and the *Record of Rites*.

As soon as his stepmother saw Shun, her heart filled with venom. [She said to her husband:] "Ever since you went to Liaoyang and left me in charge of things, your first wife's child has been unfilial, always holding wine parties in the eastern court, never using his study in the western court, night after night going out with bad sorts and never coming home. He's sold off lands and gardens and has even studied some black magic so that he didn't die when beaten with the rod. Now if King Yao should hear of it, even I might not escape blame. To settle things, give me a bill of divorce and tell me to leave your sight."

Ku-sou said to his wife: "For some reason or other, his life is very strong, so how could we hurt him? But if you have a plan, then just speak up—I'll leave the punishment to you."

Ku-sou's second wife said to him: "If we don't punish him, there is nothing more to say; but if we do, it will be a simple matter." Within two or three days the second wife came up with a plan. She told Ku-sou: "I see that the empty granary in the back courtyard has been falling apart for the past two or three years. Tell your son Shun to repair the granary, then set fires on all four sides and burn him to death."

Ku-sou told his wife: "Though you are a woman, you are skillful in coming up with plans." Ku-sou called his son Shun: "I see that the granary in the back

3. The Hindu god of thunder.

yard has been falling down for two or three years; if you fixed the granary, would you not be doing your duty to the family?"

When Shun heard him mention repairing the granary, he knew it was a plot of his stepmother's, but he mixed up a bucket of mortar, then folded his hands and said to his stepmother: "The mortar is freshly made and won't set; I need two straw hats."

Ku-sou's second wife said to him: "It's your good-for-nothing repairing the granary—he needs two straw hats. When he gets up on the granary, no matter whether he's got two hats or forty, he'll still get burned to death."

Shun had just gotten up on top of the granary when flames started up at the southwest corner. The first torch was set by his stepmother, the next by Ku-sou, and the third was by none other than his little stepbrother Hsiang. The three fires were about to scorch his feet; he saw red flames reaching to the sky and black smoke shutting out the view of the sky and earth. Fearing for his life, Shun took the two straw hats as wings and flew down from the granary. Shun was a righteous king, hence the god of the soil picked him up so that he wasn't burned and not a hair of his head was hurt. He returned to his study, reciting first the *Analects* of Confucius and the *Classic of Filial Piety*, then read the *Classic of Odes* and the *Record of Rites*.

When his stepmother once again saw Shun, her heart was filled with venom. [She said to her husband:] "Ever since you went to Liaoyang and left me in charge of things, your first wife's child has been unfilial—always having parties in the eastern court, never opening the study in the western court, night after night going out with bad sorts and not coming home. He's sold off lands and gardens and learned some sort of black magic so that he won't die even when beaten with the rod or burned by three fires. If King Yao should learn of this, then even I might not escape blame. To settle things, give me a bill of divorce and tell me to get out of your sight."

Ku-sou replied to his wife: "For some reason, his life is very strong, so how can we deal with him? But if you have a plan, speak up and I'll leave the punishment entirely to you."

His wife replied: "If we don't punish him, there will be nothing more to say; but if we do, it will be a simple matter." Before ten days had passed, the second wife came up with a plan. "I see there is a dry well in front of the house which hasn't had water for two or three years. Tell that son Shun of yours to clean out the well; then take big stones to plug it up with and so crush him to death."

Ku-sou replied to his wife: "Though you are a woman, you are skillful in making up plans." In a loud voice, he called his son: "The dry well in front of your Dad's house has been without water for two or three years. If you cleaned out the well so that it would give water, wouldn't you be doing your duty to the family?"

When Shun heard him say to clean out the well, he understood in his heart. He then took off his clothes, knelt down and bowed at the wellside, then got into the well and started removing mud. The god Indra in the upper world secretly sent down five hundred silver coins and put them in the well. Shun then put the silver coins in an earthen jar and had his stepmother take them out. After several times, he called up to his father and mother: "The well is full of water and the money is gone. Mother, couldn't you let me out and give me something to eat?"

When his stepmother heard what he had said, she lied to Ku-sou saying: "It's your no-good saying that we shouldn't use his money; if we use his money, he'll come out and tell the magistrate. Should we not kill him?"

Ku-sou then blocked up the well with big stones. His second wife whole-heartedly urged her husband to kill the first wife's son and give him no way to leave the hole. But her husband didn't heed her and just covered over the well.

The god Indra changed himself into a yellow dragon and led Shun though a passage toward the well of the neighbor on the east side. Shun called up and by luck met an old woman getting water, who replied: "Who's that in the well?"

Shun said: "The unfilial son from the house to the west." The old woman then knew that it was Shun and hauled him out. Shun bowed to her, crying; the old woman gave him clothes, dressed him, and gave him a dish of food to eat. She told him: "Don't you go home, but rather go to the grave of your very own mother and you will certainly see her appear."

After she had spoken, Shun went off to find his mother's grave. He saw her very form and cried tears of blood. His mother said to him: "Don't go home, son. Your tasks are yet unfinished. Just go to Mount Li[4] in the southwest to farm and you will certainly win great honor."

Shun took his mother's advice and after leaving her made his way into the mountains, where he saw over a hundred acres of empty land, and in his heart he sighed. Seeds and a draft-ox were nowhere to be found. But Heaven knew that he was very filial and sent a herd of pigs to plow the ground and break up the clods with their tusks, and all the birds to bring seeds and plant them; and Heaven sent a fine rain. That year the harvest did not ripen throughout the world, but Shun alone had a bountiful harvest and got several hundred bushels of grain.

In his heart he yearned for home and planned to repay his parents' goodness. He walked to the banks of the Yellow River where he saw a herd of deer and sighed: "Those who have human bodies are not so lucky as the roving deer."[5] While he was crying, he saw several merchants and asked: "Is all well with the Yao family in Chi commandery?"

The merchants replied, "There are thousands of families named Yao—who

4. There are at least five or six places in north and central China called Mount Li and which claim association with the legend of Shun; many of these also claim to save Shun's well.

5. Presumably because the deer are not separated from their families.

knows how your relatives are! But there is a Yao family, we've heard, which sent their son to clean out the well; the stepmother hated him, and she and her husband killed him by blocking up the well. Ever since then the father has lost the sight of his eyes, and the mother has become witless and carries firewood to the market. There is also a little brother who has become daft, who is very poor, and who begs for food, without a home to go back to. We only know of this one family and know nothing of others named Yao." Shun immediately knew that these were his parents and younger brother. In his heart he thought but said nothing.

Since Shun had come to Mount Li, ten years had gone by quickly. He took his grain and went to his home town. When he arrived in the market, he saw his stepmother carrying firewood to the market to exchange for rice. She met Shun selling grain in the market; Shun recognized her and sold her some grain. When Shun got his stepmother's money, he pretended forgetfulness, put it back in her grain sack, and left. And so it happened more than once. Ku-sou thought it strange and said to his second wife: "Is this not my son Shun?"

His wife said: "Buried at the bottom of a hundred-foot well, blocked up with big stones, and covered with earth, how could he have lived?" Ku-sou said: "Please take me to the market."

His wife took him to the market, and he met the young man selling grain and said to him: "What kind of saint are you that you should forgo your profit over and over?"

Shun said: "I did so because you were advanced in years."

The old man, recognizing his voice, said: "This sounds just like my son Shun's voice, doesn't it?"

Shun said: "That's right." Then he went forward and embraced his father's head and cried silently. Shun wiped his father's tears away with his tongue, and his eyes suddenly regained their sight. His mother also regained her wits, and his brother could speak. When the people of the marketplace saw this, there were none who did not sigh with deep emotion.

Shun then took his parents back home. Ku-sou, realizing his son's extreme filial piety, then assembled his neighbors and relatives, and unthinkingly took out his knife to kill his second wife.

Shun folded his hands and respectfully addressed his father: "I beg you to consider that if you kill Mother, then I will not have been filial."

The neighbors were deeply moved; no one had heard of such a thing. After his father granted her her life, they were all happy and the whole world spread his fame. The Emperor Yao heard of him and gave him his two daughters in marriage. The elder one was O-huang, and the younger was Nü-ying. Yao then abdicated his throne to Emperor Shun. Nü-ying gave birth to Shang-chün, who was no good; Shun then abdicated his throne to Yü of Hsia.

There is a poem that says:

When Ku-sou blocked up the well his eyes went blind,
And Shun ever after farmed on Mount Li.
He took his grain to market at Chi-tu and met his parents;
He licked his father's eyes with his tongue, and they regained their
  sight.

Another poem says:

Filial and obedient to his parents, beloved of Heaven,
Shun cleared out the well and found the silver;
His parents piled up rocks and crushed Shun,
But Heaven in sympathy opened a passage to the house on the east.

Transformation Text on the Boy Shun's Extreme Filial Piety, one scroll
Translated by Richard W. Bodman

268

How Liu Chih-yüan Bade San-niang Good-bye and Joined the Army in T'ai-yüan

from *Ballad of the Hidden Dragon*, Chapter 2

Anonymous (12th century?)

Li Hung-yi[1] ripped Chih-yüan's fine clothes to rags and gave him a cotton gown and trousers to wear. Then he ordered him to tend the peach orchard. The Hidden

This text is an example of a genre called the medley (*chu-kung-tiao*, literally, "various modes"). The medley is a dramatic type of storytelling that developed toward the end of the eleventh century and flourished particularly under the Chin dynasty of the Jürchen. Like so many other genres of popular literature that came after the Buddhist-influenced transformation texts (see selections 266 and 267) of the T'ang and Five Dynasties periods, the medley was prosimetric in form, the verse portions being sung and the prose portions being spoken. The medley was a solo performance in which a single artist, accompanied by percussion or a string instrument, both told the story and spoke all of the quoted dialogue. The verse portions of the medley were sung to various tunes or arias (*ch'ü-tiao*) arranged in a sequence according to fixed musical rules. A group of tunes in one mode (*kung-tiao*) were considered to be a suite (*t'ao-shu*). In spite of their once great popularity as an oral performing art, only three, or perhaps four, written medleys are extant. The majority of these survive only in fragments and were recovered only in this century, demonstrating once again the usual fate of folk and popular literature in a society that was so thoroughly dominated by the elitist values of Confucian literati. The present text is no exception, having been unearthed from the sands of Kharokhoto by the Russian explorer, Petr Kuzmitch Kozlov, during his expedition of 1907–1908. It is significant that this important discovery took place around the same time that Aurel Stein and Paul Pelliot were

Dragon[2] did not know it was a plot and that the big fellow already waited for him in a dark place.

(Chung-lü-tiao, *mu-yang-kuan*)[3]

The clouds came restlessly and went
Only a little rising moon appeared.
Unguessably wicked were Hung-hsin's[4] plans.
He waited there for Liu Chih-yüan
As slowly the hour deepened into late night.
A short time after the watchman's second drum
A fresh wind blew upon men's cheeks.

The wall was tumbled on the northwest side
And suddenly, there, appeared another hero.
He leaped the ruined wall as nimble as could be
And poised to run to the thatched hut.
Hung-yi was delighted.
The fellow was fit for death.
And all his grievances would be avenged!

(Coda) "No man has a rear-looking eye to see his danger through."
    Li Hung-yi cannot restrain his rage.
    He will smite with his club his enemy's back
    And break him quite in two.

---

recovering transformation texts and other types of lost popular literature from a cave at Tun-huang, also far from the political center of China at the edge of the Central Asian desert.

The subject of this medley is Liu Chih-yüan who was the first emperor of the Later Han dynasty (947–950), a short-lived house founded during the chaotic period of the Five Dynasties. It deals exclusively with the hero's youth before he became emperor. The first three chapters briefly describe the bitter lot of the Liu family. When Liu Chih-yüan's father, a soldier, was killed in battle, his widowed mother fled from a local famine with her two little sons and later remarried. Liu Chih-yüan has a falling-out with his half brothers and leaves home. In his wanderings, he has a fight with two village ruffians who turn out to be the brothers of Li San-niang ("Third Daughter of the Li's"). Li San-niang's father decides to marry his daughter off to Liu Chih-yüan when he sees an aura around the head of the sleeping Liu, a sign of the future emperor. The medley goes on to relate his second marriage to the daughter of a prominent military figure and his career as a soldier. The fragmentary text then skips to chapters 11 and 12 where an account is given of the happy reunion of Liu Chih-yüan, Li San-niang, and their son after a separation of thirteen years. It also recounts the gathering together of the entire Liu family whose numerous members had been scattered all over the country.

1. One of Liu Chih-yüan's brothers-in-law.

2. Liu Chih-yüan, the emperor-to-be of the Later Han dynasty (947–50).

3. Untranslated notations such as this give the mode (*kung-tiao*) and tune (*ch'ü-tiao*) title to which the following verse sections would have been sung.

4. Li Hung-hsin, Liu Chih-yüan's other brother-in-law.

Hung-yi in rage
Gripped the stick so tight it gave a puff of smoke.
A man of stone
Would be felled by such a stroke.

Struck such a blow on the back, the man was helpless. All seven feet of him toppled to the earth with a heavy crash!

(Hsien-lü-tiao, *tsui-lo-t'o*)

Hung-yi with an angry curse
Put all his strength into his hands.
Down fell the other, his heart full of hate,
Wishing he were dead, so great the pain.

Hung-yi stooped, dragged the stranger up, and looked at him.
In the light of the moon, he recognized the face.
It *wasn't* the pauper Liu Chih-yüan,
He looked more carefully—it was Li Hung-hsin!

Hung-yi between fright and smile, Hung-hsin between pain and patience. "I was afraid that you, big brother, would not be able to down that paupered devil. That's why I came to watch you." It has been true from the beginning of time that the net of Heaven stretches everywhere. Its meshes are wide, but nothing escapes it. In a moment, they saw Chih-yüan followed by several men. They all came smelling of wine. Hung-yi grabbed him: "Our father and mother are dead but a few days. How dare you drink!" The villagers replied: "We only drink to keep from crying." But the brothers would not let be. When morning came, they bound Liu Chih-yüan with rope and would have taken him to court, but San-weng[5] got wind of it.

(Huang-chung-kung, *shuang-sheng tieh-yün*)

Li Hung-hsin and Li Hung-yi
Bound the Hidden Dragon
And together began an endless din:
"Since he came to our home as a son-in-law
He's looked upon us as children's toys.
We'd say go this way and he'd go that!
Always wrangling!

"We told him to mind the orchard, uncle,
And back he came soggy drunk.
We clouted him and he got mad
And picked a fight with us!
Uncle, judge who is right and who is wrong."

5. Li San-weng, brother of Li San-chuan, or Li the Learned, who is Liu Chih-yüan's father-in-law.

When San-weng heard their words,
He shouted angrily: "Quiet, you cattle!

(Coda) "You both pick on him whenever you can
Yet now complain *he's* mannerless—
Well, which of *you* is a gentleman?"

"If you take him to court," said San-weng, "I'll fix you before the judge!" Bystanders threatened him too, so Hung-yi gave up. Several days passed and the brothers laid another plot. They sent Liu Chih-yüan to sleep in the thatched stable saying they thought the cow would soon calve. Even San-niang was unaware of their plot and Chih-yüan did not suspect them. When the deep of night had come, he slept soundly inside the stable.

(Nan-lü-kung, *ying-t'ien-ch'ang*)

Chih-yüan was depressed and sad at heart,
His tears flowed like rain.
Time and again he sighed at length
And secretly, he thought:
"Here am I, Ancestor-to-be [of the Han dynasty]
Born to a prominent family.
We lost our wealth,
I left my mother and all my kin,
Heaven led me to this place.
My father-in-law was very kind,
He asked me to marry his daughter
And was happy he could help.

"My wife and I are the fish and the stream.
Her parents we never did resent,
But alas! Disaster! They both died.
Li Hung-hsin and Li Hung-yi have
Nursed their hatred and harshly treated me.
San-weng is fond of me and guards me from much harm,
But surely one day I'll be caught up by their plots.

(Coda) "My troubles riddle as hard as the *Classic of Filial Piety!*[6]
I love my San-niang; I wish to leave but cannot.
Yet if I stay, can I bear our lot?"

Held by San-niang's love
He will grow old but never leave her.

6. According to tradition, the *Classic of Filial Piety (Hsiao-ching)*, was compiled on the basis of the conversations between Confucius and his disciple Tseng Tzu. One wonders why this should be used to describe a knotty problem.

> Thinking of the hatred of those two
> He cannot leave here fast enough.

No way out has he. When will his sorrows cease? Late at night the Hidden Dragon fell asleep. Outside the door, Li Hung-yi listened cautiously and his heart grew cruel as he began his wicked work.

(P'an-she-tiao, *ma-p'o-tzu*)

> Hung-yi judged it had passed the second watch.
> The bright moon [sparkled] like an autumn river.
> Hung-yi approached so silently
> One could have heard a light pin drop.
> For a while he sat by the cow-pen,
> Long he stayed and cocked his ear but finally was pleased.

> He remembered: "In the wine-shop . . .
> O, how I was knocked about!
> And then he was brought
> Into the family as a son-in-law—
> My father himself protected him!
> But now, how can he escape!
> He soundly sleeps, his snore is thunderlike.
> This thorn in my eye will soon be plucked out
> And after today I shall be glad again."

(Coda) He's got him in a cow-shed covered with thick thatch.
> To burn it down is simple,
> Just bar the gate, toss the torch, and let the fire catch!

>> P'ang Chüan[7] himself was not as cruel
>> As this rustic wolf.
>> Huang Ch'ao[8] is merciful as Buddha
>> Compared to Hung-yi,
>> Alas! The Emperor-to-be
>> Must end his life in the flames.

(Shang-chiao, *ting-feng-p'o*)

> Liu Chih-yüan sleeps soundly and wakes not,
> Snoring as the tigers roar amidst the hills.
> How can San-niang know
> She may never meet her love again!

7. P'ang Chüan, envious, perfidious, and cruel general from the state of Wei during the period of the Warring States (403–221 B.C.E.).

8. Huang Ch'ao, the leader of a peasant rebellion toward the end of the T'ang dynasty. He perished in 884 C.E.

This is not a pretense and not a dream,
His shade is destined to return to the Yellow Springs![9]

Just then Li Hung-yi
Cups his ear and listens carefully.
He hesitates, he vacillates,
(Still, how can Chih-yüan save himself?)
And then as he touches torch to hut,
Suddenly a noise is heard that startles the great oaf.
He quickly jerks his head to look:

(Coda) The stars have moved, the dipper's turned
And then it was third watch again.
Now will the Emperor's fortune show itself!
Clouds there were not nor even fog
Yet of a sudden it began to rain!

His sufferings were the same as Kuang Wu's.[10] His escape as miraculous as Chin Wang's.[11] The rain quenched the fire. Chih-yüan awoke and though he knew Hung-yi had done it, he dared not complain. Next day Chih-yüan harnessed the ox and donkey to their cart to work near the Temple of Three Religions.[12] At noon, he rested for a while in the temple and slept. Soon a group of older villagers came there for respite from the summer heat. Li San-weng was among them.

(P'an-she-tiao, *ch'in-yüan-ch'un*)

Liu Chih-yüan tied both ox and ass,
He did not think about the cart
But climbed the temple steps.
So troubled was he these many days past
He threw himself down in a heap
To sleep for a little while.
San-weng was standing by
And looked upon him anxiously,
His brows were knit.
"Here is a plight to wound the heart:
Just this. A beautiful jade from Ching-shan hill
Buried here deep in the mud!"

9. Yellow Springs, the Chinese Hades.
10. After a violent civil war, the Emperor Kuang-wu regained the throne for the Han dynasty (25 C.E.).
11. Chin Wen-kung (Duke Wen of Chin), whose name was Ch'ung-erh, lived in the seventh century B.C.E. during the Spring and Autumn era.
12. A syncretic sect that simultaneously believed in Buddhism, Taoism, and Confucianism.

As the old man stood there saddened,
Suddenly was heard a clap of thunder from the sky
And all were startled by the crash.
Then they saw the lightning flash
And it frightened them to death:
It shook their souls out till none was left.
Then something caught their eyes
And they raised their heads to look:
In such a wild, ill-omened storm
The tender grain is battered down
And everywhere there'll be a desert
And famine-stricken folk.

(Coda) The good Dragon of the clouds
Has sent his devils with this rain.
Black clouds stretched across the skies
To pour the Four Seas down again.

The lightning darted silver snakes. The thunder pealed an iron gong, the winds dashed against the sky, and the heavy rain was a torrent. The ox and donkey, frightened, snapped the hemp rope, ran away, and disappeared to who knows where. San-weng shouted a warning to Chih-yüan who raced to catch the beasts, but they had gone. When it grew dark, Liu Chih-yüan did not dare return to the village.

(Kao-p'ing-tiao, *ho-hsin-lang*)

When Chih-yüan heard San-weng's shout, he jumped,
Left San-weng, and hurried from the shrine.
He cared not that his leather shoes got soiled
But searched all through the lake of mud.
Along the way he murmured to himself a thousand times:
"These two sons of piebald donkeys
Will tie me to the mulberry tree
And straightway I'll get fifty stripes."

Now, history has come to the end of T'ang
And reached the age of Five Dynasties.
The people have lost their way; the multitudes are sorely oppressed
But rich and famous men show bravery and brilliance,
And new-come heroes are hard and firm.
In T'ai-yüan[13] district they brand their young recruits.
Chih-yüan wants to join but still he vacillates.
Not that he is of two minds
But is it strange that he should be pulled two ways at once?
So sad, so hard it is to leave San-niang!

13. A city in Shansi province.

When evening came, Liu Chih-yüan dared not return to the village. He wished to steal secretly away and join the army in T'ai-yüan. But his affection for San-niang is great; he cannot leave her. Under the bright moon, he could find sufficient reason neither for going nor staying, and he sighed again and again.

(Tao-kung, *chieh-hung*)

Wringing his hands and rubbing his fingers,
Chih-yüan beneath the moon
Heaved a deep sigh and talked to himself:
"Could I have avoided kicking and boxing?
Even no trouble at all causes trouble between Hung-yi and me,
Each of us irks the other so.
How much worse it will be now,
For I have lost both ox and ass!
If I return to the village, what will they say?
I am afraid to face Hung-hsin and Hung-yi.
I urge you, all young men and youths,
Try as best you can with each of your lives
To avoid becoming a son-in-law such as I.

"While her parents were yet alive
All things were good and living easy.
Since their death the others have harried my wife and me.
Those men and their wives are never still,
They find fault with everything in us.
You can ruin any good man by slicing away at him
Till he struggles for his very breath.
I was so long poor, and not once rich,
They said that this could never change.
Just a beggar owning nothing but a hearty appetite.
Can a man stand five score insults such as these?
Can anything good ever be cut from such cloth?

(Coda) "Throughout the village, grown men and young girls too
    Gave me a nickname, will they never stop?
    Everyone calls me Beggar Liu."

It was slightly past the second watch when Liu Chih-yüan secretly returned. He had come to bid San-niang good-bye.

(Hsien-lü-tiao, *sheng-hu-lu*)

Beneath the moon moved Mr. Liu like a wisp of smoke,
His mouth still full of complaints
Because he hadn't found the ox and ass.
Holding back his alarm, containing his fear,

He tiptoed forward and traveled
Roundabout through the orchard.

"I say good-bye to my San-niang;
I go to T'ai-yüan.
When I'm in and branded
We'll be together again.
I walk but know not if I move little or much.
So strong are the feelings of husband and wife
This is like leaping a fence or scaling a wall
While tied by a rope to one leg."

(Coda) Just then he approached the cattle-shed
To slip from sight, but slip he could not
For someone grabbed him by the arms instead.

It frightened the Hidden Dragon to death. Who has seized him? He turned his
head—it was his wife San-niang: "Husband, why do you come so late? My brothers
and their wives with clubs lie in wait for you." Chih-yüan told her the whys and the
wherefores: "Tonight, I came just to say good-bye secretly, for I couldn't come openly
to see you."

(Cheng-kung, *chin-mo-tao*)

Startled, he turned in fear
And saw it was San-niang who caught him:
"I tell you, my husband,
The work was hard enough before
But after you left this morning
I could hardly wait for dark.
Oh, how anxious I grew!
There was still no trace of you
And my brothers and their wives were in such a rage!
They're waiting for you now and will give you no quarter."
What emotion!
As Chih-yüan listened to San-niang's words
His tears flowed like a spring.
He replied: "In the Temple of Three Religions,
I hid myself to escape the heat.
When I had fallen fast asleep
It began to rain as though a cistern had overturned.
When I awoke neither ox nor ass could be found
And half the slope had turned into a lake.
I searched for the beasts till evening came;
In the dark of night I could not come through the main gate,
So I leaped the wall to see my bride.

(Coda) "It will be hard to live in Sha-t'o village[14]
But stay, bear with your troubles, and farm the land.
For I must go to Ping-chou[15] and take a soldier's brand."

Dripping tears, San-niang replied: "If you go to T'ai-yüan, how will I get through the days?" Chih-yüan replied: "The governor of nine districts[16] is raising an army now and I go to join it. I came here only to say good-bye." When San-niang heard this, she felt a knife in her heart: "I am already several months with child. I had to tell you."

(Chung-lü-tiao, *mu-ta-sui*)

Li San-niang's black eyebrows knit,
She covered her sad face with cupped hands.
Then her delicate fingers caught Liu Chih-yüan's ragged clothes:
"If you go to T'ai-yüan to take the soldiers' brand,
Come back soon, and carry me away from here.
I am three months gone, remember, please!
Li Hung-yi and Li Hung-hsin are wolf and tiger.
'Topsy-turvy' and 'Prickle-stick'[17] long since have earned their evil names!
I have to stay and face their angry looks and squinted eyes.
Even the gods here are not at peace,
And the signs of the Heavens are at sixes and sevens.

"No lie leaves my mouth,
Whatever I promise, I'll keep my word:
I am your wife while I live,
I'll still be your wife when I die.
No matter what foolishness they may talk
I'll never heed any one of them.
I'll never be faithless,
Meng Chiang-nü[18] will be my model.

"Do not worry! When they tell me to find another life,
I'll shout them away.
Only when I cannot stand their beating me,

14. Village of Sha-t'o Turks. Like many rulers of northern Chinese dynasties during the past two millennia, Liu Chih-yüan (Kao Tsu of the Later Han dynasty) was of Altaic descent.
15. Ping-chou, province and later imperial capital of Liu Chih-yüan's dynasty, was located in present-day Shansi province.
16. Of Ping-chou province.
17. Liu Chih-yüan's colorfully named sisters-in-law.
18. Meng Chiang-nü, the model of Chinese wifely faithfulness. When the emperor Ch'in Shih Huang-ti (third century B.C.E.) built the so-called Great Wall against the northern "barbarians," all young and able men were recruited to work on it. Meng's husband was among them. When winter came, Meng wished to bring warm clothing to him, but she found only his bones at the Wall.

Only when I no longer can endure it,
And when it is impossible to escape,
I'll cut my throat or hang myself
But die I will—somehow."

She finished her words and her tears dropped like pearls.
Teardrops wet her silken clothes.
She whispered crying, she crying whispered
But dared not loudly cry.
Whoever had blood in him or ate food—
No, even were he carved in stone or iron cast—
He would be moved.

(Coda) She is a pear-blossom drenched in spring rain,
An empress sobbing her grief beneath the moon.
How does she behave?
Like Hsiang Fei, who speckled the bamboo
With tears she shed on Great Shun's grave.[19]

   Her eyebrows, even furrowed by grief, were so delicate that Hsi-tzu, the Prince of
Wu's mistress, had none as lovely. Her face, even drenched in tears, was yet more
beautiful than Ch'i-shih, Han Kao-tsu's love. "My husband, as long as you are in
T'ai-yüan, I'll do nothing but stand by the door and wait for you. Sir, tarry a while,
I'll go for money for your trip." A while passed, but she didn't come back, so Chih-
yüan in turn went to look.

   (Huang-chung-kung, *k'uai-huo-nien*)

"My wife has not yet come back and she's been gone too long.
She lets me wait in the deep of night which shows no sign of anyone."
Stealthily he crept inside and went to his wife's room.
The double doors were locked. He put his head in the window to look.
He saw San-niang.

She held a great ax. What did she care for death!
No one lives twice,
So death comes but once.
From ancient times till now
Few had more contempt for death than she,
And even Meng Chiang she surpassed in fidelity.

(Coda) Her tumbled hair lay on the table top
She raised the ax and frightened Liu to death!
Before he could even move—kerchop!

---

19. A legend is told that two wives of Shun, the legendary Chinese ruler (traditional
dates 2255–2205 B.C.E.), speckled the bamboo with the tears which they shed over their
husband's grave.

Chiang-nü at the Great Wall was never this faithful, nor was Yü-fei[20] at Kai-hsia as virtuous. But what of San-niang's life?

The blow of the ax had only cut off a lock of her black hair. She wrapped it in a robe of black and violet figured silk, opened the door, and handed both to young Liu. "I pray you'll never forget me." She saw him to the wall of the compound.

(P'an-she-tiao, *shao-pien*)[21]

When yin and yang first parted to form Heaven and Earth
The separation was very hard,
But do not imagine it was more difficult
Than what this husband and wife did now.
Tonight they cannot bear to leave each other.
Let us exaggerate a little—
They were like Su Hsiao-ch'ing with her student Shuang Chien in the post-
    house when she saw him to the River Ch'ien-t'ang.[22]
They were as Hsü, the commandant, surrounded by Sui troops giving his half
    of the mirror to Princess Yüeh-ch'ang at Huang-p'o.[23]
They were like the Hegemon leaving his mistress Yü at Kai-hsia,
Like the Cowherd and the Spinning Maid parting after the seventh evening of
    the seventh month.[24]

20. Yü-fei, the favorite of Hsiang Yü, who struggled with Liu Pang for hegemony in China at the end of the third century B.C.E. The scene of his parting with Yü-fei at Kai-hsia (in present-day northern Anhwei) is one of the most beloved themes of Chinese storytelling and drama. Hsiang Yü perished by his own hand when he saw that his battle was lost. The allusion is invoked again near the end of the following song.

21. *Shao-pien* in its lyric (*tz'u*) form is known for its great length and prosy rhythms. The singer has doubtlessly chosen this melody for just that reason "to exaggerate a little."

22. The sing-song girl Su Hsiao-ch'ing and her lover, the student Shuang Chien, enjoyed their deep love until he had to leave and pass examinations in the capital. He did not return for a long time, but Su did not want anybody else. The owner of the brothel, however, sold the girl to a rich traveling merchant. Sitting in his boat, Su sang sad songs about her fate and one of them she wrote on the wall of the Golden Mountain monastery when they passed it. In the meantime, Shuang became rich and famous in the capital. Once when walking around the monastery, he found the poem and recognized Su's handwriting. He found her and happily married her.

23. There is a legend about the princess Yüeh-ch'ang, the younger sister of the emperor Hou-chu from the Ch'en dynasty (557–589), and her husband Hsü Te-yen. The territory of Ch'en being surrounded by the army of Sui dynasty, Hsü had to go to battle and leave his wife. The princess broke a bronze mirror, gave half to her husband, and told him to go the fifteenth day of the first lunar month to the market in the capital. If he found her half which she would keep until market day and then sell, she would be somewhere nearby. The Ch'en dynasty perished and the two were separated for a long time. But on the fixed day, Hsü went to the market, located his wife's half of the mirror, finally found princess Yüeh-ch'ang, and they were joined in love until the time of their death.

24. A myth based upon the union of the constellation of the Herdboy and Spinning Damsel, which is supposed to occur in the seventh of the seventh lunar month. The lovers living in the stars could meet only once a year.

And the rain and clouds parted as they did
When the beloved goddess of Wu-shan left Sung Yü in his grief.[25]

"If sold, my robe of figured silk can furnish money for your trip," said San-
    niang.
Her generosity is as great as the mountain.
A moment before she had let down her cloud of black hair
And cut off a lock of it with the ax.
She hands it now to young Liu saying:
"Remember often tonight's love."
Should you recall examples from the past
Of such affectionate partings,
I think no grief in all the world
Could be compared with theirs.
Her pain was so great, again and again the tear pearls fell.
The earth was mourning, Heaven was plunged in sorrow,
The sun itself gave no light.
If Buddha of the Eternal Smile were witness, he too would frown.

(Coda) A mandarin duck driven from its mate,
    Lien-li[26] trees cut asunder,
    Uncaring Hung-hsin and Hung-yi have made
    The lonely *luan* bird and solitary phoenix separate.

   Hung-hsin was a fence as high as the sky. Hung-yi was a wind-screen reaching the
earth. "Prickle-stick" was the awl to undo their love-knot. "Topsy-turvy" was the saw
which cut the *lien-li* trees with interlocked branches. The whole day they plan to drive
Chih-yüan from their house and cause husband and wife to live apart. Chih-yüan and
San-niang had just said good-bye to each other when suddenly they heard a shout.

   (Hsieh-chih-tiao, *shua-san-t'ai*)

Li San-niang and Liu Chih-yüan—
A couple who had scarce begun to live together.
Her tears were as many as the raindrops.
"An old grief is seldom dispersed by a new one."
"When you arrive at Ping-chou
Send back for me.
Don't make me wait too long by the door,
Think often on tonight's parting,
Sir, recall everything of our past."

---

25. Clouds and rain are symbolic of sexual relationship. Allusion to a famous sensual poem,
"The Goddess," by Sung Yü (third century B.C.E., see selection 149).
   26. Intertwined.

Suddenly there was a loud shout
Which startled husband and wife.
Li Hung-yi dressed all differently:
(His face about to burst with rage)
A shiny black turban, his tunic girt by a cord,
Leather boots for which two rabbits had once been brought to grief.
The sash about his middle
Was three feet wide, of ornamented purple silk.
His shirt was woven of coarse hemp.

In his hand he held a club
Which in the past had knocked down five rough fighters.
His ears stood out like dried-out mulberry leaves.
His nose, arrogant, eyes deep set inside his face.
His thighs were big, his buttocks huge,
He had a quick and ox-lipped mouth
Which drank the crudest village wine without a pucker.
He cursed Liu Chih-yüan:
He called his mother a gallows bird
And him a spine-broken pauper
Who had seduced his little sister—just a child.

(Coda) He opened his mulberry-eating, sesame-chewing mouth
With a shout that matched an ox's bellow,
Which not only Chih-yüan trembled to hear
But the unicorn itself would have fled in fear.

Both brothers raised their clubs to harm the future Emperor.
Both their wives hiked up skirts and raced to belabor the Empress.
Alas! The time had not come for phoenix and mate.
How sad! The swallow and sparrow cheat them.

(Nan-lü-kung, *ying-t'ien-ch'ang*)

Li Hung-yi and his brother fly into a rage,
Their strength was the wolf's, the tiger's strength.
They raise their clubs
And wildly shout:
"You useless pauper! Not content to lose the ox and ass
You even had the cheek
To come back to the compound and lead your wife astray!
Get out this moment and you'll save your life,
If you wait, both our clubs are raised against you!"

Both brothers were rough enough at all times
And more so now for they could not resist their wives' chatter,

Like a field of magpies all let loose at once.
They insulted their brother-in-law
Until the Hidden Dragon could stay no longer
But had to leave the compound.
Angrily he cried: "One day I'll come on the wind and thunder
And carry back my San-niang!

(Coda) "I go! I go away! I leave at once!"
Chih-yüan watched her and she watched him
As gradually they drew apart.
Both wept:
The one for he was saddened, the other for she was sick at heart.

Chih-yüan, leaving, cried angrily to the other couples: "One day I'll reach my goal and I'll never forgive you!" The brothers laughed: "When you are famous, we'll snuff up three pecks and three pints of vinegar." And their wives added: "We'll eat three pecks and three pints of salt."

(Huang-chung-kung, *ch'u-tui-tzu*)

Chih-yüan shouted: "Now I am in shadow,
But as the storm is followed by bright sunbursts
So I'll return to take my beauty back.
Then will I show vengeance to my enemies and kindness to my friends!"

Hung-yi and Hung-hsin repeated their oath:
"When you are famous, we'll sniff up three measures of vinegar!"
The brothers' wives added their bit to be unpleasant:
"When you're honored and make your name
We'll certainly eat our three measures of salt!"

(Coda) "Don't hope to raise the parasol of rank
Nor sit in a saddle and conduct the drill,
If the cold doesn't get you then hunger will!"

When they had finished, both couples seized San-niang and dragged her into the compound. Liu Chih-yüan set out alone on the old path to T'ai-yüan. Next day, he came to Ping-chou and asked the inhabitants for information. They told him where to find the army camp and advised him to visit Brigade-general Yüeh Chin. The ranks had not yet been filled. Following this advice, Chih-yüan went to the camp [. . . .] The ceremonial visit being finished, next came competition in drawing the bow. Chih-yüan rejected one bow as too soft. The general, in anger, had the (stiffest) bow of the brigade brought out from the arsenal to be drawn.

(Chung-lü-tiao, *fu-ni-shang*)

Officers and the commander-in-chief
Watched Chih-yüan and their faces were pleased.

He stood like a pine.
Like a pine he stood,
His body seven feet high, his presence majestic and awesome.
All disciplines of military art he had accomplished
And drilled in them for many years.
The time had come [. . .]²⁷
To serve his palace and protect his home.

The noble hero drew the bow as though it were but rotten wood,
Displaying well his mighty strength.
His voice rang like a bell,
Like a bell rang his voice
As he thundered his replies
With his back rigidly to the west
And his face squarely to the east.
Whirling the iron mace, he makes the north wind blow.
Wrestling, who can match him?
Swinging the mace back and forth
He startles the commander-in-chief.

(Coda) Brigadier Yüeh is nearly startled to death
As he watches Liu Chih-yüan. For it seems as though
An eight-clawed dragon draws that mighty birch bow.

    The general saw above Chih-yüan's head a red glow and struggling dragons twined together. To himself he said with a sigh: "Someday this man's wealth and honor will be limitless." Thereupon he gave him a jar of wine, three strings of cash, and gave him a furlough in the camp. Later he called Li Hsin, his vice-commander, and ordered him secretly to act as go-between. "I have a daughter of marriageable age not yet betrothed and I seek a husband for her. What I tell you, you must do and I won't admit any excuse." Li Hsin understood. He privately visited Chih-yüan and told him about the marriage offer from the Brigade-general's family. The Hidden Dragon wept and told the vice-commander about his wife San-niang.

(Hsieh-chih-tiao, *yung-yü-lo*)

When Chih-yüan heard Li Hsin's words
He clasped his hands, gave a bow and said:
"My little San-niang in Sha-t'o village is awaiting news of me.
She cut me off a lock of her hair
And when I left, she gave me something for the trip.
Secretly she made me a present of her lock together with her garment of
    ornamented silk.

---

27. The woodblock print is damaged here and below near the end of the chapter.

When I'm branded to the army, if I take another wife,
She surely will hear of it."

"Today I want to make you a groom," said Li Hsin,
"This betrothal, our commander is bound he'll have.
His daughter's beauty is the equal of Ch'ang-o,[28]
Her face surpasses that of Lo-p'u.[29]
The family would not ask you directly.
'One remembers present favors and forgets past faithfulness,'
They said of old and say it now.
What matter if a principle suffers?
With a new wife it's easy to forget the old."

"Already I have a wife, how dare I marry once again?" Li Hsin replied with a smile:
"Sir, how simple you are! Sir, don't you know when the camp gate is shut, the general
is king? If you don't comply, disaster will be upon you!" Chih-yüan sighed deeply.
The only thing left to do was to accept the betrothal gifts.

(P'an-she-tiao, *ch'in-yüan-ch'un*)

Li Hsin delivered his message,
The groom was fearful because a general was his go-between.
Chih-yüan could not escape,
He accepted the betrothal gifts,
With his face contorted in grief and his brows drawn down.
[. . . . .]
[. . . . .] who is who.
How can one know [. . . . . .] Ch'in [. . . . . .]
[. . . . .] Ch'i.

His speech now proves deceptive.
Like a needle in cotton,
Like poison in honey.
"No need to mention T'ang Tun-chuan[30] in the past,
Or speak of Tsung-tao,[31] who once divorced his wife.
For now I am more perfidious than Huang Ch'ao,[32]
I am heartless as P'ang Chüan.

28. Ch'ang-o, a great beauty, stole the elixir of immortality and fled with it to the moon.
Folk legend says she still lives there.
29. Another legendary beauty, also called Lo-fu, heroine of the ballad "Mulberry up the
Lane" (see selection 164).
30. T'ang Tun-chuan and his story are unknown.
31. Wang Tsung-tao left his first wife because of another woman. The story is told in quite
different ways in novels and dramas.
32. The infamous rebel.

My heart is a nest of vipers, of scorpions, of snakes,
I am a Li Mien[33] who joined the rebels,
I am Wang K'uei[34] who married twice."

(Coda) He wrung his hands: "Far off in your village,
Wife, if you can hear my voice,
Forgive my ingratitude for your favors
But this time I have no choice."

> The cloudy hair of her head
> He rejects like dust from his feet;
> The tenderness shown on the pillow
> Is no more than an autumn breeze which passed his ear.
> Not only does Chih-yüan break his first vow,
> But will forsake his first wife for the new one.

As soon as Chih-yüan agreed to the marriage, the vice-commander's wives, Lady Li and Lady Wang, became speakers for the girl.

End of Chapter the Second
How Chih-yüan Bade San-niang Good-bye and Joined the Army in T'ai-yüan
Translated by M. Doležalová-Velingerová and J. I. Crump

33. The stories of Li Mien and P'ang Chüan (compare note 7 above) are not adequately known, but are obviously being referred to here as examples of treachery and infidelity.
34. Wang K'uei, symbol of man's perfidy. He married a sing-song girl who gave him all her money to support him during his studies. When he became an official, he married another.

269
Master Tung's Western Chamber Romance
Tung Chieh-yüan (fl. c. 1190–1208)

Chapter 2

(Hsien-lü-tiao mode)

Trimming the Silver Lamp

> Stopping before the steps, the young monk gushed:
> "What a fearful sight:

The medley (*chu-kung-tiao*) is a prosimetric form of oral storytelling that stands midway between narrative and drama. It appears to have been created toward the end of the twelfth century in the entertainment quarters of the Northern Sung capital, Pien-ching, and quickly spread to other parts of China, but its popularity began to wane within a century of its birth.

Tumultuous dust seals the sky;
Fluttering banners conceal the sun;
A shower of fine earth rains down from all directions!
Gongs are clashing; drums are rolling;
Lances and swords surge pell-mell
All around our temple!

"One glimpse at the chief bandit
Is enough to freeze you with terror.
He wears a scarlet turban covered with
Pearls, like rice clinging to the sides of a vat,
Two suits of lion-hide armor,
A pair of green boots
And his mount is a dragonlike
Curly-maned Ch'ih-t'u.[1]

Coda

"A yellow birch crossbow arches over his arm,
A mountain-cleaving ax, big as a winnowing fan,
  rests on his shoulder,
He's none other than Flying Tiger Sun, the bridge-guarding
  general!"

Several mode names and tune titles of the melody reflect the ultimate Buddhist and western (i.e., Central and South Asian) origins of the musical elements of the genre. For example, Master Wen-hsü was a T'ang period monk who gave popular lectures, and *p'an-she* is the Chinese transcription of the Sanskrit word for "five" (*pañca*), hence *P'an-she-tiao* means "Fifth Mode."

Master Tung's Western Chamber Romance (*Tung Chieh-yüan hsi-hsiang chu-kung-tiao*), in contrast to the rough, earthy quality of the medley on Liu Chih-yüan (see selection 268), is of exceptional literary value and shows how the medley can also exist in a more refined form. The contrast between these two medleys demonstrates a recurring paradigm: Chinese literary genres tend to be created in the popular milieu but are later taken up by the literati and become increasingly polished.

The present medley, based on the famous T'ang period classical-language short story, "The Story of Ying-ying" (see selection 252), is very different from its source in language, form, and style. The medley version is written in a mixture of vernacular and classical language, and is much more elaborate and detailed than the short story. For example, the entire second chapter given here is a vivid and lengthy description of a battle that is barely alluded to in the T'ang short story. The author's fertile imagination is demonstrated in his creation of the warrior monks who are instrumental in quelling the rebellion of local troops that threaten the safety of Ying-ying and her mother, who have taken refuge in their temple. The monks are particularly interesting, yet unprecedented in the tradition of the short story and its subsequent adaptations.

Next to nothing is known of the author. Indeed, we do not even know his real name, Chieh-yüan being but an honorific title (nominally Prefectural [Provincial] Graduate with Highest Honors).

1. The name of a famous charger owned by Lü Pu (second century C.E.), the Three Kingdoms warrior.

[Prose]

During the T'ang dynasty, troops were stationed in the P'u prefecture. The year of our story, the commander of the garrison, Marshal Hun, died. Because the second-in-command, Ting Wen-ya, did not have firm control of the troops, Flying Tiger Sun, a subordinate general, rebelled with five thousand soldiers. They pillaged and plundered the P'u area.

How do I know this to be true? It is corroborated by "The Ballad of the True Story of Ying-ying." The "Ballad" says:

> Bridge-side garrison loses its chief,
> Banners and halberds topple in a heap.
> Ere a new head is announced,
> Soldiers mutiny and crowd into town.
> Husbands proffer silk and jade,
> So wives from injury may escape.
> But how can the beauties flee and hide
> When everywhere rebels gallop and riot?
> Mothers cry and wail to heaven;
> Holding daughters they part with ornaments.
> Abandoning rouge to lessen their charm,
> Maidens seem effigies, pale and wan.

(Cheng-kung mode)

Master Wen-hsü, ch'an

[The young monk continued:]
> "Reverend elders,
> Cease your commotion, and
> Hear me while I explain:
> Marshal Hun Chen
> Recently passed away.
> The bridge-guarding Wen-ya is a profligate.
> He's incompetent;
> His troops mutinied and
> Proceeded to terrorize the countryside.
> City walls and moats, one after the other, are overrun and destroyed.

> "The insurgents loot and plunder; they
> Seize women and girls.
> None dare oppose them, since
> Rioters don't know right from wrong,
> White from black.
> In the town of P'u, the southern district and the northern ward have
>   been burned to ashes;

> Booty is carted away;
> Highways and byways
> Are mounds of corpses and seas of blood.

Licorice Root

> "They wreak a terrible havoc.
> Oh, they wreak a terrible havoc.
> The rebel chief's
> Crimes are as vast as the sky.
> Intrepid, fearless,
> He does battle in a heavy coat of mail.
> With his military might
> He thinks he can overthrow the T'ang.
> It will be pure luck if he leaves us alone.
> But if not, how can we resist?

Removing the Cotton Garment

> "How can we resist?
> The thought confounds me.
> We're really in a fix—
> Do I hear more troops approach? . . ."

Coda

> Within an hour,
> Waves of soaring dust have fully eclipsed the sun;
> Five thousand bandits throng outside.

[Prose]

The monks had no time to make any preparations. All they could do was to close the temple gate. The bandits beat on the gate with their swords and sent arrows into the temple. One of them shouted: "We don't want anything else; we just want a meal." The abbot said to the monks: "I think we had better open the gate and invite them in. They can stay in the prayer halls and on the verandahs. After giving them a meal, we can soften them up with bribes so that they will not hurt us. Otherwise, I am afraid they may force their way in and kill us all. Does my suggestion appeal to you?"

The monk Chih-shen, the superintendent, replied: "Inviting the bandits in will not harm *us* in any way. But at present we have in the temple Madam Ts'ui's daughter Ying-ying, who is a beautiful girl. If the bandits saw her, they would certainly kidnap her. Minister Ts'ui had many relatives and friends who enjoy imperial favors and occupy important positions. Once Ying-ying is captured, we shall certainly suffer for it. For, although it would be the bandits who had seized her, the fault would be ours for having opened the gate to them. When we are charged with complicity, what can we say in our own defense?"

(Ta-shih-tiao mode)

Kun Section of [the Elaborate Melody] Yi-chou

> In the prayer hall
> The monks discussed
> Whether they should invite the bandits in.
> The superintendent said no,
> And gave his reasons in detail:
> "What shall we do
> If the rebels
> Should capture Ying-ying?
> When the news becomes known
> We're sure to share the fate of vanishing waters."
>
> "What can be done then?" the abbot asked.
> "The bandits are at the gate, and
> We've no way to fight them."
> From the ranks a monk
> Thundered out his angry cry:
> "Have no fear, abbot.
> You other monks, you three hundred and more,
> Jabbering is all you do.
> Despite your size, you're helpless babes.
> Your chow has been wasted on you, you good-for-nothings."

Coda

> Lifting his frayed Buddhist robe,
> Raising his three-foot consecrated sword,
> He said: "Let me put my life on the line and fight this horde of
>   thieves."

[Prose]

Who was this monk? He was none other than Fa-ts'ung. Fa-ts'ung was a descendant of a tribesman from western Shensi. When he was young he took great pleasure in archery, fencing, hunting, and often sneaked into foreign states to steal. He was fierce and courageous. When his parents died, it suddenly became clear to him that the way of the world was frivolous and trivial, so he became a monk in the Temple of Universal Salvation.

"My mind is made up. As long as we are menaced, I will not sit back and watch. For such is not the way of a humane person. If my valiant brothers will help me, we can easily defeat the rebels. In fact, they will dissolve on their own, like a shaken grain stalk snapping into bits. Actually, only two or three mutineers have a seditious intent; the rest have been tricked into following. While they see the spoils before their eyes they are blind to the dire consequences waiting around the corner. If I can explain to them the gains and the losses, most of them will lose their desire to fight and will disperse."

(Hsien-lü-tiao mode)

An Embroidered Belt

> He didn't know how to read sūtras;
> He didn't know how to follow rituals;
> He was neither pure nor chaste
> But was indomitably courageous . . . .
> Formerly he had often killed
> Without batting an eye.
> After becoming a monk,
> He left his iron cudgel
> Unsharpened for years.
> His consecrated sword
> Had slain tigers and dragons.
> But once he tired of shedding blood,
> It hung neglected
> On the wall.
>
> The sword's ram-horn hilt was sealed to the sheath by grime,
> Its icy blade and point had dulled.
> Fa-ts'ung called out: "Fellow monks,
> Who will follow me?
> Have no fear,
> I guarantee there'll be no risk."
> To himself he thought:
> "Today I'll have meat to eat and
> My cudgel will sharpen itself on the thieves."
> He stood by the verandah
> And counted the gathering monks:
> "Tough and fierce men
> Who dare to fight.
> You need only shout to cheer me on.
> No danger will befall you.

Coda

"Just open the gate and aid me with war yells,
And I'll mow down the thieves with my sword.
Let them be pastry fillings for our meal!"

[Prose]

A penchant to kill
Has changed into a desire to save;
A former ruffian
Is now a praiseworthy hero.

Fa-ts'ung urged loudly: "For our religion and for each other, we should do our utmost. Those who dare help me fight, go to the right of the hall." In a short time nearly three hundred monks gathered by the hall with cudgels and swords in their hands. They said to Fa-ts'ung: "We are willing to follow you and fight to the death."

(Shuang-tiao mode)

Wen-ju-chin

When you looked close you'd see
Fa-ts'ung had a ferocious mien:
Defiant, bold,
Somewhat irregular and somewhat strange.
His bull-like torso was hefty,
His tiger waist supple and long.
He wore a three-foot consecrated sword and
Carried an iron cudgel.
His horse was
An elephant without tusks.
Wearing a tight-fitting cloth corselet, he had
No armor, no helmet.
A full eight feet,
He was splendidly imposing.
A Buddhist Tzu-lu!²
A tonsured Chin-kang!³

His followers, more than two hundred,
Used weapons
Rarely seen.

2. Confucius' disciple. In *The Analects*, the Master says: "Yu [Tzu-lu] is more inclined to bravery than I."
3. A protective deity.

Some had deep-set eyes;
Some looked savage and fierce.
Some brandished kitchen cleavers,
Rolling pins;
Some banged on temple drums and gongs.
They wore prayer pennants for armor,
Begging-bowls as helmets.
A few novices with disheveled hair
Dashed out of their cells in
Dark brown clerical gowns.
Giving rein to pent-up valor,
They shouted: "We too want
To fight on the battleground till the bitter end."

Coda

Unwilling to follow Tripiṭaka to search for scriptures,[4]
This lot shouldered brooms and canes to
Trail a homicidal monk!

[Prose]

Before the superintendent could caution prudence, Fa-ts'ung had already led his followers to the gate. Seeing the impressive enemy strength, he knew he could not defeat them easily. At once he dismounted and ascended the belfry to address the rebels in the hope of undermining their morale.

(P'an-she-tiao mode)

Spring in the Chin Garden

Closely dotting the vast fields,
Iron halberds pierced the sky;
Embroidered banners reflected the sun;
They formed the backdrop for
A mounted officer
Whose red brocade military cape covered
A suit of oil-glossy, jet-black armor.
Flat-nosed, hare-lipped, with
Thick eyebrows and large eyes,
The general carried on his shoulder a gigantic Ku-ting sword,[5]
Magnificent as a god,
He had a barrel chest, a bulky torso,
Massive thighs, thick buttocks and waist.

4. See selections 259 and 270.
5. A sword wrought in Ku-ting, near P'u-yang district in Hopei.

Virile, alert,
He playfully prodded with his sword the jeweled stirrup of his
    mount.
And the warriors in his command?—
It's always difficult to describe
The panache of true heroes—
Some were short, some were tall,
Some thin, some fat,
But all were flawlessly stalwart and brave.
If you counted carefully,
They were less than six thousand,
But certainly five thousand and more.

Flowers above the Wall

In neat formations,
They tightly encircled
The temple's five-mile estate.
A third of them wore black cotton leggings;
Half had yellow silk wadded jackets.

Their drums rumbled *tung-tung*.
The din of their horns spiraled and whirled.
Their banners danced in the wind, like brilliant tongues of fire.
The combat-urgers made earth-stunning, deafening roars;
The battle-criers uttered sky-lifting yells and shouts.

How could the temple withstand such an onslaught?
Solidly built,
Its walls were like stone ramparts.
The iron-bound gate was impregnable.
An almost impossible feat to get inside
And molest the monks.

Song of Che Tree Branches

Steel axes and swords hacked and hewed.
What cacophony, what confusion.
Politely Fa-ts'ung said to
The rebel general:
"We have no treasures,
Or food or fodder,
How can we offer adequate hospitality
To the immense troops in your command?

Kun Section of [the Elaborate Melody] God of Longevity

> "The court will soon hear of
> Your treasonous deeds.
> Armies will be dispatched
> To quell you.
> You're making a grave mistake.
> When it's too late, even remorse won't help.
> Think over what I say."

> The rebel general
> Was outraged by these words.
> "You bald-pated criminal, fit to be flogged,
> How dare you contravene your lord's will?
> We don't mean to
> Impose on you monks.
> Why should your unchaste lips make such a fuss?

A Fast Melody

> "We don't want to take your temple.
> We don't want to get your gold.
> My men are tired and need a rest.
> So why close your gate?
> Of all the monks only you behave like a tiger, a leopard, and
> Plague your father with tiresome chatter.

Coda

> "Your hands should be cut off,
> Brains knocked out,
> Ears chopped off, and with legs tied,
> You ought to be hung upside down from the lintel till doomsday!"

[Prose]

Fa-ts'ung said: "Compose yourself, compose yourself. We shall comply with your wishes. Since there are a few thousand of you, I shall be grateful if you would retreat about a hundred paces, so that when the food is ready you can file in slowly, in an orderly way."

The general said: "Now that you agree to help us, I would be in the wrong if I didn't cooperate."

Thereupon he ordered his troops to retreat a hundred paces. In the meantime, Fa-ts'ung came down from the belfry and mounted his horse.

(Huang-chung-tiao mode)

The Restless Oriole, ch'an-ling

> When the soldiers heard the order
> They retreated two or three hundred paces.
> Someone removed the crossbar, the padlock,
>> and threw open the two panels of the temple gate.
> Fa-ts'ung shouted:
> "Follow me!" and
> With this call
> All the monks plunged through the gate.
> Such a bizarre army was never seen before.
>
> Rash,
> Fearless,
> They thought nothing of their five thousand foes.
> Fa-ts'ung, holding his cudgel level with the ground,
> Raised his voice and menacingly yelled:
> "Treasonous rebels!
> Send someone out to fight!
> There's no need for you to sink staves,
>> drive in posts, and make camp.

Ssu-men-tzu

> "Our country hasn't treated you ill.
> Reckon for yourselves:
> The emperor gives you your uniforms, your food, and your pay.
> You don't know how lucky you are.
> Shame! Disgrace!
> The time is peaceful with no strife.
> Shame! Disgrace!
> You receive your wages without having to work.
>
> "At Marshal Hun's death,
> You broke into a lawless mob.
> You terrorized the people; you robbed them
>> of their wealth and goods.
> Now you want to ransack my temple.
> Shame! Disgrace!
> The food you demand I'll refuse—
> Shame! Disgrace!—
> I'd rather feed it to my ass.

Willow Leaves

> "Why make a racket here?
> You'd be better off guarding your mother's tomb.
> I know what I say, I don't mean to frighten you,
> My sons, it's time to surrender and yield.

Coda

> "Wise or unwise,
> I'll let you go.
> If you don't leave
> You'll taste the gall of my sixty-pound cudgel."

[Prose]

Fa-ts'ung, galloping on his horse, shouted: "I wish to see the commanding general." An officer rode forth from the ranks and said to him: "You are a Buddhist monk, you should be chanting sūtras and meditating. Why are you here threatening and menacing us?"

Fa-ts'ung replied: "You are soldiers and officers; our country pays you to keep peace on the frontier. You and your families receive food rations at the end of every month, and every season you are given new clothes. Not only are you spared the pain of hunger and cold, you are allowed to enjoy the bliss of family life. Now, temporarily deprived of guidance, you forget the great favor our country has conferred upon you; mercilessly you persecute innocent people and leave the whole prefecture in ruins. The court is not far; it will be informed presently; troops will arrive any moment. You yourselves will be reduced to pools of blood on the battlefield and your families will be condemned for complicity. After you are dead and your clans exterminated, what good is the loot? I think it would be wise for you to reflect on this."

Spurring his horse forward, the rebel officer retorted: "So, besides refusing us food, you have the impudence to harangue my men!"

(Ta-shih-tiao mode)

Jade-Winged Cicada

> When the officer heard Fa-ts'ung's words,
> Even if he had been a Buddha, he would have been enraged.
> He ground and nearly broke his great wolflike teeth.
> He scanned his men:
> "Trusted soldiers,
> Do as I bid.
> Help me with just one shout, and
> In one round I'll capture the bald-pated lout."
> At this the rebels

Rolled their drums and
Vigorously waved their multicolored flags.

Their yells penetrated the sky.
In unison they blew their decorated horns.
Worried clouds shielded the sun as
The air of battle reached the firmament.
The officer growled: "You, monk,
Quit your madness and just wait:
Hold on to your cudgel;
Sit tight on your saddle;
Meditate on the Western Paradise.
In seconds I'll perform the charitable deed
Of sending you there
With ten thousand strokes of my sword."

Coda

Before you could cover your ears, his horse had dashed ahead.
A rainbow of dust trailed behind the hooves.
The rebel aimed his sword straight at the monk's nose.

[Prose]

A clashing sound was heard. Was the monk dead?

(Ta-shih-tiao mode)

Kun Section of [the Elaborate Melody] Yi-chou ch'an-ling

Hell wind rises.
The field is packed with lances and armor.
The air of battle darkens the sky.
Soldiers of six divisions yell and shout.
Before the banners, two mounted warriors fight.
The monk Fa-ts'ung,
Deftly defending himself,
Raises his cudgel to his eyebrow.
A clashing sound—
He wards off the slashing Ku-ting sword.

Dragonlike chargers, tigerlike warriors.
The cudgel twirls, the sword strikes,
In ways prescribed by *Martial Arts*.[6]
This combat will separate
The victor from the loser.

6. *Six Scabbards* (*Liu t'ao*), a pre-T'ang work on military craft.

After three rounds
The rebel begins to tire.
What does he do?
He adopts a defensive posture and hides behind his sword.
It will be impossible now for him to overcome the monk.

A Red Gauze Garment

Doggedly he fights on,
Desperately he perseveres.
He's like a rabbit facing an eagle,
      a mouse running into a cat.
When finally he manages
A slight advantage
He tries to
Escape to his ranks.
Just then another mounted warrior flies forth,
Holding a spear twelve feet long,
Dressed with bizarre extravagance that seems to
Add to his brutal ferocity.

The valiant monk
Has mastered the military arts well.
Though the moment he fends off the spear the sword is upon him,
He remains confident, relaxed,
Calm, undaunted,
Serene, and cool.
His eyes are sharp, his movements brisk;
His steed charges swiftly, his blows are precise and sure.
Circling round him, the two rebels pant and gasp.
They want to quit
But dread their men's jeers.

Coda

Fa-ts'ung's heart pounds violently.
He's furious; his eyes are heptagons, octagons.
The two rebels dare not approach him.

[Prose]

Six arms,
The one holding the cudgel is the strongest.
Three warriors,
The one wearing a helmet withdraws to rest.
The sword-wielder leaves the struggle,
The spear-thruster carries on the fight.

(Cheng-kung mode)

Master Wen-hsü

>Having recovered his strength,
>The sword-wielder puts on his armor again.
>No threats are exchanged,
>No question asked,
>He lunges toward the monk to unhorse him.
>The monk dodges and grasps the rebel's belt.
>With no pity and
>All his strength
>He yanks the rebel over to his own horse
>And smashes him down across the pommel of his saddle.

>A shrill wail—
>The rebel is sliding, head down, through his belt!
>Too weary to
>Remount his tired horse,
>Unable to keep up even the pretense of a hero,
>He decides to flee.
>Steering clear of
>The monk,
>He sprints south to save his skin.

Licorice Root

>How to catch him?
>How to catch him?
>When Fa-ts'ung sees him escape,
>His anger flares up.
>Feigning to give chase,
>He screams and yells thunderously.
>Actually he doesn't budge;
>His screams alone are terrifying enough.
>All the rebels stare with unblinking eyes:
>"This bald monk is unbelievably fierce!"

Coda

>The monk now noisily taunts:
>"You bandits, you criminals, how dare you rebel?
>If anyone else is crazy enough to fight, come out this instant."

[Prose]

>Embroidered vanguard banners
>Set loose in the wind hundreds of miles of morning clouds.

Rousing military drums
Exploded from the ground a thousand claps of thunderbolts.
One general was so incensed that he took up the challenge. Who was he?
Who was he?

(Hsien-lü-tiao mode)

Adorning Crimson Lips

This general
Is famous for his bravery.
Dissatisfied with his rank
He wants to rule the whole country.

Robust, ferocious:
People freeze when he appears.
Fa-ts'ung says to himself:
"I'll bet he always looks
Annoyed and angry."

The "hai-hai" Song

Roly-poly, a portly belly,
Triangular eyes, enormous nose, thick fleshy lips,
His forehead is wide, his chin is broad, he has winged eyebrows,
And a red beard.
Hai-hai.

Wind Blowing Lotus Leaves

Wearing a military cape with clouds and geese embroidered in gold,
A pair of green, wolf-skin boots,
He's superbly fitted out.
The scarlet turban
On his head
Is decorated profusely with pearls.

The Inebriated Tartar Woman

He wears two suits of armor.
His courage is unsurpassed—
Single-handedly he'd take on ten thousand foes.
He's nicknamed Flying Tiger Sun.

Coda

Carrying an iron-shafted crossbow,
A quiver with a hundred pairs of steel arrows,
He shoulders a mountain-cleaving ax as big as a winnowing fan.

[Prose]

> A moment ago this bandit held sway on the highway;
> Suddenly a challenger entered the chess game.[7]

(P'an-she-tiao mode)

A Pock-Marked Old Lady

> Flying Tiger is brave,
> Fa-ts'ung is stalwart.
> Flying Tiger likes to fight,
> Fa-ts'ung refuses to yield.
> Flying Tiger's out to sack the temple.
> Fa-ts'ung's determined to crush the rebels.
> Fa-ts'ung has a plan to subdue the insurgents,
> Flying Tiger has a scheme to overthrow the throne.
>
> Fa-ts'ung uses an iron cudgel,
> Flying Tiger uses a steel ax.
> One smites the monk with his ax,
> One attacks the Tiger with his cudgel.
> Flying Tiger excels in offensive jabs,
> Fa-ts'ung's superb with defensive parries.
> Fa-ts'ung has the upper hand,
> Flying Tiger tries to escape.

Coda

> Fa-ts'ung wins;
> Flying Tiger loses.
> Fa-ts'ung shouldn't have pursued—
> Flying Tiger draws his crossbow.

[Prose]

Fa-ts'ung thought he really had won, but actually Flying Tiger feigned defeat. Flying Tiger thrust his ax into the saddle, put his boots through the stirrups, and raised his dragon-tendon crossbow. He oiled the release and cranked the brass gear. Even in the wind his arrows could pierce an aspen tree from a hundred paces, so how could he possibly miss the seven-foot monk?[8]

---

7. Similar parallel-line descriptions occur frequently in Chinese stories of the Robin Hood type. The lines are inappropriate here as neither Fa-ts'ung nor Flying Tiger Sun is a highwayman. Master Tung seems to have simply borrowed them from the other tradition.

8. Earlier, Fa-ts'ung is said to be seven-and-a-half and eight feet tall. Such inconsistency is not infrequent in this medley.

(Cheng-kung mode)

Master Wen-hsü

> The general's flight
> Is a ruse.
> Fa-ts'ung shouldn't have given chase.
> In chasing
> He falls into a trap. . . .
> Pressing his feet on the stirrups,
> Flying Tiger rears nimbly.
> A clap of thunder—
> An arrow leaves the bowstring and
> Flies forward like a lightning bolt.

> Fa-ts'ung
> Sees this
> From afar.
> Truly a seasoned
> Fighter, he's
> Completely unruffled.
> With quick reflexes,
> He pulls at the reins,
> Leans forward on his saddle, and
> Halts his white-bellied bay.

Coda

> Opening wide his murderous eyes,
> He lifts, his *ta-chiang* whip.[9]
> Crash—the whip intercepts and breaks the arrow.

[Prose]

> An iron whip was raised: a great python leaped into the air.
> A steel arrow was blocked: a meteor plummeted to the ground.

The rebels were petrified. Flying Tiger said to them: "The monk has no armor. Although I failed to defeat him at close range, you can overpower him from where you are. If he chases after me again, shoot your arrows at him in unison; that will certainly finish him off."

Fa-ts'ung thought: "The bandits seem to have something up their sleeves. Moreover, my horse is exhausted and cannot fight on much longer." He told

---

9. "Beat-the-[opposing]-general whip." The term seems to be a coinage expressing the purported use of this weapon.

his followers: "Retreat and guard the temple: I shall break through the lines to carry out a plan I have."

(Chung-lü-tiao mode)

Catching a Snake in a Comical Way

> Looking ahead, Fa-ts'ung
> Sees a tremendous throng of rebels
> Brandish their spears and lances on the field
> In a threatening way.
> Before the ranks, a general sits on a stallion,
> An ax on his shoulder and
> A peevish scowl on his face.
>
> The rebels press forward to
> Cut at the passing monk.
> But every thrust is cleverly warded off.
> Fat-ts'ung is invulnerable.
> No one can match his skills.
> Flying Tiger despairs at his
> Dexterity, his sharp vision,
>   his ability to slither away and escape.

Coda

> The rebels muse:
> "Before we can stretch out our hands,
> This damned quick, shaven-headed criminal
> Has slipped by."

[Prose]

The fierce monk:

> Fighting singly,
> Is as brave as Hsiang Yü at Nine-Mile Mount.[10]
> Battling alone,
> Is as bold as Kuan Yü at White Horse Hill.[11]

He charges into the thick of Flying Tiger's troops without giving a thought to his life.

---

10. Hsiang Yü, the Prince of Ch'u (third century B.C.E.), contended for the throne against Liu Pang and was besieged by his enemies at Nine-Mile Mount, near present-day T'ung-shan district in Kiangsu.

11. Kuan Yü, a general of the third century C.E., slew his opponent Yen Liang in a battle at Pai-ma kang (White Horse Hill), near present-day Hua district in Honan.

(Hsien-lü-tiao mode)

Yi-hu-ch'a

> Though the rebels are numerous,
> They promptly fall back before the monk.
> They are like lambs confronting a tiger,
> Beasts surprised by a wolf.
> Their arrows are useless,
> The monk's cudgel is an impenetrable shield.
> Sky-rocking wails shoot up in the wake of his horse's hooves,
> Bile and blood splash on the dusty ground.
>
> In half an hour the monk breaks the lines;
> His fearlessness is truly magnificent.
> Covered with spilled blood—
> In emergencies certain things can't be helped—
> He looks like the monk of Yao-chou,
> After a bout with the fierce Scholar Meng.[12]
> Perhaps I shouldn't say this—he's exactly like
> A cock having just
> Emerged from a cunt.

[Prose]

Unable to defeat the rebels alone, Fa-ts'ung broke out through the enemy lines. The rebels then surrounded the temple and Flying Tiger Sun cried at the gate: "First, I want to give my men some food. Second, I know Madam Ts'ui and her family are here and I want Ying-ying. If you give her to me, we shall withdraw; otherwise, calamity will befall you this instant." His words were reported to the Ts'uis. Ying-ying was terrified.

(Ta-shih-tiao mode)

Jade-Winged Cicada

> Braving the lines, whipping his horse,
> Fa-ts'ung flees to the southwest.
> He hasn't time to worry
> That his followers
> Aren't protected
> By cuirasses or armor.
> The rebels shower arrows at them
> Without a moment's respite.

---

12. Apparently this alludes to a story popular in Tung's time. The story is no longer extant.

Of more than three hundred monks
Seventy or eighty percent are
Killed before they can knock on the temple gate.

A few senior monks
Die serenely from their wounds.
The prior is stricken by a sword;
His blood oozes through his muslin robe.
A number of injured cenobites,
Though at first buoyed up by the Buddha,
    are finally trampled to death by the horses.
One slow-moving priest,
Captured by a lieutenant,
Turns ashen
In fright,
Like a figure of wax.
From under the banners Flying Tiger bawled:
    "Drive him hither for interrogation."

Coda

The rebels think to drag him by the hair, but alas,
    his head has been shaved.
Pulling him by his mendicant robe,
They yank him toward their general's horse.

[Prose]

Flying Tiger asked: "Why do you refuse me a single meal?"

The monk replied: "The abbot was willing to invite you, but the superinten-dent argued that you might kidnap the beautiful Ying-ying who is keeping vigil in our temple over her deceased father, the late Prime Minister Ts'ui. He said that if this happened, there would be grave consequences as the minister had many influential friends."

Flying Tiger laughed: "What Fa-ts'ung just said was true, then; there really is a Ying-ying!"[13] He thought to himself: "Since Ting Wen-ya likes nothing better than wine and women, if I have Ying-ying put on makeup and a gorgeous dress, and offer her to Ting, I am sure he would be overjoyed. We can join forces to occupy the entire P'u area, and once this is done, we can defeat any troops the court may dispatch against us."

---

13. This is curious as nowhere has Fa-ts'ung mentioned the existence of Ying-ying. An exchange between Fa-ts'ung and Flying Tiger Sun might have been inadvertently left out by the copyist who made what was to become the origin of all existing editions of this medley.

(Cheng-kung-tiao mode)

Licorice Root

>Having heard the monk,
>Having heard the monk,
>Flying Tiger strokes his blond beard[14] and
>Relaxes his peevish frown.
>A few underlings transmit his order
>To the men to quicken their attack.
>He himself shouts at the gate:
>"Listen, you monks,
>Obey me and I'll withdraw; otherwise
>You'll have to suffer the consequence.

Removing the Cotton Garment

>"If you give me Ying-ying, I'll remove my troops;
>If not, I'll destroy you instantly.
>I've wasted enough time
>And enough words with you!

Coda

>"Even if your temple were wrapped in steel
>And couldn't be broached, I could always
>Block the gate and set it on fire."

[Prose]

The monks are frightened. Fa-pen takes the injured monks to Madam Ts'ui to tell her what has happened. When she hears the report, she faints. Alarmed, Hung-niang[15] and Ying-ying try to revive her. After a long time they succeed. Ying-ying weeps and says: "Please do not worry about me, Mother, as you have Father's coffin to care for. Allow me to give myself up to the rebels. Though I shall be humiliated, you will be left your remaining years, and the temple, the monks will likewise be spared. You must not let others be harmed just so that I may be saved from shame."

(Tao-kung mode)

Chieh-hung

>The sudden report
>Frightened Ying-ying's soul away from her body.
>"It seems inevitable that

14. Earlier, the beard is red (see p. 1166). Flying Tiger must be from northwest China and of Central Asian (Indo-European or Indo-Iranian) extraction.

15. Ying-ying's maid.

My family will be torn apart.
Father has died, and
While we mourn him, we're besieged by these rebels.
Alas,
Brother Huan-lang is still a boy. . . ."
Just then she heard strident voices
Clamor for her.
A thousand knives cut into her heart.
The widowed mother and her daughter
Had no place to seek help.

Ying-ying reflected on the situation:
"Only by a miracle
Could I escape.
As things stand,
There's little hope of that.
If I go with the rebels
Who'd care for
My aged mother?
This worries me even more.
Though the earth is wide, the sky is high, there's no shelter for me.
I'm completely at the mercy of a horde of bandits.
I can worry about neither chastity nor filial piety.
I must make clear to Mother
That if she tries to save me
There'll be three calamities:

Coda

"One, her life will be in danger;
Two, the monks will be killed;
Three, the magnificent temple will be burned."

[Prose]

Madam Ts'ui wept: "It is proper that a mother love her children with all her might, and it is natural that she care for them with the most profound affection. If you give yourself up to the rebels, what would be the good of my living on? I am sixty; if I die now I would have had a long life. But you are still young and unmarried. If you die, you would die a spinster, leaving no one behind." When she had finished, she let go of herself and wailed.

(Ta-shih-tiao mode)

Music for Returning to the Capital

Ying-ying and her mother
Held on to each other and cried.

Their loud wailing
Threw the monks into great confusion.
"It's more than likely that
Mother and I will both be killed this time.
I'd like to commit suicide,
But I'm afraid the rebels,
Frustrated in their desires,
Would burn the temple in revenge.
If I give myself up,
Posterity will learn of my shame;
Not only will I be
A laughing-stock for thousands of years to come,
My father's name will be disgraced as well.

"What am I
To do?
While Mother and the abbot
Discuss and ponder,
Some of the monks
Are urging reverently—
With touched palms—
For my delivery to the thieves.
It'd be difficult to dissuade them.
They're so insistent. . . .
All right, I will die, and
To appease
The rebels
My corpse can be offered
To their lawless swords.
They can strike me ten thousand times.
At least in death
My reputation will be intact!"

Coda

She lifted her gown and prepared to jump from the steps.
All became immobile, dazed with alarm—
Someone laughed and clapped his hands.

[Prose]

Fa-ts'ung's valor
Fails to defeat the rebels,
A weakling's plan
Succeeds in subduing the bandits.

Ying-ying was about to jump; she was about to jump! Madam Ts'ui and Hung-niang restrained her. Suddenly, peals of laughter were heard; everyone looked around. Who laughed?

(Huang-chung-kung mode)

Year of Happiness

> Ying-ying and her mother were beside themselves with anguish;
> Others shared their grief.
> Suddenly someone spoke out claiming that
> He could defeat the rebels.
> All turned and looked.
> A young scholar
> Matchless in beauty
> Emerged from the crowd of monks
>
> Over twenty years old,
> Five feet tall,
> Trim eyebrows, lovely eyes,
> Straight nose, strong teeth.
> His lips were red as rouge,
> His face, a luminous moon.
> Compared with him
> P'an An and Sung Yü [16] were ugly ruffians.

Dancers' Exit

> All recognized him to be Chang.
> A monk tugged at his robe and
> Whispered: "Young gentleman,
> This is not like chanting poetry in your study!
> You should've seen the rows and rows of rebels.
>
> "Are you mad or insane?
> How can you make good your boastful claim?
> You saw how hard Fa-ts'ung fought
> With Flying Tiger on the battleground.
> And even he had to flee before he was overcome.

Willow Leaves

> "Your muscles and bones are as delicate as a girl's,
> How can you wield a sword?
> You have no strength in your arms or legs,
> How can you ride a horse?

16. Epitomes of masculine beauty and literary talent.

"Your fingers are like bamboo shoots,
How can you let fly an arrow?
You are slight and frail,
How can you support a hauberk?

Coda

"Even holding a brush tires you out,
Yet you claim you can make the troops withdraw.
Tell me, what's your plan?"

[Prose]

Who laughed? Who laughed? Everyone looked around; it was Chang. Chang said: "Women have no presence of mind; whenever danger arises, they only weep. And you monks, you, too, have not been very resourceful. Obviously you have not come up with a way to deter the rebels; you merely wait to be slaughtered. But if you follow my suggestion, you can certainly defeat them." The abbot Fa-pen knew that Chang was endowed with a rare intelligence, so that he might well have an unusual plan. He went up to Chang and said: "Indeed we have no way to escape our predicament. Since you, sir, have an unusual scheme, please help us."

Chang smiled and replied: "You and your followers are disciples of the Buddha; do you not understand that life is the origin of death and death paves the way for your next life? Life and death are natural phenomena of human existence. Even Shakyamuni[17] himself had to die! Moreover, the concept of retribution is indigenous to Buddhism; it is expounded clearly in your scriptures. If, in your previous incarnation, you did evil to the bandits, it is natural that they should seek revenge now, and there is no escape for you. But, if, on the other hand, you never harmed them, then they are not your enemies in this life, and you have no reason to be afraid."

The abbot said: "You are quite right, sir. Actually, I only begrudge the destruction of our temple. When they were built, the gate, prayer halls, verandahs, bell towers, and library cost more than one million pieces of silver. A fire would reduce them to a heap of ashes. I wish that, just for the sake of accumulating merits, you would prevent this from happening."

Chang smiled even more broadly: "When you preach, reverend abbot, you explicate the *Diamond Sūtra*. You seem, however, to be ignorant that even our bones, our flesh, our skin and hair are not our own. Our spirit is our true self; our body is but a temporary abode. When death arrives, our spirit leaves, and the four elements which make up our body disintegrate. Those who are dearest to us, our wives and children, cannot follow us; possessions most

17. The historical Buddha.

precious to us, our gold and pearls, must be left behind. And now you manifest such a proprietary attachment to the prayer halls and bell towers!"

The abbot retorted: "True, true, we who preach the Dharma do not care whether we live or die, and we are actually quite indifferent to the destruction of a temple. But it does pain us to see a daughter forcibly taken away from her mother. It is only for this reason that I am asking for your help."

Chang then said: "Madam Ts'ui has never bestowed any kindness upon me, and I was not acquainted with the late minister. There has never been any communication between the Ts'ui family and me, so why should I save them?"

"If you do not save Ying-ying, and Madam Ts'ui refuses to surrender her, the enraged rebels will no doubt attack us with great force. What will *you* do then?"

"You need not worry about me, I can protect myself. You would do well to devise a way to protect *yourself*."

The abbot tried another tack: "You are a Confucian, sir, and you uphold the principle of charity and justice. A charitable person loves humanity and abhors that which threatens it; it thus follows that you would want to remove this present threat. An upholder of justice respects order and detests those who subvert it; so, clearly, you would want to dispel the unruly rabble. Now a young woman and her widowed mother are both at the point of committing suicide, yet you sit here and laugh at them. Is this a charitable person's manifestation of love for humanity? On a different plane, these mutinous soldiers have ruthlessly harried innocent people; you see it but make no attempt to curb them. Is this how an upholder of justice shows his respect for order? In antiquity, Duke Chung of Cheng did not restrain Shu-tuan when Shu-tuan behaved incorrectly as a younger brother;[18] the Marquis of Wei did not save the Marquis of Li when the latter was attacked by Ti barbarians;[19] they were both censured in the *Spring and Autumn Annals*. Sir, you have a scheme to repel the mutineers but you refuse to disclose it. Judged by the criterion implicit in *Spring and Autumn*, your conduct is greatly amiss. Decide for yourself whether I am right."

Chang smiled again and said: "Reverend abbot, your knowledge of Confucian teaching is indeed superficial. The Master once said: 'When a gentleman is brave but behaves improperly, confusion will result. When a small man is

18. Shu-tuan attempted to usurp the dukedom from his older brother Duke Chung, who for a long time took no action to stop him.

19. During the Spring and Autumn Era (770–481 B.C.E.) the state of Wei had hegemony for a time over nine other states of which Li was one; the Marquis of Wei was therefore bound by treaty to render whatever help he could to the Marquis of Li. When Ti barbarians invaded the state of Li, not only did the Marquis of Wei refuse to dispatch troops to expel the invaders, but he also treated the Marquis of Li shabbily when the latter fled to Wei.

brave but behaves improperly, banditry will result.' Thus, a gentleman shuns actions that are brave but lack propriety. In the present situation, although I am fearless, so long as the parties involved do not ask for it, it would be improper for me to offer help. Furthermore, the Master said: 'When propriety is observed, pupils seek their teachers; teachers do not go about looking for pupils.' Clearly, it is beneath a gentleman to recommend himself."

(P'an-she-tiao mode)

A Pock-Marked Old Lady

> Again and again the abbot tried to persuade Chang:
> "Sir, you're being perverse.
> Everyone is distressed
> But you; you're in high spirits."
> Chang laughed with glee:
> "Reverend teacher, how dense you are!
> Surely you must know, since it's recorded
>   in your Buddhist scriptures and not
> In my Confucian books:
>
> Where there is life, there is death;
> Only when birth desists will extinction cease!
> Death, like life, is part of human existence.
> It needn't be feared. . . .'
> There are more than five thousand rebels outside.
> But even if they were as fierce as the God of Water and the God of
>   Wrath,
> So long as I'm alive
> You'll not be captured.

Coda

> "I don't need to mount a horse,
> I don't need an inch of weapon,
> I don't need to fight in battles,
> One look from me will reduce the five thousand bandits
>   to messes of fat and blood."

[Prose]

When the abbot transmitted Chang's words to Madam Ts'ui, she replied: "Is that so?"[20] With decorum she introduced herself to Chang and said, sobbing:

(Hsiao-shih-tiao mode)

---

20. This, of course, refers to the previous prose passage in which Chang says that it is beneath a gentleman to recommend himself.

The Center of the Flower Moves

"The rebels
Demand my daughter Ying-ying, and
Whatever can we do?
We, piteous
Widow and orphan,
Put ourselves in your hands."
Chang responded with a smile:
"Honorable Madam, pray sit down.
Set your heart at ease.
There's nothing to fear.

"I'm not boasting;
I do have a plan which will
Defeat the rebels immediately.
The troops will withdraw,
The temple will stay intact,
The monks will be spared, and
You, your family and servants—all fifty of you—
Will not be hurt in any way. . . .
But when this is done
You mustn't start treating me like a stranger again."

[Prose]

Madam Ts'ui said: "Of course not, of course not; your apprehension is quite
unnecessary. I only hope you will not consider my offer unworthy: once the
catastrophe is averted and we are safe, I should like to have you as a son."[21]
(etc., etc.)[22]

Chang told the abbot: "Send a messenger to inform the rebels that Ying-
ying has agreed to their demand. She is taking leave of her mother and her
father's coffin, and making herself presentable. She will be ready in a moment.
Ask them to be patient and to please relax their attack somewhat."

The rebels slackened their harassment.

Chang then said: "Mutinous troops cannot be swayed with words; insurgent
hordes should not be tackled with mere force. They must be subdued by authority."

21. The term may mean making someone a son by giving him the hand of one's daughter,
or adopting someone as a son and hence making him the brother of one's daughter. The
ambiguity, fully intended by Master Tung, makes later events possible.
22. "Et cetera," and "and so forth," set in smaller print than the rest of the text is probably
meant to indicate to the performing singer-narrator that at this point he may or is expected to
add further elaboration.

The abbot and Madam Ts'ui asked simultaneously: "Who has authority?"

"I have a friend who was a Confucian scholar in his youth. Later, he distinguished himself in military campaigns and suppressed many rebellions. He has a just heart and an awe-inspiring countenance. When he was made a governor, all the thieves and brigands left his province. When he was appointed to the frontiers, barbarian horsemen ceased to encroach on our land. From these accomplishments one knows that he must be an invincible warrior replete with goodness and virtue, and that he must command devotion from the people and respect from his troops. Though his surname is Tu, and his given name Ch'üeh, people call him 'White Horse General,' since he often rides a white stallion on the battlefield. He is at present the Commanding General of P'u pass. And because of the unwavering loyalty his men have for him, no one has dared to offend him. General Tu and I are intimate friends, and I have here a draft of a letter addressed to him. Please read it, Madam."

In brief the letter said:

Your humble friend Chang Kung sends this missive to Your Excellency, the Commanding General:

In haste, I shall not embellish my prose; before Your Excellency, I shall come immediately to my entreaty. An unfortunate event has occurred: Marshal Hun of P'u prefecture recently passed away. His brigadier general, Ting Wen-ya, lost control of the troops, so that certain regiments mutinied and proceeded to ravage the countryside. As villages and towns are burned, moaning and wailing reverberate throughout the entire region. All citizens are threatened with death and torture; they are in desperate straits like a man hung from his heels. Your Excellency is blessed with unusual farsightedness; you are revered by all who know you. You are famous for your protection of the people and for your courage in combat. In face of the present upheaval, I know you will not stay behind in your fortress and allow the rebels to indulge their savagery. Indeed, Your Excellency seems the only one who can stop this menacing anarchy. Please make haste, since undue hesitation may cause widespread chaos. Once you come, you will easily destroy the rebel leaders and the rest will surrender; the people will be saved and peace will be restored. When the court hears of this, an imperial edict will commend you for your meritorious achievement. If, on the contrary, you refuse to dispatch your troops, then surely you will be censured for your cowardice. At present the insurgents have surrounded the Temple of Universal Salvation, and I have no way to escape. So it is with some urgency that I beseech you to serve your country and to save your unworthy friend. Trapped in the mouth of death I look forward eagerly to your reply. I shall be exceedingly grateful to you for vouchsafing me a second life.

Once again your humble friend Chang Kung salutes Your Excellency, the Commanding General.[23]

Translated by Li-li Ch'en

23. In the next chapter, we learn that Chang had already given a copy of the letter to Fa-ts'ung when he went forth to fight the rebels. After breaking through their lines, Fa-ts'ung gives the letter to General Tu. The latter arrives in due course with his troops who swiftly subdue the rebels.

270

The Story of How the Monk Tripiṭaka of the Great Country of T'ang Brought back the Sūtras

Anonymous (13th century?)

One: [Title missing]

[Chapter One is missing.]

Two: En Route They Encounter the Monkey Pilgrim [1]

The group of six monks began their journey that same day. The Dharma Master said: "Now we shall proceed to the West[2] traversing a million tricents. Let each of us be very careful." The lesser masters all responded affirmatively.

One day at about noon they were passing through a certain country when

The texts of this novelette were lost in China but two editions are mentioned in a catalog of the holdings of Kōzanji temple in Japan from 1633 and they are considered to have been in the country for some time even then. In the second decade of the twentieth century, two Chinese scholar expatriates, Wang Kuo-wei (see selection 147) and Lo Chen-yü, identified them as having been published during the Southern Sung dynasty. Modern Chinese editions of the two texts derive directly from copies brought back to China by Lo. Our text is based on the one considered to be the older of the two but is supplemented, when appropriate, by the other.

The story is definitely related to the great novel of the Ming dynasty, *Monkey* or *Journey to the West* (*Hsi-yu chi*, see selection 259). The two versions shared common characters and incident frames. Most notable are the Monkey Pilgrim and Deep Sand Demon; the references to the Pool of the Queen Mother of the West; and the visit to the Country of Women. This is the first extensive fictional treatment of Hsüan-tsang's travels to the Western Regions with his band of pilgrim disciples and may be regarded as the embryonic predecessor of the famous Ming novel.

1. "Pilgrim" might more literally be rendered as "novice monk," but the Chinese term in question, *hsing-che*, may also mean "itinerant [monk]."

2. More literally, "to the Western Paradise" or "India, [which lies in the] West."

they happened to see a scholar dressed in a white robe coming directly from the East. He greeted the monks: "Ten thousand blessings! Ten thousand blessings! Now, where are you monks bound for? Could it be that you're going to the West again to get the sūtras?"

The Dharma Master joined his palms in greeting and said: "This humble monk has a mission: since the sentient beings of the Eastern Lands are still ignorant of the Buddha's Law, I am to get the sūtras."

The scholar responded: "Reverend Monk, you have gone in two previous lives to get the sūtras and each time you have encountered difficulties along the way. If you are going again this time you will die a thousand deaths."

The Dharma Master asked: "How could you know this?" The scholar said: "I am none other than the bronze-headed, iron-browed king of the eighty-four thousand monkeys of the Purple Cloud Grotto on the Mountain of Flowers and Fruits. I have come now to help the reverend monk procure the sūtras. We shall traverse a million tricents and pass through thirty-six countries. There will be many places where we encounter difficulties."

The Dharma Master rejoined: "If this is so, one may deduce that there is a karma uniting the past, present, and future, and that the sentient beings of the Eastern Lands will reap great benefits."

At this point the Dharma Master began to refer to the scholar as Monkey Pilgrim.

The group of seven monks set out together the next day. Monkey Pilgrim helped them in every way and left us this poem:

> So many tricents of traveling to reach that side,
> I come now before the Dharma Master to help;
> With one mind/heart we seek the Buddha's true doctrine,
> Together we go to India's "Chicken Foot Mountain."[3]

The Dharma Master Tripiṭaka made a verse in reply:

> This day was predestined in previous lives,
> That this morning I should meet a great worthy;
> Though ahead may lie demon-infested places,
> I look to this godly manifestation to bring me to the Buddha.

Three: Entering the Palace of Mahābrahmā[4] Devarāja[5]

On the journey, when the Dharma Master arrived at the River of Scalding Water, he asked the Monkey Pilgrim: "How old are you?" "I have seen the

---

3. *Kukkuṭapāda.*
4. "Great Brahmā," king of the eighteen Brahmalokas (heavens of form).
5. "Heavenly King."

Yellow River clear nine times," answered Pilgrim. The Dharma Master couldn't help smiling, then he said with great surprise: "A youngster like you and already telling lies?"

Pilgrim replied: "I am young, but I have lived through thousands of generations. I know that your reverence went twice in previous lives to get the sūtras in India and met disaster along the way. Do you remember where you died twice before, reverend sir?" The Master replied that he did not, and Pilgrim continued: "At that time your reverence was not yet fully knowledgeable of the Buddha's Dharma; your karma was not yet complete and hence these things happened to you."

The Dharma Master said: "If you have seen the Yellow River clear nine times, you must know about Heaven and Hell?" Pilgrim replied: "How could I not know about them?" The Dharma Master asked: "What's happening up in heaven today?" Pilgrim said: "Today Vaiśravana[6] of the North, the Mahābrahmā Devarāja, is offering a maigre feast in his Crystal Palace." "May I go along to attend the maigre feast with your mighty assistance?" the Dharma Master asked.

Pilgrim ordered the monks to close their eyes. Then he made magic spells. Quite a long time passed before they opened their eyes again, and all seven of them were in the Palace of Mahābrahmā Devarāja of the North.

They saw thousands of fragrant flower arrangements, and vegetarian dishes and fruits of myriad kinds. Drums resounded sonorously and there was a loud clatter of "wooden fishes" being struck. Five hundred arhats,[7] their eyebrows reaching down to the corners of their mouths,[8] were all assembled in the palace listening attentively to the various Buddhas lecturing on the Dharma.

Suddenly the assembly were aware of the scent of human beings, and the Mahābrahmā Devarāja asked: "Why do we smell this vulgar odor of human beings?" A venerable arhat replied: "Today the monk Hsüan-tsang from the great country of T'ang in the world below has come to the maigre feast in the Crystal Palace with his six companions and hence there is this human odor."

Thereupon Mahābrahmā Devarāja said to the arhats: "This man was a monk in three incarnations. He is proficient in the Buddha's teachings."

Then Hsüan-tsang, the Dharma Master from the mundane world, was invited to ascend the platform and to lecture on the sūtras. He was asked to mount the crystal pulpit, but he could not. An arhat said: "No mortal can

6. One of the four Buddhist Lokapāla, Guardians of the Four Quarters, but here he is being casually identified with Mahābrahmā, king of a group of gods in the Brahmaloka, who derives from the chief of the Hindu pantheon.

7. Saints.

8. Indicative of great age.

ascend that pulpit. Let him mount the incense platform." This was easily accomplished.

The arhats said: "We thank the Master for coming to the palace today. Does the master excel in explaining sūtras?" Hsüan-tsang replied: "If it is a sūtra, I can explain it. If it is not, I do not." "Can you explain the *Lotus Sūtra?*" the arhat asked. Hsüan-tsang replied: "That's easy."

Thereupon the five hundred arhats, the Mahābrahmā Devarāja, and in all a company of over a thousand gathered to listen to the sūtra. Hsüan-tsang recited flawlessly without pausing for breath. Like pouring water from a vase, he clarified the obscurities of the text. Everyone praised his marvelous delivery.

When the feast was over and all were taking their leave, the arhats said: "The reverend monk has twice gone to India in search of the sūtras, but because he was not thoroughly versed in the Buddha's Way he was swallowed up each time by the Spirit of the Deep Sand and lost his life. Now, fortunately, he has been able to come to this palace and, through the intercession of Devarāja, he can go forward by appealing to the Buddha's Dharma and avoid many calamities."

The Dharma Master and Monkey Pilgrim approached the Devarāja and begged for his help. The Devarāja granted them a cap of invisibility, a golden-ringed staff, and a begging-bowl. After accepting these three boons, the Dharma Master said farewell, then turned to the Monkey Pilgrim and asked: "How can we get back to the mortal world?" Pilgrim replied: "Before the Dharma Master speaks of returning to the world below, he had better ask the Devarāja how we can save ourselves from the monsters and disasters which lie ahead of us." The Dharma Master returned to Mahābrahmā and asked as Monkey had suggested. The Devarāja responded: "When you meet calamity, point toward the Heavenly Palace from afar and shout 'Devarāja' once, and you will be saved." The Dharma Master accepted his instructions and bowed farewell.

Monkey Pilgrim and the Master took leave of the five hundred arhats and the Taoist adepts who had come to the gathering. At this time the arhats all came out to see the Dharma Master and his company off, and prayed that he might get the sūtras and one day soon return to their midst. Then, joining their palms, the arhats made a short hymn of praise:

> The Crystal Palace feast is over, swiftly we return;
> Unfolding our arms, we easily follow the wind.
> Yet know our brotherhood of five hundred
> Once walked afoot in the world of men.

The Dharma Master gave a poem in reply:

Sentient beings of the Eastern Lands, lacking the Buddha's karma,
With one heart/mind pray that we not delay our quest;
In the Heavenly Palace we were granted three boons,
To become our precious jewels for quelling demons on the road ahead.

Four: Entry in Incense Mountain⁹ Temple

On their meandering journey they came to Incense Mountain. It was the land of the "Thousand-armed Thousand-eyed Bodhisattva"¹⁰ and was also the place where the Bodhisattva Mañjuśrī perfected himself. When the travelers looked up, they saw a plaque with an inscription: "Incense Mountain Temple." The Dharma Master and Monkey Pilgrim could not resist going through the gate to rest. On either side of the entrance were hoary guardian gods with fierce demeanor and commanding awe. As the Dharma Master looked at them he began to sweat with fear; the hairs of his body stood out like barbs.

Monkey Pilgrim said: "Let's go in and look around, Master." They went in and came to the main hall. No one was there. There was nothing but an ancient, empty hall with soaring hiproofs, grasses growing in profusion, and a soughing wind. The Dharma Master was startled at the desolation. Monkey Pilgrim knew what the master was thinking, so he said: "Don't be alarmed, Master, at the desolation of the Western Route. This is a different world, after all. What lies ahead are places peopled by tigers, wolves, snakes, and rabbits. We will not be able to speak with the people whom we meet and there will be myriad kinds of terror. From here on, in all the human settlements, there is only heterodoxy." The master heard this and bowed his head with a grim smile. They walked through the temple grounds, looking around, then exited from the opposite side.

They traveled another hundred tricents and Monkey Pilgrim said: "Master, the land which lies beyond is the Snake Country." And indeed, they saw snakes of all sizes coiling together in a numberless mass of confusion. The larger snakes had heads over sixteen feet high; those of the smaller snakes were over eight feet high. Their glaring eyes and ferocious fangs were like lanterns and spears. They exhaled fiery breath. When the Dharma Master saw this sight, he fell back with fright. "Don't be afraid, Master," said Monkey Pilgrim. "This is called the Country of Snakes, and there are lots of snakes of various sizes here. But none of the snakes here are vicious, because they all possess the Buddha nature. They won't injure anybody or anything." The Dharma Master said: "If that is so, I shall not fear and will rely on the awesome might of my little disciple." And he advanced.

When the large and small snakes saw the file of seven advance, they

9. Gandhamādana.
10. The compassionate savior, Avalokiteśvara (Kuan-yin).

completely cleared the road. Closing their eyes and lowering their heads, they indicated their obeisance while the men passed by. They harmed no one.

On the pilgrims went for some forty tricents, passing through the snake territory. Then Monkey Pilgrim said: "Tomorrow we shall pass through Lion Wood and Tree People countries." The Dharma Master said: "Speak no more of it! Let us only pray that we get safely through." The seven paused to rest, their sweat poring down them like rain. The Dharma Master composed a poem:

> We passed through the territory of snakes several tens of tricents;
> The pure dawn rose on the lonely Incense Mountain.
> Ahead lie demons and troubles
> As we seek for sentient beings the Buddha's truth.

Five: Passing the Lion Wood and the Country of Tree People

Arising early, the seven went perhaps ten tricents when Monkey Pilgrim announced: "Master! Ahead lies the Lion Wood." Before he finished speaking they arrived at the Lion Wood. There they saw coming out of the woods to receive them unicorns rushing forward speedily and towering lions waving their heads and swinging their tails in majestic roars. In their mouths were fragrant flowers which they brought to express their devotion. Joining his palms, the Dharma Master went forward to meet them. The lions raised their heads in greeting. For more than fifty tricents, there were unicorns everywhere. Then they came to a forsaken place. There the Dharma Master said farewell to the Lion King.

Monkey Pilgrim said: "Master, ahead of us lies the country of the Tree People." After they entered that country, there were only withered thousand-year-old trees, ageless rocks, pines and cypresses like dragons, contorted rock forms like tigers. They observed that in the middle of the mountains was a village temple, but there seemed to be no monks there. All they saw were roosters that seemed like phoenixes and mountain dogs that seemed like dragons. Outside the gate was a pair of golden bridges. Beneath the bridges was a gilded stream. They watched the red sun set in the west, but found no place for travelers to stay. Monkey Pilgrim said: "Let us go on. Let us not be afraid!" On they went for fifty or sixty tricents until they found a small inn. And there they spent the night, all seven of them.

The next morning the seven stretched and yawned: "This is really a strange place for us to have spent the night!" A disciple was sent to buy some food for breakfast. The innkeeper said: "There are sorcerers hereabouts. Come back soon!" The Dharma Master was unconvinced. The little disciple went to buy the food but had still not returned by noon. The Dharma Master said: "I'm worried! My little disciple went to buy food and hasn't returned yet. It's already noon! Could it be that he has really been bewitched by some sorcerer of these parts?" Monkey Pilgrim replied: "Wait while I go and look around myself, all right?" The Dharma Master replied: "Very good! Very good!"

Monkey Pilgrim went several tricents, asking along the way, until he saw a dwelling. A fishing boat was moored to a tree, and outside the door hung a straw raincoat. But the little disciple had been magically transformed into a donkey and was tethered at the front of the cottage. When the donkey saw Monkey Pilgrim coming, he gave a long, drawn-out "hee-haw!" Monkey Pilgrim said to the owner of the cottage: "Did one of our little disciples who went out to buy food pass by here?" The owner of the cottage replied: "This morning a little disciple came here. I used magic to turn him into a donkey. You see him here." Monkey Pilgrim immediately became very angry. Now, the cottager had a new bride and, though she was just sixteen, she was very beautiful and fetching in her demeanor. She was more lovely than the fabled Hsi-shih. Monkey Pilgrim worked his own magic and transformed the woman into a bundle of green grass which he placed beside the donkey's mouth. The cottager asked: "Where did my new bride go?" Monkey Pilgrim replied: "She is that bundle of grass by the donkey's mouth." The cottager said: "So you too practice sorcery? I didn't think anyone else could do this. Now, sir, I beg of you to bring back my new bride!" Monkey Pilgrim replied: "You bring back my little disciple at the same time." The cottager blew some water out of his mouth and the donkey became a disciple once again. Monkey did the same thing and the bundle of green grass became a woman.

Monkey Pilgrim said: "My master and six monks will pass through here soon. Don't you dare use sorcery on them. If you do, I shall have to mow down all the grass of your house." The cottager came forward and bowed: "I will not dare to disobey." Trembling in fright, he made a poem of apology:

> The disciple from morning until now
> Was a donkey changed by sorcerer's art;
> From today I raise my hands in praise of the arhat
> To avert calamity from my door.

Thereupon Monkey Pilgrim left behind a poem:

> Don't use sorcery to harm travelers!
> I have seen the Yellow River clear nine times.
> When next my master comes this way,
> Be honestly sincere and welcome him.

Six: Passing Long Ditch and Great Serpent Peak

The pilgrims arrived at the valley of the fire-spitting White Tiger Spirit. Coming closer they encountered a great ditch. The four steep entrances were pitch-black and they heard a roar of thunder. They could not advance. The Dharma Master held up his golden-ringed staff and, flourishing it toward the distant heavenly palace, yelled: "Devarāja! Help us in our afflictions!" Suddenly a shaft of light shot out from the staff five tricents long. It slashed through the long ditch and soon they were able to get across.

Next they came to Great Serpent Peak. There they saw a gigantic serpent like a dragon. It likewise was not harmful to humans. Then they crossed the pit of the fire-spitters. Down, down into the fiery pit they looked and saw a pile of dry bones over forty tricents long. The Dharma Master asked Monkey Pilgrim: "What are those white withered bones piled up there like snow on a mountain?" Monkey Pilgrim replied: "This is the place where the Heir Apparent, Ming Huang ('Brightly August'), changed his bones." The Dharma Master, hearing this, joined his palms and bowed his head in reverence.

Next they suddenly came to a prairie fire which reached to the heavens. It sent off such a huge amount of smoke and sparks that the pilgrims could not proceed. The Dharma Master shone the light of his begging-bowl toward the fire and yelled: "Devarāja!" The fire died out immediately and the seven pilgrims crossed this pit. When they were halfway across, Monkey Pilgrim said: "Master, did you know this peak is inhabited by a white tiger spirit? It often appears as a vixen, demon, or goblin and even eats people." The Master replied: "I didn't know!" After a while they could see a spume of ominous-looking smoke rising behind the peak and from the cloud thus formed fell a mixture of rain, snow, and sleet. In the cloudy mist there was a woman dressed all in white.

She wore a white bodice of gauze, a white gauze skirt with a white belt, and held in her hands a single white peony. Her face was as pretty as a white lotus, her ten fingers like precious jades. Observing the form of the ogress, Monkey Pilgrim had his suspicions confirmed. "Master, don't go any farther," said Monkey Pilgrim. "It's surely an ogress. Wait till I go up and ask who she is." Monkey Pilgrim took one look at her and shouted in a loud voice: "What place are you from, demon? What shape is beneath your facade? If you are a sprite or a goblin, why don't you hurry back to your lair? If you are an ogress, hurriedly hide your traces. But, if you are the daughter of a human being, then tell me your name and surname. And be quick about it! If you procrastinate and don't speak, I shall reduce you to dust and powder!" Hearing the pilgrim's ferocious tone of voice, the white-clad woman slowly advanced, smiled coyly, and inquired whither the master and his disciples were going. Monkey Pilgrim said: "Ask no more! We travel for the sake of the sentient beings of the Eastern Lands. And you must be none other than the White Tiger Spirit of the Fire-spitting Pit."

Hearing this, the woman's mouth gaped open and she screamed loudly, while at the same moment her skin burst open revealing claws, long fangs, a tail, and a feline head. She was fifteen feet long. In another instant the whole mountain was filled with white tigers. Monkey Pilgrim transformed his golden-ringed staff into a gigantic yakṣa[11] whose head touched the sky and whose feet straddled the earth. In his hands he grasped a demon-subduing cudgel. His body was blue as indigo, his hair red as cinnabar; from his mouth a fiery gleam shot forth a hundred yards long. At the same time, the White Tiger Spirit advanced with a roar to do battle, but she was repulsed by the Monkey Pilgrim. After a short while, Monkey Pilgrim asked if the tiger spirit was ready to submit. She replied, "Never!" Monkey said: "If you will not submit, you will find an old monkey in your stomach!"

The tiger spirit heard what he said yet did not surrender right away. But no sooner had he yelled "Monkey!" than a monkey in the White Tiger Spirit's stomach responded. The tiger spirit was forced to open her mouth and spit out the monkey. When it landed on the ground in front of her, it became twelve feet long with flashing eyes. The White Tiger Spirit spoke: "I still will not submit!" Monkey replied: "Then you will find another in your stomach!" Again, he caused the tiger spirit to open her mouth and spit out another monkey which landed in front of her. And again the tiger spirit said: "I still do not submit!" Monkey replied: "There are countless old monkeys in your stomach now, and even if you spit them out all day today until the next, all this month until the next, all this year until the next, all this life until the next, you will not be rid of them!" This made the tiger spirit angry. She was again afflicted by Monkey when he transformed himself into a great stone in her stomach which gradually grew in size. Though she tried to spit it out, she couldn't. Her stomach split asunder and blood poured from her seven orifices.[12] Monkey called upon the yakṣa to slaughter the big White Tiger Spirit ruthlessly, and the yakṣa pulverized its bones and obliterated its last vestiges.

The monk pilgrims, having withdrawn their magic, rested for a time before resuming the journey. They left a poem:

> The pit of fire-spitters and the White Tiger Spirit,
> All that lot are vanquished, and peace and safety reign.
> Now, the supernatural power of Monkey Pilgrim is displayed,
> Protecting the monkish pilgrims across the great ditch.

Seven: Entering Nine Dragon Pond

They proceeded to Nine Dragon Pond. Monkey Pilgrim said: "Look, Master! This is the abode of the nine-headed lizard-dragons. They often cause mischief and harm humans. Be careful, Master!" Suddenly, vast stretches of nasty waves reared up and white foam thundered endlessly. For a thousand tricents

---

11. Demon.
12. Two eyes, two ears, two nostrils, one mouth.

of raven river flowed myriad ranks of black combers. There were the nine-headed dragons roaring, their fiery whiskers shooting out rays of light as they advanced. Monkey Pilgrim transformed the cap of invisibility into a curtain which obscured the sky, and sucked all the thousand tricents of water into the begging-bowl. Then he transformed the magic staff into an iron dragon. Regardless of night or day the two sides fought. Monkey Pilgrim straddled the nine-headed dragons. "I want to pull out the sinews from your spine to present to my master as a belt." The nine dragons surrendered. All had the sinews of their spines pulled out and all suffered in addition eight hundred blows with the iron cudgel on their backs. "From now on, be good; and if you resume your former bad actions, you will all be annihilated." The dragons were exhausted half to death. They hid their traces and disappeared. Monkey Pilgrim braided a belt from the sinews and gave it to the Dharma Master to tie around his waist. As soon as the Master of the Law put it on, he could walk as fast as flying, and when he came to any difficult place, he would leap over it. The dragons' sinews were possessed of supernatural power. With them one could assume any shape. Later, when Tripiṭaka returned to the Eastern Lands the belt went back up of its own accord to the Heavenly Palace. This is what monks nowadays refer to as "watered-satin-brocade fabric." With it, the Master of the Law did many wondrous things. There is a poem:
[Poem missing.]

Eight: [Title Missing.]

[First Part Missing]
". . . what sort of creature I am?" The reply was: "I do not." Deep Sand said: "I am the one who devoured you twice before, monk. Slung from my neck are all your dry bones!" The monk said: "You are most unenlightened! If you don't reform this time, I shall cause you and your lot to become extinct!" Deep Sand joined his palms in reverence and begged forgiveness and mercy. While Deep Sand howled, Tripiṭaka was alarmed. The only thing he could see was red dust whirling in profusion and white snow swirling. After quite a while, he saw a few rays of light. Deep Sand roiled higher, and a sound like thunder roared. In the distance could be seen a golden bridge with two silver rails along its sides. All along it was the spirit of Deep Sand whose body stretched thirty feet and who held it steady with his arms. The Master and the seven pilgrims crossed over the sandy depths on the golden bridge.

Deep Sand Spirit joined his palms and saw them on their way. The Dharma Master said: "Thank you for your help. When I return to the Eastern Lands I shall repay your kindness. But don't do any more evil from now on." The kindred spirits on both sides joined palms and bowed, repeatedly voicing their acquiescence.

Deep Sand came forward and chanted a poem:

> I have been submerged in the deep sand for five hundred springs;
> My relatives have suffered many calamities.
> My two arms embracing the golden bridge allow the master to pass;
> I beg him to intercede for the liberation of this dark spirit.

The Dharma Master replied with his own poem:

> Twice have I been devoured by you.
> I see my withered bones and ask their former shapes,
> But I shall free you now to live out your remaining years,
> And count you among my own in the Eastern Lands.

Monkey Pilgrim's poem said:

> Thank you for your change of heart—away from deviancy.
> Your golden bridge with silver has let us pass in peace;
> When we return to the Eastern Lands and perfect ourselves,
> I'll recommend you, Deep Sand, to the Buddha himself.

Nine: Entering the Country of Hārītī [13]

On they traveled for several tens of tricents. Human habitations were rare and inns were few. Crossing a mountain they found the going rough, almost impossible. No birds flew there in that place nor did they know what lay therein.

They came upon a main road but still they saw no one. Another hundred tricents they went without a sign of dwellings or shops.

There was a country which they entered and they saw an abandoned temple devoid of monks. On the city streets they encountered a few people whom they asked: "Where are we?" But the people spoke not a word, much less replied to their questions. Seeing this, the Dharma Master became alarmed. The band of seven found a place to stay.

The next day at dawn they sought unsuccessfully to buy some rice. Though they asked people, they received no reply. They went from one end of the town to the other and entered all the buildings. All they saw were myriads of three-year-old children. As soon as the king of that land saw the Dharma Master and his band, he expressed great devotion. The entire country burned incense and came out to welcome them. The king inquired: "Monk, where do you wish to go?" The Dharma Master replied: "For the sake of the sentient beings of the Eastern Lands, we go to India to seek the sūtras." The king was delighted to hear this and, palms joined in piety, he donated to them a picul

---

13. Hārītī is her Sanskrit name. Her Chinese name means "Mother of Ghostly Children." Converted to Buddhism, she becomes a protectress of the faith.

of rice, a bushel of pearls, two thousand gold pieces, and two bundles of embroidered cloth to offset the expenses of their journey. He also ordered a vegetarian feast which was excellent in every way. The pilgrim band of seven thanked the king profusely for his generosity.

The king asked: "Have you known of our country?" The Dharma Master replied: "No, your majesty." The king continued: "We are not far from India." The Dharma Master asked further: "Your majesty, how is it that the people here seem so insensitive? We addressed numerous people in our progress through the city, but not a single one replied. Moreover, there were no adults, only three-year-olds. Why should there be countless children and no parents?" The king laughed: "My dear monk, in your westward travels, has no one ever told you of the country of Hārītī ('Mother of Ghostly Children')?" When he heard this, the Dharma Master was astonished: "You mean that we seven have been talking to ghosts?" The king continued: "I pray you meet with no calamities on your journey. On your return please stop with us again for refreshment." The Dharma Master and his companions were embarrassed. They made a poem which they left behind:

> Who would have known this was the country of Hārītī?
> Just when we were famished we were given a monkish feast,
> And pearls and rice for our travel expenses;
> We shall fetch sūtras to repay our debt of gratitude.

The Hārītī side gave a poem also:

> Inns are far and few hereabouts;
> One asks passersby, but there is no reply.
> From here you can almost see India to the west,
> But keep your heart and person as pure as water.
>
> Rise early, retire late, and praise the Buddha;
> At dawn and dusk, pray and burn incense.
> Returning from fetching sūtras you'll surely pass by here,
> Then we shall meet you with respect and have you stay a few days.

Ten: Passing Through the Country of Women

The whole troop of monks arrived and took a bath, cleansing their bodies. The place was totally desolate and no habitation could be seen. Though there were tigers, wolves, and reptiles there, when they saw humans they presented no harm whatsoever.

Next there was a country where there were no people at all, but only broken-down houses and dilapidated fences about. They walked a bit farther and gradually began to see a few farmers tilling their fields and planting grain. The Dharma Master said: "Although this area has the look of a settled place that is divided into provinces and counties, doubtless there are but few people. Up till now these four or five farmers are the only people we have seen." When the farmers saw the pilgrims, they looked at each other in surprise. The Dharma Master made a poem:

> Desolate provinces, deserted counties—no place of habitation;
> Day after day we monks walk and at night sleep on the ground.
> The farmers we saw today are rare sights to this monk's eyes,
> So that finally he can smile a little bit.

Monkey Pilgrim's poem went:

> Say no more of empty lands and people-less places;
> If these districts were deserted, who would till them?
> Master does not know about the human labor of tilling fields.
> This Prince lives at West City Wall;
> Mornings he comes to work the fields,
> Evenings he spends in a Heavenly Palace, resting in cavernous halls.
> Continuing our journey on the road ahead, we succumb to no other desire,
> And avoid troubled thoughts of the Eastern Land, awaiting our return.

They continued their journey with increased speed until they came to a torrent whose waters were in flood. The Dharma Master was perplexed. Monkey Pilgrim said: "You have only to ask permission to proceed and it will be granted!" "Devarāja!" With that one shout of the pilgrim, the waters of the river ceased flowing and the waves dried up in their course. The master and his band walked across joining their palms in veneration. It was for good karma in a previous life that Heaven aided him now.

Continuing their travels, they encountered another barren land. Onward they marched for several tens of tricents and then rested at a village. The Dharma Master remarked: "Up ahead there is no sign of human habitation. What place could it be?" Monkey Pilgrim replied: "I have gone ahead and investigated. There's no need for sighs of apprehension."

After another hundred tricents, they came to a country which was bristling with people and trade. When they entered the country, they saw a sign over a gate: "Country of Women." The pilgrims asked permission to have audience with the queen. The queen asked them: "How is it that you monks have come here?" The Dharma Master replied: "We received a command from the T'ang emperor to come to the West and fetch sūtras to create fields of blessing for the sake of all sentient beings of the Eastern Lands." The queen joined her palms and, out of devotion, ordered a vegetarian feast prepared. The pilgrims all sat down to the feast but were unable to eat anything. The queen inquired: "Why do you not eat the food?" The pilgrims rose and respectfully replied: "We thank your majesty for giving us this feast. But since there is so much sand in it, the food will not go down." The queen said: "Permit me to inform you, oh monk, that our country had none of the five grains. They only began to grow when Buddhists from the Eastern Lands came and prepared vegetarian feasts. Since the grain is all gathered from a few places in the land, that is why there is so much sand. When you monks return to the Eastern Lands, I pray you will have some grain sent to us!" The Dharma Master rose and left a poem:

> Although the queen had the intention to offer a pure feast,
> Too much sand made it hard to swallow;
> On the day we return from fetching sūtras in India,
> We will instruct the Eastern Lands to make grain offerings for you.

After seeing the poem, the queen invited Dharma Master and his band to the inner palace for rewards. Upon entering, the monkish pilgrims observed that fragrant flowers were everywhere heaped up like the seven precious things. Sixteen-year-old maidens stood in two ranks. They were very beautiful. Their eyes were like stars, eyebrows like willow fronds, lips like vermilion, teeth like pomegranates, cheeks like peaches, hair like cicada's wings. Their garments sparkled. Their words were soft. Indeed they were entirely unlike ordinary mortals. As soon as they saw the monkish pilgrims enter, all began to smile, and looking shyly up from lowered eyes darkened with kohl, they advanced and bowed in greeting: "Reverend sirs, this is the Country of Women. There are no males here. Now that we have seen you pilgrims, we shall have a temple constructed here and invite you seven to live in it. Further, all the women of our country will come to the temple morning and night, offer incense, and hear sūtras to learn about the law of the Buddha. Many seeds of goodness can be planted. And at the same time the women will be able to see their predestined husbands. How does your reverence feel about this?" The Dharma Master replied: "I serve the sentient beings of the Easter Lands; how could we remain here in a temple?" The queen responded: "Reverend sir, my dear brother, have you not heard the saying of the ancients: 'Man only passes through this world once in this life'? Moreover, if you stay here you shall become our ruler. Would that not be a pleasantly romantic life?"

The monk firmly refused and prepared to leave. The two ranks of women wept pearly tears and knitted their darkened brows in perplexity. They said to one another: "After they leave, when will we ever see men again?"

The queen took five night-shining pearls and a white horse, and gave them to the monks for use on their journey. The monkish pilgrims joined their palms and expressed their thanks. They left a poem:

> We pray your majesty to preserve your goodness;
> How long does the illusive, ephemeral world abide?

If one does not realize the vanity of mundane thoughts,
One may spend a thousand kalpas[14] in the depths of Avīci[15] Hell.
Dote not on raven tresses and peach-blossom faces;
Dawdle not with love of pretty figures and oriole brows.
When the great limit of life approaches, where can we hide,
And where shall our skeletons have need of garments?

The queen and the assembled women scattered fragrant flowers for the Master and his pilgrim band as they left the city. A poem says:

This land is a separate world of fairies,
Who send you on your way to India;
If you would know the queen's name and surname.
She is none other than Mañjuśrī Samantabhadra.[16]

Eleven: Entering the Pool of the Queen Mother

They had traveled onward several hundred more tricents when the Dharma Master involuntarily gasped. Monkey Pilgrim remarked: "Master, keep going a little longer. Just fifty tricents ahead is the pool of the Queen Mother of the West." The Dharma Master inquired: "Have you ever been there?" Monkey Pilgrim replied: "When I was eight hundred years old, I went there and stole some peaches that I ate. Now I'm twenty-seven thousand years old and I haven't been back since." The Dharma Master noted: "I hope that if the peaches of immortality are ripe now you could steal a few for us to eat." Monkey Pilgrim replied: "Because I stole ten peaches to eat when I was eight hundred years old, I was captured by the Queen Mother and given eight hundred blows on my left side and three thousand blows on the right with an iron cudgel. Then I was exiled to the Purple Cloud Grotto on the Mountain of Flowers and Fruits. Even today my sides hurt and now I definitely don't dare to steal any more peaches!" The Dharma Master responded: "This pilgrim is a Taoist immortal from the highest heaven. First he told us he had seen the Yellow River clear nine times and I was going to say he was lying. Now I hear him say he came to this place when he was young to steal peaches and I suppose it's the truth."

As they proceeded, they suddenly saw an enormous rock cliff towering ten thousand fathoms and in another glance they saw a stone platter which was four or five tricents across. And there were two pools which were tens of tricents around their rectangular perimeters. They contained vast amounts of water and no birds flew over them. No sooner had the band of seven sat down

14. Eras.
15. The lowest of the eight great *naraka* ("hot hells"); the hell of uninterrupted suffering.
16. The names of two Bodhisattvas (saviors).

and were just relaxing than their gazes wandered up the face of the immense rock wall. Far above they could see a number of peach trees which showed glistening colors amid their dark foliage. Their tops touched the azure heavens; the leaves of their heavily laden branches floated on the surface of the pool. The Dharma Master exclaimed: "Aren't these the peaches of immortality?" Monkey Pilgrim cautioned: "Please speak softly. No shouting. This is the pool of the Queen Mother. When I was young I played the thief here, and I still feel fear." The Dharma Master said: "Why not just go and steal one?" Monkey Pilgrim replied: "These peach trees sprout a thousand years after planting. They blossom in three thousand years and produce a fruit in ten thousand years. The fruit requires ten thousand more years to ripen. He who eats one gains three thousand years of life." The Master remarked: "No wonder you're so long-lived!" Monkey Pilgrim continued: "There are more than ten peaches on the tree now, but there are gods of the earth who are posted here especially to protect them. There is no way to steal the peaches." The Master teased: "Your supernatural powers are stupendous. If you were to go, what could prevent you?" Before his words were finished three peaches of immortality fell down into the pool. The Master was startled by the splash and he asked: "What fell down?" Monkey Pilgrim replied: "Don't be alarmed, Master. It was just a few ripe peaches of immortality which fell into the pool." The Master said: "Can we find them and eat them?"

Monkey Pilgrim took the golden-ringed staff and shook it three times in the direction of the huge, flat stone. A small child with a greenish face appeared. His fingernails were as sharp as a hawk's claws and from his gaping mouth the teeth showed as he emerged from the pool. Pilgrim asked: "How old are you?" The child answered: "Three thousand years." Pilgrim replied: "I have no use for you." Again he rapped five times and a child appeared whose face was as round as the full moon. He wore embroidered clothes and a headdress with tassels. Pilgrim asked: "How old are you?" The child replied: "Five thousand years." Pilgrim replied: "I will not use you." And once more he rapped several times with the staff. Another child appeared all of a sudden. Monkey Pilgrim asked: "How old are you?" "Seven thousand years," the child replied. Pilgrim put down the golden-ringed staff and made the child get on his hand. Then he asked: "Monk! Will you eat this?" The monks were terrified and fled. Pilgrim whirled his hand with the child in it a number of times and the child became a milky jujube which he popped into his mouth.

Later, when the pilgrims were returning to the T'ang court of the Eastern Lands, Monkey spit out the seed at Hsi-ch'uan,[17] and to this day ginseng grows there.

A figure appeared in the sky and recited this poem:

17. Western Szechwan.

A youngster from the Mountains of Flowers and Fruits
Came here and misbehaved once upon a time;
And now our heavenly ears hear a familiar voice,
The former thief has come once again.

Twelve: Entering the Country of Heavy Scent

The Master and his disciples continued onward and suddenly saw a place with
a sign saying: "Country of Heavy Scent." All they saw were aloe trees stretching
in rows for tens of thousands of tricents. Large and small, they were everywhere and there were oldsters whose branches touched the clouds high above.
Tripiṭaka said: "There wouldn't be forests like this in our land of T'ang, I
suppose?" He then left behind a poem:

> This country called Heavy Scent supports no human race,
> High and low the forest's emerald tops stretch on for thousands of rods;
> Farther on we'll come to the country of Vara,[18]
> As on we march to India in the west to fetch the Buddhist sūtras.

Thirteen: Entering the Country of Vara

They entered the country of Vara and found it to be a paradise all to itself.
Beautiful women with proper manners. Houses all neat and tidy. Boisterous
lads tussled and toddlers played at kick-the-ball. Lions and dragons chanted
hymns together, and the pedestal of the Buddha's stone statue reverberated
with the tiger's roar. The atmosphere of this country was felicitous; the sights
to see were extraordinary indeed. There is a praise poem:

> Vara Land is a paradise all to itself;
> Beautiful maids and well-kept homes fill the place.
> Big lads and little boys alike
> Know the T'ang monk's troubles in going to India.
> Sentient beings of the Eastern Lands have yearned so very long:
> Three years and no word, their tears fall streaming down.
> The Emperor Ming Huang
> Sent Hsüan-tsang to fetch the sūtras for the sake of Great T'ang.
> On a lengthy journey to where the sun sets,
> Invited by the subtly pure Dharma King.[19]

---

18. The Chinese transcription is Po-lo. This may be an abbreviated form of Po-lo-na, the
Chinese transcription of Varanasi, which appears in the real Tripiṭaka's travel account.
  19. The Buddha.

Fourteen: Entering the Country of Utpala [20]

The pilgrims arrived at the country of Utpala. They saw wisteria twining, flowers blossoming for countless miles. Everywhere there were blooming plants. Tripiṭaka asked Monkey Pilgrim: "Where are we?" Monkey Pilgrim replied: "This is the country of Utpala. It is altogether an auspicious country and the atmosphere is filled with the scent of Utpala trees and Bodhi flowers. These trees are not cultivated but flourish here naturally. They know neither spring nor summer, winter nor autumn. The blossoms are always on the boughs, colorful and fragrant. There are no fierce winds nor searing hot days. Snow and cold come not, nor is there night. There is only endless spring." The Master asked: "How could there be no night?" Pilgrim replied: "There are no seasons in the Buddha's heaven. The red sun sinks not in the west. Children grow not old and there is no sorrow for death. They live twelve hundred years and never lack food. Those who come to this land return to a hundred good incarnations. They come when they are twenty and return when they are older than anyone knows. Tens of generations live together, so they do not have to commemorate their deceased ancestors. While mulberry fields become oceans and mountains become streams, time passes in the outside world. But a day spent in the Buddha's heaven is as a thousand days. By the way, Master, India is near! We shall arrive shortly." The pilgrims chanted another poem:

> Utpala, your divinely auspicious omens are all complete,
> But who would think this place so near to Western Heaven?
> Diligently have we come here, seeking the teachings in the sūtras;
> India quite clearly lies just ahead.

Fifteen: Entering India [21] and Crossing the Sea

The Dharma Master and his band traveled onward. Monkey Pilgrim remarked: "Master, you did not know it, but yesterday we reached our destination. It has taken us three years, but this is western India, and nearby is Chicken Foot Mountain." They proceeded for three more days until they came to the gates of a city. Above the gate was a sign announcing: "India."

20. Supposedly a kind of blue lotus or water lily, the plant is clearly described as a tree in the following sentences. Obviously the author has mistranscribed *Yu-t'an-po-lo* (*Udambara*, a type of fig tree) as *Yu-po-lo* (*Utpala*).

21. One of the most common Chinese transcriptions of the name "India" (derived from the word "Indus," a great river of the South Asian subcontinent) is T'ien-chu. The ostensible signification of the characters employed is "Heaven[ly] Bamboo." Often the name is prefixed by *Hsi*, i.e., "[in the] west," and the syllable *-chu* is just as often abbreviated. This leads to the further confusion of India with the "Western Heaven/Paradise," as in the present chapter and throughout this story.

Entering the city, they observed bustling neighborhoods filled with an auspicious atmosphere and the busy traffic of people, horses, and sedan-chairs. The fragrance of incense filled the air, flowers and fruits were abundant, and there were sights which were entirely new to mundane eyes. Next, they saw a temple called Prosperous Immortals Temple which they entered and where they were received by the monk in charge of guests. There were over five thousand monks in residence. Next they called on the abbot, and they were also introduced to the cook. Inside the temple grounds, flowers waved enticingly, and spreading canopies were hung in festooned profusion. All the Buddhist paraphernalia were complete and the seven jewels were inlaid on all objects.

A golden bell sounded and the vegetarian meal was served forthwith. The Dharma Master said to his disciples: "I'm completely unfamiliar with the flavors of this meal." Monkey Pilgrim responded: "This is the food partaken of by the Buddha of the Western Heaven. It is different from ordinary fare. How could it be familiar to you who are an ordinary mortal?" The monkish pilgrims partook and were imbued with the four major elements.[22]

At evening the abbot engaged the Dharma Master in conversation while they enjoyed tea all around. "Why is it that you have hastened this great distance?" the monks asked the Dharma Master. The Dharma Master arose as he replied: "I received a command from the Emperor of T'ang for the sake of the sentient beings of the Eastern Lands who have yet to receive the teachings of the Buddha to hasten especially to this country and ask for the great vehicle." As the monks of the temple listened to these words, they lowered their heads and smiled sarcastically. One of them said: "We of Prosperous Immortals Temple, for countless thousands of years and myriads of generations, have yet to hear of the Buddha's law. You say you seek that law, yet where is it to be found? Where is the Buddha? You are a fool!" The Dharma Master replied: "If the Buddha's law is not to be found here, why is there a temple here and so many monks?" The monk replied: "We who are here teach the sūtras all year round and individually understand the import of the Buddha's law. Why should we seek further?" The Dharma Master replied frankly: "This is a fairyland. Its inhabitants are most intelligent. Tell me where I shall find the place where the Buddha's law is taught." The reply was: "The Buddha dwells in Chicken Foot Mountain. One may gaze at it from here. It is the famous mountain to our west which emits a strange, holy light. No people go there nor can birds fly to it." The Dharma Master asked: "Why do people not go there?" The reply was: "Between here and there is a thousand tricents and more of water, and from the other shore to the mountain again is more than five hundred tricents. The waters of the stream are turbulent and countless are its waves. At the peak of the mountain is a single gate, and that is where the

22. The four *mahābhūta* (earth, water, fire, and wind).

Buddha resides. A sheer cliff a thousand tricents high confronts the pilgrim who would reach the gate. Unless your reverence can fly, you won't get there." The Dharma Master lowered his head dejectedly as he heard these words. Then he asked Monkey: "There are myriad tricents of mountain and a thousand tricents of water between us and the place where the Buddha dwells. How can we get across?" Monkey Pilgrim replied: "Let me devise another plan by tomorrow."

When dawn came, Monkey Pilgrim said: "The Buddhism of this place has come about naturally. Master, you should offer incense with the greatest sincerity, sit on a mat in meditation, direct your prayers to the Western Indian Chicken Foot Mountain, and beg for the Buddha's guidance."

The Master did exactly as Monkey had said and begged with all his heart. The monks of Prosperous Immortals Temple gathered around to observe as the Dharma Master and his six disciples burned incense and prayed toward Chicken Foot Mountain. Their united voices moved all who heard to tears. This same day the Emperor of T'ang and all the people of his country thought longingly of Tripiṭaka and lamented. Abruptly, the world became so dark that people couldn't see each other's faces. Then after a short while thunder resounded and myriad rays of light flashed. The sound was as deafening as great cymbals clashed by one's ears. After quite a while, it gradually grew light. And lo, on the prayer mat appeared a stack of sūtras. All the monks of the temple joined their palms and exclaimed: "This monk is truly a saint!"

Tripiṭaka bowed respectfully to the sūtras and discovered upon checking that there were five thousand and forty-eight volumes, all whole and complete. Only the *Heart Sūtra* was lacking. The Dharma Master gathered them up and the seven carried them to the horse for transport. They set out on their return journey, bidding farewell to the Indian community of monks. The inhabitants of the entire city saw them off, wishing the Dharma Master and his band safety on their long journey with its many obstacles, hoped that they would be able to preserve the profound scriptures so as to return to the T'ang court and carry out their edifying task. Everyone wept as they left. As the seven set out, they made this poem:

> Of enormous length was our journey to fetch the sūtras,
> But we seven now help each other as we turn homeward bound;
> Indeed, responding to the many woes of the people in the Eastern
>   Lands,
> May T'ang's emperor Ming Huang live ten thousand years!
> We'll establish a sūtra library with many temples and cloisters,
> And cast seven and more images of the Buddha;
> The dark world of Deep Sand and its host of spirits,
> Relying on this deed, can now cross that karmic ford.

India and the Western Heaven are both the Buddha,
Where even a year-old child is versed in the scriptures;
This trip lacks only the *Heart Sūtra*,
And when we see that Dragon Countenance we'll give him all the rest.

Sixteen: Returning They Arrive at Fragrant Grove Temple and Receive the Heart Sūtra

On the return journey from India they reached the country of P'an-lü after ten months on the road. There they stayed overnight at a place called "Fragrant Grove Town."

It was the third watch of the night when the Dharma Master suddenly dreamed that a spirit informed him: "Tomorrow someone will give you the *Heart Sūtra* and assist you on your return to the court." After some time, the Dharma Master awoke with a start and said to Monkey Pilgrim: "I have just had a very strange dream!" Monkey Pilgrim said: "Your dream indicates that we shall see the sūtra."

Soon their eyes smarted and their ears stung. Far off and directly in front of them they saw propitious clouds rising resplendently with a benign effulgence. A monkish form could gradually be discerned within the cloud. He seemed to be about fifteen years old. His face was very proper and he held a staff with golden rings. He took out the *Heart Sūtra* from the sleeve of his gown and said to the Dharma Master: "I'm giving you the *Heart Sūtra*. Guard it carefully on your return to the court. The power of this sūtra penetrates to the palaces of Heaven above and to the depths of Hell below. Its yin and yang are measureless, so do not transmit it lightly. Thus sentient beings whose karmic blessings are slight should not receive it."

Bowing with head to the ground, the Dharma Master responded to the Buddha: "My whole purpose is dedicated to the sentient beings of the Eastern Lands, and now that my karma is fortunately achieved why should I not transmit it?" Once again the Buddha spoke from within the clouds: "As soon as this sūtra is opened, bright lights will flash, ghosts will weep and spirits will howl, winds and waves will quiet of themselves, and the sun and moon will cease to shine! How could you possibly give it to anyone else?"

"I am deeply grateful! I am deeply grateful!" the Dharma Master repeated apologetically. Once more the Buddha addressed him: "I am Dīpaṃkara Buddha.[23] Today I have come to give you the *Heart Sūtra*. When you return to the T'ang court, you are to give this message to the emperor: He should quickly have temples built throughout the empire, increase the initiations of monks and nuns, and promote respect for the Buddha's Dharma. It is now the

---

23. The "Fixing Light Buddha" or "Buddha of Lights."

fourth month and I am giving you the *Heart Sūtra*. On the fifteenth day of the seventh month,[24] it will be time for you, Dharma Master, and your band of seven to return to the celestial halls. Remember what I have said, and on the fifteenth rise early and bathe yourself. Say farewell to the T'ang emperor, for at noon the 'Lotus-Plucking Barge' will arrive. There will also be golden lotus-flower seats and auspicious rainbow-colored clouds. Twelve mellifluously voiced youths will escort you with incense, flowers, and decorated banners. They will adorn you with the seven precious gems, welcoming you seven to return to Heaven. But the invitation from Heaven has a time limit and you must not dally! Listen well to what I have told you and keep it firmly implanted in your mind!"

The Dharma Master and his group of seven wept and bowed in gratitude as Dīpaṃkara Buddha guided his cloud upward and away toward the West.

The monkish band of seven etched these events on their hearts. Then, prepared to continue their journey, they completed this poem:

> Returning from India carrying sūtras for Eastern Lands
> Traveling ten months now, we came to Fragrant Grove;
> Merits of three lives our karma fulfilled,
> Carefully we attended to the words of truth bestowed upon us,
> Ancient Dīpaṃkara Buddha appeared in a cloud,
> Then speedily we prepared our return journey;
> For it's said that on the fifteenth of the seventh month
> All seven of us monkish pilgrims will return to the halls of Heaven.

Seventeen: They Reach Shensi, Where the Wife of the Householder Wang Kills His Son[25]

On their return journey, they arrived at Ho-chung prefecture. There was a householder there named Wang who had always done good works and was then thirty-one years old. After his first wife died he married a woman of the Meng family.

His son by his first wife was called Daffy, and there was a son by Madame Meng as well called Stay-put. One day the householder, remembering the kindness of his deceased parents and the love of his late wife, offered a memorial service for their souls. Then, he spoke with Madame Meng: "I'm going abroad to do business now. You take good care of Daffy for

---

24. It is significant that the monks' ascension should fall on this date, for it is All Souls' Day, a festival often referred to as Ullambana that is reserved for the deliverance of hungry ghosts. See selection 266, note 1 and pp. 1124 ff.

25. For an analysis of this most unusual chapter, see Victor H. Mair, "Parallels Between Some Tun-Huang Manuscripts and the 17th chapter of the Kōzanji *Journey to the West*," *Cahiers d'Extrême-Asie*, 3 (1987), 41–53. The resemblances to the "Transformation Text on the Boy Shun's Extreme Filial Piety" (selection 267) are particularly striking.

me. The boy was very young when he lost his mother and still does not understand things. Please treat him as lovingly as though he were your own son."

Then he divided up his wealth into two portions: "One portion is for you and the children to live on here at home, and one portion I shall take to trade in foreign lands. When I return we shall give a great thanksgiving feast open to all, and a generous almsgiving on behalf of our deceased ancestors and in order to accumulate good karma." After he gave these directions to his wife, he selected an auspicious day to set out on his journey. As his wife saw him off at the gate, he repeatedly enjoined her to look after Daffy and not be negligent.

After her husband had been gone for half a year he met a man he knew who was returning and gave him a letter for home, a suspended drum, a decorated cushion, colorfully embroidered clothes, and all kinds of toys to take back with him. When Madame Meng received the letter and read it, she learned that everything was to be given to Daffy. "Over and over about how I should care for Daffy, but not a word about my Stay-put!"

After reading the letter Madame Meng became terribly angry. She tore up the letter, smashed the toys, and began to think about killing Daffy.

One day she said to her maid, Spring Willow: "I want to kill Daffy. Do you have any suggestions?" Spring Willow replied: "That's easy. We have a great iron caldron in the house. Have Daffy sit down inside, then put the thirty-pound iron lid over it. Next, build a fierce fire beneath it and roast him. That's sure to kill him." "That's great!" said Madame Meng.

The next day they did as they had planned. They had Daffy sit down in the caldron and shut him in with the lid. Then they roasted him for three days and three nights over a fierce fire. On the fourth day, they lifted the iron lid only to see Daffy stand up inside the caldron and greet his stepmother. Madame Meng asked: "What are you doing here?" Daffy replied: "You put me in here, mother. Then the iron caldron changed into a lily pad on which I sat, surrounded by the cool waters of a pond. I could sleep or just sit there. It was very comfortable."

When she heard this Madame Meng turned worriedly to Spring Willow to talk things over some more: "We've got to quickly think of some way to kill him! I'm afraid that when my husband returns Daffy will tell him what we've done!" Spring Willow said: "Tomorrow, hide an iron hook in your hand and have Daffy go with you to the back garden to eat cherries. When he opens his mouth use the iron hook to tear out his tongue at the root. Then, even when your husband returns, the boy won't be able to speak."

The next day according to plan they sent him to the garden and tore out his tongue with the hook, splattering blood all over the ground.

The day after that when they got up and yelled "Daffy!" they found that he was able to talk as before. Madame Meng asked him: "How can this be?"

Daffy replied: "A person came in the middle of the night who said he was 'Ambrosia King Buddha.' He had a medicinal object in his hand and rejoined my tongue at the root."

Again Spring Willow advised Madame Meng: "There's a storehouse out back. Have him guard the storehouse. Lock him inside and let him starve to death." A month after doing this they opened the storehouse to see Daffy stand up and greet his stepmother. Madame Meng said: "The other day when the maid locked the storehouse I had no idea you were inside. Have you had anything to eat this month?" Daffy replied: "Whenever I was hungry or thirsty, doe's milk naturally came down from the air."

Spring Willow said: "Right now the river out front is in flood. Have Daffy go up on top of a tower to look at the river, then push him off into the boundless torrent. When your husband returns, just say he leaped into the stream himself and was drowned. That should avert any danger to us."

When Madame Meng saw that the water was billowing high, she did as suggested. She had Daffy go up on the tower to look at the water and Spring Willow gave him a push from behind, throwing Daffy down into the torrent. Madame Meng looked on and said: "This time he's dead!"

At the moment she came down from the tower a messenger suddenly appeared at the gate who announced that the householder had learned en route that Daffy had fallen in the river and been drowned and was returning home weeping at every step. As soon as the householder entered the gate, he began beating his breast, weeping and lamenting.

Because of Daffy's extreme filialness, a day was selected for performing a memorial service to liberate his soul and a great maigre feast was prepared to which all were invited.

Dharma Master Tripiṭaka was returning with the sūtras from Rājagṛha and his whole party of seven monks came to the householder's maigre feast. But neither the Master nor Monkey Pilgrim ate even one bite. The householder asked them: "Since you honorable monks have come to the feast, why is it you aren't eating anything?" The Dharma Master replied: "I'm drunk today and all I want to have is some fish broth. I don't want to eat anything else at all." When the householder heard this, he thought he would receive no good karma if he did not get the monk what he desired, so he ordered a servant to go out and buy a fish. The Dharma Master said: "I won't eat a small fish. It must be a big fish, a hundred-pounder, then I can eat it."

The servant went to the fishmonger's and was indeed able to buy a fish weighing about a hundred pounds. When he brought it back home, he announced to the householder that he was successful and the householder asked the Dharma Master how he would like it prepared. The Dharma Master replied: "Lend me a knife. I'll prepare it myself." The rich man passed a knife to the Dharma Master who addressed the assembled guests and the house-holder: "If there had not been this maigre feast today, it would have been this fish's karma to have committed a serious crime." The householder asked: "What crime has it committed?" The Dharma Master said: "The other day this fish swallowed your eldest son, Daffy, who is now still alive in its stomach." When the assembled guests heard this, they all gathered around. Then, with one stroke the Dharma Master cut the fish into two halves. Daffy came out and began speaking just as before. The householder embraced his son. His joy and amazement were tremendous as the father joined his palms and respectfully thanked the Dharma Master: "If it had not been possible for your reverence to be here today, father and son would never have met face to face again." Everyone was joyous. In thanks for this fortunate deliverance the householder made a verse:

> While I traded nearly three years abroad,
> Madame Meng had only evil intentions at home;
> Although they threw Daffy into the flood,
> A great fish swallowed him into its stomach whole.

> And because in the course of today's maigre feast,
> The monk complained he was still too drunk;
> He demanded a large fish to cook himself,
> Father and son could meet again and believe in karma.

The Dharma Master declared: "This fish shall be taken back to the Eastern Lands and become a wooden fish in a Buddhist temple. And, whenever a maigre feast is held, it will be tapped on the stomach with a stick."
   He made another poem:

> Madam Meng gave vent to evil thoughts;
> She pushed the boy into the river,
> But thanks to the good karma of the memorial feast
> Father and son have met again.

The assembled guests then made a poem:

> Thanks to the Dharma Master's good karma today,
> The householder's Daffy is reborn;
> He will be no different from Madam Meng and Stay-put,
> But will be fed and clothed just like them.

   After the Dharma Master's group of seven left in the middle of the religious play, it took them ten days to reach the capital of T'ang.
   Soldiers patrolling the eastern route to the capital found out that the Dharma Master had brought the sūtras back and was already in the environs of the capital. They submitted a memorial to Emperor Ming Huang reporting it. At the time it was hot summer, but the emperor dispatched a great sedan-chair to meet them a hundred tricents from the city. The Dharma Master and

his group of seven met the emperor and thanked him for his kindness. Ming Huang and the Dharma Master rode together in the same carriage to the court. It was the last week of the sixth month.

Every day there were maigre feasts in the court and temples were ordered established in every province to welcome the Buddha's Dharma. The emperor personally received the *Prajñāpāramitā-hṛdaya* or *Heart Sūtra*. It was as if his eyes had been painted in:[26] he ordered incense to be burned at shrines inside and outside the palace and flowers strewn to welcome the sūtra.

On the seventh day of the seventh month, the Dharma Master sent up a memorial to the throne:

> Your humble subject wishes to address your majesty: When I received the *Heart Sūtra* at Fragrant Grove, I heard a voice from Heaven which said that on the fifteenth of this month I should return there.

The Emperor of Great T'ang responded as tears fell on his dragon robes: "Invitations from Heaven cannot be postponed; I can't force you to remain here." The Dharma Master said: "My reason for getting the sūtras and for overcoming all the difficulties and monsters on the journey was to benefit the sentient beings of the Eastern Lands. In order to thank all the gods who helped me on my way beginning with the Deep Sand Spirit, I want to have memorial services celebrated at all the temples." The emperor replied: "As the Dharma Master requests, I will have seven statues of the Buddha made to protect the halls of the temples."

During the fifth quarter hour of the noon watch on the fourteenth, honorary rank was conferred upon the Dharma Master. Then the emperor expressed his thanks: "Your reverence traveled three years to India in the West to bring back one set of sūtras and in all your incarnations you have received the sūtras three times. I therefore give you the title 'Dharma Master Tripiṭaka.' "[27]

During the fifth quarter hour of the noon watch on the fifteenth, a barge for collecting lotuses was sent down from the Heavenly Palace and Dīpaṃkara Buddha was manifest in the clouds. Announcing that he had better not tarry any longer, the Dharma Master bade a hasty good-bye to the emperor. The seven boarded the barge and, looking due west, they ascended into the heavens and became immortals. Nine dragons rose up into the mist and ten phoenixes came out to welcome them. A thousand cranes offered them felicitations and there were flashing lights of transcendence.

Because the emperor had not been able to give thanks for these marvels, he

26. There is an old tradition in China and in other countries influenced by Indian culture that the painting in of the pupils on a work of art is the final enlivening touch of the creator. The tradition is still alive today in Tawian where there are priests who make a living out of activating idols (god figures) in this manner.

27. Tripiṭaka (literally, "Three Baskets") refers to the tripartite division of the Buddhist canon.

sponsored another great maigre feast at which all the assembly burned incense in thanks and in memory of Tripiṭaka. The emperor along with the crown prince and all the officials went around all four city gates weeping, and in order that Tripiṭaka's name should always be remembered they made this poem:

> Today the Dharma Master has gone to the Heavenly Palace,
> He walks on lotus petals as he goes;
> Our entire country benefits greatly from this,
> The Eastern Lands avoid falling into worldly snares.

Emperor T'ai Tsung[28] later enfeoffed Monkey Pilgrim as "Great Sage of Bronze Muscles and Iron Bones."

Translated by Charles J. Wivell

28. Since the action is set in Emperor Ming Huang's time throughout the story, this reference to Emperor T'ai Tsung, during whose time the real Tripiṭaka lived, seems likely to have been added by some later writer.

271
Expository Tale on King Wu's Expedition Against Chow

Anonymous (c. 1321–1323)

Scroll 1

From the Three Emperors and Five Kings down to Hsia, Shang, and Chou,
The Ch'in, Han, and the Three Kingdoms Wu, Wei, and Liu,

King Chow (see section VII of selection 148) was the tyrannical last ruler of the Shang or Yin dynasty. He was overthrown by King Wu, founder of the Chou dynasty. The prosimetric fictionalization of the story as recounted here is in the genre known as "expository tale" or "plain tale" (*p'ing-hua*), a form of popular storytelling which succeeded the transformation text (*pien-wen*, see selection 266) and which, like the latter, had close ties both to the performing arts and to the development of the vernacular short story and novel in China. Indeed, this particular plain tale is the most important precursor of the late sixteenth-century novel *Romance of the Investiture of the Gods* (*Feng-shen yen-yi*). Typically, the original editions of plain texts have illustrations on the upper thirds of their pages. This shows a direct link with the transformation texts which were also intimately tied to narrative visual aids. The *Expository Tale on King Wu's Expedition Against Chow* was printed sometime between 1321 and 1323, during the Mongol Yüan dynasty, in what is now the city of Chien-yang in the southeastern province of Fukien. The genre itself must have evolved during the course of the Sung period.

The present selection offers approximately the first third of the expository tale. In it King Chow's brutality, caused by his utter intoxication with the bewitching Ta-chi, is exposed. This sets the stage for King Wu's intervention against him described in the latter part of the tale.

The Chin, the Sung,[1] the Liang, the North and South dynasties,
The Sui, T'ang, the Five Dynasties, the Sung,[2] and Chin complete.

It was said that King T'ang of Yin, whose name was Yü Lü, whose style T'ien-yi, was the fourteenth generation descendant of Lord Hsieh. His father was Kuei. He appointed Yi-yin as his premier and banished Chieh.[3] Hence he was honored posthumously with the title of T'ang which was given to those who put an end to cruelties. He enthroned himself only after he was thrice invited to the throne. And after a revolution, a nation was formed and was named Shang. Then King T'ang issued various orders: he selected a new New Year's Day in the lunar calendar, adopted the color white as an auspicious sign, built menagerie-parks, and ordered that in laying a trap for animals three sides of the net must be lowered, leaving only one of its sides standing so as to allow the animals to buck into it of their free will. All feudal princes admired King T'ang and thirty-six states came to submit themselves. It happened that a drought lasted for seven years. King T'ang reproved himself for six things and burned himself in a wood of mulberry. Then followed a heavy downpour of rain and peace for all under heaven. King T'ang ruled his country for thirteen years before his demise. The duration of Shang was six hundred and twenty-nine years, in which thirty-one rulers were enthroned. The last ruler was King Chow, the son of King Yi, who was also named Hsin and Shou. He was the last descendant of King T'ang. There is a poem:

> King Chow of Shang came with peace,
> Citizens within the four seas gave cheers,
> Because of Ta-chi he led a voluptuous life,
> And a war was provoked.

Also another one:

> There were many vicissitudes in the world,
> Which caused the Western Earl to start an expedition,
> State affairs were decided in orgies,
> Therefore the state was not peaceful.

King Chow was a born genius, and the other kings and rulers were not to be compared with him. He could recite old classics from hundreds of authors, count sheep without error, and was able to defend himself against ten thousand men; he had a big, bellowing voice; his handwriting followed the "Eight Divisions" style;[4] he had the capacity to drink a thousand cups of wine; he had a good command of strong bows and he had also horses. When King Chow

1. The Liu Sung dynasty (420–478).
2. The Chao Sung dynasty (960–1276), divided into Northern Sung (960–1126) and Southern Sung (1127–1276).
3. The corrupt and tyrannical last ruler of the Hsia dynasty.
4. A style of calligraphy which was actually devised during the Han period.

first came to reign he was forty-seven and was a capable ruler. He had a vast empire including thirty-six states and more than a hundred and sixty counties. The feudal princes came to pay tribute to his court twice a year, and all the barbarous tribes were subdued. The domain he controlled extended eastward to the sea, westward to Ch'in Ch'uan, southward to Chiu Ch'i, and northward to Sha T'o.[5]

King Chow was good enough to keep many loyal officials, civil as well as military, at his court. He appointed Pi-kan as his Premier and Great Admonishing Minister, Wei Tzu as Court Adviser, Fei Chung as Great Marshal, and Fei Lien as First Military Governor. He also had Eight Earls and the feudal princes, and an Officer Administering the Court named Hung Yao.

Chiang Huan-ch'u, the first Eastern Earl, was designated to Ch'ing-chou; Chi Ch'ang, the second Western Earl, was designated to Ch'i-chou; Yang Yüeh-ch'i, the third Southern Earl, was designated to Ching-chou; Ch'i Yang-kuang, the fourth Northern Earl, was designated to Yu-chou; Ch'u T'ien-yu, the fifth Northeastern Earl, was designated to Yang-chou; Huo Chung-yen, the sixth Southwestern Earl, was designated to Hsü-chou; Chang Fang-kuo, the seventh Southeastern Earl, was designated to Chi-chou; and Hu Ching-ta, the eighth Northwestern Earl, was designated to Ping-chou.

These Eight Earls were all loyal assistants of King Chow's predecessors. The late king honored them as elder brothers, and King Chow respected them as earls (uncles). On his birthday King Chow would set up the portrait of his predecessor and on both sides of it were portraits of the Eight Earls. Then he would pour libations in front of them just as he did before the portrait of his predecessor. The reason for this rite was that these earls were loyal officials who had enthroned four kings including King Chow himself. There is a poem:

> Kings were enthroned by these Eight Earls,
> Loyal officials without depravity,
> On birthdays and occasions of celebration
> They came to prostrate themselves before the most honored.

The first ten years of King Chow's reign was a period of tranquility and peace. Therefore he was honored by all as Yao and Shun, the most exemplary rulers in ancient history.

It happened that one day Queen Chiang invited King Chow to a party, and she announced that she would go to the Jade-Maiden Temple to worship the maiden next day and ordered her attendants to bathe before the tour began.

5. Ch'in Ch'uan refers to the far western areas occupied by the ancestors of the First Emperor of the Ch'in dynasty (see selection 225). Chiu Ch'i probably refers to the nine affluents of the Yangtze River. The Sha-t'o were a confederation of Turkic peoples active along the northern reaches of China during the latter part of the Northern and Southern Dynasties and during the Sui and T'ang periods. Several states during The Five Dynasties and Ten Kingdoms period were founded by Sha-t'o Turks. See selection 268, note 14.

King Chow heard this and asked the queen where she was going. The queen replied, "I will go to the Jade-Maiden Temple. The maiden is an immaculate virgin and now she has become a goddess. Whenever the first and the fifteenth day of the month come, I go to her to fulfill my vow." King Chow said, "Why should I not go, too?"

On the next day King Chow issued a decree, ordering all ministers in the palace to go to the Jade-Maiden Temple with them. The procession arrived at the temple, and King Chow and Queen Chiang entered. During the ceremony, King Chow noticed the image of the damsel of unique beauty and meditated, "There is no one in my palace who resembles this Jade-Maiden."

King Chow did not return to his palace, but stayed in the temple for three days, gazing at the damsel. He said to the image, "Your beauty is seldom equaled in this world." The temple was illuminated. King Chow sat drinking face to face with the maiden. She could not speak because she was made of clay. Then he summoned Fei Chung and asked, "The maiden is of clay, how can I make her talk?" Fei Chung replied, "Your Majesty should stay in the temple alone and send away all your ministers." King Chow followed this advice.

It was midnight. King Chow found himself alone in the temple. He saw the Jade-Maiden carried by a group of attendants to the hall. He was very pleased and gave her welcome. The maiden said, "What are you doing, my Lord, staying here all through the night?" The king said, "On account of the arrival of the queen at the temple, and of your peerless beauty, I sincerely wish to meet you." The maiden replied, "I am a daughter of the fairies, and Your Majesty is the king of mankind. How can we love each other? There is an old saying: 'Fairies take no wives and maidens have no husbands.' My Lord, please go quickly lest we be reprimanded." "How?" the king asked. The maiden was forced to answer, "After a hundred days, I will see my Lord, but please go away." "What is the pledge?" demanded the king. The maiden gave him a sash, saying that that was the pledge. The king received it. Suddenly he smelled something fragrant, heard the jingling of some bracelets, and perceived a colorful mist in the air. He rushed forward to embrace the maiden but he woke up to find it was only a dream. He calmed himself down for a moment and saw merely an earthen idol and not a human being. But he really had the sash, which he scrutinized under the candle flames till very late, with deep regret.

King Chow still sat in the temple. He could do nothing except think of the maiden. Fei Chung came and advised the king, "Why don't you return to the palace?" The king informed him of what he had heard from the maiden. Fei Chung said, "Wait for a hundred days, and perhaps the maiden will come to see my King. Please go back to the palace." The king followed this advice but thought of the maiden every day.

After the lapse of a hundred days, the maiden did not come. Thereupon,

King Chow summoned Fei Chung and asked him, "The maiden pledged that she would see me. But I get no news from her now. Why does she not come?" Fei Chung replied, "Your Majesty does nothing but think of her; how can she come? Pray do not think of her any more. I am afraid Your Majesty will be sick. Will Your Majesty follow the suggestion of your humble servant which will compensate for the loss Your Majesty has suffered and make Your Majesty happy?" "What can make me happy?" inquired the king. Fei Chung said, "Your Majesty can put a proclamation outside the palace gate, ordering all virgins to come to the palace. Anyone who is considered fit for the post of a superintendent in your harem shall be highly rewarded. And could there be no one among the group who can equal the maiden? Your Majesty can choose to your heart's content. What is Your Majesty's opinion?" "I will follow your advice," said the king.

The king then ordered all virgins from every family, shop, street, village, town, district, prefecture, and state to come to the palace to dedicate themselves. In a little more than a month, thousands and thousands of them came, but not one of them could compete with the maiden. The king was distressed and thought of her all the more.

Realizing that the king was unhappy, Hung Yao, the Officer Administering the Court, suggested to the king, "If Your Majesty desires to have a girl who can equal the maiden and that the girl should be found in some official's family nourished by Your Majesty, Your Majesty may command all officials, big and small, to offer their beauties, and among them there must be one who is more beautiful than the maiden." The king exclaimed, "Good idea!" Then the king posted an order again on the palace gate, instructing all officials from various parts to send in their family beauties. And any family who dared to hide their beauties would be punished by death.

Thus, no officials dared to violate the regulation and sent in their family beauties. It happened that an official named Su Hu, who was the prefect of Hua-chou, had a daughter. She was eighteen years of age, of unique beauty, and was named Ta-chi. The father dared not hide his daughter and therefore accompanied her on her tour to the capital.

In a few days, father and daughter arrived at the ancient En district, which is the present Huo Chia, and settled down in the post-house. Su Yen, the prefect of En-chou, invited them to a dinner in his office.

It was very late in the night when the beautiful Ta-chi was sleeping in her quarters in the post-house. Suddenly there rose a strong wind, and a fox, nine-tailed and golden-haired, climbed into the post-house. It approached the sleeping beauty and drew away air from the nostrils of the girl as well as her marrow. Then the body of the girl was empty and very thin. The fox then blew air into the body, thus changing the soul of the girl, making her bewitching. It was Ta-chi. Her skin was snow-white, her face was not powdered and her hair not trimmed. She looked like a fairy from the moon, and her beauty was indescribable. The girl did not seem to have been exposed to the sun and wind from her early childhood, and therefore she was bright and shiny and was extremely animated after she was altered by the fox.

Next morning the father was very much surprised to discover that his daughter was so charming when he ordered the attendants to dress her. The father was much exalted but did not utter a word. He only thought to himself, "My daughter is likely to be queen." Then they continued the journey. Su Yen escorted them.

They approached Chao Ko, King Chow's capital. Su Yen went in the palace and said to the king, "Listen, my Lord. Prefect Su Hu from Hua-chou offers his daughter. I am instructed to inform my Lord." The king then summoned Fei Chung, "The prefect of Hua-chou is going to offer his daughter; go to receive them."

Fei Chung went out and met Su Hu and saw the girl's beauty. He went back to the king, "The girl is charming." The king immediately sent for the father and daughter. They arrived and bent forward. The king said, "You are equals and exempted from ceremonies."

The king was very much pleased after he saw the girl and gave her a golden crown, skirts, phoenix-hairpins, and other ornaments. After she was dressed, she looked like the maiden. The king was extremely happy and ordered her to stay in the Fairy-Receiving Palace. Su Hu, the girl's father, having been honored with the title of Royal Father-in-law, was given a residence and had the right to share the glories of the king.

The king liked Ta-chi very much. During a dinner party, Ta-chi discovered a piece of sash which was fastened to the king and asked, "Where did my Lord obtain this lovely sash?" The king smiled and replied, "I was with the maiden some nights ago and she gave it to me as a pledge." Ta-chi was jealous, "I am afraid that my Lord may be enchanted by the maiden. My Lord should order someone to destroy the image and burn the temple, for the temple is useless." The king said, "I will follow your suggestion, burn the temple, and destroy the maiden."

King Chow did not pay attention to his state affairs for a hundred days and only enjoyed himself with Ta-chi in the Fairy-Receiving Palace. Though he was advised several times, he did not listen.

One day Queen Chiang gave birth to a prince, who was later proclaimed Prince Ching Ming and was named Yin Chiao. He was the God of the Cycle, T'ai Sui,[6] sent by heaven to bring calamity to King Chow because of his blasphemy.[7]

One day Ta-chi said to the king, "What will my Lord think of ordering that

6. Jupiter.

7. There are sixty years in a Chinese calendrical cycle, and a special star-deity presides over each year. To act in accordance with the orientation of that year brings good fortune.

anyone in the nation who has valuables should offer them to decorate the palace chambers and to serve as my playthings?" The king followed her suggestion, and posted an order on the gate commanding anyone who had precious things to offer them to the palace and not to hide them. The order lasted for more than a hundred days.

One day a minister said to the king, "Your Majesty, a good man is going to offer his valuables, and he is waiting outside." The king called the man in and asked, "What is your name?" "My name is Hsü Wen-su. I live in White Water Cave in Chung-nan Mountain as a hermit," said the man. "What arc you going to offer me?" asked the king. "I am going to offer Your Majesty a precious sword," replied the man. "This sword is not a precious one. What is the use of it?" said the king. "Listen, Your Majesty, this sword can control all witches and ghosts among men. If they meet this sword, they would be frightened and cannot escape," said Wen-su. "What monsters stay in my place?" said the king. "I see some evil airs billowing upward in Your Majesty's palace. Your Majesty had better hang this sword on the wall in the inner chamber. If a human being sees it, he will not be frightened, but if a spirit sees it, it will scream. My Lord may strike it with this sword and no spirit will ever haunt your palace. I see a witch in my Lord's palace. Please believe what I say and destroy the spirit with this sword, otherwise I will have it back," explained Wen-su. The king took the sword into the rear chambers.

Ta-chi came to see the king who then followed her to stay in her palace. After having had three cups of wine, she asked, "My Lord has ordered precious things to be brought in, and what precious things have you got lately? Fetch them for me." The king said, "There is one." And he ordered the sword to be brought to Ta-chi. It would have been good for Ta-chi had she not seen the sword but, on the contrary, she saw it and screamed and ran away abruptly for ten or twenty paces, frightened. The king saw her running away and asked, "Why do you run away?" Ta-chi, seeing the sword as a big snake running after her, thought to herself, "Though it looks like a snake, yet I am afraid I am suspected of being a witch, I must find some pretext." She had an inspiration and said to the king, "I am not afraid of the sword. But my Lord had better put it into another chamber." The king yielded to her and ordered the sword to be taken away.

Then the king asked, "What happened?" Ta-chi said, "My lord, I am not afraid of the sword. But my elder sister came to beckon me to attend the fairy party and I am preparing to go. I am now saying good-bye to my Lord but thinking of my Lord's affection for me." "Who is your elder sister?" asked the king. "The Moon Fairy is my elder sister. She knew that my Lord had the intention of deserting me, therefore she came to call me to go to the party. If my Lord has no use of me, then, please let me go. Originally I was a fairy in paradise, but owing to the commission of a sin, I have been sent down to earth." Ta-chi wept after finishing her explanation. The king was not willing to desert her, saying, "I do not blame you for your wrong behavior. Compared with you, how does the Moon Fairy look?" "My sister looks like a fairy, not an ordinary person. She has a pure heart. Her countenance remains unchanged after a lapse of thousands and thousands of years. How can mortals who are entangled in love and desire be compared with a transcendent being? And my countenance can hardly compare with hers," said Ta-chi. The king was impressed and did not care about Ta-chi's running and about the sword, which he put in the ancestral temple.

The king asked Ta-chi again, "How can I meet your sister?" Ta-chi replied, "If my Lord desires to see my sister, please listen to my advice." The king said, "Tell me." Ta-chi said, "A terrace three hundred feet high should be built in the palace and named Moon-Playing Terrace with Star-Plucking Tower. A hundred pavilions should be built upon the terrace and a thousand houses should be built below it. And a banquet should be set up on the terrace whenever the fifteenth night of the first moon arrives. Thus, my Lord can meet my sister." The king was extremely glad to hear this.

Next morning the king presided over the court and said, "I want to construct terraces and castles. How will you arrange it?" Fei Chung and Hung Yao said, "Your Majesty, the whole nation belongs to you. The work can be done." The king asked them again, "How are you going to do it?" The two replied, "If Your Majesty wants to have the work done, we can send for the Eight Earls to come to a discussion, and the work can be done." The king followed this suggestion and sent for the Eight Earls.

The king's envoys went to summon the Eight Earls with this decree. The one who came to Ch'i-chou was complimented by Chi Ch'ang in the suburbs. After Chi Ch'ang had read the order, he was terribly shocked and said, "The king is going to act unreasonably and is apt to create chaos. But how can I oppose him in view of the royal decree I have just received?" Therefore he summoned his senior Great Ministers, Kao, the Duke of Pi, and Shih, the Duke of Chao, and other attendants, a hundred in number, to follow him to see King Chow.

Within a few days, the procession arrived at the boundary of Yin Fu near the T'ung Kuan Pass. Chi Ch'ang saw a column of smoke billowing up against the sky and told the envoy who accompanied him, "The cycle of today is *wu-wu*; there will surely be a strong wind at the *szu* hour.[8] The rain will stop at noon." The envoy did not believe it.

During their conversation, dark clouds overshadowed the sky, a wild wind gradually arose, and fog and clouds covered up all sides. In an instant, there came thunder and lightning and a downpour of rain. In a moment rivers appeared on the plains and ditches were overrun by waves. However, the rain stopped and the clouds dispersed at noon. The plants were shooting up.

All were in the woods. Suddenly they discovered an old grave. Chi Ch'ang

8. 9–11 a.m.

prophesied, "There must be rain today. This grave will destroy itself and from it a hero will come out." No sooner had he finished speaking than the old grave destroyed itself. The envoy was very glad and said that it was extraordinary.

Chi Ch'ang stared at the destroyed grave and saw a woman's corpse which looked like a living being. But her belly had been blasted open by the thunder and a child was crying inside. Chi Ch'ang ordered the child to be taken out of the grave and this was done. But the followers did not know why a child should be born there. Only Chi Ch'ang knew it.

Chi Ch'ang and the envoy passed a ridge and met a Taoist whose name was Yün-chung Tzu ("Master of the Clouds"). After they had exchanged salutes, they heard the crying of a baby. Yün-chung Tzu asked, "Whose baby is crying?" Chi Ch'ang told his friend what had happened and the Taoist said, "Do not throw away the child. In eighteen years, the child will definitely assist you in destroying the tyrannous Chow." Chi Ch'ang understood what he meant and gave the child to the Taoist. Yün-chung Tzu said again, "The child has no name; we can name him Son of Thunder-shock (Lei Chen Tzu), for he is a fierce god who will destroy King Chow."

Chi Ch'ang said good-bye to his Taoist friend and continued the journey with the envoy. In a few days, they approached the capital and Chi Ch'ang met the other seven earls. And they discussed their impending meeting with the king.

Next morning, they all arrived at the palace, and after giving cheers to the king, bowed low. The king announced, "I want to build a terrace in the palace, which will be three hundred feet high, on top of which will be a hundred pavilions and below which will be a thousand houses. Therefore I summon you for a conference so that my design may be executed." Chi Ch'ang went forward to advise, "My Lord, please do not build the terrace, for it will consume the energies of the people and harm the agricultural products. My Lord, why do you not follow the good examples of Yao and Shun and have a peaceful world? Shun set a good example in promoting filial piety to other nations, and Yü is credited with control over the floods, helping thousands and thousands of people to escape calamity. Yü even had the virtue of giving away his throne to others. Why not, my Lord, think it over and give up the idea of constructing the terrace, and discard that wench? Otherwise the people may suffer a great deal. Why not, my Lord, follow the example of your predecessors? And now, my Lord, trust not what Ta-chi says. Alas, it will ruin our country and our families!" The king heard this and vacillated. Ta-chi flattered the king and said, "My Lord, trust Chi Ch'ang and do not build the terrace. I hope my Lord will put me in a secluded chamber and I certainly will die. What else can they expect from me?" The king consoled her, "I will see to it. Do not worry."

The king summoned Fei Chung and said to him, "I want to build the terrace and Chi Ch'ang advises me not to, but Ta-chi is crazy about it. What is the solution?" Fei Chung said, "My Lord, if the terrace is not to be built, there will be nothing to display the glories of a great nation." The king was much exalted and posted an order on the palace gate.

The king said, "How many men should be needed?" "Five million men," said Fei Chung. This was approved. Then the king ordered the circumference of the field to be measured, and instructed the Eight Earls to start work and that anyone who should delay his work would be punished. Therefore the earls did their best and within one year the construction was accomplished. The citizens were greatly troubled and all pined for a redeemer. The king did not pay attention to the suffering of the people and he ignored the admonitions of his officials, civil and military. An East Stag Terrace and a West Stag Terrace were being built. The decoration of their insides harmonized with that of their outsides and all the walls were ornamented with gold, jade, and precious gems. The construction was so extremely magnificent that even the palaces in heaven could not compare with it. Below the terraces were planted various flowers and rows of precious trees, and a thousand halls and houses were also built. There is a poem:

> The Eight Earls did their best in constructing
> Towers and terraces which were splendid and rare.
> King Chow arranged sumptuous feasts there,
> Who cares for the people in ashes and mire?

One day, the king set up a feast on the terrace and invited all his ministers to dine with him. Chi Ch'ang ran a great risk when he advised the king, "My king leads such a voluptuous life that the nation may be ruined. Has my Lord not heard that Yao had a son named Tan Chu ("Cinnabar Red"), who was so immoral and led such a voluptuous life that his father gave away his throne to Shun? And Shun in turn also had a bad son named Shang Chün who also led such a voluptuous life that his father gave his throne to Yü. When King Chieh came to power, he enjoyed himself amid beauties and with what we call mountains of meat and pools of wine. He caused naked boys to play licentiously with nude virgins. He lost his country because he was ruthless. My Lord, please do not follow the immoral kings but follow the good deeds of the virtuous rulers, Yao and Shun, then we shall have no ensuing troubles." The king said, "I rule my country like this." Chi Ch'ang remonstrated, "How can my Lord consider the building of the terraces as an administrative function of the government? It wastes millions of dollars and makes thousands of people suffer. Why not, my Lord, give the money and the materials which have been used in the building of terraces to the farmers and the laborers? My Lord's treasury is full and we are wealthy. What my Lord has done is rebellious to the will of heaven and not compliant with the wishes of the people. It will be inauspicious if my Lord goes on like this." The king asked, "How?" Chi

Ch'ang said, "My Lord, please listen to me. There will be a catastrophe in our country in twenty years and there will be one man who will be your rival." The king was exasperated and yelled at Chi Ch'ang, "Enough of you and your foreboding that I shall die at the hands of one man in twenty years!"

The king then asked Ta-chi, "Do you know my fate?" And then he asked Chi Ch'ang, "When will you die?" Chi Ch'ang answered, "I shall die peacefully in bed in twenty years." The king was very angry and ordered Chi Ch'ang to be decapitated, shouting, "You say you will die peacefully after twenty years, but I want to see you die now by dismembering your body." The guards got the Western Earl, seized and pushed him aside. Could Chi Ch'ang save his life? There is a poem:

> Millions of dollars spent in building terraces and towers,
> The King's deeds were condemned by heaven and earth,
> Should he hearken to Chi Ch'ang's words with discernment,
> He would never lose his power and be put to death.

Hardly had the king decided to behead Chi Ch'ang when Chiang Huan-chu, the Eastern Earl, came forward to advise, "My Lord, you are wrong. Please listen to me and quiet down. This man was a loyal minister in the court of three kings, was highly esteemed by them, and from ancient times up to the present there has been no sword which is suitable for the beheading of a feudal prince. I hope my Lord will inquire into the matter and spare him. The man also has a good knowledge of yin and yang in the creation of the universe and knows the evil and good of the earth. For these reasons I have the audacity to beg this favor of my Lord." The king ordered his attendants to shove Chi Ch'ang before him and asked, "You know the creation of the earth and are able to foretell a man's good or bad fortune and his future richness or poverty. Now you are ordered to foretell something for me, to say whether anything will happen to me. If you prove to be a prophet, I will spare your life." Chi Ch'ang did not worry about himself, for he knew that he would not die until the age of ninety-seven and would be posthumously honored as king, so he now predicted that something strange would soon happen. The king did not believe it but ordered a minister to go out to investigate and told his attendants to keep an eye on Chi Ch'ang.

At noon, the strange things happened: a wild wind arose from the southeast and carried away stones and sands. Tiles and trees were blown away. A clay man and a clay horse, both from a temple, were strolling along in the market. The minister came back and said to the king, "My Lord, what Chi Ch'ang foretold has happened." While the king was still pondering the matter, the clay man and the clay horse returned to the temple. There is a poem:

> Chi Ch'ang was able to divine the gale,
> Clay man and clay horse in market took a stroll,

The people marveled at such strange things,
And you could divine Chow's weakness within his firm countenance.

The king, therefore, ordered Chi Ch'ang to be released.

Next day, the Eight Earls bade farewell to the king and went out of the palace gate. Chi Ch'ang came to tell them, "The king will lose the reins of government in fifteen years." They were about to part when Fei Chung arrived. Chi Ch'ang said to him, "You are a flatterer, and you know that Ta-chi has stirred up a turmoil and caused much harm to the people." The earls then departed, but Fei Chung bore a grudge against Chi Ch'ang for what he had said.

One day, the king and Ta-chi dined together in the Star-Plucking Tower. Ta-chi asked the king, "My Lord, what valuables can be obtained in this world for me to play with?" The king said, "Where should the valuables be found?" Fei Chung came over and said, "My Lord, I know one man who has valuables suitable for your mistress." The king asked, "Who has valuables?" Fei Chung answered, "I know that Chi Ch'ang, the Western Earl, has a pair of gorgeous bracelets of jade which are priceless. They answer the wishes of the person who wears them. They can change the weather as desired and can make one healthy and maintain one's youth. They are genuine treasures." Ta-chi was overjoyed and said to the king, "I want to wear those bracelets; what do you think?" The king said, "This is easy, but who can run this errand for me?" Fei Chung said, "I am willing to do it. But if my Lord sends another man on this mission, I am afraid he will be allured by the gold and jewels of the Western Earl and thus not be willing to bring those bracelets." Ta-chi said, "What you say is appropriate." And she gave a hundred taels of gold to Fei Chung.

Fei Chung thanked the king and started on the journey. In a few days he sent someone to inform Chi Ch'ang of his coming. Chi Ch'ang heard this and went out of the city of Ch'i-chou to welcome the envoy. After exchanging salutes, the two entered the city and went into the government office to burn incense. Chi Ch'ang then read the holy decree and entertained Fei Chung. Fei Chung said, "I am ordered by the king to come here for a treasure." "What treasure?" asked Chi Ch'ang. "Gorgeous bracelets of jade," answered Fei Chung. Chi Ch'ang heard this and thought to himself, "This must be Fei Chung's design." The earl gave Fei Chung the bracelets and said, "These are not ordinary, but are marvelous treasures. They will make one who wears them healthy and youthful, and make him change any time. A sick man might recover if he wore them. They can drive away evils and monsters. If an elf sees them, he will be frightened and run off."

Fei Chung received the bracelets, bade farewell to Chi Ch'ang, and went back to the capital to report to the king. The king asked, "How about the bracelets?" Fei Chung handed the bracelets to the king who, seeing the treasure glistening and colorful, was very glad. The king beckoned Fei Chung to go to the rear chamber where Ta-chi welcomed him. After three cups of wine, the king ordered Fei Chung to present the bracelets to Ta-chi. Ta-chi was extremely glad and ordered, "Give them to me." She screamed and feel flat on the ground when she opened the handkerchief and saw the bracelets. She was breathless and her limbs were heavy. Were they fatal to Ta-chi's life? There is a poem:

> Marvelous were the bracelets brought from the West;
> It was the scheme of Fei Chung who had a grudge against Chi Ch'ang.
> When they were presented to Ta-chi,
> She fell to the ground in a swoon.

The king picked her up from the ground and, after a considerable lapse of time, Ta-chi recovered and said, "Take the bracelets away." The king asked, "What kind of sickness have you?" Ta-chi dared not tell the truth but had to resort to subterfuge and said, "My Lord, I have had heart attacks in the past and today I had one again. The bracelets are not good. Please give them to Queen Chiang." The king said, "I will follow your suggestion."

Queen Chiang received the bracelets and wore them. She felt more energetic and sound, and nothing happened to her. The king was informed of this. On that day, Ta-chi summoned Fei Chung surreptitiously, gave him a hundred taels of gold and said, "You draw up a plan. How can I drive away Queen Chiang?" Fei Chung said, "I have a plan." Ta-chi said, "What plan?" Fei Chung said, "Tomorrow will be Queen Chiang's birthday. You go to the first chamber to pay your respects to her. When she sees you she will be angry, then you dishevel your hair and go to the king telling him that Queen Chiang has struck you. The king will trust you and send for the queen. You then call someone to hide a dagger in the skirt of the queen and you can say to the king, 'The queen intended to murder me. You see, she dropped her dagger on the floor. She knows you like me, hence she wants to kill me.' Then the king will believe you and will indict the queen." Ta-chi said, "That's a good stratagem. Please go now."

Ta-chi followed the plan designed by Fei Chung and went to pay her respects to the queen next day. Indeed the queen was angry and scolded Ta-chi, "Are you not ashamed of yourself? Why do you come to see me, you wench?" Ta-chi mussed her hair and went to report to the king, crying. The king asked, "What makes you cry?" Ta-chi replied, "The queen hit me." The king was exasperated and sent for the queen.

The king asked, "What did you strike Ta-chi for?" The queen answered, "I have not hit her." During the king's inquiry, Ta-chi called someone to hide a dagger under the foot of the queen and said to the king, "The queen intended to kill my Lord." The king was angry and the queen said, "How could I intend to harm my Lord." The king said, "Why then do you hide a dagger under your foot?" The queen could not defend herself and only wept.

The king, not clear about the matter himself, was exasperated, and in the Star-Plucking Tower together with Ta-chi issued a holy decree ordering that the queen be given simple garments, kept secluded, and humiliated. The queen heard this and was angry. She reprimanded the king in disregard of her safety, "Ruthless and lewd ruler, you trust evil persons and seclude me. You are hated by the gods and human beings, and there shall be no place for you on this earth. You shall perish at the point of thousands and thousands of daggers. For what reasons do you hate me?" The king was extremely angry and rose abruptly, pushed the maid aside, and got hold of the queen. Disregarding her situation, the queen scolded the king again, "Formerly, King Chieh of Hsia died at the Drum Gate because he was ruthless. Now you give way to your wench and stir up troubles in the nation." No sooner had the queen finished speaking than the king, catching hold of her clothes and dark hair, pushed her down from the building to her death. A poem said:

> Queen Chiang admonished Chow against perversity,
> Her sincere reproof grated on his ear;
> Furious with anger was the ruthless ruler,
> Who pushed her down from the building with disheveled hair.

The king ordered her corpse to be buried beneath the seventh wu-t'ung tree[9] in the back garden. The pair of gorgeous jade bracelets, which Ta-chi pretended to forget, was also buried. The king, who did not care about the consequences, entertained himself with Ta-chi every day. And no one dared to admonish the king.

Time flew like an arrow and ten years quickly passed. There is a poem:

> Shadows of flowers move swiftly under the eaves,
> Time flies with a snap of the fingers;
> A goblet of wine had not emptied nor the singing ended,
> When the rooster-keeper reported a shift of the sundial.

Now the Prince Yin Chiao, the son of Queen Chiang, who was one year old at the time of the queen's death and was fostered by some palace maids, was ten years of age. He was five feet tall, brilliant, and was of an ardent disposition. The king did not care for him.

Realizing that the prince was gradually growing up, Ta-chi was frightened and thought, "A maid-of-honor will certainly inform the prince about the death of his mother. That is the trouble. I will send for Fei Chung surreptitiously." Fei Chung arrived at court. Ta-chi asked, "Do you remember an affair ten years ago?" Fei Chung said, "Which affair?" Ta-chi said, "At the

---

9. *Sterculia platanifolia* (see selection 114, note 1).

time of Queen Chiang's death, her son was one year old. Ten years have already passed, and the prince must have reached the adolescent state. I am afraid the former maids of the queen will inform the prince about the death of his mother, and therefore the prince will retaliate. How can I solve this trouble?" Fei Chung said, "I have a plan which will make you feel at ease." Ta-chi said, "What plan?" Fei Chung said, "It will be perfectly safe if the queen's maids can be eliminated." Ta-chi said, "How can they be eliminated?" Fei Chung said, "You go to see the king at dusk and pretend to be sad. The king will ask you why and you merely say, 'The maids of Queen Chiang insult me and I cannot tolerate it. You can eliminate them.' The king will say, 'How can I eliminate them?' Then you say, 'I suggest my Lord should build a wine pond and a meat forest, and find a place for a serpent-caldron and burning iron. My Lord should then instruct the maids of the queen to fight each other. Those who win should be pushed into the wine pond to drink themselves to death; those who are defeated should be tossed into the serpent-caldron and be bitten to death by snakes, lizards, and scorpions; and those who survive should be pushed into a fire pit, or tied up on a burning brass pillar and be burned to death.' This method can eliminate the maids. No one will inform the prince about the matter, and your worries will be removed." Ta-chi said, "Leave me now." Then Fei Chung departed.

In the evening, Ta-chi went to see the king with a sad face. The king was surprised and asked, "What makes you unhappy?" Pretending, Ta-chi said, "Listen, my Lord, the subordinates of the queen insult me under her prestige and I want to get rid of them." Ta-chi explained her plan, "My Lord should build a wine pond and a meat forest in the court and install a serpent-caldron and a burning pillar of iron. Then my Lord will order the maids to fight each other. Those who win shall be pushed into the pond and drink themselves to death, and those who lose shall be tossed into the caldron and be bitten by snakes and scorpions. And those who are found guilty shall be tied up on the brass pillar." The king granted her request and ordered everything be installed accordingly.

The king and Ta-chi drank in the Star-Plucking Tower. The former maids of the queen, who were all splendidly dressed, were summoned to the building and were instructed to take off their elaborate clothes except for the waist bands. Then the king ordered them to fight duels. The wind blew and they appeared naked. Ta-chi and the king amused themselves by watching the game. Those who won were sunk in the wine pond, and those who lost were flung into the serpent-caldron and bitten to death by snakes and scorpions. Those who were found guilty were tied up on the burning pillar and burned to death. The king was so ruthless that he destroyed thus thousands of lives and he amused himself with Ta-chi disregarding the unceasing crying of the chambermaids. The whole nation knew of his cruelty. A poem said:

The king was bewitched by a licentious fox,
Wine pond and meat forest he did install;
When his capital Chao Ko fell,
Would he understand the will of heaven and repent all?

Translated by Liu Ts'un-yan

Drama

272

The Monk Pu-tai and the Character for Patience

Attributed to Cheng T'ing-yü (fl. 1250)

Stage Business Key

Parentheses and lower case italics, e.g., (*Recites*): stage business as indicated in *Yüan-ch'ü hsüan* edition.

Braces and lower case italics, e.g., {*and the* hsiao-tan}: stage business as indicated in *Ku-chin tsa-chü* edition not in *Yüan-ch'ü hsüan* edition.

This is a complete Yüan drama (*tsa-chü*) showing all the typical features of the genre. The verses are sung by a single actor per act (a vestige of its origins in prosimetric storytelling) to various standard arias (*ch'ü*), the names of which are not always completely transparent and hence left untranslated here. Aside from the attribution to Cheng T'ing-yü, this play has also been ascribed to Meng Shou-ch'ing.

It should be noted that the sinograph (i.e., "character") used to write the word for "patience" (*jen*) is made up of a component that signifies "knife blade" resting on another component that signifies "heart." According to a spurious kind of folk "etymology" that is extremely popular in China, the notion of "patience" is implied in this juxtaposition of components. A more genuine analysis of the sinograph would recognize that the "knife blade" component actually functions as a phonetic indicator and that the "heart" component functions as a semantic classifier. The word *jen* originally meant "to be callous, unfeeling, unsympathetic." Later, it came to mean "to endure" and, still later, "patience, forbearance."

Translator's note: I owe a great debt to Li Tche-houa who sent me an inscribed copy of his *Le Signe de Patience et Autres Pièces du Théâtres des Yüan* in 1964 — "… en témoinage du nôtre commun amour pour le théâtre des Yüan." I used his work in my teaching for twenty-five years, always indicating to students the multitude of hints about Yüan staging to be found in it. In 1991 I read the play with students again and this time decided to do a version complete with

Brackets and lower case italics, e.g., [*He turns*]: translator's additions and explanations

Lower case bold roman, e.g., **Wife, you know not . . .** : lines only in *Ku-chin
tsa-chü* edition.

Prologue

(*Secondary role costumed as* ĀNANDA *enters*)

ĀNANDA:

(*Recites*)

The Illumined Nature hath no need
To hold the silent flower,[1]
Perceptive Minds need not read
From palm-leaf[2] texts.
Hard ice converts to water in the sun.
Moonglow still lights the sky
When the moon itself is gone.

I am the monk Ānanda. Our Buddha convened a meeting of all the
Arhats[3] on Mount Ling to explain the sūtras and speak of the Law. The
Wolf Star from above (who is in fact the thirteenth arhat) paid scant
heed to our Buddha's teachings—his mind was for that while occupied
with thoughts of the Dusty World. This infraction should have seen him
confined in Feng-tu of the Nether Regions. But great compassion welled
up in our Buddha, who merely banished him to be born a human into
the Liu clan of Pien-liang—by name, one Liu Chün-tso. Because he
feared this human soul might be deluded about the True Way, Buddha
has sent the Future Buddha, Maitreya, in the guise of the monk Pu-tai
("Cloth Sack"), to convert him. In addition, Buddha has sent Fu-hu
("Crouching Tiger"), the Ch'an[4] Master, to be incarnated as Liu The
Ninth. They will first turn this soul back to repentence and send him to
Yüeh-lin Monastery to perfect himself. Buddha will cause the Senior of
that monastery, Ting-hui, to lecture him on doctrines of Mahāyāna
("Greater Vehicle") Buddhism.

---

the added stage directions and suggestions I had prepared for earlier classes. I hope it will prove
helpful to yet another generation of Yüan drama students.

1. The phrase *nien-hua wei-hsiao* [(Buddha) held the flower and (Kaśyapa) smiled] is a
Ch'anist (Zen) "transmission story." Buddha once held a flower in his fingers and said nothing
(as a way of teaching). Kaśyapa alone smiled — meaning he understood the lesson. Hence, the
"silent flower." This same quatrain is used as an entrance verse for Buddhist characters in
other dramas.

2. Indian scriptures were traditionally written on this medium.

3. Buddhist saints.

4. I.e., Zen, from Sanskrit *dhyāna* ("meditation").

This human need only renounce wine, lust, wealth, and anger; if he dispense with concepts of right and wrong, and truly practice right actions, then I believe I can save him:

(*Recites*)

For a wrong thought
Sent to the World of Dust;
Being human, he will lust
After worldly wealth and honor.
Yet by the grace of Future Buddha
The Law will be learned.
When all the needed merit has been earned,
Back to the Lotus Throne
All will be returned.

(*Exit*)

(*Enter* LIU CHÜN-TSO *leading* WIFE, CHILDREN {ching},[5] SERVANTS)

(*Speaks*)

CHÜN-TSO: I am Liu Kuei, known as Liu Chün-tso of Pien-liang. There are four in my family: my wife, née Wang, and I who am forty years old. My wife has given me a son and a daughter. The boy is called Fo-liu and my daughter is known as Seng-nu'er.[6] Though I'm worth a couple of strings of cash, on my best day I would spend neither farthing nor pence. Any time I have to part with a string of cash, it feels as though it were ripped out of my hide, But, it is precisely because I've been so tightfisted and frugal that I've managed to collect such a fortune.

However, now it is winter and the White Blessings of the state are swirling and fluttering everywhere. The wealthy with their glowing stoves in their warm quarters are indulging themselves—enjoying the beauty of snow and drinking warm wine. Why am I, Liu Chün-tso, not willing to indulge *myself* thus? Because I fear bankrupting my family's patrimony!

WIFE: Sir, they do say, "Wind and snow are Heaven on the side of the taverner." However that may be, should we not at least take a few cups?

TSO: **Wife, you know not whereof you speak; when you spend one cash, you never know if you will get it back again.** I want not to do as you wish, but that would be churlish. Ah, well, have it your way. We'll spend, so be it, so be it! We'll be lavish and drink!

WIFE: Sir, certainly a few cups would be pleasant.

---

5. Unless the children are so considered, no *ching* character appears in the Prologue. The *ching* (comic or villain) is one category of role type in a Yüan drama.

6. Both names have a Buddhist ring to them.

TSO: Servants, fetch some wine; your mistress and I would drink. Bring it along. [*Aside, sotto voce*] But not too much, mind. A couple of cups will do.

SERVANTS: Understood! (*They pass the cups*)

WIFE: Sir, please take the first cup.

TSO (*Drinks the wine*): Bring another cup! Wife, you take this one.

WIFE: (*Drinks down the cup*) More wine.

SERVANT: There is no more, Ma'am.

WIFE: We've toasted twice and there's no more wine!? Break out some more.

TSO: That's enough wine. Remember, the ancients said, "Drink wine less, heed business more." Now I'm going into the pawnshop to see what custom there may be.

(*Secondary role,* LIU CHÜN-YU, {*dressed in rags*} *enters and recites*)

YU:

> My knowledge includes all
> That happens in the world;
> My fate is inferior to all
> The men who inhabit it.

I am Liu Chün-yu from Loyang. Since I have a fair amount of learning, I have come to this place for employment. But now my purse and hampers are both empty and winter weather has begun—heavy snow has fallen and I have nothing to clothe myself with and nothing in my belly. [*Pantomimes peering about*] This appears to be the residence of someone of consequence. I shall seek him out and beg food and warm tea. But here I am on his doorstep and I can think of no plan except to chant the Buddhist mendicants' song, "The Lotus Falls." . . . [*Chants*]

> One spring past
> Another follows fast. . . . . .

[*Speaks*]

Ah, alas, sky and earth are spinning . . . !

(*He pantomimes falling*)

TSO: Wife, while we have been drinking, someone has fallen from the cold on our doorstep! Children, help that gentleman into the house and bring coals to heat wine for him. . . .

[*Children pantomime assisting* YU *and fetching coals*]

[*Aside*] Ah, but, Liu Chün-tso, think carefully about this. . . . [*To his* WIFE] You know I am not one of kindly sensibilities; ordinarily I would pay little heed to ten men felled by the frost, much less one. But this one man has moved me strangely. I must speak with him. . . . Sir, have you recovered?

YU: I'm somewhat better, now. . . .

TSO: Then tell me, sir, where do you come from? What is your name and surname? And how did you come to drop with the cold on my doorstep? Please tell me about it.

YU: My lord, my surname is Liu, my given name is Chün-yu. I come from Loyang. Being a scholar, I was pursuing my studies here. There was nothing in my purse and hampers and I had no clothes to wear. My stomach was empty when I saw my lord here drinking. I could think of nothing else to do, so I began chanting "The Lotus Falls." Before I knew it I had fainted on your honor's doorstep. Indeed, had it not been for your honor I should have lost my life.

TSO: (*Aside*) Now, think carefully about this, Liu Chün-tso. You asked where he came from and he replied Loyang; his family name is Liu and he is called Chün-yu. Does not the proverb say:

Two kinds of blooms on the same tree;
From the same family, you and he.

Because he has touched my heart. . . . (*Turns to* YU) Tell me, Liu Chün-yu, I have it in mind to make you my sworn brother, what think you of that?

YU: Please, your honor, do not make fun of me.

TSO: I am not making fun.

YU: But, if that's true, you need hardly speak of brotherhood—I should be happy to "serve at your stirrup and saddle" in your home!

TSO: So be it then, brother. I am your elder brother as I would be were we of the same blood—and this is your sister-in-law. Pay her your respects.

YU: (*Bows his respects*) Sister-in-law, please be seated and accept my twofold bows.

WIFE: Please, uncle, dispense with ceremonies.

TSO: [*Beckoning*] Children, come pay your respects to your uncle. (CHILDREN *bow*)

YU: I can hardly accept such honor; no more ceremony.

WIFE: Sir, continue your conversation with your brother while I go in and see to tea and refreshments.

(*Exit*)

TSO: Having acknowledged your adoption this day, there is something I would speak to you about.

YU: Brother, you may speak of anything to me.

TSO: A while ago you fell in a heap in the snow and, had it not been for me, I scarcely think you would have come away with your life. Further, I made you my brother, and you may now be saying to yourself, here is a gentleman devoted to generosity—but you would be mistaken. Your brother's fortune is his because he rose early and worked late, he was frugal and labored long . . . and this is no easy thing to achieve. I would have you hear how things were. . . .

YU: Brother, do tell me how it was and I will listen.

TSO:

Hsien-lü, Shang-hua Shih[7]

(Sings)

Nowadays men respect the garment, not the man:
Whether or not I willed it
Gold has been my friend, not men.
A moment ago
In the bitter wind, in the whirling snows
You fell beside the highroad
And all but froze.

(Speaks)

My brother, I am wealthy but I took as a brother an impoverished man. Think on it, do—

(Sings)

I am as rich
As you are poor.

YU: And I was clad only in rags. Would not that fact alone make my elder brother a laughing-stock?

TSO:

Yao-pien

(Sings)

Your poverty is such
That your livelihood was straitened,
Your life impoverished.
My wealth is such
That I possess pearls, gold,
And all the money my coffers can hold.

7. The title of the song he sings. If a sung passage does not carry the title of an aria at its head, then it is sung to the tune of the preceding aria.

(*Speaks*)

Brother, abroad or at home I expect you to work without cease.
YU: I understand.
TSO:

(*Sings*)

But for now,
Make yourself comfortable
In our pawnshop.

(*Speaks*)

Goodness of heart alone caused me to make you my brother; but my
wealthy friends will say, "See Liu Chün-tso! On his best day he would
spend neither farthing nor pence—such was his stingy frugality, yet now
he takes on an idler!"

(*Sings*)

This act alone
Has made me the butt of others' laughter.
So be it! So be it!
For once I've broken a lifelong ban—
Undertaken to sustain an idle man!

(*Exeunt*)

Act One

(LIU CHÜN-YU *leading* SERVANTS *enters*)

[*Servants remain on stage until* LIU CHIU'ERH *enters. Another group of extras
enters with the monk* PU-TAI, *exits just before he does, and then constitutes
the crowd following* LIU CHIU'ERH]

YU: I am Liu Chün-yu and almost half a year has passed since elder brother
made me his sworn younger brother. He is usually so stingy that he
would spend neither farthing nor pence. The paying out of debts and the
collecting of obligations is all in my hands now.

Today is my brother's birthday. Ordinarily he would be reluctant to
celebrate, but I've taken it upon myself to have a lamb on the spit and
fruits and wines set out. If I tell him all this is a gift from friends,
neighbors, or fellow merchants, he'll be happy enjoying them, but if he
knew I had bought these festive items, it would pierce him to the heart.
Servants, are the fruit and wine properly set out?
SERV: All as required, sir.

YU: Since all is in order, I'll show my brother and sister-in-law in. [*He goes to entrance, stage right and bows*] Brother, sister please come in. . . .

(*Enter* TSO *and* WIFE *accompanied by* CHILDREN)

TSO [*Facing audience*]: I am Liu Chün-tso. It has been full half a year since I took on my sworn brother and he has proven to be most diligent—working for the household and earning his living, early to rise and late to bed, paying out debts and collecting obligations. He has been my heart's delight. Wife, this is my birthday as you know. As you also know I never celebrate the day. So do not mention it to our younger brother Chün-yu lest he wish to lay on festivities and quite likely bankrupt our fortune in the process.

WIFE: Well, I wonder just why our brother has called us? Go and speak to him.

[*All turn to Face* YU]

(TSO *pantomimes seeing* YU)

YU: Brother, please be seated. This being the anniversary of your birth. I arranged for a little wine and refreshments—and let me now perform the twofold bow, the better to show my brother what is in my heart.

TSO: [*Resigned*] Hai! Wife, look you. As I feared, he knows and has arranged a feast. You can be sure he'll bankrupt us! Alas, I shall die from the pain . . . !

YU: No, brother! You must understand—all these things were supplied by friends, neighbors, and fellow merchants. I have just finished thanking them and sent them off—not one copper of the household fortune has been spent! Now, here we have a complete banquet set out on our tables, so brother, sister, I beg you, drink a few cups.

TSO: Oh, well, if that's the case. . . . But you should have told me straight off! Yes, yes, by all means let's drink. . . . Just a few, mind!

WIFE: Oh, sir, you are always so parsimonious. How much does a drink cost . . . ?

YU: [*To the* SERVANTS] Bring in the wine; I must pass my brother his birthday cup to wish him wealth and long life. [*Raises cup in toast*] May your years continue as long as the cypress lives.

TSO: I am obliged to you, brother . . .

Hsien-lü, Tien-chiang Ch'un

(*Sings*)

My thanks, dear friend.
He wishes me good fortune, high age.
His hopes for longevity

Of cypress and pine he would convey;
He arose this early on my natal day.

Hun-chiang Lung

The horn goblets are passed about;
I seem to see the Eastwind making
The jalousies dance.
Music and beat echoing in heaven, I hear,
And even more
Does the flute and the *sheng*[8] enchant the ear.

YU: Drink the full cup off!
TSO: Brother, this is fine wine.

(*Sings*)

See how
Warm spring wine
Glitters in my cup of Jade;
How incense smoke swirls
From golden burners
Shaped like the sign for longevity.

(*Speaks*)

Tell those who would set animals free[9]

[*Sound of Buddhist chanting has been growing offstage*]

(*Sings*)

To be silent and at peace out there,
Not raise their hubub here. . . .

YU: [*Addressing* SERVANTS] Tell those creature-releasers to move off a bit and
not make their noises here. . . .
TSO:

(*Speaks*)

Brother, do you know how I amassed my fortune, eh? . . .

(*Sings*)

I spent not, but scrimped carefully,
Thus, now this wealth, and luxury.

8. A circular reed mouth organ of ancient Southeast Asian origin.
9. A common custom of Buddhist believers by which it is thought they may gain good
karma.

(*Enter* PU-TAI *leading a troupe of girls and boys*)

PU:

(*Chants*)

Buddha, Buddha, Buddha,
Namu Amida Buddha!

(*He laughs and chants a gāthā*[10])

Walking with my bag of cloth,
Sitting with my bag of cloth.
Putting my cloth bag aside
Rids me of delusive pride!

Come, earthbound ones! Come follow this humble monk and I will make you all a Buddha, make each of you the Founder! I am the Abbot of Yüeh-lin Temple in Feng-hsiang prefecture and have walked this far because here lives a certain Liu Chün-tso—a very wealthy man. But alas! the man is greedy, covetous, grasping, and stingy. He will "spend neither farthing nor pence." [*Spoken to ape* TSO's *tone when he makes this boast*] I have come a-purpose to convert him, and here is his very threshold. Ho there, miserly Liu Chün-tso! (*He laughs*)

YU: Brother, I wonder who is making all the fuss outside? I'll investigate. (*Pantomimes seeing* PU-TAI) My! *There's* a fat monk for you!

PU: (*Laughing*) You there, un-frozen beggar, is our miser here?

YU: [*Aside*] How did *he* know I fell frozen upon my brother's very doorstep?

PU: Is your miser at home?

YU: [*Attempting to keep a straight face*] I shall tell my brother. (*Pantomimes seeing* TSO *and then breaks into laughter*) Brother, I shall certainly die laughing!

TSO: Why are you laughing so?

YU: You ask now why I laugh, but if you go to the door and look, you'll be laughing, too.

TSO: Well, I certainly want to see this. (*Pantomimes seeing* PU-TAI)

PU: Well? Mr. Miser, Liu Chün-tso?

TSO: (*Laughing* [*uncontrollably*]) Ai-yah, what a fat monk! I shall die laughing!

PU: Who are you laughing at, then?

TSO: Why you, of course!

PU:

(*Reciting gāthā*)

10. Sacred Buddhist verse. "Namu Amida Buddha!" in the previous line means "Praise be to Amitābha Buddha!"

You laugh at what I have not,
I laugh at what you've got.
When Old Mortality commands,
All go to him with empty hands!

TSO: In truth, brother, I *am* laughing myself to death! I wonder what he feeds upon to make him so fat?

Yu Hu-lu

(*Sings*)

[*Sings aria with chuckling overtones*]

Suddenly looking up at him
I collapse with mirth and nearly fall.

PU: Remain where you are, my children.
TSO:

(*Sings*)

He leads and puts the boys and girls
Through their paces.

(*Speaks*)

But let me guess why he's so fat. . . .

(*Sings*)

[*Here, the singing has a sarcastic timbre*]

Monks' fasting fare—so dainty, so delicious. . . .

PU: Offer me a fasting meal.
TSO:

(*Sings*)

Perhaps the meals they beg from the faithful
Fatten Ch'an monks wondrous well.
His waist as huge as a storage-bin
With three foot bulges of belly-skin.

Poor elephants, camels, leopards and lions. . . .

PU: What are those animals doing in here?
TSO:

(*Sings*)

If you rode them you'd break their spines!

PU: [*In exaggerated hurt tone*] I fear he's mocking this poor monk!

(*Sings*)

This *poor* monk!—
A ton of meat even with the fat trimmed off!

(*Speaks*)

I wonder what he eats?

(*Sings*)

Now I ponder a comparison for him.

PU: What will you compare me with, then?
TSO:

(*Sings*)

He's plump Hsüan Tsung with a tonsured pate.

(*Speaks*)

See here, monk, your corpulence has put me in mind of two men from the past. . . .

PU: What two are they?
TSO:

(Sings)

You are as fat as the Ouigur An Lu-shan,[11]
Or again, like fat Tung Cho of the Han.

(*Speaks*)

You are so fat, standing in the door to my pawnshop, those who knew will simply say, look, there's a fat monk; those who did not

(*Sings*)

Would say the God of Wealth[12] brings again
More treasure to the wealthiest of men!

PU: Liu Chün-tso, your dull mind and flesh-dimmed eyes cannot distinguish the good, for I am the Buddha Śākyamuni!
TSO: Who is Śākyamuni!?
PU: *I* am the Buddha Śākyamuni.

11. See selections 180 and 181.
12. Usually depicted as enormously rotund.

TSO: You?! Śākyamuni? No, no, too much is lacking. . . .

Na-cho Ling

(*Sings*)

You're so obese you could never have
Sacrificed any of that to feed the eagle.
Your great thick thighs
Would have straddled in vain
The slender reed to cross the River.
Where on your glistening razored pate
Could little birds build their nests?[13]

PU: Alas, you from the World of Dust heed not the teaching of Maitreya.
TSO:

(*Sings*)

We heed not Maitreya;
Could it be that
Is why we eat so much
But do not get so fat?

PU: Liu Chün-tso, I am no ordinary monk; I am a Master of the Dhyāna School, and between one sunrise and the next I can cover three hundred tricents!
TSO:

(*Sings*)

I doubt you could circumambulate the Temple
Nor bow your respects to the Trinity,

(*Speaks*)

For you, sir are so round and fat . . .

(*Sings*)

You would, of a certainty,
Roll right out the monastery gate
And up into the sky.

---

13. A devout Indian king (the Buddha in a previous incarnation) offered his body to an eagle about to eat a dove. Tradition has it that Bodhidarma (the founder of Ch'an / Zen in China) crossed the Yangtze floating on a reed. The Buddha was once so absorbed in meditation that birds built their nests in his hair.

PU: Liu Chün-tso, give me at least one monkish meal!
TSO:

> (*Sings*)
>
> Oh, for that great hollow to be full
> Who can calculate such an amount?
>
> (*Speaks*)
>
> Mr. Monk, there is one good thing about your great weight.

PU: And what would that be?
TSO:

> (*Sings*)
>
> You'll never faint from lack of fat to draw on
> Nor have a racing heart
> For lack of things to gnaw on.

PU: Liu Chün-tso my holiness is great and my sanctity strong—I am the living Buddha!
TSO:

Chi-sheng Ts'ao

> (*Sings*)
>
> Your wisdom you claim is great.
> Alas, you have little stomach—
> For tolerance, that is.[14]
>
> (*Speaks*)
>
> Monk, hear me now . . .
>
> (*Sings*)
>
> Could one conceive of you
> As the ailing Vimalakīrti who
> So early took his Dhyāna[15] seat?
> Or again,
> Gaunt Ānanda finding final cause and effect?
> Nor scarcely
> Imagine you as sick Shen Yüeh

---

14. A play on words; *tu-liang* ("tolerance") is homophonous with *tu-liang* ("belly capacity").
15. Ch'an or Zen, i.e., meditation.

Who shaved his head to become a monk. [16]

(*Speaks*)

But you should know this, oh monk; half of me is disquieted and half of me knows fear. . . .

PU: What causes you disquiet? What makes you fear?

TSO:

(*Sings*)

Disquieted to imagine you,
South of the Southern Sea,
Unable to carry the Willow Vase. [17]
Fearful lest you,
West of the Western Heavens,
Sit upon the Lotus Seat
And smash the thing complete?!

PU: Liu Chün-tso, give me a single abstainer's meal and I will teach you the lessons of Mahāyāna Buddhism!

TSO: What is this Mahāyāna Buddhism?

PU: Furnish me with paper, brush-pen, ink, and inkstone, and I will teach you what it is.

TSO: We have no paper . . .

YU: Yes we do, brother—I'll bring you a piece. . . . [YU *fetches paper, pen, inkstick, and grinding slab, probably from propman;* TSO *tries to conceal the fact that* YU *has paper and makes him return it to propman. Could be an extended piece of humorous business*]

TSO: [*Exasperated at* YU] Brother, a sheet of paper costs a copper; at this rate you will ruin us!

PU: [*Interrupting*] No matter . . . you have no paper. Just bring me the brush and inkstone, and I shall write the lesson of the Greater Vehicle on your palm.

TSO:

(*While* YU *pantomimes grinding ink*)

Tsui-chung T'ien

(*Sings*)

16. Shen Yüeh (see selection 31) is sometimes noted as "tightening his belt" after an illness. To my knowledge, he never became a monk, though he was very much interested in Buddhist scholarship and culture.

17. One form that images of the compassionate Bodhisattva (savior figure), Kuan-yin (Avalokiteśvara), take.

> I watch as he grinds extravagantly
> My fine Black Dragon's Horn . . .

(PU *pantomines taking the brush and dipping it in the ink*)

> And see him stain the snowy rabbit-hairs. . . .[18]

PU: Give me your hand, now, and I shall write the lesson of Mahāyāna.

TSO: Here, my hand.

PU: (*Pantomimes writing on the [left] palm*) Liu Chün-tso, here, then, is the great lesson of Mahāyāna.

TSO: (*Looking at his hand and laughing*) This is very droll indeed!

> (*Sings*)

> I see that he has written
> The character for "heart."
> Atop it he placed the one for "blade."[19]

PU: This character means "be patient," "forbear," and this is your personal *vade-tecum*—a treasure to go with you forever.

TSO:

> (*Sings*)

> Treasure to go with me, so you say,
> Treasure perhaps, but I will have to pay. . . .

PU: What do you have to pay for?

TSO:

> (*Sings*)

> At least a half-bowl of water and a cake of soap.
> Since candor is better than clever words,
> Thank you, oh Bodhidharma! Soon,
> Thanks to your wastefulness,
> I'll need your begging-bowl and mendicant's dress!

PU: Liu Chün-tso, give me one abstinence meal.

YU: Brother, we are so wealthy; what have you to fear by giving him one alms-meal?

TSO: Good brother, don't you see the size of his belly? It would take two bushels of uncooked rice to fill that!

YU: [*Turning to the monk*] We have no meatless dishes.

---

18. The brush, that is (see selection 235).

19. Tso's literacy must be of a low level, because he does not seem to recognize that the two simple components form the common sinograph for "patience" (see the first unnumbered note above).

PU: I am not asking for vegetarian dishes. I also eat meat and drink wine.

TSO: What kind of a monk eats meat and drinks?

YU: Give him meat and drink.

TSO: [*Reluctantly*] Very well. . . . Pour a cup for him. (YU *pantomimes pouring a cup of wine* [*with* TSO *watching closely*]) Keep it shallower! That's too full!

PU: Let me have it, then. (*He pours out a libation*). Namu Amida Buddha.

TSO: What a waste! Let's be a bit more frugal with the libation! D'you know it takes a hundred kernels of rice to make a single drop of wine!? Let's not slop that libation around so!

PU: Liu Chün-tso, let me beg another cup. . . .

TSO: [*Interrupting—trying to forestall his brother*] There's no more wine!

YU: Brother, give him another cup.

> [*While this has been going on, the children who came on stage with the monk have quietly slipped out between the hangings instead of by usual exit around curtain, stage left*]

TSO: Oh, all right, do it. (YU *pours the wine*). So? Take it, drink, drink, drink!

PU: This one's for my disciples.

TSO: (*Turns his head, pantomimes looking*) Where are they?

PU: [*Points to distract* TSO] Over there! {*Presto!*} [PU *also slips out between the hangings when* TSO *and* YU *turn to look*][20]

TSO: Where? [*Turns back to monk*] Monk, there's nobody th . . . , [TSO *looks about him*] Now, even *he's* gone!

YU: Where did the monk go, brother?

TSO: Well, now that's strange. . . .

Ho-hsi (or) Hou-t'ing-hua

(*Sings*)

He tricked me into turning my head;
He could not have walked a step
As I filled the jade cup
To give him his toast—
Ya, ya, ya!
He disappeared in a streak of golden light!

(*Speaks*)

It was really strange.

(*Sings*)

20. It appears that the use of hangings in this fashion is most common in dramas dealing with the supernatural.

Now I think on it
He must be
A magician from the Southern Sea;
Down yonder,
He makes his audiences
Gape with wonder.

(*Speaks*)

Brother, we were just having a bit of wine and this great fat monk bursts
in to break up our party. . . .

YU: Ah, well, "mad monks and demented Taoists," you know. Pay no attention
to him; let's go inside for a glass of wine.

TSO: Now that the fat monk's gone, I certainly don't need this character on my
hand. Have some water brought.

YU: [*To servants*] Fetch water for the master to wash his hands. [*A bowl
is brought*]

TSO: (*Pantomimes washing his hands*) I can't seem to wash this off—bring me
some soap, too.

YU: [*Obtains soap from propman*] Here's a piece.

TSO: (*Pantomimes scrubbing his hands*) But why does it grow more visible as I
wash? Bring me a towel. [*Folded cloth is brought.* TSO *pantomimes
wiping his hand vigorously while he unfolds cloth, revealing many "jen"
characters which have earlier been drawn on the concealed folds*] Yah!
brother, why are there more characters the more I rub? The whole towel
is full of them! [*Shows unfolded cloth to audience*]

YU: That's odd. . . .

TSO: That's *strange!*

Chin-chan'erh

(*Sings*)

This ink was not mixed with glue,
Nor pricked in as broidery or tatoo.
Why then can I not
Wash it away, rub it out, brush it off?
That monk
Who came to vex me, fastened
The character so firmly on. . . .

Out front on the highroad,
Or in the alley at the back,
Should I ever meet him again
I'll have two brawny men,

Bumbailiffs, take him
Off to court where a deputy's
Heavy staff will break him!

YU: Why worry about him, brother?

TSO: But you must admit it was strange! Oh, well, let us sit a while in the pawnshop. (*The* ching, *dressed as Liu* CHIU'ERH *enters* [*With a crowd*])

CHIU'ERH: Ah, friends, you stay where you are. I'll be back when I get the whole string of cash that son of a whore, Liu Chün-tso, did me out of. [*Turns in the direction of* TSO *and* YU *and calls out*] Liu Chün-tso! Miser! You cheated me out of one string of cash and I'll get it back from you somehow!

YU: I must go see who is raising such a row. (*Pantomimes seeing* CHIU'ERH)

CHIU'ERH: [*Shouting*] Hey, Liu Chün-yu, you panhandler! The miser in your house did me out of a whole string of cash and I'm here to find out why he hasn't returned it to me.

YU: See here, you bone-poor whoreson. It's one thing to come here about money, but throwing epithets around—if my brother hears you he'll be very angry. I'll go see him now. (*Pantomimes seeing* TSO) Brother, there's a miserable beggar, Liu Chiu'erh, at our gate claiming you shorted him a string of cash.

TSO: Come inside, brother, I'll see to him (*Pantomimes seeing* CHIU'ERH) Why are you stirring up such a fuss in my gateyard, Liu Chiu'erh?

CHIU'ERH: Miser! Give me back the string you owe me.

TSO: See what my fate has become—first that fat monk giving me trouble and now, up pops this pennyless son-of-a-whore! Liu Chiu'erh, you're shouting to everyone that a wealthy man like me has cheated you, a pauper, out of one miserable string of cash . . . !

CHIU'ERH: If you have so much money it's because you've swindled the likes of me before. I dare you to come out of your pawnshop . . . !

TSO: I dare you to come in and get me!

CHIU'ERH: [*Advancing on* TSO] All right, here I am. . . . What're you going to do about it?!

TSO: (*Pantomimes hitting* CHIU'ERH) I'll hit you, that's what. (CHIU'ERH *pantomimes dropping dead*) I'm supposed to owe you money? No use lying there trying to cozen me. . . . Oh! I'm choked with rage!

YU: Don't get as wild as he is, brother, please sit down. You, there! Get up and get out of here. When you ask for money you don't go around badmouthing people! [*Pauses and examines* CHIU'ERH] (*Pantomimes being startled*) Brother! you struck him and his breath has gone from him and he's dead!

TSO: Look at that clown! I pushed him on the chest and he falls over dead? I don't believe it!

YU: **See for yourself.**

TSO: Step aside, brother. This no good is just trying to make much out of little. (*Pantomimes shouting at him*) Liu Chiu'erh, even if I did owe you, there's a right way to ask about money, but you slandered me. Get up! Get up! (*Places his hand in front of* CHIU'ERH's *mouth*) Good brother . . . , he really is dead!

Ho-hsi (or) Hou-t'ing Hua

(*Sings*)

> I did but tap him on the chest,
> And *p'ei!* down he fell down dead
> On the cobbles of the road.
> What matter your penniless soul
> Has fled?
> Ai,
> But you have frightened
> The soul of wealth almost to death.

> See how the cold mucus
> Drips from his nostrils;
> Blood has flowed from his seven portals,
> Leaving hands and feet turned frigid,
> As the rigor of death made them rigid.

(*Speaks*)

> For a paltry string of cash I took his life. Now I'll have to pay with mine. Oh, brother, look on me with pity, save my life.

YU: Rest easy, brother, I will manage this death for you [*He touches the body*] This man's body is still warm just below his heart, he shouldn't be dead—let me see. (*He looks closely*) Brother, here printed on his breast is that character meaning "patience."

TSO: One side, I must see this. . . . (*He pantomimes looking closely*) [*In despair*] It is . . . , the character for "forbearance" is printed clearly there!

Yi Wang-sun

(*Sings*)

> The character inverted there's the same
> As the one so resistant on my palm.

(*Speaks*)

Brother, look. The one in my hand and that on his chest are identical!

(*Sings*)

With not a single stroke misplaced?
Both of them the exact same size.

(*Speaks*)

If I am taken to court and there examined,

(*Sings*)

I may as well confess to the charge. . . .

YU: Be at ease, brother, I will stand in your stead. . . .
TSO: You can't be a substitute for me—

(*Sings*)

For look again . . . !
My palm with its character plain
Refutes with ease
And gives the lie to all my pleas.

(*Speaks*)

Brother, I must turn over all the resources of my house as well as my sweet wife and helpless children to your care. Manage them well, I beg you, as I must flee for my life.
PU: (*Pantomimes rushing on stage*) Liu Chün-tso, you have beaten a man to death! Where could you flee?!
TSO: Master! Save your disciple. . . .

Chin-chan'erh

(*Sings*)

From this day on my clouded eyes,
Seeing only money,
Will be cleared.
My money-loving heart will now discern
The lofty and the low.
Today I'll relinquish all my wealth
And worship your "Three Treasures"[21] only.

PU: I taught thee forebearance, how could you have killed a man?

---

21. The Buddha, his law (*dharma*), and the Buddhist community (*saṃgha*).

TSO:

> (*Sings*)
>
> Ever since the character for patience
> Was written on my hand
> And to this very day,
> It has summoned up
> Before my eyes my karma and its effects.

PU: Then are you prepared to abandon your home and follow me?
TSO:

> (*Sings*)
>
> Your disciple will never
> Let his greedy heart devote itself to money,
> Nor let again
> Fires of secular passions
> Burn in his belly.
> I'll emulate the master who
> Carries nought up his sleeve
> But fresh, cool air;
> I'll study my master—
> My carrying pole will bear soon
> No fardels weightier than
> The glowing moon.

PU: I taught you to be patient; why were you not? Could you not forbear to
strike this Liu the Ninth?

> (*Chants gāthā*)
>
> Forbearance is to forbear.
> Patience gained
> Is patience to use.
> Small things weigh as great
> If either one you lose.

> If I restore that man to life, will you follow me?

TSO: Oh, Master, if you could but bring him back to life, I would follow you
anywhere and forever leave my home.
PU: [*Solemnly and with emphasis*] What you have sworn to, never recant.
(*He turns to* CHIU'ERH [*Makes gestures with hands*]) Presto! Liu
Chiu'erh. . . .
CHIU'ERH: (*Stands up and gazes at the crowd around him*) Well! That was a
good sleep!

PU: Namu Amida Buddha.

CHIU'ERH: Liu Chün-tso, return me my string of cash.

TSO: Brother, give him one, quickly! (YU *pantomimes giving* CHIU'ERH *a string of cash*)

CHIU'ERH: So, you're returning my cash after all! Brothers, I'm a string of cash to the good. [*To crowd*] Come and drink with me!

(*Exit*)

TSO: [*Sotto voce*] (*To* YU) Brother, how much *did* you give him?

YU: Why, a string, one thousand.

TSO: [*Exasperated but resigned*] Hai . . . alas! I'm sure you could have got by with five hundred. . . .

YU: **A life has been saved and he thinks of money!**

PU: Come, Liu Chün-tso, leave home and come with me.

TSO: Master have a heart! How can I leave all this wealth, property, my sweet wife, and dependent children? Let your disciple just build a contemplation shack at the bottom of his garden. That way I'll have left home by staying home—I shall have three vegetarian meals a day and chant "Namu Amida Buddha." Surely this will be enough . . . ?

PU: I see you are not ready to leave the world. . . . Very well, then, in all things use forbearance and chant "Namu Amida Buddha."

TSO: Master, your disciple understands. Brother, I am turning over all our household assets to you. Treat my children with care.

YU: You may rest easy, brother; I shall take all responsibilities on my shoulders.

TSO:

Chuan-sha {*wei*}

(*Sings*)

At this moment
I hold the debts of a hundred families,
Pawned property of thirty more.

(*Speaks*)

Thus was I with money—

(*Sings*)

Day and night, body and soul
Have I broken on gold,
Lavished on gardens, house,
Towers, and pavilions.

But now I build a little thatched hut
To study the sūtras and perfect my virtue.
To fear no longer plundering thieves,
Fires, floods, or life's tempests and waves.

(*Speaks*)

Think well on this Liu Chün-tso . . .

(*Sings*)

I see that inconstant times, fickle fortune,
Cannot guard you to old age.

(*Looks at the character in his palm*)

I look upon this sign for patience
And thank Master for his teaching.

PU: Be forbearing in everything. . . .
TSO: Oh, fear not, fear not, I shall forbear. . . . {*Repeats three times*}

(*Sings*)

In those who covet wealth,
This character has its counterpart.
Desire, the lethal dagger,
Lies heavy on the impatient heart!

(*Exit*)

PU: So, who could foresee that Liu Chün-tso, vouchsafed a Small Revelation,
would leave home[22] at home? I shall wait until he has shed all thoughts
of this world and then return to convert him.

(*Chants gāthā*)

To study the true way
Is to balance your carrying pole
And ascend a hill.
Think not the road too long,
Nor return uncertain.
The load will soon transmogrify;
The carrier will be suspended
Between the earth and sky.

(*Exit*)

---

22. To become a monk, as it were.

YU: The Master's left and my brother has retired to meditate, leaving all to me. Well, I must be off to collect debts within the city and without.

(*Exit*)

Act Two

(TSO *enters*)

TSO: [*Wearing a simple novice robe in contrast to the rich garments of a wealthy merchant*] I am Liu Chün-tso following the religious directions of my teacher. I have had a meditation hut built in our rear garden; each day I eat three abstemious meals and recite "Namu Amida Buddha." The days and months have passed so rapidly that . . .

Nan-lü, Yi-chih Hua

(*Sings*)

Orioles and swallows now wing
Over the flowery creek,
Ducks already swim in the lotus pond
As now across chrysanthemum skies,
Geese fly in from far frontiers,
On plum-bloom ridge still croak
Ravens of the cold.
I think upon
The best of times throughout the year.
A snap of the fingers—spring is gone,
A turn of the head—fall is here.

I believe my will to seek
Fame and fortune is gone, is past.
I've smashed those manacles
Of gold, of jade at last.
Control of my mind is now complete;
Secured against apes' passion,
Reined in against stallion heat.

Liang-chou Ti-ch'i

I sweep my doorstep every day,
Burn incense, pray.
This I much prefer
To buying kindling,

Weighing provender,
Managing my house.

(*Speaks*)

Ah, Liu Chün-tso, what would have become of you had it not been for
the Master?!

(*Sings*)

Thanks to all the Bodhisattvas,
To all the Higher Forms;
Reverence to the Master of my salvation.
They saved me from
The law of kings and condign punishment.
I swore in deceit,
My finger pointing to heaven,
Yet my body and my soul,
Thanks to him,
Were freed.

I, I, I render thanks to you,
Patient Ch'an-master from the Snowy Peak.
Who, who, who taught me well
The deathless precepts from the Lotus Seat
And limitless lessons of the law.
I came, came, came, and built
My thatched meditation hut to dwell
Without fear or fret and live
The eremite's life.

Should the flame of folly burn again,
I can set my mind at rest—
Freed from the lure of worldly things.
Rosary beads between my fingers,
I sit here wordless, letting peace abide,
As petals flutter by me, one by one,
Throughout the mists of eventide.

(*Speaks*)

Namu Amida Buddha. I sit here at peace. (*Enter* CHILD {*and the* hsiao-
tan})[23]

CHILD: I am Liu Chün-tso's child. Father is meditating in the rear garden;
uncle is keeping my mother company and drinking wine. I've come to

23. The *Ku-chin tsa-chü* text has the wife (*hsiao-tan* [secondary female role]) enter at this
time: this cannot be right.

tell our father so. [*Pantomimes knocking on door and shouting*] Open,
open up!

TSO: Who calls "open up"?

Ma Yü-lang

(*Sings*)

I have lowered the spotted bamboo blind,
All within is silent, no clamor heard,
Why put up with even the squeaking of a single door . . . ?

CHILD: Open up!

TSO:

(*Sings*)

Now I cease to think and speculate;
When I've looked
I'll listen and I'll wait.

CHILD: Open up!

TSO:

Kan Huang-en

(*Sings*)

Perhaps it is my young wife
Whose threshold I've not crossed
These many days.
I light incense of fragrance rare,
Hastily adjust the clothes I wear,
Clutch my rosary. . . .

[*He readies himself to greet his wife*]

CHILD: Open up!

TSO:

(*Sings*)

Perhaps someone has come bringing
Clear, fresh water. . . .
I approach the steps,
Stand beside the window,
Near the curtain gauze.

> Or, again, does someone come to me
> With an offer of fresh tea?

CHILD: Open up!

TSO:

> (*Speaks*)

> Who comes here, then . . . ?

Ts'ai-ch'a Ko

> (*Sings*)

> My eyes are dazzled by the day. . . .
> Has, perhaps, some Bodhisattva come . . . ?

CHILD: Open up!

TSO: (*Pantomimes opening door and seeing* CHILD)

> (*Sings*)

> Yah! it is my foolish little one;
> Spoiled, but so well loved.
> Doubtless his mother has given him
> A scarce-deserved slap, and he
> Runs for his doting father's sympathy.

> (*Speaks*)

> Child, why have you come?

CHILD: If nothing were the matter I would never have come, but ever since you began meditating here, our mother and uncle have been together all the time, drinking wine. I only came to tell you. . . .

TSO: Oh? Is this true? Your mother has been keeping your uncle company in our house and drinking wine? [*He advances on the* CHILD]

CHILD: [*Defensively*] It's true, I wouldn't lie to you!

TSO: (*Pantomimes anger*) Why that half-frozen pauper! What kind of behavior is this from you?! When I remember hauling you out of the snow-drift and saving your hide . . . and making you a sworn brother . . . giving you free run of the house . . . and all my wealth entrusted to you! I should take this hand and. . . . (*Pantomimes seeing the character for "patience" on his palm*) Hai! . . . no, son, run along and play. . . .

CHILD: Come home, daddy.

TSO:

Mu-yang Kuan

(*Sings*)

Do not trouble the mind of your father,
Perhaps your eyes were blurred. . . .

CHILD: There was nothing wrong with my eyes, I saw it. . . .
TSO:

(*Sings*)

Perhaps uncle was walking with a neighbor. . . .

CHILD: No, it was *not* someone else; it was mother drinking wine with uncle.
TSO:

(*Sings*)

Are you telling the truth . . . ?

CHILD: The truth. . . .
TSO:

(*Sings*)

Tell no lies to me!

CHILD: I wouldn't dare. . . .
TSO: (*Pantomimes becoming angry*)

(*Speaks*)

If it's the truth, I'll never put up with that . . . !

(*Sings*)

For no heavy iron chain would do,
No double cangue that murderers wear,
Nor would it help to lay my case
Before the purest-hearted judge. . . .

(*Speaks*)

I would never put up with that!

(*Sings*)

Be calm! But you must understand,
I will cruelly kill you
With my own hand.

(*Exeunt omnes*)

(YU *and* WIFE *enter*)

YU: I am Liu Chün-yu to whom my brother trusted his home and family to care for while he retired to his meditation hut in the garden. How happy am I, how joyful!

WIFE: You say well, cousin. Come, I've had wine and refreshment prepared, let us take a few cups together, my dear, as we should.

YU: I should very much enjoy that. . . . Let me close the bedroom door and we'll drink [*They sit together on the bench*], **and see who shows up.** (*They pantomime drinking*)

TSO: (*Enters [Holding large knife]*) I had no blade ready to hand but took one from the kitchen and here I am at the door. Let me stop and listen.

WIFE: Cousin, this house and family, early and late, owes much to you. . . . Drink up.

YU: Ah, sister, I shall not forget your favors as long as I live. . . . Please, sister. . . .

TSO: [*Aside*] So! It's true! This is what has been going on! My rage will kill me!

K'u Huang-t'ien

(*Sings*)

Seeing the window-blind drawn
Anger seized my heart.
If this door is not opened
I shall kick it in!

Against my will,
Anger mounts in my breast
As my grip tightens on this knife.

(*Pantomimes peering in, speaks*)

I must try to see. . . .

WIFE: Cousin, have another cup.

TSO:

(*Sings*)

The pair are seated on the couch. . . .

(*Speaks*)

Open up!

YU: Someone has come.

(*Exit*)[24]

---

24. It would seem that he slides between the drapes as PU enters and stays there until PU's *Presto!* makes him appear from behind the hangings.

(PU *enters in secret*)

[*He enters around curtain stage right, slides behind one hanging and comes out. He is seen moving across center stage, disappears behind the other hanging (stage left) and stays there for the rest of the scene until* TSO *begins to sing* HUNG SHAO-YAO]

WIFE: (*Pantomimes opening door*) Good sir, have you come back to your home?

TSO:

(*Sings*)

I open the chamber door
And rest against it.
But I've taken these two in adultery
With my own hand. . . .

WIFE: [*Retreats from him while looking at knife*] Two in adultery!? Then, where is the other? [*Turns and shouts*] Help, anyone! He's going to kill me!

TSO:

(*Sings*)

What boots it now to cry out!
Why raise your voice and shout?

(*Pantomimes seizing her as she cries "help!"*)

Hah! Yes, come you all!
I have one of the adulterous pair.

(*Pantomimes pushing her*)

But come, I would speak to both.

[*He has been holding knife in left hand while he pushes her with his right. At this point he takes knife in right hand so the character—concealed up til now—faces audience*]

(*Pantomimes seeing the character on the handle of the knife*)

Yah! Suddenly the trace
Of "patience" appears again—
All its strokes in place!

Wu-yeh T'i

(*Sings*)

Here I see the dark smudge
Printed upon the steel knife's grip.

Ah, heavens!
I'm strangled by my fated enemy—
That character for patience!

WIFE: [*Scornfully*] The good religious convert! Committing murder! Help, Liu Chün-tso is murdering me!

TSO:

(*Sings*)

Cease your cries, your hubbub.
We'll not speak of the king's law
But of household morality. . . .

WIFE: Liu Chün-tso, let us not mention, then, how someone who left his home to read holy scriptures, would suddenly now commit murder!

TSO:

(*Sings*)

There is no
Black habit on me,
Nor dyed monks' robes,
Nor yet has the metal razor blade
Tonsured my fine, black hair. . . .
So wrap yourself no more
In such impertinent robes, woman,
I am your husband!
And in this house
You must act my spouse!

(*Speaks*)

No, I'll not kill you. . . . Where has the other adulterer gone . . . ?

WIFE: I'll leave you to find him.

(*Exit*)

(PU *sneezes* [25] *from behind the hanging*)

TSO: So that's where the cur has hidden himself. I'll take care of him. . . ! [*Starts toward the division between hangings*]

Hung Shao-yao

(*Sings*)

First I'll seize him by his sash
And haul him in front of me.

25. The *Ku-chin tsa-chü* edition has "puffs."

Never again will he dodge or duck,
Nor slip and slide away. . . !

PU: [*From behind the hanging*] Liu Chün-tso, are you showing forbearance?
[*Comes out from behind hanging*]
TSO: (*Pantomimes seeing* PU)

(*Sings*)

This brings my head up sharply;
One startled glance
And I am shocked as my two hands
Drop to my sides.
Would that a knife-blade
Might pierce my heart!

PU: So? And what character has a knife blade piercing the heart, Liu Chün-tso?
TSO: (*Pantomimes thinking*) A knife blade on the heart . . .

(*Sings*)

Oh, again he seeks
The roots of patience!
I sought to seize
From behind the wall hangings,
Her adulterous accomplice,
Instead he seems to come
Before my eyes from
The very corners of the earth.

(*Speaks*)

I thought I would capture her confederate. To my astonishment, my
Master is here. This gives one pause. . . .

P'u-sa Liang-chou

(*Sings*)

His nose and the other's—
Two types on this portrait.
My Master's appears, not her accomplice's.

I kowtow in haste and salute you.
You may give me pause,
But you are the Bodhisattva
Who rescued me from danger and strife.
I all but did the wicked deed just now.

Now I must dispose of my ten thousand cash;
She whom my parents chose for my wife
I must marry to another.
Then all ties will be broken!

Forbearance or not, my mind
Must examine this with care!

PU: Do it, Liu Chün-tso, sever your family ties and come with me.
TSO:

(*Speaks*)

He wants me to leave my wife and family

(*Sings [an aside]*)

I cannot,
But I shall make him believe
What is said only to deceive!

PU: I urged you to patience; you not only rejected that, but almost did murder with dagger in hand. Let's say no more about "leaving home while home"; I want you truly to leave with me now.

TSO: I wish with all my heart to follow you, Master, but what of my ten thousand household duties, my sweet wife, my dependent children? There is no one to care for all those things—if there were, I would go with my Master immediately!

PU: [*Slowly, knowing he will trap him*] Liu Chün-tso, you say you would leave if there were someone to take over your duties. If such a one should appear, would you follow me? Give me your word. **Presto! In Buddha's name** . . . [*Makes gesture which summons* YU *instantly on stage: Probably another entry from between the hangings where he has been waiting*]

YU: (*Enters*) Here I am, Liu Chün-yu. . . . I have just returned from collecting monies and came to see brother Chün-tso. (*Pantomimes seeing him*) Brother, here I am back from collecting debts owed us. . . .

TSO: [*Ruefully*] I wish you'd been a bit delayed. . . !

PU: [*On a note of triumph*] So! Here's the very person who can manage all your affairs. *Now*, you will come away with me.

TSO: [*Trying to ignore* PU, *he turns to* YU *and speaks eagerly*] How did it go with the collection?

YU: I got it all.

TSO: Good fellow! I made no mistake thinking you could manage things. But there's something I must ask you. . . .

PU: [*Interrupting, he thinks* TSO *will bring up adultery*] Forbear, Liu Chüntso! Invoke the name of Buddha!

TSO: [*Hastily*] Yes, yes, Namu Amida Buddha. . . .

Mu-yang Kuan

(*Sings*)

What is the weight of the silver ingots?

YU: Of differing weights; some just an ounce and others almost an ounce and a half.

TSO:

(*Sings*)

But with gold and silver
There is honest weight and false.

YU: The gold is good red gold and the silver, pure white silver.

TSO:

(*Sings*)

Were the payments made in good heart,
Or grudgingly given?

YU: All were paid willingly; had they not been so, I would have settled the debt though I carried off their last cooking pot!

TSO:

(*Speaks*)

That's right, "Even charity forgives not debt."—Namu Amida Buddha! [*Eagerly*] Let me look at one of the ingots, brother.

(YU *passes an ingot to* TSO *and the character "jen" appears on it*)

[*He receives oversized ingot with blank side facing audience, puts it in his other hand with written side out for the audience to see*]

TSO:

(*Startled, sings*)

I had only to touch the gold,
And, lo, the image appeared;
Without benefit of woodblock
Or brushed on ink!

PU: That character demands that you forbear.

TSO:

(*Sings*)

The Master tells me
The character demands itself.

YU: [*Offers* TSO *another ingot*] Here's a better one. . . .
TSO:

(*Sings*)

Take it back!
As much as I would like to,
I dare not fondle that metal!

PU: [*Recalling everyone to the business at hand*] Liu Chün-tso, the one who can manage your affairs has been produced. Follow me now and leave your home. Hear this:

(*Recites gāthā*)

Yearn not for silver or gold again,
Forget sweet nights of husband and wife.
What price a Great Dipper full of money when
Old Mortality comes to take your life
And pass your gold on to other men?
Abandon household impediment,
Follow your Master to Enlightenment.

Once you were Liu Chün-tso, miser, but I will turn you into a monk "Seated by the window, indifferent to all things."

TSO: Enough, enough, enough! Ever since I made Chün-yu my sworn brother I have been happy. Yet I struck down a man for a string of cash, pursued a nonexistent adulterer, and all but killed another. Today I hand over the affairs of the house, my sweet wife, and dependent children while I follow the Master and leave my home. They are all in your hands, brother; look after them well for me while I follow my Master—enough, enough!

Huang-chung coda

(*Sings*)

I now speak of Three Births,
A decade of Dusty Dreams.
Now I will sip "Seven cups of the tea that makes
Cool breezes blow across the armpits."

I say with neither boast nor pride
Mine was the first family of our town.

I now have drunk the wine of poverty,
Sipped the tea of idlers.
I can laugh to see the miser
Mired in his own affairs,
Sigh to see him slight the law.
My thanks, Master, you have rescued me.

All my worldly goods,
My wife and children are in your care,
My brother, my thanks that you accept the trust.
No longer do I count in thousands,
Ten thousands no longer measure.
Deep in the hills I will suppress the mind
Once preoccupied with cares,
So that in a monk's hut
A heart committed to devotion
Will flourish in its place.

PU: Praise Buddha!
TSO:

Speaks)

As my master commands—every day I shall intone Namu Amida Buddha.

(*Sings*)

And in the end
Right and wrong shall be meaningless
And I will enjoy sheer happiness!

PU: Little did we imagine that Liu Chün-tso would experience another Small Revelation and thereafter would turn over all his worldly goods to follow me to Yüeh-lin Monastery. There I will teach him the disciplines of Mahāyāna Buddhism.

(*Exit*)

Act Three

(*Enter the Ch'an Master* TING-HUI. *Recites*)

TING:

Who speaks words to unlock the eternal
Is blessed of the gods.
Perceptive nature can transmit
Lord Buddha's Light.

I donned monk's robes, but still
I only bear my fellowman goodwill.

This humble monk is the Ch'an Master, Ting-hui, of Yüeh-lin Monastery in the city of Pien-liang. Let me observe that Buddhism teaches us Primal Chaos was separated into Three Worlds and the Four Kinds of sentient beings were produced. These thereupon began the transmigrations—life and death, each equally vain. We are as ants on a revolving millstone, birds that have hurled themselves into nets and springes, who, after repeated *kalpas*[26] still do not understand their true natures. Women have become men who have become women; humans die to become sheep; sheep die to become men—even as we discard or change garments, so do we change face and form. Men and women of intelligence seek to escape from the web. It is difficult to gain human form, difficult to know the Laws of Buddhism, difficult to be born in the Middle Kingdom. One should practice the Law and avoid falling into the Way of Evil. Our Buddha spread his teaching from the West by one Bodhisattva after another until there were twenty-eight in all. The first was Bodhidharma, the second, Hui-k'o, the third, Seng-ts'an, the fourth, Tao-hsin, the fifth, Hung-hen, and the sixth, Hui-neng.[27]

Buddhism spread over the Central Kingdom[28] by a series of thirty-six patriarchs, five of whom founded the Five Sects and the Five Schools with their orthodox doctrines. What then are the Five Schools? Lin-chi, Yün-men, Ts'ao-hsi, Fa-yen, and Wei-shan. The Five Sects are Nan-shan, Tzu-en, T'ien-t'ai, Hsüan-shou, and Pi-mi.

(*Recites gāthā*)

I say: studying the Law
Is defending the citadel—
In daylight you ward off "Six Thieves,"
At night mind your vigilance well.
If generals hand good orders down,
Harvest by harvest, year by year
Ultimate peace is finally grown.

This day have I received directions from our Buddha that nearby lives a man named Liu, called Chün-tso. Formerly this one was addicted to wealth and property and longed for glory and honor—he was unwilling to submit to monastic discipline. But he has been singled out by the Buddha to read the sūtras and worship Buddha, to pray and to meditate. But here it is already the hour for lessons and he has not yet shown up.

26. Eons or ages, consisting of 432,000,000 years each.
27. The traditional list of the first six patriarchs of Ch'an / Zen Buddhism in China.
28. China.

[*Calls offstage*]

Liu Chün-tso, you are missing your lesson!

TSO: [*Dressed as a monk, wearing oversized prayer beads and possibly a tonsored wig*] (*Enters chanting*) Namu Amida Buddha. I am Liu Chün-tso who left his home to follow the Master. Now, each day I read sūtras and worship Buddha. The Master appointed his chief disciple to attend to my practices and whenever my mind wanders to the profane world, he knows it and raps me smartly. I should go to him now. [*Pantomimes seeing* TING-HUI]

TING: Liu Chün-tso, I was charged with seeing to your purity of heart, the lessening of your desires, the rigorousness of your abstention and fasting. I was to see that your thoughts should not return to the profane world, and if they did, you were to be given fifty strokes with the bamboo. In all things were you to observe *forbearance!* Hear you now, patience is the greatest of all virtues:

(*Recites gāthā*)

[*As he chants this gāthā he speaks more and more slowly and begins to nod: as he reaches the end, saying "Praise Buddha, patience, patience," he falls asleep*]

The quality of patience is not strange;
A life of patience is a life of peace.
Make patience part of your morality;
Patience is the key to immortality.

Praise——Buddha, praise—Buddha—patience . . . patie . . . (*Falls asleep*)

TSO: Yes, yes! Namu Amida Buddha, Namu Amida Buddha . . . patience . . . pa—[*Aside*] Oh, he's fallen asleep! (*Sighs*) Hai . . . ! Liu Chün-tso, when I first followed the Master here, I would praise Buddha every day. But, though Buddha was on my tongue, in my heart lay the ten thousand strings of cash which are my fortune. I wonder how those strings're doing . . . ?

TING: (*Shouts*) Pooh! Liu Chün-tso, who ever saw ten thousand strings in a Ch'an meditation chamber? Hah, it is well said: "Nothing can you take with you save your own karma." I am under the orders of our Master to teach you to meditate, to resurrect your spirit—and I shall succeed! So cease these wild and disordered thoughts. You must concentrate them in a dense and massive way—as though afflicted by a severe disease. You must eat and not notice tastes, drink and not notice flavors—as though you were paralyzed, drunk! Distinguish not east from west, nor south from north. When you achieve this, I promise you, your heart's blossoming and awakening to your origins will follow, and wordless you will stand at the nexus of life and death. Death and life are grave matters and

Old Mortality is swift. When ten men ascend a mountain, each will succeed only by his own effort. It is well said:

[*He chants slower and slower until he reaches "Praise Buddha," etc., when he falls asleep*]

(*Chants gāthā*)

Each man lives a dream of his own,
Full of change and perturbation.
Each man believes his dream
Was his own creation.
The breath is full of ecstasy.
He is bewitched, subverted,
Who vows to regulate his soul,
Nirvana is his final goal.

. . . Praise Buddha, praise Buddha, patience, pa . . . . (*Falls asleep*)

TSO: Yes, yes, Praise Buddha—Namu Amida Buddha . . . . Ah, he's fallen asleep again! Oh, heavens! Household wealth counts for little when I think of it . . . but giving up that flower of a wife. . . .

TING: (*Wakens*) Pooh! Liu Chün-tso, what Ch'an meditation chamber ever saw a flower of a wife? Our Master would have you cultivate your virtue and discover your true nature; lock up the ape of the mind and the stallion of temperament. . . . Oh, thou stupid man. . . .

[*He chants this more and more slowly, and by the end he is nodding and falls asleep again*]

(*Chants*)

Care for yourself,
For yourself take care.
If you do it not, who would dare?
Take daily burdens on your back,
Lest you fall in with devils, have a care.
From the spark of wit calamity grew,
The evil you've done it is useless to rue.
Busybodies vainly seek out cares—
I laugh at them for the burden's not theirs,
Nor do they retreat in the face of dispute.
"Harm him profit me," they're a million kinds!
Cares shatter bowels of steel, iron minds—
Deep are the roots of karma that bind
The eye on this world that's turning blind.
Escape from brasier or soup pot is hard.

Old Yama[29] lacks the feelings of man;
In the final moments, it's too late to care—
Though you may try as hard as you can!

Oh, Liu Chün-tso, praise Buddha. . . . Praise Buddh . . . patience . . .
pa . . . . (*He sleeps*)

TSO: Yes, yes, Praise Buddha, patience, patience! Namu Amida Buddha—
Namu Amida Buddh. . . . Oh, he's fallen asleep again. Never mind
that flower of a wife . . . , but what has become of my children,
handsome as Moholo. . . .[30]

TING: (*Wakens*) Pooh! Liu Chün-tso, who ever heard of children beautiful as
Moholo in the meditation chamber of a Ch'anist? Our Master has
charged you to undertake pious practices. To do this you must first
concentrate your wisdom.[31]

With concentrated wisdom as a base you cannot go astray. "Concentration" is the basis of wisdom and "wisdom" is the practice of concentration. Thus, when one is wise, concentration is part of that wisdom;
when one has concentrated, wisdom is part of that concentration. . . .
When you understand this, you have attained concentrated wisdom.
[*He is becoming more and more perfunctory and monotonous; these are
elementary lessons he has repeated time and again*] Neophytes say only
"be wise and concentration will ensue." But concentrated wisdom resembles a lamp's brightness: when the lamp exists so does brightness; lacking
a lamp, darkness ensues. A lamp, then, is the essence of brightness, and
brightness is the function of lamps. Now, though we use different terms,
essence and function are one. This is the heart of concentrated wisdom.
. . . Praise Buddha, praise Buddha, patience, patience. . . .

TSO: (*Takes off his prayer-beads and hurls them*) Teacher! I have lost my patience. . . !

(*Sings*)

Having leapt clear of
The boundaries of Thou and I,
The domain of Right and Wrong,

(*Speaks*)

Master, I think of my wife and children and . . .

(*Sings*)

Since I took leave of them,
It is a canker on the heart.

29. King of the underworld.
30. A doll. The name derives from Sanskrit *mahoraga* ([image of] a deity).
31. Note that this is the Ch'an / Zen Master's name-in-religion.

This world of Red Dust[32] and
Wars of white ants are now but
A Yellow Millet Dream—[33]
But impatience and irritation
Battle each other in my head.

TING: Hear me, Liu Chün-tso. Your transcendent soul will become as transparent as the Great Void; your corporeal self with its five constituents
will perish as though it had been a dream. When you have developed
the Inner Eye, you will know that your person was but a flower in the
void. You will go directly to the absolute, bypassing forever life and
destruction. The world of taint and passion is easy of access; the karma
leading to Buddhahood is difficult to achieve. To those who do not
understand the Primal Cause, all causality appears random. The vastness
of our ambiance obscures the Forest of Merit; violence of passion's
flames destroys the seeds of Bodhi-wisdom. If your contemplation of the
Way is as genuine as the manifestation of your emotions, then the Law
of Buddha will forever be before your eyes. If you do unto others as you
do unto yourself, you will be delivered from all taint of Dusty Cares.[34] It
is well said:

(*Recites gāthā*)

Invoke the name of Buddha:
Empowered by the grace of Maitreya's words,
The Hill of Daggers, Forests of Swords[35]
Are made to disappear.
Take upon thyself and expiate
Those wrongs properly laid on thee.
Wait not upon the final day,
For then thou shalt be
Engaged in another way!

Praise Buddha, praise Buddha . . . forbear, forbear!

TSO:

[TSO *now speaks more and more slowly and finally falls asleep*] Yes, yes!
Praise Buddha. . . . Namu Amida Buddha . . . namu . . . amida . . . .

32. The mundane world.
33. An old tale of ephemeral and illusory glory.
34. Every sentence of this paragraph contains at least one Buddhist technical term or
doctrinal concept. TING's speech is intended as a mechanical parody of a religious sermon.
35. Tortures in hell.

TING: He sleeps. Now shall he be given a Small Revelation! Presto! [*He gestures with his hands: wife and children appear from between the hangings*] Let a spectral vision of his fixations[36] appear!

(*Enter* WIFE *and* CHILDREN)

WIFE: I am Liu Chün-tso's wife and I have been sent to see him (*Pantomimes seeing* TSO) Husband. . . .

TSO: Wife, how have you come here!? [*He is asleep throughout this episode and speaks as if in a dream*]

WIFE: Sir, I brought the children to see you.

TSO: Oh, wife, I nearly died of longing for you . . . .

Yen'erh Lo

(*Sings*)

Whether I will it or not
My emotions wound me
And bruise me with sadness.
We have known such happiness
From marriage and family. . . .
Then it came to pass
That hedge-monk came to us, alas. . . .

WIFE: What have you to fear from him?

TSO: Alas, wife, you could not know. . . .

Te-sheng Ling

(*Sings*)

He hopes to take a cudgel
To mated mandarin ducks;
Never would he play the pipes
To reunite phoenixes.

WIFE: The pain of what you say will kill me, sir.

TSO:

(*Sings*)

You ask when grief will cease.
And not a day goes by
I do not recall your sweet love. . . .

36. Obstacles lying in the way to Nirvana.

[*She has concealed her hands up to this point. Tso now holds one of them and then turns the back of it toward the audience displaying the character "jen" which was already painted there. She stares at it, startled*] (*The character appears on her hand*)

WIFE: Look! The character for "patience" now is printed on my hand!
TSO:

(*Sings*)

As I ponder it now,
I feel that character's blade
On my very own heart is laid.
And despite myself, I fear,
Oh, wife I hold dear,
There is no better artifice
To break once loving hearts than this!

WIFE: The children are with me . . . come to see you, too. . . .
TSO:

Shui Hsien-tzu

(*Sings*)

Oh, dear children,
I have missed you so!

[*He draws each child to him and lays his hand on the forehead of each*]

I touch them on the brow,
Each by the corner of his eyelid.

(*The character for "patience" appears on the foreheads of the children*)

[*He looks at each child in turn and sings*]

Oh, cursed character
Which shows me to be little blessed
And much maligned!
It is as though that character had
Magic power to hang a moon and a sun
In a calabash, with a flick of the wrist.

Ah, wife! How often have I looked
Upon your finger-tips—
How seldom on the back of your hand!

(*He examines the character on everyone*)

As Liu Ch'en was disjoined
From the Goddesses of Mount T'ien-t'ai.[37]
The boy has the character upon his brow,
The girl, hers on her temple.

(*He examines another "jen"*)

Forbearance, indeed!
I am not reconciled!
Your knife blade has severed the heart-strings
Connecting father and child!

[TING *has been overseeing the scene and now makes a commanding gesture*]

TING: Vanish! (WIFE *and* CHILDREN *exeunt* [*through one set of hangings*])
Presto! [*He gestures again and* PU, *wives, and children appear through the other set of hangings*]

(PU *and wives and children enter, walk once around the stage and exeunt*)

TSO: [*He has wakened now*] (*Pantomimes watching this circuit*) Teacher, was that not my Master?
TING: Yes, and my Master, too.
TSO: And who were the women?
TING: The were my teacher's wives.
TSO: And who were the children?
TING: They were the Master's children.
TSO: (*Pantomimes anger*) Now, there's a fine monk for you! He has me divorce my wife, abandon my children, and give up my entire fortune to follow him. This is enough to make me die of anger. [*With great emphasis*] Don't let this come as a surprise, Master: I will no longer quit the world—I'm going home now!

Ch'uan Po-cho

(*Sings*)

Now I see that he
Is less observant than I.
All right ! Let that be!

---

37. The allusion is to one of several Rip Van Winkle stories. Liu and friend cannot find their way back to the lovely mountain genies who entertained them so delightfully. The allusion is inapposite.

Does it make you more powerful
That I should be brought to ruin?
I own paddy and ponds,
Fish tanks and marshes full of reeds.
Traveler's inns, oil presses,
Wine shops and teahouses;
Also, I like a satin brocade,
Lavishly painted compounds,
Each house complete with colonnade.
I was the richest man of all
Within our town.
They could speak of nought else—
Those who knew me then and know me still—
The day that I surrendered to your will!

(*Speaks*)

We did but take a little wine together when my brother said to me,
"There's a fat monk at the door. . . ."

Ch'i Ti-hsiung

(*Sings*)

I left the living quarters,
The pawnshop, and saw
That monk of yours
Who had eaten so much he grew
Inexcusably fat.
He it was who tricked
The honored Mr. Liu into it—
Over the edge of this firepit!

TING: Patience!
TSO:

(*Speaks*)

Not I alone would be furious. . . .

(*Sings*)

But were I the Buddha himself,
I would tumble in anger's heat
Down from the Lotus Seat. . . .

Mei-hua Chiu

He it was who tricked me thus,
Who made me desert my wife,
Who caused me to abandon my offspring—
While he had got himself two wives!
How should this hedge-monk
Come hither and trouble
You, Ch'an Master, with my training?

TING: Patience, do not agitate yourself. . . .
TSO:

(*Sings*)

You may not be angered,
But for me, I must.

TING: Patience, be not hasty. . . .
TSO:

(*Sings*)

You are not hasty; haste is for me.
In my life before, I burned
Not a single stick of incense;
He had me pay homage facing south.

All my life I loved brisk trade;
Now he has me seated
On the chair of contemplation.
He it was who has taken credit
For religious conversion of this man;
While the Master remains the model hypocrite. . . .
Explain this, teacher, if you have the wit!

(*Speaks*)

Teacher, this "celibate" has himself two wives!

Hsi Chiang-nan

(*Sings*)

Oh, heavens, he has tricked me
To scatter my riches—!
How then can I return home?
Who would have thought,

Who ever heard of uxorious Buddhist monks?
I think now of my simple wife
Repining on our threshold—
I shall return at once—
She need no longer scratch
With ever-shortened hairpin
On the mossy wall,
Keeping count
Of the days of our separation
As they mount.

TING: Liu Chün-tso, if you no longer will live a life of contemplation, where will you go?

TSO: Master, forgive me, but I will indeed no longer lead the religious life. This very day I return to Pien-liang.

TING: If you would return, you had best start today what will prove to be a long journey . . .

TSO: [*Begins walking figure eight indicating journey*]

Yüan-yang Sha

(*Sings*)

If I had learned he had two wives
To take beneath the golden drapes,
Would I agree to sink my ship of gold
Among these astonishing waves?
He begot progeny to guide and hold,
But left my family broken and gone.
I had better quit this monastery,
Returning now, shame-faced, to Pien-liang.

The setting sun bathes dying grass
As I look back and sigh in vain;
I try to reach my native heath
To return this shame-blushed face.

After today what sect do I need?
What preachment will I ever heed?

(*Exit*)

TING: Hai! who would have thought that this Small Revelation would send Liu Chün-tso hurrying back to Pien-liang? This trip he will meet temptations of wine, lust, wealth, and anger; see the gulf between "I" and "Thou," the "Right" and the "Wrong." However, when he has seen greed, malice, ignorance, and evil, then will he meet the Master and convert, for he will finally have achieved the Way.

(Recites gāthā)

Our Buddha founded the Five Sects.
Who seeks enlightenment chooses the Ch'an,
When merit and acts are both complete,
He and the Future Buddha meet.

(Exit)

Act Four

(The ching Liu JUNG-TSU made up as Old Man enters with children)

JUNG-TSU: I am a citizen of Pien-liang. My surname is Liu and my given name is Jung-tsu and I am eighty years old. My grandchildren are many, my fields and their crops are numerous—in fact, I am the wealthiest man in Pien-liang. My father once told me that my grandfather, Liu Chün-tso, was led away to a religious life by a fat monk. On the palm of grandfather's hand was the character for "patience"—in fact, that was how he could be identified; to this very day we have kept in our house a towel with many characters for "patience" on it. We pay our respects, young and old, to that towel as though it were my grandfather himself. This being the festival of Ch'ing-ming,[38] I have brought the cloth to the empty tomb we had built for my grandfather, and I shall sacrifice paper money for him there.

(Exit)

(Enter TSO)

TSO: I am none other than Liu Chün-tso. I can't believe I let that shave-pate rogue trick me the way he did! But I will soon be home again . . . .

Chung-lü, Fen Tieh-erh

(Sings)

He has left me without
A carping word to say.
It is incredible—
I was totally deceived
By that lying Ch'an monk.

38. The grave-sweeping festival held in the spring.

For nought did I abandon
My family wealth, bright as a copper dipper.
Wife and offspring must have imagined me
Sitting content on the Lotus Seat.
I think and am distressed—
How many others were brought low
When this miser's recompense was manifest.

Tsui Ch'un-feng

So deeply do I hate that monk
The fire in my heart
Will never dim.
Deceived by the demon of madness
That fat monk brought with him,
I won't emulate the pious monk P'ang
And sink *my* treasure in the sea;
Nor sing like a phoenix as did Sun Teng
On Mount Su-men.
I never will
Like Hsieh An-chih
Sleep on the Eastern Hill
Awaiting the proper time to fill
My destined post.[39]

(*Speaks*)

I left the monastery several days ago and here I am at my family's graveyard. [*He stops abruptly and looks about him*] Ah, let me look again—it seemed so unfamiliar I nearly passed it by. However, this *is* our plot, indeed. Let me go in and look.

Ying Hsien-k'o

(*Sings*)

Now I walk beside our family tombs,

(*Speaks*)

But why are they so overgrown and unkept?

(*Sings*)

39. This spate of self-explanatory allusions is typical of certain concentrated lyrical moments in Chinese drama.

Bramble thorns have grown on them.

[*Stops and looks upward and all around him*] And surely there were no trees this size here when I left.

(*Sings*)

When I left, this pine, this cypress
Were not higher than my head.
What has made them grow
So much so fast?
Perhaps more rain has fallen here?
But still, a scant three months
Have passed since I left home—
Could they attain
Their present size
Just from abundant rain?

(*Speaks*)

I shall go in and walk among the tombs. [*Pantomimes walking and looking*] Well, I've been walking half a day and now I'd like to sit a while. [*Pantomimes sitting*]

JUNG-TSU: [*Enters with children*] I have reached our graveyard. [*Pantomimes seeing* TSO] But who is that young man sitting there? I shall approach and ask. Tell me, young man, what are you doing here?

TSO: [*Somewhat pugnaciously*] Since this is my family's cemetery, I scarcely think I need your permission to sit in it.

JUNG-TSU: [*Aside*] A cheeky young fellow! [*Addresses* TSO] This is *our* family plot: not only are you sitting in it, but you have the nerve to claim it's yours!

TSO: [*Aside*] Here's an ill-mannered old man! [*Addresses* JUNG-TSU] Am I not allowed to sit in my own graveyard?

JUNG-TSU: You claim it is yours, perhaps you could explain. . . . I'll listen.

TSO:

Shang Hsiao-lou

(*Sings*)

I shall explain, old rustic,
In order that you should not
Hail this before some magistrate!
That land around our funerary lions,
Our stone-carved goats,
Who said you, now,

Could put that open land to plow?

JUNG-TSO: Well, if this is your cemetery, suppose you tell me exactly how much cropland you own hereabouts?

TSO:

(*Sings*)

In this little pot-full of land
There are only five sixth-acres.

But you're a doughty,
Thick-skinned fellow, indeed,
To have gone your way,
At your sole command,
And plowed up my very cemetery land!

JUNG-TSU: But it's *my* land.

TSO: No, it is *my* land!

JUNG-TSU: Since you're so positive it's yours, perhaps you can tell me how the tombs are arranged.

TSO:

(*Sings*)

Pride of place is given
To the family founder—
This is no cozy home !
If you try to cut me off,
I will seek official trial;
I'll carry my complaint
Loudly and with speed,
Then what will happen when
I do the deed?

[*He advances threateningly toward* JUNG-TSU]

JUNG-TSU: Why, you insolent rogue! Do you dare strike me?

TSO: If I hit you, then what?

(*Sings*)

Now I've lost all patience!
Anger rushes to the fore
And I would lay violent hold of him . . . .

[*He raises his hands to seize* JUNG-TSU's *tunic, then stops and recovers himself*]

Stop! Stop! Stop!

That would just compel
That cursed character
To appear on his lapel!

(*Speaks*)

All right. If it's your cemetery, what is your surname?

JUNG-TSU: My name is Liu.

TSO: So be it, your name is Liu, but from what Liu family do you come?

JUNG-TSU: The family of Liu Chün-tso.

TSO: [*He's beginning to sound hesitant*] But which Liu Chün-tso?

JUNG-TSU: He was the Liu Chün-tso who was led off by some fat monk to a life of religion.

TSO: (*Aside*) But that would be me! (*Turns to* JUNG-TSU) What relation was that man to you?

JUNG-TSU: He was my grandfather.

TSO: How are these graves arranged, then?

JUNG-TSU: Well, this spot right here is the empty tomb of my grandfather.

TSO: [*Pointing*] And this one?

JUNG-TSU: That is the tomb of my grandfather's brother, Liu Chün-yu.

TSO: Could that be the Liu Chün-yu who fell, frozen, into a snowdrift?

JUNG-TSU: [*Aside*] Ai-ya! How could this rascal say something like that!?

TSO: [*Pointing to another tomb*] And who is this?

JUNG-TSU: That's the tomb of my father.

TSO: And was he Fo-liu?

JUNG-TSU: [*Aside*] He has a nerve using my father's milk-name![40]

TSO: And who's place is this? [*Points*]

JUNG-TSU: My aunt's.

TSO: Do you mean little Seng-nu?

JUNG-TSU: It sounds almost as though you collected the baby-hair of my family!

TSO: Did you know your grandfather, Chün-tso?

JUNG-TSU: No, I never saw him.

TSO: Then open your eyes and you will! I am your grandfather!

JUNG-TSU: [*Sarcastically*] And I'm your uncle! What do you mean, my grandfather?

TSO: If what I tell you now is so, then acknowledge me; if what I tell you is untrue, disown me.

JUNG-TSU: Speak, I'm ready to listen.

TSO: It was on my birthday. That fat monk wrote on the palm of my hand the character for "patience" which I could neither wash nor rub off. Instead, the character became rubbed and imprinted again and again on the towel. He led me off but I left behind that cloth with the characters on it—do you still have it?

40. Baby name.

JUNG-TSU: There is such a cloth, but perhaps not the one you mean.

TSO: Bring it here and let me identify it.

[*There should be some business here with producing the towel*]

JUNG-TSU: Here's the towel; now you identify it.

TSO: (*Scrutinizes the towel*) This is indeed mine. In case you have any doubts, look at this character on my palm. Is it not identical to those on the cloth? [*Holds out palm and cloth toward audience*]

JUNG-TSU: You must be my grandfather, then! Children! Come, pay your respects to your great-grandfather . . . . (*All kneel and bow*) Where have you been, grampa?

TSO: Everyone, rise.

Man-t'ing Fang

    (*Sings*)

> Well! Here you all are—
> All saluting me,
> My very own, my own, my very,
> Very warm and noisy children!
> Now then, who among these
> Generations below me,
> Is the oldest, pray?

JUNG-TSU: I am the oldest.

TSO:

    (*Sings*)

> He with the nest of silky white hair,

    (*Speaks*)

[*Pointing*] And who is this one?

JUNG-TSU: Grandsir, that's my niece.

TSO:

    (*Sings*)

> But this niece
> Should be old enough
> To be my mama!

    (*Speaks*)

And this one?

JUNG-TSU: He's your great-grandson, of course!

TSO:

(*Sings*)

My great-grandson!
Yet he looks old enough
To be my elder brother!

[*Here is where he somehow registers his enlightenment for the first time*]

These oddities reveal too clearly
Life must seem
Always evanescent as
The South Branch dream.[41]

JUNG-TSU: Grandfather, tell us, why are you not old at all?

TSO: If you were willing to invoke the name of Buddha as I do, you would not grow older.

JUNG-TSU: How should I invoke the name of Buddha?

TSO: Just do as I do now, "Namu Amida Buddha". . . . Hai! Liu Chün-tso. . . . You didn't understand that your Master was well intentioned! I went with the Master a scant three months ago, but in the World of Dust, over a century has passed. But, what to do now? I can find neither the gate that leads forward nor the one leading back. Oh, Master, come save your disciple!

Shih-erh Yüeh

(*Sings*)

Oh, Master, speed here and save me!
How will these events end?
Time flowed like the river;
Days and months darted by as does a shuttle.
Though word and deed never matched,
I did use my lips to say
The names of Buddha.

Yao-min Ko

Yah, vainly did I call
The names of gods,
And heedless, the name
Of Buddha was on my tongue.
But at least I've learned
What Chuang Tzu knew,

41. See selection 253.

Singing and thumping his pot.[42]
Master, what if you have arisen to the heavens,
Then what will become of me?

(*Speaks*)

Enough, enough! I've had all I want of this life!

(*Sings*)

I may as well end what's left
And dash my head against this pine. . . .

(*He attempts to dash his head against a tree but* PU [*enters by way of hangings and*] *prevents him*)

PU: Liu Chün-tso, do you see clearly yet?
TSO: Oh, Master, your disciple is finally awake.
PU: My disciple, your true karma is finally run so you are at last able to believe!
TSO:

(*Sings*)

You speak the truth, heigh-ho,
And all because there were many
Characters for "patience."

(*Speaks*)

If you had not come just when you did, Master,

(*Sings*)

A single moment would know
That character printed
Thirty times in a row!

PU: Hear me, Liu Chün-tso. . . . You are no ordinary mortal. You were, in another world, the thirteenth arhat, Piṇḍola. Nor was your wife a mortal—she was a transformation of Li-shan Lao-mu.[43] Your children were the Golden Lad and the Jade Girl.[44] But because you once longed for the secular, you were sent to the world of men to experience wine, lust, greed, and anger, and the distinctions of "thou" and "me." But your merit suffices and your works are done, so you may now return to your origins and to the Way of the Buddha to be an arhat forever. Do you recognize me, now?
TSO: No, Master, I don't. Who are you?

42. See selection 9. This is an allusion to Master Chuang's behavior when his wife died.
43. Old Mother of Mount Li, a matriarchal figure of popular religion.
44. Idealized children of legend.

PU:

(*Chants*)

Neither am I the ancestor, Bodhidharma,
Nor yet Tripiṭaka.
I am Maitreya taking the form
Of the monk with the cloth sack.

TSO: (*Making reverence*) Namu Amida Buddha . . . .

Sha-wei

(*Sings*)

Although I was sent back to the world,
I did in fact become a Buddha.
I left home once to escape catastrophe,
But who could know it would come to this—
Back home I still found Eternal Bliss!

(*Exeunt omnes*)

T'I-MU: A Beggar Shows the Way to a Miser
CHENG-MING: The Monk Pu-tai and the Record of the Character for Patience[45]

Translated by J. I. Crump

45. *T'i-mu* ("topic") and *Cheng-ming* ("proper name") regularly appear at the end of Yüan playscripts.

273
Injustice to Tou Ǒ

Act 3

Kuan Han-ch'ing (c. 1220–c. 1307)

(*Enter the officer in charge of execution*)

OFFICER: I am the officer in charge of execution. Today we are putting a criminal to death. Officers, guard the roads. Do not let any passersby loiter.

The story of Tou Ǒ has been told in many different versions and is still presented in Peking opera under the title *Snow in Midsummer*. All of the supernatural phenomena that occur when

(*Enter attendant. They beat the drum and gong three times. The executioner enters, waving a flag, carrying a sword, and guarding* TOU Ŏ *in a cangue*)

EXECUTIONER: Move faster, move faster! The officer in charge of execution has long since gone to the place of execution.

TOU Ŏ: (*Sings first lyric*)

> For no reason, I am found guilty by Imperial law;
> Unexpectedly, I suffer punishment.
> My cry of injustice startles Heaven and Earth!
> In a moment, my drifting soul goes to Yama's palace.[1]
> Why shouldn't I blame Heaven and Earth?

(*Sings second lyric*)

> The sun and moon hang aloft by day and by night;
> Ghosts and spirits hold the power over our lives and deaths.
> Heaven and Earth should distinguish the pure from the foul;
> But how they have mixed up Bandit Chih and Yen Yüan![2]

Tou Ŏ dies are taken from earlier sources, but through his literary artistry, Kuan Han-ch'ing (see selection 130) first brought them together in a fashion that has made this the most memorable work in which they are to be found. The verse portions of Kuan's play are especially fine. *Injustice to Tou Ŏ* is written in early Mandarin, as is all Yüan drama, which means that it is full of colloquial speech.

A brief synopsis of the play is as follows: Scholar Tou sells his only daughter, aged seven, to Mistress Ts'ai, a money-lender, for a few ounces of silver so that he can travel to the capital to sit for the imperial examinations. Thirteen years later, Tou Ŏ, who was married to Mistress Ts'ai's son, is now mourning his death as a young widow of twenty. Old Chang and his son, Donkey Chang, come courting Mistress Ts'ai and Tou Ŏ respectively. The two men force their way into the house and demand compensation for having previously saved Mistress Ts'ai from being strangled by an evil quack doctor. Mistress Ts'ai seems willing to remarry, but Tou Ŏ refuses out of faithfulness to the memory of her late husband. Donkey Chang plans to do away with Mistress Ts'ai so that he can have his way with Tou Ŏ after the old lady is dead. When Tou Ŏ makes some mutton-tripe soup for her mother-in-law, Donkey Chang puts poison in it. Old Chang drinks the poisoned soup by mistake and dies. Donkey Chang accuses Tou Ŏ of having murdered his father and has her dragged into court. There a forced confession is extracted from her after she is flogged. She is sentenced to death and executed. The three-year drought brought on by Tou Ŏ's unjust execution brings to the district a high official, who happens to be Tou Ŏ's father, on an inspection tour. As he reviews the documents of her trial by candlelight, Tou Ŏ's ghost appears to him and asks for retribution. The unfortunate young woman's case is reopened, she is cleared of guilt, and the real culprit is punished.

The third act, presented here, is the execution scene. In it Tou Ŏ passionately calls on Heaven and Earth to rectify the great injustice inflicted upon her. The supernatural phenomena that come to pass in response to her invocation transform a single woman's fight against her enemies into a battle of good and evil, thus enlarging the scope of the play and endowing it with cosmic significance. This selection typifies the skill and power of Kuan as a playwright.

1. The palace of Yama, king of the nether world in popular Buddhism.
2. Both were of the Spring and Autumn period. Chih was a notorious robber, and Yen

The good suffer poverty and short life;
The wicked enjoy wealth, nobility, and long life.
Even Heaven and Earth have come to fear the strong and oppress the
    weak.
They, after all, only push the boats following the current.[3]
Oh Earth, as you fail to discriminate between good and evil,
    How can you function as Earth?
Oh Heaven, in mistaking the sage and the fool,
    You are called Heaven in vain!

EXECUTIONER: Move on faster; we are late.
TOU Ŏ: (*Sings third lyric*)
    I am twisted by this cangue
    Till I tilt to the left and stagger to the right;
    The crowd pushes me backward and forward.
    I, Tou Ŏ, wish to say something to you, brother.

EXECUTIONER: What do you want to say?
TOU Ŏ: (*Sings*)
    If we go through the main street, I shall bear you a grudge;
    If we go through the back street,
    I will have no grievance, though I die.
    Do not refuse me by saying, "The back road is too long."

EXECUTIONER: Now that you are going to the execution ground, if you have
    any relatives you would like to see, it would be all right for you to
    see them.
TOU Ŏ: (*Sings fourth lyric*)
    Unhappily I am all alone and have no relatives;
    So I can only endure in silence, and sigh in vain.

EXECUTIONER: Do you mean to say that you don't even have parents?
TOU Ŏ: I have only a father, who went to the capital thirteen years ago to take
    the Examination. There has not been any word from him since. (*Sings*)

    I have not seen my father for over ten years.

EXECUTIONER: Just now you asked me to take you by the back street. What is
    your reason?
TOU Ŏ: (*Sings*)
    I fear that on the main street my mother-in-law would see me.
EXECUTIONER: You cannot even take care of your own life now. Why should
    you worry about her seeing you?

Yüan, a Confucian disciple, was a virtuous person who died young in poverty. Later these two
persons represented the extreme bad and good.
    3. Meaning "to help without sincerity; to offer help to those who are already lucky."

TOU Ŏ: If my mother-in-law sees me in a cangue and lock, going to the execution ground to be killed, (*Sings*)

Won't she die from anger for nothing?
Won't she die from anger for nothing?
I tell you, brother,
It is good to do favors for people in times of peril.

TS'AI: Oh Heaven, isn't this my daughter-in-law?

EXECUTIONER: Old woman, stand back.

TOU Ŏ: Since my mother-in-law is here, ask her to come closer. Let me say a few words to her.

EXECUTIONER: You old woman over there, come near. Your daughter-in-law wants to say something to you.

TS'AI: My child, this pains me to death!

TOU Ŏ: Mother, when Donkey Chang put the poison in the mutton-tripe soup, he really wanted to kill you and then force me to be his wife. He never expected you to give the soup to his father to eat, and thus kill him instead. Because I was afraid you would get into trouble, I confessed, under pressure, to murdering my father-in-law. Today I am going to the execution ground to be killed. Mother, in the future, during the winter season, on New Year and other festivals, and on the first and fifteenth of each month, if you have any spare gruel, pour half a bowl for me; and if you have paper money to spare, burn some for me. Do this for the sake of the personal dignity of your late son.

(*Sings fifth lyric*)

Think of Tou Ŏ, who wrongly was found guilty;
Think of Tou Ŏ, whose head and body were severed;
Think of Tou Ŏ, who, in the past, worked in your house.
Oh mother, do all of these for the sake of Tou Ŏ's face,
    Since she has no father or mother.

(*Sings sixth lyric*)

Think of Tou Ŏ, who served you all these years;
At festivals, offer me a bowl of cold gruel,
Burn some paper money for my headless corpse.
Regard this as offering sacrifice to your own late son.

TS'AI: (*Weeping*) Child, don't worry. I shall remember all this. Ah Heaven, this kills me.

TOU Ŏ: (*Sings*)

Oh mother, do not cry or fret or complain to high Heaven.
It is I, Tou Ŏ, who has no luck,
And who has to suffer in confusion such great injustice.

EXECUTIONER: (*Shouts*) You old woman over there, stand back! The hour has come.

(*Tou Ŏ kneels and the executioner unlocks the cangue*)

TOU Ŏ: I wish to say to your honor, that if you would agree to one thing, I would die content.

EXECUTION OFFICER: Say what you have on your mind.

TOU Ŏ: I want a clean mat to stand on. Also, I want a piece of white silk, twelve feet long, to hang on the flagpole. If I have really been wronged, when the knife strikes and my head falls, a chestful of warm blood, without a drop staining the ground, will fly up to the piece of white silk.

EXECUTION OFFICER: I agree to this; it's nothing of importance.

(*The executioner fetches the mat and* TOU Ŏ *stands on it. He also fetches a piece of white silk and hangs it on the flagpole*)

TOU Ŏ: (*Sings seventh lyric*)
It is not that I, Tou Ŏ, make irrational wishes;
Indeed the wrong I suffer is profound.
If there is no miraculous sign to show the world,
Then there is no proof of a clear, blue Heaven.
I do not want half a drop of my blood to stain the earth;
All of it will go to the white silk hanging on the eight-foot flagpole.
When people see it from four sides,
It will be the same as the blood of Ch'ang Hung[4] turning into a green stone,
Or the soul of Wang-ti[5] residing in a crying cuckoo.

EXECUTIONER: What else do you have to say? If you don't tell his honor now, when are you going to tell?

TOU Ŏ: (*Kneels again*) Your honor, this is the hottest time of summer. If Tou Ŏ has been truly wronged, after her death Heaven will send down three feet of auspicious snow to cover her corpse.

EXECUTION OFFICER: In such hot weather, even if you had grievances reaching to Heaven, you still couldn't call down one snowflake. Surely this is talking nonsense!

TOU Ŏ: (*Sings eighth lyric*)
You say that hot summer is not a time for snow.

---

4. Ch'ang Hung was an official of the Chou dynasty who was unjustly killed. According to legend, after his death his blood turned into a green stone.

5. According to legend, Tu Yü, styled Wang-ti, was king of the Shu state toward the end of the Chou dynasty. He abdicated in favor of his prime minister because of the latter's success in controlling the flood. Wang-ti himself then retired to the Western Mountain and later turned into a cuckoo which cries in the spring, and people grieve for it.

Have you not heard that frost formed in June because of Tsou Yen?[6]
If I have a chestful of wronged feelings that spurt like fire,
It will move snow to tumble down like cotton,
And keep my corpse from exposure.
What need is there of white horses and a white carriage,[7]
To escort my funeral through the ancient path and wild trail?

(TOU Ŏ *again kneels*)

Your honor, I, Tou Ŏ, truly die unjustly. I ask that from this day this
    Ch'u-chou[8] district should suffer from drought for three years.
EXECUTION OFFICER: Slap her! What a thing to say!
TOU Ŏ: (*Sings ninth lyric*)
You say that Heaven cannot be counted on,
It has no sympathy for the human heart;
You don't know that Heaven does answer men's prayers.
Otherwise, why did sweet rain fail to fall for three years?
It was all because of the wrong suffered by the filial daughter at Tung-
    hai.[9]
Now is the turn of your Shan-yang district![10]
It is all because officials care not for justice,
People in turn are afraid to speak out.

EXECUTIONER: (*Waving a flag*) Why is the sky suddenly overcast? (*Sound of
    wind is heard from backstage*) What cold wind!
TOU Ŏ: (*Sings tenth lyric*)
The wandering clouds darken for my sake,
The mournful wind whirls on my behalf.
My three prayers will make things completely clear.

(*Weeps*) Mother, wait till snow falls in June and drought lasts for three
years; (*Sings*)

Then, and only then, the innocent soul of Tou Ŏ will be revealed.

(*The executioner strikes, and* TOU Ŏ *falls*)

6. Frost formed in the sixth month of the year because of Tsou Yen's unjust death. Tsou
Yen was a loyal official of the Warring States period. When he suffered unjust imprisonment,
he cried to heaven; frost occurred—even in the warm month of June. This unnatural event is
understood to be a sign of heaven's displeasure.
7. In the Later Han period, Chang Shao died, and his friend Fan Shih came from afar and
attended the funeral in a white (the color of death and mourning in China) carriage drawn by a
white horse. Later this allusion comes to mean a funeral.
8. The area from which Mistress Ts'ai hails.
9. An allusion to the source of the basic story in *Injustice to Tou Ŏ*, which is taken from the
biography of Yü Ting-kuo in the *History of the Han*.
10. Where the action of this play occurs.

EXECUTION OFFICER: What! It is indeed snowing. How strange!

EXECUTIONER: I, for my part, say that usually when I execute people, the ground is full of blood. The blood of this Tou Ŏ, however, all flew onto the twelve feet of white silk and not a single drop is on the ground. This is truly wondrous.

EXECUTION OFFICER: There must be injustice in this death sentence. Two of her wishes have already come true. There is no knowing whether her talk of a three-year drought will come true or not. We shall wait and see how it turns out. Attendants, there is no need to wait for the snow to stop; now take her corpse away and return it to Mistress Ts'ai.

(All answer. Exeunt, carrying the corpse)

Translated by Chung-wen Shih

274

The Lute

Scene 33

Kao Ming (c. 1305–1359)

ACOLYTE: *(Played by the mo[1] actor, enters and recites in* shih[2] *form)*
Old in years, content in heart, I live without a care.

The playwright, Kao Ming, was a scholar-official who created in *The Lute* (*P'ip'a chi*) a masterpiece consisting of beautiful songs, vivid characters, and a forceful moral message. This is one of the very first plays written in the romance (*ch'uan-ch'i*; for the origin of this term, see selection 249), a form of drama that emerged during the fourteenth century from southern drama (*nan-hsi*) to become a model for later playwrights of this genre. In contrast to northern plays such as Yüan drama (*tsa-chü*), which are livelier and somewhat raucous, southern romances tend to be slower and more languorous, both musically and theatrically.

A bright and conscientious scholar, Ts'ai Po-chieh, has spent his youth in study for the civil service examinations, the traditional means by which one became a member of the highly esteemed and powerful official class. When the final examination in the capital is announced, he is reluctant to travel there to participate in it because of his filial devotion. His parents are aged and he balks at leaving them with no other support than that of his young wife, Wu-niang. It is only out of obedience to his father, who insists that he attempt to win glory for the family, that Ts'ai finally sets out for the capital. Once there, he wins first place in the examinations. Now the most coveted marital catch in the empire, he is coerced by the powerful prime minister Niu, supported by the emperor, into marrying his daughter and taking up residence in his mansion.

While Ts'ai lingers on in the capital, finding it impossible to return home, his hometown is ravaged by famine. Wu-niang's valiant struggles to provide her parents-in-law with food are in vain and they die one after another, first the mother, then the father. She sets out for the capital to find her husband and inform him of his parents' deaths. Along the way she plays her *p'i-p'a* ("balloon guitar," a pear-shaped lute imported to China from Persia more than two thousand

Hemp clothes and straw mat are fine enough for me.
So many people tell me they'll leave the world and come;
But on this hallowed ground not one of them do I see.[3]

I am an acolyte in this Amitabha[4] Monastery. Today we're having an assembly of the Pure Land sect. People from all over are coming, some to save the souls of their dead parents, others to seek protection for their own lives. What a beautiful monastery this is! How does it look?

(*He continues in parallel prose*)

Just see the ornateness of the Buddhist temple, the dignity of the lotus throne. Like a craggy mountain, the great hall—its golden walls gleam. Winding round and round, the passageways—in bright colors they're painted. The high pagoda rises a thousand stories, breaking into the clouds above; high in the sky is heard the intermittent sound of clear bells that hang in its eaves. The towers decorated with seven jewels shine like crystal in the rays of the sun. All through the day constantly echo pealing bells.

Pine trees protect the Buddhist monastery;
The dust of the world can't penetrate here.
Bamboo surrounds this Buddhist retreat;
Bright sunlight can't cast a glare.

The majesty of the wise countenances of these arhats[5] can compare to that of the millions of Buddhas at Snow Mountain.[6] The purity of the austere conduct of these bhikshus[7] is like that of the thousands of followers who lived in Jetavana Park.[8] Amid banners, see how high the stone altar is raised! All is quiet in the flower courtyard—only the sounds of those at

---

years ago) and sings as she begs for alms. This is a typical *modus vivendi* for *p'i-p'a* players, many of whom were blind, in old China. Wu-niang also carries with her the portraits of her parents-in-law and these objects become very important in later scenes of the play for bringing the couple back together. Finally reunited, they return, along with Mistress Niu, to Ts'ai Po-chieh's home village, to carry out the traditional three years of mourning by his parents' graveside. The play closes at the end of this mourning period, with Ts'ai about to return to the capital to resume his official career after he and his two wives have received an imperial commendation for their filial and virtuous conduct.

1. Subordinate male role and stage manager.
2. Genre of poetry ("classical poetry") having lines with equal numbers of syllables, usually five or seven (see selection 22ff.).
3. The poem is by Ling Ch'e (746–816).
4. Presiding deity of the western Pure Land, a Buddhist paradise.
5. Saints.
6. The reference to the Buddhas of Snow Mountain has not been traced.
7. Monks.
8. A beautiful monastery built by a faithful king for Śākyamuni (the historical Buddha) during his lifetime.

chess. Enough talk of this pure monastery; let me tell of the dignified assembly hall. See the ethereal vision of pearled pennants and jeweled canopies. Off and on sound the musical stones and golden bells. All nine grades of red lotuses are set in dragon-shaped vases; in this Pure Land, though years may pass, never does one age.[9] Crimson buds of flame blossom on the thousand branches of phoenix candles—constantly illuminating the Buddhist heaven both night and day. In perfect order, the pages of the Buddhist texts are turned together; with a rustling sound, the divine flowers scatter down on the congregation.[10] In this forest of sandalwood trees is burned "pure clean incense" and "way and virtue incense." In the temple kitchen is offered up "joys of meditation food" and "pleasure in the Law food." Each person seems to be an inhabitant of the immortal islands; everyone has purified his consciousness and perception. As they beat the drum of the Great Law and sound the conch of the Great Law, immortal music is performed. The sweet dew gate is opened, the sweet dew city entered; spirits lost in the shades attain speedy deliverance.[11] We send word to those who sojourn in the sea of travail, "Come to the assembly at Ling-shan."[12]

Because of the big assembly today, there may be high officials and other important people coming here to visit. I'll take out the register and try to solicit some money to help with our expenses. The words are just out of my mouth, and already I see two patrons coming!

(*Two rogues, played by the* ching[13] *and* ch'ou[14] *actors, enter and sing to the tune* Lü-lü chin)

Making trouble wherever we go,
Two rascals are we.
Not a scrap of food left over at home;
So what could keep us there?
All our lives we've played the fool,
And now we can't repent.
We've wandered here to the "forest of monks,"
This Buddhist assembly to see.

9. The Pure Land sect of Buddhism believed that those born into the various levels of the Pure Land would never grow old.

10. Flowers are said to fall from the sky when a Buddhist master expounds the scriptures in a particularly brilliant manner.

11. The "sweet dew gate" is a reference to the practice of providing hungry ghosts with food and drink; "sweet dew city" describes the clarity of the master's discourse. Both help lost souls to advance in the spiritual world.

12. The lines refer to a famous assembly held at Vulture Peak in India.

13. Secondary or subordinate role, male or female, often comic.

14. Subordinate role, male or female, generally comic.

ACOLYTE: Gentlemen, please sit down and have some tea.

CHING and CH'OU: Does this assembly cost very much?

ACOLYTE: Yes, indeed! Please excuse me for annoying you with a request, but since Heaven has blessed us with this visit by two such worthy gentlemen, I can't help asking you to donate a little something—just to help out with the expenses.

CHING: Let's have a look at the subscription book! Brother, money is, after all, just a thing of chance—so why not spend it?

CH'OU: Right you are! People like us never pass a day without spending several strings of cash.

CHING: I'll donate five ingots.

CH'OU: Me too!

CHING and CH'OU: Of course we didn't bring cash with us here. In a little while you can come with us and we'll give it to you.

ACOLYTE: Thank you, gentlemen!

CHING: Look! Do you see over there? There's a woman coming. She's not bad looking either!

CH'OU: Yes, I see a woman with a lute on her back. She looks like your sister!

ACOLYTE: As they say, these two can "see clearly even at a distance."

WU-NIANG: (*Enters and sings to the previous tune*)

> The road I travel,
> How hard to bear!
> No money left,
> Destitute and helpless,
> I play my lute,
> Beg alms from those I meet.
> To save the souls of my parents-in-law from deep burial,
> I've come to this Buddhist assembly.

I've finally reached Loyang! They say that the Amitabha monastery is having an assembly today, So I've come to beg a few cents and use them to pray for the souls of my parents-in-law.

ACOLYTE: Don't come any closer, little lady!

CHING and CH'OU: What do you have there?

WU-NIANG: These are portraits of my parents-in-law.

CHING and CH'OU: Where do you come from?

WU-NIANG: (*Sings to the tune* Hsiao-chin chang)

> Listen and I'll tell you:
> I'm the wife of a well-bred man,
> Yet it was he who brought me down.
> He went to take the examinations,

And never returned to his hometown.
In famine's ravage,
I lost my parents-in-law;
I made the grave for them myself.
Now I'm on my way to seek my husband.

(CHING and CH'OU: Where is your husband?)

I seek and don't know—
Where is he now?

CHING: What's the lute for?
WU-NIANG: I'll play some songs, beg for alms, then go into the temple and pray
    for the souls of my parents-in-law.
CHING and CH'OU: What songs can you play? Can you play "Yeh-ssu-erh?"
WU-NIANG: I don't know that one.
CHING and CH'OU: Can you play "Pa-ch'iao-shou?"
WU-NIANG: I don't know that either. I only know a few songs about filial piety.
ACOLYTE: These two gentlemen have been giving out money here and saying,
    "Why not spend it?" You go ahead and play for them, and they'll give
    you a generous reward.
WU-NIANG: (*Recites to the lyric*[15] Chiang-nan hao)

In raising children
How toilsome are the first three years!
Before the child can talk and walk,
How the parents suffer!

(*With an action, she sings to the previous tune*)

In raising children
Most difficult are the ten months of pregnancy,
And the three wearisome years of carrying them in one's arms, on one's
    back.
Everyone knows how parents sacrifice their own comfort for their
    children's sake,
Perform thousands and thousands of toilsome duties.
Really, in a thousand ways they show their loving care,
In a thousand ways show their loving protection.
If the slightest discomfort bothers their child,
The parents worry and fuss, don't know where to turn,
Until he's well again.
Then when he's well again, their joy returns anew.

15. Genre of poetry (*tz'u*) having lines with irregular numbers of syllables (see selections
107ff).

CHING and CH'OU: Well played! That was great.

ACOLYTE: It sure was!

CHING and CH'OU: When you've got money, why not spend it? We'll give you a nice jacket.

(*They perform an action*)

WU-NIANG: (*Recites to the previous lyric*)

Day by day the child grows,
And so grows the happiness of his parents.
They teach him to walk and to talk, they teach him proper conduct,
And long for the day when he'll be a man.

(*She sings to the previous tune*)

When the child takes his first few steps,
Mother and father exchange a happy glance.
Slowly he learns to walk and talk;
He hankers after food and drink
From morning to night.
Always their anxious thoughts are upon him,
So many, many worries!
They choose for him a good tutor,
But worry that their son may be stupid and slow.
And if he shows but a little talent,
With what joy do they reward him!

CHING and CH'OU: Well played!

ACOLYTE: Very fine!

CHING and CH'OU: When you have money, why not spend it? We'll give you another jacket.

(*They perform an action*)

ACOLYTE: These two must be crazy!

CHING and CH'OU: Play some more!

WU-NIANG: (*Recites to the previous lyric*)

How diligently they teach him—
History in the evening, classics in the morning,
With the hope that he'll bring glory to parents and ancestors,
Achieve fame with a single examination.

(*She sings to the previous tune*)

Classics in the morning, history at night,
Composition of poetry and prose—
All for the spring exam to which they urge him on,

In the hope that he'll bring glory to parents and ancestors,
And raise their status in the world.
Always their anxious thoughts upon him,
They think of the day he'll wear a belt of gold round a purple robe.
While their son is on the road,
They fear he's eating only wind and sleeping in dew.
From spirits and diviners they seek out news,
Secretly calculate the time of his return.

CHING and CH'OU: Well played! Well played! When you have money, why not spend it? Here's another jacket for you!

ACOLYTE: How tattered and torn their clothes are underneath! Would you mind my asking—what are you thinking of to take off your jackets when it's so cold?

CHING and CH'OU: So it's cold! We won't let that ruin our style. People like us who are used to spending lots of money are never afraid of the cold. Another song!

ACOLYTE: I wonder what they'll give her next.

WU-NIANG: (*Recites to the previous lyric*)

The son sets out;
Surely he'll soon return.
For if one son commits the Five Sins,[16] another is filial,
Each will meet his just reward.

(*She sings to the previous tune*)

The son who keeps father and mother in his heart
Will hasten to return to his family home,
Remembering how baby crows feed their parents.
Don't take my husband as your model
And do wrong to your parents!
It's often said of parenthood,
Only when one has children himself does he realize how kind his
   own father was.
One son commits the Five Sins;
Another obeys and serves his parents.
If they don't meet with their just rewards,
How unfair of Heaven and earth!

CHING and CH'OU: You play and sing very well, but we don't have anything left to give you.

ACOLYTE: I knew it!

CHING and CH'OU: (*Acting as if cold*) We'd look pretty silly going home like this.

---

16. The Five Sins of Buddhism include killing one's mother or father.

CH'OU: This acolyte here will be glad to give us some clothes. (*They grab the acolyte*) So! This acolyte tricked our clothes away from us!

ACOLYTE: You gave them away yourselves. How can you say I tricked you?

CHING and CH'OU: When we told her she played well, you agreed with us. You kept encouraging us—wouldn't you call that a trick?

ACOLYTE: Young lady, please return their clothes—what would you want with them anyway?

WU-NIANG: Here, take them back.

CHING and CH'OU: Though it's true that "If you have money, why not spend it?" it's hard to bear such cold!

CH'OU: I told you that you sang and played very well, but when I think it over, it wasn't any good at all. If you have any doubt, then sing again and we'll see!

WU-NIANG: I can't sing any more.

CHING: Of course not! She wouldn't dare.

(*Exit poem*)

CH'OU:

Brother, we're not people who hanker after power and wealth.

ACOLYTE:

It was useless to ask them for alms.

WU-NIANG:

Could it be that these clothes don't belong to you at all?

CHING and CH'OU:

Quite right! We haven't a pair of trousers to our name!

(*The* ching, ch'ou, *and* ACOLYTE *exit*)

WU-NIANG: "Every second of man's life is determined by destiny." I came here to beg a few coins to use to pray for the souls of my parents-in-law, never knowing that I'd meet with those two madmen to annoy me so. I see off in the distance a crowd of men and horses; it must be an official coming here. I'd better stand in attendance.

(TS'AI, *on horseback, along with the* STEWARD, *and another* ATTENDANT *played by the* ch'ou *actor, enter*)

TS'AI: (*Sings to the tune* Lü-lü chin)

The times are hard,
Fate how perverse!
For my parents on the road,
I fear disaster.

STEWARD and ATTENDANT: (*Continue the song*)

> This is the Amitabha monastery;
> Stop the carriage!

(*They sing the chorus together*)

> With hearts devout, to pray to the Lotus Throne,
> We come to join the Buddhist assembly.

STEWARD: (*Pushes* WU-NIANG *aside*) Get out of sight! A high official approaches.

(*He strikes her*)

WU-NIANG: (*With an action*) "When you pass under low eaves, you have to bow your head."

(*She exits*)

TS'AI: (*Dismounts, enters the temple, and sees the portraits*) What is this painting doing here?

ATTENDANT: There was a nun here a minute ago—maybe she left it.

TS'AI: Call her back to get it.

ATTENDANT: Sister, come get your painting!
　　(*He performs an action*) She's gone off—I can't see her.

TS'AI: Well, if we can't find her, then we'll keep it for her.

(*The* STEWARD *takes the painting*)

ABBOT: (*Played by the* ching *actor, enters and sings to the previous tune*)

> Wine I can drink,
> And I gobble up my meatless meals.
> I drink till I'm smashed,
> Then find a new acolyte to cuddle.
> When I expound scriptures and recite prayers,
> I'm really at a loss.
> So learned gentlemen, I beg you,
> Stay away from this Buddhist assembly!

(TS'AI *and the* ABBOT *greet each other*)

TS'AI: My father and mother are on their way here, and I'm worried about their safety and health on the road. I've come to seek protection for them; I wish you to read some scriptures to ensure their safety.

ABBOT: I see. Please offer incense and communicate your desire.

TS'AI: (*Offers incense and sings to the tune* Chiang-erh shui)

> Before Buddha I testify:
> This petition of Ts'ai Yung please consider.

Does all go well with my parents on the road?
Only the great compassion of the Bodhisattva can keep them safe.

(*They sing the chorus together*)

Dragons and angels have heard your request;
Dragons and angels will shelter and protect,
Shelter and protect them as mountains they climb, rivers they cross.

ABBOT: (*Sings to the same tune*)

Before Buddha I testify;
Listen to my heart's desire.
Please give protection to the parents of Ts'ai Yung.
On your ineffable powers we rely.

(*They repeat the chorus above*)

STEWARD: (*Sings to the same tune*)

My Master's days are filled
With endless distress and doubt,
For he worries over his parents on the road.
Such filial love will surely move the spirits above.

(*They repeat the chorus above*)

ATTENDANT: (*Sings to the same tune*)

I heard of this assembly here,
And came to have some fun.
Dish me out some vegetables and bread,
Or I'm off to the kitchen to get them myself!

(*They repeat the chorus above*)

(*Exit poem*)

ABBOT:

If it's so destined in your life, Buddha's blessings are bestowed.

TS'AI:

Let my parents' journey have no hardship, no delay.

STEWARD:

"Chancing upon this bamboo temple, I held conversation with a monk,

ATTENDANT:

Found freedom from my empty life, if but for half a day."[17]

(*All exit*)

17. The two lines are from a poem by Li She (fl. 806).

WU-NIANG: (*Enters and sings to the tune* Lü-lü chin)

> Who was that
> But Ts'ai Po-chieh!
> Attendants led the way
> As the First Winner[18] came near.
> I think the portraits of his parents
> Are now in his keeping.
> It seems that Heaven seeks to reunite us,
> And this Buddhist assembly is the start.

I asked the gentleman who was here just now, and it was none other than Ts'ai Po-chieh! How wonderful! It seems we will be able to meet again. It must have been he who took the portraits of my parents-in-law. Now I'll go to his house and see what happens. It may be we can really be reunited! Ah! It really seems Heaven is bringing us together again! Just as they say, "If the old fisherman hadn't led the way, how could I have viewed these billowing waves?"[19]

(*She exits*)

Translated by Jean Mulligan

18. At the highest level of the civil service examinations.
19. This saying, common in southern-style drama, describes the working of fate to lead one to a desired goal.

275
The Lichee and the Mirror

(Excerpt)

Anonymous (mid-16th century)

CH'EN SAN: Little sister, what are you going to do with that basin of water?
MAID: I am taking it to the mistress so she can wash her face.
CH'EN: Let me take it to her for you.

The Lichee and the Mirror (Li ching chi) is the earliest and best-known play of the dozens of titles that survive for the genre known as Pear Garden Drama (*Li-yüan hsi*). Pear Garden Drama, now considered to be a type of Ming romance (*ch'uan-ch'i*), originated in Chuanchou (Ch'üan-chou) and spread to Chin-chiang, Lung-hsi, Amoy, and Taiwan. It also became popular among

    (CH'EN *takes the basin of water and goes offstage*)

MAID: How come you're so anxious to be a servant? Aren't you afraid the mistress will scold you if you take the water to her?

    (*The* MAID *goes off and* CH'EN *reappears*)

CH'EN: (*Sings to the tune "Golden Filigree"*)

    As I take this basinful of water into her boudoir,
    I feel partly happy,

---

overseas Chinese communities in Southeast Asia. This kind of drama preserves old features of instrumentation and lyric tunes. The movements of the actors are strictly regulated, and some are clearly patterned after those of puppets. *The Lichee and the Mirror* survives in a number of editions, the earliest extant dating to 1566. Ultimately, the play may have its roots in the fifteenth-century folk drama of southern Fukien.

    The Lichee and the Mirror relates the story of Ch'en San (Third Ch'en) and Wu-niang (Fifth Lass) which had long been popular in southern Fukien and eastern Kwangtung provinces. Indeed, *Ch'en San Wu-niang* is the customary title for this play as it is performed in the Pear Garden Drama repertoire. Many other types of local performing arts in Kwangtung and Fukien provinces have made this story a mainstay of their repertoires as well. The author of the 1566 edition of *The Lichee and the Mirror* remains unknown, and the story is obviously the collective cultural property of a whole large region of China that has been reworked many times by countless hands. Perhaps the most remarkable aspect of this enormously popular play is that it was written neither in Classical Chinese nor in Mandarin, but in the southeastern Sinitic topolect known as Minlam (one of the so-called Wu [or Ngwa] languages). The language of the play, which includes several dialectical variations, is therefore quite difficult to understand.

    A brief synopsis of the play is as follows:

    Ch'en San (full name Ch'en Po-ch'ing), who hails from Chuanchou, is accompanying his older brother on a long trip to Kuang-nan in Yunnan province where the latter is going to take up an official position. Their way passes through Chaochou (Chao-chou) and there Ch'en San meets Wu-niang (full name Huang Pi-chü) at the Lantern Festival (Yüan-hsiao, the fifteenth day of the first lunar month). Needless to say, they fall in love with each other at first sight. Wu-niang's parents, Huang Chiu-lang (Huang the Ninth) and his wife, promise their daughter in marriage to the wealthy Big Lin. On the day that the matchmaker comes to present betrothal gifts to the Huang family, Wu-niang smashes the gifts and beats off the matchmaker.

    The next year, Ch'en San comes back to Chaochou. Wu-niang is leaning over a balcony enjoying the warmth of summer and thus the two lovers meet once again. She tosses down a lichee branch and a handkerchief as a pledge of her affection. Thereupon Ch'en San pretends to be a mirror polisher. He intentionally breaks a precious mirror belonging to the Huang family and sells himself into slavery to them to repay the loss. After repeated inquiries, Wu-niang finally learns Ch'en San's real background. Her maid, named Yi-ch'un, plays a crucial role in helping the two to get together. They elope but are soon caught and Ch'en San is thrown into jail. His brother, Ch'en Po-hsien, who by now has been elevated to the high rank of Executive Censor of Kwangtung and Kwangsi provinces, comes to his rescue and so the two lovers are reunited once again.

    The short scene selected here is perhaps the most memorable of the play and is considered to be risqué according to the standards of the Chinese stage. It shows Ch'en San, who is masquerading as a servant, looking on while Wu-niang washes her face.

And partly afraid.
My heart is filled with suffering
That I dare not reveal;
My feelings are tremendously confused,
But she has not the slightest suspicion.

(WU-NIANG *calls the* MAID *and she appears*)

MAID: It's Ch'en San. . . .

WU-NIANG: You wench! I asked you to bring me a basin of water to wash my face. What do you mean by letting Ch'en San bring it?

MAID: When you asked me to go fetch the water, I happened upon your mother who told me to do some other things.

WU-NIANG: What did mother ask you to do?

MAID: She had me go tend to the tea. I was afraid that you needed the water right away, so I had Ch'en San bring it.

WU-NIANG: Despicable wench! Bring me the hot water so I can wash my face!

CH'EN: Let me take it over to her.

MAID: You make me laugh!

CH'EN: Well, go ahead and laugh then.

MAID: It's disgraceful!

CH'EN: Not to me.

(WU-NIANG *starts to wash herself while* CH'EN SAN *looks on*)

WU-NIANG: Yi-ch'un, I'd like to wash my face. What's Ch'en San doing standing there?

MAID: [*To* CH'EN SAN] Our mistress wants to wash her face and wishes that you would go away.

CH'EN: Your mistress can wash her face by herself. I'm just waiting here to serve her.

WU-NIANG: Scoundrel! I want to wash my face. Who needs you to wait on them? Go away!

(CH'EN SAN *goes off but comes back again to watch her*)

WU-NIANG: Yi-ch'un, who's over there watching me while I wash myself?

MAID: It's Ch'en San.

WU-NIANG: The scoundrel! How dare he watch me while I'm washing my face? Yi-ch'un, pretend that you don't know he's there and throw this water in his face. We'll see if he goes away then.

MAID: Dear mistress, this basin is so full of water. If I splash it on him, aren't you afraid he'll catch cold?

WU-NIANG: It's up to you how you handle it.

MAID: I'm afraid he'll scold me if I splash him.

WU-NIANG: Vixen! At least dump half of it on him.

MAID: Dear mistress, since you're so concerned about Ch'en San, you might as well not splash him at all.

(*Together,* WU-NIANG *and the* MAID *throw the water on him*)

CH'EN: Hey! Who made me all soaked like this?
MAID: We didn't know you were sitting there.
CH'EN: Little sister, you really can't tell black from white.
MAID: Who told you to peep at the mistress while she was washing?
CH'EN: (*Sings to the tune of "Red Presentation Jacket"*)

When I carefully reflect on what happened,

(CH'EN SAN *understands*)

I realize this was something you two schemed up.

Translated by Victor H. Mair

276
The Peony Pavilion

Scene 7: The Schoolroom

T'ang Hsien-tsu (1550–1616)

CH'EN TSUI-LIANG:

Droning verses, re-revising
    lines composed last spring,
pondering, my belly filled,
    the taste of the noontime tea;
ants climb up the table leg
    to skirt the inkslab pool,
bees invade the window
    to raid the blooms in my vase.

The Peony Pavilion, written in 1598, is a southern-style drama (see the introductory notes to selections 274 and 277) consisting of fifty-five scenes. It celebrates the power of passion and was part of the new, humane current of thought that appeared during the waning years of the Ming dynasty. The schoolroom scene selected here is one of the two most famous scenes of the play and one of the few that is still performed. The play is much too long to be performed in toto for modern audiences.

The plot is that of a typical romantic comedy: boy meets girl; there are obstacles to their love due to family opposition coupled with a fortuitous separation and/or the machinations of some boorish rival; the obstacles are overcome; and the play concludes with a celebration of reunion. The theme of *The Peony Pavilion* is especially fantastic: Bridal Tu, the heroine, is resurrected

Here in the Prefect's residence I, Ch'en Tsui-liang, have "hung my bed curtain" so that I may instruct the daughter of the house, following family tradition, in the *Classic of Odes*. The mistress, Madam Tu, is treating me with the greatest kindness. Now that breakfast is over I shall immerse myself for a while in the *Odes*.

(*He intones*)

"*Kuan-kuan* cry the ospreys
on the islet in the river.
So delicate the virtuous maiden,
a fit mate for our Prince,"[1]

"Fit," that is to say, "fit"; "mate," that is to say, "seeking." (*He looks about*) How late it gets, and still no sign of my pupil. Horribly spoiled. Let me try three raps on the cloud board. (*He raps the cloud board*) Fragrance, summon the young mistress for her lesson.

(*Enter* BRIDAL TU, *followed by* SPRING FRAGRANCE *bearing books*)

BRIDAL TU:

Jao Ti Yu

Lightly adorned for morning,
to library leisurely strolling,
unconcerned I face
table's gleam by window's brightness.

SPRING FRAGRANCE:

Words of Worth from the Ancients
—What a deadly thought

---

from death by her lover for whom she has pined away and died. She first experiences love only in dreams, then as a shade in the nether world, and finally as a real wife in the flesh. Bridal Tu's lover is Liu Meng-mei ("Dreaming of Plum," the name he has taken in memory of his dreamy assignation with her) who comes from a good family. He is a handsome, gifted scholar, but not simply conventional, for he also has the courage to follow his instincts that are born of his devotion to Bridal Tu. Her father is Tu Pao, an official who is a Confucian rationalist and cannot believe that his daughter could come back to life through the strength of love.

The romanized transcriptions before the verse portions of the text refer to different aria patterns.

T'ang Hsien-tsu, the playwright, passed the metropolitan examinations at age thirty-three and began his career as a dramatist while serving in Nanking as a secretary under the board of ceremony. For more information concerning him, see selection 98.

1. The first stanza of the first poem in the *Classic of Odes* (see selection 22). Actually a folk love lyric, this, like many more of the *Odes*, was traditionally interpreted in didactic fashion as expressing popular esteem for a benevolent prince. James Legge's Victorian period translation is used here both to accord with this kind of interpretation and for the sake of its by now somewhat fustian quality (compare with selection 16).

but when I'm through

I'll be able to teach the parrot to order tea.

(*They greet* CH'EN)

BRIDAL: Our best respects, esteemed sir.

FRAGRANCE: We hope you're not vexed, esteemed sir.

CH'EN: As the *Rites* prescribe, "It is proper for a daughter at first cockcrow to wash her hands, to rinse her mouth, to dress her hair, to pin the same, to pay respects to her father and mother." Once the sun is up then each should attend to her affairs. You are now a pupil and your business is to study: you will need to rise earlier than this.

BRIDAL: We shall not be late again.

FRAGRANCE: We understand. Tonight we won't go to bed so that we can present ourselves for our lesson in the middle of the night.

CH'EN: Have you rehearsed the portion of the *Odes* I presented yesterday?

BRIDAL: I have, but await your interpretation.

CH'EN: Let me hear you.

BRIDAL (*Recites*):

> "*Kuan-kuan* cry the ospreys
> on the islet in the river.
> So delicate the virtuous maiden,
> a fit mate for our Prince."

CH'EN: Now note the interpretation.

> "*Kuan-kuan* cry the ospreys":

the osprey is a bird; "*kuan-kuan*," that is to say, its cry.

FRAGRANCE: What sort of cry is that?

(CH'EN *imitates the call of the osprey;* FRAGRANCE *ad libs an imitation of* CH'EN *imitating the osprey*)

CH'EN: This bird being a lover of quiet, it is on an island in the river.

FRAGRANCE: Quite right. Either yesterday or the day before, this year or last year some time, an osprey got trapped in the young mistress's room and she set it free, and I said to myself, if I try to catch it again, I *land* in the river.

CH'EN: Rubbish. This is a "detached image."

FRAGRANCE: What, a graven image? Who detached it?

CH'EN: To "image," that is to say, to introduce thoughts of. It introduces the thought of the "delicate virtuous maiden," who is a nice, quiet girl waiting for the Prince to come seeking her.

FRAGRANCE: What's he seeking from her?

CH'EN: Now you are being impudent.

BRIDAL: My good tutor, to interpret the text by means of the notes is something I can do for myself. I should like you rather to instruct me in the overall significance of the *Classic of Odes*.

CH'EN:

Tiao Chiao Erh

Of all six Classics
the *Classic of Odes* is the flower
with "Airs" and "Refinements" most apt for lady's chamber:
for practical instruction
Chiang-yüan[2] bears her offspring
"treading in the print of God's big toe";
warning against jealousy
shine the virtues of queen and consort.

And then there are the

"Song of the Cockcrow,"
the "Lament for the Swallows,"
"Tears by the Riverbank,"
"Longings by the Han River"
to cleanse the face of rouge:
in every verse an edifying homily
to "fit a maid for husband and for family."

BRIDAL: It seems to be a very *long* classic!

CH'EN: "The *Odes* are three hundred, but their meaning may be expressed in a single phrase":

no more than this,
"to set aside evil thoughts,"
and this I pass to you.

End of lesson. Fragrance, fetch the "four jewels of the scholar's study" for our calligraphy.

FRAGRANCE: Here are paper, ink, brushes, and inkstone.

CH'EN: What sort of ink is this supposed to be?

BRIDAL: Oh, she brought the wrong thing. This is "snail black," for painting the brows.

CH'EN: And what sort of brushes?

BRIDAL: (*Laughing*) Mascara brushes.

CH'EN: Never did I see such things before! Take them away, take them away. And what sort of paper is this?

2. See selection 22, poem no. 245.

BRIDAL: Notepaper woven by the Tang courtesan Hsüeh T'ao.[3]

CH'EN: Take it away, take it away. Bring such as was woven by the noble inventor of paper, the ancient Ts'ai Lun. And what sort of inkstone? Is it single or double?

BRIDAL: It's not single, it's married.

CH'EN: And the "eye" patterns on it—what sort of eyes?

BRIDAL: Weeping eyes.[4]

CH'EN: What are they weeping about?—Go change the whole lot.

FRAGRANCE: (Aside) Ignorant old rustic! (To CH'EN) Very well. (She brings a new set) Will these do?

CH'EN: (Examines them) All right.

BRIDAL: I believe I could copy some characters. But Fragrance will need your hand, sir, to guide her brush.

CH'EN: Let me see how you write. (As BRIDAL writes, he watches in amazement) Never did I see writing of this quality! What is the model?

BRIDAL: The model is "The Beauty Adorns Her Hair with Blossoms," the style transmitted by the Lady Wei of Chin times.

FRAGRANCE: Let me do some characters in the style of "The Maid Apes Her Mistress."

BRIDAL: Too early for that.

FRAGRANCE: Master, I beg leave to be excused—to leave the room and excuse myself. (She exits)

BRIDAL: Esteemed tutor, may I inquire what age your lady has attained?

CH'EN: She has reached exactly sixty.

BRIDAL: If you would let me have the pattern, I should like to embroider a pair of slippers to congratulate her.

CH'EN: Thank you. The pattern should be from Mencius, "To make sandals without knowledge of the foot."

BRIDAL: Fragrance isn't back yet.

CH'EN: Shall I call her?

(He calls thrice)

FRAGRANCE: (Enters) Clapping like that—I'll give him the clap!

BRIDAL (Annoyed): What have you been doing, silly creature?

FRAGRANCE: (Laughing) Peeing. But I found a lovely big garden full of pretty flowers and willows,[5] lots of fun.

---

3. See selection 54.

4. Inkstones of a highly prized variety made at Tuan-hsi in Kwangtung were decorated with patterns of "eyes" carved to follow the natural grain of the stone. If the "eyes" were not clear-cut "bright eyes," they were known as "weeping eyes," or worse, "dead eyes."

5. "Flowers and willows": this euphemism for "syphilis" reinforces the "clap" of her previous speech. We are no doubt to assume that Bridal remains innocent of these suggestions of her maid, aimed at Tutor Ch'en.

CH'EN: Dear, dear, instead of studying she is off to the garden. Let me fetch a
bramble switch.

FRAGRANCE: What do you want a bramble switch for?

Tiao Chiao Erh

How can a girl
take the examinations and fill an office?

All it's for is to

read a few characters and scrawl a few crow's-feet.

CH'EN: There were students in ancient times who put fireflies in a bag or read
by the moon.

If you use reflected moonlight
you'll dazzle the toad up there;
as for fireflies in a bag
just think of the poor things burning!

CH'EN: Then what about the man who tied his hair to a beam to keep from
nodding off, or the scholar who prodded himself awake with an awl in
the thigh?

FRAGRANCE: If you were to try

tying your hair to a beam
you wouldn't have much left
and pricking your thighs
you'd be even scabbier than you are.
What's so glorious about that?

(A *flower vendor's cry comes from within*)

Listen, young mistress,

a flower vendor's cry
drowns out the drone of studies.

CH'EN: Again she distracts the young lady. This time I shall really beat her.
(He *moves to do so*)

FRAGRANCE: (Dodging)

Try and beat me then,
poor little me—
tutor to young ladies
scaring this poor malefactor
within an inch of her life!

(She *grabs the bramble switch and throws it to the floor*)

BRIDAL: You wicked creature, kneel at once for such rudeness to the tutor. (FRAGRANCE *kneels*) Since this is her first offense, sir, perhaps it will be enough if I give her a scolding:

Tiao Chiao Erh

> Your hands must not touch the garden swing,
> nor your feet tread the garden path.

FRAGRANCE: We'll see about that!

BRIDAL: If you answer back, we shall have to

> scorch with an incense stick
> these lips of yours that blow breezes of malice,
> blind with a sewing needle
> these eyes that blossom into nothing but trouble.

FRAGRANCE: And what use would my eyes be then?

BRIDAL: I insist that you

> hold to the inkstone,
> stand fast by the desk,
> attend to "It is written in the *Odes*,"
> be there when "the Master says,"
> and do not let your thoughts wander.

FRAGRANCE: Oh, do let's wander a little!

BRIDAL: (*Seizes her by the hair*) Do you want as many

> weals on your back
> as there are hairs on your head?
> I'll have you show respect for the "comptroller of the household"
> —the stick Madam Tu my mother keeps in her room!

FRAGRANCE: I won't do it again.

BRIDAL: You understand then?

CH'EN: That will be enough, we shall let her go this time. Get up.

(FRAGRANCE *rises to her feet*)

> Except she lacks ambition for the fame of office,
> instruction of the girl pupil parallels the boy's.

Only when your lessons are completed may you return to the house. Meanwhile, I shall exchange a few words with your father.

BRIDAL, FRAGRANCE, CH'EN: What a waste of

this new red gauze on the sunlit window.

(CH'EN *exits*; FRAGRANCE *points scornfully at his retreating back*)

FRAGRANCE: Ignorant old ox, dopey old dog, not an ounce of understanding.

BRIDAL: (*Tugs at her sleeve*) Stupid creature, "a tutor for a day is a father for a lifetime"; don't you understand he has the right to beat you? But tell me, where is this garden of yours?

(FRAGRANCE *refusing to speak,* BRIDAL *gives an embarrassed laugh and asks again*)

FRAGRANCE: (*Pointing*) Over there, of course!

BRIDAL: What is there to look at?

FRAGRANCE: Oh, lots to look at, half a dozen pavilions, one or two swings, a meandering stream one can float wine cups down, weathered T'aihu rocks on the other bank. It's really beautiful, with all those prize blooms and rare plants.

BRIDAL: How surprising to find such a place! But now we may go back to the house.

(*Envoi*)

BRIDAL:

> Catkins floated on the breeze
> in the Hsieh family court

FRAGRANCE:

> thwarted is my desire to become
> a butterfly in the western garden.

BRIDAL:

> Ask not what sorrows follow spring
> for they are limitless.

BRIDAL, FRAGRANCE:

> Take for a while this loan
> of green shade for your strolling.

Translated by Cyril Birch

277

The Peach Blossom Fan

Part I, Scene 1

The Storyteller

SECOND MONTH, 1643

K'ung Shang-jen (1648–1718)

(*Enter* HOU FANG-YÜ *in the robes of a scholar*)

HOU: (*Sings*)

> On Grieve-Not Lake beside the Poet's Tower,[1]
> The weeping willows burgeon once again.
> The sun is setting: hill and river blend
> In perfect beauty, and the traveler is tempted
> To drink, recalling beauties long ago,
> Painted and powdered in the southern courts.
> Sad thoughts come with twilight, while the swallows
> Frolic regardless of the fall of kings.

The Peach Blossom Fan, completed in 1699, relates the downfall of the Ming dynasty in highly poetic language. The play depicts the corrupt abandon of the court while the Manchus were swiftly swallowing up China. Yet, in the midst of all the degradation, there was still great cultivation and sensibility in certain circles.

Though somewhat effete, Hou Fang-yü (see selection 233) is a brilliant young spokesman for the Revival Club, a group of scholar-loyalists opposed to those court officials who are selling out to the Manchus. He falls in love with a beautiful singing girl, Li Hsiang-chün ("Fragrant Princess"), a woman of strong character who is remarkable for her devotion to her lover and her delicacy of sentiment. The story revolves around events in the south where there was an abortive restoration of Ming rule at Nanking after the loss of the north. Thus it is appropriate that the play was written in the southern style which contrasts strongly with the theater of the northern style (basically Yüan drama and its successors). Southern-style plays typically have a large cast of characters instead of just the four in Yüan drama that focus primarily on a single lead role. Contrasting groups of characters alternate in different scenes. They may sing solo, duet, or in chorus; the singing role is by no means restricted to a single character. There are also many more scenes in a southern-style play than in northern plays. *The Peach Blossom Fan*, for example, has forty plus a Prologue and an Epilogue. Often four or five evenings would be required for the complete production of a southern-style drama. The scenes in southern drama vary greatly in length and complexity though there are standard themes that make love scenes, martial scenes, and comic scenes almost obligatory. All of this, and much more, is present in *The Peach Blossom Fan* which ends with a Taoist ceremony of mourning for the fallen dynasty, the remaining loyalists having resolved to seclude themselves in the hills rather than serve the alien regime. The play gets its name from the bloodstains on Li Hsiang-chün's fan which were converted into peach blossoms by a skillful artist.

Liu Ching-t'ing, the famous storyteller who performs in this scene, is also featured in selection 208 (the second item).

(*Recites*)

Hushed is the courtyard, cold the kitchen stove;
And I have risen late from heavy slumber.
Though flowers bloom, fatigue invades the limbs,
And while it rains at every dawn of day,
And trees around the royal tombs decay,
The river swollen with the melted snows
Washes away the palace's foundations.
I write new poems grieving for the past;
An exile's sorrow, dreaming dreams of home.
Where will the swallows choose to nest this year,
In my village home far west of the misty waters?

(*Speaks*) My name is Hou Fang-yü, and I am a native of Kuei-te in the heart of the empire. I am descended from a long line of scholars and officials; my father and grandfather were Ministers of State, and both set up their standards in the Eastern Forest.[2] Trained in poetry and the classics, I have won distinction in the world of letters and allied myself with the Revival Society. My early writings were influenced by those master spirits Pan Ku and Sung Yü; in maturity I am drawing nearer to Han Yü and Su Tung-p'o.[3] I have written in praise of wine in the Yüeh-hua Palace, despite my reluctance to plant more flowers in the garden at Loyang.[4] Since finishing my examinations last year, I have been staying on the shore of Grieve-Not Lake. But the clouds of war continue to cover us, and the news from home is scarce. It is mid-spring and the green grass stretches to the dim horizon, but where shall I find a companion for my homeward journey? The yellow dust rises from the earth, but here I sit in solitary exile. Oh! Grieve Not, Grieve Not! How can I fail to grieve? Fortunately, my literary friends Ch'en Chen-hui and Wu

1. Grieve-Not Lake and the Poet's Tower (built for the fourth-century poet Sun Ch'u) were located just to the west of the city wall of Nanking.

2. The Tung-lin or Eastern Forest Party was a school of intellectuals who organized opposition to the corrupt dictatorship of the eunuch Wei Chung-hsien and his secret police. The Fu-she Society for the revival of ancient learning was an offshoot of the Eastern Forest Party whose aim was to "make friends by means of literature" and help its members prepare for the civil service examinations. Wu Ying-chi, who appears in this play, in historical fact recorded over two thousand members of this influential society, here translated as the "Revival Club."

3. Pan Ku, died 92 C.E., eminent historian (see selection 226); Sung Yü, third-century B.C.E. statesman and poet whose works form part of the *Elegies of Ch'u* (see selections 148 and 149); Han Yü, 768–824, poet and essayist, leader of the influential "ancient-style movement" of the T'ang period (see selection 53); Su Tung-p'o or Su Shih, 1037–1101, leading poet and essayist of the Sung period (see selection 156).

4. Hou Fang-yü uses these allusions to compare himself with the poet Tsou Yang (c. 206–129 B.C.E.), guest in the Yüeh-hua Palace built by Prince Hsiao of Liang, and with the poet Shih Ch'ung (died 300 C.E.), owner of a famous garden outside Loyang.

Ying-chi are staying over Ts'ai Yi-so's bookshop. We often meet and cheer each other's solitude. Today we shall gather at the Fair City Monastery and enjoy the splendor of the plum blossoms. I must start immediately or I shall be late. (*He proceeds to sing*)

New warmth invades the breeze,
Mist 'whelms the river glade.
We stroll through flowery leas
With wine in jars of jade.
Thrilled by a sudden flute
The pilgrim's heart is mute.
Don't pass by Swallow Lane:
New owners are repainting
The lintels of your friends
Who will not come again. (*Exit*)

(Enter CH'EN CHEN-HUI and WU YING-CHI)

CH'EN: (*Sings*)

The royal power is fading from Nanking;
The war flags wave, the drums of battle beat.
One dreads to cross the river, though it flows
So placidly through willow groves and orchards.

[*Each announces his name*]

CH'EN: What is the latest news of the roving bandits?
WU: Yesterday I saw an official report. After defeating the national armies, the bandits are drawing near the capital. Tso Liang-yü, the Earl of Ning-nan, has retreated to Hsiang-yang, and central China is totally unprotected. The fate of the dynasty is sealed. We might as well enjoy the spring while it lasts.
CH'EN and WU together: (*Singing*)
Spring floods the air, but wind and rain
Have scattered petals of the pear,
And so dawn seems dishevelled and in pain.

HOU: (*Reentering*) Greetings! So the two of you came betimes.
WU: Of course. We could not bear to keep you waiting.
CH'EN: I sent my servants ahead to sweep the monastery courtyard and serve refreshments.
SERVANT: (*Entering in haste*) When it is cold, the wine's not warm enough; when flowers bloom, the trippers are too many. . . . We arrived too late, Your Honor. Let us all go home.
CH'EN: What do you mean, too late?

SERVANT: Master Hsü from the Wei Palace is giving a party in honor of the blossoms. The whole monastery is crammed with his guests.

HOU: Let us go up the river then, and visit the beauties of the Water Pavilion.

WU: Why trouble to go so far? Do you know that brilliant minstrel Liu Ching-t'ing of T'ai-chou? He is highly esteemed by such connoisseurs as the Ministers Fan Ching-wen and Ho Ju-ch'ung, and I hear that he lives nearby. On this languid spring day, would it not be pleasant to listen to him?

CH'EN: That is also a good suggestion.

HOU: (*Angrily*) Pockmarked Liu was a toady of Juan Ta-ch'eng, Bearded Juan, the eunuch's adopted son. I would rather avoid such a creature.

WU: Apparently you do not know the facts. Since the despicable Juan persisted in patronizing singers and dancers and flattering the powerful at court instead of resigning, I wrote an impeachment exposing his crimes and demanding his punishment. When at last his troupe of artists discovered that he was a member of the treacherous Ts'ui and Wei cliques, they all walked out on him in the middle of a performance, and Pockmarked Liu was among them. In my opinion Liu deserves our respect.

HOU: I should never have expected to find such high principles in a man of that sort. Let us pay him a visit. (*They proceed together*)

HOU, WU, and CHEN together: (*Singing*)
Random pipe-notes in the Courts of the Transcendents
Where the secluded Alchemist
Watches "the vast sea turn into mulberry groves."[5]

SERVANT: Here we are. I'll knock at the door. (*Shouts*) Is Pockmarked Liu at home?

CH'EN: Fie, fie! He is a celebrity: you should address him as *Master* Liu.

SERVANT: Master Liu, open the door!

(*Enters Liu, a* ch'ou *or comedian type with a white beard, a skullcap, and a blue gown*)

LIU: (*Sings*)

Green moss and weeds grow rank and high
Beside my long-locked door.
Woodsmen and fishingfolk amble nigh
To praise the times of yore.

(*Seeing the visitors, he exclaims*) Oh Masters Ch'en and Wu! Forgive my ignorance of your arrival. Who is the gentleman you have brought along with you?

---

5. The sea's giving place to mulberry groves is a common Taoist (i.e., "Alchemist") metaphor for the mutability of all phenomena.

CH'EN: This is our friend Hou Fang-yü of Honan, whose fame is in the ascendant. He has long admired your art and hopes to hear you.

LIU: I am overwhelmed. Pray be seated and drink some tea. (*They sit, and* LIU *continues*) You gentlemen are such fine scholars, so familiar with the *Records of the Grand Historian*, the *Comprehensive Mirror*,[6] or whatever; what pleasure or instruction could you hope to gain from my vulgar discourse? (*He points at his courtyard and sings*)

In the forsaken garden, a withered pine leans over a broken wall;
On the fragrant grass of the palace ruins, the silky showers fall.
The Six Great Dynasties' decay[7] brings thoughts too sad to render;
In telling tales I often weep, because my heart's too tender.

HOU: You are excessively modest. Please favor us with a sample of your skill.

LIU: Since you honor me with your company, I dare not disappoint you. But I fear that my crude versions of history and blind man's tales are unworthy of your ears, so I shall comment on a chapter of Confucius's *Analects* instead.

HOU: How strange! One would hardly expect you to choose such a theme.

LIU (*Laughing*): You scholars discuss the *Analects*, why shouldn't I? Today you will judge my slender claim to learning. (*Recites*)

"I dwell among green hills: you ask me why.
My soul at ease, I smile without reply.
The peach petals are swept along the stream
To other lands outside this mortal dream."[8]

(*He claps his "wakener-board" and continues, speaking*) I shall tell how the crime of three powerful clans who conspired against their ruler was exposed. I shall also tell how wondrously Confucius succeeded in the reform of music. The great doctrine of the Way was on the wane. Avarice and covetousness were deeply embedded in the heart of man. On returning to Lu from the state of Wei, our great Sage began to restore the true principles of music. So profoundly were performers affected by the result that they were ashamed to realize they had been serving the wrong masters, and abandoned those tribes of malefactors. The theaters of the mighty, which had been full of glowing color and

6. The *Records of the Grand Historian* (*Shih chi*) is by Ssu-ma Ch'ien (145 to c.90 B.C.E., see selection 225) who, after his reformation of the calendar, took up and completed the monumental work begun by his father, the history of China from the earliest ages to his own time. The *Comprehensive Mirror for Aid in Government* (*Tzu-chih t'ung-chien*) was the history of China by Ssu-ma Kuang, 1019–1086.

7. The Six Dynasties were those which from the third through the sixth centuries maintained their capital at Chien-k'ang, modern Nanking.

8. A poem by the great T'ang master Li Po, 701–762 (see selection 45).

vibrant melody, were deserted in a twinkling. Truly fearsome, truly marvelous was the influence of the Sage! (*He sings to drum accompaniment, keeping rhythmic time*)

The great Sage of antiquity was most versatile in magic;
He could sway the wind and rain,
And turn handfuls of peas into armies of warriors.
When he saw that the turbulent nobles
Had lost all sense of propriety in their dancing and music,
He played a subtle trick on them.
Hence the lowest of slaves
Began to behave like the highest of heroes.

(LIU *claps his board and continues, speaking*) The first player to leave for the state of Ch'i was good Master Chih. And why did he leave for Ch'i? I'll tell you. (*He drums and sings*)

Alas, he exclaimed,
Why should I ring the bell for these three clans?
I must have been blind to wallow in such mire.
I shall leave at once,
Setting forth with long, swift strides towards the northeast;
There I shall join my old comrades and win fresh laurels.
I shall play for the delight of Master K'ung[9] himself,
Who forgot the flavor of meat
For three months after hearing my performance.
And the virtuous Duke Ching
Will also be moved to tears by my art.
Even if the usurpers have swallowed
The heart of a leopard and the gall of a bear,
I doubt if they would pursue me to Ch'i,
The land of Chiang T'ai-kung's descendants![10]

(LIU *claps his board and continues speaking*) The second master's name was Kan. He left for the state of Ch'u. The third master, Liao, retired to the state of Ts'ai. The fourth one was Ch'üeh, who went to the state of Ch'in. Why did these three leave? I'll tell you. (*He drums and sings*)

All these musicians, who played at every banquet,
Had lost their leader now;
One by one they embarked on a new career.

9. Confucius.
10. Chiang T'ai-kung, twelfth century B.C.E. legendary octogenarian who consolidated the Chou dynasty. He was said to exercise authority over the spirits of the unseen universe, and hence was often depicted over doors to frighten away evil spirits.

The second master said: "See the usurper
Grasp his rice-bowl in the hall!
Why should we blow trumpets
And beat drums for his entertainment?
Our leader has left for the state of Ch'i;
Nobody can make him return.
As for me, I propose to play for Hsiung Yi, the King of Ch'u,
Committing myself to his powerful protection."
The third master said: "Though the state of Ts'ai,
South of the river, is not extensive,
It is near the capital
And in the heart of the central plain."
The fourth master gazed toward the south and said:
"I can see a new imperial spirit
Rising from the state of Ch'in,
Which has strong armies and fortifications;
Thither I shall take my lute."
All three of them pointed at the usurpers and said:
"We have endured your tyranny too long;
Henceforth we shall make you wince at the sound of our names."

(LIU *claps his board and continues speaking*) One drummer named Fang Shu went to the Yellow River region, and another named Wu to the Han River region. The junior leader's name was Yang and the gong-beater's name was Hsiang, and these repaired to the seacoast. The manner of their leaving was different. I'll tell you. (*He drums and sings*)

Altogether there were four drummers and gong-beaters.
"Our theater remains in confusion," said they,
"And we have no desire to stay.
Disgusted with our fiendish patrons,
We shall seek employment elsewhere,
Even though it is unlikely that we shall fare better.
Let us sail a light boat to the Peach Blossom Spring.[11]
At least we may win renown
As fishermen of the lakes and rivers."

(LIU *claps his board and continues speaking*) These four made the wisest decision. Hearken to their speech! (*He drums and sings*)

11. The expression "Peach Blossom Spring" was coined by the poet and essayist, T'ao Ch'ien (265–420; see selection 204), and became a metaphor for a place of retirement where the sage could live happily, far from the noise and turmoil of the world. The allusion is of course anachronistic here, coming as it does from the lips of a contemporary of Confucius.

"The trees of coral soar a hundred feet, vermilion in the sunlight;
The crystal palace of the sea-god is built on a terrace of pearls.
The Dragon King will invite us to a banquet
Where golden boys and jade girls excel earthly mortals.
Phoenix flutes and ivory pipes
Will be tuned to the dragon's most exquisite melodies;
For this time, *others* will play while *we* shall listen.
Though the usurpers may try to pursue us down the rivers,
There will be thousands of leagues between us
In which they will lose their way.
We need not fear to be friendless
Among the mountains and distant waters,
For all men within the four seas
And beyond the horizon are our comrades.
We should tear the paper windowpane
And look at the real world.
We have saved ourselves from the abyss by divine inspiration.
Even if sea becomes land, and land sea,
The vision of our Sage endures in the Six Canons.[12]

(*Standing up,* LIU *speaks*) Thank you for listening! I have shown what
    trifling talents I possess.
CH'EN: Superb! None of our modern pundits could express himself so well.
    You are indeed a consummate artist.
WU: Since leaving Juan, Liu has not cared to seek another patron. This last
    recital was autobiographical.
HOU: I perceive he has a noble character, untainted by worldliness. He is truly
    one of us. Storytelling is merely one of his minor accomplishments.
CH'EN, WU, and HOU together: (*Singing*)

The deep red dust[13] is suddenly clear,
And all shines bright as snow.
The warm spring light is suddenly chill;
The Sage solves all below.

(*They laugh and continue*)

---

   12. The oldest enumeration of Chinese classics gave only five *ching: Classic of Changes* (*Yi
ching*), *Classic of Documents* (*Shu ching*), *Classic of Odes* (*Shih ching*), *Record of Rites* (*Li chi*),
and *Spring and Autumn Annals* (*Ch'un ch'iu*). The *Record of Music* (*Yüeh chi*) was later added
as the sixth classic, but it is usually classed as one of the chapters of the *Record of Rites.*
   13. The mundane world.

Your mocking satire, our delight,
Each phrase at once caress and bite,
The triple beat of Yü-yang drum
To judgment come![14]

LIU: (*Sings*)

Please come another day;
And if to Peach Blossom source
You fail to find the way,
To this old fisherman have recourse.

WU: Which of your other colleagues left the house of Juan?
LIU: We are all dispersed. Only the master-singer Su K'un-sheng remains in this neighborhood.
HOU: I should like to meet him too, and hope you will both pay me a visit.
LIU: Of course we should be most honored.

(*Each sings a line of the following quatrain*)

LIU:

After my song is sung, the sun is setting.

CH'EN:

The fragrance of fallen petals fills the courtyard.

WU:

Terraces and towers seem myriad blades of grass.

HOU:

Spiritual discourse and imperial strategy melt into the void.

Translated by Chen Shih-hsiang and Harold Acton
with the collaboration of Cyril Birch

---

14. The "triple beat of Yü-yang drum" alludes to the drumming to whose accompaniment Mi Heng cursed the tyrant Ts'ao Ts'ao in the time of the Three Kingdoms (third century C.E.).

278
The Mortal Thoughts of a Nun

from a popular drama

Anonymous (before 1700)

A young nun am I, sixteen years of age;
My head was shaven in my maidenhood.

For my father, he loves the Buddhist sūtras,
And my mother, she loves the Buddhist priests.

Morning and night, morning and night,
I burn incense and I pray, for I
Was born a sickly child, full of ills.
So they sent me here into this monastery.

Amitābha! Amitābha![1]
Unceasingly I pray.
Oh, tired am I of the humming of the drums and the tinkling of the
    bells;
Tired am I of the droning of the prayers and the crooning of the priors;
The chatter and the clatter of unintelligible charms,
The clamor and the clangor of interminable chants,
The mumbling and the murmuring of monotonous psalms.
Prajñāpāramitā, Mayura-sūtra,
        Saddharmapuṇḍarīka[2]
            Oh, how I hate them all!

While I say Mitābha,
        I sigh for my beau.
While I chant *saparah,*
        My heart cries, "Oh!"
While I sing *tarata,*
        My heart palpitates so!

Ah, let me take a stroll,
Let me take a stroll!

This is a traditional scene from K'un-ch'ü (southern-style opera) that appears in several of the
better known plays of the repertoire.
1. The Buddha of the Western Pure Land (paradise).
2. The names of important Buddhist scriptures.

(*She comes to the Hall of the Five Hundred Lohans,*[3] *where there are clay figures of the Buddhist saints, known for their distinctive facial expressions*)

Ah, here are the Lohan,
What a bunch of silly, amorous souls!
　　Every one a bearded man!
How each his eyes at me rolls!

Look at the one hugging his knees!
　　His lips are mumbling my name so!
And the one with his cheek in hand,
　　As though thinking of me so!
That one has a pair of dreamy eyes,
　　Dreaming dreams of me so!

　　But the Lohan in sackcloth!
What is he after,
　　With his hellish, heathenish laughter?
With his roaring, rollicking laughter,
　　Laughing at me so!
　　　　　　　—Laughing at me, for
When beauty is past and youth is lost,
　　Who will marry an old crone?
When beauty is faded and youth is jaded,
　　Who will marry an old, shriveled cocoon?

The one holding a dragon,
　　He is cynical;
The one riding a tiger,
　　He is quizzical;
And that long-browned handsome giant,
　　He seems pitiful,
For what will become of me when my beauty is gone?

These candles of the altar,
　　They are not for my bridal chamber.
These long incense containers,
　　They are not for my bridal parlor.
And the straw prayer cushions,
　　They cannot serve as quilt or cover.

　　Oh, God!
Whence comes this burning, suffocating ardor?

3. Saints; worthies; advanced disciples of the Buddha Śākyamuni. *Lohan* is an abbreviated Chinese transcription of Sanskrit *arhat.*

Whence comes this strange, infernal, unearthly ardor?
I'll tear these monkish robes!
    I'll bury all the Buddhist sūtras;
I'll drown the wooden fish,[4]
    And leave all the monastic *putras!*[5]

I'll leave the drums,
    I'll leave the bells,
        And the chants,
        And the yells,
And all the interminable, exasperating, religious chatter!

I'll go downhill, and find me a young and handsome lover—
Let him scold me, beat me!
    Kick or ill-treat me!
I will *not* become a Buddha!
I will *not* mumble *mita, prajna, para!*

Translated by Lin Yutang

---

4. Carved, hollow wood blocks for beating time in Buddhist ceremonies.
5. Some of the Sanskritic-sounding terms used by the young nun are intentional deformations meant to express contempt for the religion which constrains her.

PRINCIPAL CHINESE DYNASTIES AND PERIODS

Hsia (not fully verified)	c. 2100–c. 1600 B.C.E.
Shang or Yin (largely verified)	c. 1600–c. 1028
Chou	c. 1027–256
Western Chou	c. 1100–771
Eastern Chou	c. 770–256
Spring and Autumn period	722–468
Warring States period	403–221
Ch'in	221–207
Han	206 B.C.E.–220 C.E.
Western or Former Han	206 B.C.E.–8 C.E.
Hsin (New)	9–23
Liu Hsüan (Han)	23–25
Eastern or Later Han	25–220
Three Kingdoms	220–265
Wei (North China)	220–265
Shu (Szechwan)	221–263
Wu (Lower Yangtze Valley)	222–280
Chin	265–420
Western Chin	265–316
Eastern Chin	317–420
Southern and Northern Dynasties	420–589
Sixteen Kingdoms (North China)	304–439
Northern Dynasties [1]	386–581
Northern Wei (Tabgatch)	386–534
Eastern Wei	534–550
Western Wei	535–557
Northern Ch'i	550–577
Northern Chou	557–581
Southern Dynasties [2]	420–589
Sung (Former or Liu)	420–479
Ch'i	479–502
Liang	502–557

Note: B.C.E. and C.E. stand for Before the Common Era and the Common Era. They coincide with B.C. and A.D.

1. The Northern Dynasties were dominated by non-Sinitic groups.

2. Wu and Eastern Chin plus the Southern Dynasties are collectively known as the Six Dynasties.

Ch'en	557–589
Sui	581–618
T'ang	618–684, 705–907
Chou (Empress Wu)	684–705
Five Dynasties[3]	907–960
Later Liang	907–923
Later T'ang	923–936
Later Chin	936–946
Later Han	947–950
Later Chou	951–960
Sung (Later or Chao)	960–1279
Northern Sung	960–1127
Southern Sung	1127–1279
Liao (Khitan)	916–1125
Western Liao	1125–1201
Western Hsia (Tangut)	1032–1227
Chin (Jürchen)	1115–1234
Yüan (Mongol)	1260–1368
Ming	1368–1644
Ch'ing (Manchu)	1644–1911 C.E.

3. The Five Dynasties, dominated by non-Sinitic peoples, coexisted with a series of smaller and even more ephemeral Ten Kingdoms.

ROMANIZATION SCHEMES FOR MODERN STANDARD MANDARIN

Wade-Giles	Pinyin	Wade-Giles	Pinyin
a[h]	a	ch'ien	qian
ai	ai	chih	zhi
an	an	ch'ih	chi
ang	ang	chin	jin
ao	ao	ch'in	qin
cha	zha	ching	jing
ch'a	cha	ch'ing	qing
chai	zhai	chiu	jiu
ch'ai	chai	ch'iu	qiu
chan	zhan	chiung	jiong
ch'an	chan	ch'iung	qiong
chang	zhang	cho	zho
ch'ang	chang	ch'o	cho
chao	zhao	chou	zhou
ch'ao	chao	ch'ou	chou
che	zhe	chu	zhu
ch'e	che	ch'u	chu
chei	zhei	chü	ju
chcn	zhen	ch'ü	qu
ch'en	chen	chua	zhua
cheng	zheng	ch'ua	chua
ch'eng	cheng	chuai	zhuai
chi	ji	ch'uai	cluai
ch'i	qi	chuan	zhuan
chia	jia	ch'uan	chuan
ch'ia	qia	chüan	juan
chiang	jiang	ch'üan	quan
ch'iang	qiang	chuang	zhuang
chiao	jiao	ch'uang	chuang
ch'iao	qiao	chüeh	jue
chieh	jie	ch'üeh	que
ch'ieh	qie	chui	zhui
chien	jian	ch'ui	chui

WADE-GILES	PINYIN	WADE-GILES	PINYIN
chun	zhun	huai	huai
ch'un	chun	huan	huan
chün	jun	huang	huang
ch'ün	qun	hui	hui
chung	zhong	hun	hun
ch'ung	chong	hung	hong
e[h], ě	e	huo	huo
ei	ei	i	yi
en	en	jan	ran
erh	er	jang	rang
fa	fa	jao	rao
fan	fan	jeh	re
fang	fang	jen	ren
fei	fei	jeng	reng
fen	fen	jih	ri
feng	feng	jo	ro
fo	fo	jou	rou
fou	fou	ju	ru
fu	fu	juan	ruan
ha	ha	jui	rui
hai	hai	jun	run
han	han	jung	rong
hang	hang	ka	ga
hao	hao	k'a	ka
hei	hei	kai	gai
hen	hen	k'ai	kai
heng	heng	kan	gan
ho	he	k'an	kan
hou	hou	kang	gang
hsi	xi	k'ang	kang
hsia	xia	kao	gao
hsiang	xiang	k'ao	kao
hsiao	xiao	ke, ko	ge
hsieh	xie	k'e, k'o	ke
hsien	xian	ken	gen
hsin	xin	k'en	ken
hsing	xing	keng	geng
hsiu	xiu	k'eng	keng
hsiung	xiong	kou	gou
hsü	xu	k'ou	kou
hsüan	xuan	ku	gu
hsüeh	xue	k'u	ku
hsün	xun	kua	gua
hu	hu	k'ua	kua
hua	hua	kuai	guai

WADE-GILES	PINYIN	WADE-GILES	PINYIN
k'uai	kuai	me	me
kuan	guan	mei	mei
k'uan	kuan	men	men
kuang	guang	meng	meng
k'uang	kuang	mi	mi
kuei	gui	miao	miao
k'uei	kui	mieh	mie
kun	gun	mien	mian
k'un	kun	min	min
kung	gong	ming	ming
k'ung	kong	miu, miou	miu
kuo	guo	mo	mo
k'uo	kuo	mou	mou
la	la	mu	mu
lai	lai	na	na
lan	lan	nai	nai
lang	lang	nan	nan
lao	lao	nang	nang
le[h]	le	nao	nao
lei	lei	ne	ne
leng	leng	nei	nei
li	li	nen	nen
lia	lia	ni	ni
liang	liang	niang	niang
liao	liao	niao	niao
lieh	lie	nieh	nie
lien	lian	nien	nian
lin	lin	nin	nin
ling	ling	ning	ning
liu	liu	niu	niu
lo, luo	luo	no	nuo
lou	lou	nou	nou
lu	lu	nu	nu
lü	lü, lyu	nü	nü, nyu
luan	luan	nuan	nuan
lüan	lüan, lyuan	nüeh	nüe, nyue
lüeh	lüe, lyue	nung	nong
lun	lun	o, ŏ, e	e
lün	lün, lyun	ou	ou
lung	long	pa	ba
ma	ma	p'a	pa
mai	mai	pai	bai
man	man	p'ai	pai
mang	mang	pan	ban
mao	mao	p'an	pan

WADE-GILES	PINYIN	WADE-GILES	PINYIN
pang	bang	shou	shou
p'ang	pang	shu	shu
pao	bao	shua	shua
p'ao	pao	shuai	shuai
pei	bei	shuan	shuan
p'ei	pei	shuang	shuang
pen	ben	shui	shui
p'en	pen	shun	shun
peng	beng	shuo	shuo
p'eng	peng	so	suo
pi	bi	sou	sou
p'i	pi	ssu, szu	si
piao	biao	su	su
p'iao	piao	suan	suan
pieh	bie	sui	sui
p'ieh	pie	sun	sun
pien	bian	sung	song
p'ien	pian	ta	da
pin	bin	t'a	ta
p'in	pin	tai	dai
ping	bing	t'ai	tai
p'ing	ping	tan	dan
po	bo	t'an	tan
p'o	po	tang	dang
p'ou	pou	t'ang	tang
pu	bu	tao	dao
p'u	pu	t'ao	tao
sa	sa	te	de
sai	sai	t'e	te
san	san	tei	dei
sang	sang	teng	deng
sao	sao	t'eng	teng
se	se	ti	di
sen	sen	t'i	ti
seng	seng	tiao	diao
sha	sha	t'iao	tiao
shai	shai	tieh	die
shan	shan	t'ieh	tie
shang	shang	tien	dian
shao	shao	t'ien	tian
she	she	ting	ding
shei	shei	t'ing	ting
shen	shen	tiu	diu
sheng	sheng	to	duo
shih	shi	t'o	tuo

WADE-GILES	PINYIN	WADE-GILES	PINYIN
tou	dou	t'u	tu
t'ou	tou	tuan	duan
tsa	za	t'uan	tuan
ts'a	ca	tui	dui
tsai	zai	t'ui	tui
ts'ai	cai	tun	dun
tsan	zan	t'un	tun
ts'an	can	tung	dong
tsang	zang	t'ung	tong
ts'ang	cang	tzu	zi
tsao	zao	tz'u	ci
ts'ao	cao	wa	wa
tse	ze	wai	wai
ts'e	ce	wan	wan
tsei	zei	wang	wang
tsen	zen	wei	wei
ts'en	cen	wen	wen
tseng	zeng	weng	weng
ts'eng	ceng	wo	wo
tso	zuo	wu	wu
ts'o	cuo	ya	ya
tsou	zou	yai	yai
ts'ou	cou	yang	yang
tsu	zu	yao	yao
ts'u	cu	yeh	ye
tsuan	zuan	yen	yan
ts'uan	cuan	yin	yin
tsui	zui	ying	ying
ts'ui	cui	yu	you
tsun	zun	yü	yu
ts'un	cun	yüan	yuan
tsung	zong	yüeh	yue
ts'ung	cong	yün	yun
tu	du	yung	yong

LIST OF PERMISSIONS

The editor and publisher acknowledge with thanks permission granted to reproduce in this volume the following material previously published elsewhere. Every effort has been made to trace copyright holders, but if any have been inadvertently overlooked, the publisher will be pleased to make the necessary arrangement at the first opportunity.

In an anthology of this magnitude, which includes over four hundred published and unpublished items by more than a hundred contributors, keeping track of copyrights and permissions has been an insurmountable task. A few of the previously published translations have appeared in several places, have been out of print then back in print again, or have been retranslated expressly for this volume. Other translations that were prepared for this anthology have since appeared elsewhere. Some copyrights are held by the translators or their heirs, others by the publishers, and still others have changed ownership one or more times. Several of the older works are in the public domain. Some translators required only attribution at the conclusion of their works; others requested identification in the list of permissions.

Special thanks go to Professor Anne Birrell for permitting generous use of her translations and notes for the following: Anon., "We Have Chosen a Timely Day," and Anon., "Crows on City Walls," from *Popular Songs and Ballads of Han China* (Hawaii University Press, 1993), and Ssu-ma Hsiang-ju, "Cock-Phoenix, Hen-Phoenix," Li Yen-nien, "A Song," attributed to Hsi-chün, "Lost Horizon," Anon., "Song of the Viet Boatman," Anon., "Mulberry up the Lane," Anon., from the "Nineteen Old Poems," Anon. or attributed to Ts'ai Yung, "Watering Horses at a Long Wall Hole," Fu Hsüan, "Pity Me!," Anon., "A Peacock Southeast Flew," and Pao Chao, "Magic Cinnabar" from *New Songs from a Jade Terrace* (Penguin Classics, 1986).

Li Po, "Up into the Clouds Music," "Late Bloomer at the Front of My Garden," "To Send to Tu Fu as a Joke," "Drinking Alone in the Moonlight," "A Suite in the *Ch'ing-p'ing* Mode," and Meng Hao-jan, "Spring Dawn" from Elling O. Eide, *Poems by Li Po* (Lexington, KY: Anvil Press, 1984) are reprinted by kind permission of Elling O. Eide.

The following selections from *The Poetry of Li Shang-yin: Ninth Century Baroque Chinese Poet* (1969) were trans. by James J. Y. Liu: Li Shang-yin, "Boasting of

My Son" and "Master Chia," reprinted by permission of the University of Chicago Press.

Chapter 31 ("On Ghosts") from *The Ethical and Poetical Works of Mo Tzu* trans. by Yipao Mei (Hyperion Press, 1973). Title in public domain.

Selection from *Journey to the West,* trans. by Anthony C. Yu, reprinted by permission of the translator and the University of Chicago Press.

Selections from *The Collected Songs of Cold Mountain,* trans. by Red Pine. Copyright (c) 1983 by Copper Canyon Press. Used by permission of Copper Canyon Press, P.O. Box 271, Port Townsend, WA.

Selections from *Tao Te Ching: The Classic Book of Integrity and the Way* and *Wandering on the Way: Early Taoist Tales and Parables of Chuang Tzu,* trans. and edited by Victor H. Mair, are used by permission of Bantam Books, a division of Bantam, Doubleday, Dell Publishing Group.

Selection from *The Secret History of the Mongols,* trans. and edited by Francis Woodman Cleaves, reprinted by permission of the publishers: Harvard University Press, Cambridge, Mass.: Copyright (c) 1982 by the Harvard Yenching Institute.

K'ang-hsi, "Lines in Praise of a Self-chiming Clock," from *Emperor of China: Self-Portrait of K'ang-hsi,* trans. by Jonathan Spence and published by Knopf, appears courtesy of Jonathan Spence.

Selections of P'u Sung-ling, *Strange Tales from Make-Do Studio,* trans. by Victor H. Mair and Denis C. Mair, appears by permission of Foreign Languages Press, San Francisco, CA.

"On the Cicada: In Prison" by Lo Pin-wang, and "Poem Written in Answer to His Majesty's Question: 'What is There in the Mountains?'" from *The Poetry of the Early T'ang,* trans. by Stephen Owen, copyright (c) 1977 by Yale University Press, is reprinted permission of Yale University Press.

Two chapters from the *Kuan Tzu,* attributed to Kuan Chung, "Inner Workings" and "Duties of the Student," trans. by W. Allyn Rickett, will appear in *Guanzi: Political, Economic, and Philosophical Essays from Early China, Volume Two.*

Compiled by Liu Hsiang, *Intrigues of the Warring States* appears with kind courtesy of James I. Crump, Jr.

"Written on a Cold Evening," "Songs of Depression," "Don't Read Books!" and "Watching a Village Festival," from *Heaven My Blanket, Earth My Pillow: Poems by Yang Wan-Li,* trans. by Jonathan Chaves, are reprinted by permission of Tanko Sha, New York.

Su Shih, "Red Cliff," numbers 1 and 2, Wang Hsi-chih, Preface to *Collected Poems from the Orchid Pavilion,* Chang Tai, "The Relic of King Aśoka Temple," and Chou Mi, "Observing the Tidal Bore," from *Reminiscences of Wu-lin,* appear by kind permission of translator Richard Strassberg and the University of California Press. The selections appear in *Inscribed Landscapes,* edited by Richard Strassberg, the University of California Press.

"Expository Tale on King Wu's Expedition Against Chow" is taken with permission from Liu Ts'un-yan, *Buddhist and Taoist Influences on Chinese Novels. Vol. 1. The Authorship of the Feng-shen yen-i* (Wiesbaden: Harrasowitz, 1962).

Liu Yin, "Miscellaneous Poems on Rural Life," Yüan Chüeh, "Shipboard Song," Li

Chapter 2 from *Ballad of the Hidden Dragon*, trans. by M. Doleželová-Veringová and J. I. Crump, published by Clarendon Press (1971).

The Literary Review (Fairleigh Dickinson University) for poems translated by Sam Hamill.

Various poems from *Sunflower Splendor*, eds. Wu-chi Liu and Irving Yucheng Lo, originally published by Indiana University Press (1975) and reprinted by Anchor.

Four poems from James Robert Hightower, trans. and comm., *The Poetry of T'ao Ch'ien*, published by Clarendon Press (1970).

Three poems from Jeanne Larsen, trans., *Brocade River Poems: Selected Works of the Tang Dynasty Courtesan Xue Tao*, published by Princeton University Press (1987).

"Letter in Reply to Liu Yi-chang," trans. by Victor H. Mair, is reprinted by permission from *Renditions*, 9 (Spring, 1978) (Chinese University of Hong Kong, Research Center for Translation), pp. 81–84.

"The Sins of Mahādeva," trans. by Victor H. Mair, formerly appeared in *Asian Folklore Studies*, 45.1 (1986) (Nagoya), pp. 19–32.

Poems by Juan Chi, Ch'en Tzu-ang, Chang Chiu-ling, and Li Po trans. by Victor H. Mair are from the translator's *Four Introspective Poets*, published by Arizona State University Center for Asian Studies (1987).

The Story about K'ung Jung is from Richard B. Mather, trans., *Shih-shuo Hsin-yü: A New Account of Tales of the World*, published by University of Minnesota Press (1976).

"Written on Seeing the Flowers, and Remembering My Daughter" is from F. W. Mote, *The Poet Kao Ch'i, 1336–1374*, Princeton University Press (1962).

"To Meng Hao-jan," "Climbing Pien-chüeh Temple," and "Second Song for the Worship of the Goddess" from *The Great Age of Chinese Poetry: The High T'ang* (c) 1981 by Yale University Press.

"On a Visit to Ch'ung-chen Taoist Temple," trans. by Kenneth Rexroth and Ling Chung, is from their *Women Poets of China*, published by New Directions in 1972.

Act 3 of *Injustice to Tou O*, trans. by Chung-wen Shih, is included here with the permission of Cambridge University Press, who published it in 1972.

"Great Preface," trans. by Steven Van Zoeren, is from his *Poetry and Personality*, Stanford University Press (1991).

Shen Fu, *Six Chapters from a Floating Life*, chapters 1 and 3, trans. by Lin Yutang, from *The Wisdom of China and India*, published by Random House (1942); originally published in *The Importance of Living* (John Day). Various other selections have also been taken from *The Importance of Living*.

Book 2, *Confucian Analects*, trans. by Ezra Pound, was published in 1933 by Peter Owen.

"The Ballad of Mulan" is from Arthur Waley, trans., *The Temple and Other Poems*, published by George Allen and Unwin (1923).

The following appear by permission of Columbia University Press:

"The Shrew," "A Burial Mound for Flowers," and "The Woman's Kingdom," from *Chinese Literature: Popular Fiction and Drama* (1973) trans. and edited by H. C. Chang.

Other Works in the Columbia Asian Studies Series

Chūshingura: The Treasury of Loyal Retainers, tr. Donald Keene. Also in paperback ed.   1971

The Zen Master Hakuin: Selected Writings, tr. Philip B. Yampolsky   1971

Chinese Rhyme-Prose: Poems in the Fu Form from the Han and Six Dynasties Periods, tr. Burton Watson. Also in paperback ed.   1971

Kūkai: Major Works, tr. Yoshito S. Hakeda. Also in paperback ed.   1972

The Old Man Who Does as He Pleases: Selections from the Poetry and Prose of Lu Yu, tr. Burton Watson   1973

The Lion's Roar of Queen Śrīmālā, tr. Alex and Hideko Wayman   1974

Courtier and Commoner in Ancient China: Selections from the History of the Former Han by Pan Ku, tr. Burton Watson. Also in paperback ed.   1974

Japanese Literature in Chinese, vol. 1: Poetry and Prose in Chinese by Japanese Writers of the Early Period, tr. Burton Watson   1975

Japanese Literature in Chinese, vol. 2: Poetry and Prose in Chinese by Japanese Writers of the Later Period, tr. Burton Watson   1976

Scripture of the Lotus Blossom of the Fine Dharma, tr. Leon Hurvitz. Also in paperback ed.   1976

Love Song of the Dark Lord: Jayadeva's Gītagovinda, tr. Barbara Stoler Miller. Also in paperback ed. Cloth ed. includes critical text of the Sanskrit.   1977

Ryōkan: Zen Monk-Poet of Japan, tr. Burton Watson   1977

Calming the Mind and Discerning the Real: From the Lam rim chen mo of Tsoṅ-kha-pa, tr. Alex Wayman   1978

The Hermit and the Love-Thief: Sanskrit Poems of Bhartrihari and Bilhaṇa, tr. Barbara Stoler Miller   1978

The Lute: Kao Ming's P'i-p'a chi, tr. Jean Mulligan. Also in paperback ed.   1980

A Chronicle of Gods and Sovereigns: Jinnō Shōtōki of Kitabatake-Chikafusa, tr. H. Paul Varley.   1980

Among the Flowers: The Hua-chien chi, tr. Lois Fusek   1982

Grass Hill: Poems and Prose by the Japanese Monk Gensei, tr. Burton Watson   1983

Doctors, Diviners, and Magicians of Ancient China: Biographies of Fang-shih, tr. Kenneth J. DeWoskin. Also in paperback ed.   1983

Theater of Memory: The Plays of Kālidāsa, ed. Barbara Stoler Miller. Also in paperback ed.   1984

The Columbia Book of Chinese Poetry: From Early Times to the Thirteenth Century, ed. and tr. Burton Watson. Also in paperback ed.   1984

Poems of Love and War: From the Eight Anthologies and the Ten Long Poems of Classical Tamil, tr. A. K. Ramanujan. Also in paperback ed. 1985

The Columbia Book of Later Chinese Poetry, ed. and tr. Jonathan Chaves. Also in paperback ed.   1986

The Tso Chuan: Selections from China's Oldest Narrative History, tr. Burton Watson   1989

Waiting for the Wind: Thirty-six Poets of Japan's Late Medieval Age, tr. Steven Carter   1989

Selected Writings of Nichiren, ed. Philip B. Yampolsky   1990

STUDIES IN ASIAN CULTURE

20. *Songs for the Bride: Women's Voices and Wedding Rites of Rural India,* by W. G. Archer; eds. Barbara Stoler Miller and Mildred Archer   1986
21. *A Heritage of Kings: One Man's Monarchy in the Confucian World,* by JaHyun Kim Haboush   1988

COMPANIONS TO ASIAN STUDIES

Approaches to the Oriental Classics, ed. Wm. Theodore de Bary   1959
Early Chinese Literature, by Burton Watson. Also in paperback ed.   1962
Approaches to Asian Civilizations, eds. Wm. Theodore de Bary and Ainslie T. Embree   1964
The Classic Chinese Novel: A Critical Introduction, by C. T. Hsia. Also in paperback ed.   1968
Chinese Lyricism: Shih Poetry from the Second to the Twelfth Century, tr. Burton Watson. Also in paperback ed.   1971
A Syllabus of Indian Civilization, by Leonard A. Gordon and Barbara Stoler Miller   1971
Twentieth-Century Chinese Stories, ed. C. T. Hsia and Joseph S. M. Lau. Also in paperback ed.   1971
A Syllabus of Chinese Civilization, by J. Mason Gentzler, 2d ed.   1972
A Syllabus of Japanese Civilization, by H. Paul Varley, 2d ed.   1972
An Introduction to Chinese Civilization, ed. John Meskill, with the assistance of J. Mason Gentzler   1973
An Introduction to Japanese Civilization, ed. Arthur E. Tiedemann   1974
Ukifune: Love in the Tale of Genji, ed. Andrew Pekarik   1982
The Pleasures of Japanese Literature, by Donald Keene   1988
A Guide to Oriental Classics, eds. Wm. Theodore de Bary and Ainslie T. Embree; 3d edition ed. Amy Vladeck Heinrich, 2 vols.   1989

INTRODUCTION TO ASIAN CIVILIZATIONS
Wm. Theodore de Bary, Editor

Sources of Japanese Tradition, 1958; paperback ed., 2 vols., 1964
Sources of Indian Tradition, 1958; paperback ed., 2 vols., 1964; 2d ed., 2 vols., 1988
Sources of Chinese Tradition, 1960; paperback ed., 2 vols., 1964

NEO-CONFUCIAN STUDIES

Instructions for Practical Living and Other Neo-Confucian Writings by Wang Yang-ming, tr. Wing-tsit Chan   1963
Reflections on Things at Hand: The Neo-Confucian Anthology, comp. Chu Hsi and Lü Tsu-ch'ien, tr. Wing-tsit Chan   1967
Self and Society in Ming Thought, by Wm. Theodore de Bary and the Conference on Ming Thought. Also in paperback ed.   1970
The Unfolding of Neo-Confucianism, by Wm. Theodore de Bary and the Conference on Seventeenth-Century Chinese Thought. Also in paperback ed.   1975
Principle and Practicality: Essays in Neo-Confucianism and Practical Learning, eds. Wm. Theodore de Bary and Irene Bloom. Also in paperback ed.   1979

The Syncretic Religion of Lin Chao-en, by Judith A. Berling — 1980

The Renewal of Buddhism in China: Chu-hung and the Late Ming Synthesis, by Chün-fang Yü — 1981

Neo-Confucian Orthodoxy and the Learning of the Mind-and-Heart, by Wm. Theodore de Bary — 1981

Yüan Thought: Chinese Thought and Religion Under the Mongols, eds. Hoklam Chan and Wm. Theodore de Bary — 1982

The Liberal Tradition in China, by Wm. Theodore de Bary — 1983

The Development and Decline of Chinese Cosmology, by John B. Henderson — 1984

The Rise of Neo-Confucianism in Korea, by Wm. Theodore de Bary and JaHyun Kim Haboush — 1985

Chiao Hung and the Restructuring of Neo-Confucianism in Late Ming, by Edward T. Ch'ien — 1985

Neo-Confucian Terms Explained: Pei-hsi tzu-i, by Ch'en Ch'un, ed. and trans. Wing-tsit Chan — 1986

Knowledge Painfully Acquired: K'un-chih chi, by Lo Ch'in-shun, ed. and trans. Irene Bloom — 1987

To Become a Sage: The Ten Diagrams on Sage Learning, by Yi T'oegye, ed. and trans. Michael C. Kalton — 1988

The Message of the Mind in Neo-Confucian Thought, by Wm. Theodore de Bary — 1989

MODERN ASIAN LITERATURE SERIES

Modern Japanese Drama: An Anthology, ed. and tr. Ted. Takaya. Also in paperback ed. — 1979

Mask and Sword: Two Plays for the Contemporary Japanese Theater, by Yamazaki Masakazu, tr. J. Thomas Rimer — 1980

Yokomitsu Riichi, Modernist, Dennis Keene — 1980

Nepali Visions, Nepali Dreams: The Poetry of Laxmiprasad Devkota, tr. David Rubin — 1980

Literature of the Hundred Flowers, vol. 1: *Criticism and Polemics*, ed. Hualing Nieh — 1981

Literature of the Hundred Flowers, vol. 2: *Poetry and Fiction*, ed. Hualing Nieh — 1981

Modern Chinese Stories and Novellas, 1919–1949, ed. Joseph S. M. Lau, C. T. Hsia, and Leo Ou-fan Lee. Also in paperback ed. — 1984

A View by the Sea, by Yasuoka Shōtarō, tr. Kären Wigen Lewis — 1984

Other Worlds, Arishima Takeo and the Bounds of Modern Japanese Fiction, by Paul Anderer — 1984

Selected Poems of Sō Chōngju, tr. with intro. by David R. McCann — 1989

The Sting of Life: Four Contemporary Japanese Novelists, by Van C. Gessel — 1989

Stories of Osaka Life, by Oda Sakunosuke, tr. Burton Watson — 1990

The Bodhisattva, or Samantabhadra, by Ishikawa Jun, tr. with intro. by William Jefferson Tyler — 1990

The Travels of Lao Ts'an, by Liu T'ich-yun, tr. Harold Shadick. Morningside ed. — 1990

Designer: Jennifer Dossin

Text: Electra

Compositor: Maple-Vail

Printer: Maple-Vail

Binder: Maple-Vail